Essentials of Psychology

Essentials of Psychology

ROBERT A. BARON

RENSSELAER POLYTECHNIC INSTITUTE

With the special assistance of
Michael J. Kalsher
Rensselaer Polytechnic Institute

ALLYN AND BACON

Boston   London   Toronto   Sydney   Tokyo   Singapore

Vice President and Publisher, Social Sciences: Susan Badger
Development Editors: Elizabeth Brooks, Sue Gleason
Editorial Assistants: Laura Ellingson, Erika Stuart
Executive Marketing Manager: Joyce Nilsen
Production Administrator: Susan McIntyre
Copy Editor: Jay Howland
Editorial-Production Service: Lifland et al., Bookmakers
Text Designer: Meral Dabcovich/Visual Perspectives
Cover Administrator: Linda Knowles
Photo Research: Laurel Anderson/Photosynthesis
Prepress Buyer: Linda Cox
Manufacturing Buyer: Megan Cochran
Electronic Composition: Michele Locatelli, Charles Provancher

All chapter opening collages were created by Nancy Gibson-Nash.

Photo credits appear on page xxix, which constitutes a continuation of the copyright page.

 Copyright © 1996 by Allyn & Bacon
A Simon & Schuster Company
Needham Heights, MA 02194

Library of Congress Cataloging-in-Publication Data

Baron, Robert A.
    Essentials of psychology / Robert A. Baron ; with the special assistance of
Michael J. Kalsher.
        p.   cm.
    Includes bibliographical references and indexes.
    ISBN 0-205-17450-7
    1. Psychology.   I. Kalsher, Michael J.   II. Title.
BF121.B3   1995
150—dc20   95-12236
                                                              CIP

Printed in the United States of America
10 9 8 7 6 5 4 3 2 1   00 99 98 97 96 95

To H. J. and Daisy,
who have more room in their hearts than anyone else I know,
and
to Sandra,
*who certainly inherited **that** family trait!*

Contents-at-a-Glance

Contents

1 Psychology: Its Nature, Scope, and Methods   1

2 Biological Bases of Behavior: A Look Beneath the Surface   43

3 Sensation and Perception: Making Contact with the World Around Us 79

4 *Consciousness:*
Awareness of Ourselves
and the External World **121**

5 *Learning:* *How We're*
Changed by Experience **157**

CONTENTS xi

6
Memory: Of Things
Remembered . . . and
Forgotten   *193*

HUMAN MEMORY: THE INFORMATION-
PROCESSING APPROACH   194

7 Cognition and Intelligence   229

8 Human Development: From Child to Adult   281

9 Motivation and Emotion 333

CONTENTS

12 Psychological Disorders:
Their Nature and Causes 445

13 Therapy: Diminishing the Pain of Psychological Disorders

14 Social Thought and Social Behavior

Appendix
Statistics: Uses—and
Potential Abuses

To the Student

WHY PSYCHOLOGY MATTERS: REFLECTIONS OF A LONG-TERM BELIEVER

In the mid 1970s, when I was on the faculty of Purdue University, I had a friend named Sam. Sam was an analytical chemist and one of the most brilliant people I have ever known. But what Sam didn't know about *people* would fill several books. Let me give you an example.

Sam was perpetually having problems with his department's copy room. Many jobs he sent there were not done on time—a real problem for him since he constantly worked against tight deadlines. After listening to Sam moan about this problem over and over again, I asked him the following questions: (1) Did he ever bring his really important jobs to the copy room himself rather than sending them down with his secretary? (2) Did he ever thank the people involved when copies were ready on time? Sam was puzzled by my questions. He couldn't see any purpose in visiting the copy room in person, and his attitude about on-time jobs was simple: Why should he thank someone for simply doing his or her job?

When I suggested that both of these steps might help, Sam seemed doubtful. But he was open-minded, so he promised to give them a try. Several weeks later, he reported that they did seem to help. In fact, he said, after he thanked the copy-room staff in person a few times, a miraculous change occurred: They began to put his work on top of the stack rather than on the bottom. Sam was happy about this change, but confused about *why* it had occurred. When I described the basic principles of reinforcement to him, he listened in rapt attention. Here, I could tell, was something entirely new for Sam, world-class scientist though he was. Yes, Sam was brilliant, but as he himself admitted, he almost never thought about people.

I haven't seen my friend Sam in many years, but I'm tempted to dedicate this book to him. To me, he is a perfect illustration of the importance of psychology and of why everyone—top-notch scientists included—needs a basic, working knowledge of it. Psychology, I have long believed, is much more than a scientific field or a collection of findings and principles: It is also an invaluable perspective for understanding ourselves, other people, our relationships, and just about everything else that really matters to most of us most of the time. It is, in short, an eminently useful field, with important practical benefits for anyone wise enough to use it, or at least to adopt it as a personal framework. So it's no exaggeration to state that I strongly believe in the theme of this book: *making psychology part of your life*. Psychology should be part of everyone's education and, ultimately, everyone's life. With it, and the knowledge it provides, we gain insight into virtually every aspect of our experience. Without it, we must struggle along like my friend Sam, constantly puzzled by our own reactions, others' behavior, and many aspects of daily existence.

Because of my strong convictions about the practical as well as the scientific value of psychology, this text is designed to do more than simply present a broad and up-to-date introduction to the field. It seeks to bring the usefulness of psychology sharply into focus, to illustrate its relevance and application to daily life—everyone's daily life. In order to attain this goal, I've incorporated many helpful features, summarized on the following pages.

SPECIAL FEATURES RELATED TO THE BOOK'S MAJOR THEME

Built into every chapter, these features give you a framework for organizing—and retaining—text material.

Chapter Openings

At the beginning of every chapter, you will be engaged by interesting questions about the topics ahead. From there, I lay out a "road map" for the chapter, pointing the way through the contents ahead, helping you to preview the material to come.

Also, in every chapter I use personal experiences wherever appropriate to illustrate the relevance of psychology's principles and findings to what goes on every day. Students have consistently praised this feature.

increas...
inked.

consider an example from my
bers of my own family reacted to a
vent was the news that my grandfather had dev
of cancer. Curiously, the person least affected by the diagno
grandfather himself; he remained calm and collected, despite the impl
for him personally. Why? Because, as he told me, he felt that he had do
part; he had done everything he could to stay healthy. In contrast, my gra
mother took the news badly—but not just because of the discovery of the il
ness. Shortly before the examination in which doctors detected the cancer, she
had given my grandfather a hard time about wasting time and money getting
annual checkups. In particular, she felt that he paid too many visits to his life-
friend Herb, who also happened to be his personal physician. Each time
nt for one of these check-ups, she had complained, Herb would tell him
thing: "Good news, you're the picture of health—see you next time."
rtainty of my grandfather's future, coupled with
hed he gra

Perspectives on Diversity

As our world grows smaller via electronics, communications, and transportation, today's students must understand the different perspectives on diversity and how they evolved. I try to help you understand these issues with integrated diversity sections such as these . . .

Chapter 2	The Biological Basis of Gender Differences
Chapter 4	Culture and the Interpretation of Dreams
Chapter 6	Culture and Memory: Remembering What Fits with Our Cultural Schemas
Chapter 9	The Role of Cultural Factors in Aggression: The Social Context of Violence
Chapter 12	Taking Account of Cultural Factors in Psychological Disorders: Improvements in the DSM-IV

are calm and relaxed, pain may be reduced. We'll explore the influence of other contextual factors—including culture—on the experience of pain in **Perspectives on Diversity** below.

PERSPECTIVES ON DIVERSITY

Culture and the Perception of Pain

I magine the following scene: You are in the midst of an ancient tribal ceremony. Nearly a hundred warriors are seated cross-legged on the ground of a smoke-filled lodge. Their attention is riveted on two persons, an old man and a young one, standing face to face at the center of the room. Only a low, rhythmic drumbeat breaks the silence. Sunlight through the lodge's apex penetrates the smoke, revealing what comes next. Using an eagle's talon, the old man rips the skin above the younger man's chest, then inserts lengths of bone horizontally through each of the wounds. Amazingly, the young man's stoic expression remains unchanged. Loops of rope are then secured around the bones, and the young man is hoisted into the air, where he is allowed to dangle—until the bones tear through the skin or he becomes unconscious.

Sound like a sadistic late-night horror show? It's actually a description of *"swinging to the pole,"* a ceremony practiced by the Lakota Sioux and Cheyenne tribes in which warriors demonstrated their courage and ability to withstand tremendous pain. This ceremony and similar ones in other cultures have led to intriguing questions about the nature of pain (Weisenberg, 1982). Although we commonly view pain as something automatic and universal, large cultural differences exist in the interpretation and expression of pain, as illustrated in the "swinging" scene above. But what is the basis for these differences?

At first glance it is tempting to conclude that cultural differences in *pain threshold*—physical differences—are the cause. After all, many of us could never endure such torture. However, no consistent experimental evidence supports this view (Zatzick & Dimsdale, 1990). Instead, observed cultural differences in the capacity to withstand (or not withstand) pain seem to be perceptual in nature and to reflect the powerful effects of social learning (Morse & Morse, 1988). For example, honor and social standing among the Bariba of West Africa are tied closely to stoicism and the ability to withstand great pain (Sargent, 1984). Thus, both Bariba men and women are expected to suffer pain silently. And as you might expect, their language contains few words for the expression of pain. Additional environmental factors may also play a role in determining our perceptions of pain. For example, some evidence suggests that persons exposed to harsh living or working conditions become more stoical than those who work or live in more comfortable circumstances (Clark & Clark, 1980).

Taken together, the evidence suggests that pain may, in fact, be universal—at least in some respects. Specifically, differences in pain perception seem to result from the powerful effects of social learning, not from physical differences.

Endorphins, the opiatelike chemicals our body produces, discussed in chapter 2, may also interact with the spinal "gate" to lessen sensations of pain (Akil et al., 1984; Millan, 1986). Researchers have found that certain areas of the spinal cord are highly enriched in opiate receptors and endorphin-containing neurons; thus, these substances may close the spinal gate by inhibit-

Endorphins: Opiatelike substances produced by the body.

Making Psychology Part of Your Life

Appearing at the end of each chapter, these sections help you apply the chapter's principles to everyday living. On their own, these pages are an excellent set of reminders about skills you can use daily. Examples include . . .

The Point of It All

These sections explain the impact of psychological findings and their practical applications, helping to answer the question "Why study psychology?"

Key Concept pages

These full-page, graphically appealing sections fully illustrate or summarize difficult concepts to give you a better grasp of chapter material.

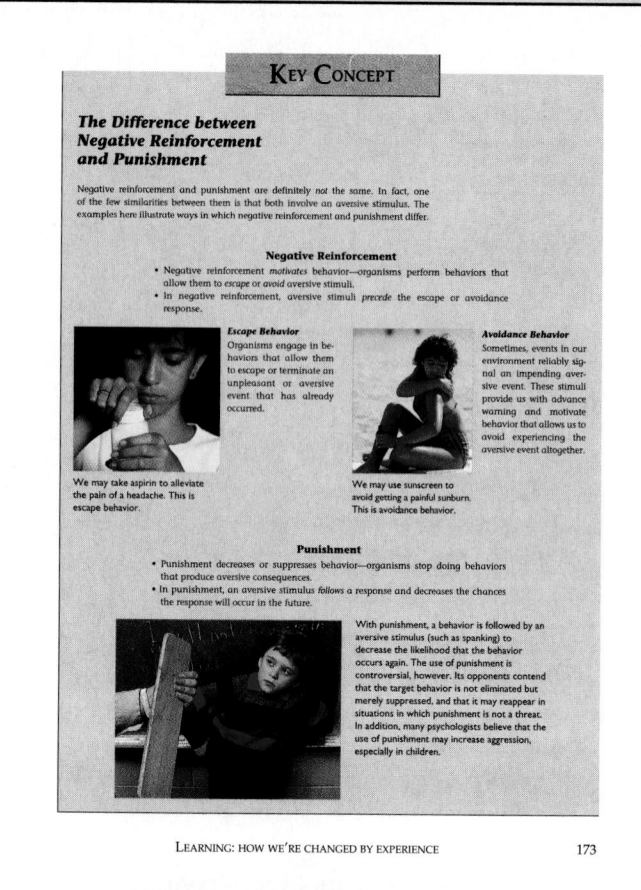

Key Questions

By answering the Key Questions, you will be preparing yourself thoroughly for tests and quizzes. Strategically placed at the end of major sections, they reinforce chunks of information by questioning you on key points.

KEY QUESTIONS

- What is the aim of health psychologists?
- What is behavioral medicine?
- To what can many of today's leading causes of premature death be attributed?

Learning Objective 11.2
Understand the basic nature and causes of stress, including the general adaptation syndrome and the cognitive appraisal process.

Learning Objective 11.3
Describe how stress can affect health and task performance and cause burnout.

Learning Objectives

At the beginning of each major section, learning objectives preview your goals for successfully studying that section.

Teaching Graphs

Certain figures include recognizable "teaching labels" pointing out the key results and helping you understand and interpret research findings.

Summary and Review of Key Questions

This summary reviews the chapter by heading, answers the Key Questions posed throughout the chapter, and lists key terms for study.

Critical Thinking Questions

Exercises in critical thinking are interwoven throughout, both within the text and at the end of each chapter.

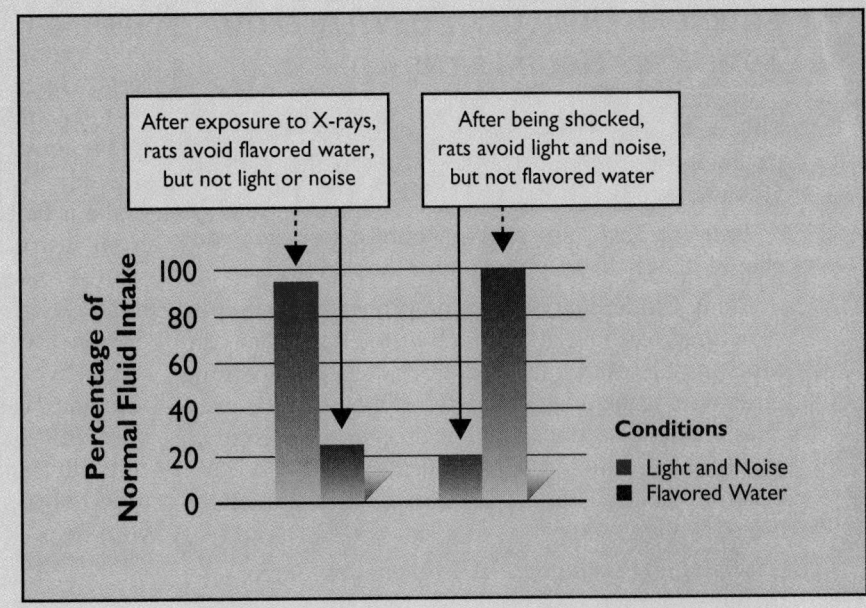

After exposure to X-rays, rats avoid flavored water, but not light or noise

After being shocked, rats avoid light and noise, but not flavored water

Conditions
■ Light and Noise
■ Flavored Water

Note the boxes with explanations of findings and interpretations of data.

SUMMARY AND REVIEW OF KEY QUESTIONS

CLASSICAL CONDITIONING: LEARNING THAT SOME STIMULI SIGNAL OTHERS

• *What is learning?*

Learning is any relatively permanent change in behavior (or behavior potential) produced by experience.

• *What is classical conditioning?*

Classical conditioning is a form of learning in which neutral stimuli (stimuli initially unable to elicit a particular response) come to elicit that response through their association with stimuli that are naturally able to do so.

• *On what factors does acquisition of a classically conditioned response depend?*

Acquisition of a conditioned response is dependent on temporal arrangement of the CS–UCS pairings, intensity of the CS and the UCS relative to other background stimuli, and familiarity of any potentially conditioned stimuli that are present.

• *What is extinction?*

Extinction is the process through which a conditioned stimulus that is no longer paired with an unconditioned stimulus gradually ceases to elicit a conditioned response. However, the conditioned response can be quickly restored through reconditioning.

• *What is the difference between stimulus generalization and stimulus discrimination?*

Stimulus generalization allows us to apply our learning to other situations; stimulus discrimination allows us to differentiate among similar but different stimuli.

• *Is classical conditioning equally easy to establish with all stimuli for all organisms?*

Because of biological constraints on learning that differ among species, types of conditioning readily accomplished by some species are only slowly acquired—or not acquired at all—by others.

• *How are conditioned taste aversions acquired?*

Conditioned taste aversions are typically established when a food or a beverage (conditioned stimulus) is paired with a stimulus that naturally leads to feelings of illness (unconditioned stimulus). Conditioned taste aversions can be established after a single CS–UCS pairing.

• *How do modern views of classical conditioning differ from earlier perspectives?*

Modern views of classical conditioning emphasize the important role of cognitive processes.

• *What is blocking?*

In blocking, conditioning to one stimulus is prevented by previous conditioning to another stimulus.

• *What are flooding and systematic desensitization?*

Flooding and systematic desensitization are procedures used to extinguish fears established through classical conditioning. In flooding, a person is forced to come into contact with fear-eliciting stimuli without an avenue of escape. Cases in which fearful thoughts are too painful to deal with directly are treated by systematic desensitization—a progressive technique designed to replace anxiety with a relaxation response.

• *Do classical conditioning principles have practical applications in solving problems of everyday life?*

Basic principles of classical conditioning have been used to solve a variety of everyday problems, including phobias (learned fears) and unexplained instances of drug overdose.

KEY TERMS: *learning, p. 158; classical conditioning, p. 159; stimulus, p. 159; unconditioned stimulus (UCS), p. 160; unconditioned response (UCR), p. 160; conditioned stimulus (CS), p. 160; conditioned response (CR), p. 160; acquisition, p. 161; delayed conditioning, p. 161; trace conditioning, p. 161; simultaneous conditioning, p. 161; backward conditioning, p. 161; extinction, p. 164; reconditioning, p. 164; spontaneous recovery, p. 164; stimulus generalization, p. 164; stimulus discrimination, p. 164; biological constraints on learning, p. 165; conditioned taste aversion, p. 166; phobias, p. 169; flooding, p. 169*

OPERANT CONDITIONING: LEARNING BASED ON CONSEQUENCES

• *What is operant conditioning?*

In operant conditioning, organisms learn the relationships between certain behaviors and the consequences they produce.

• *Which operant techniques strengthen behavior? Which ones weaken behavior?*

Both positive and negative reinforcement strengthen or increase behavior. In contrast, punishment and omission training are techniques that suppress or weaken behavior.

• *What are examples of primary reinforcers and conditioned reinforcers?*

Primary reinforcers include food, water and sexual pleasure; conditioned reinforcers include money, status, and praise.

• *What is the Premack principle?*

The Premack principle suggests that more preferred activities can be used to reinforce less preferred activities.

• *In what way is shaping useful?*

Shaping is useful for establishing new responses by initially reinforcing successive approximations, which are behaviors that increasingly resemble the desired behavior.

• *What is chaining?*

Chaining is a procedure used to establish a complex sequence or chain of behaviors. The final response in the chain is shaped first; then, working backwards, earlier responses in the chain are reinforced by the opportunity to perform the last response in the chain, which leads to a reward.

• *What are schedules of reinforcement?*

Schedules of reinforcement are rules that determine the occasion on which a response will be reinforced. Schedules of reinforcement can be time-based or event-based, fixed or variable. Each schedule of reinforcement produces a characteristic pattern of responding.

• *When is the use of a continuous reinforcement schedule desirable?*

A continuous reinforcement schedule is useful for establishing new behaviors; partial or intermittent schedules of reinforcement are more powerful in maintaining behavior.

• *What is a discriminative stimulus?*

A discriminative stimulus signals the availability of reinforcement if a specific response is made. When a behavior occurs consistently in the presence of a discriminative stimulus, it is said to be under stimulus control.

• *What evidence supports the involvement of cognitive factors in operant conditioning?*

Studies of learned helplessness and contrast effects support the conclusion that cognitive factors play an important role in operant conditioning.

• *Why is knowledge of operant conditioning important?*

Procedures based on operant conditioning principles can be applied to help solve many problems of everyday life.

KEY TERMS: *operant conditioning, p. 171; reinforcement, p. 171; positive reinforcers, p. 171; Premack principle, p. 171; negative reinforcers, p. 172; punishment, p. 172; omission training, p. 172; shaping, p. 175; chaining, p. 175; schedules of reinforcement, p. 176; continuous reinforcement schedule, p. 177; fixed-interval schedule, p. 177; variable-interval schedule, p. 177; fixed-ratio schedule, p. 177; variable-ratio schedule, p. 177; discriminative stimulus, p. 179; stimulus control, p. 179*

OBSERVATIONAL LEARNING: LEARNING FROM THE BEHAVIOR AND OUTCOMES OF OTHERS

• *What is observational learning?*

Observational learning is the acquisition of new information, concepts, or forms of behavior through exposure to others and the consequences they experience.

• *What factors determine the extent to which we acquire new information through observational learning?*

In order for observational learning to be effective, we must pay attention to those modeling the behavior, remember the modeled speech or action, possess the ability to act on this memory, and have the motivation to do so.

• *In what forms of behavior does observational learning play a role?*

Observational learning plays a role in many types of behavior, including aggression.

• *In what ways can observational learning be used to solve problems of everyday life?*

Observational learning can play an important role in work settings—for example, in training workers to interact more effectively with people from different cultural backgrounds.

KEY TERM: *observational learning, p. 185*

CRITICAL THINKING QUESTIONS

APPRAISAL	At the present time, many psychologists are moving increasingly toward a cognitive view of the learning process. Do you think this movement is appropriate, or is there still a role for operant principles?
CONTROVERSY	Growing evidence suggests that animals do indeed form mental representations of their environments that are analogous to those formed by human beings. Does this mean that animals think? What are your views on this issue? What are the implications of this theory of animal learning?
MAKING PSYCHOLOGY PART OF YOUR LIFE	Knowing something about important principles of learning is very useful to persons who wish to get into shape or lose weight. But these are only two ways in which knowledge of learning can be applied to help people. Can you think of others?

Learning Aids: A Lot of Help from Some Very Good Friends

This text is accompanied by a complete learning package for students. The key parts of this package are described below.

Practice Tests are multiple-choice tests for each chapter that help prepare you for the real thing.

Study Guide Plus offers a comprehensive, carefully structured learning guide to all of the important concepts in this text. Organized around chapter learning objectives, it includes a variety of book-specific exercises, review sections, and exercises to strengthen your critical thinking and application skills. A computerized Study Guide with graphics and animations is also available.

Studying Psychology: A Manual for Success by Robert T. Brown, is a brief how-to manual designed to help you develop the skills needed to succeed in psychology and in other college-level courses. The down-to-earth techniques and ideas in this manual will help you develop effective strategies for studying, listening, learning from lectures, and preparing for exams.

Evaluating Psychological Information: Sharpening Your Critical Thinking Skills, Second Edition, by James Bell, focuses on helping you evaluate research as you build critical thinking skills through step-by-step exercises.

World of Psychology is a brief series of current articles on diversity from the *Washington Post*. Highly interesting, topical, and provocative, these articles will help build critical thinking skills.

Psychology and Culture, edited by Walter Lonner and Roy Malpass, is a broad-based book of readings that serves as an introduction to the role of culture and ethnicity in human behavior. It features original articles by experts in the field.

Sound Guide for Psychology is a unique audio study aid that reinforces text concepts and helps you review, rehearse, and take practice tests.

PsychScience by Syan, Inc., offers computer simulations that put you in the same classic situations as some of the most noted psychologists and their subjects. These include 12 interactive modules for IBM and Macintosh computers. Additional computerized study aids and a CD-ROM are also available.

Some Final Comments . . . and a Request for Help

Friends who know me well often describe me as a "high sensation-seeker," and I think they are right:

I'm not one who likes to sit back, put my feet up, and take a rest. I am always getting involved in new projects. Given this fact, my taking on an "essentials" text isn't at all surprising—a "stand-pat" approach is just not my style. But this text was not written just for the sake of change; rather, it reflects my desire to make a better book to respond to helpful feedback from instructors and students, and—just as important—to make it obvious to readers, no matter what their background or interests, that psychology really does matter! As always, only you, my readers, can tell me whether, and to what extent, I've succeeded in achieving these goals. So please do write, call, or fax me with your comments and suggestions. I'll listen carefully, and the odds are good that they will be reflected in the next edition. Thanks in advance for your help.

Robert A. Baron
303 Lally
Rensselaer Polytechnic Institute
Troy, New York 12180-3590
(518) 276-2864
FAX: (518) 276-8661
E-mail: Baronr@rpi.edu

To My Colleagues

ARE SEMESTERS GETTING SHORTER OR DOES IT JUST SEEM THAT WAY?

If your experience is anything like mine, you've sometimes felt overwhelmed by the amount of material to be covered in introductory psychology. "How will I ever get through all these chapters in a semester?" you may have wondered. I've had precisely that experience while teaching the course in summer sessions. And although I've never offered introductory psychology in a school on the quarter system, I can only imagine what a nightmare that can be. So, one important reason for preparing this book is my recognition of the fact that there are many situations in which a briefer text can come in handy.

A second reason is that I've learned, largely through discussions with many colleagues, that some want to hold reading assignments to a minimum. There are many situations in which this is useful: for example, when dealing with students whose academic preparation is not very strong or with students whose interests clearly do not center on psychology—like the engineering students at my own university. In such cases, shorter reading assignments leave more room for projects and class discussion; and these activities, in turn, are often just what's needed to make the course a more enjoyable experience for these students.

With these thoughts in mind, I've sought to write a book that "covers all the bases"—including all the major content that most psychologists consider part of the core of our field—but at the same time is somewhat shorter than full-length books. The result is a text of about 600 pages—considerably shorter than many other introductory psychology texts. Although length has been reduced, I want to emphasize that this has not been achieved at the cost of essential content. On the contrary, I've attained these reductions primarily by following two strategies: (1) combining topics and chapters and (2) holding nonessential detail to a minimum. Chapter 8, which covers all aspects of human development, is a clear example of the first strategy. Here, I've covered child, adolescent, and adult development in a single chapter instead of in two separate units. Similarly, I've included coverage of intelligence in the chapter on cognition instead of in a chapter of its own. With respect to the second strategy, I've tried to hold nonessential detail to a minimum throughout the book. For example, in

describing specific experiments, I've often focused on the major findings and their implications rather than on details of experimental procedure.

I also want to emphasize, however, that *Essentials of Psychology* is not a "stripped-down version" of a full-length text. On the contrary, it is as broad in scope and as up to date in content as I could make it. Each chapter contains references from 1994 and even 1995; and I've included coverage of many new topics at the cutting edge of our field. A small sample of these topics follows.

CURRENT TOPICS

Evolutionary Perspective

Ethical Issues in the Practice of Psychology

Interpreting Diverse Results: Meta-Analysis and the Search for an Overall Pattern

Multiple (Cognitive) Resource Theory

Warning Labels: When Are They Effective?

New Findings on the Effects of Pleasant Fragrances on Behavior

Potential Benefits of Increased Self-Consciousness

Dreams of Absent-Minded Transgression: Their Role in Quitting Smoking and Reducing Alcohol Consumption

Stimulus Control of Behavior and Protecting the Environment

Operant Conditioning and Seatbelt Use

Memory for the Time When a Past Event Occurred

Repression of Memories of Childhood Sexual Abuse

The Oversight Bias in Reasoning

Artificial Intelligence and Neural Networks

Information Processing and Cognitive Development

Adolescent Invulnerability

Successful Development in High-Risk Environments

Effects of Mood on Information Processing

Gender Differences in Social Behavior and Mate Selection

The Neuroscience Approach to Intelligence

Sensation Seeking

The Potential "Downside" of High Self-Esteem

Stress from Natural and Human-Caused Disasters

Changing Risky Behaviors

DSM-IV

Posttraumatic Stress Disorder

Chronic Mental Illness and the Homeless

Settings for Therapy

Prevention of Psychological Disorders

Tilts in Social Cognition: Automatic Vigilance, Motivated Skepticism

Troubled Relationships: When Love Dies

Effects of Being in a Good Mood on Physicians' Judgments

Antisocial Personality Disorder and Weak Reactions to Negative Stimuli

New Evidence on the Effects of Punishment on Criminal Behavior

Techniques for Enhancing the Accuracy of Eyewitness Testimony

SUPPLEMENTS FOR INSTRUCTORS

Instructor's Resource Manual   The Instructor's Resource Manual provides step-by-step instructions, as well as ready-to-duplicate handouts for over 125 activities and demonstrations. It also includes detailed notes on lecture launchers, Chapter-at-a-Glance tables that show how to organize the many supplementary materials available for each chapter, and an array of additional teaching aids.

Transparencies   Over 140 transparencies from both the text and other sources supplement your teaching. Developed in consultation with instructors who teach large sections, they will help you save time as you introduce and reinforce key chapter principles. An additional set of supplemental transparencies is also available.

Allyn and Bacon Testing Services   The testing resources at instructors' disposal include the following:

- *Test Bank I* contains over 2000 factual, applied, and conceptual multiple-choice questions, each rated for difficulty and referenced by page number.

- *Test Bank II* with 1500 more alternate items.

- *Computerized Test Bank* ESATEST III, the best available state-of-the-art test generation software program, is available free to adopters for both IBM (DOS and Windows) and Macintosh computers.

- *Call-in and FAX Testing* Call in your test request, and the Allyn and Bacon testing center will send you a finished, ready-to-duplicate test within 48 hours or FAX you a test for rush service.

 *Just-in-Time Custom Publishing* gives you the option of building a textbook or supplement to fit your own curriculum. This unique and exciting program allows you to select materials from a database of psychology texts, other published sources, and your own materials to create a custom book from Baron or a supplement for your class. Ask your Allyn and Bacon representative for more details, including class size requirements.

CNN *CNN Video III*, from Allyn and Bacon and Cable News Network, directly correlates video clips with the text material. Just check the CNN listing in the Instructor's Resource Manual and turn on the corresponding segment. All new, these up-to-the-minute, relevant CNN stories are perfect for launching lectures, sparking classroom discussion, or encouraging critical thinking.

Allyn and Bacon Video Library offers an impressive selection of videos from such sources as *Films for the Humanities* and *Annenberg/CPB* for qualified adopters.

Acknowledgments

SOME WORDS OF THANKS

Writing, as my family well knows, is a solitary activity that occurs largely behind closed doors. Converting an author's words into a book, however, requires the help of many persons. In preparing this text, I have been aided by a large number of talented people—too many, in fact, to thank here. However, I do wish to express my appreciation to those whose help has been most valuable.

First and foremost, I offer sincere thanks to my good friend and colleague Michael J. Kalsher, who played the primary role in preparing several chapters. It's no exaggeration to say that his help has been invaluable, and I rank it—and his friendship—as precious commodities, indeed!

I also wish to express my thanks to the many colleagues who read and commented on various portions of the manuscript. Their comments and suggestions were exceptionally constructive and certainly played a key role in the final content and form of this book. These reviewers are:

Professor Norman Austin
Monroe Community College

Professor Janice Beal
Prairie View A&M University

Professor Deborah Best
Wake Forest University

Professor Jerry Bruce
Sam Houston State University

Professor James Calhoun
University of Georgia

Professor William Calhoun
University of Tennessee

Professor Lynda Dogen
North Harris County College

Professor William Dwyer
Memphis State University

Professor Louis Fusilli
Monroe Community College

Professor Grace Galliano
Kennesaw State College

Professor Dashiel Geyen
University of Houston—Downtown

Professor William Gibson
Northern Arizona State University

Professor Alan Glaros
University of Missouri—Kansas City

Professor Wayne Hall
San Jacinto College—Central

Professor Tracy Henley
Mississippi State University

Professor John Hensley
Tulsa Junior College

Professor Charles Hinderliter
University of Pittsburgh

Professor Carol Huntsinger
College of Lake County

Professor Charles Kaiser
College of Charleston

Professor Richard King
UNC—Chapel Hill

Professor Clixie Larson
Utah Valley State College

Professor Charles Levinthal
Hofstra University

Professor Paul Levy
University of Akron

Professor Joseph Lowman
UNC—Chapel Hill

Professor Richard Marrocco
University of Oregon

Professor Cameron Melville
McNeese State University

Professor Ed Merrill
University of Alabama

Professor Gordon Pitz
SIU—Carbondale

Professor Joseph Porter
Virginia Commonwealth University

Professor Adrian Rapp
North Harris County College

Professor Michael Robbins
University of Utah

Professor Jerome Rosenberg
University of Alabama

Professor Peter Rowe
College of Charleston

Professor Richard Serkes
Tulsa Junior College—Metro Campus

Professor Catherine Seta
Wake Forest University

Professor Robert Siegler
Carnegie Mellon University

Professor Mary Helen Spear
Prince George's Community College

Professor Granville Sydnor
San Jacinto College—North

Professor James Thomas
University of Nebraska—Omaha

Professor Ross Thompson
University of Nebraska

Professor John Williford
County College of Morris

In addition, I am indebted to the following colleagues who kindly completed our preliminary survey and thus provided much useful data:

Professor William Barber
Eastern Washington University

Professor Kathleen Gibson
Macomb Community College

Professor Jerry Gilbert
Chemeketa Community College

Professor Randy Gold
Cuesta College

Professor Peter Graham
Pensacola Junior College

Professor David Grilly
Cleveland State University

Professor Frances Hill
University of Montana

Professor Judith Kruppenbacher
Ohlone College

Professor Kathy Lorenzo
Macomb Community College

Professor Peter Maneno
Normandale Community College

Professor Marilyn Milligan
Santa Rosa Junior College

Professor Benjamin Newburg
Kent State University

Professor John Nield
Utah Valley State College

Professor Lee Schrock
Kankakee Community College

Professor Michael Schuller
Fresno City College

Professor Darlene Smith
Cuesta College

Professor Jack Spawn
Citrus College

Professor Alice Tate
Kankakee Community College

I also extend my personal thanks to Susan Badger. Officially, she is my editor, and she certainly fulfills that role with style, grace, and efficiency. In addition, I have no doubt that her talent, expertise, and sound judgment are major "pluses" for this book, Allyn and Bacon, and the entire publishing industry. Working with her is always challenging—and I do like to be challenged!

It's a pleasure to express my appreciation to Beth Brooks, my developmental editor. Beth's intelligence and creativity are matched only by her patience. I deeply appreciate her high level of commitment to this book and gratefully acknowledge her many contributions to it.

Next, I'd like to thank Susan McIntyre, my production editor, for her outstanding help in keeping the project on track and pulling all the loose ends together.

I also extend thanks to Jay Howland, for a careful, intelligent, and thought-provoking job of copy editing. Her questions always keep me on my toes—and help me clarify important points that might otherwise "slip between the cracks."

And speaking of "slipping through the cracks," I want to take this opportunity to offer my heartfelt thanks to Jane Hoover for her outstanding work in coordinating many elements of the production process, for the third edition of *Psychology* as well as for this book. Her help was truly invaluable, and I can only hope that I will be fortunate enough to work with her again in the future.

In addition, I want to thank Sue Gleason for her excellent help with the front matter. I think the new "walkthrough" for students, which she conceptualized, is an effective means of acquainting readers with the special features of this book and will increase the benefits they gain from those features.

Finally, my thanks go to several friends and colleagues for their outstanding work on various ancillaries. The ancillaries are essential to helping students learn—a personal goal throughout my twenty-six years of college teaching—so I'm truly indebted to these people for their help. Mark Garrison has produced what I believe is the most complete and useful set of instructor materials ever published. Cathy Seta, John Seta, and Paul Paulus have prepared an outstanding study guide. Finally, Celia Reaves and Charles Hinderliter have prepared superior test items to accompany the text.

To all these truly excellent people, and to many others, too, I offer my warm personal regards.

PHOTO CREDITS

10, left: Janeart, Ltd./The Image Bank. 10, right: Frank Siteman/Stock • Boston. 14: P. Ward/Stock • Boston. 19: © 1993/Gamma. 20: © David Young-Wolff/PhotoEdit. 26: © 1994 David J. Sams/Texas Inprint. 33: Steve Winter/Black Star. 34: © Louis Bencze/AllStock. 39: © Robert E. Daemmrich/The Image Works. 45: © Biophoto Associates/Science Source. 51: © 1990 Kevin Morris/AllStock. 55: Monkmeyer Press/Grant. 56: Julie Fiez and Steven Petersen. 57: © 1990/Custom Medical Stock Photo. 70: © Robert E. Daemmrich/The Image Works. 72: CNRI/Science Photo Library, Photo Researchers, Inc. 73: Porter/The Image Works. 74: © Charles Gupton/AllStock. 84: Peter Menzel/Stock • Boston. 85: J. L. Weber/Peter Arnold, Inc. 93: PhotoEdit. 97: Alexander Tsiaras/Stock • Boston. 102: © Gerard Vandystadt/Photo Researchers, Inc. 107, top: Robert Harbison. 107, center: © Robert E. Daemmrich/Tony Stone Images, Inc. 107, bottom left: © 1989 Bill Ross/AllStock. 107, bottom right: © J & M Ibbotson/AllStock. 109, top left: © 1991 Tommy L. Thompson/Black Star. 109, top right: © Steve Marts/AllStock. 109, bottom, left and right: Rob Pretzer. 117: © Jim Sully/The Image Works. 128: Migdale/Stock • Boston. 130: © John Coletti. 131: © Tony Stone/Worldwide. 133: Michal Heron/Woodfin Camp & Assoc. 139: © 1985 Christopher Arnesen/AllStock. 145: Steven Underwood Photography. 148: Westenberger/Gamma. 150, top right: M. Ferri/The Stock Market. 150, top left: Allan Tannenbaum/Sygma. 150, bottom left: Monkmeyer Press. 150, bottom right: The Stock Market. 167: © Stan Wayman/Photo Researchers, Inc. 170: Dr. Benjamin Harris. 171: © David Madison 1987. 172: © Tony Freeman/PhotoEdit. 173, top left: © Stephen Frisch/Stock • Boston. 173, top right: © Richard Hutchings/PhotoEdit. 173, bottom: Kevin Horan/Stock • Boston. 175: Nina Leen/Time Warner Inc. 176: © Gerald Davis, Contact Press Images/Woodfin Camp & Assoc. 177: © Robert E. Daemmrich/Tony Stone Worldwide, Ltd. 186: Robert Harbison. 189: © Charles Gupton/AllStock. 196, top: © 1989 Kent Wood/AllStock. 196, middle: Steven Underwood Photography. 196, bottom: © David Young-Wolff/PhotoEdit. 197: © David Young-Wolff/PhotoEdit. 199: © 1989 Kent Wood/AllStock. 203: Brian Smith. 209: © Shahn Kermani/Gamma Liaison. 213, top left: © 1989 Kent Wood/AllStock. 213, top right: Steven Underwood Photography. 213, bottom: © David Young-Wolff/PhotoEdit. 214: Wide World Photos. 223: Stephen Marks. 231, left and right: Bridgeman Art Library. 240, top: © Robert E. Daemmrich Photos/Stock • Boston. 240, middle: Robert Harbison. 240, bottom: © Will & Deni McIntyre/Photo Researchers, Inc. 247: © Ed Kashi 1984. 249: Corroon/Monkmeyer Press. 250: © Peter Pearson/Tony Stone Images, Inc. 253: CNN. 256, top: Jim Pickerell. 256, middle: Laima Druskis/Stock • Boston. 256, bottom: F. Baldwin/Photo Researchers, Inc. 263: Merrim/Monkmeyer Press. 267, top: © Paul Chesley/Tony Stone Worldwide, Ltd. 267, middle: © Robert E. Daemmrich/Stock • Boston. 267, bottom: © Jon Riley/Tony Stone Images, Inc. 271: Mario Ruiz/Picture Group. 272: © Porterfield/Chickering, Photo Researchers, Inc. 273: © 1987 Arnold Zann/Black Star. 276: Robert Harbison. 283, left: Francis Leroy, Biocosmos/Science Photo Library, Photo Researchers. 283, middle: © Lennart Nilsson/Bonniers. 283, right: © Lennart Nilsson/Bonniers. 286: Courtesy of J. Campos, B. Bertenthal, and R. Kermoian. 289: Tom McCarthy/Stock South. 291: © Andy Sacks/Tony Stone Images, Inc. 293: © David Young-Wolff/PhotoEdit. 302: © Martin Rogers/Stock • Boston. 305: Bill Gillette/Stock • Boston. 306: J. Gerard Smith/Monkmeyer Press Photo. 308: Robert Harbison. 309, top right: Robert Harbison. 309, middle right: Robert Harbison. 309, middle left: Robert Harbison. 309, bottom right: © Charles Gupton/The Stock Market. 312: © 1989 Ed Kashi. 314: Robert A Baron. 315: © Ed Kashi. 325: © Natsuko Utsumi/Gamma Liaison. 326: © John Coletti. 335: © Shahn Kermani/Gamma Liaison. 337: Duomo Photography. 338, top right: Stephen Marks. 338, bottom left: K. Reininger/Black Star. 343: © Susan Lapides/Woodfin Camp & Assoc. 345: Underwood Photography. 353: Superstock. 356, top: © Robert E. Daemmrich/TSW-Click/Chicago Ltd. 356, bottom: © Robert E. Daemmrich/Stock • Boston. 358: © Hans Halberstadt/Photo Researchers, Inc. 360: © Bonnie Kamin 1988. 365: © Joel W. Rogers. 372: The Granger Collection, New York. 376: Underwood Photo Archives, SF. 380, left: © Dan Bosler/Tony Stone Images, Inc. 380, right: © Lou Jones 1994. Shooting Star. 381: Shooting Star. 386: Culver Pictures, Inc. 390: Gamma Liaison. 392: Richard Hutchings/Photo Researchers, Inc. 394, middle left: B. Aron/Photo-Edit. 394, middle right: Gamma Liaison. 394, bottom: F. Baldwin/Photo Researchers, Inc. 399: © 1987 Joel W. Rogers. 400: Stephen Marks. 406: © Robert Harbison. 410: AP/Wide World Photos. 412, top: David Madison 1992. 415: Robert Harbison. 429: © Everton/The Image Works. 432: © Ed Kashi 1993. 435: Stephen Marks. 438: Robert Harbison. 440: Elena Dorfman. 446: Baum/Monkmeyer Press. 447: © Chip Clark 1993. 448: Northwind Photo Archives. 449: © Anis Hamdani/Gamma Liaison. 451, upper right: The Granger Collection. 451, lower left: © James Wilson/Woodfin Camp & Assoc. 454: © Michael Newman/PhotoEdit. 457: © Gordon Willitt/Tony Stone Worldwide/Chicago Ltd. 460: The Bridgeman Art Library. 461: Reuters/Bettmann. 465, left: UPI/Bettmann. 465, right: UPI/Bettmann. 468: Russ Kinne/Comstock. 474, upper left: Grunnitus/Monkmeyer Press. 474, lower right: Courtesy of the Genain estate. 478: © M. Antman/The Image Works. 486: Mary Evans/Sigmund Freud Copyrights. 490: © Richard Howard 1986. 492: W. Spunbarg/PhotoEdit. 493: © Catherine Ursillo/Photo Researchers, Inc. 497: © James Wilson/Woodfin Camp & Assoc. 500: Robert E. Daemmrich/Stock • Boston. 501, top: © Mary Evans/Sigmund Freud Copyrights. 501, middle: © Richard Howard 1986. 501, bottom: © Chris Cheadle/Tony Stone Images, Inc. 506: Robert A. Baron. 507: © James Wilson/Woodfin Camp & Assoc. 508: Adam Hart-Davis/Science Photo Library, Photo Researchers, Inc. 512: © Peter Southwick/Stock • Boston. 515: Steven Underwood Photography. 529: © Susan Lapides/Woodfin Camp & Assoc. 531: Robert Harbison. 532: © Peter Vadnai/The Stock Market. 536, right: Shooting Star. 538: © 1991 Lawrence Migdale/Photo Researchers, Inc. 545, top and bottom: Courtesy of the Milgram estate. 547: Robert Harbison. 548, top: Sylvan Grandadam/Photo Researchers, Inc. 548, middle: © David J. Sams/Tony Stone Images, Inc. 548, bottom: © Bill Wisser/Liaison International. 550: © Jan Halaska/Photo Researchers, Inc. 552, left: © John Curtis/Off Shoot. 552, right: © Catherine Karnow/Woodfin Camp & Assoc. 554: SuperStock. 558: © 1993 Rob Badger. 559: Robert Harbison.

Essentials of Psychology

Psychology:

Its Nature, Scope, and Methods

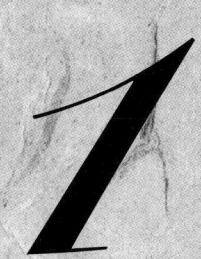

*D*o the things other people do and say ever surprise you? Are you sometimes puzzled by your own thoughts, feelings, or reactions? Do you wonder what you'll be like in five years or ten years? Or think about how you compare with other persons in terms of your intelligence, personality traits, happiness, or psychological adjustment? If so, then welcome to the club: Most people spend a lot of time pondering just such issues.

What most of us do on a part-time basis with respect to our own lives and experiences, psychologists pursue as a full-time career. They seek to obtain scientific information on virtually every imaginable aspect of human behavior—everything from

Ironically, Barnum's and Bailey's respective kids—Sid and Marty—both ran away one night to join corporate America.

OFTEN, WE'RE PUZZLED BY OTHERS' BEHAVIOR

Are you ever surprised by other people's actions? This is one reason why many persons are interested in the field of psychology.
(*Source:* THE FAR SIDE copyright 1993 FAR-WORKS, INC./ Dist. by UNIVERSAL PRESS SYNDICATE. Reprinted with permission. All rights reserved.)

how our senses function and how our memories operate to why we fall in love, what factors or conditions motivate us to work hard, and why we become depressed. In fact, as you can see in Table 1.1, the field of psychology is so broad in scope that I am confident of the following fact: Psychologists are currently studying every question about human behavior you have ever contemplated—and many you have probably not yet considered.

One major goal of this book, therefore, is acquainting you with the knowledge psychologists have attained through the systematic study of human behavior. There are many specialties in psychology, and psychologists in these subfields have focused on different aspects of behavior—for example, on memory, human development, and psychological disorders, to name just three major areas of the field. Reflecting this fact, each chapter will focus on a different aspect of behavior. But since I want to present an *integrated* view of psychology, I'll often indicate how these various aspects of behavior are related, and how ideas and concepts reported in one portion of the book are related to those in other portions.

A second, and equally important, goal stems from my belief that psychology is not only a scientific field of study—it is also an eminently *useful* and *practical* one. In other words, I firmly believe that you can profit greatly from applying to your own life the information presented in this text. In keeping with this view, I will consistently call attention to the practical aspects of psychology's findings, and how, perhaps, you can apply them. Thus, an important theme of this book is **Making Psychology Part of Your Life**, and you'll see this theme reflected in many ways in every chapter.

Before I can turn to the findings of modern psychology and its potential uses, however, it's important to provide you with some basic facts about the nature and scope of the field. One important reason for doing so is suggested by the findings of psychological research on memory and thinking (covered in chapters 6 and 7). This research indicates that having a mental framework in which to place new information makes it easier to understand, remember, and use. In view of these findings, I'll use the rest of this chapter for the purpose of providing you with a "mental scaffold" for studying psychology—a framework that will help you to understand new information as it is presented. This framework will consist of several distinct parts.

TABLE 1.1	**TOPIC/ISSUE**	**CHAPTER**
The Breadth of Psychological Research	Why do some people have so much difficulty regulating their weight?	2
	How can we perform two activities at once—such as driving while talking to a friend?	3
As shown here, psychologists are currently investigating almost every imaginable aspect of human behavior.	What is hypnotism? Is everyone susceptible to it?	4
	Can we learn simply by watching others?	5
	How accurate is the testimony provided by eyewitnesses?	6
	How do children acquire a sense of morality?	8
	Do people become less intelligent as they age?	8
	Can changes in our facial expressions influence our moods?	9
	What are the most important dimensions of personality—the most central traits?	10
	Why are some people so much more resistant to stress than others?	11
	What is schizophrenia? What are its causes?	12
	Does psychoanalysis really work? Or are there more effective kinds of therapy?	13
	Can our attitudes be changed by information of which we are not aware?	14

CHAPTER 1

First, I'll provide a brief summary of psychology's history and offer an overview of its scope and nature today. In this context, I'll call special attention to psychology's growing concern with a multicultural perspective. I'll also answer several key questions about the nature of psychology often asked by students encountering it for the first time (for example, is it really scientific?). Second, I'll say a few words about modern psychologists—who they are and what they do. Third, and perhaps most important, I'll describe the methods used by psychologists in their research. These are the techniques used to gain new insights into various aspects of behavior. At this point, I'll also address some of the ethical issues faced by psychologists in their research and in the practice of their profession. Next, I'll describe the organization of this text, some special features it contains, and how these can help your studying. Finally, I'll consider the question of what you, as an individual, will gain from your first exposure to psychology. Included here will be a discussion of **critical thinking**—the ability to make objective judgments about statements and claims, judgments based on careful reasoning and close scrutiny of available facts. As you'll see throughout this text, critical thinking is an essential ingredient in psychology, and learning to think like a psychologist (at least where questions about behavior are concerned) is one of the most important benefits you will gain from this text and from your first course in this field.

PSYCHOLOGY: *What It Is and How It Developed*

What, exactly, is psychology? As you'll soon see, the definition has changed and evolved during its relatively short history. Today we define **psychology** as *the science of behavior and cognitive processes.* In other words, psychologists are concerned with obtaining scientific information on everything we (and other living organisms) think, feel, and do. They examine observable behavior, cognitive processes, physiological events, social and cultural influences, and hidden and largely unconscious processes. They also look at the complex interactions between all of these different factors in order to understand behavior.

How did the field of psychology come to exist? In movies and television shows, scientists are sometimes represented as magnificent loners—geniuses who work in isolation and develop major breakthroughs out of their own creative spirit. While this sometimes occurs, another pattern is more frequent: Progress flows naturally from what went before. Modern psychology is no exception to this general rule. When it emerged as an independent field of study in the late nineteenth century, it had important roots in several other disciplines, ranging from philosophy on the one hand to biology and physiology on the other.

PHILOSOPHY AND SCIENCE: *The Dual Roots of Modern Psychology*

From philosophy came two important influences: (1) the logical underpinnings of science, or ideas concerning the ways in which we can acquire valid knowledge about the natural world, and (2) ideas concerning the relationship between mind (mental events) and body. With respect to the philosophy of science, two very important ideas were *empiricism,* the view that knowledge can be gathered through careful observation, and *rationalism,* the view that

Learning Objective 1.1
Describe the roots of psychology.

Learning Objective 1.2
Compare and contrast structuralism, functionalism, and behaviorism.

Learning Objective 1.3
Describe the growth and development of psychology in the twentieth century.

Learning Objective 1.4
Compare and contrast the key perspectives within modern psychology.

Critical Thinking: Careful assessment of available evidence in order to evaluate claims and statements in an objective and reasoned manner.

Psychology: The science of behavior and cognitive processes.

Learning Objective 1.5
Discuss the implications of
growing cultural diversity for
psychology.

Learning Objective 1.6
Answer the questions "Is psychology really scientific?" and
"Is psychology merely common
sense?"

knowledge can be gained through logic and careful reasoning. During the eighteenth and early nineteenth centuries these two traditions combined with other lines of philosophical thought to yield the basic ground rules of modern science. Psychology took shape as an independent field of study when a number of scientists with training in such fields as biology, physiology, and medicine concluded that the methods of science could be applied to the understanding of many aspects of behavior.

Turning to the mind-body issue, seventeenth-century philosophers rejected the idea that mind and body are separate (a view known as *dualism*) and suggested, instead, that they interact: Mental events can influence physical ones and physical events can influence mental ones. This view, known as *interactionism*, is a key principle in modern psychology, as you'll see when we consider the complex relationship between feelings and thought in chapter 9.

In short, psychology emerged when (1) ideas in philosophy—especially ideas about how new knowledge can be acquired and about the relationship between mind and body—and (2) progress in several scientific fields combined to create an environment in which the idea of the scientific study of human behavior could emerge.

As is true of all new fields, however, psychology did not spring into existence fully formed; nor was there agreement among its early founders as to just what the new science should be or what it should study. On the contrary, early psychologists disagreed sharply about these issues. Since these disagreements played an important role in shaping the nature of our modern field, I'll touch on them briefly.

PSYCHOLOGY: *Some Early Views*

Perhaps a useful way of illustrating important shifts in how psychologists have defined their field is to imagine a conversation between three major figures in the history of the field. Wilhelm Wundt was the founder of the first psychological laboratory (1879); William James wrote an early influential text, *Principles of Psychology,* and had a lasting impact on the field; and John B. Watson founded an approach that dominated the field until well into the twentieth century. (Please note that this conversation is purely imaginary. There is no indication that these people ever met face to face. If they had, however, they might well have made comments such as these.)

WUNDT: In my opinion, psychology should focus on the study of conscious experience. Our task is that of analyzing sensations, feelings, and images into their most basic parts, just as chemists analyze complex substances. In that way, we'll come to understand the nature of the human mind—what it is. We can accomplish this through introspection—asking individuals to describe what is going on in their own minds as they perform various tasks or have specific experiences.

JAMES: I disagree. The mind isn't static. It is always changing. Also, it is useful—probably the most useful thing we possess. So the key task for psychology should be understanding how the mind functions in everyday life—how it works, and how it helps us adapt to a complex and ever-changing world. To understand the human mind, we have to study how it functions. We need to know how people form habits, how they form their ideas of their own selves, and how they experience emotions. Identifying the basic components of the mind is interesting, but it provides only part of the total picture.

WATSON: You're both all wet. We can't see "mind" or "conscious experience." All we can observe is overt behavior. And people can't report accurately what goes on in their "minds"— whatever those are! The idea of using introspection as a research method to build our new science is ridiculous. Overt behavior is the only thing we can observe or measure scientifically, so that should be the focus of psychology.

As you can readily see, these three individuals held sharply contrasting beliefs about the nature of psychology. Wundt was the chief advocate of **structuralism**: the view that psychology should focus on conscious experience and on the task of analyzing such experience into its basic parts. In contrast, James was a vigorous supporter of **functionalism**: the view that psychology should study the ways in which the ever-changing stream of conscious experience helps us adapt to, and survive in, a complex and challenging world. And Watson was the foremost spokesperson for **behaviorism**: the view that psychology should focus solely on observable, overt activities, ones that can be measured in a scientific manner. Events and processes going on "inside,"such as thoughts, images, feelings, and intentions, have no place in the field.

Which view prevailed? For many years, Watson's behaviorism was dominant—the view that psychology should focus solely on aspects of behavior that can be directly observed and measured. Indeed, for almost sixty years psychology was defined, by and large, as the science of behavior. While this strong emphasis on observable behavior persists, the scope of modern psychology broadened considerably during the 1960s and 1970s, to include many topics Watson and other early behaviorists would *not* have included in the field. What are these topics, and how did psychology evolve into its present, eclectic, form? To see, let's briefly consider the history of psychology during the twentieth century.

PSYCHOLOGY DURING THE TWENTIETH CENTURY: *How It Developed and Grew*

Watson unfurled the banner of behaviorism as the decade of the Roaring Twenties began. Yet much important work had already been completed by psychologists prior to that time. For example, tests designed to measure intelligence and other human characteristics had already been devised and been put to practical use (Binet & Simon, 1905). Sigmund Freud had already published many aspects of his famous theories on human personality and psychological disorders (Freud, 1901, 1915). And much had already been learned about the functioning of our senses (Fechner, 1860) and the operation of human memory (Ebbinghaus, 1913).

In the decades that followed, the pace of progress within psychology accelerated sharply. During the 1930s and 1940s, C. L. Hull, B. F. Skinner, and other behaviorists uncovered much new information about learning and related topics (Hull, 1943; Skinner, 1953). Important work on conformity, leadership, and other aspects of social behavior was performed during the same period (e.g., Lewin, 1947; Sherif, 1935). In the 1950s the scope of psychology expanded greatly, and major advances were made in knowledge about human development (Piaget, 1954), motivation (McClelland et al., 1953), functioning of the human brain (Lashley, Chow, & Semmes, 1951), and many other topics.

The 1960s brought the emergence of many new interests and subfields. One of these is *environmental psychology*—the study of how behavior is affected by the physical world around us. Another is *psychology and law*—a

Structuralism: An early view suggesting that psychology should focus on conscious experience and on the task of analyzing such experience into its basic parts.

Functionalism: An early view of psychology suggesting that psychology should study the ways in which the ever-changing stream of conscious experience helps us adapt to a complex and challenging world.

Behaviorism: The view that psychology should study only observable behavior.

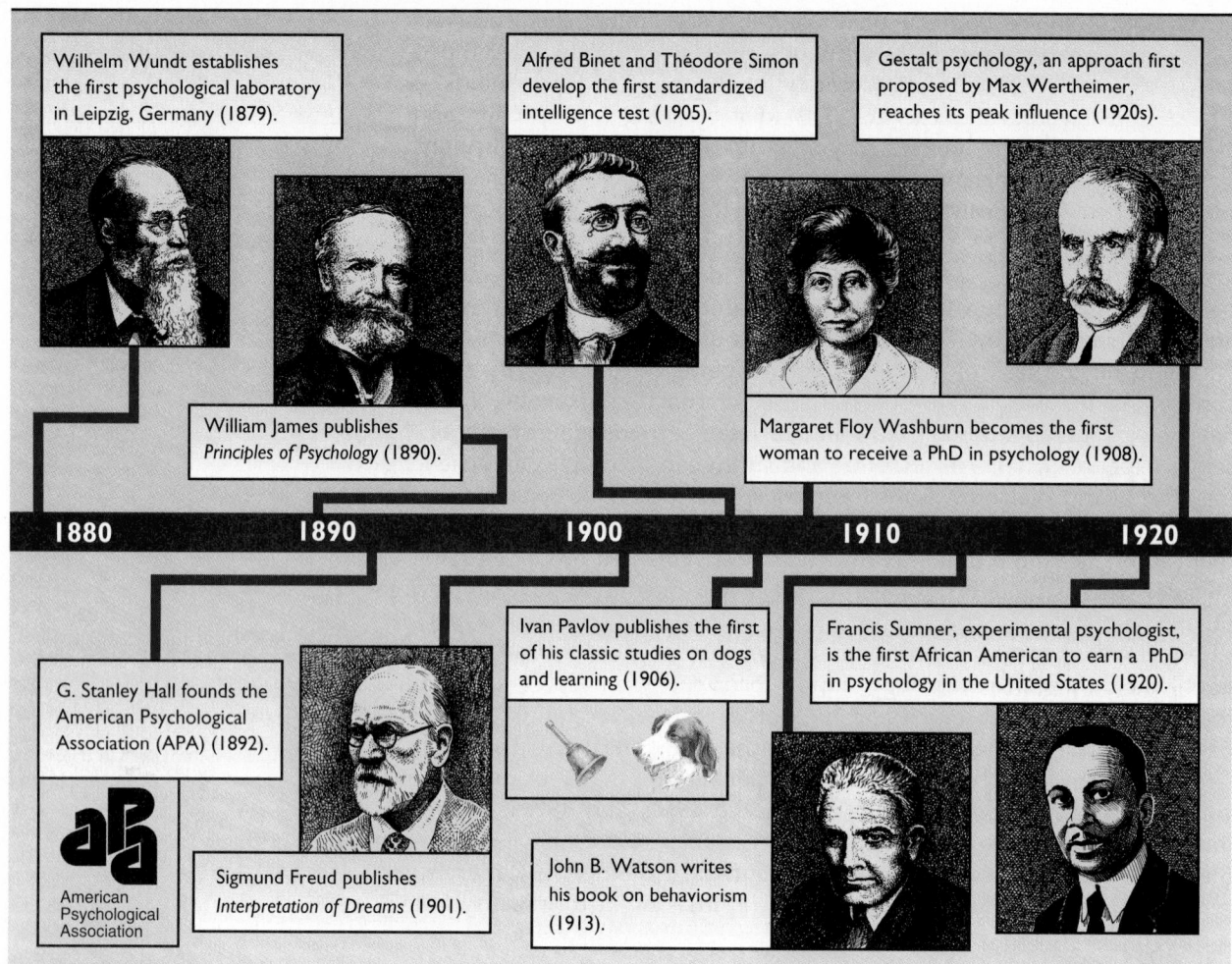

Wilhelm Wundt establishes the first psychological laboratory in Leipzig, Germany (1879).

Alfred Binet and Théodore Simon develop the first standardized intelligence test (1905).

Gestalt psychology, an approach first proposed by Max Wertheimer, reaches its peak influence (1920s).

William James publishes *Principles of Psychology* (1890).

Margaret Floy Washburn becomes the first woman to receive a PhD in psychology (1908).

1880   1890   1900   1910   1920

Ivan Pavlov publishes the first of his classic studies on dogs and learning (1906).

Francis Sumner, experimental psychologist, is the first African American to earn a PhD in psychology in the United States (1920).

G. Stanley Hall founds the American Psychological Association (APA) (1892).

American Psychological Association

Sigmund Freud publishes *Interpretation of Dreams* (1901).

John B. Watson writes his book on behaviorism (1913).

FIGURE 1.1

Milestones in the Development of Modern Psychology

field that focuses on how basic psychological processes (memory, perception, social influence) can, and do, affect the legal process (see chapter 6). Rapid progress also continued in existing areas of research.

During the 1970s and 1980s, psychology, in a sense, came fully into its own. It gained increasing recognition as an active and valuable branch of science. Moreover, its scope expanded even further with the emergence of such new fields and specialties as *adult development* (development and change during the adult years; see chapter 8), *gender differences* (differences between the sexes; see chapters 2 and 7), and *health psychology* (the impact of various psychological factors on physical health; see chapter 11). As a result, psychology has now expanded its scope to study virtually every question about human behavior you can possibly imagine—and then some.

By design, this capsule overview of the history of the field is extremely brief. However, the information I've presented should provide you with at least a rough idea of how the field has grown and developed during the twentieth century (see Figure 1.1).

MODERN PSYCHOLOGY: SOME KEY PERSPECTIVES

Earlier, I defined psychology as the science of behavior and cognitive processes. Psychologists seek to obtain systematic information about all aspects of behavior—with behavior being very broadly defined—through the use of

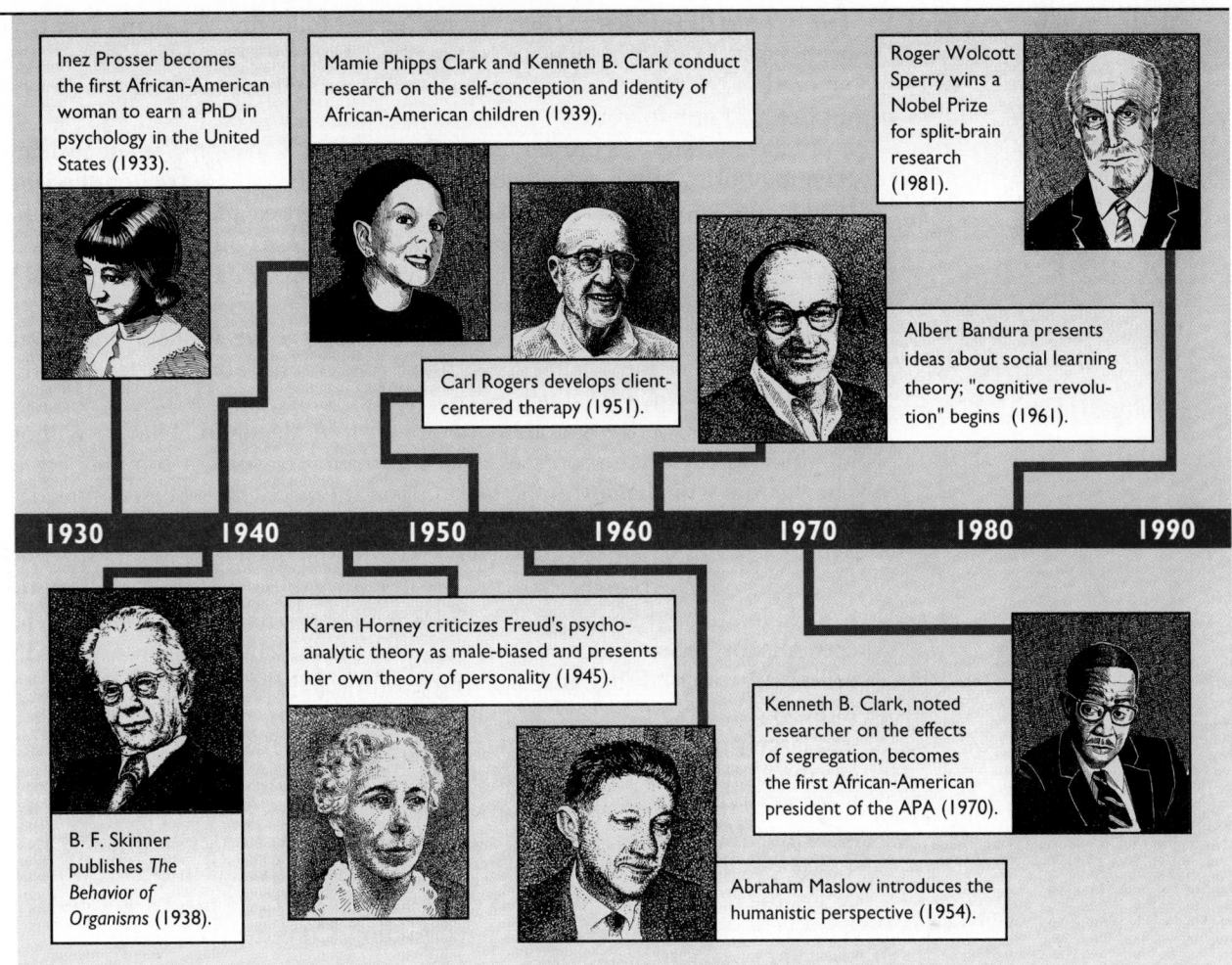

Inez Prosser becomes the first African-American woman to earn a PhD in psychology in the United States (1933).

Mamie Phipps Clark and Kenneth B. Clark conduct research on the self-conception and identity of African-American children (1939).

Roger Wolcott Sperry wins a Nobel Prize for split-brain research (1981).

Carl Rogers develops client-centered therapy (1951).

Albert Bandura presents ideas about social learning theory; "cognitive revolution" begins (1961).

1930   1940   1950   1960   1970   1980   1990

Karen Horney criticizes Freud's psycho-analytic theory as male-biased and presents her own theory of personality (1945).

Kenneth B. Clark, noted researcher on the effects of segregation, becomes the first African-American president of the APA (1970).

B. F. Skinner publishes *The Behavior of Organisms* (1938).

Abraham Maslow introduces the humanistic perspective (1954).

scientific methods. In order to obtain complete and accurate answers to the complex questions with which they grapple (refer back to Table 1.1), psychologists have found it useful to study behavior from several different perspectives. The most important of these are described next.

THE BEHAVIORAL PERSPECTIVE   In an important sense, the behaviorist tradition is still very much alive and well in modern psychology. Indeed, most psychologists agree that only aspects of behavior that can be carefully measured, either directly or indirectly, have a place in a scientific field of psychology. Further, most agree that only concepts that can be related to observable aspects of behavior are useful from the point of view of a science-oriented psychology. For example, consider the question of what motivates people to work hard—to expend effort on their jobs. This is a key question studied by *industrial/organizational psychologists,* who are interested in all aspects of behavior in work settings. As you'll see in chapter 9, we can't observe such *work motivation* directly; it is an internal state that we assume exists inside people and affects their overt behavior—for example, how long and hard they work at a given task. But we *can* observe both the conditions we believe may influence motivation, such as the extent to which good performance is rewarded, and changes in overt behavior that appear to be linked to motivation, such as actual output, number of errors, and so on. In sum, modern psychology still focuses a great deal of attention on overt behavior, so this remains an important perspective within the field.

THE COGNITIVE PERSPECTIVE Consider the following incident. You have been asked to write a letter of recommendation for someone. How do you proceed? Probably, by thinking about this individual and bringing many incidents to mind. From these you try to extract some basic themes (e.g., she is intelligent; she is conscientious). Notice that you don't select just any themes or bring any incidents to mind. Rather, since this is a letter of recommendation, you tend to focus on positive experiences and events—ones that will help you write a good, supportive letter. Because you can only include in the letter information you recall, the workings of your memory are crucial to carrying out this task in the way you (and your friend) desire.

This and countless other events indicate that if we wish to understand people and how they behave, we must pay careful attention to **cognitive processes**: the ways in which people think, remember, decide, and so on. Indeed, many would argue that attempting to understand behavior without attention to cognitive processes is akin to trying to solve a complex jigsaw puzzle from which many of the most important pieces have been removed.

THE PSYCHODYNAMIC PERSPECTIVE Do dreams have any meaning? Why do people often experience slips of the tongue, saying, for example, "I could have killed him!" when they meant to say "I could have kissed him"? What accounts for bizarre forms of behavior often attributed to "psychological disorders" or "mental illness"? According to the **psychodynamic perspective**, these and many other puzzling aspects of behavior stem from continuous, and largely unconscious, struggles among hidden forces deep within our personalities. The most famous advocate of this perspective, of course, was Sigmund Freud, a scholar whose views we'll discuss at several points in this book (chapters 10, 12, and 13). However, even psychologists who disagree strongly with Freud's theories of human personality and mental disorders accept the notion that behavior is often affected by forces, urges, and tendencies largely outside our conscious recognition. Consideration of these, too, is a part of modern psychology.

THE HUMANISTIC PERSPECTIVE Is there such a thing as *free will*? For behaviorists this question is irrelevant, since they contend that behavior is *determined* by a wide range of internal and external factors. Other psychologists, however, believe that such factors do *not* rigidly shape our actions, feelings, or thoughts. Rather, they contend, we can choose how to behave, regardless of the pressures exerted by the environments in which we live. Further, psychologists who adhere to the **humanistic perspective** emphasize the importance of tendencies toward *personal growth*—tendencies in each of us to try to become the best person we can be. Only when external obstacles interfere is the growth process interrupted; in such cases, humanistic psychologists contend, we may experience various psychological disorders stemming from disruption of our normal growth.

While some psychologists find the optimism of the humanistic perspective appealing, many feel that the approach is somewhat vague and difficult to test. However, it has called attention to several key issues, such as the importance of a favorable self-concept and the importance of continued growth and development throughout life. Thus, in these respects humanistic psychology has been influential, and it is certainly part of the rich tapestry of modern psychology.

THE BIOPSYCHOLOGICAL OR NEUROSCIENCE PERSPECTIVE What happens inside your body when you think, listen to music, grow hungry, or become angry? And what takes place when you dream, experience anxiety, become sexually aroused, or simply read a text such as this one? Obviously, *something*

Cognitive Processes: Mental activities involving the acquisition, representation, storage, retrieval, or use of information.

Psychodynamic Perspective: An approach suggesting that many aspects of behavior stem from hidden forces within our personalities.

Humanistic Perspective: A perspective in modern psychology suggesting that human beings have free will and are not simply under the control of various internal and external factors.

CHAPTER 1

must be occurring in all these cases; we are living beings, and every experience we have must be accompanied, at some level, by biological events. Activity in our brains and other parts of the nervous system, hormones released by our glands and the bodily changes these induce—such processes are intimately linked to everything we do, think, feel, or say (Carlson, 1993). Psychologists have long recognized this fact and generally agree that understanding these biological roots is an essential component of the field.

THE EVOLUTIONARY PERSPECTIVE   Does behavior stem primarily from inherited tendencies and related biological factors, or primarily from experience and learning? This question—often described as the *nature-nurture controversy*—has long been of interest to psychologists. Early behaviorists, of course, adopted a strict "nurture" position: They argued that behavior is entirely shaped by experience and the effects of learning. Indeed, in a famous quotation, Watson boasted that he could make any healthy infant into virtually any kind of adult simply by controlling all of its experiences (Watson, 1924, p. 194).

Modern psychologists generally reject such extreme views and adopt a much more balanced position with respect to the nature-nurture controversy. They realize that like all other species on our planet, human beings have an evolutionary history, which equips them with inherited tendencies or dispositions. It would be surprising if such tendencies played little or no role in our behavior. And in fact, growing evidence suggests that inherited dispositions do, indeed, exert important effects. Recognition of this fact has led to the emergence of the field of **evolutionary psychology**—a branch of psychology that studies the adaptive problems humans have faced over the course of evolution, and the behavioral mechanisms that have evolved in response to such environmental pressures (e.g., Nisbett, 1990).

Evidence pointing to the potentially important role of genetic or evolutionary factors in human behavior is provided by several different lines of research. For example, recent research on *mate preference*—the characteristics individuals seek in potential romantic partners—indicates that males and females may differ in some intriguing ways. For example, females tend to place greater emphasis on such characteristics as dominance and status, while males place greater emphasis on youth and physical attractiveness (Kenrick, Neuberg, Zierk, & Krones, 1994). This difference is consistent with an evolutionary perspective suggesting that females invest greater resources in bearing children than males do in fathering them. Thus, with regard to being successful at passing one's genes on to the next generation, it makes sense for females to seek mates who will be able to provide the resources needed for child rearing (mates high in status or dominance). For males, in contrast, it makes sense to seek mates who are young and healthy, and so capable of bearing many offspring. I should emphasize that while findings pointing to such differences are consistent with an evolutionary approach, they do not in any way prove that it is accurate.

Other evidence offering support for the role of genetic factors is provided by the study of identical twins separated early in life. Despite the fact that such persons are raised in sharply contrasting environments, they tend to show an amazing amount of similarity with respect to many aspects of behavior, including personality traits, interests, and even attitudes (e.g., Keller et al., 1992). We'll review additional evidence pointing to the potentially important role of genetic factors in human behavior in later chapters (see chapters 2, 8, 12, and 13).

THE SOCIOCULTURAL PERSPECTIVE   Imagine the following situation. An American real estate agent is asked to find a suitable home for a high-ranking executive of a Japanese company that has just opened a large plant in the

Evolutionary Psychology: A branch of psychology that studies the adaptive problems humans faced over the course of evolution and the behavioral mechanisms that evolved in response to these environmental pressures.

United States. Confidently, she takes the executive and his wife to see a house in the fanciest subdivision in town. As they enter the subdivision, the executive becomes nervous; and as they approach the house, both he and his wife become visibly upset. In fact, they tell the agent that they do not wish to see the house but would prefer to see another one located on the opposite side of town. The real estate agent is puzzled, because this house seems to be precisely what the executive and his wife are seeking. Why do they refuse to consider it? Later she finds out: the executive's boss lives in this subdivision, just down the block. From the Japanese perspective, buying a house in the same location would be viewed as inappropriate; in fact, it could be interpreted as an insult by the higher-ranking executive!

This incident provides one illustration of the fact that culture is a very important determinant of human behavior. In many cases, individuals' perceptions, feelings, and actions are strongly influenced by the social and cultural systems in which they live. In order to fully understand many aspects of behavior, therefore, one must take such factors into account. Psychologists have become increasingly aware of this fact in recent years and, as a result, have adopted an increasingly multicultural perspective on all of the topics that they study (e.g., Smith & Bond, 1993). We'll return to some of the implications of this perspective below. (See Table 1.2 for an overview of these different perspectives.)

> ## KEY QUESTIONS
>
> - What is the definition of modern psychology?
> - How did early psychologists—the structuralists, functionalists, and behaviorists—differ in their ideas about the nature of psychology?
> - What are the key differences among the various perspectives adopted by psychologists—the behavioral, cognitive, psychodynamic, humanistic, biopsychological, evolutionary, and sociocultural perspectives?

PSYCHOLOGY IN A DIVERSE WORLD:
THE MULTICULTURAL PERSPECTIVE

When I was a high school junior, the world was a very different place. One crucial way in which it differed from the world of today involved much lower levels of cultural or ethnic diversity. Perhaps a few statistics will bring the scope of this change into focus:

- In 1960, approximately 90 percent of the people living in the United States were of European descent; in the mid 1990s, this figure is about 80 percent, and is dropping quickly; it is projected that by the year 2050, it will decrease to only 53 percent.
- In just a few years (by 2000), no single group will constitute a majority in California, the most populous state in the United States; similar situations will be reached in several other states (e.g., New York) a few years after that.

PERSPECTIVE	FOCUS/MAJOR INTERESTS
Behavioral	Focuses on overt, observable behavior; concepts are viewed as useful only if they can be related to overt behavior.
Cognitive	Focuses on cognitive processes such as memory, thinking, decision making. Often adopts an information-processing approach.
Psychodynamic	Emphasizes the role of internal forces and conflicts in behavior. Views many actions, and many forms of psychological disorders, as stemming from unconscious impulses or forces.
Humanistic	Emphasizes the importance of tendencies toward personal growth. Assumes that individuals have free will with respect to their own behavior.
Biopsychological	Relates behavior to biological and physiological events and processes, especially those occurring in the nervous system.
Evolutionary	Suggests that behavior is shaped to some extent by inherited tendencies and dispositions. Often focuses on the task of determining the relative importance of genetic factors and experience with respect to specific aspects of behavior.
Sociocultural	Focuses on the impact of cultural factors on various aspects of behavior. Recognizes that behavior is often strongly determined by such factors.

TABLE 1.2

Major Perspectives of Modern Psychology

As indicated here, modern psychology includes many different perspectives or approaches within its boundaries.

- As recently as 1970, more than 98 percent of the people living in such countries as France, Germany, and Italy were native-born; today this figure has dropped to somewhere just over 90 percent and continues to decrease in the face of massive migration from Eastern Europe, Africa, and Asia.

In short, many countries around the world now find themselves confronting much higher levels of cultural and ethnic diversity in their populations than was true in the past. In addition, the shift toward a true world economy in recent decades has led to dramatic increases in business contacts across national boundaries. When this is added to unprecedented levels of foreign travel, it is clear that more people from different cultures are in contact with one another now than at any time in the past.

What are the implications for psychology of this growing cultural diversity? In the view of many psychologists, they are nothing short of profound. For various historical reasons, psychology has, until recently, been primarily a North American and European–based field. Indeed, today, when there are more than 500,000 psychologists worldwide (Sexton & Hogan, 1992), almost one-third of them live and work in the United States. Further, a very large proportion of ongoing research is conducted in North America and Europe (Rosenzweig, 1992). Given these facts, it is not surprising that most of the key figures in psychology's past were Americans or Europeans. And, reflecting the state of the world as well as strong barriers against achievement by women and various minorities, a large proportion of these persons were white males. I should hasten to add that there were notable exceptions to this general rule. Women such as Mary Whiton Calkins made key contributions to the field. Calkins developed the method of paired associates, an important technique for studying memory; in 1905, she became the fourteenth president of the American Psychological Association (APA). And despite the existence of seemingly insurmountable barriers, minorities, too, numbered among the ranks of productive early psychologists. In 1920, Francis Sumner became the first African American to receive a PhD in psychology. Albert Sidney

WOMEN AND MINORITIES IN PSYCHOLOGY'S EARLY DAYS

Despite major barriers that operated against their obtaining higher education, women and minorities made important contributions to psychology in its early decades. Shown here are Mary Whiton Calkins (1863–1930) and Albert Sidney Beckham (1897–1964).

Beckham, another African American, conducted important early studies on intelligence and its relation to success in various occupations. By and large, however, the history of psychology has, until recently, been the history of a field in which the vast majority of active members were both white and male.

As you can probably guess, this situation has changed radically in the past two decades. At present, women are receiving a majority of the new advanced degrees in psychology. And while the representation of minorities among psychologists has not increased in a similar manner, there is at least a growing **multicultural perspective** within the field: growing attention to the concerns of minority groups, as well as increasing interest in all aspects of cultural diversity (e.g., Smith & Bond, 1993). This interest has taken the form of an increased volume of research on the effects of ethnic and cultural factors on many aspects of behavior. Indeed, there is hardly an area of psychology in which research on such issues is not currently being conducted.

In addition, growing concern with multicultural diversity on the part of psychologists has led to the formulation of guidelines for providing psychological services (for example, counseling) to ethnically and culturally diverse populations (American Psychological Association, 1993). These guidelines note that psychologists must recognize cultural diversity and take full account of it in all their activities. For example, psychologists must provide information to clients in forms and languages that those from different ethnic or cultural groups can understand; they must be certain that psychological tests are valid for use with various cultural groups; and they must recognize ethnicity and culture as important factors in the understanding of psychological processes, including psychological disorders. In short, the guidelines insist that practicing psychologists be sensitive to cultural, ethnic, and linguistic differences, and that they build awareness of these differences into all their professional activities.

This growing concern with cultural diversity does not imply that the situation is perfect, however—far from it. Recent evidence indicates that although there has been major change, there is still room for improvement. In one recent study, Gannon and her colleagues (1992) examined almost 5,000 articles published in major psychological journals between 1970 and 1990 to determine whether barriers against women had decreased during that period. Some of their results were highly encouraging. For example, as shown in Figure 1.2, the proportion of articles in which a female was first author increased dramatically during this period. Similarly, the use of sexist language (for example, using "he" to refer to both males and females) dropped to almost zero during these years. However, there was still some indication of sex bias even in 1990: Sex of participants was not specified in some articles, sexist language was used, and findings with one gender were extended to the other in an inappropriate fashion. Approximately 29 percent of the articles published in 1990 showed one or more of these flaws.

Similarly, while there has been increasing research interest in the problems faced by minorities, a recent survey of publications in major psychological journals (Graham, 1992) indicates that the proportion of articles dealing with African Americans peaked in 1972 and decreased substantially after that date. What accounts for this drop? According to Graham, several factors may have played a role, including a reluctance to conduct socially sensitive research (for example, research comparing blacks and whites on various dimensions); the relatively small number of African-American psychologists (African Americans constitute only about 3.4 percent of new PhDs in psychology); and psychologists' growing interest in other topics, such as cognition and the effects of aging. Whatever the reason, it is clear that the volume of research on African Americans and other ethnic or cultural minorities has not kept pace with psychologists' increasing recognition of the importance of

Multicultural Perspective: In modern psychology, a perspective that takes note of the fact that many aspects of behavior are strongly influenced by factors related to culture and ethnic identity.

Chapter 1

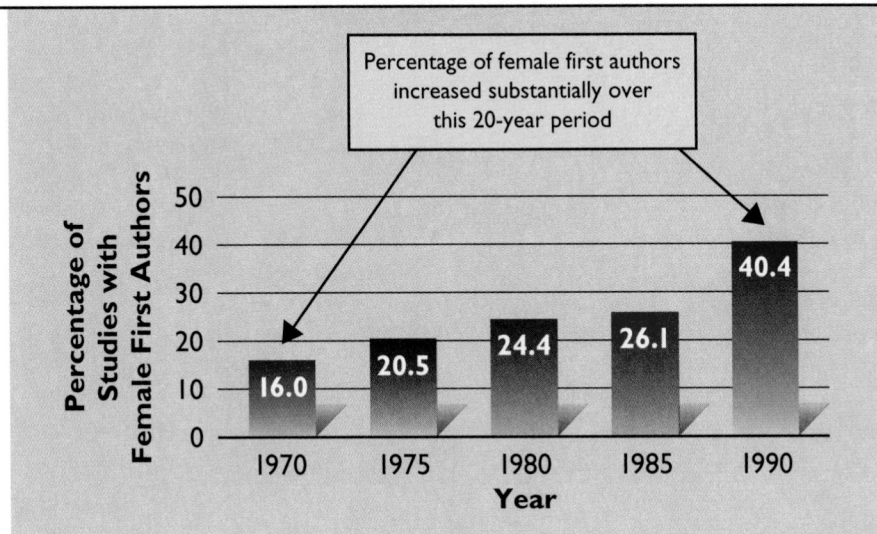

FIGURE 1.2

Women: A Growing Role in Psychology

As shown here, the proportion of articles in major psychological journals authored by women increased substantially between 1970 and 1990.
(*Source:* Based on data from Gannon et al., 1992.)

such differences. Only time will tell whether this situation will change. A change would appear to be well justified, for as noted by Graham (1992, p. 638): "In contemporary society, most of the population is not white and middle class. Neither should the subject populations in the journals of our discipline continue to be so disproportionately defined."

PSYCHOLOGY: *Some Basic Questions*

Definitions, it has often been said, are made to be challenged. Given that fact, we'll now consider some of the questions you may have about my suggestion that psychology be viewed as the science of behavior and cognitive processes.

IS PSYCHOLOGY REALLY SCIENTIFIC? To start at the beginning, let's address a question I have sometimes heard from students in my own classes: Is psychology really scientific? Even today, some people seem to feel that this is not a science in the same sense as chemistry, physics, or biology. Such reservations may stem mainly from a basic misunderstanding about the meaning of the word *science*.

Some people assume that the term *science* refers to specific fields of study, such as chemistry or physics, and that only these are truly scientific in nature. In fact, the word actually refers mainly to a general approach to acquiring knowledge—one involving the use of certain methods plus adherence to several key values or standards. The methods consist primarily of *systematic observation* and direct *experimentation* and will be described in detail in a later section. The standards involve commitment to such goals as objectivity (evaluating information on the basis of its merits rather than according to one's personal preferences), accuracy (gathering information as carefully and precisely as possible), and skepticism (accepting findings as true only after they have been verified over and over again and all inconsistencies have been resolved).

As you can see, these methods and values are largely independent of the content of any specific field. In fact, they can be used to study a wide range of topics. In determining whether a field is or is not scientific, then, the crucial question is this: Does the field make use of scientific methods and accept scientific values? To the extent it does, it may be viewed as scientific in nature.

All psychological researchers, regardless of the techniques they use, are firmly committed to the scientific method and to the values of science.

To the extent it does not, it should be seen as basically nonscientific in its approach. In short, it is the methods and values, not the topics being studied, that are essential.

Given the criteria just described, is psychology really scientific? My answer is a firm *yes*. In their efforts to understand behavior and cognitive processes, psychologists rely heavily on scientific methods and adhere closely to the standards mentioned above. For this reason it is appropriate to define psychology as "the science of behavior and cognitive processes," because in their research psychologists are firmly committed to the scientific method and to the values of science. The topics they seek to study certainly differ from those in older and more traditional fields of science, but the approach they follow is basically the same. And that, as I have already noted, is really the central issue.

IS PSYCHOLOGY MERELY COMMON SENSE?   In a very real sense, everyone is an amateur psychologist. We all think about our own behavior, and that of other persons, on a regular basis. Because we do, we often feel that we already know the answers to many of the questions studied by psychology, and that we can predict the results of psychological research on this basis. Are such impressions correct? In other words, is psychology merely a rehashing of what our common sense and informal experience already tell us? Before you conclude this is so, consider these two points.

First, if you stop and think about it for a moment, you'll quickly realize that common sense isn't quite as useful a guide to human behavior as you might initially assume. Often it yields contradictory answers about important issues. For example, according to common sense, "absence makes the heart grow fonder" (separation strengthens bonds of affection). But common sense also notes, "out of sight, out of mind" (separation weakens bonds of affection). Can both be true? Perhaps, but common sense doesn't explain why or how. As another example, consider these two statements: "birds of a feather flock together" (similar persons are attracted to one another), and "opposites attract" (dissimilar persons are mutually attracted). Again, we are left with contradictory suggestions. This is where a scientific field like psychology comes into its own. Through systematic research, it can help determine whether any of these commonsense suggestions are true. Going further, it can also find out why such effects occur—why, for example, the more similar two persons are, the more they tend to like each other. (As I'll note in chapter 14, this is actually the case—there's very little support for the view that opposites attract; Smeaton, Byrne, & Murnen, 1989.)

Second, before concluding that many of the findings of psychology are merely common sense, you should consider a phenomenon known as the hindsight, or "I-knew-it-all-along," effect. This refers to our tendency to assume, on learning of some event, that we knew it would happen all along and that therefore it is not all that surprising (Mazursky & Ofir, 1990). Why do we tend to do this? Because doing so puts us in a favorable light in our own eyes. After all, if we perceive that new information is not really very new and that, in fact, we knew it (or at least would have predicted it) all along, this confirms the vast scope of our personal wisdom.

In any case, because of the hindsight effect, people often perceive the results of psychological research as something they would have predicted if asked in advance. In fact, however, several studies indicate that when people are asked to predict the results of actual research, they are often dead wrong. So before you decide that the knowledge gathered by psychologists is usually something you really knew all along (or something your grandmother could have told you if you had asked), remember that in such cases, as in many others, hindsight is often a lot better than foresight (Wasserman, Lempert, & Hastie, 1991).

PSYCHOLOGY: Who and What

*H*aving defined the field of psychology and addressed some questions about its basic nature, let's turn to two related topics: who psychologists are and what they actually do.

Learning Objective 1.7
Describe the background and training of psychologists. Describe the specialties that exist within psychology.

WHO: The Background and Training of Psychologists

The terms *psychiatrist* and *psychologist* are quite similar, so it is not surprising that many persons think they mean the same thing. Actually, they refer to two different groups of professionals. Psychiatrists are physicians who, after completing medical studies, specialize in the treatment of mental disorders. In contrast, psychologists receive their training in graduate programs of psychology, where they earn both a master's degree and, in most cases, a PhD. The latter degree usually requires a minimum of four to five years of study. In addition, psychologists who choose to specialize in certain areas of their field, such as the treatment of psychological disorders, must also complete one or more years of practical experience in a hospital, clinic, school, or business. Throughout their graduate education, psychologists focus mainly on the principles and findings of their field. However, most also complete extensive training in statistics, in research methods, and in related fields such as physiology, sociology, or management sciences.

It should be clear, then, that psychologists and psychiatrists receive different kinds of training. So why are the two fields often confused? In part because many psychologists specialize in the diagnosis, study, and treatment of psychological (mental) disorders. As a result, they focus on many of the same problems and perform many of the same activities as psychiatrists. In fact, members of the two fields often work closely together in the same mental health facilities. Since only some psychologists focus on mental disorders, the two fields overlap only partially and remain largely independent.

Now that we've clarified the difference between psychologists and psychiatrists, here are a few facts about psychologists themselves:

1. The most recent available data indicate that there are now more than 120,000 psychologists in the United States alone (Fowler, 1993).

2. Of these, more than 40 percent are female. This represents a marked increase in the proportion of females; as recently as the 1950s only about 10 percent of all psychologists were women (APA, 1993).

3. As a group, psychologists are relatively young. Almost half received their PhD degree between 1970 and 1979. Thus, most psychologists are in their thirties or forties.

4. More than 3,000 doctoral degrees are awarded in psychology each year (Rosenzweig, 1992).

WHAT: Specialties within Psychology

Before going further, stop and answer the following question: What exactly do psychologists do? If you are like most people, you probably said "conduct therapy," "help people with problems," or perhaps "conduct research." In a sense, the first two replies are not inaccurate, for nearly half of all psychologists are *clinical* or *counseling* psychologists, and they do indeed focus on mental problems and disorders. But there are many other specialties within psychology, so in reality psychologists do many different things and investigate a wide range of topics. Here is a brief description of several of psychology's major subfields:

Clinical Psychology: Studies the diagnosis, causes, and treatment of mental disorders. For example, clinical psychologists have recently devised effective forms of treatment for reducing aggression among highly assaultive children (e.g., Bienert & Schneider, 1993).

Counseling Psychology: Assists individuals in dealing with many personal problems that do not involve psychological disorders. For example, counseling psychologists assist individuals in career planning and in developing more effective interpersonal skills.

Development Psychology: Studies how people change physically, cognitively, and socially over the entire life span. For example, developmental psychologists have found that the patterns of attachment children form to their parents can influence the nature of the romantic relationships they form as adults (Vormbrock, 1993).

Educational Psychology: Studies all aspects of the educational process, from techniques of instruction to learning disabilities. For example, educational psychologists are working to develop classroom procedures designed to help minority children in the United States overcome the environmental disadvantages they face.

Cognitive Psychology: Investigates all aspects of cognition—memory, thinking, reasoning, language, decision making, and so on. For example, cognitive psychologists have recently found evidence suggesting that the reason we can't remember events that happen to us before we are about three years old is that we lack a clearly developed self-concept prior to this age (Howe & Courage, 1993).

Industrial/Organizational Psychology: Studies all aspects of behavior in work settings—selection of employees, evaluation of performance, work motivation, leadership. For example, industrial/organizational psychologists have found that work performance often de-

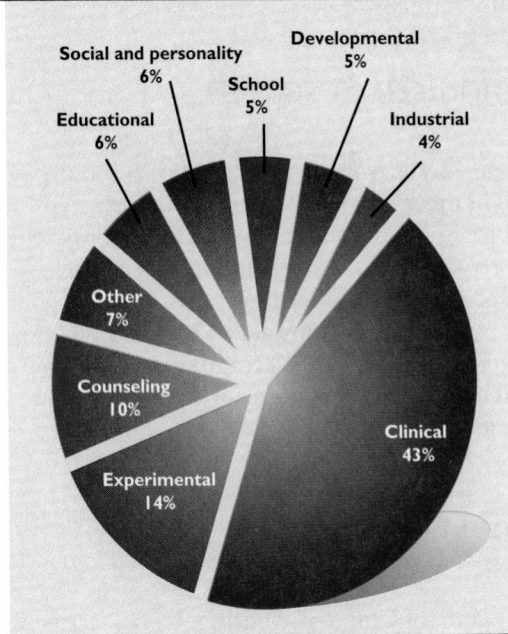

FIGURE 1.3

Subfields of Psychology

Approximate percentages of psychologists working in different subfields or specialties.
(*Source:* Based on membership of divisions of APA given in 1993 *Membership Register.*)

creases sharply when employees feel that they are being treated unfairly—that they are receiving fewer benefits than they deserve. Indeed, professional basketball players who feel underpaid actually score fewer points than those who feel that their salaries are fair (Harder, 1992).

Psychobiology (Physiological Psychology): Investigates the biological bases of behavior—the role of biochemical events within our nervous systems and bodies in everything we do, sense, feel, or think. For example, psychobiologists have recently investigated the possible role in gender differences in behavior of subtle differences in the structure of female and male brains (Law, Pellegrino, & Hunt, 1993).

Social Psychology: Studies all aspects of social behavior and social thought—how we think about and interact with others. For example, social psychologists have recently found that while both women and men use *complaints* to change others' behavior, the two genders use this technique in slightly different ways (Klotz & Alicke, 1993).

Experimental Psychology: Studies all aspects of basic psychological processes such as perception, learning, and motivation. For example, research by experimental psychologists has recently added much to our understanding of attention—the process of directing portions of our information-processing capacity to specific stimuli. This knowledge, in turn, is now being applied to the design of more effective warnings about various hazards (e.g., Duffy, Kalsher, & Wogalter, 1993).

The proportion of all psychologists currently working in each of these fields is shown in Figure 1.3. The exact percentages are not crucial; rather, keep in mind two facts: (1) Psychologists do a number of very different things; and (2) despite the existence of many subfields or specialties, psychology remains a unified field with shared values, goals, and overall methods.

KEY QUESTIONS

• How are psychologists trained?
• What are the major subfields of psychology?

ADDING TO WHAT WE KNOW:
The Process of Psychological Research

So far in this chapter, I have considered some basic questions about psychology and have indicated why, in my view, it can be defined as a scientific field. Now let's turn to what is perhaps the most important question in this chapter: How do psychologists perform the task of adding to our knowledge about behavior and cognitive processes? How do they move beyond common sense in seeking answers to puzzling questions about human behavior? Psychologists use several different techniques for conducting systematic research. This section will describe the most important of these procedures. The next section will examine some of the complex ethical issues these procedures sometimes raise.

NATURALISTIC OBSERVATION: Scientists as Explorers

Almost everyone finds the giant panda of China fascinating. Here, at least in outward appearance, is a teddy bear come to life. For many years zoos throughout the world sought eagerly to add these appealing animals to their collections. Unfortunately, these efforts usually produced disappointing results. The pandas, when finally obtained, seemed to pine away in captivity. Even worse, they adamantly refused to mate, despite the best efforts of the experts and the pandas' keepers. Given the small and declining numbers of pandas present in the wild, these events seemed to spell disaster for a species most people would very much like to preserve. Could anything be done to change this situation? There seemed only one way to find out: observe the pandas in their natural habitat to learn more about their behavior and about what could be done to save them from extinction. In short, this seemed to be a situation in which research should be conducted through **naturalistic observation**—systematic study of behavior in natural settings. Fortunately, efforts along these lines (Schaller, 1986) have added greatly to our knowledge of giant pandas. Scientists have spent months observing the pandas in the mountainous regions of western China where they live and, from such study, have extracted information about pandas' diet and mating habits that may prove useful in assuring their survival.

As this example suggests, naturalistic observation is often used to study animal behavior. However, it is sometimes applied to human beings as well. For example, an ingenious study of this type conducted by Murdoch and Pihl (1988) observed the behavior of male patrons drinking beer or liquor in randomly selected bars. Information on the number of drinks the men consumed and resulting changes in their reactions to others offered intriguing insights into the effects of alcohol on behavior in at least one setting.

I should add that sometimes the data obtained through naturalistic observation are relatively informal, and this can reduce their scientific value. However, the fact that subjects are studied in natural settings and so are likely to act in the ways they normally do is an important advantage that makes this method useful in some contexts.

CASE STUDIES: Generalizing from the Unique

As you already know from your own experience, human beings are unique: Each possesses a distinctive combination of traits, abilities, and characteris-

Naturalistic Observation: A research method in which various aspects of behavior are carefully observed in the settings where such behavior naturally occurs.

tics. Given this fact, is it possible to learn anything about human behavior generally from detailed study of one or perhaps a few persons? Several famous figures in the history of psychology have contended that it is. Thus, they have adopted the **case method,** in which detailed information is gathered on specific individuals. For example, Freud based his entire theory of personality on the case method. Is the case method really useful? In the hands of talented researchers such as Freud, it does seem capable of yielding valuable insights about behavior. Moreover, when the behavior involved is very unusual, the case method can be quite revealing. In chapter 6 you'll see how detailed study of several unique cases has added greatly to our understanding of the biological bases of memory. These cases involve individuals who have experienced specific kinds of damage to the brain and, as a result, show certain kinds of memory deficits. By studying the pattern of such memory losses, psychologists have been able to piece together a more complete picture of how memories are stored in the brain (Graf & Schachter, 1985; Squire, 1991). So, despite its obvious drawbacks—for example, the possibility that researchers' emotional attachments to people with whom they work closely for months or even years can reduce their objectivity—the case method does appear to have its uses. When used with considerable caution, it can prove helpful in the investigation of at least some aspects of behavior.

SURVEYS: *The Science of Self-Report*

You are probably already familiar with another research method often used by psychologists—the **survey method**. This involves asking large numbers of individuals to complete questionnaires designed to yield information on specific aspects of their behavior or attitudes. Such surveys (or polls) are often conducted to measure a wide range of attitudes and behaviors. Examples include surveys on health care reform in the United States or economic reform in Russia, voting preferences prior to elections, consumer reactions to various products, health practices, and public compliance with safety regulations.

Surveys are often repeated over long periods of time in order to track shifts in public opinions or actual behavior. For example, some surveys of job satisfaction—individuals' attitudes toward their jobs—have continued for several decades. And changing patterns of sexual behavior and sexual attitudes have been tracked by the Kinsey Institute since the 1940s.

The survey method offers some very real advantages. Large amounts of information can be gathered with relative ease, and shifts over time can be readily noted. And when conducted carefully, surveys can provide highly accurate predictions with respect to the outcome of elections and other events. However, the disadvantages are also quite apparent. People may fail to respond accurately or truthfully, providing answers that place them in a favorable light rather than ones that reflect their true views. In addition, the results of surveys are useful only if the persons questioned are truly representative of larger groups to whom the findings are to be generalized. For example, imagine that a survey conducted with 10,000 young men and women indicates that more than 90 percent are strongly in favor of allowing total nudity on public beaches. Should you throw away your bathing suit as an unnecessary nuisance? Perhaps. But not if you learn that all 10,000 persons who responded to the survey are subscribers to a magazine devoted solely to the joys of nudism. The fact that they are raises serious questions about the extent to which they are representative of the larger group to whom we wish to generalize—the entire adult population. The moral is clear: Unless the people who respond to a survey are similar to a larger group to whom we wish to extend the results, such generalizations are on very shaky grounds.

THE GIANT PANDA

In recent years, naturalistic observation has been used effectively to gain valuable information about the habits of the giant panda. This knowledge is crucial if pandas are to be saved from extinction.

Case Method: A method of research in which detailed information about individuals is used to develop general principles about behavior.

Survey Method: A research method in which large numbers of people answer questions about aspects of their views or their behavior.

PSYCHOLOGY: ITS NATURE, SCOPE, AND METHODS

THE CORRELATIONAL METHOD: Knowledge through Systematic Observation

Prediction—the ability to forecast future events from present ones—is an important goal of science; psychologists, too, often seek to make predictions. Consider, for instance, how useful it would be if we could predict from current information such future outcomes as a person's success in school or various occupations, effectiveness as a parent, length of life span, or likelihood of developing a serious mental disorder. How can this goal be attained? One answer involves efforts to determine whether various aspects of the world (termed *variables* because they can take different values) are related to one another. That is, we try to determine whether changes in one variable are associated with changes in another so that, for example, as one rises, the other does too. The stronger such relationships (*correlations*), the more successfully one variable can be predicted from the other. (The Appendix provides more information about correlations and how they are computed.)

As you already know from your own experience, some events are indeed closely related to others and so can be used as effective predictors of them. For example, meteorologists (scientists who specialize in the prediction of weather) have found that the greater the number of disturbances on the face of the sun (sunspots), the more unsettled the world's weather will be in the coming months in several different respects. Similarly, it has been observed that the greater the number of hours of violent television shows watched by children, the greater their likelihood of behaving aggressively as teenagers (Eron, 1987).

While these examples involve only two variables, you should bear in mind that in many cases accurate predictions can be obtained only when several factors (and the correlations between them) are taken into account at once. For example, if you wish to predict the likelihood that specific persons will rise to positions of leadership in their careers, you will probably have to consider many different factors, including personal characteristics (for example, their interest in serving as leaders as well as their intelligence, flexibility, and persuasiveness); opportunities for leadership in the fields they plan to enter; the needs of the groups they may possibly lead; the potential leaders' gender; and many other variables as well (Mumford et al., in press). How do psychologists use correlations in their research? How do they search for relationships between variables in order to be able to make accurate predictions about important aspects of behavior? Perhaps the best way of illustrating the nature and value of this research approach—known as the **correlational method**—is through an actual example.

Correlational Method: A research method in which investigators observe two or more variables in order to determine whether changes in one are accompanied by changes in the other.

Hypothesis: In psychology, a prediction about behavior that is to be investigated in a research project.

THE CORRELATIONAL METHOD: AN EXAMPLE
Imagine that a researcher wished to test the following **hypothesis,** an as yet untested prediction about some aspect of behavior: The faster people speak, the more successful they are at persuasion. In other words, the researcher wants to find out whether fast talkers are indeed more convincing than slow ones. How could the investigator proceed? While there are many possibilities, one would be to measure the speed of speech of many would-be persuaders in a wide range of contexts—politics, sales, and so on. In each of these contexts, the researcher would also obtain some measure of the success of the persuaders—for example, the percentage of votes each candidate receives, the amount of merchandise each salesperson sells, and so on. If fast talkers are really more persuasive than slower ones, results might indicate that these two variables (speed and persuasiveness) are positively correlated: The faster candidates and salespersons speak, the greater their success. The researcher would prob-

CHAPTER 1

OBSERVED RELATIONSHIP	POSSIBLE UNDERLYING CAUSE
(1) The more people weigh, the higher their salaries.	_____ _____
(2) The greater the degree of crowding in cities, the higher the crime rate.	_____ _____
(3) The colder the winter, the greater the number of births the next fall.	_____ _____

Some Correlations That Don't Imply Causation

All of the relationships listed here have actually been observed. However, none indicates that the two factors involved are causally linked. Can you determine why? (Answers are given below the table.)

Possible answers to Table 1.3: (1) Weight and earnings both increase with age and experience. (2) Crowding and crime are both related to poverty. (3) Cold weather makes people stay indoors and increase their tendency to cuddle—with predictable results.

ably also use appropriate statistical procedures (see the Appendix) to measure the strength of this relationship; the stronger the correlation, the more accurately each variable can be predicted from the other. Correlations can range from –1.00 to +1.00; the greater their departure from 0.00, the stronger the relationship between the variables being considered. So if the researcher found a correlation of +0.80 between speed of speech and success in influencing others, this would indicate a stronger link between these two variables than a correlation of +0.30. Similarly, a correlation of –0.60 would indicate a stronger relationship than one of –0.20. In this case, however, the negative sign indicates that the faster people speak, the *less* successful they are at persuasion.

The correlational method offers several major advantages. For one thing, it can be used to study behavior in many real-life settings. For another, it is often highly efficient and can yield a large amount of interesting data in a short time. Moreover, it can be extended to include many different variables at once. Thus, in the simple study described above, information on the physical attractiveness, age, height, and gender of the political candidates, salespersons, and so on might also be obtained. Then these variables could also be related to success in persuasion, to determine if they too influence this outcome. (See the Appendix for further discussion of such procedures.)

Unfortunately, however, the correlational method suffers from one major drawback that lessens its appeal, at least to a degree: *The findings it yields are not conclusive with respect to cause-and-effect relationships.* That is, the fact that two variables are correlated (even highly correlated) does not guarantee that there is a *causal* link between them—that changes in the first cause changes in the second. Rather, in many cases, the fact that two variables tend to rise or fall together simply reflects the fact that both are caused by a third variable.

For example, suppose that our researcher finds a positive correlation between the speed at which politicians talk and the percentage of votes they receive in elections. Does this mean that speed of speech causes voters to prefer certain candidates? Perhaps. But it may also be that fast-talking candidates know more about the issues than slower-talking ones. If this is the case, then the relationship between speed of speech and the outcome of elections is somewhat misleading. Both speed of speech and success at winning elections are actually related to a third factor—knowledge of the issues. Perhaps this key point can be clarified by a few additional examples of correlations that do not indicate causation. These are listed in Table 1.3. Can you identify the third factors that may underlie each relationship shown in the table?

> ### KEY QUESTIONS
>
> • What is the basic nature of naturalistic observation, the case method, and the survey approach?
>
> • What is the basic nature of the correlational method of research?
>
> • Why is it true that correlations do not prove causation?

EXPERIMENTATION: *Knowledge through Systematic Intervention*

While psychologists use all of the research methods described so far, they often prefer the approach we will now consider: **experimentation** (or *the experimental method*). This involves efforts to determine if variables are related to one another by systematically changing one (or more) and observing the effects of such variations on the other (or others). There are several reasons why psychologists prefer this basic approach, but perhaps the most important is this: In contrast to the other methods we have considered, experimentation yields relatively clear-cut evidence on causality. If systematic variations in one factor produce changes in another (and if additional conditions we'll soon consider are also met), we can conclude with reasonable certainty that there is a causal link between the factors: that changes in one caused changes in the other. Establishing such causality is extremely valuable from the perspective of one major goal of science: *explanation*. Briefly, scientists do not wish merely to describe the world around them and the relationships between different variables or factors in it. They also wish to be able to explain why such relationships exist—why, for example, people find some gauges easier to read than others, why individuals with certain personality traits are more likely than others to suffer heart attacks, why some people gain weight readily while others do not. Experimentation, because it often yields information useful in answering such questions, is frequently the method of choice in psychology. But bear in mind that there are no hard-and-fast rules in this regard. Rather, most psychologists select the research technique that seems most suited to the topic they wish to study and the resources available to them.

EXPERIMENTATION: ITS BASIC NATURE   Reduced to its bare essentials, the experimental method involves two basic steps: (1) The presence or strength of some variable believed to affect behavior is systematically altered, and (2) the effects of such alterations (if any) are measured. The logic behind these steps is as follows: If the factor varied does indeed influence behavior or cognitive processes, then individuals exposed to different levels or amounts of that factor should differ in terms of their behavior. Thus, exposure to a small amount of the variable should result in one level of behavior, exposure to a larger amount should result in a different level, and so on.

The factor systematically varied by the researcher is termed the **independent variable**, while the aspect of behavior or cognitive processes studied is termed the **dependent variable**. In a simple experiment, then, different groups of participants are exposed to contrasting levels of the independent variable (such as low, moderate, and high). The participants' behavior is then carefully measured to determine whether it does in fact vary with different levels or amount of the independent variable. If it does—and if two other conditions described below are met—the researcher can tentatively conclude that the independent variable does indeed cause changes in the aspect of behavior being studied.

To illustrate the basic nature of experimentation in psychological research, let's return to the question we considered earlier: Are fast talkers more persuasive than slow ones? A researcher who decides to employ the experimental method to study this topic might begin with the hypothesis that the faster people talk (at least up to a point), the more persuasive they are. In such research, the independent variable would be the speed at which would-be persuaders speak, and the dependent variable would be some measure of the persuaders' success in influencing their audiences.

There are many different ways of testing the hypothesis that fast talkers are more persuasive than slow ones, but for the sake of illustration, let's

Experimentation: A research method where investigators systematically alter one or more variables in order to determine whether such changes will influence some aspect of behavior.

Independent Variable: The variable that is systematically altered in an experiment.

Dependent Variable: The aspect of behavior that is measured in an experiment.

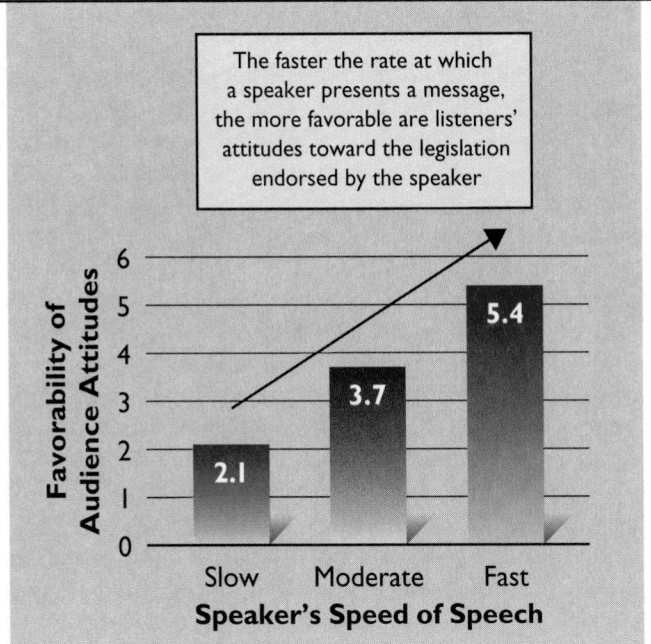

The faster the rate at which a speaker presents a message, the more favorable are listeners' attitudes toward the legislation endorsed by the speaker

FIGURE **1.4**

Results of a Simple Experiment

The results shown here indicate that the faster would-be persuaders speak, the greater their impact on the attitudes of an audience.

assume that the researcher arranges to have an assistant deliver a speech designed to alter listeners' views on a specific issue: legislation to limit the use of chemicals known to deplete the earth's ozone layer. The speaker would then present this speech to different groups of participants at contrasting speeds. For example, for participants in one group, the speech would be presented at a slow pace (150 words per minute); for those in another group, it would be presented at a moderate pace (170 words per minute); and for those in the third group, it would be presented at a fast pace (190 words per minute). Then some measure of audience members' attitudes toward the legislation would be obtained. If rate of speech does affect persuasion, then results something like those shown in Figure 1.4 might be obtained. As this figure shows, the faster the persuader speaks, the more favorable are the audience members' attitudes toward the pending legislation. We must assume, by the way, that individuals in the three groups start out with similar attitudes toward the legislation; if they do not, serious complications can arise in the interpretation of any results that are obtained. (Actually, several studies have been conducted to investigate the relationship between speed of speech and persuasion. I'll mention the results of these studies below.)

EXPERIMENTATION: TWO REQUIREMENTS FOR ITS SUCCESS   Earlier, we saw that before we can conclude that an independent variable has caused some change in behavior, two conditions must be met. The first condition involves **random assignment of participants to experimental conditions**. According to the principle of random assignment, all participants in an experiment must have an equal chance of being exposed to each level of the independent variable. The reason for this rule is simple: If participants are *not* randomly assigned to each group, it may later be impossible to determine whether differences in their behavior stem from differences they brought with them, from the impact of the independent variable, or from both. For instance, continuing with our study of speed of speech and persuasion, imagine that participants in the study are drawn from two different groups: first-year law students and a group of high school dropouts enrolled in a special course designed to provide them with basic vocational skills. Now imagine that because of differ-

Random Assignment of Participants to Experimental Conditions: Assuring that all research participants have an equal chance of being assigned to each of the experimental conditions.

ences in the two groups' schedules, most of the participants exposed to the slow talker are law students, while most of the people exposed to the fast talker are high school dropouts. Suppose that results indicate that participants exposed to the fast talker show much more agreement with the views expressed than participants exposed to the slow talker. What can we conclude? Not much, because it is entirely possible that the difference stems from the different mixes of participants in the two experimental conditions. In the slow-talker condition, 85 percent of the participants are law students and 15 percent are high school dropouts, while in the fast-talker condition, the opposite is true. Since law students may be somewhat harder to persuade than high school dropouts, we can't really tell why these results occurred. Did they derive from differences in the persuaders' rate of speech? From different proportions of the two groups of participants in each condition? Both factors? It's impossible to tell. To avoid such problems, it is crucial that all subjects have an equal chance of being assigned to each experimental group.

The second condition referred to above may be stated as follows: Insofar as possible, all other factors that might also affect participants' behavior, aside from the independent variable, must be held constant. To see why this is so, consider what will happen if, in the study on speed of speech and persuasion, different speakers are used in the two conditions. Further, imagine that one of these speakers—the fast talker—has a pleasant, cultivated voice, while the slow talker has an irritating voice and a thick, unpleasant accent. Now assume that participants express greater agreement with the fast talker than the slow one. What is the cause of this result? The difference in the speakers' speed of speech? Differences in the pleasantness of their voices? Both factors? Obviously, it's impossible to tell. In this situation the independent variable of interest (speed of speech) is *confounded* with another variable—pleasantness of the speaker's voice—that is not a planned part of the research. That is, another factor changes as the independent variable changes, so we can't tell whether any effects observed are produced by the independent variable or this other factor. When such confounding occurs, the findings of an experiment are largely uninterpretable. (See Figure 1.5.)

EXPERIMENTER EFFECTS AND DEMAND CHARACTERISTICS: HOW TO GET POSITIVE RESULTS WITHOUT REALLY TRYING Before concluding this discussion of experimentation, we should consider two additional pitfalls lying in wait for careless researchers. The first of these is the risk of **experimenter effects**—the fact that sometimes researchers can influence the behavior of subjects without intending to do so. Such effects can occur in several ways. First, researchers usually have expectations about how participants in their studies may behave. These expectations, in turn, may influence their behavior toward participants and so alter the results obtained. For example, if an experimenter expects fast talkers to be more persuasive than slow ones, she may nod or smile at participants when they express agreement with the speaker's views in the fast-speech condition, but show disapproval when they express agreement in the slow-speech condition. The result: Her reactions may influence participants and lead to greater agreement with the speaker's views in the fast-speech than in the slow-speech condition.

A second potential snare for unwary researchers is the fact that experimenters can sometimes communicate the hypothesis behind the study to participants. Once they do, participants' behavior may be affected even if the researchers have no direct contact with them and cannot provide subtle cues of approval and disapproval such as those described above. The effects of such communication are known as **demand characteristics**, since they place subtle demands on participants to "help" the researcher by confirming his or her hypothesis. Research findings indicate that experimenter effects and

Experimenter Effects: Unintentional influence exerted by researchers on research participants.

Demand Characteristics: Implicit pressure on research participants to act in ways consistent with a researcher's expectations.

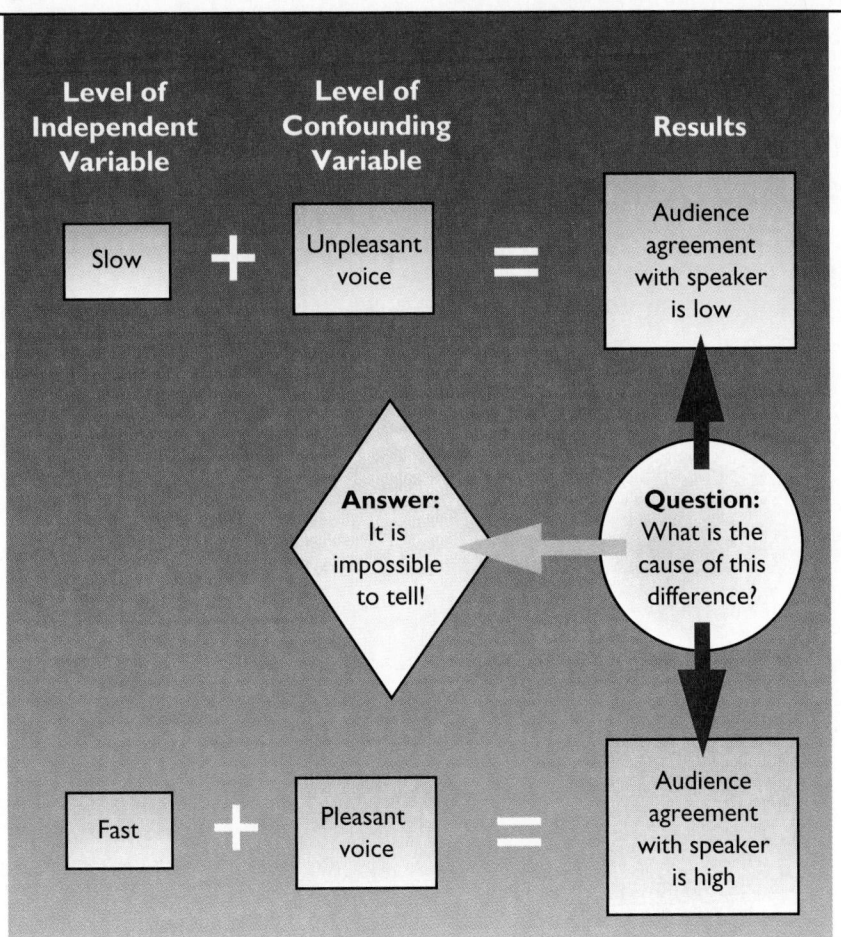

FIGURE **1.5**

Confounding of Variables: A Fatal Flaw in Experimentation

In an imaginary study designed to investigate the effects of speed of speech on persuasion, the person who speaks quickly has a pleasant, cultivated voice, while the person who speaks slowly has an irritating voice and unpleasant accent. As a result, two variables—speed of speech and pleasantness of speech—are *confounded*. Because of this fact, it is impossible to interpret the results.

demand characteristics can both exert powerful effects on participants' behavior. Thus, it is crucial that these effects be minimized in all psychological research. One way of doing this is through a **double-blind procedure**. Here, persons who have contact with participants (often research assistants) are unfamiliar with the hypothesis under investigation and don't know the condition to which participants have been assigned. Under these conditions, they can't readily communicate the hypothesis being studied and can't have clear expectations about how a given participant "should" behave. Another technique for avoiding experimenter effects and demand characteristics is to minimize direct contact between participants and the researcher. This can be accomplished through the use of computerized procedures, in which subjects receive instructions and perform experimental tasks by means of a computer terminal. Through these and related procedures, the impact of several potential pitfalls can be reduced and the validity or accuracy of experimental findings enhanced. For an overview of the correlational and experimental methods of research, please see the **Key Concept** on page 26.

INTERPRETING RESEARCH RESULTS:
Statistics as a Tool

Once an experiment has been completed, researchers must turn to the next crucial task: interpreting the results. Suppose that in the study we have been

Double-Blind Procedure:
Procedure in which neither the persons collecting data nor research participants have knowledge of the experimental conditions to which they have been assigned.

Correlational and Experimental Research Methods

Question: Do people act more aggressively when the temperature goes up?

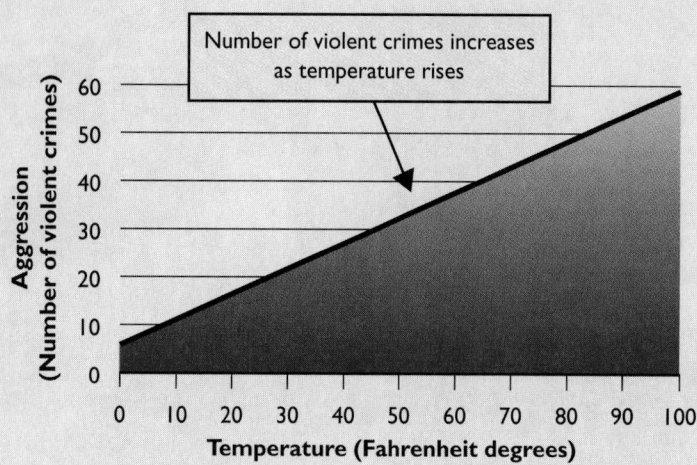

Number of violent crimes increases as temperature rises

Correlational Method

- Records of temperature are obtained for each day for two years in several large cities.
- The number of violent crimes committed on these days is also recorded.
- These two sets of numbers are correlated.

Conclusion: As temperature rises, aggression increases.

Experimental Method

- Participants are exposed to comfortably cool (72°F) or very hot (90°F) conditions.
- After thirty minutes of exposure to one of these conditions, members of each group are given an opportunity to aggress against a stranger by evaluating his or her work. (Poor ratings will prevent this person from being reappointed to a position as a research assistant.)
- Mean ratings assigned to the stranger's work are obtained for the two experimental groups and compared.

Conclusion: Exposure to uncomfortably high temperatures increases aggression. Since temperature was systematically varied, there is some evidence of a causal link between heat and aggression.

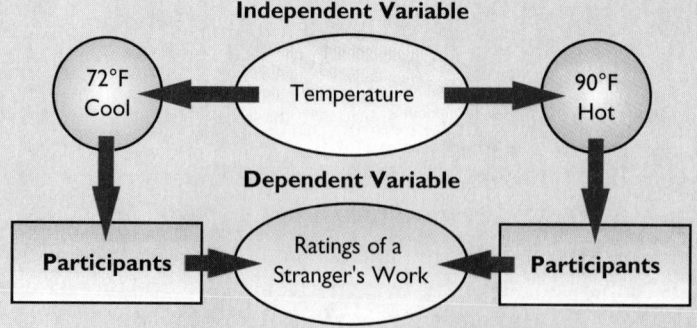

Independent Variable

72°F Cool ← Temperature → 90°F Hot

Dependent Variable

Participants → Ratings of a Stranger's Work ← Participants

Findings:
Persons exposed to higher temperatures gave lower ratings (acted more aggressively)

discussing throughout this section, results like those in Figure 1.4 are obtained: The faster speakers talk, the more successful they are at persuading listeners. How much confidence can we place in these results? In other words, are the differences observed real ones—ones that would be observed again if the study were repeated with other participants? This is a crucial question, for unless we can be confident that the differences are real, the results really tell us little about human behavior.

One way of dealing with this question, of course, would be to repeat the study over and over again. This would do the trick, but, as you can well imagine, it would be costly in terms of time and effort. Another approach is to use **inferential statistics**. This is a special form of mathematics designed, in part, to evaluate the likelihood that a given pattern of findings, such as differences between experimental groups, is due to chance alone. Thus, to determine whether the findings of a study are indeed real (are unlikely to have occurred by chance alone), psychologists perform appropriate statistical analyses on the data they collect. If these analyses suggest that the likelihood of obtaining the observed findings by chance is low (usually, fewer than five times in a hundred), the results are described as being *significant*. Only then are they interpreted as being of value in the task of understanding some aspect of behavior.

Please note: The likelihood that a given pattern of findings is a chance event is never zero. This probability can be very low—for example, one chance in ten thousand or even one chance in a million—but there is always some possibility, however small, that a pattern occurred by chance. For this reason, actual replication of results by different researchers in different laboratories is usually necessary before the findings of any research project can be accepted with confidence, even if statistical analysis indicates that the findings are unlikely to be a chance event. Still, inferential statistics is a valuable tool of tremendous help to psychologists in evaluating research findings.

META-ANALYSIS AND THE SEARCH FOR AN OVERALL PATTERN Before concluding this discussion, I should mention yet one more complexity in the process. Because the results of a single experiment are rarely sufficiently clear to warrant strong conclusions, most hypotheses are subjected to independent tests by many different researchers. When they are, the results are not always consistent. Some studies may find support for a given hypothesis while others do not. For example, imagine that over the years fifty different studies are conducted to examine the effects of speed of speech on persuasion. Of these, thirty-five yield results supporting the hypothesis that the faster people talk, the greater their success in influencing others. However, ten report exactly the opposite findings, and five report no difference in persuasiveness between slow and fast talkers. How can we reach any firm conclusions in this situation? In other words, how can we combine the results obtained by all these studies to determine whether speed of speech really does or does not influence persuasion? In recent years a very powerful technique for doing precisely this has been developed. This technique is known as **meta-analysis** (e.g., Dillard, 1991; Eagly, Makhijani, & Klonsky, 1992) and has gained increasing acceptance among researchers in all areas of psychology. The complex statistical procedures of meta-analysis are far beyond the scope of this discussion. In essence, however, these procedures combine the results of many different studies in order to estimate both the direction and the magnitude of the effects of independent variables of interest. For example, a meta-analysis on the results of the fifty studies on speed of speech and persuasion would combine the findings of all of these investigations in order to determine whether, across all fifty, speed has any effect on persuasion. Meta-analysis is especially useful because it helps to counteract the all-too-human

Inferential Statistics: Statistical procedures that provide information on the probability that an observed event is due to chance.

Meta-Analysis: Statistical procedures for combining the results of many studies in order to determine whether their findings provide support for specific hypotheses.

tendency to be strongly influenced by results that are especially interesting or well presented. It utilizes statistical formulas that are free from such influences to combine the results of all available studies. Incidentally, meta-analysis of the many studies that have investigated the effect of speed of speech on persuasion indicate that fast talkers do indeed appear to be more persuasive than slow ones (Smith & Shaffer, 1991).

In sum, because of their commitment to scientific skepticism, psychologists are reluctant to accept the results of any research project—even their own—as valid. Only when the data have been subjected to appropriate mathematical (statistical) analysis and significant effects have been obtained do psychologists view experimental findings as useful in understanding various aspects of behavior. And only when the results of many different studies, combined through meta-analysis, point to specific conclusions, are these accepted as valid and informative.

THE ROLE OF THEORY IN PSYCHOLOGICAL RESEARCH

Now that we have considered basic aspects of the research process in psychology, we can turn to a question students often ask: Just how do psychologists come up with the ideas for all those studies anyway? As you can probably guess, there is no simple answer, for several factors play a role. Some research projects are suggested by informal observation of the world around us. Psychologists take note of some puzzling aspect of behavior or cognition and plan investigations to increase their understanding of them. At other times the idea for a research project is suggested by the findings of earlier studies. Successful experiments do not simply answer questions; they often raise additional ones as well. Thus, the problem facing psychologists is usually not that of coming up with interesting ideas for research. Rather, the difficulty is in choosing among the many intriguing possibilities. Perhaps the most important single basis for research in psychology, however, is formal theories.

Theories represent efforts by scientists in any field to answer the question "Why?" In more formal terms, theories consist of two major parts: (1) basic concepts, and (2) statements concerning relationships between these concepts. Scientists use these parts to generate testable propositions—ones that can be examined in actual research and found to be either true or false. The development of accurate theories is a major goal of all sciences, and psychology is no exception to this rule (Howard, 1985; Popper, 1959). Psychologists, like other scientists, wish not merely to observe or describe the phenomena they study (that is, aspects of behavior); they wish to explain them as well. Thus, a great deal of research in psychology consists of efforts to construct, refine, and test specific theories. Perhaps the best way of illustrating the central role of theory in ongoing research is, again, through a concrete example.

Consider the following: When individuals make a decision, they tend to stick to it even in the face of growing signs that it was wrong. For example, they remain in romantic relationships even after these continue to yield more pain than joy. Or they continue to "throw good money after bad" by repairing an automobile that requires one repair after another. This pattern is sometimes known as "escalation of commitment," and we'll consider it in more detail in chapter 7 (Garland & Newport, 1991).

Certainly, knowing about this tendency is useful in itself. It allows us to predict what may happen in situations where people invest resources or effort in failing courses of action: All things being equal, they will continue to stick to their initial bad decisions. Further, it also suggests the possibility of intervening in some manner to prevent such outcomes. For example, informing people about this tendency to throw good money after bad may prove

Theories: In science, frameworks for explaining various phenomena. Theories consist of two major parts: basic concepts and assertions concerning relationships between these concepts.

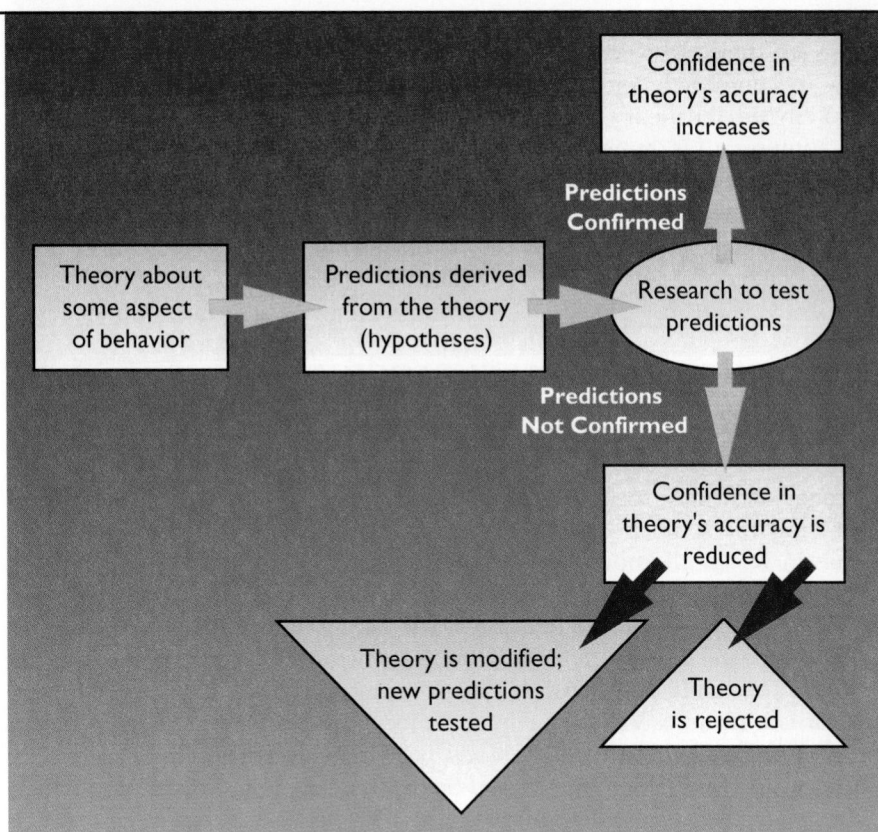

FIGURE **1.6**

The Role of Theory in Psychological Research

Once a theory has been formulated, predictions derived from it are tested through research. If these predictions are confirmed, confidence in the theory's accuracy is increased. If they are disconfirmed, confidence in the theory's accuracy is reduced. The theory may then be modified so as to generate new predictions, or, ultimately, be rejected.

helpful in lessening its occurrence. These two outcomes—prediction and intervention (or control)—are major goals of science. Knowing about the occurrence of escalation of commitment, however, does not explain why it occurs. It is at this point that theory enters the picture, for as noted above, providing such explanation is its foremost goal.

In fields such as physics or chemistry, theories often take the form of mathematical equations. While this is also true to some extent in psychology, many of the theories we will consider in later chapters involve verbal statements. For example, a theory designed to account for escalation of commitment might state: "When individuals make decisions that result in losses, they are reluctant to admit their mistake, for this admission causes them to 'lose face' (look foolish) in the eyes of others. As a result, they feel they have no choice but to stick to their original commitment in order to make up for initial losses and so justify their decision." Note that this theory, like all others, consists of the two parts mentioned above: basic concepts (such as losses, pressures to justify past actions) and assertions about the relationships between these concepts (as losses mount, pressures to justify previous decisions intensify).

Once a theory has been formulated, a critical process begins (see Figure 1.6). First, predictions are derived from the theory. These predictions, known as *hypotheses,* are formulated in accordance with basic principles of logic. Then the hypotheses are tested in actual research. If they are confirmed, confidence in the theory's accuracy is increased. If, instead, such predictions are disconfirmed, confidence in the theory's accuracy is

KEY QUESTIONS

- What is the basic nature of experimentation?
- Why must participants in an experiment be randomly assigned to different conditions?
- What is confounding in an experiment?
- What are experimenter effects and demand characteristics?
- What are the basic components of theories?
- Why must the results of an experiment be statistically significant to be informative?
- What is meta-analysis?

reduced. The theory itself may be altered so as to generate new predictions. These are subjected to test and the process continues. If the modified predictions are confirmed, confidence in the revised theory is increased. If they are disconfirmed, the theory may be modified again or, ultimately, rejected.

It's important to remember that theories are useful only to the extent that they lead to testable predictions. If a theory does not generate hypotheses that can be examined in actual research, it cannot be viewed as scientific in nature.

ETHICAL ISSUES IN PSYCHOLOGICAL RESEARCH

Learning Objective 1.10
Discuss the major ethical issues that psychologists face in their research with humans and animals.

Learning Objective 1.11
Discuss the major ethical issues that psychologists face in the practice of psychology.

Strange as it may seem, the phrase "psychological research" has an ominous ring for some people. When they hear it, they visualize unsettling scenes in which all-knowing psychologists somehow force unwary subjects to reveal their deepest secrets and wildest fantasies. Do such concerns have any basis in fact? Is psychological research really harmful to the people and animals who participate in it, and therefore unethical?

While I certainly don't wish to gloss over a complex and serious issue, my answer is a firm *no*. Virtually all psychological research conducted today is performed in accordance with ethical principles acceptable both to society and to science. Indeed, in the United States (the location of more psychological research than any other country), both the federal government and the American Psychological Association have established stringent standards for conducting behavioral research with both humans and animals. These standards seek to guarantee the safety, privacy, and well-being of all research participants and are strictly enforced in universities and other organizations in which research takes place by special review panels called Institutional Review Boards. These boards review all proposed research projects, and such projects can proceed only when final approval is granted. Government agencies and private foundations that fund psychological research will not provide funding for projects until they have received Institutional Review Board approval. Given these safeguards, it seems clear that the frightening picture of psychological research sketched above has little connection to reality.

Despite such precautions, however, two ethical issues deserving of our attention persist. One has to do with the use of deception—withholding information about a study from research participants or, in some cases, giving false information about it. The other has to do with the use of animals in psychological research.

DECEPTION: *Is It Ever Appropriate for Psychologists to Lie to Research Participants?*

Suppose that before becoming involved in a research project, participants were informed that the purpose was to determine how readily they could be influenced by a stranger. Then, suppose they were actually exposed to efforts by another person to change their attitudes or their behavior. Would the study yield any valid results? In all probability, it would not. Having learned that they would soon be exposed to influence, many participants would probably dig in their heels and resist—even if, without this information, they might have yielded. Similarly, imagine that before taking part in a study concerned with willingness to help others in an emergency, participants were informed of this purpose. If they were then exposed to a simulated emergency, could anything be learned about their reactions to such events? Again, probably not, for the knowledge that this aspect of their behavior was being studied might well alter their reactions.

In situations such as these, many psychologists feel that it is appropriate to withhold information about a study from participants, or even to give them misleading information, on a temporary basis. The reason behind such procedures—which are known as **deception**—is straightforward: Researchers believe that if participants have complete information about the purposes and procedures of an investigation, their behavior will be changed from what it would otherwise be and the study will fail to yield any valid new information.

Yet, employing deception raises important ethical issues. Deception, even when temporary, may result in some type of harmful outcome for the persons exposed to it (Kelman, 1967). For example, they may experience discomfort, stress, negative shifts in their self-esteem, or related effects. In addition, there is the question of whether scientists, committed to the search for knowledge, should place themselves in the position of deceiving persons kind enough to assist them in this undertaking.

Given such possibilities, is it ever appropriate to employ temporary deception in psychological research? I have often faced this question myself, because in many of my own studies, it seemed clear that if participants received full information about the purposes of the research, their behavior would be changed by this information. For example, several of my recent experiments have focused on the question of whether pleasant fragrances can affect people's behavior—for example, influencing their performance on various tasks or, by putting them in a positive mood, thus increasing their willingness to help others (e.g., Baron, 1990; Baron & Bronfen, 1994). In such cases I, like many other psychologists, have concluded that it is appropriate to temporarily withhold some information from research participants. However, this is only acceptable if two important conditions are met: (1) **Informed consent** is employed—before agreeing to take part in a study, subjects must be provided with information about all the events and procedures it will involve and also must be informed that they are free to participate or not participate and can withdraw from the research at any time (American Psychological Association, 1992). (2) Thorough **debriefing** is provided—after the study is over, subjects must be provided with full information about all of its aspects and purposes. Both informed consent and thorough debriefing are required by the ethical standards for conducting behavioral research mentioned earlier, so these are essentially built into the process.

Despite this fact, however, not all psychologists accept the view that deception is sometimes acceptable in research projects (Baumrind, 1985). These critics feel that the use of such procedures reduces participants' faith in science generally, and in psychology in particular, and so jeopardizes continued public support for psychological research. While such arguments cannot be ignored, existing evidence seems to point to more optimistic conclusions. When surveyed, an overwhelming majority of participants report that they view temporary deception as acceptable and do not resent its use (Rogers, 1980; Smith & Richardson, 1985). Further, individuals who have participated in studies involving deception do not report more negative feelings about psychological research than those who have not and do not express lower levels of trust in others (Sharpe, Adair, & Roese, 1992). Finally, it appears that even relatively brief informed consent forms—ones that do not go into great detail about the procedures of a study—can be quite effective in providing individuals with the information they need in order to decide whether to participate. Indeed, recent findings indicate that relatively brief forms are just as

Deception: Withholding information about a study from participants. Deception is used in situations where the information that is withheld is likely to alter participants' behavior.

Informed Consent: Participants' agreement to take part in a research project after they are provided with information about the nature of such participation.

Debriefing: In psychological research, the provision of complete and accurate information about a study to participants after they have taken part in it.

useful in this context as longer and more detailed ones (Mann, 1994). Of course, even in the light of such findings it is unwise to take the safety or suitability of deception for granted (Rubin, 1985). On the contrary, psychologists must always be on guard to protect the rights and well-being of all individuals who, by offering their time, effort, and cooperation, help to advance the frontiers of psychological knowledge.

RESEARCH WITH ANIMALS:
Is It Acceptable?

If you were given a tour through the research facilities of any large psychology department, you would soon encounter rooms filled with rats, pigeons, or monkeys, plus equipment used in studying their behavior. At the present time approximately 8 percent of all research projects in psychology are conducted with animal subjects—primarily rodents, such as white rats (Beckstead, 1991). There are several compelling reasons for this state of affairs.

First, and probably foremost, it is often impossible (for health or safety reasons) to conduct certain types of research with human participants. For obvious ethical and legal reasons, researchers cannot perform operations on healthy human beings in order to study the role of various parts of their brains in important aspects of behavior. And researchers cannot place human beings on diets lacking in certain nutrients to determine how such deficits influence their learning, or give them addicting drugs to study the neural basis for substance abuse. Under certain conditions, however, it is permissible to employ such procedures with animals.

Other reasons for conducting research with animals include their relatively short life spans, which make investigations of various aspects of development (changes over time) more feasible, and the fact that they can be bred over many generations so as to be genetically homogeneous. Such homogeneity, in turn, makes it easier to investigate the impact of many different variables on behavior, since individual differences relating to genetic factors are minimized. Finally, knowledge of animal behavior can be of great practical value. For example, understanding the behavior of pests can help us to combat them more effectively, perhaps without the use of dangerous chemicals.

In view of these and other important considerations, many psychologists believe that it is appropriate to conduct at least some research projects with animals. Moreover, I should note that most psychological projects conducted with animals involve absolutely no harm or discomfort to the animals; indeed, in many cases they involve such procedures as observing the animals' social interaction with members of their own species or the rate at which they learn to perform various activities. Despite this fact, however, research with animals has generated intense controversy. Supporters of animal rights contend that the procedures employed in research with animals often expose them to harsh or cruel treatment. Most of these protests have been directed against medical research, in which, for example, animals may be injected with lethal microbes or given potentially dangerous drugs. And vigorous objections have been raised against the use of animals in the development and testing of commercial products such as cosmetics. As you might guess, most people find this last type of research especially objectionable—far less acceptable than research in which the results may, potentially, contribute to human health and welfare (Beckstead, 1991). Although psychologists do not typically conduct medical or marketing research, they too have been criticized for exposing animals to dangerous or harmful treatments in their studies of various aspects of behavior.

ANIMAL RESEARCH: THE DEBATE

Research with animals is only a small part of psychological research, but it is invaluable for exploring many topics, including learning, attachment, and social behavior.

As you can readily see, this is a complex issue, with no simple solutions. It does seem cruel to expose animals to conditions that are deemed unsafe or unethical for humans. Yet important breakthroughs have often been produced by such research. For example, studies conducted by psychologists with animals have contributed to the development of effective forms of therapy for treating emotional problems, the control of high blood pressure, the reduction of chronic pain, the rehabilitation of persons with neuromuscular disorders (such as disorders that prevent normal walking), and an enhanced understanding of the neural mechanisms underlying memory loss, senility, and various addictions (Miller, 1985).

Do such benefits justify research with animals—even research that exposes subjects to conditions that could not be used with humans? Clearly, this is a value judgment, outside the realm of science. However, many psychologists believe that if every possible precaution is taken to minimize harm or discomfort to subjects, this is a case where the potential benefits do outweigh the very real costs. It is for you as an individual to decide whether—and in what circumstances—you agree.

ETHICAL ISSUES IN THE PRACTICE OF PSYCHOLOGY

While psychologists often confront complex ethical issues when conducting research, I would be remiss if I did not mention that they may also face such issues in the normal practice of their profession—when delivering psychological services to clients. Indeed, given that a large majority of psychologists are engaged in applied work rather than in research, the ethical issues they face in such work are probably far more common than the ones described earlier.

A survey of practicing psychologists (Pope & Vetter, 1992) indicates that, as you might well expect, there are many different situations in which ethical issues or dilemmas arise. The most frequent of these center on questions of *confidentiality*—situations in which psychologists receive information from their clients that professional ethics require them to hold confidential, but which they also feel obligated to reveal to legal authorities. For example, one psychologist reported a distressing situation in which a client reported being raped but could not get police to believe her story. Shortly afterward, another client of the same psychologist admitted committing this crime (Pope &

CONFIDENTIALITY AND ETHICS

Ethical standards require that psychologists hold in strict confidence information divulged by their clients during therapy. However, what happens when such information involves illegal actions? Should therapists reveal their knowledge to legal authorities? There is no easy or simple answer to such dilemmas.

Vetter, 1992, p. 399). Clearly, the psychologist in question faced a difficult ethical dilemma. What would *you* do in the same situation? (We don't know what the psychologist ultimately decided to do, because this person chose to keep the decision itself confidential.)

Another frequent cause of ethical concern involves situations in which psychologists find themselves in dual or conflicted relationships with clients. That is, the psychologist's professional role as healer is somehow inconsistent with other relationships he or she may have with a client. For example, one therapist reported an incident in which he sought to file a complaint against very noisy neighbors, only to discover that the owner of the property was one of his patients. Considerable ethical concern also centers on sexual issues—instances in which psychologists are attracted to their clients or vice versa. Clearly, the professional role of therapist (and strong guidelines of the American Psychological Association) forbids sexual relationships between therapists and clients; yet such attraction still occurs and can be very distressing to all parties concerned.

These are just a few of the ethical dilemmas and problems faced by psychologists in their efforts to assist individuals. Many others, ranging from concerns over providing expert testimony in criminal trials through the use of advertising to build one's practice, exist as well. In short, efforts to help individuals cope with life problems and psychological disorders raise many ethical issues and require adherence to the highest professional standards. Truly, then, working as a psychologist can be a demanding job.

KEY QUESTIONS

- Why is the use of deception in psychological research controversial?

- What ethical issues are raised by research with animals?

- What ethical dilemmas do psychologists often face in their work?

USING THIS BOOK: *A Note on Its Features*

Are all textbooks alike? I don't believe so. Rather, I feel that textbooks, like individuals, are all unique and reflect the experience, perspectives, and goals of their authors. I've already mentioned my goals for this book: providing you with a broad yet integrated overview of the findings of modern psychology, *and* calling your attention to how you, personally, can benefit from this knowledge. In order to reach these goals, I've incorporated a number of special features into this book. In keeping with my earlier comments about "mental frameworks," I'll describe these briefly here so that you'll have a better idea of what's coming and an awareness of how to make maximum use of these features.

First, I've taken several steps to make the text easier to read and more convenient to use. Each chapter begins with an outline and ends with a summary. Within the text, key terms are printed in **dark type like this** and are accompanied by a definition. These terms are also defined in a running marginal glossary, as well as in a glossary at the end of the book. In addition, important principles that lie at the heart of the field of psychology are highlighted under the heading **Key Questions**. If you understand and retain these, you will be off to a very good start in your efforts to profit from this first course in psychology. All figures and tables are as clear as possible, and most contain special labels and notes designed to help you interpret them. Finally, to help you understand concepts that many students find difficult to grasp, special **Key Concept** pages illustrate these ideas in an attractive format.

Second, in keeping with the theme of **Making Psychology Part of Your Life**, I've included numerous references to my *own* life—instances in which I, personally, made use of the principles and findings of psychology. I believe that these references will get you thinking about ways in which the topics and materials discussed are relevant to your own experiences, so please watch for them throughout the book.

Third, this text includes several types of special sections I think you'll find both interesting and useful. One type is labeled **The Point of It All**. These sections seek to accomplish two goals. First, they will help you to see the "big picture"—to understand why specific topics are important and why psychologists are interested in them. Second, they describe actual ways in which the findings and principles of psychology are currently used to solve a wide range of practical problems. All chapters conclude with a section entitled **Making Psychology Part of Your Life**. These sections indicate how you personally can apply the information presented to enhance your own life. Finally, because of psychology's growing concern with the role of cultural and ethnic diversity, all chapters contain special sections entitled **Perspectives on Diversity**. These sections examine the impact of ethnic and cultural factors on many aspects of behavior and, I believe, will bring psychology's commitment to a multicultural perspective firmly into focus.

I hope that these and other features of this text will help you to understand psychology—and help me share with you my excitement about this field. In any case, may your first contact with psychology be as stimulating, enjoyable, and beneficial as mine was many years ago.

USING THE KNOWLEDGE IN THIS BOOK: Some Tips on How to Study

*T*hree topics that have long been of major interest to psychologists are learning, memory, and motivation. (We'll consider them in detail in chapters 5, 6, and 9.) Indeed, all three can probably be listed among the topics about which psychology currently knows most. From your perspective as a college student, this is a positive state of affairs, for all three are closely related to one activity you must perform—and perform well—as a college student: studying. After all, you must be motivated to study, must learn new materials, and must remember them accurately in order to succeed. Knowledge gained by psychologists can be very useful to you in accomplishing these tasks. In this section I'll draw on existing knowledge about learning, memory, and motivation in order to offer some concrete tips on how you can get the most out of the time you spend studying.

1. *Begin with an overview.* Research on memory indicates that it is easier to retain information if it can be placed within a cognitive framework—in other words, if it is clear how different pieces of information or topics relate to one another. So when you begin to study, it is very helpful to start with an overview. Examine the outline provided at the start of each chapter and thumb through the chapter itself once or twice. That way, you'll know what to expect and will already have an initial framework for holding the information in mind when you get down to more serious studying.

2. *Eliminate (or at least minimize) distractions.* In order for information to be entered into memory accurately, close attention to such input is necessary; it won't make sense or flow into your mind unless you focus on it. This implies that you should take care to avoid distractions—stimuli or events that will disrupt your attention and cause you to focus on something other than your studying. So when you get down to serious studying, try to do it in a quiet, secluded place. Turn off the television or radio, put those magazines out of sight, and unhook your telephone. You may find this hard to do, but remember: If you don't eliminate distractions, it will take you longer to cover the same ground. And where studying is concerned, efficiency—covering the most you can in the shortest period of time—is a key goal.

3. *Recognize the limitations of your own span of concentration.* Students sometimes tell me that they have studied for one of their exams "for eight hours without a break." Perhaps; but I know that I couldn't study that long without stopping. We are, after all, human; and this means that we get hungry or bored after performing one activity for a long time. How long should you study without taking a break? People differ greatly on this dimension. However, it is important to recognize your own span of concentration and to avoid exceeding it. Yes, you should certainly try to stretch it a bit: this kind of self-discipline can help you increase the length of your study sessions. But no, you should not try to study for many hours without a break. Your learning efficiency will decrease, and you will get diminishing returns from forcing yourself to continue well beyond your own personal limits.

4. *Set specific, challenging, but attainable goals for your studying.* Industrial/organizational psychologists have long been concerned with the topic of work motivation—willingness to expend effort on various tasks (Locke & Latham, 1990). One of the key findings of their research is that setting certain kinds of goals can help greatly in this regard. When individuals set specific goals, ones that are challenging yet attainable, both motivation and task performance often increase. What does this mean with respect to studying? First, that you should set concrete goals for each session—for example, "I'll read twenty pages and review my class notes," or "I'll read an entire chapter." Merely telling yourself "I'll do as much as I can" is far less effective. Second, you should set challenging but feasible goals. If you know that you can't sit still for more than an hour, then it is silly to set as a goal "I'll read two chapters." You simply won't be able to do so before you get restless and can't continue. It is much more effective to set somewhat difficult goals that you can, with effort, attain. Such goals are within your reach, and you can experience a sense of accomplishment when you attain them. So begin by setting appropriate goals; you will almost certainly increase your motivation!

5. *Reward yourself for progress.* As you'll see in chapter 5, people often perform various activities to attain external rewards, ones administered to them by others. But in many cases we provide our own rewards. We pat ourselves on the back for accomplishments, eat a favorite dessert as a reward for dieting successfully all week, and so on. You can put this process to good use where studying is concerned. Studying is certainly hard work. So, after completing an assignment or reaching one of your self-set goals, you should definitely give yourself a reward. What rewards should you select? This depends on what you like. The basic rules are simply these: (a) Provide yourself with something you enjoy, whatever that may be; and (b) do so only after you have completed your studying and reached the goals you set.

6. *Engage in active, not passive, studying.* As you probably know, it is quite possible to sit in front of a book or set of notes for hours without accomplishing much—except daydreaming. And even when you keep your mind on what you read, it is difficult to remember it if all you do is follow the printed words. Many studies on memory and related aspects of cognition suggest that in order truly to master new information, we must do more than merely be exposed to it. We must also think about it, relate it to information we already know, ask questions about it, and so on (Baddeley, 1990; Craik & Tulving, 1975). With respect to studying, this implies that when you read new material, you should think actively about it as you progress. Ask questions about it, try to generate examples of the principles or concepts covered, and relate the material to what you already know. Taking notes on key points and reviewing these later can also be helpful. (This is one reason why I have included **Key Questions** in this text.) Finally, you should actively review your notes and the material, quizzing yourself in various ways.

Following these guidelines sounds like a lot of effort. But doing so can greatly increase the effectiveness with which you study. Moreover, once you gain practice with these procedures and form good study habits, the whole process will tend to get easier. The ultimate result, then, will be that you learn and remember more information in shorter periods of time. Certainly, reaching that outcome is well worth the effort.

Practice in Critical Thinking: The Hidden Bonus in Introductory Psychology

I f I asked a large group of students to indicate why they had enrolled in introductory psychology, I'd obtain a wide range of answers. Among the most common, though, would be replies such as these: "I wanted to know more about people," "I want to know more about myself," "I thought it would be interesting." In other words, most would indicate that they enrolled in the course because of its content. They expected to learn a lot of interesting facts about people—things they didn't know before taking the course.

Such expectations are fully warranted; you will acquire a great deal of intriguing information about behavior and cognitive processes from this book and from your course. Yet there is another major benefit you will derive from your first exposure to psychology—one that is often overlooked. In a phrase, not only will you acquire facts about psychology, you will also learn to think critically about human behavior. To illustrate this hidden value of introductory psychology, we must first define the term *critical thinking* (Paul, 1990).

First, let's note what critical thinking is not. Critical thinking does not mean negative, fault-finding, nit-picking thinking. It does not imply an automatic rejection of all arguments, hypotheses, or theories. What it does involve is the ability to cast a skeptical mental eye on claims, assertions, and arguments until they are carefully assessed and objectively examined. In other words, critical thinking means the ability to resist being stampeded, emotionally or otherwise, into accepting statements or arguments that are not actually supported by the facts. (See Table 1.4 for a summary of key aspects of critical thinking.)

For example, suppose that one day you pick up a newspaper and notice the following headline: "Personality Flaws Keep People from Promotion." You read on and learn that according to a management "expert," people who demonstrate certain personal characteristics—such as constant complaining, being a loner, or being arrogant and overconfident—don't get promotions. "More people lose jobs or promotions because of personality problems than from an inability to do the work," states the expert. How should you react to these claims? Your first reactions may be, "Hmm . . . that makes sense. I'd better watch out for these problems in my own behavior." If you stop and think more carefully, however, you may ask questions such as these: How does the expert know that these things keep people from getting promotions? What data did he or she collect? How do you measure complaining, being a loner, or being overconfident? What kind of jobs were involved? Are these traits really the ones that matter most? In other

TABLE 1.4	ASPECT	VALUE/PURPOSE
Critical Thinking: Some Basic Components *Critical thinking* involves considerable cognitive effort. However, since it can help you avoid serious errors of judgment, bad decisions, and many other pitfalls, it is a skill well worth developing.	Define the issue or problem clearly, including key terms.	You can't think clearly about an issue unless you know just what it involves.
	Examine all relevant evidence; avoid jumping to premature conclusions.	Avoid the temptation to go with "gut-level feelings." Better decisions and judgments can be made if all available evidence is taken into account.
	Carefully consider assumptions and biases.	All arguments are based on assumptions. These must be brought out into the open so you can determine their validity.
	Avoid the tendency to oversimplify.	Simple answers or solutions are very misleading and ignore important complexities.
	Avoid the tendency to overgeneralize.	Avoid leaping from a single event or experience to all related events or experiences.

words, you would approach the whole issue with a healthy degree of skepticism—and reserve judgment until you have better answers to your questions.

But what, specifically, does introductory psychology have to do with development of the capacity for critical thinking? In fact, a great deal. First, such critical thinking is part and parcel of the scientific approach in our field. Time and time again in this text, we'll consider instances in which common sense suggests a simple answer to an important question about behavior—an answer which is then shown to be false by systematic research. In the absence of science-based critical thinking, the commonsense conclusion, false as it is, might well persist. Indeed, the question of its accuracy might never even be raised. Therefore, many examples of critical, scientific thinking will appear in later chapters.

Second, discussions of such topics as memory, decision making, problem solving, and creativity will provide you with new insights into these important processes—and especially with insights into the many forms of bias and error that can affect them. Realizing that your memory can indeed play tricks on you and that your decisions can be influenced by many forms of bias will help alert you to these potential problems. And as one old saying goes, "Forewarned is forearmed."

Third, and perhaps most important, exposure to psychology will provide you with experience in thinking critically about behavior. My experience tells me that many persons who are quite capable of thinking clearly and critically about the physical world lapse

into far less careful and sophisticated patterns of thought when they contemplate their own feelings, others' behavior, or their social relationships. As you'll see throughout this book, critical thinking can be applied to virtually any topic—including all aspects of behavior. Thus, once you become proficient at it, you can apply it to almost any situation or question you encounter in later life.

As you will see, your first course in psychology will provide you with much practice in critical thinking. And this is definitely a skill you will take with you—and use—long after the course and this book are just memories of days long past.

The ability to avoid believing everything you read is one important aspect of critical thinking.

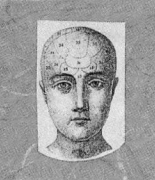

Psychology: What It Is and How It Developed

- **What is the definition of modern psychology?**

Psychology is defined as the science of behavior and cognitive processes.

- **How did early psychologists—the structuralists, functionalists, and behaviorists—differ in their ideas about the nature of psychology?**

Structuralists thought that psychology should identify the basic parts of consciousness. Functionalists believed that psychology should focus on the adaptive value of the human mind. Behaviorists felt that psychology should focus primarily on observable behavior.

- **What are the key differences among the perspectives adopted by psychologists—the behavioral, cognitive, psychodynamic, humanistic, biopsychological, evolutionary, and sociocultural perspectives?**

The behavioral perspective focuses on observable aspects of behavior. The cognitive perspective focuses on the nature of cognitive processes. The psychodynamic perspective suggests that many aspects of behavior stem from hidden forces within our personalities. The humanistic perspective suggests that human beings have free will and are not under the control of internal and external factors. The biopsychological perspective focuses on the biological processes underlying behavior. The evolutionary perspective focuses on the role of inherited tendencies in behavior. The sociocultural perspective focuses on the role of cultural factors in human behavior.

- **How do psychologists take account of cultural differences in conducting research and providing psychological services?**

Until recently, psychology devoted little attention to cultural or ethnic differences. Now, however, this situation has changed greatly, and such differences are the focus of an increasing amount of research attention.

- **Why can psychology be considered scientific in nature?**

Psychology is scientific in nature because it adopts the methods and values of science in its efforts to understand behavior.

- **What makes modern psychology much more than "common sense"?**

Psychology is more than common sense because the results of systematic research are a much more reliable guide to understanding human behavior than informal observation.

KEY TERMS: *critical thinking, p. 3; psychology, p. 3; structuralism, p. 5; functionalism, p. 5; behaviorism, p. 5; cognitive processes, p. 8; psychodynamic perspective, p. 8; humanistic perspective, p. 8; evolutionary psychology, p. 9; multicultural perspective, p. 12*

Psychology: Who and What

- **How are psychologists trained?**

Psychologists receive their advanced training in graduate departments of psychology. Most receive a PhD after at least five years of advanced study.

- **What are the major subfields of psychology?**

There are many subfields in psychology, including cognitive psychology, developmental psychology, social psychology, psychobiology, and industrial/organizational psychology. All share a commitment to advancing our knowledge of behavior through scientific means.

Adding to What We Know: The Process of Psychological Research

- **What is the basic nature of naturalistic observation, the case method, and the survey approach?**

Naturalistic observation involves observing various aspects of behavior in natural settings. The case method involves collecting detailed information about individuals in order to develop general principles about behavior. In the survey method of research, large numbers of people answer questions about aspects of their views or their behavior.

- **What is the basic nature of the correlational method of research?**

In the correlational method of research, efforts are made to determine whether relationships (correlations) exist between variables—that is, whether changes in one variable are accompanied by changes in another.

- **Why is it true that correlations do not prove causation?**

Correlations do not prove causation because changes in two variables may stem from the effects of a third variable; the two variables may not influence each other directly.

- **What is the basic nature of experimentation?**

Experimentation involves systematically altering one or more variables in order to determine whether changes in the variable(s) affect behavior.

- **Why must participants in an experiment be randomly assigned to different conditions?**

Participants in an experiment must be randomly assigned to different conditions because if they are not, it is impossible to determine whether differences between the conditions stem from the independent variable or from differences among the participants.

• *What is confounding in an experiment?*

Confounding occurs when one or more variables other than the independent variable are permitted to vary across conditions of an experiment.

• *What are experimenter effects and demand characteristics?*

Experimenter effects refer to unintentional influence exerted by researchers on research participants. Demand characteristics refer to implicit pressure on research participants to act in ways consistent with a researcher's expectations.

• *What are the basic components of theories?*

Theories consist of basic concepts and statements concerning relationships between these concepts.

• *Why must the results of an experiment be statistically significant to be informative?*

Results of an experiment must be statistically significant to be informative because only then is the probability that they were obtained by chance alone very low.

• *What is meta-analysis?*

Meta-analysis is the use of statistical procedures for combining the results of many different experiments.

KEY TERMS: *naturalistic observation, p. 18; case method, p. 19; survey method, p. 19; correlational method, p. 20; hypothesis,* *p. 20; experimentation, p. 22; independent variable, p. 22; dependent variable, p. 22; random assignment of participants to experimental conditions, p. 23; experimenter effects, p. 24; demand characteristics, p. 24; double-blind procedure, p. 25; inferential statistics, p. 27; meta-analysis, p. 27; theories, p. 28*

ETHICAL ISSUES IN PSYCHOLOGICAL RESEARCH

• *Why is the use of deception in psychological research controversial?*

The use of deception in psychological research is controversial because some psychologists believe that it violates the rights of research participants and may, potentially, be harmful to them.

• *What ethical issues are raised by research with animals?*

Research with animals raises ethical issues with regard to the harm they may experience and the suggestion that they are often exposed to harsh or dangerous treatment in research having commercial rather than scientific goals.

• *What ethical dilemmas do psychologists often face in their work?*

Psychologists often face ethical dilemmas concerning sexual attraction and client confidentiality.

KEY TERMS: *deception, p. 31; informed consent, p. 31; debriefing, p. 31*

CRITICAL THINKING QUESTIONS

APPRAISAL	Most psychologists view their field as being scientific in nature. Do you agree? Explain why you accept or reject this view.
CONTROVERSY	Research with animals is a very controversial topic. Some people believe that it is never appropriate to conduct such research, while others feel that such research is often justified. What are your views on this issue? Is research with animals ever justified? If so, when? If not, why?
MAKING PSYCHOLOGY PART OF YOUR LIFE	Now that you know the basic ground rules of psychological research, do you think this knowledge will lead you to evaluate claims about human behavior differently than in the past? Think of one statement about people you have read in newspapers or magazines or heard on television in recent days; in the light of appropriate research methods, do you think it is accurate?

Biological Bases of Behavior:

A Look Beneath the Surface

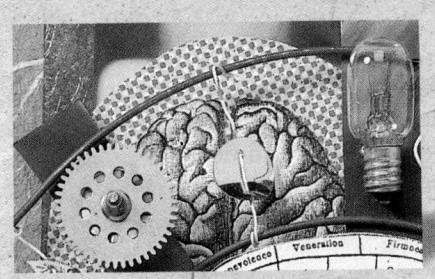

Congress declared the 1990s the "decade of the brain." Why? In part, to recognize the tremendous progress scientists have made toward unlocking the human brain's many secrets. Rapid advancements in technology have enabled researchers to look inside the nervous system of living people to discover important relationships between structures and functions of the brain and behavior. Although such advances would have been considered science fiction only a generation ago, today they are a

reality. Moreover, exciting new discoveries in this area continue to occur at an astonishing pace. As we proceed through this chapter, you'll see that the 1990s are, indeed, an exciting period in the history of psychology.

Scientific study dedicated to unlocking the mysteries of biology and behavior is called **biopsychology** (Pinel, 1993). This term is appropriate because it accurately reflects the very broad scope of current efforts to understand how important aspects of behavior and cognition are related to complex biological processes. For example, perhaps you have wondered about such questions as these: What happens inside our bodies when we experience joy, anger, or sexual desire? How can our brains store memories of events that took place years or even decades ago? What happens when we dream? Make plans? Imagine future events or outcomes? How is our sexual orientation determined? Clearly, all these activities must be related to biological events within our bodies; but what, precisely, are these events? Biopsychologists, too, are deeply interested in such questions. And although they do not yet have all the answers, they are making tremendous progress toward answering many important questions in this decade of the brain.

Biopsychologists also recognize that the brain does not exist in isolation, but rather performs in concert with elements of our physical and social environment. Armed with the tools of modern technology, scientists are now discovering how biological processes interact with environmental factors to determine how we think, feel, and behave—sometimes, but not always, for the best, as we'll see later in this chapter. Fortunately, a rapidly growing body of evidence suggests that environmental factors can sometimes offset the effects of nature. Thus, while biological factors are powerful, they are not immutable.

We'll begin our discussion of biopsychology by examining the structure and function of neurons, the building blocks of the nervous system. As you'll soon see, understanding how neurons function—and especially how they communicate with one another—provides important insights into such diverse topics as how drugs exert their effects and how, perhaps, serious forms of mental illness develop. Next, we will turn to the structure and function of the nervous system, devoting special attention to the brain, the marvelous organ that is ultimately responsible for consciousness—and for the fact that you are now reading and understanding these words! Discussion of the structure and function of the brain will lead us to several fascinating topics, including the surprising fact that the two sides of the brain are actually specialized for the performance of somewhat different tasks. After this, we will turn briefly to the endocrine system, internal glands regulated by the nervous system that play an important role in key aspects of behavior. We'll conclude our discussion by reviewing recent evidence regarding the role of genetic factors in determining several important aspects of human behavior, physical and mental disorders, and even sexual orientation.

Biopsychology: *The branch of psychology concerned with discovering the biological bases of our thoughts, feelings, and behaviors.*

NEURONS: Building Blocks of the Nervous System

Why do the words "It's time for supper!" produce rumbles in our stomachs, strong feelings of hunger, and a dash to the dinner table? In other words, how can information reaching our ears produce bodily reactions, sensations of hunger, and overt actions relating to these? The answer involves the activity of **neurons**—cells within our bodies that are specialized for the tasks of receiving, moving, and processing information.

NEURONS: Their Basic Structure

Neurons are tremendously varied in appearance. Yet most consist of three basic parts: (1) a *cell body*, (2) an *axon*, and (3) one or more *dendrites*. **Dendrites** carry information toward the cell body, whereas **axons** carry information away from it. Thus, in a sense, neurons are one-way channels of communication. Information usually moves from dendrites or the cell body toward the axon and then outward along this structure. A simplified diagram of a neuron and actual neurons are shown, magnified, in Figure 2.1.

In many neurons the axon is covered by a sheath of fatty material known as *myelin*. The myelin sheath (fatty wrapping) is interrupted by small gaps.

Learning Objective 2.1
Describe the basic structure of the neuron.

Learning Objective 2.2
Explain how neurons function and how synaptic transmission occurs.

Learning Objective 2.3
Discuss the effects of neurotransmitters.

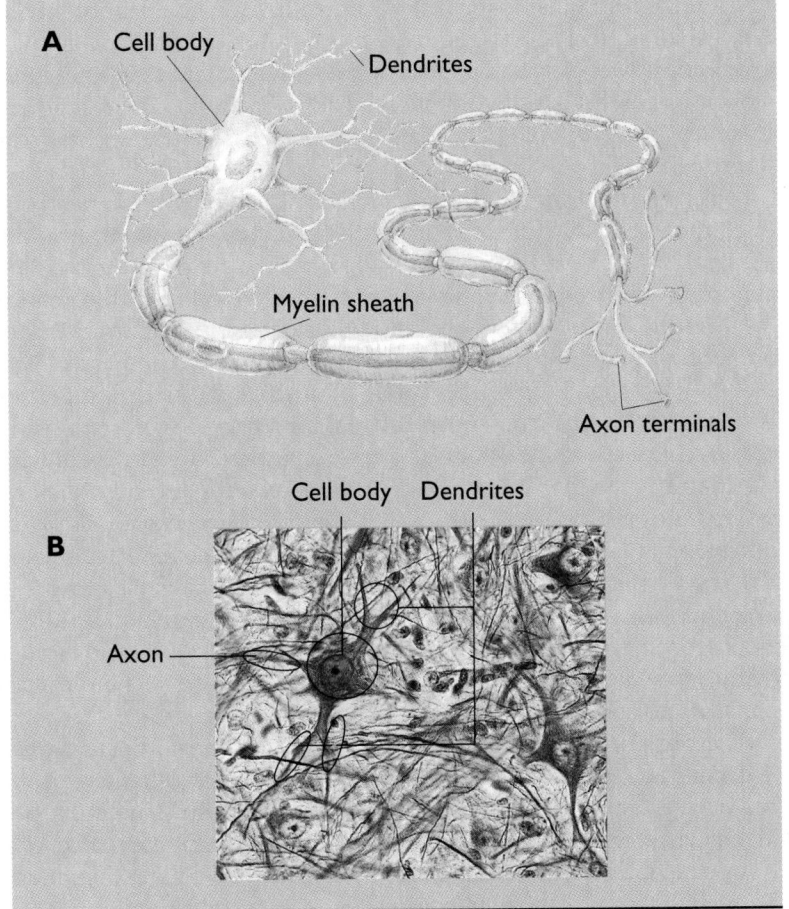

FIGURE **2.1**

Neurons: Their Basic Structure

(A) Neurons appear in many forms, but all possess the basic structures shown here: a cell body, an axon (with axon terminals), and one or more dendrites. (B) Actual human neurons, greatly magnified.

Neurons: Cells specialized for communicating information, the basic building blocks of the nervous system.

Dendrites: The parts of neurons that conduct the action potential toward the cell body.

Axons: The parts of the neurons that conduct action potential away from the cell body.

Both the sheath and the gaps in it play an important role in the neuron's ability to transmit information, a process we'll consider in detail shortly. The myelin sheath is actually produced by another basic set of building blocks within the nervous system, **glial cells**. Glial cells, which outnumber neurons by about ten to one, form the myelin sheath by sending out parts that wrap around axons.

Near its end, the axon divides into several small branches. These, in turn, end in round structures known as **axon terminals** that closely approach, but do not actually touch, other cells (other neurons, muscle cells, or gland cells). The region at which the axon terminals of a neuron closely approach other cells is known as the **synapse**. The manner in which neurons communicate with other cells across this tiny space is described below.

NEURONS: *Their Basic Function*

As we consider how neurons function, two questions arise: (1) How does information travel from point to point within a single neuron, and (2) how is information transmitted from one neuron to another or from neurons to other cells of the body?

COMMUNICATION WITHIN NEURONS: THE ACTION POTENTIAL The answer to the first question is complex but can be summarized as follows. When a neuron is at rest, there is a tiny electrical charge (–70 millivolts) across the cell membrane. That is, the inside of the cell has a slight negative charge relative to the outside. This electrical charge is due to the fact that several types of ions (positively and negatively charged particles) exist in different concentrations outside and inside the cell. As a result, the interior of the cell acquires a tiny negative electric charge relative to the outside. This *resting potential* does not occur by accident; the neuron works to maintain the resting potential by actively pumping positively charged ions back outside if they enter while retaining negatively charged ions in greater concentrations than are present outside the cell.

When the neuron is stimulated, either directly (by light, heat, or pressure) or by messages from other neurons, the situation may change radically. If the stimulation is of sufficient magnitude—if it exceeds the *threshold* of the neuron in question—complex biochemical changes occur in the cell membrane. As a result of these changes, some types of *positively charged ions* are briefly allowed to enter the neuron through specialized pores called *ion channels* more readily than before. This influx of positive ions reduces and then totally eliminates the resting potential. Indeed, for a brief period of time, the interior of the cell may actually attain a positive charge relative to the outside.

After a very brief period (1 or 2 milliseconds), the neuron then actively pumps the positive ions back outside and allows other ions, which flowed outside via their own ion channels, to reenter. As a result, the resting potential is gradually restored, and the cell becomes ready to "fire" once again. Together, these swings in electric charge—from negative to positive and back again—are termed the **action potential**. And it is the passage of this electrical disturbance along the cell membrane that constitutes the basic signal within our nervous system.

Note, by the way, that the action potential is an *all-or-none response*. Either it occurs at full strength or it does not occur at all; there is nothing in between. Also, the speed of conduction is very rapid in neurons possessing a myelin sheath. In a sense, the action potential along myelinated axons jumps from one small gap in the sheath to another—openings known as **nodes of Ranvier**. Speeds along myelinated axons can reach 270 miles per hour!

Glial Cells: *Cells in the nervous system that surround, support, and protect neurons.*

Axon Terminals: *Structures at the end of axons that contain transmitter substances.*

Synapse: *A region where the axon of one neuron closely approaches other neurons or the cell membrane of other types of cells such as muscle cells.*

Action Potential: *A rapid shift in the electrical charge across the cell membrane of neurons. This disturbance along the membrane communicates information within neurons.*

Nodes of Ranvier: *Small gaps in the myelin sheath surrounding the axons of many neurons.*

Another basic category of signals within neurons—called **graded potentials**—results from the external physical stimulation of the dendrite or cell body (please refer back to Figure 2.1). Unlike the all-or-nothing nature of the action potential, the magnitude of a graded potential varies in proportion to the size of the stimulus that produced it. Thus, a loud sound produces a graded potential of greater magnitude than a softer sound. Because graded potentials weaken quickly, they function primarily to convey incoming information over short distances; usually along the dendrite toward the neuron's cell body. Neurons typically receive information from many other cells—often thousands of them. As a result, it is the overall pattern of graded potentials reaching the cell body that determines whether or not an action potential will occur. The **Key Concept** on page 48 diagrams the nervous system's information transmission mechanism.

COMMUNICATION BETWEEN NEURONS: SYNAPTIC TRANSMISSION   Earlier we saw that neurons closely approach, but do not actually touch, other neurons (or other cells of the body). How, then, does the action potential cross the gap? Existing evidence points to the following answer.

When a neuron "fires," the action potential produced travels along the membrane of the axon to the axon terminals located at the end of the axon. Within the axon terminals are many structures known as **synaptic vesicles**. Arrival of the action potential causes these vesicles to approach the cell membrane, where they fuse with the membrane and then empty their contents into the synapse (see Figure 2.2 on page 49). The chemicals thus released—known as **neurotransmitters**—travel across the tiny synaptic gap until they reach special receptor sites in the membrane of the other cell.

These receptors are complex protein molecules whose structure is such that transmitter substances fit like chemical keys into the locks they provide. Specific transmitters can deliver signals only at certain locations on cell membranes, thereby introducing precision into the nervous system's complex communication system. Upon binding to their receptors, neurotransmitters either produce their effects directly, or function indirectly through the interaction of the neurotransmitter and its receptor with other substances. It's important to note that neurotransmitters are not released exclusively into synapses; they can also be released into body fluids, which carry them to many other cells. As a result, their effects may be quite far-reaching and are not necessarily restricted to other, nearby neurons.

Whether directly or indirectly, neurotransmitters produce one of two effects. If their effects are *excitatory* in nature, they cause a *depolarization* in the membrane of the second cell, making it more likely for the cell to fire. Or the transmitter substances may produce *inhibitory* effects. In this case, they actually *hyperpolarize* (increase the negative electrical charge of) the cell membrane of the second cell, thereby making it less likely that the cell will fire.

At this point you may be wondering about an obvious question we haven't yet considered: What happens to neurotransmitters after they cross the synapse? The answer is relatively clear. Either they are taken back for reuse in the axon terminals of the neuron that released them, a process known as *reuptake*, or they are deactivated by various enzymes present at the synapse.

It is important to note that in my comments so far, I have greatly simplified reality by describing a situation in which one neuron contacts another across a single synapse. In fact, this is rarely, if ever, the case. Most neurons actually form synapses with many others—ten thousand or more in some cases. Thus, at any given moment, most neurons are receiving a complex pat-

Graded Potential: A basic type of signal within neurons that results from external physical stimulation of the dendrite or cell body. Unlike the all-or-nothing nature of action potentials, graded potentials vary in proportion to the size of the stimulus that produced them.

Synaptic Vesicles: Structures in the axon terminals that contain various neurotransmitters.

Neurotransmitters: Chemicals, released by neurons, that carry information across the synapse.

Communication in the Nervous System: Putting It All Together

The key to understanding communication in the nervous system is to understand that information transmission depends on the movement of positively and negatively charged ions across the membrane that covers the neuron.

As shown in the diagram, a resting neuron has a slight negative charge (–70 millivolts) across the cell membrane (the inside is negative relative to the outside). The nervous system expends a great deal of energy to maintain this state of readiness. This is because the neuron's cell membrane is not a perfect barrier—it leaks a little, allowing some particles to slip in and others to slip out.

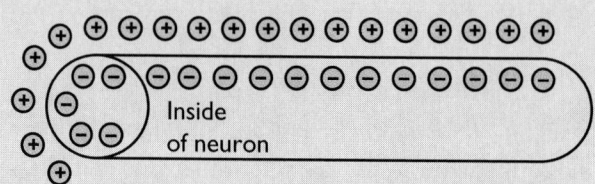

Steps in the Transmission Mechanism

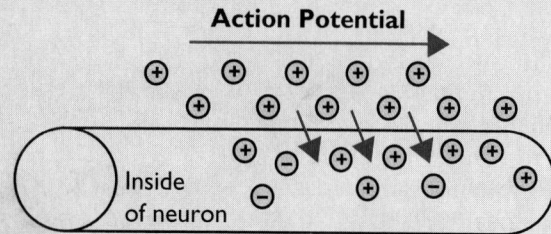

1. When the neuron is stimulated either by an external stimulus or by another neuron, positively charged particles enter the membrane through specialized *ion channels*, thereby momentarily eliminating the negative charge just inside the neuron's membrane. Movement of this disturbance along the membrane constitutes the action potential.

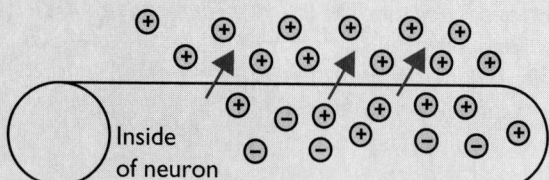

2. After a brief period, positively charged particles are actively pumped back outside of the neuron's membrane via the ion channels.

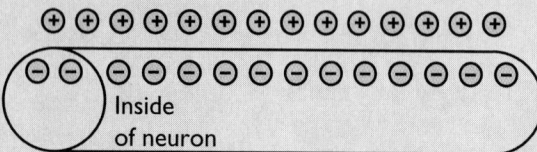

3. As a result of this active process, the inside of the neuron's membrane regains its negative charge (–70 millivolts) relative to the outside, and the cell is ready to "fire" once more. The passage of this electrical disturbance along the cell membrane serves as the basis for communication in the nervous system.

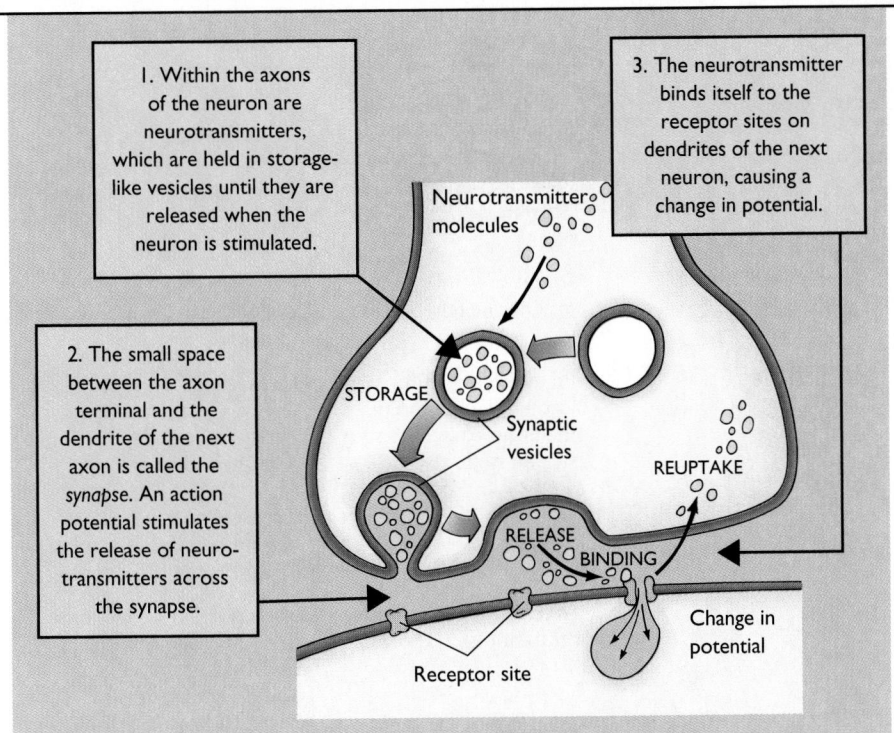

FIGURE 2.2

1. Within the axons of the neuron are neurotransmitters, which are held in storage-like vesicles until they are released when the neuron is stimulated.

3. The neurotransmitter binds itself to the receptor sites on dendrites of the next neuron, causing a change in potential.

2. The small space between the axon terminal and the dendrite of the next axon is called the *synapse*. An action potential stimulates the release of neuro-transmitters across the synapse.

Neurotransmitter molecules

STORAGE

Synaptic vesicles

REUPTAKE

RELEASE   BINDING

Change in potential

Receptor site

Synaptic Transmission: An Overview

The axon terminals found on the ends of axons contain many *synaptic vesicles*. When an action potential reaches the axon terminal, these vesicles move toward the cell membrane. Once there, the vesicles fuse with the membrane and release their contents (*neurotransmitters*) into the synapse.

tern of excitatory and inhibitory influences from many neighbors. Whether a neuron conducts an action potential or not, then, depends on the total pattern of this input (for example, whether excitatory or inhibitory input predominates). Further, the effects of excitatory and inhibitory input can be cumulative over time, in part because such effects do not dissipate instantaneously. Thus, if a neuron that has recently been stimulated, but not sufficiently to produce an action potential, is stimulated again soon afterwards, the two sources of excitation may combine so that an action potential is generated. In one sense, then, neurons act as tiny *decision-making* mechanisms, firing only when the pattern of information reaching them is just right. The fact that individual neurons affect and are, in turn, affected by many others strongly suggests that it is the total pattern or network of activity in the nervous system that is crucial. As we will see in later discussions, it is this intricate web of neural excitation that generates the richness and complexity of our conscious experience.

KEY QUESTIONS

- What is biopsychology?
- What does a neuron do? What are the parts of a neuron?
- What are action potentials?
- How do neurons communicate with one another?

NEUROTRANSMITTERS: Chemical Keys to the Nervous System

The fact that transmitter substances produce either excitatory or inhibitory effects might seem to suggest that there are only two types of neurotransmitters. In fact, there are at least nine universally recognized substances known to function as neurotransmitters, and forty or more peptides (amino acid combinations) *appear* to function as neurotransmitters. Several known neurotransmitters and their functions are summarized in Table 2.1 (on page 50).

Although the specific role of many transmitter substances is largely unknown, several have been investigated extensively. For example, *acetylcholine*

TABLE 2.1

Neurotransmitters: A Summary

Neurons have been found to communicate by means of many different *neurotransmitters*. This table presents several known neurotransmitters, where they are found, and their known or suspected effects on the body.

NEUROTRANSMITTER	LOCATION	EFFECTS
Acetylcholine	Found throughout the central nervous system, in the autonomic nervous system, and at all neuromuscular junctions.	Involved in muscle action, learning, and memory.
Norepinephrine	Found in neurons in the autonomic nervous system.	Primarily involved in control of alertness and wakefulness.
Dopamine	Produced by neurons located in a region of the brain called the substantia nigra.	Involved in movement, attention, and learning. Degeneration of dopamine-producing neurons linked to Parkinson's disease. Too much dopamine has been linked to schizophrenia.
Serotonin	Found in neurons in the brain and spinal cord.	Plays a role in the regulation of mood and in the control of eating, sleep, and arousal. Has also been implicated in the regulation of pain and in dreaming.
GABA (gamma-aminobutyric acid)	Found throughout the brain and spinal cord.	GABA is the major inhibitory neurotransmitter in the brain. Abnormal levels of GABA have been implicated in sleep and eating disorders.

is an important neurotransmitter found throughout the nervous system. Current evidence indicates that acetylcholine is the neurotransmitter at most junctions between motor neurons (neurons concerned with muscular movements) and muscle cells. Thus, anything that interferes with the action of acetylcholine can produce paralysis. Acetylcholine is also believed to play a role in attention, arousal, and memory processes. Scientists believe that the severe memory loss characteristic of persons suffering from *Alzheimer's disease* results from a degeneration of cells that produce acetylcholine. Examinations of the brains of persons who have died from this disease show unusually low levels of this substance (Coyle, Price & DeLong, 1983).

ENDORPHINS   Perhaps the most fascinating findings about neurotransmitters and their effects are the result of a surprising discovery first reported in the mid-1970s (Hughes et al., 1975). At that time many researchers who were studying the impact of *morphine* and other opiates discovered that there were special receptor sites for such drugs within the brain. This was indeed intriguing: Why should such receptors exist? The answer was quick in coming: Naturally occurring substances that closely resemble morphine in chemical structure were soon isolated deep within the brain. These substances, known as *endorphins*, seemed to act as neurotransmitters, stimulating specialized receptor sites. But this finding, in turn, raised another question: Why should the brain produce

KEY QUESTIONS

• What are the effects of neurotransmitters?
• What problems can be solved using knowledge of neurotransmitters?

such substances? Research has now suggested one possibility: Endorphins are released by the body in response to pain or vigorous exercise and so help reduce sensations of pain that might otherwise interfere with ongoing behavior (Fields & Basbaum, 1984). Additional evidence indicates that endorphins, more precisely known as *opioid peptides*, also serve to intensify positive sensations—for example, the "runner's high" many people experience after vigorous exercise. As a longtime runner, I can attest to the powerful and pleasant effects exerted by these substances. Indeed, nothing seems to ease the tension of a tough workday better than a long run at the end of the day.

In short, it appears that the brain possesses an internal mechanism for moderating unpleasant sensations and magnifying positive ones, and that the effects of morphine and other opiates stem, at least in part, from the fact that these drugs stimulate this naturally existing system.

This fact, and related evidence, has led to research efforts aimed at identifying drugs to alter synaptic transmission for practical purposes. Growing evidence suggests that understanding the process of synaptic transmission may be the key to successful treatment of a variety of disorders, including addictions to alcohol and other drugs.

ENDORPHINS: NEUROTRANS-MITTERS AS PAIN RELIEVERS?

Endorphins are released by the body in response to pain and may also intensify positive bodily sensations, as in the "runner's high."

THE NERVOUS SYSTEM: *Its Basic Structure and Functions*

*I*f neurons are the building blocks, then the **nervous system** is the structure they, along with other types of cells, combine to erect. Since this system regulates our internal bodily functions and permits us to react to the external world in countless ways, it deserves very careful attention. In this section I will describe the basic structure of the nervous system and will introduce several techniques psychologists use to study its complex functions.

THE NERVOUS SYSTEM: *Its Major Divisions*

Although the nervous system functions as an integrated whole, it is often viewed as having two major portions—the **central nervous system** and the **peripheral nervous system**. Figure 2.3 (on page 52) diagrams these and other divisions of the nervous system.

THE CENTRAL NERVOUS SYSTEM The central nervous system (CNS) consists of the brain and the spinal cord. Since I'll soon describe the structure of the brain in detail, we won't examine it here. The spinal cord runs through the middle of a bony column of hollow bones known as *vertebrae*. You can feel these by moving your hand up and down the middle of your back.

The spinal cord has two major functions. First, it carries sensory information via *afferent* nerve fibers from receptors throughout the body to the brain and conducts information via *efferent* nerve fibers from the brain to muscles and glands. Second, it plays a key role in various *reflexes*. These are seemingly automatic actions evoked rapidly by particular stimuli. Withdrawing your hand from a hot object or blinking your eye in response to a rapidly approaching object are common examples of reflex actions. In their simplest form, reflexes involve neural circuits in which information from various receptors is carried to the spinal cord, where it stimulates other neurons known as *interneurons*. These then transmit information to muscle cells, thus

Learning Objective 2.4
Describe the major divisions of the nervous system.

Learning Objective 2.5
Describe the major techniques for studying the nervous system.

Learning Objective 2.6
Know how imaging techniques have increased our understanding of brain/behavior relationships.

Nervous System: The complex structure that regulates bodily processes and is responsible, ultimately, for all aspects of conscious experience.

Central Nervous System: The brain and the spinal cord.

Peripheral Nervous System: The portion of the nervous system that connects internal organs and glands, as well as voluntary and involuntary muscles, to the central nervous system.

FIGURE 2.3

Major Divisions of the Nervous System

The nervous system consists of several major parts.

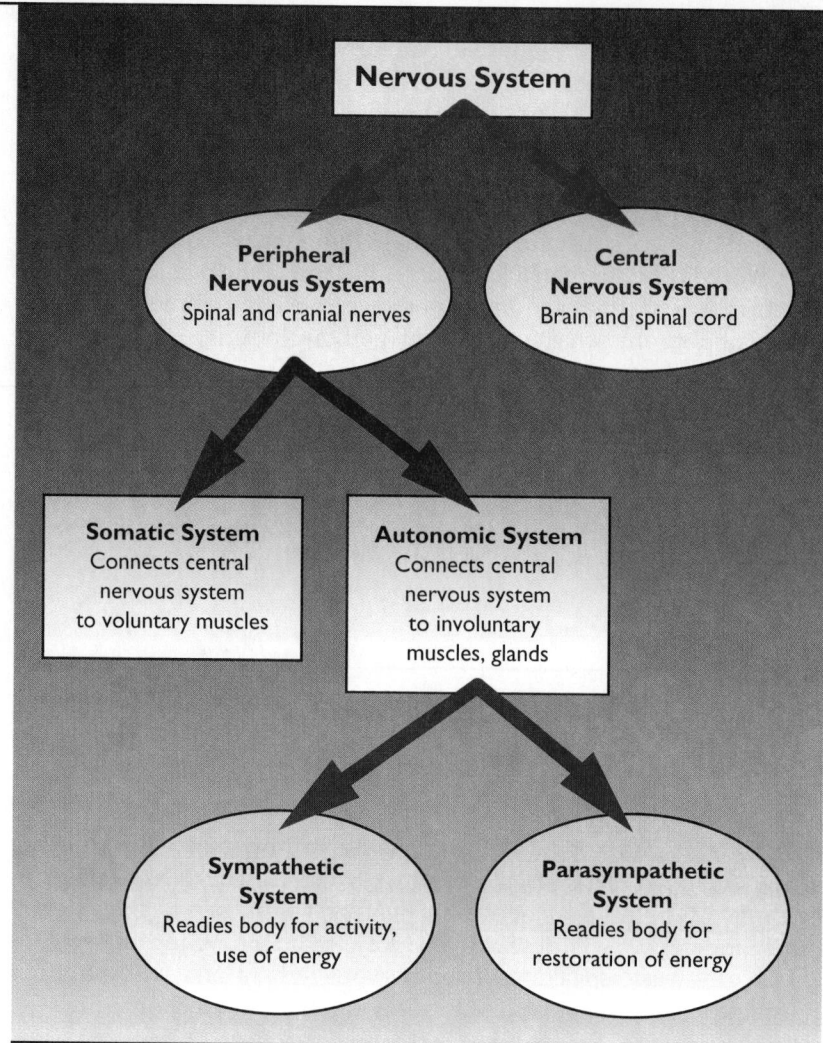

Somatic Nervous System: *The portion of the peripheral nervous system that connects the brain and spinal cord to voluntary muscles.*

Autonomic Nervous System: *The part of the peripheral nervous system that connects internal organs, glands, and involuntary muscles to the central nervous system.*

Sympathetic Nervous System: *The portion of the autonomic nervous system that readies the body for expenditure of energy.*

Parasympathetic Nervous System: *The portion of the autonomic nervous system that readies the body for restoration of energy.*

producing reflex actions. But please take note: Reflexes are usually much more complex than this. Hundreds or even thousands of neurons may influence a reflex, and input from certain areas of the brain may be involved as well. However they arise, spinal reflexes offer an obvious advantage: They permit us to react to potential dangers much more rapidly than we could if we had to consider intellectually how to respond.

THE PERIPHERAL NERVOUS SYSTEM The peripheral nervous system consists primarily of *nerves*, bundles of axons from many neurons, which connect the central nervous system with sense organs and with muscles and glands throughout the body. Most of these nerves are attached to the spinal cord; these *spinal nerves* serve all of the body below the neck. Other nerves known as *cranial nerves* extend from the brain. They carry sensory information from receptors in the eyes and ears and other sense organs; they also carry information from the central nervous system to muscles in the head and neck.

The peripheral nervous system has two further subdivisions: the **somatic** and **autonomic nervous systems**. The somatic nervous system connects the central nervous system to voluntary muscles throughout the body. Thus, when you engage in almost any voluntary action, such as ordering a pizza or reading the rest of this chapter, portions of your somatic nervous system are involved. In contrast, the autonomic nervous system connects the central

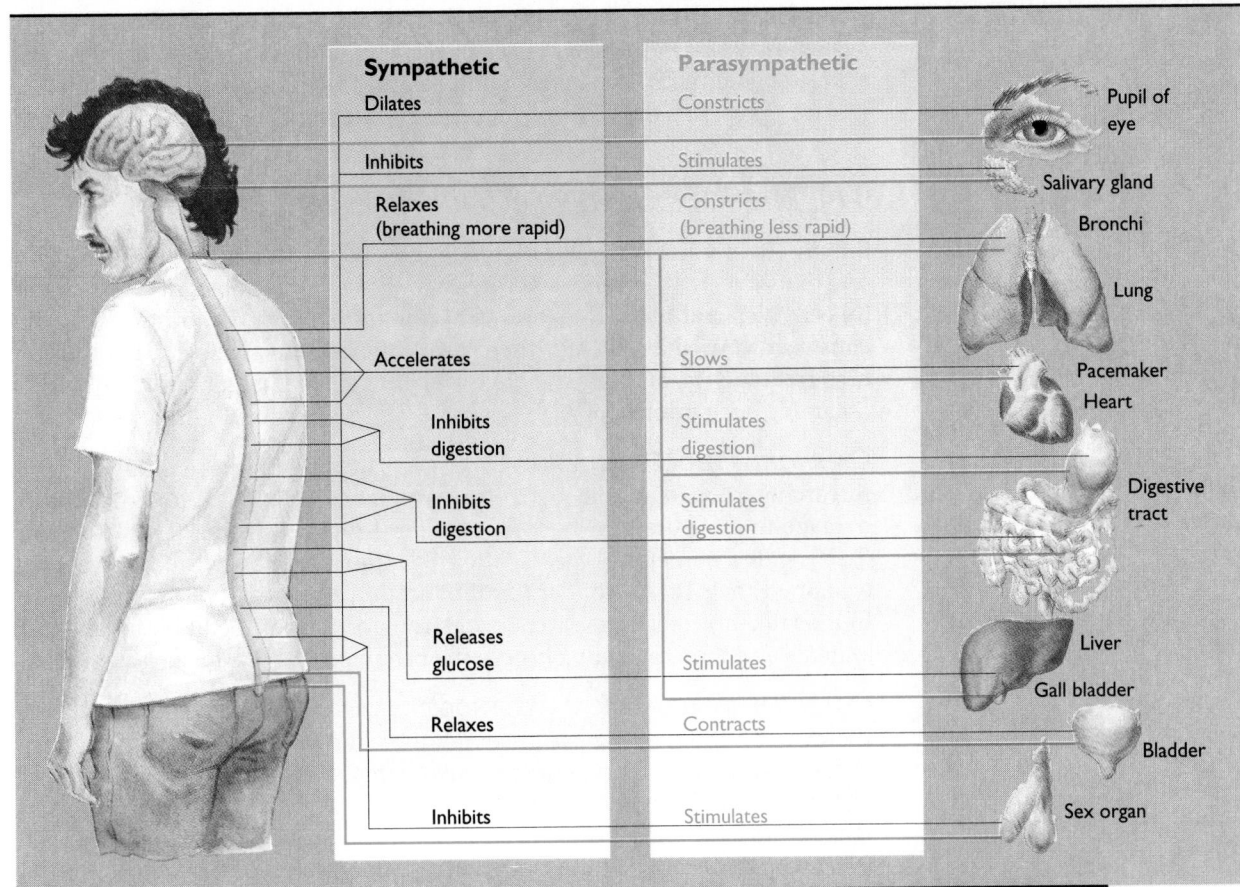

Sympathetic	Parasympathetic	
Dilates	Constricts	Pupil of eye
Inhibits	Stimulates	Salivary gland
Relaxes (breathing more rapid)	Constricts (breathing less rapid)	Bronchi
		Lung
Accelerates	Slows	Pacemaker Heart
Inhibits digestion	Stimulates digestion	Digestive tract
Inhibits digestion	Stimulates digestion	
Releases glucose	Stimulates	Liver
		Gall bladder
Relaxes	Contracts	Bladder
Inhibits	Stimulates	Sex organ

FIGURE 2.4

nervous system to internal organs and glands and to muscles over which we have little voluntary control—for instance, the muscles in our digestive system.

Still, we can't stop dividing things here. The autonomic nervous system, too, consists of two distinct parts. The first is known as the **sympathetic nervous system**. In general, this system prepares the body for using energy, as in vigorous physical actions. Thus, stimulation of this division increases heartbeat, raises blood pressure, releases sugar into the blood for energy, and increases the flow of blood to muscles used in physical activities. The second portion of the autonomic system, known as the **parasympathetic nervous system**, operates in the opposite manner. It stimulates processes that conserve the body's energy. Activation of this system slows heartbeat, lowers blood pressure, and diverts blood away from skeletal muscles (for example, muscles in the arms and legs) and to the digestive system. Figure 2.4 summarizes many of the functions of the autonomic nervous system.

At first glance it might appear that these two parts of the autonomic system compete with one another in a head-on clash. In fact, this is far from the case. The sympathetic and parasympathetic systems actually function in a coordinated manner. For example, after a person eats a large meal on a warm day, the parasympathetic system stimulates digestion while at the same time the sympathetic system increases sweating in order to eliminate excess heat. Similarly, both systems are involved in regulating changes in sexual organs during sexual relations.

The Autonomic Nervous System: An Overview

The autonomic nervous system consists of two major parts: the sympathetic and the parasympathetic nervous systems. Some of the functions of each are shown here.

KEY QUESTIONS

- What structures comprise the central nervous system?
- What is the function of the spinal cord?
- What two systems make up the peripheral nervous system? What are the roles of these two systems?
- What are the functions of the sympathetic and parasympathetic nervous systems?
- How do psychologists study the nervous system?
- How are PET scans used to study the activity of the brain?

Before concluding, I should emphasize that while the autonomic nervous system plays an important role in the regulation of internal bodily processes, it does so mainly by transmitting information to and from the central nervous system. Thus, it is the CNS, ultimately, that runs the show.

THE NERVOUS SYSTEM: *How It Is Studied*

Suppose that you are a psychologist interested in creating a map of the brain, one that reveals the brain structures and processes involved in various mental activities and behaviors. How do you get the information from which to construct your map? While there are no simple answers to this question, biopsychologists and others have devised several ingenious methods for obtaining such information.

OBSERVING THE EFFECTS OF DAMAGE   In one of the earliest methods, researchers observed the behavior of persons who had suffered obvious damage to their brain or nervous system through accident. Then, following their death—sometimes years after the injury had occurred—researchers examined their brains to identify the location and extent of the brain injury. In a related approach, researchers destroy portions of the brain in laboratory animals and then carefully observe the behavioral effects of such damage.

PSYCHOPHARMACOLOGICAL METHODS: INTRODUCING DRUGS INTO THE BRAIN   Psychologists have also mapped the brain's functions by using minute quantities of drugs to produce damage at specific brain sites, or to stimulate or anesthetize specific groups of neurons. If, for example, a drug that anesthetizes neurons is introduced into an area believed to play a role in speech production, we might expect the person's ability to speak to decrease while the drug's effects persist.

ELECTRICAL RECORDING AND BRAIN STIMULATION   If a particular part of the brain plays a role in some form of behavior, this part should be active during that behavior. Consistent with this reasoning, neuroscientists attempt to study the nervous system by recording electrical activity within the brain. Sometimes this involves measuring the electrical activity of the entire brain by means of electrodes placed on the skull—a procedure called **electroencephalography**, or **EEG**. In other cases it involves the precise implantation of tiny electrodes in specific locations to *record* the activity of a single neuron or groups of neurons. A related technique utilizes the *delivery* of small electric currents to specific brain areas. By means of the accurate implantation of tiny electrodes, researchers can stimulate specific areas of the brain to investigate their role in various forms of behavior. Researchers also use EEG and related procedures to determine the precise location and timing of mental events. Moreover, intriguing new evidence suggests that these procedures soon may be used to diagnose a variety of cognitive disorders, including Alzheimer's disease (Polich, 1993).

IMAGES OF THE LIVING BRAIN: MRIs, SQUIDs, AND PETs   Perhaps most exciting, however, are an alphabet soup of techniques that provide detailed images of the living brain's structures and functions. The first of these techniques is **magnetic resonance imaging**, or **MRI**. Here, images of the brain are obtained by means of a strong magnetic field. Hydrogen atoms, found in all living tissue, emit measurable waves of energy when exposed to such a field. In MRI, these waves are measured and combined to form images of the brain. These MRI images are impressively clear and therefore extremely useful in diagnosing many brain disorders. A high-speed version of MRI known as *functional MRI* captures detailed images of the brain in action.

Electroencephalography (EEG): A technique for measuring the electrical activity of the brain via electrodes placed at specified locations on the skull.

Magnetic Resonance Imaging (MRI): A method for studying the intact brain in which images are obtained by exposing the brain to a strong magnetic field.

A second recently developed imaging device is called **SQUID**—short for **superconducting quantum interference device**. SQUID produces images based on its ability to detect tiny changes in magnetic fields in the brain. Apparently, when neurons fire, they create an electric current. Electric currents, in turn, give rise to magnetic fields that the SQUID interprets as neural activity. Researchers have used SQUIDs to map various brain functions, including construction of a topographical map in the hearing part of the brain. The SQUID tonal map closely resembles a musical scale; one tiny group of cells reacts to a middle C note, an adjacent group to a C sharp, and so on—much like the keys on a piano.

A third high-tech method neuroscientists use to snoop on the living brain is **positron emission tomography**, or **PET**, scans. PET scans provide information regarding the metabolic activity of the brain—how active its various parts are at a given point in time. PET scans do this by measuring blood flow in various neural areas, or by gauging the rate at which glucose, the brain's fuel, is metabolized. Individuals undergoing PET scans are injected with small amounts of harmless radioactive isotopes attached to either water or glucose molecules. Blood flow (containing the radioactive water molecules) is greatest in the most active areas of the brain. Similarly, glucose is absorbed by brain cells in proportion to their level of activity, with the most active cells taking in the greatest amount of glucose. As a result, PET scans allow scientists to map activity in various parts of a person's brain as she or he reads, listens to music, or engages in a mental activity such as solving math problems. Needless to say, such images can contribute much to our understanding of the role of various portions of the brain in many forms of behavior. For more information on practical uses of imaging techniques please refer to the **Point of It All** section.

MRI: A HIGH-TECH TOOL TO PEEK INSIDE THE BODY

Magnetic resonance imaging provides detailed images of the body's internal structures and is especially useful in diagnosing brain disorders.

THE POINT OF IT ALL

High-Tech Snoopers: Putting Brain-Imaging Devices to Work

Advances in technology have made it possible to create dynamic images of the living brain. This, in turn, has allowed researchers to apply these techniques in intriguing ways. One application involves performing brain scans on normal persons and on persons with a variety of mental disorders to detect differences in the activity of their brains (Resnick, 1992). For example, as we'll see in chapter 12, *obsessive-compulsive disorder* is characterized by persistent, uncontrollable intrusions of unwanted thoughts and urges to engage in ritualistic behaviors. PET scans of persons with obsessive-compulsive disorder consistently show increased activity in several areas of the brain, including the frontal lobe of the cerebral cortex—a brain region believed to be involved in impulse control and response inhibition. Following successful pharmacologic or psychosurgical treatment, PET scans of these patients' brains show decreased activity in these areas. These findings suggest that imaging techniques

SQUID (Superconducting Quantum Interference Device): An imaging device that captures images of the brain through its ability to detect tiny changes in magnetic fields in the brain.

Positron Emission Tomography (PET): An imaging technique that detects the activity of the brain by measuring glucose utilization or blood flow.

FIGURE **2.5**

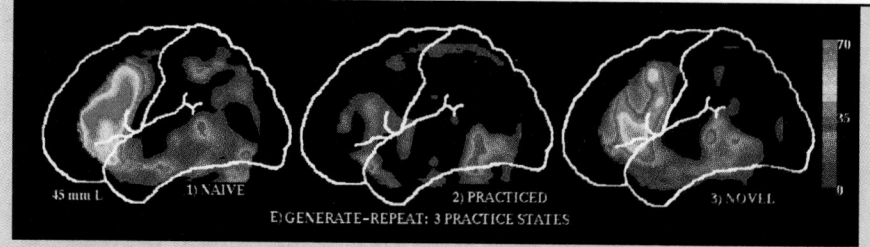

E) GENERATE-REPEAT: 3 PRACTICE STATES

PET Scanners: A Research Tool for Exploring Important Brain Processes

Brain imaging tools are proving to be important research tools—in this case, for determining how the pattern of activity in the brain changes with experience on a language task.

(*Source:* Fiez & Petersen, 1993.)

may play a useful role in monitoring the effects of treatments for a variety of mental disorders.

Imaging techniques may also reveal how the brain delegates mental tasks. In one study, researchers used a PET scanner to monitor participants' brains while they performed a fairly simple task—signing their name with their dominant hand (Nadis, 1992). The PET scan showed a low level of activity in a region of the cortex—the region of the brain associated with higher cognitive functions such as thinking, planning, and reasoning. In contrast, a high level of activity was present in the basal ganglia, an area responsible for coordination of motor activity. When participants were asked to write their name with their *nondominant* hand, however, an opposite pattern emerged: decreased activity in the basal ganglia, but increased activity in the brain's cortex. This simple example reveals an important principle regarding how the brain delegates its resources: When we undertake a novel or complex task, a greater overall amount of mental effort is required—especially in the brain's cortex. Later, as we master a task, less mental effort is required, and responsibility for the task is shifted away from the cortex to more automatic brain regions.

Recent evidence suggests that this principle seems to apply to other aspects of information processing as well, including how the brain delegates language-processing tasks (Fiez & Petersen, 1993; Posner & McCandliss, 1993). For example, in one study researchers asked participants to say aloud an appropriate verb for each of several nouns (e.g., baseball–throw and money–spend) at three different times: before they had experience with the task (naive condition); after they had several opportunities to practice with the same set of nouns (practiced condition); and following practice with the task, but with a new set of nouns (novel condition). As shown in Figure 2.5, a PET scan of their brains revealed that the brain delegates language-processing tasks based on experience: Higher activity in the brain's cortex was observed during the naive and novel conditions, but not in the practiced condition. The findings of these and related studies demonstrate that modern imaging techniques are useful tools for increasing our understanding of important brain behavior relationships.

THE BRAIN: *Where Consciousness Is Manifest*

Learning Objective 2.7
Identify the structures and functions of the parts of the brain.

*I*f there can be said to be a "governing organ" of the body, it is definitely the brain. And what an amazing structure it is! Into slightly more than three pounds the brain crams an array of functions and capacities that even today computer scientists envy. After all, what computer, no matter how huge or advanced, is currently capable of (1) storing seemingly *unlimited* amounts of information for years or decades, (2) rewriting its own programs in response

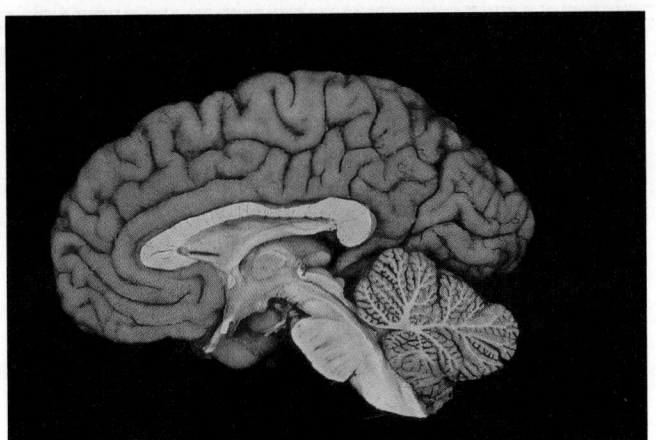

THE HUMAN BRAIN

An actual human brain split in half
reveals its inner structure.

to new input and experience, and (3) simultaneously controlling a vast number of complex internal processes and external activities? Moreover, even if such a computer existed, it could not, as far as we can tell, reproduce the emotional experiences, imagery, insights, and creativity of the human brain.

The brain is a complex structure and can be described in many different ways. Often, though, it is divided—for purposes of discussion—into three major components: portions concerned with basic bodily functions and survival; portions concerned with motivation and emotion; and portions concerned with such complex activities as language, planning, foresight, and reasoning.

SURVIVAL BASICS: The Brain Stem

Let's begin with the basics: the structures in the brain that regulate the bodily processes we share with many other life forms on earth. These structures are located in the *brain stem*, the portion that begins just above the spinal cord and continues into the center of this complex organ (refer to Figure 2.6 on page 58).

Two of these structures, the **medulla** and the **pons,** are located just above the point where the spinal cord enters the brain. Major sensory and motor pathways pass through both of these structures on their way to higher brain centers or down to effectors (muscles or glands) in other parts of the body. In addition, both the medulla and the pons contain a central core consisting of a dense network of interconnected neurons. This is the **reticular activating system,** and it has long been viewed as a part of the brain that plays a key role in sleep and arousal—a topic I'll discuss in greater detail in chapter 4. Recent evidence, however, indicates that the reticular activating system is also concerned with many seemingly unrelated functions, such as muscle tone, cardiac and circulatory reflexes, and attention (Pinel, 1993). Thus, referring to it as a single "system," which implies a unitary function, is somewhat misleading.

The medulla also contains several *nuclei*—collections of neuron cell bodies—that control vital functions such as breathing, heart rate, and blood pressure, as well as coughing and sneezing.

Behind the medulla and pons is the **cerebellum** (refer again to Figure 2.6). It is primarily concerned with the regulation of motor activities, serving to orchestrate muscular activities so that they occur in a synchronized fashion. Damage to the cerebellum results in jerky, poorly coordinated muscle functioning. If such damage is severe, it may be impossible for a person to stand, let alone to walk or run. Recent evidence suggests the cerebellum may play a role in nonmotor cognitive activities as well (e.g., Daum et al., 1993).

Medulla: *A brain structure concerned with the regulation of vital bodily functions such as breathing and heartbeat.*

Pons: *A portion of the brain through which sensory and motor information passes and which contains structures relating to sleep, arousal, and the regulation of muscle tone and cardiac reflexes.*

Reticular Activating System: *A structure within the brain concerned with sleep, arousal, and the regulation of muscle tone and cardiac reflexes.*

Cerebellum: *A part of the brain concerned with the regulation and coordination of basic motor activities.*

FIGURE 2.6

Basic Structure of the Human Brain

In this simplified drawing, the brain has been split down the middle to show its inner structure.

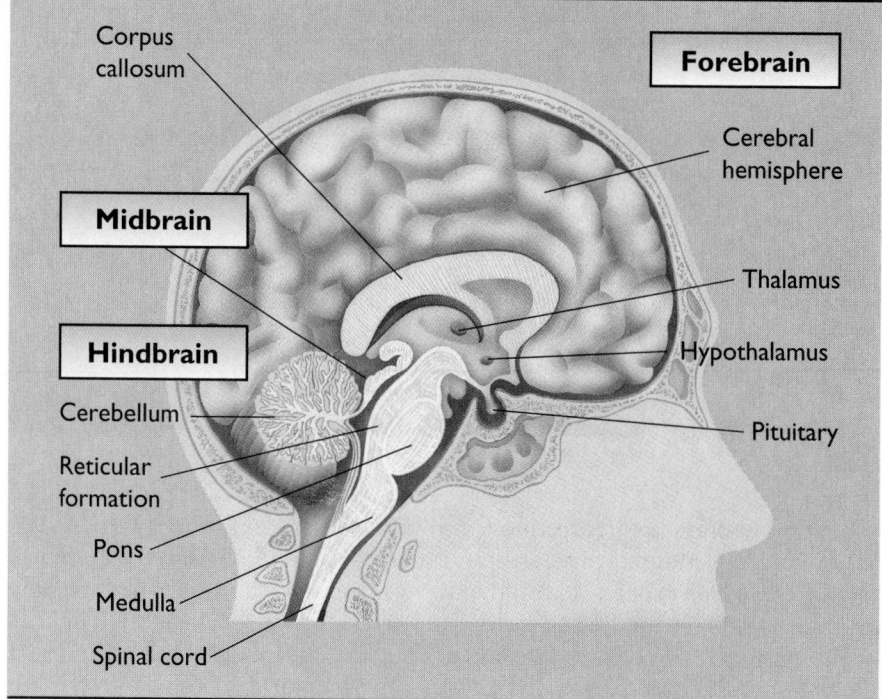

Above the medulla and pons, near the end of the brain stem, is a structure known as the **midbrain**. It contains an extension of the reticular activating system as well as primitive centers concerned with vision and hearing: the *superior colliculi* (vision) and the *inferior colliculi* (hearing). The midbrain also contains structures that play a role in such varied functions as the pain-relieving effects of opiates and the guidance and control of motor movements by sensory input.

EMOTION AND MOTIVATION: THE HYPOTHALAMUS, THALAMUS, AND LIMBIC SYSTEM

Ancient philosophers identified the heart as the center of our emotions. While this poetic belief is still reflected on many valentine cards, modern science indicates that it is wrong. If there is a center for appetites, emotions, and motives, it actually lies deep within the brain in several interrelated structures.

Perhaps the most fascinating of these is the **hypothalamus**. Less than one cubic centimeter in size, this tiny structure exerts profound effects on our behavior. First, it regulates the autonomic nervous system, thus influencing reactions ranging from sweating and salivating to the shedding of tears and changes in blood pressure. Second, it plays a key role in *homeostasis*—the maintenance of the body's internal environment at optimal levels. Portions of the hypothalamus seem to play a role in the regulation of eating and drinking, primarily through an impact on metabolism. For example, animals that have suffered damage to the ventromedial hypothalamus tend to overeat, because their bodies show a greatly increased tendency to store calories as fat. As a result, they must keep eating to maintain sufficient stores of available energy in their blood to meet immediate requirements (Gray & Morley, 1986; Powley et al., 1980). Certain neurotransmitters (neuropeptide Y), when

Midbrain: A part of the brain containing primitive centers for vision and hearing. It also plays a role in the regulation of visual reflexes.

Hypothalamus: A small structure deep within the brain that plays a key role in the regulation of the autonomic nervous system and of several forms of motivated behavior such as eating and aggression.

directly injected into portions of the hypothalamus, also stimulate prolonged overeating and obesity in rats (Stanley & Gillard, 1994). Damage to the lateral hypothalamus reduces food intake, probably because of a more general reduction in responsiveness to all sensory input. In other words, subjects with lesions in the lateral hypothalamus seem to lose interest in many stimuli, including food and drink. (Please see Chapter 9 for further discussion of the regulation of eating and of several eating disorders.)

The hypothalamus also plays a role in other forms of motivated behavior such as mating and aggression. It exerts this influence, at least in part, by regulating the release of hormones from the **pituitary gland,** which we'll consider in more detail in our discussion of the endocrine system.

Above the hypothalamus, quite close to the center of the brain, is another important structure, the **thalamus**. This structure consists of two football-shaped parts, one in each hemisphere. This has sometimes been called the great relay station of the brain, and with good reason. The thalamus receives input from all of our senses except olfaction (smell), performs some preliminary analyses, and then transmits the information to other parts of the brain.

Finally, we should consider a set of structures that together are known as the **limbic system**. The functions of this system—and the question of whether it should even be considered a unitary system—are still unclear. There is some indication, though, that the structures that make up the limbic system play an important role in emotion and in motivated behavior such as feeding, fleeing, fighting, and sex.

THE CEREBRAL CORTEX: THE HUB OF COMPLEX THOUGHT

The **cerebral cortex**—the thin outer covering of the brain—seems to be the part of the brain responsible for our ability to reason, plan, remember, and imagine. In short, this structure accounts for our impressive capacity to process and transform information.

The cerebral cortex is only about one-eighth of an inch thick, but it contains billions of neurons, each connected to thousands of others. The predominance of cell bodies gives the cortex a brownish-gray appearance. Because of its appearance, the cortex is often referred to as gray matter. Beneath the cortex are myelin-sheathed axons connecting the neurons of the cortex with those of other parts of the brain. The large concentrations of myelin gives this tissue an opaque appearance, and hence it is often referred to as white matter. It is important to note that the cortex is divided into two nearly symmetrical halves, the *cerebral hemispheres*. Thus, many of the structures described below appear in both the left and right cerebral hemispheres. As we'll soon see, however, this similarity in structure is not entirely matched by similarity in function. The two hemispheres appear to be somewhat specialized in the functions they perform.

The cerebral hemispheres are folded into many ridges and grooves, which greatly increase their surface area. Each hemisphere is usually described, on the basis of the largest of these grooves or *fissures*, as being divided into four distinct regions or lobes.

THE FRONTAL LOBE Occupying the area of the brain nearest the face, the **frontal lobe** is bounded by the deep *central fissure*. Lying along this fissure, just within the frontal lobe, is the *motor cortex*, an area concerned with the control of body movements (see Figure 2.7 on page 60). Damage to this area does not produce total paralysis. Instead, it often results in a loss of control over fine movements, especially of the fingers. This illustrates an important

Pituitary Gland: An endocrine gland that releases hormones to regulate other glands and several basic biological processes.

Thalamus: A structure deep within the brain that receives sensory input from other portions of the nervous system and then transmits this information to the cerebral hemispheres and other parts of the brain.

Limbic System: Several structures deep within the brain that play a role in emotional reactions and behavior.

Cerebral Cortex: The outer covering of the cerebral hemispheres.

Frontal Lobe: The portion of the cerebral cortex that lies in front of the central fissure.

FIGURE 2.7

Major Regions of the Cerebral Cortex

The cerebral cortex is divided into four major lobes (left drawing). Specific areas in these lobes are concerned with sensory and motor functions (right drawing).

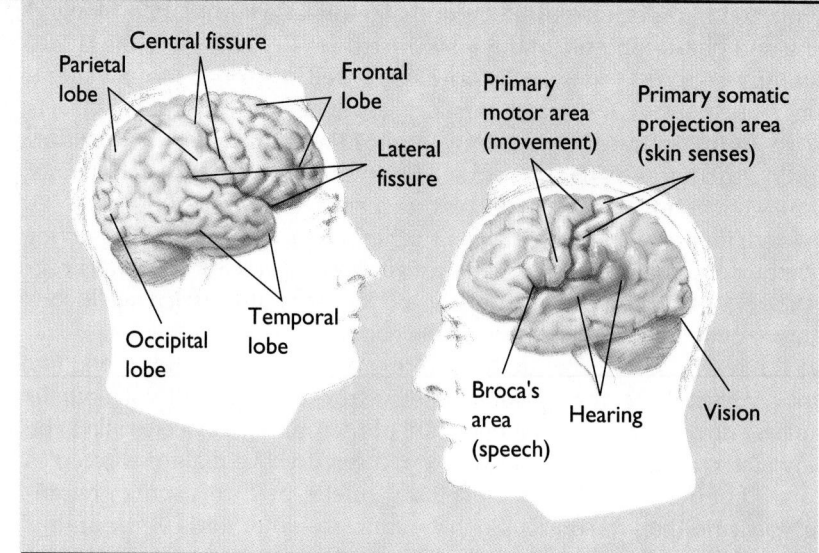

fact about the human brain: While a specific area may normally perform a given function, other regions can often take up the slack if an area is damaged and may gradually come to perform the same functions. Such *plasticity*, as it is often termed, is greater at a young age than after maturity, but it seems to operate to some extent throughout life.

THE PARIETAL LOBE Across the central fissure from the frontal lobe is the **parietal lobe**. This contains the *somatosensory cortex*, to which information from the skin senses—touch, temperature, pressure, and so on—is carried. (Refer to Figure 2.7.) Discrete damage to this area produces a variety of effects, depending in part on whether injury occurs to the left or right cerebral hemisphere. If damage involves the left hemisphere, individuals may lose the ability to read or write, or they may have difficulty knowing where parts of their own body are located. In contrast, if damage occurs in the right hemisphere, individuals may seem unaware of the left side of their body. For example, a man may forget to shave the left side of his face.

THE OCCIPITAL LOBE The **occipital lobe** is located near the back of the head. Its primary functions are visual, and it contains a sensory area that receives input from the eyes. Damage to this area often produces a "hole" in the person's field of vision: Objects in a particular location can't be seen, but the rest of the visual field is unaffected. Interestingly, in cases of severe damage to the occipital lobes, people may report complete loss of vision, yet respond appropriately to certain visual stimuli as if they *had* seen them. As with other brain structures, injury to the occipital lobe may produce contrasting effects depending on which cerebral hemisphere is affected. Damage to the occipital lobe in the right hemisphere produces loss of vision in the left visual field, whereas damage to the occipital lobe in the left hemisphere produces loss of vision in the right visual field.

THE TEMPORAL LOBE Finally, the **temporal lobe** is located along the side of each hemisphere (see Figure 2.7). The location makes sense, for this lobe is concerned primarily with hearing and contains a sensory area that receives input from the ears. Damage to the temporal lobe, too, can result in intriguing symptoms. When such injuries occur in the left hemisphere, people may

Parietal Lobe: A portion of the cerebral cortex, lying behind the central fissure, that plays a major role in the skin senses: touch, temperature, and pressure.

Occipital Lobe: A portion of the cerebral cortex involved in vision.

Temporal Lobe: The portion of the cerebral cortex that is involved in hearing.

lose the ability to understand spoken words. When damage is restricted to the right hemisphere, they may be able to recognize speech but may lose the ability to recognize other organizations of sound—for example, melodies, tones, or rhythms.

It is interesting to note that when added together, areas of the cortex that either control motor movements (*motor cortex*) or receive sensory input (*sensory cortex*) account for only 20 to 25 percent of the total area. The remainder is known as *association cortex* and, as its name suggests, is assumed to play a role in integrating the activities in the various sensory systems and in translating sensory input into programs for motor output. In addition, the association cortex seems to be involved in complex cognitive activities such as thinking, reasoning, and remembering. However, evidence concerning its role in these functions is incomplete at best (Pinel, 1993).

LANGUAGE AND THE CEREBRAL CORTEX

We have noted that many complex mental activities seem to take place in the cerebral cortex. If this is indeed the case, then it should be possible to identify areas of the cortex that are responsible for language—the abilities to speak, read, write, and so on. Not surprisingly, much research has been directed to this topic, and investigators have made considerable progress in understanding where and how the brain handles language. In the discussion that follows, I'll first outline a relatively simple model initially proposed to explain the neural bases of language. Then I'll provide a rough sketch of a more accurate picture that has emerged more recently (Peterson et al., 1989).

THE WERNICKE-GESCHWIND MODEL   Writing in the mid-nineteenth century, Paul Broca suggested that an area of the left frontal lobe, just in front of the primary cortex, played a key role in this process. Specifically, he noted that damage to this area left people able to understand speech but with reduced capacity to produce it. Broca concluded that this area of the brain contained memories for the sequence of muscular movements needed for fluent speech.

Some years later, in 1874, another researcher, Karl Wernicke, suggested that a second area, located in the left temporal lobe just behind the primary auditory cortex, also played a key role in language. Wernicke noticed that damage to this region left people able to speak but with reduced understanding of spoken or written words. In other words, such persons could speak fluently, but they could not readily understand what was said to them.

Almost one hundred years later, Geschwind combined these suggestions, plus other data, into a unified model known as the **Wernicke-Geschwind theory** (Geschwind, 1972). According to this model, both areas of the cortex identified by Broca and Wernicke, pathways connecting them, and several other regions including the primary visual cortex and the primary motor cortex function together in the production and comprehension of language. By way of illustration, here is how the theory describes what happens in the brain when language is actually used—when, for example, you engage in a conversation with another person. According to the Wernicke-Geschwind model, auditory signals triggered by the other person's speech are received by your primary auditory cortex and conducted to Wernicke's area, where they are comprehended. Neural information then moves from Wernicke's area to Broca's area via a pathway known as the *arcuate fasciculus*. In Broca's area, information about the muscular movements needed to produce speech is activated. This, in turn, is transmitted to the primary motor cortex, which stimulates muscles in your larynx and elsewhere. The result: overt speech occurs (see Figure 2.8 on page 62).

Wernicke-Geschwind Theory: A theory of how the brain processes information relating to speech and other verbal abilities. Although the theory has generated a considerable amount of research, recent evidence suggests that it does not provide an adequate picture of this process.

FIGURE **2.8**

The Wernicke-Geschwind Model of Human Speech

The Wernicke-Geschwind model of speech suggests that information received by the ears is transmitted to the primary auditory cortex (1). From there it moves to Wernicke's area, where it is comprehended. Neural information is then sent from this area to Broca's area (2). There it activates information concerned with the muscular movements needed to produce speech. When this information is transmitted to the motor cortex (3), actual speech occurs (4).

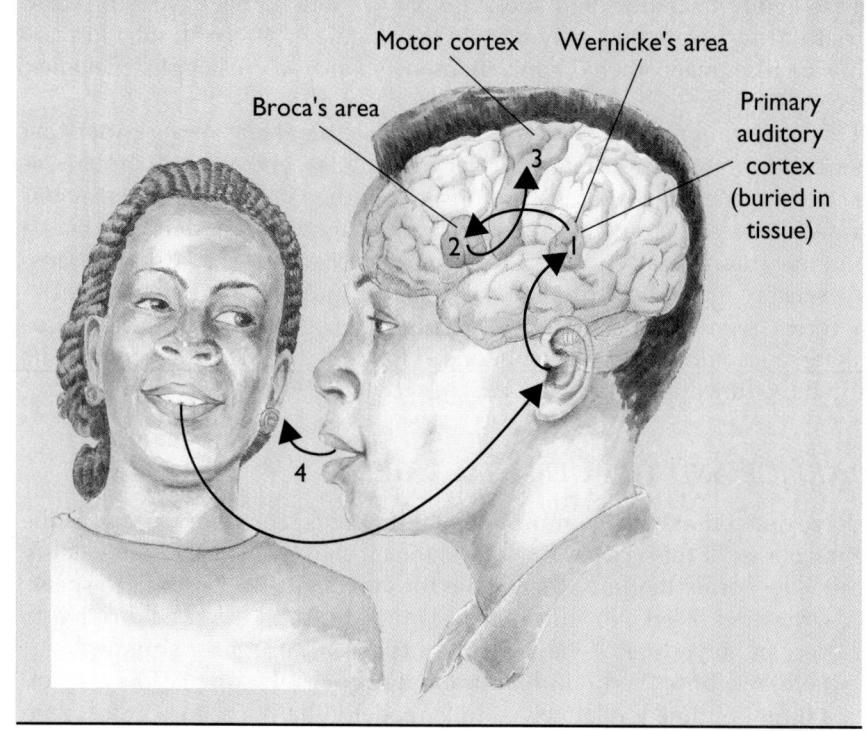

EVIDENCE RELATING TO THE WERNICKE-GESCHWIND MODEL Is this model accurate? Does it really describe the sequence of events within the brain that permits us to understand and use language? Growing evidence suggests that it does not. Careful study of persons suffering from some form of *aphasia*—brain damage–produced disturbances in the ability to use or comprehend language—argues against accepting this model as accurate. First, consider what happens when parts of the cortex are removed for medical reasons. In some cases, operations have removed areas viewed as crucial by the Wernicke-Geschwind model. Despite this fact, many patients show little disruption in their language skills, thereby calling basic assumptions of the theory into question (Rasmussen & Milner, 1975).

Second, scans of the brains of individuals suffering from language-related problems rarely if ever show damage in either Broca's or Wernicke's area. This has been the case even when patients showed language deficits quite similar to the ones originally used to establish the importance of these areas (Naeser et al., 1981).

Finally, when the brains of persons who have suffered accidental or disease-related damage during life are examined after their deaths or during medical operations, predictions of the Wernicke-Geschwind model concerning how the location of such damage should be related to language deficits are again not confirmed. For example, one study examined the brains of 214 persons who had experienced lesions in Broca's and Wernicke's areas, and not one demonstrated the kind of language deficits predicted by the model (Hecaen & Angelergues, 1964).

Together, these findings suggest that the model proposed by Geschwind should not be viewed as accurate. But if the Wernicke-Geschwind theory is incorrect, how is language represented in the brain? A more modern view is briefly described next.

KEY QUESTIONS

- What structures comprise the brain stem? What are their functions?
- What are the functions of the hypothalamus and the thalamus?
- What is the result of damage to the ventromedial hypothalamus? To the lateral hypothalamus?
- What is the role of the cerebral cortex?
- How is language processed in the brain?

PARALLEL MODELS OF THE NEURAL BASIS OF LANGUAGE   The Wernicke-Geschwind theory is sometimes described as a *serial* model—it suggests that neural events relating to language occur one step at a time and along one route. Many psychologists believe that such models are flawed and instead suggest that language and other complex mental processes may be more accurately represented by *parallel* models—ones suggesting that neural information can move along several routes at once and be processed simultaneously in different ways in different areas of the brain. Given the incredible complexity of language, such models seem to make very good sense. More importantly, however, they are supported by a growing body of evidence (Peterson et al., 1989).

LATERALIZATION OF THE CEREBRAL CORTEX: Two Minds in One Body?

A simple visual inspection of the two halves of the human brain would lead casual observers to conclude that they are mirror images of one another. Yet a large and rapidly growing body of evidence suggests that the cerebral hemispheres of the human brain are quite different—at least with respect to their function.

In other words, the brain shows a considerable degree of **lateralization of function**. Each hemisphere seems to be specialized for the performance of somewhat different tasks. Speech is one of the most important of these. For a large majority of human beings, this crucial process is located primarily in the *left* hemisphere (Benson, 1985). In fact, taken as a whole, research on lateralization of brain functions points to the following conclusions: In many persons, though by no means all, the left hemisphere specializes in verbal activities like speaking, reading, and writing and in logical thought and the analysis of information. The right hemisphere specializes in the control of certain motor movements, in synthesis (putting isolated elements together), and in the comprehension and communication of emotion. Many studies employing diverse methods and procedures support these basic conclusions.

For purposes of summarizing, it is most convenient to divide these studies into two major categories: investigations conducted with noninjured persons and studies conducted with persons whose cerebral hemispheres have been isolated from each other through surgery.

RESEARCH WITH INTACT (NONINJURED) PERSONS

In some respects, the most convincing evidence for lateralization of function in the cerebral hemispheres is provided by research employing the drug *sodium amytal*. When injected into an artery on one side of the neck, this drug quickly anesthetizes the cerebral hemisphere on that side. During the few minutes that elapse before the anesthesia passes, a person can be tested on a number of different tasks. Studies using these procedures indicate that for most individuals, the left hemisphere possesses much more highly developed verbal skills than the right hemisphere. For example, when the right hemisphere is anesthetized, participants can—through the functioning of their left hemispheres—recite letters of the alphabet or days of the week, name familiar objects, and repeat sentences. In contrast, when the left hemisphere is anesthetized and only the right hemisphere is available, participants experi-

Learning Objective 2.8
Describe the different roles of the two hemispheres of the cerebral cortex.

Lateralization of Function: Specialization of the two hemispheres of the brain for the performance of different functions.

ence considerably more difficulty in performing such tasks. Further, the more complex the tasks, the greater the deficits in performance (Milner, 1974).

Additional evidence for lateralization of brain function is provided by studies using PET scan procedures. These studies indicate that when individuals speak or work with numbers, activity in the left hemisphere increases. In contrast, when they work on perceptual tasks—for instance, tasks in which they compare various shapes—activity increases in the right hemisphere (e.g., Springer & Deutsch, 1985). Interestingly, additional research suggests that while individuals are making up their minds about some issue, activity is higher in the left than in the right hemisphere (Cacioppo, Petty, & Quintanar, 1982). However, once logical thought is over and a decision has been made, heightened activity occurs in the right hemisphere, which seems to play a larger role in global, nonanalytic thought.

RESEARCH WITH SPLIT-BRAIN PARTICIPANTS: *Isolating the Two Hemispheres*

Under normal conditions, the two hemispheres of the brain communicate with each other primarily through the **corpus callosum,** a wide band of nerve fibers that passes between them. Sometimes, though, it is necessary to sever this link—for example, in order to prevent the spread of epileptic seizures from one hemisphere to the other. Careful study of individuals who have undergone such operations provides intriguing evidence on lateralization of function of the brain (Gazzaniga, 1984, 1985; Sperry, 1968).

For example, consider the following demonstration. A man whose corpus callosum has been cut is seated before a screen and told to stare, with his eyes as motionless as possible, at a central point on the screen. Then simple words such as *tenant* are flashed across the screen so that the letters *ten* appear to the left of the central point and the letters *ant* appear to the right. What does the man report seeing? Before you guess, consider the following fact: Because of the way our visual system is constructed, stimuli presented to the *left* visual field of each eye stimulate only the *right* hemisphere of the brain; items on the *right* side of the visual field of each eye stimulate only the *left* hemisphere (please refer to Figure 2.9).

Now, what do you think the split-brain man reports? If you said "ant," you are correct. This would be expected, since only the left hemisphere, which controls speech, can answer verbally. However, when asked to *point* to the word he saw on a list of words, the man reacts differently: He points with his left hand to the word *ten*. So the right hemisphere has indeed seen and recognized this stimulus; it simply can't describe it in words.

Perhaps even more dramatic evidence for the existence of differences between the left and right hemispheres is afforded by situations in which each cerebral hemisphere is provided with different information. For example, consider this simple demonstration. In one study, pictures of two objects were presented on a screen. One picture was presented only to the left visual field, while the other was presented only to the right visual field (refer again to Figure 2.9). Then participants were asked to reach into two bags, simultaneously, and select the objects shown. Before withdrawing their hands from the bags, participants were asked to describe what each hand held. Almost invariably, they named the object shown to the right visual field which, of course, stimulated the verbally advanced left hemisphere. Imagine their surprise when, on looking in their hands, they found that they actually held two different objects—the ones flashed on the screen.

Corpus Callosum: A band of nerve fibers connecting the two hemispheres of the brain.

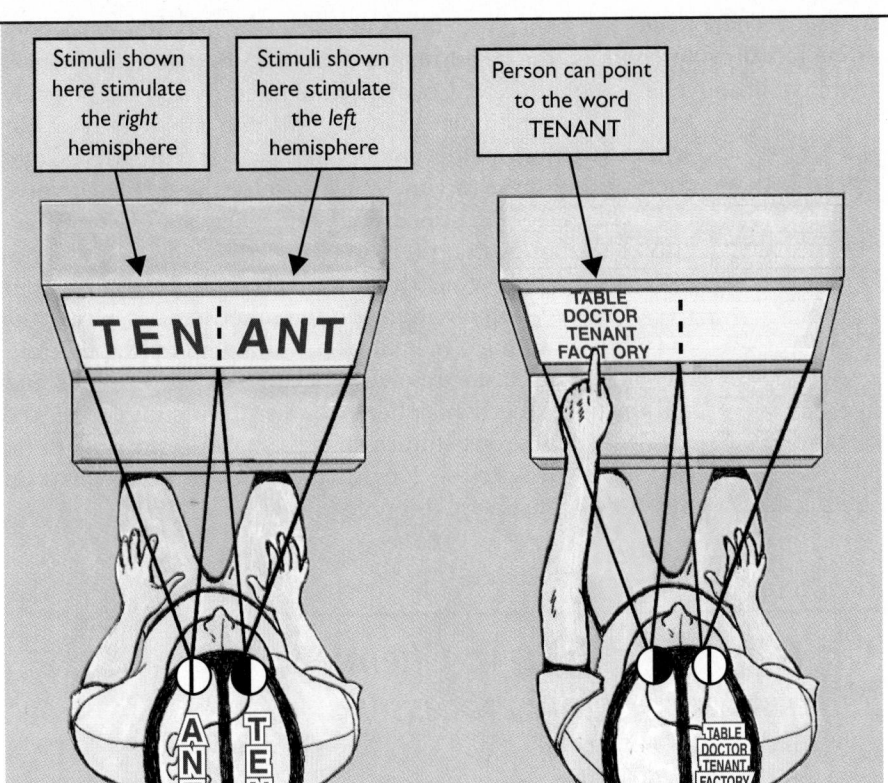

Stimuli shown here stimulate the *right* hemisphere

Stimuli shown here stimulate the *left* hemisphere

Person can point to the word TENANT

TEN ANT

TABLE
DOCTOR
TENANT
FACT ORY

FIGURE 2.9

Some Intriguing Effects of Severing the Corpus Callosum

If a simple word such as *tenant* is shown to a person whose corpus callosum has been severed, the letters *ten* stimulate only the right hemisphere while the letters *ant* stimulate only the left hemisphere. The person then reports seeing *ant* (left drawing). This is because only the left hemisphere can respond to the verbal question "What do you see?" If shown a list of words and asked to point to the one seen previously, however, the split-brain person can do so correctly; he or she points to *tenant* with the left hand (right drawing). This indicates that the right hemisphere recognizes this word and can respond to it in a nonverbal manner (that is, by pointing).

PUTTING THE BRAIN BACK TOGETHER AGAIN: MULTIPLE RESOURCE THEORY
The two hemispheres of the brain show differences that are often striking (Zaidel, 1994). The existence of these differences raises interesting questions about how these separate systems coordinate their efforts to produce consciousness—the perception of continuity we have in relation to the world around us. The manner in which the brain orchestrates interaction between the two sides of the brain, however, is not always easily predicted. Some information-processing tasks require the combined efforts of both hemispheres of the brain, whereas others are carried out independently by one side of the brain.

Several recent investigations suggest that the extent of cooperation between the two sides of the brain is based on the relative costs and benefits—or efficiency—of doing so (Hellige, 1993). One particularly important factor appears to be the difficulty of the task; performance on cognitively difficult tasks is enhanced through cooperation *between* the brain's hemispheres, whereas simple tasks are carried out more efficiently *within* a single hemisphere (Banich & Belger, 1990). In addition, evidence suggests that the brain delegates its resources not only between its two hemispheres but also *within* each hemisphere (Boles, 1992). To test the possibility of multiple resources within each side of the brain, Boles and Law (1992) used a *dual-task procedure* in which study participants performed two tasks presented to one side of the brain simultaneously. Half the task pairs were constructed such that each task used the *same* cognitive resource; for the other half, pairs consisted of tasks that used different cognitive resources.

The results were consistent with the idea that each side of the brain contains multiple cognitive resources. A decrease in performance (such as increased reaction time) was observed for task pairs that used the *same* cognitive resource. In contrast, the performance of task pairs that used *different* cognitive resources was not affected. Consider how these results might apply to a real-life example: Imagine that you are steering a car while listening to the emotional voice of your distraught friend riding next to you. While both of these tasks involve the right side of the brain, separate resources are used to recognize spatial position (where your car is going) and emotion. As a result, your driving ability is unlikely to suffer from this task combination. On the other hand, steering the car while scanning a mental image of a map may spell trouble, since both tasks involve checking spatial positions and call on the same hemispheric resource. To summarize, the results of numerous studies suggest that it *is* possible to do two things at once—as long as the tasks do not depend on the same hemispheric resource.

KEY QUESTIONS

- Are the left and right hemispheres of the brain specialized for the performance of different tasks?
- What evidence supports the existence of hemispheric specialization?
- Why is it possible to perform more than one activity at once, such as listening to the radio while driving?

THE ENDOCRINE SYSTEM: *Chemical Regulators of Bodily Processes*

Learning Objective 2.9
Describe how the endocrine system regulates bodily processes.

Learning Objective 2.10
Identify the various factors that influence the premenstrual syndrome.

Learning Objective 2.11
Discuss the role of biology in the behavior of males and females.

*E*arlier, I mentioned that the hypothalamus plays a key role in the activities of important glands. These are the **endocrine glands,** which release chemicals called **hormones** directly into the bloodstream. Hormones exert profound effects on a wide range of processes related to basic bodily functions. Of special interest to psychologists are *neurohormones*—hormones that interact with and affect the nervous system. Neurohormones, like neurotransmitters, influence neural activity. However, because they are released into the circulatory system rather than into synapses, they exert their effects more slowly, at a greater distance, and often for longer periods of time than neurotransmitters. The locations of the major endocrine glands are shown in Figure 2.10.

The relationships between the hypothalamus and the endocrine glands are complex. Basically, though, the hypothalamus exerts its influence through the *pituitary gland* (refer to Figure 2.10). This gland is located just below the hypothalamus and is closely connected to it. The pituitary is sometimes described as the master gland of the body, for the hormones it releases control and regulate the actions of other endocrine glands.

The pituitary is really two glands in one, the *posterior pituitary* and the *anterior pituitary*. The posterior pituitary releases hormones that regulate reabsorption of water by the kidneys and, in females, the production and release of milk. It is the anterior pituitary that releases the hormones that regulate the activity of other endocrine glands. One such hormone, ACTH, stimulates the outer layer of the adrenal gland, the *adrenal cortex*, causing it to secrete cortisone. Cortisone, in turn, affects cells in many parts of the body. The pituitary also secretes hormones that affect sexual development, govern the functioning of the sexual glands (regulating the amount of hormones they release), and help control basic bodily functions relating to metabolism and excretion.

A dramatic illustration of the importance of hormones secreted by the endocrine glands is provided by a disorder known as the *congenital adrenogenital syndrome (CAS)*. In this condition excessive levels of adrenal androgens (hormones that typically exist in higher concentrations in males than females) are produced. In males, this disorder merely accelerates the onset of puberty. In females, however, the syndrome has much more disturb-

Endocrine Glands: *Glands that secrete hormones directly into the bloodstream.*

Hormones: *Substances secreted by endocrine glands that regulate a wide range of bodily processes.*

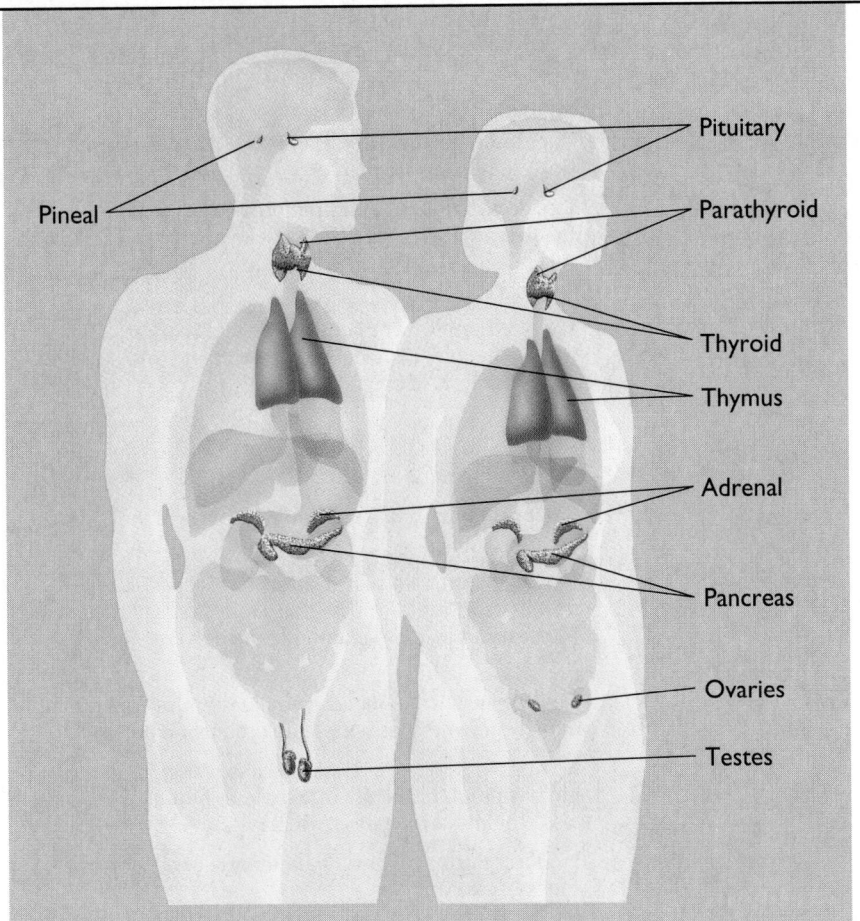

FIGURE 2.10

Location of the Endocrine Glands

Endocrine glands are found in several locations throughout the body. The hormones they release exert important effects on many bodily processes.

Pituitary

Pineal

Parathyroid

Thyroid

Thymus

Adrenal

Pancreas

Ovaries

Testes

ing effects. A female suffering from this disorder is born with external sexual organs that are distinctly masculine in appearance. If her condition is recognized at birth and she receives corrective surgery plus hormonal treatment designed to reduce levels of androgens, the girl's development may proceed normally. If, however, she does not receive treatment until her teen years, she may retain some masculine characteristics; she may describe herself as a tomboy, prefer boys' clothes, and express little interest in babies or future maternity (Ehrhardt & Meyer-Bahlberg, 1981). Since many other females also demonstrate such tendencies, however, the meaning of these findings is somewhat difficult to interpret.

In another disorder, known as the *adrenogenic insensitivity syndrome*, the cells of genetic males lack receptors for androgens. Such persons are born with genitals that are distinctly female, and they develop as what appear to be normal females. As noted by Money and Ehrhardt (1972), their childhood play, goals, sexual behavior, and maternal interests all conform to patterns traditionally seen among females. However, these individuals are unable to have children, since they lack ovaries and other internal female sexual organs. Treatment for such persons includes surgical enlargement of the vagina and psychological counseling to help them cope with the fact that because of their condition, they cannot become pregnant.

Together, the adrenogenital syndrome and adrenogenic insensitivity syndrome suggest that hormones secreted by the endocrine glands, and especially by the *gonads*, or sex glands, exert important effects on social and cognitive as well as physical development. However, as we'll see in chapter

BIOLOGICAL BASES OF BEHAVIOR: A LOOK BENEATH THE SURFACE

67

TABLE 2.2	GLAND	EFFECTS OR FUNCTIONS IT REGULATES
The Endocrine System: A Summary of Its Major Effects The various hormones released by the endocrine glands play major roles in body processes.	**Adrenal Glands** Adrenal medulla	Produces *epinephrine* and *norepinephrine*. Both play an important role in reactions to stress (e.g., increased heartbeat, raised blood pressure).
	Adrenal cortex	Produces hormones that promote release of sugar stored in the liver. Also regulates the excretion of sodium and potassium.
	Gonads Ovaries	Produce hormones responsible for secondary sex characteristics of females (e.g., breast development); also regulate several aspects of pregnancy.
	Testes	Produce hormones responsible for secondary sex characteristics of males (e.g., beard growth); also affect sperm production and male sex drive.
	Pancreas	Produces hormones (e.g., insulin, glucagon) that regulate metabolism.
	Parathyroid	Produces hormones that regulate levels of *calcium* and *phosphate* within the body (these substances play an important role in functioning of the nervous system).
	Pituitary Gland Anterior	Controls activity of gonads; regulates timing and amount of body growth; stimulates milk production in females.
	Posterior	Releases hormones that control contractions of uterus during birth and the release of milk from mammary glands; also regulates excretion of water.
	Thyroid	Produces *thyroxin*, which regulates rate of metabolism and controls growth.

8, the development of *gender identity*—individuals' recognition of their sex and the effects of such recognition on later development—is influenced by many social and environmental variables. Thus, the possible role of biological factors in this process should be viewed with considerable caution. Nevertheless, these syndromes underscore the importance of the endocrine glands and the various different hormones they secrete. Table 2.2 summarizes the major endocrine glands and their effects.

HORMONES AND BEHAVIOR: *Is the Premenstrual Syndrome Real?*

In general, the endocrine system functions similarly in females and males. There is one major exception to this pattern, however: Gonadal hormone levels remain fairly constant in males but change markedly in a rhythmic manner in young to middle-aged adult females. These changes are associated with the *menstrual cycle* and occur regularly over about twenty-eight days. As you probably know, this cyclicity is related to shifts in fertility.

Because shifts in gonadal hormones during the course of this cycle are very large, it has been assumed that these shifts may be related, in some fashion, to behavior or emotions. And indeed, many women report that their moods, energy level, and even sexual desire do seem to alter over the course of their menstrual cycle. For some women, these changes are most pronounced in the days just before the start of menstruation—an effect known as the *premenstrual syndrome* (PMS for short) (Hopson & Rosenfeld, 1984). Are these changes real? Perhaps, but research evidence suggests that in many cases they may be smaller and less clear-cut than is often assumed. In fact, it appears that in many cases, reports of shifts in mood, energy, and symptoms may be more closely related to *beliefs* about such changes than to actual changes themselves. For example, in one revealing study (McFarland et al., 1989), women who believed strongly in the existence of PMS remembered experiencing more physical symptoms and mood shifts just before or during menstruation than they actually had at these times. (Their memories for such reactions were compared with entries in daily diaries—in which they recorded physical symptoms and moods every day.)

These findings by no means imply that shifts in hormonal levels do not influence moods or behavior; on the contrary, other evidence indicates that such effects do occur (Pinel, 1993). However, the results obtained by McFarland and her colleagues indicate that the psychological and physical impact of hormones can be strongly influenced by expectations, beliefs, and other cognitive factors. It is hard to imagine a more compelling illustration of the fact that the biological processes that give rise to our conscious experience are, indeed, complex. For information on the possible role of biological factors in sex differences, please see the **Perspectives on Diversity** section.

> ### KEY QUESTIONS
>
> - How does the endocrine system influence aspects of our behavior?
> - Do cognitive factors play a role in premenstrual syndrome?
> - Are there gender differences in brain size? In cognitive abilities?
> - What role does the endocrine system play in shaping gender-specific behaviors?

PERSPECTIVES ON DIVERSITY

The Biological Basis of Gender Differences

Throughout this chapter, we've noted that basic biological processes underlie many aspects of our cognition and behavior. One age-old biological fact of life that has sparked a great deal of controversy in recent years, however, is sex. At issue is the relative contribution of a person's sex to differences in the way that men and women think, feel, and behave. During the past several decades, research has focused on identifying social and cultural factors that might explain the origin of these differences. If environmental factors—including social and cultural forces—could be shown to be the culprits, so the argument goes, then changing these factors should lead to the elimination of many gender-related differences. Consistent with these predictions, many gender-related differences *have* narrowed over the past few decades, reflecting changes in socialization, education, and employment practices that have occurred in this country.

Yet recent research suggests that differences in certain cognitive processes and behaviors of males and females still remain (e.g., Berenbaum & Hines, 1992; Law, Pellegrino, & Hunt, 1993). For example, men tend to score higher on tests of spatial ability, such as the ability to mentally rotate three-dimensional figures, and show greater language lateralization (hemispheric specialization) for processing verbal material than women do. Women, on the other hand, tend to hold a slight advantage over men on certain verbal tasks. How do psychologists attempt to explain such differences? One possibility is sex differences in the size of their brains.

SEX DIFFERENCES IN BRAIN STRUCTURE AND COGNITIVE PROCESSES

Recent evidence suggests that men and women do, in fact, differ in brain structure. For example, several studies have discovered sex differences in the size of certain brain structures, including the corpus callosum (Clarke et al., 1989). The corpus callosum is made up of more than 200 million nerve fibers and is the main link between the two hemispheres of the brain. Thus, it is not

**HORMONES: SHAPING
GENDER-SPECIFIC BEHAVIORS**

Researchers are studying the effects
of basic biological processes—
including hormonal influences—on
the development of sex-typed
behaviors among children.

surprising that researchers would suspect the involvement of this structure in a variety of cognitive processes. In one recent study, Hines and her colleagues (1992) used MRI, a brain-imaging technique, to measure the size of several regions of the corpus callosum in twenty-eight women. Then they obtained measures of the women's cognitive abilities, including a verbal test and a test of language lateralization. They hypothesized that areas of the corpus callosum reported to be larger in women than in men would be positively related to the women's scores on tests on which women typically score higher (the verbal test). In contrast, they predicted that areas reported to be larger in men than in women would be negatively related to the women's scores on tests on which men typically score higher (language lateralization). The results supported their predictions: There was a significant positive relationship between the women's scores on the verbal test and the size of a corpus callosum region reported to be larger in women. In contrast, a negative relationship was observed between scores on the language lateralization measure and the size of an area reported to be larger in men than in women. I should emphasize that these results are preliminary and should be interpreted with caution. They do not prove that differences in brain structure are the cause of the cognitive differences observed in this study. Still, they are provocative in that they raise interesting questions regarding the relationship between sex differences in brain structure and sex differences in cognitive processes and behavior.

THE ROLE OF HORMONES IN GENDER-RELATED BEHAVIORS

If the results of the preceding study are accurate, what then is the basis for sex differences in brain structure? Recent evidence suggests that basic biological processes that occur very early in our development—in fact, before we are born—may be involved. Earlier I touched on the curious genetically based disorder termed congenital adrenogenital syndrome (CAS), which appears to produce in girls behavior patterns typical of boys, due to high levels of adrenal androgens. Although it appears that these behaviors result from hormonal influences present before birth, it is also possible that environmental influences play a role as well. To illustrate this, consider a recent study by Berenbaum and Hines (1992). These researchers assessed differences in children's preferences for three types of toys: traditional boys' toys, girls' toys, or toys that were gender-neutral. The participants in the study were boys and girls between the ages of three and eight—including girls with CAS. At issue was the question of which toys the children would prefer to play with if given equal access to all three types. The results showed that CAS girls spent significantly more time playing with boys' toys than girls who did not have CAS. In fact, their preferences closely matched those of the boys.

An alternative explanation for these results is that parents of the CAS girls may have encouraged their daughters to behave like boys. In other words, because of their masculine features and tendencies at birth, parents of the CAS girls may have inadvertently treated them in a masculine fashion. Similarly, the other parents may have encouraged gender-specific behaviors in their children as well. However, measures taken to assess this possibility showed there were no differences among parents in their tendencies to encourage their children to behave in gender-specific ways. In short, these results suggest that biological processes may play a significant role in important aspects of human development.

HEREDITY AND BEHAVIOR

*T*he basic theme of this chapter is straightforward: that behavior and consciousness are manifestations of complex biological processes within our bodies. If this is true, and virtually all psychologists assume that it is, then it certainly makes sense to consider the relationship of **heredity**—biologically determined characteristics—to behavior. After all, many aspects of our biological nature are inherited; so in an indirect manner, and always through the filter of our experience and environmental factors, heredity can indeed influence behavior (Rushton, 1989a and 1989b). In this final section, then, we'll examine several aspects of heredity that appear to be relevant to understanding the biological bases of behavior.

GENETICS: *Some Basic Principles*

Every cell of your body contains a set of biological blueprints that enable it to perform its essential functions. This information is contained in **chromosomes,** strandlike structures found in the nuclei of all cells. Chromosomes are composed of a substance known as DNA, short for deoxyribonucleic acid. DNA, in turn, is made up of several simpler components arranged in the form of a double helix—something like the twisting water slides found by the sides of large swimming pools. Chromosomes contain thousands of **genes**—segments of DNA that serve as basic units of heredity. Our genes, working in complex combinations and in concert with forces in the environment, ultimately determine many aspects of our biological makeup (see Figure 2.11 on page 72).

Remarkable progress has been made toward detecting genetic involvement in a variety of physical and mental disorders. For example, researchers recently discovered the gene that causes **Huntington's disease,** a rare, progressive neuromuscular disorder. Persons afflicted with Huntington's disease experience a gradual onset of uncontrollable, jerky movements in their limbs. Unfortunately, there is at present no cure for Huntington's disease (Pinel, 1993). Children of an affected person have a 50 percent chance of inheriting the gene that causes this disorder. Ironically, the onset of symptoms usually appears after age forty—long after many parents have their children, and therefore too late for them to reconsider their decision. Although scientists are not yet sure how the gene actually causes the disease, it is now possible to detect its presence before the onset of symptoms and, more importantly, in time to let parents avoid passing the lethal gene to their children.

Merely possessing a particular gene, however, does not ensure that a specific effect will follow. Genes do not control behavior or other aspects of life directly—they exert their influence only indirectly through their influence on chemical reactions in the brain or other organs. These reactions, in turn, may depend on certain environmental conditions. For example, consider **phenylketonuria (PKU),** a genetically based disorder in which persons lack the enzyme necessary to break down *phenylalanine*—a substance present in many foods. Affected persons on a normal diet tend to accumulate phenlalanine in their bodies. This, in turn, interferes with normal development of the brain and leads to mental retardation, seizures, and hyperactivity (Nyhan, 1987). Altering environmental conditions, however, can prevent this chain of events. Hospitals now routinely screen infants' blood for high levels of phenylalanine. If PKU is detected during the first few weeks of life, babies placed on a diet low in phenylalanine do not develop the PKU symptoms. Dietary restrictions can then be relaxed in late childhood after the majority of brain development is complete.

Most human traits, however, are determined by more than one gene. In fact, hundreds of genes acting in concert with environmental forces may be involved in shaping complex physical or cognitive abilities (Lerner, 1993; McClearn et al., 1991). At this point you are probably wondering, "Then how

Learning Objective 2.12
Outline the basic principles of genetics.

Learning Objective 2.13
Discuss the different research strategies employed to determine the importance of genetic and environmental factors in behavior.

Heredity: Biologically inherited characteristics.

Chromosomes: Threadlike structures containing genetic material, found in nearly every cell of the body.

Genes: Biological "blueprints" that shape development and all basic bodily processes.

Huntington's Disease: A genetically based fatal neuromuscular disorder characterized by the gradual onset of jerky, uncontrollable movements.

Phenylketonuria (PKU): A genetically based disorder in which a person lacks the enzyme to break down phenylalanine, a substance present in many foods. The gradual buildup of phenylalanine contributes to subsequent outcomes that include mental retardation.

FIGURE **2.11**

DNA: Mapping Our Genetic Heritage

Chromosomes are composed of DNA (deoxyribonucleic acid). Each human cell contains twenty-three pairs of chromosomes. The twenty-third pair determines sex. In males, the twenty-third pair contains one X and one Y chromosome (shown here); in females, the twenty-third pair contains two X chromosomes.

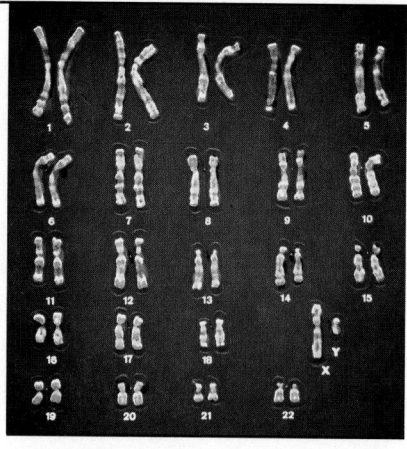

do psychologists tell which aspects of behavior are determined by genetic versus environmental factors—by heredity or by experience?" This question has been the source of debate among psychologists for many years and is often referred to as the *nature-nurture controversy*, an issue we will consider in greater detail below and again in subsequent chapters.

Most cells in the human body contain forty-six chromosomes, existing in pairs (refer to Figure 2.11). When such cells divide, the chromosome pairs split; then, after the cells have separated, each chromosome replicates itself so that the full number is restored. This kind of cell division is known as **mitosis**. In contrast, sperm and ova—the male and female sex cells, or *gametes*—contain only twenty-three chromosomes. Thus, when they join to form a fertilized ovum from which a new human being will develop, the full number (forty-six) is attained. For each of us, then, half of our genetic material comes from our mother and half from our father.

These basic mechanisms explain why persons who are related resemble one another more than persons who are totally unrelated, and also why the closer the familial tie between individuals, the more similar they tend to be physically. The closer such links are, the greater the proportion of chromosomes and genes family members share. And since genes determine many aspects of physical appearance, similarity increases with closeness of relationship. Thus, siblings (children of the same parents) tend to be more alike than cousins (the children of siblings). In the case of identical twins, or *monozygotic twins*, a single fertilized egg splits in two and forms two children. Because identical twins share all of their genes, they are usually remarkably similar in appearance. They are surprisingly similar in other respects as well, including their religious beliefs, their television viewing preferences, their grief responses (e.g., Segal & Bouchard, 1993), and even their risk for divorce. Psychologists have long known that there is an increased risk of divorce among the children of divorced parents, and data reported recently by McGue and Lykken (1992) indicate that genetic factors may play a role in this outcome. Briefly, they found that if one identical (monozygotic) twin was divorced, the probability that her or his twin would also divorce was higher than was true for nonidentical (dizygotic) twins. This suggests that there may be inherited tendencies that contribute to the likelihood of divorce. We'll consider what these might be in a more detailed discussion of this study (see chapter 8).

DISENTANGLING GENETIC AND ENVIRONMENTAL EFFECTS: *Research Strategies*

Mitosis: Cell division in which chromosome pairs split and then replicate themselves so that the full number is restored in each of the cells produced by division.

Efforts to assess the relative roles of genetic and environmental effects on complex forms of behavior have often involved comparisons between identical twins who were separated early in life and raised in contrasting environments. As we've already noted, since such twins have identical genes, any differences between them must be due to contrasting experiences and environments. And to the extent that identical twins demonstrate similarity in various behaviors, despite being raised in different environments, the greater

the contribution of genetic factors to such behaviors. Research of this type (e.g., Bouchard, 1987; Bouchard et al., 1990) has yielded some surprising findings. Even identical twins reared in very different environments show remarkable similarities (Lykken et al., 1992).

Perhaps the most startling evidence for such similarity is provided by a study conducted by Arvey and his colleagues (1989). These researchers asked thirty-four sets of identical twins to complete standard measures of job satisfaction—liking for their current jobs. Each pair of twins (average age forty-two) had been separated since they were only a few months old and had spent most of their lives in different homes, leading different lives. Despite this fact, and despite the fact that they held different jobs, there was a significant degree of similarity in their rated satisfaction: The higher the satisfaction reported by one twin, the higher the satisfaction reported by the other. Moreover, this relationship was not reduced even when corrections were made for possible similarities in the twins' jobs. (If they held similar jobs, then it would not be surprising for them to report similar levels of satisfaction.) Arvey and his colleagues suggest these results may stem from tendencies to be positive and enthusiastic—characteristics already known to be partly determined by genetic factors (Tellegen et al., 1988). In other words, because of genetic factors, some people tend to experience positive moods more often than others, and these positive moods contribute to their level of satisfaction with their work.

Whatever the mechanism involved, it seems clear that there may be a genetic component in many aspects of behavior, including, surprisingly, sexual orientation. For example, Bailey and Pillard (1991) studied 161 gay men, each of whom had an identical twin, a fraternal brother, or an adopted brother. Bailey and Pillard reasoned that if homosexuality has a genetic component, then the identical twin brothers of the gay men would be most likely to also be gay. Results supported this hypothesis: 52 percent of the identical twins were both gay, compared to 22 percent of the fraternal twins, and 11 percent of the adopted brothers. Similar results have also been reported among women (Bailey & Pillard, 1993). In addition, other findings suggest that certain genes may be directly involved in the determination of sexual preference (Hamer et al., 1993). While these and related findings indicate that genetic factors may play a role in sexual preference, it is important to note that they are definitely *not* the entire story; environmental factors, too, exert important effects on this complex process.

KEY QUESTIONS

- How do genetic factors influence behavior?
- What are some examples of genetically based diseases?
- What evidence supports the possibility that genetic factors influence aspects of our behavior?

Traumatic Brain Injury: Using Psychology to Enhance Quality of Life

I f you were asked to guess the odds that you will be involved in a life-threatening accident during your lifetime, what would you guess? You may be surprised to learn they are fifty-fifty. In fact, one of the biggest threats facing young adults is severe trauma to some portion of their nervous systems—from severe blows sustained in contact sports such as hockey or football, to injuries sustained in automobile crashes. Because of the prevalence of these traumas, the chances are likely that you may even know someone who has suffered such an injury.

After having read this chapter, you should have no trouble understanding why a discussion of brain injuries is included here. There is an intimate relationship between the nervous system and the capacity to think, feel, and behave, and damage to the brain will have corresponding effects on all of these abilities. In other words, the consequences of injury to the brain aren't confined to the *physical* repercussions of injury-producing events, but often result in profound *psychological* ones as well. Indeed, some people who have sustained such injuries report that in certain respects, living with a damaged brain can be a fate *worse* than death.

The term often used to refer to severe instances of head injury, *traumatic brain injury (TBI)*, emphasizes that the brain has been damaged secondary to extreme forces applied to the skull and its contents (Prigatano, 1992). The damages that result from TBI are often diffuse and variable in scope. Some portions of the damage may be extensive enough to be discovered by brain-imaging devices, whereas others may be microscopic and thus escape detection. The damage also tends to extend to regions throughout the brain, making it difficult for psychologists and other health professionals to predict with precision the type or extent of psychological disturbances that are likely to occur. This, in turn, makes it difficult to design effective treatments for persons who have sustained a TBI (Armstrong, 1991).

Reports of the disturbances affecting TBI patients show several common features. Interestingly, though, each disturbance is associated with curious inconsistencies. For example, the most prevalent consequence of a brain injury is irritability, the tendency to become easily annoyed or upset. As many as 70 percent of TBI patients exhibit this tendency. Ironically, the extent of irritability does *not* appear to be related to the extent of damage to the brain. A similar inconsistency is related to another common feature of TBI—motivation. Although TBI patients typically become apathetic following brain injury, they may suddenly become explosively angry. Finally, TBI patients tend to lack a sense of self-awareness regarding their condition, but may become quite disturbed when their new limitations are pointed out to them (Prigatano, 1992).

What is the basis for the observed inconsistencies in behavior patterns associated with TBI? The root cause appears to be an inability to cope with environmental demands that these persons could have handled with ease prior to their injury. For instance, they may have a difficult time solving even simple problems, and as a result, they often become frustrated and emotionally overwhelmed.

Based on this discovery, psychologists have developed rehabilitation programs that attempt to accommodate the unique circumstances of brain-injured people (Armstrong, 1991). Indeed, the most successful programs to date focus on creating environments that are flexible to the needs of each person, depending on the nature of their disability. One of the most important ingredients in a successful treatment program appears to be structure: an environment arranged to reduce frustration and increase the probability the person's efforts to cope will meet with success. For example, a common source of frustration among brain-injured persons is the inability to anticipate future events. Providing a structure that allows these persons to focus their efforts one step at a time increases the chances they will meet with success. This sets the stage for greater accomplishments later on. Another

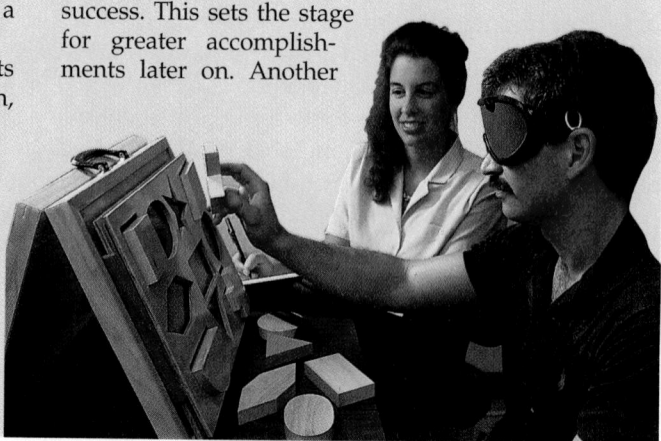

Injuries to the brain can often produce widespread physical and psychological problems. New insights into the relationship between biological processes and behavior have led to exciting new programs to enhance the quality of life of brain-injured people.

advantage of imposing structure is that it limits the number of things these persons must attend to at one time, and thereby reduces the confusion (and frustration) TBI patients experience while making choices. A final—but critical—ingredient of successful treatment of TBI has to do with how the intervention is applied; the chances of success are increased when treatment begins soon after the injury, when family members are actively involved, and when the procedures are applied consistently over time.

In short, thanks to advances in understanding the complex interaction between biological processes and behavior, psychologists can improve the quality of life among persons who have suffered traumatic brain injury. It's important to realize, however, that the approach outlined here helps persons who have suffered TBI to deal with their disabilities more effectively—it does not *restore* their former physical and cognitive abilities. Therefore, the most effective way to prevent TBI from happening to you is to avoid dangerous situations, such as driving drunk or riding with someone who has been drinking, and to be consistent in using protective equipment, such as safety belts or helmets, when appropriate.

SUMMARY AND REVIEW OF KEY QUESTIONS

NEURONS: BUILDING BLOCKS OF THE NERVOUS SYSTEM

- **What is biopsychology?**

Biopsychology is the branch of psychology concerned with discovering the biological processes that give rise to our thoughts, feelings, and actions.

- **What does a neuron do? What are the parts of a neuron?**

A neuron is a cell specialized for receiving, processing, and moving information. It is made up of a cell body, an axon, and one or more dendrites.

- **What are action potentials?**

Action potentials are rapid changes in the electrical properties of the cell membranes of neurons. They constitute the basic mechanism by which information travels through the nervous system.

- **How do neurons communicate with one another?**

Neurons communicate across the tiny gaps that separate them by means of neurotransmitters.

- **What are the effects of neurotransmitters?**

Neurotransmitters produce one of two effects: Excitatory effects cause a depolarization in the nerve cell membrane, making it more likely that a graded potential will be generated; inhibitory effects hyperpolarize the cell membranes, making it less likely that the cell will fire.

- **What problems can be solved using knowledge of neurotransmitters?**

Growing evidence suggests that knowledge of neurotransmitter systems can be applied to solve important practical problems, including drug and alcohol abuse and certain mental disorders.

KEY TERMS: biopsychology, p. 44; neurons, p. 45; axon, p. 45; dendrites, p. 45; glial cells, p. 46; axon terminals, p. 46; synapse, p. 46; action potential, p. 46; nodes of Ranvier, p. 46; graded potentials, p. 47; synaptic vesicles, p. 47; neurotransmitters, p. 47

THE NERVOUS SYSTEM: ITS BASIC STRUCTURE AND FUNCTIONS

- **What structures comprise the central nervous system?**

The central nervous system includes the brain and the spinal cord.

- **What is the function of the spinal cord?**

The spinal cord carries sensory information from receptors in the body to the brain via afferent nerve fibers and carries information from the brain to muscles and glands via efferent nerve fibers. It also plays an important role in reflexes.

- **What two systems make up the peripheral nervous system? What are the roles of these two systems?**

The peripheral nervous system consists of the somatic and autonomic nervous systems. The somatic nervous system connects the brain and spinal cord to voluntary muscles throughout the body; the autonomic nervous system connects the central nervous system to internal organs and glands and to muscles over which we have little voluntary control.

• *What are the functions of the sympathetic and parasympathetic nervous systems?*

The sympathetic nervous system prepares the body for using energy; the parasympathetic nervous system activates processes that conserve the body's energy.

• *How do psychologists study the nervous system?*

Psychologists use several methods to study the nervous system, including observation of the effects of brain damage, electrical or chemical stimulation of the brain, and several modern imaging techniques.

• *How are PET scans used to study the activity of the brain?*

PET scans have been used to show how the brain's activities change in response to experience in certain language tasks. The brain appears to expend less energy as it masters a task.

KEY TERMS: *nervous system, p. 51; central nervous system, p. 51; peripheral nervous system, p. 51; somatic nervous system, p. 52; autonomic nervous system, p. 52; sympathetic nervous system, p. 52; parasympathetic nervous system, p. 52; electroencephalography (EEG), p. 54; magnetic resonance imaging (MRI), p. 54; SQUID (superconducting quantum interference device), p. 55; positron emission tomography (PET), p. 55*

THE BRAIN: WHERE CONSCIOUSNESS IS MANIFEST

• *What structures comprise the brain stem? What are their functions?*

The brain stem—including the medulla, pons, and cerebellum—is concerned primarily with the regulation of basic bodily functions. The cerebellum, however, may be involved in higher cognitive processes.

• *What are the functions of the hypothalamus and the thalamus?*

The hypothalamus and the thalamus are brain structures involved in the regulation of motivated behavior and emotion.

• *What is the result of damage to the ventromedial hypothalamus? To the lateral hypothalamus?*

Damage to the ventromedial hypothalamus increases food intake because of its dramatic impact on metabolism. Damage to the lateral hypothalamus reduces food intake.

• *What is the role of the cerebral cortex?*

The cerebral cortex is the hub for higher mental processes such as thinking, planning, reasoning, and memory.

• *How is language processed in the brain?*

Language processing in the brain is most consistent with parallel models, which suggest that neural information moves along several routes and is processed simultaneously in different brain regions.

KEY TERMS: *medulla, p. 57; pons, p. 57; reticular activating system, p. 57; cerebellum, p. 58; midbrain, p. 58; hypothalamus,*

p. 58; pituitary gland, p. 59; thalamus, p. 59; limbic system, p. 59; cerebral cortex, p. 59; frontal lobe, p. 59; parietal lobe, p. 60; occipital lobe, p. 60; temporal lobe, p. 60; Wernicke-Geschwind theory, p. 61

LATERALIZATION OF THE CEREBRAL CORTEX: TWO MINDS IN ONE BODY?

• *Are the left and right hemispheres of the brain specialized for the performance of different tasks?*

In most persons, the left hemisphere specializes in verbal activities and in logical thought and analysis. The right hemisphere specializes in the comprehension and communication of emotion and in the synthesis of information.

• *What evidence supports the existence of hemispheric specialization?*

Evidence for hemispheric specialization has been obtained from studies of people with intact brains and from research on split-brain individuals.

• *Why is it possible to perform more than one activity at once, such as listening to the radio while driving?*

Within each hemisphere of the brain, cognitive processes may operate independently, allowing us to do two tasks at once—as long as the tasks do not depend on the same cognitive resource.

KEY TERMS: *lateralization of function, p. 63; corpus callosum, p. 64*

THE ENDOCRINE SYSTEM: CHEMICAL REGULATORS OF BODILY PROCESSES

• *How does the endocrine system influence aspects of our behavior?*

Hormones released by the endocrine glands exert far-reaching effects on bodily processes and, in turn, on important aspects of behavior.

• *Do cognitive factors play a role in premenstrual syndrome?*

Research findings suggest that women's beliefs and expectations concerning the premenstrual syndrome may, in fact, play a more important role than gonadal hormones.

• *Are there gender differences in brain size? In cognitive abilities?*

Some evidence suggests a relationship between sex differences in the size of regions of the corpus callosum and sex differences in several cognitive abilities, including verbal fluency and language lateralization.

• *What role does the endocrine system play in shaping gender-specific behaviors?*

Genetically based hormonal disturbances such as CAS may play a role in shaping gender-specific behaviors.

KEY TERMS: *endocrine glands, p. 66; hormones, p. 66*

HEREDITY AND BEHAVIOR

• How do genetic factors influence behavior?

Genetic factors influence behavior via genes—"biological blueprints" located on chromosomes. Chromosomes contain thousands of genes that shape development and all basic bodily processes, which in turn affect physical characteristics and aspects of behavior.

• What are some examples of genetically based diseases?

Two well-known genetically based diseases are Huntington's disease and phenylketonuria (PKU).

• What evidence supports the possibility that genetic factors influence aspects of our behavior?

Research comparing identical twins raised apart suggests that genetic factors play a role in many aspects of behavior.

KEY TERMS: *heredity, p. 71; chromosomes, p. 71; genes, p. 71; Huntington's disease, p. 71; phenylketonuria (PKU), p. 71; mitosis, p. 72*

CRITICAL THINKING QUESTIONS

APPRAISAL	Throughout this chapter, you've seen that our thoughts, feelings, and actions all stem from basic biological processes. Do you think that all of our conscious experience can be reduced to electrochemical events? If so, why? If not, offer an alternative view.
CONTROVERSY	Growing evidence suggests that sexual orientation may be linked to genetic processes and may not simply be a lifestyle choice. Given this strong possibility, what ethical and social implications does this hold? A related issue pertains to the possibility that scientists will soon be able to determine if genetic abnormalities are present in the developing fetus. What ethical issues does this raise? What are your views on these issues?
MAKING PSYCHOLOGY PART OF YOUR LIFE	Perhaps you know someone who has suffered traumatic brain injury. Now that you understand the difficult path such a person faces during rehabilitation, can you think of ways in which you can use the information in this chapter to improve the TBI patient's quality of life?

Sensation and Perception:

Making Contact with the World Around Us

*H*ave you ever wondered why certain smells trigger scenes long forgotten? Why does bathwater that initially "scalds" feel soothing only moments later? Do you know why the moon appears large on the horizon but smaller overhead? Do you believe in ESP? If you've wondered about issues like these, you're already aware that making sense of the world around us is a complicated business. Indeed, the mystery of how we sense and interpret events in our environment constitutes one of the oldest fields of study in psychology. Careful psychological research conducted over decades has shown that we do not understand the external world in a simple, automatic way. Rather, we actively construct our interpretation of sensory information through several complex processes.

To clarify how we make sense of the world around us, psychologists distinguish between two key concepts: sensation and perception. The study of **sensation** is concerned with the initial contact between organisms and their physical environment. It focuses on describing the relationship between various forms of sensory stimulation (including electromagnetic, sound waves, pressure) and how these inputs are registered by our sense organs (the eyes, ears, nose, tongue, and skin).

In contrast, the study of **perception** is concerned with identifying the processes through which we interpret and organize sensory information to produce our conscious experience of objects and object relationships. It is important to remember that perception is not simply a passive process of decoding incoming sensory information. If this were the case, we would lose the richness of our everyday stream of conscious experiences.

The dual processes of sensation and perception play a role in virtually every topic we will consider in later chapters. For this reason, we will devote careful attention to them here. We'll begin by exploring in detail how the receptors for each sensory system transduce raw physical energy into an electrochemical code. As we'll soon note, our sensory receptors are exquisitely designed to detect various aspects of the world around us. As part of our discussion, we'll consider the role of cultural factors in one very important aspect of our sensory processes—the sensation of pain. Next, we'll turn our attention to the active process of perception. Here, we'll focus on how the brain integrates and interprets the constant flow of information it receives from our senses. In our discussion of perception, we'll also consider the relative contributions of heredity and experience to our perception of the world around us. Finally, we'll conclude by examining the evidence supporting one intriguing aspect of perception—the possibility of extrasensory perception, or *psi*.

SENSATION: *The Raw Materials of Understanding*

*T*he sight of a breathtaking sunset, the taste of ice-cold lemonade on a hot day, the piercing sound of heavy metal music, the soothing warmth of a steamy bath—exactly how are we able to experience these events? As you may recall from chapter 2, all of these sensory experiences are based on complex processes occurring within the nervous system. This fact highlights an intriguing paradox: Although we are continually bombarded by various forms of physical energy, including light, heat, sound, and smells, our brain cannot directly detect the presence of these forces. Rather, it can only respond to intricate patterns of action potentials conducted by *neurons*, special cells within our bodies that receive, move, and process sensory information. Thus, a critical question is how the many forms of physical energy impacting our sensory systems are converted into signals our nervous system can understand.

Highly specialized cells known as **sensory receptors**, located in our eyes, ears, nose, tongue, and elsewhere, are responsible for accomplishing this coding task. Thus, sights, sounds, and smells that we experience are actually the product of **transduction**, a process in which the physical properties of stimuli are converted into neural signals that are then transmitted to our brain via specialized sensory nerves. To illustrate how our nervous system makes

Sensation: *Input about the physical world provided by our sensory receptors.*

Perception: *The process through which we select, organize, and interpret input from our sensory receptors.*

Sensory Receptors: *Cells specialized for the task of transduction—converting physical energy (light, sound) into neural impulses.*

Transduction: *The translation of physical energy into electrical signals by specialized receptor cells.*

sense out of the surging sea of physical energies in our environment, we'll begin by focusing on two critical concepts: *thresholds* and *sensory adaptation*.

SENSORY THRESHOLDS: *How Much Stimulation Is Enough?*

Although we are immersed in sensory information, we thrive rather than drown. Our bodies seem well prepared to deal with this ocean of information; so well prepared that when deprived of all sensory input—in a condition termed *sensory deprivation*—our bodies may produce hallucinations to fill the void (Sekuler & Blake, 1990). But what is the slightest amount of stimulation that our sensory systems can detect? In other words, how much physical stimulation is necessary in order for us to experience a sensation? Actually, it turns out to be impressively low for most aspects of sensation. For example, we can hear a watch tick twenty feet away in a quiet room; we can smell a single drop of perfume in an empty three-room apartment; and on a clear dark night, we can see a lighted candle thirty miles away (Galanter, 1962).

Although our receptors are remarkably efficient, they do not register all the information available in the environment at any given moment. We are able to smell and taste certain chemicals but not others; we hear sound waves only at certain frequencies; and our ability to detect light energy is restricted to a relatively narrow band of wavelengths. The range of physical stimuli that we and other species can detect seems to be designed in a way that maximizes survival potential (Coren & Ward, 1989).

ABSOLUTE THRESHOLDS: "WAS IT REALLY THERE?" For more than a century, psychologists have conducted studies to determine the level of sensitivity in each sensory system. To do this, they have used a variety of procedures called *psychophysical methods*. These procedures allow psychologists to determine the smallest magnitude of a stimulus that can be reliably discriminated from no stimulus at all 50 percent of the time; this is called the **absolute threshold**. To understand how absolute thresholds for our sensory systems have been explored, consider the following example. Suppose researchers at the Jaw Breaker Chewing Gum Company have discovered a new way to make the flavor in gum last forever. The process is simple and inexpensive but has a minor flaw: A critical ingredient, substance SOUR, escapes detection when in low concentrations, but in larger concentrations makes the gum taste terrible.

To determine the absolute threshold for detection of SOUR, Jaw Breaker researchers select several concentrations; the lowest is clearly below threshold (nobody tastes the SOUR), and the highest causes the tasters to spit out the gum. Then volunteers chew many samples of gum with different concentrations of SOUR. The concentration at which the volunteers detect SOUR 50 percent of the time is the absolute threshold, suggesting that the concentration of SOUR in the final product should fall *below* this level.

ABSOLUTE THRESHOLDS: SOME COMPLICATIONS We often assume there is a direct relationship between the presence of a physical stimulus and the resulting sensation. Thus, given a stimulus of sufficient intensity, we should always be able to detect its presence. Unfortunately, as shown in the SOUR example, this relationship is not so simple. Why? One reason is that our sensitivity to stimuli changes from moment to moment. A stimulus we can detect at one time will not necessarily be detected later. For this reason, psychologists have arbitrarily defined the absolute threshold as that magnitude of physical energy we can detect 50 percent of the time.

Learning Objective 3.1
Distinguish between sensation and perception.

Learning Objective 3.2
Describe how researchers study sensory thresholds and the factors that influence sensory thresholds.

Absolute Threshold: The smallest amount of a stimulus that we can detect 50 percent of the time.

Although this definition takes account of fluctuations in our sensitivity to various stimuli, it does not explain *why* such fluctuations occur. There are actually several reasons. First, aspects of our body's functions are constantly changing in order to maintain our body's internal environment at optimal levels, a state termed *homeostasis*. It is not surprising that as a result of these changes, the sensitivity of our sensory organs to external stimuli also varies. Second, motivational factors such as the rewards or costs associated with detecting various stimuli also play a role. For example, the outcome of the SOUR study might have changed if the participants had been faced with the prospect of being fired for a "wrong" decision.

Signal detection theory suggests that complex decision mechanisms are involved whenever we try to determine if we have or have not detected a specific stimulus (Swets, 1992). For instance, imagine that you are a radiologist. While scanning a patient's X-ray, you think you detect a faint spot on the film, but you're not quite sure. What should you do? If you conclude that the spot is an abnormality, you must order more scans or tests—an expensive and time-consuming alternative. If further testing reveals an abnormality, such as cancer, you may have saved the patient's life. If no abnormality is detected, though, you'll be blamed for wasting resources and unnecessarily upsetting the patient. Alternatively, if you decide the spot is *not* an abnormality, then there's no reason to order more tests. If the patient remains healthy, then you've done the right thing. If the spot is really cancerous tissue, however, the results could be fatal.

Your decision in this scenario is likely to be influenced by the rewards and costs associated with each choice alternative. Because of the potentially deadly consequences, you may be tempted to order more tests—even if the spot on the X-ray is extremely faint. But what if you are new on the job and you have just gone deeply into debt buying a house for your growing family? The fear of making a foolish decision that could cost you your job may weigh more heavily in the balance; you may not report the spot unless you are quite certain you saw it.

In summary, deciding whether we have detected a given stimulus is not always easy. These decisions often involve much more than a simple determination of the relationship between amount of physical energy present in a stimulus and the resulting psychological sensations.

DIFFERENCE THRESHOLDS: ARE TWO STIMULI THE SAME OR DIFFERENT?

A good cook tastes a dish, then adds salt to it, then tastes it again to measure the change. This illustrates another basic question relating to our sensory capacities: How much change in a stimulus is required before a shift can be noticed? Psychologists refer to the amount of change in a stimulus required for a person to detect it as the **difference threshold**. Obviously, the smaller the change we can detect, the greater our sensitivity. In other words, the difference threshold is the amount of change in a physical stimulus necessary to produce a **just noticeable difference (jnd)** in sensation. As it turns out, our ability to detect differences in stimulus intensity depends on the magnitude of the initial stimulus; we easily detect even small changes in weak stimuli, but we require much larger changes before we notice differences in strong stimuli. If you are listening to your favorite tunes at a low sound intensity, even small adjustments to the volume are noticeable. But if you are listening to very loud music, much larger changes are required before a difference is apparent. As you might guess, we are also more sensitive to changes in some types of stimuli than to changes in others. For example, we are able to notice very small shifts in temperature (less than one degree Fahrenheit) and in the pitch of sounds (a useful ability for people who tune musical instruments), but we are somewhat less sensitive to changes in loudness or in smells.

Signal Detection Theory: A theory suggesting that there are no absolute thresholds for sensations. Rather, detection of stimuli depends on their physical energy and on internal factors such as the relative costs and benefits associated with detecting their presence.

Difference Threshold: The amount of change in a stimulus required before a person can detect the shift.

Just Noticeable Difference (jnd): The smallest amount of change in a physical stimulus necessary for an individual to notice a difference in the intensity of the stimulus.

Subliminal Perception: The presumed ability to perceive a stimulus that is below the threshold for conscious experience.

Stimuli below Threshold: Can They Have an Effect? For decades **subliminal perception** has been a source of controversy. The question is whether we can sense or be affected by subthreshold stimuli that remain outside our conscious awareness (Greenwald, 1992; Merikle, 1992). Subliminal perception first captured the public's attention in the 1950s when a clever marketing executive announced he had embedded subliminal messages like "Eat popcorn" and "Drink Coke" into a then popular movie. Supposedly, the embedded messages were flashed on the movie screen so briefly (a fraction of a second) that audience members were not aware of them. Popular press reports claimed that sales of both products in theater lobbies increased substantially right after the messages (Brean, 1958). Although the executive later confessed to the hoax (no messages were actually presented), many people remained convinced that subliminal messages could be powerful sources of persuasion.

During the 1980s, public attention was again drawn to the issue of subliminal perception when concerned parents and religious leaders expressed outrage over the presence of "evil messages" recorded backward (this is known as backward masking) and embedded into songs on rock albums. The issue came to a head in a highly publicized trial in which the heavy metal band Judas Priest was accused of embedding subliminal satanic messages promoting suicide on their album *Stained Class*. The subliminal messages—which told listeners to "do it"—were alleged to be instrumental in the shotgun suicides of two young men. The judge in the case dismissed the charges against the rock band, citing a lack of scientific evidence that the subliminal messages actually *caused* the shootings (*Vance et al. v. Judas Priest et al.*, 1990).

Is it possible that subliminal satanic messages can lead unsuspecting youthful listeners down a path of loose morality and aberrant behavior? One key to understanding subliminal perception seems to lie in carefully defining what we mean by "subthreshold." For example, participants in a study by Niedenthal (1990) were asked to view a series of cartoon characters. Before each cartoon slide, a face expressing either joy or disgust was presented for 2 milliseconds—too briefly for the participants to be consciously aware of its presence. Later, participants viewed a second set of cartoons, some they'd seen previously (*targets*) and new ones they had not seen (*distractors*). As before, a face was briefly presented before each cartoon—but for half of the target slides, a change was made. Target cartoons that had initially been paired with a smiling face were now paired with a frowning face, and vice versa. Niedenthal reasoned that if the joy or disgust presented had influenced subjects' initial perception of the target cartoons, then a consistent emotion should facilitate their ability to recognize the cartoons later on. As predicted, participants recognized the target cartoons faster when the emotion expressed (joy or disgust) was consistent with the emotion expressed during the initial trials. Thus, the stimuli in Niedenthal's study were below threshold in terms of conscious awareness—but not in terms of participants' ability to respond to them.

Another critical issue to consider is the way in which subthreshold stimuli are evaluated. In chapter 1 we discussed the importance of controlled experimentation to rule out possible alternative explanations for certain findings. For example, consider the current explosion of self-help materials that offer to help you lose weight, stop smoking, get smarter, or improve your memory. Their manufacturers often claim that the effectiveness of these products is due to the presence of subliminal messages. Are these claims true? The results of careful research suggest that the answer is no (Greenwald et al., 1991; Urban, 1992). Instead, improve-

> ### KEY QUESTIONS
>
> - What is the primary function of our sensory receptors?
> - What does the term *absolute threshold* refer to?
> - Why is signal detection theory important to a discussion of sensory processes?
> - What is the role of sensory adaptation in sensation?

ments appear to stem from other factors, such as motivation and expectations—not from the effects of subliminal perception.

SENSORY ADAPTATION: "It Feels Great Once You Get Used to It!"

I have vivid memories of summer camping trips I took as a young boy with my friends. On particularly hot afternoons we would cool off with a dip into an icy mountain lake or stream. Although the initial shock of the icy water was overpowering, it eventually felt refreshing. This experience illustrates the process of **sensory adaptation**, the fact that our sensitivity to an unchanging stimulus tends to decrease over time. When we first encounter a stimulus, like icy water, our temperature receptors fire vigorously. Soon, however, they fire less vigorously, and through the process of sensory adaptation, the water then feels just right.

SENSORY ADAPTATION

Have you ever jumped into the icy waters of a mountain lake or the ocean? At first the water feels freezing, but later it feels refreshing. This an example of sensory adaptation.

Sensory adaptation has some practical advantages. If it did not occur, we would constantly be distracted by the stream of sensations we experience each day. We would not adapt to our clothing rubbing our skin, to the feel of our tongue in our mouth, or to bodily processes such as eye blinks and swallowing. However, sensory adaptation is not always beneficial and can even be dangerous. For instance, after about a minute our sensitivity to most odors drops by nearly 70 percent. Thus, in situations where smoke or harmful chemicals are present, sensory adaptation may actually reduce our sensitivity to existing dangers. In general, though, the process of sensory adaptation allows us to focus on changes in the world around us, and that ability to focus on and respond to stimulus change is usually what is most important for survival.

Now that we've considered some basic aspects of sensation, let's examine in detail each of the major senses.

VISION

Sensory Adaptation: Reduced sensitivity to unchanging stimuli over time.

Cornea: The curved, transparent layer through which light rays enter the eye.

Pupil: An opening in the eye, just behind the cornea, through which light rays enter the eye.

Iris: The colored part of the eye that adjusts the amount of light that enters by constricting or dilating the pupil.

*L*ight, in the form of energy from the sun, is part of the fuel that drives the engine of life on earth. Thus, it is not surprising that we possess exquisitely adapted organs for detecting this stimulus: our eyes. Indeed, for most of us, sight is the most important way of gathering information about the world. Figure 3.1 shows a simplified diagram of the human eye.

THE EYE: Its Basic Structure

How is light energy converted into signals our brain can understand? The answer lies in the basic structure of the eye. It is in the eye that light energy is converted into a neural code understandable to our nervous system. Light rays first pass through a transparent protective structure called the **cornea** and then enter the eye through the **pupil**, a round opening whose size varies with lighting conditions: the less light present, the wider the pupil opening (refer to Figure 3.1). These adjustments are executed by the **iris**, the colored

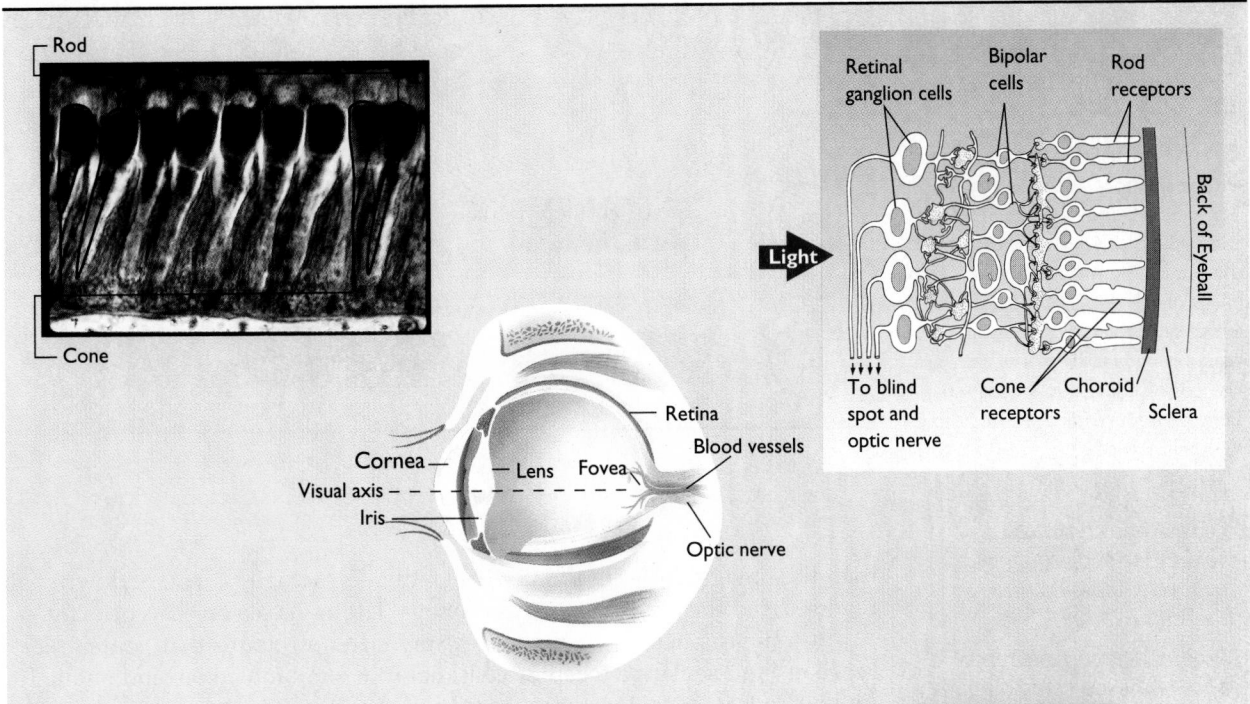

FIGURE 3.1

The Human Eye

Light filters through layers of retinal cells before hitting receptors (rods and cones), located at the back of the eye and pointed away from the incoming light. The rods and cones pass an electrical impulse to bipolar cells, which relay it to the ganglion cells. The axons of these cells form the fibers of the optic nerve.

part of the eye, which is actually a circular muscle that contracts or expands to let in varying amounts of light. After entering through the pupil, light rays pass through the **lens**, a clear structure whose shape adjusts to permit us to focus on objects at varying distances. When we look at a distant object the muscles of the lens relax, allowing the lens to become thinner and flatter; when we look at a nearby object they contract, making the lens thicker and rounder. Light rays leaving the lens are projected on the **retina** at the back of the eyeball. As illustrated in Figure 3.2 the lens bends light rays in such a way

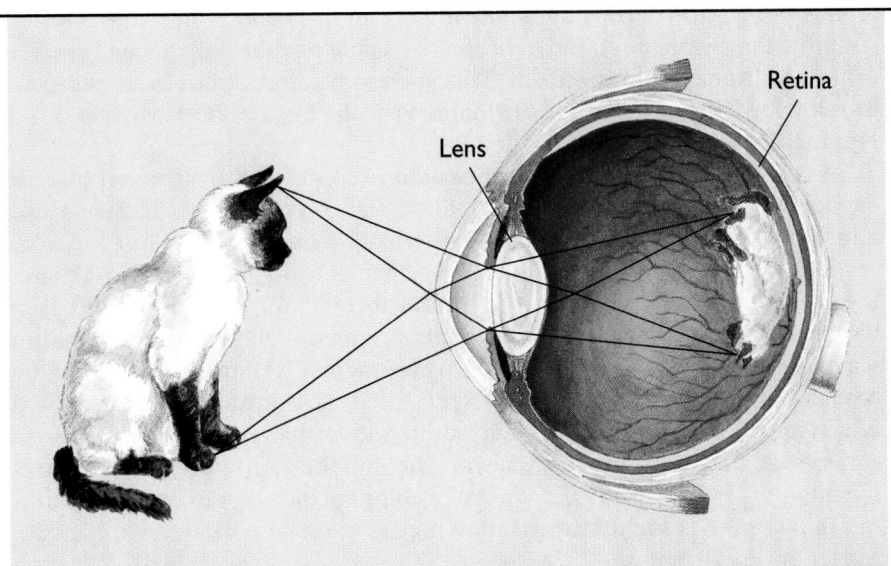

FIGURE 3.2

The Upside-Down and Reversed Image Projected onto the Retina

The lens bends light rays entering the eye so that the image projected onto the retina is upside down and reversed: Light rays from the top of an object are projected onto receptors at the bottom of the retina, and light rays from the left side of an object are projected onto receptors on the right side of the retina. Our brain rearranges this information and enables us to see the object correctly.

FIGURE 3.3

The Blind Spot

To find your blind spot, close your left eye and focus your right eye on the A. Slowly move the page toward and away from your right eye until the dot on the right disappears. The image of this dot is now being projected onto the blind spot—the region of the retina where there are no rods or cones. Now, follow the same procedure for the B and the C. What do you see?

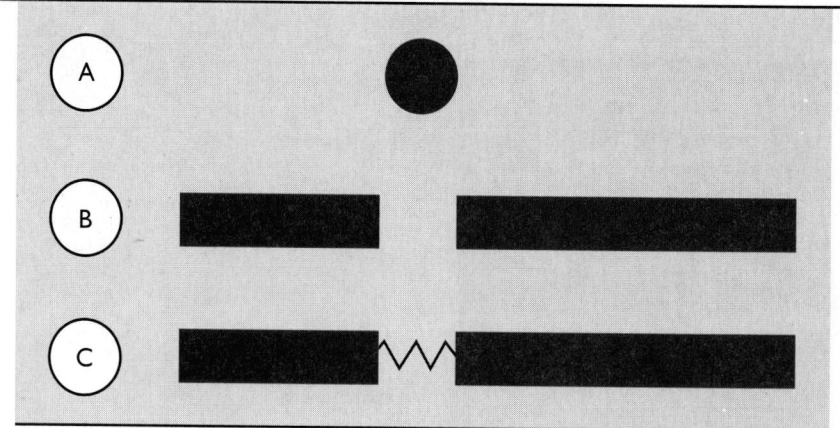

Lens: *A curved structure behind the pupil that bends light rays, focusing them on the retina. (p. 85)*

Retina: *The surface at the back of the eye containing the rods and cones. (p. 85)*

Cones: *Sensory receptors in the eye that play a crucial role in sensations of color.*

Rods: *One of the two types of sensory receptors for vision found in the eye.*

Fovea: *The area in the center of the retina in which cones are highly concentrated.*

Optic Nerve: *A bundle of nerve fibers that exit the back of the eye and carry visual information to the brain.*

Blind Spot: *The point in the back of the retina through which the optic nerve exits the eye. This exit point contains no rods or cones and is therefore insensitive to light.*

Wavelength: *The peak-to-peak distance in a sound or light wave.*

Hue: *The color that we experience due to the dominant wavelength of a light.*

Brightness: *The physical intensity of light.*

Saturation: *The degree of concentration of the hue of light. We experience saturation as the purity of a color.*

that the image projected onto the retina is actually upside down and reversed; but the brain reverses this image, letting us see objects correctly.

The retina is actually a postage-stamp-sized structure that contains two types of light-sensitive receptor cells: about 6.5 million **cones** and about 100 million **rods**. Cones, located primarily in the center of the retina in an area called the **fovea**, function best in bright light and play a key role both in color vision and in our ability to notice fine detail. In contrast, rods are found only outside the fovea and function best under lower levels of illumination, so rods help us to see in a darkened room or at night. At increasing distances from the fovea, the density of cones decreases and the density of rods increases. Once stimulated, the rods and cones transmit neural information to other neurons called *bipolar cells*. These cells, in turn, contact other neurons, called *ganglion cells*. Axons from the ganglion cells converge to form the **optic nerve** and carry visual information to the brain. Interestingly, no receptors are present where this nerve exits the eye, so there is a **blind spot** at this point in our visual field. Try the exercise in Figure 3.3 to check your own blind spot.

LIGHT: *The Physical Stimulus for Vision*

At this point we will consider some important facts about light, the physical stimulus for vision. First, the light that is visible to us is only a small portion of the electromagnetic spectrum. This spectrum ranges from radio waves at the slow or long-wave end to cosmic rays at the fast or short-wave end (see Figure 3.4).

Second, certain physical properties of light contribute to our psychological experiences of vision. **Wavelength**, the distance between successive peaks and valleys of light energy, determines what we experience as **hue**, or color. As shown in Figure 3.4, as wavelength increases from about 400 to 700 nanometers (a nanometer is one-billionth of a meter), our sensations shift from violet through blue (shorter wavelengths), green, yellow, orange (medium wavelengths), and finally red (longer wavelengths). The intensity of light, the amount of energy it contains, is experienced as **brightness**. The extent to which light contains only one wavelength, rather than many, determines our experience of **saturation**; the fewer the number of wavelengths mixed together, the more saturated or "pure" a color appears. For example, the deep red of an apple is highly saturated, whereas the pale pink of an apple blossom is low in saturation.

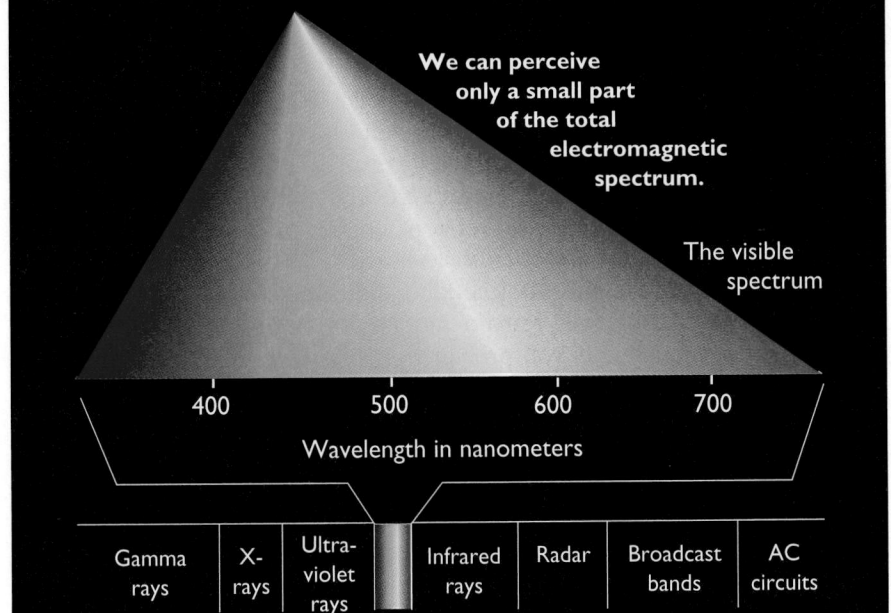

FIGURE 3.4

The Electromagnetic Spectrum

Visible light occupies only a narrow band in the entire spectrum.

We can perceive only a small part of the total electromagnetic spectrum.

The visible spectrum

| 400 | 500 | 600 | 700 |

Wavelength in nanometers

| Gamma rays | X-rays | Ultra-violet rays | | Infrared rays | Radar | Broadcast bands | AC circuits |

BASIC FUNCTIONS OF THE VISUAL SYSTEM: *Acuity, Dark Adaptation, and Eye Movements*

Our visual system is remarkably sensitive and can detect even tiny amounts of light. However, another important aspect of vision is **acuity**, the ability to resolve fine details. Two types of visual acuity are measured. The first is *static visual acuity (SVA)*, our ability to discriminate different objects when they are stationary or static, as on the familiar chart at an eye doctor's office. The second measure of acuity is *dynamic visual acuity (DVA)*, our ability to resolve detail when the test object and/or the viewer is in motion (Houfman, House, & Ryan, 1981). In general, our ability to discriminate objects decreases as the *angular velocity*—the speed at which an object's image moves across our retina—of the object increases. This aspect of our visual capacity is important in, for example, a professional baseball player's ability to detect a sizzling fastball out of the corner of his eye on his way to hitting a grand slam home run. If you wear eyeglasses or contact lenses designed to improve your visual acuity, chances are that your visual deficit stems from a slight abnormality in the shape of your eye. If your eyeball is too long, you suffer from **nearsightedness**, in which you see near objects clearly, but distant objects appear blurry. This occurs because the image entering your eye is focused slightly in front of the retina rather than directly on it. Similarly, in **farsightedness**, your eyeball is too short and the lens focuses the image behind the retina.

Another aspect of visual sensitivity is **dark adaptation**, the increase in sensitivity that occurs when we move from bright light to a dim environment, such as a movie theater. The dark-adapted eye is about 100,000 times more sensitive to light than the light-adapted eye. Actually, dark adaptation occurs in two steps. First, within five to ten minutes, the cones reach their maximum sensitivity. After about ten minutes, the rods begin to adapt; they complete this process in about thirty minutes (Matlin & Foley, 1992).

Eye movements also play a role in visual acuity. To appreciate the importance of the ability to move your eyes, just imagine how inefficient it would

Learning Objective 3.3
Describe the basic structure of the eye and the properties of light.

Learning Objective 3.4
Describe how the visual system works and how we process visual information.

Acuity: The visual ability to see fine details.

Nearsightedness: A condition in which the visual image of a distant object is focused slightly in front of the retina rather than directly on it. Therefore distant objects appear fuzzy or blurred, whereas near objects can be seen clearly.

Farsightedness: A condition in which the visual image of a nearby object is focused behind rather than directly on the retina. Therefore close objects appear out of focus, while distant objects are seen clearly.

Dark Adaptation: The process through which the visual system increases its sensitivity to light under low levels of illumination.

be to read a book or play your favorite sport if your eyes were stuck in one position. In order to change the direction of your gaze, you would have to move your entire head.

Eye movements are of two basic types: *version movements*, in which the eyes move together in the same direction, and *vergence movements*, in which the lines of sight for the two eyes converge or diverge. As we'll discover later in this chapter, vergence movements are crucial to our ability to perceive distance and depth. Three types of version movements are *involuntary movements*, *saccadic movements*, and *pursuit movements*.

At the end of this sentence, stop reading and stare at the last word for several seconds. Did your eyes remain motionless or did they tend to move about? The eye movements you probably experienced were *involuntary*; they occurred without your conscious control. These movements assure that the stimuli reaching our rods and cones are constantly changing. Like other sensory receptors, those in our retina are subject to the effects of sensory adaptation; if involuntary movements did not occur, we would experience temporary blindness whenever we fixed our gaze on any object for more than a few seconds.

Saccadic movements are fast, frequent jumps by the eyes from one fixation point to the next. Saccadic movements are apparent in reading or driving. Careful research has shown that both the size of the jumps and the region seen during each fixation maximize the information we glean while reading (McConkie et al., 1989; McConkie & Zola, 1984; Just & Carpenter, 1987). Moreover, the saccadic movements of good readers move smoothly across the materials being read; those of poor readers are shorter and move backward as well as forward (Schiffman, 1990). Finally, *pursuit movements* are smooth eye movements used to track moving objects, as when you watch a plane fly overhead and out of sight.

COLOR VISION

A world without color would be sadly limited, for color—vivid reds, glowing yellows, restful greens—is a crucial part of our visual experience. For many people, though, some degree of color deficiency is a fact of life. Nearly 8 percent of males and 0.4 percent of females are less sensitive than the rest of us either to red and green or to yellow and blue (Nathans, 1989). And a few individuals are totally color blind, experiencing the world only in varying shades of white, black, and gray. Intriguing evidence on how the world appears to people suffering from color weakness has been gathered from rare cases in which individuals have normal color vision in one eye and impaired color vision in the other (e.g., Graham & Hsia, 1958). One such woman indicated that to her color-impaired eye, all colors between red and green appeared yellow, while all colors between green and violet seemed blue.

There are two leading theories to explain our rich sense of color. The first, **trichromatic theory**, suggests that we have three different types of cones in our retina, each of which is maximally sensitive, though not exclusively so, to a particular range of light wavelengths—a range roughly corresponding to blue (450–500 nanometers), green (500–570 nanometers), or red (620–700 nanometers). Careful study of the human retina suggests that we do possess three types of color receptors, although as Figure 3.5 shows, there is a great deal of overlap in each receptor type's sensitivity range (DeValois & DeValois, 1975; Rushton, 1975). According to trichromatic theory, our ability to perceive colors result from the joint action of the three receptor types. Thus, light of a particular wavelength produces differential stimulation of each receptor type, and it is the overall pattern of stimulation that produces

Saccadic Movements: Quick movements of the eyes from one point of fixation to another.

Trichromatic Theory: A theory of color perception suggesting that we have three types of cones, each primarily receptive to particular wavelengths of light.

CHAPTER 3

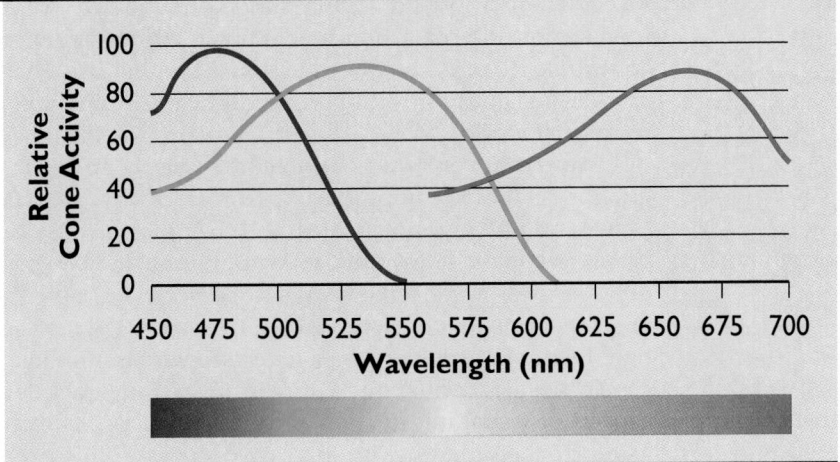

FIGURE 3.5

Three Types of Receptors Contribute to Our Perception of Color

Color vision appears to be mediated by three types of cones, each maximally sensitive, but not exclusively so, to wavelengths corresponding to blue (450–500 nm), green (500–570 nm), and red (620–700 nm).

our rich sense of color. This differential sensitivity may be due to genes that direct different cones to produce pigments sensitive to blue, green, or red (Nathans, Thomas, & Hogness, 1986).

Trichromatic theory, however, fails to account for certain aspects of color vision, such as the occurrence of **negative afterimages**—sensations of complementary colors that occur after one stares at a stimulus of a given color. For example, after you stare at a red object, if you shift your gaze to a neutral background, sensations of green may follow. Similarly, after you stare at a yellow stimulus, sensations of blue may occur.

The **opponent-process theory** addresses phenomena such as afterimages more effectively than trichromatic theory, by accounting for what happens after the cones in the retina transmit their information to the bipolar and ganglion cells. Opponent-process theory suggests that we possess six kinds of cells that play a role in sensations of color (DeValois & DeValois, 1975). Two of these handle red and green: One is stimulated by red light and inhibited by green light, whereas the other is stimulated by green light and inhibited by red. This is where the phrase *opponent process* originates. Two additional types of cells handle yellow and blue: One is stimulated by yellow and inhibited by blue, while the other shows the opposite pattern. The remaining two types handle black and white—again, in an opponent-process manner. Opponent-process theory can help explain the occurrence of negative afterimages (Jameson & Hurvich, 1989). The idea is that when stimulation of one cell in an opponent pair is terminated, the other is automatically activated. Thus, if the original stimulus viewed was yellow, the afterimage seen would be blue. Each opponent pair is stimulated in different patterns by the three types of cones. It is the overall pattern of such stimulation that yields our complex and eloquent sensation of color.

Although these theories competed for many years, scientists now know that both are necessary to explain our impressive ability to respond to color. Trichromatic theory explains how color coding occurs in the cones of the retina, whereas opponent-process theory accounts for processing in higher-order nerve cells (Coren & Ward, 1989; Hurvich, 1981; Matlin & Foley, 1992).

VISION AND THE BRAIN: *Processing Visual Information*

Our rich sense of vision does not result from the output of single neurons, but instead from the overall pattern of our sensory receptors. In other

Negative Afterimage: A sensation of complementary color that we experience after staring at a stimulus of a given hue.

Opponent-Process Theory: A theory that describes the processing of sensory information related to color at levels above the retina. The theory suggests that we possess six types of neurons, each of which is either stimulated or inhibited by red, green, blue, yellow, black, or white.

- What is the physical stimulus for vision?
- How do psychologists explain color perception?
- Why is visual perception a hierarchical process?
- What are the basic building blocks of visual perception?

Feature Detectors: *Neurons at various levels within the visual cortex that respond primarily to stimuli possessing certain features.*

Simple Cells: *Cells within the visual system that respond to specific shapes presented in certain orientations (horizontal, vertical, etc.).*

Complex Cells: *Neurons in the visual cortex that respond to stimuli moving in a particular direction and having a particular orientation.*

Hypercomplex Cells: *Neurons in the visual cortex that respond to complex aspects of visual stimuli, such as width, length, and shape.*

Prosopagnosia: *A rare condition in which brain damage impairs a person's ability to recognize faces.*

words, there is more to vision than meets the eye. But how, then, do the simple action potentials of individual neurons contribute to our overall conscious experience? To help answer this question, let's consider how the brain "invents" our visual world.

Until recently scientists believed that visual scenes in our environment were impressed onto our retinas, much like images on photographic plates, and then sent directly to the brain. We now know this view is wrong, however. The visual world we perceive results from a complex division of labor that only *begins* in the retina. In other words, it is only light that enters our eyes—we really see with our brains.

The brain processes visual information hierarchically. Groups of neurons analyze simpler aspects of visual information and send their results to other groups of neurons for further analysis. At successive stages in this process, increasingly complex visual information is analyzed and compiled—eventually producing the coherent and flowing scenes that constitute perception of the world around us (Zeki, 1992).

Our understanding of the initial stages of this process was greatly advanced by the Nobel Prize–winning series of studies conducted by Hubel and Wiesel (1979). These researchers conducted studies on **feature detectors**—neurons at various levels in the visual cortex that respond primarily to stimuli possessing certain features. Their work revealed the existence of three types of feature detectors. One group of neurons, known as **simple cells,** responds to bars or lines presented in certain orientations (horizontal, vertical, and so on). A second group, **complex cells,** responds maximally to moving stimuli such as a vertical bar moving from left to right, or to a tilted bar moving from right to left. Finally, **hypercomplex cells** respond to even more complex features of the visual world, such as length, width, and even aspects of shape, like corners and angles. These cells may fail to respond to a thin bar moving from right to left, but may respond strongly to a thick bar moving from lower to higher regions of the visual field. Or they may respond to a shape containing a right angle but fail to respond to one containing an acute angle.

Additional clues suggesting that the brain processes visual information hierarchically come from case studies of persons with visual disorders like **prosopagnosia,** a condition in which people can no longer recognize faces, but still retain relatively normal vision in other respects (Goldberg, 1992). The existence of this kind of disorder suggests that the visual system operates much like a computer, assembling bits of visual information at various locations in the brain—and not like a camera. Prosopagnosia results from damage to specific areas within the visual cortex and surrounding areas. This "computer" model explains why we can lose certain visual abilities—like recognizing faces—while others, including the ability to perceive form, motion, or color remain largely unaffected (Mestre et al., 1992; Zeki, 1992). Using modern imaging techniques, scientists are beginning to unravel how we "see" the world around us. These tools create detailed visual images that help researchers pinpoint areas of the brain that, when damaged, result in predictable visual abnormalities.

Taken together, these findings have important implications for our understanding of visual perception. First, they suggest that the visual system is quite *selective*; certain types of visual stimuli stand a greater chance of reaching the brain and undergoing further processing. Second, since nature is rarely wasteful, the existence of cells specially equipped to detect certain features of the external world suggests that these features may be the building blocks for many complex visual abilities, including reading and identifying subtly varied visual patterns such as faces. Finally, as illustrated by disorders such as prosopagnosia, "seeing" the world is a complex process—one that requires precise integration across many levels of our visual system.

HEARING

The murmur of laughing voices, the roar of a jet plane, the rustling of leaves, and that quintessential sound of the late twentieth century—the "beep, beep" of a personal computer—clearly we live in a world full of sound. And, as with vision, human beings are well equipped to receive many sounds in their environment. A simplified diagram of the human ear is shown in Figure 3.6; refer to it as you proceed through the discussion below.

THE EAR: Its Basic Structure

Try asking a friend, "When did you get your pinna pierced?" The response will probably be a blank stare. **Pinna** is the technical term for the visible part of our hearing organ, the *ear*. However, this is only a small part of the entire ear. Inside the ear is an intricate system of membranes, small bones, and receptor cells that transform sound waves into neural information for the brain. The *eardrum*, a thin piece of tissue just inside the ear, moves ever so slightly in response to sound waves striking it. When it moves, the eardrum causes three tiny bones within the *middle ear* to vibrate. The third of these bones is attached to a second membrane, the *oval window*, which covers a fluid-filled, spiral-shaped structure known as the **cochlea**. Vibration of the oval window causes movements of the fluid in the cochlea. Finally, the movement of fluid bends tiny *hair cells*, the true sensory receptors of sound. The neural messages they create are then transmitted to the brain via the *auditory nerve*.

Learning Objective 3.5
Describe the basic structure of the ear and the characteristics of sound.

Learning Objective 3.6
Describe two theories of pitch perception.

Learning Objective 3.7
Explain how we are able to localize sound.

Pinna: *The external portion of the ear.*

Cochlea: *A portion of the inner ear containing the sensory receptors for sound.*

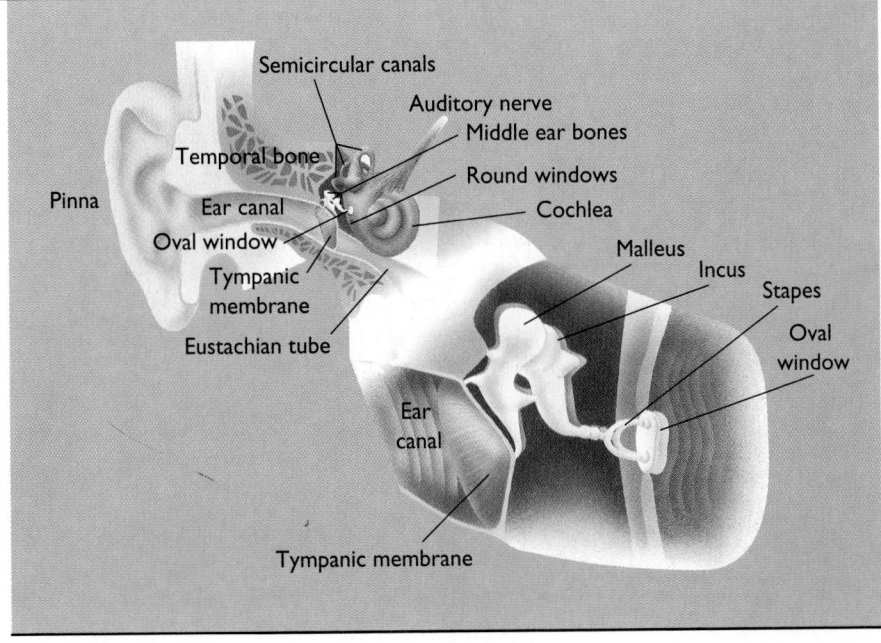

FIGURE 3.6

The Human Ear

A simplified diagram of the human ear. Sound waves (alternating compressions and expansions in the air) enter through the external auditory canal and produce slight movements in the eardrum. This motion, in turn, produces movements in fluid within the cochlea. As this fluid moves, tiny hair cells shift their position, thus generating the nerve impulses we perceive as sound.

SENSATION AND PERCEPTION: MAKING CONTACT WITH THE WORLD

SOUND: *The Physical Stimulus for Hearing*

In discussing light, we noted that relationships exist between certain of its physical properties, such as wavelength and intensity, and psychological aspects of vision, like hue and brightness. Similar relationships exist for sound, at least with respect to two of its psychological qualities: *loudness* and *pitch*.

Sound waves consist of alternating compressions of the air, or, more precisely, of the molecules that compose air. The greater the *amplitude* (magnitude) of these waves, the greater their loudness to us; see Figure 3.7. The rate at which air is expanded and contracted constitutes the *frequency* of a sound wave, and the greater the frequency, the higher the **pitch**. Frequency is measured in cycles per second, or hertz (Hz), and humans can generally hear sounds ranging from about 20 Hz to about 20,000 Hz. In **Making Psychology Part of Your Life**, at the end of this chapter, we'll explore how the loudness of your stereo headset can dramatically affect your ability to hear certain sound frequencies.

A third psychological aspect of sound—its **timbre**—refers to a sound's quality. This quality depends on the mixture of frequencies and amplitudes that make up the sound. For example, a piece of chalk squeaking across a blackboard may have the same pitch and amplitude as a note played on a clarinet, but it will certainly have a different quality. In general, the timbre of

Pitch: *The characteristic of a sound that is described as high or low. Pitch is mediated by the frequency of a sound.*

Timbre: *The quality of a sound, resulting from the complex makeup of a sound wave; timbre helps us to distinguish the sound of a trumpet from that of a saxophone.*

FIGURE 3.7

Physical Characteristics of Sound

Our perception of sounds is determined by three characteristics. *Loudness* depends on the amplitude or the height of the sound waves; as amplitude increases, the sound appears louder. *Pitch* is determined by the frequency of the sound waves; the number of sound waves that pass a given point per second. *Timbre* refers to the quality of the sound we perceive and is the characteristic that helps us distinguish the sound of a flute from the sound of a saxophone.

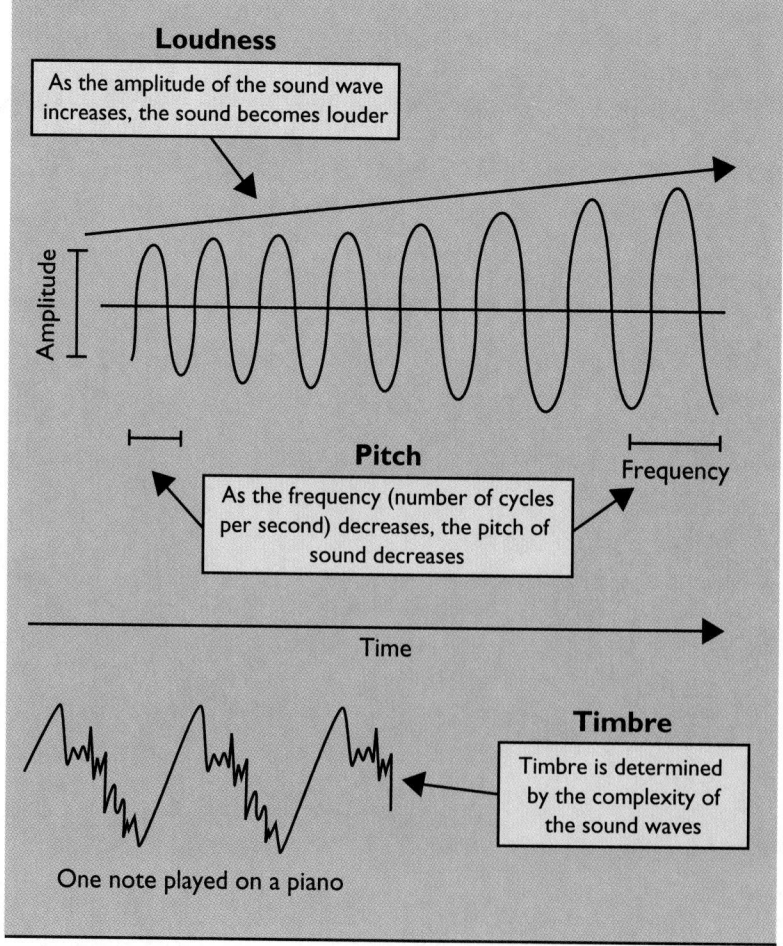

a sound is related to its complexity—how many different frequencies it contains. However, other physical aspects of the source of the sound may be involved as well, so the relationship is not a simple one (refer to Figure 3.7).

PITCH PERCEPTION

When we tune a guitar or sing in harmony with other people, we demonstrate our ability to detect differences in pitch. Most individuals can easily tell when two sounds have the same pitch and when they are different. But how does a person manage to make such fine distinctions? Two explanations, based on two different mechanisms, seem to provide the answer.

Place theory (also called the *traveling wave theory*) suggests that sounds of different frequencies cause different places along the *basilar membrane* (the floor of the cochlea) to vibrate. These vibrations, in turn, stimulate the hair cells—the sensory receptors for sound. Actual observations have shown that sound does produce pressure waves and that these waves peak, or produce maximal displacement, at various distances along the basilar membrane, depending on the frequency of the sound (Békésy, 1960). High-frequency sounds cause maximum displacement at the narrow end of the basilar membrane near the oval window, whereas lower frequencies cause maximal displacement toward the wider, farther end of the basilar membrane (see Figure 3.8). Unfortunately, place theory does not explain our ability to discriminate among very low-frequency sounds—sounds of only a few hundred cycles per second—since displacement on the basilar membrane is nearly identical for these sounds. Another problem is that place theory does not account for our ability to discriminate sounds whose frequencies differ by as little as 1 or 2 Hz; basilar membrane displacement for these sounds is nearly identical.

Frequency theory suggests that sounds of different pitch cause different rates of neural firing. Thus, high-pitched sounds produce high rates of activity in the auditory nerve, whereas low-pitched sounds produce lower rates. Frequency theory seems to be accurate up to sounds of about 1,000 Hz—the maximum rate of firing for individual neurons. Above that level, the theory must be modified to include the *volley principle*: the assumption that sound

SOUND WAVES: THE PHYSICAL STIMULUS FOR HEARING

Like light, sound has a range of intensities—from very soft to very loud.

Place Theory: A theory suggesting that sounds of different frequency stimulate different areas of the basilar membrane.

Frequency Theory: A theory of pitch perception suggesting that sounds of different frequencies, heard as differences in pitch, induce different rates of neural activity in the hair cells of the inner ear.

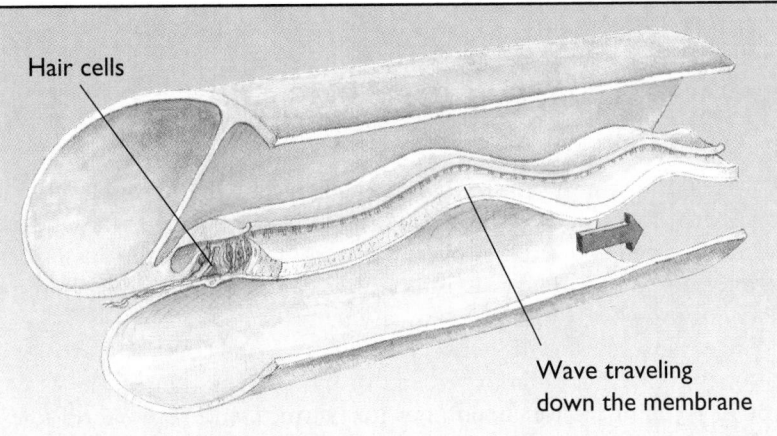

Hair cells

Wave traveling down the membrane

FIGURE 3.8

The Basilar Membrane

The cochlea is unwound and cut open to reveal the basilar membrane, which is covered with thousands of hair cells. Pressure waves in the fluid filling the cochlea cause oscillations to travel in waves down the basilar membrane, stimulating the hair cells.

receptors for other neurons begin to fire in volleys. For example, a sound with a frequency of 5,000 Hz might generate a pattern of activity in which each of five groups of neurons fires 1,000 times in rapid succession—that is, in volleys.

Since our daily activities regularly expose us to sounds of many frequencies, both theories are needed to explain our ability to respond to this wide range of stimuli. Frequency theory explains how low-frequency sounds are registered, whereas place theory explains how high-frequency sounds are registered. In the middle ranges, between 500 and 4,000 Hz, the range that we use for most daily activities, both theories apply.

SOUND LOCALIZATION

You are walking down a busy street filled with many sights and sounds. Suddenly a familiar voice calls your name. You instantly turn in the direction of this sound and spot one of your friends. How do you know where to turn? Research on **localization**—the ability of the auditory system to locate the source of a given sound—suggests that several factors play a role.

The first is the fact that we have two ears, placed on opposite sides of our head. As a result, our head creates a *sound shadow*, a barrier that reduces the intensity of sound on the "shadowed" side. Thus, a sound behind us and to our left will be slightly louder in our left ear. The shadow effect is strongest for high-frequency sounds, which have difficulty bending around the head, and may produce a difference in intensity of 30 decibels or more in the ear farthest away (Phillips & Brugge, 1985). The placement of our ears also produces a slight difference in the time it takes for a sound to reach each ear. Although this difference is truly minute—often less than one millisecond—it provides an important clue to sound localization.

What happens when sound comes from directly in front or directly in back of us? In this instance, we often have difficulty determining the location of the sound source, since the sound reaches our ears at the same time. Head movements can help resolve a problem like this. By turning your head, you create a slight difference in the time it takes for the sound to reach each of your ears—and now you can determine the location of the sound and take appropriate action (Moore, 1982).

In summary, our auditory system is ideally constructed to take full advantage of a variety of subtle cues. When you consider how rapidly we process and respond to such information, the whole system seems nothing short of marvelous in its efficiency.

KEY QUESTIONS

- What is the physical stimulus for hearing?
- How do psychologists explain pitch perception?
- How do we localize sound?

TOUCH AND OTHER SKIN SENSES

What is the largest sensory organ you possess? If you said anything except "my skin," think again. The skin is the largest sensory organ and produces the most varied experiences: everything from the pleasure of a soothing massage to the pain of injury. Actually, there are several skin senses, including touch (or pressure), warmth, cold, and pain.

Since there are specific sensory receptors for vision and hearing, it seems reasonable to expect this to be true for the various skin senses as well—one type of receptor for touch, another for warmth, and so on. And microscopic examination reveals several different receptor types, which led early re-

Localization: The ability of our auditory system to determine the direction of a sound source.

searchers to suggest that each receptor type produced a specific sensory experience. Several researchers attempted to test this prediction. They located sensitive patches of their own skin, then snipped these patches out and examined them under a microscope. The results were disappointing; specific types of receptors were *not* found at spots highly sensitive to touch, warmth, or cold. Other studies have also shown that many different types of receptors often respond to a particular stimulus. Therefore, the skin's sensory experience is probably determined by the total pattern of nerve impulses reaching the brain.

The physical stimulus for sensations of touch is a stretching of or pressure against the receptors in or near the skin. But have you ever wondered why certain areas are more sensitive than others? As it turns out, the receptors in skin are not evenly distributed; the touch receptors in areas highly sensitive to touch, such as the face and fingertips, are much more densely packed than receptors in less sensitive areas, such as our legs (see Figure 3.9). In addition, areas of the skin with greater sensitivity also have greater representation in higher levels of the brain.

Most of us have experienced the soft texture of a baby's skin, the sleek feel of silk, or the grittiness of sandpaper. In most instances we discover the tex-

Learning Objective 3.8
Discuss the nature of the skin senses.

Learning Objective 3.9
Describe the implications of the gate-control theory of pain.

Learning Objective 3.10
Know how culture influences our perception of pain.

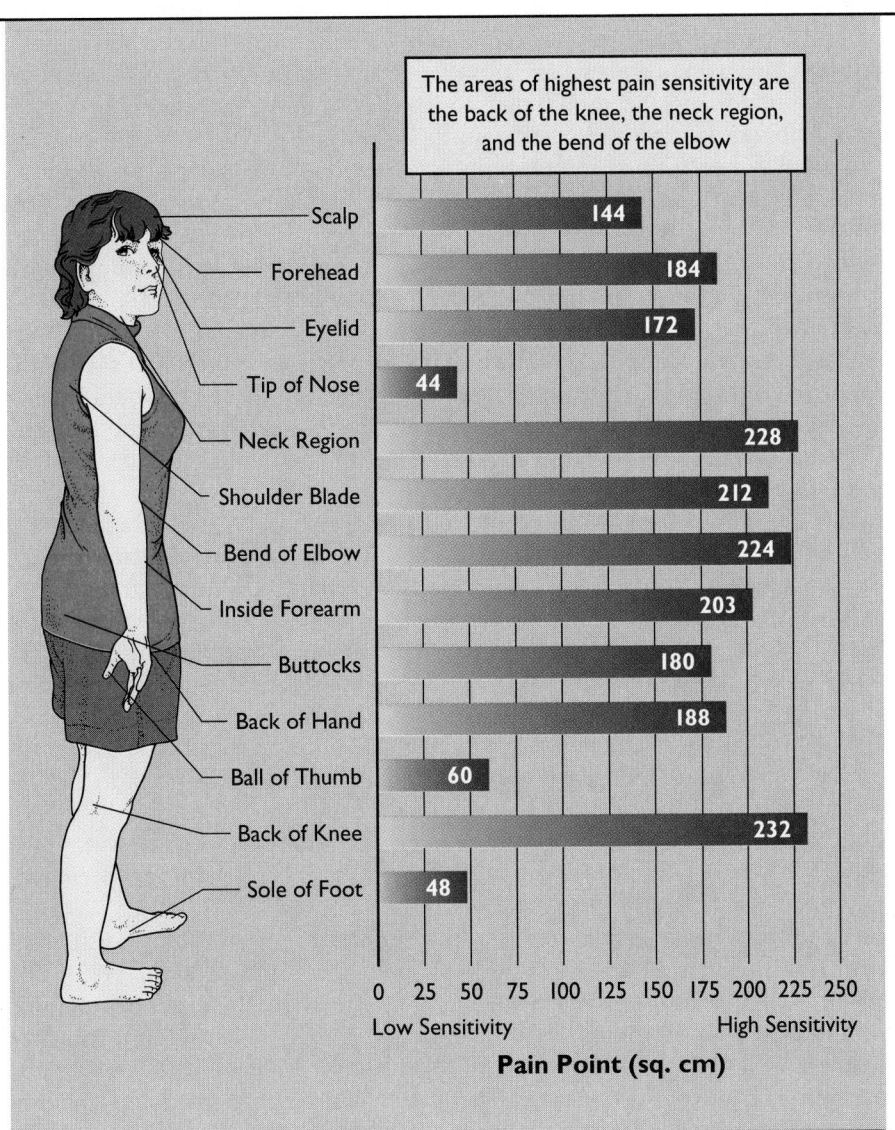

The areas of highest pain sensitivity are the back of the knee, the neck region, and the bend of the elbow

Region	Pain Point (sq. cm)
Scalp	144
Forehead	184
Eyelid	172
Tip of Nose	44
Neck Region	228
Shoulder Blade	212
Bend of Elbow	224
Inside Forearm	203
Buttocks	180
Back of Hand	188
Ball of Thumb	60
Back of Knee	232
Sole of Foot	48

0 25 50 75 100 125 150 175 200 225 250
Low Sensitivity   High Sensitivity

Pain Point (sq. cm)

FIGURE 3.9

The Distribution of Pain Sensitivity over Various Regions of the Skin

Pain receptors are not distributed evenly on our skin.

ture of an object through active exploration—using our fingertips or other sensitive areas of our body. Psychologists distinguish between *passive touch*, in which an object comes in contact with the skin, and *active touch*, in which we place our hand or other body part in contact with an object. We are considerably more accurate at identifying objects through active than through passive touch, in part because of feedback we receive from the movement of our fingers and hands when exploring an object (Matlin & Foley, 1992). Our understanding of active touch has been especially important in the development of reading aids for blind persons. For example, the **Braille alphabet** (a series of raised dots recognizable through touch) is much easier for blind persons to identify than raised versions of standard letters.

PAIN: *Its Nature and Control*

Pain plays an important adaptive role; without it, we would be unaware that something is amiss with our body or that we have suffered some type of injury. Determining the mechanisms for pain sensation has been particularly difficult, because unlike the other sensory processes that we have studied, pain sensation has no specific stimulus (Besson & Chaouch, 1987). However, sensations of pain do seem to originate in *free nerve endings* located throughout the body: in the skin, around muscles, and in internal organs. Apparently, painful stimuli cause damage to body tissues. The tissues, in turn, release chemical substances, including a neurotransmitter called *substance P*, that stimulate specialized pain neurons; the messages from these neurons are responsible for our sensations of pain.

Actually, two types of pain seem to exist. One can best be described as quick and sharp—the kind of pain we experience when we receive a cut. The other is dull and throbbing—the pain we experience from a sore muscle or an injured back. The first type of pain seems to be transmitted through large myelinated sensory nerve fibers (Campbell & LaMotte, 1983). You may recall from chapter 2 that impulses travel faster along myelinated fibers, and so it makes sense that sharp sensations of pain are carried via these fiber types. In contrast, dull pain is carried by smaller unmyelinated nerve fibers, which conduct neural impulses more slowly. Both fiber types synapse with neurons in the spinal cord that carry pain messages to the thalamus and other parts of the brain (Willis, 1985).

The discovery of the two pain systems described above led to the formulation of an influential view of pain known as the **gate-control theory** (Melzack, 1976). Gate-control theory suggests that there are neural mechanisms in the spinal cord that sometimes close, thus preventing pain messages from reaching the brain. Apparently, pain messages carried by the large fibers cause this "gate" to close, while messages carried by the smaller fibers—the ones related to dull, throbbing pain—cannot. This may explain why sharp pain is relatively brief, whereas an ache persists. The gate-control theory also helps to explain why vigorously stimulating one area to reduce pain in another sometimes works (Matlin & Foley, 1992). Presumably, tactics such as rubbing the skin near an injury, applying ice packs or hot-water bottles, and even acupuncture stimulate activity in the large nerve fibers, closing the spinal "gate" and reducing sensations of pain.

This theory has also been revised to account for the importance of several brain mechanisms in the perception of pain (Melzack & Wall, 1982). For example, our current emotional state may interact with the onset of a painful stimulus to alter the intensity of pain we experience. The brain, in other words, may affect pain perception by transmitting messages that either close the spinal "gate" or keep it open. The result: When we are anxious (as many persons are when sitting in a dentist's chair), pain is intensified; and when we

Braille Alphabet: *Representation of letters by a system of raised dots, used in reading materials for blind persons.*

Gate-Control Theory: *A theory suggesting that the spinal cord contains a mechanism that can block transmission of pain signals to the brain.*

CHAPTER 3

are calm and relaxed, pain may be reduced. We'll explore the influence of other contextual factors—including culture—on the experience of pain in **Perspectives on Diversity** below.

PERSPECTIVES ON DIVERSITY

Culture and the Perception of Pain

I magine the following scene: You are in the midst of an ancient tribal ceremony. Nearly a hundred warriors are seated cross-legged on the ground of a smoke-filled lodge. Their attention is riveted on two persons, an old man and a young one, standing face to face at the center of the room. Only a low, rhythmic drumbeat breaks the silence. Sunlight through the lodge's apex penetrates the smoke, revealing what comes next. Using an eagle's talon, the old man rips the skin above the younger man's chest, then inserts lengths of bone horizontally through each of the wounds. Amazingly, the young man's stoic expression remains unchanged. Loops of rope are then secured around the bones, and the young man is hoisted into the air, where he is allowed to dangle—until the bones tear through the skin or he becomes unconscious.

Sound like a sadistic late-night horror show? It's actually a description of *"swinging to the pole,"* a ceremony practiced by the Lakota Sioux and Cheyenne tribes in which warriors demonstrated their courage and ability to withstand tremendous pain. This ceremony and similar ones in other cultures have led to intriguing questions about the nature of pain (Weisenberg, 1982). Although we commonly view pain as something automatic and universal, large cultural differences exist in the interpretation and expression of pain, as illustrated in the "swinging" scene above. But what is the basis for these differences?

At first glance it is tempting to conclude that cultural differences in *pain threshold*—physical differences—are the cause. After all, many of us could never endure such torture. However, no consistent experimental evidence supports this view (Zatzick & Dimsdale, 1990). Instead, observed cultural differences in the capacity to withstand (or not withstand) pain seem to be perceptual in nature and to reflect the powerful effects of social learning (Morse & Morse, 1988). For example, honor and social standing among the Bariba of West Africa are tied closely to stoicism and the ability to withstand great pain (Sargent, 1984). Thus, both Bariba men and women are expected to suffer pain silently. And as you might expect, their language contains few words for the expression of pain. Additional environmental factors may also play a role in determining our perceptions of pain. For example, some evidence suggests that persons exposed to harsh living or working conditions become more stoical than those who work or live in more comfortable circumstances (Clark & Clark, 1980).

Taken together, the evidence suggests that pain may, in fact, be universal—at least in some respects. Specifically, differences in pain perception seem to result from the powerful effects of social learning, not from physical differences.

CULTURE AND PAIN

Pain is a universal sensation, but pain perception can be strongly influenced by one's culture.

Endorphins, the opiatelike chemicals our body produces, discussed in chapter 2, may also interact with the spinal "gate" to lessen sensations of pain (Akil et al., 1984; Millan, 1986). Researchers have found that certain areas of the spinal cord are highly enriched in opiate receptors and endorphin-containing neurons; thus, these substances may close the spinal gate by inhibit-

Endorphins: Opiatelike substances produced by the body.

ing the release of excitatory substances for neurons carrying information about pain (Snyder, 1977; Neale et al., 1978).

Drugs such as morphine can also be effective in relieving pain. Physicians often avoid prescribing these medications or administer them in levels too small to provide any benefit, because of the drugs' potentially addictive properties. However, under certain conditions and under close medical supervision, morphine can be used safely to relieve pain (Melzack, 1990). Apparently, context is the key: The chances of addiction are high when morphine is taken for "recreational" purposes, but low when it is taken for pain.

In cases of persistent excruciating pain, people sometimes seek relief through measures as extreme as surgery to sever nerve pathways. But because our perception of pain stems from both physical and psychological causes (Fernandez & Turk, 1992), psychologists have developed less drastic means of relief, collectively termed *cognitive-behavioral procedures*. Evidence suggests that changing our thoughts and feelings—as well as our overt responses—before, during, and after painful episodes can dramatically influence our perceptions of pain (Turk & Rudy, 1992). Although the specific mechanisms accounting for the success of cognitive-behavioral procedures remain unclear, an important element seems to be the extent to which we think negative thoughts while in pain. Some intriguing research has shown that reducing or interrupting such thoughts can greatly improve our ability to cope with pain (Chaves & Brown, 1987; Turner & Clancy, 1986). As a long-time runner, I have used these and related techniques to deal with the pain associated with certain types of training. For example, I'm careful *not* to focus on the discomfort I sometimes feel and to think, instead, about other things. Of course, I'm careful to avoid overdoing it: Pain can be a warning sign that we are pushing our bodies to—and beyond—their limit. Woe to the athlete, runner or otherwise, who totally ignores these warnings! Other techniques that involve cognitive mechanisms, such as hypnosis, distraction, and social modeling, have also been successfully applied to relieve pain (Bellisimo & Tunks, 1984; Craig & Prkachin, 1978).

KEY QUESTIONS

- What is the physical stimulus for touch?
- Where does the sensation of pain originate?
- What is the basis for cultural differences in pain perception?

SMELL AND TASTE: *The Chemical Senses*

Learning Objective 3.11
Explain the basic principles and findings relating to the chemical senses—smell and taste.

*A*lthough smell and taste are separate senses, we'll consider them together for two reasons. First, both respond to substances in solution—that is, substances that have been dissolved in a fluid or gas, usually water or air. Second, in everyday life, smell and taste are interrelated.

SMELL AND TASTE: *How They Operate*

SMELL   The stimulus for sensations of smell consists of molecules of various substances contained in the air. Such molecules enter the nasal passages, where they dissolve in moist nasal tissues. This brings them in contact with receptor cells contained in the *olfactory epithelium* (see Figure 3.10). Human beings possess only about 10 million of these receptors. (Dogs, in contrast, possess more than 200 million receptors.) Nevertheless, our ability to detect smells is impressive. To appreciate this, consider a "scratch-and-sniff" smell

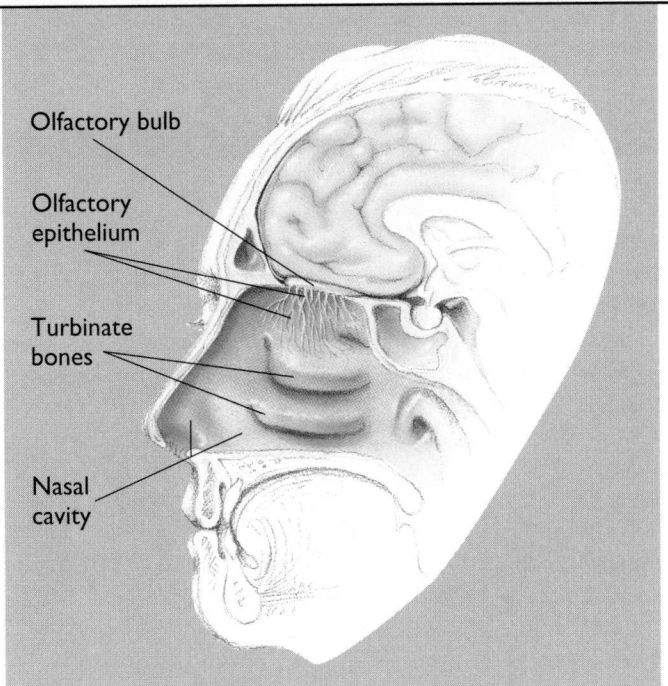

FIGURE 3.10

Olfactory bulb

Olfactory
epithelium

Turbinate
bones

Nasal
cavity

Location of Receptors for Smell

Receptors for our sense of smell are located in the olfactory epithelium, at the top of the nasal cavity. Molecules of odorous substances are dissolved in moisture present in the nasal passages. This brings them into contact with *receptor cells* whose neural activity gives rise to sensations of smell.

survey in which six different odors were embedded separately onto panels measuring about 1.75 by 1.25 inches. Amazingly, less than 1 ounce of each odor was needed to place these smells onto 11 million copies of the survey (Gibbons, 1986; Gilbert & Wysocki, 1987).

Our olfactory senses are restricted, however, in terms of the range of stimuli to which they are sensitive, just as our visual system can detect only a small portion of the total electromagnetic spectrum. Our olfactory receptors can detect only substances with molecular weights—the sum of the atomic weights of all atoms in an odorous molecule—between 15 and 300 (Carlson, 1994). This explains why we can smell the alcohol contained in a mixed drink, with a molecular weight of 46, but cannot smell table sugar, with a molecular weight of 342.

Several theories have been proposed for how smell messages reach the brain. *Stereochemical theory* suggests that substances differ in smell because they have different molecular shapes (Amoore, 1970; 1982). Unfortunately, support for this theory has been mixed; nearly identical molecules can have extremely different fragrances, whereas substances with very different chemical structures can produce very similar odors (Engen, 1982; Wright, 1982). Other theories have focused on isolating "primary odors," similar to the basic hues in color vision. But these efforts have been unsuccessful, because there is often disagreement in people's perceptions of even the most basic smells.

TASTE   The sensory receptors for taste are located inside small bumps on the tongue known as *papillae.* Within each papilla is a cluster of *taste buds* (see Figure 3.11 on page 100). Each taste bud contains several receptor cells. Human beings possess about 10,000 taste buds. In contrast, chickens have only 24, while catfish would win any taste-bud–counting contest: They possess more than 175,000, scattered over the surface of their body. In a sense, they can "taste" with their entire skin (Pfaffmann, 1978).

People generally believe that they can distinguish a large number of flavors in foods. But in fact, there appear to be only four basic tastes: sweet,

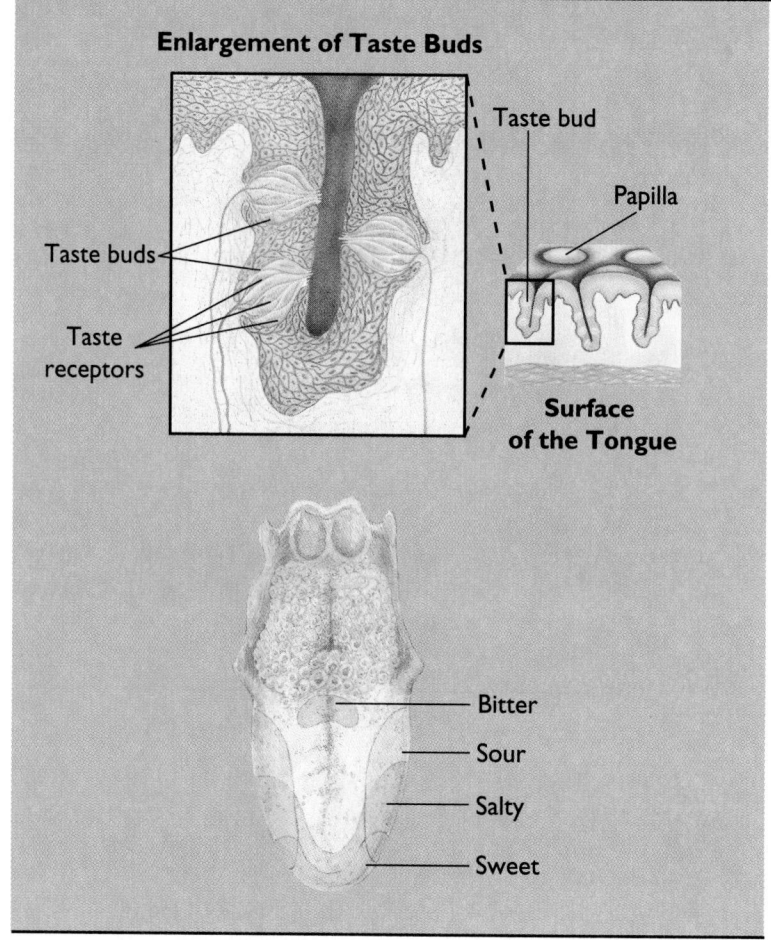

FIGURE 3.11

Sensory Receptors for Taste

Taste buds are located inside small bumps on the surface of the tongue known as papillae. Within each taste bud are individual receptor cells. Also shown here are the areas of the tongue most sensitive to the four basic tastes: sweet, salty, sour, and bitter.

salty, sour, and bitter (see Figure 3.11). Why, then, do we perceive many more? The answer lies in the fact that we are aware not only of the taste of the food but of its smell, its texture, its temperature, the pressure it exerts on our tongue and mouth, and many other sensations. When these factors are removed from the picture, only the four basic tastes remain.

SMELL AND TASTE: Some Interesting Findings

Perhaps because they are more difficult to study, smell and taste have received far less attention from researchers than vision and hearing. However, this does not imply that these senses are not important. Indeed, individuals who have lost their sense of smell (a state known as *anosmia*) often become deeply depressed; some even commit suicide (Douek, 1988).

Despite the relative lack of research effort, many interesting facts have been uncovered about smell and taste. For example, it appears that we are not very good at identifying different odors (Engen, 1986). When asked to identify thirteen common fragrances (such as grape, smoke, mint, pine, and soap), individuals were successful only 32 percent of the time. Even when brand-name products or common odors are used, accuracy is still less than 50 percent. Some research suggests that we lack a well-developed representational system for describing olfactory experiences (Engen, 1987). In other words, we may recognize a smell without being able to name the odor in question—a condition sometimes called the "tip-of-the-nose" phenomenon

(Lawless & Engen, 1977; Richardson & Zucco, 1989). And some experiments have shown that when odorants are associated with experimenter-provided verbal and visual cues, participants' long-term ability to recognize odors is enhanced (Lyman & McDaniel, 1986; 1987).

Actually, although our ability to identify specific odors is limited, our memory of them is impressive (Schab, 1991). Once exposed to a specific odor, we can recognize it months or even years later (Engen & Ross, 1973; Rabin & Cain, 1984). This may be due, in part, to the fact that our memory for odors is often coded as part of memories of a more complex and significant life event (Richardson & Zucco, 1989). For example, the delicious aroma of freshly made popcorn may elicit images of your favorite movie theater.

Knowledge about the chemical senses, especially smell, can also have important practical implications—a fact that has not escaped manufacturers of scented products. In the United States alone, sales of fragranced products exceed $19 billion annually (Foderaro, 1988). Commercial success has led to numerous claims regarding the potential benefits of fragrance. For example, practitioners of a field called *aromatherapy* claim that they can successfully treat a wide range of psychological problems and physical ailments by means of specific fragrances (Tisserand, 1977). Moreover, a growing number of companies have installed equipment that introduces various fragrances into the heating and air-conditioning systems of their buildings. Supposedly, the fragrances yield a variety of benefits: Fragrances such as lemon, peppermint, and basil lead to increased alertness and energy, whereas lavender and cedar promote relaxation and reduced tension after high-stress work periods (Iwahashi, 1992). Although little scientific evidence for such claims exists, the concept poses an intriguing question: Can fragrance influence human behavior in measurable ways? A growing body of evidence indicates the answer is yes. Several studies indicate that persons wearing perfume or cologne to job interviews can strongly affect the ratings they receive—but not always positively (Baron, 1983, 1986). Other evidence suggests that simply introducing pleasant fragrances into the air of work settings (known as *ambient fragrance*) can often produce beneficial effects (Baron & Bronfen, 1994; Baron & Thomley, 1994; Warm, Dember, & Parasuraman, 1991). For example, in a recent series of studies (Baron & Bronfen, 1994), pleasant fragrances (lemon, floral) were either introduced or not introduced into rooms where people worked on various cognitive tasks (for example, decoding written messages). The presence of a pleasant aroma increased performance on these tasks and also increased participants' willingness to help another person who requested their assistance. Indeed, participants exposed to pleasant fragrances were more likely to complete and return a questionnaire on their own time, days or even weeks after participating in the study. Together, these and related findings suggest that pleasant fragrances enhance people's current moods, and so exert a wide range of effects on their behavior.

KEY QUESTIONS

- What is the physical stimulus for smell?
- Where are the sensory receptors for taste located?
- Are there practical benefits to introducing pleasant scents into the workplace?

KINESTHESIA AND VESTIBULAR SENSE

One night while driving, you notice flashing lights on the roadside ahead. Because traffic has slowed to a crawl, you get a close look at the situation as you pass by. A state trooper is in the process of administering a sobriety test to the driver of a car he has pulled over. The driver's head is tilted back at an angle, and he is trying to touch each of his fingers to his nose but is having

Learning Objective 3.12
Explain the nature of the sensory systems involved in our sense of balance and body movements.

great difficulty doing so. This example illustrates the importance of our *kinesthetic* and *vestibular senses*—two important but often ignored aspects of our sensory system.

Kinesthesia is the sense that gives us information about the location of our body parts with respect to each other and allows us to perform movements—from simple ones like touching our nose with our fingertips to more complex ones required for gymnastics, dancing, or driving an automobile. Kinesthetic information comes from receptors in joints, ligaments, and muscle fibers (Matlin & Foley, 1992). When we move our body, these receptors register the rate of change of movement speed as well as the rate of change of the angle of the bones in our limbs, then transform this mechanical information into neural signals for the brain. We also receive important kinesthetic information from our other senses, especially vision and touch. To demonstrate how your kinesthetic sense system draws on other senses, try the following experiment: Close your eyes for a moment and hold your arms down at your sides. Now without looking, touch your nose with each of your index fingers—one at a time. Can you do it? Most people can, but only after missing their nose a time or two. Now, try it again with your eyes open. Is it easier this way? In most instances it is, because of the added information we receive from our visual sense.

Whereas kinesthesia keeps our brain informed about the location of our body parts with respect to each other, the **vestibular sense** gives us information about body position, movement, and acceleration—factors critical for maintaining our sense of balance (Schiffman, 1990). We usually become aware of our vestibular sense after activities that make us feel dizzy, like amusement park rides that involve rapid acceleration or spinning motions.

The sensory organs for the vestibular sense are located in the inner ear (see Figure 3.12). Two fluid-filled **vestibular sacs** provide information about the body's position in relation to the earth by tracking changes in linear movement. When our body accelerates (or decelerates) along a straight line, as when we are in a bus that is starting and stopping, or when we tilt our head or body to one side, hair cells bend in proportion to the rate of change in our motion. This differential bending of hair cells causes attached nerve fibers to discharge neural signals that are sent to the brain.

THE VESTIBULAR SENSE

A spinning ice skater provides an example of rotational acceleration around one of the three axes monitored in the semicircular canals.

FIGURE **3.12**

The Structures Underlying Our Sense of Balance

Shown here are the organs of our kinesthetic and vestibular senses. Structures in the two *vestibular sacs* provide information about the positions of the head and body with respect to gravity by tracking changes in linear movement, whereas those in the *semicircular canals* provide information about *rotational acceleration* around three principal axes.

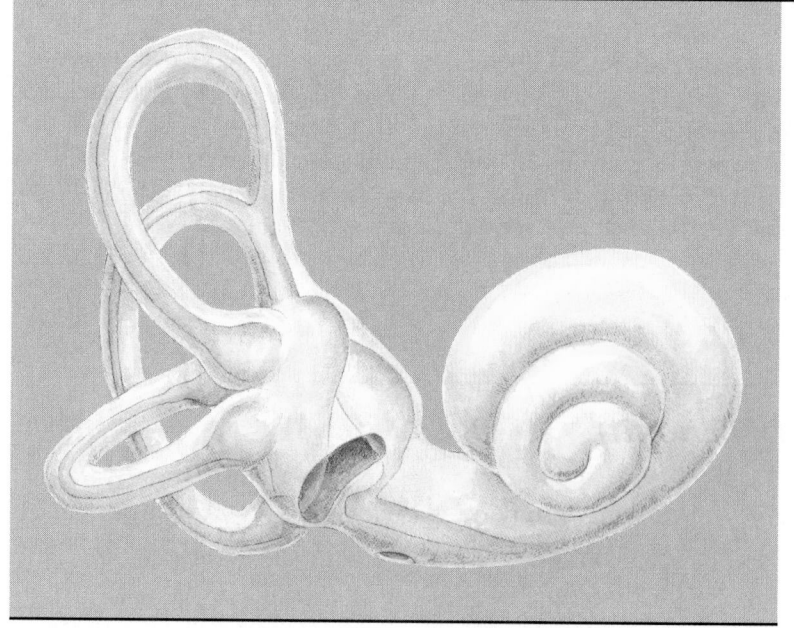

Three fluid-filled **semicircular canals,** also in the inner ear, provide information about rotational acceleration of the head or body along three principal axes. Whenever we turn or rotate our head, the fluid in these canals begins to move and causes a bending of hair cells. Since these structures are arranged at right angles to each other, bending is greatest in the semicircular canal corresponding to the axis along which the rotation occurs.

Note that the vestibular system is designed to detect changes in motion rather than constant motion. For example, it helps us to detect the change in acceleration that accompanies takeoff in an airplane, but not the constant velocity that follows.

We also receive vestibular information from our other senses, especially vision—a fact that can produce queasy consequences if the information from these senses is in conflict (Jefferson, 1993). Developers of a realistic "Back to the Future" ride at Universal Studios in Florida discovered this fact when riders in their DeLorean simulator became nauseous. Apparently, the visual effects were not synchronized with the movements the riders felt. Once reprogrammed, however, the simulator conveyed the developers' initial intent—the sensation of flying through space and time.

KEY QUESTIONS

- What information does the kinesthetic sense provide to the brain?
- What information does the vestibular sense provide to the brain?

PERCEPTION: *Putting It All Together*

Up to this point we have focused on the sensory processes that convert raw physical stimulation into usable neural codes. But you may be wondering how this array of neural action potentials contributes to the richness of conscious experience. Stop for a moment and look around you. Do you see a meaningless swirl of colors, brightnesses, and shapes? Probably not. Now turn on the radio and tune it to any station. Do you hear an incomprehensible babble of sounds? Certainly not (unless, of course, you've tuned to a foreign-language or heavy metal station). In both cases, you "see" and "hear" more than the raw sensations that stimulate the receptors in your eyes, ears, and other sense organs; you see recognizable objects and hear understandable words or music. In other words, transmission of sensory information from sensory receptors to the brain is only part of the picture. Equally important is the process of perception—the way in which we *select*, *organize*, and *interpret* sensory input to achieve a grasp of our surroundings. The remainder of this chapter concerns some basic principles that influence perception.

PERCEPTION: *The Focus of Our Attention*

Based on the preceding discussion, you may realize that your attention, or mental focus, captures only a small portion of the visual and auditory stimuli available at a given moment, while ignoring other aspects. But what about information from our other senses? By shifting the focus of our attention, we may suddenly notice smells, tastes, and tactile sensations that were outside our awareness only moments ago. For example, if you're absorbed in a good book or watching a suspenseful movie, you may not notice the delightful aroma of a freshly baked pie—at least until the cook says, "Dessert is ready!"

Kinesthesia: The sense that gives us information about the location of our body parts with respect to each other and allows us to perform movements.

Vestibular Sense: Our sense of balance.

Vestibular Sacs: Fluid-filled sacs in our inner ear that provide information about the positions and changes in linear movement of our head and body.

Semicircular Canals: Fluid-filled structures that provide information about rotational acceleration of the head or body around three principal axes of rotation.

One thing is certain: We cannot absorb all of the available sensory information in our environment. Thus, we *selectively attend* to certain aspects of our environment while relegating others to the background (Johnston & Dark, 1986). Selective attention has obvious advantages, since it allows us to maximize information gained from the object of our focus while reducing sensory interference from other, irrelevant sources (Matlin & Foley, 1992). Unfortunately, selective attention to one thing may mean neglecting another. For a firsthand understanding of the power of selective attention, watch someone who is completely absorbed in a suspenseful novel or a thrilling sports event. Studies have shown that people can focus so intently on one task that they fail to notice other events occurring simultaneously—even very salient ones (Becklen & Cerone, 1983; Cherry, 1953). We are, however, faced with many everyday situations in which we must cope with multiple conflicting inputs. Think back to the last time you were at a crowded party with many conversations going on at once. Were you able to shut out all voices except for that of the person you were talking to? Probably not. Our attention often shifts to other aspects of our environment, such as a juicy bit of conversation or a mention of our own name (Moray, 1959). This is often referred to as the *cocktail party phenomenon* and illustrates one way in which we deal with the demands of divided attention.

Although we control the focus of our attention, at least to some extent, certain characteristics of stimuli can cause our attention to shift suddenly. Features such as contrast, novelty, stimulus intensity, color, and sudden change tend to attract our attention. Indeed, advertisers have capitalized on attention-getting strategies for years. Additionally, if you recall the discussion of signal detection theory early in this chapter, it should not surprise you that the focus of our attention is dramatically affected by higher-level cognitive processes; in other words, motivation and expectancy factors have a lot to do with selective attention.

As it turns out, our attentional processes play a crucial survival role in aspects of our everyday lives by alerting us to immediate natural dangers in our environment—enabling us, for example, to leap back onto the curb when we glimpse a speeding car out of the corner of our eye. You can probably imagine hundreds of ways in which attentional processes help you to avoid peril. But what about hazards for which there are no sensory cues available? One of the most deadly examples of such a hazard is radioactivity. The radioactive particles emitted by certain materials are colorless and odorless and thus cannot be detected through our normal sensory receptors; even a limited exposure, however, can have deadly consequences. In such cases, people need *warnings*—information displays that attempt to influence behavior through the information they present. A growing body of evidence indicates that warnings can be effective in inducing people to act more safely, but only when the warnings take careful account of both sensory and perceptual processes. For example, they must be designed so that they are readily noticed, and they must present information in a manner consistent with the ways in which we typically organize and interpret sensory input (Kalsher, Clarke, & Wogalter, 1993; Wogalter & Young, 1993). Unfortunately, many warnings fail to take account of these basic principles, and so are less effective than they might otherwise be. For example, the warning placed on alcoholic beverages in the United States is so small that many drinkers do not notice it or cannot read it, and it presents information that many do not find personally relevant (such as the fact that pregnant women should not drink alcohol because it may contribute to birth defects). To avoid such problems, all warnings should be designed to take account of basic knowledge about sensation and perception provided by psychological research.

PERCEPTION: Some Organizing Principles

Look at the illustrations in Figure 3.13. Instead of random smatterings of black and white, you can probably discern a familiar figure in each. But how does our brain allow us to interpret these confused specks as a dog and a horseback rider? The process by which we structure the input from our sensory receptors is called *perceptual organization.* Aspects of perceptual organization were first studied systematically in the early 1900s by **Gestalt psychologists**—German psychologists intrigued by certain innate tendencies of the human mind to impose order and structure on the physical world and to perceive sensory patterns as well-organized wholes rather than as separate, isolated parts (*Gestalt* means "whole" in German). These scientists outlined several principles that describe the way we organize basic sensory input into whole patterns (gestalts). Some of these are described below. You could say that the Gestalt psychologists changed our perceptions about the nature of perception.

FIGURE AND GROUND: WHAT STANDS OUT?   By looking carefully at Figure 3.14 (on page 106), you can experience a principle of perceptual organization known as the **figure-ground relationship**. What this means, simply, is that we tend to divide the world around us into two parts: *figure*, which has a definite shape and a location in space; and *ground*, which has no shape, seems to continue behind the figure, and has no definite location. The figure-ground relationship helps clarify the distinction between sensation and perception. While the pattern of sensory input generated in our receptors remains constant, our perceptions shift between the two figure-ground patterns in Figure 3.14; thus, we may see either the young or the old woman, but not both. Note that the principles of perceptual organization apply to the other senses, too. For instance, consider how the figure-ground relationship applies to audition: During a complicated lecture, you become absorbed in whispered gossip between two students sitting next to you; the professor's voice becomes background noise. Suddenly you hear your name and realize the professor has asked you a question; her voice has now become the sole focus of your attention, while the conversation becomes background noise.

GROUPING: WHICH STIMULI GO TOGETHER?   The Gestaltists also called attention to a number of principles known as the **laws of grouping**—basic

> **Gestalt Psychologists:** *German psychologists intrigued by our tendency to perceive sensory patterns as well-organized wholes rather than as separate, isolated parts.*
>
> **Figure-Ground Relationship:** *Our tendency to divide the perceptual world into two distinct parts: discrete figures and the background against which they stand out.*
>
> **Laws of Grouping:** *Simple principles describing how we tend to group discrete stimuli together in the perceptual world.*

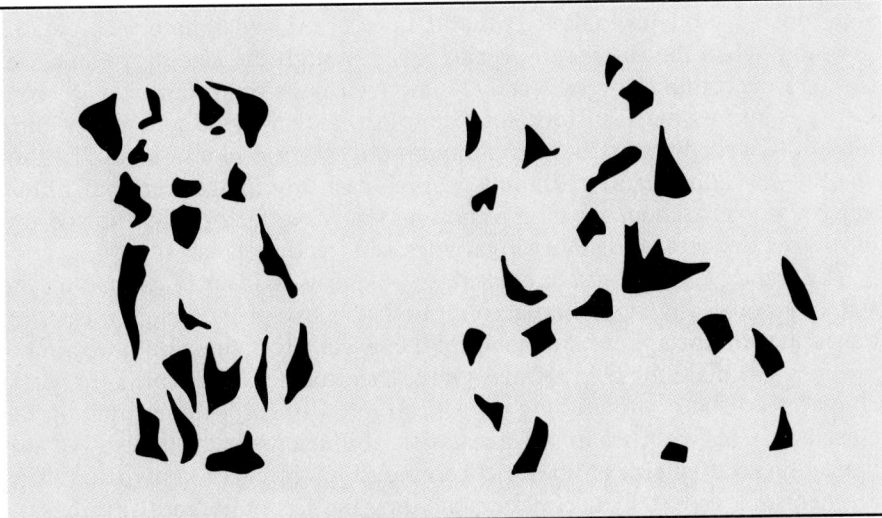

FIGURE 3.13

Perceptual Organization

Look carefully at each of these figures. What do you see? Our perceptual processes often allow us to perceive shapes and forms from incomplete and fragmented stimuli.

FIGURE 3.14

A Demonstration of Figure-Ground

What do you see when you look at this drawing? You probably see either an old woman or a young woman. Since this is an ambiguous figure, your perceptions may switch back and forth between these two possibilities.

ways in which we group items together perceptually. Several of these laws, including a more recently discovered perceptual grouping principle called *common region* (Palmer, 1992), are illustrated on the **Key Concept** page. As you can see, laws of grouping do offer a good description of our perceptual tendencies.

The principles outlined by Gestalt psychologists are not, however, hard-and-fast rules. They are merely descriptions of ways in which we perceive the world around us. Whether these principles are innate, as the Gestaltists believed, or learned, as some newer evidence suggests, is still open to debate. In any case, principles of perceptual organization are readily visible in the natural world, and they are effective in helping us organize our perceptual world.

CONSTANCIES AND ILLUSIONS: *When Perception Succeeds—and Fails*

Perception, we have seen, is more than the sum of all the sensory input supplied by our eyes, ears, and other receptors. It is the active selection, organization, and interpretation of such input. It yields final products that differ from raw, unprocessed sensations in important ways. Up to now, this discussion has focused on the benefits of this process. But perception, like any other powerful process, can be a double-edged sword. On the one hand, perception helps us adapt to a complex and ever-changing environment. On the other hand, perception sometimes leads us into error. To see how, let's consider *constancies* and *illusions*.

PERCEPTUAL CONSTANCIES: STABILITY IN THE FACE OF CHANGE   Try this simple demonstration. Hold your right hand in front of you at arm's length. Now, move it toward and away from your face several times. Does it seem to change in size? Probably not. Now hold your left hand in front of your face at a distance of about 20 cm (about 8 inches); again, move your right hand in and out. Does it seem to change in size now? Again, probably not. The purpose of this demonstration is to illustrate the principles of perceptual **constancies**—our tendency to perceive aspects of the world as unchanging despite changes in the sensory input we receive from them. The principle of **size constancy** relates to the fact that the perceived size of an object remains the same when the distance is varied, even though the size of the image it casts on the retina changes greatly. Under normal circumstances, such constancy is impressive. Consider, for example, seeing a friend you are meeting for lunch walking toward you, although still several blocks away. Distant objects—including cars, trees, and people—cast tiny images on your retina. Yet you perceive them as being of normal size. Two factors seem to account for this tendency: size-distance invariance and relative size.

The principle of *size-distance invariance* suggests that when estimating the size of an object, we take into account both the size of the image it casts on our retina and the apparent distance of the object. From these data we almost instantly calculate the object's size. Only when the cues that normally reveal an object's distance are missing do we run into difficulties in estimating the object's size (as we'll see in our discussion of illusions that follows). We also notice the **relative size** of an object compared to objects of known size. This mechanism is especially useful for estimating the size of unfamiliar things.

Constancies: *Our tendency to perceive physical objects as unchanging despite shifts in the pattern of sensations these objects induce.*

Size Constancy: *The tendency to perceive a physical object as having a constant size even when the size of the image it casts on the retina changes.*

Relative Size: *A visual cue based on comparison of the size of an unknown object to one of known size.*

Gestalt Principles of Organization

Figure-Ground

Tendency to view the world in two parts: *figure*, which has definite shape and location in space; and *ground*, background stimuli with no specific shape or location in space

Laws of Grouping

Law of Similarity

Tendency to perceive similar items as a group

Law of Proximity

Tendency to perceive items located together as a group

Law of Common Region

Tendency to perceive objects as a group if they occupy the same place within a plane

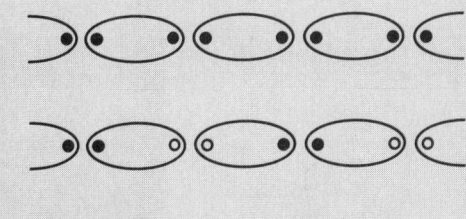

Law of Good Continuation

Tendency to perceive stimuli as part of a continuous pattern

Law of Closure

Tendency to perceive objects as whole entities, despite the fact that some parts may be missing or obstructed from view

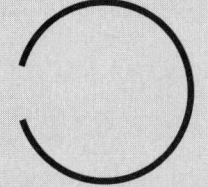

Law of Simplicity

Tendency to perceive complex patterns in terms of simpler shapes

But size is not the only perceptual feature of the physical world that does not correspond directly with the information transmitted by our sensory receptors. The principle of **shape constancy** refers to the fact that the perceived shape of an object does not alter as the image it casts on the retina changes. For example, all of us know that coins are round; yet we rarely see them that way. Flip a coin into the air: Although you continue to perceive the coin as being round, the image that actually falls onto your retina constantly shifts from a circle to various forms of an ellipse.

The principle of **brightness constancy** refers to the fact that we perceive objects as constant in brightness and color even when viewed under different lighting conditions. Thus, we will perceive a sweater as dark green whether indoors or outdoors in bright sunlight. Brightness constancy apparently prevails because objects and their surroundings are usually lighted by the same illumination source, so changes in lighting conditions occur simultaneously for both the object and its immediate surroundings. As long as the changes in lighting remain constant for both object and surround, the neural message reaching the brain is unchanged. Brightness constancy breaks down, however, when changes in lighting are not equivalent for both the object and its surroundings (Sekuler & Blake, 1990).

Although most research on perceptual constancies has focused on size, shape, and brightness, constancy pervades nearly every area of perception, including our other senses. For example, imagine listening to elevator music while riding on an elevator en route to a dental appointment on the thirtieth floor of an office building. When one of your favorite oldies from the mid-1970s begins, you can't believe what they've done to "your song." Nonetheless, you are still able to recognize it, despite differences in its loudness, tone, and pitch.

Whatever their basis, perceptual constancies are highly useful. Without them, we would spend a great deal of time and effort re-identifying sensory information in our environments each time we experienced the information from a new perspective. Thus, the gap between our sensations and the perceptions provided by the constancies is clearly beneficial.

ILLUSIONS: WHEN PERCEPTION FAILS Perception can also, however, provide false interpretations of sensory information. Such cases are known as **illusions**, a term used by psychologists to refer to incorrect perceptions. Actually, there are two types of illusions: those due to physical processes and those due to cognitive processes (Matlin & Foley, 1992). Illusions due to distortion of physical conditions include *mirages*, in which you perceive things that aren't really there—like the water you often seem to see on the dry road ahead of you. Our focus, however, will be on the latter type of illusions—those involving cognitive processes.

Countless illusions related to cognitive processes exist, but most fall into two categories: illusions of *size* and illusions of *shape* or *area* (Coren et al., 1976). Natural examples of two well-known size illusions are presented in Figure 3.15 and as you can see, their effects are powerful. But why do illusions occur? What causes our interpretation of such stimuli to be directly at odds with physical reality? Recent evidence suggests that illusions generally have multiple causes (Schiffman, 1990). However, one explanation is provided by the *theory of misapplied constancy*. It suggests that when looking at illusions, we interpret certain cues as suggesting that some parts are farther away than others. Our powerful tendency toward size constancy then comes into play, with the result that we perceptually distort the length of various lines (refer to Figure 3.16). Learning also plays an important role in illusions, as shown in the architectural examples of the *Müller-Lyer illusion* in Figure 3.16. Past experience tells us that the corner shown in the photo on the right

Shape Constancy: The tendency to perceive a physical object as having a constant shape even when the image it casts on the retina changes.

Brightness Constancy: The tendency to perceive objects as having a constant brightness even when they are viewed under different conditions of illumination.

Illusions: Instances in which perception yields false interpretations of physical reality.

CHAPTER 3

FIGURE 3.15

Illusions of Size

Natural examples of two powerful illusions of size. (A) The horizontal-vertical illusion stems from our tendency to perceive objects higher in our visual field as more distant. This illusion helps explain why the St. Louis Gateway Arch falsely appears taller than it is wide (its height and width are actually equal). (B) In the Ponzo illusion, the object in the distance appears larger, although both objects are actually the same size.

is usually farther away than the corner in the photo on the left. Since the size of the retinal image cast by the vertical lines in both photos is identical, we interpret the vertical line as longer in the photo on the right. Moreover, learning seems to affect the extent to which our perception is influenced by illusions, since many visual illusions decline in magnitude following extended exposure—although they do not decline altogether (Greist-Bousquet, Watson, & Schiffman, 1990).

Another type of illusion is that of *shape* or *area*. If you've ever wondered why the moon looks bigger at the horizon (about 30 percent bigger!) than

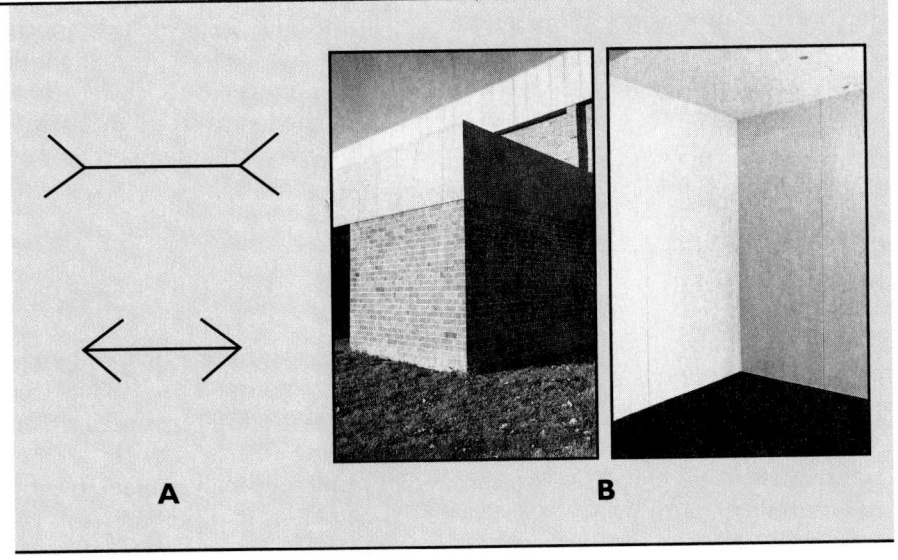

FIGURE 3.16

The Müller-Lyer Illusion

(A) In the Müller-Lyer illusion, lines of equal length appear unequal; the line with the wings pointing outward looks longer than the line with the wings pointing inward. (B) Now carefully examine the vertical line in each photograph. Which line is longer? Most people perceive the vertical line in the photo on the right as longer, although careful measurement shows they are exactly the same length!

FIGURE 3.17

Illusions of Area or Shape

Illusions of area or shape can be quite powerful. (A) In this drawing, known as the Poggendorf illusion, which of the three lines on the right continues the line on the left? Check your answer with a ruler. (B) In this drawing, are the horizontal lines straight or bent in the middle? Again, check for yourself. (C) Finally, in this drawing, are the letters tilted or vertical? When you check, you'll see why sometimes you can't believe what you think you see.

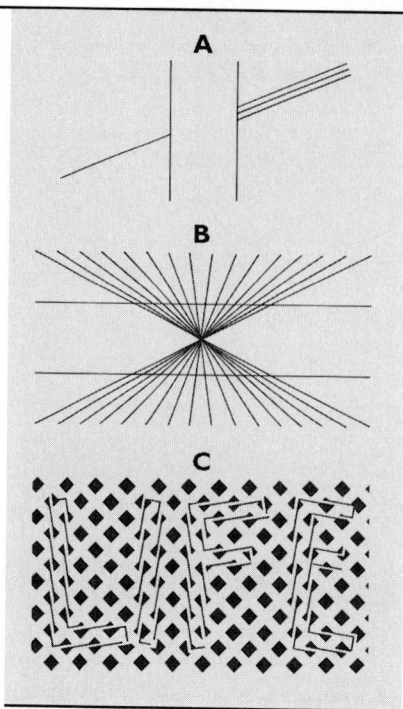

at its highest point in the sky, then you are familiar with the most famous area illusion—the *moon illusion*. Why does the moon illusion occur? In part, because when the moon is near the horizon, we can see that it is farther away than trees, houses, and other objects. When it is overhead at its zenith, such cues are lacking. Thus, the moon appears larger near the horizon because there are cues available that cause us to perceive that it is very far away. Once again, our tendency toward size constancy leads us astray.

Like illusions of size or area, shape illusions (see Figure 3.17) can influence perception—sometimes producing unsettling consequences. Consider a real-world example involving the *Poggendorf illusion* (see drawing A in Figure 3.17). In this illusion, a line disappears at an angle behind a solid figure, reappearing at the other side— at what seems to be the incorrect position. As reported by Coren and Girgus (1978), in 1965 two airplanes were about to arrive in New York City, and because of the Poggendorf illusion, they perceived that they were on a collision course. Both pilots changed their path to correct for what they perceived as an error, and thus collided. The result was four deaths and forty-nine injuries—all because of an illusion.

One final point: illusions are not limited to visual processes. Indeed, there are numerous examples of illusions for our other sensory modalities, including touch and audition (Sekuler & Blake, 1990; Shepard, 1964). One well-known illusion that you can demonstrate for yourself is that of touch temperature. First place one hand in a container of hot water and the other hand in cold water. Then place *both* hands in a container of lukewarm water. What do you feel? Most people experience a dramatic difference in perceived temperature between the two hands; the hand initially placed in hot water feels the lukewarm water as cool, whereas the hand initially placed in cold water feels it as hot. How do we explain this illusion? When we touch an object, the temperature of the area of our skin in contact with it shifts toward that of the object's surface. So, when we perceive an object to be warm or cool, our experience stems partly from the temperature difference between the object and our skin, not solely from the actual temperature of the object.

SOME KEY PERCEPTUAL PROCESSES: *Pattern and Distance*

It can be argued that perception is a practical process, for it provides living organisms with information essential to survival in their normal habitat. The specific nature of this information varies greatly with different species. For example, frogs must be able to detect small moving objects in order to feed on insects, whereas porpoises require sensory input that enables them to navigate turbulent and murky ocean waters. Nonetheless, it is probably safe to say that virtually all living creatures need information concerning (1) what's out there and (2) how far away it is. Humans are no exception to this general rule, and we possess impressive perceptual skills in both areas.

PATTERN RECOGNITION: WHAT'S OUT THERE? The ability to read the words on this page depends on the ability to recognize small black marks as letters and collections of such marks as words. How do we accomplish this task? An early explanation for this phenomenon was the *template-matching theory*. According to this theory, we have many **templates**, or specific patterns, stored in our memories for various visual stimuli that we encounter. Thus, if a visual stimulus—say a letter—matches one of the templates, we recognize it; if it does not, we search for another that does match. As you may have already guessed, this theory is impractical, since it requires that we store an almost infinite number of these templates in our memories in order to be able to recognize even variants of the same letter. Additionally, the template-matching theory does not explain our ability to read at rates exceeding hundreds of words per minute or to recognize visual stimuli almost instantly, even when they're viewed from different perspectives (Pinker, 1984).

A related but more viable explanation, referred to as *prototype-matching theory*, suggests that we automatically compare each letter (and perhaps word) to abstract representations of these stimuli in our memories known as **prototypes**. According to this view, we have a prototype in memory for each letter of the alphabet, based on all examples of the letter previously encountered. Thus, recognition is dependent on finding a correct match between the stimulus letter or word and a previously seen prototype. Please note that a prototype is not an exact match or a template for some visual stimulus, but a general pattern that lets us recognize a letter even when it is distorted. While some evidence supports this view (e.g., Franks & Bransford, 1971), the physiological details of this theory are not well developed (Matlin & Foley, 1992). For example, it is not yet clear how these stimuli are internally represented in our cognitive structure.

Two other approaches are the bottom-up and top-down theories of pattern recognition. As their names imply, these adopt somewhat opposite perspectives on the basic question of how we recognize patterns of visual stimuli. The *bottom-up approach* suggests that our ability to recognize specific patterns, such as letters of the alphabet, is based on simpler capacities to recognize and combine correctly lower-level features of the letters, such as lines, edges, corners, and angles. For example, our ability to recognize an A and distinguish it from other letters depends on activation of *feature detectors*, which when stimulated activate other neurons that may be described as *letter detectors*. Bottom-up theories suggest that pattern recognition is constructed from simpler perceptual abilities through a discrete series of steps (Marr, 1982). Unfortunately, bottom-up theories based on feature analysis do not explain well how people perceive ambiguous stimuli. For example, in Figure 3.18 (on page 112), we can see either a vase or faces, despite the fact that the stimulus pattern remains the same in both instances.

In contrast, the *top-down approach* emphasizes the fact that our expectancies play a critical role in shaping our perceptions. We often proceed in accordance with what our past experience tells us to expect, and therefore we don't always analyze every feature of most stimuli we encounter. Although top-down processing can be extremely efficient (think about the speed with which you can read this page), it can also lead us astray. Nearly everyone has had the experience of rushing over to another person who appears to be an old friend, only to realize he or she is actually a stranger. In

Templates: *Specific patterns stored in our memories for various visual stimuli that we encounter.*

Prototypes: *Representations in memory of various objects or stimuli in the physical world.*

FIGURE 3.18

Bottom-Up Theories Do Not Explain Perception of Reversible Figures

Bottom-up theories based on feature analysis cannot explain how we can see both faces and a vase in this reversible ambiguous figure, since the actual stimulus features remain constant.

such cases, our tendency to process information quickly from the top down can indeed produce errors.

Which of these theories is correct? Current evidence indicates that both play a role in pattern recognition (Matlin & Foley, 1992). When we have strong expectations or we are in a familiar context, we often opt for speed and adopt a top-down approach. However, when we are dealing with unfamiliar situations or stimuli, bottom-up processing often dominates. In many situations, both processes may occur at once. In summary, our efforts to make sense out of the world around us tend to take whatever form is most efficient in a given context.

DISTANCE PERCEPTION: HOW FAR AWAY IS IT? Our impressive ability to judge depth and distance occurs because we make use of many different cues in forming such judgments. These cues can be divided into two categories, *monocular* and *binocular*, depending on whether they can be seen with only one eye or require the use of both eyes.

Monocular cues to depth or distance include the following:

1. *Size cues:* The larger the image of an object on the retina, the larger the object is judged to be; in addition, if an object is larger than other objects, it is often perceived as closer.

2. *Linear perspective:* Parallel lines appear to converge in the distance; the greater this effect, the farther away an object appears to be.

3. *Texture gradient:* The texture of a surface appears smoother as distance increases.

4. *Atmospheric perspective*: The farther away objects are, the less distinctly they are seen—smog, dust, haze get in the way.

5. *Overlap* (or interposition): If one object overlaps another, it is seen as being closer than the one it covers.

6. *Height cues* (aerial perspective): Below the horizon, objects lower down in our field of vision are perceived as closer; above the horizon, objects higher up are seen as closer.

7. *Motion parallax:* When we travel in a vehicle, objects far away appear to move in the same direction as the observer, whereas close objects move in the opposite direction. Objects at different distances appear to move at different velocities.

Monocular Cues: *Cues to depth or distance provided by one eye.*

As you can see, much of our ability to perceive depth is based on the use of *monocular cues*. However, we also rely heavily on **binocular cues**—depth information based on the coordinated efforts of both eyes. Binocular cues for depth perception stem from two primary sources:

1. *Convergence*: In order to see close objects, our eyes turn inward, toward one another; the greater this movement, the closer such objects appear to be.
2. *Retinal disparity* (binocular parallax): Our two eyes observe objects from slightly different positions in space; the difference between the two images is interpreted by our brain to provide another cue to depth.

The lists of monocular and binocular cues are by no means exhaustive. By using the wealth of information provided by these and other cues (Schiffman, 1990), we can usually perceive depth and distance with great accuracy.

KEY QUESTIONS

- Why is selective attention important?
- Why is it important to consider sensation and perception in the development of warnings?
- What role do the Gestalt principles play in perceptual processes?
- What are perceptual constancies?
- What are the bottom-up and top-down theories of pattern recognition?
- How are we able to judge depth and distance?

THE PLASTICITY OF PERCEPTION: To What Extent Is It Innate or Learned?

*I*magine a man blind from birth whose sight is suddenly restored through a miraculous operation. Will his visual world be the same as yours or mine? Will it be orderly and consistent with his expectations? Or will he experience a chaotic swirl of colors, brightnesses, and meaningless shapes? This intriguing question has often served as the basis for exploring the nature-nurture controversy. In other words, to what extent are aspects of perception learned or hereditary?

Learning Objective 3.17
Discuss the evidence that suggests that perception is innate or learned.

PERCEPTION: *Evidence That It's Innate*

Evidence that perception is innate stems from two lines of research. The first involves people like the one described above—people born blind (or blinded soon after birth) whose sight is later restored through medical procedures. If perception is innate, then such persons should be able to see clearly immediately after recovery from surgery. Although cases like this are few in number and the results often vary, many of these individuals can make at least partial sense out of the visual world soon after their sight is restored. For example, they can detect and follow moving objects, suggesting that some aspects of visual perception may indeed be innate (Von Senden, 1960). However, certain complications require us to be cautious in making even limited interpretation of these findings. For example, it is difficult to know precisely when recovery from a medical procedure is sufficient to allow for "normal" vision. This leaves open the question of when the patient should be tested for perceptual abilities.

Additional evidence suggesting that perception is innate is provided by research with very young subjects, such as babies only a few hours or days old. Studies have explored numerous perceptual abilities, particularly audi-

Binocular Cues: *Cues to depth or distance provided by the use of both eyes.*

tory and visual abilities, that are present at birth or shortly afterward (Schiffman, 1990). In one such study, infants slightly more than three days old were exposed to squares of colored light (blue, green, yellow, red) and to gray light of equal brightness. The results showed that infants spent more time looking at every one of the colored stimuli than at the gray—an indication that ability to perceive color is present soon after birth (Adams, 1987).

In another study, Balogh and Porter (1986) exposed newborns only a few hours old to one of two aromas—ginger or cherry—for about twenty-four hours. One odor was present on a gauze pad in each infant's bassinet. After the initial exposure, two pads, each containing a different smell, were placed in each bassinet, and the amount of time the infant spent orienting toward each one during brief test periods was observed. Female infants showed a marked preference for the familiar odor—the one to which they had previously been exposed—while male infants showed no preference. It is not certain why this gender difference occurred; other research suggests, however, that at all ages females are superior to males in identifying specific odors (Doty et al., 1984). Thus, our perception of smell may also be present at or soon after birth. In any case, studies like these suggest that some aspects of perception are innate or at least that they appear early in life.

PERCEPTION: *Evidence That It's Learned*

On the other hand, there is considerable evidence for the view that key aspects of perception are learned. In a famous series of studies, Blakemore and Cooper (1970) raised kittens in darkness except for brief periods, during which the kittens were exposed to either horizontal or vertical stripes. When later released from their restricted environment, the kittens showed what seemed to be permanent effects of their earlier experience. Those exposed only to vertical lines would respond to a long black rod when it was held in an upright position, but ignored it when it was held horizontally. In contrast, kittens exposed only to horizontal lines would respond to a rod only when it was held in a horizontal position, ignoring it when it was presented vertically. Despite the fact that the kittens' visual systems were undamaged—at least in any measurable physical sense—their restricted visual experience appeared to produce permanent perceptual deficits.

Additional evidence for the role of learning in perception comes from studies in which human volunteers wear special goggles that invert their view of the world and reverse right and left. Such persons initially experience difficulty in carrying out normal activities with their goggles on, but soon adapt and do everything from reading a book to flying a plane (Kohler, 1962). These findings, and others, suggest that we do indeed learn to interpret the information supplied by our sensory receptors.

MUST WE RESOLVE THE NATURE-NURTURE CONTROVERSY?

The findings we've reviewed thus far offer no simple resolution to the nature-nurture issue; other studies involving both animals and humans are equally inconclusive. Some studies show that certain aspects of visual perception seem to be present without previous sensory experience, whereas other aspects develop only through experience with the external world (Wiesel, 1982).

Confronted with this mixed evidence, most psychologists accept that perception is influenced both by innate factors *and* by experience. For example, consider the strange case of Virgil—a fifty-year-old man who regained his sight after forty-five years of blindness (Sacks, 1993). The fact that Virgil could immediately detect visual features, such as letters, objects and colors, suggested the influence of nature. However, Virgil could not "see" in the true sense. Learning even simple visual relationships required great effort, since most of his knowledge of the world had come to him through the sense of touch.

In sum, perception is plastic in the sense that it can be, and often is, modified by our encounters with physical reality. However, perception may also be strongly affected by innate tendencies and principles. So the answer to the question "Must we resolve the nature-nurture controversy?" is a resounding *no*, since it is clear that learning *and* biology both play critical roles in perception.

KEY QUESTION

- How are the concepts of nature and nurture related to perception?

EXTRASENSORY PERCEPTION: Perception without Sensation?

*H*ave you ever wondered if we have a "sixth sense"? In other words, can we gain information about the external world without use of our five basic senses? Many persons believe we can and accept the existence of **extrasensory perception**—literally, perception without a basis in sensation. The first and most basic question we can ask about ESP is "Does it really exist?" Recently this question has been recast by Bem and Honorton (1994) in terms of a hypothetical process known as **psi**. These researchers define psi as unusual processes of information or energy transfer that are currently unexplained in terms of known physical or biological mechanisms. In short, psi underlies and forms the basis for what has previously been described as ESP. Thus, in the discussion that follows, we'll use this newer term, psi, instead of the older term, ESP.

What precisely is psi? And is there any evidence for its existence? In the section that follows, we will discuss some of the evidence on this intriguing topic.

Learning Objective 3.18
List the different types of extrasensory perception and describe the evidence for and against the existence of psi.

PSI: What Is It?

Parapsychologists, those who study psi and other *paranormal events*, or events outside our normal experience or knowledge, suggest there are actually several distinct forms of psi (or ESP). One form of psi is *precognition*, the ability to foretell future events. Fortunetellers and even stock market analysts often earn their livings from the supposed ability to make such predictions. *Clairvoyance*, the ability to perceive objects or events that do not directly stimulate your sensory organs, is another form. While playing cards, if you somehow know which one will be dealt next, you are experiencing clairvoyance. *Telepathy,* a skill used by mind readers, involves the direct transmission of thought from one person to the next. Another phenomenon often associated with psi is *psychokinesis*, the ability to affect the physical world purely through thought. Bending spoons or moving objects with your mind or performing feats of levitation (making objects rise into the air) are examples of psychokinesis.

Extrasensory Perception (ESP): *Perception without a basis in sensory input.*

Psi: *Unusual processes of information or energy transfer that are currently unexplained in terms of known physical or biological mechanisms. Included under the heading of psi are such supposed abilities as telepathy (reading others' thoughts) and clairvoyance (perceiving unseen objects or unknowable events).*

Parapsychologists: *Individuals who study psi and other paranormal events.*

Psi: Does It Really Exist?

The idea of a mysterious sixth sense is intriguing, and many people are passionately convinced of its existence (Bowles & Hynds, 1978). But does it really exist? Most psychologists are skeptical about the existence of psi for several reasons. The first, and perhaps the most important, reason for doubting its existence is the repeated failure to replicate instances of psi; that is, certain procedures yield evidence for psi at one time but not at others. Indeed, one survey failed to uncover a single instance of paranormal phenomena that could be reliably produced after ruling out alternative explanations such as fraud, methodological flaws, and normal sensory functioning (Hoppe, 1988). Moreover, it appears that the more controlled studies of psi are, the less evidence for psi they provide (Blackmore, 1986).

Second, present-day scientific understanding states that all aspects of our behavior must ultimately stem from biochemical events, yet it is not clear what physical mechanism could account for psi. In fact, the existence of such a mechanism would require restructuring our view of the physical world. Nevertheless, major changes in our knowledge are still occurring, and it is still possible that a mechanism accounting for psi could be discovered.

Third, much of the support for psi has been obtained by persons already deeply convinced of its existence. As we noted in chapter 1, scientists are not immune to being influenced in their observations by their own beliefs. Thus, while studies suggesting that psi exists may represent a small sample of all research conducted on this topic, perhaps only the few experiments yielding positive results find their way into print; perhaps the many "failures" are simply not reported.

Recent evidence, however, has caused researchers to reexamine their beliefs in this respect, largely because of studies employing the *ganzfield procedure*—a procedure used to test for telepathic communication between a *sender* and a *receiver.* Using this procedure, parapsychologists have attempted to eliminate flaws that caused scientists to criticize much of the earlier research on psi. Receivers in the ganzfield procedure are placed in a comfortable chair in a soundproof room. Translucent Ping-Pong ball halves are taped over the receivers' eyes, and headphones are placed over their ears. A red floodlight directed toward the eyes produces a homogenous visual field, and white noise is played through the headphones to mask any outside noises.

The sender is usually secluded in a separate room and asked to concentrate on a "target" visual stimulus, such as a photograph or a brief videotape. Simultaneously, the receiver provides an ongoing verbal report of mental images that he or she experiences. After about thirty minutes, the receiver is presented with several stimuli and, without knowing which was the "target" stimulus on which the sender concentrated, is asked to rate the extent to which each stimulus matches the imagery he or she experienced during the ganzfield period. If a high proportion of the receivers' ratings are assigned to "target" stimuli, it is assumed to be evidence for psi. A recent evaluation of studies that used the ganzfield procedure suggest that receivers are significantly more accurate in selecting target stimuli than would be explained by chance (Bem & Honorton, 1994). While even critics of psi theories are intrigued by the results of these studies, the critics remain skeptical and await the results of additional research in this area (Hyman, 1994).

KEY QUESTION

• How do most psychologists view the possibility of extrasensory perception, or psi?

The Danger of Stereo Headsets: Let's Turn Down the Volume

If you've experienced the clamor of traffic during rush hour, the deafening roar of a jet taking off, or the piercing blast of a jackhammer digging up city streets, you're already familiar with the growing problem of *noise pollution*. Noise has become a pervasive part of everyday living, and increasing evidence suggests that noise pollution affects aspects of our physical and mental health, task performance, and social behavior (Matlin & Foley, 1992).

Although many sources of noise in our environment are beyond our control, people often bring hearing-related problems on themselves. Psychologists and other health professionals are becoming increasingly concerned with the rapid increase in use of portable stereo headset radios and CD players. Millions of these devices are sold each year in the United States, primarily to young people (Monroe, 1990). One problem with their use is that these headsets produce sound intense enough to cause varying degrees of hearing loss (Rice, Breslin, & Roper, 1987).

Three types of hearing loss are usually distinguished: *temporary threshold shift* (TTS), a short-term and reversible elevation of the level at which sounds are first heard; *permanent threshold shift* (PTS), nonreversible hearing loss from long-term exposure to noise; and *acoustic trauma*, permanent hearing loss stemming from brief exposure to extremely intense noise, such as an explosion (Jones & Broadbent, 1987). Even brief exposure to certain levels of sound intensity can cause a measurable shift in hearing ability. For example, exposure to 90-decibel sound levels—the level of noise that might be present in a crowded restaurant—can produce a TTS of nearly 20 decibels after only one and one-half hours of sound exposure.

So why all the fuss over the use of stereo headsets? Consider, for example, the results of a study by Navarro (1990) in which researchers examined fifty portable stereo headsets to determine if they had the potential to damage hearing. The decibel levels were measured at three volume settings: one-third, two-thirds, and full volume. The results showed that headsets produce an average of 87 decibels at one-third of their full volume, 100 decibels at two-thirds, and 108 decibels at full volume. Thus, it should be clear that portable stereo headsets have the potential to produce serious hearing loss even at seemingly low volume settings, particularly among persons who listen to them often and for extended periods of time. Indeed, some evidence suggests that habitual use of portable headsets at high volumes does result in temporary threshold shifts and *tinnitus*, or ringing of the ears, and increases the risk of permanent hearing loss (Lee et al., 1985; Rice, Breslin, & Roper, 1987).

So next time you get the urge to crank up the volume of you portable headset while walking, jogging, or doing some other activity—do yourself a favor by turning down the sound. The hearing you save may be your own.

Stereo headsets, one source of noise that *can* be controlled, have the potential to cause permanent damage to the ears.

SUMMARY AND REVIEW OF KEY QUESTIONS

SENSATION: THE RAW MATERIALS OF UNDERSTANDING

- **What is the primary function of our sensory receptors?**

Sensory receptors transduce raw physical energy into neural impulses, which are then interpreted by the central nervous system.

- **What does the term absolute threshold *refer to?***

The absolute threshold is the smallest magnitude of a stimulus that can be detected 50 percent of the time.

- **Why is signal detection theory important to a discussion of sensory processes?**

Signal detection theory helps to separate sensitivity from motivational factors.

- **What is the role of sensory adaptation in sensation?**

Sensory adaptation allows us to focus on important changes in our environment.

KEY TERMS: *sensation, p. 80; perception, p. 80; sensory receptors, p. 80; transduction, p. 80; absolute threshold, p. 81; signal detection theory, p. 82; difference threshold, p. 82; just noticeable difference (jnd), p. 82; subliminal perception, p. 82; sensory adaptation, p. 84*

VISION

- **What is the physical stimulus for vision?**

The physical stimulus for vision consists of the electromagnetic waves that stimulate the rods and cones on the retina.

- **How do psychologists explain color perception?**

Two theories that explain how we perceive color are trichromatic theory and opponent-process theory.

- **Why is visual perception a hierarchical process?**

Visual perception is a hierarchical process because at successive stages of the process, increasingly complex visual information is analyzed and compiled.

- **What are the basic building blocks of visual perception?**

The basic building blocks of visual perception begin with feature detectors and continue with integration of characteristic stimuli at higher levels in the brain.

KEY TERMS: *cornea, p. 84; pupil, p. 84; iris, p. 84; lens, p. 86; retina, p. 86; cones, p. 86; rods, p. 86; fovea, p. 86; optic nerve, p. 86; blind spot, p. 86; wavelength, p. 86; hue, p. 86; brightness, p. 86; saturation, p. 86; acuity, p. 87; nearsightedness, p. 87; farsightedness, p. 87; dark adaptation, p. 87; saccadic movements, p. 88; trichromatic theory, p. 88; negative afterimage,*

p. 89; opponent-process theory, p. 89; feature detectors, p. 90; simple cells, p. 90; complex cells, p. 90; hypercomplex cells, p. 90; prosopagnosia, p. 90

HEARING

- **What is the physical stimulus for hearing?**

Sound waves that stimulate tiny hair cells in the cochlea are the physical stimulus for hearing.

- **How do psychologists explain pitch perception?**

Place theory and frequency theory help explain how we perceive pitch.

- **How do we localize sound?**

The sound shadow created by the head causes sound to reach one ear slightly faster than the other. This small time difference helps us localize the source of sound.

KEY TERMS: *pinna, p. 91; cochlea, p. 91; pitch, p. 92; timbre, p. 92; place theory, p. 93; frequency theory, p. 93; localization, p. 94*

TOUCH AND OTHER SKIN SENSES

- **What is the physical stimulus for touch?**

The physical stimulus for touch is a stretching of or pressure against receptors in the skin.

- **Where does the sensation of pain originate?**

Sensations of pain originate in free nerve endings throughout the body.

- **What is the basis for cultural differences in pain perception?**

Cultural differences in pain perception appear to be the result of learning—not physical differences.

KEY TERMS: *Braille alphabet, p. 96; gate-control theory, p. 96; endorphins, p. 97*

SMELL AND TASTE: THE CHEMICAL SENSES

- **What is the physical stimulus for smell?**

The physical stimulus for sensations of smell are molecules that stimulate receptors in the nose.

- **Where are the sensory receptors for taste located?**

The sensory receptors for taste are located in papillae on the tongue.

- **Are there practical benefits to introducing pleasant scents into the workplace?**

Pleasant scents in the workplace can have positive effects on workers' attitudes and behaviors.

KINESTHESIA AND VESTIBULAR SENSE

• *What information does the kinesthetic sense provide to the brain?*

Kinesthesia informs the brain about the location of body parts with respect to each other.

• *What information does the vestibular sense provide to the brain?*

The vestibular sense provides information about body position, movement, and acceleration.

KEY TERMS: *kinesthesia, p. 103; vestibular sense, p. 103; vestibular sacs, p. 103; semicircular canals, p. 103*

PERCEPTION: PUTTING IT ALL TOGETHER

• *Why is selective attention important?*

Selective attention reduces the interference from irrelevant sensory sources.

• *Why is it important to consider sensation and perception in the development of warnings?*

The effectiveness of warnings depends on both sensory and perceptual processes.

• *What role do the Gestalt principles play in perceptual processes?*

The Gestalt principles of perceptual organization help us to structure the input from our sensory receptors.

• *What are perceptual constancies?*

Perceptual constancies refer to our ability to perceive aspects of the world as unchanging despite variations in the information reaching our sensory receptors.

• *What are the bottom-up and top-down theories of pattern recognition?*

The bottom-down theory suggests that pattern recognition stems from our ability to recognize and combine basic visual features. In contrast, the top-down theory emphasizes the role that expectations play in shaping our perceptions.

• *How are we able to judge depth and distance?*

Judgments of depth and distance result from both binocular and monocular cues.

KEY TERMS: *Gestalt psychologists, p. 105; figure-ground relationship, p. 105; laws of grouping, p. 105; constancies, p. 106; size constancy, p. 106; relative size, p. 106; shape constancy, p. 108; brightness constancy, p. 108; illusions, p. 108; templates, p. 111; prototypes, p. 111; monocular cues, p. 112; binocular cues, p. 113*

THE PLASTICITY OF PERCEPTION: TO WHAT EXTENT IS IT INNATE OR LEARNED?

• *How are the concepts of nature and nurture related to perception?*

Both nature and nurture are important determinants of the ways we perceive the world around us. Nature refers to genetic influences on perception, whereas nurture refers to the relative effects of the environment and learning.

EXTRASENSORY PERCEPTION: PERCEPTION WITHOUT SENSATION?

• *How do most psychologists view the possibility of extrasensory perception, or psi?*

Most psychologists remain skeptical about its existence and await the results of further careful research.

KEY TERMS: *extrasensory perception (ESP), p. 115; psi, p. 115; parapsychologists, p. 115*

CRITICAL THINKING QUESTIONS

APPRAISAL	Many psychologists would agree that conscious experience is nothing more than the result of the brain's efforts to integrate information received from the senses. Do you agree? Why? If not, offer an alternative view.
CONTROVERSY	Recent studies employing the ganzfield procedure have eliminated many of the methodological flaws present in earlier research and have demonstrated weak, but consistent, evidence for psi. Does psi exist? Or is it more likely that subsequent research will uncover methodological flaws in these studies?
MAKING PSYCHOLOGY PART OF YOUR LIFE	Knowing something about the way in which we receive and process sensory information is useful for a variety of practical reasons. For example, knowing that sensitivity to smell decreases rapidly through habituation is critical, especially if you have just detected the odor of a poisonous gas! Can you think of other ways in which you can benefit from such knowledge?

Consciousness:

Awareness of Ourselves and the External World

4

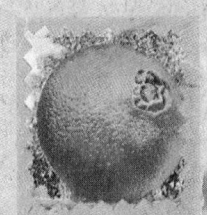

*D*o you feel more alert and energetic at some times during the day than at others? Have you ever daydreamed in class so that later you had no idea what the teacher or professor said? Have you ever stood in front of a mirror brushing your teeth while your thoughts were a thousand miles away? If so, you already know that we all experience different **states of consciousness**—levels of awareness of internal and external stimuli—every day. And when we go to sleep at night (perchance to dream!) or take some drug that affects the way we feel, these changes are even more dramatic in scope. Being familiar with these shifts, however, doesn't necessarily help us understand them. Can we really do two or more things at the same time, and if so, how? *Why* are we more alert at some times during the day than at others? What happens when we fall asleep? What, precisely, *are* dreams? And how do various drugs affect our emotions, perceptions, and cognition?

Given the obvious impact of states of consciousness on many aspects of our behavior, they are clearly an important topic for the field of psychology. You may be surprised to learn, therefore, that from about the 1920s until as recently as the 1960s, consciousness was largely ignored by psychologists. In fact, it was viewed by some as a slightly shady topic—one to be avoided by serious scientists. Many factors contributed to this unsettling state of affairs, but perhaps the most important was the dominance of behaviorism. As you may recall from chapter 1, Watson and other early behaviorists believed that psychology should focus only on overt, observable actions. Since consciousness cannot be directly seen or measured, they literally ruled it out as a legitimate topic of research.

Needless to state, this is no longer the case, and in recent decades consciousness has reemerged as an important topic of study. I say "reemerged" because, as noted in chapter 1, some early psychologists—the structuralists—viewed consciousness as the core topic on which psychology should focus.

Although consciousness has returned as a topic of systematic research in psychology only during the past few decades, we have already acquired a great deal of interesting—and often provocative—knowledge about it. Much of this information will be summarized in this chapter. We'll begin by considering the biological roots for at least some of our shifting patterns of consciousness: *biological rhythms*. These are naturally occurring, cyclical changes in many basic bodily processes and mental states that occur over the course of a day or longer periods of time. Next, we'll consider several aspects of what might be described as normal, *waking consciousness*. Here, we'll examine three major topics: (1) *controlled* and *automatic processing*, shifts between conscious attention to our current behavior and the kind of "automatic pilot" that seems to operate when we perform well-practiced actions such as grooming or driving; (2) the nature and impact of *daydreams* and *fantasies*; and (3) changing levels of *self-consciousness*, the degree to which we focus on ourselves rather than the external world. Next, we'll turn to what is perhaps the most profound, regular shift in consciousness we experience: *sleep*. Finally, we'll examine two external factors that sometimes produce important shifts in consciousness: *hypnosis* and the effects of various *consciousness-altering drugs*.

BIOLOGICAL RHYTHMS: *Tides of Life—and Conscious Experience*

*S*uppose that you must schedule an appointment for a very important interview. The interviewer has a number of time slots available, so you can choose to meet with her at almost any time of day. What time will you select? Probably you have little difficulty in making a choice. Most of us are well aware of the fact that we are at our best—most alert and energetic—at certain times of the day. Thus, all other things being equal, you'll probably schedule the meeting for a time when you know that you're most likely to make a good impression (Monk & Folkard, 1983).

The existence of such shifts in our alertness or energy is one illustration of what psychologists and other scientists term **biological rhythms**—regular fluctuations in our bodily processes (and therefore in consciousness) over

States of Consciousness: Varying degrees of awareness of ourselves and the external world.

Biological Rhythms: Cyclic changes in bodily processes.

time. Many of these fluctuations occur over the course of a single day and are known as **circadian rhythms** (from the Latin words for "around" and "day"). As we'll soon see, such rhythms can exert important effects on us in many respects. Other biological rhythms take place within shorter periods of time; they are known as *ultradian rhythms*. For example, many people become hungry every two or three hours (at least while they are awake). And during sleep, periods of dreaming seem to occur at roughly ninety-minute intervals. Finally, some biological rhythms occur over longer periods, such as the menstrual cycle experienced by women, which spans approximately twenty-eight days. Such rhythms often have a relationship to states of consciousness. Since circadian rhythms have received most research attention, I'll focus primarily on these, describing their basic nature, individual differences among them, and some practical implications of their existence.

CIRCADIAN RHYTHMS: *Their Basic Nature*

Most people are aware of fluctuations in their alertness, energy, and moods over the course of a day. Do such circadian shifts reflect actual changes in underlying bodily states? A large amount of evidence suggests that they do (e.g., Moore-Ede, Sulzman, & Fuller, 1982). Careful study has revealed that many bodily processes do indeed show daily cyclical changes. To mention just a few, it has been found that the production of various hormones fluctuates across the day; their levels are high at some points in time but much lower at others. Similarly, for many persons, core body temperature, blood pressure, and several other processes are highest in the late afternoon or evening and lowest in the early hours of the morning—although, as we'll see below, large individual differences in this respect exist.

These cyclic fluctuations in basic bodily functions are reflected in performance on many tasks. Tasks requiring physical activity are performed best at times when body temperature and other processes are at or near their peaks. The same is true for simple cognitive (mental) tasks. However, as the complexity of cognitive tasks increases, the closeness of the link between them and circadian rhythms seems to weaken. This fact is indicated clearly by the results of a study by Daniel and Potasova (1989). These researchers asked workers at a chemical factory to perform several different tasks. One was a tapping task that required rapid hand movements. Another was a relatively simple cognitive task in which participants searched for a target letter among a series of letters and, when they found it, pushed a button as quickly as possible. A third task required complex mental effort; it involved making grammatical transformations on a series of sentences. Participants' body temperature was recorded at several times during the day. As shown in Figure 4.1 (on page 124), there was a clear relationship between body temperature and performance on the tapping task. This relationship also held true for the simple visual search task. The relationship disappeared, however, for the complex sentence transformation. This pattern of findings suggests that daily fluctuations in body temperature may have a stronger impact on relatively simple tasks than on more complex cognitive ones.

CIRCADIAN RHYTHMS: *What Mechanism Underlies Them?*

If bodily processes, mental alertness, and performance on many tasks fluctuate regularly over the course of the day, it seems reasonable to suggest that we possess some internal biological mechanism for regulating such changes.

Circadian Rhythms: Cyclic changes in bodily processes occurring within a single day.

FIGURE 4.1

Circadian Rhythms, Body Temperature, and Task Performance

On both a tapping task and a relatively simple cognitive task, performance rose and fell with daily changes in body temperature. However, there was no relationship between body temperature and performance on a more complex cognitive task. (*Source:* Based on data from Daniel & Potasova, 1989.)

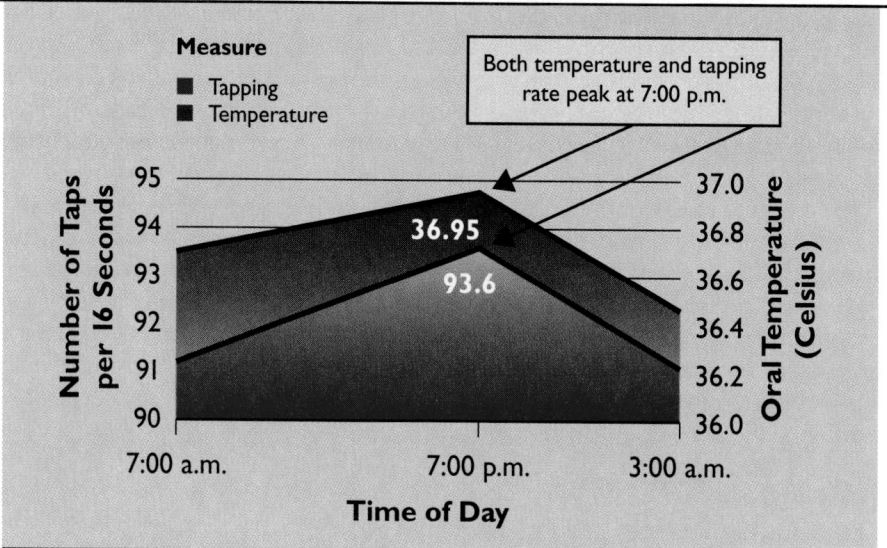

In other words, we must possess a biological clock that times various circadian rhythms. While there is not as yet total agreement on the nature of this clock, many scientists believe that it is located in a portion of the hypothalamus—specifically, in the **suprachiasmatic nucleus** (Moore & Card, 1985). This nucleus responds to visual input from the eyes and either stimulates or inhibits activity in the pineal gland. This gland, in turn, secretes *melatonin*, a hormone with far-reaching effects. Melatonin exerts a sedative effect, reducing activity and increasing fatigue.

Exposure to daylight stimulates the suprachiasmatic nucleus, and this in turn reduces the secretion of melatonin. In contrast, darkness enhances it. Interestingly, only exposure to fairly intense light (three to five times that of ordinary room lighting) is sufficient to stimulate the suprachiasmatic nucleus. Thus, if you spent all of your time in a dimly lit environment, your biological clock would respond as if you were living in perpetual night. Melatonin secretion would be increased, and you would probably feel quite tired most of the time. Perhaps this is one reason why many people report feeling depressed if they cannot get a dose of sunlight at least occasionally during the winter months, a reaction known as **seasonal affective disorder (SAD)** (Rosenthal, 1985).

Evidence that the suprachiasmatic nucleus acts as a biological clock is provided by research indicating that when it is damaged or when neural pathways connecting it to the eyes are destroyed, circadian rhythms tend to disappear totally (Moore & Card, 1985).

Another intriguing fact is that when left to its own devices, our internal biological clock seems to operate on a twenty-five-hour rather than a twenty-four-hour day. This is indicated by research in which volunteers have lived in caves or other environments totally removed from clocks, the rising and setting of the sun, and other cues we normally use to keep track of time. Under these conditions, most persons seem to shift to a "day" of about twenty-five hours (Moore-Ede, Sulzman, & Fuller, 1982). In other words, each day they rise and go to sleep a little later, and all their activities shift accordingly. Their basic bodily functions, too, seem to shift from a twenty-four-hour cycle to this slightly longer one.

Suprachiasmatic Nucleus: *A portion of the hypothalamus that seems to play an important role in the regulation of circadian rhythms.*

Seasonal Affective Disorder (SAD): *Depression experienced during the winter months, supposedly stemming from a lack of exposure to sunlight.*

INDIVIDUAL DIFFERENCES IN CIRCADIAN RHYTHMS: *Of Larks and Owls*

Before reading further, please answer the questions in Table 4.1. How did you score? If you answered "Day" to eight or more questions, the chances are good that you are a morning person (a lark). If, instead, you answered "Night" to eight or more questions, you are probably a night person (an owl). Morning people feel most alert and active early in the day, while night people experience peaks in alertness and energy in the afternoon or evening. Such differences are more than purely subjective. Studies comparing larks and owls indicate that the two groups differ in several important ways. For example, morning people have a higher overall level of adrenaline than night people; thus, they seem to operate at a higher overall level of activation (e.g., Akerstedt & Froberg, 1976). Similarly, as you might expect, morning people experience peaks in body temperature earlier in the day than night people (Wallace, 1993). While morning people have temperature peaks before noon, night people often experience their peaks in temperature in the evening, around 6:00 p.m. or even later.

In addition, some findings suggest that larks and owls also differ with respect to relatively subtle fluctuations in cognitive states. Not surprisingly, morning people report feeling more alert and do better on many cognitive tasks early in the day. In contrast, night people report feeling more alert and do better on such tasks later in the day. More surprising is the fact that these two groups also differ with respect to times at which they are most susceptible to *hypnotism*—a topic we'll consider later in this chapter. Morning people seem to be most susceptible to hypnosis in the morning and early afternoon, while night people are most susceptible to hypnosis in the afternoon and evening (Wallace, 1993).

DISTURBANCES IN CIRCADIAN RHYTHMS: *Jet Lag and Shift Work*

Under normal conditions, the existence of circadian rhythms poses no special problems. Most people are aware of their personal highs and lows and try to schedule their activities accordingly. Unfortunately, though, there are cir-

Respond to each of the following items by circling either "Day" or "Night."		
1. I feel most alert during the	Day	Night
2. I have most energy during the	Day	Night
3. I prefer to take classes during the	Day	Night
4. I prefer to study during the	Day	Night
5. I get my best ideas during the	Day	Night
6. When I graduate, I prefer to find a job during the	Day	Night
7. I am most productive during the	Day	Night
8. I feel most intelligent during the	Day	Night
9. I enjoy leisure-time activities most during the	Day	Night
10. I prefer to work during the	Day	Night

TABLE 4.1

Are You a Lark or an Owl?

If you answer "Day" to eight or more of these questions, you are probably a morning person. If you answer "Night" to eight or more, you are probably a night person. (*Source:* Based on items from Wallace, 1993.)

cumstances under which circadian rhythms may get badly out of phase with our daily activities.

The first of these situations occurs as a result of modern travel—especially by jet plane. When individuals cross several time zones, they often experience considerable difficulty in adjusting to their new location. The reason for this is clear: Their internal biological clocks are calling for one level or type of activity, while the external world is calling strongly for another one. I experienced such effects recently myself, when I returned home after a month in France. My plane left Paris at 1:00 p.m. and, because of the six-hour time difference, arrived in New York at 2:45 p.m. I caught another plane two hours later and finally got home at about 7:00 that evening. Although my clock read 7:00 p.m., my biological clock was reading 1:00 a.m., and I was *tired*. I forced myself to stay up until about 10:30 p.m. (4:30 a.m. according to my biological clock) and fell asleep immediately. However, I awoke again about three hours later, because my internal biological clock was reading "7:30 a.m.—time to get up." These effects gradually disappeared over the course of the next six days, as my internal biological clock readjusted to my own time zone.

A second cause of difficulties with respect to circadian rhythms is *shift work*. Here, individuals must work at times when they would normally be sleeping (say midnight to 8:00 a.m.). To make matters worse, shift workers often face a schedule in which they work on one shift for a fairly short period (say a week), get two days off, and then work on another shift. The results are, for many people, quite unsettling. Even if you've never had a job involving shift work, you have probably experienced such effects after winter or spring break. During these vacation periods, you may have stayed up late and slept in every day. Then, when you returned to school, you probably found readjusting to early morning classes a drag, to say the least. Shift workers, who must constantly reset their biological clocks, suffer even stronger effects, such as high levels of fatigue and serious sleep disorders. In addition, growing evidence suggests that they may suffer other adverse effects, such as increased rates of heart disease and ulcers; increased rates of automobile and industrial accidents; and increased use of alcohol, sleeping pills, and other drugs, relative to non–shift workers (Angerspach et al., 1980; Liddell, 1982). The economic loss resulting from these effects is staggering and was once estimated at more than $70 billion in the United States alone (Bickford, 1988). Fortunately, research on shift work suggests several steps that can help to counter these effects. For example, it appears that a pattern in which employees spend seven days on each shift and then change to a later (rather than earlier) shift can improve both job performance and satisfaction (Cziesler, Moore-Ede, & Coleman, 1982). This occurs because, in general, it is easier for people to *delay* their biological clocks than to advance them. Through these and related steps, the adverse effects of shift work can be reduced—a beneficial outcome for both employees and companies.

KEY QUESTIONS

• What are biological rhythms?

• How long is the cycle for many of our bodily processes?

• What are larks and owls?

• What effects do jet lag and shift work have on circadian rhythms?

WAKING STATES OF CONSCIOUSNESS: *Everyday Experience*

One of the first things I learned about teaching was this: No matter what you are saying and no matter how interesting it is, only part of the class is listening at any given time. Why? One answer relates to the topic of this chapter: While many members of the class are paying attention to your words, others are lost in their own thoughts, daydreaming, planning dinner, and so on. After a while, they may tune in again on what you're saying, but then may shift back into some other state of consciousness. Such fluctuations are a normal part of life, for during our waking hours, we shift frequently between contrasting states of consciousness. This section focuses on several of these recurring or routine states of consciousness.

CONTROLLED AND AUTOMATIC PROCESSING: *The Limits of Attention*

Have you ever tried to carry on conversations with two different people at once? If so, you already know a basic fact about human consciousness: Our attentional or *information-processing* capacities are quite limited. We simply don't have the ability to focus on several different stimuli or events at once. Rather, we find it necessary to shift back and forth between events that we wish to make the center of our current attention. If this is so, how do we manage to perform two or more activities at once, for example, combing our hair while thinking about the day's coming events? The answer seems to involve the fact that there are two contrasting ways of controlling ongoing activities—different levels of attention to, or conscious control over, our own behavior (Logan, 1985, 1988).

The first level is the "automatic pilot" to which I referred at the start of this chapter, when I asked whether you have stood in front of a mirror grooming while your thoughts were far away. Psychologists call this level **automatic processing** because it involves the performance of activities with relatively little conscious awareness. Such processing seems to make little demand on our attentional capacity. Thus, several activities, each under automatic control, can occur at the same time (Shiffrin & Schneider, 1977; Shiffrin & Dumais, 1981). You are demonstrating automatic processing when you drive your car and listen to the radio at the same time. Automatic processing, with respect to a given activity, tends to develop with practice, as the components of the activity become well learned and associated with specific stimulus conditions.

In contrast, **controlled processing** involves more effortful and conscious control of behavior. While it is occurring, you direct careful attention to the task at hand and concentrate on it. Obviously, processing of this type does consume significant attentional capacity. As a result, only one task requiring controlled processing can usually be performed at a time.

Research on the nature of automatic and controlled processing suggests that they differ in several important respects. First, as you might guess, behaviors that have come under the control of automatic processing are performed more quickly and with less effort than ones that require controlled processing (Logan, 1988; Newell & Rosenbloom, 1981). In addition, automatized acts, but not controlled ones, can be initiated without conscious intention; they are seemingly triggered automatically, by specific stimulus conditions or events (Norman & Shallice, 1985). In fact, it may be difficult to inhibit automatized actions once they are initiated. Finally, within limits, neither the accuracy nor the speed of automatic processing is strongly affected by *attentional load*—the number of different items, objects, or operations with which we must deal.

This fact was demonstrated for the first time by Schneider and Shiffrin (1977) in a famous series of experiments. In one of these studies, participants were asked to search for numbers contained in a list of letters. On some trials they searched for a single target (for instance, the number 7). On others, they searched for as many as four different targets at once (such as the numbers 1,

Automatic Processing:
Processing of information with minimal conscious awareness.

Controlled Processing:
Processing of information with relatively high levels of conscious awareness.

Many complex tasks can't be performed automatically; they require our full attention and absorb a large portion of our information-processing capacities.

4, 7, 8). After many practice trials, participants were able to search for the four targets almost as quickly as they could search for one. This was interpreted as evidence for the fact that the participants had shifted to automatic processing in performing this task.

Taking these differences into account, it is clear that neither controlled nor automatic processing necessarily has an edge; both offer a mixture of advantages and disadvantages. As we have seen, automatic processing is rapid and efficient but relatively inflexible. Controlled processing is slower but is more flexible and open to change. Clearly, both have a place in our efforts to deal with information from the external world. One final point: automatic and controlled processing are not hard-and-fast categories, but rather ends of a continuum.

In sum, it seems that we have a strong tendency to adopt automatic processing whenever feasible. Given our limited capacity for attending to many simultaneous stimuli and for processing information generally (see chapters 6 and 7), this tendency offers major benefits. At the same time, though, our readiness to use our automatic pilot can exact important costs. Whatever the balance between the relative pluses and minuses, the important point to remember is this: Even during waking activities, we can and often do shift back and forth between contrasting levels of awareness or consciousness.

DAYDREAMS AND FANTASIES:
Self-Induced Shifts in Consciousness

Sigmund Freud once stated, "A happy person never fantasizes; only an unsatisfied one" (1908, p. 136). If that comment is true, most of us must be very unhappy, for most of us regularly have **daydreams** or **fantasies**—imaginary events or scenes that we experience while we are awake (Singer, 1975). Further, it is clear that for many people such experiences can be quite intense, blotting out the external world at least temporarily. But what do people daydream about? And do these self-generated shifts of consciousness serve any function? It is on these questions that we will now focus.

THE CONTENT OF DAYDREAMS AND FANTASIES: MAJOR THEMES   What was the content of your last daydream? If you are like most people, it can probably be placed under one of the these headings: success or failure (you imagined receiving straight A's or failing an important test); aggression or hostility (you fantasized about evening the score with someone who angered you); sexual or romantic fantasies; guilt (you tortured yourself once again over something you should or shouldn't have done); or problem solving (you imagined yourself working on some task or solving some problem). Of course, many other themes exist; these are merely the most common ones.

While a majority of persons report daydreaming at least occasionally, large individual differences exist with respect to this activity. First, people differ greatly in the frequency with which they daydream or fantasize (Lynn & Rhue, 1986). While some report spending up to half their free time in this activity, others indicate that they rarely have fantasies or daydreams (Silva & Kirsch, 1992). Second, the intensity of such experiences also varies greatly. Some persons report that their fantasies and daydreams are so vivid and

Daydreams: *Imaginary scenes or events that occur while a person is awake.*

Fantasies: *Imaginary events or scenes that a person experiences while awake.*

lifelike that they are almost real and may even become confused with reality. If such experiences are not readily controlled by the persons who have them, they may be said to border on being **hallucinations**—vivid perceptual experiences that occur in the absence of an external stimulus. Such experiences are usually associated with severe psychological disorders, but they occasionally occur among non–mentally ill individuals as well (Bentall, 1990). For most persons, however, fantasies and daydreams are much less intense and far less involving.

DAYDREAMS AND FANTASIES: WHAT FUNCTION DO THEY SERVE? If people spend a considerable amount of time engaging in daydreams and fantasies—changing their own consciousness, if you will—then these activities must serve some useful function. But what, precisely, do they accomplish? No clear-cut answer to this question has as yet emerged, but existing evidence points to several interesting possibilities.

First, daydreams and fantasies may serve as a kind of safety valve, permitting persons to escape, however briefly, from the stresses and boredom of everyday life. Perhaps this is one reason why many students tend to daydream in class or while reading their textbooks. (Not this one, I hope!)

Second, daydreams and fantasies often provide us with a ready means of altering our own moods, primarily in a positive direction. If you've ever felt happier after a daydream filled with desirable activities and events, you are already familiar with such benefits (Forgas & Bower, 1988).

Third, it is possible that daydreams and fantasies help people find solutions to actual problems in their lives. By imagining various behaviors and the outcomes they may produce, we can examine potential courses of action carefully and from the safe perspective of our own minds. This can help us formulate useful plans of action.

Finally, fantasies may play an important role in the self-regulation of behavior. By imagining negative outcomes, people may strengthen their inhibitions against dangerous or prohibited behaviors (Bandura, 1986). Similarly, by dreaming about potential rewards, people may enhance their own motivation and performance. In sum, fantasies and daydreams may be much more than a pleasant diversion; they may actually yield substantial benefits to those who choose to induce them.

SELF-CONSCIOUSNESS: *Some Effects of Looking Inward*

What do you do when you pass a mirror? If you are like most people, you stop, however briefly, and examine your appearance. When you do, you are also, in a sense, changing your current state of consciousness. Before you passed the mirror, you were probably thinking about something other than yourself. Now, at least while you stand in front of the glass, your thoughts are focused on yourself. Psychologists term this focus **self-consciousness**, and they have uncovered much about its causes and effects. We'll first consider one influential theory concerning self-consciousness and then turn to some of the surprising effects of entering this state.

THE CONTROL THEORY OF SELF-CONSCIOUSNESS: SELF-REGULATION OF BE-HAVIOR Think for a moment about how the thermostat in your house or apartment works. In essence, it continuously compares the level of temperature you have set to the actual temperature in the room. When the temperature is too cold or too hot, the thermostat closes a circuit that turns on the

Hallucinations: Sensory experiences that occur in the absence of external stimuli yet have the full force of impact of real events or stimuli.

Self-Consciousness: Increased awareness of oneself as a social object or of one's own values and attitudes.

furnace or air conditioner. In what they term the **control theory of self-consciousness**, Carver and Scheier (1981, 1990) suggest that self-consciousness operates in a similar manner. Once we focus our attention on ourselves, we compare our current state with important goals and values. If the gap between reality and these goals and values is too large, we make adjustments in our behavior to move closer to the desired states. In this sense, self-consciousness is an important component in the self-regulation of our behavior.

Scheier and Carver (1986, 1987) and many other psychologists (e.g., Britt, 1992) also draw a distinction between two forms of self-consciousness: *private self-consciousness* and *public self-consciousness*. Private self-consciousness is our tendency to reflect on private aspects of the self—our own feelings, attitudes, and values. In contrast, public self-consciousness has to do with our tendency to think about aspects of the self that are presented to others—how we appear in others' eyes. When you look into a mirror or at a photograph of yourself, you almost certainly experience public self-consciousness; after all, you are seeing yourself (physically) the way others do. But if seeing your own reflection causes you to think about how you are feeling or about what kind of person you really are, you may experience heightened private self-consciousness too. In fact, in much research on self-awareness, experimenters cause participants to experience this state by having them work on various tasks in front of a mirror or with a camera aimed in their direction. Many different studies offer support for the basic assumptions of the control theory proposed by Carver and Scheier. Thus, this theory seems to be a useful framework for thinking about the nature of self-consciousness and its impact on behavior.

FACTORS THAT PRODUCE HEIGHTENED SELF-CONSCIOUSNESS That mirrors and cameras induce heightened self-consciousness is obvious. Many other factors, however, may cause us to enter this state of consciousness. One of these can best be described as a personal tendency or disposition to become self-conscious. Some persons, in other words, spend more time thinking about themselves—their feelings and reactions, the kind of impression they are making on strangers—than others. Where do you fall on this dimension? To find out, answer the questions in Table 4.2.

These are items from a psychological test designed to measure both private and public self-consciousness (Scheier & Carver, 1986). As you can

HEIGHTENED SELF-CONSCIOUSNESS

What do you do when you pass a mirror? If you are like most people, you glance at your reflection—experiencing increased awareness of yourself and your appearance.

TABLE 4.2	

Private Self-Consciousness

Are you high in private self-consciousness? To find out, add the numbers you entered for items 1, 3, 4, 5, 6, and 8; then subtract the numbers you entered for items 2 and 7. The higher your score, the more you tend to be aware of your own inner feelings and reactions. (*Source:* Based on items from Britt, 1992).

Indicate how characteristic or uncharacteristic of you each of these items is by placing a number in the blank space next to each.

0 = extremely uncharacteristic
1 = uncharacteristic
2 = neither characteristic nor uncharacteristic
3 = characteristic
4 = extremely characteristic

_____ 1. I'm always trying to figure myself out.

_____ 2. Usually, I'm not very aware of myself.

_____ 3. I think about myself a lot.

_____ 4. I'm often the subject of my own fantasies or daydreams.

_____ 5. I usually pay close attention to my inner feelings.

_____ 6. I'm aware of the way my mind works when I try to solve a problem or reason something out.

_____ 7. I never reflect on myself.

_____ 8. I frequently examine my own motives.

probably guess, the items in Table 4.2 measure private self-consciousness; people who score high on these items have a greater than average tendency to think about themselves and their inner feelings or reactions (Britt, 1992). Other items on the self-consciousness scale measure public self-consciousness.

Another factor that influences self-consciousness is the familiarity of a given situation. In general, the more familiar and comfortable with a situation people are, the greater their tendency to think about themselves while in it, and so the greater their self-consciousness.

A third factor that strongly influences self-consciousness is our current mood. Research findings indicate that persons experiencing either happy or sad moods are more likely to focus their attention inward than are persons in a neutral mood, presumably because they wish to understand their feelings and the factors responsible for them (Salovey, 1992).

> **Control Theory of Self-Consciousness:** *A theory suggesting that people compare their current behavior and states with important goals and values. They then alter their behavior to close any gaps they observe.*
>
> **Choking under Pressure:** *The tendency to perform less well at times when pressures for excellent performance are especially high.*

THE EFFECTS OF SELF-CONSCIOUSNESS: REDUCED PERFORMANCE BUT INCREASED SELF-INSIGHT That we often experience self-consciousness is obvious: This state is a regular part of daily life. But what are the effects of this inward focus? Research on this topic suggests that they are something of a mixed bag. On the negative side of the ledger is a phenomenon known as **choking under pressure** (Baumeister & Scher, 1988). This term refers to the fact that sometimes people do worse when confronted with strong pressures to perform than on other occasions. For example, athletes who do very well in practice, when pressure is low, may choke up during important games or contests. Growing evidence indicates that heightened self-consciousness may contribute to such effects. The reasoning goes something like this. Many highly skilled activities are performed under automatic control. For example, consider typing. Once you have mastered this skill, you don't think about the keys. If you do, such cognition may actually interfere with your performance and cause you to make errors. Similar effects occur with respect to many other skilled actions, from skiing and diving to pitching a baseball and swinging a golf club. When people performing such actions think too much about what they are doing, their performance may suffer. Unfortunately, heightened self-consciousness—such as that induced by a huge audience of cheering fans—leads to precisely this kind of thought. The result: performance suffers. Several studies offer support for this reasoning (e.g., Baumeister & Steinhilber, 1984). So in some cases, at least, it appears that increased self-consciousness can prove costly indeed.

This is not the entire story, however. There are also potential benefits from entering a state of increased self-consciousness. In particular, it appears that doing so can sometimes increase *self-insight*—the understanding we have of ourselves and our major characteristics (e.g., Hixon & Swann, 1993; Swann et al., 1992). This is not always the case, however; other evidence indicates that if we think about ourselves too much, we can become confused and experience reduced rather than increased self-insight (Wilson & Schooner, 1991). But, in general, it appears that self-reflection *is* an important ingredient in increased self-knowledge.

CHOKING UNDER PRESSURE

Performing in front of a large crowd can cause many people—even professional athletes—to experience increased self-consciousness. This, in turn, can sometimes interfere with performance.

> ### KEY QUESTIONS
>
> - What is the difference between automatic processing and controlled processing?
> - What are daydreams and fantasies, and what functions do they serve?
> - What happens when we focus our attention inward?
> - What effect does increased self-consciousness have on the performance of skilled activities?

SLEEP: *The Pause That Refreshes?*

Learning Objective 4.5
Describe the basic nature of sleep, how sleep is studied, and the potential functions of sleep.

Learning Objective 4.6
Describe the sleep disorders.

Learning Objective 4.7
Survey the basic facts about dreams and discuss their nature from the psychoanalytic, cognitive, and physiological viewpoints.

What single activity occupies more of your time than any other? While you may be tempted to say "studying" or "working," think again. If you are like most people, the correct answer is probably **sleep**. A majority of human beings spend fully one-third of their entire lives asleep, and for some the proportion is even higher (Dement, 1975; Webb, 1975). Any activity that occupies so much of our time must be important, so efforts to understand the nature of sleep have continued in psychology for several decades. What has this research revealed? What happens when we sleep and when we dream? And what are the functions of these processes? These are some of the questions we will now explore.

SLEEP: *How It Is Studied*

Everyone would agree that when we sleep, we are in a different state of consciousness than when we are awake. But what is sleep really like? This is a difficult question to answer, since during sleep we are generally less aware of ourselves and our surroundings than at other times. For this reason, asking people about their own experience with sleep is not a very useful technique for studying it. Fortunately, another, much more informative approach exists. As a person moves from a waking state to deep sleep, complex changes in the electrical activity of the brain occur. These changes can be measured with great precision, and the resulting **electroencephalogram** (EEG) reveals much about the nature of sleep. Thus, in much research on this process, volunteers are fitted with electrodes so that researchers can study their EEGs as well as other changes in bodily functions such as respiration, muscle tone, heart rate, and blood pressure. The changes that occur as the volunteers fall asleep and continue sleeping are then recorded. In this way researchers can obtain revealing information about the normal course of sleep as well as about factors affecting it.

SLEEP: *Its Basic Nature*

Sleep: A process in which important physiological changes (including shifts in brain activity and slowing of basic bodily functions) are accompanied by major shifts in consciousness.

Electroencephalogram (EEG): A record of electrical activity within the brain. EEGs play an important role in the scientific study of sleep.

Alpha Waves: Brain waves that occur when individuals are awake but relaxed.

Delta Waves: High-amplitude, slow brain waves that occur during several stages of sleep, but especially during Stage 4.

What has sleep research revealed? Perhaps the best way of answering is by describing the changes in brain activity and other bodily processes that occur during a single night of sleep. As we will soon see, these changes reveal a regular progression through several different stages. In a sense, these are part of our normal circadian rhythms, so it is reasonable to view sleep as an additional portion of this overall pattern.

When you are fully awake and alert, your EEGs contain many *beta waves*: relatively high-frequency (14 to 30 Hz), low-voltage activity. As you enter a quiet, resting state (for example, just after getting into bed and turning out the light), beta waves are replaced by **alpha waves**: EEG activity that is somewhat lower in frequency (8 to 13 Hz) but slightly higher in voltage. As you begin to fall asleep, alpha waves are replaced by even slower, higher-voltage **delta waves**. The appearance of delta waves seems to reflect the fact that increasingly large numbers of neurons are firing together, in a synchronized manner.

Although such phrases as "drifting off to sleep" suggest that the onset of sleep is gradual, it is actually quite sudden. One instant you are awake and aware of your surroundings; the next you are asleep, no longer experiencing such awareness. Sleep is not entirely an either-or type of phenomenon, however. EEG records obtained from thousands of volunteers in sleep research indicate that sleep can actually be divided into four different stages. The tran-

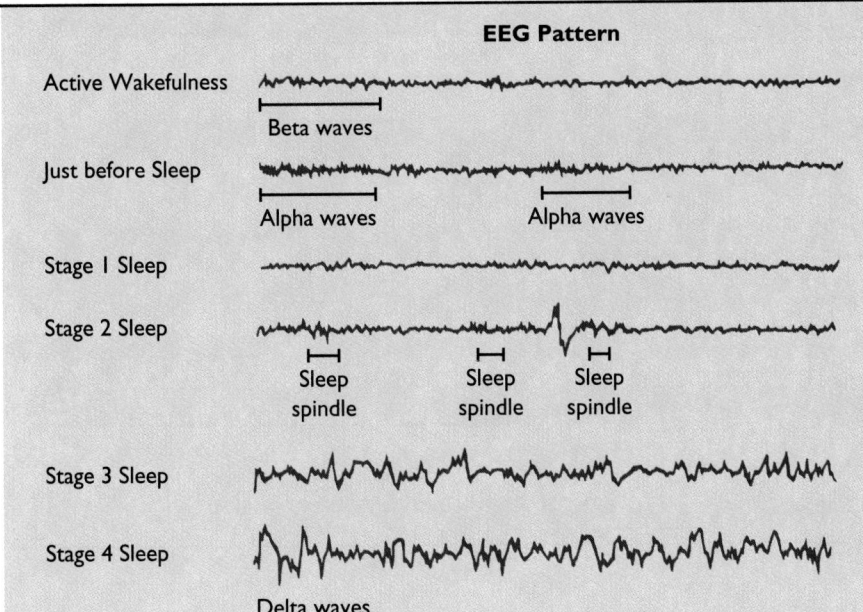

EEG Pattern

Active Wakefulness — Beta waves

Just before Sleep — Alpha waves   Alpha waves

Stage 1 Sleep

Stage 2 Sleep — Sleep spindle   Sleep spindle   Sleep spindle

Stage 3 Sleep

Stage 4 Sleep — Delta waves

FIGURE 4.2

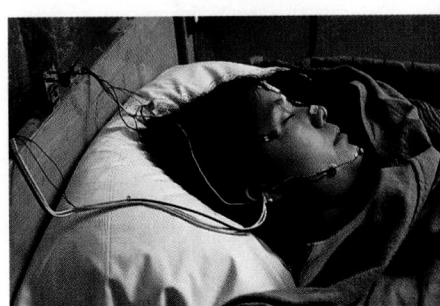

Sleep Stages

As an individual falls asleep, the electrical activity of her or his brain changes in an orderly manner. Note the contrasting patterns of activity shown before sleep begins and during each of the succeeding stages.

sition from wakefulness to sleep occurs with the onset of Stage 1 sleep. During this stage, a mixed but relatively slow, low-voltage EEG pattern emerges. Breathing slows, muscle tone decreases, and the body generally relaxes. At this point, individuals can still be readily awakened by external stimuli. If they are not, they move into Stage 2 (Webb, 1975). During this stage the brain emits occasional short bursts of rapid, high-voltage waves known as sleep spindles. In Stage 2, sleepers are much more difficult to awaken than they were during Stage 1. Stage 2 is followed by Stages 3 and 4. As shown in Figure 4.2, these stages are marked by the increasing appearance of slow, high-voltage delta waves, and by a further slowing of all major bodily functions (Dement, 1975). Almost everyone shows the same pattern of shifts in falling asleep; indeed, departures from this pattern are often a sign of physical or psychological disorders (e.g., Empson, 1984).

So far, the picture I have presented probably sounds consistent with your own subjective experience of sleep; you change from being awake to being more and more deeply asleep. About ninety minutes after the process begins, however, several dramatic changes occur. First, most persons enter a highly distinct phase known as **REM (rapid eye movement) sleep**. During this phase, the electrical activity of the brain changes rapidly; it now closely resembles that shown when people are awake. Delta waves disappear, and fast, low-voltage activity returns. Second, sleepers' eyes begin to move about rapidly beneath their closed eyelids. Third, there is an almost total suppression of activity in body muscles. Indeed, muscle relaxation is so great that a state bordering on paralysis seems to exist. Yet at the same time, males may experience erections and females corresponding changes in their sexual organs. This combination of signs of activation along with signs of profound relaxation has led some researchers to describe REM sleep as *paradoxical* in nature, and in several respects this description seems apt.

These observable shifts in brain activity and bodily processes are accompanied, in many cases, by one of the most fascinating phenomena of sleep: *dreams*. An individual awakened during REM sleep often reports dreaming. In some cases, eye movements during such sleep seem to be related to the content of dreams (Dement, 1974). It is as if the individual is following the action in a dream with his or her eyes. The relationship between rapid eye

REM Sleep: A state of sleep in which brain activity resembling waking restfulness is accompanied by deep muscle relaxation and movements of the eyes. Most dreams occurring during periods of REM sleep.

FIGURE 4.3

Time Spent in Various Stages of Sleep during a Single Night

Periods of REM sleep alternate with other stages of sleep during the night. The duration of the REM periods tends to increase toward morning, while the amount of time spent in Stage 4 decreases.

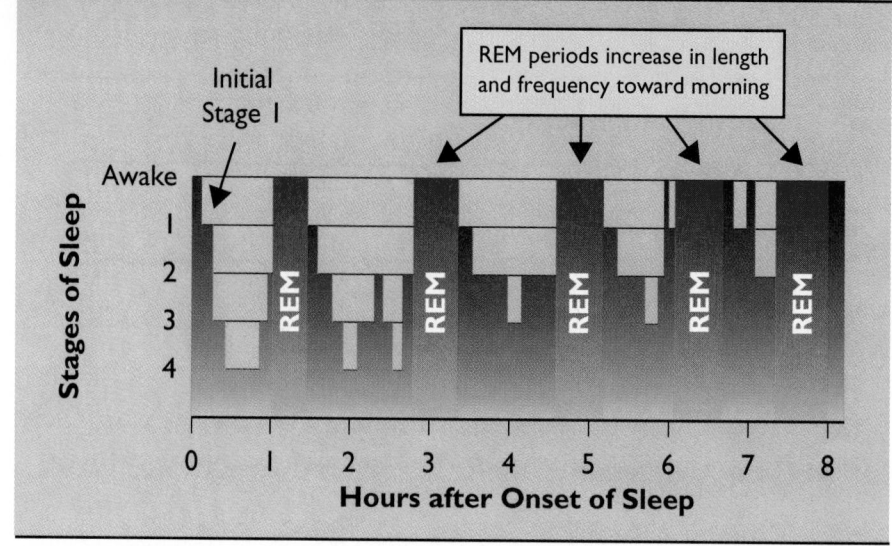

movements and dream content is uncertain, however, so it is best to view this as an intriguing but as yet unverified possibility.

Periods of REM sleep continue to alternate with the other stages of sleep throughout the night. The duration is variable, but the REM periods tend to increase in length toward morning, while the amount of time spent in Stage 4 tends to decrease (see Figure 4.3). Thus, while the first REM period may last only five to ten minutes, the final one—from which many people awake—may last thirty minutes or more (Hartmann, 1973; Kelly, 1981).

SLEEP: *What Functions Does It Serve?*

Any activity that fills as much of our lives as sleep must serve important functions. But what, precisely, are these? What benefits do we gain from the hours we spend asleep? Several theories exist.

The first, and perhaps most obvious, is the restorative or recuperative theory, which suggests that sleep provides the rest we require to recover from the wear and tear of the day's activities. While this view seems consistent with our subjective impressions (we often report feeling irritable and out of sorts after a poor night's sleep), there is little direct evidence for it. Even prolonged deprivation of sleep does not seem to produce large or clear-cut effects on behavior. For example, in one demonstration seventeen-year-old Randy Gardner stayed awake for 264 hours and 12 minutes—eleven entire days! His motivation for doing so was simple: He wanted to earn a place in the *Guinness Book of Records,* and he did. Although he had some difficulty staying awake this long, he remained generally alert and active throughout the entire period. After completing his ordeal, Randy slept a mere 14 hours. Then he returned to his usual 8-hour cycle. Further, he seemed to suffer no lasting physical or psychological harm from his long sleepless period.

More systematic studies of the effects of sleep deprivation have been conducted with both animals and people (e.g., Rechtschaffen et al., 1983). With respect to humans, several long-term studies have been performed in which volunteers gradually reduce their nightly sleep (for example, by thirty minutes every two or three weeks). These procedures continue until the volunteers report that they do not want to reduce their sleep any further. Results indicate that most people can reduce their amount of sleep to about five hours per night (Mullaney et al., 1977). No reductions in their performance on various tasks, no negative shifts in mood, and no harmful effects on health seem to result from such reductions. The major changes observed involve sleep itself. After reducing their sleep to five hours or less, participants demonstrate what has been described as increased *sleep efficiency*. They fall asleep very quickly, and they spend a higher proportion of time in Stage 4 sleep. It is as if they have learned to compress their sleep into a shorter period of time. In sum, research on sleep deprivation does not offer strong support for the view that sleep serves primarily a restorative or recuperative function.

A second theory on the function of sleep emphasizes the relationship of sleep to basic circadian rhythms. According to this view, sleep is merely the neural mechanism that evolved to encourage various species, including human beings, to remain inactive during those times of day when they do not usually engage in activities related to their survival. As one well-known sleep researcher (Webb, 1975) has put it, sleep is nature's way of keeping us quiet at night—a dangerous time for our ancestors and, given crime statistics, for us, too.

Yet another possibility is that only certain components of sleep are crucial. For example, it has been suggested that perhaps it is REM sleep that is essential to our health and well-being, and that being deprived of such sleep will induce harmful effects. Unfortunately, efforts to test this possibility have yielded mixed results. On the one hand, a few studies have indicated that selectively depriving individuals of REM sleep (by waking them whenever their EEGs indicate that they have entered this phase) may interfere with their ability to retain newly learned information (McGrath & Cohen, 1978). These findings suggest that REM sleep may play an important role in the integration of newly acquired information with existing memories and knowledge. On the other hand, some studies indicate that the only effect of depriving individuals of REM sleep is to increase the amount of such sleep they have on subsequent nights (Webb & Agnew, 1967).

So where does all this leave us? Does sleep really serve important functions? Or is it merely a holdover from our more primitive past, like male facial hair or the appendix? Most sleep researchers reject this conclusion. They believe that sleep probably serves both the restorative and the circadian functions noted above (Borbely et al., 1989). In support of this reasoning, some findings suggest that the amount of time people spend in slow-wave sleep is related to how long they have been awake, while the amount of time they spend in REM sleep is related mainly to circadian rhythms—the daily cycles of activity and rest (Webb, 1975). Further, there is an important relationship between sleep and waking moods. The more effectively people sleep, the more positive are their waking moods, and the less anxiety they experience (Berry & Webb, 1985). So, in sum, sleep does seem to serve important functions for us. Falling asleep is a function of both restorative and circadian factors, and sleep itself fulfills needs related to both.

KEY QUESTIONS

- What is an EEG?
- What distinguishes the major stages of sleep?
- What happens during REM sleep?
- What are the effects of sleep deprivation?
- What functions does sleep serve?

SLEEP DISORDERS: *No Rest for the Weary*

Do you ever have trouble falling or staying asleep? If so, you are in good company: Almost 40 percent of adults report that they sometimes have this problem—generally known as **insomnia** (Bixler et al., 1979). Further, such problems seem to increase with age and are somewhat more common among women than men. While many people report insomnia, it is not clear that the problem actually exists in all cases. When the sleep habits of people who claim to be suffering from insomnia are carefully studied, it turns out that many of them sleep as long as people who do not complain of such problems (Emp-

Insomnia: Disorder involving the inability to fall asleep or remain asleep.

son, 1984). As pointed out by Trinder (1988), this does not necessarily imply that such persons are faking their disorder or complaining about a problem they don't really have. For example, while the amount of sleep they obtain is within what experts consider to be normal limits (6.5 hours or more per night), this may still not be enough to meet their individual needs. Further, the quality of their sleep may be disturbed in ways not yet measured in research. Still, such arguments aside, it does appear that many people who believe that their sleep is somehow inadequate may actually be getting as much sleep, and sleeping about as well, as others who don't report such problems.

Unfortunately, no totally effective cure for insomnia exists. However, you may well find the following tactics helpful:

1. Read something pleasant or relaxing just before going to sleep.
2. Arrange your schedule so you go to sleep at the same time each night.
3. Take a warm bath, massage, or other relaxing treatment at bedtime.
4. If you find yourself tossing and turning, get up and read, work, or watch television until you feel drowsy. Lying in bed for hours worrying about loss of sleep is definitely *not* the answer.
5. Don't worry. Almost everyone experiences difficulty falling asleep sometimes, so don't be overly concerned unless the problem persists for more than a few days.

By the way, despite the promises of advertisements, sleeping pills—prescription as well as nonprescription—are *not* an effective sleep aid. They may induce sleep at first, but tolerance to them develops quickly so that larger and larger doses are soon needed. Further, some drugs used for this purpose interfere with REM sleep, and this can lead to other sleep disturbances.

Unfortunately, insomnia is far from the only problem associated with sleep. Several other *disorders of initiating and maintaining sleep* (DIMS for short) exist. First, there are disorders of arousal. The most dramatic of these is **somnambulism**—walking in one's sleep. This is less rare than you might guess; almost 25 percent of children experience at least one sleepwalking episode (Empson, 1984). A second, related disorder is **night terrors**: Individuals, especially children, awaken from deep sleep with signs of intense arousal—such as a racing pulse and rapid respiration—and powerful feelings of fear. Yet they have no memory of any dream relating to these feelings. Night terrors seem to occur primarily during Stage 4 sleep. In contrast, *nightmares*, which most of us have experienced at some point, occur during REM sleep and often can be vividly recalled. Both somnambulism and night terrors appear to be related to disturbances in the functioning of the autonomic nervous system, which plays a key role in regulating brain activity during sleep.

Another, especially disturbing, type of sleep disorder is **apnea**. Persons suffering from sleep apnea actually stop breathing while they are asleep. Needless to say, this causes them to wake up. Since this process can be repeated literally hundreds of times during the night, apnea can seriously affect the health of persons suffering from it.

Have you ever felt yourself twitch suddenly as you were sleeping or while falling asleep? If so, you have had a small taste of what people suffering from another sleep disorder—*nocturnal myoclonus*—experience. Such persons endure periodic and repeated episodes of body twitching throughout the night. Little wonder that their sleep is greatly disturbed.

Finally, there are several disorders known as **hypersomnias**, in which affected persons appear to sleep too much. The most serious of these is **narcolepsy**, a condition in which individuals suddenly fall deeply asleep in the midst of waking activities. Such attacks are sometimes accompanied by almost total paralysis and are often triggered by a strong emotion. Thus,

Somnambulism: A sleep disorder in which individuals actually get up and move about while still asleep.

Night Terrors: Extremely frightening dreamlike experiences that occur during non-REM sleep.

Apnea: Cessation of breathing during sleep.

Hypersomnias: Disorders involving excessive amounts of sleep or an overwhelming urge to fall asleep.

Narcolepsy: A sleep disorder in which individuals are overcome by uncontrollable periods of sleep during waking hours.

when a person with narcolepsy becomes excited or upset, he or she may suddenly fall down in a deep sleep. I once had a colleague who suffered from this problem. During a lecture he would sit down, lean forward, and suddenly be asleep—often in the middle of a sentence. Students in his classes found this disturbing, to say the least.

What causes such sleep disorders? For some persons, insomnia seems to involve disturbances in the internal mechanisms that regulate body temperature. As noted in our discussion of circadian rhythms, core body temperature usually drops to low levels during sleep. This conserves energy and permits many bodily functions to proceed at reduced rates. In persons suffering from insomnia, however, these mechanisms fail to operate normally, with the result that the body temperatures of insomniacs remain relatively high (Sewitch, 1987).

Other causes of sleep disorders may involve disturbances of the biological clock within the hypothalamus (the suprachiasmatic nucleus). This clock interacts with other structures of the brain—such as serotonin-producing portions of the reticular activating system and parts of the forebrain just in front of the hypothalamus—to regulate all circadian rhythms, including the sleep-waking cycle. Any disturbance in these complex and delicately balanced mechanisms, then, can result in sleep disorders.

DREAMS: Stimulation in the Midst of Sleep

Without a doubt, the most dramatic aspect of sleep is **dreams**—jumbled, vivid, sometimes enticing and sometimes disturbing images that fill our sleeping minds. What are these experiences? Why do they occur? Psychologists are still seeking final answers to these puzzling questions, but we already know much more about dreams than was true only a few decades ago. Here, we'll first consider some basic facts about dreams, then turn to three contrasting views concerning their nature and function.

DREAMS: SOME BASIC FACTS Try answering each of the following questions. Then consider the answers given—which reflect current knowledge about the nature of these encounters with the workings of our own nervous systems.

1. *Does everybody dream?* The answer seems to be yes. While not all people remember dreaming, EEG recordings and related data indicate that everyone experiences REM sleep. Moreover, if awakened during such periods, even people who normally don't recall dreaming may report vivid dreams.

2. *How long do dreams last?* Many people believe that dreams last only an instant, no matter how long they may seem. In fact, though, dreams seem to run on "real time": The longer they seem to last, the longer they really are (Dement & Kleitman, 1957).

3. *Can external events be incorporated into dreams?* Common sense suggests that they can, and this idea seems to be correct, at least to a degree: External events are sometimes incorporated into dreams. For example, Dement and Wolpert (1958) sprayed water on sleeping people who were experiencing REM sleep. Then they woke them up. In more than half the cases, participants reported water in their dreams.

4. *If a man experiences an erection or a woman experiences vaginal secretions during sleep, does this mean that the sleeper is having a sexy dream?* The answer to this one seems to be no. When male and female volunteers are awakened at such times, they are no more likely to report dreams with sexual content than they would be at other times (Karacan et al.,

Dreams: *Cognitive events, often vivid but disconnected, that occur during sleep. Most dreams take place during REM sleep.*

1966). So signs of sexual arousal during dreams seem to be a mere by-product of other bodily events occurring during dreaming.

5. *Do dreams really express unconscious wishes?* Many people believe that they do, but there is no convincing evidence for this view. Please see the discussion of this topic below.

6. *When people cannot remember their dreams, does this mean that they are purposely forgetting them, perhaps because they find the content of their dreams too disturbing?* Probably not. Research on why people can or cannot remember their dreams indicates that this is primarily a function of what they do when they wake up; for instance, whether they lie quietly in bed, actively trying to remember the dream, or leap up and start the day's activities. While we can't totally rule out the possibility of some kind of repression—that is, of active, motivated forgetting—there is little evidence for its occurrence.

Now that we've considered some basic facts about dreams, let's turn to several views concerning their nature and function.

DREAMS: THE PSYCHODYNAMIC VIEW   Perhaps the most dramatic answers to the questions posed at the start of this section are those proposed by Sigmund Freud. He felt that dreams provide an important means of probing the unconscious—all those thoughts, impulses, and wishes that lie outside the realm of conscious experience. In dreams, he believed, we can give expression to impulses and desires we find unacceptable during our waking hours. Thus, we can dream about gratifying illicit sexual desires or about inflicting painful tortures on persons who have made us angry, although we actively repress such thoughts during the day.

Freud contended that no matter how vague, jumbled, or strange dreams may seem to be, they always contain important messages. Often these are disguised, either in the dreams themselves or in our memories of them. But if we search diligently enough, we will be able to uncover them. Freud incorporated detailed analysis of dreams into his treatment of patients suffering from a wide range of psychological problems. He claimed that this often provided him with just the insight he needed to understand and help them. His reports of such interpretations make provocative reading—but, alas, there is virtually no scientific evidence for their accuracy, or for Freud's more general assertions about dreams. He left us with no clear-cut rules for interpreting dreams and no way of knowing whether such interpretations are accurate. Further, as we'll note in the **Perspectives on Diversity** section below, dreams, and their meanings, may be strongly influenced by cultural factors; dreams differ greatly not only from one person to another, but from culture to culture. In view of these facts, few psychologists are currently willing to accept the view that dreams offer a unique means for exploring the unconscious. Instead, most accept one of the alternative views we will now consider.

PERSPECTIVES ON DIVERSITY

Culture and the Interpretation of Dreams

Manifest Content: In Freud's theory, the overt or reported content of dreams.

Latent Content: In Freud's theory, the hidden content of dreams.

As mentioned earlier, Freud believed that dreams contain important messages from the *unconscious*—that they reflect impulses and thoughts that are hidden from our view while we are awake. More specifically, he contended that the **manifest content** of a dream—what we actually remember about it—may not, at first glance, reveal its **latent content**—the underlying, hidden meaning. How can the latent content of dreams be determined? Freud's answer: through careful application of his theories!

For example, consider Freud's interpretation of dreams that were reported to him by several of his male patients. In these dreams the patients' fathers were somehow harmed, much to the patients' grief and horror. In fact, when describing such dreams, some patients would lose control and burst into tears. How did Freud interpret these dreams? In his view, dreams serve a wish-fulfilling function, allowing people to express desires they cannot express while awake. Within this framework, dreams in which male patients' fathers are harmed represent unconscious anger or resentment toward their parents. According to Freud, these feelings, in turn, stem from what he termed the Oedipus complex—the male's jealousy about his father's sexual relationship with his mother.

These are certainly provocative suggestions, but are they actually correct? One way to find out would be to determine whether males in cultures other than the one in which Freud worked (nineteenth-century Vienna) also report such dreams. If they do, then support could be obtained for the view that the Oedipus complex is universal, and for Freud's interpretation of such dreams.

Such research has been conducted, and in general it has failed to confirm the universality of "Oedipus complex" dreams. For example, in one famous study, Malinowksi (1927) found that boys in the Trobriand culture of New Guinea often reported dreams in which their maternal uncles (their mothers' brothers), not their fathers, were hurt. Why did they have such dreams? Their uncles certainly didn't have sexual relationships with their mothers, so what was the root of the hidden resentment toward their uncles expressed in these dreams? One possibility is suggested by the fact that in Trobriand culture, maternal uncles, not fathers, are the ones who train and discipline boys. So it seems possible that the dreams reported by Trobriand boys reflect resentment toward the adult males who discipline them. This interpretation is strengthened by the facts that Trobriand boys do *not* have such dreams about their fathers, while none of Freud's Viennese patients have such dreams about their uncles. Put in other terms, in Viennese culture, the two roles "mother's lover" and "source of discipline" are filled by a single person: boys' fathers. In Trobriand culture, in contrast, these two roles are filled by different persons: boys' fathers and maternal uncles. Comparing the two cultures permits us to determine which of these roles is related to a specific kind of dream (Segall et al., 1990).

In sum, the findings of cross-cultural research indicate that Freud may well have been correct in suggesting that dreams can sometimes function as an outlet for expressing unacceptable impulses, but that he was wrong in suggesting that dreams' content is universal across all cultures. Rather, it appears that the content of dreams—and their specific meaning—is strongly influenced by the dreamer's culture. Further, comparing dreams in different cultures can help us to understand the dreams' meaning and the impact of cultural factors on them. Even at this very basic level, therefore, adopting a multicultural perspective is valuable and informative.

CULTURE AND DREAMS

If dreams represent universal human themes, as Freud asserted, then they should be similar in all cultures. Research with the Trobriand culture in New Guinea has shown that they are not.

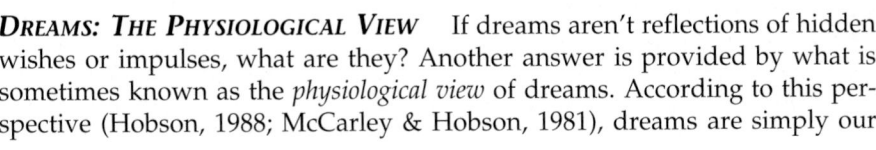

DREAMS: THE PHYSIOLOGICAL VIEW   If dreams aren't reflections of hidden wishes or impulses, what are they? Another answer is provided by what is sometimes known as the *physiological view* of dreams. According to this perspective (Hobson, 1988; McCarley & Hobson, 1981), dreams are simply our subjective experience of what is, in essence, random neural activity in the brain. Such activity may reflect ongoing information-processing tasks, as described below, or may occur simply because a minimal amount of stimulation is necessary for the normal functioning of the brain and nervous system. In other words, dreams merely represent efforts by our cognitive systems to make sense out of this neural activity (Foulkes, 1985; Hobson, 1988). As Hobson has put it, the brain "is so . . . bent on the quest for meaning that it attributes and even creates meaning when there is little or none to be found in the data it is asked to process."

DREAMS: THE COGNITIVE VIEW A third view carries somewhat further these suggestions concerning our cognitive systems' efforts to interpret neural activity during sleep. This perspective, proposed by Antrobus (1991), suggests that two facts about REM sleep are crucial to understanding the nature of dreams: (1) During REM sleep areas of the brain in the cerebral cortex that play a key role in waking perception, thought, and regulation of motor processes are highly active; (2) yet, at the same time, there is massive inhibition of input from sensory systems and muscles (which, as you may recall, are suppressed during REM sleep). As a result, Antrobus (1991) reasons, the cortical structures or systems that normally regulate perception and thought have only their own output as input. The result is that this activity forms the basis for the imagery and ideas in dreams.

Does this mean that dreams are meaningless? Not at all. Since they represent interpretations of neural activity by our own brains, they reflect aspects of our memories and waking experience. Convincing evidence for this connection between dreams and important events in our lives is provided by the fact that people attempting to make important changes in their own behavior—for example, to quit smoking or drinking—often report having **dreams of absent-minded transgression**—DAMIT dreams for short (e.g., Gill, 1985). In such dreams, people suddenly notice that they are smoking or drinking, and that they have slipped into this behavior in an absent-minded or careless manner—without planning to do so. This realization leads to feelings of panic or guilt in the dream. In many cases, the dreamers awake at that point, feeling very disturbed.

A study conducted by Hajek and Belcher (1991) yielded intriguing data on the nature of such dreams and their relationship to waking behavior. These researchers asked several hundred persons enrolled in a stop-smoking program to report on the kind of dreams they had before and during the program. They found that about 33 percent of the participants reported having DAMIT dreams while trying to quit, and that they had not had such dreams in the past, while still smoking. Further, and of even greater importance, it was found that having such dreams was positively related to participants' success at quitting smoking. A higher proportion of those who reported such dreams were still not smoking one year after the training program.

Why was the occurrence of DAMIT dreams related to success in efforts to refrain from smoking? Hajek and Belcher (1991) suggest that the guilt and panic produced by such dreams are so unpleasant that they help strengthen smokers' resolve to break their habit. The fact that smoking in these dreams is *not* accompanied by the pleasurable feelings of smoking helps to strengthen such effects. To the extent this interpretation is correct, it suggests not only a clear link between what is happening in people's lives at the

KEY QUESTIONS

- What are some common types of sleep disorders?

- During what sleep stage do dreams usually occur?

- What was Freud's explanation for the occurrence of dreams?

- What does the physiological view of dreams suggest?

- What does the cognitive view of dreams suggest?

- What is the effect of cultural factors on dreams?

Dreams of Absent-Minded Transgression: *Dreams in which persons attempting to change their own behavior, as in quitting smoking, see themselves unintentionally slipping into the unwanted behavior.*

moment and the contents of their dreams, but a link between the content of dreams and subsequent behavior. In this sense, the content of dreams does have meaning; and, what's more, such meaning may have strong effects on dreamers' overt behavior.

HYPNOSIS: *Altered State of Consciousness or Social Role Playing?*

At one time in the past, every traveling fair and circus included at least one hypnotist among its performers. The hypnotist would ask for volunteers from the audience and then, before the eyes of hundreds of onlookers, would put these people in what seemed to be a deep trance. Once they were hypnotized, the volunteers would be made to do an assortment of amazing—and sometimes embarrassing—things. They might be told to imagine that they were someone else, or even an animal. Under the hypnotist's commands they would then act this part. Or, having been told that a glass of ammonia contained delightful perfume, they would proceed to sniff it with apparent delight. Sometimes they would be given instructions to perform strange actions after they were awakened from their trance, whenever the hypnotist said a particular word or clapped his hands. Later, the volunteers would obey these previously issued commands, even though they claimed they could not remember the hypnotist's instructions.

Are such seemingly amazing feats actually possible? In other words, is **hypnosis** real? And if so, what is it, and how does it work?

HYPNOSIS: *What It Is and Who Is Susceptible to It*

Let's start with two basic questions: (1) How is hypnotism performed? (2) Is everyone susceptible to it? With respect to the first, standard hypnotic inductions usually involve *suggestions* by the hypnotist that the person being hypnotized feels relaxed, is getting sleepy, and is unable to keep his or her eyes open. Speaking continuously in a calm voice, the hypnotist suggests to the subject that she or he is gradually sinking deeper and deeper into a relaxed state—not sleep, but a state in which the person will not be able to do, think, or say anything without input from the hypnotist. Another technique involves having a person concentrate on a small object, often one that sparkles and can be rotated by the hypnotist. Hypnosis is definitely not sleep, by the way. EEG recordings of a hypnotized person resemble those of normal waking, not any of the sleep stages described earlier (Wallace & Fisher, 1987).

Now for the second question: Can anyone be hypnotized? The answer seems clear: Large individual differences in hypnotizability exist. About 15 percent of adults are highly susceptible (as measured by their response to a graded series of suggestions by the hypnotist); 10 percent are highly resistant; the rest are somewhere in between. In addition, it appears that several traits are related to hypnotic susceptibility (Lynn & Rhue, 1986; Silva & Kirsch, 1992). Specifically, persons who are susceptible to hypnotism tend to:

- Have vivid, frequent fantasies
- Be high in visual imagery

Learning Objective 4.8
Describe hypnosis and the views on the nature of hypnosis.

Hypnosis: An interaction between two persons in which one (the hypnotist) induces changes in the behavior, feelings, or cognitions of the other (the subject) through suggestions. Hypnosis involves subjects' expectations and their attempts to conform to the role of the hypnotized person.

- Be high in the trait of absorption—the tendency to become deeply involved in sensory and imaginative experiences
- Be dependent on others and seek direction from them
- Expect to be influenced by hypnotic suggestions and believe that these will have a powerful effect on them
- Experience more or stronger *dissociative experiences*—experiences in which some portion of the self or memory is split off from the rest

The greater the extent to which individuals possess these characteristics, the greater, in general, is their susceptibility to hypnosis. Recent evidence suggests that this is the case because such persons, to a greater extent than others, can readily imagine the effects suggested by the hypnotist and so tend to translate these into their own behavior (Silva & Kirsch, 1992). You might want to pause here and ask yourself the following question: To what extent do *you* possess the characteristics listed above? To the degree you do, you may be a suitable subject for hypnosis.

It is interesting to note that persons suffering from *bulimia,* a serious eating disorder involving repeated cycles of bingeing and purging, score higher on standard measures of hypnotizability than other persons. Indeed, in one recent study, fifteen out of seventeen bulimics scored very high in hypnotizability—at a level found in only 10 to 15 percent of the general population (Covino et al., 1994). Why are bulimics relatively easy to hypnotize? One possibility is that they are more likely than others to have dissociative experiences—a finding confirmed by recent studies (e.g., Covino et al., 1994). We'll consider other possibilities for the high hypnotizability of bulimics in our discussions of this disorder in chapters 9 and 12.

HYPNOSIS: *Contrasting Views about Its Nature*

Now let's consider a more complex question: What does hypnosis involve? In other words, what changes—if any—does it produce in consciousness and other psychological processes? Systematic research has led to the formulation of two major theories of the nature of hypnosis.

THE SOCIAL-COGNITIVE OR ROLE-PLAYING VIEW
The first of these views suggests that the seemingly strange and mysterious effects of hypnosis can best be understood by reference to the relationship between hypnotized persons and the hypnotist. Specifically, this theory argues that hypnotized persons are actually playing a special *social role*—that of *hypnotic subject*. Having seen movies and read stories about hypnosis, most people have a clear idea of what it supposedly involves. They believe that when hypnotized they will lose control over their own behavior and will be unable to resist strong suggestions from the hypnotist. When exposed to hypnotic inductions (instructions to behave in a certain way or to experience specific feelings), therefore, many people tend to obey, since this is what the social role they are enacting suggests *should* happen. Further, they often report experiencing the changes in perceptions and feelings that they *expect* to experience (e.g., Lynn, Rhue, & Weekes, 1990; Spanos, 1991).

It's important to note that this does not mean that persons undergoing hypnosis engage in conscious efforts to fool others. On the contrary, they sincerely believe that they are experiencing an altered state of consciousness and that they have no choice but to act and feel as the hypnotist suggests. Thus, in an important sense, their behavior and their reports of their experiences while hypnotized are genuine (Kinnunen, Zamansky, & Block, 1994). These behaviors and experiences, however, reflect beliefs about hypnosis and the role of hypnotic subject as much as—or perhaps even more than—the special skills of the hypnotist or the effects of hypnosis on consciousness.

THE NEODISSOCIATION THEORY The second major theory of hypnosis is very different. The **neodissociation theory** suggests that hypnosis operates by inducing two kinds of splits or *dissociations* in consciousness (Bowers, 1990; Hilgard, 1977). The first of these, *dissociated experience*, involves the erection by hypnosis of an amnesia-like barrier that prevents experiences during hypnosis from entering normal consciousness. The second split, known as *dissociated control*, implies a split in normal control over behavior. Persons who have been hypnotized, the theory argues, obey suggestions from the hypnotist in a direct, uncritical fashion; the higher centers of control or *will* are essentially cut out of the picture. According to Hilgard (1977), then, persons who have been hypnotized are in an altered state of consciousness in which one part of their mind accepts suggestions from the hypnotist, while the other part (which Hilgard terms "the hidden observer") observes the procedures without participating in them. So, for example, if hypnotized persons are told to put their arms into icy water but told that they will experience no pain, they will obey and will report no discomfort. However, if asked to describe their feelings in writing, they may indicate that they did experience feelings of intense cold (Hilgard, 1979). So it seems as if one part of consciousness obeys hypnotic suggestions while another does not.

Which of these theories is correct? While support for both views exists (e.g., Miller & Bowers, 1993), most psychologists believe that the social-cognitive view is more accurate. It appears that most of the unusual or bizarre effects observed under hypnosis can readily be explained in terms of hypnotized persons' belief in the effects of hypnotism and their efforts—not necessarily conscious—to behave in accordance with their expectations and the hypnotist's suggestions. Several forms of evidence lend support to this conclusion.

EVIDENCE FOR THE SOCIAL-COGNITIVE VIEW OF HYPNOSIS First, consider the potential effects of hypnosis on memory. Can hypnotism help people remember events they have forgotten? This is an important question, for as we'll see in chapter 6, hypnotism is sometimes used to help eyewitnesses to crimes "remember" events they have observed (Loftus, 1993). Critics of such procedures suggest that, in fact, hypnotism does not improve memory: All it does is induce hypnotized persons to remember what the hypnotist suggests they *should* remember. However, research on this issue indicates that when offered rewards for being accurate, hypnotized persons can do so, despite suggestions from the hypnotist (Murrey, Cross, & Whipple, 1992). These findings suggest that hypnotism does not produce actual changes in memory; rather, it simply suggests to hypnotized persons what they should remember—a conclusion consistent with the social-cognitive view.

Additional evidence for the social-cognitive view is provided by studies focused on the question of whether hypnotism produces actual changes in perception—for example, whether hypnotism can induce people to perceive stimuli that aren't there or render them incapable of perceiving stimuli that are present (Miller & Bowers, 1993; Spanos et al., 1990). Again, the weight of existing evidence suggests that when such effects occur, they do not stem from real changes in perception; rather, they arise out of efforts by hypnotized persons to behave as they think the hypnotist wants them to behave.

In sum, existing evidence offers considerable support for the conclusion that the effects of hypnosis stem mainly from efforts (perhaps unconscious ones) by hypnotized persons to meet the expectations of the hypnotist, plus

Neodissociation Theory: A theory of hypnosis suggesting that hypnotized individuals enter an altered state of consciousness in which consciousness is divided.

KEY QUESTIONS

- What is hypnosis?
- What does the social-cognitive view of hypnosis suggest?
- What does the neodissociation theory of hypnosis suggest?

their beliefs concerning the powerful impact of hypnotism. This does not imply that hypnotism is a fraud or involves actual faking. On the contrary, in describing their experiences when hypnotized, most persons appear to be quite truthful (Kinnumen, Zamansky, & Block, 1994). What existing evidence *does* suggest, in brief, is that hypnotism is better understood in terms of such processes as influence and demand characteristics (see chapter 1) than in terms of mystical powers of hypnotists.

CONSCIOUSNESS-ALTERING DRUGS: *What They Are and What They Do*

Learning Objective 4.9
Describe what consciousness-altering drugs are and what they do.

Learning Objective 4.10
Compare and contrast the different perspectives on why people abuse drugs.

Learning Objective 4.11
List the characteristics of depressants, stimulants, opiates, and hallucinogens.

Drugs are big business in the late twentieth century. Each day, many millions of human beings use drugs to change the way they feel—to alter their moods or states of consciousness. Much of this use of consciousness-altering drugs is completely legal; indeed, many people take such drugs under a physician's supervision. In many other instances, however, people turn to drugs that are illegal, or use legal ones to excess, in the absence of medical advice. Thus, drug use—and abuse—is certainly a serious social problem in the 1990s. In this final section, therefore, we'll consider several issues relating to the use of consciousness-altering drugs.

CONSCIOUSNESS-ALTERING DRUGS: *Some Basic Concepts*

First, what are **drugs**? One widely accepted definition states that they are compounds that, because of their chemical structure, change the structure or function of biological systems (Grilly, 1989). *Consciousness-altering drugs,* therefore, are drugs that produce changes in consciousness when introduced into the body (Wallace & Fisher, 1987).

Suppose you went to your family medicine cabinet and conducted a careful inventory of all the drugs present. How many would you find? Unless your family is very unusual, quite a few. To the extent these drugs were prescribed by a physician and were used for medical purposes, taking them would probably be appropriate. The term **drug abuse**, therefore, is usually restricted to instances in which people take drugs purely to change their moods, and in which they experience impaired behavior or social functioning as a result of doing so (Wallace & Fisher, 1987).

Unfortunately, when people consume consciousness-altering drugs on a regular basis, they often develop **dependence**—they come to need the drug and cannot function without it. Two types of dependence exist. One, **physiological dependence**, occurs when the need for the drug is based on organic factors, such as changes in metabolism. This type of dependence is what is usually meant by the term drug addiction. However, people can also experience **psychological dependence**, in which they experience strong desires to continue using the drug even though, physiologically, their bodies do not need it. As we'll soon see, several psychological mechanisms probably contribute to such dependence. Physiological and psychological dependence often occur together and magnify individuals' cravings for and dependence on specific drugs.

Drugs: Chemical substances that change the structure or function of biological systems.

Drug Abuse: Instances in which individuals take drugs purely to change their moods, and in which they experience impaired behavior or social functioning as a result of doing so.

Dependence: Strong physiological or psychological need for particular drugs.

Physiological Dependence: Strong urges to continue using a drug based on organic factors such as changes in metabolism.

Psychological Dependence: Strong desires to continue using a drug even though it is not physiologically addicting.

Continued use of a drug over a prolonged period of time often leads to drug **tolerance**—a physiological reaction in which the body requires larger and larger doses in order to experience the same effects. Drug tolerance has been observed in connection with many consciousness-altering drugs and often increases the dangers of using these substances. In some cases, use of one drug increases tolerance for another; this is known as **cross-tolerance**.

PSYCHOLOGICAL MECHANISMS UNDERLYING DRUG ABUSE: *Contrasting Views*

On the face of it, drug abuse is a puzzling form of behavior. Recreational use of drugs, after all, carries considerable risk of harm, and long-term drug abuse usually undermines the physical and psychological health of those who adopt such practices. Why, then, do so many people engage in this behavior? Let's consider some contrasting explanations.

THE LEARNING PERSPECTIVE: REWARDING PROPERTIES OF CONSCIOUSNESS-ALTERING DRUGS

Several explanations for why people use consciousness-altering drugs derive from basic principles of learning—principles we'll consider in detail in chapter 5. One approach suggests that people use such drugs because doing so feels good; in other words, the effects produced by the drugs are somehow rewarding (Wise & Bozarth, 1987). Evidence supporting this view is provided by many studies indicating that animals will self-administer many of the same drugs that people abuse, presumably because they find the effects of these drugs rewarding (Young & Herling, 1986).

On the other side of the coin, use of consciousness-altering drugs has also been attributed to the fact that these substances reduce *negative* feelings, such as stress, anxiety, or physical discomfort. Thus, people take drugs to reduce negative feelings rather than simply to generate positive ones (Tiffany, 1990). This explanation is especially applicable to cases in which individuals have become physiologically dependent on a drug; the negative symptoms they experience when it is no longer consumed—known as *withdrawal*—may provide a powerful incentive to obtain the drug again at all costs.

THE PSYCHODYNAMIC PERSPECTIVE: COPING WITH UNCONSCIOUS FEARS AND DESIRES

As we saw in chapter 1, the psychodynamic perspective views human behavior as stemming from unconscious conflicts among hidden aspects of personality. This perspective points to another, and very different, explanation for drug abuse: Perhaps individuals use drugs to reduce or at least conceal the anxiety generated by such inner turmoil. While this is an intriguing idea, it is very difficult to test empirically. Thus, it currently receives little attention from psychologists.

THE SOCIAL PERSPECTIVE: DRUG ABUSE AND SOCIAL PRESSURE

A third perspective suggests that drug abuse can be understood largely in terms of social factors. According to this view, individuals—especially adolescents and young adults—use consciousness-altering drugs because it is the "in" thing to do. They observe their friends using these substances and experience pressure—subtle or overt—to join them (Mann, Chassin, & Sher, 1987). You may well have experienced such pressure yourself; if so, you know hard it can be to resist. We'll examine social influence in detail in chapter 14.

THE COGNITIVE PERSPECTIVE: DRUG ABUSE AS AUTOMATIC BEHAVIOR

Another, and very intriguing, perspective on the use of consciousness-altering drugs has been proposed by Tiffany (1990). He suggests that in many cases, drug abuse represents a kind of automatic processing on the part of the

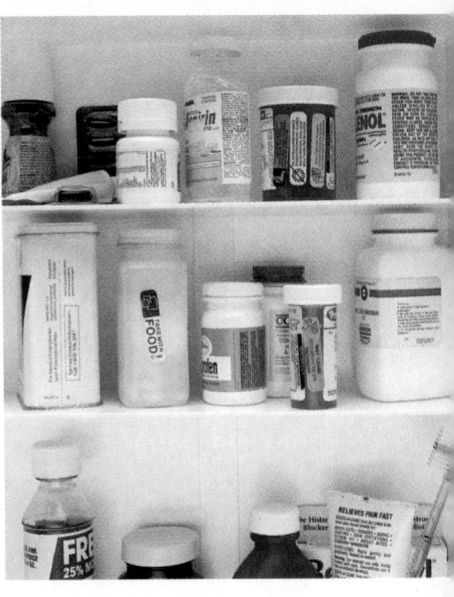

DRUGS AT HOME

Does your medicine cabinet look like this one? Most people have a variety of consciousness-altering drugs in their homes.

Tolerance: Habituation to a drug, causing larger and larger doses to be required to produce effects of the same magnitude.

Cross-Tolerance: Increased tolerance for one drug that develops as a result of taking another drug.

persons involved. As individuals use various drugs, Tiffany contends, the cognitive systems controlling many aspects of obtaining the drugs and consuming them take on the character of automatic processes. As we discussed earlier in this chapter, this implies that drug use becomes quick and relatively effortless, occurs without conscious intention, is difficult to inhibit, and may even take place in the absence of conscious awareness. Thus, once they have used a drug on a considerable number of occasions, individuals may find themselves responding almost automatically to external cues—for example, a specific environment in which the drug has often been enjoyed, such as a bar, or specific sights and smells associated with drug use, such as the aroma of a burning cigarette. In a similar manner, they may respond automatically to internal cues or emotions, such as wanting to celebrate or feeling tired or out of sorts. These cues may trigger people's tendencies to use drugs, and they may find themselves doing so before they realize it, even without any strong urge to take a drug.

Do you remember the DAMIT dreams—dreams of absent-minded transgression—reported by many persons trying to give up tobacco or alcohol? The content of such dreams captures the kind of automatic drug use suggested by Tiffany. Note that according to Tiffany (1990), strong urges or cravings are not necessary for drug use to occur; such behavior may be initiated in the absence of these urges by appropriate internal or external stimuli.

Tiffany's model has not yet been subjected to extensive test. However, many findings concerning drug abuse appear to be consistent with it. For example, it has often been noted that individuals who were once addicted to a drug and stopped using it are more likely to relapse into using it when experiencing high levels of stress than at other times (Bliss et al., 1989). Tiffany explains these relapses by suggesting that at such times, individuals must use part of their cognitive resources to deal with the stress, thus leaving fewer resources to focus on continued abstinence. The result: they resort to patterns of automatic processing, and this leads them to their drug relapse. Despite such indirect support, Tiffany's (1990) theory must be subjected to additional, systematic testing before it can be accepted. Still, it seems to offer important insights into the nature of drug abuse and drug addiction. As such, the theory deserves further careful attention.

KEY QUESTIONS

• Why do people use drugs?

• What are physiological and psychological dependence on drugs?

• How does the learning perspective explain drug abuse?

• How does the social perspective explain drug abuse?

• How does the cognitive perspective explain drug abuse?

CONSCIOUSNESS-ALTERING DRUGS: An Overview

While many different drugs affect consciousness, most seem to fit under one of four major headings: *depressants, stimulants, opiates,* or *psychedelics and hallucinogens.* Please note that these categories are based on the psychological effects of various drugs, not their chemical nature. Several drugs can exert similar effects on mood or consciousness but have fundamentally different chemical formulas, and some drugs with similar chemical formulas can exert very different psychological effects (Pinel, 1993).

DEPRESSANTS Drugs that reduce both behavioral output and activity in the central nervous system are called **depressants**. Perhaps the most important of these is *alcohol,* undoubtedly the most widely consumed drug in the world. Small doses of alcohol seem, subjectively, to be stimulating—they induce feelings of excitement and activation. Larger doses, however, act as a depres-

Depressants: Drugs that reduce activity in the nervous system and therefore slow many bodily and cognitive processes. Depressants include alcohol and barbiturates.

sant. They dull the senses so that feelings of pain, cold, and other forms of discomfort become less intense. This is why alcohol was widely used to deaden the pain of medical operations before more effective anesthetics became available. Large doses of alcohol also interfere with coordination and normal functioning of our senses, often with tragic results for motorists, and may disrupt information processing in several respects. Alcohol also lowers social inhibitions. After consuming large quantities of this drug, people often become more prone to engage in dangerous forms of behavior and more generally unrestrained in their words and actions. Alcohol may produce its pleasurable effects by stimulating special receptors in the brain. Its depressant effects may stem from the fact that it interferes with the capacity of neurons to conduct nerve impulses, perhaps by affecting the cell membrane directly.

Barbiturates, which are contained in sleeping pills and relaxants, constitute a second type of depressant. First manufactured in the late nineteenth century, these drugs depress activity in the central nervous system and reduce activation and mental alertness. How these effects are produced is not certain, but existing evidence suggests that barbiturates may reduce the release of excitatory neurotransmitters by neurons in many different locations. Initially, high doses of barbiturates can produce feelings of relaxation and euphoria—a kind of drunkenness without alcohol. They often go on to produce serious confusion, slurred speech, memory lapses, and reduced ability to concentrate. Wide swings of emotion, from euphoria to depression, are also common. Extremely large doses can be fatal, because they result in paralysis of centers of the brain that regulate respiration. This is a real danger, since tolerance to barbiturates gradually develops, so individuals find it necessary to increase the doses they consume to obtain the same effects.

Because some barbiturates induce sleep, people often try to use them to treat sleep disorders such as insomnia. However, these drugs do not seem to produce normal sleep. In particular, REM sleep is suppressed and may rebound after individuals stop taking the drugs.

STIMULANTS Drugs that produce the opposite effects, feelings of energy and activation, are known as **stimulants**. Included in this category are **amphetamines** and **cocaine**. Both of these stimulants inhibit the reuptake of the neurotransmitters dopamine and norepinephrine. As a result, neurons that would otherwise stop firing continue to respond. Such drugs raise blood pressure, heart rate, and respiration—all signs of activation or arousal produced by the sympathetic nervous system. In addition, stimulants yield short periods of pleasurable sensations, twenty to forty minutes during which users feel incredibly powerful and energetic. Users pay dearly for such feelings, however, for as the drug wears off they often experience an emotional crash marked by strong anxiety, depression, and fatigue.

In the past, cocaine was widely hailed as a valuable medical drug and was added to many patent medicines. Freud believed that it was useful in treating such varied illnesses as asthma, indigestion, and even addiction to alcohol or morphine. But continued use of cocaine can produce harmful effects, including a loss of appetite and intense feelings of anxiety, so it is clearly a dangerous drug.

Cocaine is usually consumed by *snorting*, a process in which it is inhaled into each nostril. There it is absorbed through the mucous lining directly into the bloodstream. Cocaine can also be swallowed, usually in liquid form, but this produces weaker effects. When cocaine is heated and treated chemically, a form known as **crack** is produced. This can be smoked, and when it is, the drug affects the brain almost instantly. This produces a high during which individuals experience powerful feelings of energy, confidence, and excitement. While cocaine is not usually considered to be addicting, it often pro-

Barbiturates: Drugs that act as depressants, reducing activity in the nervous system and behavior output.

Stimulants: Drugs that increase activity in the nervous system, including amphetamines, caffeine, and nicotine.

Amphetamines: Drugs that act as stimulants, increasing feelings of energy and activation.

Cocaine: A powerful stimulant that produces pleasurable sensations of increased energy and self-confidence.

Crack: A cocaine derivative that can be smoked. It acts as a powerful stimulant.

duces strong psychological dependence. And crack appears to have even stronger effects of this type. In order to obtain it, heavy users turn to prostitution, theft, and anything else they can think of that will provide enough money for the next "hit," or dose.

Other stimulants in common use include *caffeine*, found in coffee, tea, and many soft drinks, and *nicotine*, found in tobacco.

RIVER PHOENIX (1970–1993)

This actor's life was tragically cut short by a lethal combination of drugs.

OPIATES Among the most dangerous drugs in widespread use are the **opiates**. These drugs include *opium, morphine, heroin,* and related synthetic drugs. Opium is derived from the opium poppy; remember the scene in *The Wizard of Oz* when Dorothy falls asleep amidst a field of beautiful poppies? Morphine is produced from opium, while heroin is obtained from morphine. Opiates produce lethargy and a pronounced slowing of almost all bodily functions. These drugs also alter consciousness, producing a dreamlike state and, for some people, intensely pleasurable sensations. The costs associated with these pleasurable sensations are high, however. Heroin and other opiates are extremely addicting, and withdrawal from them often produces agony for former users. Growing evidence indicates that the brain produces substances (*opioid peptides* or *endorphins*) closely related to the opiates in chemical structure and contains special receptors for them (Phillips & Fibiger, 1989). This suggests one possible explanation for the discomfort experienced by opiate users during withdrawal. Regular use of opiates soon overloads endorphin receptors within the brain. As a result, the brain ceases production of these substances. When the drugs are withdrawn, endorphin levels remain depressed. Thus, an important internal mechanism for regulating pain is disrupted (Reid, 1990).

Tolerance for opiates such as heroin increases rapidly with use, so physiological addiction can occur very quickly. The withdrawal symptoms that result when addicts cannot obtain the drug are truly agonizing. Indeed, they are so painful that addicts will go to incredible lengths, and take incredible risks, in order to obtain a steady supply of the drug.

PSYCHEDELICS AND HALLUCINOGENS Perhaps the drugs with the most profound effects on consciousness are the **psychedelics**, drugs that alter sensory perception and so may be considered mind-expanding, and **hallucinogens**, drugs that generate sensory perception for which there are no external stimuli. The most widely used psychedelic drug is *marijuana*. Known use of marijuana dates back to ancient times; indeed, it is described in a Chinese guide to medicines dating from 2737 B.C. Marijuana was widely used in the United States and elsewhere for medical purposes as late as the 1920s. It could be found in almost any drugstore and purchased without a prescription, like aspirin today. It was often prescribed by physicians for headaches, cramps, and even ulcers. Starting in the 1920s, however, the tide of public opinion shifted, efforts were made to make the drug illegal, and by 1937 marijuana was outlawed completely in the United States. When smoked or eaten, as when baked into cookies or cakes, marijuana produces moderate arousal in the form of increased blood pressure and pulse rate; a perceived increase in the intensity of various stimuli, such as sounds, colors, tastes, and smells; and distortion in the sense of time, such as a feeling that more time has elapsed during a given period than is actually the case. Unfortunately, marijuana also interferes with the ability to judge distances, an effect that can lead to serious accidents when users of the drug drive a car or operate other equipment. Other effects reported by some, but not all, users include reduced inhibitions, increased sexual pleasure (which may simply reflect increased sensitivity to all sensations), and feelings of relaxation. Some findings, but by no means

Opiates: *Drugs that induce a dreamy, relaxed state and, in some persons, intense feelings of pleasure. Opiates exert their effects by stimulating special receptor sites within the brain.*

Psychedelics: *Drugs that alter sensory perception and so may be considered mind-expanding.*

Hallucinogens: *Drugs that profoundly alter consciousness, such as LSD.*

CHAPTER 4

all, also suggest that marijuana use may interfere with memory (Miller, Cornelius, & McFarland, 1978).

Marijuana is in widespread use throughout the world, mostly as a recreational drug. Unfortunately, there have been few studies of its long-term effects. The research that has been performed reports few adverse effects (e.g., Page, Fletcher, & True, 1988). Yet continued use of marijuana poses certain dangers. First, as already noted, the perceptual distortions it produces can result in tragedy when users attempt to drive or operate power machinery. Also, because it is still illegal in many nations, marijuana is often blended with other substances, so users never know exactly what they are getting. Third, there is some indication that long-term use of marijuana may result in shifts in personality toward passivity and a general lack of motivation (Baumrind, 1984). These potential risks should be carefully weighed against the potential pleasures some people report finding in this drug.

Much more dramatic effects are produced by *hallucinogens*—drugs that produce vivid hallucinations and other perceptual shifts. Of these, the most famous is **LSD** (lysergic acid diethylamide), or *acid*. After taking LSD, many persons report profound changes in perceptions of the external world. Objects and people seem to change color and shape; walls may sway and move; and many sensations seem more intense than normal. There may also be a strange blending of sensory experiences known as *synesthesia*. Music yields visual sensations, while colors produce feelings of warmth or cold.

Such effects may sound exciting or even pleasant, but many others produced by LSD are quite negative. Objects, people, and even one's own body may seem distorted or threatening. Users may experience deep sorrow or develop intense fear of close friends and relatives. Perhaps worst of all, the effects of this drug are unpredictable; there is no way of determining in advance whether LSD will yield mostly pleasant or mostly unpleasant sensations. In fact, the same person may experience radically different effects at different times. Unless you are willing to gamble with your own health, therefore, LSD is certainly a drug to avoid. An overview of various drugs and their effects is provided by the **Key Concept** on page 150.

> ### KEY QUESTIONS
>
> - What are the effects of depressants?
> - What are the effects of stimulants?
> - What are the effects of opiates?
> - What are the effects of psychedelics and hallucinogens?
> - What factors determine the behavioral effects of a given drug?

A Note on the Psychology of Drugs' Effects

In my comments so far, I may have given you the impression that drugs always produce specific effects. Before concluding, I should point out that this impression would not be fully accurate. While specific drugs do generally produce the effects described above, their impact may vary, depending on many other factors.

First, the impact of drugs is often determined by expectations. If users expect a drug to produce certain effects (increase their sex drive, reduce their inhibitions, put them in a good mood), such effects are much more likely to occur than if users do not anticipate them.

Second, drug effects depend on users' physical state. Some people are naturally more tolerant of various drugs than others. In addition, the influence of a specific drug may depend on whether the person taking it is fatigued or well rested, whether he or she has recently eaten, and many other factors.

Third, the effects of various drugs depend on previous experience. First-time users of alcohol or tobacco generally report very different reactions to

LSD: A powerful hallucinogen that produces profound shifts in perception; many of these are frightening in nature.

Effects of Consciousness-Altering Drugs

Depressants

Reduce behavioral output and activity in the central nervous system

Alcohol

- Deadens pain
- Reduces coordination
- Interferes with normal functioning of senses
- Reduces social inhibitions

Barbiturates

- Reduced mental alertness
- Sleep
- Confusion
- Euphoria
- Memory lapses, inability to concentrate
- Suppression of REM sleep

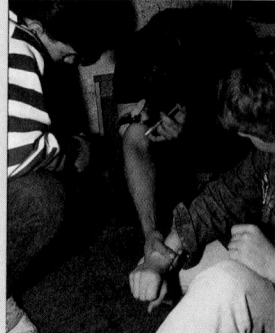

Stimulants

Induce feelings of energy and activation

Amphetamines

- Elevation of blood pressure, heart rate, respiration
- Feelings of alertness, energy, followed by depression as effects wear off

Caffeine

- Mild feelings of increased alertness
- Mild diuretic effect (increased urination)

Cocaine and Derivatives (including Crack)

- Feelings of tremendous power and energy
- Intense pleasurable sensations
- Psychological dependence (cocaine)
- Powerful addiction (crack)

Opiates

Produce lethargy and pronounced slowing of almost all bodily functions; induce a dreamlike state and pleasurable sensations

Opium

- Deadens pain
- Produces dreamlike state
- Highly addicting
- Causes pleasurable sensations, feelings

Heroin

- Like opium and morphine, but pleasurable sensations are intensified; described by some users as "a whole body orgasm"
- Extremely addicting

Morphine

- Similar to opium but even more pronounced

Psychedelics and Hallucinogens

Psychedelics alter sensory perception; sometimes viewed as mind-expanding. Hallucinogens generate sensory perceptions for which there are no external stimuli

Psychedelics (e.g., Marijuana)

- Moderate arousal
- Increased intensity of various stimuli
- Distortions in sense of time
- Diminished ability to judge distances
- Feelings of increased sexual pleasure for some persons
- Feelings of relaxation

Hallucinogens (e.g., LSD)

- Profound changes in perceptions of external world
- Blending of sensory experiences
- Objects seem to change shape
- Ordinary situations may become threatening or frightening
- Effects of drugs vary greatly on different people

these substances than people who have used them for quite some time. The same thing is true for many other drugs that alter mood or consciousness.

Finally, the influence of a given drug depends on what other drugs users are also taking. In medicine, careful physicians check on the possibility of drug interactions, in which the impact of a drug is altered by the presence of other drugs, before issuing prescriptions. People who take various illegal drugs, however, rarely consider possible interactions between them—sometimes with tragic results.

MAKING PSYCHOLOGY PART OF YOUR LIFE

Meditation: A Technique for Inducing Potentially Beneficial Shifts in Consciousness

For centuries, travelers from the West who visited India returned with tales of amazing feats performed by *yogis*—members of special religious orders who seemed to possess incredible powers. Such persons, it was reported, could walk barefoot over hot coals and lie on beds of nails without experiencing pain. Perhaps even more astounding, some seemed able to enter a self-induced trance in which they could bring their own hearts to a virtual stop!

Were such reports actually true? Existing evidence is mixed, at best, but one fact *is* clear: There are indeed techniques through which at least some individuals can produce important shifts in consciousness and enter a state in which they are less responsive than usual to the external world (Shapiro, 1980). Several techniques for producing such changes exist, but among these *meditation* is by far the most popular.

Meditation involves procedures designed to produce altered states of consciousness in which awareness of and contact with the external world are reduced. Many different varieties of meditation exist. One technique that attained widespread popularity during the 1970s is known as *transcendental meditation* (TM for short). Practitioners of TM repeat a word or set of words, known as their *mantra*, over and over again, focusing their attention entirely on this activity and on the mantra rather than on the world around them. If they find their thoughts beginning to wander to something else, they attempt to bring them back to the mantra. This requires considerable cognitive discipline, but this skill must be learned if meditation is to be successful.

Why should anyone bother to meditate? Are there any real benefits from this procedure? Research designed to investigate the physiological effects of meditation suggests that there are. Such research indicates that during meditation, and especially during TM, significant and potentially beneficial changes do occur in basic biological processes. For example, in one well-known study on the effects of TM, Wallace and Ben-son (1972) found that during meditation people's oxygen consumption decreased, their heartbeat slowed, and they showed stronger alpha brain waves (see Figure 4.4 on page 152). In other words, they experienced several signs of relaxation and reduced tension. While some researchers suggest that one can obtain similar effects simply by resting (Holmes, 1984), others contend that greater and more general shifts in physiological processes are produced by meditation (Benson & Friedman, 1985). Additional evidence indicates that after adopting TM, many people report finding it easier to give up the use of various drugs, including marijuana, amphetamines, and barbiturates (Marzetta, Benson, & Wallace, 1972). So meditation does seem to have several potential benefits.

Can you enjoy such benefits yourself, without special training and without joining a religious group that makes meditation the center of its philosophy? Yes; transcendental meditation is a relatively simple technique and requires only a few minutes each day. To put it into practice, follow these steps:

1. *Find a quiet, isolated location.* TM doesn't require lots of time, but it *does* require you to focus your attention inward, away from the outside world. So the first requirement is that you find a quiet physical location where you can be alone for twenty minutes to half an hour.

2. *Choose an appropriate mantra.* Meditation derives historically from Buddhism and Hinduism. Thus, in its original form, TM involved choosing a mantra from religious writings. This is not necessary; your mantra can be almost any word or phrase on which you can concentrate.

3. *Meditate.* Repeat your mantra silently, over and over again, and focus your attention only on this word. The hardest part of meditation is learning to keep your thoughts from slipping away from the mantra and back to the normal worries, cares, and concerns of everyday

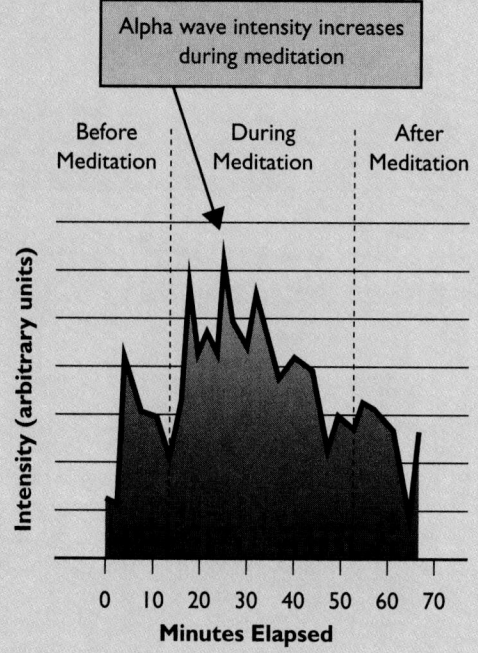

FIGURE 4.4 — Physiological Changes during Meditation

During meditation individuals experience changes in several basic physiological processes. Oxygen consumption decreases and the intensity of alpha waves increases.
(*Source:* Based on data from Wallace & Benson, 1972.)

Oxygen consumption drops during meditation

Alpha wave intensity increases during meditation

Before Meditation | During Meditation | After Meditation

Oxygen Consumption per Minute (cubic cm)

Minutes Elapsed

Intensity (arbitrary units)

Minutes Elapsed

---

life. At first you may find this difficult, but if you practice and really try, you can acquire such discipline.

4. *Continue meditating for fifteen to twenty minutes.* As you master the skill of focusing your attention on the mantra and screening out other distracting thoughts, gradually increase your period of meditation to fifteen or twenty minutes. (Initially, five to ten minutes will suffice.) If possible, meditate several times each week, especially on days when you feel stressed.

What benefits can you expect to obtain from meditating? Research findings suggest that benefits may include reduced feelings of tension, increased ability to express your feelings freely, and reduced levels of anxiety (Greenberg, 1991). Of course, TM is not for everyone, and if you find it difficult or unappealing, you should consider other techniques for gaining these benefits. If you do find meditation to your liking, however, you may wish to make it part of your daily life.

BIOLOGICAL RHYTHMS: TIDES OF LIFE—AND CONSCIOUS EXPERIENCE

- **What are biological rhythms?**

Biological rhythms are regular fluctuations in our bodily processes.

- **How long is the cycle for many of our bodily processes?**

Many of our bodily processes take place on a twenty-four-hour cycle, regulated by a biological clock that is located in a portion of the hypothalamus and affected by visual input.

- **What are larks and owls?**

Larks are people whose circadian rhythms make them most alert and active early in the day; owls tend to experience their peaks later in the day.

- **What effects do jet lag and shift work have on circadian rhythms?**

Travel across time zones and shift work can produce disturbances in circadian rhythms. Knowledge of circadian rhythms suggests effective ways of countering such disturbances.

KEY TERMS: states of consciousness, p. 122; biological rhythms, p. 122; circadian rhythms, p. 123; suprachiasmatic nucleus, p. 124; seasonal affective disorder, p. 124

WAKING STATES OF CONSCIOUSNESS: EVERYDAY EXPERIENCE

- **What is the difference between automatic processing and controlled processing?**

We are capable of performing many activities without directing conscious attention to them. Such automatic processing does not require much, if any, of our limited attention capacity. In contrast, controlled processing requires conscious attention and does use information-processing capacity.

- **What are daydreams and fantasies and what functions do they serve?**

Daydreams and fantasies are alterations in consciousness commonly experienced while we are awake. They may serve several useful functions, such as providing temporary escape from stress and boredom and improving our moods.

- **What happens when we focus our attention inward?**

When we focus our attention on ourselves, we enter a state of self-consciousness, in which we compare our current state with important goals and values.

- **What effect does increased self-consciousness have on the performance of skilled activities?**

Self-consciousness can reduce performance on skilled tasks; however, it is also an important first step toward increased self-insight.

KEY TERMS: automatic processing, p. 127; controlled processing, p. 127; daydreams, p. 128; fantasies, p. 128; hallucinations, p. 129; self-consciousness, p. 129; control theory of self-consciousness, p. 131; choking under pressure, p. 131

SLEEP: THE PAUSE THAT REFRESHES?

- **What is an EEG?**

An EEG is a recording of electrical activity in the brain, which can be used for studying sleep.

- **What distinguishes major stages of sleep?**

As we sleep, we pass through several different stages in which changes occur in brain activity and awareness of the external world.

- **What happens during REM sleep?**

During REM sleep the EEG shows a pattern similar to that of waking, but the activity of body muscles is almost totally suppressed. Most dreams occur during REM sleep.

- **What are the effects of sleep deprivation?**

Although people undergoing sleep deprivation report feeling tired and irritable, they can function quite well even after long periods without sleep.

- **What functions does sleep serve?**

Growing evidence indicates that sleep serves important functions that are related to restoration of bodily resources and circadian rhythms.

- **What are some common types of sleep disorders?**

Insomnia is difficulty in falling asleep; somnambulism is walking in one's sleep; narcolepsy is a tendency to fall suddenly into a deep sleep in the midst of waking activities.

- **During what sleep stage do dreams usually occur?**

Dreams occur primarily during REM sleep.

- **What was Freud's explanation for the occurrence of dreams?**

Freud believed that dreams reflect our suppressed thoughts, wishes, and impulses.

- **What does the physiological view of dreams suggest?**

The physiological view suggests that dreams reflect the brain's interpretation of random neural activity occurring during sleep.

- **What does the cognitive view of dreams suggest?**

The cognitive view suggests that dreams result from the fact that many systems of the brain are active during sleep while input from muscles and sensory systems is inhibited.

- **What is the effect of cultural factors on dreams?**

Cross-cultural research indicates that the content and meaning of dreams are strongly influenced by the dreamer's culture.

KEY TERMS: *sleep, p. 132; electroencephalogram (EEG), p. 132; alpha waves, p. 132; delta waves, p. 132; REM sleep, p. 133; insomnia, p. 135; somnambulism, p. 136; night terrors, p. 136; apnea, p. 136; hypersomnias, p. 136; narcolepsy, p. 136; dreams, p. 137; manifest content, p. 138; latent content, p. 138; dreams of absent-minded transgression, p. 140*

HYPNOSIS: ALTERED STATE OF CONSCIOUSNESS OR SOCIAL ROLE PLAYING?

- **What is hypnosis?**

Hypnosis involves a condition in which individuals are highly susceptible to suggestions from others.

- **What does the social-cognitive view of hypnosis suggest?**

The social-cognitive view suggests that the effects of hypnosis stem from the hypnotized person's expectations and his or her efforts to play the role of hypnotized subject.

- **What does the neodissociation theory of hypnosis suggest?**

The neodissociation theory suggests that hypnotism involves splits in consciousness; hypnotized persons are unaware of experiences during hypnosis and cannot exert normal control over their behavior.

KEY TERMS: *hypnosis, p. 141; neodissociation theory, p. 143*

CONSCIOUSNESS-ALTERING DRUGS: WHAT THEY ARE AND WHAT THEY DO

- **Why do people use drugs?**

People often use drugs to alter their states of consciousness, as well as for medical reasons.

- **What are physiological and psychological dependence on drugs?**

Physiological dependence involves strong urges to continue using a drug because of organic factors such as changes in metabolism. Psychological dependence involves strong desires to continue using a drug even though it is not physiologically addicting.

- **How does the learning perspective explain drug abuse?**

The learning perspective suggests that drug abuse occurs because people find the effects of consciousness-altering drugs rewarding or because these drugs help to lessen stress, anxiety, and other negative feelings.

- **How does the social perspective explain drug abuse?**

The social perspective suggests that people abuse drugs because of strong social pressures to do so.

- **How does the cognitive perspective explain drug abuse?**

The cognitive perspective proposes that drug abuse may be at least in part an automatic behavior triggered by the presence of external cues.

- **What are the effects of depressants?**

Depressants reduce both behavioral output and activity in the central nervous system. Important depressants include alcohol and barbiturates.

- **What are the effects of stimulants?**

Stimulants produce feelings of energy and activation. Amphetamines and cocaine are examples of stimulants.

- **What are the effects of opiates?**

Opiates produce lethargy and pronounced slowing of almost all bodily functions, but also induce intense feelings of pleasure in some persons. Morphine and heroin fall within this category.

- **What are the effects of psychedelics and hallucinogens?**

Psychedelics such as marijuana alter sensory perception, while hallucinogens such as LSD produce vivid hallucinations and other bizarre perceptual effects.

- **What factors determine the behavioral effects of a given drug?**

A specific dose of a given drug may have very different effects for the same person at different times, depending on such factors as the person's expectations, his or her physical state, and other drugs he or she has taken recently.

KEY TERMS: *drugs, p. 144; drug abuse, p. 144; dependence, p. 144; physiological dependence, p. 144; psychological dependence, p. 144; tolerance, p. 145; cross-tolerance, p. 145; depressants, p. 146; barbiturates, p. 147; stimulants, p. 147; amphetamines, p. 147; cocaine, p. 147; crack, p. 147; opiates, p. 148; psychedelics, p. 148; hallucinogens, p. 148; LSD, p. 149*

CRITICAL THINKING QUESTIONS

APPRAISAL	Today, most psychologists believe that states of consciousness can be studied in a scientific manner. Do you agree? Or do you feel that this is stretching the banner of science beyond the breaking point? Why do you hold the opinion that you do?
CONTROVERSY	Hypnotism is one of the most controversial topics of research in modern psychology. Many psychologists doubt that hypnosis represents an altered state of consciousness, while others believe that it does. What are your views on this issue?
MAKING PSYCHOLOGY PART OF YOUR LIFE	Now that you have some basic understanding of biological rhythms, states of consciousness, self-consciousness, and the nature of sleep, try to think of ways in which you can put this knowledge to practical use. For example, what steps might you take to schedule your day so as to take advantage of high points in your own circadian rhythms? How can you help assure that you get a good night's sleep as often as possible? List at least three ways in which you can benefit from your increased understanding of various states of consciousness.

Learning:

How We're Changed by Experience

*H*ave you ever gotten ill after eating a favorite food—and wondered why, even years later, just the thought of it makes you feel sick? How do animals at Sea World learn to perform complex sequences of behaviors, while your dog does not seem to comprehend even simple commands like "sit"? Does watching violence on television cause children to perform violent acts? Why do gamblers continue to put money into slot machines, even after losing a bundle? If you've wondered about issues like these, then you are already familiar with one of the most basic topics in psychology—*learning*. Indeed, the learning process is crucial to all organisms, including people, since it helps us adapt to changing conditions in the world around us.

In this chapter we'll examine several basic principles that help to explain how many forms of behavior are affected by experience. Psychologists refer to these effects on behavior as learning. Specifically, they define **learning** as *any relatively permanent change in behavior, or behavior potential, produced by experience*. Several aspects of this definition are noteworthy. First, the term *learning* does not apply to temporary changes in behavior such as those stemming from fatigue, drugs, or illness. Second, it does not refer to changes resulting from maturation—the fact that you change in many ways as you grow and develop. Third, learning can result from *vicarious* as well as from direct experiences; in other words, you can be affected by observing events and behavior in your environment as well as by participating in them (Bandura, 1986). Finally, the changes produced by learning are not always positive in nature. As you well know, people are as likely to acquire bad habits as good ones.

There can be no doubt that learning is a key process in human behavior. Indeed, it appears to play an important role in virtually every activity we perform—from mastering complex skills to falling in love. Although the effects of learning are diverse, many psychologists believe that learning occurs in several basic forms: *classical conditioning*, *operant conditioning*, and *observational learning*. We'll begin with *classical conditioning*, a form of learning in which two stimulus events become associated in such a way that the occurrence of one event reliably predicts the occurrence of the other. Classical conditioning is the basis for many learned fears and also helps explain how we acquire taste aversions. Next, we'll turn to *operant conditioning*, a form of learning in which organisms learn associations between behaviors and their consequences. Here, we'll see how psychologists have applied basic operant principles to promote certain behaviors, such as using safety belts, conserving energy, and recycling. Finally, we'll explore *observational learning*, a form of learning in which organisms learn by observing the behaviors—and the consequences of the behaviors—of others around them.

CLASSICAL CONDITIONING: *Learning That Some Stimuli Signal Others*

Learning Objective 5.1
Describe classical conditioning and survey the basic principles of classical conditioning.

Learning Objective 5.2
Discuss what the research on acquired taste aversion has told us about the traditional principles of classical conditioning.

Learning: Any relatively permanent change in behavior (or behavior potential) resulting from experience.

Consider the following situation: During a particularly hectic semester, you find yourself with a class schedule that leaves absolutely no time for lunch. After a few days, you lose your ability to concentrate during your afternoon classes because all you can think about is food. A friend tells you about a vending area where she buys microwaveable snacks, including popcorn. As it turns out, this solution works out well; you love popcorn, it is ready in only a few minutes, and you find that it is even possible to do other things while the popcorn is popping—like cram for tests—since a loud beep from the microwave signals when the popcorn is done. When you open the door of the microwave, the delightful aroma of freshly popped popcorn rushes out, causing you to salivate in anticipation of eating it. After several days, however, your mouth waters immediately after the beep, before you actually open the door to the microwave. Why should this occur? After all, at this point you can neither see nor smell the popcorn. The reason is actually fairly simple: Since the beep is always followed by the aroma and taste of the popcorn, the beep comes to serve as a signal. Just hearing the beep, you expect

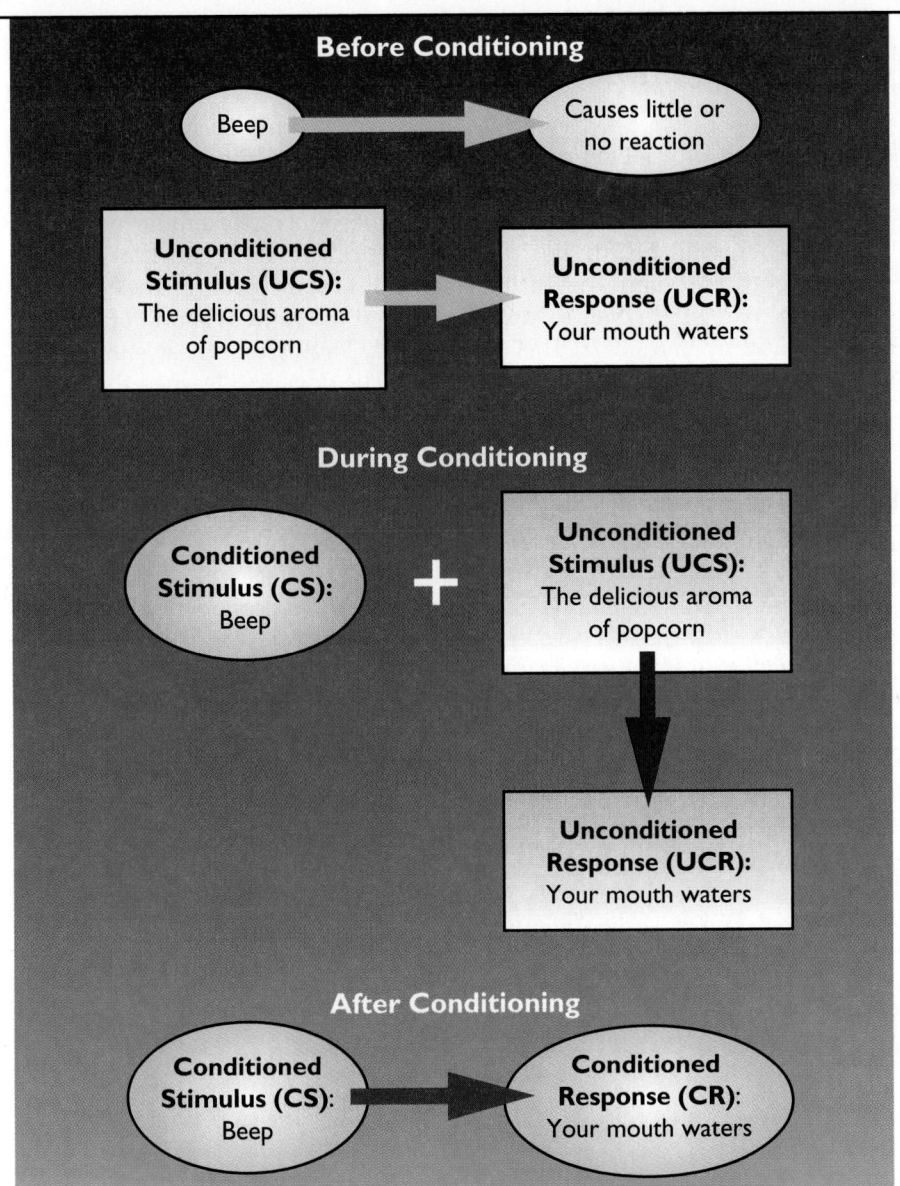

Before Conditioning

Beep → Causes little or no reaction

Unconditioned Stimulus (UCS): The delicious aroma of popcorn → Unconditioned Response (UCR): Your mouth waters

During Conditioning

Conditioned Stimulus (CS): Beep + Unconditioned Stimulus (UCS): The delicious aroma of popcorn → Unconditioned Response (UCR): Your mouth waters

After Conditioning

Conditioned Stimulus (CS): Beep → Conditioned Response (CR): Your mouth waters

FIGURE 5.1

Classical Conditioning: A Simple Example

At first, the sound of the microwave's beep may startle you and cause you to look toward its source, but it will probably not cause you to salivate. However, after the beep has been paired with the aroma and taste of the popcorn on several occasions, you may find that you salivate to the beep alone. This "mouth-watering" reaction is a result of classical conditioning.

the smell and taste of the popcorn to follow, and you react accordingly (see Figure 5.1).

The situation just described is a common example of **classical conditioning**, the first type of learning that we will consider. In classical conditioning, a physical event—termed a **stimulus**—that initially does not elicit a particular response gradually acquires the capacity to elicit that response as a result of repeated pairing with a stimulus that *can* elicit a reaction. Learning of this type is quite common and seems to play a role in such varied reactions as strong fears, taste aversions, some aspects of sexual behavior, and even racial or ethnic prejudice (Baron & Byrne, 1994). Classical conditioning became the subject of careful study in the early twentieth century, when Ivan Pavlov, a Nobel Prize–winning physiologist from Russia, identified it as an important behavioral process.

Classical Conditioning: A basic form of learning in which one stimulus comes to serve as a signal for the occurrence of a second stimulus. During classical conditioning, organisms acquire information about the relations between various stimuli, not simple associations between them.

Stimulus: A physical event capable of affecting behavior.

Learning Objective 5.3
Describe the cognitive perspective on classical conditioning.

Learning Objective 5.4
Discuss the ways in which classical conditioning can be used in therapy.

Unconditioned Stimulus (UCS): In classical conditioning, a stimulus that can elicit an unconditioned response the first time it is presented.

Unconditioned Response (UCR): In classical conditioning, the response elicited by an unconditioned stimulus.

Conditioned Stimulus (CS): In classical conditioning, the stimulus that is repeatedly paired with an unconditioned stimulus.

Conditioned Response (CR): In classical conditioning, the response to the conditioned stimulus.

PAVLOV'S EARLY WORK ON CLASSICAL CONDITIONING: *Does This Ring a Bell?*

In one of those strange twists of fate that seem so common in the history of science, Pavlov did not set out to investigate classical conditioning. Rather, his research focused on the process of digestion in dogs. During his investigations he noticed a curious fact: Similar to the popcorn example described above, the dogs in his studies often began to salivate when they saw or smelled food but before they actually tasted it. Some even salivated at the sight of the pan where their food was kept or at the sight or sound of the person who usually brought it. This suggested to Pavlov that these stimuli had somehow become signals for the food itself: The dogs had learned that when the signals were present, food would soon follow.

Pavlov quickly recognized the potential importance of this observation and shifted the focus of his research accordingly. The procedures that he now developed were relatively simple. Dogs were placed in an apparatus similar to that shown in Figure 5.2. On *conditioning trials,* a neutral stimulus that had previously been shown to have no effect on salivation—a bell, for example—was presented. This was immediately followed by a second stimulus known to produce a strong effect on salivation: dried meat powder placed directly into the dog's mouth. The meat powder was termed the **unconditioned stimulus (UCS)**, because its ability to produce salivation was automatic and did not depend on the dog's having learned the response. Similarly, the response of salivation to the meat powder was termed an **unconditioned response (UCR)**; it too did not depend on previous learning. The bell was termed a **conditioned stimulus (CS)**, because its ability to produce salivation depended on its being paired with the meat powder. Finally, salivation in response to the bell was termed a **conditioned response (CR)**.

FIGURE 5.2

Pavlov's Apparatus for Studying Classical Conditioning

Pavlov used equipment similar to this in his early experiments on classical conditioning. He attached a tube to a dog's salivary gland, which had been surgically moved to the outside of the dog's cheek to allow easy collection of saliva. He then measured the number of drops of saliva that occurred naturally when a bell was sounded. Next, he measured the number of drops of saliva that occurred when a bell was sounded along with the presentation of food. Pavlov found that after repeated presentations of the bell followed by food, the dog's saliva increased as soon as the bell was sounded, indicating that it had learned to associate the food and the bell.

The basic question was whether the sound of the bell would gradually elicit salivation in the dogs as a result of its repeated pairing with the meat powder. In other words, would the bell elicit a conditioned response when it was presented alone? The answer was clearly *yes*. After the bell had been paired repeatedly with the meat powder, the dogs salivated upon hearing it, even when the bell was not followed by the meat powder.

CLASSICAL CONDITIONING: *Some Basic Principles*

Let's turn now to the principles that govern the occurrence of classical conditioning.

ACQUISITION: THE COURSE OF CLASSICAL CONDITIONING   In most instances, classical conditioning is a gradual process in which a conditioned stimulus gradually acquires the capacity to elicit a conditioned response as a result of repeated pairing with an unconditioned stimulus. This process—termed **acquisition**—often occurs as shown in panel A of Figure 5.3 (on page 162). At first conditioning proceeds quite rapidly, increasing as the number of pairings between conditioned and unconditioned stimulus increases. However, there is a limit to this effect; after a number of pairings of CS and UCS, acquisition slows down and finally levels off.

Although psychologists initially believed that conditioning was determined primarily by the number of conditioned-unconditioned stimulus pairings, we now know that this process is affected by other factors. As shown in Figure 5.4 (on page 163), one such factor is *temporal arrangement* of the CS–UCS pairings. Temporal means time-related: the extent to which a conditioned stimulus precedes or follows the presentation of an unconditioned stimulus. The first two temporal arrangements shown, **delayed conditioning** and **trace conditioning**, are examples of what is termed *forward conditioning*, since the presentation of the conditioned stimulus (light) always precedes the presentation of the unconditioned stimulus (shock). They differ, however, in that the CS and the UCS overlap to some degree in *delayed* conditioning, but not in *trace* conditioning. Two other temporal arrangements are **simultaneous conditioning**, in which the conditioned and unconditioned stimuli begin and end at the same time; and **backward conditioning**, in which the unconditioned stimulus precedes the conditioned stimulus.

The results of systematic research suggest that *delayed conditioning* is generally the most effective method for establishing a conditioned response. This is because the conditioned stimulus often plays an important role in predicting forthcoming presentations of the unconditioned stimulus (Lieberman, 1990). To illustrate this point, consider the following example: You are taking a shower when suddenly the water turns icy cold. Your response—a startle reaction to the cold water—is an unconditioned response. Now imagine that just before the water turns cold, the plumbing makes a slight grinding sound. Because this sound occurs just before the icy water, delayed conditioning can occur. If this situation is repeated several times, you may acquire a startle reaction to the slight grinding sound; it serves as a conditioned stimulus. In contrast, suppose you do not hear the sound until after the water turns cold, as in backward conditioning, or until the precise instant at which it turns cold, as in simultaneous conditioning. In these cases, you would probably not acquire a startle reaction to the grinding sound, since it provides no information useful in predicting the occurrence of the icy water.

Conditioning also depends on the *conditioned stimulus–unconditioned stimulus interval*: the time interval between presentations of the two stimuli. Extremely short intervals—less than 0.2 second—rarely produce conditioning.

Acquisition: The process by which a conditioned stimulus acquires the ability to elicit a conditioned response through repeated pairings of an unconditioned stimulus with the conditioned stimulus.

Delayed Conditioning: A form of forward conditioning in which the presentation of the conditioned stimulus precedes, but overlaps with, the presentation of the unconditioned stimulus.

Trace Conditioning: A form of forward conditioning in which the presentation of the conditioned stimulus precedes and does not overlap with the presentation of the unconditioned stimulus.

Simultaneous Conditioning: A form of conditioning in which the conditioned stimulus and the unconditioned stimulus begin and end at the same time.

Backward Conditioning: A type of conditioning in which the presentation of the unconditioned stimulus precedes and does not overlap with the presentation of the conditioned stimulus.

FIGURE 5.3

The Course of Conditioning

The strength of the conditioned response rapidly increases during *acquisition* (panel A). The process of *extinction* begins once the conditioned stimulus is no longer paired with the unconditioned stimulus (panel B). As shown in panels C and D, extinction can be disrupted through the processes of *spontaneous recovery* and *reconditioning*. Finally, although not shown in the figure, if no subsequent conditioned stimulus–unconditioned stimulus pairings occur, the conditioned response will decrease once again.

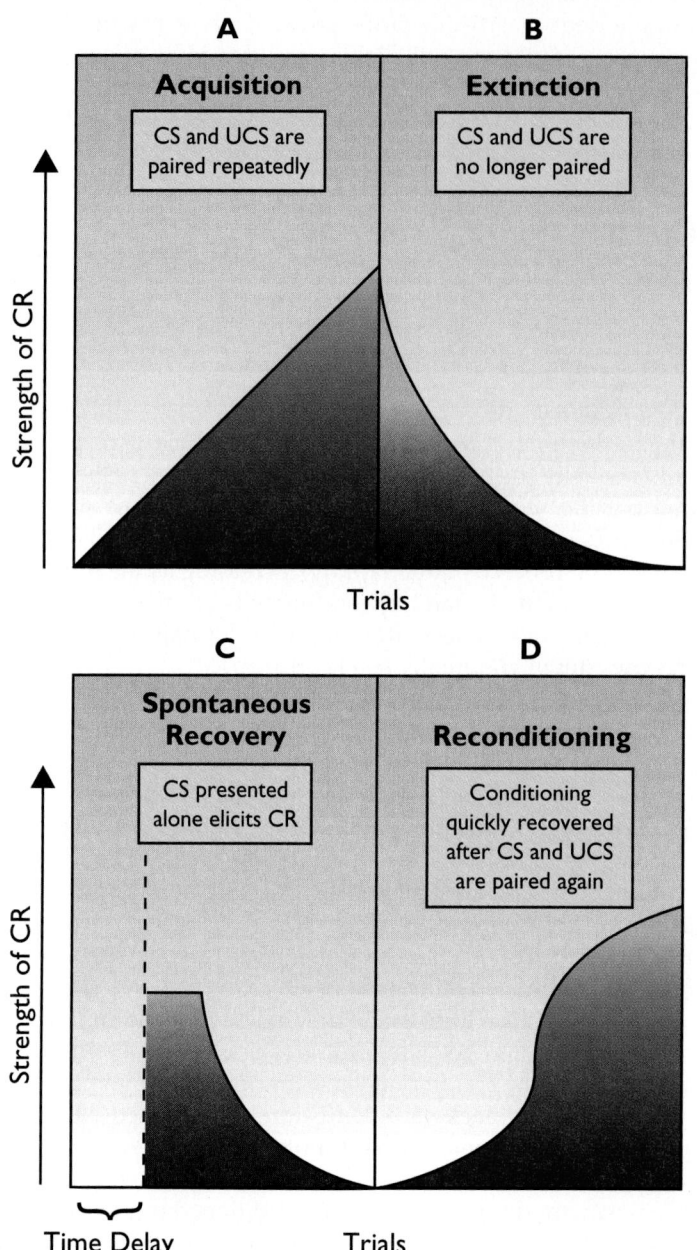

A
Acquisition
CS and UCS are paired repeatedly

B
Extinction
CS and UCS are no longer paired

Strength of CR

Trials

C
Spontaneous Recovery
CS presented alone elicits CR

D
Reconditioning
Conditioning quickly recovered after CS and UCS are paired again

Strength of CR

Time Delay   Trials

In animal research, the optimal CS–UCS interval seems to be between 0.2 and 2 seconds; longer intervals make it difficult for animals to recognize the conditioned stimulus as a signal for some future event (Gordon, 1989).

In general, conditioning is faster when the *intensity* of either the conditioned or unconditioned stimulus increases. However, it is not necessarily the absolute intensity of a stimulus that is most important to the conditioning process, but rather its intensity relative to other background stimuli. A study by Kamin (1965) helps illustrate this point. In this study, the conditioned stimulus was not a discrete stimulus; instead it was a contrast created by a reduction in the usual level of background noise. All subjects in the study (laboratory rats) were first exposed to "white noise" at a level of 80 decibels. Then the subjects were divided into groups that received varying reductions in this noise level as the conditioned stimulus. The reduction in noise was

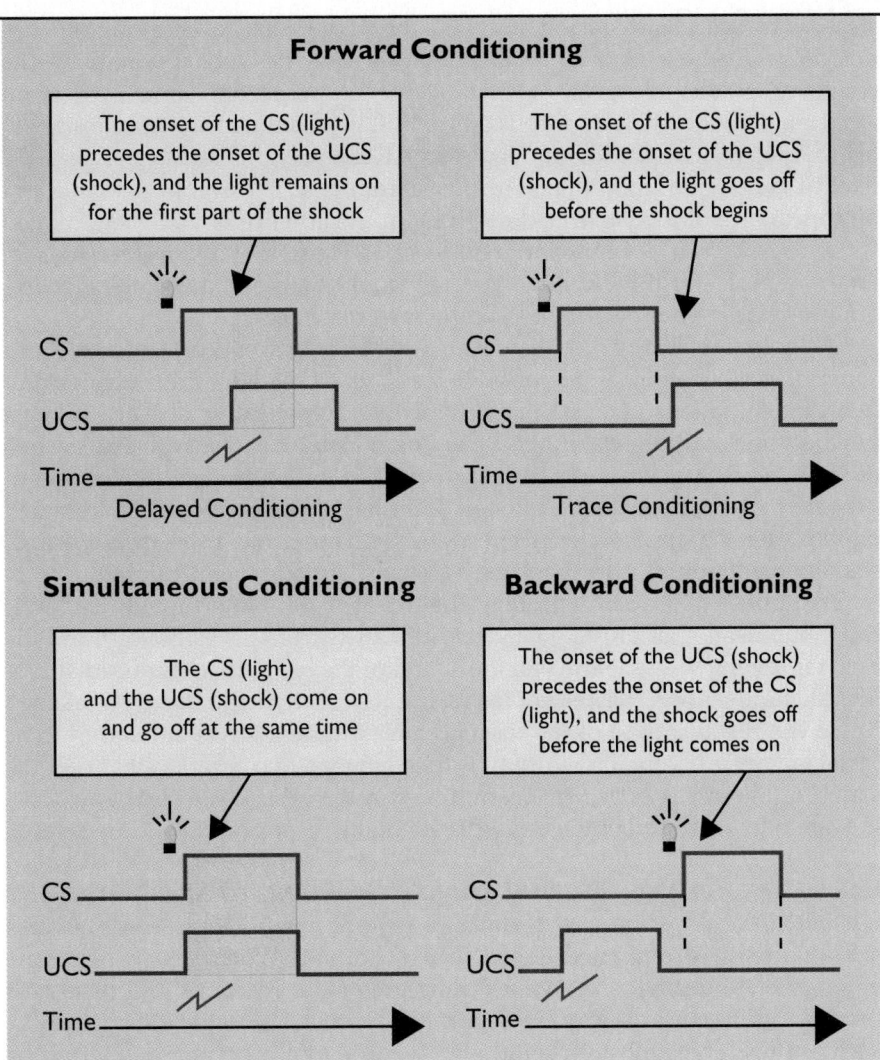

Forward Conditioning

The onset of the CS (light) precedes the onset of the UCS (shock), and the light remains on for the first part of the shock

CS

UCS

Time

Delayed Conditioning

The onset of the CS (light) precedes the onset of the UCS (shock), and the light goes off before the shock begins

CS

UCS

Time

Trace Conditioning

Simultaneous Conditioning

The CS (light) and the UCS (shock) come on and go off at the same time

CS

UCS

Time

Backward Conditioning

The onset of the UCS (shock) precedes the onset of the CS (light), and the shock goes off before the light comes on

CS

UCS

Time

FIGURE 5.4

Temporal Arrangement of the CS and UCS Affects the Acquisition of a Conditioned Response

Four CS–UCS temporal arrangements commonly used in classical conditioning procedures are shown. *Temporal* means time-related: the extent to which a conditioned stimulus precedes or follows the presentation of an unconditioned stimulus. *Delayed conditioning* generally produces the most rapid learning. *Simultaneous conditioning* and *backward conditioning* are usually the least effective procedures.

always followed by an unconditioned stimulus, an electrical shock. The rats receiving the largest reduction in noise level as a conditioned stimulus—which interestingly was also the least intense level of noise in absolute terms—demonstrated the greatest evidence of conditioning. The results of this study show that conditioning is more likely when conditioned stimuli stand out, relative to other background stimuli.

Finally, *familiarity* can greatly affect conditioning. In contrast to the laboratory, where stimuli selected for study are often novel, many of the potential conditioning stimuli found in the environment are familiar to us. Thus, our day-to-day experiences often teach us that certain stimuli, such as the background noise usually present in an office setting, do not predict anything unusual. In other words, we learn that these stimuli are largely irrelevant, which makes future conditioning of them difficult (Baker & Mackintosh, 1977).

EXTINCTION: ONCE CONDITIONING IS ACQUIRED, HOW DO WE GET RID OF IT?

You are one of several executives in a large marketing firm. You and your coworkers have been working night and day to prepare a proposal crucial to the survival of the firm, and things are not going well. Over the past week the president of the company has chewed you out at least a dozen times. Now, whenever you hear the unmistakable sound of his approaching footsteps, your heart starts racing and your mouth gets dry, even though he has not yet reached your office. Fortunately, the story has a happy ending—the company's directors are impressed by the proposal, and your boss is no longer angry when he enters your office. Will you continue to react strongly to his footsteps? In all likelihood, you won't. Gradually, his footsteps will cease to elicit the original conditioned response from you. The eventual decline and disappearance of a conditioned response in the absence of an *un*conditioned stimulus is known as **extinction** (refer back to Figure 5.3). Extinction plays an important role, for if it did not occur, we would soon become walking collections of useless—but persistent—conditioned responses.

The course of extinction, however, is not always entirely smooth. Let's consider the behavior of one of Pavlov's dogs to see why this is true. After many presentations of a bell (conditioned stimulus) in the absence of meat powder (unconditioned stimulus), the dog no longer salivates in response to the bell. In other words, extinction has occurred. But if the conditioned stimulus (the bell) and the unconditioned stimulus (the meat powder) are again paired after the conditioned response of salivation has been extinguished, salivation will return very quickly—a process termed **reconditioning.**

Or suppose that after extinction, the experiment is interrupted: Pavlov is caught up in another project that keeps him away from his laboratory, and the dog, for several weeks. Now will the sound of the bell, the conditioned stimulus, elicit salivation? The answer is yes, but the reaction will be in a weakened form. The reappearance of the reaction after a time interval is referred to as **spontaneous recovery.** If extinction is then allowed to continue—that is, if the sound of the bell is presented many times in the absence of meat powder—salivation to the sound of the bell will eventually disappear.

GENERALIZATION AND DISCRIMINATION: RESPONDING TO SIMILARITIES AND DIFFERENCES Suppose that because of several painful experiences, a child has acquired a strong conditioned fear of hornets: Whenever she sees one or hears one buzzing, she shows strong emotional reactions and heads for the hills. Will she also experience similar reactions to other flying insects, such as flies? She almost certainly will, because of a process called **stimulus generalization**, the tendency of stimuli similar to a conditioned stimulus to elicit similar conditioned responses (Honig & Urcuioli, 1981; Pearce, 1986). As you can readily see, stimulus generalization often serves a useful function. In this example, it may indeed save the girl from additional stings. The red lighted signals that we encounter at certain intersections while driving also illustrate the important function served by stimulus generalization: Even though these signals often vary in brightness or shape, we learn to stop in response to all of them, and it's a good thing we do.

Although stimulus generalization can serve an important adaptive function, it is not always beneficial and in some cases can be dangerous. For example, because of many pleasant experiences with parents and other adult relatives, a young child may become trusting of all adults through stimulus generalization. Unfortunately, this process will not be beneficial if it extends to certain strangers. You can understand why stimulus generalization can be maladaptive—even deadly. Fortunately, most of us avoid such potential problems through **stimulus discrimination**—a process of learning to respond to certain stimuli but not to others. Perhaps a recent incident from my own life will illustrate this concept. About a year ago a friend was badly bitten by a dog. Until that incident she had no fear of dogs. Because she was so frightened by the attack, I was concerned that the incident would generalize to other breeds of dogs—perhaps even to her own dog. Fortunately, because of stimulus discrimination, this didn't happen; she becomes fearful only when she encounters the breed of dog that bit her.

Extinction: The process through which a conditioned stimulus gradually loses the ability to elicit conditioned responses when it is no longer followed by the unconditioned stimulus.

Reconditioning: The rapid recovery of a conditioned response to a CS–UCS pairing following extinction.

Spontaneous Recovery: Following extinction, return of a conditioned response upon reinstatement of CS–UCS pairings.

Stimulus Generalization: The tendency of stimuli similar to a conditioned stimulus to elicit a conditioned response.

Stimulus Discrimination: The process by which organisms learn to respond to certain stimuli but not to others.

CLASSICAL CONDITIONING: *Exceptions to the Rules*

When psychologists began the systematic study of learning, around the turn of the century, they noticed that some species could master certain tasks more quickly than others could. Such findings sparked little interest, though, because early researchers saw their task as that of establishing general principles of learning—principles that applied equally well to all organisms and to all stimuli. For several decades it was widely assumed that such principles existed. Beginning in the 1960s, however, some puzzling findings began to accumulate. These results suggested that not all organisms learn all responses or all associations between stimuli with equal ease.

The most dramatic evidence pointing to such conclusions was reported by Garcia and his colleagues (Braverman & Bronstein, 1985; Garcia, Hankins, & Rusiniak, 1974). In perhaps the most famous of these studies, Garcia and Koelling (1966) allowed two groups of rats to sip saccharin-flavored water from a device that emitted a bright flashing light and a loud clicking noise (conditioned stimuli) whenever the rats licked the water. While both groups were drinking, one group of rats was exposed to X-rays that later made them sick (an unconditioned stimulus), and the other group received painful shocks to their feet (an unconditioned stimulus). Traditional principles of classical conditioning suggest that *both* groups of rats should have learned to avoid all three stimuli—the flavored water, the bright light, and the clicking noise. After all, for both groups, these stimuli were followed by a strong unconditioned stimulus (either X-rays or a painful shock). But this was not what Garcia and Koelling found. Rats exposed to the painful shock learned to avoid the light and noise, but not the flavored water; rats that were made to feel ill learned to avoid the flavored water, but not the light or noise (see Figure 5.5 on page 166). In short, it seems that rats—and other organisms—are predisposed to associate nausea and dizziness with something they've consumed (the flavored water) and to associate pain with something they've seen or heard (the bright light and clicking noise). Similar findings from many different studies (e.g., Braverman & Bronstein, 1985) suggest that acquisition of a conditioned response does *not* occur with equal ease for different stimuli.

Another intriguing outcome that emerged from Garcia and Koelling's study is also noteworthy: Although the rats who received the X-rays did not get sick immediately, they still acquired an aversion to the flavored water. This finding contradicted the widely held belief that classical conditioning can occur only if the unconditioned stimulus follows the conditioned stimulus within a very short interval.

Further research has also shown that in regard to conditioning, important differences exist among species. Because of these **biological constraints on learning**, types of conditioning readily accomplished by some species are only slowly acquired by others. And often, the types of conditioning most readily accomplished by one species are the very ones it needs to survive in its normal habitat (Shettleworth, 1993). For example, rats eat a varied diet and are most active at night. Thus, it is especially useful for them to be able to associate specific tastes with later illness, since in many cases they can't see the foods they eat. In contrast, birds depend heavily upon vision for finding food. For a bird it is more useful to be able to form associations between visual cues and later illness (Wilcoxon, Dragoin, & Kral, 1971).

KEY QUESTIONS

- What is learning?
- What is classical conditioning?
- On what factors does acquisition of a classically conditioned response depend?
- What is extinction?
- What is the difference between stimulus generalization and stimulus discrimination?
- Is classical conditioning equally easy to establish with all stimuli for all organisms?
- How are conditioned taste aversions acquired?

Biological Constraints on Learning: *Tendencies of some species to acquire some forms of conditioning less readily than other species do.*

FIGURE 5.5

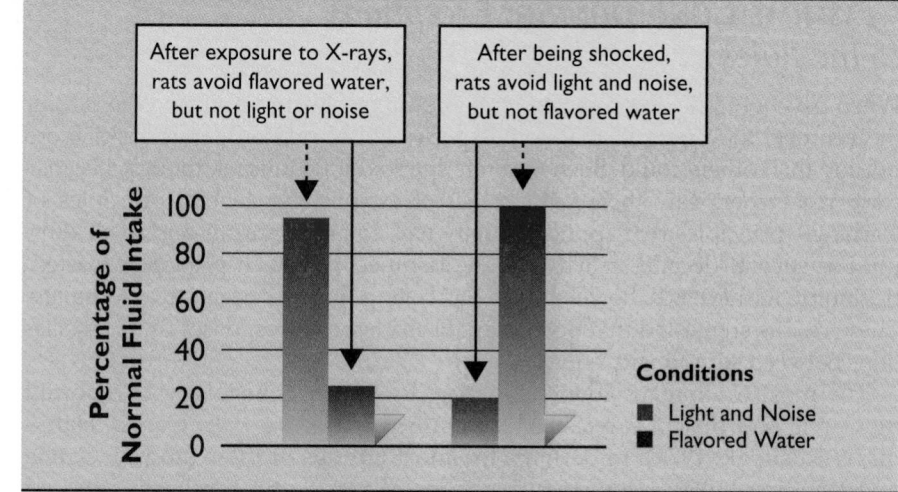

After exposure to X-rays, rats avoid flavored water, but not light or noise

After being shocked, rats avoid light and noise, but not flavored water

Biological Constraints and Characteristics of the CS and UCS Affect the Acquisition of a Conditioned Response

Rats quickly acquired an aversion to a flavored water when it was followed by X-rays that made them ill, but they did *not* readily acquire an aversion to the flavored water when it was followed by an electric shock. In contrast, rats learned to avoid a light–noise combination when it was paired with shock, but not when it was followed by X-rays. These findings indicate that classical conditioning cannot be established with equal ease for all stimuli and for all organisms.
(*Source:* Based on data from Garcia & Koelling, 1966.)

One of the clearest demonstrations of an exception to the rules of traditional classical conditioning involves what is termed conditioned taste aversion. We'll explore this interesting aspect of learning in the **Point of It All** section.

THE POINT OF IT ALL

Conditioned Taste Aversions: Breaking All the Rules?

Y ou are at a dinner party, and the host has prepared lasagna, a favorite dish you haven't tasted in ages. The first few bites are delicious, but as the meal progresses you begin to feel dreadful. For the next two days you have a fever and can't keep anything down. Months later you still experience the awful feelings whenever you see, smell, or even think about lasagna. You've developed a **conditioned taste aversion** to your formerly favorite dish.

Conditioned taste aversions are important for survival, because they inhibit the repeated ingestion of dangerous and toxic substances in animals' natural environment. And surveys show that food or beverage aversions are quite common among humans; most people report at least one such learned aversion (Logue, Ophir, & Strauss, 1981; Logue, Logue, & Strauss 1983). While many conditioned taste aversions result from overindulgence, some are established when we eat just before the onset of an illness like the flu (Garb & Stunkard, 1974). Interestingly, many people report that even though they are convinced that a particular food or beverage was not the cause of the illness that followed, they continue to experience a taste aversion to that substance. This evidence suggests that such aversions are unusually strong and can occur despite our thoughts about the cause of our illness (Seligman & Hager, 1972).

Research also shows that the way in which these powerful associations are established differs from most classical conditioning in several important respects. First, a conditioned taste aversion can usually be established with a single CS–UCS pairing, termed *one-trial learning*, in contrast to the many pairings involved in most Pavlovian conditioning. Second, conditioned taste aversions have been reported when the conditioned stimulus was presented hours before the occurrence of the unconditioned stimulus. In contrast, most instances of conditioning require a CS–UCS interval of not more than a few seconds. Finally,

Conditioned Taste Aversion: A type of conditioning in which the UCS (usually internal cues associated with nausea or vomiting) occurs several hours after the CS (often a novel food), leading to a strong CS–UCS association in a single trial.

conditioned taste aversions are extremely resistant to extinction; some evidence suggests that they may last a lifetime (Garb & Stunkard, 1974; Logue, 1979).

Unfortunately, conditioned taste aversions can create serious problems for some individuals. For example, radiation and chemotherapy used to treat cancer often cause nausea or vomiting as a side effect (Burish & Carey, 1986). Thus, cancer patients may acquire taste aversions to foods ingested before therapy sessions. Several studies have in fact shown that conditioned taste aversions are common among patients receiving chemotherapy (Bernstein, 1978). These effects help explain the lack of appetite often reported by such patients.

Radiation and chemotherapy patients can take a number of steps to reduce the likelihood of developing a conditioned taste aversion. First, the strength of a conditioned response depends partly on the temporal relationship between the conditioned and the unconditioned stimulus. Thus patients receiving chemotherapy should arrange their meal schedules to decrease the chances of establishing an association between ingestion of the food and illness; the interval between their meals and chemotherapy should be as long as possible. Second, since in most classical conditioning, the strength of a conditioned response is directly related to novelty, patients should also eat familiar foods, avoiding novel or unusual foods before therapy. Because familiar foods have already been associated with feeling good, it is less likely that cancer patients will acquire an aversion for these foods. Finally, since the strength of a conditioned response is related to the intensity of the conditioned stimulus, patients should eat bland foods and avoid strongly flavored ones.

Understanding of acquired taste aversions has also been used to help Western ranchers solve a serious problem—the loss of sheep and cattle to predators such as wolves and coyotes (Garcia, Rusiniak & Brett, 1977; Gustavson et al., 1974). By establishing a conditioned taste aversion for cattle and sheep, ranchers have been able to save livestock without having to kill the predators. To create the taste aversion, ranchers lace small amounts of mutton or beef with lithium chloride, a substance that causes dizziness and nausea. The predators eat the bait, become sick several hours later, and, as a result, learn to avoid sheep or cattle.

The point of it all, then, is that a solid understanding of processes like learned taste aversion—a clear exception to traditional rules of classical conditioning—can be applied in solving important real-life problems.

LEARNED TASTE AVERSIONS: PUTTING CLASSICAL CONDITIONING TO WORK

Classical conditioning has been used to solve many practical problems, including saving ranchers' livestock from predators.

CLASSICAL CONDITIONING: A Cognitive Perspective

During his early conditioning experiments, Pavlov (1927) observed a curious thing. A dog was conditioned to the ticking of a metronome, which had been previously paired with the presentation of food. When the metronome was turned off, the dog sat in front of the machine and proceeded to whine and beg. Why? If conditioning involves only the development of an association between conditioned and unconditioned stimuli, then the dog should have responded only when the conditioned stimulus was presented. The fact that the dog appeared to beg for the ticking sound suggests that classical conditioning involves more than just association. In fact, this and several related findings point to the following conclusion: Regular pairing of a conditioned stimulus with an unconditioned stimulus provides subjects with valuable predictive information; it indicates that whenever a conditioned stimulus is presented, an unconditioned stimulus will shortly follow. Thus, as conditioning proceeds, subjects acquire the *expectation* that a conditioned stimulus will be followed by an unconditioned stimulus.

In this context, the dog's behavior is easy to understand. During conditioning, the dog learned that the ticking of the metronome signaled the delivery of food. Then, without any warning, this fickle machine stopped working. Obviously, something had to be done to get it started, so the dog acted on its expectancies: It whined and begged for the metronome to tick again. That cognitive processes involving expectation play a role in classical conditioning is a thesis supported by several types of evidence (Rescorla & Wagner, 1972). First, conditioning fails to occur when unconditioned and conditioned stimuli are paired in a random manner. With random pairings, subjects cannot acquire any firm expectation that an unconditioned stimulus will indeed follow presentation of a conditioned stimulus. Therefore, for conditioning to occur, the CS–UCS pairing must be consistent.

Second, the cognitive thesis is supported by a phenomenon known as *blocking*—the fact that conditioning to one stimulus may be prevented by previous conditioning to another stimulus. For example, suppose that a dog is initially conditioned to a tone. After repeated pairings with presentation of meat powder, the tone becomes a conditioned stimulus, capable of causing the dog to salivate. Then a second stimulus, a light, is added to the situation. It too occurs just before the presentation of food. If classical conditioning occurs in an automatic manner, simply as a result of repeated pairings of a conditioned stimulus with an unconditioned stimulus, then the light too should become a conditioned stimulus: It should elicit salivation when presented alone. In fact, this does not happen. Why? Again, an explanation in terms of expectancies is helpful. Since the meat powder is already predicted by the tone, the light provides no new information. Therefore, it is of little predictive value to the subjects and fails to become a conditioned stimulus.

These findings suggest that classical conditioning involves much more than the formation of simple associations between specific stimuli. Indeed, modern views of conditioning conceive of it as a complex process in which organisms form rich representations of the relationships among a variety of factors—including many aspects of the physical setting or context in which the conditioned and unconditioned stimuli are presented (Rescorla, 1988; Swartzentruber, 1991).

I should add that this cognitive perspective on classical conditioning has also been extended to several of its basic aspects. For example, one theory of stimulus generalization suggests that memory and other cognitive processes play an important role (Pearce, 1986; Shettleworth, 1993). During conditioning, organisms form a representation in memory of the stimuli that preceded the unconditioned stimulus. When they then encounter different stimuli at later times, they compare these with the information stored in memory. The greater the similarity between current stimuli and such memory representations, the stronger the response now evoked. In short, both memory and active comparison processes play a role in what might at first seem to be an automatic function.

The suggestion that cognitive processes are important in human classical conditioning is not surprising. After all, we all have expectancies about what events go together or are likely to follow one another. But it may surprise you to learn that processes like memory and active comparison also occur in animals. Although this possibility would have been unheard of even as recently as the 1970s, growing evidence suggests that animals, like humans, form mental representations of events in the world around them (Cook, 1993; Wasserman, 1993). We'll consider cognitive processes in greater detail in chapter 7.

CLASSICAL CONDITIONING: *Turning Principles into Action*

Much of the discussion in this chapter has focused on basic principles of classical conditioning, many of them derived from laboratory research involving animals. Before concluding, however, I should call attention to the fact that knowledge of these principles has been put to many practical uses to help people.

One of the earliest applications was reported in a study, now a classic in psychology, conducted by John B. Watson and his assistant, Rosalie Raynor, in 1920. Watson and Raynor (1920) demonstrated that human beings can sometimes acquire strong fears—termed **phobias**—through classical conditioning. In their study, an eleven-month-old child named Albert was shown a white laboratory rat. His initial reactions to the rat were positive: He smiled and attempted to play with it. Just as he reached out for the rat, though, an iron bar was struck to make a loud noise right behind his ear. Albert jumped, obviously very upset by the startling noise. After several more pairings of the rat (conditioned stimulus) and the loud noise (unconditioned stimulus), Albert cried hysterically and tried to crawl away whenever he saw the rat—even when it was not accompanied by the noise.

Fortunately, knowledge of how phobias like little Albert's occur has led to the development of several effective procedures for reducing these reactions (Davey, 1992). In one procedure, termed **flooding**, a person suffering from a specific fear may be forced to confront the fear-eliciting stimulus without an avenue of escape (Gordon, 1989; Morganstern, 1973). For example, a therapist may persuade a person who has an irrational fear of heights to walk onto a high bridge and may keep the person there for a while—under careful supervision, of course. Because no harm results from this experience, the person may eventually become less fearful of heights. In cases where fear-provoking thoughts are too painful to deal with directly, *systematic desensitization—* a progressive technique designed to replace anxiety with a relaxation response—has proven effective (Wolpe, 1958; 1969). A person undergoing this procedure is asked to describe fearful situations. Then, starting with the least anxiety-producing situation, the person alternately visualizes situations and relaxes. Gradually, the individual learns to relax while imagining situations that are increasingly more threatening. Chapter 13 will discuss these procedures in more detail.

Knowledge of conditioning processes has also led to another intriguing application. Research evidence suggests that some instances of drug overdose can be explained, at least in part, through aspects of classical conditioning. For example, it is well known that certain drugs become less effective over time. But why does this occur? One possibility is that when a person uses drugs in a particular context, the stimuli in that environment become conditioned stimuli and come to elicit a conditioned response (Siegel, 1983, 1984). Interestingly, for certain addictive drugs, this conditioned response can be just the opposite of the unconditioned response. With morphine, for example, although the unconditioned response is a decreased sensitivity to pain, the conditioned response to a conditioned stimulus associated with the drug is increased sensitivity to pain (Siegel, 1975). Apparently, these conditioned stimuli signal the body to prepare for morphine by suppressing the response to it (Chance, 1988). An experiment conducted by Siegel and his colleagues (Siegel, Hinson, Krank, & McCully, 1982) supported this theory. In the study, rats received

Phobias: *Intense, irrational fears of objects or events.*

Flooding: *A procedure for eliminating conditioned fears that is based on principles of classical conditioning. During flooding an individual is exposed to fear-inducing objects or events. Since no unconditioned stimulus then follows, extinction of fears eventually takes place.*

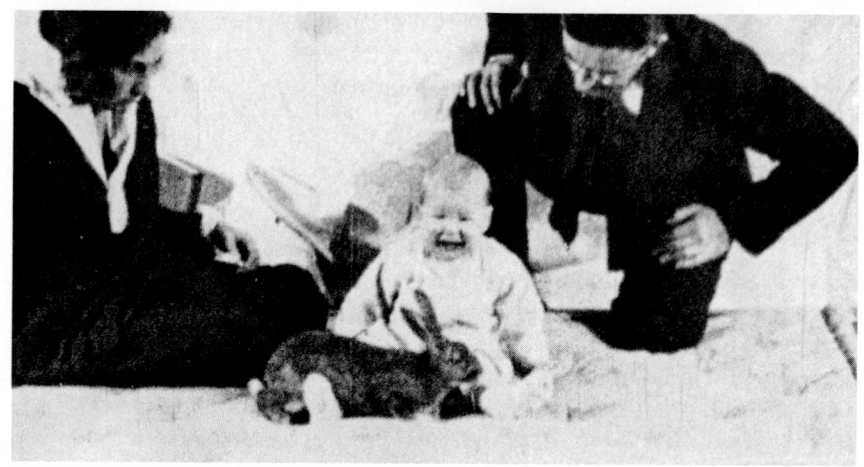

CLASSICAL CONDITIONING: A HUMAN EXAMPLE

John B. Watson and his graduate assistant Rosalie Raynor used classical conditioning to teach "Little Albert" to fear various small, furry objects. What ethical problems were involved in these studies?

injections of either heroin or placebo on alternating days, in alternating environments. Then all subjects received a single high—potentially fatal—dose of heroin. One group received this dose in the heroin environment, the other group in the placebo environment. A control group that had previously received only placebo were also injected with the high dose of heroin. The results? First, more subjects with previous drug experience survived than control group subjects; apparently, tolerance resulted from the early nonlethal injections. Second, and more interesting, mortality differed between the other two groups: Mortality was highest among those receiving the injection in the environment previously associated with the placebo—*not* heroin. These results suggest that cues associated with the heroin environment served as conditioned stimuli and prepared the rats' bodies partially to counteract the effects of the lethal injection; the placebo environment did not provide such cues. Indeed, drug users who have nearly died following drug use commonly report something unusual about the environment in which they took the drug (Siegel, 1984). Often these environmental differences are quite subtle, a fact that emphasizes the powerful effects produced by conditioning.

These results may also have implications for drug treatment. Recent evidence has shown that the environments to which former drug users return often contain cues that may produce drug-related conditioned responses, such as withdrawal symptoms and drug cravings (Ehrman et al., 1992). Knowledge of classical conditioning processes may help health professionals arrange environments that minimize relapse among former drug users—by eliminating the cues that trigger conditioned responses.

KEY QUESTIONS

- How do modern views of classical conditioning differ from earlier perspectives?
- What is blocking?
- What are flooding and systematic desensitization?
- Do classical conditioning principles have practical applications in solving problems of everyday life?

OPERANT CONDITIONING: *Learning Based on Consequences*

Learning Objective 5.5
Explain the basic nature and principles of operant conditioning.

*I*t was the first day of school, and Jeff was already off to a bad start. Barely there an hour, he had already landed himself in the principal's office. Before starting the first grade, Jeff had always gotten his way. Although they knew it was wrong, his parents eventually gave into his demands because of the tantrums Jeff was sure to throw if they did not. Now Jeff's behavior had become unbearable—even in school.

Much to Jeff's surprise, however, his teacher did not react to his misbehaviors as he expected. In fact, each time Jeff misbehaved, he received "time out"—a few minutes in a quiet corner of the room, away from his classmates. At first Jeff tried his usual routine: He kicked and screamed all the way to the corner. After all, this strategy always worked at home. The teacher's reaction to these outbursts, however, remained consistent, despite the fact that Jeff's tantrums initially worsened. Interestingly, Jeff's outbursts seemed to lose some of their steam as the weeks went by. Jeff also began to notice that on days when he was well behaved, the teacher smiled at him more and rewarded his good behavior with cartoon stickers or special jobs, such as passing out papers. After just a few weeks, Jeff's outbursts disappeared completely.

What happened here? The answer is probably obvious: Jeff's behaviors changed consistent with the nature of the consequences they produced. Behaviors that produced positive consequences increased in frequency, whereas those that were ignored or resulted in time out decreased. In short, the teacher had used *operant* (or *instrumental*) *conditioning* to change Jeff's behavior.

THE NATURE OF OPERANT CONDITIONING: *Consequential Operations*

In situations involving **operant conditioning**, the probability that a given response will occur changes depending on the consequences that follow it. Psychologists generally agree that these probabilities are determined through four basic procedures, two of which strengthen or increase the rate of behavior and two of which weaken or decrease the rate of behavior. Procedures that *strengthen* behavior are termed *reinforcement*, whereas those that *suppress* behavior are termed *punishment*.

REINFORCEMENTS There are two types of **reinforcement**: positive reinforcement and negative reinforcement. *Positive reinforcement* involves the impact of **positive reinforcers**—stimulus events or consequences that strengthen responses that precede them. In other words, if a consequence of some action increases the probability that the action will occur again in the future, that consequence is functioning as a positive reinforcer. Some positive reinforcers seem to exert these effects because they are related to basic biological needs. Such *primary reinforcers* include food when we are hungry, water when we are thirsty, and sexual pleasure. In contrast, other events acquire their capacity to act as positive reinforcers through association with primary reinforcers. Among such *conditioned reinforcers* are money, status, grades, trophies, and praise from others.

Preferred activities can also be used to reinforce behavior, a principle referred to as the **Premack principle**. If you recall hearing "You must clean your room before you can watch TV" when you were growing up, then you're already familiar with this principle. Jeff's teacher could use the Premack principle to reinforce a *less* preferred behavior—like doing school work or behaving appropriately—with a *more* preferred activity, such as playing outside during recess. As you can guess, the Premack principle is a powerful tool for changing behavior.

Please note that a stimulus event that functions as a positive reinforcer at one time or in one context may have a different effect at another time or in another place. For example, food may serve as a positive reinforcer when you are hungry, but not when you are ill or just after you finish a large meal.

USING REINFORCEMENT ON THE FOOTBALL FIELD

Some college football teams use helmet stickers to reward good plays. According to the principles of operant conditioning, if the stickers increase the probability that the desired action occurs again, they are functioning as positive reinforcers. What positive reinforcers do you respond to?

Learning Objective 5.6
List the various schedules of reinforcement and define their effects.

Operant Conditioning: A process through which organisms learn to repeat behaviors that yield positive outcomes or permit them to avoid or escape from negative outcomes.

Reinforcement: The application or removal of a stimulus to increase the strength of a behavior.

Positive Reinforcers: Stimuli that strengthen responses that precede them.

Premack Principle: The principle that a more preferred activity can be used to reinforce a less preferred activity.

LEARNING: HOW WE'RE CHANGED BY EXPERIENCE

THE PREMACK PRINCIPLE: A POWERFUL BEHAVIOR CHANGE TECHNIQUE

The Premack principle is a powerful tool to encourage desired behaviors—including eating one's veggies!

Learning Objective 5.7
Describe the research that supports the cognitive perspective on operant conditioning.

KEY QUESTIONS

- What is operant conditioning?
- Which operant techniques strengthen behavior? Which ones weaken behavior?
- What are examples of primary reinforcers? and conditioned reinforcers?
- What is the Premack principle?

Negative Reinforcers: Stimuli that strengthen responses that permit an organism to avoid or escape from their presence.

Punishment: The application or removal of a stimulus so as to decrease the strength of a behavior.

Omission Training: A procedure in which a response is weakened through the removal of a desired object or activity.

Also, at least where people are concerned, many individual differences exist. Clearly, a stimulus that functions as a positive reinforcer for one person may fail to operate in a similar manner for another person. We will return to this important point later on in this chapter.

Negative reinforcement involves the impact of **negative reinforcers**—stimuli that strengthen responses that permit an organism to avoid or escape from their presence. Thus, when we perform an action that allows us to escape from a negative reinforcer that is already present or to avoid the threatened application of one, our tendency to perform this action in the future increases. Some negative reinforcers, such as intense heat, extreme cold, or electric shock, exert their effects the first time they are encountered, whereas others acquire their impact through repeated association.

There are many examples of negative reinforcement in our everyday lives. For example, imagine the following scene. On a particularly cold and dark winter morning, you're sleeping soundly in a warm, comfortable bed. Suddenly, the "alarm clock from hell" begins to wail from across the room. Although getting out of your cozy bed is the last thing on your mind, you find the noise intolerable. What do you do? If you get up to turn off the alarm—or, on subsequent mornings, get up early to avoid hearing the sound of the alarm altogether—your behavior has been *negatively* reinforced. In other words, your tendency to perform actions that allowed you to escape from or avoid the sound of the alarm clock has increased. Another everyday example of negative reinforcement occurs when parents give in to their children's tantrums—especially in public places, such as restaurants and shopping malls. Over time, the parent's tendency to give in may increase, because doing so stops the screaming.

To repeat, then, both positive and negative reinforcement are procedures that strengthen or increase behavior. Positive reinforcers are stimulus events that strengthen responses that precede them, whereas negative reinforcers are aversive stimulus events that strengthen responses that lead to their termination or avoidance.

PUNISHMENT AND OMISSION TRAINING In contrast to reinforcement, *punishment* and *omission training* are procedures that weaken or decrease the rate of behavior. In **punishment**, behaviors are followed by aversive stimulus events termed *punishers*. In such instances, we learn not to perform these actions since aversive consequences—punishers—will follow. Imagine that you are driving home in a hurry, exceeding the speed limit. A sick sensation creeps into your stomach as you become aware of flashing lights and a siren. A state trooper has detected your speeding. Your eyes bug out when you see how much the ticket will cost you; and after paying that fine, you obey the posted speed limit. This is an example of the impact of *punishment*—an unpleasant outcome follows your speeding, so the chances that you will speed in the future decrease. The **Key Concept** page summarizes the differences between negative reinforcement and punishment, about which there is often much confusion.

Omission training is the term used to describe the weakening of a response through the removal of something pleasurable. For example, parents frequently attempt to combat certain behaviors of their teenagers by removing their privileges, like access to the family car for weekend dates. Thus, both punishment and omission training are procedures that weaken or decrease behavior. Table 5.1 (on page 174) summarizes positive reinforcement, negative reinforcement, punishment, and omission training.

The Difference between Negative Reinforcement and Punishment

Negative reinforcement and punishment are definitely *not* the same. In fact, one of the few similarities between them is that both involve an aversive stimulus. The examples here illustrate ways in which negative reinforcement and punishment differ.

Negative Reinforcement

- Negative reinforcement *motivates* behavior—organisms perform behaviors that allow them to *escape* or *avoid* aversive stimuli.
- In negative reinforcement, aversive stimuli *precede* the escape or avoidance response.

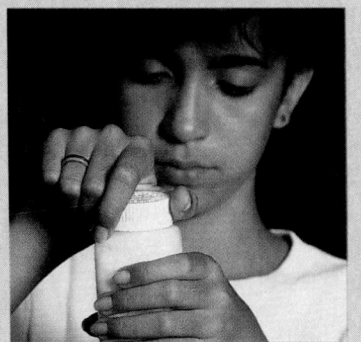

We may take aspirin to alleviate the pain of a headache. This is escape behavior.

Escape Behavior

Organisms engage in behaviors that allow them to escape or terminate an unpleasant or aversive event that has already occurred.

We may use sunscreen to avoid getting a painful sunburn. This is avoidance behavior.

Avoidance Behavior

Sometimes, events in our environment reliably signal an impending aversive event. These stimuli provide us with advance warning and motivate behavior that allows us to avoid experiencing the aversive event altogether.

Punishment

- Punishment decreases or suppresses behavior—organisms stop doing behaviors that produce aversive consequences.
- In punishment, an aversive stimulus *follows* a response and decreases the chances the response will occur in the future.

With punishment, a behavior is followed by an aversive stimulus (such as spanking) to decrease the likelihood that the behavior occurs again. The use of punishment is controversial, however. Its opponents contend that the target behavior is not eliminated but merely suppressed, and that it may reappear in situations in which punishment is not a threat. In addition, many psychologists believe that the use of punishment may increase aggression, especially in children.

PROCEDURE	STIMULUS EVENT	EFFECTS	BEHAVIORAL OUTCOMES
Positive reinforcement	Application of desirable (appetitive) stimulus (e.g., food, sexual pleasure, praise)	Strengthens responses that precede occurrence of stimulus	Organisms learn to perform responses that produce positive reinforcers
Negative reinforcement	Removal or postponement of undesirable (aversive) stimulus (e.g., heat, cold, harsh criticism)	Strengthens responses that permit escape from or avoidance of stimulus	Organisms learn to perform responses that permit them to avoid or escape from negative reinforcers
Punishment	Application of undesirable (aversive) stimulus	Weakens responses that precede occurrence of stimulus	Organisms learn to suppress responses that lead to unpleasant consequences
Omission training	Removal of desirable (appetitive) stimulus	Weakens responses that precede occurrence of stimulus	Organisms learn to suppress responses that lead to the removal of pleasant consequences

TABLE 5.1

Positive Reinforcement, Negative Reinforcement, Punishment, and Omission Training: An Overview

Positive and negative reinforcement are both procedures that strengthen behavior. Punishment and omission training are procedures that weaken behavior.

Learning Objective 5.8
List the various ways operant conditioning has been applied to practical problems.

OPERANT CONDITIONING: Some Basic Principles

In classical conditioning, organisms learn associations between stimuli: Certain stimulus events predict the occurrence of others that naturally trigger a specific response. In addition, the responses performed are generally *involuntary*. In other words, they are *elicited*—pulled out of the organism—by a specific unconditioned stimulus in an automatic manner; for example, salivation to the taste of food, blinking the eyes in response to a puff of air.

In operant conditioning, in contrast, organisms learn associations between particular *behaviors* and the consequences that follow them. Additionally, the responses involved in operant conditioning are more voluntary and are *emitted* by organisms in a given environment. In order to understand the nature of this form of conditioning, then, we must address two basic questions: (1) Why are certain behaviors emitted in the first place? (2) Once they occur, what factors determine the frequency with which they are repeated?

SHAPING AND CHAINING: GETTING BEHAVIOR STARTED AND THEN PUTTING IT ALL TOGETHER
In order to study operant conditioning under laboratory conditions, psychologists often use two basic types of apparatus. The first is a maze, or runway. Here, subjects (usually rats) must learn which ways to turn in order to receive some reward, usually food, at the end of the maze. Since making correct responses yields a rewarding consequence, the speed and accuracy of such responses usually increases over successive trials.

The second type of equipment is known as a *Skinner box*, after its originator, B. F. Skinner. Skinner is a major figure in the history of psychology, well known both for his research and his outspoken support of a behavioristic viewpoint that he termed the *experimental analysis of behavior*. We will consider his substantial contributions to psychology at several points in this chapter. Animals (usually rats or pigeons) in a Skinner box must press a lever or peck a key in order to obtain small pellets of food. Since this is the only response that yields reinforcement, it quickly increases in frequency, and subjects may spend long periods of time working for their reward. A device called a cumulative recorder, developed by Skinner, registers each response at the time it occurs and so provides a permanent record of how the rate of a particular response, whether pecks or presses, changes over time. Although technologically simple by today's standards, Skinner's tools allowed him to observe systematically the relationship between simple responses and the consequences they produced, thus leading to the discovery of important principles that we'll consider later in this discussion.

The responses that occur in mazes and Skinner boxes are both simple and natural for the organisms involved; rats often run through tunnels and pecking is common among pigeons. But how can behaviors that organisms *don't* spontaneously emit be established? The answer involves a procedure known as shaping, which was first systematically studied by Skinner. In essence, **shaping** is based on the principle that a little can eventually go a long way. Subjects receive a reward for each small step toward a final goal—the target response—rather than only for the final response. At first, actions even remotely resembling the target behavior—termed *successive approximations*—are followed by a reward. Gradually, closer and closer approximations of the final target behavior are required before the reward is given. This sounds simple, but does it actually work? Absolutely. For example, when a baby suddenly blurts out the sound "Mmmuuhh," the parents are ecstatic: They immediately lavish attention and affection on the child and do so each time the baby repeats the sound; all the baby's other relatives do the same. But what happens over time? Although initially the family responds enthusiastically to any sound the child makes, gradually they respond only to sounds that approximate actual words. Shaping, then, helps organisms acquire, or construct, new and more complex forms of behavior from simpler behavior.

What about even more complex sequences of behavior, such as the exciting water routines performed by dolphins and killer whales at Sea World? These behaviors can be cultivated by a procedure called **chaining**, in which trainers establish a sequence, or chain, of responses, the last of which leads to a reward. Trainers usually begin chaining by first shaping the final response. When this response is well established, the trainer shapes responses earlier in the chain, then reinforces them by giving the animal the opportunity to perform responses later in the chain, the last of which produces the reinforcer.

Shaping and chaining have important implications for human behavior. For example, when working with a beginning student, a skilled dance teacher or ski instructor may use shaping techniques to establish basic skills, such as performing a basic step or standing on the skis without falling down, by praising simple accomplishments. As training progresses, however, the student may receive praise only when he or she successfully completes an entire sequence or chain of actions, such as skiing down a small slope.

Shaping and chaining techniques can produce dramatic effects. But can they be used to establish virtually any form of behavior in any organism? If you recall our earlier discussion of biological constraints on classical conditioning, you can probably guess the answer: no. Just as there are biological constraints on classical conditioning, there are constraints on forms of learning based on consequences, or shaping. Perhaps this is most clearly illustrated by the experience of two psychologists, Keller and Marian Breland (1961), who attempted to put their expertise in techniques of operant conditioning to commercial use by training animals to perform unusual tricks and exhibiting them at state fairs. At first, things went well. Using standard shaping techniques, the Brelands trained chickens to roll plastic capsules holding prizes down a ramp and then peck them into the hands of waiting customers; they taught pigs to deposit silver dollars into a piggy bank. As time went by, though, these star performers gradually developed some unexpected responses. The chickens began to seize the capsules and pound them against the floor, and the pigs began to throw coins onto the ground and root them

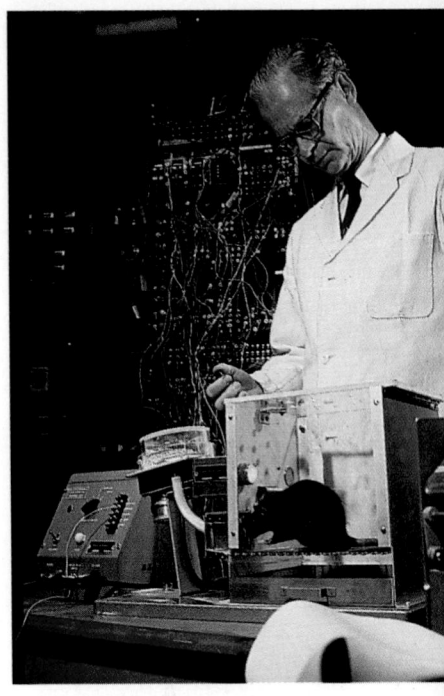

B. F. Skinner with His Skinner Box

Animals in the Skinner box learn to press a lever or peck a key in order to obtain small pellets of food. The animals' responses are recorded by a device called a *cumulative recorder*.

Shaping: A technique in which closer and closer approximations of desired behavior are required for the delivery of positive reinforcement.

Chaining: A procedure that establishes a sequence of responses, which lead to a reward following the final response in the chain.

SHAPING AND CHAINING

The dual processes of shaping and chaining help explain the development of complex behaviors in animals, including these water-skiing squirrels.

Schedules of Reinforcement: Rules determining when and how reinforcements will be delivered.

about instead of making "deposits" in their bank. In short, despite careful training, the animals showed what the Brelands termed *instinctive drift*—a tendency to return to the type of behavior they would show under natural conditions. So operant conditioning, like classical conditioning, is subject to biological constraints. While the power of positive and negative reinforcers is great, natural tendencies are important, too, and can influence the course and results of operant conditioning in many cases.

THE SIZE OF REINFORCEMENT AND DELAY: BIGGER OR SMALLER, SOONER OR LATER Operant conditioning usually proceeds faster as the *magnitude* of the reward that follows each response increases. But does this mean the absolute size of each reward or does it mean the number of rewards received? One study shows that if two groups of rats receive the same absolute amount of reward for each response, but one group receives this amount in a greater number of smaller pieces, the group receiving more pieces will respond faster (Campbell, Batsche, & Batsche, 1972). This suggests that the rats prefer to receive smaller, more numerous rewards rather than larger, fewer ones.

Reward delay also affects operant conditioning, with longer delays producing poorer levels of performance. A study by Capaldi (1978), for example, examined how reward delay affected running behavior in two groups of rats. Although both groups received the same amount and quality of food on each trial, one group received the reward immediately and the other group received it after a ten-second delay. As you might guess, subjects in the immediate-reward group performed better than subjects in the delayed-reward group.

The effects of reward delay—also termed *delay discounting*—are also evident in humans. Research has generally shown that the ability to delay gratification increases as we get older (Green et al., 1994). As you might expect, children are often more likely than adults to choose smaller, immediate rewards over rewards of greater value that they must wait to receive. But adults, too, often demonstrate a lack of self-control by choosing immediate rewards—even if the delayed consequences for doing so are aversive. Smokers, for instance, often choose the immediate pleasures they derive from smoking over the potentially negative consequences they may suffer later, such as cancer. Alcoholic beverages can also affect the way in which we evaluate short-term versus delayed consequences (Steele & Josephs, 1990). For example, drinking too much the night before an exam may reduce the influence of inhibiting cues associated with long-term consequences, such as failing the next day's test, and may increase the influence of environmental cues associated with short-term consequences, such as friends or good music.

SCHEDULES OF REINFORCEMENT: DIFFERENT RULES FOR DELIVERY OF PAYOFFS Through experience, you may already realize that under natural conditions reinforcement is often an uncertain event. Sometimes a given response yields a reward every time it occurs, but sometimes it does not. For example, smiling at someone you don't know may produce a return smile and additional positive outcomes. On other occasions it may be followed by a suspicious frown or other rejection. Similarly, putting a coin in a soda machine usually produces a soft drink. Sometimes, though, you merely lose the money.

In these cases, the occurrence or nonoccurrence of reinforcement seems to be random or unpredictable. In many other instances, though, it is governed by rules. For example, paychecks are delivered on certain days of the month; free pizzas or car washes are provided to customers who have purchased a specific amount of products or services. Do such rules—known as **schedules of reinforcement**—affect behavior? Several decades of research by Skinner and other psychologists suggest that they do. Many different types of schedules of reinforcement exist (Ferster & Skinner, 1957; Honig & Staddon, 1977). We'll concentrate on several of the most important ones here.

The simplest is called the **continuous reinforcement schedule**, in which every occurrence of a particular behavior is reinforced. For example, if a rat receives a food pellet each time it presses a lever, or a small child receives twenty-five cents each time he ties his shoes correctly, both are on a continuous reinforcement schedule. As you might imagine, continuous reinforcement is useful for establishing or strengthening new behaviors.

Other types of schedules, however, termed *partial* or *intermittent reinforcement*, are often more powerful in maintaining behavior. In the first of these, known as a **fixed-interval schedule**, the occurrence of reinforcement depends on the passage of time; the first response made after a specific period has elapsed brings the reward. When placed on schedules of this type, people generally show a pattern in which they respond at low rates immediately after delivery of a reinforcement, but then gradually respond more and more as the time when the next reward can be obtained approaches. A good example of behavior on a fixed-interval schedule is provided by students studying. After a big exam, little if any studying takes place. As the time for the next test approaches, the rate of such behavior increases dramatically.

Reinforcement is also controlled mainly by the passage of time in a **variable-interval schedule**. Here, though, the period that must elapse before a response will again yield reinforcement varies around some average value. An example of behavior on a variable-interval schedule of reinforcement is provided by employees whose supervisor checks their work at irregular intervals. Since the employees never know when such checks will occur, they must perform in a consistent manner in order to obtain positive outcomes, such as praise, or avoid negative ones, such as criticism. This is precisely what happens on variable-interval schedules: Organisms respond at a steady rate without the kind of pauses observed on fixed-interval schedules. An important procedure that is arranged according to a variable-interval schedule is random drug testing of individuals in safety-sensitive jobs—people whose impaired performance could endanger the lives of others, such as airline pilots or operators at nuclear reactor sites. Because they cannot predict the day on which the next test will occur, these individuals may be more likely to refrain from using drugs that could impair their on-the-job performance.

Reinforcement is determined in a very different manner on a **fixed-ratio schedule**. Here, reinforcement occurs only after a fixed number of responses. Individuals who are paid on a piecework basis, in which a fixed amount is paid for each item produced, are operating according to a fixed-ratio schedule. Generally, such schedules yield a high rate of response, though with a tendency toward a brief pause immediately after each reinforcement. The pauses occur because individuals take a slight breather after earning each unit of reinforcement. People who collect bottles, cans, and other recyclable materials for the money they bring are behaving according to a fixed-ratio schedule.

Finally, on a **variable-ratio schedule**, reinforcement occurs after completion of a variable number of responses. Since organisms confronted with a variable-ratio schedule cannot predict how many responses are required before reinforcement will occur, they usually respond at high and steady rates. The effect of such schedules on human behavior is readily apparent in gambling casinos, where high rates of responding occur in front of slot machines and other games of chance.

SCHEDULES OF REINFORCEMENT AT WORK

Migrant workers are paid on a fixed-ratio schedule. Because each worker's pay depends on the amount of produce picked, this type of schedule generally yields a high rate of response. Which type of payment schedule would you prefer?

Continuous Reinforcement Schedule: A schedule of reinforcement in which every occurrence of a particular behavior is reinforced.

Fixed-Interval Schedule: A schedule of reinforcement in which a specific interval of time must elapse before a response will yield reinforcement.

Variable-Interval Schedule: A schedule of reinforcement in which a variable amount of time must elapse before a response will yield reinforcement.

Fixed-Ratio Schedule: A schedule of reinforcement in which reinforcement occurs only after a fixed number of responses have been emitted.

Variable-Ratio Schedule: A schedule of reinforcement in which reinforcement is delivered after a variable number of responses have been performed.

Variable-ratio schedules also result in behaviors that are highly resistant to extinction—ones that persist even when reinforcement is no longer available. In fact, resistance to extinction is much higher after exposure to a variable-ratio schedule of reinforcement than it is after exposure to a continuous reinforcement schedule. This phenomenon is known as the *partial reinforcement effect* and seems to occur for the following reason. Under a variable-ratio schedule, many responses are not followed by reinforcement. Many golfers are well acquainted with the partial reinforcement effect; for each great shot they hit, they hit many more poor ones, yet they continue to play the game.

Suppose that a golfer fails to hit even one good shot over the course of an entire season—will she continue to play? The chances are good that she will. When reinforcement is infrequent and intermittent in its delivery, people or other organisms may continue to respond because it is difficult for them to recognize that reinforcement is no longer available. In short, they fail to realize that no amount of responding will do any good (Mowrer & Jones 1945).

As summarized in Figure 5.6 and evident throughout the preceding discussion, different schedules of reinforce-

KEY QUESTIONS

- In what way is shaping useful?
- What is chaining?
- What are schedules of reinforcement?
- When is the use of a continuous reinforcement schedule desirable?

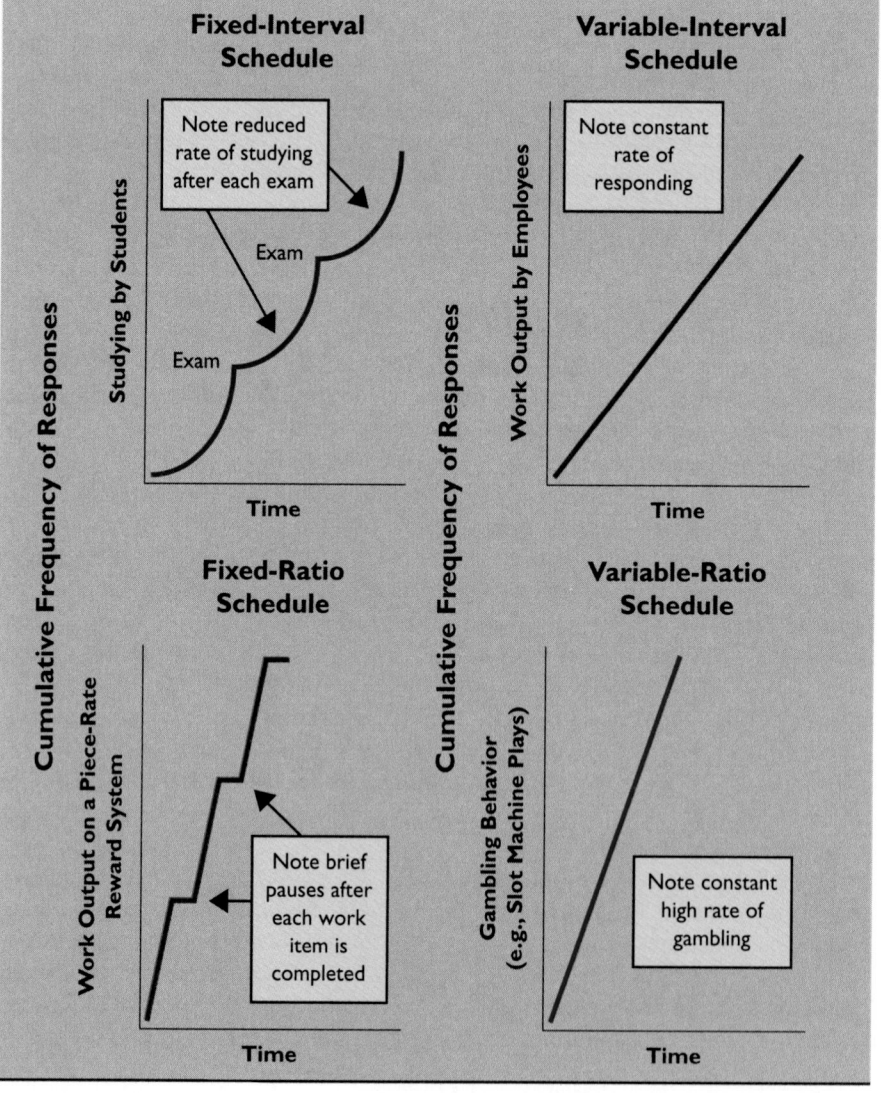

FIGURE 5.6

Schedules of Reinforcement: A Summary of Their Effects

Rates of responding vary under different schedules of reinforcement. The steeper each line in the graph, the higher the rate at which responses are performed.

ment produce distinct patterns of responding. Each schedule helps describe how the delivery of consequences affects our behavior. However, consequences are not the only determinants of behavior. Stimuli that precede our behavior and signal the availability of certain consequences are also important.

Stimulus Control of Behavior: Signals about the Usefulness (or Uselessness) of Responses   Imagine you are a rat in a Skinner box. Over the past few days, you have learned to press a lever in order to receive food pellets. One morning you notice the presence of a light in the box that is turned on and off with some regularity. The light is actually a signal: You will be rewarded with food if you press the lever when the light is on, but not when the light is off. Over time, you learn to press the lever in the presence of the light—termed a **discriminative stimulus**—but not when the light is turned off. In short, your lever-pressing behavior has come under **stimulus control** of the light: You are obeying the light's signal as to whether lever pressing should be performed or omitted (Skinner, 1938).

Stimulus control has important implications for people, too. For example, one type of graphic discriminative stimulus, the *Mr. Yuk sticker*, has been used to prevent accidental poisonings among small children who can't yet read warning labels or understand the dangers of many household products. How do Mr. Yuk stickers work? Initially parents place the stickers on all poisonous products in their home and explain to their children that Mr. Yuk means "No, don't touch." Then, each time a child attempts to handle a product containing the sticker, he or she receives a scolding. Soon Mr. Yuk comes to signal the availability of unpleasant consequences, and children quickly learn to avoid products with Mr. Yuk stickers.

You may have guessed by now that stimulus control can be a powerful tool for changing many aspects of behavior. Psychologists recognize this fact and have incorporated this principle into programs designed to promote a variety of environmentally responsible behaviors, including recycling (Austin et al., 1993; Dwyer et al., 1993).

For example, in one recent study, researchers designed an intervention based on stimulus control to promote recycling of paper wastes among office workers on a university campus (Kalsher et al., 1993). Initial observations showed that the office environments in which these persons worked actually discouraged the recycling of paper wastes. The employees' trash bins were located next to their desks or workstations. In contrast, recycling bins were located in dingy basements or on another floor of the building. Thus, the trash cans and recycling bins served as *discriminative stimuli* that signaled the availability of very different consequences: Throwing paper into the trash was quick, easy, and convenient; in contrast, the recycling bins signaled a long walk, lost time, and a great deal of inconvenience.

Kalsher and his colleagues redesigned the office environments to be more conducive to recycling. They equipped campus offices with sets of colored bins for the purpose of sort-separating three types of recyclable paper waste (please refer to Figure 5.7 on page 180). Colorful posters placed above each set of bins gave specific instructions for correct placement of the paper wastes. Finally, brochures describing the program were distributed to each employee to ensure that employees knew the appropriate recycling procedures. Results showed that the program was successful: Both the average daily weight of paper recycled and the percentage of paper correctly sorted into the bins increased dramatically following the program. Moreover, the program did not require the use of money or other extrinsic rewards. In short, stimulus control has important implications for solving a variety of problems in everyday life.

Discriminative Stimulus: *Stimulus that signals the availability of reinforcement if a specific response is made.*

Stimulus Control: *Consistent occurrence of a behavior in the presence of a discriminative stimulus.*

FIGURE 5.7

Stimulus Control in Action: Promoting Recycling Behaviors

Poster used to prompt correct placement of paper wastes. The bins depicted in the poster were colored to correspond to each bin's purpose—red for white paper, yellow for colored paper, and blue for computer paper.
(*Source*: Kalsher et al., 1993.)

OPERANT CONDITIONING: *A Cognitive Perspective*

Do cognitive processes play a role in operant conditioning as they do in classical conditioning? This continues to be a point on which psychologists disagree. Skinner and his supporters have contended that there is no need to introduce cognition into the picture: If we understand the nature of the reinforcers available in a situation and the schedules on which they are delivered, we can accurately predict behavior. But many other psychologists—a majority, it appears—believe that no account of operant conditioning can be complete without attention to cognitive factors (e.g., Colwill, 1993). Several types of evidence support this conclusion.

First, and perhaps most dramatic, is the existence of a phenomenon known as *learned helplessness:* the lasting effects produced by exposure to situations in which nothing an organism does works—no response yields reinforcement or provides escape from negative events. After such experience, both people and animals seem literally to give up. And here is the unsettling part: If the situation changes so that some responses will work, they never discover this fact. Rather, they remain in a seemingly passive state and simply don't try (Seligman, 1975; Tennen & Eller, 1977). Learned helplessness has important implications. As we'll see in later chapters, learned helplessness may play a key role in depression, a serious psychological disorder. Although it is not clear why learned helplessness occurs (McReynolds, 1980), it seems impossible to explain it entirely in terms of contingent relations between individual responses and the consequences they produce. Rather, some evidence suggests that organisms learn a general expectation of helplessness that transfers across situations, even if they do gain control over their environment (Maier & Jackson, 1979). The onset of learned helplessness seems to stem from our perceptions of control; when we begin to believe that we have no control over our environment or our lives, we stop trying to improve our situations (Dweck & Licht, 1980). For example, many children growing up in urban slums perceive they have little control over their environment and even less hope of escaping it. As a result of learned helplessness, they may simply resign themselves to a lifetime of disenfranchisement, deprivation, and exclusion.

Second, several studies indicate that in some cases people's beliefs about schedules of reinforcement may exert stronger effects on behavior than do the schedules themselves. For example, in one study (Kaufman, Baron, & Kopp, 1966), three groups of participants performed a manual response on a variable-interval schedule; the period between reinforcements varied, but averaged one minute. One group was told the schedule would be in effect. Two other groups were given false information: one was told that they would be rewarded every minute, a fixed-interval schedule; the other was told that they would be rewarded after an average of 150 responses, a variable-ratio schedule. Although all groups actually worked on the same schedule, large differences in their behavior emerged. Those who thought they were working on a variable-ratio schedule showed a high rate of responses: 259 per minute. Those told they would be rewarded on a fixed-interval schedule showed a very low rate of 6 responses per minute; and those who were correctly informed that they would work on a variable-interval schedule showed an intermediate rate of 65 responses per minute. As suggested by Bandura (1986, p. 129), people's behavior may sometimes be more accurately predicted from their beliefs than from the actual consequences they experience.

Third, evidence suggests that our behavior is influenced not only by the level of rewards we receive, but by our evaluation of rewards relative to our experiences with previous rewards. Studies have shown that shifts in the amount of reward we receive can dramatically influence performance, a temporary behavior shift termed the *contrast effect* (e.g., Crespi, 1942; Flaherty & Largen, 1975; Shanab & Spencer, 1978). For example, when laboratory animals are shifted from a small reward to a larger reward, there is an increase in their performance to a level greater than that of subjects consistently receiving the larger reward. This increase is known as a positive contrast effect. Conversely, when subjects are shifted from a large reward to a smaller reward, their performance decreases to a level lower than that of subjects receiving only the smaller reward—a negative contrast effect. But positive and negative contrast effects are transient. Thus, the elevated or depressed performances slowly give way to performance levels similar to those of control animals that receive only one level of reward. The existence of contrast effects indicates that level of reward alone cannot always explain our behavior and that experience with a previous level of reward—and consequent expectancies—can dramatically affect our performance. Contrast effects also help explain certain instances of our everyday behavior. For example, following an unexpected raise in salary or a promotion, a person is initially elated, and his or her performance skyrockets—at least for a while. Then, after the novelty wears off, performance falls to levels equal to that of others already being rewarded at the same level.

Finally, evidence suggests that cognitive processes play an important role in learning among animals, as well. In a classic study by Tolman and Honzik (1930), rats were trained to run through a complicated maze. One group, the reward group, received a food reward in the goal box at the end of the maze on each of their daily trials. A second group, the no-reward group, never received a reward. The third group, the no-reward/reward group, did not receive a food reward until the eleventh day of training. As illustrated in Figure 5.8 (on page 182), rats in the reward group showed a steady improvement in performance, decreasing the number of errors they made in reaching the goal box. Rats in the no-reward group showed only a slight improvement

FIGURE 5.8

The Role of Cognitive Processes in Learning

Performance for rats in the no-reward/reward group improved dramatically immediately after the introduction of the food reward. Because the improvement was so dramatic, these data suggest that the animals "learned" something during previous trials—even though they received no reward for their efforts. Tolman used this as evidence for the importance of cognitive processes in learning, suggesting that the rats may have formed a "cognitive map."
(*Source*: Based on data from Tolman & Honzik, 1930.)

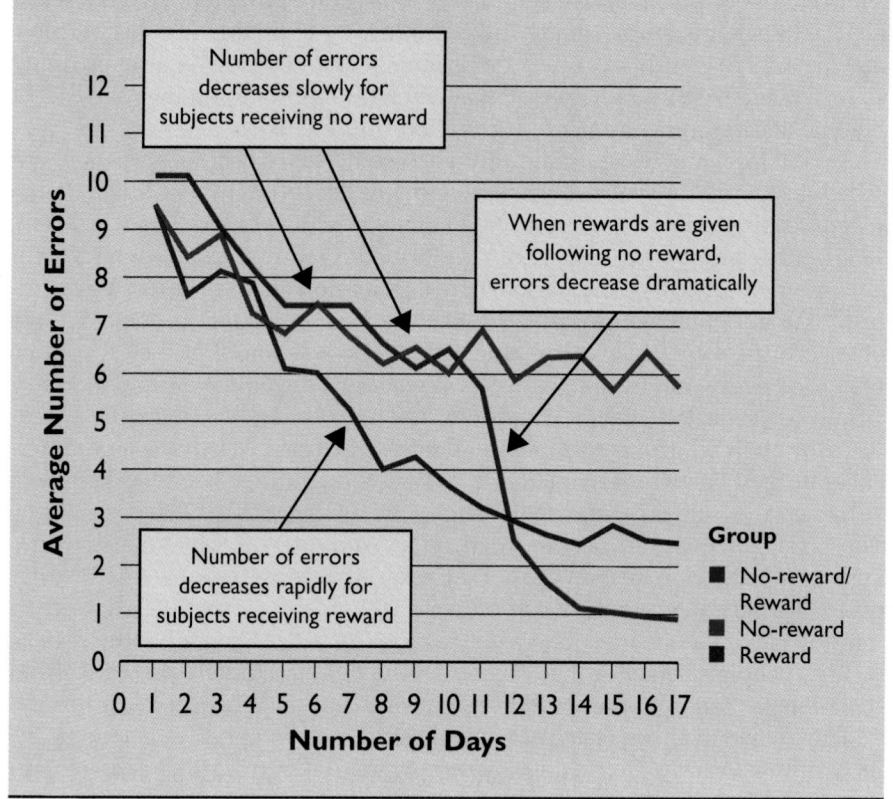

Number of errors decreases slowly for subjects receiving no reward

When rewards are given following no reward, errors decrease dramatically

Number of errors decreases rapidly for subjects receiving reward

Group
■ No-reward/Reward
■ No-reward
■ Reward

in performance. Rats in the no-reward/reward group showed performance similar to those in the no-reward group—for the first ten days. However, their performance improved dramatically immediately after the introduction of the food reward. In fact, their performance was as good as that of rats who had been rewarded for their performance all along.

How do we account for these results? An explanation based on reinforcement alone is not sufficient; the improvement in performance of the third group was too sudden. Obviously, the rats had learned something in the previous trials. Tolman and others point to these data, and the results of other studies (e.g., Colwill & Rescorla, 1985; 1988), as evidence for the importance of cognitive processes in learning. In fact, Tolman theorized that the rats may have formed what he termed a *cognitive map*—a mental representation of the maze. Although the existence of such maps has not yet been clearly established (e.g., Dyer, 1991; Wehner & Menzel, 1990), a large body of evidence supports the view that under certain conditions, animals form mental representations of their environment that include spatial and temporal features of stimuli they encounter (Poucet, 1993). Although we do not yet fully understand their precise nature, one thing is clear: Cognitive processes play an important and active role in animal learning.

APPLYING OPERANT CONDITIONING: Can We Make a Difference?

Because positive and negative reinforcement exert powerful effects on behavior, procedures based on operant conditioning have been applied in many practical settings—so many that it would be impossible to describe them all here. An overview of some of these uses will suffice, though.

First, principles of operant conditioning have been applied to the field of education. One of the most impressive operant-based teaching techniques is termed *precision teaching* (Lindsley, 1992). In this approach the "precision teacher" rarely lectures; instead, she performs like a coach, organizing materials and methods for the students to teach themselves and each other. The learners are taught to measure and chart their own daily progress on standard charts. The charts provide students with immediate feedback and facilitate more efficient learning. The tools and methods used in precision teaching permit even primary-grade students to project, improve, and summarize their own learning (Bates & Bates, 1971).

Another educational application of operant techniques involves the use of computers in the classroom—often termed *computer-assisted instruction*, or *CAI*. In CAI, students interact with sophisticated computer programs that provide immediate reinforcement of correct responses. The programs are paced according to each student's progress and permit the student to enter branch programs for special help in areas of weakness. Some evidence suggests that students may learn to take greater responsibility for their own performance under CAI than under teacher-led instruction, because they view computers as impersonal and therefore fairer. CAI technology includes the use of computer-based simulation exercises that allow students to apply what they've learned in the classroom to solve problems under realistic conditions. With the color graphics, synthesized speech, and other effects available on increasingly sophisticated equipment, CAI instruction may add excitement and enhance motivation for learning.

A second intriguing area of application of operant conditioning is in connection with eating disturbances such as *anorexia nervosa* (see chapter 9). Persons suffering from this disorder literally starve themselves. How can operant techniques be used to deal with this problem? Consider an individual who has been hospitalized because her unwillingness to eat is seriously affecting her health. In order to help this person, we might first ask her to monitor her eating behavior carefully and then identify something she likes, such as watching a favorite television program. Then we would make this activity available only when she eats a minimum amount of food. At first, the patient would have to eat only a small amount of food in order to gain access to a television. In accordance with the principles of shaping, however, the amount she must eat would gradually be increased. Such procedures, when used as part of a comprehensive treatment plan, have been successful (Bemis, 1987; Schmidt, 1989).

Third, principles of operant conditioning have been applied in interventions for solving socially significant issues in our communities, such as crime, energy conservation and recycling, health care issues, consumer affairs, and safety promotion (Greene et al., 1987). For example, experts tell us that more than half of the 50,000 deaths that occur on our highways each year could be prevented by the consistent use of safety belts. Yet many drivers and their passengers do not use the belts, despite the existence of safety-belt mandates in most states. A large body of evidence suggests that operant principles can be used effectively to increase the use of safety belts (e.g., Geller et al., 1987, 1989; Hagenzeiker, 1991). In one study, Kalsher et al. (1989) tested safety-belt incentives and disincentives at two large naval bases. At the incentive base, the license-plate numbers of drivers observed buckled up were entered into weekly drawings for prizes donated by local merchants, including a grand prize of a tropical vacation. The disincentive program, in contrast, consisted of a media blitz publicizing an existing safety-belt mandate and threatening consequences for noncompliance ranging from a warning ticket to a complete loss of on-base driving privileges. Would the "carrot" of pleasant consequences or the "stick" of aversive consequences be more effective? As it turned out, the increase in safety-belt use for the disincentive base was highest initially, but long-term follow-up showed that the two approaches were equally effective for motivating safety-belt use.

Interestingly, much of the increase observed at the disincentive base was due to safety-belt observations taken on vehicles entering the navy base, where a marine guard was present. If you recall our discussion of stimulus control, then you've probably guessed that the presence of the guard served as a *discriminative stimulus*—one that signaled the prospect of a particular consequence: a ticket for not being buckled up.

Fourth, operant conditioning principles have been applied to a severe disorder in which individuals inflict injury on themselves—*self-injurious behavior, or SIB* (Carr, 1977; Lovaas, 1982). SIB occurs frequently in individuals with mental retardation or autism, and manifests itself in a variety of forms, including head hitting, self-biting, severe scratching, eye gouging, and even hair pulling, known as trichotillomania (Maurice & Trudel, 1982). How can care givers use operant techniques to treat self-injury? First, by determining the factors that maintain its occurrence. Using a unique observational assessment procedure, Iwata and his colleagues discovered that individuals engage in self-injury for a variety of reasons (Iwata et al., 1982). Some individuals engage in SIB to attract the attention of people around them, whereas others do so to avoid or terminate demands placed on them. Still others engage in SIB as a form of self-generated sensory reinforcement. Iwata and colleagues' assessment procedure has led to the development of many effective techniques to treat this unsettling form of behavior (e.g., Iwata et al., 1990; Pace et al., 1993; Van Houten, 1993).

Finally, techniques of operant conditioning have been applied to many issues and problems in work settings—for example, to improve the performance of sales personnel and waiters (e.g., Luthans, Paul, & Baker, 1981; George & Hopkins, 1989) and in the development of flexible work schedules (Winett & Neale, 1981). These techniques have also helped improve the performance of work groups. For example, Petty, Singleton, and Connell (1992) demonstrated that a group incentive program improved the productivity of employees in a division of an electric utility company, thereby reducing the cost of electricity to its customers. Moreover, employees perceived that the incentive plan increased teamwork and encouraged greater employee involvement in decision making. Perhaps the most intriguing use of operant principles in work settings, though, has involved efforts to answer an age-old question: Why are some persons more effective in the role of leader or manager than others? Researchers have carefully observed and then analyzed the actual on-the-job behavior of managers within the framework of operant conditioning (e.g., Komacki, 1986). The results indicate that effective managers are ones who pay close attention to their subordinates' performance and then provide contingent rewards and punishments. This approach may sound like common sense, but in fact it doesn't come naturally in many work settings. Often, instead of yielding rewards, good performance is "recognized" by higher expectations and therefore more work and tougher challenges. Clearly, both organizations and their workers can profit greatly from closer attention to basic principles of operant conditioning.

KEY QUESTIONS

- What is a discriminative stimulus?
- What evidence supports the involvement of cognitive factors in operant conditioning?
- Why is knowledge of operant conditioning important?

OBSERVATIONAL LEARNING:
Learning from the Behavior and Outcomes of Others

Y̲ou are at a formal dinner party. Next to your plate are five different forks, including two of a shape you've never seen before. Which ones do you use for which dishes? You have no idea. In order to avoid making a complete fool of yourself, as the first course arrives, you watch the other guests. When several reach unhesitatingly for one of the unfamiliar forks, you do the same. Now, thank goodness, you can concentrate on the food.

Even if you have not had an experience quite like this, you have probably encountered situations in which you have acquired new information, forms of behavior, or even abstract rules and concepts from watching other people. Such **observational learning** is a third major way we learn, and it is a common part of everyday life (Bandura, 1977, 1986). Indeed, a large body of research findings suggest it can play a role in almost every aspect of behavior as these examples illustrate:

- A couple watches a television program that shows step by step how to remodel a bathroom. The following day, the couple sets out to remodel their own.
- A child watches his parents wash dishes, do the laundry, cook meals, and go to their jobs each morning. From such experience, he forms an impression that married couples share the responsibilities of running a household.

In these and countless other instances, we appear to learn vicariously, merely by watching the actions of other persons and the consequences others experience.

More formal evidence for the existence of observational learning has been provided by hundreds of studies, many of them performed with children. Perhaps the most famous of these studies are the well-known "Bobo doll" experiments conducted by Bandura and his colleagues (e.g., Bandura, Ross, & Ross, 1963). In these studies one group of nursery-school children saw an adult engage in aggressive actions against a large inflated Bobo doll. The adult who was serving as a model knocked the doll down, sat on it, insulted it verbally, and repeatedly punched it in the nose. Another group of children were exposed to a model who behaved in a quiet, nonaggressive manner. Later, both groups of youngsters were placed in a room with several toys, including a Bobo doll. Careful observation of their behavior revealed that those who had seen the aggressive adult model often imitated this person's behavior: They too punched the toy, sat on it, and even uttered verbal comments similar to those of the model. In contrast, children in the control group rarely if ever demonstrated such actions. While you may not find these results surprising, they may be significant in relation to the enduring controversy over whether children acquire new ways of aggressing through exposure to violent television programs and movies. We'll return to this issue below. For the moment, let's consider the nature of observational learning itself.

OBSERVATIONAL LEARNING: *Some Basic Principles*

Given that observational learning exists, what factors and conditions determine whether, and to what extent, we acquire behaviors, information, or con-

Learning Objective 5.9
Define observational learning and discuss common instances of its occurrence.

Learning Objective 5.10
Discuss how observational learning can be used to prepare employees for cross-cultural assignments.

Observational Learning: The acquisition of new information, concepts, or forms of behavior through exposure to others and the consequences they experience.

cepts from others? According to Bandura (1986), who is still the leading expert on this process, four factors are most important.

First, in order to learn through observation you must direct your *attention* to appropriate *models*—that is, to other persons performing an activity. And, as you might expect, you don't choose such models at random but focus most attention on people who are attractive to you; on people who possess signs of knowing what they're doing, such as status or success; and on people whose behavior seems relevant to your own needs and goals (Baron, 1970).

Second, you must be able to *remember* what the persons have said or done. Only if you can retain some representation of their actions in memory can you perform similar actions at later times or acquire useful information from them.

Third, you need to be able to convert these memory representations into appropriate actions. Bandura terms this aspect of observational learning *production processes*. Production processes depend on (1) your own physical abilities—if you can't perform the behavior in question, having a clear representation of it in memory is of little use; and (2) your capacity to monitor your own performance and adjust it until it matches that of the model.

Finally, *motivation* plays a role. We often acquire information through observational learning but do not put it into immediate use in our own behavior. You may have no need for the information, as when you watch someone tie a bow tie but have no plans to wear one yourself. Or the observed behaviors may involve high risk of punishment or be repugnant to you personally, as when you observe an ingenious way of cheating during an

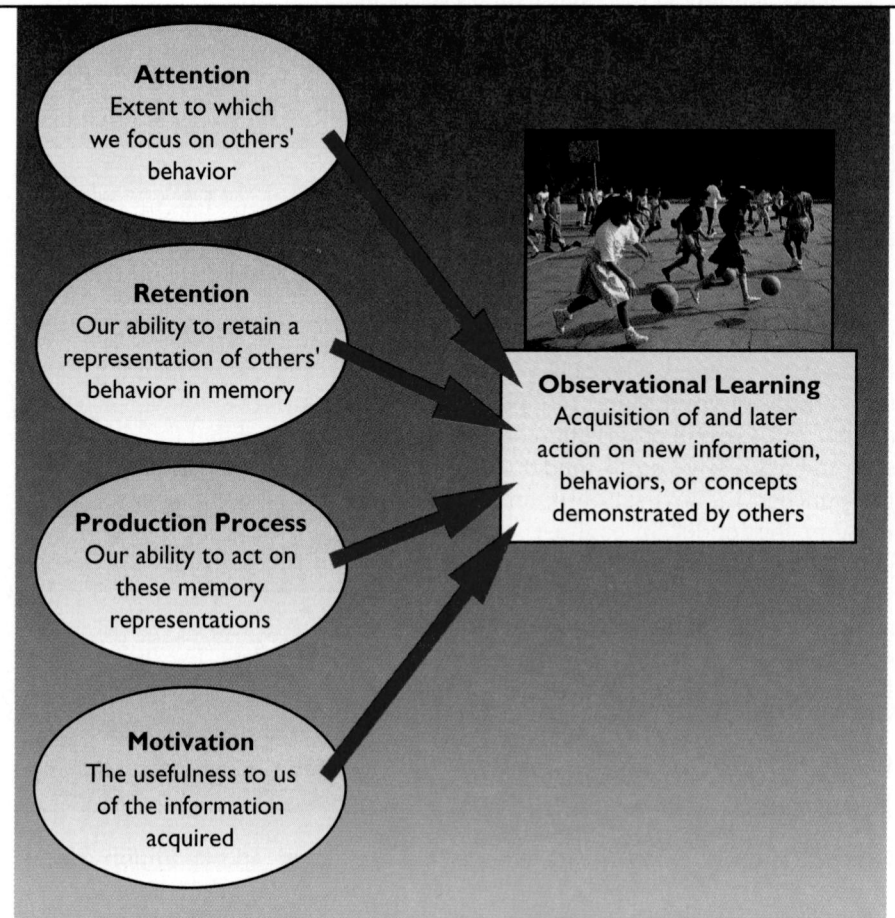

FIGURE 5.9

Key Factors in Observational Learning

Observational learning is affected by several factors or subprocesses. The most important of these are summarized here.

Attention
Extent to which we focus on others' behavior

Retention
Our ability to retain a representation of others' behavior in memory

Production Process
Our ability to act on these memory representations

Motivation
The usefulness to us of the information acquired

Observational Learning
Acquisition of and later action on new information, behaviors, or concepts demonstrated by others

exam but don't want to try it yourself. Only if the information or behaviors acquired are useful will observers put them to actual use. Figure 5.9 summarizes factors affecting observational learning.

As you can see, observational learning is a complex process—far more complex than mere imitation—and plays an important role in many aspects of behavior. This point is perhaps most forcefully illustrated by the controversy that has persisted in psychology, and in society as a whole, since the early 1960s: whether children, and perhaps even adults, are made more aggressive by long-term exposure to violence on television shows or in movies.

OBSERVATIONAL LEARNING AND AGGRESSION

A large body of evidence suggests that aggression may indeed be learned through observation (Baron & Richardson, 1994; Centerwall, 1989; Snyder, 1991; Wood, Wong, & Chachere, 1991). Apparently, when children and adults are exposed to new ways of aggressing against others—techniques they have not previously seen—they may add these new behaviors to their repertoire. Later, when angry, irritated, or frustrated, they may put such behaviors to actual use in assaults against others.

Of course, exposure to media violence, whether on the evening news or in movies or television programs, has other effects as well. It may convey messages that violence is an acceptable means of handling interpersonal difficulties; after all, if heroes and heroines can do it, why not viewers? It may elicit additional aggressive ideas and thoughts, convincing viewers, for example, that violence is even more common than it is (Berkowitz, 1984). And it may also lessen emotional reactions to aggression and the harm it produces, so that such outcomes seem less upsetting or objectionable (Thomas, 1982). When these effects are coupled with new behaviors and skills acquired through observational learning, the overall impact may contribute to an increased tendency among many persons to engage in acts of aggression (Eron, 1987).

It is important to note that not all findings support such conclusions (Freedman, 1986; Widom, 1989) and that the effects of exposure to media violence, when they occur, seem to be modest in scope. Given the fact that many children spend more time watching television and playing violent video games than they do any other single activity, however, the potential influence of such experience on behavior seems worthy of careful attention.

Research has also studied the effects of television on behavior in other areas of life. For instance, in one large-scale study, Geller (1988) examined automobile safety-belt use among stars on prime-time television shows for three years (1984–86). In general, the results of this study showed that the major television networks were, at least initially, irresponsible in their broadcasting practices. Drivers and their passengers were rarely shown belted, and the most probable consequences of crashes for unbelted vehicle occupants, serious injury or death, were almost never depicted. In response to this, Geller and his students initiated a nationwide campaign designed to bring public attention to the nonuse of safety belts by television stars. As part of this campaign, they encouraged children to write letters to their television heroes, requesting that they use safety belts. In one instance, more than 800 students from Olympia, Washington, wrote buckle-up requests to Mr. T, a star on a popular action program called "The A-Team." Interestingly, Mr. T increased from no belt use in 1984 to over 70 percent belt use in 1985, following the letter-writing campaign.

KEY QUESTIONS

- What is observational learning?
- What factors determine the extent to which we acquire new information through observational learning?
- In what forms of behavior does observational learning play a role?
- In what ways can observational learning be used to solve problems of everyday life?

It is noteworthy that safety-belt use on television shows *increased* over the three-year period of the study, consistent with changes in national safety-belt use statistics. Because television shows enjoy such a massive viewing audience, often millions of viewers, efforts to depict exemplary behavior among network stars—like safe driving—could potentially save millions of lives.

Observational learning, then, plays an important role in many aspects of behavior—including our language and customs. The following **Perspectives on Diversity** section explores this point further.

PERSPECTIVES ON DIVERSITY

Learning to Avoid Culture Shock

R ecently, psychologists have applied principles of observational learning to help solve a problem of growing concern: preparing people for the "culture shock" that can sometimes occur when they live and work in another country with a different language and unfamiliar customs.

As the United States and other nations move toward a global economy, companies throughout the world are faced with a difficult challenge. They must prepare their employees for a business environment that requires a broad range of skills and the ability to interact effectively with people from other cultures (Adler & Bartholomew, 1992; Feldman & Tompson, 1993). Dramatic differences in language, customs, and lifestyle often lead to unintended misunderstandings between persons from different cultural backgrounds. Behaviors that are acceptable and encouraged in one country may be offensive and intolerable to persons from another country. Indeed, ignorance of cultural differences has long been cited as a chief cause of misunderstandings between persons of different cultural backgrounds (Harris, 1979).

The scope of such differences was called sharply—and repeatedly—to my attention during a recent extended visit to France. One difference in particular stands out in my memory. In the United States, children treat adults in a casual manner; indeed, they often call them by their first name. In France, the situation is very different. Children are required to show a high degree of politeness toward adults. For example, whenever French children came within about ten feet of me, they would stop, bow slightly, and say "Good day, sir!" before running by. How different things were when I visited the Museum of Natural History in New York during the Christmas holidays. The museum was literally swarming with youngsters, and I lost count of the number who stepped on my feet or pushed me out of the way as they ran by. Imagine the reactions of French visitors to the United States when confronted with such behavior!

To soften the effects of such cultural gaps, companies that conduct business abroad have scrambled to develop cross-cultural training programs. The goal of these programs is to help a company's representatives toward more appropriate, sensitive, and consistent behavior in their cross-cultural interactions. Initial efforts to prepare employees for cross-cultural assignments focused on a cognitive approach, in which trainees received factual information about a particular country (Fielder et al., 1971).

More recently, however, experts in the area of cross-cultural training have advocated an "experiential" approach based on behavioral modeling (Black & Mendenhall, 1990). In the behavioral modeling approach, trainees first watch films in which models exhibit the correct behaviors in a problem situation. Then they participate in a situation role-playing exercise to test their knowledge. Finally, they receive constructive feedback regarding their performance.

Are such programs effective? Research findings suggest that the answer is yes. In one study, Harrison (1992) compared the effectiveness of several approaches to cross-cultural training. One experimental group received culture-relevant information only; another received behavioral modeling training only; a third received both components; and a fourth was a no-training control group. The results showed that participants who received both forms of training—information and behavioral modeling—performed best on measures of culture-specific knowledge and on a behavioral measure.

These findings, and those of other related studies, illustrate the important role that observational learning plays in alleviating the effects of culture shock. Observational learning initially enables us to perform behaviors appropriate to our own cultures, but later helps us to adapt to the demands of a rapidly changing world.

MAKING PSYCHOLOGY PART OF YOUR LIFE

Getting in Shape: Applying Psychology to Get Fit and Stay Fit

Need to get back into shape? Or lose a pound or twenty? Why not make learning principles a part of your fitness system? Establishing your fitness program using the principles discussed in this chapter will help you hit the diet and exercise trail running.

First, it is important to set your sights realistically. Don't try to lose all twenty pounds in one week or run ten miles the first time out. Why not? Recall reinforcement and punishment: Setting impossible goals will lead to failure, and failure will actually punish your efforts, making it even more difficult to stay with your program. If you've tried to stick with a diet or exercise program in the past and failed because of this, you can probably appreciate the point.

Instead, set yourself up for small wins by taking advantage of the principle of *shaping*—rewarding yourself with modest rewards for successive steps toward your ultimate exercise and weight-reduction goals. Then slowly increase the amount of exercise that you do or the amount of weight that you lose, building on each of your previous successes. Also, take care to choose rewards that are desirable but consistent with your goals. For example, if you are trying to lose weight, reward yourself with a movie or pants with a smaller waist size—not with a hot fudge sundae.

Third, specify the amount and intensity of the exercise you will do or the amount of weight you intend to lose—and write it down. Some people find that it is helpful to chart their progress in order to give themselves accurate and immediate feedback that will serve to reinforce or punish their behavior. Also, by placing the chart in a prominent place for yourself and your friends and family to see, you can take advantage of both positive and negative reinforcement. For example, you can work to receive the positive attention that will come your way when your chart shows progress. Negative reinforcement may also help you, because by posting your progress publicly you can work to avoid the negative comments you may get if you are tempted to "take a day off . . . just because."

Fourth, *stimulus control* can help set the stage for healthy responses. Avoid situations where you may be tempted to consume unhealthy food or beverages. Instead, go to places that are likely to occasion healthy responses. For example, by joining a health club, YMCA, or other *active* organization, you will be more likely to exercise and eat healthy.

Finally, take advantage of the principles of observational learning by identifying people with traits and skills that you admire. By observing and then emulating their behavior, you may become more efficient in reaching your goals.

Charting the progress of an exercise or weight loss program may help keep you on track because it provides accurate and immediate feedback.

CLASSICAL CONDITIONING: LEARNING THAT SOME STIMULI SIGNAL OTHERS

- **What is learning?**

Learning is any relatively permanent change in behavior (or behavior potential) produced by experience.

- **What is classical conditioning?**

Classical conditioning is a form of learning in which neutral stimuli (stimuli initially unable to elicit a particular response) come to elicit that response through their association with stimuli that are naturally able to do so.

- **On what factors does acquisition of a classically conditioned response depend?**

Acquisition of a conditional response is dependent on temporal arrangement of the CS–UCS pairings, intensity of the CS and the UCS relative to other background stimuli, and familiarity of any potentially conditioned stimuli that are present.

- **What is extinction?**

Extinction is the process through which a conditioned stimulus that is no longer paired with an unconditioned stimulus gradually ceases to elicit a conditioned response. However, the conditioned response can be quickly restored through reconditioning.

- **What is the difference between stimulus generalization and stimulus discrimination?**

Stimulus generalization allows us to apply our learning to other situations; stimulus discrimination allows us to differentiate among similar but different stimuli.

- **Is classical conditioning equally easy to establish with all stimuli for all organisms?**

Because of biological constraints on learning that differ among species, types of conditioning readily accomplished by some species are only slowly acquired—or not acquired at all—by others.

- **How are conditioned taste aversions acquired?**

Conditioned taste aversions are typically established when a food or a beverage (conditioned stimulus) is paired with a stimulus that naturally leads to feelings of illness (unconditioned stimulus). Conditioned taste aversions can be established after a single CS–UCS pairing.

- **How do modern views of classical conditioning differ from earlier perspectives?**

Modern views of classical conditioning emphasize the important role of cognitive processes.

- **What is blocking?**

In blocking, conditioning to one stimulus is prevented by previous conditioning to another stimulus.

- **What are flooding and systematic desensitization?**

Flooding and systematic desensitization are procedures used to extinguish fears established through classical conditioning. In flooding, a person is forced to come into contact with fear-eliciting stimuli without an avenue of escape. Cases in which fearful thoughts are too painful to deal with directly are treated by systematic desensitization—a progressive technique designed to replace anxiety with a relaxation response.

- **Do classical conditioning principles have practical applications in solving problems of everyday life?**

Basic principles of classical conditioning have been used to solve a variety of everyday problems, including phobias (learned fears) and unexplained instances of drug overdose.

KEY TERMS: learning, p. 158; classical conditioning, p. 159; stimulus, p. 159; unconditioned stimulus (UCS), p. 160; unconditioned response (UCR), p. 160; conditioned stimulus (CS), p. 160; conditioned response (CR), p. 160; acquisition, p. 161; delayed conditioning, p. 161; trace conditioning, p. 161; simultaneous conditioning, p. 161; backward conditioning, p. 161; extinction, p. 164; reconditioning, p. 164; spontaneous recovery, p. 164; stimulus generalization, p. 164; stimulus discrimination, p. 164; biological constraints on learning, p. 165; conditioned taste aversion, p. 166; phobias, p. 169; flooding, p. 169

OPERANT CONDITIONING: LEARNING BASED ON CONSEQUENCES

- **What is operant conditioning?**

In operant conditioning, organisms learn the relationships between certain behaviors and the consequences they produce.

- **Which operant techniques strengthen behavior? Which ones weaken behavior?**

Both positive and negative reinforcement strengthen or increase behavior. In contrast, punishment and omission training are techniques that suppress or weaken behavior.

- **What are examples of primary reinforcers and conditioned reinforcers?**

Primary reinforcers include food, water and sexual pleasure; conditioned reinforcers include money, status, and praise.

- **What is the Premack principle?**

The Premack principle suggests that more preferred activities can be used to reinforce less preferred activities.

- **In what way is shaping useful?**

Shaping is useful for establishing new responses by initially reinforcing successive approximations, which are behaviors that increasingly resemble the desired behavior.

- **What is chaining?**

Chaining is a procedure used to establish a complex sequence or chain of behaviors. The final response in the chain is shaped first; then, working backwards, earlier responses in the chain are reinforced by the opportunity to perform the last response in the chain, which leads to a reward.

- **What are schedules of reinforcement?**

Schedules of reinforcement are rules that determine the occasion on which a response will be reinforced. Schedules of reinforcement can be time-based or event-based, fixed or variable. Each schedule of reinforcement produces a characteristic pattern of responding.

- **When is the use of a continuous reinforcement schedule desirable?**

A continuous reinforcement schedule is useful for establishing new behaviors; partial or intermittent schedules of reinforcement are more powerful in maintaining behavior.

- **What is a discriminative stimulus?**

A discriminative stimulus signals the availability of reinforcement if a specific response is made. When a behavior occurs consistently in the presence of a discriminative stimulus, it is said to be under stimulus control.

- **What evidence supports the involvement of cognitive factors in operant conditioning?**

Studies of learned helplessness and contrast effects support the conclusion that cognitive factors play an important role in operant conditioning.

- **Why is knowledge of operant conditioning important?**

Procedures based on operant conditioning principles can be applied to help solve many problems of everyday life.

KEY TERMS: *operant conditioning, p. 171; reinforcement, p. 171; positive reinforcers, p. 171; Premack principle, p. 171; negative* *reinforcers, p. 172; punishment, p. 172; omission training, p. 172; shaping, p. 175; chaining, p. 175; schedules of reinforcement, p. 176; continuous reinforcement schedule, p. 177; fixed-interval schedule, p. 177; variable-interval schedule, p. 177; fixed-ratio schedule, p. 177; variable-ratio schedule, p. 177; discriminative stimulus, p. 179; stimulus control, p. 179*

OBSERVATIONAL LEARNING: LEARNING FROM THE BEHAVIOR AND OUTCOMES OF OTHERS

- **What is observational learning?**

Observational learning is the acquisition of new information, concepts, or forms of behavior through exposure to others and the consequences they experience.

- **What factors determine the extent to which we acquire new information through observational learning?**

In order for observational learning to be effective, we must pay attention to those modeling the behavior, remember the modeled speech or action, possess the ability to act on this memory, and have the motivation to do so.

- **In what forms of behavior does observational learning play a role?**

Observational learning plays a role in many types of behavior, including aggression.

- **In what ways can observational learning be used to solve problems of everyday life?**

Observational learning can play an important role in work settings—for example, in training workers to interact more effectively with people from different cultural backgrounds.

KEY TERM: *observational learning, p. 185*

CRITICAL THINKING QUESTIONS

APPRAISAL	At the present time, many psychologists are moving increasingly toward a cognitive view of the learning process. Do you think this movement is appropriate, or is there still a role for operant principles?
CONTROVERSY	Growing evidence suggests that animals do indeed form mental representations of their environments that are analogous to those formed by human beings. Does this mean that animals think? What are your views on this issue? What are the implications of this theory of animal learning?
MAKING PSYCHOLOGY PART OF YOUR LIFE	Knowing something about important principles of learning is very useful to persons who wish to get into shape or lose weight. But these are only two ways in which knowledge of learning can be applied to help people. Can you think of others?

Memory:
Of Things Remembered . . .
and Forgotten

Memory, people often say, is a very funny thing, and our life experiences tend to confirm this particular bit of folklore. Have you ever forgotten a phone number you looked up in the directory before you managed to dial it? Have you ever taken a wrong turn while driving because your memory told you that your destination was off in one direction, only to learn, later, that it was really in the opposite one? Has your mind ever gone blank when you were about to introduce two people to each other, or during an exam? Nearly everyone has had such experiences. In these situations we come face to face with the imperfect nature of **memory**—our cognitive system for storing and retrieving information.

Yet while memory is clearly far from perfect, it is also very impressive in several respects. We often retain vivid—and accurate—memories of events and scenes from months, years, or even decades in the past. On a recent visit to my parents' home, I came across a copy of my high school yearbook. I hadn't seen it for many years, yet I found that I easily recognized virtually every face in the book—people I hadn't seen in more than three decades. In a similar manner, most people who learned how to ride a bicycle as children can do so successfully as adults, even if many years have passed since their last ride. In these and other respects, memory truly *is* impressive.

Because it is clearly a crucial aspect of cognition, memory has long occupied a central place in psychological research. In fact, memory was the focus of some of the earliest systematic work in the field—studies conducted more than one hundred years ago by Hermann Ebbinghaus (1885). Using himself as a subject, Ebbinghaus memorized and then recalled hundreds of nonsense syllables— meaningless combinations of letters, such as teg or pxt. Some of his findings about the nature of forgetting have withstood the test of time and are valid even today. For example, he found that at first we forget materials we have memorized quite rapidly. Later, forgetting proceeds more slowly.

While Ebbinghaus's studies were ingenious in many respects, modern research on memory has gone far beyond these simple beginnings. It is probably safe to say that psychologists now know more about memory than about any other basic aspect of cognition. To provide you with an overview of this diverse and intriguing body of knowledge, we'll proceed in the following manner. First, we'll consider a basic model of human memory—one that is currently accepted by many psychologists. This model suggests that we actually possess three distinct memory systems. After describing the model, we'll examine each of these systems in turn, indicating how each carries out the basic tasks of memory: (1) entering information into storage, (2) retaining such input for varying periods of time, and (3) retrieving it when it is needed. Next, we'll explore the operation of memory in natural contexts—how memory operates in daily life, outside the confines of the experimental laboratory. We will focus on such issues as *autobiographical memory,* or memory of events and experiences in our own lives; *distortion and construction* in memory; and *eyewitness testimony.* We'll conclude by examining several memory disorders and what these disorders (plus other research) tell us about the biological nature of memory.

HUMAN MEMORY: The Information-Processing Approach

*H*ave you ever operated a personal computer? If so, you already know that computers, like people, have memories. In fact, most have two different types of memory: a temporary, working memory (known as random access memory), and a larger, and more permanent memory in which information is stored for longer periods of time (a hard drive). Do the memories of computers operate like those of human beings? Almost certainly not. Consider the following differences. Unless you correctly specify the precise nature and location of information you want to find, computers are unable to recover it. They merely flash an error message such as "Invalid path." In contrast, you can often find information in your own memory even on the basis of a partial description. Similarly, if information is lost from a computer, it is often permanently gone. In contrast, you can fail to remember a fact or information at one time but then remember it readily at another. And you can often remem-

Memory: The capacity to retain and later retrieve information.

CHAPTER 6

ber part of the information you want, even if you can't remember all of it. To repeat: human memory and computer memory are definitely *not* identical (Lewandowsky & Murdock, 1989).

Despite this fact, however, many researchers have concluded that there is sufficient similarity between computer memory and human memory for the former to serve as a rough working model for the latter. Both of these types of memory, after all, must accomplish the same basic tasks: (1) **encoding**, or converting information into a form that can be entered into memory; (2) **storage**, or retaining information over varying periods of time; and (3) **retrieval**, or locating and accessing specific information when it is needed at later times. Please don't misunderstand: The fact that computers and human memory deal with the same basic tasks in no way implies that they operate in an identical manner. They certainly do not. Thus, you should view this **information-processing approach** primarily as a useful means for drawing a bead on the key issues. It is a convenient way of discussing memory—not a fully developed representation of how memory operates.

Human Memory: One Influential Model—and an Emerging New Approach

Having issued these cautions, I should quickly note that in psychology the study of memory has proceeded, since the late 1960s, largely within the context of the information-processing approach. Thus, it makes good sense to organize much of this chapter around that basic theme. Further, several important models of memory rest firmly on this basic approach. Of these, a model proposed by Atkinson and Shiffrin (1968) has been perhaps the most influential.

The Modal Model: Three Kinds of Memory Systems   The Atkinson-Shiffrin model is sometimes described as the *modal*, or most representative, model. Its most central feature is the contention that in fact we possess not one but *three* distinct memory systems. One of these, known as *sensory memory*, provides temporary storage of information brought by our senses. If you've ever watched someone wave a flashlight in a dark room and perceived what seemed to be trails of light behind it, you are familiar with the operation of sensory memory.

A second type of memory is known as *short-term memory* (STM). Short-term memory holds relatively small amounts of information for brief periods of time, usually thirty seconds or less. This is the type of memory system you use when you look up a phone number and dial it immediately.

Our third memory system, *long-term memory*, allows us to retain vast amounts of information for very long periods of time. For example, consider the following incident (Marek, 1975). Once, just before the beginning of a concert, the noted conductor Arturo Toscanini was approached by a member of the orchestra who said that the lowest note on his bassoon was broken. Toscanini thought for a moment and then replied, "It is all right; that note does not occur in tonight's concert." In other words, in just a few moments he had mentally run through the entire score for all the instruments! Clearly, from the point of view of duration and capacity, long-term memory can be impressive. As we'll soon see, though, its key problem is retrieval: finding a specific piece of information in this huge storage system.

How does information move from one memory system to another? We'll return to this complex question in more detail below, but here I can note that the modal model (Atkinson & Shiffrin, 1968) suggests the operation of *active control processes* that act as filters, determining which information will be retained. Information in sensory memory enters short-term memory when it

Learning Objective 6.1
Explain why the information-processing approach uses the computer as a model for human memory.

Learning Objective 6.2
List the basic components of the modal model of memory.

Learning Objective 6.3
Compare and contrast the modal model with the parallel distributed processing perspective.

Learning Objective 6.4
List the characteristics of three types of information stored in memory.

Encoding: The process through which information is converted into a form that can be entered into memory.

Storage: The process through which information is retained in memory.

Retrieval: The process through which information stored in memory is located.

Information-Processing Approach: An approach to understanding human memory that emphasizes the encoding, storage, and later retrieval of information.

becomes the focus of our attention; sensory impressions that do not engage attention fade and quickly disappear. So, where memory is concerned, **selective attention**—our ability to pay attention to only some aspects of the world around us while largely ignoring others—often plays a crucial role.

In contrast, information in short-term memory enters long-term storage through *elaborative rehearsal*—when we think about its meaning and relate it to other information already in long-term memory. (Figure 6.1 provides a summary of the Atkinson and Shiffrin model.)

Parallel Distributed Processing: An Emerging Perspective While the modal model and related views remain important in psychology, other influential perspectives on memory exist as well (Craik & Lockhart, 1972). Of these, perhaps the one now receiving the greatest amount of attention is the

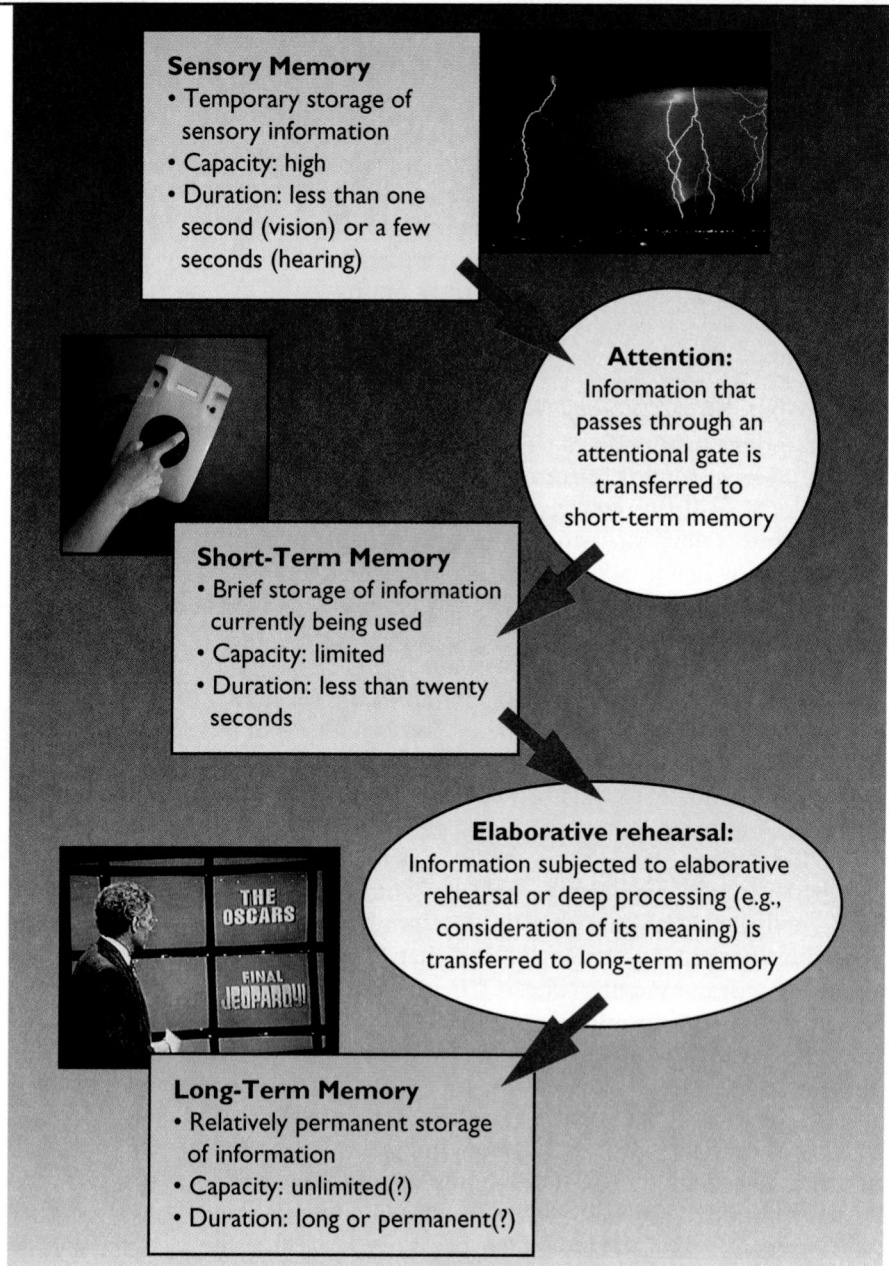

FIGURE **6.1**

One Widely Accepted Model of Memory

According to a model proposed by Atkinson and Shiffrin (1968), we actually possess three distinct memory systems. Information moves between these through *active control processes* such as attention and elaborative rehearsal.

Sensory Memory
• Temporary storage of sensory information
• Capacity: high
• Duration: less than one second (vision) or a few seconds (hearing)

Attention: Information that passes through an attentional gate is transferred to short-term memory

Short-Term Memory
• Brief storage of information currently being used
• Capacity: limited
• Duration: less than twenty seconds

Elaborative rehearsal: Information subjected to elaborative rehearsal or deep processing (e.g., consideration of its meaning) is transferred to long-term memory

Long-Term Memory
• Relatively permanent storage of information
• Capacity: unlimited(?)
• Duration: long or permanent(?)

Selective Attention: Our ability to pay attention to only some aspects of the world around us while largely ignoring others.

parallel distributed processing model (Lewandowsky & Murdock, 1989). According to this model, information is not processed in the step-by-step manner proposed by the Atkinson-Shiffrin model. In other words, it does not move from sensory to short-term and from short-term to long-term memory. Rather, the parallel distributed processing model suggests that information is actually processed simultaneously in several different parts of our total memory system. These parts or units operate in parallel, working on the same information at once. This means that many copies or representations of given information are present simultaneously at numerous locations within memory and can be accessed from any of these.

Why do many psychologists find this model so appealing? Because something like parallel processing of information is in fact necessary to account for many daily activities involving memory. For example, consider reading. This task, which most of us can perform with ease, includes recognizing the vertical, horizontal, and curved lines that combine to make up letters, identifying letters themselves, understanding words, and comprehending combinations of words. It is difficult to see how all these tasks could be performed so quickly and smoothly in the absence of something like parallel processing. In short, we must possess some mechanism for processing complex information from what we read *and* complex information already stored in memory at once.

So models of memory based on parallel processing seem consistent with the ways in which memory actually operates—and also, as we'll see in a later section, with growing evidence about the functioning of the human brain. To the extent that it helps us establish such links between cognitive and neural activity, the parallel distributed processing perspective may prove to be a valuable one.

TYPES OF INFORMATION IN MEMORY

If memory is a system (or, as we have seen, a set of systems) for retaining information, the next question is obvious: What types of information does it store? The world, and our experience in it, is incredibly diverse, so this is a more complex question than you might at first assume. After careful study, however, psychologists have concluded that most, if not all, information in memory can be classified as falling into one of three distinct categories.

The first is **semantic memory**: the sum total of each person's general, abstract knowledge about the world. What is the population of the United States? Is France larger or smaller than Brazil? Are shrimp crustaceans or mollusks? And, whatever their place in the animal kingdom, how long does it take to cook them? The answers to these and countless other questions are contained in semantic memory. Persons who win large prizes on television quiz shows are ones who have managed to expand the scope of their semantic memory beyond that of most other human beings. Semantic memory allows us to represent and mentally operate on objects or situations that are not present to our senses. As one expert on memory puts it (Tulving, 1993, p. 67), "The owner of a semantic memory system can think about things that are not here now."

A second type of information we retain involves specific events that we have experienced personally. This is known as **episodic memory** (or sometimes as *autobiographical memory*), and it is these memories that allow us, in a sense, to travel back in time. When was the last time you went to a movie? How did you feel on the day of your most recent graduation? What was it like to drive a car for the first time? Information pertaining to these and countless other aspects of your own experience are contained in episodic memory.

Another way to understand the difference between semantic and episodic memory is to think about the conscious experiences associated with them. When we retrieve information from episodic memory, we experience this as

SEMANTIC MEMORY IN ACTION

People who are highly successful on television quiz shows, like *Jeopardy*, have stored a tremendous amount of general knowledge in their semantic memories.

Parallel Distributed Processing Model: A model suggesting that our memory systems process information in several different ways simultaneously.

Semantic Memory: The content of our general, abstract knowledge about the world.

Episodic Memory: Memories of events that we have experienced personally (sometimes termed autobiographical memory).

the act of remembering; in a sense, we experience again something that happened to us in the past. In contrast, when we retrieve information from semantic memory, we realize that we know this information—we can bring it to mind. This is quite different from the conscious experience of remembering events in our lives (Tulving, 1993).

Finally, we retain information relating to the performance of various tasks. Do you know how to ice skate? Tie a necktie? Play the saxophone? If so, then you are well aware of the operation of our third type of memory, known as **procedural memory**. Procedural memories are the result of the basic learning processes discussed in chapter 5. In contrast to semantic and episodic memories, these memories are difficult to put into words; indeed, as we saw in chapter 4, trying to do so and becoming overly self-conscious can interfere with smooth performance. Yet such memories are extremely important, for without them we would be unable to retain many skills once they are learned.

As you can readily guess, we often require—and use—information of all three types at once. Consider a student taking a final examination. Obviously, she is drawing on facts stored in semantic memory. In addition, she is using complex motor skills such as writing, which are represented in procedural memory. And as she takes the exam, she may think about experiences with other examinations. For example, she may remember that recently she actually lowered her grade on an exam by changing many correct answers to wrong ones. As she recalls this, she may refrain from revising several answers. In this and many other situations, all three types of information are used at once.

SENSORY MEMORY: *Gateway to Consciousness*

Learning Objective 6.5
Explain the characteristics and functions of sensory memory.

Procedural Memory: A memory system that retains information we cannot readily express verbally—for example, information necessary to perform skilled motor activities such as riding a bicycle.

Sensory Memory: A memory system that retains representations of sensory input for brief periods of time.

You are waiting in a busy airport. Many different activities are occurring around you. People are rushing about; passengers are moving through security gates; people are talking, laughing, crying, hugging. You glance at a large video monitor containing flight information. You look away, but then, almost instantly, you look back to it. Something seemed different—what was it? Groaning, you realize that your flight has been delayed—again. Discouraged, you settle back in your chair for an even longer wait.

This incident may seem at first to have more to do with the difficulties of modern travel than with memory; but think again: What made you glance back at the screen? The answer involves what is in a sense our simplest memory system: **sensory memory**. This system holds representations of information from our senses very briefly—just long enough, it appears, for us to determine that some aspect of this input is worthy of further attention. Without such memory, you would have had no reason to look back at the video monitor. As soon as your eyes moved away from it, all traces of the screen and its contents would have vanished. In this and countless other situations, sensory memory is useful indeed. Without it, we'd be able to react only to those stimuli reaching us at a given instant.

How much can sensory memory hold? And how long does such information last? Existing evidence suggests that the capacity of sensory memory is quite large—indeed, it may hold fleeting representations of virtually everything we see, hear, taste, smell, or feel (Reeves & Sperling, 1986). These representations are retained for only brief periods, however. Visual sensory memory seems to last for less than a second, while acoustic sensory memory lasts for no more than a few seconds (Cowan, 1984). Convincing evidence for these conclusions was first gathered by Sperling (1960) in a series of now well-known experiments.

In one of these studies, participants were shown nine letters arranged in rows of three on a card. These stimuli were shown very briefly—for only 50 milliseconds (0.05 second). Participants were then asked to report all the letters they could remember. Under these procedures, their memory was not impressive: They could recall only about four or five of the nine letters shown. However, they reported the impression that right after seeing the card, they could remember all of the letters; the visual image faded quickly, however, so by the time participants had named four or five letters, the rest were completely gone. To determine if this was actually happening, Sperling devised an ingenious technique. Immediately after presentation of the letters, he sounded a tone that was either high, medium, or low in pitch. The high tone meant that participants should report the first row, the medium tone indicated that they should report the second, and so on. Results were clear: Under these conditions, participants demonstrated near-perfect scores. Just how quickly does such information fade? To answer this question, Sperling repeated the above procedures, but delayed presentation of the tone for various periods of time. Results indicated that sensory memory is indeed brief. When the tone was delayed only 0.10 second (100 milliseconds), participants' performance dropped sharply; when it was delayed for an entire second, their ability to remember the letters all but disappeared.

These findings, confirmed in many later studies, point to two conclusions. Sensory memory exists, and it can store an impressive amount of information. But it is very short-lived. Where sensory memory is concerned, then, it appears to be a matter of "now you see (hear) it, now you don't."

VISUAL SENSORY MEMORY

Visual sensory memory holds an image, such as a flash of lightning, for only a fraction of a second—just long enough for us to determine if it is worthy of further attention.

> ### KEY QUESTIONS
>
> - What kind of information does sensory memory hold?
> - How long do representations of the external world last in sensory memory?

SHORT-TERM MEMORY: *The Workbench of Consciousness*

*I*magine that you are in an ethnic restaurant tasting foods you've never had before. One of the dishes is truly delicious, so you ask the waiter for its name in his native language. He tells you, and you repeat it several times until you get it right. A couple of minutes later, you decide to write it down so you won't forget. You get out your pen and paper—only to find that it is already too late: You've forgotten the name of the dish. Have you ever had an experience like this? If not, remember the last time you looked up a phone number and forgot it while in the act of dialing; or the last time you met someone, only to forget his or her name within seconds of hearing it. Such experiences point to the existence of our second memory system: **short-term memory**, which holds a limited amount of information for a brief period of time. Despite its limitations, short-term memory, like sensory memory, is very important. Indeed, many experts view it as a kind of workbench for consciousness—a system for temporarily holding information you are using or processing right now. Thus, another term for short-term memory is *working memory.*

Learning Objective 6.6
Describe the evidence for the existence of a short-term memory system and its basic operation.

Short-Term Memory: A memory system that holds limited amounts of information for relatively short periods of time.

EVIDENCE FOR THE EXISTENCE OF SHORT-TERM MEMORY

Everyday experience strongly supports the existence of short-term memory and the view that it is distinct from long-term memory. But before turning to some of the basic characteristics of this memory system, let's also look briefly at some of the scientific evidence for its presence.

THE SERIAL POSITION CURVE   Suppose that someone read you a list of unrelated words and asked you to recall as many as possible in any order you wished. Which words would you be most likely to remember? Research findings indicate that you would be more likely to remember words at the beginning and at the end of the list than words in the middle (see Figure 6.2). Why does this effect, known as the **serial position curve**, occur? One possible answer involves the existence of two memory systems. Presumably, you remember the last words you heard quite well—a *recency* effect—because they are still in short-term memory when you are asked to recall them. And you remember the words at the start of the list because they have already been entered into long-term memory. Words in the middle, in contrast, have vanished from short-term memory and are not yet fully present in long-term memory. Several different studies have obtained results consistent with this reasoning (Postman & Phillips, 1965). The serial position curve concept, then, provides support for the existence of two distinct memory systems.

THE WORD-LENGTH EFFECT   A related finding is that lists of short words are often recalled more successfully than lists of long words—a finding known as the *word-length effect*. Recent evidence (e.g., Cowan et al., 1992) indicates that this is due to the fact that memory representation of some words deteriorates during the time it takes to pronounce other words aloud during recall. This finding, too, points to the existence of a short-term memory system.

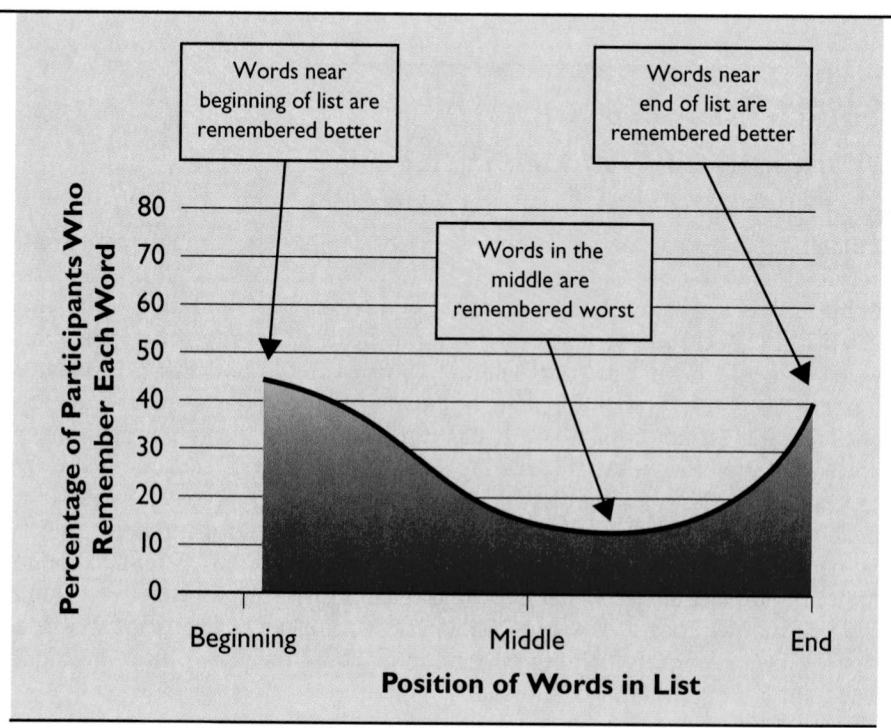

FIGURE 6.2

The Serial Position Curve

When people try to recall a list of unrelated words, they usually remember more words from the beginning and end of the list than from the middle. This serial position curve provides evidence for the existence of two distinct memory systems: short-term and long-term memory.

Serial Position Curve: The greater accuracy of recall of words or other information early and late in a list than words or information in the middle of the list.

ACOUSTIC AND SEMANTIC CODING   Additional evidence for the distinction between short-term and long-term memory comes from studies indicating that people have more difficulty in immediate recall of words or letters whose names sound alike, such as P, D, V, C, and T than of ones whose names sound different, such as K, Y, Z, W, and R (e.g., Wickelgren, 1965). This finding suggests that information is entered into immediate short-term memory in terms of acoustic coding—how it sounds. In contrast, when asked to recall words over longer periods, people have more difficulty remembering ones that sound different but are similar in meaning (such as big, huge, broad, long, tall) than ones that are dissimilar in meaning but sound alike (such as man, mad, cap, can). These latter findings suggest that information may be entered into long-term memory primarily in terms of its meaning. While other evidence suggests that this distinction is not as clear-cut as was once believed (Baddeley, 1990), the fact that information is coded differently when remembered for short periods of time than when remembered for longer ones supports the existence of two distinct memory systems.

In sum, despite some recent controversy concerning the existence of short-term memory (e.g., Crowder, 1993), considerable evidence offers support for the conclusion that we do indeed possess such a memory system (Cowan, Wood, & Borne, 1994).

SHORT-TERM MEMORY: *Its Basic Operation*

Now let's turn to some of the basic features of short-term memory. What kind of information does it hold? How much? And for how long?

In sensory memory, information is represented in a form similar to that reported by our senses. But information is represented somewhat differently in short-term memory. In short-term memory most verbal input, both the words we read and the words others speak, seems to be stored acoustically, by how it sounds (Salame & Baddeley, 1982). There is some indication, however, that information is also represented semantically, in terms of its meaning. When asked to recall words they have just memorized, people often confuse ones with similar meanings as well as ones that sound alike. So, it appears that we can store information in different ways in short-term memory.

Second, how much can this memory system hold? The answer seems to be something like seven to nine separate pieces of information. However, each of these "pieces" can contain several separate bits of information—bits that are somehow related and can be grouped together into meaningful units. When this is the case, each piece of information is described as a **chunk**, and the total amount of information held in chunks can be quite large. For example, consider the following list of letters: IBFIMBWBMATWIAC. After hearing or reading it once, would you remember it? Probably not. But imagine that, instead, the letters were presented as follows: FBI, IBM, BMW, TWA, CIA. Could you remember them now? The chances are much better that you could, because now you could combine them into meaningful chunks—acronyms for famous organizations. Because of the process of *chunking*, short term memory can hold a large amount of information, even though it can retain only seven to nine separate items at once.

Third, how long does information in short-term memory system last? The answer is clear: not very long. Unless it is actively *rehearsed* (repeated again and again), information entered into short-term memory fades quickly. Indeed, if individuals are prevented from rehearsing—for example, by being asked to count backwards—the information may be almost totally gone within twenty seconds (e.g., Peterson & Peterson, 1959).

Chunk: Stimuli perceived as a single unit or a meaningful grouping. Most people can retain seven to nine chunks of information in short-term memory at a given time.

- How long is information retained in short-term memory?
- What support does the serial position curve offer for the distinction between short-term memory and long-term memory?
- What additional evidence supports the distinction between short-term and long-term memory?

Additional evidence suggests that the greater the extent to which rehearsal is prevented, for example, by tasks even more distracting than counting backwards, the more rapid is the fading of short-term memory (Reitman, 1974). Further, most people seem aware of this important fact: When left to their own devices, a large majority of people actively rehearse information they wish to retain in short-term memory. The moral of such findings is clear. If you want to keep a phone number, a license plate, a new acquaintance's name, or any other piece of information in short-term memory, there's only one solution: rehearse, rehearse, and then rehearse some more.

LONG-TERM MEMORY: The Storehouse of Consciousness

Learning Objective 6.7
Explain the operation of long-term memory.

Can you remember your first trip to the dentist? Your first-grade teacher? Your first date? Even though these events occurred long ago, the chances are good that you have vivid memories of them. The fact that you do points to the existence of a third memory system—one that permits us to store vast quantities of information in a relatively permanent manner. This is known as **long-term memory**, and evidence concerning its accuracy is nothing short of startling. For example, in one study, Standing, Canezio, and Haber (1970) presented 2,560 color slides to participants at the rate of one slide every ten seconds. Later, they presented slides in pairs, each pair consisting of one slide participants had already seen and one they had not. The participants' task was to point to the slides they had seen earlier. Despite the enormous number of items shown, they were accurate almost 90 percent of the time!

Yet we have all had experiences in which we could not remember some item or piece of information, no matter how hard we tried. To make matters worse, at such times we often feel that the fact, name, or item we want is somewhere "in there" but lies just beyond our reach. This is known as the **tip-of-the-tongue phenomenon**, and research findings indicate that it is quite real. When individuals are given the definition of an uncommon English word such as *sampan, geode,* or *charisma* and report that they can almost think of the word, they are quite successful in supplying its first letter and indicating how many syllables it has (Brown & McNeill, 1966). To add to our frustration at such times, we often find ourselves repeatedly coming up with related but incorrect responses (Reason & Lucas, 1984). These tend to be words that are more common than the one we want, and as we think of them repeatedly, they tend to strengthen still further until they totally block all efforts to remember the word we really want. If we then give up, however, some kind of search often continues, and later, quite unexpectedly, the missing item suddenly appears in consciousness. These everyday experiences indicate that the information being sought is indeed present in memory but can't be located. As we'll soon see, *retrieval* is a crucial process where long-term memory is concerned; after all, information that can't be found is as useless to us, in a practical sense, as information that is no longer present.

So we are left with a mixed picture of long-term memory. On the one hand, it is impressive in its capacity to store huge quantities of information for long periods of time. On the other hand, it often lets us down just when we seem to need it most—for example, while we are taking exams or delivering an important speech. How does this memory system operate? How is

Long-Term Memory: A memory system for the retention of large amounts of information over long periods of time.

Tip-of-the-Tongue Phenomenon: The feeling that we can almost remember some information we wish to retrieve from memory.

information entered into long-term memory and later retrieved? These are among the questions we'll now consider.

LONG-TERM MEMORY: *Its Basic Operation*

The first question we should address is this one: How does information enter long-term memory from short-term memory? The answer seems to involve a process we have already discussed: rehearsal. In this case, though, the rehearsal does not consist simply of repeating what we wish to remember, as in restating a phone number over and over again. Rather, for information to enter long-term memory, **elaborative rehearsal** seems to be required. This is rehearsal requiring significant cognitive effort; it can include thinking about the meaning of the new information and attempting to relate it to information already in memory (see Figure 6.3). For example, if you wish to enter the facts and findings presented in a section of this chapter into long-term memory, it is not sufficient merely to state them over and over again. Instead, you should think about what they mean and how they relate to things you already know.

If elaborative rehearsal is required for information to enter long-term memory, then anything that interferes with such rehearsal should also interfere with long-term memory. Many factors produce such effects, but one with which many people have had direct experience is alcohol. Informal observation suggests that when consumed in sufficient quantities, this drug interferes with long-term memory, and research findings lend support to this claim: Alcohol does seem to impair human memory (Birnbaum & Parker, 1977). Specifically, it seems to interfere with the processes through which information is entered into long-term memory. We'll return to this topic in more detail in a discussion of eyewitness testimony later in this chapter (Yuille & Tollestrup, 1990).

LEVELS OF PROCESSING: COGNITIVE EFFORT AND LONG-TERM MEMORY We have been focusing on the concept of elaborative rehearsal as it relates to long-term memory; but now let's consider one of the alternative models of memory (alternatives to the modal model) we mentioned earlier: the **levels of processing view,** first introduced by Craik and Lockhart (1972). These

THE ROLE OF REHEARSAL

In order to pass from short-term to long-term memory, information must be rehearsed repeatedly.

Elaborative Rehearsal: Rehearsal in which the meaning of information is considered and the information is related to other knowledge already present in memory.

Levels of Processing View: A view of memory suggesting that the greater the effort expended in processing information, the more readily it will be recalled at later times.

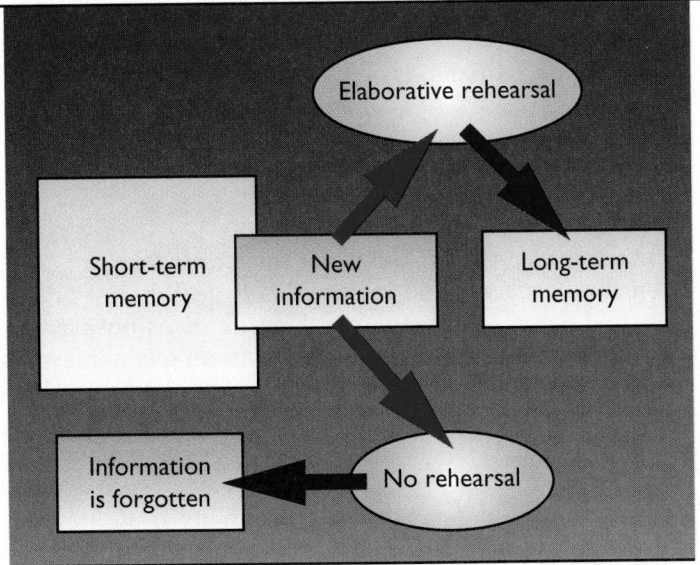

FIGURE 6.3

Entering Information into Long-Term Memory

In order for information to move from short-term memory to long-term memory, *elaborative rehearsal* is required. Such rehearsal involves thinking about the meaning of new information and attempting to relate it to information already in memory. If this cognitive effort is not expended, the new information may fail to enter long-term memory and be rapidly forgotten.

researchers suggested that rather than concentrating on the structure of memory and the different systems it involves, it might be more useful to concentrate on the processes that contribute to remembering. They noted that information can be processed in several different ways, ranging from relatively superficial *shallow processing* through more effortful and lasting *deep processing*. Shallow processing might consist of merely repeating a word or making a simple sensory judgment about it—for example, do two words or letters look alike? A deeper level of processing might involve somewhat more complex comparisons—for example, do two words rhyme? A much deeper level of processing would include attention to meaning—for example, do two words have the same meaning? Does a word make sense when used in a specific sentence?

Considerable evidence suggests that the deeper the level of processing that takes place when we encounter new materials, the more likely the materials are to enter long-term memory. For example, in a well-known study, Craik and Tulving (1975) presented unrelated words and asked participants one of three kinds of questions about each word: Was the word written in capital or lower-case letters? Did the word rhyme with another word? Did the word fit within a given sentence? After answering a large number of such questions, participants were asked whether each word in a list was one they had already seen or was new. Results offered clear support for the levels of processing view. The deeper the level of processing performed by subjects, the slower their responses—but the more accurate their decisions.

Why does deeper and more effortful processing of information lead to better long-term memory? One possibility is that such cognitive effort leads us to encode more features of the items in question. This, in turn, makes it easier to locate the information later. Supporting this view is the fact that, in general, when people not only see a series of objects but actually perform some action on them, they can later remember the names of the objects better in a test of free recall—a test in which they are simply asked to recall as many of the objects as possible (Nilsson & Cohen, 1988).

While such findings are compatible with the levels of processing model, there are still some difficulties with this model that cannot be overlooked. For example, it is difficult to specify in advance just what constitutes a deep versus a shallow level of processing. Second, it is not clear that a person can read a word over and over again and not be aware of, or think about, its meaning. In fact, several forms of processing (such as acoustic and semantic) may occur at once. So it is difficult to speak about discrete levels of processing.

Despite such problems, there can be little doubt that the levels of processing view has added to our understanding of long-term memory, and especially to our knowledge of how information is entered into this system.

RETRIEVAL: *Locating Information in Long-Term Memory*

As noted earlier, the limitations of short-term memory are all too obvious: It has limited capacity, and information is quickly lost unless it is continually rehearsed. Long-term memory, of course, does not have these problems. It has a seemingly limitless capacity, and it can retain information for very long periods, perhaps indefinitely. Is it, then, a perfect memory system? Definitely not. All too often we are unable to remember information we need just when we need it. Only later—maddeningly!—does it sometimes appear effortlessly in our mind (Payne, 1987). What is the cause of such difficulties? The answer involves the process of *retrieval*—our ability to locate information that has previously been stored in memory.

Where long-term memory is concerned, it is difficult to separate retrieval from the issue of *storage*—the way information is initially placed in long-term memory. Storage plays an important role in determining how readily information can later be retrieved. In general, the better organized materials are, the easier they are to retrieve (Bower et al., 1969). One key to the effective retrieval of information from long-term memory, then, is *organization*. Organizing information requires extra effort, but it appears that the benefits in terms of later ease of retrieval make this effort well worthwhile.

RETRIEVAL CUES: STIMULI THAT HELP US REMEMBER   Imagine that after an absence of several years, you return to a place where you used to live. On your arrival memories of days gone by come flooding back, with no apparent effort on your part to bring them to mind. You remember incidents you had totally forgotten, conversations with people you haven't seen in years, even the weather during your last visit. Have you ever had this kind of experience? If so, you are already familiar with the effects of what psychologists term **retrieval cues**. These are stimuli that are associated with information stored in memory and so can help bring it to mind at times when it cannot be recalled spontaneously. Such cues can be aspects of the external environment—a place, sights or sounds, even smells. Indeed, some evidence suggests that odors are particularly effective in evoking memories of events in our lives (Richardson & Zucco, 1989).

Many studies point to the important impact of retrieval cues on long-term memory. Perhaps the most intriguing research on this topic involves what is known as **context-dependent memory**: the fact that material learned in one environment is more difficult to remember in a very different context than it is in the original one. A study performed by Godden and Baddeley (1975) ingeniously illustrates context-dependent memory.

In this study, participants were practiced deep-sea divers. They learned a list of words either on the beach or beneath fifteen feet of water; then they tried to recall the words either in the same environment in which they had learned them or in the other setting. Results offered striking evidence for the impact of context—in this case, physical setting. Words learned on land were recalled much better in this location than under water, and vice versa. Interestingly, such effects were not found with respect to recognition—merely deciding whether or not they had seen the words before (Godden & Baddeley, 1980). Thus, it appears that context-related retrieval cues are beneficial primarily with respect to actual recall. Additional findings suggest that it is not necessary to be in the location or context where storage into long-term memory occurred; merely imagining this setting may be sufficient (Smith, 1979). In other words, we seem capable of generating our own context-related retrieval cues.

Finally, even our own internal states can serve as retrieval cues in some cases. The concept of **state-dependent retrieval** refers to the fact that it is often easier to recall information in long-term memory when our internal state is similar to that at the time the information was first learned than when these states are different. For example, suppose that while studying for an exam you drink lots of coffee. Thus, the effects of caffeine are present while you memorize the materials in question. On the day of the test, should you also drink lots of coffee so that the effects of caffeine will again be present? Will these effects act as a retrieval cue and enhance your memory? The results of several studies indicate that this will indeed be the case (Eich, 1985). Again, as in the case of context-related memory, state-dependent retrieval seems to apply only to free recall; recognition is not necessarily enhanced.

In sum, many different stimuli can serve as retrieval cues. Which ones do we actually use, and which are most helpful? According to the **encoding specificity principle** (Tulving & Thomson, 1973), this depends on what

Retrieval Cues: *Stimuli associated with information stored in memory that can aid in its retrieval.*

Context-Dependent Memory: *The greater ease of recall of information entered into memory in one context or setting in that same context than in others.*

State-Dependent Retrieval: *Retrieval of information stored in long-term memory cued by aspects of one's physical state.*

Encoding Specificity Principle: *The fact that only cues encoded at the time information is entered into memory can later contribute to the retrieval of such information.*

- How does information move from short-term to long-term memory?
- What does the levels of processing view suggest about the relationship between cognitive effort and memory?
- What are retrieval cues?

information we enter into memory in the first place. If, when learning some information, you encode certain aspects of your physical surroundings as part of the "package," these will later serve as useful retrieval cues. If your internal state is part of what is encoded, then this will later serve as an effective retrieval cue. The key point seems to be a close match between the conditions under which you first acquire some information and the conditions under which you attempt to recall it. The specific nature of individual retrieval cues seems to be of less importance.

FORGETTING FROM LONG-TERM MEMORY

Learning Objective 6.8
Compare and contrast the trace decay hypothesis and the interference view of forgetting.

Learning Objective 6.9
Discuss the factors that influence prospective memory.

When are we most aware of memory? Typically, when it fails—when we are unable to remember information that we need at a particular moment. Given this fact, it is not surprising that the first systematic research on memory, conducted by Ebbinghaus, was concerned with forgetting. As you may recall, Ebbinghaus experimented on himself and studied the rate at which he forgot nonsense syllables. The results of his investigations suggested that forgetting is rapid at first but slows down with the passage of time.

Modern research has generally confirmed Ebbinghaus's findings where meaningless materials such as nonsense syllables are concerned, but suggests that we are much better at remembering other and more meaningful types of information. For example, Bahrick (1984) asked college professors to identify the names and faces of former students who had taken a single course with them. Even after more than eight years, the professors were quite successful in recognizing the students' names and in matching their names with photos of them. Similarly, it is clear that many complex skills, such as swimming, driving a car, or riding a bicycle, are retained over long periods of time, even if we have little opportunity to practice them. In contrast, other skills—ones requiring associations between specific stimuli and responses, called discrete skills—are subject to much greater degrees of forgetting. Thus, a few months after learning how to perform a procedure for reviving heart attack victims, most individuals have forgotten many of the steps and actions it involves (McKenna & Glendon, 1985). And many other complex skills, such as typing, show a similar pattern. What, then, accounts for forgetting? Why is information firmly entered in long-term memory sometimes lost, at least in part, with the passage of time? Several explanations have been offered; here we'll focus on the two that have received the most attention. After that, we'll examine a sharply contrasting view of forgetting—*repression*—and its bearing on the tragedy of childhood sexual abuse (Loftus, 1993).

THE TRACE DECAY HYPOTHESIS: *Forgetting with the Passage of Time*

Perhaps the simplest view of forgetting is that information entered into long-term memory fades or decays with the passage of time. This suggestion is consistent with our informal experience: Often, information we acquired quite some time ago is more difficult to remember than information learned only recently. Yet considerable evidence suggests that decay is probably not the key mechanism in forgetting.

First, consider a famous study conducted by Jenkins and Dallenbach (1924). They asked two participants to learn a list of ten nonsense syllables. In one condition, both individuals then went directly to sleep. In another, they continued with their normal activities. The participants' recall of the nonsense syllables was tested after one, two, four, and eight hours. Results indicated that forgetting was more rapid when the participants stayed awake than when they went to sleep. These findings argue against the suggestion that forgetting is primarily the result of gradual decay of information over time.

Can you see any problems with this study that raise doubts about its seemingly straightforward results? Here's one problem: Participants who went to sleep learned the nonsense syllables in the evening; those who stayed awake learned them in the morning. Thus, differences in circadian rhythms may have played a role in the obtained results. Indeed, sleep during the day does not seem to reduce forgetting as reported by Jenkins and Dallenbach.

However, other research, in which animals have been kept awake but prevented from moving about and engaging in normal activities, also indicates that forgetting is not merely a matter of the passage of time. In one such study, for example, Minami and Dallenbach (1946) taught cockroaches to avoid a dark compartment by giving them an electric shock whenever they entered it. After the subjects had mastered this simple task, they were either restrained in a paper cone or permitted to wander around a darkened cage at will. Results again argued against the trace decay hypothesis: Roaches permitted to move about showed substantially more forgetting over a given period of time.

FORGETTING AS A RESULT OF INTERFERENCE

If forgetting is not a function of the passage of time and the weakening of materials stored in memory, then what *is* its source? The answer currently accepted by most psychologists focuses on *interference* between items of information stored in memory. Such interference can take two different forms (see Figure 6.4). In **retroactive interference**, information currently being learned interferes with information already present in memory. If learning the rules of a new board game causes you to forget the rules of a similar game you learned to play

Retroactive Interference: *Interference with retention of information already present in memory by new information being entered into memory.*

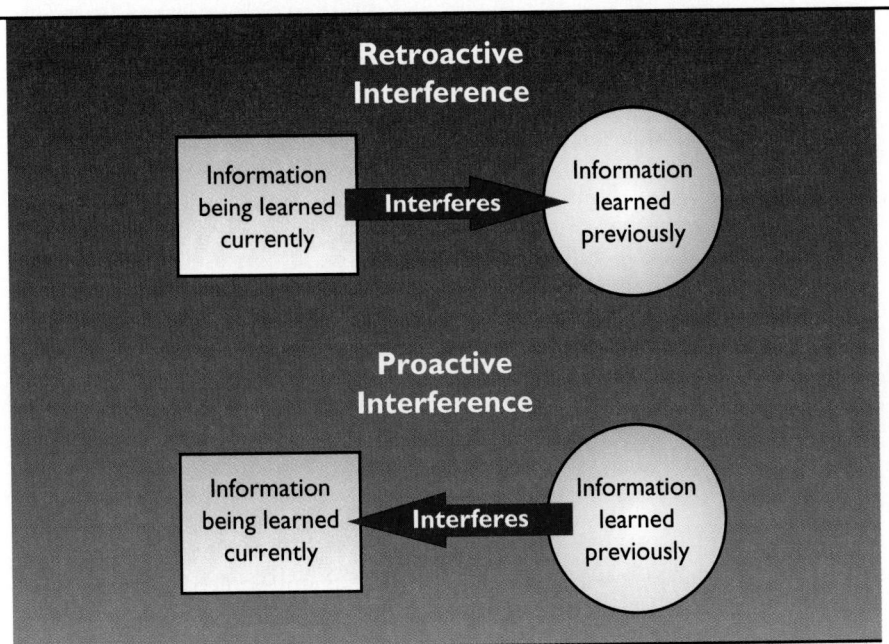

FIGURE 6.4

Retroactive and Proactive Interference: Important Factors in Forgetting

In *retroactive interference*, information currently being learned interferes with retention of previously acquired information. In *proactive interference*, information learned previously interferes with retention of new information.

Retroactive Interference

Information being learned currently — **Interferes** → Information learned previously

Proactive Interference

Information being learned currently ← **Interferes** — Information learned previously

last year, you are experiencing the effects of retroactive interference. In contrast, the second form of interference, **proactive interference**, occurs when previously learned information interferes with information you are acquiring at present. If information you have mastered about how to operate an old VCR interferes with your ability to operate a new one that has very different controls, you are experiencing the impact of proactive interference.

A large body of evidence offers support for the view that interference plays a key role in forgetting from long-term memory (e.g., Tulving & Psotka, 1971). For example, in many laboratory studies, the more similar the words or nonsense syllables participants are to learn from different lists, the more interference among them, and the poorer the participants' ability to remember these materials (Gruneberg, Morris, & Sykes, 1988). What remains unclear, however, is precisely *how* interference causes forgetting. Does it actively push information out of memory? Or does it merely impede our ability to retrieve information? A final answer to such questions must await the completion of additional research.

Please see the **Point of It All** section for information about *repression*, a third potential cause of forgetting from long-term memory.

THE POINT OF IT ALL

Repression: Do We Sometimes Forget Because We Want to Forget?

I n 1991, George Franklin Sr. was convicted of sexually attacking and then murdering an eight-year-old girl who was a friend of his daughter. The crime had occurred in 1969—more than twenty years earlier. How had he escaped prosecution for all these years, and why was he finally placed on trial so long after this tragic crime? The answer is that in 1990 his daughter Eileen came forward and accused her father of being the murderer. Further—and directly related to our discussion of forgetting—she claimed that she had not come forward sooner because she had not remembered these events until shortly before she made her accusations. How could she "forget" such traumatic events for so long a period?

One answer is provided by a third theory of forgetting from long-term memory—the theory of **repression**. According to this theory, which plays a key role in Freud's views of personality and mental illness (as we'll see in chapters 10 and 12), traumatic events such as the one described above are so shocking that all memory of them is forced from consciousness—*repressed*—into hidden recesses of the unconscious. There, the memories lie hidden until they are brought back into consciousness by some specific event, for example, by the probings of a therapist. In short, the theory of repression suggests that we forget certain information and experiences because we find them too frightening or threatening to bear.

The existence of repression is widely accepted by psychologists and psychiatrists, as well as by society generally (Loftus & Herzog, 1991). Thus, Eileen Franklin's charges carried great weight with the jury who tried her father—so much weight, in fact, that he was convicted primarily on this evidence.

Repression has featured prominently in many dramatic trials focusing on charges of *early childhood sexual abuse*. In these trials, repression has been offered as an explanation for the fact that the victims failed to remember these terrible experiences until many years after they occurred. Only when these individuals were exposed to careful questioning by trained therapists did memories of their abuse during early childhood come flooding back into con-

Proactive Interference:
Interference with the learning or storage of current information by information previously entered into memory.

Repression: A theory of forgetting that suggests that memories of experiences or events we find threatening are sometimes pushed out of consciousness so that they can no longer be recalled.

CHAPTER 6

sciousness. Such trials, and the accounts of the persons involved, certainly make for dramatic reading. Indeed, in recent years, many public figures—entertainers, famous athletes, and even Miss America—have reported the sudden emergence of traumatic memories of childhood abuse.

The growing frequency of these reports raises a question: Are the frightening "memories" always—or even usually—accurate? Did the persons who report them actually experience the devastating events? This is a complex question, because in many cases the alleged events occurred so long ago that concrete objective evidence of their occurrence is difficult to obtain. In addition, as noted by Loftus (1993), a leading expert on memory, there are several reasons for viewing at least some of these claims with a healthy degree of skepticism.

First, and most important, there is still very little scientific evidence for the existence of repression. Most support for the theory of repression derives from case studies. While these are often quite impressive, they do not, as we saw in chapter 1, generally provide conclusive evidence on the issues they address. Indeed, existing evidence for the existence of repression is so weak that one researcher (Holmes, 1990, p. 97) has suggested that use of the concept of repression in psychological reports should be preceded by the following statement: "*Warning: The concept of repression has not been validated with experimental research and its use may be hazardous to the accurate interpretation of behavior.*"

Second, the fact that many therapists believe strongly in the existence of repression and its role in psychological disorders indicates that in some instances, at least, therapists may act in ways that lead clients to report repressed memories even if they don't really have them. For example, a therapist who believes in the powerful impact of repressed memories might say something like this: "You know, in my experience a lot of people who are struggling with the same kind of problems as you had painful experiences as kids—they were beaten or even molested. I wonder if anything like that ever happened to you?" Faced with such questions and the *demand characteristics* they imply (refer to chapter 1), clients may begin to search their memories for traces of traumatic early events. This search, in turn, may sometimes lead them to generate memories that weren't there or to distort ones that do exist. As we'll see later in this chapter, growing evidence suggests that memories can be generated or altered in precisely this fashion (e.g., Haugaard et al., 1991; Loftus & Coan, in press).

Third, even if they are not undergoing therapy and do not hear their therapist suggest repressed memories, many people may be influenced by media accounts indicating that both early sexual abuse and repressed memories of these experiences are quite common. Following exposure to such accounts, persons suffering from depression, sexual dysfunction, or other psychological problems may be all too ready to attribute these difficulties to traumatic childhood events that they can no longer remember.

I am not suggesting that repressed memories never exist or that they can't be accurate. There is certainly no doubt that childhood sexual abuse is a disturbingly frequent occurrence (Kutchinsky, 1992). However, there do seem to be sufficient questions concerning both the nature and the occurrence of repression, and sufficient evidence that even memories of traumatic events can be unintentionally fabricated, to suggest the need for caution. Many reports of repressed memories of early sexual abuse may indeed be accurate. But careful research indicates that memory is sometimes highly susceptible to distortion by misleading questions or false information (Loftus, 1992). Even worse, once such errors and distortions of memory occur, they may be accepted as truth by the person involved.

Thus, as Loftus (1993) has put it, we must careful to avoid letting false memories of early childhood abuse take on the certainty of unalterable fact. Falling into this trap, it seems, could ultimately be as dangerous and unfair to ostensible perpetrators as closing our eyes to the existence and frequency of abuse was, in the past, to its victims.

REPRESSION AND MEMORY

In the 1991 trial of George Franklin, his daughter testified that she had witnessed the murder that took place more than twenty years earlier. She claimed that the memory had been repressed since the traumatic event took place.

PROSPECTIVE MEMORY: Forgetting to Do What We're Supposed to Do

So far, we have focused on what can be termed *retrospective forgetting*—an inability to remember specific information entered into memory at an earlier time. Such forgetting is important, but often it is not the most annoying type we experience. Much worse, from this perspective, are those occasions on which we forget to keep an appointment or forget to perform some chore or errand we promised to complete. Such incidents involve **prospective memory**—remembering that we are supposed to perform some action at a certain time. Such memory has important practical implications. Missing an important meeting can have serious consequences for a person's career; forgetting to take a prescribed medication at certain times of the day can adversely affect a person's health (Ley, 1988).

Why do we experience such forgetting? The answer seems to involve at least two factors. First, such forgetting is closely related to motivation. We tend to forget appointments or errands that are relatively unimportant to us or that we view as unpleasant burdens, while remembering the ones we judge to be important or pleasurable (Winograd, 1988). For example, many dentists have to phone their patients the day before to remind them of their appointments; whereas few hairdressers find this necessary.

Second, prospective memory, like other forms of memory, involves the impact of retrieval cues. We remember to perform those activities that we build into the structure of our days in such a way that we are reminded of them by various cues. Thus, we remember to go to the supermarket, the dry cleaners, and the bank on the way home by taking a route that passes each of these establishments; the route itself provides vivid reminders for prospective memory. Other cues we use for prospective memory are internal, relating to the passage of time (Harris & Wilkins, 1982). At first we check our watch or nearby clocks frequently, to "calibrate" our internal time-measuring mechanism. In the middle of the waiting period, we perform fewer checks. Later, as the time for performing some activity—such as removing a cake from the oven or departing for a meeting—approaches, we check clocks and watches with increasing frequency. The result: we have a continuing series of cues to remind us of the activity we must perform (Ceci, Baker, & Bronfenbrenner, 1988). If retrieval cues are absent, however, prospective memory may fail us.

KEY QUESTIONS

- Why does forgetting from long-term memory occur?
- What is retroactive interference?
- What is proactive interference?
- What does existing evidence suggest about the role of repression in forgetting?
- What is prospective memory?

MEMORY IN NATURAL CONTEXTS

Learning Objective 6.10
Discuss the operation of autobiographical memory and how it is studied.

Much of the research mentioned so far has involved the performance of relatively artificial tasks: memorizing nonsense syllables, lists of words, or lists of numbers. While we do have to remember some such items in real life, this kind of research seems fairly remote from many situations in daily life. In this section, we'll turn to the operation of memory in natural contexts and see how it operates in our daily lives (Loftus, 1991).

AUTOBIOGRAPHICAL MEMORY: Remembering the Events of Our Own Lives

Prospective Memory: Remembering to perform certain activities at specific times.

How do we remember information about our own lives—*autobiographical memory*? Also known as *episodic memory*, this topic has long been of interest to psychologists and has been studied in several different ways. For example, Baddeley and his colleagues (Kopelman, Wilson, & Baddeley, cited in Baddeley, 1990) have developed an *Autobiographical Memory Schedule*, in which individuals are systematically questioned about different periods of their lives. Questions about childhood ask them to supply the names of their teachers and friends and addresses at which they lived and to describe incidents in their early lives. Additional questions are asked about other periods in their lives. The information obtained is then checked for accuracy against objective records, and in this way, the accuracy of autobiographical memory can be assessed.

DIARY STUDIES: RECALLING THE DAILY EVENTS OF OUR LIVES   Another technique for studying autobiographical memory involves efforts by individuals to keep detailed diaries of events in their own lives (Linton, 1975). In one such study, the Dutch psychologist Willem Wagenaar (1986) kept a diary for six years. On each day he recorded one or two incidents, carefully indicating who was involved, what happened, where it happened, and when it took place. He rated each incident in terms of whether it was something that happened frequently or rarely, and he also indicated the amount of emotional involvement he experienced. During the course of the study, he recorded a total of 2,400 incidents. Then he tested his own memory for each, over a period of twelve months. To do so, he took each incident and, after cueing himself with one piece of information, tried to recall the rest. Thus, he might provide the *who*, and then try to recapture the *what*, *where*, and *when*. Of course, he randomly selected the cue; for some incidents it involved *what*, for others *where*, and so on.

The findings Wagenaar (1986) reported are intriguing. First, he found that cues relating to who, what, and where were about equally effective in prompting memory. Information about when an incident took place, however, was far less useful. This not surprising. Can you remember where you were last June 12 or October 15? Probably not, unless these dates are personally significant for you—your birthday or anniversary, for instance. But you probably have a much better chance of remembering where you were during a particular incident if you know whom you were with or what you were doing.

In addition, and as expected, Wagenaar found that the more cues he provided to himself, the more successful he was in answering correctly. Thus, if he knew who, what, and when, he was more successful in supplying the where than if he knew only who or what alone. He also found, again far from surprisingly, that incidents that were unusual, emotionally involving, or pleasant were easier to recall than ones that were unpleasant. Finally, he appeared to forget fewer items than did other persons who have conducted similar studies (e.g., Linton, 1975), perhaps because he used a more detailed procedure for recording incidents and remembering them—one that provided him with more retrieval cues.

Please keep in mind that there was only one subject in Wagenaar's (1986) study, and that the study was essentially observational in nature. As noted in chapter 1, while such research is often informative, it cannot establish causal relations or test hypotheses with the same degree of precision as experimentation. But Wagenaar's project, and the results of similar studies, indicate that autobiographical memory is affected by many of the same variables—such as retrieval cues and emotional states—that have been found to affect memory for abstract information presented under controlled laboratory conditions. This is valuable information in itself, and it suggests that further efforts to investigate autobiographical memory may indeed prove fruitful.

Learning Objective 6.11
Describe the nature of infantile amnesia.

Learning Objective 6.12
Discuss the evidence for and against the existence of flashbulb memories.

Learning Objective 6.13
Explain how schemas influence memory distortion and memory construction.

MEMORY FOR TIMES OF PAST EVENTS: WHEN DID YOU DO WHAT YOU REMEMBER DOING?

Consider the following events:

Your last visit to the dentist

The most recent presidential election

Your most recent date

The last time you ate Chinese food

Your most recent midterm exam

Can you place these events in chronological order from the one that occurred earliest to the one that occurred most recently? Of course—in fact, this sounds like a very trivial request. But the fact that you can do this with such ease and certainty points to an important fact about autobiographical memory: It involves a strong sense of time. Looking back over our lives, we do not see a jumble of unrelated events. Rather, we perceive a "story" that unfolds in time, with one event following another. We have a sense of how long ago each event occurred—its distance from the present. We know its general location in the patterns of our life; for example, that it happened while we were in high school rather than college. And we know each event's relative position, whether it occurred before or after other events in our lives (Friedman, 1993).

How do we manage to keep track of time in this impressive manner? Research findings offer support for the following conclusions. As events occur, they are associated in memory with general contextual information and with other events. For example, consider your memories of your first date. At the time this event took place and information about it was entered into memory, it was associated with information about the environment (for example, you had just moved to a new house, it was a blazingly hot day) and about your own internal state (you were just recovering from the flu, you were feeling anxious about entering a new school), and so on. Later, when you think about your first date, you retrieve this contextual information along with information about the date. Since you know when you moved, that it is hot only in the summer, and that you tend to worry about the coming school year only during August, you immediately have lots of useful information at your disposal (e.g., Brown, Shevell, & Rips, 1986; Friedman, 1993). And this kind of information forms the basis for our ability to determine fairly accurately the timing of past events. Apparently, it is by examining past events in the context of a wealth of other information about our own lives and a rich knowledge of social, natural, and personal time patterns that we know when events took place. Please see the **Key Concept** page for an overview of the different kinds of memory.

INFANTILE AMNESIA: FORGETTING THE EVENTS OF OUR EARLIEST YEARS

What is your earliest memory? If you are like most people, it probably dates from your third or fourth year of life, although some persons seem capable of recalling events that occurred when they were as young as two (Usher & Neisser, in press). This inability to recall events that happened to us during the first two or three years of life is known as **infantile amnesia** (Howe & Courage, 1993) and is, in one important sense, quite puzzling. It is obvious that we do retain information we acquired during the first years of life, for it is then that we learned to walk and to speak. Why, then, is autobiographical memory absent for this period? Why are we unable to recall events that happened to us at specific times and in specific places? Until recently, two explanations were widely accepted. According to the first, autobiographical memory is absent early in life because the brain structures necessary for such memories are not sufficiently developed at this time (Moscovitch, 1985). A second possibility involves the absence of language skills. Since we can't verbalize

Infantile Amnesia: Inability to remember the first two or three years of life, probably because we did not possess a well-developed self-concept during that period.

Different Kinds of Memory: An Overview

Primary Memory Systems

Sensory Memory

Holds information from our senses for brief periods of time.

An image of a flash of lightning is held in visual sensory memory for just a fraction of a second.

Short-Term Memory

Holds a limited amount of information—about seven to nine "chunks"—for short periods of time—less than a minute.

Short-term memory allows us to remember a phone number we have just looked up long enough to dial it.

Long-Term Memory

Holds seemingly unlimited amounts of information for long periods of time—perhaps indefinitely.

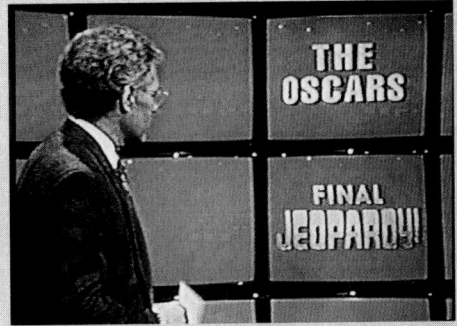

The wide range of information representing correct answers to quiz show questions is held in long-term memory.

Aspects of Long-Term Memory

Prospective Memory

Memory for actions that we are supposed to perform at a certain time.

Autobiographical Memory

Memory for information about our own lives including information about the *who, what, where,* and *when* of events we have experienced.

Memory for the Timing of Past Events

Memories for when various events in our own lives occurred.

Flashbulb Memories

Memories of where we were or what we were doing at the time of significant or unusual events.

THE CHALLENGER EXPLOSION

For many of us, the tragic explosion of the space shuttle *Challenger* represents a *flashbulb memory*—we remember where we were and what we were doing when we heard the news in 1986. Can you think of other flashbulb memories?

very effectively during the first two years of life, and since language plays a key role in long-term memory, it is not surprising that we cannot remember specific events from this period (Baddeley, 1990).

More recent findings, however, suggest that neither of these explanations is entirely accurate. Contrary to widespread belief, infants appear to possess relatively well-developed memory abilities. For example, as we'll see in chapter 8, babies can imitate actions shown by an adult even after a twenty-four-hour delay (Meltzoff, 1990). Similarly, they show considerable retention of both nontraumatic and traumatic events (e.g., Goodman et al., 1991).

In view of such findings, it does not seem reasonable to explain infantile amnesia in terms of infants' lack of memory abilities. What, then, does account for this phenomenon? According to Howe and Courage (1993), the answer lies in the fact that it is not until somewhere between our second and third birthday that most of us develop a clear *self-concept*. And without this concept, these researchers contend, we lack the personal frame of reference necessary for autobiographical memory. In other words, we cannot remember events that happened to us because we have no clear sense of ourselves as distinct individuals.

When do we acquire a clear self-concept? Not until we are about two years of age. Prior to this time, for example, babies show considerable interest in their own reflection in a mirror, but will not attempt to rub a spot of rouge off their nose when they see it in their reflection. By the time they are eighteen months to two years of age, in contrast, they do attempt to rub off the spot, thus indicating that they recognize their own physical features (Lewis et al., 1989).

In sum, recent evidence suggests that infantile amnesia may actually be a misleading term. Our inability to report autobiographical memories from the first few years of life seems to reflect the absence of a clearly defined self-concept during this period, *not* deficits in our memory systems. In light of this evidence, it may be more appropriate to refer to this gap in our autobiographical memories not as a period of infantile amnesia, but rather as a period of infantile nonself.

FLASHBULB MEMORIES: MEMORIES THAT DON'T FADE—OR DO THEY?

Think back over the last year: What was the most surprising or unusual event that you can remember hearing about? (My personal choice: televised scenes of a large number of police cars following O. J. Simpson's white Bronco on the highways of Los Angeles.) Can you also remember what you were doing and where you were when you first learned about whatever event you choose? If so, then you have a personal, first-hand example of what Brown and Kulik (1977) term **flashbulb memories**—vivid memories of what we were doing at the time of an emotion-provoking event.

Are such memories accurate? Can we really remember what we were doing or where we were at the time of surprising events? Growing evidence suggests that this is one of those cases in which our subjective impressions concerning our own memory are wrong. The surprising thing about flashbulb memeories is not that they are so accurate but rather that they are actually quite inaccurate (Neisser, 1991). For example, in one study on this topic, students were asked, the day after the space shuttle *Challenger* exploded, how they had first heard this news. Three years later, the same persons were asked to recall this information again.

Most were sure that they could remember; but in fact, about one-third of their accounts were completely wrong. Why do such errors occur? Perhaps because the strong emotions present when flashbulb memories are formed may interfere with accurate encoding, and so lead to later errors (Forgas & Bower, 1989). Whatever the mechanism, it is clear that flashbulb memories are another intriguing aspect of autobiographical memory.

KEY QUESTIONS

- What is autobiographical memory?
- What is infantile amnesia?
- What are flashbulb memories?

Flashbulb Memories: Vivid memories of what we were doing at the time of an emotion-provoking event.

DISTORTION AND CONSTRUCTION IN MEMORY OF NATURAL EVENTS

A friend who has seen a popular movie describes it to you. It sounds appealing, so you go to see it. When you do, you discover that the plot is very different from what your friend described. Your friend changed, omitted, or even added important events to the story. What has happened? One possibility is that your friend's description of the film has fallen prey to two basic types of errors that frequently affect memory in natural contexts: *distortion*—alterations in what is remembered and reported—and *construction*—the addition of information that was not actually present or, in some cases, the creation of "memories" of events or experiences that never took place.

DISTORTION AND THE INFLUENCE OF SCHEMAS
We have all had experience with memory distortion. For example, when we look back on our own behavior in various situations, we often tend to perceive it in a favorable light; we remember saying or doing things we feel we *should* have said or done, even if we didn't actually say or do them. Similarly, when thinking about other persons, we often remember them as closer to our stereotypes of the groups to which they belong than they actually are.

Distortions in memory also occur in response to false or misleading information provided by others. If someone's comments suggest some fact or detail that is not present in our memories, we may add that fact or detail to our memories (Loftus, 1992). Unfortunately, such effects often occur during trials, when attorneys pose *leading questions* to witnesses—questions that lead the witnesses to "remember" what the attorneys want them to. For example, an attorney might ask, "Was the intruder's mustache light or dark colored?" —suggesting that the intruder had a mustache. A witness may not remember a mustache, and in fact the intruder may not have had a mustache. But in response to this kind of question, a witness's memory may be distorted, and he or she may "remember" seeing a mustache. We'll return to such effects in our discussion of eyewitness testimony.

What accounts for memory distortions? In many cases, they seem to involve the operation of **schemas**—cognitive structures representing individuals' knowledge and assumptions about the world (Fiske & Taylor, 1991; Rumelhart, 1975). Schemas are developed through experience and act something like mental scaffolds, providing basic frameworks for processing new information and relating it to existing knowledge. A schema can also be viewed as a packet of information consisting of a fixed core and a variable component. For example, your schema for buying something in a store has as its fixed aspect the exchange of money for some product. In addition, it allows room for variability with respect to the amount of funds involved, the specific item purchased, and so on.

Once schemas are formed, they exert strong effects on the way information is encoded, stored, and then retrieved. These effects, in turn, can lead to important errors or distortions in memory. Perhaps such effects are most apparent with respect to encoding. Current evidence suggests that when schemas are initially being formed—for example, when you are first learning about the activities, roles, and responsibilities of being a college student— information inconsistent with the newly formed schema is easier to notice and encode than information consistent with it. Such inconsistent information is surprising and thus seems more likely to become the focus of attention. In contrast, after the schema has been formed and is well developed, information consistent with it becomes easier to notice and hence recall (Stangor & Ruble, 1989) (see Figure 6.5 on page 216). It is the operation of schemas that, in part, accounts for the fact that in many cases we are more

Schemas: *Cognitive frameworks representing our knowledge about aspects of the world.*

FIGURE **6.5**

Schemas: How They Affect the Encoding of Information into Memory

When schemas are being formed, inconsistent information is easier to notice and encode than information that is consistent with the schemas. After schemas are well developed, however, the opposite is true.

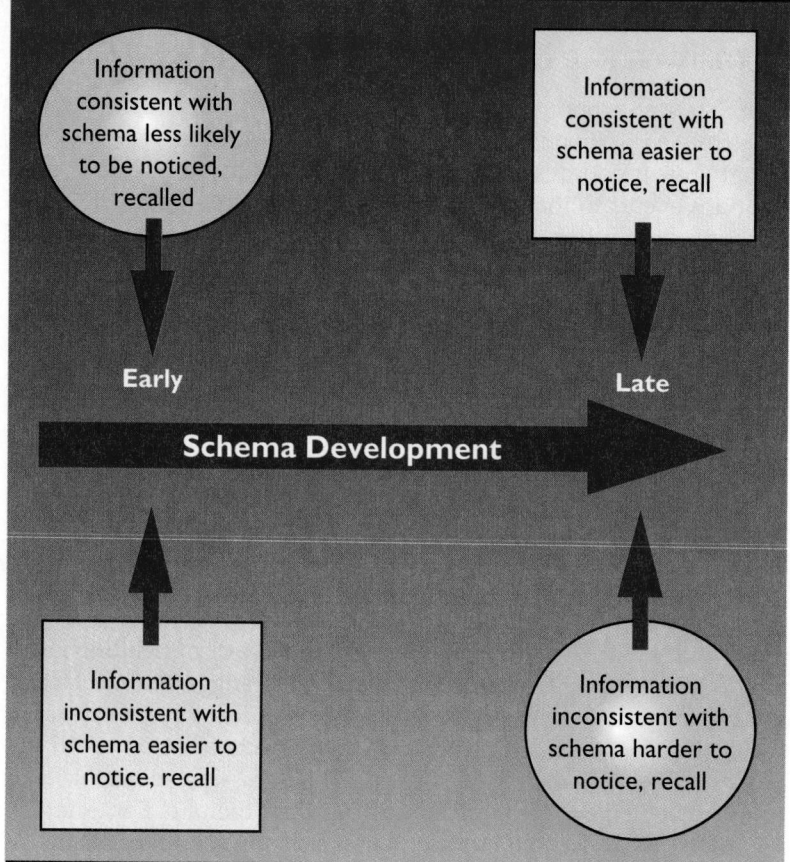

likely to notice and remember information that supports our beliefs about the world than information that challenges them.

So, what role might schemas play in your friend's faulty account of the movie? Suppose the film is about a group of scientists working to discover a cure for a fatal disease, but one of the scientists is secretly working for a large drug company that wants to obtain the cure for its own use. Yet your friend fails to mention this crucial fact. Why? Perhaps because the idea of a scientist selling out for personal gain is inconsistent with your friend's strongly established schema for scientists. This may not be the cause of the error in this particular case, but it is indicative of the way in which schemas can lead to distortion in long-term memory.

Do people living in different cultures develop different schemas? And do such differences influence their memory? For information on these issues, see the **Perspectives on Diversity** section.

PERSPECTIVES ON DIVERSITY

Culture and Memory: Remembering What Fits with Our Cultural Schemas

S chemas play an important role in memory and in human cognition generally. These mental frameworks are acquired through experience and, once formed, strongly influence what aspects of the external world get our attention,

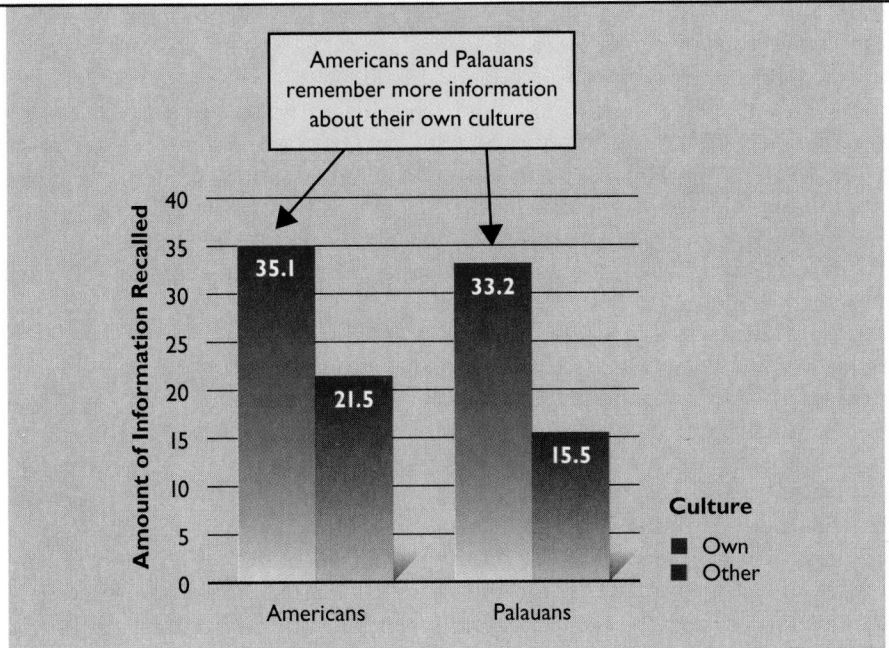

Americans and Palauans remember more information about their own culture

FIGURE 6.6

Culture and Memory

After reading letters containing information about funerals in two cultures, persons from each culture remembered more information about their own culture than about the other one. These findings suggest that *cultural schemas* formed through experience with one's own culture can strongly influence what information is entered into long-term memory and later retrieved from it.
(*Source:* Based on data from Pritchard, 1991.)

what information gets entered into memory, and what is later retrieved from memory storage. Since schemas develop out of experience, it seems only reasonable to expect that they would reflect the cultures in which people live. People growing up in different cultures have different experiences in many areas of life, so their schemas for these areas, too, may differ. For example, persons raised in Western cultures may have very different mental frameworks for courtship, work relationships, and entertainment than persons raised in Asian or African cultures. And these contrasting schemas, in turn, may exert powerful effects on what people notice and remember in a given situation.

Direct evidence for the impact on memory of such culture-linked frameworks has been obtained in several studies (e.g, Shore, 1991). In one such investigation, for example, Pritchard (1991) asked high school students in the United States and in Palau (a small Pacific island nation) to read two letters written by a woman to her sister. In the letters the woman described events surrounding a typical funeral in each culture. Since funerals differ greatly in the United States and Palau, Pritchard expected that participants would find the letter about their own culture more familiar than the one about the other culture. Moreover, since information in the letter about their own culture would fit with their cultural schema for funerals, it would be easier for the students to enter that information into memory and to recall it at a later time.

To test this hypothesis, Pritchard (1991) asked the participants from both cultures to tell everything they could remember about the letters shortly after reading them. The number of distortions in participants' accounts were also scored. As shown in Figure 6.6, results provided clear support for the hypothesis that participants would find it easier to remember information relating to their own culture than information relating to an unfamiliar culture.

These findings, and those of many related studies (e.g., Segall et al., 1990) indicate that cultural factors do indeed play an important role even in such basic psychological processes as memory. The culture in which we grow up can strongly shape the mental frameworks we use to understand the world around us, and hence many important aspects of our behavior.

MEMORY CONSTRUCTION Unfortunately, distortion is not the only type of error that can affect memory of everyday events. Such memory is also affected by *construction*: our tendency to fill in the details when recalling natural events, or even to remember experiences we never actually had. I recently had a startling experience with construction in my own memory when I visited my parents. I asked my father what had become of my great-grandfather's uniform, the one he wore when he was a soldier in Europe in the 1890s. My father was puzzled and asked how I knew about the uniform. When I answered that I remembered seeing it on many occasions when I was a child, he reported that this was impossible: The uniform was thrown away when *he* was a teenager, many years before I was born. I was shocked, because I vividly recalled seeing it. I realize now, though, that despite what my memory told me (and still tells me!) I never laid eyes on it.

The mystery of my great-grandfather's uniform is fairly trivial, but the effects of memory construction can sometimes be far more important. For example, in a widely publicized court case, two young women accused their father, Paul Ingram of Olympia, Washington, of having sexually abused them for many years when they were children. Very little confirming evidence was available for the women's stories, and Ingram at first denied the charges. Under repeated questioning by police and attorneys, however, he began to report "recovered memories" of these crimes. Were these memories accurate? Or did Ingram construct them in response to the repeated suggestion that he had committed the crimes? To find out, a trained psychologist, Richard Ofshe, made up a completely false story in which Ingram forced his son and daughter to have sex (Loftus, 1993; Ofshe, 1992). Ofshe then presented this story to Ingram, urging him to try to remember these events. At first Ingram denied any knowledge of these events. But later he reported that he could remember them; indeed, he gradually developed detailed "memories" for events that were entirely fabricated!

This is a very dramatic illustration of the fact that under the power of suggestion, people may often construct memories of events that never took place (Loftus, 1993). Moreover, the occurrence of such memory construction is confirmed by many studies involving less traumatic events, such as people's remembering loud noises at night that never occurred (Weekes et al., 1992) or remembering that they voted in an election when they actually did not (Abelson, Loftus, & Greenwald, 1992). Unfortunately, young children seem to be especially susceptible to suggestions, readily constructing detailed memories of events that never took place when prompted by repeated questions from adults (Goleman, 1993). As you can see, this finding has important implications for cases in which children are either victims or witnesses of crimes such as sexual abuse.

What accounts for the occurrence of memory construction? One possible answer involves processes at work during encoding. When we enter information into memory, we may store the information itself but omit details about context—how and when the information was obtained. This may have been the case with my imagined memories of my great-grandfather's uniform. When I was a child, I heard many descriptions of it from my father and grandmother. Later, I remembered this information, but not the fact that it was based on verbal descriptions rather than on seeing the uniform itself.

Whatever the precise mechanisms involved, it is clear that under appropriate conditions—repeated prompting or questioning—people may construct memories of events that never occurred or experiences they never had. When this occurs in a court of law, the potential for injustice is truly disturbing. Please read on for more information about this important topic.

Eyewitness Testimony: Is It as Accurate as We Believe?

Eyewitness testimony—evidence given by persons who have witnessed a crime—plays an important role in many trials. At first glance, this makes a lot of sense: What better source of information about the events of a crime could there be than persons who actually saw them? After reading the previous discussions of potential sources of errors, distortion, and construction in memory, however, you may already be wondering about an important question: Is such testimony as accurate as many people believe?

The answer provided by careful research is straightforward: In general, eyewitnesses to crimes are far from infallible. On the contrary, they often falsely identify innocent persons as criminals (Wells, 1993), make mistakes about important details about a crime (Loftus, 1991), and even sometimes report "remembering" events they did not actually see (Haugaard et al., 1991). As a result of such errors, innocent persons may be convicted of crimes they did not commit—or, conversely, persons guilty of serious crimes may be wrongly cleared of the charges against them. Indeed, recent evidence indicates that the single largest factor accounting for such miscarriages of justice is faulty eyewitness testimony (Wells, 1993). Can anything be done to enhance eyewitnesses' accuracy? Fortunately, several procedures seem useful in this regard.

Enhancing the Accuracy of Eyewitness Testimony: Some Useful Techniques One promising approach involves improvements in the procedures used to question eyewitnesses—improvements based on current scientific knowledge of memory (Geiselman et al., 1985). Techniques that seem useful in this regard include asking witnesses to report everything, even partial information, and asking them to describe events from several different perspectives in several different orders, not just the order in which the events occurred. Research on memory suggests that these techniques should enhance recall, and in fact, when they are used, witnesses' accuracy increases by up to 50 percent in some cases (Fisher & Geiselman, 1988).

Interestingly, other findings indicate that merely asking eyewitnesses repeatedly to try to recall what they saw does not help (Turtle & Yuille, 1994). While such repeated attempts at recall do yield increased memory for details of a crime, errors also increase; so there is no net gain in accuracy. Only if such efforts to remember are repeated within a short period of time—something that rarely happens in actual criminal proceedings—is there any measurable benefit (Roediger & Wheeler, 1993; Scrivner & Safer, 1988; Turtle & Yuille, 1994).

Another technique that *does* seem to help, however, is asking eyewitnesses to imagine themselves back at the scene and to reconstruct as many details as possible. This seems to provide witnesses with additional retrieval cues, and so enhances memory (Malpass & Devine, 1981).

Eyewitness testimony and hypnotism: Does hypnosis improve accuracy? Perhaps the most dramatic—and controversial—technique used to improve the accuracy of eyewitnesses is hypnosis. In several highly publicized cases, eyewitnesses have been hypnotized in an effort to increase the amount of information they remember. While media reports often claim that hypnotism was helpful in such cases, there is actually little or no evidence for this conclusion. Eyewitnesses have occasionally been able to report new information while under hypnosis, but it is unclear whether such effects stemmed from being hypnotized or from differences in the way they were questioned while in this state. For example, while hypnotized, some witnesses have been forcefully

Eyewitness Testimony: Information provided by witnesses to crimes or accidents.

instructed to "make a real effort" to remember. This kind of urging, rather than the hypnotism itself, may have been responsible for improvements in memory—if they actually occurred. So, it seems reasonable to conclude that where memory enhancement is concerned, hypnosis promises more than it delivers.

To conclude: existing evidence suggests that eyewitnesses are not as accurate a source of information as the public, attorneys, police, and juries often assume. Several techniques can assist such persons in bringing to mind information they have noticed and encoded; but if information was never entered into memory in the first place, such procedures will not prove helpful. In many cases, then, it is best to view eyewitness testimony as an imperfect and potentially misleading source of information about reality.

KEY QUESTIONS

- What factors underlie memory distortion?
- How does culture influence memory?
- What factors are responsible for memory construction?
- How accurate is eyewitness testimony?

THE BIOLOGICAL BASES OF MEMORY: How the Brain Stores Knowledge

Learning Objective 6.14
Discuss the biological bases of amnesia and other memory disorders.

Learning Objective 6.15
Discuss the modern view on the storage and processing of information within the brain.

*L*et's begin with a simple but compelling assumption: When you commit information to memory, something must happen in your brain. Given that memories can persist for decades, it seems reasonable to suggest that this "something" involves relatively permanent changes within the brain. Where, precisely, do these occur? And what kind of alterations are they? These questions have fascinated—and frustrated—psychologists and other scientists for decades. Only recently have even partial answers begun to emerge.

AMNESIA AND OTHER MEMORY DISORDERS: Keys to Understanding the Nature of Memory

The study of **amnesia**, or loss of memory, has added greatly to our understanding of the biological bases of memory. Amnesia is far from rare. Among human beings, it can stem from accidents that damage the brain, from drug abuse, or from operations performed to treat various medical disorders. Two major types exist. In **retrograde amnesia**, memory of events prior to the amnesia-inducing event is impaired. Thus, persons suffering from such amnesia may be unable to remember events from specific periods in their lives, such as events they experienced between the ages of eighteen and twenty-two. In **anterograde amnesia**, in contrast, individuals cannot remember events that occur *after* the amnesia-inducing event. For example, if they meet someone for the first time after the onset of amnesia, they cannot remember this person the next day, or even a few minutes after being introduced.

Amnesia: Loss of memory stemming from illness, accident, drug abuse, or other causes.

Retrograde Amnesia: The inability to store in long-term memory information that occurred before an amnesia-inducing event.

Anterograde Amnesia: The inability to store in long-term memory information that occurs after an amnesia-inducing event.

H.M. AND THE ROLE OF THE MEDIAL TEMPORAL LOBES Let's begin with the dramatic case of H.M.—an individual whose amnesia has been studied by psychologists ever since the 1950s. In 1953, at the age of twenty-seven, H.M. underwent an operation to remove the medial portion of both temporal lobes of his brain. The reason for this operation was to stop seizures; H.M. suffered from an extreme form of epilepsy and was experiencing at least one major seizure each week. The operation almost completely cured H.M.'s seizures, but it produced both retrograde and anterograde amnesia (Milner,

Corkin & Teuber, 1968). H.M.'s retrograde amnesia was relatively minor; he could remember all of the past with the exception of the most recent one or two years. His anterograde amnesia, however, was profound. For example, he could not remember people he met after his operation even if he encountered them over and over again. When his family moved to a new home, he could not find his way back to it, even after several months of practice. He could read the same magazine over and over again with continued enjoyment, because as soon as he put it down, he forgot what it contained.

H.M. seemed quite normal in many respects, however. He could carry on conversations, repeat seven numbers from memory, and perform simple arithmetic tasks without paper and pencil. Together, these findings suggested that both his short-term and long-term memory systems were intact. His major problem seemed to be an inability to transfer new information from short-term memory to long-term memory. As a result, it was as if he had become suspended in time on the day in 1953 when he regained his health but lost the ability to store new information. Additional evidence, obtained from studying H.M.'s performance on a wide range of tasks, points to a slightly different conclusion: He *can* transfer information from short-term to long-term memory (Graf & Schachter, 1985), but is incapable of noticing or reporting this fact.

What, precisely, does the case of H.M. tell us about the biological bases of memory? Since it was portions of his temporal lobes that were removed, these findings suggest that these lobes—or structures within them—play a key role in our memory systems. In particular, the temporal lobes seem to be crucial in the **consolidation of memory**: the process of shifting new information from short-term to longer-term storage. Research has confirmed this conclusion and has identified one structure in the temporal lobes—the *hippocampus*—as crucial in this respect.

DECLARATIVE MEMORY AND THE HIPPOCAMPUS Earlier in this chapter, I drew a distinction between *semantic* and *episodic* memory on the one hand and *procedural* memory on the other. As I hope you'll recall, both semantic and episodic memory involve our ability to recall information that we know—to bring it into consciousness and, if necessary, to describe it. Procedural memory, in contrast, is the kind of memory on which skillful behaviors—everything from riding a bike to playing golf—are based. While we can't put the information stored in this kind of memory into words, we know quite well that we possess it. Where does the hippocampus, a portion of the temporal lobes, fit into the picture? Converging lines of research conducted with humans and animals point to the conclusion that the hippocampus plays a key role in the first two kinds of memory, which are often grouped under the term *declarative memory*, or **explicit memory**, since we can describe their contents verbally. However, the hippocampus does not seem to play a role with respect to the second type of memory, sometimes termed **implicit memory**. This latter memory system is related to other areas of the brain, specifically, the neocortex, striatum, and amygdala (Tulving & Schachter, 1990).

Many different forms of evidence offer support for this view of the potential role of the hippocampus in memory (Squire, 1991). Some of the most fascinating studies, however, have focused on people suffering from amnesia. Many amnesics, it turns out, have experienced damage to the hippocampus. And their performance on tasks involving declarative or explicit memory seems to suffer as a result of these injuries. In contrast, their ability to perform some tasks involving implicit memory is not impaired (Knowlton, Ramus, & Squire, 1992; Schachter, Church, & Treadwell, 1994).

Addtional evidence points to an even broader role of the hippocampus in memory (Squire & McKee, 1992). Specifically, it appears that the hippocam-

Consolidation of Memory: *The process of shifting new information from short-term to long-term storage.*

Explicit (Declarative) Memory: *A memory system that permits us to express the information it contains verbally. It includes both semantic and episodic memory.*

Implicit Memory: *A memory system that stores information that we cannot express verbally; sometimes termed procedural memory.*

pus somehow binds together distributed sites of activaton in the neocortex with sites of activation in other regions of the brain, such as the medial temporal lobe. Such connections are needed for the formation of memories. When the hippocampus is damaged, these links cannot be formed. The result is that "out of sight" does equal "out of mind"—no lasting storage of information brought to the brain from the senses can occur. At present, much available evidence is consistent with such conclusions. However, further research is necessary before definite conclusions can be reached concerning the functions of the hippocampus in human memory.

AMNESIA AS A RESULT OF KORSAKOFF'S SYNDROME   Individuals who consume large amounts of alcohol for many years sometimes develop a serious illness known as **Korsakoff's syndrome**. The many symptoms of Korsakoff's syndrome include sensory and motor problems as well as heart, liver, and gastrointestinal disorders. In addition, the syndrome is often accompanied by both anterograde amnesia and severe retrograde amnesia: Patients cannot remember events that took place even many years before the onset of their illness. Careful medical examinations of such persons' brains after their death indicate that they have experienced extensive damage to portions of the diencephalon, especially to the thalamus and hypothalamus. This suggests that these portions of the brain play a key role in long-term memory. Convincing evidence for this conclusion is provided by the case of N.A.

N.A. was serving in the Air Force when he experienced a tragic accident. His roommate was making thrusts with a miniature fencing sword when N.A. suddenly turned around in his chair. The foil penetrated his right nostril and damaged his brain. The results of this accident were both immediate and striking. N.A. suffered extreme retrograde amnesia; he could not remember any events, personal or otherwise, from the past two years. What was the cause of his memory deficit? A brain scan revealed that N.A. had suffered damage to the mediodorsal nucleus of the thalamus. (We discussed the nature of such scans in chapter 2.) While other causes of N.A.'s problem cannot be entirely ruled out, these findings suggest that the mediodorsal nucleus may play an important role in long-term memory.

THE AMNESIA OF ALZHEIMER'S DISEASE   One of the most tragic illnesses to strike human beings in the closing decades of life is **Alzheimer's disease**. This illness, which afflicts some 5 percent of all people over sixty-five, begins with mild problems, such as increased difficulty in remembering names, phone numbers, or appointments. Gradually, however, patients' condition worsens until they become totally confused, are unable to perform even simple tasks like dressing or grooming themselves, and experience an almost total loss of memory. Indeed, in the later stages patients may fail to recognize their spouse or children. Careful study of the brains of deceased Alzheimer's patients has revealed that in most cases they contain tiny bundles of *amyloid beta protein,* a substance not found in similar concentrations in normal brains. Growing evidence (Yankner et al., 1990) suggests that this substance causes damage to neurons that project from nuclei in the basal forebrain to the hippocampus and cerebral cortex (Coyle, 1987). These neurons transmit information primarily by means of the neurotransmitter *acetylcholine,* so it appears that this substance may play a key role in the functioning of memory. Further evidence that such acetylcholine-based systems are crucial is provided by the fact that the brains of Alzheimer's patients contain lower than normal amounts of acetylcholine. In addition, studies with animal subjects in which the acetylcholine-transmitting neurons are destroyed suggest that this does indeed produce major dislocations in memory (Fibiger, Murray, & Phillips, 1983).

Korsakoff's Syndrome: An illness caused by long-term abuse of alcohol that often involves profound retrograde amnesia.

Alzheimer's Disease: An illness primarily afflicting individuals over the age of sixty-five and involving severe mental deterioration, including retrograde amnesia.

In sum, evidence obtained from the study of memory disorders indicates that specific regions and systems within the brain play central roles in our ability to transfer information from short-term to long-term storage and to retain it in long-term memory for prolonged periods of time.

MEMORY AND THE BRAIN: *A Modern View*

To return to the key questions: Where are memories stored within the brain? What changes within the brain underlie the long-term storage of information? With respect to the first question, the answer seems to be that information is stored in several different locations. Evidence indicates that there are at least two different storage systems within the brain—one for declarative or explicit memory and the other for procedural or implicit memory—and that different structures and regions are primarily associated with each. In addition, it appears that our brains process information simultaneously at several different locations rather than in a linear, step-by-step manner. If information processing occurs in several locations at once, it seems reasonable to assume that representations of the information exist in multiple places. So, again, where does the brain store specific memories? The most reasonable answer seems to be in multiple locations and in multiple forms.

Now for the second question: How, precisely, is such information actually stored? Apparently, through several subtle biochemical processes within the brain. It appears that the formation of long-term memories involves alterations in the rate of production or release of specific neurotransmitters. Such changes increase the ease with which neural information can move within the brain and may produce *localized neural circuits*. Evidence for the existence of such neural circuits, or *neural networks*, is provided by research in which previously learned conditioned responses are eliminated when microscopic areas of the brain are destroyed—areas that, presumably, contain the neural circuits formed during conditioning (Thompson, 1989). Long-term memory may also involve changes in the actual structure of neurons—changes that strengthen communication across specific synapses (Teyler & DiScenna, 1984). For example, there is some indication that after learning experiences, the shape of dendrites in specific neurons may be altered, and that these shifts may facilitate the neurons' responsiveness to neurotransmitters. Some of these changes may occur very quickly, while others may require considerable amounts of time. This, perhaps, is one reason why newly formed memories are subject to disruption for some period after they are formed (Squire & Spanis, 1984).

In sum, it appears that we are now entering an exciting period; armed with new and sophisticated research techniques, psychologists and other scientists may finally be able to unravel the biochemical code of memory. When they do, the potential benefits for persons suffering from amnesia and other memory disorders will probably be immense.

MEMORY FAILURE: ALZHEIMER'S DISEASE

Damage to specific neurons in the brain is implicated in Alzheimer's disease, one of the most tragic illnesses to afflict older people.

KEY QUESTIONS

- Why does the study of memory disorders provide insights into the biological bases of memory?
- What are retrograde amnesia and anterograde amnesia?
- What role does the hippocampus play in explicit memory?
- According to recent evidence, what biological factors may play a role in the occurrence of Alzheimer's disease?

Improving Your Memory: Some Useful Steps

H ow good is your memory? If you are like most people, your answer is probably "Not good enough!" At one time or another, most of us have wished that we could improve our ability to retain facts and information. Fortunately, with a little work, almost anyone can learn to remember more information more accurately. Systematic research on memory, such as that described in this chapter, offers several useful suggestions for accomplishing this goal. Here are some you can readily put to use.

1. *Really think about what you want to remember.* If you wish to enter information into long-term memory, it is important to think about it: ask questions about it, consider its meaning, and examine its relationship to information you already know. Doing so will help make the new information part of your existing knowledge frameworks and will increase the chances of its entry into long-term memory. This kind of thinking calls for considerable cognitive work, but it's worth the effort because it will increase your retention.

2. *Pay attention to what you want to remember.* Quick: Whose face appears on a ten-dollar bill? On a twenty? A fifty? If you live in the United States, you have seen these images many, many times, yet there is a good chance that you can't remember. Why? The answer is simple: You haven't paid close attention to this information. While you have certainly paid attention to the numbers on the corners of each of these bills each time you have seen or had one, the faces in the center are another story. In any case, if you can't remember information such as this, to which you've been exposed on countless occasions, think how difficult it is to remember other information to which you direct little attention. The moral is clear: If you want to remember something, you must first make it the center of your attention.

3. *Use visual imagery.* You've probably heard the old saying, "A picture is worth a thousand words." Where memory is concerned, this is sometimes true. Research indicates that it is often easier to remember information associated with vivid mental images (Gehring & Toglia, 1989; Pavio, 1969). If you wish to improve your memory, therefore, you can put this basic principle to use. In fact, imagery plays a central role in several well-known *mnemonics*, or strategies for improving memory. One of these, the *method of loci*, involves the following steps. Suppose you want to remember a series of points for a speech you will soon make. First, imagine walking through some familiar place, say your own home. Then form a series of images in which each item you wish to remember is placed in a specific location. Perhaps the first point is, "The greenhouse effect is a reality." You might imagine a large, steamy greenhouse containing plants right outside your front door. For the next point, "Destruction of the tropical rain forest is contributing to the greenhouse effect," you might imagine a large cut-down palm tree lying in your living room. And so on. Now, by taking an imaginary walk through your house, you should be able to see each of these images and so remember the points in your speech.

4. *Give yourself extra retrieval cues.* As I hope you remember, a key problem with long-term memory involves retrieving stored information. You can help yourself in this area through the use of retrieval cues. One type of cue is the *context* in which the information was first acquired. In other words, pause for a moment and try to remember the situations or surroundings in which you first entered the information into memory. Often, remembering the context will help you to retrieve the information you seek. For example, maybe you are attempting to remember the name of a restaurant. Try as you may, you can't bring the name to mind. If you pause and think about the location of the restaurant, how you first heard about it, what it looks like from the outside, the name may quickly follow.

5. *Develop your own shorthand codes.* You may have learned the names of the nine planets by means of a simple procedure known as the first-letter technique, in which the first letter of each word in a simple phrase stands for an item you wish to remember. In the case of the planets, one such phrase is "Mary's Violet Eyes Make John Stay Up Nights Pondering" (Mercury, Venus, Earth, Mars, Jupiter, Saturn, Uranus, Neptune, Pluto). This can be a very useful technique; indeed, more than half of first-year medical students report using it when studying anatomy (Gruneberg, 1978). If you need to remember lists of items, you can readily come up with your own sentences to represent them. And of course, the more meaningful or familiar a sentence is to you, the more helpful it will be.

6. *Develop your own cognitive scaffolds.* One basic finding of research on memory is that organized information is much easier to remember than unorganized information. If you wish to retain a large array of facts, dates, or terms, it is very helpful to organize them in some manner. Organization provides a framework to which new information can be attached—a kind of mental scaffold. This is one reason why each chapter of this book begins with an outline and ends with a detailed summary. Together, they provide the "big pic-

ture"—an overview of the chapter's content. And this in turn can be very helpful to you in your studying.

I could list additional techniques for enhancing your memory, but most would be related to the ones I've already described. Whichever techniques you se-lect, you will find that making them work does re-quire some degree of effort. In memory training, as in any other effort at self-improvement, the old saying "No pain, no gain" tends to hold true.

SUMMARY AND REVIEW OF KEY QUESTIONS

HUMAN MEMORY: THE INFORMATION-PROCESSING APPROACH

- *According to modern models of memory, what three memory systems do we possess?*

Several models of human memory indicate that we pos-sess three distinct memory systems: sensory memory, short-term memory, and long-term memory.

- *How does parallel processing of information differ from step-by-step, or linear, processing?*

Parallel processing occurs in different parts of the total memory system at the same time. Step-by-step process-ing occurs first in one part and then in another.

- *What kinds of information are stored in memory?*

Semantic memory holds general information about the world. Episodic memory holds information about expe-riences we have had in our own lives. Procedural mem-ory holds nonverbal information that allows us to perform various motor tasks, such as riding a bicycle or playing the piano.

KEY TERMS: *memory, p. 194; encoding, p. 195; storage, p. 195; retrieval, p. 195; information-processing approach, p. 195; selec-tive attention, p. 196; parallel distributed processing model, p. 197; semantic memory, p. 197; episodic memory, p. 197; pro-cedural memory, p. 198*

SENSORY MEMORY: GATEWAY TO CONSCIOUSNESS

- *What kind of information does sensory memory hold?*

Sensory memory holds fleeting representations of our sensory experiences.

- *How long do representations of the external world last in sensory memory?*

Representations in sensory memory generally last less than one second.

KEY TERM: *sensory memory, p. 198*

SHORT-TERM MEMORY: THE WORKBENCH OF CONSCIOUSNESS

- *How long is information retained in short-term memory?*

Short-term, or working memory, retains information for a few seconds.

- *What support does the serial position curve offer for the distinction between short-term memory and long-term memory?*

The serial position curve shows that words near the beginning and the end of a list are remembered better than those in the middle. This finding indicates that the words near the beginning have been placed in long-term memory while those near the end are still in short-term memory.

- *What additional evidence supports the dis-tinction between short-term and long-term mem-ory?*

The distinction between short-term and long-term memory is also supported by the finding that people have more difficulty keeping words or letters that sound alike in short-term memory than ones that do not sound alike. In addition, it is supported by the find-ing that lists of short words are often recalled better than lists of long words.

KEY TERMS: *short-term memory, p. 199; serial position curve, p. 200; chunk, p. 201*

LONG-TERM MEMORY: THE STOREHOUSE OF CONSCIOUSNESS

- *How does information move from short-term to long-term memory?*

Information moves from short-term memory to long-term memory through the process of elaborative re-hearsal.

- **What does the levels of processing view suggest about the relationship between cognitive effort and memory?**

The levels of processing view suggests that the more cognitive effort we expend in processing information, the better it will be remembered.

- **What are retrieval cues?**

Retrieval cues are stimuli associated with information stored in long-term memory; they help us bring such information to mind.

KEY TERMS: *long-term memory, p. 202; tip-of-the-tongue phenomenon, p. 202; elaborative rehearsal, p. 203; levels of processing view, p. 203; retrieval cues, p. 205; context-dependent memory, p. 205; state-dependent retrieval, p. 205; encoding specificity principle, p. 205*

FORGETTING FROM LONG-TERM MEMORY

- **Why does forgetting from long-term memory occur?**

Forgetting from long-term memory appears to result primarily from interference, not from the weakening of memories over time.

- **What is retroactive interference?**

In retroactive interference, information being learned now interferes with information already in memory.

- **What is proactive interference?**

In proactive interference, information already in memory interferes with acquisition of new information.

- **What does existing evidence suggest about the role of repression in forgetting?**

Although there is widespread belief that repression of traumatic memories occurs, there is little scientific evidence supporting this belief. Individuals who suddenly "remember" painful events from long ago may not be providing accurate descriptions of actual events.

- **What is prospective memory?**

Prospective memory involves remembering to perform certain activities at specific times.

KEY TERMS: *retroactive interference, p. 207; proactive interference, p. 208; repression, p. 208; prospective memory, p. 210*

MEMORY IN NATURAL CONTEXTS

- **What is autobiographical memory?**

Autobiographical memory involves remembering information about our own lives.

- **What is infantile amnesia?**

Infantile amnesia refers to our inability to recall events from the first three years of life, probably primarily because we did not yet possess a well-defined self-concept.

- **What are flashbulb memories?**

Flashbulb memories are memories connected to dramatic events in our lives. Contrary to popular belief, they are not highly accurate.

- **What factors underlie memory distortion?**

Memory distortion arises for several reasons, including our tendency to interpret our own behavior in a favorable light, the influence of leading questions, misinformation from others, and the impact of schemas.

- **How does culture influence memory?**

Culture exerts strong effects on memory through the operation of cultural schemas. People generally find information relating to their own culture easier to remember than information relating to other cultures.

- **What factors are responsible for memory construction?**

Memory construction often occurs in response to suggestions from others, or when we fail to encode information about how and when information stored in memory was acquired.

- **How accurate is eyewitness testimony?**

Because of memory distortion and construction and other factors, eyewitness testimony is not as accurate as is widely believed. Although several techniques can increase the accuracy of eyewitnesses' accounts of crimes they have observed, hypnosis does not appear to be among these.

KEY TERMS: *infantile amnesia, p. 212; flashbulb memory, p. 214; schemas, p. 215; eyewitness testimony, p. 219*

THE BIOLOGICAL BASES OF MEMORY: HOW THE BRAIN STORES KNOWLEDGE

- **Why does the study of memory disorders provide insights into the biological bases of memory?**

The study of various memory disorders provides important insights into the biological bases of memory because such disorders are often related to damage to specific regions of the brain.

- **What are retrograde amnesia and anterograde amnesia?**

Retrograde amnesia involves loss of memory of events prior to the amnesia-inducing event. Anterograde amnesia is loss of memory for events that occur after the amnesia–inducing event.

- **What role does the hippocampus play in explicit memory?**

Growing evidence indicates that the hippocampus plays a crucial role in explicit memory by forming temporary links among active sites in the brain. Other portions of the brain are important for implicit memory.

- *According to recent evidence, what biological factors may play a role in the occurrence of Alzheimer's disease?*

Amnesia associated with Alzheimer's disease seems to result from damage to neurons that transmit information by means of the neurotransmitter acetylcholine.

KEY TERMS: *amnesia, p. 220; retrograde amnesia, p. 220; anterograde amnesia, p. 220; consolidation of memory, p. 221; explicit memory, p. 221; implicit memory, p. 221; Korsakoff's syndrome, p. 222; Alzheimer's disease, p. 222*

CRITICAL THINKING QUESTIONS

APPRAISAL	At the present time, most psychologists accept the view that studying human memory from an information-processing perspective is very useful. Do you agree? Or do you believe that this view omits important aspects of memory?
CONTROVERSY	The concept of *repressed memories* has long enjoyed widespread acceptance among psychologists and the general public. Yet there is little research evidence for such effects. What are your views? Is continued belief in repression justified? Or should we discard this concept as being of little value?
MAKING PSYCHOLOGY PART OF YOUR LIFE	Knowing something about how memory operates is very useful from one obvious perspective: It can suggest ways for you to improve your memory. But this is not the only way in which you can benefit from such knowledge. Can you think of others? (Hint: What does your new knowledge about memory tell you about trusting your own, even in situations where you are confident that it is accurate?)

Cognition
and Intelligence

*O*ne of the reasons I love being a psychologist is that I get paid to do something I've always enjoyed naturally—observing other people. For example, many years ago, as a high school student, I noticed that some of my classmates were outstanding students—they regularly received the top grades on tests—but that they were "clueless" in other ways. They were shy and awkward at parties, couldn't do the latest dances, and had no idea how to fix their cars. This observation led me to the following conclusion, one psychologists have long accepted: There may actually be many kinds of intelligence, or different facets of intelligence, and each may draw on somewhat different cognitive abilities.

It is on these cognitive abilities—key aspects of our higher mental processes—that I'll focus in the present chapter. Specifically, I'll begin by examining what psychology currently knows about **cognition,** including such important cognitive processes as *thinking, reasoning, decision making, problem solving,* and *creativity.* Next, because it has recently been the subject of a great deal of research in psychology, I'll address the question of whether animals, too, are capable of these cognitive processes—whether they, like human beings, can think, reason, and so on. Finally, because it provides the basis for much of the activity occurring in cognitive processes, I'll also examine *language* in some detail, focusing on its basic nature, how it develops, and whether it is something we share with other species on Earth.

After considering these important aspects of cognition, I'll return to the issue raised above: individual differences in cognitive abilities. Psychologists usually refer to such individual differences in cognitive abilities using the term *intelligence,* and because of its many practical implications, they have devoted a great deal of attention to this topic. To acquaint you with the findings of almost a century of systematic research on intelligence, I'll discuss several issues: the nature of intelligence, how it's measured, and the potential contributions of heredity and environment to individual differences in this key dimension. In addition, I'll describe some intriguing new evidence concerning possible *gender differences* in intelligence and the potential role of biological factors in such differences.

THINKING: *Forming Concepts and Reasoning to Conclusions*

Learning Objective 7.1
Discuss the two strategies that psychologists have adopted to investigate the nature of thought: concepts and images.

Learning Objective 7.2
Explain the difference between formal and everyday reasoning processes.

Learning Objective 7.3
Know the basic sources of bias in reasoning.

Cognition: The activities involved in thinking, reasoning, decision making, memory, problem solving, and all other forms of higher mental processes.

What are you thinking about right now? If you've answered the question, then it's safe to say that at least to some extent you are thinking about the words on this page. But perhaps you are also thinking about a snack, the movie you saw last night, the argument you had with a friend this morning—the list could be endless. At any given moment, consciousness contains a rapidly shifting pattern of diverse thoughts, impressions, and feelings. In order to understand this complex and ever-changing pattern, psychologists have often adopted two main strategies. First, they have focused on the basic elements of thought—how, precisely, aspects of the external world are represented in our thinking. Second, they have sought to determine the manner in which we *reason*—how we attempt to process available information cognitively in order to reach specific conclusions.

BASIC ELEMENTS OF THOUGHT: *Concepts and Images*

What, precisely, does thinking involve? In other words, what are the basic elements of thought? While no conclusive answer currently exists, it appears that *concepts* and *images* may play an important role.

CONCEPTS: CATEGORIES FOR UNDERSTANDING EXPERIENCE   What do the following objects have in common: apples, bananas, strawberries? You probably have no trouble in replying: They are all fruits. Now, how about these

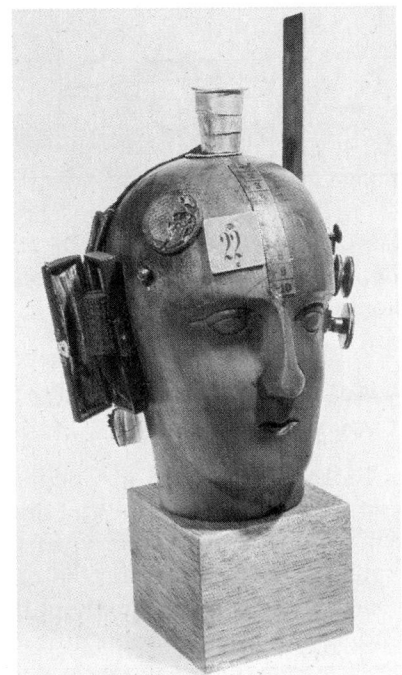

Prototypes are the best or clearest examples of concepts. For the concept *art*, which of the examples shown here is more prototypical?

items: a Honda Accord, an elevator, and a tractor? Perhaps it takes a bit longer to answer, but soon you realize that they are all vehicles. The items in each of these groups look different from one another, yet in a sense you perceive—and think about—them as similar, at least in certain respects. The reason you find the task of answering these questions relatively simple is that you already possess well-developed concepts for both groups of items. **Concepts** are mental categories for objects, events, experiences, or ideas that are similar to one another in one or more respects. They allow us to represent a lot of information about diverse objects, events, or ideas in a highly efficient manner.

Psychologists often distinguish between artificial and natural concepts. **Artificial concepts** are ones that can be clearly defined by a set of rules or properties. Thus, a tomato is a fruit because it possesses the properties established by botanists for this category. Not surprisingly, artificial concepts are quite useful in many areas of mathematics and science. In contrast, **natural concepts** are ones that are fuzzy around the edges; they have no fixed or readily specified set of defining features. Yet they more accurately reflect the state of the natural world, which rarely offers us the luxury of hard-and-fast, clearly defined concepts.

Natural concepts are often based on **prototypes**—the best or clearest examples (Rosch, 1975). Prototypes emerge from our experience with the external world, and new items that might potentially fit within their category are compared with them. The more attributes such items share with an existing prototype, the more likely they are to be included within a concept. For example, consider the following natural concepts: *clothing, art*. For clothing, most people think of shirts, pants, or shoes. They are far less likely to mention wet suits, mink coats, or coats of armor. Similarly, for art, most people think of drawings, sculptures, and paintings, such as the Mona Lisa, shown on the left. Fewer think of artworks such as the laser light show at Disney World or the kind of project shown in the photo at the right.

Learning Objective 7.4
Discuss the research findings concerning animal cognition.

Concepts: Mental categories for objects or events that are similar to one another in certain respects.

Artificial Concepts: Concepts that can be clearly defined by a set of rules or properties.

Natural Concepts: Concepts that are not based on a precise set of attributes or properties, do not have clear-cut boundaries, and are often defined by prototypes.

Prototypes: The best or clearest examples of various objects or stimuli in the physical world.

FIGURE 7.1

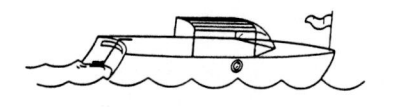

Mental Scanning of Visual Images

When shown a drawing such as this one and then asked questions about it, most people take longer to estimate the distance between the flag and the rudder than between the flag and the porthole. (*Source:* Based on an illustration used by Kosslyn, 1980.)

In everyday situations, therefore, concept membership is not an all-or-nothing decision; rather, it is graded, and items are recognized as fitting within a category to a greater or a lesser degree (Medin & Ross, 1992).

IMAGES: MENTAL PICTURES OF THE WORLD   Look at the drawing in Figure 7.1. Now cover it up with a piece of paper and answer the following questions:

1. Was there a flag? If so, in what direction was it fluttering?
2. Was there a handle attached to the rudder?
3. Was there a porthole? On which side of the boat?

Probably you could answer all of these questions quite easily. But how? If you are like most people, you first formed a visual image of the boat. Then, when asked about the flag, you focused on that part of your image. Next, you were asked to think about the rudder, at the opposite end of the boat. Did you simply jump to that end of the boat or scan the entire image? Research findings indicate that you probably scanned the entire image: After being asked about some feature near the front of the boat, it takes most people longer to answer a question about a feature near the back than a feature somewhere in the middle (Kosslyn, 1980). Such findings suggest that once we form a mental image, we think about it by scanning it visually just as we would if it were an object we were actually looking at. Other findings support this conclusion. For example, when asked to estimate the distance between two locations on a familiar university campus, people take longer to make such judgments the farther apart the places are (Baum & Jonides, 1979).

Our use of visual images in thinking, however, is not precisely like actual vision (Pylyshyn, 1981). For instance, in one study, participants were asked to imagine carrying either a cannonball or a balloon along a familiar route (Intons-Peterson & Roskos-Ewoldsen, 1988). Not surprisingly, it took them longer to complete their imaginary journeys when carrying the heavy object. So perhaps we don't simply "read" the visual images we generate; if we did, participants in this study should have been able to move through the imagined route equally fast in both conditions. The results of this study suggest that visual images are actually embedded in our knowledge about the world, and are interpreted in light of such knowledge rather than simply scanned.

Whatever the precise mechanisms by which they are used, mental images serve important purposes in thinking. People report using them for understanding verbal instructions, by converting the words into mental pictures of actions; for increasing motivation, by imagining successful performance; and for enhancing their own moods, by visualizing positive events or scenes (Kosslyn et al., 1991). Clearly, then, they constitute another basic element of thinking.

KEY QUESTIONS

- What are concepts?
- What is the difference between an artificial concept and a natural concept?
- What are the basic elements of thought?

REASONING: *Transforming Information to Reach Conclusions*

Reasoning: Cognitive activity that transforms information in order to reach specific conclusions.

A task we face frequently in everyday life is **reasoning**: drawing conclusions from available information. More formally, reasoning involves making cognitive transformations of appropriate information in order to reach specific conclusions (Galotti, 1989). How do we perform this task? And to what extent are we successful at it—in other words, how likely are the conclusions we reach to be accurate or valid?

FORMAL VERSUS EVERYDAY REASONING   First, it's important to draw a distinction between *formal reasoning* and what might be described as *everyday reasoning*. In formal reasoning, all the required information is supplied, the problem to be solved is straightforward, there is typically only one correct answer, and the reasoning we apply follows a specific method. One important type of formal reasoning is **syllogistic reasoning**—reasoning in which conclusions are based on two propositions called *premises*. For example, consider the following syllogism:

> *Premise:* All people who love chocolate are excessively kind.
> *Premise:* Saddam Hussein loves chocolate.
> *Conclusion:* Therefore, Saddam Hussein is excessively kind.

Is the conclusion correct? According to the rules of formal reasoning, it is. But you may find it hard to accept—and the reason for the problem should be obvious. At least one of the premises is incorrect: There is no strong evidence that all people who love chocolate are extremely kind. This simple example illustrates an important point: Formal reasoning can provide a powerful tool for processing complex information, but *only* when its initial premises are correct.

In contrast to formal reasoning, *everyday reasoning* involves the kind of thinking we do in our daily lives: planning, making commitments, evaluating arguments. In such reasoning some of the premises are implicit, and others may not be supplied at all; the problems involved often have several possible answers, which may vary in quality or effectiveness; and the problems themselves are not self-contained—they relate to other issues and questions of daily life. Everyday reasoning, then, is far more complex and far less definite than formal syllogistic reasoning. Since it is the kind we usually perform, however, it is worthy of careful attention.

REASONING: SOME BASIC SOURCES OF ERROR   How good are we at reasoning? Unfortunately, not as good as you might guess. Several factors, working together, seem to reduce our ability to reason effectively.

The confirmation bias: Searching for positive evidence. Imagine that over the course of several weeks, a person with deeply held convictions *against* the death penalty encounters numerous magazine articles; some report evidence confirming the usefulness of the death penalty, while others report evidence indicating that it is ineffective in terms of deterring crime. As you can readily guess, the person will probably remember more of the information that supports the anti–death penalty view. In fact, there is a good chance that he or she will read only these articles, or will read them more carefully than the ones arguing in favor of capital punishment. To the extent that this happens, it demonstrates the **confirmation bias**—our strong tendency to test conclusions or hypotheses by examining only, or primarily, evidence that confirms our initial views (Baron, 1988; Klayman & Ha, 1987). Because of the confirmation bias, individuals often become firmly locked into flawed conclusions; after all, when this bias operates, it prevents people from even considering information that might call their premises, and thus their conclusions, into question (see Figure 7.2 on page 234).

The oversight bias: Overlooking important information. During the 1992 presidential election, critics of then-candidate Bill Clinton were relentless in

Syllogistic Reasoning: A type of formal reasoning in which two premises are used as the basis for deriving logical conclusions.

Confirmation Bias: The tendency to pay attention primarily to information that confirms existing views or beliefs.

FIGURE **7.2**

The Confirmation Bias

The confirmation bias leads individuals to test conclusions or hypotheses by examining primarily—or only—evidence consistent with their initial views. As a result, these views may be maintained regardless of the weight of opposing evidence.

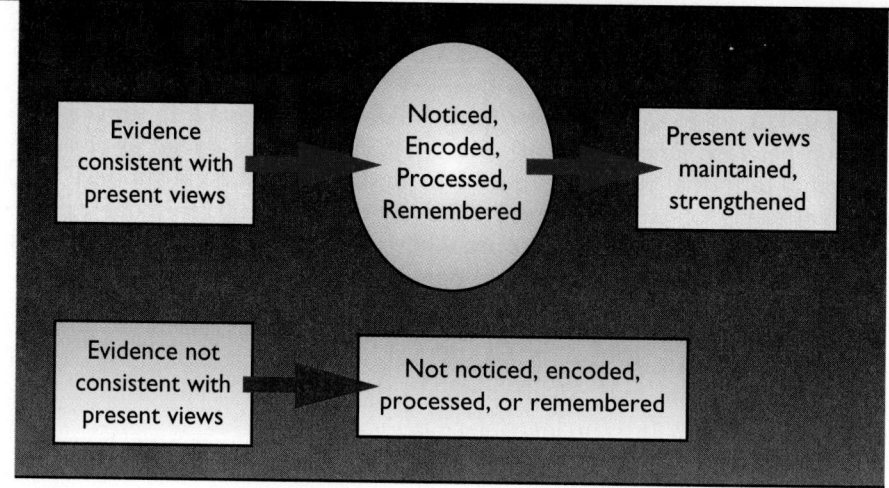

emphasizing his character flaws and relative inexperience in foreign policy. Supporters tended to ignore this information, instead focusing on positions he took on issues they perceived as more important, such as the status of this nation's economy. This example illustrates the **oversight bias**: We are selective in overlooking flaws depending on the perceived importance of the issue at hand. Even experts, it seems, are prone to this type of error. In a recent study, Wilson and his collegues (1993) asked two groups of scientists to evaluate descriptions of several fictitious studies in terms of their scientific merit. All of the studies described contained obvious flaws. Now for the interesting part: There were actually two versions of each study. The pairs of versions were identical except that in one the topic of the study was *important* (for example the effects of alcohol on cardiovascular disease), whereas in the other the topic was relatively *unimportant* (the effects of alcohol on heartburn). As predicted by the oversight bias, the experts rated descriptions of studies of *important* topics as having greater merit than the descriptions of studies of unimportant topics—even though all the descriptions were *equally* flawed (please refer to Figure 7.3).

Hindsight: The "I knew it all along" effect revisited. Have you ever heard the old saying "Hindsight is better than foresight"? What it means is that after specific events occur, we often feel as though we could have or actually did predict them. This is known in psychology as the **hindsight effect** (Hawkins & Hastie, 1990). A dramatic real-life illustration of this effect is provided by the launch of the Hubble space telescope in the spring of 1990. Shortly after the telescope reached orbit, it was discovered to have a serious defect. Within a few days of this discovery, several officials stated that they had known that this might happen all along; in fact, the problem resulted from a failure to conduct certain tests of the telescope that they had personally recommended.

Were these individuals correct? Existing evidence on the hindsight effect casts considerable doubt on this possibility. In many studies, conducted in widely different contexts, learning that an event occurred causes individuals to assume that they could have predicted it more accurately than is actually the case (Fischoff, 1975; Mitchell, Russo, & Pennington, 1989).

Can anything be done to counteract the hindsight effect? There are several possibilities. For example, if people are asked to explain a reported outcome along with other possible outcomes that did *not* occur, they are better able to

Oversight Bias: The tendency to overlook flaws if the overall topic or issue is perceived as important.

Hindsight Effect: The tendency to assume that we would have been better at predicting actual events than is really true.

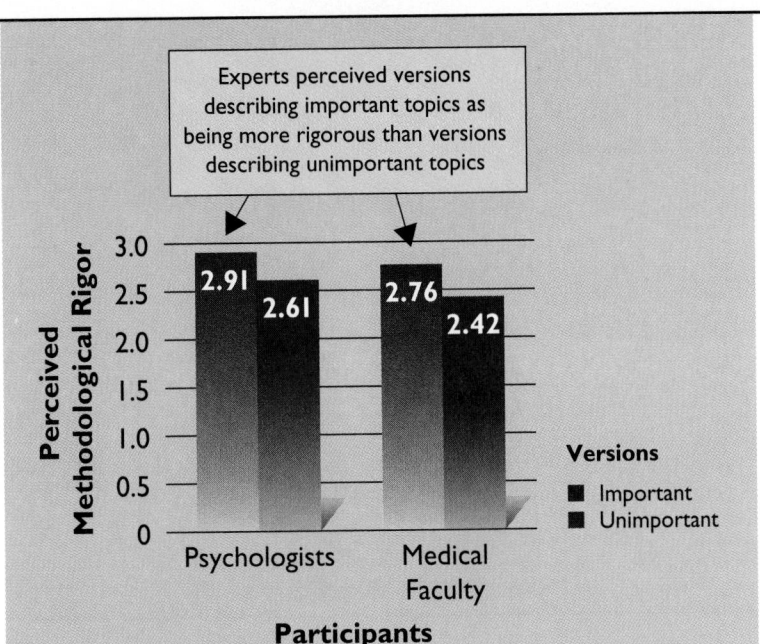

Experts perceived versions describing important topics as being more rigorous than versions describing unimportant topics

FIGURE 7.3

The Oversight Bias: Overlooking the Unimportant

The oversight bias seems to affect experts, too. As shown here, perceived importance of the topic affected scientists' evaluations of the rigor of the research. Scientists rated the important versions higher than the unimportant versions in terms of their scientific rigor—despite the fact that both versions were equally flawed.
(*Source:* Based on data from Wilson et al., 1993.)

recall their actual views before learning of the event, and this reduces the hindsight effect (Davies, 1987; Slovic & Fischoff, 1977). We can also reduce the hindsight effect by calling attention to the fact that others were surprised by the event and that it was indeed truly difficult to predict (Wasserman, Lempert, & Hastie, 1991). In sum, it does appear that we can combat our strong tendency to assume that we are better at predicting events than is actually justified. To the extent that we avoid such tendencies, our ability to reason effectively may be enhanced.

Let's now turn to a topic that has been the subject of a great deal of research in psychology during the past decade—the possibility that animals, too, possess cognitive abilities.

ANIMAL COGNITION: *Tails of Intelligence*

That human beings possess cognitive abilities such as thinking, reasoning, and planning is obvious. But how about animals—do they have similar abilities? Until now, our discussion in this chapter has implied that cognitive processes are primarily a human attribute. After all, it is difficult for most of us to picture animals thinking or performing other complex mental activities. And for many years, the view that only humans think prevailed among behavioral researchers as well.

Several developments, however, have forced scientists to reconsider their positions on this issue. First, as noted in chapter 5, behavioral researchers throughout this century have encountered many instances of animal learning that are difficult to explain solely through conditioning processes (e.g., Capaldi & Miller, 1988; Tolman & Honzik, 1930). Second, growing evidence suggests that animals *do* form complex mental representations of their environments, an attribute that helps them adapt to changing conditions they often face in nature (Cook, 1993; Shettleworth, 1993). Finally, initial studies of animal cognition often involved tasks that required physical skills beyond

FIGURE 7.4

Animal Cognition: A Sample Test Environment

The upper portion of the figure shows the apparatus used to assess the baboon's ability to rotate visual stimuli mentally. Subjects were trained to use the joystick to manipulate stimuli displayed on a fourteen-inch color monitor. The bottom portion of the figure shows an example of a sample stimulus (left) and two comparison stimuli (right).

[*Source:* From an article by J. Vauclair, J. Fagot, & W. D. Hopkins, in *Psychological Science*, Vol. 4 (1993). Reprinted with the permission of Cambridge University Press.]

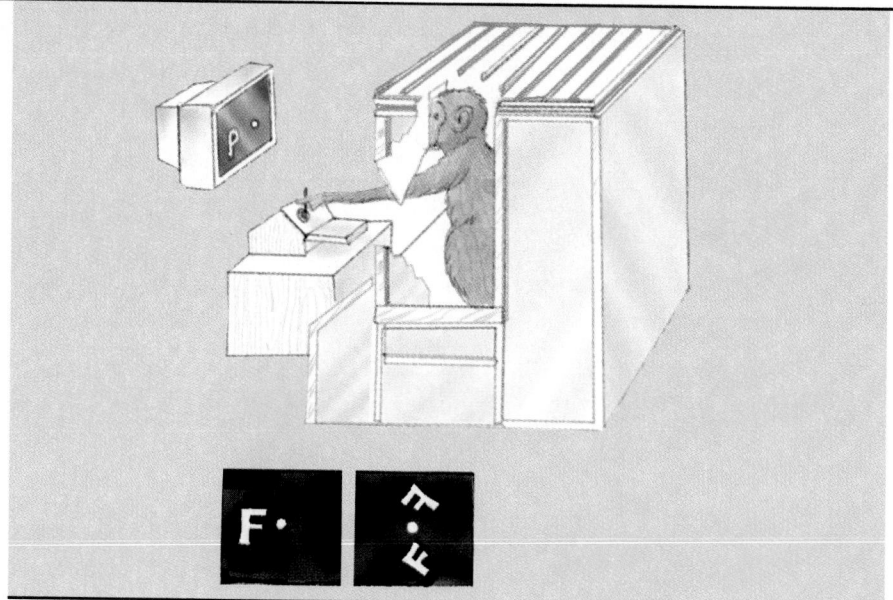

the capabilities of most species of animals. Scientists now concede that these procedures are not appropriate for studying the cognitive processes of animals (Hulse, 1993).

To determine whether animals and humans possess similar cognitive abilities, researchers have recently devised procedures that allow direct comparisons between them. For example, a cognitive ability that has been well established in human beings—but not in nonhuman species—is the ability to perform mental rotation of visual forms (Shepard & Metzler, 1971). To test mental rotation, people first view a *sample stimulus*—say the letter R. They are then shown two *comparison stimuli*—rotated versions of the same stimulus and its mirror image. Their task is to determine which of the comparison stimuli matches the sample. To do so, participants must first mentally rotate both stimuli to a normal position before they can conclude which of the stimuli matches the sample. The amount of time required to report the correct stimulus usually varies directly with the amount of mental rotation required.

To test whether baboons are also capable of mentally rotating visual stimuli, Vauclair, Fagot, and Hopkins (1993) recently developed a procedure appropriate to the abilities of baboons (refer to Figure 7.4). First the baboons view a "sample" shape (e.g., the letter F) that is flashed briefly on a screen. Then they see two comparison shapes that are rotated 0, 60, 120, 180, 240, or 300 degrees. One of the comparison shapes always matches the sample; the other is its mirror image. The baboons' task is to use a joystick to select the comparison shape that matches the sample. Each correct response produces a small food reward.

The results of this procedure show that baboons can, in fact, mentally rotate visual stimuli, an ability that many researchers had believed was beyond the capacity of nonhuman species. Moreover, baboons' performance varies directly with the degree of rotation of the comparison stimuli—a finding that closely mirrors the performance of their human counterparts on the same task. In short, these results, as well as those of related studies (e.g., Wasserman, 1993), show that when appropriate methods are used, animals demonstrate cognitive abilities that are similar in many respects to those of humans.

KEY QUESTIONS

- What is the process of reasoning? How does formal reasoning differ from everyday reasoning?

- What forms of error and bias can lead to faulty reasoning?

- What are three lines of evidence that led scientists to reconsider the possibility that some animals and humans possess similar cognitive abilities?

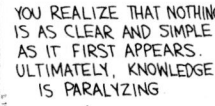

HEURISTICS: QUICK BUT FALLIBLE DECISION TOOLS

Calvin recognizes that decision making is hard work. Like many people, Calvin may resort to heuristics—rules of thumb that reduce the amount of effort required—to help him make quicker, but not necessarily better, decisions. (*Source:* CALVIN AND HOBBES copyright 1987 & 1993 Watterson. Dist. by UNIVERSAL PRESS SYNDICATE. Reprinted with permission. All rights reserved.)

MAKING DECISIONS: *Choosing Among Alternatives*

As the preceding section indicates, reasoning can often be hard work. In certain respects, though, it is less difficult than another cognitive task you perform many times each day: **decision making**. Throughout our waking hours, life presents a continuous stream of choices; what to wear, what to eat, what school to attend, what job to accept, whether to continue or end a long-term relationship—the list of everyday decisions is endless.

If you were a perfectly rational decision maker, you would make each of these choices in a cool, almost mathematical way, taking into consideration (1) the utility or value to you of the outcomes each alternative might yield and (2) the probability that such results would actually occur. As you know from your own life, though, people don't usually reason in such a systematic manner. Instead, decisions are often made informally, on the basis of hunches, intuition, or the opinions of others. Let's consider several factors that influence the decision-making process, making it less rational or effective than might otherwise be the case.

HEURISTICS: *Using Quick—But Fallible—Rules of Thumb to Make Decisions*

Where cognition is concerned, human beings definitely follow the path of least resistance whenever possible. Since making decisions is hard work, it is only reasonable to expect people to take shortcuts in performing this activity, as Calvin demonstrates in the cartoon. One group of cognitive shortcuts is known as **heuristics**—rules of thumb that reduce the effort required, though they may not necessarily enhance the quality or accuracy of the decisions reached (Kahneman & Tversky, 1982). Heuristics are extracted from past experience and serve as simple guidelines for making reasonably good choices quickly and efficiently. We'll focus on the three heuristics that tend to be used most frequently.

AVAILABILITY: WHAT COMES TO MIND FIRST? Let's start with the **availability heuristic**: the tendency to make judgments about the frequency or likelihood of events in terms of how readily examples of them can be brought to mind. This shortcut tends to work fairly well, because the more readily we can bring various events to mind, the more frequent they generally are; but it can lead us into error as well.

A good example of the availability heuristic in operation is provided by a study conducted by Tversky and Kahneman (1974). They presented lists of names like the one in Table 7.1 (on page 238) to participants and then

Learning Objective 7.5
Describe the use of heuristics in decision making.

Learning Objective 7.6
Describe the influences of framing on decision making.

Learning Objective 7.7
Explain how we can become committed to bad decisions.

Decision Making: The process of choosing among various courses of action or alternatives.

Heuristics: Mental rules of thumb that permit us to make decisions and judgments in a rapid and efficient manner.

Availability Heuristic: A cognitive rule of thumb in which the importance or probability of various events is judged on the basis of how readily they come to mind.

TABLE 7.1		

Louisa May Alcott	Henry Vaughan	Allan Nevins
John Dickson Carr	Kate Millet	Jane Austen
Emily Dickinson	Eudora Welty	Henry Crabb Robinson
Thomas Hughes	Richard Watson Gilder	Joseph Lincoln
Laura Ingalls Wilder	Harriet Beecher Stowe	Emily Brontë
Jack Lindsay	Pearl Buck	Arthur Hutchinson
Edward George Lytton	Amy Lowell	James Hunt
Margaret Mitchell	Robert Lovett	Erica Jong
Michael Drayton	Edna St. Vincent Millay	Brian Hooker
Edith Wharton	George Jean Nathan	

The Availability Heuristic in Operation

Does this list contain more men's or women's names? The answer may surprise you: The number of male and female names is about equal. Because of the *availability heuristic*, however, most people tend to guess that female names are more numerous. Since the women listed are more famous, it is easier to bring their names to mind; this leads to overestimates of their frequency.

asked them whether the lists contained more men's or women's names. Although the numbers of male and female names were equal, nearly 80 percent of the participants reported that women's names appeared more frequently. Why? Because the women named in the lists were more famous, their names were more readily remembered.

The availability heuristic also influences many persons to overestimate the chances of being a victim of a violent crime, being involved in an airplane crash, or winning the lottery. Because such events are given extensive coverage in the mass media, individuals can readily bring vivid examples of them to mind. The result: they conclude that such outcomes are much more frequent than they actually are (Tyler & Cook, 1984).

REPRESENTATIVENESS: ASSUMING THAT WHAT'S TYPICAL IS ALSO LIKELY
Imagine that you've just met your next-door neighbor for the first time. On the basis of a brief conversation, you determine that he is neat in his appearance, has a good vocabulary, seems very well-read, is somewhat shy, and dresses conservatively. Later, you realize that he never mentioned what he does for a living. Is he more likely to be a business executive, a dentist, a librarian, or a waiter? One quick way of making a guess is to compare him with your idea of typical members of each of these occupations. If you proceed in this fashion, you may conclude that he is a librarian, because his traits seem to resemble those of your image of the prototypical librarian more closely than the traits of waiters, dentists, or executives. If you reasoned in this manner, you would be using the **representativeness heuristic**. In other words, you would be making your decision on the basis of a relatively simple rule: The more closely an item—or event, or object, or person—resembles the most typical examples of some concept or category, the more likely it is to belong to that concept or category.

Unfortunately, the use of this heuristic sometimes causes us to ignore forms of information that could potentially prove very helpful. The most important of these is information relating to *base rates*—the relative frequency of various items or events in the external world. Returning to your new neighbor, there are many more businessmen than male librarians. Thus, of the choices given, the most rational guess might be that your neighbor is a businessman. Yet because of the representativeness heuristic, you might falsely conclude that he is a librarian (Tversky & Kahneman, 1974).

ANCHORING-AND-ADJUSTMENT: REFERENCE POINTS THAT MAY LEAD US ASTRAY
The day I received my driver's license, I began to shop for my first car. After a long search, I found the car of my dreams. The major question, of course, was "How much will it cost?" A totally rational person would have located this information in the *Blue Book*, which lists the average prices paid

Representativeness Heuristic: A mental rule of thumb suggesting that the more closely an event or object resembles typical examples of some concept or category, the more likely it is to belong to that concept or category.

for various used cars in recent months. But given our strong tendency to follow the path of least resistance (and the fact that the Blue Book is not readily available everywhere), I tried a different approach. I asked the seller what he wanted for the car, then proceeded to bargain from there. At first glance, this may seem like a reasonable strategy. But think again: If you adopt this approach, you have allowed the seller to set a *reference point*—a figure from which your negotiations will proceed. If this price is close to the one in the *Blue Book*, well and good. If it is much higher, though, you may end up paying more for the car than it is really worth—as I did in this example.

In such cases, decisions are influenced by what is known as the **anchoring-and-adjustment heuristic**: a mental rule of thumb for reaching decisions by making adjustments in information that is already available. The basic problem with the anchoring-and-adjustment heuristic is that the adjustments made are often insufficient in magnitude to offset the impact of the original reference point. In this case, the reference point was the original asking price. In other contexts, it might be a performance rating assigned to an employee, a grade given to a term paper, or a suggested asking price for an automobile or a new home (Northcraft & Neale, 1987). Please see the **Key Concept** on page 240 for an overview of several of the heuristics we have discussed.

FRAMING AND DECISION STRATEGY

Imagine that a rare tropical disease has entered the United States and is expected to kill 600 people. Two plans for combating the disease exist. If plan A is adopted, 200 people will be saved. If plan B is adopted, the chances are one in three that all 600 will be saved but two in three that no one will be saved. Which plan would you choose?

Now consider the same situation with the following changes. Again, there are two plans. If plan C is chosen, 400 people will definitely die; if plan D is chosen, the chances are one in three that no one will die, but two in three that all 600 will die. Which would you choose now?

If you are like most respondents to these scenarios, you probably chose plan A in the first example, but plan D in the second example (Tversky & Kahneman, 1981). Why? Plan D is just another way of stating the outcomes of plan B, and plan C is just another way of stating the outcomes of plan A. Why, then do you prefer plan A in the first example but plan D in the second? Because in the first example, the emphasis is on lives saved, while in the second, the emphasis is on lives lost. In other words, the two examples differ in what psychologists term **framing**—presentation of information about potential outcomes in terms of gains or in terms of losses. When the emphasis is on potential gains (lives saved), research indicates that most people are *risk averse*. They prefer avoiding unnecessary risks. Thus, most choose plan A. In contrast, when the emphasis is on potential losses (deaths), most people are *risk prone*; they prefer taking risks to accepting certain losses. As a result, most choose plan D. In sum, the way in which information is framed can have major effects on our decisions.

ESCALATION OF COMMITMENT: *Getting Trapped in Bad Decisions*

Have you ever heard the phrase "throwing good money after bad"? It refers to the fact that in many situations, persons who have made a bad decision tend to stick to it even as the evidence for its failure mounts. They may even commit additional time, effort, and resources to a failing course of action in order to turn the situation around. This tendency to become trapped in bad

Anchoring-and-Adjustment Heuristic: A cognitive rule of thumb for decision making in which existing information is accepted as a reference point but then adjusted in light of various factors.

Framing: Presentation of information concerning potential outcomes in terms of gains or losses.

Factors That Influence the Decision-Making Process

Heuristics

Rules of thumb extracted from past experience that serve as guidelines for making decisions quickly and efficiently—but not infallibly.

Availability Heuristic

The tendency to make judgments about the frequency or likelihood of events in terms of how readily examples of them can be brought to mind.

Because lotto winners are given extensive media coverage, people can readily bring examples of these winners to mind. They falsely conclude that such outcomes are much more frequent than they really are.

Representativeness Heuristic

A rule of thumb suggesting that the more closely an event or object resembles typical examples of some concept or category, the more likely it is to belong to that concept or category.

Because of the representativeness heuristic, you might be tempted to label these youths as gang members.

Anchoring-and-Adjustment Heuristic

A rule of thumb in which existing information (the anchor) is accepted as a reference point but then adjusted—usually insufficiently—in light of various factors.

Familiarity with the anchoring-and-adjustment heuristic could save you a bundle—in this case, thousands of dollars when you're negotiating the price of a new home.

decisions, known as **escalation of commitment**, helps explain why many investors hold onto what are clearly bad investments and why individuals remain in troubled marriages or relationships (Brockner & Rubin, 1985).

But why does escalation of commitment occur? Staw and Ross (1989) have suggested that it probably stems from several different factors. Early in the escalation process, initial decisions are based primarily on *rational* factors. People choose particular courses of action because they believe that these will yield favorable outcomes. When things go wrong and negative results occur, it is at first quite reasonable to continue. After all, temporary setbacks are common, and there may also be considerable costs associated with changing an initial decision before it has had a chance to succeed (Staw & Ross, 1987).

As negative outcomes continue to mount, however, *psychological* factors come into play. Persons responsible for the initial decision may realize that if they back away from or reverse it, they will be admitting that they made a mistake. Indeed, as negative results increase, these individuals may experience a growing need for *self-justification*—a need to justify both their previous judgments and the losses already endured. Recent evidence suggests that individuals tend to stick with failing courses of action only when they have to justify these either to themselves (private self-justification) or to others (public self-justification) (Bobocel & Meyer, 1994).

In later phases of the process, external pressures stemming from other persons or groups affected by the bad decision may come into play. For example, individuals who did not originally make the decision but have gone along with it may now block efforts to reverse it because they too have become committed to actions it implies. Figure 7.5 summarizes the escalation process and several factors that play a role in its emergence and persistence.

Fortunately, researchers have found that under certain conditions people are less likely to escalate their commitment to a failed course of action (please

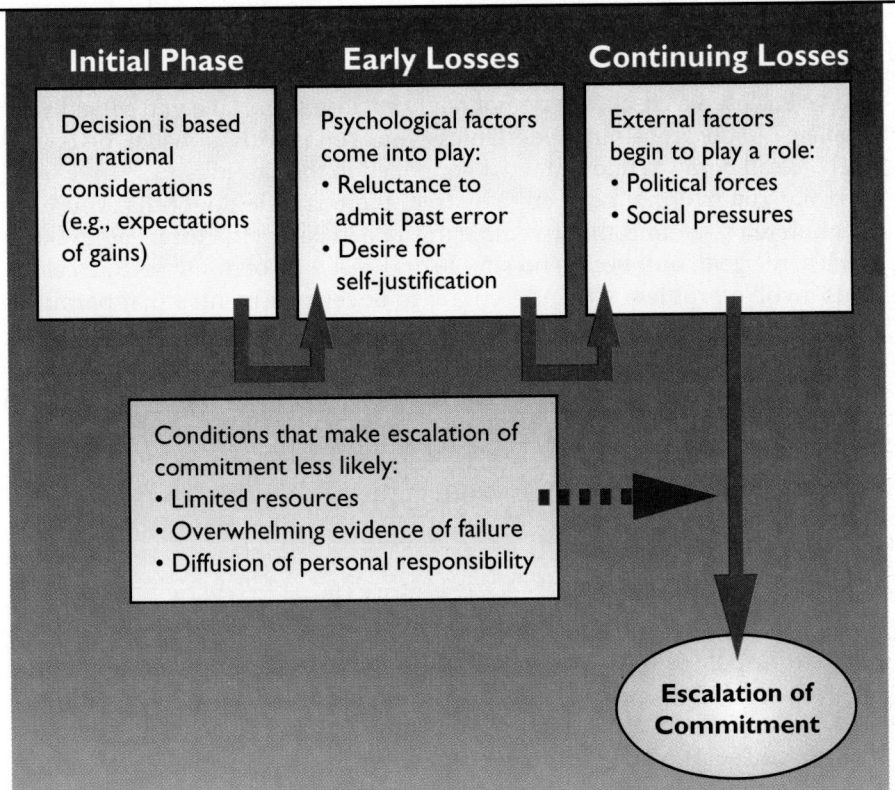

FIGURE **7.5**

Escalation of Commitment: An Overview

Early in the escalation process, there may be a rational expectation of a positive outcome. As losses occur, however, people are reluctant to admit their errors and seek self-justification. Later, external factors may strengthen tendencies to stick to the initial bad decision. However, other conditions may reduce the likelihood of escalation of commitment. (*Source:* Based on suggestions by Staw & Ross, 1989, and Garland & Newport, 1991.)

Escalation of Commitment: The tendency to become increasingly committed to bad decisions even as losses associated with them increase.

refer to Figure 7.5). First, people are likely to refrain from escalating commitment when available resources to commit to further action are limited and the evidence of failure is overwhelmingly obvious (Garland & Newport, 1991). Thus, an individual or group can decide in advance that when losses reach certain limits, no further resources will be squandered. Second, escalation of commitment is unlikely to occur when people can *diffuse their responsibility* for being part of a poor decision (Whyte, 1991). In other words, the less people feel personally responsible for making bad decisions, the less they may be motivated to justify their mistake by investing additional time or money. Thus, the tasks of making decisions and implementing them should be assigned to different persons. Together, these steps can help both individuals and groups avoid getting trapped in costly spirals that magnify the harmful effects of poor decisions. (See chapter 14 for more information on the effects of *diffusion of responsibility*.)

KEY QUESTIONS

- What are heuristics?
- What are the availability, representativeness, and anchoring-and-adjustment heuristics, and what roles do they play in reasoning?
- What is framing, and how does it relate to decision making?
- How does escalation of commitment affect decision making?

PROBLEM SOLVING AND CREATIVITY: *Finding Paths to Desired Goals*

Learning Objective 7.8
Survey the different techniques that can be used for solving problems.

Learning Objective 7.9
Discuss factors that can interfere with effective problem solving.

Learning Objective 7.10
Discuss what psychologists know about the nature of creativity.

Learning Objective 7.11
Discuss the important issues confronting the field of artificial intelligence.

*I*magine that you are a parent whose son is attending college in another state. You've asked him to keep in touch by phone and mail, but nearly a month has gone by without a word. You're a worrier, so you phone him repeatedly; all you get is his answering machine. What do you do? Several possibilities exist. You can call some of his friends and ask them to urge him to get in touch with you. You can try leaving a message that, you hope, will cause him to phone. Or—and here's the interesting one—you can try something like this: You write a letter to your son. In your letter, you mention that you've enclosed a check, but do not really enclose one. Have you solved your problem? In all probability, yes. Unless your son is truly unusual, he is very likely to call home to find out what happened to the check!

While you may not have any children, there is little doubt that you have encountered situations that resemble this one in basic structure: you'd like to reach some goal, but there is no simple or direct way of doing so. Such situations involve **problem solving**—efforts to develop responses that permit us to attain desired goals. In this section we'll examine several problem-solving techniques and factors that sometimes interfere with effective problem solving. In addition, we'll explore *creativity*—the ability to produce new and unusual solutions to various problems.

TECHNIQUES FOR SOLVING PROBLEMS: *From Trial and Error to Heuristics*

Perhaps the simplest problem-solving approach is **trial and error**, a technique that you have no doubt used yourself. Trial and error involves trying different responses until, perhaps, one works. Sometimes this is all you can do—you don't have enough information to adopt a more systematic approach. But such an approach is not very efficient, and it offers no guarantee that a useful solution will actually be found.

A second general approach to solving problems involves the use of **algorithms**. These are rules for a particular kind of problem that will, if followed,

Problem Solving: *Efforts to develop or choose among various responses in order to attain desired goals.*

Trial and Error: *A method of solving problems in which possible solutions are tried until one succeeds.*

Algorithm: *A rule that guarantees a solution to a specific type of problem.*

yield a solution. For example, imagine that you are supposed to meet a friend at a Chinese restaurant. Try as you may, you can't remember the name of the restaurant. What can you do? One approach is to get out the yellow pages and see if this refreshes your memory. If it doesn't, you can try calling all the restaurants listed to ask if your friend made a reservation (which you know she was planning to do). Following this algorithm—"Call every restaurant in the book"—will work; but it is time-consuming and inefficient. A much more effective way of solving many problems is to use an appropriate *heuristic*.

Heuristics, as you'll recall, are rules of thumb we often use to guide our cognition. With respect to problem solving, heuristics involve strategies suggested by prior experience—ones we have found useful in the past. These may or may not work in the present case, so a solution is not guaranteed. But what heuristics lack in terms of certainty they gain in efficiency: They often provide useful shortcuts. In the case of the forgotten Chinese restaurant, you might begin by assuming that your friend probably chose a restaurant close to where she lives. This simple rule could eliminate many of the most distant restaurants and considerably simplify your task.

One heuristic we often employ is known as **means-ends analysis** (or sub-goals analysis). This involves dividing the problem into a series of smaller pieces or sub-problems. By solving each of these, we can reduce the distance between our original state and the goal in a step-by-step fashion.

Finally, we sometimes attempt to solve problems through the use of **analogy**—the application of techniques that worked in similar situations in the past. For example, imagine that while driving through an unfamiliar town, you are suddenly seized by an uncontrollable desire for a Big Mac. You don't know your way around this town, but you know from past experience that McDonald's restaurants are often located near busy interstate highways. Applying this knowledge, you follow signs showing the way to the nearest interstate. If you are then rewarded by the sight of the famous golden arches, you have solved the problem through analogy.

FACTORS THAT INTERFERE WITH EFFECTIVE PROBLEM SOLVING

Sometimes, despite our best efforts, we are unable to solve problems. In many cases our failure stems from obvious causes, such as lack of necessary information or experience. Similarly, as we'll soon see, we may lack internal frameworks that allow us to represent the problem situation fully and effectively. As a result, we don't know which variables or factors are most important, and we spend lots of time "wandering about," using an informal type of trial-and-error strategy (Johnson, 1985). In other cases, though, difficulties in solving problems seem to stem from more subtle factors. Let's consider some of these now.

FUNCTIONAL FIXEDNESS: PRIOR USE VERSUS PRESENT SOLUTIONS Suppose you want to use the objects shown in Figure 7.6 (on page 244) to attach the candle to a wall so that it can stand upright and burn properly. What solution(s) do you come up with? If you are like most people, you may mention using the tacks to nail the candle to the wall or attaching it with melted wax (Duncker, 1945). While these techniques may work, they overlook a much more elegant solution: emptying the box of matches, tacking the box to the wall, and placing the candle on it (see Figure 7.7 on page 245). Described like this, the solution probably sounds obvious. Then why don't most people think of it? The answer involves **functional fixedness**—a strong tendency to think of using objects only in ways they have been used before. Since most of

Means-Ends Analysis: A technique for solving problems in which the overall problem is divided into parts and efforts are made to solve each part in turn.

Analogy: A strategy for solving problems based on applying solutions that were previously successful with other problems similar in underlying structure.

Functional Fixedness: The tendency to think of using objects only as they have been used in the past.

FIGURE 7.6

Solving Complex Problems

How can you attach the candle to a wall so that it stands upright and burns normally, using only the objects shown here?

us have never used an empty box as a candle holder, we don't think of it in these terms and so fail to hit on this solution. Interestingly, if the matchbox is shown empty, people are much more likely to think of using it as a candle holder (Weisberg & Sulls, 1973); so it doesn't take much to overcome such mental blind spots. Unless we can avoid functional fixedness, our ability to solve many problems can be seriously impaired.

MENTAL SET: STICKING TO THE TRIED AND TRUE Another factor that often gets in the way of effective problem solving is **mental set**. This is the tendency to stick with a familiar method of solving particular types of problems. Since past solutions have in fact succeeded, this is certainly reasonable, at least up to a point. Difficulties arise, however, when this tendency causes us to overlook other, more efficient approaches. The powerful impact of mental set was first demonstrated by Luchins (1942) in what is now a classic study. Luchins presented participants with the problems shown in Table 7.2, which involve using three jars of different sizes to measure amounts of water. If you work through the first two or three items, you will soon discover that you can solve them all by following this simple formula: Fill jar B, and from it fill jar A once and jar C twice. The amount of water remaining is then the desired amount.

KEY QUESTIONS

- How do psychologists define problem solving?
- Through what two mechanisms are problems usually solved?
- What role do heuristics play in problem solving?
- What factors can interfere with effective problem solving?

TABLE 7.2

Mental Set: Another Potential Deterrent to Problem Solving

How can you use three jars, A, B, and C, each capable of holding the amounts of liquid shown, to end up with one jar holding the exact amount listed in the right-hand column? See the text for two possible solutions.

| | AMOUNT HELD BY EACH JAR | | | |
PROBLEM	JAR A	JAR B	JAR C	GOAL (AMOUNT OF WATER DESIRED)
1	24	130	3	100
2	9	44	7	21
3	21	58	4	29
4	12	160	25	98
5	19	75	5	46
6	23	49	3	20
7	18	48	4	22

Because this formula works for all items, participants in Luchin's study tended to stick with it for all seven problems. But look at item 6: It can be solved in a simpler way. Just fill jar A, and then from it fill jar C. The amount remaining in jar A is precisely what's required (20 units). There is also a simple solution for item 7; see if you can figure it out. Do you think many of the participants in Luchin's study noticed these simpler solutions? Absolutely not. When they reached item 6, almost all continued to use the tried-and-true formula and overlooked the more efficient one.

Similar effects occur in many other contexts. For example, commuters often continue to take the same crowded roads to work each day because they have always done so; they don't even consider alternate routes that might seem less direct but are actually easier to travel. In these and many other situations, sliding into mental ruts can indeed prove costly.

FIGURE **7.7**

Functional Fixedness: How It Interferes with Problem Solving

Because of functional fixedness, surprisingly few people think of using the tacks to attach the box to the wall as a candle holder.

CREATIVITY: *Innovative Problem Solving*

Following the battle of Marengo in 1805, at which he won a great victory, Napoleon asked his chef to prepare a special celebration dinner. Unfortunately, the poor chef had very little to work with—nothing but a chicken, some onions, mushrooms, tomatoes, and wine. What could he do? Drawing on his culinary expertise, he created a new dish that has become a classic of French cooking: Chicken Marengo.

Most people would say that the chef's solution to this problem showed **creativity**—cognitive activity that results in a new or novel way of viewing or solving a problem (Solso, 1991). Further, most people would agree that creativity is desirable; after all, it is from creativity that major inventions, scientific breakthroughs, and great works of music, literature, and art derive.

CREATIVITY: ITS BASIC NATURE
Although it is tempting to assume that creativity springs suddenly from flashes of inspiration or other heroic sources, psychologists who have studied it conclude that in fact creativity involves a series of specific steps.

First, creativity involves considerable *preparation*. A person who develops a creative solution to an important problem generally spends long periods of time immersed in the problem, gathering knowledge relevant to it, and working on it. As Thomas Edison once remarked, "Success is ninety-eight percent perspiration and only two percent inspiration."

Second, creative solutions often emerge after a period of *incubation*—an interval during which the persons involved stop working actively on the problem and turn to other matters. Incubation periods may provide people with an opportunity to recover from the fatigue generated by the intense preparation phase. And as noted in chapter 4, during incubation additional work on the problem may be occurring even outside the realm of consciousness, such as during sleep.

Third, creativity does often involve a sudden *illumination*, or insight. At such times, individuals report that they suddenly see, perhaps only in partially developed form, the first glimmer of a solution they have been seeking for months or even years. This is how James Watson and Francis Crick, the scientists who discovered the structure of the DNA molecule, describe the

Mental Set: *The impact of past experience on present problem solving; specifically, the tendency to retain methods that were successful in the past even if better alternatives now exist.*

Creativity: *Cognitive activity resulting in new or novel ways of viewing or solving problems.*

experience; suddenly, they saw that it *must* be something like a double helix, with one strand intertwined with the other. Recent evidence on this topic suggests that flashes of insight probably involve cognitive restructuring of the problem situation (Durso et al., 1994).

Illumination, however, is not the end of the process. Considerable *refinement* must often follow. The idea must be worked out, translated into testable form, then actually tested. Only when mounting evidence indicates that it does work is the creative solution carried to its final conclusion.

MEASURING CREATIVITY How can creativity be measured or assessed? Panels of judges often attempt to assess creativity in everything from designs for buildings to poetry, high fashion, and even doctoral dissertations; yet there is no single agreed-upon psychological test for measuring creativity.

One measure of creativity developed by Guilford (1967) is based on the distinction between convergent and divergent thinking. **Convergent thinking** applies existing knowledge and rules of logic to the task of narrowing the range of potential solutions and zeroing in on a single correct answer. While such thinking is productive in many situations, it does not appear to foster true creativity. In contrast, **divergent thinking** moves outward from conventional knowledge or wisdom into unexplored paths and unconventional solutions. It is from such thinking that creative breakthroughs seem to derive. In Guilford's *divergence production test*, individuals are asked to list the number of uses they can generate for common objects—for example, bricks. The more uses a person can list, and the more unusual these are, the higher the score. Thus, responses like "build a wall" or "make a chimney" are scored as being lower in creativity than ones like "grind them up to make emergency face powder" or "give them to people going to work on Mars to use as shoes." The very strangeness of the unusual answers reflects thinking that breaks out of the ordinary cognitive channels most of us follow most of the time.

ARTIFICIAL INTELLIGENCE: *Can Machines Really Think?*

When I took my first course in computer science, in 1964, the professor painted a glowing picture of the future capabilities of computers. The prediction that sticks in my mind most vividly, though, is his promise that within ten years we would be able to talk to computers directly, in everyday English. Now, more than thirty years later, I've yet to see someone sit down and converse readily and easily with a computer. Yet I'm optimistic that this *will* happen, and very soon.

If someday soon we'll be able to hold ordinary conversations with computers, and if they can already do many other things we usually attribute to human intelligence, an interesting question arises: If computers can accomplish these tasks, would it make sense to say that are intelligent? This question lies at the heart of the study of **artificial intelligence (AI)**—a branch of science in which psychologists and other scientists examine the capacity of computers to demonstrate performance that, if it were produced by human beings, would be described as showing intelligence. (We will explore the nature of intelligence in more detail later in this chapter.)

How much intelligence do computers actually show? Actually, quite a lot. Since modern computers can carry out millions of computations per second—a capability far beyond that of mere mortals—it is not surprising that they are better than people at doing repetitive tasks requiring speed and accuracy. Computers are commonly used, in the automobile industry for example, to perform tasks that range from welding seams to installing wind-

Convergent Thinking:
Thinking that applies existing knowledge and rules of logic so as to zero in on a single correct solution to a problem.

Divergent Thinking:
Thinking that moves outside conventional solutions or knowledge in an effort to develop novel solutions to a problem.

Artificial Intelligence: A branch of science that studies the capacity of computers to demonstrate performance that, if it were produced by human beings, would be described as showing intelligence.

shields (Munakata, 1994). With the help of various scanning devices, computers also perform important perceptual tasks, such as detecting flaws in many different products (Robotics Institute, 1984). Since computers are tireless and can make accurate judgments with amazing speed, they are better suited for such tasks than human beings. Artificial intelligence researchers are also working toward the development of computers that can actually fool people into believing they are conversing with a human being (Loebner, 1994; Shieber, 1994). In one annual contest, a human judge converses via computer terminal with two other terminals: one operated by another human, the other by a computer. Under certain conditions—for example, when the topic of discussion is carefully restricted—computers have actually been able to fool the human judge (Epstein, 1992)!

Computers can also be efficient problem solvers. For instance, computers have been programmed to play chess very well—and in fact have recently beaten some of the very best human players. As you might guess, they do this primarily by relying on their great speed and memory (Elmer-Dewitt, 1985). Thus, each time an opponent makes a move, the computer can rapidly consider all possible counters plus their likely effects. And new programs allow computers to play chess the way expert human beings do—on the basis of long-range strategies that take account of an opponent's style and apparent weaknesses.

However, as I mentioned earlier, efforts to demonstrate computer intelligence with regard to language have had somewhat mixed results. This has caused artificial intelligence researchers—and professors like the one I had in my first course in computer science—to revise their initial predictions that development of intelligent computers was "just around the corner." On one hand, the language abilities demonstrated by computers are remarkable. For example, banks, credit unions, and credit-card companies now regularly use computerized voice-recognition systems to handle certain types of business transactions, such as provision of account balances. Even more impressive, though, are computers that can converse with their operators and carry out a variety of tasks, including booking airline reservations. These complex machines possess large vocabularies, understand syntax well enough to be able to understand simple instructions, and know when to ask relevant questions if they do not understand or do not have enough information to act (Rensberger, 1993). On the other hand, though, it has proven frustratingly difficult to teach computers to grasp many of the subtleties of human speech that we acquire through our everyday experience (Munakata, 1994). And many ordinary tasks that most people take for granted, such as shopping at the mall or understanding simple conversations, exceed the capabilities of even the most powerful modern computers.

In response to these and related issues, researchers have designed computers that imitate the way in which the brain—perhaps the most powerful computer in the universe—operates. Whereas most computers process information in a sequential fashion, the brain processes the input from all of the senses simultaneously through a complex network of highly connected neurons. The new computer systems, termed **neural networks**, are structures consisting of highly interconnected elementary computational units that work together in parallel (Denning, 1992; Levine, 1991). The primary advantage of neural networks comes not from the individual units themselves, but from the overall pattern resulting from millions of these units working together. In addition, neural networks have the capacity to learn from experience and adjust the strength of the output from individual units based on new information. Although research on neural networks is still in its infancy, scientists have learned a great deal from these structures regarding how the brain operates.

ARTIFICIAL INTELLIGENCE: PUTTING COMPUTERS TO WORK

The field of artificial intelligence (AI) has made rapid progress in creating computers and other "intelligent" devices capable of performing a wide variety of tasks. But are such machines truly intelligent?

Neural Networks: Computer systems modeled after the brain and made up of highly interconnected elementary computational units that work together in parallel.

Where does all this leave us with respect to artificial intelligence? Most psychologists who specialize in this field would readily admit that early predictions about the capacities of computers to show such characteristics as intention, understanding, and consciousness were greatly overstated (Levine, 1991; Searle, 1980). However, they note that computers are indeed exceptionally useful in the study of human cognition and can, in certain contexts, demonstrate performance that closely resembles that of intelligent human beings. Although you may not soon meet a robot who can speak with you in a fluent manner like the ones in films, the chances are good that computers and other machines will continue to become more "intelligent" with the passage of time.

KEY QUESTIONS

- What steps are involved in the creative process?
- What is divergent thinking?
- What is artificial intelligence?

LANGUAGE: *The Communication of Information*

Learning Objective 7.12
Compare and contrast the different views of language development and describe the basic milestones of language development.

Learning Objective 7.13
Describe the contrasting views on the relationship between language and thought.

Learning Objective 7.14
Discuss the research on animal language and communication.

At present most scientists agree that what truly sets us apart from other species of animals is **language**—our ability to use an extremely rich set of symbols, plus rules for combining them, to communicate information. While the members of all species do communicate with one another in some manner, and while some may use certain features of language, the human ability to do so far exceeds that of any other organism on earth. We'll now examine the nature of language and its relationship to other aspects of cognition.

LANGUAGE: *Its Basic Nature*

Language uses symbols for communicating information. In order for a set of symbols to be viewed as a language, however, several additional criteria must be met. First, information must actually be transmitted by the symbols—the words and sentences must carry *meaning*. Second, although the number of separate sounds or words in a language may be limited, it must be possible to combine these elements into an essentially infinite number of sentences. Third, the meanings of these combinations must be independent of the settings in which they are used. In other words, sentences must be able to convey information about other places and other times. Only if all three of these criteria are met can the term *language* be applied to a system of communication.

THE DEVELOPMENT OF LANGUAGE

Throughout the first few weeks of life, infants have only one major means of verbal communication: crying. Within a few short years, however, children progress rapidly to speaking whole sentences and acquire a vocabulary of hundreds or even thousands of words. Some of the milestones along this remarkable journey are summarized in Table 7.3. Although we'll consider other developmental issues in more detail in chapter 8, we'll now turn to two questions relating to the development of language: What mechanisms play a role in this process? And how, and at what ages, do children acquire various aspects of language skills?

Language: A system of symbols, plus rules for combining them, used to communicate information.

THEORIES OF LANGUAGE DEVELOPMENT: SOME CONTRASTING VIEWS   The *social learning view* of language development suggests one mechanism for the rapid acquisition of language. This view proposes that speech is acquired

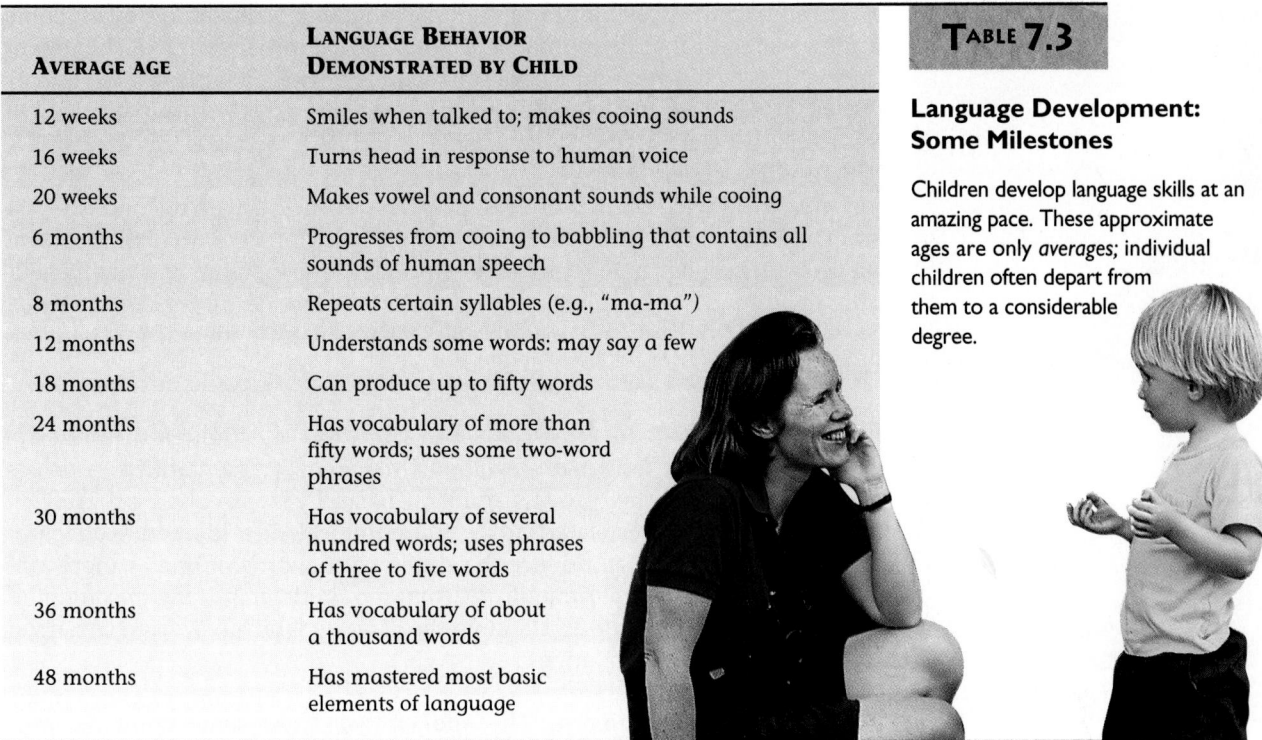

AVERAGE AGE	LANGUAGE BEHAVIOR DEMONSTRATED BY CHILD
12 weeks	Smiles when talked to; makes cooing sounds
16 weeks	Turns head in response to human voice
20 weeks	Makes vowel and consonant sounds while cooing
6 months	Progresses from cooing to babbling that contains all sounds of human speech
8 months	Repeats certain syllables (e.g., "ma-ma")
12 months	Understands some words: may say a few
18 months	Can produce up to fifty words
24 months	Has vocabulary of more than fifty words; uses some two-word phrases
30 months	Has vocabulary of several hundred words; uses phrases of three to five words
36 months	Has vocabulary of about a thousand words
48 months	Has mastered most basic elements of language

TABLE 7.3

Language Development: Some Milestones

Children develop language skills at an amazing pace. These approximate ages are only *averages*; individual children often depart from them to a considerable degree.

through a combination of operant conditioning and imitation (please refer to chapter 5). Presumably, children are praised or otherwise rewarded by their parents for making sounds approximating those of their native language. Moreover, parents often model sounds, words, or sentences for their children. Together, it is contended, these basic forms of learning contribute to the rapid acquisition of language.

A sharply different view has been proposed by the noted linguist Noam Chomsky (1968). According to Chomsky, language acquisition is at least partly innate. Human beings, he contends, have a *language acquisition device*—a built-in neural system that provides them with an intuitive grasp of grammar. In other words, humans are prepared to acquire language and do so rapidly for this reason.

Finally, a *cognitive theory* offered by Slobin (1979) recognizes the importance of both innate mechanisms and learning. This theory suggests that children possess certain information-processing abilities or strategies that they use in acquiring language. These are termed *operating principles* and seem to be present, or to develop, very early in life. One such operating principle seems to be "Pay attention to the ends of words"—children pay more attention to the ends than to the beginnings or middles of words. This makes sense, since in many languages suffixes carry important meanings. Another principle is "Pay attention to the order of words." And indeed, word order in children's speech tends to reflect that of their parents. Since word order differs greatly from one language to another, this, too, is an important principle.

Which of these theories is correct? At present, all are supported by some evidence, but none seems sufficient by itself to account for all aspects of language development. For example, contrary to what the social learning view suggests, it appears that parents do not directly reinforce their children for correct syntax or grammar often enough to shape such skills through conditioning (Hirsch-Pasek, Treiman, & Schneiderman, 1984). Yet in every culture children's speech resembles that of their parents in many important ways, so imitation does seem to play an important role.

A First Step toward Language Development

Most children say their first spoken words by their first birthday. After this milestone, their vocabulary grows rapidly.

Phonological Development: Development of the ability to produce recognizable speech.

Semantic Development: Development of understanding of the meaning of spoken or written language.

Grammar: Rules within a given language indicating how words can be combined into meaningful sentences.

Babbling: An early stage of speech development in which infants emit virtually all known sounds of human speech.

Phonological Strategies: Simplifications used by young children to facilitate the task of producing recognizable speech.

Fast Mapping: A process through which children attach a new word to an underlying concept on the basis of a single encounter with it.

Turning to the possibility of an innate language acquisition device, some findings suggest that there may be a *critical period* for language development during which children find it easiest to acquire various language components (Elliott, 1981). If for some reason children are not exposed to normal speech at this time, they may find it increasingly difficult to master language (De Villiers & De Villiers, 1978).

Given this mixed pattern of evidence, it is probably safest to conclude that language development is the result of a complex process involving several aspects of learning, many cognitive processes, and perhaps various genetically determined mechanisms as well. Additional evidence is clearly needed before more precise conclusions about mechanisms of language development can be reached.

Basic Components of Language Development   Although the underlying mechanisms of language development remain to be clarified, much is known about how this process unfolds. Basically, it involves progress in three distinct but interrelated areas: **phonological development**—development of the ability to pronounce the sounds and words of one or more languages; **semantic development**—learning to understand the meaning of words; and **grammar**—understanding the rules by which words are arranged into sentences in a given language.

Phonological development: The spoken word. At some point between three and six months, babies begin **babbling**. At first babbling contains a rich mixture of sounds, virtually every sound used in human speech. By nine or ten months, however, the range of babbling narrows and consists mainly of sounds used in the language of the child's native culture. From this point to the production of the first spoken word is a relatively short step, and most children accomplish it by their first birthday.

After the appearance of the first word, vocabulary increases rapidly. However, many children apply **phonological strategies**, or techniques for simplifying the pronunciation of many words; for example, they may delete unstressed syllables so that "banana" becomes "nana" or the name "Melissa" becomes "Missy." Pronunciation improves rapidly during the preschool years, but some refinements continue throughout childhood; for example, learning to change the stressed syllable when words add endings (*prac*tical to practi*cal*ity, *hu*mid to hu*mid*ity).

Semantic development: The acquisition of meaning. By age six, most children have a vocabulary of more than 14,000 words. This means they add an average of about nine new words to their vocabulary each day—in part by asking their parents to name everything in sight (Clark, 1973). Some researchers suggest that children accomplish this feat through a process called **fast mapping**: They "map" a new word to an underlying concept as a result of a single exposure. This is fast indeed; consider how many times you, as an adult, must encounter a word in a foreign language before you can enter it into your vocabulary.

The first words acquired by children are *object words*, which apply to specific objects in the world. These are followed by *action words*, which describe specific activities. Children's use of specific words does not always conform to adults' usage, however. Initially, a child may use a noun such as "door" and a verb such as "open" to refer to the same action: opening the door. It is not until they are two to two and a half that most children begin to use *state words*, ones describing transient conditions, such as "dirty", "clean", "hot", or "cold".

As children increase their vocabulary, they often demonstrate several interesting forms of error. First, they show *mismatches*, instances in which a new word is attached to an inappropriate concept. For example, they may relate the word "new" to something they dislike and "old" to something they want, as in "I want *old* candy, not *new* candy." In addition, they often show *underextensions*, in which a term is applied to a smaller range of objects or events than its true meaning, or *overextensions*, in which a term is applied to a wider range than appropriate. An underextension might be use of the word "apple" to refer only to red ones; overextension might be application of the word "car" to any and all vehicles. Finally, children often coin new words; they may refer to a hammer as "hitter," for instance.

Grammatical development.   Every language has *grammar*, a set of rules dictating how words can be combined into sentences. Children must learn to follow these rules, as well as to utter sounds that others can recognize as words. At first, grammar poses little problem, since early speech is *holophrastic*—that is, young children use single words to express complex meanings. Thus, "Eat!" may mean "I want to eat" or "Mommy is eating." By the time most children are two, they progress to *telegraphic* speech, omitting less-important words. An example: "Daddy cookie" may mean "Give Daddy a cookie" or "Daddy, bring me some cookies."

Between two and three, most children begin to use simple sentences consisting of three words. *Mean utterance length*, the average length of the sentences children use (Brown, 1973), increases to about three or four words between the ages of three and six; and more complex grammatical forms also appear, including use of conjunctions such as "and" and connected clauses—"Dad picked me up at school and we went for hamburgers." The use of increasingly complex forms in everyday speech continues to develop throughout childhood and is not complete until early adolescence.

In sum, language development is definitely a continuing feature of cognitive development throughout childhood. Given the complexity of language aquisition, and its central role in many aspects of cognition, this is far from surprising.

Key Questions
• What abilities are involved in the production of language?
• How does language develop in humans?
• What are the basic components of language development?

Language and Thought: *Do We Think What We Say or Say What We Think?*

Although we often have vivid mental images, as we saw earlier in this chapter, most of our thinking seems to involve words. This fact raises an intriguing question: What is the precise relationship between language and thought? One possibility, known as the **linguistic relativity hypothesis**, suggests that language actually shapes or determines thought (Whorf, 1956). According to this view, people who speak different languages may perceive the world in different ways because their thinking is determined, at least in part, by the words available to them. For example, Eskimos, who have many different words to describe snow, may actually perceive this aspect of the physical world differently from English-speaking persons, who have only one word.

The opposing view is that thought shapes language. This position suggests that language merely reflects the way we think—how our minds work. Which position is more accurate? While the issue is far from resolved, existing evidence seems to argue against the linguistic relativity approach (Miura & Okamoto, 1989). If this view were correct, people who speak a language that has few words to describe colors should have greater difficulty in perceiving various colors than people who speak a language rich in color words. But research designed to test such possibilities has generally failed to support

Linguistic Relativity Hypothesis: The view that language shapes thought.

them. In one experiment, Rosch (1973) studied natives of New Guinea. Their language, Dani, has only two color names: *mola*, for bright, warm colors, and *mili*, for dark, cool ones. Rosch found that despite this fact, Dani speakers perceived colors in much the same manner as persons who speak English, a language containing many color words.

So, while it may be easier to express a particular idea or concept in one language than another, this apparently does not mean that our thoughts or perceptions are strongly shaped by language. On the contrary, basic aspects of human perception and thought seem to be very much the same around the world, regardless of spoken language.

LANGUAGE IN OTHER SPECIES

Members of nonhuman species communicate with one another in many ways. Bees do a complex dance to indicate the direction of and distance to a food source; birds sing songs when seeking to attract a mate; seagoing mammals such as whales communicate with one another through complex patterns of sounds. But what about language? Are we the only species capable of using this sophisticated means of communication? Until the 1970s, there seemed little question that this was so.

During the 1940s, for instance, Keith and Cathy Hayes raised a chimpanzee named Vicki from infancy in their home and provided her with intensive speech training; but she was able to utter only a few simple words, such as "mama," "papa," and "cup." These disappointing results were due, in part, to the fact that nonhuman primates (and other animals) lack the vocal control necessary to form words and, hence, *spoken* language. However, the ability to speak is not essential for the use of language. After all, deaf persons can still communicate by writing or sign language. The fact that a chimp could not learn to speak, then, did not rule out the possibility that chimps or other animals could learn to use some form of language.

The findings reported by several teams of researchers seemed to indicate this might be so. For example, Beatrice and Allen Gardner succeeded in teaching Washoe, a female chimp, to use and understand nearly 200 words in American Sign Language (ASL), which is used by many deaf persons (Gardner & Gardner, 1975). Research with gorillas yielded similar results (Patterson, 1978).

Still, many psychologists argued that the animals in these studies, while exhibiting impressive learning, were not really demonstrating use of language (Davidson & Hopson, 1988; Terrace, 1985). Close examination of the procedures used to train and test the animals suggested that their trainers may often unintentionally have provided subtle cues that helped them respond correctly to questions. It also appeared that in some cases trainers overinterpreted the animals' responses, reading complex meanings and intentions into relatively simple signs. Finally, it remained unclear whether animals are capable of grasping several basic features of human languages, such as *syntax*—the rules by which words are arranged to form meaningful sentences, and *generativity*—the ability to combine a relatively limited number of words into unique combinations that convey a broad range of meanings.

ANIMAL LANGUAGE: LOOK WHO'S TALKING NOW Recent studies of other species of animals, including bonobos (a rare type of chimpanzee) and dolphins, have begun to address these and related issues. For example, consider the language abilities demonstrated by a bonobo named Kanzi (Linden, 1993). While attempting to teach Kanzi's mother to use an artificial language made up of abstract visual symbols, psychologist Sue Savage-Rumbaugh noticed that Kanzi (then an infant) learned several symbol-words just by watching.

Researcher Sue Savage-Rumbaugh has taught Kanzi, a chimp, to communicate using symbols on a special keyboard. Kanzi is unusual because he can also respond to spoken commands like "Please bring me the flashlight."

Intrigued by the possibilities raised by this discovery, Savage-Rumbaugh and her colleagues continued to train Kanzi in this informal way—speaking to him throughout the day while simultaneously pointing to the corresponding word symbols on portable language boards they carried with them.

Since then, Kanzi has demonstrated a grasp of grammatical concepts, and he comprehends several hundred spoken words (Savage-Rumbaugh et al., 1992). More importantly, though, the use of strict control procedures has ruled out the possibility that Kanzi was responding to subtle cues from his trainers, a criticism leveled against many early demonstrations of animals' use of language.

But what about more complex features of language? Are animals capable of grasping these concepts, too? Psychologist Louis Herman believes the answer is yes. Herman and his colleagues taught a female dolphin named Akeakamai—or Ake for short—an artificial language in which hand gestures are the words (Herman, Richards, & Wolz, 1984). Each gesture symbolizes either an *object* such as "Frisbee," an *action* such as "fetch," or a *description of position* such as "over" or "left." Ake has learned more than fifty of these gesture-words. These researchers have also discovered that Ake is capable of comprehending more complex features of language, including word order and syntax in word sequences up to five gestures. For example, RIGHT BASKET LEFT FRISBEE FETCH instructs Ake to take the Frisbee on her left to the basket on her right. More impressively, though, when familiar gestures are rearranged to form novel commands—ones Ake has never seen before—she continues to respond correctly.

In short, growing evidence suggests that language may not be a uniquely human possession, but rather a continuum of skills that different species of animals exhibit to varying degrees. And it is clear that dolphins and other species of animals are capable of comprehending features of language that go beyond the forms of behavior observed in the earlier studies of animal language.

KEY QUESTIONS

- What is the linguistic relativity hypothesis?
- Do animals possess language?

INTELLIGENCE: Its Nature and Measurement

*I*n everyday life, we make judgments about where other people—and we ourselves—stand along many different dimensions: attractiveness, ambition,

Learning Objective 7.15
Compare and contrast the different views on the nature of intelligence.

Learning Objective 7.16
Discuss the findings as to whether there are differences between males and females in cognitive abilities.

Learning Objective 7.17
Describe the different measures of human intelligence and discuss their positive and negative features.

Learning Objective 7.18
Describe the concepts of test reliability and validity and the different types of reliability and validity.

Learning Objective 7.19
Describe the findings related to cultural bias in intelligence tests and the efforts to design culture-fair tests to overcome this bias.

patience, charm, and energy, to name just a few. Among these dimensions, one of the most important clearly is **intelligence**—the ability to think abstractly and learn readily from experience (Flynn, 1987). Why do we consider people's relative position along this dimension to be so important? Partly because we believe intelligence predicts many important aspects of behavior: how quickly people can master new information and tasks; how well they will understand and adapt to new situations; how successful they will be in school, in various kinds of training, and in life generally. As we'll soon see, these commonsense notions are correct, at least to a degree: The higher persons score on various measures of intelligence, the better able they are to accomplish many different tasks (Ceci, 1991; Matarazzo, 1992).

In this section we'll first consider several contrasting views of intelligence. Then we'll turn to the question of how this important characteristic can be measured. In this context, we'll consider some of the basic requirements of *any* tests designed to assess individual differences in *any* aspect of psychological functioning. Finally, we'll address the evidence as to the relative contributions of environmental and genetic factors to intelligence.

HUMAN INTELLIGENCE: Some Contrasting Views

What is intelligence? Every person has her or his own definition, and psychologists too, disagree about this issue (e.g., Glazer, 1993; Sternberg, 1985). Most would include in their definitions of intelligence the ability to think abstractly and learn readily from experience, but beyond these basics, there is little consensus. Let's examine several schools of thought about the nature of intelligence to see how they differ.

INTELLIGENCE: UNIFIED OR MULTIFACETED?

Is intelligence a single characteristic, or does it consist of several distinct parts? In the past, psychologists who studied intelligence often disagreed sharply on this issue. In one camp were scientists who viewed intelligence as a general, unified capacity—a single characteristic or dimension along which people vary. An early supporter of this view was Spearman (1927), who believed that performance on any cognitive task depended on a primary general factor, which he named g, and one or more specific factors (s) relating to that particular task. Spearman based this view on the observation that people who scored high or low on one kind of test of intelligence tended to score at a similar level on other tests, too.

In contrast, other experts believed that intelligence is composed of many separate cognitive abilities that operate more or less independently. One of the strongest proponents of this position was Thurstone (1938), who suggested that intelligence is a composite of seven distinct primary mental abilities. Included in his list were *verbal meaning*—understanding of ideas and word meanings; *number*—speed and accuracy in dealing with numbers; and *space*—the ability to visualize objects in three dimensions. Thurstone believed that assessment of a person's intelligence required measurement of all seven abilities. Related theories (e.g., Gardner, 1983; Guilford, 1967, 1985) have divided intelligence into other patterns of components, but the basic underlying idea remains the same: Intelligence is *multifaceted*.

Not all views of intelligence are divided sharply on this issue, however. In fact, one influential perspective, proposed by Cattell (1963, 1987), adopts a more integrated approach. According to Cattell, intelligence consists of two major components: *fluid intelligence* and *crystallized intelligence*. **Crystallized intelligence** refers to those aspects of intelligence that involve drawing on pre-

Intelligence: The ability to think abstractly and to learn readily from experience.

Crystallized Intelligence: Aspects of intelligence that draw on previously learned information to make decisions or solve problems.

viously learned information to make decisions or solve problems. Classroom tests, vocabulary tests, and many social situations involve crystallized intelligence. In contrast, **fluid intelligence** involves the abilities to form concepts, reason, and identify similarities. In short, fluid intelligence is more intuitive and involves forming new cognitive structures rather than making use of existing ones. Research focusing on these two types of intelligence suggests that fluid intelligence may peak in early adulthood, while crystallized intelligence increases across the life span (Lerner, 1990; Willis & Nesselroade, 1990).

Where does the pendulum of scientific opinion rest today? Somewhere in the middle. At present, most psychologists believe that intelligence involves *both* a general ability to handle a wide range of cognitive tasks and problems *and* a number of more specific abilities. In a sense, though, modern thinking about the nature of intelligence has largely moved beyond the *unitary versus multifaceted* issue and now addresses very different questions relating to the role of *information processing* in intelligence.

THE INFORMATION-PROCESSING APPROACH: BASIC COMPONENTS OF INTELLIGENT THOUGHT As we'll see repeatedly in this book, psychologists have applied an *information-processing perspective* to understanding many aspects of human behavior—everything from the nature of memory and cognitive development through key aspects of motivation (see chapters 6, 8, and 9). It is not surprising, then, that this approach has also been applied to understanding the nature of intelligence. According to an information-processing perspective, to understand intelligence we must understand the cognitive strategies used by individuals who score high or low on this dimension. In other words, we must define intelligence in terms of basic aspects of cognition, a topic we considered earlier in this chapter (Matarazzo, 1992; Naglieri & Das, 1990). This perspective has already led to important new insights about intelligence. For example, consider a theory proposed by Sternberg (1985, 1986).

According to Sternberg's theory, known as the **triarchic theory** of intelligence, there are actually three types of human intelligence (see Figure 7.8 on page 256). The first, known as **componential intelligence**, emphasizes effectiveness in information processing. Persons high on this dimension are able to think critically and analytically. Thus, they usually excel on standard tests of academic potential and make excellent students. In contrast, the second type, **experiential intelligence**, emphasizes insight and the ability to formulate new ideas. Persons high on this dimension excel at zeroing in on what information is crucial in a given situation and at combining seemingly unrelated facts. This is the kind of intelligence shown by many scientific geniuses and inventors, such as Einstein, Newton, and—some would say—Freud. Johannes Gutenberg, for example, inventor of the movable type that first made large-scale production of books possible, combined the mechanisms for producing playing cards, pressing wine, and minting coins into his invention.

Finally, there is what Sternberg terms **contextual intelligence**. Persons high on this dimension are intelligent in a practical, adaptive sense. They quickly recognize what factors influence success on various tasks and are competent at both adapting to and shaping their environment. Successful people in many fields excel in this capacity.

Sternberg has also expanded his theory to bridge the gap between intelligence and personality, the topic we'll consider in chapter 10 (Sternberg, 1988, 1989). In this expanded view, known as *mental self-government*, Sternberg notes that in addition to the three types of intelligence described above, we must also consider *intellectual styles*—ways in which people actually use the three types in solving the problems of everyday life.

Fluid Intelligence: Aspects of intelligence that involve forming concepts, reasoning, and identifying similarities.

Triarchic Theory: A theory suggesting that there are actually three distinct kinds of intelligence.

Componential Intelligence: The ability to think analytically.

Experiential Intelligence: The ability to formulate new ideas or to combine seemingly unrelated information.

Contextual Intelligence: The ability to adapt to a changing environment.

FIGURE **7.8**

Sternberg's Triarchic Theory of Intelligence

According to Sternberg's triarchic theory, there are three distinct types of intelligence: *componential*, *experiential*, and *contextual*.

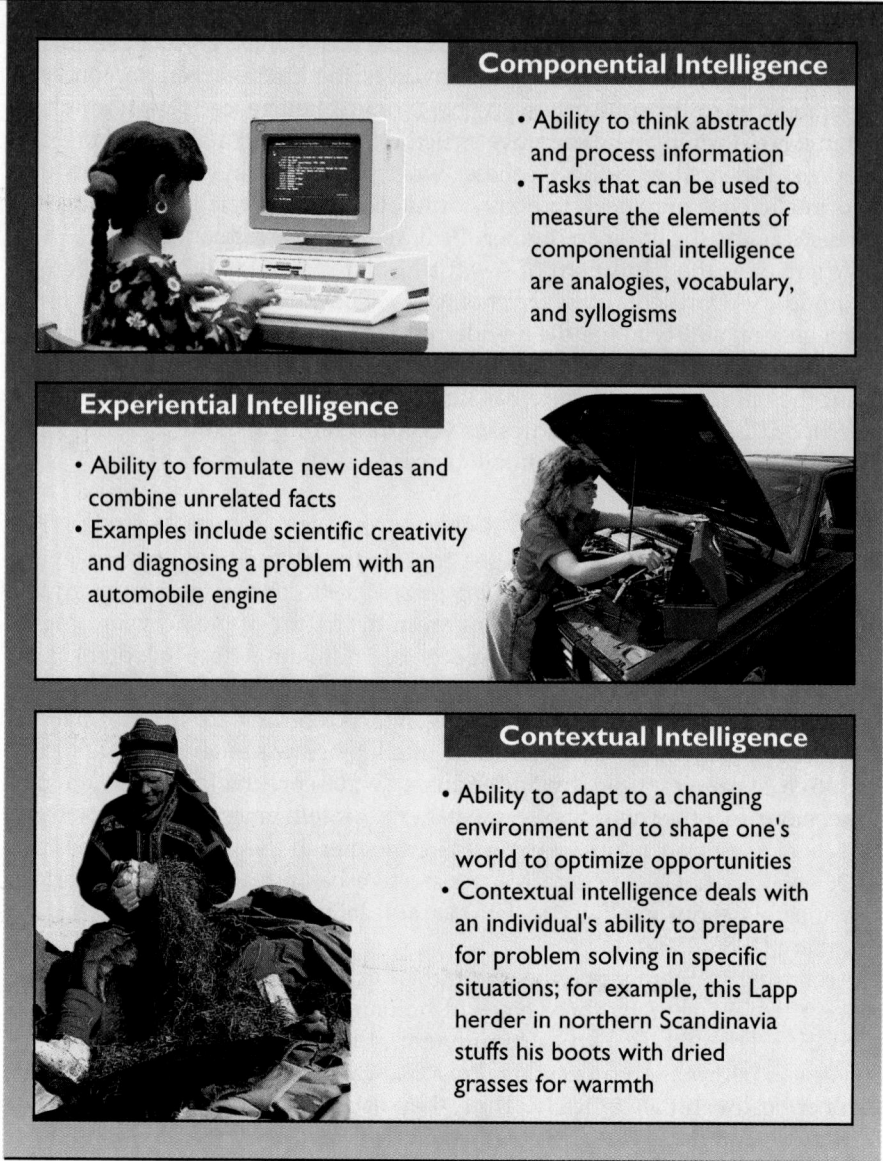

Componential Intelligence

- Ability to think abstractly and process information
- Tasks that can be used to measure the elements of componential intelligence are analogies, vocabulary, and syllogisms

Experiential Intelligence

- Ability to formulate new ideas and combine unrelated facts
- Examples include scientific creativity and diagnosing a problem with an automobile engine

Contextual Intelligence

- Ability to adapt to a changing environment and to shape one's world to optimize opportunities
- Contextual intelligence deals with an individual's ability to prepare for problem solving in specific situations; for example, this Lapp herder in northern Scandinavia stuffs his boots with dried grasses for warmth

Whether or not Sternberg's theories are confirmed by future research, they are representative of a new approach to the study of intelligence that draws heavily on basic knowledge about cognition generally. Clearly, this is a promising perspective.

THE NEUROSCIENCE APPROACH: INTELLIGENCE AND NEURAL EFFICIENCY
Highly intelligent persons are often described as being "quick," people who can respond rapidly to changing situations and new events. This everyday usage points to another possible perspective on intelligence—one emphasizing neural factors, such as more rapid or efficient processing of information within the brain. In fact, such an approach has gained increasing attention among psychologists, mainly because a growing body of evidence suggests that intelligence may be closely linked to physiological processes—especially ones going on in the nervous system and brain (e.g., Matarazzo, 1992). What kind of evidence points to such connections? A good illustration is provided by a study conducted recently by Reed and Jensen (1993).

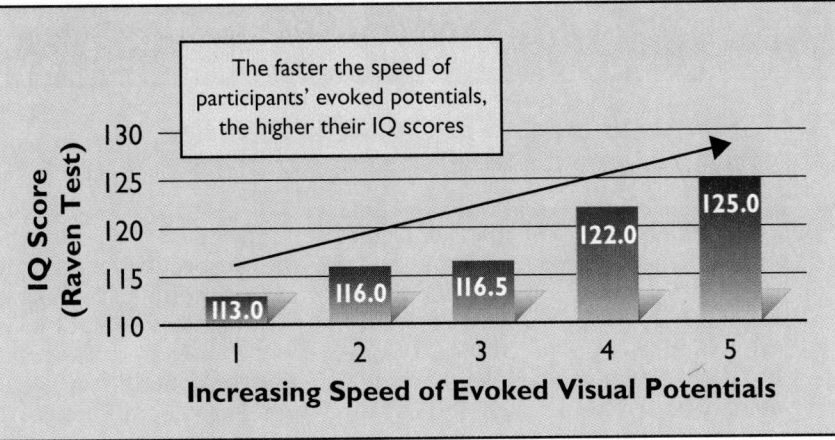

FIGURE 7.9

The Physiological Basis of Intelligence

The faster their nerve impulses in response to visual stimuli, the higher research participants scored on one test of intelligence. These findings, and many others, suggest that intelligence may rest in part on the efficiency with which individuals' brains process information. (*Source*: Based on data from Reed & Jensen, 1993.)

These researchers recorded electrical responses (evoked potentials) in the brains of 147 male volunteers when they were presented with a visual stimulus. The investigators obtained the average latency (delay) with which these potentials followed presentation of the visual stimuli for each volunteer and then divided the latency by the length of the volunteer's head to obtain a measure of the speed with which nerve impulses were conducted in his visual system. They then correlated these data with the volunteers' scores on one written test of intelligence (the Raven Matrices, a test we'll consider in a later section). As shown in Figure 7.9, results were startling: The higher this measure of neural speed, the higher was the participant's intelligence.

Other research has examined metabolic activity in the brain during cognitive tasks (e.g., Haier et al., in press). Presumably, if intelligence is related to efficient brain functioning, then the more intelligent people are, the less energy their brains should expend while working on various tasks. This prediction has been confirmed: The brains of persons scoring highest on written measures of intellectual ability *do* expend less energy when these individuals perform complex cognitive tasks. The data in these studies has been gathered by means of the PET technique of brain imaging described in chapter 2.

Finally, and perhaps most surprising of all, it has been found that there is a link between brain structure and intelligence (Andreasen et al., 1993). Specifically, scores on standard measures of intelligence such as the *Wechsler Adult Intelligence Scale* (discussed later in this chapter) are related to the size of certain portions of the brain, including the left and right temporal lobe and the left and right hippocampus (Andreasen et al., 1993). Moreover, this is true even when individuals' overall physical size is statistically controlled so that it cannot play a role in these findings.

In sum, it appears that the improved methods now available for studying the brain and nervous system are beginning to establish the kind of links that psychologists have long suspected between intelligence and these structures. Such research is very recent, and there is not yet enough of it to warrant firm conclusions. Still, it does appear that we are on the verge of establishing much firmer links between intelligence—a crucial aspect of mind—and body than have ever existed before. For additional information on the possible role of brain structure and function in intelligence—and especially in possible gender differences in intelligence—please see **Perspectives on Diversity** on page 258.

KEY QUESTIONS

- What is intelligence? Is intelligence a unitary or a multifaceted characteristic?
- What is the focus of the information-processing approach to intelligence?
- What is Sternberg's triarchic theory of intelligence?
- How are biological factors involved in intelligence?

Gender Differences in Cognitive Abilities: Do They Exist?

I t is widely assumed that females have higher verbal abilities than males, and that males surpass females with respect to mathematics and tasks that involve *spatial relations*—the movement of objects in space, or visualization of such movements. Do these differences actually exist? Research on this issue has continued for several decades, so by now there is an extensive body of evidence on which to base conclusions. Recent meta-analyses on these data indicate that while some differences do appear to exist between females and males with respect to various cognitive abilities, such differences are generally smaller than gender stereotypes suggest (Feingold, 1992b; Hyde & Linn, 1988; Hyde, Fennema, & Lamon, 1990). In addition, in recent years there has been a tendency for such differences to decrease in magnitude, especially among adolescents (Feingold, 1992b). Finally, the differences that occur seem to appear among young children and then to decrease or totally vanish during adolescence. Some differences in certain cognitive abilities seem to be present among adults, but as noted by Feingold (1992b, p. 109), this finding may be due to the fact that adults in many of these comparisons were born before the 1960s—at a time when gender stereotypes were much stronger than has been true since the advent of the women's movement. Thus, it seems possible that even these remaining differences will decrease or disappear in the future. A summary of research evidence concerning cognitive differences between males and females is presented in Table 7.4.

GENDER DIFFERENCES IN COGNITIVE ABILITIES: A NOTE ON THEIR POSSIBLE ORIGINS

Most psychologists believe that many of the observed differences between males and females stem largely from cultural and social factors, such as contrasting socialization practices for girls and boys, and from the pervasive influence of gender stereotypes and gender roles (Deaux, 1993; Etaugh & Liss, 1992; Stoppard & Gruchy, 1993). Yet this is not the entire story. Growing evidence suggests that *biological factors*, too, may play an important role. This does not in any way imply that differences between females and males are predetermined

---

TABLE 7.4	COGNITIVE ABILITY	GENDER DIFFERENCES
Gender Differences in Cognitive Abilities	Vocabulary	No appreciable difference.
	Reading	Girls score higher than boys, but this difference disappears in adolescence.
Differences between females and males appear to be relatively small in most cases; differences also tend to decrease with age.	Spelling	Girls score higher than boys.
	General information	Males score higher at all ages.
(*Source:* Based on data from Feingold, 1992b.)	Mathematics	Girls outperform boys in the first two years of high school; this difference disappears by the time they are seniors.
	Spatial visualization	Boys score slightly higher than girls, and this difference persists through adolescence.
	Perceptual speed	Females score higher than males at all ages.
	Memory	No difference between males and females.

or unmodifiable—far from it. Rather, it simply indicates that there may be biological factors that tend to predispose females and males toward somewhat different patterns of cognitive functioning in some situations.

You may recall that in chapter 2 we noted that there may be subtle differences between the brains of females and males (Berenbaum & Hines, 1992; Law, Pellegrino, & Hunt, 1993). For example, some of this evidence suggests that the structure of the *corpus callosum*—the broad band of neurons that connects the two hemispheres of the brain—may differ in females and males. Moreover, such differences may be related to subtle differences in cognitive abilities between the sexes—for example, higher verbal fluency among females. Additional evidence for the role of biological factors in gender differences comes from studies of persons who have experienced damage to one cerebral hemisphere (Kaufman, 1990). This research indicates that males and females may show somewhat different effects from such damage (see Figure 7.10). For example, in one recent study (Turkheimer & Farace, 1992), damage to the *left* hemisphere produced deficits in verbal aspects of intelligence in

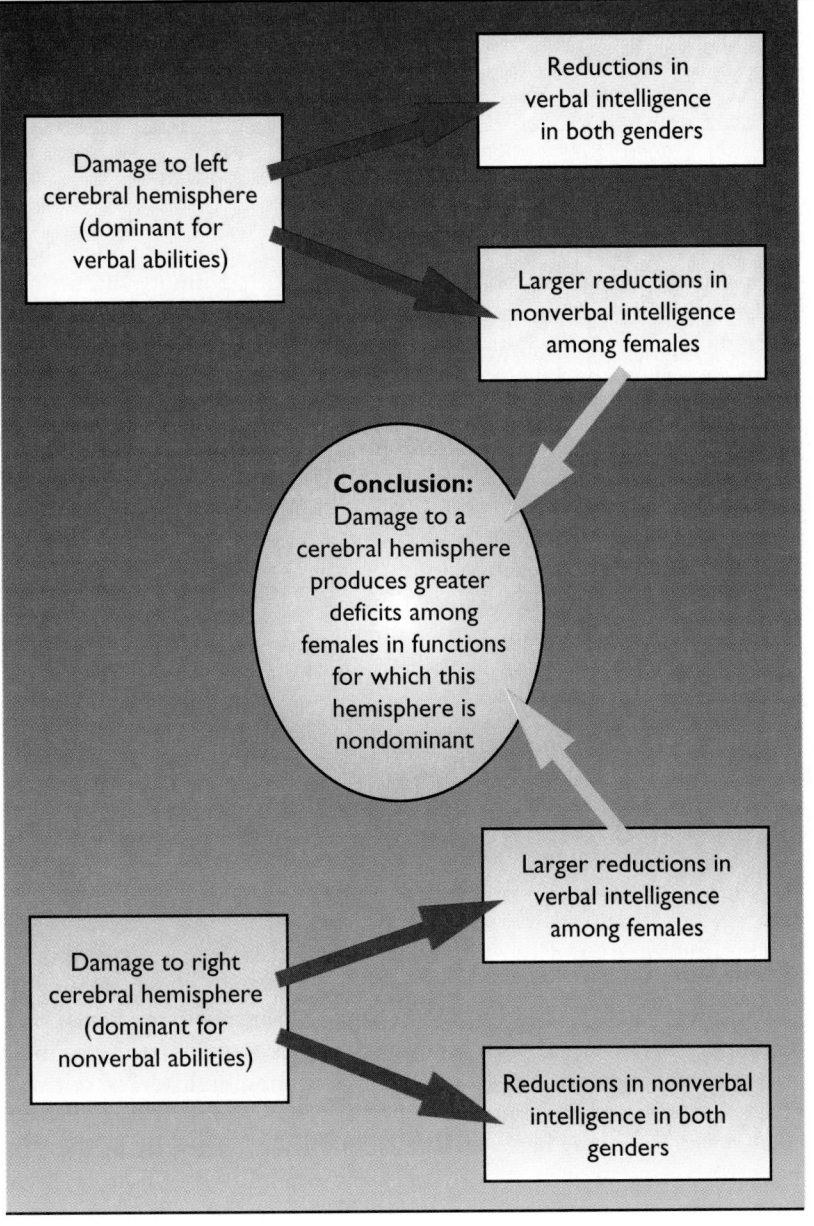

FIGURE 7.10

Contrasting Effects of Brain Damage among Females and Males

Damage to the left cerebral hemisphere produces deficits in verbal intelligence for both males and females. However, reductions in other aspects of intelligence are larger for females. Further, damage to the right hemisphere produces larger deficits in verbal intelligence among females. Together, these findings suggest that females show higher levels of *bilateral processing* than males.
(*Source:* Based on findings reported by Turkheimer & Farace, 1992.)

both males and females. However, reductions in other, *nonverbal* aspects of intelligence, such as the ability to complete missing parts of pictures, were larger in females than in males. In contrast, damage to the *right* hemisphere, which generated deficits in non-verbal aspects of intelligence for both sexes, produced larger deficits in *verbal* aspects of intelligence among females. Since in most persons the left hemisphere plays a primary role in verbal abilities and the right hemisphere plays a primary role in nonverbal abilities, these findings suggest that damage to a given cerebral hemisphere produces larger deficits among females than males in the cognitive functions *for which that hemisphere is nondominant* (refer back to Figure 7.10). This conclusion, in turn, is consistent with the view that females show higher levels of *bilateral processing* than males do; that is, females, more than males, process incoming information in both hemispheres of the brain.

By now the main point is probably clear: There do appear to be subtle differences between the brains of females and males, and these differences may influence some aspects of cognitive functioning and overt behavior. But please keep the following statement firmly in mind: Biological tendencies are only one of many different factors affecting behavior and are *not* irresistible or unmodifiable influences. Indeed, where complex forms of behavior are concerned, biological tendencies are almost certainly influenced by social and situational variables.

MEASURING HUMAN INTELLIGENCE

In 1904, when psychology was just emerging as an independent field, members of the Paris school board approached Alfred Binet with an interesting request: Could he develop an objective method for identifying children who were mentally retarded, so they could be removed from the regular classroom and given special education? Binet was already at work on related topics, so he agreed, enlisting the aid of his colleague, Theodore Simon.

In designing this test, Binet and Simon were guided by the belief that the items used should be ones children could answer without special training or study. They felt that this was important because the test should measure the ability to handle intellectual tasks—*not* specific knowledge acquired in school. Therefore, Binet and Simon decided to use items of two basic types: ones so new or unusual that none of the children would have prior exposure to them, and ones so familiar that almost all youngsters would have encountered them in the past. For example, children were asked to perform the following tasks:

Follow simple commands or imitate simple gestures.

Name objects shown in pictures.

Repeat a sentence of fifteen words.

Tell how two common objects are different.

Complete sentences begun by the examiner.

The first version of the test was published in 1905 and contained thirty items. Much to Binet and Simon's pleasure, it was quite effective: With its aid, teachers would readily identify children in need of special assistance. Encouraged by this success, Binet and Simon broadened the scope of their test to measure variations in intelligence among children of normal intelligence. The revised version, published in 1908, grouped items by age, with six items at each level between three and thirteen years. Items were placed at a particular age level if about 75 percent of children at that age could pass them correctly.

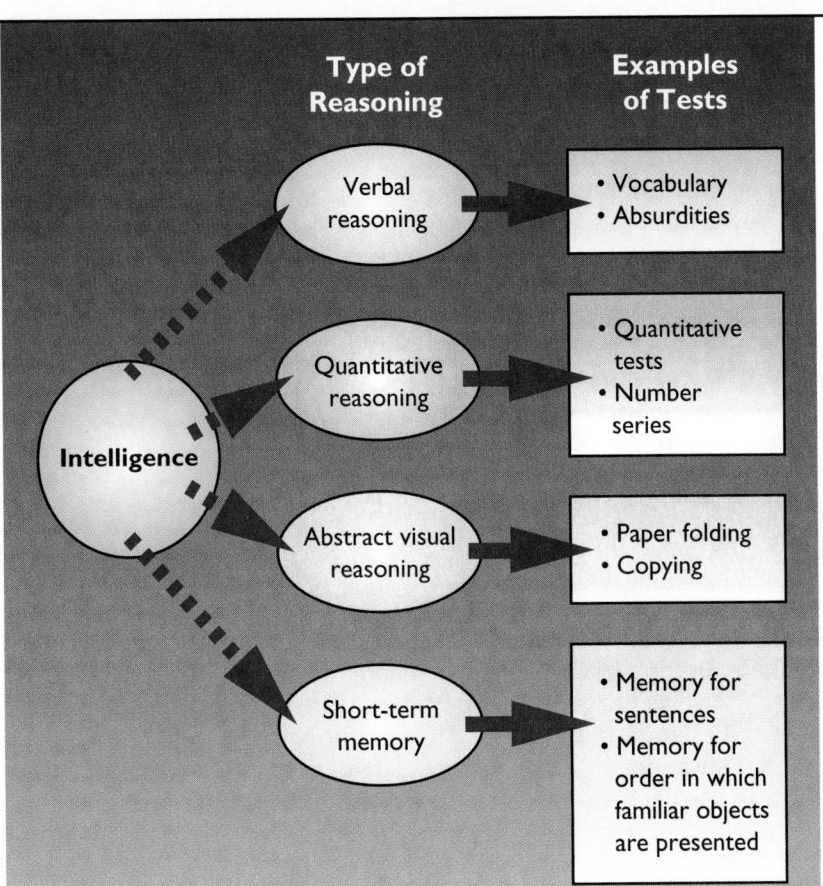

Type of Reasoning → **Examples of Tests**

Intelligence

Verbal reasoning → • Vocabulary • Absurdities

Quantitative reasoning → • Quantitative tests • Number series

Abstract visual reasoning → • Paper folding • Copying

Short-term memory → • Memory for sentences • Memory for order in which familiar objects are presented

FIGURE 7.11

The Stanford-Binet Test

A recent version of the Stanford-Binet test measures intelligence with a composite score made up of four scores for broad types of mental activity: verbal reasoning, quantitative reasoning, abstract visual reasoning, and short-term memory. Each of the scores is obtained through a series of subtests that measure specific mental abilities.

Binet's tests were soon revised and adapted for use in the United States by Lewis Terman, a psychologist at Stanford University. The **Stanford-Binet test**, as it came to be known, gained rapid acceptance and was soon put to use in many settings. Over the years it has been revised several times (see Figure 7.11 for a description of a recent version, published in 1986). One of the features of the Stanford-Binet that contributed to its popularity was that it yielded a single score assumed to reflect an individual's level of intelligence—the now famous IQ.

IQ: ITS MEANING THEN AND NOW   Originally, the letters **IQ** stood for *intelligence quotient*, and a quotient is precisely what such scores represent. To obtain an IQ, an examiner divides an individual's mental age by his or her chronological age, then multiplies by 100. For this computation, mental age is based on the number of items a person passes correctly on the test. Test takers are awarded two months for each correct item. If an individual's mental and chronological ages are equal, an IQ of 100 is obtained. Numbers above 100 indicate that an individual's intellectual age is greater than her or his chronological age; in other words, the individual is more intelligent than typical youngsters of this age. In contrast, numbers below 100 indicate that the individual is less intelligent than her or his peers.

Perhaps you can already see one obvious problem with this type of IQ: At some point, mental growth levels off or stops, while chronological age continues to grow. As a result, IQ scores begin to decline after the early teen

Stanford-Binet Test: A popular test for measuring individual intelligence.

IQ: A numerical value that reflects the extent to which an individual's score on an intelligence test departs from the average for other people of the same age.

years! Partly because of this problem, IQ scores now have a different meaning. They simply reflect an individual's performance on an intellectual test relative to that of persons the same age.

THE WECHSLER SCALES   As noted above, the tests developed by Binet and later adapted by Terman and others remained popular for many years. They do, however, suffer from one major drawback: All are mainly verbal in content. As a result, they pay little attention to the fact that intelligence can be revealed in nonverbal activities as well. For example, an architect who visualizes a majestic design for a new building is obviously demonstrating intelligence. Yet no means of assessing such abilities was included in early versions of the Stanford-Binet test.

To overcome this and other problems, David Wechsler devised a set of tests for both children and adults that include nonverbal, or *performance*, items as well as verbal ones, and that yield separate scores for these two components of intelligence. The Wechsler tests are perhaps the most frequently used individual intelligence tests today. Table 7.5 presents an overview of the subtests that make up one of the Wechsler scales, the *Wechsler Adult Intelligence Scale-Revised* (WAIS-R for short).

Wechsler believed that differences between scores on the various subtests could be used to diagnose serious mental disorders. Research on this possibility, however, has yielded mixed results. Some findings suggest that a Verbal IQ significantly higher than a Performance IQ can indicate damage to the left hemisphere, while the opposite pattern can indicate damage to the right hemisphere (Aiken, 1991). However, this is not always the case, and

TABLE 7.5	**TEST**	**DESCRIPTION**
Subtests of the Wechsler Adult Intelligence Scale	**VERBAL TESTS**	
	Information	Examinees are asked to answer general information questions, increasing in difficulty.
This widely used test of adult intelligence includes the subtests described here.	Digit span	Examinees are asked to repeat series of digits read out loud by the examiner.
	Vocabulary	Examinees are asked to define thirty-five words.
	Arithmetic	Examinees are asked to solve arithmetic problems.
	Comprehension	Examinees are asked to answer questions requiring detailed answers; answers indicate their comprehension of the questions.
	Similarities	Examinees indicate in what way two items are alike.
	PERFORMANCE TESTS	
	Picture completion	Examinees indicate what part of each picture is missing.
	Picture arrangement	Examinees arrange pictures to make a sensible story.
	Block design	Examinees attempt to duplicate designs made with red and white blocks.
	Object assembly	Examinees attempt to solve picture puzzles.
	Digit symbol	Examinees fill in small boxes with coded symbols corresponding to a number above each box.

other evidence is usually required before conclusions can be reached about possible brain damage. Other findings indicate that patterns of scores on the Wechsler tests may be linked to various psychological disorders. For example, chronic schizophrenics have higher Verbal IQs than Performance IQs, while persons suffering from a disorder known as the *antisocial personality disorder* (see chapter 12)—a disorder marked by a lack of conscience and impulsive, often violent behavior—have higher Performance than Verbal IQs (Kunce, Ryan, & Eckelman, 1976). Once again, though, not all studies have confirmed such findings, so they must be interpreted with caution.

A Wechsler test for children—the *Wechsler Intelligence Scale for Children* (or WISC)—has also been developed. Here, too, efforts have been made to determine whether differences in scores on the various subtests indicate certain kinds of disorders, such as personality and learning disorders (Hubble & Groff, 1982). For example, some findings indicate that children who score high on certain subtests, such as Picture Completion and Object Assembly, but lower on other tests (Arithmetic, Information, and Vocabulary) are more likely to be suffering from a learning disability than children with other patterns of scores (Aiken, 1991). However, not all findings point to such conclusions, so the value of the WISC for this purpose remains uncertain.

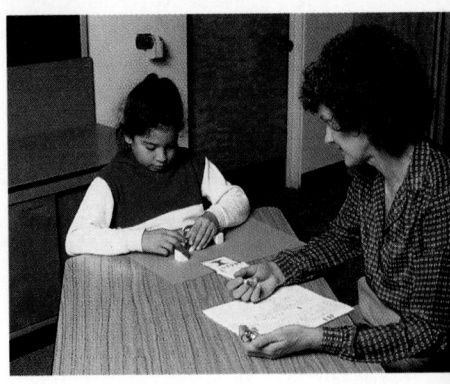

THE WISC–R

Developed by David Wechsler, the WISC–R (a revised form of the WISC) is one of the most widely used intelligence tests for children.

GROUP TESTS OF INTELLIGENCE Both the Stanford-Binet and the Wechsler scales are *individual* tests of intelligence: They are designed for use with one person at a time. Obviously, it would be much more efficient if *group* tests could be administered to large numbers of people at once. The need for such tests was driven home at the start of World War I, when the armed forces in the United States were suddenly faced with the task of screening several million recruits. In response to this challenge, psychologists such as Arthur Otis developed two tests: *Army Alpha* for persons who could read and *Army Beta* for persons who could not or who did not speak English. These early group tests proved highly useful. For example, they were used to select candidates for officer training school.

In the succeeding decades many other group tests of intelligence were developed. Among the more popular of these are the *Otis tests,* such as the Otis-Lennon School Ability Test (Otis & Lennon 1967), the *Henmon-Nelson Tests* (Nelson, Lamke, & French, 1973), and the *Cognitive Abilities Test* (CAT) (Thorndike & Hagen, 1982). All are available in versions that can be administered to large numbers of persons. The advantages offered by such tests soon made them very popular, and they were put to routine use in many school systems during the 1940s and 1950s. But in the 1960's, as you probably already know, this practice was called into question and became the focus of harsh criticism. There were many reasons for this controversy, including the suggestion that such tests were unfair, in several respects, to children from disadvantaged backgrounds—especially youngsters from various minority groups. We'll return to these objections below. Now, however, we'll consider two other issues relating to the use of these—or *any*—psychological tests: *reliability* and *validity*.

RELIABILITY AND VALIDITY: Basic Requirements for All Psychological Tests

Suppose that in preparation for a summer at the beach, you decide to go on a diet in order to lose 10 pounds. Your current weight is 135, and for two weeks you skip desserts and engage in vigorous exercise. Then you step onto your bathroom scale to see how much progress you've made. To your shock, the needle reads 139; you've actually *gained* 4 pounds! How can this be? Perhaps you made a mistake. So you step back on the scale. Now it reads 134. You get off and step onto it again; now it reads 136. At this point, you realize the truth: Your scale (thank goodness!) is *unreliable*—the numbers it shows change even though your weight, obviously, can't change from one second to the next.

This is a simple illustration of a very basic point. In order to be of any use, measuring devices must have high **reliability**—they must yield the same result each time they are applied to the same quantity. If they don't, they are essentially useless. The same principle applies to psychological tests, whether they are designed to measure intelligence or to assess any other characteristic. They too must be reliable to be of any value. But how do we know whether, and to what extent, this is the case? In fact, several different methods for guaging a test's reliability exist.

INTERNAL CONSISTENCY: DO THE ITEMS ON A TEST MEASURE THE SAME THING? If we wish to develop a test that measures a single psychological characteristic, such as intelligence, then it is important to establish that all the test items actually measure this characteristic—that the test has what psychologists describe as *internal consistency*. One criterion for internal consistency of a test is known as **split-half reliability**. Determining split-half reliability involves dividing the test into two equivalent parts, such as the first and second halves or the odd- and even-numbered items, and then comparing the scores on each. If the test really measures intelligence, then the correlation between the scores on both halves should be positive and high. If it is not, then some of the items may be measuring different things, and the test is unreliable in one important sense. There are several statistical formulas for measuring internal consistency. The most widely used is known as *coefficient alpha*, and it simultaneously considers all of the possible ways of splitting into halves the items on a test. Since this process is done on computers, it is very efficient, and coefficient alpha has become one standard measure of a test's internal consistency.

CONSISTENCY ACROSS TIME: TEST-RETEST RELIABILITY A test that yields very different scores when taken by the same persons at different times is of little value if the characteristic it measures is one that is stable over time, such as intelligence. Thus, another type of reliability, **test-retest reliability**, is also important. One way to measure this is to give the test to the same group of persons on more than one occasion and to compare the scores. The more similar these are, the higher the test's reliability.

One obvious problem with the test-retest method is that people's scores on a retest may increase simply because they have taken the test again—because of *practice effects*. To reduce this problem, psychologists often use *alternate forms* of the same test—two different forms that cover the same material at the same level of difficulty. Figure 7.12 provides an overview of both split-half reliability and test-retest reliability.

VALIDITY: DO TESTS MEASURE WHAT THEY CLAIM TO MEASURE? On a recent visit to one of our local malls, I noticed a new machine outside one of the stores. The front of the machine read "Test Your Sex Appeal!" I was fascinated, so I read further. Additional information on the front panel indicated that by inserting a quarter and pushing some buttons, users would receive a score indicating their appeal to members of the opposite sex. Do you think this machine was really capable of measuring sex appeal? The answer is obvious: no! In all probability, the machine measured nothing whatsoever—

Reliability: The extent to which any measuring device yields the same results when applied more than once to the same quantity.

Split-Half Reliability: The extent to which an individual attains equivalent scores on two halves of a psychological test.

Test-Retest Reliability: The extent to which a psychological test yields similar scores when taken by the same person on different occasions.

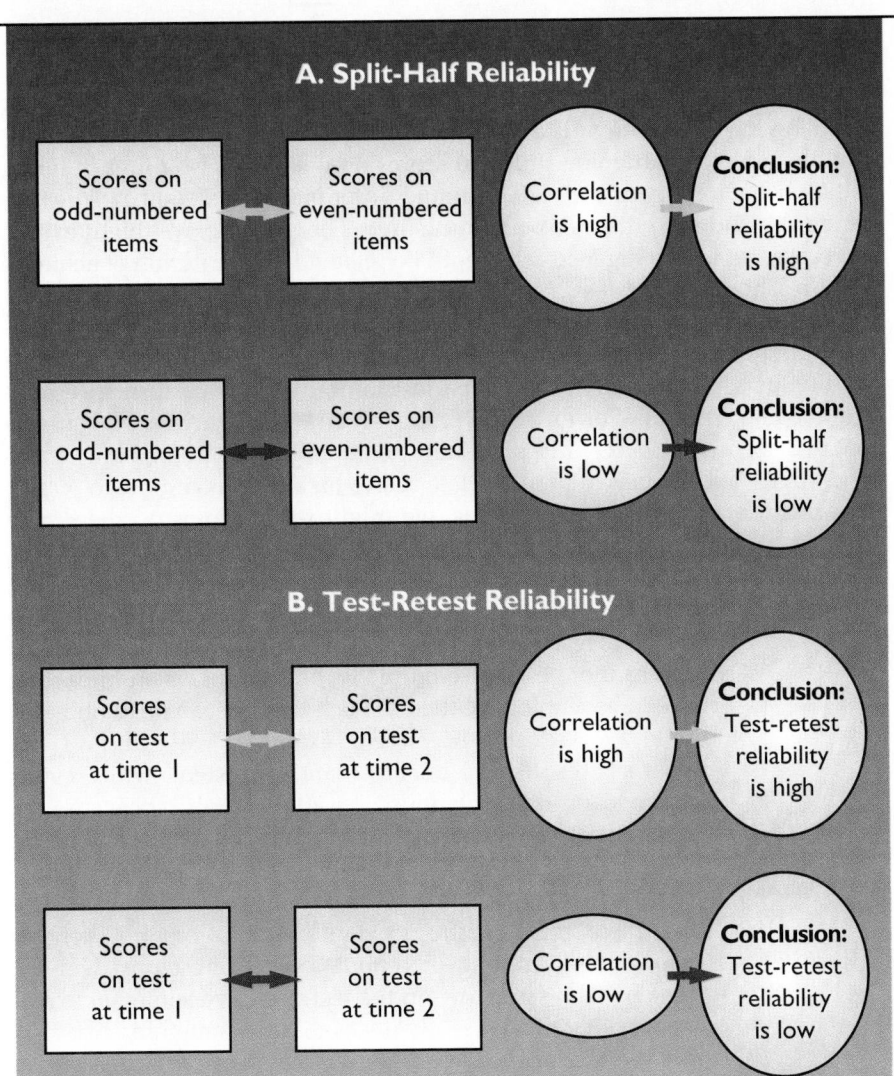

FIGURE 7.12

A. Split-Half Reliability

| Scores on odd-numbered items | ⟷ | Scores on even-numbered items |

Correlation is high → Conclusion: Split-half reliability is high

| Scores on odd-numbered items | ⟷ | Scores on even-numbered items |

Correlation is low → Conclusion: Split-half reliability is low

B. Test-Retest Reliability

| Scores on test at time 1 | ⟷ | Scores on test at time 2 |

Correlation is high → Conclusion: Test-retest reliability is high

| Scores on test at time 1 | ⟷ | Scores on test at time 2 |

Correlation is low → Conclusion: Test-retest reliability is low

Reliability: A Basic Requirement of Psychological Tests

In order to be useful, psychological tests must be reliable. Two types of reliability are illustrated here: (A) *split-half reliability* (a type of *internal consistency*) and (B) *test-retest reliability.*

except, perhaps, willingness to believe silly claims. Psychologists describe such machines—and any other measuring device that claims to measure something it does not—as being low in **validity**: the ability to measure what the devices are supposed to measure.

The same principle applies to psychological tests: They, too, are useful only to the extent that they really measure the characteristics they claim to assess. Thus, an intelligence test is useful only to the extent that it really measures intelligence. How can we determine whether a test is valid? By examining several different aspects of the test. One of these is known as **content validity**: the extent to which the items on a test sample the behaviors we can reasonably assume are related to the characteristic in question. For example, if an intelligence test consisted of measurements of the length of people's earlobes or of the sharpness of their teeth, we could probably assume that it was low in content validity: These measurements do not seem to be related to what we mean by the term *intelligence*. If, instead, the test measured the breadth of a person's vocabulary or his or her ability to solve various kinds of puzzles, as discussed earlier in this

Validity: *The extent to which tests actually measure what they claim to measure.*

Content Validity: *The extent to which the items on a test sample the skills or knowledge needed for achievement in a given field or task.*

chapter, we would have more faith in the test's content validity: The items do seem to be related to various aspects of intelligence.

Another type of validity, known as **criterion-related validity**, is based on the following assumption: If a test actually measures what it claims to measure, then persons attaining different scores on it should also differ in terms of their behavior. Specifically, they should differ in terms of some *criterion*, or standard, relating to the trait being measured. For example, we might expect that scores on an intelligence test would be related to the criterion of achievement in school, or that of success in various occupations.

Two kinds of criterion-related validity that are often measured by psychologists are **predictive validity** and **concurrent validity**. To measure predictive validity, psychologists use scores on a test to predict *later* performance relative to some criterion. For example, scores on an intelligence test taken *now* are used to predict success in some kind of training program. To measure concurrent validity, psychologists relate scores on a test taken now to *present* performance on some criterion. Thus, we might relate scores on the test to students' current performance in school.

Key Questions

- What was the first individual test of intelligence, and what did its score signify?
- What steps have psychologists taken to devise tests that measure more than just verbal aspects of intelligence?
- What are some positive and negative aspects of group tests of intelligence?
- What is test reliability, and how do psychologists assess it?
- What is validity? Are there different ways to assess validity?

A third type of validity—**construct validity**—is a bit more complex. This type of validity has to do with the extent to which a test measures a psychological concept or variable that cannot be assessed directly, but that plays an important role in psychological theory. Such validity can be established in any of several ways. For example, we can find out whether results on our test are consistent with results obtained on other obvious or well-established measures of the same *construct*—that is, the same variable or concept. Suppose we develop a test that we believe measures the tendency to take risks. If persons who score high on our test also have more traffic accidents and are more likely to belong to sky-diving or mountain-climbing clubs than are persons who score low on the test, we have some *convergent evidence* that the test really does measure something like risk-taking tendencies. Please see the **Key Concept** page for an overview of different types of validity.

In sum, any psychological test is useful only to the extent that it is both reliable and valid—to the extent that the test yields consistent scores and that independent evidence confirms that it really does measure what it purports to measure. How do intelligence tests stack up in this respect? In terms of reliability, the answer is: quite well. Widely used tests of intelligence do yield consistent scores and do possess internal consistency. The question of validity, however, is much more controversial, especially where group tests of intelligence are concerned. The issue of validity leads us back to an issue raised earlier: Are intelligence tests suitable for use with persons from all social and cultural groups?

Criterion-Related Validity: A measure of the validity of any psychological test, determined by correlations between scores on the test and some standard of the characteristic the test supposedly assesses.

Predictive Validity: The relationship between scores on a test and later performance relative to a criterion.

Concurrent Validity: The relationship between test scores and current performance relative to some criterion.

Construct Validity: The extent to which a test measures a variable or concept described by a psychological theory.

INTELLIGENCE TESTING AND PUBLIC POLICY: *Are Intelligence Tests Fair?*

Objections to the widespread use of tests of intelligence have touched on many different points. Perhaps the most important, though, is the possibility that intelligence tests are biased against certain groups. The basis for such concerns is obvious: In the United States and elsewhere, people belonging to some ethnic or racial minorities score lower on group tests of intelligence than do other persons (Weinberg, 1989). For example, African Americans, Native Americans, and persons of Hispanic descent score lower than whites

Major Types of Test Validity

Content Validity

The extent to which items on a test are related to the characteristics or behaviors we wish to measure.

For example, the flight simulator shown here tests many behaviors that pilots must demonstrate when actually flying a plane. Because of this close linkage between test components and real flight skills, the simulator may be said to possess high content validity.

Criterion-Related Validity

The extent to which test scores are related to some accepted measure of the characteristic or behavior we wish to measure.

For example, scores on some tests of *academic aptitude* (the ability to learn the kinds of skills taught in school) are related to grades and, ultimately, to graduation. The stronger this relationship, the greater is the criterion-related validity of such tests (one of which is the well-known Scholastic Aptitude Test, or SAT).

Construct Validity

The extent to which a psychological test measures a psychological variable that can't be assessed directly and has no simple or clear-cut criteria.

For example, scores on a test of the psychological variable *stress tolerance* may be related to several other possible indicators of tolerance for stress. Persons who score high on this test may be more likely to work in high-stress occupations such as emergency room medicine than are persons who score low. And persons who score low may be more likely to experience stress-related illnesses such as heart attacks.

of European ancestry (Aiken, 1991; Cohen et al., 1988). Further, it appears that these tests may be less *valid* when used with such groups; for example, these groups' scores on the tests are less successful in predicting their future performance in school (Aiken, 1991). What factors are responsible for such differences? Many critics of intelligence tests contend that the differences stem mainly from strong **cultural bias** built into these tests. In other words, because the tests were developed by and for persons belonging to a particular culture, individuals from other cultures may be at a disadvantage when taking them.

Are such concerns valid? Careful examination of the items used on intelligence tests suggest that they are. Many items assume that all children have had the opportunity to acquire certain kinds of information. Unfortunately, this is not true for children from disadvantaged or minority backgrounds, who may never have had the chance to acquire the knowledge being tested. Thus, they cannot answer correctly, no matter how high their intelligence.

As Helms (1992) argues forcefully, however, this is only part of the problem. She notes that widely used intelligence tests also suffer from other forms of cultural bias that may be somewhat more subtle but are just as damaging for minority children. Such tests, Helms contends, incorporate unstated values that derive primarily from a *Eurocentric perspective*—an implicit acceptance of European values as the standards against which everything is judged (Helms, 1989). For example, Helms contends, European cultures accept a view she terms *dualism*—the idea that answers are either right or wrong, and that only logical thinking is to be valued. Children from European-descended cultural backgrounds accept this value, so when they take intelligence tests, they look for the one correct answer on each item. According to Helms, children from other backgrounds—for example, African-American children—may accept this value to a lesser degree, or may even accept other values that can interfere with their test performance. For instance, they may not assume that answers are right or wrong; they may spend time reasoning about the extent to which each possible answer is accurate. In other words, Helms suggests, subtle cultural factors may influence the way in which children approach intelligence tests—the tactics they use in taking the tests—and these, in turn, can influence their scores.

In an effort to eliminate cultural bias from intelligence tests, some psychologists have attempted to design *culture-fair tests.* Such tests attempt to include only items to which all groups, regardless of ethnic or racial background, have been exposed. Because many minority children are exposed to languages other than standard English, these tests tend to be nonverbal in nature. I referred to one of these, the *Raven Progressive Matrices Test* (Raven, 1977), in my earlier discussion of the biological bases of intelligence. This test consists of sixty matrices of varying difficulty, each containing a logical pattern or design with a missing part. Individuals select the item that completes the pattern from several different choices. Evidence indicates that the Raven test is a valid measure of general intelligence (Paul, 1985), but it is not clear that it—or any other supposedly culture-fair test—fully addresses the sources of cultural bias described by Helms (1992) and others. Items from another such test, the *Culture-Fair Intelligence Test,* are shown in Figure 7.13. As you can see, this test requires work with abstract figures or relations between various objects. Presumably, such items are less subject to cultural bias than are verbal items; but, again, this has not been clearly established.

Another test that has gained increasing popularity recently is the *Kaufman Assessment Battery for Children*—the K-ABC for short (Kaufman, 1983). This individually administered test is specifically designed to measure informa-

Cultural Bias: *The tendency of items on a test of intelligence to require specific cultural experience or knowledge.*

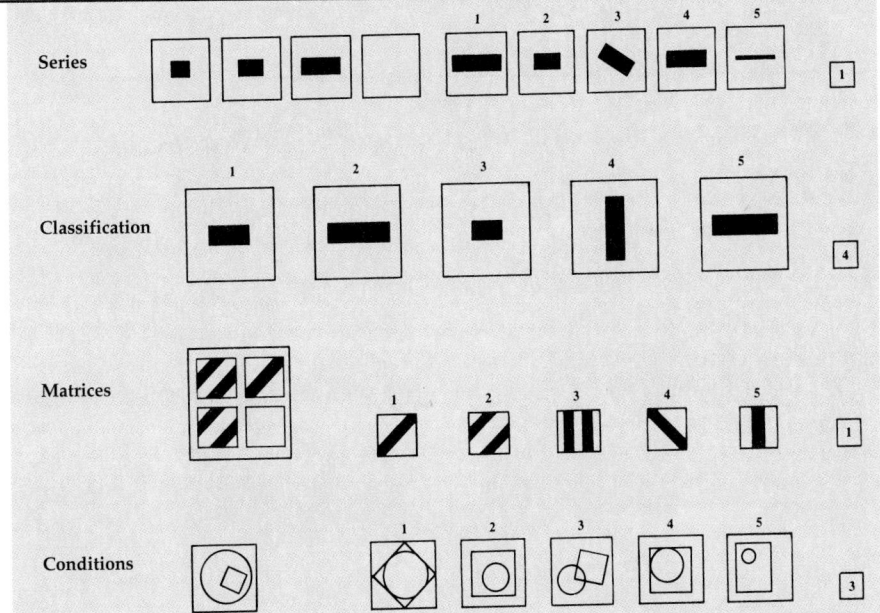

FIGURE 7.13

Sample Items from One Culture-Fair Test of Intelligence

The *Culture-Fair Intelligence Test* includes items designed to be unaffected by specific cultural knowledge or experience. The items shown here are similar to those in one such test. Unfortunately, it has proved impossible to devise a test that is totally independent of culture-related factors.

(*Source:* Based on items from the Culture-Fair Intelligence Test, Institute for Personality and Ability Testing, Inc. Copyright © 1949, 1960, by the Institute for Personality and Ability Testing, Inc. All rights reserved. Reproduced by permission.)

tion-processing capacity. In other words, it focuses on effectiveness in handling new information and minimizes the roles of language and previously acquired information or skills. It includes tasks that require *sequential processing*, such as repeating a series of digits in the same order in which they are presented, as well as ones that require *simultaneous processing*, or integrating many stimuli at once. An example of simultaneous processing is remembering the placement of various pictures on a page following a brief exposure to them. Results with this test have been promising. Differences between African Americans, Hispanics, and whites are much smaller than those on other intelligence tests. However, critics note that these smaller differences in test scores come at the expense of reduced predictive validity: Scores on the K-ABC are less successful in predicting success in school or other contexts than those on other intelligence tests. Still, this test's focus on information processing is consistent with the information-processing perspective described earlier and may represent one useful approach to solving a difficult and complex problem.

Perhaps, ultimately, the solution to the problem of designing completely culture-fair tests of intelligence will involve the development of reliable *physiological measures*—ones that assess the speed and efficiency with which human brains process information (e.g., Matarazzo, 1992). Presumably, basic aspects of brain functioning are much the same for all human beings, so it may be possible to eliminate, or at least reduce, the impact of cultural bias through such measures. I should add that at present this is merely a possibility: Research relating brain structure and function to intelligence is too new and too fragmentary to permit any firm conclusions. But at least this research offers one promising avenue for meeting a need on which all psychologists agree: the need for tests of intelligence that do not place *any* group of persons at an unfair disadvantage.

What are the practical uses to which existing tests of intelligence are put? Please see the **Point of It All** section (on page 270) for information on this issue.

KEY QUESTIONS

- Has the construction of culture-fair tests been successful?

- Is there any way to solve the problems of cultural bias?

Individual Tests of Intelligence: Their Practical Uses

Individual tests of intelligence are costly: They must be administered one-on-one by a psychologist or other trained professional. Why, then, do they continue to be widely used? The answer is that these tests have several practical uses; they provide benefits that offset their obvious costs. The most important of these uses is identification of children at the extremes with respect to intelligence: those who suffer from some degree of *mental retardation* and those who are *intellectually gifted*.

Mental retardation refers to considerably below-average intellectual functioning combined with varying degrees of difficulty in meeting the demands of everyday life (Aiken, 1991; Wielkiewicz & Calvert, 1989). As shown in Figure 7.14, mental retardation is typically described according to four broad categories: mild, moderate, severe, and profound. Individuals' level of retardation is determined by at least two factors: test scores *and* success in carrying out activities of daily living expected of persons their age.

What causes mental retardation? In some cases, it can be traced to genetic abnormalities such as **Down Syndrome**, which is caused by the presence of an extra chromosome; persons with Down Syndrome usually have IQs below 50. Mental retardation can also result from environmental factors, such as inadequate nutrition or use of drugs or alcohol by mothers during pregnancy, infections, toxic agents, and traumas resulting from a lack of oxygen during birth.

FIGURE 7.14

Degrees of Mental Retardation

Degree of mental retardation is often identified according to IQ scores on standard tests of intelligence. In general, an IQ score that falls below 70 suggests some level of retardation. IQ scores are not the only consideration, however; the individual's capacity to function adequately in everyday life is also important.

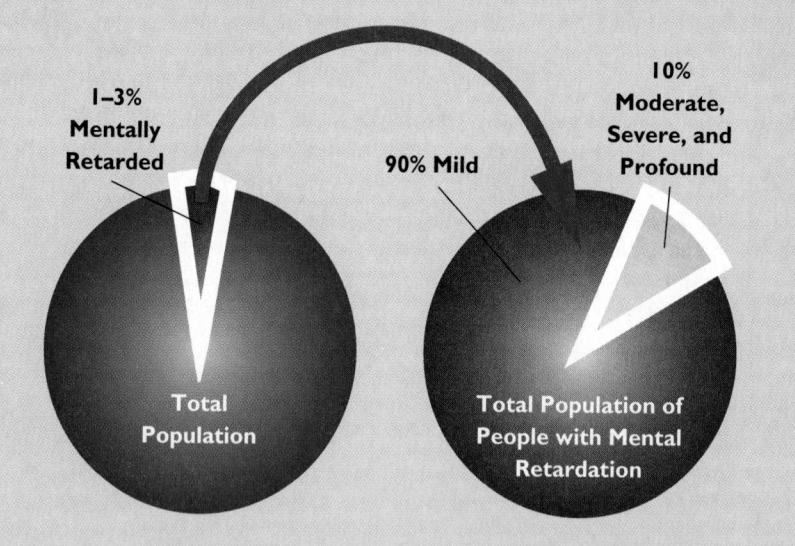

Mental Retardation: Intellectual functioning that is considerably below average.

Down Syndrome: A disorder caused by an extra chromosome and characterized by varying degrees of retardation and physical disorders.

CLASSIFICATION	STANFORD-BINET IQ SCORE	WECHSLER IQ SCORE	PERCENTAGE OF THE MENTALLY RETARDED	EDUCATIONAL LEVEL POSSIBLE
Mild	52–68	55–69	90	Sixth grade
Moderate	36–51	40–54	6	Second to fourth grade
Severe	20–35	25–39	3	Limited speech
Profound	Below 20	Below 25	1	Unresponsive to training

Most cases of mental retardation, however, cannot readily be traced to specific genetic or environmental causes. Persons in this group are usually mildly retarded, having IQs between 50 and 70.

Intelligence tests have also been used to identify the *intellectually gifted*—persons whose intelligence is far above average (Goleman, 1980; Terman, 1954). The most comprehensive study of persons with high IQs was begun by Lewis Terman in 1925. He followed the lives of 1,500 children with IQs of 130 or above to determine the relationship between high intelligence on the one hand, and occupational success and social adjustment on the other. As a group, the gifted children in Terman's study were tremendously successful: They earned more academic degrees, attained higher occupational status and salaries, experienced better personal and social adjustment, and were healthier than the average adult. These results refuted the commonly held belief that intellectually gifted persons are social or emotional "weaklings"—nerds who miss out on all the fun of life.

While many programs currently exist for children identified as mentally retarded, there is growing concern that in the United States and elsewhere, intellectually gifted children are being largely ignored (Resnick, 1993). In part, this situation is due to a rejection of the concept of *ability grouping*—dividing students into groups according to intellectual ability and designing different educational programs for each. Ability grouping was common practice in the past; in fact, it was an important part of *my* educational experience. In the sixth grade, everyone in my school took a test, which, I now realize, was a standard group test of intelligence. Because I scored high, I was placed in a special class that covered the seventh, eighth, and ninth grades in two years. Looking back, I see it as a very stimulating experience that probably played a large role in my choice of an academic career. Also, it certainly boosted my self-esteem to hear from teachers, over and over again, that I was part of a class that was "the cream of the crop" and that they expected my classmates and me to go on to do great things! Because minority groups were often underrepresented in such programs, however, accelerated classes no longer exist in many school systems. One result of this change is that many bright children, forced to proceed through programs designed for average learners, quickly become bored and discouraged (Resnick, 1993). Growing recognition of these problems—and the potential losses to society they may represent—has led recently to the reestablishment of special programs for gifted children in a few locations. Only time will tell whether this will become a general trend in education. In any case, it does illustrate one of the potential uses to which individual (or group) tests of intelligence can be put.

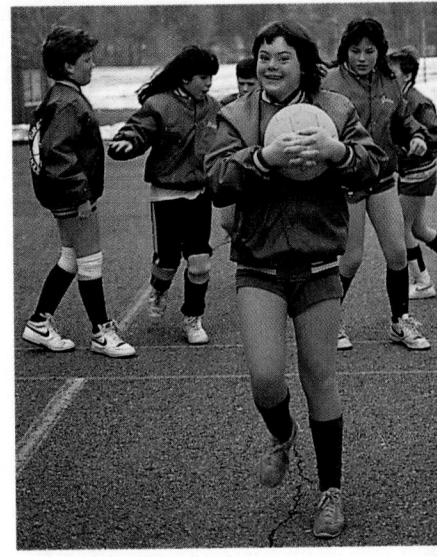

DOWN SYNDROME: A GENETIC CAUSE OF MENTAL RETARDATION

One cause of mental retardation is Down syndrome, a genetic defect that occurs when the cells in the body have an extra copy of chromosome number 21.

HUMAN INTELLIGENCE: *The Role of Heredity and the Role of Environment*

*T*hat people differ in intelligence is obvious. Indeed, we rarely need test scores to remind us of this fact. The causes behind these differences, though, are less obvious. Are they largely a matter of heredity—differences in the genetic materials and codes we inherit from our parents? Or are they primarily the result of environmental factors—conditions favorable or unfavorable to intellectual growth? I'm sure you know the answer: Both types of factors are involved. Human intelligence appears to be the product of an extremely complex interplay between genetic factors and environmental conditions

Learning Objective 7.20
Discuss the evidence for the roles of heredity and the environment in intelligence.

(Plomin, 1989; Weinberg, 1989). Let's review some of the evidence pointing to this conclusion.

EVIDENCE FOR THE INFLUENCE OF HEREDITY

Several lines of research offer support for the view that heredity plays a significant role in human intelligence. First, consider findings with respect to family relationship and measured IQ. If intelligence is indeed determined by heredity, we would expect that the more closely two persons are related, the more similar their IQs will be. This prediction has generally been confirmed (Bouchard & McGue, 1981; Erlenmeyer-Kimling & Jarvik, 1963). For example, the IQs of identical twins raised together correlate almost +0.90, those of brothers and sisters about +0.50, and those of cousins about +0.15. (Remember: higher correlations indicate stronger relationships between variables.)

Additional support for the impact of heredity on intelligence is provided by studies involving adopted children. If intelligence is strongly affected by genetic factors, the IQs of adopted children should resemble those of their biological parents more closely than those of their adoptive parents. In short, the children should be more similar in IQ to the persons from whom they received their genes than to the persons who raised them. This prediction, too, has been confirmed. While the IQs of adopted children correlate about +0.40 to +0.50 with those of their biological parents, they correlate only about +0.10 to +0.20 with those of their adoptive parents (Jencks, 1972; Munsinger, 1978). I should add, though, that not all studies have yielded such results. Further, in some investigations, the IQs of adopted children have been observed to become increasingly similar to those of their foster parents over time (Scarr & Weinberg, 1976). Such findings, of course, suggest that environmental factors, too, play an important role.

Perhaps the most intriguing evidence for the role of genetic factors in intelligence has been provided by Bouchard and his colleagues through a project called the *Minnesota Study of Twins Raised Apart* (Bouchard, 1987; Bouchard et al., 1990). In this research, Bouchard and his colleagues located a number of pairs of identical twins who were separated early in life and were raised in different homes. Since such persons were exposed to different environmental conditions (in some cases, sharply contrasting ones), a high correlation between their IQs would suggest that heredity plays a key role in human intelligence. In fact, this is what was found. The IQs of identical twins reared apart (in many cases, from the time they were only a few days old) correlate almost as highly as those of identical twins reared together. Moreover, such persons are also amazingly similar in many other characteristics, such as physical appearance, dress, mannerisms, and even personality. Clearly, such findings point to an important role of heredity in intelligence and in many other aspect of psychological functioning.

We have already considered another line of research that can be interpreted as evidence for the role of heredity in intelligence. This is the finding that various measures of the speed of neural conduction or efficiency in brain functioning are associated with scores on intelligence tests (Haier et al., in press; Reed & Jensen, 1993). As I pointed out, one interpretation of these findings is that intelligent people have efficient brains: They can accomplish the same amount of cognitive work with less physical effort. Since the physical structure of the brain, like that of other parts of the body, is strongly determined by genetic factors, it seems possible that intelligence, too, is shaped at least partly by such factors. Needless to add, such suggestions are mainly

HEREDITY AND INTELLIGENCE

Research has shown that the more closely two persons are related, the more similar their IQ scores tend to be. But does this suggest that a person's environment has no effect on intelligence?

speculative at present; additional evidence is needed before firm conclusions can be reached concerning the relationship between brain activity, the brain's physical structure, and intelligence.

EVIDENCE FOR THE INFLUENCE OF ENVIRONMENTAL FACTORS

Genetic factors are definitely not the total picture where human intelligence is concerned, however. Other findings point to the conclusion that environmental variables, too, are of great importance. One finding pointing to this conclusion is that during the second half of the twentieth century, IQ scores rose substantially around the world at all age levels (Flynn, 1987). Since it seems very unlikely that massive shifts in human heredity occurred during this period, such findings can only be interpreted as stemming from environmental factors—rising living standards, improved diets, and better educational opportunities for millions of human beings.

Second, studies of *environmental deprivation* and of *environmental enrichment* offer support for the important role of environmental factors. With respect to deprivation, it has been found that intelligence can be reduced by the absence of certain forms of environmental stimulation early in life (Gottfried, 1984). In terms of enrichment, removing children from sterile, restricted environments and placing them in more favorable settings seems to enhance their intellectual growth. For example, in one of the first demonstrations of the beneficial impact of an enriched environment on IQ, Skeels (1938, 1966) removed thirteen children (approximately two years of age) from the impoverished orphanage in which they lived and placed them in the care of a group of retarded women living in an institution. The women lavished attention on the youngsters, and after a few years Skeels noted that the children's IQs had risen dramatically—on average, 29 points. Interestingly, Skeels also obtained IQ measures of children who had remained in the orphanage and found that the average IQ among this group had actually *decreased* by 26 points—presumably as result of the impoverished environment at the orphanage. Twenty-five years later the thirteen children who had experienced the enriched environment were all doing well; most had graduated from high school, found a job, and married. In contrast, those in the original control group either remained institutionalized or were functioning poorly in society.

In addition, some special programs designed to enrich the educational experiences of children from disadvantaged backgrounds have been found to produce substantial increases in the IQ scores of participants (Royce, Darlington, & Murray, 1983). Perhaps the most famous (and controversial) of these is *Project Head Start*—a federally funded program in the United States that provides special intellectual and social skills training for young children from disadvantaged environments (Zigler & Berman, 1983). Evaluations of Project Head Start have yielded mixed results; children who participate in Project Head Start do not demonstrate lasting gains in IQ score (Haskins, 1989) but do surpass nonparticipants in other important ways. For example, Head Start graduates are less likely to fail in school or require remedial courses, and more likely to exhibit positive self-esteem than nonparticipants (McKey et al., 1985).

Evidence for the important impact on intelligence of environmental factors is also provided by the type of kinship studies described earlier. Such research indicates that for a given degree of kinship (family relationship), individuals raised in the same environment have more similar IQs than persons raised apart, in different environments. For example, the IQs of brothers and sisters raised together correlate about +0.50, whereas those of brothers and

IDENTICAL TWINS REARED APART

The IQ scores of identical twins separated at birth and raised in different home environments—such as Oskar Stohr and Jack Yufe, shown here—are highly correlated. This finding provides evidence for the impact of genetic factors on intelligence.

FIGURE 7.15

Birth Order and IQ: Confluence Theory

According to *confluence theory*, the intellectual environment in which children develop becomes less and less favorable as the number of previous children born in the family increases. As a result, the IQ of first-borns is higher than that of second-borns; the IQ of second-borns is higher than that of third-borns, and so on. Research on confluence theory suggests that these differences are quite small but do seem to exist.
(*Source:* Based on suggestions by Zajonc, 1976.)

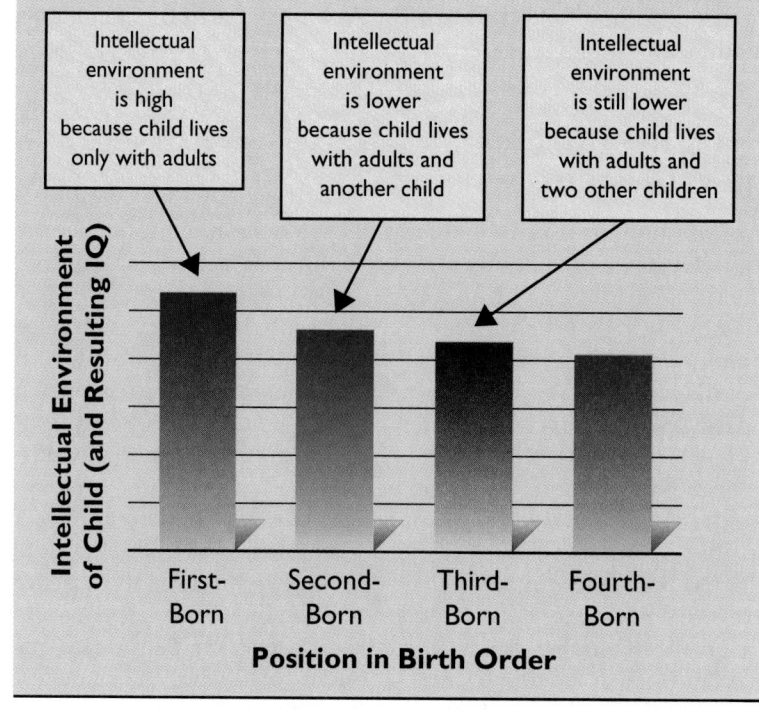

sisters raised apart correlate about +0.45. Similarly, the IQs of unrelated persons raised apart show virtually no correlation.

A fourth source of evidence for the influence of environmental factors is provided by research on birth order and intelligence. Several studies on this topic report that first-borns tend to have higher IQs than second-borns, who tend to have higher IQs than third-borns, and so on (Zajonc & Markus, 1975). The differences are not large—only a few IQ points at most—but they do seem to be real. Why do such differences exist? One possibility is suggested by a theory proposed by Zajonc (1975, 1986). According to this theory, each individual's intellectual growth depends to an important degree on the intellectual environment in which he or she develops. A first-born child benefits from the fact that for some period of time (until the birth of another child), he or she lives with two adults who provide a relatively advantaged intellectual environment. A second-born child, in contrast, lives with two adults who divide their attention with another child; thus the average level of his or her intellectual environment is somewhat "diluted." Such effects become even stronger for third-borns, and continue to grow as the number of children in a family rises (please refer to Figure 7.15).

Regardless of whether Zajonc's interpretation proves accurate, the fact that first-borns tend to have higher IQs than later-borns cannot readily be explained in terms of heredity; the genes contributed by parents should remain fairly constant across the entire birth order. Thus, the impact of environmental factors is suggested once again.

Finally, the important contribution of environmental factors to intelligence is suggested by many studies indicating that the longer students remain in school, the higher their IQ scores tend to be (Ceci, 1991). While this finding could also be interpreted as suggesting that more intelligent persons choose to remain in school, several facts point to the conclusion that staying in school may benefit intelligence. For example, it has been found that persons who attend school regularly score higher on intelligence tests than persons who attend irregularly, and that those who start school at an older than average age score lower than those who start at an average or early age. Finally, there is some indication that the worldwide increase in IQ scores to which I referred earlier stems, at least in part, from increased years in school in many countries (Ceci, 1991).

I should also note that a wide range of other environmental factors have been found to be related to IQ scores. These include nutrition, family background (for example, parents' education and income), and quality of education, to mention just a few (Bouchard & Segal, 1985). Such effects are small, but, again, they appear to be real.

ENVIRONMENT, HEREDITY, AND INTELLIGENCE: Summing Up

In sum, there is considerable evidence that *both* environmental and genetic factors play a role in intelligence. This is the view accepted by almost all psychologists, and there is little controversy about it. Great disagreement continues to exist, however, concerning the *relative* contribution of each of these factors. Do environmental factors or genetic factors play a stronger role in shaping intelligence? Or are heredity and environment of roughly equal importance? To date, efforts to answer these questions have failed to yield a clear answer. However, growing evidence from the field of *behavioral genetics* does seem to point to the possibility that genetic factors are quite important—perhaps more important in some respects than environmental ones (Plomin, 1989). As you can probably guess, many psychologists are made uneasy by the implications of these conclusions (Herrnstein, 1973; Kamin, 1978). Being concerned with human welfare, psychologists would strongly prefer to be in a position to intervene—to help enhance the intellectual capacity of all human beings. Evidence favoring a genetic basis for intelligence seems, at first glance, to rule out such possibilities. In fact, however, it does not. Genes do not fix or determine behavior; rather, genetic factors establish a range of possible responses to a given environment—a phenomenon referred to as *malleability* (Weinberg, 1989). Even if intelligence is strongly affected by genetic factors, it can still be influenced by environmental conditions. From this perspective, programs designed to enrich the intellectual environments of children from disadvantaged backgrounds may still produce beneficial results. Heredity, in short, should definitely *not* be viewed as a set of biological shackles or as an excuse for giving up on children who are at serious risk because of poverty, prejudice, or neglect.

KEY QUESTION

- What do most psychologists believe about the roles of heredity and environment in determining intelligence?

MAKING PSYCHOLOGY PART OF YOUR LIFE

Making Better Decisions

Have you ever made a bad decision—one that you later wished you could change? Unless you have led a charmed life, you probably have. Even the most intelligent people often find decision making a challenge. And errors in judgment may prove quite costly.

Given the vast complexity of the world and the diversity of options that often exist, it is unlikely that anyone can provide you with a perfect system for making correct decisions. Nevertheless, here are some cognitive guidelines for increasing the chances that many of your decisions will be good ones—or at least as free from sources of error and bias as possible.

1. *Don't trust your own memory, or beware of availability.* When we make decisions, we can do so only on the basis of the information available to us. Be careful! The information that comes most readily to mind is not always the most useful or revealing (Kahneman & Tversky, 1982). When you face an important decision, therefore, jog your memory in several ways; and, if time permits, consult written documents or sources before proceeding. As noted in chapter 6, memory often plays tricks on us, and relying on a quick scan of it when making an important decision can be risky.

2. *Don't take situations at face value, or question all anchors.* In many decision-making situations the stage is set long before we come on the scene. The asking price for a house or car is set by the seller, the number of meetings for a committee has been determined by its chair, and so on. While you can't always change such givens, you should at least recognize them for what they are and question whether they make sense. If you don't raise such questions, you will probably accept these "anchors" implicitly and then offer only minor adjustments to them (Northcraft & Neale, 1987). This can be a mistake! It may lead you to decisions that work against your best interests. So whenever and to whatever extent you can, question all proposed anchors.

3. *Remain flexible, or don't fall in love with your own decisions.* Making decisions is effortful; so once they are made, we tend to heave a sigh of relief and to stick with them—through thick and thin. Then, before we know it, we may have too much invested

to quit. In other words, we may be trapped in a situation where we ought to change our initial decision and cut our losses, but instead we continue down the path to ruin—or at least to negative outcomes (Brockner & Rubin, 1985). Don't let this happen! It's always difficult to admit a mistake, but doing so is often far better than sticking to a losing course of action.

4. *Consider all options, or is half an orange always better than none?* When you make a decision, you must choose among the available options. But what, precisely, are they? Sometimes not all options are out on the table when you begin. Thus, a useful strategy is to start by gathering as much information as you can and then to use it to generate as many potential options as possible. Doing so can often suggest choices or courses of action that you did not consider at first. For example, suppose two cooks are both preparing dishes that require an orange, yet there is only one orange available. What do they do? The obvious answer: cut it in half. But what if one cook needs only the juice and the other only the peel? Now a very different option exists: give the juice to one cook and the peel to the other. This kind of integrative option is often not apparent at first glance, so only careful consideration will suggest it (Pruitt & Rubin, 1986). A good rule to follow, then, is this: Never assume that the options with which you start are the only ones available or the best that can be devised.

We make decisions every day, some relatively trivial (such as which brand to buy in the supermarket), some relatively important (such as which job offer to accept). How can you improve *your* decision-making skills?

THINKING: FORMING CONCEPTS AND REASONING TO CONCLUSIONS

• *What are concepts?*

Concepts are mental categories for objects, events, or experiences that are similar to one another in one or more respects.

• *What is the difference between an artificial concept and a natural concept?*

Artificial concepts can be clearly defined by a set of rules or properties. Natural concepts cannot; they are usually defined in terms of prototypes—the most typical category members.

• *What are the basic elements of thought?*

Images (mental pictures of the world) and concepts are the basic elements of thought.

• *What is the process of reasoning? How does formal reasoning differ from everyday reasoning?*

Reasoning involves transforming available information in order to reach specific conclusions. Formal reasoning derives conclusions from specific premises; in contrast, everyday reasoning is less clear-cut and more complex.

• *What forms of error and bias can lead to faulty reasoning?*

Reasoning is subject to several forms of error and bias; among them are the confirmation bias, the oversight bias and the hindsight effect.

• *What are three lines of evidence that led scientists to reconsider the possibility that some animals and humans possess similar cognitive abilities?*

First, throughout this century scientists have observed many instances of behavior that cannot be attributed solely to conditioning process. Second, recent evidence shows that animals form complex mental representations of their environments that help them adapt to changing conditions. Third, when methods consistent with their abilities are used, animals demonstrate cognitive abilities similar to those of humans.

KEY TERMS: cognition, p. 230; concepts, p. 231; artificial concepts, p. 231; natural concepts, p. 231; prototypes, p. 231; reasoning, p. 232; syllogistic reasoning, p. 233; confirmation bias, p. 233; oversight bias, p. 234; hindsight effect, p. 234

MAKING DECISIONS: CHOOSING AMONG ALTERNATIVES

• *What are heuristics?*

Heuristics are informal mental rules of thumb that provide quick—but not infallible—solutions.

• *What are the availability, representativeness, and anchoring-and-adjustment heuristics, and what roles do they play in reasoning?*

The availability heuristic refers to our tendency to make judgments about the frequency or likelihood of various events in terms of how readily they can be brought to mind. The representativeness heuristic refers to the tendency to assume that the more closely an item resembles the most typical examples of some concept, the more likely it is to belong to that concept. The anchoring-and-adjustment heuristic refers to our tendency to reach a decision by making adjustments to reference points or existing information.

• *What is framing, and how does it relate to decision making?*

Decisions can be strongly affected by framing, which is the presentation of information about possible outcomes in terms of gains or losses. People are generally less certain and more inconsistent in their preferences when options are framed as losses than when they are framed as gains.

• *How does escalation of commitment affect decision making?*

Individuals often become trapped in bad decisions through escalation of commitment, an effect that derives from a reluctance to admit past mistakes and a desire to justify past losses.

KEY TERMS: decision making, p. 237; heuristics, p. 237; availability heuristic, p. 237; representativeness heuristic, p. 238; anchoring-and-adjustment heuristic, p. 239; framing, p. 239; escalation of commitment, p. 241

PROBLEM SOLVING AND CREATIVITY: FINDING PATHS TO DESIRED GOALS

• *How do psychologists define problem solving?*

Problem solving involves efforts to develop or choose among various responses in order to attain desired goals.

• *Through what two mechanisms are problems usually solved?*

Problems can be solved through trial and error or through the use of algorithms—rules that will, if followed, yield a solution.

• *What role do heuristics play in problem solving?*

Heuristics are rules of thumb suggested by our experience that we often apply to solve problems.

• *What factors can interfere with effective problem solving?*

Functional fixedness (the tendency to think of using objects only as they have been used before) and mental set (the tendency to stick with familiar methods) can interfere with effective problem solving.

- **What steps are involved in the creative process?**

Creativity seems to involve several distinct aspects: careful preparation, incubation, flashes of insight, and testing of proposed solutions.

- **What is divergent thinking?**

Creative breakthroughs seem to stem from divergent thinking—thinking that involves moving away from conventional knowledge or wisdom.

- **What is artificial intelligence?**

Artificial intelligence is an interdisciplinary field concerned with the capacity of computers to demonstrate intelligent performance.

KEY TERMS: *problem solving, p. 242; trial and error, p. 242; algorithms, p. 242; means-end analysis, p. 243; analogy, p. 243; functional fixedness, p. 243; mental set, p. 245; creativity, p. 245; convergent thinking, p. 246; divergent thinking, p. 246; artificial intelligence, p. 246; neural networks, p. 247*

LANGUAGE: THE COMMUNICATION OF INFORMATION

- **What abilities are involved in the production of language?**

Language involves the ability to use a rich set of symbols, plus rules for combining these to communicate information. It includes the abilities to produce and to comprehend speech.

- **How does language develop in humans?**

Contrasting theories of language development suggest that children acquire language through social facilitation, innate mechanisms, and cognitive mechanisms.

- **What are the basic components of language development?**

Language development involves phonological development, semantic development, and acquisition of grammar.

- **What is the linguistic relativity hypothesis?**

According to the linguistic relativity hypothesis, language actually shapes or determines thought. Existing evidence does not offer strong support for this hypothesis.

- **Do animals possess language?**

Growing evidence suggests that some species of animals, including bonobo chimpanzees and dolphins, are capable of grasping several basic aspects of language, including word order and grammar.

KEY TERMS: *language, p. 248; phonological development, p. 250; semantic development, p. 250; grammar, p. 250; babbling, p. 250; phonological strategies, p. 250; fast mapping, p. 250; linguistic relativity hypothesis, p. 251*

INTELLIGENCE: ITS NATURE AND MEASUREMENT

- **What is intelligence? Is intelligence a unitary or a multifaceted characteristic?**

While psychologists generally agree that intelligence involves the ability to think abstractly and learn from experience, there is considerable disagreement about whether it is unitary or multifaceted in nature. At present, most psychologists believe that intelligence probably involves both a general capacity to solve many types of problems and several specific abilities.

- **What is the focus of the information-processing approach to intelligence?**

In recent years many researchers have adopted the information-processing approach to intelligence: focusing on the basic cognitive processes underlying intelligence.

- **What is Sternberg's triarchic theory of intelligence?**

Sternberg's triarchic theory adopts the perspective of information processing and proposes that there are actually three distinct types of intelligence: componential, experiential, and contextual.

- **How are biological factors involved in intelligence?**

Research on the biological basis of intelligence indicates that persons scoring high on intelligence tests show faster rates of neural conduction and higher levels of metabolic efficiency in their brains than do persons who score lower on such tests. There also appear to be subtle differences between the brains of females and males, and these differences may influence some aspects of cognitive functioning and overt behavior.

- **What was the first individual test of intelligence, and what did its score signify?**

The first individual test of intelligence was the assessment devised by Binet and Simon in the early years of the twentieth century. This test yielded an IQ (intelligence quotient) score obtained by dividing a child's mental age by chronological age.

- **What steps have psychologists taken to devise tests that measure more than just verbal aspects of intelligence?**

Because intelligence can be demonstrated nonverbally as well as verbally, other widely used tests of intelligence, the Weschler Scales, obtain both a Verbal and a Performance IQ.

- **What are some positive and negative aspects of group tests of intelligence?**

Group tests of intelligence are efficient because they can be administered to large numbers of persons at once. However, serious questions have been raised concerning their use with persons from minority groups.

- **What is test reliability, and how do psychologists assess it?**

In order to be useful, any psychological test must have high reliability—it must yield very similar scores when applied more than once to the same quantity. One important form of reliability, internal consistency, is the extent to which items on the test measure the same characteristic. Another form of reliability is test-retest reliability: the extent to which scores on a test are stable over time.

- **What is validity? Are there different ways to assess validity?**

Psychological tests must also be high in validity—the capacity to measure what they claim to measure. Content validity involves the extent to which the items on a test reflect behaviors related to the characteristics that are being measured. Criterion-related validity involves the extent to which persons scoring high or low on a psychological test also differ in terms of some standard aspect. Construct validity concerns the extent to which a test actually taps psychological variables we wish to measure but can't observe directly.

- **Has the construction of culture-fair tests been successful?**

Efforts to reduce cultural bias and to construct culture-fair tests have been only partly successful. Members of some minority groups continue to score lower than whites of European decent on standard intelligence tests. This appears to be due at least in part to the cultural bias of these tests.

- **Is there any way to solve the problem of cultural bias?**

One potential solution to this problem may involve development of physiological tests of intelligence based on the speed or efficiency of information processing by individuals' brains.

KEY TERMS: *intelligence, p. 254; crystallized intelligence, p. 254; fluid intelligence, p. 255; triarchic theory, p. 255; componential intelligence, p. 255; experiential intelligence, p. 255; contextual intelligence, p. 255; Stanford-Binet test, p. 261; IQ, p. 261; reliability, p. 264; split-half reliability, p. 264; test-retest reliability, p. 264; validity, p. 265; content validity, p. 265; criterion-related validity, p. 266; predictive validity, p. 266; concurrent validity, p. 266; construct validity, p. 266; cultural bias, p. 268; mental retardation, p. 270; Down Syndrome, p. 270*

HUMAN INTELLIGENCE: THE ROLE OF HEREDITY AND THE ROLE OF ENVIRONMENT

- **What do most psychologists believe about the roles of heredity and environment in determining intelligence?**

Several lines of evidence indicate that genetic factors play a role in determining intelligence. Other evidence indicates that environmental conditions also strongly influence intelligence. Thus, most psychologists believe that intelligence is the result of a complex interplay between environmental conditions and genetic factors.

CRITICAL THINKING QUESTIONS

APPRAISAL	Human thought processes appear to be less than perfect in several important respects. For example, our reliance on heuristics can lead us to make rapid but seriously flawed decisions. What can psychologists do to help people reduce or eliminate the effects of these errors in their thinking?
CONTROVERSY	Suppose that at some future time, highly reliable measures of intelligence based on physiological functioning are developed. Do you think such measures should replace standard tests of intelligence? What advantages would they offer? Would such measures be entirely culture-free, or can you think of subtle ways in which cultural differences might influence performance on even *these* tests?
MAKING PSYCHOLOGY PART OF YOUR LIFE	Now that you understand the basic nature of cognitive processes and the many factors that affect them, can you think of ways in which you can use this knowledge to improve your problem-solving abilities? Name several specific steps you could take to become more effective in this respect.

Human Development:

From Child to Adult

*C*hange, it is often said, is the only constant. And where human beings are concerned, this is certainly true. Stop for a moment and think about the many ways in which you've changed over the course of your life, or even during the past few years. If you do, you'll be struck by both the scope and the magnitude of these alterations. In fact, in a very real sense, change is a basic part of human existence: We are all in a continuous state of flux as we move through life's journey.

The field of **developmental psychology** focuses on such change. This chapter examines some of its major findings. While the changes we experience throughout life seem countless, developmental psychologists have found it helpful to consider these shifts under three major categories: **physical growth and development, cognitive development**, and **social and emotional development**. These terms refer, respectively, to changes in the physical size and structure of our bodies; changes in our mental abilities and functioning; and changes in our emotional reactions to, and relations with, other persons. In this chapter we'll consider such changes as they occur during three major phases of life: *childhood, adolescence*, and *adulthood*.

PHYSICAL GROWTH AND DEVELOPMENT DURING CHILDHOOD

*W*hen does human life begin? From a purely biological point of view, your life as an individual began when one of the millions of sperm released by your father during sexual intercourse fertilized an ovum deep within your mother's body. The product of this union was barely 1/175 of an inch in diameter—smaller than the period at the end of this sentence.

THE PRENATAL PERIOD

After fertilization the ovum moves through the mother's reproductive tract until it reaches the womb, or uterus. This trip takes several days, and during this time the ovum divides again and again. Ten to fourteen days after fertilization, the ovum becomes implanted in the wall of the mother's uterus. For the next six weeks it is known as the **embryo** and develops at a rapid pace. By the third week a primitive heart has formed and begun to beat. By the fourth week the embryo is about one-fifth of an inch (one-half centimeter) long, and the region of the head is clearly visible. Rapid growth continues, and by the end of the eighth week the embryo is about one inch long, and a face as well as arms and legs are present; simple reflexes appear during the eighth or ninth week of life.

During the next seven months the developing child—now known as the **fetus**—shows an increasingly human form. The external genitals take shape, so sex is recognizable by the twelfth week. Fingernails and toenails form, hair follicles appear, and eyelids that open and close emerge. By the end of the twelfth week the fetus is 3 inches (7.6 centimeters) long and weighs about 3/4 ounce (21 grams). By the twentieth week it is almost 10 inches (25 cm) long and weighs 8 or 9 ounces (227–255 g).

During the last three months of pregnancy, the fetus gains about eight ounces each week and grows rapidly. By the seventh and eighth months it appears to be virtually fully formed. However, if born at this time, it may still experience difficulties in breathing, because the alveoli, tiny air sacs within the lungs, are not yet fully formed. At birth babies weigh more than 7 pounds (3.17 kilograms) on average and are about 20 inches (50.8 cm) long.

Cognitive abilities, too, appear to take shape during the prenatal period. In an ingenious series of studies, DeCasper and his colleagues (e.g., DeCasper & Fifer, 1980; DeCasper & Spence, 1986) arranged for mothers-to-be to read *The Cat in the Hat* to their unborn children two times each day during the last six weeks of pregnancy. At the end of that period, the heart rate of each fetus was

Developmental Psychology: The branch of psychology that studies all types of changes occurring throughout the life span.

Physical Growth and Development: Physical changes in the size and structure of our bodies between conception and adulthood.

Cognitive Development: Changes in cognitive abilities and functioning occurring as individuals grow older.

Social and Emotional Development: Changes in emotional experiences and expressions, and in behaviors and attitudes toward others, occurring with age.

Embryo: The developing child during the second through the eighth week of prenatal development.

Fetus: The developing child during the last seven months of prenatal development.

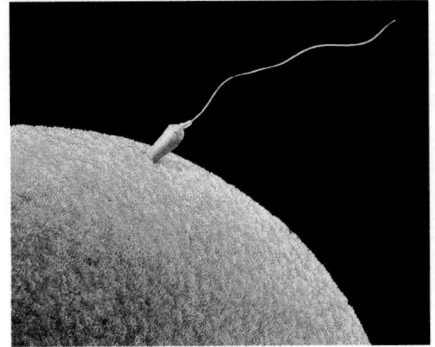 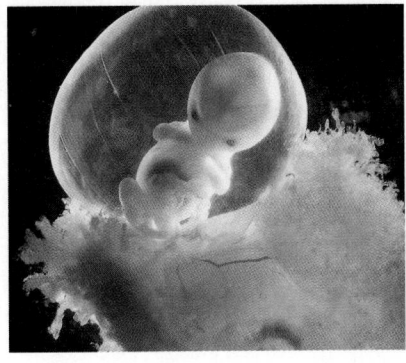 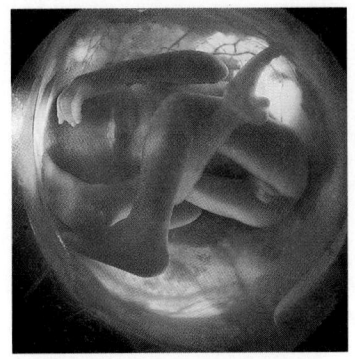

measured as recordings of the familiar story and of an unfamiliar story were played. Results indicated that the familiar story produced a slight decrease in fetal heart rate, while the unfamiliar one produced a slight increase. A decrease in heart rate often indicates increased attention, so these findings suggest that the fetuses could distinguish between the familiar and unfamiliar stories.

PRENATAL INFLUENCES ON DEVELOPMENT: WHEN TROUBLE STARTS EARLY

Under ideal conditions, development during the prenatal period occurs in an orderly fashion, and the newborn child is well equipped at birth to survive outside its mother's body. Unfortunately, however, conditions are not always ideal. Many environmental factors can damage the fetus and interfere with normal patterns of growth. Such factors are known as **teratogens**, and their impact can be devastating. Table 8.1 provides an overview of some potential teratogens and their possible effects on the developing fetus.

Learning Objective 8.1
Describe the scope of developmental psychology.

Learning Objective 8.2
List the main events of the prenatal period.

Learning Objective 8.3
Describe the course of infants' physical and perceptual development.

PHYSICAL AND PERCEPTUAL DEVELOPMENT DURING OUR EARLY YEARS

Physical growth is rapid during infancy. Assuming good nutrition, infants almost triple in weight (to about 20 pounds or 9 kg) and increase in body

TERATOGEN	POTENTIAL EFFECTS ON FETUS
Disease during pregnancy (e.g., rubella, chicken pox, mumps, syphilis, herpes, AIDS)	Blindness, deafness, heart disease, serious birth defects
Prescription and over-the-counter drugs	Premature birth, increased irritability, digestive problems
Illegal drugs	Physical malformations, respiratory disease, premature birth
Alcohol	Fetal alcohol syndrome: severely retarded growth, damage to brain and nervous system, distortions in normal shape of the face
Smoking	Spontaneous abortion, decreased birth weight and size, damage to the central nervous system

TABLE 8.1

Various Teratogens and Their Effects

Environmental factors or conditions that harm the developing fetus are known as *teratogens*. As shown here, their effects can be truly devastating.

Teratogens: Factors in the environment that can harm the developing fetus.

FIGURE 8.1

Milestones of Motor Development

Some highlights of motor development. Please note that the approximate ages shown here are only *averages*. Most children will depart from them to some extent; departures are of little importance unless they are extreme.
(*Source:* Frankenberg & Dodds, 1967.)

length by about one-third (to 28 or 29 inches, 71 to 74 cm) during the first year alone.

Newborns possess a number of simple reflexes at birth. They can follow a moving light with their eyes, suck on a finger or nipple placed in their mouth, and turn their head in the direction of a touch on the cheek. In addition, they can grasp a finger placed in their palm and will make stepping motions if held so that their feet barely touch a flat surface. Their ability to move about and reach for objects is quite limited, but this situation changes quickly. Within a few months they can sit and crawl. And, as harried parents quickly learn, most infants are quite mobile by the time they are fourteen or fifteen months old. Figure 8.1 summarizes several milestones of motor development. It's important to keep in mind that the approximate ages indicated in the figure are *average* values. Departures from them are of little importance unless they are quite extreme. After the initial spurt of the first year, the rate of physical growth slows; both boys and girls gain about 2 to 3 inches (5 to 10 cm) and 4 to 7 pounds (2 to 4 kg) per year until adolescence, when both sexes experience a growth spurt lasting about two years.

LEARNING ABILITIES OF NEWBORNS Can newborns show the kinds of learning discussed in chapter 5? Evidence concerning classical conditioning suggests that they can, but that such conditioning occurs most readily for stimuli that have survival value for babies. For example, infants only two hours old readily learn to associate gentle stroking on the forehead with a sweet solution; after these two stimuli have been paired repeatedly infants will show sucking responses to the stroking (the conditioned stimulus) (Granchrow, Steiner, & Daher, 1983). In contrast, human infants do not readily acquire conditioned fears until they are at least eight months old. Remember little Albert, discussed in chapter 5, who acquired fear of a white rat (the conditioned stimulus) after it was paired with a loud sound (the unconditioned stimulus)? He was eleven months old at the time the study was conducted.

Turning to operant conditioning, there is considerable evidence that newborns can readily demonstrate this basic kind of learning. For example, they readily learn to suck faster in order to see visual designs or hear music and human voices (Rovee-Collier, 1987). And by the time infants are two months old, they will move their head against a pressure-sensitive pillow in order to produce movements in a mobile hung above their crib (Watson & Ramey, 1972).

Additional evidence indicates that newborns are even capable of imitation. In a series of well-known studies, Meltzoff and his colleagues (Meltzoff & Moore, 1977, 1989) demonstrated that infants between twelve and twenty days of age could imitate facial gestures shown by an adult—for example, sticking out their tongue or opening their mouth. Indeed, in one well-conducted study, infants tested only a few minutes after birth showed imitation of two facial expressions: widened lips and pursed lips (Reissland, 1988).

PERCEPTUAL DEVELOPMENT How do infants perceive the world around them? Do they recognize form, see color, and perceive depth in the same manner as adults? Infants can't talk, so it is necessary to answer such questions through indirect methods, such as by observing changes in their heart rate, their sucking response, or the amount of time they spend gazing at various stimuli. For example, it has been found that after infants have seen a visual stimulus several times, they spend less time looking at it when it is presented again than they do at a new stimulus they have never seen before. This fact provides a means of determining whether infants can detect a difference between two stimuli. If they can, then after seeing one stimulus repeatedly, infants should spend less time looking at it than at a new stimulus when both are presented together. If they cannot, they should look equally at both stimuli. Studies based on this premise have determined that newborns can distinguish between different colors (Adams, 1987), odors (Balogh & Porter, 1986), tastes (Granchrow, Steiner, & Daher, 1983), and sounds (Morrongiello & Clifton, 1984). Infants as young as three days old will turn their eyes and head in the direction of a sound. Moreover, they are especially sensitive to auditory stimuli within the frequency range of normal human speech. Indeed, they can even distinguish between such similar sounds as "ba" and "ga" (Eimas & Tarter, 1979).

Infants also show impressive abilities with respect to form or pattern perception. In now classic research on this topic, Fantz (1961) showed babies six months old a variety of visual patterns. By observing how long they fixated visually on each, he determined that the babies had a clear preference for patterned as opposed to plain targets and that they seemed to prefer the human face over all the other stimuli tested.

> ## KEY QUESTIONS
>
> • What environmental factors can adversely affect the developing fetus?
>
> • What perceptual abilities are shown by infants?
>
> • At what age do infants develop the ability to perceive depth?

THE VISUAL CLIFF: STUDYING INFANT DEPTH PERCEPTION

Infants six or seven months old refuse to crawl out over the deep side of the *visual cliff*. This indicates that they can perceive depth.

Subsequent research has indicated that recognition of faces may develop even earlier. By two months of age infants prefer a face with features in normal locations over one with scrambled features (Maurer & Barrera, 1981). By three months they can distinguish between their mother's face and a stranger's, and can even tell one stranger's face from another (Barrera & Maurer, 1981a).

The ability to perceive depth, too, seems to develop rapidly in the months immediately after birth. Early studies on depth perception employed an apparatus known as the *visual cliff* (Gibson & Walk, 1960). As you can see from the photo, the patterned floor drops away on the deep side of the cliff.

A transparent surface continues across this chasm, so there is no actual drop—and no real danger. Yet human infants six or seven months old refuse to crawl across the deep side to reach their mothers, thus indicating that they perceive depth by this time. Does this perceptual ability appear prior to this age? Since younger infants can't crawl across the cliff even if they want to, it is necessary to use other methods to find out. Such research has been performed and indicates that depth perception may first appear when infants are about three months old (Fox et al., 1979; Yonas, Arterberry, & Granrud, 1987).

In sum, shortly after birth, infants have sophisticated abilities to interpret complex sensory input. How do they then integrate such information into cognitive frameworks for understanding the world? We'll consider this question shortly. Before turning to *cognitive development*, however, let's look at the basic research methods used by psychologists in their efforts to understand all aspects of human development.

BASIC METHODS FOR STUDYING HUMAN DEVELOPMENT

Learning Objective 8.4
Compare and contrast the basic methods for studying human development.

*H*ow can we obtain systematic evidence on the course of human development and the factors that affect it? Developmental psychologists employ several different methods for answering such questions. One of these methods is known as **longitudinal research** and involves studying the same individuals for extended periods of time (see Figure 8.2). For example, to determine whether children raised by their own mothers differ in cognitive development—for example, in language skills—from children raised in day-care centers, researchers might identify two groups of children being raised in these contrasting environments and then study them over several years.

Longitudinal research offers important advantages. Since the same persons are tested or observed repeatedly, individual variations in the course of development can be observed. Further, because the same persons are studied over relatively long periods of time, it may be possible to draw conclusions about how specific events influence the course of subsequent development. There are also potential disadvantages, however. First, there is the problem of *subject attrition*—the loss of some participants over the course of the project. Families may move, break up, or lose interest, causing their children to be removed from the sample. As a result, the youngsters who remain in the study may be different in important respects from those who withdraw. Another potential disadvantage is *practice effects*. People who are tested or observed repeatedly may gradually become very familiar with the kind of tasks used in the research. Again, to the extent such effects occur, the results obtained may be invalid.

Now let's consider another way of studying the mother/day-care question. Instead of following the development of two groups of youngsters for several years, we might instead simply compare children of different ages

Longitudinal Research:
Research in which the same individuals are studied across relatively substantial periods of time, such as years.

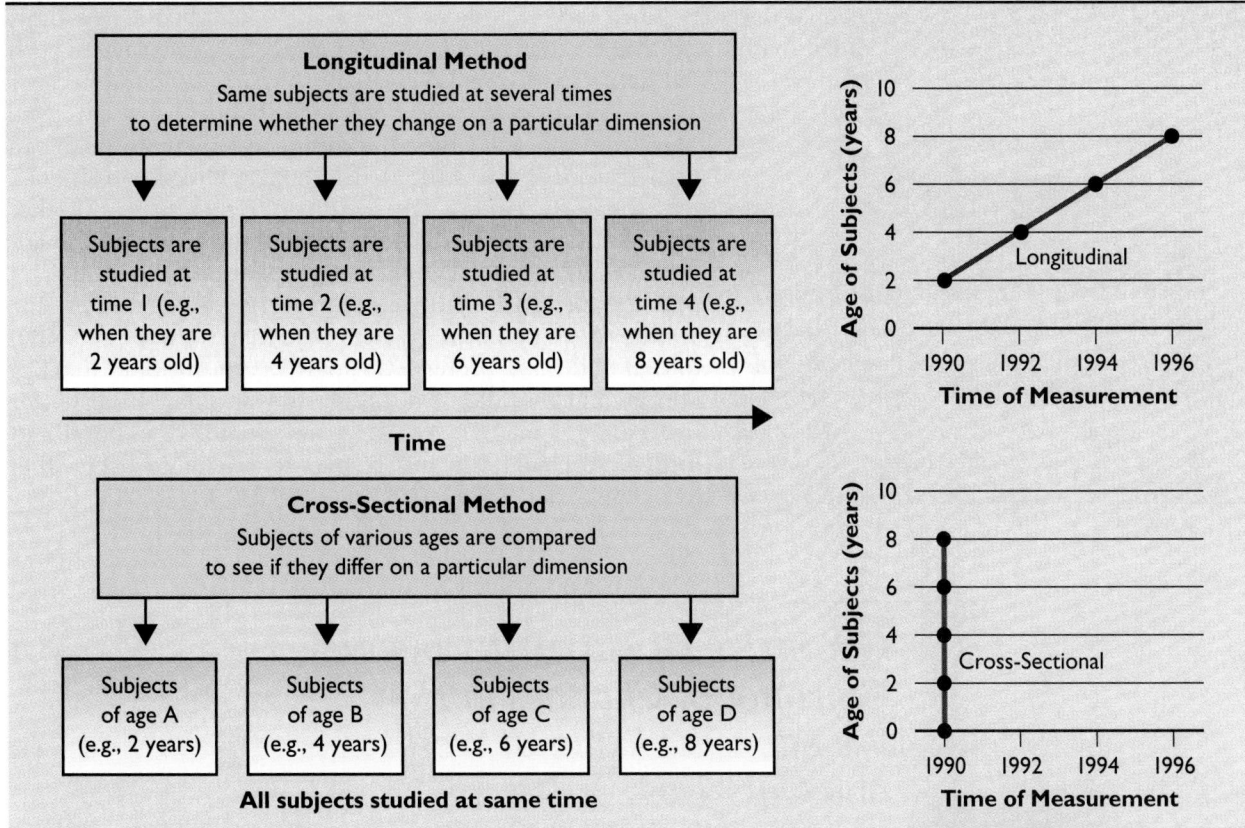

FIGURE 8.2

Basic Methods of Studying Human Development

In the *longitudinal method*, the same individuals are studied across time. In the *cross-sectional method*, persons of different ages are studied at one time.

who have been cared for by their mothers or in day-care centers. For example, we might compare three-year-olds, four-year-olds, and five-year-olds raised under each condition, to determine whether they differ with respect to cognitive development at each age. This is an example of **cross-sectional research**—research in which people of different ages are studied at the same point in time (refer to Figure 8.2).

Cross-sectional research, too, offers several advantages. It can be conducted much more quickly than longitudinal research. And since participants are tested only once, practice effects of the kind described above are minimized. Unfortunately, though, cross-sectional research also has several disadvantages. Perhaps the most important of these involves what are known as **cohort effects**. That is, differences between groups of persons of different ages may derive not merely from differences in age but from the fact that the people were born at different times and have been exposed to contrasting life experiences and cultural conditions. Such differences may be small among children who are currently three, four, and five years old. But suppose psychologists are interested in comparing people who are sixty-five, forty-five, and twenty-five. Clearly, the life experience of these groups may differ sharply, and cohort effects—not increasing age—may be responsible for any differences between them.

Faced with the mixed picture of advantages and disadvantages outlined above, developmental psychologists have sought to formulate a research approach that combines the advantages of longitudinal and cross-sectional research while minimizing the disadvantages of each. One such approach is known as the **longitudinal-sequential design**. It involves studying several samples of people of different ages over a period of years. In other words, this technique combines major aspects of both longitudinal and cross-

Cross-Sectional Research: Research comparing groups of persons of different ages in order to determine how some aspect of behavior or cognition changes with age.

Cohort Effects: Differences between persons of different ages stemming from the contrasting social or cultural conditions of the periods in which they grew up.

Longitudinal-Sequential Design: A research approach in which several groups of individuals of different ages are studied across time.

sectional research. Since each sample of participants is studied across time, changes within each can be attributed to development. But since several such samples are studied, researchers can also assess the impact of cohort effects or cultural changes by comparing persons born in different years with one another at the same age. Any differences between them can then reasonably be attributed to cohort effects—to the fact that the participants were born in different years. Another advantage of such designs is that they allow for both longitudinal and cross-sectional comparisons. If the results of both are the same, then we can be quite confident about the validity of these findings. While the longitudinal-sequential design still faces problems of participant attrition, practice effects, and the like, it does offer an additional means for untangling some of the interwoven strands of cultural and individual change. In this respect it is another useful tool available to developmental researchers.

KEY QUESTIONS

- What are they key differences between longitudinal research and cross-sectional research?

- How is longitudinal-sequential research conducted?

- What are the key advantages of each of these major research methods?

COGNITIVE DEVELOPMENT DURING CHILDHOOD: *Changes in How We Know the External World . . . and Ourselves*

Learning Objective 8.5
Understand the assumptions underlying Piaget's theory of cognitive development and describe its stages.

*D*o children think, reason, and remember in the same manner as adults? Until well into the twentieth century, it was widely assumed that they do. In the late 1920s, however, this assumption was vigorously challenged by the Swiss psychologist Jean Piaget. On the basis of careful observations of his own and many other children, Piaget concluded that in several crucial respects children do not think or reason like adults. Rather, because they lack certain abilities, their thought processes are different not only in degree but in kind. Piaget's theory of cognitive development contains many valuable insights and has guided a great deal of research. Thus, we will consider it in detail here. But it is important to realize that many psychologists no longer accept this theory as accurate. Moreover, Piaget's theory has been seriously challenged by a different approach—one based on the information-processing perspective we discussed in detail in chapter 6 (Case, 1991). So, after considering Piaget's theory and modern assessments of it, we'll turn to this newer information-processing approach to cognitive development.

PIAGET'S THEORY: *An Overview*

Stage Theory: Any theory proposing that all human beings move through an orderly and predictable series of changes.

Adaptation: In Piaget's theory of cognitive development, building mental representations of the world through interaction with it.

Assimilation: In Piaget's theory, the tendency to understand new information in terms of existing mental frameworks.

Accommodation: In Piaget's theory, the modification of existing mental frameworks to take account of new information.

Piaget's theory of cognitive development is a **stage theory**—one suggesting that all human beings move through an orderly and predictable series of changes. What force underlies our progress through these stages? According to Piaget, it is **adaptation**: the process of building mental representations of the world through direct interaction with it. Adaptation, in turn, consists of two basic components. The first of these is **assimilation**, our tendency to fit new information into existing mental frameworks—to understand the world in terms of existing concepts, schemas, and modes of thought. The second is **accommodation**, our tendency to alter existing concepts or mental frameworks in response to new information or new recognizable dimensions of the external world. Piaget suggests that it is the tension between these two components that fosters adaptation and cognitive development—our progress through ever more complex conceptions of the world around us. Now let's turn to the details of the different stages of cognitive development Piaget described.

THE SENSORIMOTOR STAGE: LEARNING TO REPRESENT THE WORLD INTERNALLY The first of Piaget's stages lasts from birth until somewhere between eighteen and twenty-four months. During this period, which Piaget terms the **sensorimotor stage,** infants gradually learn that there is a relationship between their actions and the external world. They discover that they can manipulate objects and produce effects. In short, they acquire a basic grasp of the concept of cause and effect.

Throughout the sensorimotor period, however, infants seem to know the world only through motor activities and sensory impressions. They have not yet learned to use mental symbols or images to represent objects or events. This results in some interesting effects. For example, if an object is hidden from view, four-month-olds will not attempt to search for it. For such infants, "out of sight, out of mind" seems to be true, at least under some conditions. By the time they are eight or nine months old, however, most infants will search for the hidden object. Thus, they seem to have obtained a basic idea of **object permanence,** an understanding that objects continue to exist when they are hidden from view.

THE PREOPERATIONAL STAGE: GROWTH OF SYMBOLIC ACTIVITY Sometime between the ages of eighteen and twenty-four months, Piaget contends, babies acquire the ability to form mental images of objects and events. At the same time, language develops to the point at which a young child begins to think in terms of verbal symbols—words. These developments, Piaget suggests, mark the end of the sensorimotor period and the start of the **preoperational stage.** During this stage, which lasts until about age seven, children are capable of many actions they could not perform earlier. For example, they begin to demonstrate **make-believe play,** in which they enact familiar activities, such as pretending to eat or go to sleep.

While the thought processes of preoperational children are more advanced than those in the preceding stage, Piaget emphasizes that children at this stage of cognitive development are still quite immature in several respects. First, they are limited by **egocentrism**: They have difficulty understanding that others may perceive the world differently than they do (Piaget, 1975). Children in the preoperational stage also seem to lack understanding of relational terms such as *darker, larger,* or *harder.* Further, they lack *seriation*—the ability to arrange objects in order along some dimension. Finally, and perhaps most important, they lack a grasp of what Piaget terms the principle of **conservation**—knowledge that certain physical attributes of an object remain unchanged even though the outward appearance of the object is altered. For example, imagine that a four-year-old is shown two identical lumps of clay. One lump is then flattened into a large pancake as the child watches. Asked whether the two lumps still contain the same amount of clay, the child may answer "no" (see Figure 8.3 on page 290).

THE STAGE OF CONCRETE OPERATIONS: THE EMERGENCE OF LOGICAL THOUGHT By the time they are six or seven (or perhaps even earlier, as we'll see below), most children can solve the simple problems described above. According to Piaget, a child's mastery of conservation marks the beginning of a third major stage of cognitive development—the stage of

MAKE-BELIEVE PLAY

When they engage in make-believe play, children demonstrate that they can represent everyday activities mentally. According to Piaget, they become capable of such behavior during the preoperational stage.

Sensorimotor Stage: In Piaget's theory, the earliest stage of cognitive development. It is during this stage that infants learn that there is a relationship between their actions and the external world.

Object Permanence: An understanding of the fact that objects continue to exist when they pass from view.

Preoperational Stage: In Piaget's theory, a stage of cognitive development during which children become capable of mental representations of the external world.

Make-Believe Play: Play in which children pretend to be engaging in various familiar activities, such as eating or going to sleep.

Egocentrism: The inability of young children to distinguish their own perspective from that of others.

Conservation: Principle stating that certain physical attributes of an object remain unchanged even though its outward appearance changes.

FIGURE 8.3

Is there the same amount
of clay in each ball?

Now does each piece have
the same amount of clay, or
does one have more?

Lack of Understanding of Conservation during the Preoperational Stage

A four-year-old is shown two identical lumps of clay (left). Then one lump is flattened into a large pancake (right). Asked whether the two lumps still contain the same amount of clay, the child may answer "no." Such behavior indicates that the child lacks understanding of the concept of *conservation*.

Learning Objective 8.6
Explain the assumptions of the information-processing perspective on cognitive development.

Learning Objective 8.7
Compare and contrast the attentional focus of younger and older children.

Learning Objective 8.8
Survey the various ways in which memory improves with age.

Concrete Operations: In Piaget's theory, a stage of cognitive development occurring roughly between the ages of seven and eleven. It is at this stage that children grasp such principles as conservation and the capacity for logical thought emerges.

Formal Operations: In Piaget's theory, the final stage of cognitive development, during which individuals may acquire the capacity for deductive or propositional reasoning.

Hypothetico-Deductive Reasoning: In Piaget's theory, a type of reasoning first shown during the stage of formal operations. It involves formulating a general theory and deducing specific hypotheses from it.

concrete operations. Piaget believed that this is a major turning point in cognitive development, because, in terms of his theory, children at this stage think more like adults than like younger children at earlier stages. During the stage of concrete operations, which lasts until about the age of eleven, many important skills emerge. Youngsters gain understanding of relational terms and seriation. They come to understand *reversibility*—the fact that many physical changes can be undone by a reversal of the original action. Most important, children who have reached the stage of concrete operations begin to engage in what Piaget would describe as logical thought. If asked, "Why did you and your mother go the store?" they will reply, "Because my mother needed some milk." In short, they provide a logical explanation. Younger children, in contrast, may reply, "Because afterwards, we came home."

THE STAGE OF FORMAL OPERATIONS: DEALING WITH ABSTRACTIONS AS WELL AS REALITY At about the age of twelve, Piaget suggests, most children enter the final stage of cognitive development—the stage of **formal operations.** During this period, major features of adult thought first appear. While children in the stage of concrete operations can think logically, it appears that they can do so only about concrete events and objects. In contrast, those who have attained the stage of formal operations can think abstractly; they can deal not only with the real or concrete but with possibilities—potential events or relationships that do not exist but can be imagined.

During this final stage of cognitive development, children become capable of what Piaget terms **hypothetico-deductive reasoning.** When faced with a problem, young people can formulate a general theory that includes all possible factors. From this, they can reason deductively to formulate specific hypotheses that they can then test by examining existing evidence or acquiring new evidence.

While the thinking of older children or adolescents closely approaches that of adults, however, Piaget believed that it still falls short of the adult level. Thus, older children, and especially adolescents, often use their new powers of reasoning to construct sweeping theories of religion, ethics, or politics. While the reasoning in such views may be logical, the theories are often naive, because the individuals who construct them simply don't know enough about life to do a more sophisticated job.

One final point: while people who have reached the stage of formal operations are capable of engaging in advanced forms of thought, there is no guarantee that they will actually do so. On the contrary, even adults often slip back into less developed modes of thought on some occasions (Kuhn, 1989).

PIAGET'S THEORY: A Modern Assessment

Because of their sweeping scope and broad implications, Piaget's views have been the focus of a large number of investigations designed to test their accuracy (Flavell, 1982). The results of such research suggest that the theory, although insightful, does not provide a completely accurate account of cognitive development. In particular, existing evidence suggests that Piaget's theory is incorrect—or at least requires major revision—with respect to three important issues.

THE CASE OF THE COMPETENT PRESCHOOLER   The first of these involves the cognitive abilities of very young children. A large body of evidence indicates that Piaget underestimated these abilities to a serious degree. For example, even infants 4.5 months of age seem to possess a basic grasp of object permanence (Baillargeon, 1987). Similarly, children as young as three show some understanding of the concept of conservation—the fact that certain physical attributes of an object can remain unchanged even though the outward appearance of the object is altered (Cuneo, 1980).

DISCRETE STAGES IN COGNITIVE DEVELOPMENT: MYTH OR REALITY?   Piaget proposed that cognitive development passes through discrete stages and that these are discontinuous: Children must complete one stage before entering another. Most research findings, however, indicate that cognitive changes occur in a gradual manner. Rarely does an ability entirely absent at one age appear suddenly at another. Thus, many developmental psychologists disagree with this basic aspect of Piaget's theory.

LANGUAGE AND THE SOCIAL CONTEXT OF COGNITIVE DEVELOPMENT
Young children often talk to themselves as they go about their daily activities, giving themselves instructions about what to do next. Piaget called this *egocentric speech* and suggested that it was a sign of children's cognitive immaturity. Thus, he downplayed the importance of such speech in cognitive development. The Soviet psychologist Vygotsky (1987) objected strongly to these beliefs, contending that **private speech**, as he termed it, is not egocentric. On the contrary, it occurs when young children encounter obstacles and difficulties and represents their efforts to engage in self-guidance. Vygotsky felt that this early use of language helps young children reflect on their own behavior and so plays a key role in cognitive development. The results of many studies tend to confirm these views (e.g., Bivens & Berk, 1990). Moreover, research also provides support for another of Vygotsky's contentions: the idea that social communication with caregivers plays a key role in cognitive growth. Of course, private speech and verbal communication are not the only mechanisms through which children's thinking develops. However, these factors do play a more important role than Piaget believed, so his theory appears to be inaccurate in these respects, too.

In sum, there is now general agreement among developmental psychologists that in certain respects Piaget's theory is incorrect. Despite its weaknesses, though, it altered some of our most basic ideas about the way children think and reason.

THE SOCIAL CONTEXT OF COGNITIVE DEVELOPMENT

According to Vygotsky (1987), children often learn in situations in which parents present them with cognitive tasks that are slightly too difficult for them to perform alone. The social interaction and dialogue that occur in such situations help children master new skills.

Learning Objective 8.9
Define "metacognition" and explain its importance for cognitive functioning.

KEY QUESTIONS

• According to Piaget's theory, what cognitive abilities do infants, children, and adolescents demonstrate during the sensorimotor stage, the preoperational stage, the stage of concrete operations, and the stage of formal operations?

• In what respects does Piaget's theory appear to be inaccurate?

COGNITIVE DEVELOPMENT: An Information-Processing Perspective

Although Piaget's views remain influential even today, an alternative approach to understanding cognitive development has emerged during the past two decades and gained increasing support among psychologists.

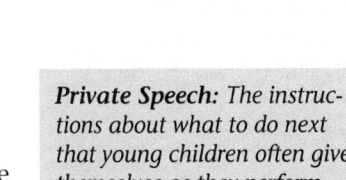

Private Speech: *The instructions about what to do next that young children often give themselves as they perform various activities.*

Known as the **information-processing approach** (see chapter 6), this view suggests that the human mind is best understood as an active information-processing system. Psychologists who adopt this approach seek to understand how children's capacities to process, store, retrieve, and actively manipulate information increase with age (Case, 1991). Because the information-processing approach is supported by a large body of scientific evidence, and because it is fully consistent with the growing emphasis on cognitive processes in all of modern psychology, it merits our careful attention.

SENSORY PROCESSING: EFFICIENCIES IN PERCEIVING THE EXTERNAL WORLD
Earlier in this chapter we saw that even newborns possess considerable ability to perceive the world around them. As you can readily guess, however, children's skills in this respect improve rapidly over the years. The information-processing approach suggests that such improvements include an increasing ability to notice fine-grained and subtle features of the external world—for example, not just the difference between a human face and a jumbled pattern, but the differences between individual faces.

In addition, cognitive growth involves the development of increasingly sophisticated cognitive frameworks, or *schemas*, for interpreting new stimuli. Research findings suggest that even newborns possess impressive abilities to form such frameworks (e.g., Langlois, Roggmann, & Reisser-Danner, 1990; Walton & Bower, 1993; Walton, Bower, & Bower, 1992). For example, newborns will look longer at a face that resembles others they have seen than at a face that is completely unfamiliar (Walton & Bower, 1993). This suggests that they have formed a mental representation of facial features to which they can compare new faces.

ATTENTION: FROM UNFOCUSED SCANNING TO FOCUSED PLANFULNESS   If you've ever observed very young children, you know that they are readily distracted. In other words, they seem unable to focus their attention exclusively on whatever task they are currently performing. As children grow older, however, they acquire an increasing ability to concentrate. Thus, by the time they are about seven years old, they can learn to tune out such distractions as music or other background stimuli (e.g., Higgins & Turnure, 1984). Since our information-processing capacities are quite limited (refer to chapters 6 and 7), this growing ability to focus on the most important aspects of a given situation offers important advantages. Unfortunately, not all children show this increasing ability to focus their attention. Youngsters suffering from **attention-deficit hyperactivity disorder** (ADHD) are unable to concentrate their attention on any task for more than a few minutes. As a result, they quickly become bored in school and cause many problems for teachers, classmates, and themselves. They talk during quiet periods, ignore social rules, leave their seats, and generally create disturbance in the classroom. They always seem to be operating on "high," and they charge through each day with excessive energy. Their behavior leaves teachers frazzled and often leads to rejection by their classmates (Henker & Whalen, 1989). It is estimated that 3 to 5 percent of all school-age children suffer from this disorder, although it is four or five times as common among boys as girls.

Fortunately, ADHD can be effectively treated with medication and through therapy in which appropriate behavior is modeled (Barkley, 1990). Family intervention, too, is important. The unruly behavior of ADHD children often strains parents' patience to the breaking point, leading parents to treat the children in a punitive manner—which tends to increase rather than decrease the wild behavior. So there is definitely hope for ADHD children, but only if they receive appropriate treatment. And assuring that they receive

Information-Processing Approach: An approach to understanding human memory that emphasizes the encoding, storage, and later retrieval of information.

Attention-Deficit Hyperactivity Disorder: A psychological disorder in which children are unable to concentrate their attention on any task for more than a few minutes.

it seems crucial: If left untreated, ADHD children often develop into hostile, impulsive adults.

ATTENTION-DEFICIT HYPERACTIVITY DISORDER

Children with *attention-deficit hyperactivity disorder* cannot focus their attention on any task for more than a few minutes. As a result, they quickly become bored and often disrupt classroom activities.

MEMORY: IMPROVING STRATEGIES, IMPROVING PERFORMANCE   Memory is a key aspect of cognition, so it is hardly surprising that it improves in many ways as children grow older. With respect to short-term memory, a key change is the increasing use of various strategies for retaining information. As noted in chapter 6, rehearsal is perhaps the most important of these. As you might expect, five- and six-year-olds are much less likely than adults to repeat information to themselves as they try to memorize it. By the time children are eight years old, however, they do engage in simple forms of rehearsal. And when they are ten or eleven, they combine various items or pieces of information and rehearse these larger chunks of information (e.g., Kunzinger, 1985).

With respect to long-term memory, it is clear that as children mature, they expand their knowledge base in numerous ways. Many researchers now believe that a key aspect of cognitive development involves expansion of *domain-specific knowledge*, knowledge pertaining to specific areas of life and activity. As domain-specific knowledge increases, new information relating to any given domain becomes more meaningful and familiar; as a result, it is processed more efficiently and enters more readily into long-term memory (e.g., Bjorklund, 1987).

Children also acquire increasingly sophisticated **scripts**, or mental representations of expected sequences of events for various situations, as they grow older. This helps them improve their *episodic memory*—memory of events in their own lives. Children as young as three can describe simple scripts for everyday activities. And recent findings indicate that even those who lack the verbal skills to describe sequences of events—children only one or two years old—can act out rudimentary scripts for various situations with toys (e.g., Bauer & Mandler, 1992). One of my own early scripts was for visits to the dentist, and it went something like this: "First you go into a room with bright lights; then you sit in a big, cold chair; and then a man in a white coat sticks things into your mouth and hurts you." You can imagine how eager I was to follow *that* script!

METACOGNITION: THINKING ABOUT—AND UNDERSTANDING—THINKING   Another important aspect of cognitive development that fits very well with the information-processing approach is **metacognition**: awareness and understanding of our own cognitive processes. Cognitive psychologists believe that in order to operate most effectively, cognitive systems such as our minds must be aware of themselves. They must be able to generate thoughts such as "I'd better read this paragraph again; I didn't understand it the first time," or "I'd better make a note of that information—it seems important, and I may want to use it later." Clearly, young children lack such insights in comparison to older children and adults. Yet they are not totally lacking where metacognition is concerned. Three-year-olds understand that thinking about other things can hinder their performance on a task (Miller & Zalenski, 1982). And by the time they are four or five, most children realize that other people can hold false beliefs (Harris, 1991) and that their own memories are limited (Miller & Zalenski, 1982).

Gradually, as they develop increasing understanding of how their own minds operate, children acquire new and more sophisticated strategies for maximizing their own efficiency. They combine various strategies for en-

KEY QUESTIONS

- According to the information-processing perspective, what does cognitive development involve?

- What changes occur in children's ability to focus their attention as they grow older?

- What strategies do children acquire for enhancing their short-term and long-term memory?

- What is metacognition?

Script: Mental representation of the sequence of events in a given situation.

Metacognition: Awareness and understanding of our own cognitive processes.

hancing attention and memory, monitor their progress toward chosen goals, and examine their own understanding of information and feedback as it is received. In short, they become increasingly capable of self-regulation with respect to their cognitive processes as well as other aspects of their behavior. Please see the **Key Concept** page for a comparison of Piaget's theory and the information-processing approach to cognitive development.

MORAL DEVELOPMENT: REASONING ABOUT "RIGHT" AND "WRONG"

Is it ever right to cheat on an exam? What about cheating on your taxes? Is it okay to remove the pollution-control system from your car in order to improve its gas mileage? As adults, we often ponder such moral questions—issues concerning what is right and what is wrong in a given context—taking careful account of many different factors. But what about children: How do they deal with such issues? This is the key question addressed in research on **moral development**—changes in the ability to reason about what is right and what is wrong in a given situation (Vitz, 1990). Perhaps the most influential theory dealing with moral development is the one proposed by Lawrence Kohlberg (1984).

KOHLBERG'S STAGES OF MORAL UNDERSTANDING   Building on views proposed by Piaget (1932/1965), Kohlberg studied boys and men and suggested that human beings move through three distinct levels of moral reasoning, each divided into two separate phases. In order to determine the stage of moral development participants had reached, Kohlberg asked them to consider imaginary moral dilemmas, situations in which competing courses of action were possible. Participants then indicated the course of action they would choose, and explained why. According to Kohlberg, it is the explanations, not the decisions themselves, that are crucial, because it is the reasoning displayed in these explanations that reveals individuals' stage of moral development. One such dilemma is as follows:

> A man's wife is ill with a rare kind of cancer. There is a drug that may save her, but it is very expensive. The pharmacist who discovered this medicine will sell it for $2,000, but the man has only $1,000. He asks the pharmacist to let him pay part of the cost now and the rest later, but the pharmacist refuses. Being desperate, the man steals the drug. Should he have done so? Why—or why not?

Let's consider each level of moral development described by Kohlberg, and the kind of reasoning he feels would be indicative of it.

Moral Development:
Changes in the capacity to reason about actions' rightness or wrongness that occur with age.

Preconventional Level (of morality): According to Kohlberg, the earliest stage of moral development, in which individuals judge morality in terms of the effects produced by various actions.

The preconventional level.   At the first level of moral development, which Kohlberg terms the **preconventional level,** children judge morality largely in terms of consequences: They perceive actions that lead to rewards as good or acceptable and ones that lead to punishments as bad or unacceptable. Within the preconventional level, Kohlberg describes two distinct phases. At Stage 1, known as the *punishment-and-obedience orientation,* children cannot grasp the existence of two points of view in a moral dilemma. As a result, they unquestioningly accept an authority's perspective as their own. For example, a child at this stage might state: "The man should steal the drug because if he lets his wife die, he'll get in trouble. He'll be blamed for not spending the money to help her." At Stage 2, known as the *naive hedonistic orientation,* children are aware of the fact that people can have different points of view in a moral dilemma. Thus, they judge morality in

Two Views of Cognitive Development

Piaget's Theory

- There is tension between these drives: assimilation and accommodation.
- Cognitive development is an invariant movement through a fixed order of *stages*.
- New cognitive abilities appear at each stage.

Sensorimotor Stage
0–2
The child begins to interact with the environment; the idea of permanence develops.

Preoperational Stage
2–6 or 7
The child begins to represent the world symbolically.

Concrete Operations Stage
7–11 or 12
The child learns to appreciate such principles as conservation; logical thought emerges.

Formal Operations Stage
12–adulthood
The adolescent becomes capable of logical thought.

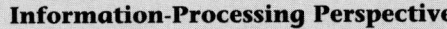

Information-Processing Perspective

- Children's capacities to process information increase with age.
- Neither the rate nor the order of these changes is invariant.
- Improvements occur with respect to each capacity.

Sensory Processing
The child gains in ability to notice subtle features of the external world.

Attention
Children's ability to focus attention and make plans increases with age.

Memory
Children acquire increasing capacity plus more sophisticated techniques for enhancing memory.

Metacognition
As children grow, their capacity to regulate their own cognitive processes increases.

terms of what satisfies their own needs or the needs of others. A child at Stage 2 might say: "The man shouldn't steal the drug unless he's so crazy about his wife that he can't live without her. He's running a big risk in stealing the drug."

The conventional level. As their cognitive abilities increase, Kohlberg reasons, children enter a second level of moral development, where they are aware of some of the complexities of the social order. People at the **conventional level** judge morality in terms of what supports and preserves the laws and rules of their society. This level, too, is divided by Kohlberg into two distinct stages. In Stage 3, known as the *good boy–good girl orientation,* people judge morality in terms of adhering to social rules or norms, but only with respect to people they know personally. They want the approval of such persons and seek it by judging morality in terms of adherence to norms or rules accepted by these persons. Thus, a child at this stage might state: "It's OK to steal the drug, because no one will think you are bad if you do. If you don't and let your wife die, you'll never be able to look anyone in the face again."

In Stage 4, known as the *social-order–maintaining orientation,* people can extend judgments of morality to include the perspectives of third persons, not just their own and those of people they know. Thus, they feel that laws must be applied equally to all, not only to friends or relatives. In the drug-stealing example, a child at Stage 4 who argues for stealing the drug might state: "The man should steal the drug since he took a marriage vow to stand by his wife. It's wrong to steal, so he should expect to pay for this action."

The postconventional level. Finally, in adolescence or early adulthood, many—though by no means all—individuals enter a third level known as the **postconventional level,** or principled level. At this stage people judge morality in terms of abstract principles and values. Again, Kohlberg suggests that there are two stages within the postconventional level. At Stage 5, known as the *social contract/legalistic orientation,* individuals are aware of the fact that any single rule system is only one of many possibilities and can envision alternatives to the existing social order. Thus, they realize that laws sometimes can be inconsistent with the rights of individuals or the interests of the majority and that such laws should be changed. Individuals at this stage of moral development might reason: "There is a law against stealing, and it represents the will of the majority—how people have decided to live together in society. By living in that society, the man agrees to maintain its laws, so stealing the drug is a violation of this agreement."

Finally, in Stage 6, known as the *universal ethical principle orientation,* individuals judge the morality of actions in terms of self-chosen ethical principles. Persons who attain this highest level of moral development believe that certain obligations and values transcend the laws of society at any given point in time. The rules they follow are abstract and are based on inner conscience rather than on external sources of authority. Individuals at Stage 6 might argue for stealing the drug as follows: "If the man doesn't steal the drug, he is putting property above human life; this makes no sense. People could live together without private property, but a respect for human life is essential." An overview of the stages described by Kohlberg is provided in Table 8.2.

EVIDENCE CONCERNING KOHLBERG'S THEORY Do we really pass through the series of stages described by Kohlberg? While not all evidence is consistent with Kohlberg's theory, many studies do support at least its broad outlines. A review of many cross-sectional studies with a total of more than 6,000 participants indicated that moral maturity, as measured by Kohlberg's

Conventional Level *(of morality): According to Kohlberg, a stage of moral development during which individuals judge morality largely in terms of existing social norms or rules.*

Postconventional Level *(of morality): According to Kohlberg, the final stage of moral development, in which individuals judge morality in terms of abstract principles.*

LEVEL/STAGE	DESCRIPTION
Preconventional Level	
Stage 1: Punishment-and-obedience orientation	Morality judged in terms of consequences.
Stage 2: Naive hedonistic orientation	Morality judged in terms of what satisfies own needs or those of others.
Conventional Level	
Stage 3: Good boy–good girl orientation	Morality judged in terms of adherence to social rules or norms with respect to personal acquaintances.
Stage 4: Social-order–maintaining orientation	Morality judged in terms of social rules or laws applied universally, not just to acquaintances.
Postconventional Level	
Stage 5: Legalistic orientation	Morality judged in terms of human rights, which may transcend laws.
Stage 6: Universal ethical principle orientation	Morality judged in terms of self-chosen ethical principles.

TABLE 8.2

Kohlberg's Theory of Moral Development: A Summary

According to Kohlberg, we move through three distinct levels of moral development.

system, does increase with age (Rest, 1986). Interestingly, in several of these studies, no participants achieved Stage 6 reasoning. This led Kohlberg to conclude that Stage 6 should be eliminated from the theory: It seems to demand a level of sophistication with respect to moral reasoning that few human beings ever achieve.

Existing evidence suggests, then, that in many cultures many persons do move through the stages described by Kohlberg. However, such progress is more variable and less universal than Kohlberg assumed. In addition, moral reasoning is strongly affected by environmental factors, such as education (Rest & Thomas, 1985), parents' child-rearing practices (Walker & Taylor, 1991), and culture. For information on the effects of culture, please see the **Perspectives on Diversity** section.

PERSPECTIVES ON DIVERSITY

Moral Development: Universal or Culture-Related?

A s described earlier in the chapter, research indicates that in technologically advanced cultures, many individuals do seem to move through the stages outlined by Kohlberg. But what about other cultures? Is the same progression apparent? Growing evidence indicates that it is not. For example, in isolated peasant and tribal communities, few if any people reach Stage 4 (Boyes & Walker, 1988). This finding does not seem to reflect communication problems, because even in these cultures research participants understand the dilemmas presented to them and view the issues raised as important and familiar (Walker, 1988). Rather, the absence of Stage 4 and subsequent stages of moral reasoning seems to be related to the absence of contact with formalized systems of government, law, and ethics. Experience with such systems seems to be needed for emergence of the later stages of moral reasoning.

Evidence for these conclusions is provided by comparison of American children and kibbutz-reared Israeli children (Fuchs et al., 1986). Because children on kibbutzim are raised in an environment where they participate regularly in the cooperative institutions of their society, we might expect that they would score higher in moral development than Americans of comparable age—and they do. Kibbutz-raised children score higher on moral development than Americans from age thirteen on, and a higher proportion eventually reach Stage 5.

Do these findings mean that Kohlberg's theory is applicable only to Western societies, with their emphasis on institutionalized moral values and individual rights? One way to find out would be to examine the development of moral reasoning in societies that are as complex as Western ones but that accept contrasting philosophical traditions—ones emphasizing a collectivistic orientation and collective solutions to individual problems.

One such society that has been studied in this respect is India (Vasudev & Hummel, 1987). In this research, moral-reasoning interviews were conducted with urban middle-class and upper-middle-class people ranging in age from eleven to over fifty. The religions of participants included Hindu, Jain, and Sikh—religions emphasizing as basic moral values nonviolence and the interrelatedness of all forms of life. Results indicated that, consistent with previous research, stage of moral development did increase with age. Indeed, about 20 percent of adults gave postconventional responses. These findings suggest that Kohlberg's theory applies to cultures other than Western ones. However, additional findings indicated that cultural factors did play an important role in shaping participants' responses. Specifically, Indian cultural traditions tend to emphasize collective solutions to moral dilemmas rather than appeals to private conscience. Thus, many participants were reluctant to select a solution to the problem of the man and the drug. Instead, they suggested, the solution should be worked out in terms of the needs of the entire society, not those of a single individual. Similar comments have also been obtained from Israeli and Chinese participants (Hwang, 1986).

What do these findings mean? One interpretation is that Kohlberg's theory does indeed tap universal dimensions of moral reasoning—dimensions that exist in all cultures. However, such reasoning occurs in a cultural context and cannot be entirely separated from it. Where morality is concerned, then, we must consider not only universal principles but important culture-based factors as well.

GENDER DIFFERENCES IN MORAL DEVELOPMENT: IS KOHLBERG'S THEORY GENDER-BIASED? Perhaps the most controversial aspect of Kohlberg's theory is the finding, reported in several early studies designed to test it, that females lag behind males in terms of Kohlberg's stages of moral reasoning (Holstein, 1976). In response to such findings, Gilligan (1982) suggested that Kohlberg's theory was gender-biased. She pointed out that Kohlberg did not include females in his original research and that his theory judges morality solely in terms of the ability to reason abstractly about moral dilemmas. In this respect, it overlooks another vital basis for moral judgments: *concern for others.* Gilligan proposed that females may move through several stages of moral development based on this factor. Thus, she argued that males and females are equal in terms of the complexity of their moral reasoning; they merely emphasize different aspects of this process.

These suggestions are intriguing, but subsequent research suggested that, in fact, males and females do not seem to differ either in their levels of moral development or in the basis for their moral reasoning (Walker & DeVries, 1985). The difference between males and females reported in early studies has not been found in more recent investigations, and, contrary to Gilligan's views, males and females do not appear to differ with respect to whether they base their moral decisions on concerns for impersonal rights or on caring for others (Walker, 1988). In sum, there is little evidence for the view that the two sexes focus on different aspects of moral dilemmas.

Despite these findings, Gilligan's concerns about Kohlberg's theory have yielded an important benefit: They call attention to the fact that evaluating moral development solely in terms of rights and justice is not enough; concern for the welfare of others must also be taken into account (Galotti, Kozberg, & Farmer, 1991).

KEY QUESTIONS

- According to Kohlberg's theory, what are the major stages of moral development through which all persons pass?
- What do research findings indicate with respect to Kohlberg's theory?
- What do research findings indicate with respect to gender differences in moral reasoning?

SOCIAL AND EMOTIONAL DEVELOPMENT DURING CHILDHOOD: Forming Relationships with Others

Cognitive development is certainly a crucial aspect of human growth. Yet it does not occur in a social vacuum. At the same time infants and children are acquiring the capacities to think, reason, and use language, they are also gaining the basic experiences, skills, and emotions that permit them to form close relationships with others and to interact with them effectively. How does such social and emotional development occur? What are some of its crucial milestones? It is on these and related questions that we'll focus next.

Learning Objective 8.11
Describe the course of children's emotional development, including temperament and attachment.

Learning Objective 8.12
Compare and contrast the various views on the development of gender identity.

EMOTIONAL DEVELOPMENT AND TEMPERAMENT

At what age do infants begin to experience and demonstrate discrete emotions? They can't describe their subjective feelings, of course, so efforts to answer these questions have focused primarily on discrete facial expressions—outward signs of distinct emotions. Research on emotional development has documented that such expressions appear within the first few months of life (Izard, 1992). Infants as young as two months old demonstrate social smiling in response to human faces. They show laughter by the time they are three or four months old (Sroufe & Waters, 1976). And other emotions, such as anger, sadness, and surprise, also appear quite early and are readily recognizable to adults.

As they grow older, children also develop increasing ability to regulate their own emotional reactions. Infants have very little capacity to regulate their own emotions, but preschoolers engage in active efforts to understand and control their own internal states. For example, they may cover their eyes or ears to avoid exposure to stimuli they find disturbing, and they may talk to themselves to reduce anxiety ("Mommy said she'd be right back"). Such abilities increase throughout the grade-school years. By the time they are ten, most children can engage in fairly sophisticated strategies for regulating their own emotions, such as lowering their expectations in order to minimize the threat of failure (Altshuler & Ruble, 1989).

TEMPERAMENT: INDIVIDUAL DIFFERENCES IN EMOTIONAL "STYLE" Do you know anyone who is always cheerful and upbeat—a true optimist?

And what about the other extreme—someone who is reserved and usually irritable and gloomy? Psychologists refer to such stable individual differences in the quality and intensity of emotional reactions as **temperament.** Growing evidence suggests that these differences are present very early in life—perhaps even at birth (e.g., Kagan & Snidman, 1991). In fact, systematic research on temperament suggests that infants can be divided into three basic categories in this respect (Thomas & Chess, 1977). The first category, about 40 percent of infants, are described as *easy children.* They quickly establish regular routines in infancy, are generally cheerful, and adapt easily to new experiences. In contrast, about 10 percent are *difficult children.* They are irregular in daily routines, are slow to accept new situations or experiences, and show many negative reactions, such as crying more than other infants. Another 15 percent or so can be described as *slow-to-warm-up children.* They are relatively inactive and apathetic and show mild negative reactions to many new situations or experiences. Finally, the remaining 35 percent of infants cannot readily be classified under one of these headings. Obviously, parents of children in the first group have a much easier time dealing with their offspring than those in the latter categories.

How stable are such differences in temperament? Research findings present a mixed picture. On the one hand, several studies indicate that some aspects of temperament—attentiveness, activity level, and irritability—are quite stable (Ruff et al., 1990). For example, in one study (Kagan, Snidman, & Arcus, 1992), researchers tested several hundred infants when they were four months old and, on the basis of these tests, classified the babies as either *high-reactive* or *low-reactive.* High-reactive infants showed fretting, crying, and a high level of motor activity when exposed to unfamiliar events (tape-recorded human voices, unpleasant tastes, moving mobiles). In contrast, low-reactive infants showed low motor activity and minimal crying in response to the same events. When the babies were fourteen months old, the researchers tested both groups again by observing their reactions as they encountered unfamiliar rooms, people, toys, and procedures (for example, placement of a blood-pressure cuff on their arm, facial and vocal disapproval from the researcher, a request to test liquid from a dropper). Results indicated that 50 percent of the high-reactive children showed a high level of fear, while only 10 percent of the low-reactive infants did so. Similar results were obtained when the children were tested again at twenty-one months of age. In related research (Kagan, Reznick, & Snidman, 1988), differences such as these have been found to remain stable into middle childhood.

On the other hand, however, additional studies indicate that long-term stability in various aspects of temperament may occur only for persons who are relatively extreme on these dimensions (Kagan, Reznick, & Gibbons, 1989). So, although temperament may be influenced by genetic factors and tends to be quite stable, it can be altered by experience and by external factors such as child-rearing practices (Otaki et al., 1986). Whatever the relative contributions of genetic and environmental factors to temperament, individual differences in temperament have important implications for social development. For example, a much higher proportion of difficult than easy children experience behavioral problems later in life (Chess & Thomas, 1984). They find it more difficult to adjust to school, to form friendships, and to get along with others. In addition, many high-reactive children demonstrate shyness as they grow older and enter an increasingly broad range of social situations. Shyness can be a

Temperament: Stable individual differences in the quality and intensity of emotional reactions.

KEY QUESTIONS

- What recognizable facial expressions are shown by infants?

- In what ways do children's abilities to regulate their own emotions develop with age?

- When do differences in temperament—consistent individual differences in the quality and intensity of emotions—first appear?

serious problem for them and may adversely influence many aspects of later social development (Kagan, Reznick, & Snidman, 1988).

ATTACHMENT: THE BEGINNINGS OF LOVE Do infants love their parents? They can't say so directly, but by the time they are six or seven months old, most babies appear to have a strong emotional bond with the persons who care for them (Ainsworth, 1973; Lamb, 1977). Infants recognize their mothers, fathers, and other caregivers, smile at them more than at other persons, seek them out, and protest when separated from them. This strong affectional tie between infants and their caregivers is known as **attachment** and is, in an important sense, the first form of love for others that we experience.

What are the origins of this initial form of love? One explanation emphasizes the role of learning. Caregivers provide for infants' physical needs, so caregivers both offer and are associated with many forms of reward. Thus, both classical conditioning and operant conditioning may play a role in the formation of attachment. While these basic forms of learning probably do contribute to attachment, however, there are strong grounds for questioning the belief that they are its most important foundations. For example, attachment relationships, once they are formed, tend to persist over long periods of time, even when the persons to whom bonds of attachments are formed are absent or no longer provide various forms of reinforcement (Ainsworth, 1969). Think about your own feelings of attachment to your mother or other loved ones; your bonds to these persons persist even if you have not seen them for many months and have not been provided with reinforcements by them during this period.

An alternative view of attachment is suggested by **ethological theory**, first proposed by Bowlby (1969). According to this theory, infants are born with a set of behaviors that elicit parental care and so increase the infants' chances of survival. These attachment-facilitating behaviors include sucking, clinging, crying, smiling, gazing at the caregiver's face, and crawling after the caregiver (once the baby learns to crawl). As infants emit these behaviors, they elicit attention and caring behavior from adults. This, in turn, forms the foundation for the development of reciprocal bonds of attachment.

Measuring attachment: Reactions to the strange situation test. How can the strength of attachment be measured? Mary Ainsworth and her colleagues (e.g., Ainsworth et al., 1978) devised an approach to this task in which researchers observe babies' behavior in situations where fear and distress are aroused. Presumably, children will seek comfort from their caregiver in this context, and the stronger their bonds of attachment, the greater the comfort they will derive from this person's presence—and the stronger their fear in his or her absence. To assess the strength of attachment, then, researchers expose babies to the sequence of events shown in Table 8.3 (on page 302). These involve the arrival of mother and baby in an unfamiliar room, entry of a stranger into the room, departure by the mother, return of the mother, and so on. (I say "mother" because most research has focused on mothers and their infants.) As each event occurs, babies' reactions are carefully observed. Do they cry when the mother leaves? How do they react when she returns? Do they appear more confident in her presence, despite the presence of a stranger? These are the kind of questions considered.

When tested in the **strange situation test**, as it is often termed, young children often show one of four different patterns. Some show **secure attachment**: They evidence discomfort when their mother leaves the room, are not comforted by the presence of a stranger, and seek contact with their mother when she returns. In contrast, other children show **avoidant attachment**: They don't cry when their mother leaves, and they don't seek contact with

Attachment: A strong affectional bond between infants and their caregivers.

Ethological Theory (of attachment): A theory suggesting that infants are born with a set of behaviors that elicit parental care and so increase the infants' chances of survival.

Strange Situation Test: A procedure for studying attachment in which mothers leave their children alone with a stranger for several minutes and then return.

Secure Attachment: A pattern of attachment in which infants actively seek contact with their mother and take comfort from her presence when they are reunited with her during the strange situation test.

Avoidant Attachment: A pattern of attachment in which infants don't cry when their mother leaves them alone during the strange situation test.

TABLE 8.3

EPISODE	PERSONS PRESENT	DURATION	EVENTS/PROCEDURES
1	Mother and baby	30 seconds	Experimenter brings mother and baby to room; leaves
2	Mother and baby	3 minutes	Baby plays; mother seated
3	Mother, baby, stranger	3 minutes	Stranger enters; talks to mother
4	Stranger and baby	3 minutes (or less)	Mother leaves room; stranger remains; offers comfort to baby
5	Mother and baby	3 minutes (or more)	Mother returns, greets baby, offers comfort
6	Baby alone	3 minutes (or less)	Mother leaves room
7	Stranger and baby	3 minutes (or less)	Stranger enters room, offers comfort
8	Mother and baby	3 minutes	Mother returns; offers comfort

Sequence of Events in the Strange Situation

The *strange situation* is used to study infants' attachment to their mothers. Researchers carefully study the infants' reactions to each of the events described here so as to determine the strength and nature of their attachment bonds to their mothers.
(*Source*: Adapted from Ainsworth et al., 1978.)

HARLOW'S STUDIES OF ATTACHMENT

Although the wire "mothers" used in Harlow's experiments provided the monkey babies with nourishment, the babies preferred the soft cloth "mothers," which provided contact comfort. What do these famous experiments demonstrate?

her when she returns. Still others show **resistant attachment**: They reject their mother angrily when she returns after separation. Finally, a fourth group shows **disorganized attachment**: disorganized or even contradictory reactions to their mother after separation. Such differences in patterns of attachment appear to be important. For example, securely attached children seem to experience fewer behavioral problems during later childhood than those showing other patterns (Fagot & Kavanaugh, 1990). Further, these different patterns of attachment seem to persist, and they may even affect the nature of romantic relationships during adult life (Simpson, 1990; Vormbrock, 1993).

Contact comfort and attachment: The soft touch of love. Have you ever known an infant who was strongly attached to a cuddly toy or even to an old blanket? My daughter Jessica certainly was; she had a stuffed monkey she slept with every night and to which she clung whenever she was upset. The fact that so many children show such behavior suggests that another factor—close physical contact between infants and their caregivers—may also play an important role in attachment. In short, attachment rests partly on the hugging, cuddling, and caresses babies receive from adults.

The research that first established this fact was conducted by Harry Harlow and his colleagues. When Harlow began this research, infant attachment was the farthest thing from his mind. He was interested in testing the effects of brain damage on learning. Since he could not perform such experiments with humans, he chose to work with rhesus monkeys. In order to prevent baby monkeys from catching various diseases, Harlow raised them alone, away from their mothers. This practice led to a surprising observation. Many of the infants seemed to become quite attached to small scraps of cloth present in their cages. They held tightly to these "security blankets" and protested strongly when they were removed for cleaning. This led Harlow to wonder whether the babies actually needed contact with soft materials. To find out, he built two artificial "mothers." One consisted of bare wire, while the other possessed a soft terrycloth cover. Conditions were then arranged so that the monkey babies could obtain milk only from the wire mother. According to the conditioning explanation of attachment, they should soon have developed a strong bond to this cold wire mother. After all, she was the source of all their nourishment. In fact, this was not what happened. The infants spent almost all of their time clinging tightly to the soft cloth-covered mother. Only when driven by pangs of hunger did they leave her to obtain milk from the wire mother. Based on these and related findings, Harlow concluded that a monkey baby's attachment to its mother rests, at least in part, on her ability to satisfy its need for *contact comfort*—direct contact with soft objects. The satisfaction of other physical needs, such as the need for food, is not enough.

Do such effects occur among human babies as well? Some studies seem to suggest that they may. For example, two- and three-year-old children placed in a strange room play for longer periods of time without becoming distressed when they have a security blanket present than when it is absent (Passman & Weisberg, 1975). In fact, they play almost as long as they do when their mother is in the room. These findings suggest that for blanket-attached children, the presence of this object provides the same kind of comfort and reassurance as that provided by their mothers. So human infants, too, may have a need for contact comfort, and the gentle hugs, caresses, and cuddling they obtain from their caregivers may play a role in the formation of attachment.

Key Questions

- What is attachment?
- How does the strange situation test measure the strength of attachment?
- How does contact comfort affect attachment?

Gender: *The Development of Gender Identity and Gender-Stereotyped Behavior*

From the moment that children are born, **gender**—the fact that they belong to one sex or the other—plays a crucial role in their lives. The first words spoken about newborns often refer to their sex. And from the instant that parents hear a nurse or physician announce "It's a girl" or "It's a boy," they begin to think about and behave toward their child in ways that differ depending on its sex. In this section we'll consider the important effects of gender on social development.

Gender Identity: Some Contrasting Views At what age does a child become aware of being a girl or a boy—of belonging to one of the two sexes? Existing evidence suggests that this process begins very early in life. By the time they are two, many children have learned to use gender labels appropriately; they refer to themselves as a boy or a girl and correctly label others as belonging to one sex or the other. However, they are still uncertain about the stability of gender. When asked, "Could you ever become a daddy?" many little girls up until the age of about three and a half say yes, and little boys indicate that they could become a mother. Between three and a half and four and a half, however, children begin to understand the stability of gender over time—**gender constancy.** Is this delay due to children's cognitive immaturity? Research evidence suggests that, in fact, it may stem from another factor: a child's lack of knowledge about genital differences between the sexes. Thus, children as young as three who are aware of genital differences show a grasp of gender constancy (Bem, 1989).

Through what process do children acquire gender identity? Several different theories have been proposed. According to *social learning theory*, two

Resistant Attachment: A pattern of attachment in which infants reject their mother and refuse to be comforted by her after she leaves them alone during the strange situation test.

Disorganized Attachment: A pattern of attachment in which infants show contradictory reactions to their mother after being reunited with her during the strange situation test.

Gender: An individual's membership in one of the two sexes.

Gender Constancy: Children's understanding that gender is stable over time.

kinds of learning are involved: observational learning and operant conditioning. Through observational learning, children gradually come to match the behaviors of same-sex individuals, especially those of their parents. Further, adults actively reinforce such imitation. As children become increasingly similar to their same-sex parent, they gradually organize recognition of their own behavior and these similarities into the idea that they are "a girl like Mommy"or "a boy like Daddy."

An alternative view of how children acquire gender identity has been proposed by Bem (1984). This approach, known as **gender schema theory,** focuses primarily on the cognitive mechanisms underlying gender identity. It suggests that acquisition of gender identity rests in part on the development of *gender schemas.* These are cognitive frameworks reflecting children's experiences with their society's beliefs about the attributes of males and females, such as instructions from their parents, observations of how males and females typically behave, and so on. Once a gender schema takes shape, it influences children's processing of a wide range of social information (Martin & Little, 1990). For example, children with a firmly established gender schema tend to categorize the behavior of others as either masculine or feminine. Similarly, they may process and recall behaviors consistent with their own gender schema more easily than behaviors not consistent with it. In short, for children possessing such schemas, gender is a key concept or dimension, one they often use in attempts to make sense out of the social world.

Which of these theories is most accurate? At present, it is difficult to choose between them; there is some evidence consistent with both, so it seems likely that both social learning and cognitive processes are involved in the formation of gender identity.

GENDER-STEREOTYPED BELIEFS AND BEHAVIOR At the same time that children are acquiring their gender identity, they also learn much more about their own society's views concerning gender. Children acquire beliefs about the supposed characteristics of males and females—gender-role stereotypes or beliefs—and they develop a basic understanding of how their society expects males and females to behave—gender-stereotyped behaviors. Unfortunately, such stereotypes are not neutral in content: At least in Western cultures, they generally attribute more admired characteristics and behaviors to males than to females. Thus, both boys and girls learn that males are—supposedly—independent, aggressive, dominant, and adventurous, and that females are—again, supposedly—emotional, gentle, submissive, and passive (Deaux, 1993; Deaux & Lewis, 1986). Research on such gender-role stereotypes suggests that they increase in strength throughout childhood (Best et al., 1977).

As you might think, stereotypes and beliefs about **gender roles,** or expected behaviors of males and females, differ greatly from one culture to another as well as across time within a given culture. Further, there has certainly been some change in gender stereotypes in many countries in recent decades. Yet such stereotypes continue to persist and to exert strong effects on developing children (e.g., Deaux, 1993).

How do children acquire gender-stereotyped beliefs and behaviors? Much of the answer involves the impact of various environmental influences, such as their families, teachers, and peers. All of these agents tend to behave in ways that strengthen beliefs that boys and girls differ in important ways and that certain activities are appropriate for boys and others for girls (McGuire, 1988; Weisner & Wilson-Mitchell, 1990). Some psychologists, however, have proposed that genetic factors, too, may play a role. For example, Eleanor Maccoby (1990), a noted developmental psychologist, proposes

Gender Schema Theory: A theory that children develop a cognitive framework, or schema, reflecting the beliefs of their society concerning the characteristics and roles of males and females; this gender schema then strongly affects the processing of new social information.

Gender Roles: Beliefs about how males and females are expected to behave in many situations.

that hormonal differences between girls and boys influence their styles of play, with boys showing rough, noisy movement and girls calm, gentle actions. Such differences, Maccoby contends, may place girls at a distinct disadvantage in mixed-gender groups. In such contexts, girls behave more politely than boys, waiting for a turn to speak—which may never come! And they often attempt to exert influence by polite requests rather than through demands or physical force. Unfortunately, males, who have learned to assert their independence in order to maintain their high status, are unlikely to respond to such tactics, with the result that girls may exert little influence. As Maccoby (1990) notes, such differences in style of social interaction are potentially important, especially during the current period of profound change, when many females are moving into positions of power and authority.

KEY QUESTIONS

- When do children acquire gender constancy—understanding of the fact that their sexual identity is stable?
- How do children acquire gender identity and gender-stereotyped beliefs?

ADOLESCENCE: *Between Child and Adult*

When does childhood end? When does adulthood start? Since development is a continuous process, there are no hard-and-fast answers to these questions. Rather, every culture decides for itself just where the dividing line falls. Many cultures mark this passage with special ceremonies; in many Western countries, however, the transition from child to adult takes place more gradually, during a period known as **adolescence**.

Adolescence has traditionally been viewed as beginning with the onset of **puberty**, a sudden spurt in physical growth accompanied by the development of sexual maturity, and as ending when individuals assume the responsibilities associated with adult life—marriage, entry into the workforce, and so on (Rice, 1992). Again, though, I wish to emphasize that when entry into adolescence occurs, how long adolescence lasts, and even whether a distinct period of adolescence is assumed to exist are all matters that are culturally defined.

CULTURE AND ADOLESCENCE

In this adolescent initiation ceremony, an Apache community celebrates a young girl's reaching puberty with an elaborate ritual.

PHYSICAL DEVELOPMENT DURING ADOLESCENCE

A sudden increase in the rate of physical growth signals the beginning of adolescence. While this growth spurt occurs for both sexes, it starts earlier for girls (at about age ten or eleven) than for boys (about age twelve or thirteen). Before this spurt, boys and girls are similar in height; in its early phases, girls are frequently taller than boys; after it is over, males are several inches taller on average than females.

This growth spurt is just one aspect of the process of puberty. Also during puberty the gonads, or sex glands, produce increased levels of sex hormones, and the external sex organs assume their adult form. Girls begin to menstruate and boys start to produce sperm. In addition to these changes, which are often referred to as *primary sexual characteristics*, both sexes undergo many other shifts relating to sexual maturity. Boys develop facial and chest hair, and their voices deepen. Girls experience breast enlargement and a widening

Adolescence: A period beginning with the onset of puberty and ending when individuals assume adult roles and responsibilities.

Puberty: The period of rapid change during which individuals reach sexual maturity and become capable of reproduction.

PUBERTY AND THE GROWTH SPURT

Girls tend to mature somewhat earlier than boys do; they experience the growth spurt one to two years sooner.

Learning Objective 8.13
Describe the characteristics of physical development during adolescence.

Learning Objective 8.14
Discuss the controversy concerning whether adolescents do or do not think like adults.

KEY QUESTIONS

- What physical changes occur during puberty?
- How does the thinking of adolescents and adults differ?
- To what extent do adolescents view themselves as invulnerable—unlikely to experience various kinds of harmful outcomes?

---

of their hips; both sexes develop pubic hair. There is great variability in the onset of sexual maturity. Most girls begin to menstruate by the time they are thirteen; but for some this process does not start until age fifteen or sixteen, and for others it may commence as early as age seven or eight. Most boys begin to produce sperm by the time they are fourteen or fifteen, but for some the process may begin considerably earlier or later. As you undoubtedly know from your own experience, many adolescents find the rapid pace of these changes disconcerting.

COGNITIVE DEVELOPMENT DURING ADOLESCENCE

Do adolescents think and reason like adults? As we saw earlier, Piaget believed that in many respects they do. Yet Piaget also contended that adolescents' thinking still falls short of that of adults in several important respects. Adolescents often use their newfound cognitive skills to construct sweeping theories about various aspects of life, but these theories are naive because of adolescents' lack of experience. Similarly, many adolescents show tendencies toward egocentrism, assuming, rigidly, that no other views but their own can be correct.

The idea that adolescents' thinking is inferior to—or at least sharply different from—that of adults is echoed by many other theorists. Elkind (1967), for one, suggested that adolescents often go seriously astray when they try to conceptualize the thoughts of other persons. For example, they fail to differentiate others' thoughts from their own. This tendency leads them to assume that they are the focus of others' attention, a phenomenon Elkind termed the *imaginary audience*. Adolescents often believe that others are focusing attention on them, and so become painfully self-conscious in many situations.

Such intriguing ideas have captured the attention of psychologists, educators, and parents for decades. But are they correct? Does the thinking of adolescents actually differ appreciably from that of adults? While some differences do appear to exist, growing evidence suggests that they are smaller than everyday experiences—and several theories—suggest (Beyth-Marom et al., in press; U.S. Office of Technology Assessment, 1991). Perhaps the most intriguing research pointing to this conclusion is that concerned with the question of whether adolescents and adults think about risk in different ways.

ADOLESCENT INVULNERABILITY: DO ADOLESCENTS THINK DIFFERENTLY THAN ADULTS DO ABOUT RISK? That adolescents engage in lots of high-risk behaviors, ranging from unprotected sex to reckless driving, is obvious. One widely accepted explanation for this fact is that young persons are characterized by what has been termed **adolescent invulnerability**—the belief that they are somehow immune from the potential harm of high-risk behaviors (Baron & Brown, 1991). Is this view correct? Surprisingly, it is not supported by all research findings. Recent studies indicate that adolescents are no more likely to view themselves as impervious to negative outcomes from risky behavior than adults (e.g., Fischoff, 1992; Quadrel, 1990; Quadrel, Fischoff, & Davis, 1993).

Why, then, are adolescents more likely to engage in high-risk behaviors? Several factors may play a role. Perhaps adolescents find the rewards associated with such actions so pleasurable that they are not deterred even by the threat of serious potential harm. Alternatively, many adolescents may belong to groups whose social norms—rules about what is and is not appropriate behavior—favor high-risk actions. In short, they engage in such actions because their friends both expect and encourage them to do so. As we'll see in chapter 11, social norms seem to play an important role in teenagers' willingness to engage in unprotected sex, even if they fully understand the risk of AIDS and other sexually transmitted diseases (e.g., Fisher & Misovich, 1989).

SOCIAL AND EMOTIONAL DEVELOPMENT DURING ADOLESCENCE

Not surprisingly, the major physical and cognitive changes occurring during adolescence are accompanied by—and closely intertwined with—equally extensive changes in social and emotional development. What are these changes? We'll examine several of the most important here.

EMOTIONAL CHANGES: THE UPS AND DOWNS OF YOUTH

Much folklore suggests that adolescents are unpredictable creatures, prone to wide swings in mood and wild outbursts of emotion. Are these assertions true? To a degree, they are. In several studies on this issue, large numbers of teenagers wore beepers and were signaled at random times throughout an entire week. When signaled, they were to enter their thoughts and feelings in a diary. Results indicated that they did in fact show frequent and large swings in mood—from the heights to the depths (Csikszentmihalyi & Larson, 1984). Moreover, these swings occurred very quickly, sometimes within only a few minutes. Older people also show shifts in mood, but theirs tend to be less frequent, slower, and smaller in magnitude. So some evidence supports the view that adolescents, at least in Western nations, are more emotionally volatile than adults.

Other widely accepted views about adolescent emotionality, however, do not appear to be correct. For example, it is often assumed that adolescence is a period of great stress and unhappiness. In fact, this does not appear to be the case. On the contrary, most teenagers report feeling quite happy and self-confident, not unhappy or distressed (Offer & Sabshin, 1984). Moreover, and again contrary to a prevailing stereotype about adolescence, most teenagers report that they enjoy relatively good relations with their parents. In other words, the so-called generation gap is much smaller and more limited in scope than many people have assumed (Galambos, 1992).

SOCIAL DEVELOPMENT: FRIENDSHIPS AND THE QUEST FOR IDENTITY

While most adolescents report mainly positive relations with their parents, family-based relationships are only a part of the total picture in the social development of adolescents. Friendships, primarily with members of one's own sex but also with members of the other sex, become increasingly important. And along with sexual maturity, of course, comes the capacity for—and interest in—romantic and sexual relationships.

Friendships confer many obvious benefits: Within these relationships adolescents practice, and improve, a wide array of social skills (Berndt, 1992) and develop the capacity for *intimacy*—the ability to share their innermost thoughts and feelings with another person. But there is a potential downside to such relationships, too. Many studies indicate that adolescents often experience intense conflict with friends—conflict that can leave serious psychological scars. And in recent years newspapers have reported many tragic events in which adolescents, filled with sexual jealousy, have attacked and even murdered their lovers or rivals—sometimes in school. In addition, adolescents can often acquire undesirable attitudes and patterns of behavior

"You're a teenager now, Lester. Your body is changing in ways that are not always easy to understand."

PHYSICAL CHANGE DURING ADOLESCENCE: SOMETIMES IT'S DISCONCERTING

The rapid pace of physical change sometimes makes adolescents feel like the character in this cartoon. (*Source: THE NEW BREED* by Randy Glasbergen. Copyright 1990, Randy Glasbergen. Reprinted by permission.)

Learning Objective 8.15
Characterize the emotional changes and social development of the adolescent.

Learning Objective 8.16
List the eight stages of life proposed by Erikson.

Learning Objective 8.17
Survey the potential problems that face an adolescent in the 1990s and the steps that can be taken to minimize some of the dangers associated with high-risk environments.

Adolescent Invulnerability:
Adolescents' belief that they are immune from the potential harm of high-risk behaviors.

ADOLESCENT FRIENDSHIPS

Friendships are an important aspect of adolescence. They can have either a positive influence, helping adolescents improve their social skills and giving them a sense of belonging, or a negative influence, encouraging undesirable attitudes and potentially harmful behaviors.

from friends (Shantz & Hartup, 1993). For example, they may be influenced to smoke, consume alcohol or other drugs, or engage in sexual relations because some of their friends do so. As Berndt (1992) notes, however, influence among adolescent friends is reciprocal, flowing in both directions, so the potential negative effects of having "wild" or risk-taking friends should not be overemphasized.

Friendships also play an important role in another key aspect of social development during adolescence—the quest for a personal identity. This process is a pivotal element in an influential theory of psychosocial development proposed by Erik Erikson (1950, 1987).

ERIKSON'S EIGHT STAGES OF LIFE

Erikson's theory deals with development across the entire life span and is, like the one proposed by Piaget, a stage theory: It suggests that all human beings pass through specific stages, or phases, of development. In contrast to Piaget's theory, however, Erikson's is concerned primarily with social rather than cognitive development. Erikson believed that each stage of life is marked by a specific crisis or conflict. Only if individuals negotiate each of these hurdles successfully can they continue to develop in a normal, healthy manner.

The stages in Erikson's theory are summarized on the **Key Concept** page. The first four occur during childhood; one takes place during adolescence; and the final three occur during the adult years. The first stage, which occurs during the first year of life, centers on the crisis of *trust versus mistrust*. Babies must trust others to satisfy their needs. If these needs are not met, a baby may fail to develop feelings of trust in others and may remain forever suspicious and wary.

The second crisis occurs during the second year of life and involves *autonomy versus shame and doubt*. During this time, toddlers are learning to regulate their own bodies and to act in independent ways. If they succeed in these tasks, they develop a sense of autonomy. But if they fail, or if they are labeled as somehow inadequate by the persons who care for them, they may experience shame and may doubt their abilities to interact effectively with the external world.

The third stage takes place during the preschool years, between the ages of three and five. The crisis then involves *initiative versus guilt*. Children at this stage, are acquiring many new physical and mental skills. Simultaneously, however, they must develop the capacity to control their impulses, some of which lead to unacceptable behavior. If they strike the right balance between feelings of initiative and feelings of guilt, all is well. However, if initiative overwhelms guilt, children may become too unruly for their own good; if guilt overwhelms initiative, they may become too inhibited.

The fourth and final stage of childhood occurs during the early school years, when children are between six and eleven or twelve years of age. This stage involves the crisis of *industry versus inferiority*. During these years, children learn to make things, use tools, and acquire many of the skills necessary for adult life. Children who successfully acquire these skills gain a sense of competence; those who do not may compare themselves unfavorably with others and suffer from low self-esteem.

Now we come to the crucial stage in Erikson's theory for this discussion of adolescence: the crisis of *identity versus role confusion*. At this time of life, individuals ask themselves, "Who am I?" "What am I really like?" "What do I want to become?" In other words, they seek to establish a clear *self-identity*— an understanding of their own unique traits and of what is really of central importance to them. These, of course, are questions individuals ask them-

Erikson's Eight Stages of Psychosocial Development

Crisis/Phase	Description
Trust versus mistrust	Infants learn either to trust the environment (if their needs are met) or to mistrust it (if their needs are not consistently met).
Autonomy versus shame and doubt	Toddlers acquire self-confidence if they learn to regulate their own bodies and act independently. If they fail or are labeled as inadequate, they experience shame and doubt. 
Initiative versus guilt	Preschoolers (3–5 years old) acquire many new physical and mental skills but must also learn to control their impulses. Unless a good balance is struck between skills and impulses, they may become either unruly or too inhibited.
Industry versus inferiority	Children (6–11 years old) acquire many skills and competencies. If they take justified pride in these, they acquire high self-esteem. If, in contrast, they compare themselves unfavorably with others, they may develop low self-esteem. 
Identity versus role confusion	 Adolescents must integrate various roles into a consistent self-identity. If they fail to do so, they may experience confusion over who they really are.
Intimacy versus isolation	Young adults must develop the ability to form deep, intimate relationships with others. If they do not, they may become socially or emotionally isolated.
Generativity versus self-absorption	During adulthood individuals must take an active interest in helping and guiding younger persons. If they do not, they may become preoccupied with selfish needs and desires.
Integrity versus despair	In the closing decades of life, individuals ask whether their lives have had any meaning. If they can answer yes, they attain a sense of integrity. If they answer no, they may experience deep despair. 

selves at many points in life. According to Erikson, though, it is crucial that these questions be answered effectively during adolescence. If they are not, individuals may drift along, uncertain of where they want to go or what they wish to accomplish. Adolescents adopt many different strategies to help them resolve their personal identity crises. They try out many different roles—the good girl/boy, the rebel, the dutiful daughter/son, the athlete—and join many different social groups. They consider many possible *social selves*—different kinds of persons they might potentially become (Markus & Nurius, 1986). Out of these experiences they gradually piece together a cognitive framework for understanding themselves—a *self-schema*. Once formed, this framework remains fairly constant and serves as a guide for the adolescent in many different contexts.

The remaining three stages in Erikson's theory relate to crises we face as adults. Since we'll consider them in our later discussion of adult development, we won't examine them here. However, they are included, and described, in the **Key Concept** on page 309.

KEY QUESTIONS

- According to Erikson's theory, what does social development involve?

- What is the most important crisis faced by adolescents?

- How do adolescents develop a clear self-schema?

ADOLESCENCE IN THE 1990s:
A Generation at Risk

Although human history is marked by repeated periods of chaos and turmoil, it can be suggested that today's adolescents face a more dangerous and threatening world than did those of preceding generations. Consider a few facts:

- Adolescents living in the United States are fifteen to twenty times more likely to die from homicide than their counterparts living in other industrialized nations.

- From 1960 to 1990, the proportion of U.S. adolescents suffering from sexually transmitted disease increased fourfold (National Center for Education in Maternal and Child Health, 1990).

- The rate of suicide among ten- to fourteen-year-olds has tripled in recent years; it has doubled among fifteen- to nineteen-year-olds (U.S. Bureau of the Census, 1991).

- Fully one-fourth of all adolescents in the United States do not live with both of their parents; among African-American children, this figure approaches 60 percent.

These and related statistics tell a sad tale. When I consider them in the light of my own experience as an adolescent during the 1950s, they take on an even deeper meaning. Although I lived in a working-class part of town, I never knew anyone whose parents were divorced. And the worst violence I ever witnessed was an occasional fistfight. The world I experienced as an adolescent was very different from the one many teenagers face today—so different that many psychologists have reached the conclusion that in the 1990s adolescents face a set of conditions and perils unlike that encountered by any recent generation (Takanishi, 1993). Let's now examine some of these problems.

DIVORCED AND PARENT-ABSENT FAMILIES At present, more than half of all marriages in the United States and many other countries end in divorce. This means that a large proportion of children and adolescents will spend at least part of their lives in a one-parent family—typically with their mothers (Norton & Moorman, 1987). Adolescents react to divorce with fear, anxiety, and feelings of insecurity about the future. Further, many blame one of the parents for the divorce: "What did she do to make Daddy leave?" "How can he desert us like this?" Some adolescents turn these feelings inward and experience considerable self-blame and guilt, sensing that they were responsible in some manner for the breakup. In addition, adolescents described as *academic underachievers*—those whose academic performance is below what their intelligence would predict (McCall, 1994)—are more likely to come from divorced than from two-parent homes.

The effects of divorce on adolescents' emotional well-being depend on many different factors, including the quality of the care they received before the divorce (Raphael et al., 1990) and the nature of the divorce, whether amicable or filled with anger and resentment. Needless to say, the more negative the feelings of the parents toward one another, the more likely the emotional harm to the adolescent.

Adolescents living in parent-absent families face another set of problems. A growing percentage of children are being born to unmarried mothers, and many of these youngsters never even know their fathers. What are the risks associated with growing up in a parent-absent (typically father-absent) family? Research findings suggest that they include increased risk for delinquent behaviors, reduced school performance, and difficulties in forming meaningful relationships—including stable romantic ones—with members of the opposite sex (Eberhardt & Schill, 1984).

DYSFUNCTIONAL FAMILIES: THE INTIMATE ENEMY During the 1950s, television shows in the United States painted a glowing picture of family life. A caring, loving mother, a kind and wise father, considerate siblings—this was the image portrayed on the screen. Even as a teenager, I knew that there was a sizable gap between these images and reality. For many of today's adolescents, however, it's not so much a gap as a chasm. Many teenagers find themselves in what are currently termed **dysfunctional families**—families that do not meet children's needs and in fact may do them serious harm (Amato, 1990; McKenry, Kotch, & Browne, 1991). Some dysfunctional families are neglectful or even engage in maltreatment of children. For example, consider what life is like for adolescents growing up in homes where one or both parents abuse alcohol or other drugs. Such youngsters can only guess what normal behavior is like, since they see very little of it at home.

Perhaps an even more disturbing form of maltreatment involves **sexual abuse**—sexual contact or activities forced on children or adolescents. Unfortunately, sexual abuse is far from rare (Kendall-Tackett, Williams, & Finkelhor, 1993); indeed, large numbers of children become the victims of such betrayal by adults every year. Sexual abuse often occurs during early childhood, but it is also an alarmingly common experience for adolescents. That it produces serious psychological harm is obvious. Symptoms common among adolescent victims of sexual abuse are depression, withdrawal, running away, substance abuse, and somatic (bodily) complaints (Morrow & Sorrell, 1989). The likelihood and magnitude of these harmful effects increase with the frequency and duration of such abuse; when the perpetrator is a close family member such as father, mother, or sibling; and when overt force is involved (Kendall-Tackett, 1991).

In sum, it is clear that because of changing social conditions, large numbers of adolescents are at considerable risk for psychological or even physical harm. Despite the adverse conditions under which they grow up, however, many of these youngsters avoid potential harm and go on to lead healthy, rewarding lives. How do they do it? This key question is being investigated in ongoing research. For information on this work and its initial conclusions, please see the **Point of It All** section.

> ### KEY QUESTIONS
>
> • What problems do adolescents face when they grow up in divorced or parent-absent families?
>
> • What problems do adolescents face when they grow up in dysfunctional families?

> ***Dysfunctional Families:*** *Families that do not meet the needs of children and in fact do them serious harm.*
>
> ***Sexual Abuse:*** *Sexual contact or activities forced on children or adolescents by other persons, usually adults.*

THE POINT OF IT ALL

Overcoming the Odds: Adolescents in High-Risk Environments

Imagine what it would be like to grow up in an environment like the one shown in the photo. Further, keep in mind that you would be desperately poor, might never have seen your father, and would have attended schools where teachers spent as much time trying to maintain order and prevent aggressive outbursts as they did teaching; that the sounds you heard at night regularly included gunshots; and that the local heroes in your neighborhood were people whose reputations rested largely on the violent acts they had committed. What kind of person would you become? There seems to be every conceivable reason for predicting that, adapting to and mirroring your surroundings, you would choose a lifestyle similar to the one you saw all around you. Yet this is not what usually happens. Despite exposure to such devastating conditions, large majorities of African-Americans and other minority groups in the United States become law-abiding citizens who hold regular jobs and are responsible spouses and parents (Taylor, 1991). How can this be so? In other words, what factors permit so many youngsters growing up in shattered inner-city neighborhoods to overcome the disadvantages of their background and become well-adjusted, productive persons?

This important question has recently come sharply into focus in the field of developmental psychology (Jessor, 1993). And although systematic research has only just begun, important conclusions have already begun to emerge. First, it seems clear that families themselves adopt and use various strategies to protect their adolescents from the risks of living in high-risk neighborhoods (Furstenberg, in press). These strategies include negotiating with schools or police when their children get into trouble; seeking out resources for their children from community-sponsored health-care facilities and other organizations; carefully monitoring their children's behavior to provide support against drug use and other dangerous behaviors modeled by friends and peers; and seeking out safer niches for their children, such as parochial schools, when neighborhood schools become too dangerous.

HIGH-RISK ENVIRONMENT: NORTHERN IRELAND

Despite the fact that millions of children around the world grow up in disadvantaged environments like this one in Northern Ireland, most of them grow up to be productive, law-abiding members of society. Psychologists are attempting to identify the factors that help such children overcome these tremendous early disadvantages.

Other research shows that parents often work with teachers and schools to establish supportive classroom climates. Parents also recognize the importance of teamwork between school and home in promoting healthy development (Anson et al., 1991). In other words, some parents in poverty-stricken neighborhoods actively cooperate with local schools to make sure that positive behaviors are encouraged in both home and school and that the messages youngsters hear in one setting are echoed in the other.

Research designed to identify the factors that help adolescents from disadvantaged backgrounds overcome their problems is relatively recent (Jessor, 1993). However, it has already helped to counter the view that children raised in difficult environments are doomed to failure and despair. On the contrary, studies completed to date or currently underway point to a much more optimistic conclusion: Given even half a chance, human beings can—and often do—rise above conditions that seemed designed to crush and maim their spirit.

ADULTHOOD AND AGING

*I*f you live for an average number of years, you will spend more than 70 percent of your life as an adult. For this reason, it is important to consider the nature and scope of the changes that occur during the adult years. Before turning to specific physical, cognitive, and social changes that occur during this longest phase of life, however, I'll pause briefly to describe two contrasting views about the nature of adult development.

ADULT DEVELOPMENT: *Internal Crises or External Life Events?*

Psychologists who have studied adult development have often adopted one of two perspectives on adult development. These are sometimes described as the *crisis (or stage) approach* and the *life-event (or timing-of-life-events) models*.

THE CRISIS APPROACH: ERIKSON'S THEORY REVISITED
We have already touched on what is certainly the most famous crisis-oriented theory of adult development, the one proposed by Erik Erikson. As you will recall, Erikson (1950, 1987) proposed that development proceeds through a series of distinct stages, each defined by a specific crisis. These crises, in turn, result from the fact that as individuals grow older, they confront new combinations of biological drives and societal demands. During adulthood, Erikson suggests, we pass through three major crises.

Describing the first of these as the crisis of *intimacy versus isolation*, Erikson refers to the fact that during late adolescence and early adulthood, individuals must develop the ability to form deep, intimate relationships with others. This does not mean mere sexual intimacy; rather, it involves the ability to form strong emotional attachments to others. In short, this first crisis of adult life centers around the capacity to love—to care profoundly and consistently for others. People who fail to resolve this crisis successfully will live their lives in isolation, unable to form truly intimate, lasting relationships.

Erikson calls the second crisis of adult life the crisis of *generativity versus self-absorption*: Individuals need to overcome selfish, self-centered concerns and take an active interest in helping and guiding the next generation. For parents, such activities are focused on their children. After the children have grown, however, the tendency toward generativity may involve serving as a *mentor*, or guide, for members of the younger generation. People who do not become parents can express generativity through providing help and guidance to many younger persons—students, coworkers, nieces, nephews, and so on. Individuals who successfully resolve this crisis and turn away from total absorption with their own lives discover new meaning. People who do not resolve this crisis, in contrast, become absorbed in their own lives and gradually cut themselves off from an important source of growth and satisfaction.

Erikson termed the final crisis of adult development *integrity versus despair*. As people reach the last decades of life, it is natural for them to look back and to ask, "Did my life have meaning?" "Did my being here really matter?" If they are able to answer affirmatively and to feel that they reached many of their goals and made positive contributions to society and others, they attain a sense of integrity. If, instead, they find their lives to be lacking on such dimensions, they may experience intense feelings of despair. As we'll see below, successful resolution of this final crisis can have important effects on how individuals come to terms with their own mortality—the inevitable fact of death—and on their psychological and physical health during the final decades of life.

Learning Objective 8.18
Compare and contrast the internal crisis versus external life-event models of adult development.

Learning Objective 8.19
Describe the physical changes that occur during early adulthood, midlife, and later life.

Learning Objective 8.20
Discuss the research on the influences of aging on cognitive performance.

Learning Objective 8.21
Outline Levinson's stage theory concerning the social changes that occur during adulthood.

Learning Objective 8.22
Summarize the major crises of adult life.

Learning Objective 8.23
Describe the similarities and differences in patterns of male and female adult development.

In sum, according to Erikson and others who view adult development in terms of discrete phases, or stages, the major force behind change is a series of crises or transitions we face as we mature and grow older. The way in which we deal with these important turning points then determines the course and nature of our future lives.

LIFE-EVENT MODELS: CHANGE IN RESPONSE TO THE OCCURRENCE AND TIMING OF KEY EVENTS A sharply different perspective on adult development is offered by *life-event (or timing-of-life-events) models*. These models suggest that people change and develop in response to specific events in their lives and to the times at which these occur. During childhood and even adolescence, such theories acknowledge, development does occur largely in accordance with a built-in biological clock. During the adult years, however, development occurs in response to important life events such as graduation from school, the start of a career, marriage, parenthood, promotions, divorce, and retirement. Thus, development becomes tied much more closely to a social clock than to a biological one.

Several life-events models divide important occurrences into two categories: events that are expected, or *normative*, and ones that are unexpected, or *nonnormative* (Neugarten, 1979, 1987). Normative events include graduation from school, marriage, parenthood during the early adult years, and retirement in later life. Nonnormative events include divorce, traumatic accidents, the sudden death of loved ones, and unexpected loss of a long-term job or position. Needless to say, normative events, although of crucial importance, are generally less stressful and less disruptive than nonnormative ones.

In sum, two contrasting perspectives about development during our adult years hold, respectively, that such change occurs in response to a series of internal conflicts, or crises, or that it occurs in response to specific life events and their timing.

PHYSICAL CHANGE DURING OUR ADULT YEARS

Looking through a family photo album—one that spans several decades—can be a very revealing experience. When you compare the earlier appearance of family members with the way they look today, the scope of the physical changes that occur during adulthood comes sharply into focus.

PHYSICAL CHANGE DURING EARLY ADULTHOOD Physical growth is usually complete by the time people leave their teens, but for some parts of the body, the process of aging actually begins long before this time. For example, the

PHYSICAL CHANGE OVER THE LIFE SPAN

As these photos of the author at ages four, seventeen, and fifty show, we all change tremendously in appearance over the course of our lives.

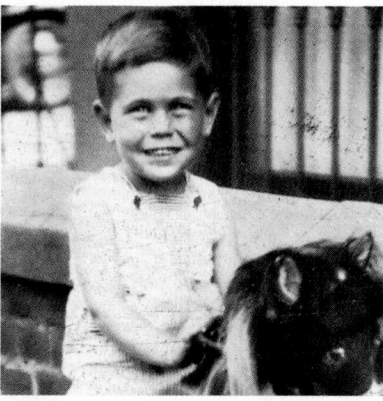

CHAPTER 8

lenses in our eyes begin to lose flexibility by the time we are only twelve or thirteen years old, and even before some people have attained full physical maturity, the tissues supporting their teeth have already begun to recede and weaken. So aging, like growth, is a continuous process that starts very early in life.

Like many biological processes, however, aging occurs slowly at first, but then proceeds more rapidly in later decades. Muscular strength, reaction time, sensory acuity, and heart action and output are all at or near their peaks through the mid-twenties, and then decline only slowly—usually imperceptibly—through the mid-thirties. Many members of both sexes do experience considerable weight gain during early adulthood, and some men undergo significant hair loss. However, by and large, physical change is both slow and minimal during this period of life.

PHYSICAL CHANGE DURING MIDLIFE By the time they are in their forties, most people are all too aware of the age-related changes occurring within their bodies. Cardiac output (the amount of blood pumped by the heart) decreases noticeably, and the walls of the large arteries lose some degree of flexibility. The performance of other major organ systems, too, declines, and an increasing number of people experience difficulties with digestion. Other changes are readily visible when middle-aged people look in the mirror: thinning and graying hair, bulges and wrinkles in place of the sleek torsos and smooth skins of youth. Large individual differences exist in the rate at which such changes occur, however, so some persons experience such changes much earlier than do others.

Among the most dramatic changes occurring during middle adulthood is the **climacteric**—a period of several years during which the functioning of the reproductive system, and various aspects of sexual activity, change greatly. While both sexes experience the climacteric, its effects are somewhat more obvious for females, the majority of whom experience **menopause**—cessation of the menstrual cycle—in their late forties or early fifties. During menopause the ovaries stop producing estrogen, and many changes in the reproductive system occur: thinning of the vaginal walls, reduced secretion of fluids that lubricate the vagina, and so on. Since ova stop being released, pregnancy is no longer possible. In the United States in the past, menopause was considered to be a stressful process for many women. Now, however, it is widely recognized that cultural factors play an important role in reactions to menopause and its effects.

Among men the climacteric involves reduced secretion of testosterone and reduced functioning of the prostate gland, which plays a role in semen formation. In many men the prostate gland becomes enlarged, and this may interfere not only with sexual functioning but with urination as well. Men often experience reduced sexual drive at this time of life, but many are still capable of fathering children.

PHYSICAL CHANGES IN LATER LIFE Average age in many countries is currently increasing at a steady pace. In the United States, for example, the proportion of the population sixty-five or older has risen from about 4 or 5 percent in 1900 to about 12 or 13 percent now; and this figure will increase to almost 20 percent when the baby-boom generation born during the 1950s and 1960s turns sixty-five. This trend brings sharply into focus the question of physical changes during the closing decades of life, for the nature and magnitude of these changes have important implications for health-care systems and therefore for national economies generally.

What picture emerges from systematic research on physical changes in later life? A somewhat encouraging one. A large proportion of Americans in their sixties, seventies, and even eighties report excellent or good health

SLOWING THE PACE OF PHYSICAL CHANGE

Physical change during our adult years is a fact of life. By remaining fit, however, we can slow this process greatly and reduce many of its adverse effects.

Climacteric: A period during which the functioning of the reproductive system, and various aspects of sexual activity, change greatly.

Menopause: Cessation of the menstrual cycle.

HUMAN DEVELOPMENT: FROM CHILD TO ADULT

(U.S. Department of Health and Human Services, 1989). Further, even in their seventies and eighties, large majorities of people do not receive hospital care during any given year (Thomas, 1992). So it appears that at least in highly developed nations like the United States, the declines in physical functioning and health people experience as they age are not as large or as devastating as stereotypes of old age suggest.

One additional—and important—point: While many physical changes do occur with increasing age, it is crucial to distinguish between those that are the result of **primary aging**—changes caused by the passage of time and, perhaps, inherited biological factors—and those that result from **secondary aging**—changes due to disease, disuse, or abuse of our bodies. Bearing this point in mind, let's briefly examine some of the physical changes that are the result of primary aging.

Several of these involve decrements in *sensory abilities*. As people age, and especially beyond midlife, they often experience declines in their senses of vision, hearing, smell and taste. Visual acuity, as measured by the ability to read letters on a standard eye-examination chart, drops off sharply after age seventy; many people experience such changes as slower dark adaptation and reduced ability to notice moving targets, such as cars on a highway (Long & Crambert, 1990). Similarly, auditory sensitivity generally decreases with age, especially among persons who have worked in noisy environments (Corso, 1977). Declines also occur in abilities to identify specific tastes and aromas, although these do not usually become noticeable until after age seventy-five (Spence, 1989). There is also a general slowing in reflexes and in responses in general, so reaction time increases with age (Spirduso & Macrae, 1990). However, there are large individual differences; a specific seventy-year-old may still respond more quickly than a specific thirty-year-old.

Some of these changes have important practical implications, especially with respect to driving, for which good vision and fast reaction time are often essential. Accident rates increase sharply for drivers above the age of seventy (see Figure 8.4) (Cerrelli, 1989). Further, when elderly dri-

Primary Aging: Aging due to the passage of time and, to some extent, inherited biological factors.

Secondary Aging: Aging due to the effects of disease, disuse, or abuse of the body.

KEY QUESTIONS

• How do stage theories such as Erikson's and life-event models explain the changes we experience during our adult years?

• What physical changes do men and women experience during early and middle adulthood?

• What physical changes occur in later life?

FIGURE **8.4**

Age and Automobile Accidents

Older drivers—those above the age of seventy—have a higher rate of accidents than drivers in their thirties, forties, and fifties. Only young drivers below the age of twenty experience higher accident rates. (*Source:* Based on data from Cerrelli, 1989.)

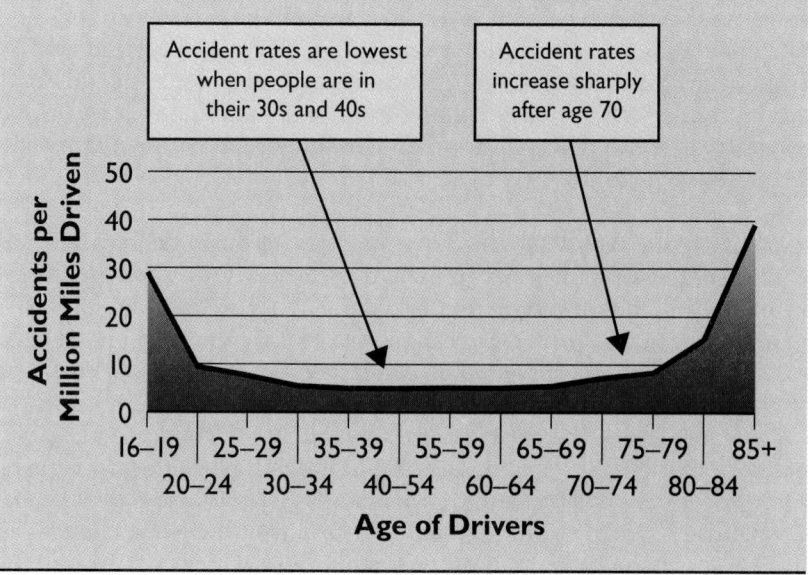

vers receive citations for traffic violations, these are more often for failing to obey traffic signs and failing to yield the right-of-way than is true of younger drivers (Stearns et al., 1985). So there is considerable evidence that declining sensory abilities increase the chances that older people will be a danger to themselves and to others.

Cognitive Change during Adulthood

Is the physical decline during adulthood matched by a decline in cognitive performance? Or can practice, a growing knowledge base, and ever-richer schemas serve to counter the effects of aging? Research findings indicate that the answer varies for different aspects of cognitive functioning.

Aging and Memory First, let's consider the impact of aging on memory. Research on short-term memory indicates that older people seem able to retain just as much information in this limited-capacity system as young ones (Poon & Fozard, 1980). However, when information in short-term memory must be processed—as, for example, when solving anagrams (scrambled words) in one's head—older persons sometimes perform more poorly than younger ones (Babcock & Salthouse, 1990).

For long-term memory, studies suggest that young people do have an edge with respect to recall, but not with respect to recognition (Hultsch & Dixon, 1990). In other words, younger persons can more readily bring to mind information stored in memory, but don't necessarily recognize a piece of information more readily than older persons when it is presented to them. Moreover, when older persons are expert in a specific area, such differences in recall tend to disappear (Charness, 1989). So, all in all, it appears that as we age, our ability to enter new information into memory in efficient ways may decrease slightly, but the capacity to bring information to mind once it has been stored remains largely unchanged (Zacks & Hasher, 1988).

The findings discussed so far are based on experiments with relatively meaningless information—nonsense syllables, anagrams, and the like. What about memory for more meaningful information—memory in everyday life? Here, findings suggest that older people often perform as well as young ones (May, Hasher, & Stoltzfus, 1993; Sinott, 1986). However, *prospective memory*—remembering to perform various actions—does decline with age for most people (Hultsch & Dixon, 1990).

So, in answer to the question "Does memory decline with age?" we can reply: Existing evidence indicates that some memory abilities, such as recall of relatively meaningless information and prospective memory, may decline with age. However, many others—especially recognition of real-life information—show little change across the entire life span.

Aging and Intelligence: Decline or Stability? In the past it was widely believed that intelligence increases into early adulthood, remains stable through the thirties, but then begins to decline as early as the forties. This view was based largely on cross-sectional research that compared the performance of persons of different ages on standard tests of intelligence. Results indicated that in general, the older persons were, the lower their scores tended to be (Schaie, 1974; Thomas, 1992). Unfortunately, as you know from our earlier discussion of research methods, cross-sectional research suffers from a serious drawback. Differences between various groups of participants can stem from factors other than their contrasting ages, such as differences in education or health. In order to eliminate such problems, more recent research on aging and intelligence has often employed a longi-

FIGURE **8.5**

Evidence for the Relative Stability of Intelligence across the Life Span

Longitudinal research indicates that intelligence is stable across virtually the entire life span. Significant declines in components of intelligence measured by standardized tests of intelligence do not occur for most persons until they are well into their seventies. (Scores for *inductive reasoning,* one important component of intelligence, are shown here.)
(*Source:* Based on data from Schaie, 1993.)

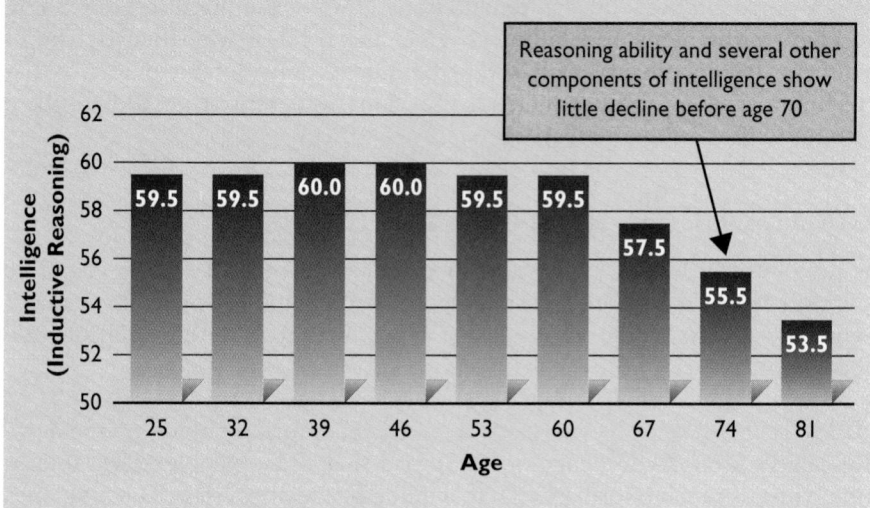

tudinal design. In such research, the same persons are tested at several different times over a period of years to see whether there are consistent changes in their performance.

The results of studies using such procedures have yielded a more positive picture than the earlier cross-sectional studies. Instead of declining sharply with age, many intellectual abilities seem to remain quite stable across the entire life span, showing little change into the sixties, seventies, or beyond. In fact, some abilities even seem to increase. For example, Schaie and his colleagues (Schaie, 1986, 1990, 1993) have tested thousands of people ranging in age from twenty-five to eighty-one at seven-year intervals. As shown in Figure 8.5, results indicate that various components (as measured by the Primary Mental Abilities Test, one standard test of intelligence) remain remarkably stable throughout adult life. Indeed, even at age eighty-one, fewer than half of the persons studied showed any declines during the preceding seven years. Only on tasks involving speed of reasoning do there appear to be consistent declines in performance. Since such drops in performance may reflect increased reaction time, there is little if any indication of a general decrease in intelligence with age.

KEY QUESTIONS

- What changes in memory occur as we age?
- How does intelligence change over the life span?

SOCIAL CHANGE IN ADULTHOOD: *Tasks and Stages of Adult Life*

During our adult years we engage in a wide range of activities and play many roles. Student, lover, spouse, parent, employee, boss, grandparent—these are only a few of the potential roles we may occupy. As we move into various roles and back and forth between them, the roles and the events they signify shape our lives and relations with others. For this reason, many psychologists who have studied adult development, and especially social development, have adopted frameworks that focus on these roles and the activities they involve. One such framework has been proposed by Levinson (1986).

LEVINSON'S STAGES OF ADULT LIFE Levinson divides the entire human life span into four distinct *eras,* each separated from the next by a *cross-era transition*—a period in which an individual makes the change from one era to the

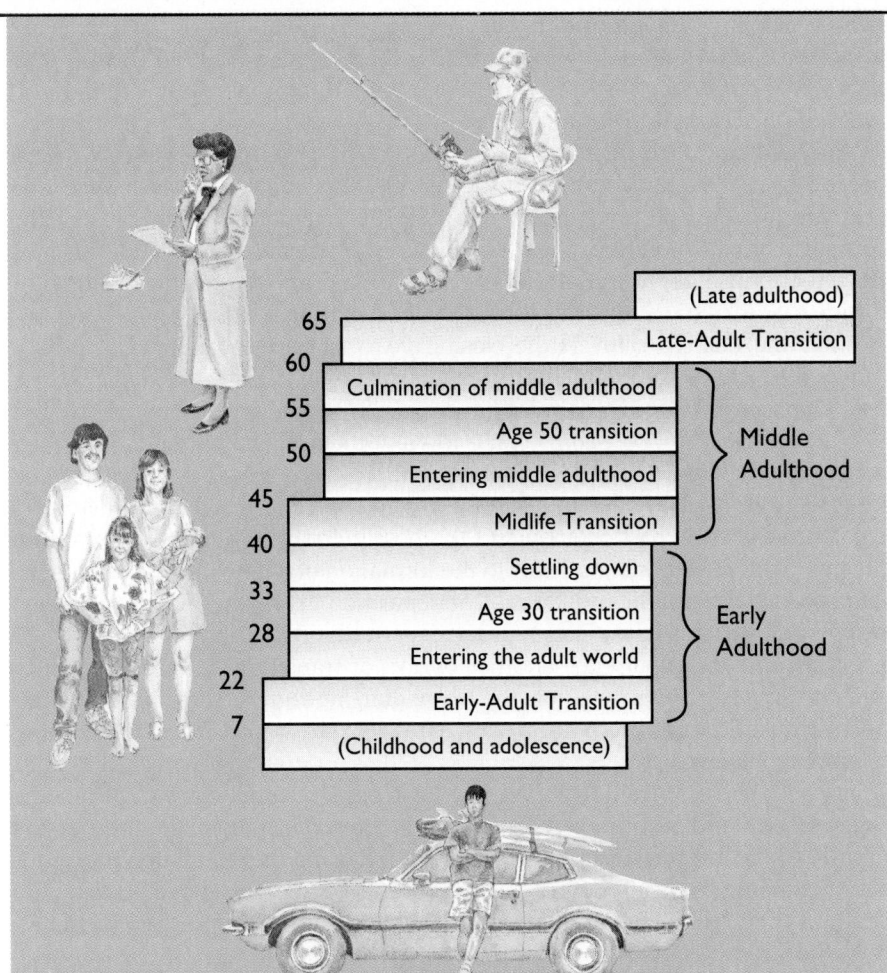

FIGURE **8.6**

Levinson's Theory of Adult Development

According to Levinson (1986), individuals move through distinct *eras* of life, each separated from the next by a turbulent *cross-era transition* period. While this theory has received a great deal of attention, its validity remains open to question.

(Late adulthood)

65 — Late-Adult Transition

60

55 — Culmination of middle adulthood

50 — Age 50 transition | Middle Adulthood

Entering middle adulthood

45

40 — Midlife Transition

Settling down

33

Age 30 transition | Early Adulthood

28 — Entering the adult world

22

Early-Adult Transition

7

(Childhood and adolescence)

next one. An important feature of Levinson's theory is the concept of **life structure**. This term refers to the underlying pattern of a person's life at a particular time: an evolving cognitive framework reflecting an individual's views about the nature and meaning of his or her life. Work and family are usually central to the life structure, but it may include other components as well—for example, a person's racial or ethnic background, or important external events that provide a backdrop for life, such as economic boom or depression. According to Levinson, individuals have different life structures at different times during their adult lives and move from one to another through transition periods lasting about five years.

The four eras identified by Levinson are summarized in Figure 8.6. As you can see, the first transition occurs between the *preadult era* (the period through adolescence) and early adulthood. This transition involves establishing one's independence, both financial and emotional. Many people pass through this transition during their college years; others accomplish it when they accept their first job or enter military service. In either case the transition is marked by such events as establishing a separate residence and learning to live on one's own.

Once this initial transition is complete, individuals enter *early adulthood.* Two key components of their life structure at this time are what Levinson terms the *dream* and the *mentor*. The dream is a vision of future accomplish-

Life Structure: In Levinson's theory of adult development, the underlying pattern or design or a person's life.

ments—what a person hopes to achieve in the years ahead. Such dreams are important sources of motivation, spurring the persons who hold them to vigorous goal-directed efforts. Mentors are older and more experienced individuals who help to guide young adults.

At about age thirty, Levinson contends, many people experience what he describes as the *age thirty transition*. At this time many people realize that they are nearing the point of no return: if they remain in their present life course, they will soon have too much invested to change. Faced with this fact, they reappraise their initial choices and either make specific changes or decide that they have indeed selected the best course.

After the relative calm of the closing years of early adulthood, a person moves into another potentially turbulent transitional period—the *midlife transition*. This generally occurs somewhere between the ages of forty and forty-five. It is a time when many people come to view themselves, at last, as the older generation. Levinson's findings suggest that for many persons this realization leads to a period of emotional turmoil. They take stock of where they have been, the success of their past choices, and the possibility of fulfilling their youthful dreams. Such reexamination leads to the formation of a new life structure—one that takes account of the individual's new position in life and may involve several new elements, such as a change in career or divorce and remarriage.

Many persons experience another period of transition between ages fifty and fifty-five. In this transition they consider modifying their life structure once again—for example, by adopting a new role in their career or by coming to view themselves as a grandparent as well as a parent. However, this transition is often less dramatic than one that occurs somewhere between the ages of sixty and sixty-five. This *late-adult transition* marks the close of the middle years and the start of late adulthood. During this transition individuals must come to terms with their impending retirement and the major life changes this will bring. As they move through this period of readjustment, their life structure shifts to encompass these changes.

LEVINSON'S THEORY: A CRITIQUE   In several respects Levinson's portrayal of development during adulthood seems to match our intuitive ideas about this process. Relatively long periods of stability are punctuated by shorter, turbulent periods in which we come to terms with changes in our goals, perspectives, and status. However, it's important to note that Levinson based his theory primarily on extensive interviews with only forty participants—all men, and all ages thirty-five to forty-five. Critics argue that this is too small and too restricted a sample on which to base such a sweeping framework (Wrightsman, 1988). In addition, it is uncertain whether Levinson's suggestions apply to women as well as men; we'll return to this point below. In conclusion, then, Levinson's theory should be viewed as an interesting but as yet unverified description of social and personality development during our adult years.

KEY QUESTIONS

- In Levinson's theory, what is the life structure, and what are the major eras of adult life?
- What criticisms have been directed against Levinson's theory?

CRISES OF ADULT LIFE

Levinson's theory can be viewed as a stage theory of adult development: It suggests that all persons pass through a series of eras and transitions. In contrast, many other researchers have focused on major *events* of adult life and how we are affected by these. Echoing a theme explored with respect to adolescents, we'll now focus on two events that can be viewed as major crises of adult life: divorce and unemployment.

DIVORCE Divorce rates in the United States and many other countries are at historically high levels. In fact, somewhere between a third and half of all first marriages end in divorce (Glick, 1989). Clearly, divorce is a very upsetting event for most persons. Families are shattered, a relationship that has lasted years or even decades is brought to an end, and the difficult process of adjusting to life alone must be begun.

What are the causes of divorce? Comparisons of couples who divorce and those who remain happily married point to a number of different factors. For example, happily married people report that they agree with their spouse on aims, goals, and even their sex life; that they genuinely like their spouse and view the spouse as a good friend; and that they share many positive experiences with their spouse (Lauer & Lauer, 1985). In addition, happily married people direct a high level of positive communication to their spouse: They express affection, approval, appreciation, and pleasure, just as they did during courtship (Bradbury & Fincham, 1992). In contrast, people who report being unhappy in their marriage indicate that they disagree with their spouse about goals, lifestyle, sex, and many other matters (Levinger, 1988). Further, they often show a negative pattern of communication in which they direct mainly criticism and blame toward their spouse (Miller, 1991). Couples who divorce also report high levels of boredom in their relationship and indicate that their spouse no longer fills their needs for affection, esteem, or approval (Badbury & Fincham, 1992; Cottrell, Eisenberg, & Speicher, 1992).

Additional factors associated with divorce include low income, a brief courtship, unrealistic expectations about the relationship, and pregnancy at the time of marriage (Kurdek, 1993). Perhaps the most surprising finding of all is that genetic factors, too, may play a role in divorce. It has long been known that people whose parents have been divorced are more likely to divorce, than those whose parents were not divorced (Glenn & Kramer, 1987). In general, it was assumed that this finding stemmed from the adverse effects of growing up in a divorced home—perhaps lower emotional stability and the absence of models of happy, long-term relationships. Such factors certainly play a role, but recent findings indicate that genetic factors may also be involved. To study this possibility, McGue and Lykken (1992) compared the divorce rates of hundreds of monozygotic (identical) twins and dizygotic (nonidentical) twins whose parents were or were not divorced. The researchers reasoned that if monozygotic twins whose twin sibling divorced were more likely to divorce than dizygotic twins whose twin sibling divorced, this would provide evidence for a genetic contribution to divorce. This is precisely what was found. McGue and Lykken (1992) also found that participants were more likely to be divorced if either their own parents or their spouse's parents had been divorced. In practical terms, in this study, if a monozygotic twin's sibling, parents, and spouse's parents were all divorced, the probability of the twin's divorcing was about 77.5 percent. In contrast, if neither the sibling nor the parents or parents-in-law were divorced, the probability that the twin would divorce was only 5.3 percent.

How can genetic factors influence divorce? McGue and Lykken (1992) suggest that individuals whose parents are divorced may inherit personal characteristics that make it difficult for them to maintain a long-term relationship. These specific characteristics remain to be identified, so this is only one among several possibilities. In any case, the findings reported by McGue and Lykken (1992) add a new perspective on divorce—one that should be carefully evaluated in future research.

UNEMPLOYMENT When asked "Who are you?" a large proportion of employed adults reply in terms of their job or their occupation (Greenberg &

Baron, 1995). Thus, it is not surprising that losing a job is very stressful for most people (Konovsky & Brockner, 1993). Unfortunately, getting laid off is an increasingly common experience for adults in the 1990s. In the United States and elsewhere, many companies have greatly reduced the size of their workforces; as a result, the term *downsizing*—which refers to such reductions—has taken on a frightening meaning. Not only are increasing numbers of people losing their jobs; when they do, it is harder for them to find other employment. In one recent survey (Time-CNN, cited in Church, 1993), 53 percent of unemployed respondents indicated that they expected long-term difficulties in obtaining future employment. Such fears appear to be well grounded: During the 1990s, American corporations have cut more than 500,000 people from their payrolls each year.

Perhaps the negative effects of being unemployed are most vividly illustrated by longitudinal research in which hundreds of recent graduates from Australian schools were studied for eight years (Winefield & Tiggemann, 1991). During this period participants in the study completed questionnaires designed to measure their self-esteem, feelings of depression, negative affect, and general health. They also reported on whether they were unemployed and recorded their level of satisfaction with their current jobs. Results were clear: Unemployed individuals reported lower self-esteem, greater depression, more negative affect, and poorer personal health than those who were employed. The differences were especially marked when unemployed participants were compared with employed persons who were satisfied with their jobs.

These and other findings indicate that losing one's job can be a highly stressful and disturbing experience—one that can threaten both physical and psychological health. Fortunately, there are steps people can take to prevent this problem and its effects. We'll examine these in the **Making Psychology Part of Your Life** section at the end of this chapter.

GENDER AND THE ADULT YEARS: *How Males and Females Differ*

Before concluding this discussion of change during our adult years, it is important to consider another—and very crucial—issue: Are there important gender differences in this process? To put it another way, do women and men pass through the same phases of development and experience similar patterns of change?

Research on this issue (Baruch, 1984; Roberts & Newton, 1987) offers something of a mixed picture. On the one hand, it appears that in early adulthood women do confront many of the same issues and tasks as men. As Levinson suggests, they also tend to formulate a dream and often choose an older and wiser mentor. However, several important differences between women and men have been uncovered. First, all the men studied by Levinson possessed a dream, but this does not seem to be true for women. Some women have a dream centered on occupational roles and achievements, others have dreams focused on relationships (for example, a dream of a happy marriage), while still others do not appear to have any well-defined dream. The largest group of all formed a *split dream* that included equal attention to careers and relationships (Roberts & Newton, 1987). In the context of Levinson's stage theory, these and other findings suggest that men and women do

---

KEY QUESTIONS

- What differences exist between the behaviors of happily married couples and those of couples who ultimately divorce?

- What are the effects of unemployment on the self-esteem and adjustment of persons who experience this crisis of adult life?

- In what ways do women and men differ in terms of development during their adult years?

experience somewhat different patterns of change and growth during their adult years.

Additional research on women's adult life has been conducted by Baruch, Barnett, and their colleagues (Baruch, 1984; Baruch, Barnett, & Rivers, 1983). These researchers conducted extensive interviews with women ages thirty-five to fifty-five. Included in their sample were married women with and without children who were employed outside the home, married women with and without children who were not employed outside the home, and divorced women with children who were employed outside the home.

Results indicated that married employed women with and without children reported the highest levels of psychological well-being. Divorced working women reported a somewhat lower level, and the lowest level was reported by married women without children who were not employed outside the home.

AGING AND DEATH: *The End of Life*

Since ancient times, human beings have searched for the "fountain of youth"—some means of prolonging youth, and life, indefinitely. But alas, such dreams have remained only illusions; while life and health can be prolonged through proper diet, exercise, and reduced exposure to various sources of stress (see chapter 11), there appears to be no way to live forever. In this section we'll consider several issues relating to the conclusion of life.

Learning Objective 8.24
Discuss the contrasting views concerning why we grow old.

Learning Objective 8.25
Provide a survey of stages in the dying and bereavement processes.

THEORIES OF AGING: *Contrasting Views about Why We Grow Old*

Many different views about the causes of aging have been proposed, but most fall under one of two major headings: wear-and-tear theories and genetic theories.

WEAR-AND-TEAR THEORIES OF AGING Wear-and-tear theories of aging suggest that we grow old because various parts of our bodies, or the cells of which they are composed, wear out. One such theory emphasizes the role of *free radicals*—atoms that are unstable because they have lost electrons. According to the theory, these highly unstable particles react violently with other molecules in cells, thus producing damage. When this damage affects DNA, free radicals can interfere with basic aspects of cell maintenance and repair. The free-radicals theory proposes that this damage cumulates over time, thus producing the declines in biological functioning associated with aging. Other wear-and-tear theories focus on different mechanisms, but the outcome—cumulative damage to cells and organs—is much the same.

Indirect evidence for wear-and-tear theories of aging is provided by individuals who repeatedly expose their bodies to harmful conditions and substances—for example, large doses of alcohol, various drugs, or harsh environments. Such persons often show premature signs of aging, presumably because they have overburdened their bodies' capacity for internal repairs.

GENETIC THEORIES OF AGING A second group of theories attributes physical aging primarily to genetic programming. According to **genetic theories of aging**,

Wear-and-Tear Theories of Aging: Theories suggesting that aging results from continuous use of cells and organs within our bodies.

Genetic Theories of Aging: Theories suggesting that aging results from genetic programming that regulates the aging process.

every living organism contains some kind of built-in biological clock that regulates the aging process. These mechanisms may be located in all cells or may operate primarily in special groups of cells within the brain. Whatever their location, such biological clocks limit the number of times various cells can reproduce. Once this number has been reached, no further cell divisions occur, and decline leading to death follows. Another genetic theory, *gene mutation theory*, suggests that genetic mutations that interfere with normal cell functioning occur throughout our lives. When these mutations reach high enough levels, death results (Cristofalo, 1988). Support for genetic theories is provided by the finding that certain cells do indeed divide only a set number of times before dying. Moreover, no environmental conditions seem capable of altering this number.

At the present time, there is not sufficient evidence to enable anyone to choose between these theories. Thus, the best scientific guess is that aging is caused by several different mechanisms and results from a complex interplay between environmental and genetic factors.

MEETING DEATH: *Facing the End of Life*

Death is inevitable: There is no fountain of eternal youth or life. But how do persons who find themselves facing their own death react? How do they come to terms with the impending end of their lives as individuals? This was the topic of a famous study conducted in the late 1960s by Elizabeth Kübler-Ross (1969). She studied terminally ill patients and, on the basis of detailed interviews with them, concluded that people pass through a series of five distinct stages.

The first stage is *denial.* In the denial phase patients refuse to believe that the end is in sight. "No, it can't be true," they seem to say. "I won't believe it." This stage is soon replaced by a second—*anger.* "Why me?" dying persons ask. "It isn't fair. Why should I die when I still want to live?" In the third stage patients show what Kübler-Ross terms *bargaining*. They offer good behavior, prayer, or other changes in their lifestyle in exchange for a postponement of death. Unfortunately, such efforts cannot alter medical realities, so when it becomes apparent that their best offers of a deal with death have not been accepted, many dying persons enter a stage of *depression*. According to Kübler-Ross, however, this is not the final stage in the process. Rather, many people move from this to another reaction she describes as *acceptance*. At this stage dying individuals are no longer angry or depressed. Instead, they seem to accept their oncoming death with dignity, and they concentrate on saying fond farewells to important persons in their life and putting their affairs in final order.

While these findings are both comforting and appealing, they have not been confirmed by other researchers. For example, Aronoff and Spilka (1984–1985) videotaped terminally ill patients at various points during their illness and examined their facial expressions for evidence of the five stages described by Kübler-Ross. They found an increase in sad expressions over time, but no evidence that the patients became calmer or happier as death approached. Other researchers have found somewhat different patterns, such as expressions of hope throughout a terminal illness (Metzger, 1980). In view of these findings, and in light of the fact that Kübler-Ross used relatively informal methods in her research, it seems best to approach her conclusions with considerable caution. They are intriguing, and they certainly hold out the hope that many of us may meet death in a composed and dignified manner. However, they cannot be viewed as valid unless they are confirmed by further careful research.

BEREAVEMENT: *Mourning the Death of Loved Ones*

My grandfather lived until he was almost ninety-three, and he was healthy and vigorous almost until the end. But one day he said something that I'll remember the rest of my life: "Bobby, I feel so sad. It's as though almost everyone I loved is gone." He was right: By the time he died, his wife, his sister, and all his friends had long since passed away. So my grandfather had more than his share of **bereavement**—grieving for the loss of persons who were dear to him.

Because bereavement is an experience most adults have, it has been studied systematically by psychologists. The results of this research indicate that when grieving for a loved one, most persons experience the following reactions (Norris & Murrell, 1990). First comes *shock*, a feeling of numbness and unreality that lasts hours or even days. This is followed by *protest and yearning*, as the bereaved person more clearly recognizes her or his loss and yearns for the deceased person. During this phase, some persons even fantasize or hallucinate that they have seen the person they are mourning; my grandfather told me that he "saw" my grandmother many mornings when he first woke up. (They had been married sixty-four years when she died.) A third stage, *disorganization and despair*, can last a year or more. During this stage, the mourning person may become apathetic and depressed; life does not seem worth living without the deceased. But in most cases, this stage is followed by *detachment, reorganization, and recovery*, as the individual establishes new roles, regains a sense of purpose in life, and psychologically picks up the pieces. Even during this stage, however, painful bouts of grieving may recur on birthdays, anniversaries, and other occasions that remind the bereaved person of his or her loss. (Figure 8.7 summarizes the major stages of bereavement.) In sum, after a prolonged period of mourning, most people do recover and go on with their lives.

KEY QUESTIONS

- How do wear-and-tear and genetic theories account for aging and death?
- According to Kübler-Ross, what stages do terminally ill persons pass through when confronting their own deaths?
- What are the major stages of bereavement?

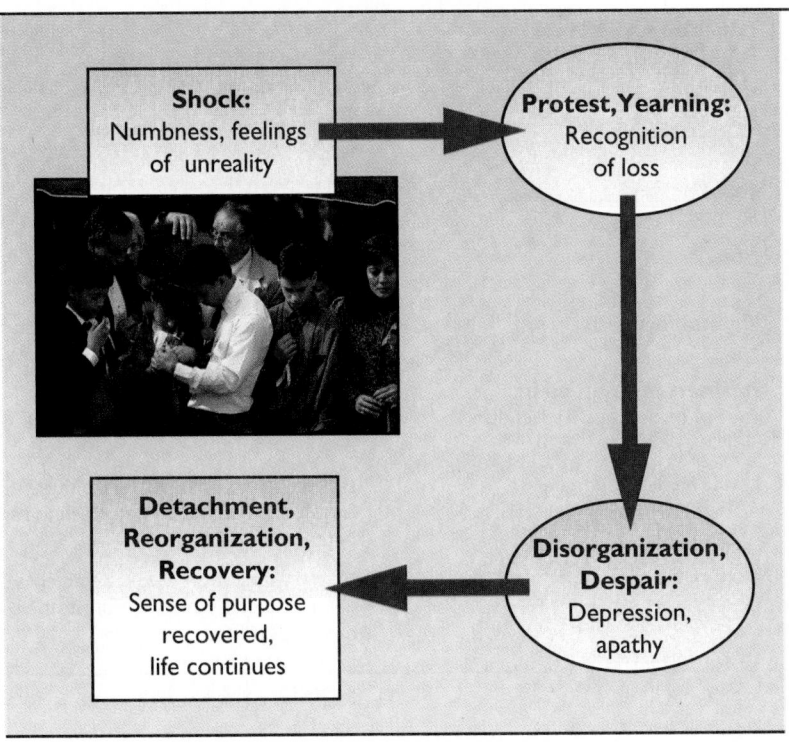

FIGURE 8.7

Major Stages of Bereavement

Persons undergoing *bereavement* seem to pass through the stages of mourning shown here.

Shock:
Numbness, feelings of unreality

Protest, Yearning:
Recognition of loss

Disorganization, Despair:
Depression, apathy

Detachment, Reorganization, Recovery:
Sense of purpose recovered, life continues

Bereavement: *The process through which individuals grieve for persons they love who have died.*

Preparing for Tomorrow's Job Market Today

I n recent years, up to 30 percent of new college graduates have either failed to find a job or finally been forced to accept one for which they were overqualified. Bellboys with BA degrees, waitresses with BS's—this is an increasingly common, and disturbing, pattern in the 1990s (Church, 1993).

Faced with the uncertainties of today's and tomorrow's job market, are there any steps you can take to increase your chances? Fortunately, there are. Several of these are summarized below. While they can't guarantee that you'll get the job you want, together they can give you an edge in an increasingly competitive economic climate (Meier, 1991).

1. *Choose a field with a future.* Echoing our theme of change in this chapter, the job market out there is changing—and with a vengeance. This means that if you want a good job, you must choose your field carefully. Specifically, you should consider a career in areas of the economy that promise to grow rapidly in the years ahead. What are these? Recent studies of the labor force have identified fields such as the ones shown in Table 8.4.

2. *Focus on small and medium-size companies.* In the past, many graduates sought jobs with prestige companies—those with a big reputation and lots of glamour. In today's job market, this is not a good strategy; for these are precisely the kinds of companies that have announced, and executed, the largest cutbacks. Focus, instead, on smaller companies. They may not seem as glamorous, but they may be a better place to launch your career.

TABLE 8.4	**JOB/CAREER**	**DESCRIPTION**
Careers with a Future	**Information Technology**	
	Computer programmers	Develop new computer programs
The careers listed here are among those expected to grow rapidly in the years ahead.	Systems analysts	Create computer applications for specific business needs
	Telecommunications managers	Specialize in the transfer of information through telephones, modems, fax machines, voice mail
	Education and Training	
	Employee trainers	Help people develop new skills needed to perform rapidly changing jobs
	Diversity managers	Help diverse groups of employees work together effectively
	Health Care	
	Family physicians	Provide primary care
	Nurse practitioners	Deal with a wide range of health problems
	Physical therapists	Specialize in helping people recover from accidents or injuries
	Business Management	
	Fifty-plus marketing specialists	Promote and sell products aimed at people over fifty
	Employee leasing agents	Help companies "lease" employees for specific projects (as opposed to hiring permanent help)
	Managed-care experts	Help organizations deal effectively with insurance companies to obtain the best health plans for employees

3. *Be ready to work for a foreign company.* In the United States and many other countries, multinational corporations that are expanding their operations are often the ones with the jobs. Working for a foreign company may mean that you must learn a new set of rules, because such companies often follow the home country's practices with respect to employees and to work. Given the continued movement toward a unified world economy, this is good experience and may open opportunities for you.

4. *Consider part-time or contract work as a way to get started.* Permanent full-time jobs with large corporations are becoming harder and harder to find, partly because large companies are cutting their own staff and hiring outsiders to do many jobs. Consider starting in this manner, because often people who are hired on a temporary, part-time, or contract basis gain an important advantage: they are the ones who get first shot at permanent full-time jobs when they develop.

SUMMARY AND REVIEW OF KEY QUESTIONS

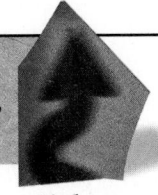

PHYSICAL GROWTH AND DEVELOPMENT DURING CHILDHOOD

• *What environmental factors can adversely affect the developing fetus?*

Diseases, drugs, alcohol, and smoking by prospective mothers are all among teratogens that can harm the developing fetus.

• *What perceptual abilities are shown by infants?*

Infants can distinguish among different colors, sounds, and tastes, and they prefer certain patterns, such as the patern of features on the human face.

• *At what age do infants develop the ability to perceive depth?*

They can perceive depth by the time they are about three months old.

KEY TERMS: *developmental psychology, p. 282; physical growth and development, p. 282; cognitive development, p. 282; social and emotional development, p. 282; embryo, p. 282; fetus, p. 282; teratogens, p. 283*

BASIC METHODS FOR STUDYING HUMAN DEVELOPMENT

• *What are the key differences between longitudinal research and cross-sectional research?*

In longitudinal research, the same individuals are studied for extended periods of time to investigate changes in their behavior. In cross-sectional research, persons of different ages are studied at the same point in time to determine whether their behaviors differ.

• *How is longitudinal-sequential research conducted?*

In longitudinal-sequential research, several samples of people of different ages are studied over a period of several years.

• *What are the key advantages of each of these major research methods?*

Longitudinal research permits observation of individual variations in development and allows for conclusions concerning the impact of specific events on the course of development. Cross-sectional research can be conducted more quickly and efficiently than longitudinal research and minimizes the possible impact of practice effects. Longitudinal-sequential research combines advantages of both longitudinal and cross-sectional research and allows for the assessment of cohort effects.

KEY TERMS: *longitudinal research, p. 286; cross-sectional research, p. 287; cohort effects, p. 287; longitudinal-sequential design, p. 287*

COGNITIVE DEVELOPMENT DURING CHILDHOOD: CHANGES IN HOW WE KNOW THE EXTERNAL WORLD . . . AND OURSELVES

• *According to Piaget's theory, what cognitive abilities do infants, children, and adolescents demonstrate during the sensorimotor stage, the preoperational stage, the stage of concrete operations, and the stage of formal operations?*

During the sensorimotor stage, infants acquire basic understanding of the links between their own behavior and the effects it produces—cause and effect. During the preoperational stage, infants can form mental representations of the external world; however, they show egocentrism in their thinking. During the stage of concrete operations, children are capable of logical thought and show understanding of conservation and reversibility. During the stage of formal operations, children and adolescents can think logically and engage in various forms of reasoning.

- *In what respects does Piaget's theory appear to be inaccurate?*

Piaget's theory is inaccurate in that it underestimates the cognitive abilities of young children, overstates the importance of discrete stages, and underestimates the importance of language and social interactions in cognitive development.

- *According to the information-processing perspective, what does cognitive development involve?*

According to this approach, cognitive development involves the increasing ability actively to process, store, retrieve, and manipulate information.

- *What changes occur in children's ability to focus their attention as they grow older?*

Children become better able to ignore distractions and to focus their attention on tasks they are currently performing.

- *What strategies do children acquire for enhancing their short- and long-term memory?*

Children acquire increased capacity to rehearse information they wish to commit to memory. They greatly expand their domain-specific knowledge, and they acquire increasingly sophisticated scripts.

- *What is metacognition?*

Metacognition is awareness and understanding of our own cognitive processes.

- *According to Kohlberg's theory, what are the major stages of moral development through which all persons pass?*

At the first, or preconventional, level, morality is judged largely in terms of its consequences. At the conventional level, morality is judged in terms of laws and rules of society. At the third, or postconventional, level, morality is judged in terms of abstract principles and values.

- *What do research findings indicate with respect to Kohlberg's theory?*

Moral reasoning does increase with age, but environmental factors such as level of education, child-rearing practices, and cultural traditions also play important roles in its development.

- *What do research findings indicate with respect to gender differences in moral reasoning?*

Contrary to initial findings, there is no evidence that males and females attain different levels of moral development or reasoning.

KEY TERMS: stage theory, p. 288; adaptation, p. 288; assimilation, p. 288; accommodation, p. 288; sensorimotor stage, p. 289; object permanence, p. 289; preoperational stage, p. 289; make-believe play, p. 289; egocentrism, p. 289; conservation, p. 289; concrete operations, p. 290; formal operations, p. 290; hypothetico-deductive reasoning, p. 290; private speech, p. 291; information-processing approach, p. 292; attention-deficit hyperactivity disorder (ADHD), p. 292; script, p. 293; metacognition, p. 293; moral development, p. 294; preconventional level, p. 294; conventional level, p. 296; postconventional level, p. 296

SOCIAL AND EMOTIONAL DEVELOPMENT DURING CHILDHOOD: FORMING RELATIONSHIPS WITH OTHERS

- *What recognizable facial expressions are shown by infants?*

Infants show smiling, anger, sadness, and surprise, among other expressions, by the time they are three or four months old.

- *In what ways do children's abilities to regulate their own emotions develop with age?*

As they grow older, children acquire increasing ability to regulate their own emotions; for example, by avoiding disturbing stimuli, by talking to themselves, or by lowering their expectations.

- *When do differences in temperament—consistent individual differences in the quality and intensity of emotions—first appear?*

Differences in temperament are present in early infancy and seem to remain relatively stable throughout life, especially for those who are relatively extreme on these dimensions.

- *What is attachment?*

Attachment refers to infants' strong emotional bond with their caregiver.

- *How does the strange situation test measure the strength of attachment?*

The strange situation test involves close observation of young children during separation from the caregiver, in the presence of a stranger, and upon the return of the caregiver in order to gauge the strength of attachment to the caregiver.

- *How does contact comfort affect attachment?*

Contact comfort—the touching, hugs, and caresses infants receive from caregivers—seems to play an important role in the formation of attachment.

- *When do children acquire gender constancy—understanding of the fact that their sexual identity is stable?*

Many children do not acquire understanding of gender constancy until they are at least four. Such understanding may occur earlier, however, if children acquire knowledge of the physical differences between the sexes.

- *How do children acquire gender identity and gender-stereotyped beliefs?*

Children apparently acquire gender identity through both social learning and development of gender schemas. Gender-stereotyped beliefs—culturally determined beliefs concerning the supposed characteristics and behaviors of males and females—are acquired largely from parents, friends, and peers. However, genetic and hormonal factors, too, may play a role in gender-specific behaviors.

KEY TERMS: *temperament, p. 301; attachment, p. 301; ethological theory, p. 301; strange situation test, p. 301; secure attachment, p. 301; avoidant attachment, p. 301; resistant attachment, p. 303; disorganized attachment, p. 303; gender, p. 303; gender constancy, p. 303; gender schema theory, p. 304; gender roles, p. 304*

ADOLESCENCE: BETWEEN CHILD AND ADULT

- *What physical changes occur during puberty?*

Puberty, the most important feature of physical development during adolescence, is a period of rapid change and growth during which individuals reach sexual maturity and become capable of reproduction.

- *How does the thinking of adolescents and adults differ?*

Research findings indicate that differences between the thinking of adolescents and that of adults are smaller in magnitude and scope than was formerly assumed. However, adolescents are more prone to such errors as imagining that they are the focus of others' attention.

- *To what extent do adolescents view themselves as invulnerable—unlikely to experience various kinds of harmful outcomes?*

Recent research indicates that adolescents do not have a greater sense of invulnerability than adults.

- *According to Erikson's theory, what does social development involve?*

Erikson's theory suggests that social development involves the resolution of a series of internal crises.

- *What is the most important crisis faced by adolescents?*

For adolescents the most important in Erikson's series of crises is that of "identity versus role confusion," which concerns establishing a clear self-identity.

- *How do adolescents develop a clear self-schema?*

Adolescents try out many roles and social selves before establishing a clear self-schema.

- *What problems do adolescents face when they grow up in divorced or parent-absent families?*

Adolescents whose parents divorce react with anxiety and insecurity; they often blame themselves for the split, and many become academic underachievers. Those raised in families from which one parent is absent are at increased risk for delinquent behaviors, reduced school performance, and difficulties in forming meaningful relationships with others.

- *What problems do adolescents face when they grow up in dysfunctional families?*

Adolescents raised in such families often suffer neglect, abuse, and/or sexual abuse.

KEY TERMS: *adolescence, p. 304; puberty, p. 304; adolescent invulnerability, p. 307; dysfunctional families, p. 311; sexual abuse, p. 311*

ADULTHOOD AND AGING

- *How do stage theories such as Erikson's and life-event models explain the changes we experience during our adult years?*

Stage theories of adult development propose that we move through distinct stages. Erikson's theory suggests that we must resolve different crises as we move through various phases of adult life. In contrast, life-event models view adult development as tied to individuals' responses to important events in their lives.

- *What physical changes do men and women experience during early and middle adulthood?*

Reduced physical functioning and decreased vigor, plus changes in appearance, are apparent in most people during middle adulthood. In addition, both men and women experience changes in their reproductive systems during midlife; these are known as the climacteric.

- *What physical changes occur in later life?*

Among the many physical changes that occur in later life are declines in sensory abilities and a slowing of reflexes.

- *What changes in memory occur as we age?*

Short-term memory does not decline with age, but recall of information from long-term memory does decline somewhat. Prospective memory, too, declines somewhat with age.

- *How does intelligence change over the life-span?*

There may be some declines in intelligence with age, but these are smaller and more limited in scope than was once widely believed.

- *In Levinson's theory, what is the life structure, and what are the major eras of adult life?*

The life structure is an underlying pattern or design we follow in our lives. It often changes as we move through a four major life eras: preadult, early, middle, and late adulthood.

- *What criticisms have been directed against Levinson's theory?*

Levinson's theory is based on a small sample of men, so it is unclear whether his conclusions apply to women as well.

- **What differences exist between the behaviors of happily married couples and those of couples who ultimately divorce?**

Happily married couples express more agreement on goals, lifestyle, and sex than unhappy couples. Further, in happy couples, spouses communicate more praise and approval to each other than is true in unhappy couples.

- **What are the effects of unemployment on the self-esteem and adjustment of persons who experience this crisis of adult life?**

Being unemployed can undermine individuals' psychological and physical well-being.

- **In what ways do women and men differ in terms of development during their adult years?**

Some women have no "dream," and many women have split dreams that focus on both careers and relationships; this is a major difference from the pattern found in men.

KEY TERMS: climacteric, p. 315; menopause, p. 315; primary aging, p. 317; secondary aging, p. 317; life structure, p. 319

AGING AND DEATH: THE END OF LIFE

- **How do wear-and-tear and genetic theories account for aging and death?**

Wear-and-tear theories suggest that aging results from continuous use of cells and organs within our bodies. In contrast, genetic theories suggest that we possess biological clocks that limit the length of our lives.

- **According to Kübler-Ross, what stages do terminally ill persons pass through when confronting death?**

Kübler-Ross found five distinct stages: denial, anger, bargaining, depression, and acceptance.

- **What are the major stages of bereavement?**

Bereavement usually involves several distinct phases: shock; protest and yearning; disorganization and despair; and detachment, reorganization, and recovery.

KEY TERMS: wear-and-tear theories of aging, p. 323; genetic theories of aging, p. 323; bereavement, p. 325

APPRAISAL	Physical, cognitive, and social development obviously occur together throughout our lives. Given this fact, does it make sense to try to study each one separately, as has often been done?
CONTROVERSY	Growing evidence indicates that children and adolescents from disadvantaged backgrounds in the United States and elsewhere are being placed at tremendous risk by the environments in which they live. This has led some persons to recommend massive government programs to help these young people. Do you think such programs could help? On what problems should they focus?
MAKING PSYCHOLOGY PART OF YOUR LIFE	On the basis of what you've learned in this chapter, what steps could you take to enhance your own physical and psychological well-being and, perhaps, increase your own life span?

DUE 7 /18

Motivation and Emotion

Why are some of us *workaholics* who thrive on endless hours of effort, while others do only the bare minimum required to get by? What makes certain movie scenes, written passages, or even articles of clothing so sexually arousing? How can we tell when another person is lying? Are there subtle cues in people's voices or facial expressions that can help us in this respect? Why does the whole world seem beautiful when we are in a good mood but unappealing when we are in a bad mood? Questions about why people act and feel the way they do relate to what might be described as the "feeling" side of life, or, as psychologists would put it, to the topics of *motivation* and *emotion*.

The term *motivation* refers to internal processes that serve to activate, guide, and maintain our behavior. Understanding motivation often helps us answer the question "Why?" as in "Why do other people behave as they do?" or "Why do they persist in certain courses of action, even when these don't seem to yield any obvious rewards?" Clearly, motivation is relevant to several of the questions raised above—the differences between workaholics and shirkaholics, the nature of sexual arousal, and so on (Silver, Mitchell, & Gist, in press).

Emotion, in contrast, refers to complex reactions consisting of (1) physiological responses such as changes in blood pressure and heart rate; (2) subjective cognitive states—the feelings we describe as joy, anger, sorrow, or sexual arousal; and (3) expressive reactions, such as changes in facial expressions or posture. It is on the last of these components—expressive reactions—that we often focus when trying to answer the question "Is that person telling the truth?" (DePaulo, 1992). Emotions play a crucial role in many aspects of behavior, including psychological disorders (see chapter 12). Further, as suggested by the question about why we tend to see the world through rose-colored glasses when we are in a good mood, emotions interact with and influence many aspects of cognition (e.g., Forgas, 1991; Smith & Shaffer, 1991).

This chapter will provide you with an overview of what psychologists currently know about these two important topics. Starting with *motivation,* we'll consider contrasting theories about its basic nature. After that, we'll examine several important forms of motivation: *hunger, sexual motivation, aggression,* and motives for *achievement* and *power.* Next, we'll turn to the topic of *emotion.* Again, we'll begin by examining several theories about its nature. Then we'll turn to the physiological bases of emotion. Third, we'll consider the expression and communication of emotion—how emotional reactions are reflected in external behavior. Finally, we'll look at the complex relationship between emotion and cognition—how feelings shape thoughts and thoughts shape feelings.

MOTIVATION: *The Activation and Persistence of Behavior*

Consider the following events:

A group of young women and men lower themselves into a dark cave and proceed to explore it. As they do, they must squeeze through openings just barely large enough for their bodies and avoid sudden drops where the cave floor plunges away into seemingly bottomless pits. They finally reemerge into the sunlight five days later, dirty and tired but happy.

A married couple drives almost one hundred miles over snow-covered roads in order to eat at a restaurant serving a type of food unavailable where they live.

How can such actions be explained? On the face of it, they are somewhat puzzling. Why would people risk life and limb exploring a cave, even though they can't hope to obtain any practical benefits by doing so? Why would anyone drive so far to eat a specific type of food (as my wife and I did when we lived in a very small university town more than one hundred miles from the nearest large city)? One answer is this: Such actions occur because the persons involved are *motivated* to perform them. In other words, they are responding to their own **motivation**—internal processes that can't be directly observed, but which activate, guide, and maintain their overt behaviors. Whenever the causes of a specific form of behavior can't be readily discerned in the immediate surroundings, many psychologists believe that it is reasonable to attribute them to various motives. While there is general agreement on this basic point, there has been considerable *disagreement*, over the years, about the basic nature of motivation. Let's consider some of these contrasting perspectives.

THEORIES OF MOTIVATION: *Diverse Views of a Complex Process*

In psychology, before there was *motivation* there was **instinct theory**. In other words, before psychologists attempted to explain behavior in terms of motives, they sought to do so through reference to various **instincts**: innate patterns of behavior that are universal in a species, independent of experience, and elicited by specific stimuli or conditions. For a time, this approach was quite popular. William James (1890), one of the founders of American psychology, included *pugnacity*, or combativeness; *acquisitiveness*, or greed; *sympathy*; and *curiosity* on his list of basic human instincts. And Sigmund Freud suggested that many complex forms of behavior—everything from aggression to love—stem from inherited, biologically based instincts.

Do instincts really play a major role in human behavior? Most psychologists doubt that they do. Moreover, most believe that instincts are not very useful from the point of view of understanding motivation. The basic problem is this: In many cases, the existence of an instinct was inferred from the very behavior it was supposed to explain. For example, take the case of *aggression*, a form of behavior we'll consider in more detail in a later section. Why do human beings, in contrast to many other species, frequently attack others of their own kind? The answer provided by James, Freud, and many others was simple: because human beings possess a powerful aggressive instinct. So far, so good. But how do we know that they possess this instinct? Because there is so much aggression. As I'm sure you can see, this is a circular process in which an instinct is inferred from observations of behavior and is then used to *explain* the occurrence of the same behavior. As recognition of this basic flaw in the instinct approach increased, support for this perspective waned, and it was soon replaced by other perspectives on motivation.

DRIVE THEORY: MOTIVATION AND HOMEOSTASIS   What do being hungry, being thirsty, being too cold, and being too hot have in common? One answer is that they are all unpleasant and cause us to do something to eliminate such feelings. This basic fact provides the basis for a second major approach to motivation: **drive theory**. According to this theory, biological needs arising within our bodies create unpleasant states of arousal—the feelings we usually describe as hunger, thirst, fatigue, and so on. In order to eliminate such feelings and restore a balanced physiological state, known as **homeostasis**, we engage in certain activities. Thus, according to drive theory, motivation is basically a process in which various biological needs push (drive) us to actions designed to satisfy these needs (see Figure 9.1 on page 336). Behaviors that work—ones that help reduce the appropriate drive—are strengthened and tend to be repeated. Those that fail to produce such effects are weakened and will not be repeated when the drive is present once again.

In its original form, drive theory focused primarily on biological needs and the aroused states, or drives, they produce. Soon, though, psychologists ex-

MOTIVATION: A USEFUL CONCEPT FOR UNDERSTANDING BEHAVIOR

Why do people engage in risky behaviors? One answer involves *motivation*—internal processes that can't be directly observed but that activate, guide, and maintain overt behavior.

Motivation: *An inferred internal process that activates, guides, and maintains behavior over time.*

Instinct Theory: *A theory of motivation suggesting that many forms of behavior stem from innate urges or tendencies.*

Instincts: *Patterns of behavior assumed to be universal in a species.*

Drive Theory: *A theory of motivation suggesting that behavior is "pushed" from within by drives stemming from basic biological needs.*

Homeostasis: *A state of physiological balance within the body.*

FIGURE **9.1**

Drive Theory: An Overview

According to *drive theory*, biological needs lead to the arousal of appropriate *drives* which activate specific forms of behavior. Actions that satisfy (reduce) these drives are strengthened and tend to be repeated when the drive is again present. Behaviors that fail to satisfy the drives are weakened.

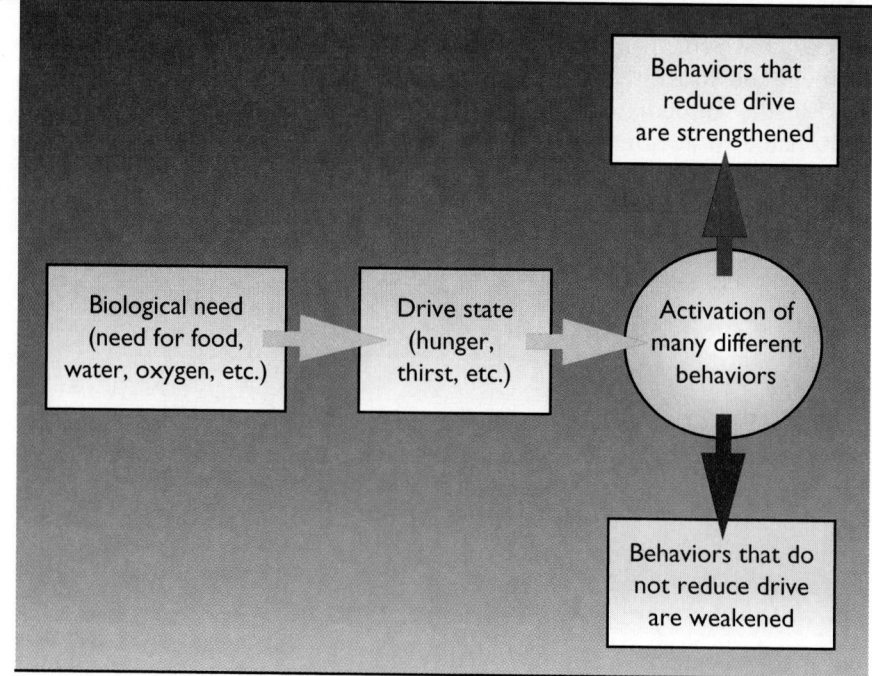

Learning Objective 9.5
Describe the factors involved in the regulation of eating, including the factors that may lead to anorexia nervosa and bulimia.

Learning Objective 9.6
Describe the relationships between hormones and sexual behavior.

Learning Objective 9.7
Survey the basic phases of human sexual behavior and list the factors that are thought to stimulate sexual arousal.

Learning Objective 9.8
Explain why there may be gender differences in sexual jealousy.

Arousal Theory: *A theory of motivation suggesting that human beings seek an optimal level of arousal, not minimal levels of arousal.*

tended this model to other forms of behavior not so clearly linked to basic needs, including drives for stimulation, for status, and for wealth and power (Weiner, 1989).

Drive theory persisted in psychology for several decades; it has not been totally discarded even today. However, there is widespread agreement among psychologists that this approach suffers from several major drawbacks. The most important problem is this: Contrary to what drive theory seems to suggest, human beings often engage in actions that tend to *increase* rather than to reduce various drives. For example, people often skip snacks and let their appetites increase in order to maximize their enjoyment of a special dinner. Similarly, many persons watch or read erotic materials in order to increase their sexual excitement, even when they don't anticipate immediate sexual gratification (Kelley & Byrne, 1992). In view of such evidence, most psychologists now believe that drive theory, by itself, does not provide a comprehensive framework for understanding human motivation.

Arousal Theory: Seeking Optimum Activation When it became clear that people sometimes seek to increase rather than to decrease existing drives, an alternative theory of motivation known as **arousal theory** was formulated (Geen, Beatty, & Arkin, 1984). This theory focuses on *arousal,* our general level of activation, which is reflected in physiological measures such as heart rate or blood pressure, muscle tension, and brain activity (Brehm & Self, 1989). Arousal varies throughout the day, from low levels during sleep to much higher ones when we are performing strenuous tasks. Arousal theory suggests that what we seek is not minimal levels of arousal, but rather *optimal arousal*—a level of arousal that is best suited to our personal characteristics and whatever activity we are currently performing. So, for example, if you are listening to soothing music, a relatively low level of arousal will be optimal. If you are competing in a sports event, a much higher one will be best.

Many studies offer at least indirect support for arousal theory. For example, there *is* often a close link between arousal and performance; see Figure 9.2 (Weiner, 1989). However, it is often difficult to determine in advance just

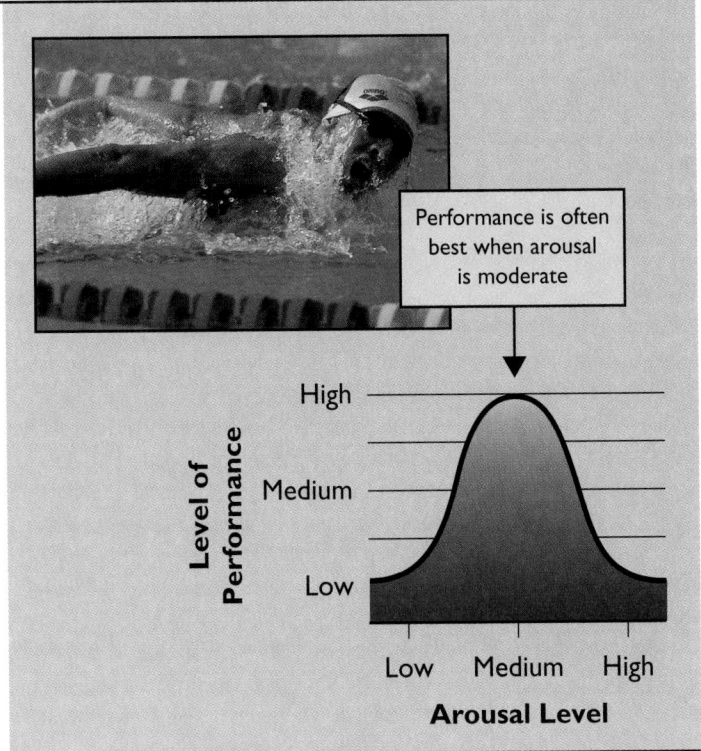

FIGURE 9.2

Arousal and Performance

Across a wide range of tasks, performance increases as arousal rises to moderate levels. Beyond some point, however, optimal levels of arousal are exceeded, and performance begins to decline.

Performance is often best when arousal is moderate

Level of Performance

High

Medium

Low

Low   Medium   High

Arousal Level

what level of arousal will be optimal for a given task or situation. Further, large individual differences exist with respect to preferred arousal level. At one extreme are individuals who prefer and seek high levels of activation (Zuckerman, 1990). At the other are persons who prefer much lower levels of arousal. Thus, while the theory does provide useful insights into the nature of motivation, it has important limitations, too.

EXPECTANCY THEORY: A COGNITIVE APPROACH   Why are you reading this book? Not, I'd guess, in order to reduce some biologically based drive. Rather, the chances are good that you are reading it because you expect that doing so will help you to reach important goals: to gain useful and interesting knowledge, to get a higher grade on the next exam, to graduate from college. In short, your behavior is determined by your *expectancies*—by your beliefs that your present actions will yield various outcomes in the future. This basic point provides the foundation for a third major theory of motivation, **expectancy theory**. This view suggests that motivation is not primarily a matter of being pushed from within by various urges; rather, it is more a question of being *pulled* from without by expectations of attaining desired outcomes. Such outcomes, known as **incentives**, can be almost anything we have learned to value—money, status, power, the admiration of others, to name just a few. In other words, while drive theory focuses mainly on the stick in the familiar carrot-and-stick notion, expectancy theory focuses more directly on the carrot. Why do people engage in complex, effortful, or even painful behaviors such as working many hours on their jobs, performing aerobic exercises, or studying long into the night? Expectancy theory answers: because they believe that doing so will yield outcomes they wish to attain.

Expectancy theory has been applied to many aspects of human motivation. Perhaps, though, it has found its most important practical use with respect to **work motivation**—the tendency to expend energy and effort on

Learning Objective 9.9
Discuss the various views on what determines or influences sexual orientation.

Learning Objective 9.10
Compare and contrast the views of the roots of aggression.

Learning Objective 9.11
Discuss individual differences in achievement and power motivation and how they are measured.

Learning Objective 9.12
Discuss the research findings concerning intrinsic motivation.

Expectancy Theory: *A theory of motivation suggesting that behavior is elicited by expectations of desirable outcomes.*

Incentives: *Rewards individuals seek to attain.*

Work Motivation: *Motivation to perform and complete various tasks.*

one's job (Locke & Latham, 1990). Research indicates that people will work hard at their jobs only when they believe that doing so will yield outcomes they desire, such as raises in pay, promotions, or increased status.

In sum, expectancy theory suggests that our motivation to engage in various activities will be high only when we expect that doing so will somehow pay off—yield outcomes or results we desire. In several respects, it is hard to imagine a more sensible statement about human motivation.

MASLOW'S NEEDS HIERARCHY: RELATIONS AMONG MOTIVES Before concluding this discussion of contrasting perspectives on motivation, it is important to consider one additional question: What specific motives influence behavior at any given time? One answer has been provided by Abraham Maslow (1970). He proposes that motives (or, as he puts it, *needs*) exist in a hierarchy, so that ones lying near the bottom of the hierarchy must be at least partially satisfied before those lying higher up can influence behavior. At the base of Maslow's **hierarchy of needs** are what he terms *physiological needs* such as the needs for food, water, oxygen, and sleep. One step above these are the *safety needs*, needs for feeling safe and secure in one's life. Above the safety needs are *social needs*, including needs to have friends, to be loved and appreciated, and to belong—to fit into a network of social relationships.

Maslow describes physiological, safety, and social needs as *deficiency needs:* They are the basics and must be satisfied before higher levels of motivation, or *growth needs,* can emerge. Above the social needs in the hierarchy are *esteem needs,* or needs to develop self-respect, gain the approval of others, and achieve success. Ambition and need for achievement, to which we'll return in a later section, are closely linked to esteem needs. Finally, at the top of the hierarchy are *self-actualization needs*. These involve the need for self-fulfillment—the desire to become all that one is capable of being. Self-actualization needs include concerns not only with one's selfish interests but also with issues that affect the well-being of others, and even of all humanity. Figure 9.3 provides an overview of Maslow's theory.

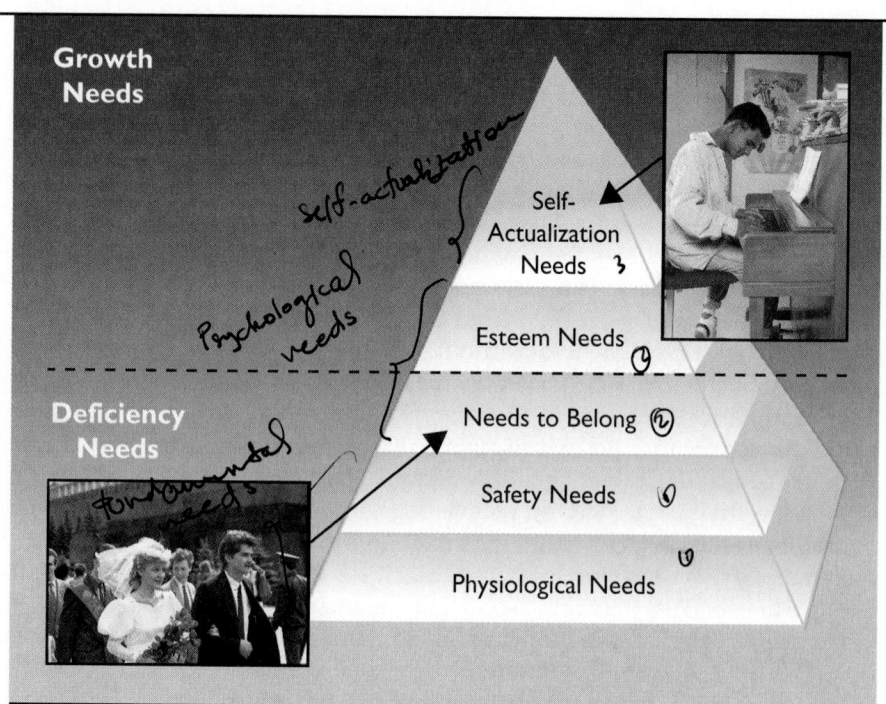

FIGURE 9.3

Maslow's Needs Hierarchy

According to Maslow (1970), needs exist in a hierarchy. Only when lower-order needs are satisfied can higher-order needs be activated.

/*Hierarchy of Needs: In Maslow's theory of motivation, an arrangement of needs from the most basic to those at the highest levels.*

Maslow's theory is intuitively appealing, but is it accurate? Do needs exist in a hierarchy, and must lower-level needs be met before higher-level ones can have a motivating effect? Research findings on these issues paint a mixed picture. Some results suggest that growth needs do come into play only after people have satisfied lower-level deficiency needs (Betz, 1982). But other findings indicate that people sometimes seek to satisfy higher-order needs even when ones lower in the hierarchy have not been met (Williams & Page, 1989). Moreover, it appears that several needs, and motivation relating to them, can sometimes be active at once (Greenberg & Baron, 1995). So, in sum, Maslow's needs hierarchy is best viewed as an interesting but largely unverified framework.

HUNGER: *Regulating Our Caloric Intake*

Mahatma Gandhi, one of the founders of modern India, once remarked, "Even God cannot speak to a hungry man except in terms of bread." By this he meant that when people are hungry, **hunger motivation**, or the urge to obtain and consume food, takes precedence over all others—a view consistent with Maslow's needs hierarchy. If you have ever had the experience of going without food for even a single day, you know from personal experience how strong and insistent feelings of hunger can be, and what a powerful source of motivation they can provide.

But where do such feelings come from? And how do we manage to regulate the amount of food we consume so that, for most persons, body weight remains fairly stable even over long periods of time? These are some of the questions psychologists have addressed in their efforts to understand the nature of hunger motivation.

THE REGULATION OF EATING: A COMPLEX PROCESS   Consider the following fact: If you consume just twenty extra calories each day (less than the amount in a single small carrot), you will gain about two pounds a year—twenty pounds in a decade. How do people keep caloric input and output closely balanced and so avoid such outcomes? What mechanisms allow for the long-term stability of body weight? The answer involves a complex system of regulatory mechanisms located in the hypothalamus, liver, and elsewhere. These systems contain special *detectors*, cells that respond to variations in the concentration of several nutrients in the blood. One type of detector responds to the amount of *glucose*, or blood sugar. Other detectors respond to levels of *protein*, and especially to certain amino acids. This is why we feel full after eating a meal high in protein, such as a thick juicy steak, even though the level of glucose in our blood remains relatively low. Finally, other detectors respond to *lipids*, or fats. Again, even if glucose levels are low, when the amount of lipids circulating in the blood is high, we do not feel hungry.

Complex as all this seems, it is still only part of the picture. In addition, eating and hunger are also strongly affected by the smell and taste of food and by feedback produced by chewing and swallowing. The impact of such factors is well documented. For example, in one series of studies, volunteers wore special equipment fitted to their teeth—equipment that permitted the researchers to obtain records of their actual chewing (Stellar, 1985). Participants also reported on their feelings of hunger and on the tastiness of the foods they ate. Results confirmed what informal observation suggests about our own eating: At first, when they were very hungry, the volunteers chewed less and swallowed more often. In other words, they consumed

Hunger Motivation: The motivation to obtain and consume food.

foods quite rapidly. As they satisfied their hunger and reported that the foods were less and less tasty, however, they chewed more and swallowed less often; their rate of intake dropped.

The sight of foods is also an important factor in eating. Foods that are attractive in appearance are hard to resist; many people eat more when presented with culinary delights than when presented with more mundane forms of food. Cultural factors, too, often play a major role in determining what, when, and how much we eat. Would you happily munch on fried grasshoppers? Sea urchin? Octopus cooked in its own ink? How about snails or snake? Depending on the culture in which you have been raised, the thought of such items may induce hunger pangs or feelings of nausea. Such contrasting reactions suggest that although hunger does indeed stem from biological needs, it is strongly influenced by learning and experience, and by cognitive factors, too (Rodin, 1984). So even this seemingly basic form of motivation is more complex than you might at first guess.

FACTORS IN OBESITY: WHY SOME PERSONS EXPERIENCE DIFFICULTY IN THE LONG-TERM REGULATION OF BODY WEIGHT

There can be little doubt that in the 1990s—at least in Western cultures—thin is in. In the United States alone, consumers spend huge sums each year on products and programs related to weight loss. What's behind this mass quest for slimness? The answer involves two powerful motives: the desire to be attractive to others and the desire to protect one's personal health. The first motive is encouraged by countless ads, movies, and television shows in which being slim is represented as an essential ingredient in physical beauty or popularity. The second motive derives from growing medical evidence indicating that being significantly overweight—a condition known as **obesity**—is indeed potentially harmful. Obesity has been linked to such serious disorders as high blood pressure, diabetes, and arthritis, to name a few (Kolata, 1985). Further, employees who are significantly overweight miss more days of work than those who are not (Goode, 1990).

Despite all this emphasis on slimness, many people experience difficulty in regulating their eating and hence their body weight. Why? Several factors seem to play a role. First, part of the problem may be learned. Many people acquire eating habits that are very likely to generate excess pounds. They learn to prefer high-calorie meals that are rich in protein and fats. Further, they learn to associate the act of eating with many different contexts and situations. If you feel a strong urge to snack every time you sit down in front if the television set or movie screen, you already know about such learning. The desire to eat can be classically conditioned (see chapter 5); that is, cues associated with eating when we are hungry can acquire the capacity to prompt eating even when we are *not* hungry.

Genetic factors, too, are important. Individuals differ greatly in terms of their *basal metabolic rate*—the number of calories their bodies require at rest within a given period of time. Persons of the same age and weight performing the same daily activities can differ widely in this regard, with the result that one person may require almost twice as many calories as the other to maintain a stable weight.

A third factor that seems to play an important role in the regulation of weight among humans involves the effects of stress. How do *you* react to stress—for example, to a big exam, a fight with your boyfriend or girlfriend, a traffic ticket? If you are like most people, your appetite probably decreases at such times. Those unpleasant feelings in the pit of your stomach make eating unattractive, at least temporarily. Overweight persons, however, often have a different reaction. They tend to eat *more* during periods of stress, even if they do not feel hungry.

Obesity: The state of being significantly overweight.

Yet another factor that seems to contribute to unwanted weight gain involves an intriguing difference between people who are obese and those who are not. Several studies indicate that overweight persons respond more strongly to external cues relating to food (Rodin & Slochower, 1976). They report feeling hungrier in the presence of food-related cues—the sight or smell of foods—than nonobese people, and they find it harder to resist eating when tasty foods are available, even if they are not hungry (Rodin, 1984).

Taking all these factors together, it is not surprising that many persons experience difficulties in regulating their own weight over the long term. There are simply too many variables or conditions that, together, can overwhelm the exquisitely balanced—and extraordinarily complex—biological mechanisms that normally keep body weight stable.

SERIOUS EATING DISORDERS: ANOREXIA NERVOSA AND BULIMIA As mentioned earlier, obesity poses a threat to personal health. Even more serious, however, are two additional conditions known together as *eating disorders*: **anorexia nervosa** and **bulimia**. (We'll consider these disorders again in chapter 12.) Persons suffering from anorexia nervosa literally starve themselves, often losing a dangerous amount of weight—15 percent or more of total body weight (Thompson, 1992). Such losses of weight can be tragically serious: Up to 5 percent of females suffering from this condition die as a result of their severe weight loss and associated problems (Hsu, 1986). Anorexia nervosa occurs ten times more frequently among women than among men, and is more common among young women in their teens and twenties than among older women. There can be little doubt that this eating disorder poses a considerable danger to the health and well-being of females in many countries.

In contrast, persons suffering from *bulimia* are generally of normal or near-normal weight; they don't suffer the extreme emaciation of persons with anorexia nervosa. However, bulimia does involve dramatic disorders in eating behavior. Bulimics maintain their normal weight through drastic means. Typically, they engage in bouts of excessive or *binge* eating, then purge themselves by self-induced vomiting or use of laxatives. Again, most persons suffering from bulimia are young women in their teens or twenties (Hinz & Williamson, 1987). Obviously, this eating disorder, too, can have profound adverse effects on personal health.

Why do so many young women—as many as 10 percent of American college women—suffer from such eating disorders? The causes are certainly complex, but one of the most important seems to be the fact that many young women are highly dissatisfied with their appearance—especially with the appearance of their bodies (Allgood-Merton & Lewinsohn, 1990). Indeed, they are much more dissatisfied in this respect than males of the same age. Their dissatisfaction, in turn, seems to stem from the emphasis many societies place on female attractiveness. When that emphasis is coupled with the powerful "thin-is-in" message conveyed by the fashion industry and mass media, it is not surprising that many young women conclude that they are overweight; after all, their bodies are much rounder than those of the fashion models and actresses who are held up as paragons of female perfection. Interestingly, many men do not find such extreme thinness in women attractive; on the contrary, they report preferring a body size somewhat larger than the one women rate as ideal (Fallon & Rozin, 1985).

Strong evidence for the role of dissatisfaction with one's body in the occurrence of anorexia and bulimia is provided by the results of several studies (e.g., Thompson, 1992; Williamson, 1990). For example, in one revealing investigation (Williamson, Cubic, & Gleaves, 1993), three groups of young women—ones diagnosed as bulimic, ones diagnosed as anorexic, and ones not suffering from any eating disorder—were asked to rate silhouettes of women ranging from

Anorexia Nervosa: An eating disorder in which individuals starve themselves and often lose a dangerous amount of weight.

Bulimia: An eating disorder in which periods of binge eating alternate with periods of self-induced purging.

ones that were emaciated to ones that were very obese. First they selected the silhouette that most accurately represented their own *current* body size, then they rated the silhouette that represented the body size they most preferred (their *ideal*). Since persons suffering from anorexia are indeed very thin, it is not surprising that anorexic persons rated their current body size as smaller than did persons in the control group. However, when **body-mass index** (current body size) was held constant statistically, a different pattern of findings emerged: Both bulimic and anorexic participants rated their current body size as larger than did control participants, and both rated their ideal as smaller than did controls. In other words, when current body weight was taken into account, both anorexics and bulimics viewed themselves as further from their ideal than persons not suffering from any eating disorder.

Several additional points help complete the picture: (1) Bulimics tend to be more preoccupied with their physical appearance than other persons (e.g., Casper, 1990); (2) bulimics are lower in social self-confidence (higher in social anxiety) than other persons (e.g., Tobin et al., 1991); and (3) bulimics' reduced self-consciousness and their heightened social anxiety are linked to lower satisfaction with their own bodies (Striegel-Moore, Silberstein, & Rodin, 1993). Together, these findings indicate that bulimics are indeed trapped in a vicious circle from which they can usually escape only with professional help (Thompson, 1992).

SEXUAL MOTIVATION: The Most Intimate Motive

Suppose that voyagers from another planet arrived on Earth and visited many large cities. What would they see? Among other things, countless signs, billboards, and advertisements focused on two topics: food and sex. As a result, the space aliens might quickly conclude that human beings are obsessed with these two topics. Since we have already considered hunger in some detail, we'll now turn to **sexual motivation**, or motivation to engage in sexual activity—clearly another very strong force in human behavior.

HORMONES AND SEXUAL BEHAVIOR: ACTIVATION AND DIFFERENTIATION As we saw in chapter 8, the onset of puberty involves rapid increases in the activity of the sex glands, or **gonads**. The hormones the gonads produce have many effects on the body. A key question from the perspective of this discussion, however, is: Do these hormones influence sexual motivation? In most organisms other than human beings, the answer seems to be yes. Sex hormones exert what are usually termed *activational effects*. In their absence, sexual behavior does not occur or takes place with a very low frequency. For example, in many animals removal of the ovaries totally eliminates female sexual receptivity. Removal of the testes in males produces similar though somewhat less clear-cut results. For many species, in short, hormones play a key role in sexual motivation.

Human beings, however, are something of an exception to this general pattern. Most women do not report large changes in sexual desire over the course of their monthly cycle, despite major shifts in the concentration of various sex hormones in their blood (Kelley & Byrne, 1992). Further, many continue to engage in and enjoy sexual relations after *menopause*, when the hormonal output of their ovaries drops sharply. And in men there is little evidence of a clear link between blood levels of sex hormones such as *testosterone* and sexual responsiveness (Byrne, 1982).

Body-Mass Index: A measure of degree of obesity, based on the ratio between height and weight.

Sexual Motivation: Motivation to engage in various forms of sexual activity.

Gonads: The primary sex glands.

This is not to say, however, that sex hormones play no role in human sexual motivation. Some women do report peaks of sexual arousal in the middle of their cycle and again prior to menstruation (Harvey, 1987). Among males, there is some evidence that testosterone levels are associated with differences in sexual arousal. For example, men with high levels of testosterone become aroused more quickly by erotic films than those with relatively low levels (Lange et al., 1980). In general, though, the link between sex hormones and sexual motivation appears to be far less clear-cut and less compelling for human beings than is true for many other species.

Other chemical substances within the body, however, may play more direct—and dramatic—roles. Recent findings suggest that when human beings are sexually attracted to another person, their brain produces increased amounts of several substances that are related to *amphetamines*. As you probably recall from chapter 4, amphetamines are stimulants, so the increased production of amphetamine-like substances such as phenylethylamine (PEA) may account for the fact that many people describe strong sexual attraction—the first stage in falling in love—as a feeling that "sweeps them away." As one researcher puts it, "love is a natural high" (Walsh, 1993), one that confirms the words of the old song, "I get a kick out of you."

In sum, while sex hormones do not seem to be as clearly linked to sexual motivation in humans as in other species, there is some scientific evidence for the view that other substances produced by our bodies do play an important role in such motivation, and even in romantic love. Does this mean that we will someday be able to produce pills that can cause us to fall in (or out of) love? Probably not; because, as we'll now see, where human beings are concerned, cognitive factors—our own thoughts, fantasies, and memories—play a very powerful role in sexual motivation. But there does seem to be a biochemistry of love, and biochemical effects, too, deserve careful attention as we try to understand the nature of human sexual motivation.

HUMAN SEXUAL BEHAVIOR: SOME BASIC FACTS   Until the 1960s the only source of scientific information about human sexual motivation was that provided by surveys. The most famous of these were the *Kinsey Reports*, published in the 1940s and 1950s. These surveys, which were based on interviews with more than ten thousand women and men, yielded many surprising facts. Half a century ago, most men and nearly half of the women reported having engaged in premarital sex (Kinsey, Pomeroy, & Martin, 1984; Kinsey et al., 1953). Further, it appeared that many couples engaged in practices that society then considered to be objectionable, such as oral sex and a wide variety of sexual positions. If there is one basic theme in the Kinsey data, though, it is this: Where sexual behavior is concerned, individual differences are enormous. Some people reported remaining celibate for years; others reported engaging in sexual relations with a large number of partners. Some reported that orgasms were a rare occurrence, but a few indicated that they experienced three or more every day.

Please note the word *reported*, however. Survey data such as those obtained by Kinsey and others are always open to question. First, who agrees to participate in a given survey? Many persons refuse, and it is impossible to tell how the findings might change if *their* patterns of sexual behavior were included.

Second, how accurate are self-reports? Do participants describe their sexual behavior and sexual motivation accurately? Or do they exaggerate, fail to provide some information, and generally seek to present themselves in a favorable light? These complex issues always leave the interpretation of survey results somewhat in doubt.

Starting in the 1960s, however, another source of information about human sexual motivation became available: direct and systematic observation of actual sexual activities. The first and still the most famous project of this kind was conducted by Masters and Johnson in the mid-1960s (Masters & Johnson, 1966). These researchers observed, filmed, and monitored the reactions of several hundred volunteers of both sexes as they engaged in sexual intercourse or masturbation. More than ten thousand cycles of arousal and satisfaction were studied. The results yielded important insights into the nature of human sexuality. Perhaps the clearest finding was the fact that both males and females move through four distinct phases during sexual behavior.

First, they enter the *excitement phase*. During this phase, many physiological changes indicative of growing sexual excitement occur. The penis and clitoris become enlarged, vaginal lubrication increases, and nipples may become erect in both sexes. If sexual stimulation persists, both women and men enter the *plateau phase*. The size of the penis increases still further, and the outer third of the vagina becomes engorged with blood, reducing its diameter. Muscle tension, respiration, heart rate, and blood pressure all rise to high levels.

After a variable period of direct stimulation, both males and females approach the *orgasmic phase*. This consists of several contractions of the muscles surrounding the genitals, along with intense sensations of pleasure. The pattern of contractions, including their timing and length, is virtually identical in females and males.

The most striking difference between the two sexes occurs during the final *resolution phase*. For males, orgasm is followed by a reduction in sexual and physiological arousal. Males then enter a *refractory period* during which they cannot be sexually aroused or experience another orgasm. Among females, in contrast, two distinct patterns are possible. They, too, may experience a reduction in sexual and physiological arousal. Alternatively, if stimulation continues, they may experience additional orgasms.

The basic pattern just described seems to apply to all human beings. However, practically everything else seems to vary from one society to another. Different cultures have widely different standards about such matters as (1) the age at which sexual behavior should begin, (2) the frequency with which it should occur, (3) physical characteristics considered attractive or sexy, (4) the particular positions and practices that are acceptable, (5) the proper time and setting for sexual relations, (6) the persons who are appropriate partners, and (7) the number of partners individuals should have at one time or in succession. So, to repeat: where human sexuality is concerned, *variability* is definitely the central theme.

HUMAN SEXUAL BEHAVIOR: WHAT'S AROUSING AND WHY Clearly, sexual motivation plays an important role in human behavior. But what, precisely, stimulates arousal? In certain respects, the same events or stimuli that produce arousal in other species. First, direct physical contacts—various forms of touching and foreplay—generate arousal. Second, there is some evidence that human beings, like other organisms, can be sexually aroused by certain naturally occurring odors.

For example, one study found that approximately 20 percent of males appear to be sexually stimulated by the scents of copulins, chemicals found in vaginal secretions (Hassett, 1978). More recently, some scientists have reported that odorless natural substances known as pheromones can produce sexual attraction and arousal in both males and females (Blakeslee, 1993). On the basis of these findings, large perfume companies have added synthetic human pheromones to products. Will wearing such perfumes make you more attractive to the opposite sex, as advertised? Since the "scientific reports" on which these claims are based are unpublished, my advice is simple: View such ads with a healthy degree of skepticism (Cain, 1988; Ehrlichman & Bastone, 1990).

One potential source of sexual motivation, however, does seem to set human beings apart from other species: real or imagined erotic stimuli and images. Unlike other species, human beings possess the capacity to generate their own sexual arousal on the basis of erotic fantasies or daydreams. And many people respond strongly to *erotic materials* containing either visual images or verbal descriptions of sexual behavior.

With respect to self-generated imagery, research findings indicate that many people can produce intense sexual arousal, even orgasm, through internally generated sexual images (Money, 1985). Further, many report using sexual thoughts or images to enhance their pleasure during sexual intercourse or masturbation, or to speed up or delay the occurrence of orgasms (Davidson & Hoffman, 1986). In these and other ways, our impressive cognitive abilities can play a major role in sexual motivation.

External erotic stimuli, too, can produce such effects. Virtually every physiological reaction and behavior recorded by Masters and Johnson during actual sexual activity can occur in response to erotic movies, tapes, or written descriptions (Kelley & Byrne, 1992). Of course, not all persons find all materials of this type equally exciting. Explicit erotic materials can be too explicit for some people's taste, so that exposure to them reduces rather than increases sexual motivation (Zillmann, 1984). However, given erotic stimuli that they *do* find attractive, most persons can be sexually aroused in this indirect manner.

If the only effects produced by erotic materials were increases in sexual motivation and perhaps sexual behavior, there would be little reason to discuss them further. Unfortunately, however, growing evidence suggests that exposure to such materials produces other effects as well—effects that many people find objectionable. First, repeated exposure to explicit erotica has been found to increase viewers' estimates of the frequency of several unusual and widely disapproved sexual practices, including *sadomasochism* (sexual practices in which participants physically hurt one another), human-animal contact, and sex between adults and children (Zillmann & Bryant, 1984). Second, exposure to explicit erotic materials seems to reduce viewers' satisfaction with their own sex lives and with their current sexual partner (e.g., Zillmann & Bryant, 1988). These findings suggest that the ready availability of erotic materials in many societies may have social consequences that were not fully anticipated when widespread sale of such materials was legalized.

PHEROMONES: A SOURCE OF SEXUAL ATTRACTION?

Some research findings suggest that pheromones—odorless substances produced by our bodies—may play a role in sexual attraction and arousal. Some colognes and perfumes supposedly have similar powers, but scientific research has not supported such claims.

GENDER DIFFERENCES IN SEXUAL JEALOUSY: A SOCIOBIOLOGICAL PERSPECTIVE

Many nonhuman species are monogamous: They mate for life. Do these animals experience jealousy if they discover their mate with another member of the opposite sex? At present, we don't know. But we *do* know that **sexual jealousy**—a negative state aroused by a perceived threat to one's valued sexual relationship with another person—is very common among our own species (Salovey, 1991; White & Mullen, 1990). As you undoubtedly know from your own experience, both women and men experience sexual jealousy. Recent findings suggest, however, that the two sexes may differ in some ways with respect to such reactions. Specifically, it appears that men may experience more intense jealousy in response to *sexual* infidelity on the part of their partners, while women may experience more intense jealousy in response to *emotional* infidelity (Buss et al., 1992). Why should this be so? The field of *socio-*

Sexual Jealousy: A negative state aroused by a perceived threat to one's sexual relationship with another person.

biology (or *evolutionary psychology* as it is sometimes known; Buss, 1990) provides one potential answer.

According to sociobiology, men should be especially upset by sexual infidelity for two reasons: (1) A man can never be perfectly certain that he is the father of his children, and (2) men invest lots of energy and resources in caring for their mates and their offspring. If a man's partner engages in sexual relations with other males, therefore, he runs the risk of investing resources in another man's children! Emotional infidelity, as long as it doesn't result in actual sexual relations, is less threatening, for obvious reasons.

What about women—why should they find emotional infidelity so disturbing? From a sociobiological perspective, the answer is as follows: Women know with certainty that they are the mothers of their children. However, throughout most of human history, women needed the assistance of a male to raise their children. Emotional infidelity threatened such support, for if a woman's mate fell in love with another woman, he might leave, taking with him his needed support and assistance. In contrast, sexual infidelity by the mate would pose no threat as long as he didn't become seriously involved with the other woman.

These are controversial suggestions, to say the least, and are certain to anger some persons. But political or social reactions aside, they are supported by the findings of several studies conducted by Buss and his colleagues (Buss et al., 1992). In one of these investigations, male and female students were asked to indicate which would upset them more: imagining that their romantic partner was forming a deep emotional attachment to another person, or learning that their partner was enjoying passionate sexual intercourse with that person. Results were clear: A large majority of the men (60 percent) reported greater distress over sexual infidelity, while a large majority of the women (83 percent) reported greater distress over emotional infidelity.

In a follow-up study, male and female participants were asked to imagine that their partner was having sexual intercourse with another person, and that their partner was falling in love with another person. While the participants were imagining these scenes, the researchers recorded their physiological reactions: activity in a facial muscle involved in frowning, pulse rate, and electrodermal activity (electrical conductivity of the skin). Again the results were clear. Males showed greater arousal and more signs of frowning when imagining sexual infidelity; females showed greater arousal and more frowning when imagining emotional infidelity.

Taken together, these findings and those of other studies (Buss, 1989) indicate that males and females may indeed differ with respect to the kinds of situations or events that make them jealous. Men seem to find sexual infidelity more disturbing than emotional infidelity, while women show the opposite pattern. Are such differences really due to the factors sociobiology emphasizes—certainty of parenthood and covering one's investments? Firm conclusions will have to await the completion of additional research.

SEXUAL ORIENTATION Estimates vary, but it appears that about 2 percent of all adults are exclusively **homosexual** in their sexual orientation: They engage in sexual relations only with members of their own sex (Kelley & Byrne, 1992). In addition, many other persons, perhaps another 2 or 3 percent of each sex, are **bisexual**: They seek out and enjoy sexual contact with members of both sexes. The remainder of the population is **heterosexual** and engages in sexual relations only with members of the opposite sex.

In the past, homosexuals of both sexes often remained "in the closet," concealing their orientation from others. Since the early 1970s, however, the situation has changed radically, and many homosexuals have engaged in vigorous

Homosexual *(sexual orientation): A sexual orientation in which individuals prefer sexual relations with members of their own sex.*

Bisexual *(sexual orientation): A sexual orientation in which individuals seek sexual relations with members of both their own and the other sex.*

Heterosexual *(sexual orientation): A sexual orientation in which individuals engage in sexual relations only with members of the other sex.*

efforts to be gain equal treatment in many areas of life—employment, housing, military service, education, and so on—even when openly avowing their orientation. This continuing struggle and the controversy surrounding it have led to renewed interest in a basic question: What factors influence or determine sexual orientation? In other words, why are some persons exclusively homosexual while most others are exclusively heterosexual? Unfortunately, research findings to date have failed to yield any firm or definite answers. All of the most obvious possibilities appear to be false. Male homosexuals do not have lower levels of male sex hormones than heterosexuals (Gladue, 1991), and increasing their levels of male sex hormones does not alter their homosexual preferences (Money, 1980). Similarly, careful study of the family backgrounds of both male and female homosexuals has failed to yield any reliable differences between these groups and heterosexuals (Hammersmith, 1982).

Another theory is that homosexuality stems from experiences during puberty (Storms, 1981). According to this view, some individuals learn to associate their emerging sexual impulses with members of their own sex and so develop homosexual preferences. At present, however, direct evidence for such effects is lacking. Moreover, many persons who are homosexual report that they had sexual fantasies and thoughts about members of their own sex long before puberty.

This latter finding is consistent with yet another possible explanation for the origin of homosexuality, one we examined in chapter 2: the view that genetic factors play an important role (Bailey & Pillard, 1991; Bailey et al., 1993; Henry, 1993). Some research findings suggest that a tendency toward homosexuality may be inherited and that it may be linked to the X chromosome all children inherit from their mothers (Hammer et al., 1993). This suggestion is consistent with the experience of many homosexuals who report that they knew from a very early age that they were "different" from most other persons. However, it is clear that environmental factors also play a role; so genetic factors and inherited tendencies are only part of the total, complex picture.

KEY QUESTIONS

- What role do sex hormones play in human sexual motivation?

- What are the major phases of sexual activity?

- What is a key difference between human beings and other species with respect to sexual arousal?

- What factors appear to play a role in determining sexual orientation?

AGGRESSIVE MOTIVATION: The Most Dangerous Motive

War. Murder. Rape. Child abuse. In the 1990s no one—neither passengers in commuter trains nor motorists on interstate highways—seems safe from acts of violence. Consider the following statistics:

- More than two million people are knifed, shot, or otherwise assaulted each year in the United States alone; more than twenty-three thousand of them die as a result of these attacks (Toufexis, 1993).

- Physical violence between spouses occurs in almost one-third of all marriages (Russell, 1988).

- Each year many thousands of children die as a result of child abuse—much of it inflicted by their own parents (Pagelow, 1984).

Such facts suggest that **aggressive motivation**—the desire to inflict harm on others—plays an all-too-common role in human affairs. Aggressive motivation often results in the occurrence of overt forms of **aggression**, or behavior directed toward the goal of injuring another living being who wishes to avoid such treatment (Baron & Richardson, 1994).

Aggressive Motivation: The desire to inflict harm on others.

Aggression: Behavior directed toward the goal of harming another living being who wishes to avoid such treatment.

THE ROOTS OF AGGRESSION: INNATE TENDENCY OR EXTERNALLY ELICITED BEHAVIOR? Is aggression an inherited and unavoidable human tendency? Freud, for one, believed that it is. After witnessing the wholesale carnage of World War I, he concluded, pessimistically, that human beings possess a powerful built-in tendency to harm others. While this view has been shared by many other scientists—for example, Konrad Lorenz, the famous *ethologist*—it is definitely *not* widely accepted by present-day psychologists (Berkowitz, 1990). Most believe that aggression, like many other forms of motivation, is elicited by a wide range of external events and stimuli. In other words, it is often "pulled" from without rather than "pushed" or driven from within. This is not to suggest that aggression has *no* biological or genetic roots. On the contrary, growing evidence indicates that such factors do play a role in the occurrence of violent crime (Gladue, 1991). For example, it has recently been reported that men convicted of impulsive crimes of violence, such as murdering strangers, have lower than normal amounts of serotonin in their brains; in contrast, those convicted of cold-blooded, premeditated aggressive crimes show normal levels of serotonin (Toufexis, 1993). This suggests that deficits in serotonin may somehow interfere with neural mechanisms that normally inhibit the outward expression of rage. In most cases, however, aggression seems to stem primarily from social and environmental factors (e.g., Bettencourt & Miller, in press).

One variable that has often been suggested as an important cause of aggressive motivation is **frustration**—the thwarting or blocking of goal-directed behavior. In other words, people experience the desire to harm others when these individuals, or perhaps others, have prevented them from obtaining what they want. The strongest statement of this view is the famous *frustration-aggression hypothesis*, which proposes that aggression always stems from frustration and that frustration always produces aggression. It is now clear that these assertions are far too sweeping in scope. Aggression often

TABLE 9.1	FACTOR	EFFECT ON AGGRESSION
Factors Influencing Aggression	High temperatures	Increase aggression
	Audience	Increases aggression when this is a strong (dominant) tendency; decreases aggression if audience disapproves of this behavior
As shown here, aggression is influenced by a wide range of social, environmental, and personal factors.	Exposure to aggressive models (others behaving aggressively)	Increases aggression
	Heightened arousal	Increases aggression when arousal is interpreted as provocation or frustration
	Alcohol	Increases aggression in large doses; reduces aggression in very small doses
	Apologies, explanations for provocative actions	Reduce aggression if accepted as sincere
	Humorous materials	Reduce aggression if they induce feelings of amusement
	Signs of pain on part of victim	Increase aggression if aggressor is very angry; reduce aggression if anger is low
	Type A behavior pattern	Increases aggression in many situations
	Presence of weapons (not used in assault)	Increases aggression because of previous association with such behavior

Frustration: *The blocking of ongoing goal-directed behavior.*

stems from causes other than frustration: direct provocation from others, exposure to others behaving in an aggressive manner, the presence of weapons or other stimuli associated with aggression, and the consumption of alcohol, to name a few (Baron & Richardson, 1994). And frustration often produces depression or resignation rather than aggression against others. So frustration is only one of many different factors that elicit aggression, and frustration seems to produce such effects only when it is unexpected and is viewed as unfair or illegitimate (Berkowitz, 1989). An overview of the many social, environmental, and personal factors that have been found to increase the likelihood or intensity of aggression is presented in Table 9.1. Even a quick review of this table suggests why reducing the level of aggression in any given society is a complex and challenging task.

What about cultural factors? Do they too play an important role with respect to the outward expression of aggressive motivation? For information on this topic, please see the **Perspectives on Diversity** section.

PERSPECTIVES ON DIVERSITY

The Role of Cultural Factors in Aggression: The Social Context of Violence

D o cultures differ with respect to the expression of aggression? Figure 9.4 provides a partial answer: As you can see, murder is much more frequent in the United States than in other industrialized nations—from ten to twenty times higher than in some nations, by some estimates (Scott, 1992). What accounts for differences like those shown in Figure 9.4? The answer is complex, but the existence of such differences suggests that cultural variables often exert powerful effects on aggression. Let's take a brief look at several of these variables.

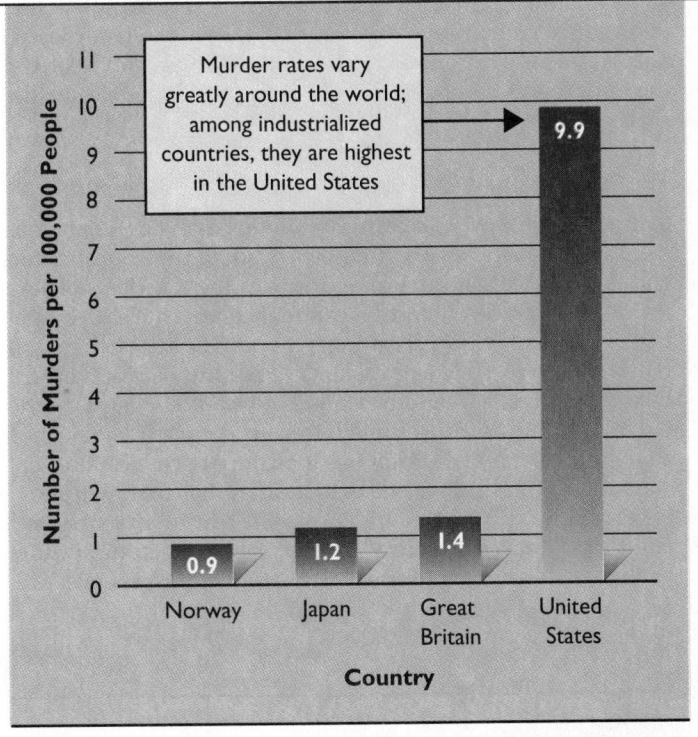

FIGURE 9.4

Cultural Differences in Aggression

As shown here, murders are much more frequent in the United States than in other industrialized nations. Differences such as these suggest that cultural factors play an important role in aggression.
(*Source:* Based on data from Scott, 1992.)

Aggression and Self-Perception: A Case in Point

In the Mexican state of Oxaca, there are two Zapotec villages located less than four miles apart. The two villages, which have existed for at least 450 years, are very similar in terms of language, religion, economics, and virtually every other aspect. Yet the murder rate in one is more than six times higher than in the other (Fry, 1990). What accounts for this difference? Careful comparison of the villages suggests that the key differences lie in contrasting *self-perceptions*. In the relatively non-violent village, residents describe themselves as peaceful, kind, and respectful of the rights of others. In the more violent village, in contrast, the people describe themselves as tough and aggressive and perceive overt acts of aggression, such as fistfights and spouse abuse, as proof of their vigor and strength. How did these contrasting views originate? The answer is lost in the mists of time, but in attempting to explain them, one investigator (Scott, 1992) suggests that the two villages were probably founded by persons with contrasting perspectives on aggression, and that the norms established in those long-vanished days have persisted up until the present, finding expression in the sharply contrasting rates of violence we now observe.

Culture and Reactions to Frustration

One especially important way in which culture influences aggression is by determining when and how reactions to frustration are expressed. In many cultures aggression is a strongly disapproved form of behavior, so persons exposed to frustration are urged to demonstrate restraint. For example, in Sri Lanka, *quiet self-control* is highly valued (Spencer, 1990). As a result, people generally refrain from aggression in response to provocations that would evoke strong retaliation from people in other cultures.

A clear illustration of the role of cultural factors in shaping reactions to frustration is provided by a study conducted by Kaufman, Gregory, and Stephan (1990). They examined the reactions of Anglo and Hispanic students in the United States to one important type of frustration: being an ethnic minority in their schools. Kaufman and his colleagues predicted that because Hispanic culture strongly emphasizes being *simpatico*—being likable, easygoing, and fun to be with—Hispanic children would demonstrate increased moodiness but *not* increased aggression when in classrooms where they were an ethnic minority. In contrast, because Anglo culture is more accepting of overt aggression, Kaufman, Gregory, and Stephan (1990) expected that Anglo children might demonstrate higher levels of aggression when they were an ethnic minority. This is precisely what was found. These and related findings illustrate the important role of culture in shaping the form and incidence of aggression in many contexts.

The Persistence of Cultural Differences in Aggression

One final point: why do cultural differences in aggression persist? One answer seems to lie in cultures' varied beliefs about the appropriateness of aggression and the different child-rearing practices these beliefs encourage. For example, a study by Osterwell and Nagano-Nakamura (1992) compared Japanese and Israeli mothers' views about aggression. The researchers found that Japanese mothers tend to view aggression as a natural part of their children's behavior, but believe that it should be expressed *within* the family, where it can be regulated and will do no serious harm. In contrast, Israeli mothers believe that aggression is mainly a response to external provocations, and they feel that it should be expressed *outside* the family rather than within it. Such contrasting beliefs about aggression influence child-rearing practices in different cultures, and these practices, in turn, help explain why cultural differences in the rate and intensity of many forms of aggression tend to persist over time (Fraczek & Kirwil, 1992).

ACHIEVEMENT AND POWER: Two Complex Human Motives

Hunger, sex, and aggression: these are motives we share with many other forms of life. There are some motives, however, that, as far as we can tell, are unique to our own species. We'll focus on two that are often closely interrelated: **achievement motivation** and **power motivation**. Achievement motivation is the desire to meet standards of excellence—to outperform others and accomplish difficult tasks (McClelland, 1961). Power motivation is the desire to be in charge, to have status and prestige and influence others (Winter, 1973). Such motives do not derive directly from basic biological factors, as do hunger, thirst, and, to some extent, sexuality. Yet they exert powerful effects on behavior in many different contexts.

ACHIEVEMENT MOTIVATION: THE QUEST FOR EXCELLENCE That individuals differ greatly in the desire for achievement is obvious. For some persons, accomplishing difficult tasks and meeting high standards of excellence are extremely important. For others, just getting by is quite enough. How can differences in this motive be measured? What are their effects? These are the issues that have received most attention in past research.

Measuring achievement and power motivation The same basic method is used for measuring both achievement and power motivation. This technique, known as the **Thematic Apperception Test (TAT)**, consists of a series of ambiguous pictures, such as an individual staring thoughtfully into space or an older person talking to a younger one. Persons completing the TAT are shown the pictures and asked to make up stories about them. The content of the stories is then evaluated by means of carefully developed keys, in order to yield scores for achievement and power motivation (McClelland, 1975). While the TAT continues to be used in its original form, Winter (1983) has also developed a technique for scoring these motives directly from any type of verbal material, without the need for ambiguous pictures or for people to make up stories about them. Winter's technique can be applied to books, speeches, or any other written material in order to obtain an index of the author's achievement and power motivation.

Effects of achievement and power motivation Do individual differences in achievement and power motivation really matter? In other words, do persons high and low in these motives have contrasting life experiences? Growing evidence suggests that they do. As you might expect, individuals high in achievement motivation tend to get higher grades in school, earn more rapid promotions, and attain greater success in running their own businesses than persons low in such motivation (Andrews, 1967; Raynor, 1970). Perhaps more surprising is the fact that persons high in achievement motivation tend to prefer situations involving moderate levels of risk or difficulty to ones that are very low or very high on these dimensions (Atkinson & Litwin, 1960). Why? The answer seems to lie in the fact that in situations involving moderate risk or difficulty there is a good chance of success, but there is also a sense of challenge. In contrast, in situations that are very high in risk or difficulty, failure is likely—and high achievement persons dislike failure intensely. Finally, situations that are very low in risk or difficulty fail to provide the challenge that persons high in achievement motivation relish.

Gender differences in achievement motivation: Do they really exist? If you ever watch old films made in the 1940s or 1950s, you may observe the following situation: A teenage girl is brighter or more competent at some

> ✓**Achievement Motivation:** *The desire to accomplish difficult tasks and meet standards of excellence.*
>
> **Power Motivation:** *Motivation to be in charge, have high status, and exert influence over others.*
>
> ✓**Thematic Apperception Test (TAT):** *A psychological test used to assess individual differences in several motives, such as achievement motivation and power motivation.*

task than a teenage boy. Yet she avoids letting him know this, because she is afraid that he will be threatened by this fact and so like her less.

Do such scenes reflect real-life events? In the past, it appears that they did. Traditional concepts of femininity seemed incompatible with high levels of competence, success, or achievement motivation on the part of women. Taking note of this fact, Horner (1970, 1972) suggested that many women actually feared success: They realized that striving for achievement could reduce their femininity in the eyes of others. She then found evidence for the existence of *fear of success* among young women. In Horner's research, female undergraduates were asked to tell a story about Anne, a young woman who found herself at the top of her medical school class. Male undergraduates were given the same task with respect to a young man named John. Almost all the men wrote stories predicting a happy and successful life for the male character. In contrast, about two-thirds of the women wrote stories predicting serious problems for Anne. She was seen as having a future in which she would be rejected by others (especially men) and would be lonely and isolated. From these findings, Horner concluded that women did indeed fear success.

Fortunately, these results were *not* replicated in subsequent investigations (Cherry & Deaux, 1975). Recent research, moreover, indicates that what the women in Horner's studies feared was not success itself, but social rejection. Thus, many psychologists now doubt that the fear of success reported by Horner ever existed at all. Her findings seem more likely to have been an artifact stemming from the specific methods she used than from any real difference between females and males with respect to feelings about success.

INTRINSIC MOTIVATION: *How (Sometimes) to Turn Play into Work*

Individuals perform many activities simply because they find them enjoyable. Everything from hobbies to gourmet dining to lovemaking fits within this category. Such activities may be described as deriving from **intrinsic motivation;** that is, we perform these activities primarily because of the pleasure they yield, not because they lead to other, external rewards. But what happens if people are given external rewards for performing such activities—if, for example, they are paid for sipping vintage wines or for pursuing their favorite hobby? Some research findings suggest that they may then actually experience reductions in intrinsic motivation. In other words, they may become *less* motivated to engage in such activities. Why? Perhaps, on considering their own behavior, such overrewarded persons conclude that they chose to perform the activities partly to obtain the external reward—the payment—provided. To the extent they reach that conclusion, they may then view their own interest as lower than was previously the case. They may shift from explaining their behavior in terms of intrinsic motivation ("I do it because I enjoy it") to explaining it in terms of external rewards ("I do it partly to obtain some kind of payment").

Many studies support this explanation. In such research, some participants were provided with extrinsic rewards for engaging in a task they initially enjoyed, while others were not. When subsequently given an opportunity to perform the task, those who received the external rewards showed reduced motivation to do so (Deci, 1975; Lepper & Green, 1978). These results have important implications for anyone seeking to motivate others by means of rewards—parents, teachers, and managers, for example. The research suggests that if the target persons already enjoy various activities, offering them rewards for performing those activities may lower their intrinsic motivation and so, ultimately, produce the paradoxical effect of reducing rather than enhancing performance!

Intrinsic Motivation: *The desire to perform activities because they are rewarding in and of themselves.*

CHAPTER 9

Fortunately, additional evidence suggests that this is not always the case, and that intrinsic and extrinsic motivation are not necessarily incompatible (Rigby et al., 1992). In fact, Deci and his colleagues (e.g., Deci & Ryan, 1985) argue that what is crucial is the extent to which individuals perceive various behaviors as *self-determined*. Intrinsically motivated behaviors are, by definition, self-determined. Extrinsically motivated actions, however, are not necessarily *non*–self-determined. If individuals find them congruent with their self-image, preferences, and values, they may view them as self-determined even though they yield extrinsic rewards. Only if such actions are perceived as ones that are not congruent with one's own preferences or wishes—as actions performed solely to gain external rewards—are rewards likely to reduce motivation.

This general principle is consistent with research findings indicating that if external rewards are viewed as signs of recognition rather than as bribes (Rosenfield, Folger, & Adelman, 1980), and if the rewards provided are large and satisfying (Fiske & Taylor, 1991), intrinsic motivation may be enhanced rather than reduced (Ryan, 1982). In view of these facts, we can conclude that paying people for doing things they enjoy can sometimes reduce their intrinsic motivation—turn play into work. But this is not always the case. When external rewards are delivered with care and in accordance with the principles just described, they can enhance rather than reduce motivation and performance.

KEY QUESTIONS

- What is aggressive motivation?
- What are achievement and power motivation?
- Do males and females differ in terms of achievement motivation?
- Under what conditions can extrinsic rewards reduce intrinsic motivation?

EMOTIONS: *Their Nature, Expression, and Impact*

Can you imagine life without **emotions**—without joy, anger, sorrow, or fear? Probably you cannot, for emotions are essential to our personal existence. Without them, we wouldn't really be ourselves.

But what are emotions? The closer we look, the more complex these reactions seem to be. There is general agreement among scientists who have studied emotions, however, that they involve three major components: (1) physiological changes within our bodies—shifts in heart rate, blood pressure, and so on; (2) subjective cognitive states—the personal experiences we label as emotions; and (3) expressive behaviors—outward signs of these internal reactions (Izard, 1992; Zajonc & McIntosh, 1992).

In the discussion that follows, we'll first look at several contrasting theories of emotion. Then we'll consider how emotions are expressed. Finally, we'll examine the complex interplay between emotions and cognition—how the way we feel influences the way we think and vice versa.

"DAWN AND HER ALTER EGO" BY MICHELLE PULEO

Can you imagine a life without emotions? Clearly, emotions are a key aspect of being human.

THE NATURE OF EMOTIONS: *Some Contrasting Views*

Among the many theories of emotion that have been proposed, three have been most influential. These are known, after the scientists who proposed

"I don't sing because I am happy. I am happy because I sing."

THE JAMES-LANGE THEORY IN OPERATION

The James-Lange theory suggests that the bird is correct: The subjective experiences we label as emotions are the result of changes within the body or overt behavior. (*Source:* Drawing by Frascino; © 1991 The New Yorker Magazine, Inc.)

Emotions: *Reactions consisting of physiological changes, subjective cognitive states, and expressive behaviors.* (p. 353)

Cannon-Bard Theory: *A theory of emotion suggesting that various emotion-provoking events simultaneously produce subjective reactions labeled as emotions and physiological arousal.*

James-Lange Theory: *A theory of emotion suggesting that emotion-provoking events produce various physiological reactions and that recognition of these is responsible for subjective emotional experiences.*

them, as the *Cannon-Bard, James-Lange,* and *Schachter-Singer* theories. A fourth theory—the *opponent-process theory*—offers additional insight into the nature of emotion and so is also deserving of our attention.

THE CANNON-BARD AND JAMES-LANGE THEORIES: WHICH COMES FIRST, ACTION OR FEELING?

Imagine that in one of your courses, you are required to make a class presentation. As you walk to the front of the room, your pulse races, your mouth feels dry, and you can feel beads of perspiration forming on your forehead. In short, you are terrified. What is the basis for this feeling? Sharply contrasting answers are offered by the Cannon-Bard and James-Lange theories of emotion.

Let's begin with the **Cannon-Bard theory**, because it is consistent with our own informal observations of our emotions. This theory suggests that various emotion-provoking events induce *simultaneously* the subjective experiences we label as emotions and the physiological reactions that accompany them. Thus, in the situation just mentioned, the sight of the audience and of your professor, pen poised to evaluate your performance, causes you to experience a racing heart, a dry mouth, and other signs of physiological arousal *and*, at the same time, to experience subjective feelings you label as fear. In other words, this situation stimulates various portions of your nervous system so that both arousal, mediated by your *autonomic nervous system* (refer to chapter 2), and subjective feelings, mediated in part by your cerebral cortex, are produced.

In contrast, the **James-Lange theory** offers a more surprising view of emotion. It suggests that subjective emotional experiences are actually the *result* of physiological changes within our bodies. In others words, you feel frightened when making your speech *because* you notice that your heart is racing, your mouth is dry, and so on. As James himself put it (1890, p. 1066): "We feel sorry because we cry, angry because we strike, and afraid because we tremble."

Which of these theories is closer to the truth? Until recent decades, most psychologists believed that the Cannon-Bard theory was more accurate. They reached this conclusion on the basis of several forms of evidence. First, surgical destruction of the sympathetic nervous system, which plays a key role in the type of physiological reactions James described, did not seem to eliminate emotional reactions (Cannon, Lewis, & Britton, 1927). Second, it appeared that many, if not all, emotional states were accompanied by highly similar patterns of physiological activity. If this was the case, then such activity could not be the basis for distinct emotional experiences such as anger, fear, joy, or sorrow.

More recently, though, the pendulum of scientific opinion has begun to swing the other way, and certain aspects of the James-Lange approach have gained increasing acceptance. Research conducted with highly sophisticated equipment indicates that different emotions are indeed associated with different patterns of physiological activity (Levenson, 1992). For example, in several studies, participants have been asked to recall experiences that evoked various emotions (e.g., Levenson et al., 1991). Careful measurement of processes regulated by the autonomic nervous system, such as heart rate and changes in skin conductance, indicated that different emotions produce contrasting patterns of reactions. In general, unpleasant emotions such as anger, fear, and sadness produce larger heart rate acceleration and larger increases in skin conductance than pleasant ones such as happiness (Levenson, 1992). However, another negative emotion, disgust, produces heart rate *deceleration*. These findings have been replicated with people in their seventies and eighties as well as with young children (Levenson et al., 1991), so they appear to be quite stable and general.

Additional support for the James-Lange theory of emotion is provided by studies of the **facial feedback hypothesis** (Laird, 1984; McCanne & Anderson, 1987). This hypothesis suggests that changes in our facial expressions sometimes produce shifts in our emotional experiences rather than merely mirroring them. In other words, as James would suggest, we feel happier when we smile, sadder when we frown, and so on. While there are many complexities in examining this hypothesis, the results of several studies offer support for its accuracy (Ekman et al., 1990; McCanne & Anderson, 1987). So there may be a substantial grain of truth in the James-Lange theory (Zajonc, Murphy, & Inglehart, 1989). Subjective emotional experiences *do* often arise directly in response to specific external stimuli, as the Cannon-Bard view suggests. However, consistent with the James-Lange theory, they can also be generated by changes in and awareness of our own bodily states—even, it appears, by changes in our current facial expressions (Ekman, 1992).

SCHACHTER AND SINGER'S TWO-FACTOR THEORY Strong emotions are a common part of daily life, but how do we tell them apart? How do we know that we are angry rather than frightened, sad rather than surprised? One potential answer is provided by a third theory of emotion. According to this view, known as the **Schachter-Singer theory**, or the *two-factor theory*, emotion-provoking events produce increased arousal (Schachter & Singer, 1962). In response to feelings of arousal, we search the external environment in order to identify the causes of such feelings. The causes we then select play a key role in determining the label we place on our arousal, and so in determining the emotion we experience. If we feel aroused after a near-miss in traffic, we will probably label our emotion as "fear" or perhaps "anger." If, instead, we feel aroused in the presence of an attractive person, we may label our arousal as "attraction" or "love." In short, we perceive ourselves to be experiencing the emotion that external cues, and our processing of them, suggest that we *should* be feeling. The theory is described as a two-factor view because it considers both arousal and the cognitive appraisal we perform in our efforts to identify the causes of such arousal.

Many studies provide support for the Schachter-Singer theory (Reisenzein, 1983; Sinclair et al., 1994). For example, in an intriguing field experiment, Dutton and Aron (1974) arranged to have male hikers meet an attractive female research assistant either while crossing a swaying suspension bridge high above a rocky gorge, or while on solid ground. Later, they asked the men to rate their attraction to the assistant. As the Schachter-Singer theory predicts, those who met her on the swaying bridge, when arousal was high, reported finding her more attractive and were more likely to actually call her for a date than those who met her on solid ground, when arousal was lower. Apparently, the male hikers interpreted their feelings of arousal as attraction to the accomplice—feelings that in her absence they might well have labeled as simple fear. Please see the **Key Concept** on page 356 for an overview of the Cannon-Bard, James-Lange, and Schachter-Singer theories.

OPPONENT-PROCESS THEORY: ACTION AND REACTION TO EMOTION Have you ever noticed that when you experience a strong emotional reaction, it is soon followed by the opposite reaction? Thus, elation is followed by a letdown, and anger is followed by calm, or even by regret over one's previous outbursts. This relationship is an important focus of the **opponent-process theory of emotion** (Solomon, 1982). The theory has two central assumptions: (1) Emotional reactions to a stimulus are followed automatically by an opposite reaction; and (2) repeated exposure to a stimulus causes the initial

Learning Objective 9.13
Compare and contrast the Cannon-Bard and James-Lange theories of emotion.

Learning Objective 9.14
Explain Schachter and Singer's two-factor theory.

Learning Objective 9.15
Discuss the assumptions of opponent-process theory.

Learning Objective 9.16
Provide a survey of the physiology of emotion and how emotion is communicated through external expressions.

Learning Objective 9.17
Discuss the relationships that exist between emotion and cognition.

Facial Feedback Hypothesis:
A hypothesis indicating that facial expressions can influence as well as reflect emotional states.

Schachter-Singer Theory
(two-factor theory): A theory of emotion suggesting that our subjective emotional states are determined, at least in part, by the cognitive labels we attach to feelings of arousal.

Opponent-Process Theory of Emotion: A theory suggesting that an emotional reaction to a stimulus is followed automatically by an opposite reaction.

Three Major Theories of Emotion

Cannon-Bard Theory

- Emotion-provoking events or stimuli (e.g., watching or participating in an exciting sports event) stimulate the nervous system.

- This stimulation results in physiological reactions (e.g., faster pulse and higher blood pressure).

- Simultaneously, this stimulation also produces the subjective cognitive states we label emotions (e.g., anxiety, joy, anger).

James-Lange Theory

- Emotion-provoking events (e.g., watching or participating in an exciting sports event) produce physiological reactions (e.g., faster pulse, higher blood pressure, increased perspiration).

- Our awareness of these reactions results in the subjective cognitive states we label emotions (e.g., anger, joy, fear). That is, we feel frightened because we notice that our heart is racing, our mouth is dry, the palms of our hands are wet, and so on.

Schachter-Singer Two-Factor Theory

- Emotion-provoking events (e.g., watching or participating in an exciting sports event) produce increased arousal.

- In response to this state of increased arousal, we search the external environment to identify possible causes for it (especially in situations where several potential causes exist).

- The emotions we experience depend on the causes we choose.

Event

Exposure to emotion-provoking events is the starting point for all major theories of emotion.

Emotions

Athletes in an emotion-provoking situation such as a close, hard-fought game have little doubt about the causes of the arousal they experience. In many other situations, however, the causes of arousal will be far less obvious.

reaction to weaken and the opponent process, or opposite reaction, to strengthen. So, for example, a politician who initially enjoys making speeches in public may experience a severe letdown after each speech is finished. With repeated experiences in delivering speeches, the pleasure she feels at addressing large crowds may weaken, while the letdown intensifies or occurs sooner after the speech is over. The result: she may gradually cut down on her public-speaking engagements.

Opponent-process theory provides important insights into drug addiction. For example, heroin users initially experience intense pleasure followed by unpleasant sensations of withdrawal. With repeated use of the drug, the pleasure becomes less intense, and unpleasant withdrawal reactions strengthen (Marlatt et al., 1988). In response, addicts begin to use the drug not for the pleasure it provides but to avoid the negative feelings that occur when they *don't* use it. In sum, according to opponent-process theory, emotional reactions often occur in action-reaction cycles, and many forms of behavior can be interpreted within this framework.

THE PHYSIOLOGY OF EMOTION

As you may recall from chapter 2, the physiological reactions that accompany emotions are regulated by the two parts of the *autonomic nervous system*. That is, activation of the *sympathetic* nervous system readies the body for vigorous activity, producing such reactions as increases in heart rate, blood pressure, and respiration. In contrast, activation of the *parasympathetic* nervous system influences activity related to restoration of the body's resources. For example, blood is diverted away from large muscles and to the digestive organs, and digestion itself is facilitated. As we saw earlier, research findings indicate that different emotions are associated with somewhat different patterns of physiological reactions; so the fact that emotions such as anger, joy, and disgust feel very different subjectively does appear to be mirrored, to some degree, in different biological reactions.

In addition, growing evidence suggests that different emotions are related to contrasting patterns of activation in the cerebral cortex (Davidson, 1992). For more than a hundred years, medical reports have indicated that persons who experience damage to the left hemisphere often develop deep depression, while those with damage to the right hemisphere show euphoria (Robinson et al., 1984). These cases suggest that positive feelings may be centered primarily in the left hemisphere, while negative ones are centered in the right hemisphere. And recent studies using recordings of electrical activity in the brain (EEGs; see chapter 2) tend to confirm this possibility. When watching films designed to elicit happiness or amusement, study participants generally show greater activation in the left than in the right cortex. In contrast, when watching films designed to elicit disgust, they show greater activation in the right cortex (Davidson, 1992; Tomarken, Davidson, & Henriques, 1990). Similar findings have even been obtained with infants less than three days old: They show greater right-side activation in response to unpleasant tastes and greater left-side activation in response to pleasant ones (Davidson & Fox, 1988).

Large individual differences in these patterns exist. For example, depressed persons show less left-frontal activation than nondepressed persons (Henriques & Davidson, 1991). Further, the inhibited children discussed in chapter 8 (those who are shy and unwilling to approach new objects or situations) show less left-frontal activation than uninhibited chil-

KEY QUESTIONS

- What is the Cannon-Bard theory of emotion?
- What is the James-Lange theory of emotion?
- What is the Schachter-Singer theory of emotion?
- What is the opponent-process theory of emotion?

dren (ones who are not shy, and who are willing to approach unfamiliar objects and people) (Davidson et al., 1991).

Together, these findings suggest that the cerebral hemispheres show a degree of specialization with respect to emotions. Positive feelings such as happiness are associated with greater activation in the left hemisphere, while negative ones such as sadness or disgust are associated with greater activation in the right hemisphere. So in brain activity as well as in heart rate and other bodily processes, there appear to be strong correspondences between our subjective emotional experiences and our physiological reactions. Mind and body are indeed one, or least intimately interlinked, as psychologists have long assumed. However, the task of deciphering the complex links between them can be accomplished only by continued thorough scientific research.

Can physiological differences among the emotions be put to practical use? For information on this topic, please see the **Point of It All** section.

THE POINT OF IT ALL

Can Physiological Reactions Be Used to Detect Lies?

R esearch findings indicate that different emotions are associated with contrasting patterns of physiological reactions and brain activity (Davidson, 1992; Levenson, 1992). If this is the case, then an interesting possibility follows: Since people often experience different emotions when lying than when telling the truth, perhaps we can use contrasting patterns of physiological reactions to assess the truthfulness of what people say. This is the central concept behind the use of *polygraphs,* or "lie detectors"—devices that record several different physiological reactions at once. The idea is that lying is more emotionally exciting than telling the truth. So if individuals show greater arousal in responding to questions about which they might be expected to lie than in responding to questions about which they have no reason to lie, perhaps it indicates that they are indeed lying. For example, suppose, using a standard lie-detector procedure known as the *control question technique,* we ask a woman suspected of a crime whether she actually committed it. She answers "No," and the needles on the polygraph show a large reaction. In contrast, when asked such *control questions* as "Have you ever lied to another person?" her reactions are much smaller. Since the reaction to the key, or *relevant,* question is larger, it might be concluded that she is lying. In contrast, innocent persons, who know they did not commit the crime, might well show a larger reaction to the control question (Saxe, 1994).

Can deception be separated from truth in this fashion? There are several grounds for considerable doubt that it can. First, so-called lie detectors really measure only *arousal;* the relationship of arousal to lying remains uncertain. Similarly, people can and do influence their physiological reactions in many ways (Lykken, 1985; Zajonc & McIntosh, 1992). For example, they can tense their muscles or change their rate of breathing. These actions and many others can change the pattern of recordings on the lie detector, yet they may have no connection to the truth of what is being said. Finally, differential reactions by persons lying and persons telling the truth would be expected to occur only to the extent that both groups believe that the polygraph works—that it really can determine whether their answers are honest or dishonest (Saxe, 1994). Since belief in the efficacy of lie detectors varies greatly across different persons, this is another important reason for doubting the usefulness of polygraph tests.

LIE DETECTORS: A RELIABLE MEASURE OF TRUTH?

Lie detectors measure changes in physiological reactions during questioning. The pattern of such changes supposedly reveals the truthfulness of a person's answers. However, growing evidence indicates that lie detectors are not reliable in determining truth.

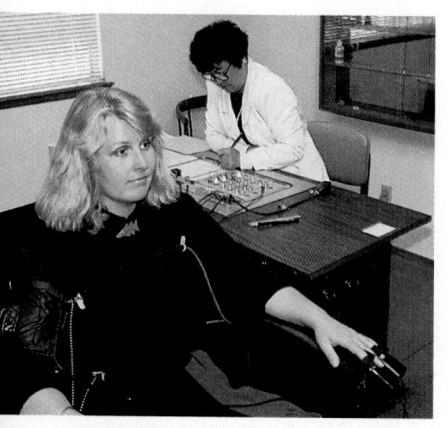

Recognizing such problems, the U.S. Congress outlawed the use of polygraph testing as a means of selecting employees (although a few businesses, such as ones providing security guards, are excluded). Further, many states have banned the use of lie detectors as evidence in court proceedings. While most psychologists concur with these actions and believe that polygraphs are of doubtful value in separating lies from truth, some research findings suggest that the accuracy of polygraphs can be increased through the use of improved procedures. In one of these, known as the *directed lie technique*, the persons being tested are instructed to lie in response to control questions so that comparisons can be made between truthful and deceitful responses. Under these conditions, it is expected that innocent persons will show larger reactions when lying in response to control questions than will guilty persons. Some research findings suggest that the accuracy of polygraph tests is indeed increased by these procedures (Honts, 1994). Still, despite such findings, most psychologists remain skeptical about the overall value of lie detectors, and continue to believe that using them to separate truth from deception can be a very risky business.

THE EXTERNAL EXPRESSION OF EMOTION: *Outward Signs of Inner Feelings*

Emotions are a private affair. No one, no matter how intimate with us they are, can truly share our subjective experiences. Yet we are able to recognize the presence of various emotions in others, and we are able to communicate our own feelings to them as well. How does such communication occur? A large part of the answer involves **nonverbal cues**—outward, observable signs of others' internal emotional states.

NONVERBAL CUES: THE BASIC CHANNELS   Several decades of research on nonverbal cues suggests that this kind of communication occurs through several basic *channels* or paths simultaneously. The most revealing of these consist of *facial expressions, eye contact, body movements and posture,* and *touching.*

Unmasking the face: Facial expressions as guides to others' emotions. More than two thousand years ago, the Roman orator Cicero stated, "The face is the image of the soul." By this he meant that feelings and emotions are often reflected in the face and can be read there from specific expressions. Modern research suggests that Cicero, and many other observers of human behavior, were correct in this belief: It *is* possible to learn much about others' current moods and feelings from their facial expressions. In fact, it appears that six different basic emotions are represented clearly, and from an early age, on the human face: anger, fear, sadness, disgust, happiness, and surprise (Ekman, 1992). Of course, this in no way implies that we are capable of showing only six different facial expressions. On the contrary, emotions occur in many combinations—for example, anger along with fear or surprise combined with happiness. Further, each emotion can vary greatly in intensity. Thus, while there are only a small number of basic themes in facial expressions, the number of variations on these themes is very large.

Until recently, it was widely assumed that basic facial expressions such as those for happiness, anger, or disgust are universal: They are recognized as indicating specific emotions by persons all over the world (e.g., Ekman & Friesen, 1975). However, a recent review of the evidence on this issue (Russell, 1994) suggests that the interpretation of facial expressions may be strongly influenced by cultural factors and that recognition of them may not be as uni-

Nonverbal Cues: Outward signs of others' emotional states. Such cues involve facial expressions, eye contact, and body language.

BODY POSTURES AND EMOTIONS

Threatening characters in classical ballet adopt angular or diagonal poses such as the one on the left much more often than friendly characters do. In contrast, friendly characters adopt rounded poses such as the one on the right much more often than threatening characters do. These findings indicate that specific postures or movements can often be a useful guide to others' emotions.

Body Language: *Nonverbal cues involving body posture or movement of body parts.*

versal as was previously assumed. In short, it appears that we must be cautious in assuming that, for example, a smile will be seen as a sign of happiness by people in cultures everywhere in the world.

Gazes and stares: The language of the eyes. Have you ever had a conversation with someone wearing dark glasses? If so, you know that this can be an uncomfortable situation. When you can't see the other person's eyes, you can't tell how she or he is reacting. Taking note of the importance of cues provided by others' eyes, ancient poets often described the eyes as "windows to the soul," and in one important sense they were right. We *do* often learn much about others' feelings from their eyes. For example, we interpret a high level of gazing from another as a sign of liking or friendliness (Kleinke, 1986). In contrast, if others avoid eye contact with us, we may conclude that they are unfriendly, don't like us, or are shy (Zimbardo, 1977).

While a high level of eye contact from others is usually interpreted as a sign of liking or positive feelings, there is one important exception to this general rule. If another person gazes at us continuously and maintains such contact regardless of any actions we perform, she or he can be said to be *staring.* Stares are often interpreted as a sign of anger or hostility, and most people attempt to minimize exposure to this particular kind of nonverbal cue if this is possible (Ellsworth & Carlsmith, 1973).

Body language: Gestures, posture, and movements. Try this simple demonstration: Try to remember some incident that made you angry—the angrier the better. Think about it for a minute. Now bring another incident to mind—one that made you feel sad—again, the sadder the better. Now compare your behavior as you recalled the two events. Did you change your posture or move your hands, arms, or legs as your thoughts shifted from the first incident to the second? The chances are good that you did, for our current mood or emotion is often reflected in the posture, position, and movement of our body. Together, such nonverbal behaviors are termed **body language**, and they can provide several useful kinds of information about others' emotions.

First, frequent body movements—especially ones in which a particular part of the body does something to another, such as touching, scratching, or rubbing—suggest emotional arousal. The greater the frequency of such behavior, the higher a person's level of arousal or nervousness seems to be (Harrigan, 1987). The specific movements made, too, can be revealing. Consider these statements "He adopted a *threatening posture*" and "She greeted him with *open arms.*" They indicate that different body orientations or postures are suggestive of particular emotional states.

Direct evidence that body postures are often interpreted in this manner is provided by research conducted by Aronoff, Woike, and Hyman (1992). These researchers first identified characters in classical ballet who played dangerous or threatening roles (for example, the Angel of Death or Macbeth) or warm, appealing roles (Juliet, Romeo). Then, they carefully examined samples of dancing by these characters in actual ballets to see if they adopted contrasting postures. Aronoff and his colleagues predicted that the threatening characters would use angular or diagonal poses more often than the friendly characters, and the friendly characters would adopt curving or rounded poses more often than the threatening characters. Both of these predictions were confirmed. Indeed, the threatening characters used diagonal poses three times as often as the friendly characters, and the friendly characters adopted rounded poses almost four times as often as the threatening characters. These and related findings suggest that large-scale body movements or postures can sometimes serve as an important source of information about others' emotions.

Finally, more specific information about others' feelings is often provided by **gestures** or *emblems*, body movements carrying a highly specific meaning in a given culture. For example, in several countries, holding one's hand with the thumb pointing up is a sign for "Okay." Similarly, seizing one's nose between the thumb and index finger is a sign of displeasure or disgust. Emblems vary greatly from culture to culture, but all human societies seem to have at least some signals of this type for greetings, departures, insults, and the descriptions of various physical states—"I'm full," "I'm tired," and so on.

Touching: The most intimate nonverbal cue. Suppose that while you were talking with another person, she or he touched you briefly. What information would this convey? How would you react? The answer to both questions is "It depends." And what it depends on is several factors relating to who does the touching—a friend or a stranger, a member of your own or of the other gender; the nature of the touching—brief or prolonged, gentle or rough; and the context in which it takes place—a business or social setting, a doctor's office. Depending on such factors, touch can suggest affection, sexual interest, dominance, caring, or even aggression. Despite these complexities, growing evidence indicates that when one person touches another in a manner that is considered acceptable in the current context, positive reactions generally result (Alagna, Whitcher, & Fisher, 1979; Smith, Gier, & Willis, 1982). Consider, for example, the results of an ingenious study by Crusco and Wetzel (1984).

These investigators enlisted the aid of waitresses who agreed to treat customers in one of three different ways when giving them their change: They did not touch the customers in any manner, they touched them briefly on the hand, or they touched them for a longer period of time on the shoulder. The researcher assessed the effects of these treatments by examining the size of the tips the customers left. Results were clear: Both a brief touch on the hand (about one-half second) and a longer touch on the shoulder (one to one and a half seconds) significantly increased tipping over the no-touch control condition. Assuming that tips increase when customers are in a positive mood, these findings are consistent with the view that being touched in a nonthreatening, appropriate manner tends to generate positive reactions.

One final point about touching: Additional studies indicate that there are important *gender differences* in this area. In a field study, Hall and Veccia (1990) observed touching between thousands of persons in many public settings—shopping malls, hotel lobbies, airports. Results indicated that overall, there was no difference between females and males in frequency of touching others. However, these investigators noted that among young persons, males touched females more often than vice versa. This difference decreased with age, and by middle age, females actually touched males more often than males touched females.

What accounts for these age-related shifts? Hall and Veccia (1990) suggest that among younger persons especially teenagers, relationships are not yet well established; and in such cases, existing gender roles encourage visible gestures of possessiveness by males. As relationships develop, however, gender roles may require more gestures of possessiveness by females. Whatever the explanation for the age reversal observed by Hall

---

KEY QUESTIONS

- What portions of the brain are associated with positive and negative emotional reactions?
- Through what nonverbal cues do we communicate emotional states to others?

Gestures: *Movements of various body parts that convey a specific meaning to others.*

and Veccia, it is interesting to note that across all ages, there appear to be no overall gender differences in touching in public settings.

EMOTION AND COGNITION: *How Feelings Shape Thoughts and Thoughts Shape Feelings*

Earlier, I asked you to remember incidents that made you feel angry and sad When you thought about these incidents, did your mood also change? Did recalling memories of these events influence the way you felt? The chances are good that it did, for in many instances, our thoughts seem to exert strong effects on our emotions. This relationship works in the other direction as well. Being in a happy mood often causes us to think happy thoughts, while feeling sad tends to bring negative memories and images to mind. In short, there appear to be important links between *emotion* and *cognition*—between the way we feel and the way we think. Let's take a brief look at some of the scientific evidence for the reality—and the importance—of these links (e.g., Forgas, 1991; in press).

HOW AFFECT INFLUENCES COGNITION
Does **affect**, our current mood, influence the way we think; that is, how we process information about ourselves or the external world? The findings of many different studies indicate that our current moods do indeed influence many aspects of cognition. First, it has been found that our moods, or *affective states* as they are often termed (Isen, 1987), strongly influence our perception of ambiguous stimuli. In general, we perceive and evaluate these stimuli more favorably when we are in a good mood than when we are in a negative one (e.g., Fiske & Neuberg, 1990; Isen & Shalker, 1982). For example, when asked to interview applicants whose qualifications for a job are ambiguous, research participants assign higher ratings to applicants when in a positive mood (such as when they have just received favorable feedback or won a small prize) than when they are in a negative mood (when they have just received negative feedback) (Baron, 1987, 1993).

Second, positive and negative moods exert a strong influence on memory. In general, information consistent with our current mood is easier to remember than information inconsistent with it (Forgas, 1991). Positive and negative affect have also been found to influence the way in which information is organized in memory. Persons experiencing positive affect seem to include a wider range of information within various memory categories than do persons in a neutral or negative mood (Isen & Daubman, 1984). Those experiencing positive affect also provide more unusual associations to neutral words and rate objects that are not very typical of a given category as more representative of it than do persons who are not in a positive mood. For example, they rate the word *elevator* as more typical of the category "vehicle" than do persons in a negative mood (Baron, Rea, & Daniels, 1992; Isen et al., 1985).

Third, our current moods often influence the process of decision making. Would you be more willing to adopt relatively risky courses of action when in a good mood or when in a bad mood? Informal observation suggests "when in a good mood." Research findings, however, indicate that the situation is a bit more complicated than this. Persons experiencing positive affect are indeed more likely to make risky decisions, but only when the potential losses involved are small or very unlikely to occur (Arkes, Herren, & Isen, 1988). They are actually *less* willing to take risks when potential losses are

√ **Affect:** *A person's current mood.*

362   CHAPTER 9

important or likely to occur—perhaps because they don't want to take a chance on reducing their current positive feelings.

Fourth, persons in a good mood are sometimes more creative than those in a negative mood. They are more successful in performing tasks involving creative problem solving, such as coming up with novel uses for everyday objects, than are persons in a neutral mood (Isen, Daubman, & Nowicki, 1987). For example, in a recent study, Estrada, Isen, and Young (in press) gave some physicians a small gift of candy but did not give others this gift. Then, the physicians worked, in their own offices, on a test of creativity—one in which they tried to find a word related to three other words (e.g., *club*, *gown*, *mare*; answer: *night*). Results indicated the physicians who were in a good mood because of the gift they received scored higher than those in a neutral mood.

Finally, research findings indicate that being in a good mood can sometimes increase our susceptibility to persuasion (Mackie & Worth, 1989). In other words, we are more likely to be influenced by a persuasive message directed at us when we are in a good mood than when we are in a less positive mood. Additional evidence indicates that this tendency may result both from the fact that being in a good mood reduces our ability to formulate counterarguments against persuasive messages (Mackie & Worth, 1989) and from the fact that when we are in a good mood, we are less motivated to engage in careful processing with respect to such messages (Smith & Shaffer, 1991).

Overall, then, it seems clear that emotions, or even relatively minor shifts in current moods, can strongly influence important aspects of cognition.

How Cognition Influences Affect   Most research on the relationship between affect and cognition has focused on how feelings influence thought. However, there is also compelling evidence for the reverse—the impact of cognition on affect. I mentioned one aspect of this relationship in discussing the two-factor theory of emotion (Schachter & Singer, 1962). This is the theory that suggests that often we don't know our own emotions directly; rather, since our internal reactions are often somewhat ambiguous, we look outward—at our own behavior or other aspects of the external world—for clues about what we are feeling. In such cases, the emotions or feelings we experience are strongly determined by the interpretation or cognitive labels we select.

A second way in which cognition can influence emotions is through the activation of *schemas* containing a strong affective component. For example, if we label an individual as belonging to some group, the schema for this social category may suggest what traits she or he probably possesses. In addition, it may also tell us how we *feel* about such persons. Thus, activation of a strong racial, ethnic, or religious schema or *stereotype* may exert powerful effects on our current feelings or moods.

Third, our thoughts can often influence our reactions to emotion-provoking events by determining how we interpret or appraise those events. For example, imagine that you are standing in line outside a theater and a woman bumps into you. Will you react with anger? This depends strongly on your interpretation of her act. If you decide that she is trying to shove you, the chances are high that you will become angry. If, instead, you conclude that she merely tripped on the sidewalk, you probably won't experience such feelings or take defensive action.

Finally, consider the impact of *expectancies* on our emotional reactions. Growing evidence indicates that when individuals hold expectations about how they will react to a new event or stimulus, these expectations shape their perceptions of and feelings about the event or stimulus when it actually occurs (e.g., Wilson et al., 1989). Thus, if you expect to dislike a new food, you probably will. If you expect to enjoy a film or a joke, the chances are good that you will have positive reactions to these stimuli when you actually encounter them. Perhaps even more surprising, expectations can even shape our later memories of how we felt about events. A dramatic illustration of such effects is provided by a study conducted by Wilson and Klaaren (1992).

They phoned some persons who had signed up to participate in an experiment and told them that it was a lot of fun, but they did not give other participants these positive expectations. When the participants arrived for the study, half the people in each group watched a film under pleasant conditions (they sat in a comfortable chair). The others watched the same film under unpleasant conditions (they sat in a hard chair and were required to keep their chin on a headrest). Three to four weeks later, all participants were phoned and asked if they would be willing to be in the study once again. Results indicated that expectations played a key role in participants' responses. Those who had expected to enjoy the film were significantly more likely to volunteer again, *regardless of whether they had participated under pleasant or unpleasant conditions*. Wilson and Klaaren (1992) interpreted these findings as indicating that expectations may sometimes override actual experience; indeed, in an important sense, expectations may *become* our reality! In such cases, one aspect of cognition is a more important determinant of our emotions than reality itself.

KEY QUESTIONS

- What is the impact of our affective states on memory?
- What other effects do our affective states exert on cognitive processes?
- How do cognitive processes influence our affective states?

MAKING PSYCHOLOGY PART OF YOUR LIFE

Getting Motivated: Some Practical Techniques

A t one time or another, almost all of us feel that getting motivated to do the things we should do is difficult if not impossible. Are there any techniques you can use to help overcome this kind of *behavioral inertia*? Industrial/organizational psychologists have focused a great deal of attention on this question in the context of *work motivation*—the motivation to perform various tasks. The results of their research suggest that one technique is especially helpful: *goal setting*, or establishing specific levels of performance or achievement that individuals should strive to attain (Locke & Latham, 1990). You probably already use goal setting informally, but here are several guidelines that will help you maximize its benefits.

1. *Set specific goals.* First, be careful to set very specific goals. This means indicating precisely what will be defined as adequate performance. For example, if you are preparing for an exam, don't set yourself the general goal of "reading all the material twice." Instead, decide how many pages you must read *each day* in order to be ready for the test. Then be sure to stick to this specific goal.

2. *Set challenging goals.* Don't fall into the trap of setting your goals so low that meeting them is trivial. People seem to be motivated to a much greater extent by goals that are challenging than by ones that are too easy to attain. So set your goals high enough that they stretch your ability to reach them.

3. *Set attainable goals.* But don't fall into the opposite trap—setting your goals so high that you can't possibly reach them. When this happens, it's easy to get discouraged and give up. The trick is to choose goals that are difficult enough to present a challenge but not so difficult that failure is guaranteed. Remember the discussion of achievement motivation? High achievers tend to prefer goals of moderate but not excessive difficulty; you should, too.

4. *Reward yourself for reaching each goal.* Often, people forget to reward themselves for reaching each goal. As soon as one goal is attained, they rush full steam ahead to the next one. This is a mistake! When choosing your goals, also identify rewards you will give yourself for reaching them. For example, in studying for a test, plan to give yourself a break, a candy bar, or some other treat after you finish each chapter. Doing so can be a big help in terms of keeping your momentum going.

5. *Become committed to your goals.* Once you establish your goals, it's important you accept them as *goals*—ones you are really committed to reaching. If

you don't have such commitment, it's too easy to change the goals, to ignore them, or, again, just to give up altogether. So be sure to adopt your goals as ones you are committed to reaching, as real standards for your behavior.

6. *Build feedback into the process.* A final question you should ask yourself before you begin is this: "How will I know when I've reached each goal?" This sounds simple, but in some instances it's more complicated than it seems. For example, in writing a term paper, you can set a specific goal, such as "I'll do five pages each night." In this case the feedback is obvious: You know you've reached the goal when you have a pile of five completed pages in front of you. But for other tasks you may have to turn to other persons for feedback. For example, suppose that you've decided to work on getting along better

with your roommate. How will you know when you've made real progress? One way is to set very specific goals, such as "I won't get into arguments over the groceries, or over cleaning the apartment." But it may also be necessary to ask the roommate directly whether she or he perceives any changes in your behavior. The main point is that feedback is essential for goal setting to work, so be sure to build this kind of information into the process.

Industrial/organizational psychologists have studied techniques for helping people increase their motivation, in both their work and their personal lives.

Summary and Review of Key Questions

Motivation: The Activation and Persistence of Behavior

- *According to drive theory, what is the nature of motivation?*

Drive theory suggests that motivation is a process in which various biological needs push (drive) us to actions designed to satisfy those needs.

- *According to arousal theory, what is the nature of motivation?*

Arousal theory suggests that organisms seek optimal levels of arousal, not minimal levels of arousal.

- *What is the major concept of expectancy theory?*

Expectancy theory suggests that behavior is motivated by expectancies concerning the outcomes that will result from specific actions.

- *What is Maslow's needs hierarchy theory?*

Maslow's needs hierarchy theory suggests that needs exist in a hierarchy and that higher-level needs cannot be activated and thus serve as a source of motivation until lower-level needs have been satisfied.

- *What factors play a role in the regulation of eating?*

Eating is regulated by complex biochemical systems within the body and is also affected by the sight of food, feedback from chewing and swallowing, and cultural factors.

- *What factors contribute to obesity?*

Many variables contribute to obesity, including eating habits, reactions to stress, basal metabolic rate, and responses to food-related cues.

- *What are anorexia nervosa and bulimia?*

Anorexia nervosa and bulimia are two serious eating disorders. Persons suffering from anorexia starve themselves and experience extreme weight loss. Persons suffering from bulimia engage in binge eating followed by purging.

- *What role do sex hormones play in human sexual motivation?*

Sex hormones seem to play only a subtle and relatively minor role in human sexual motivation. However, other chemicals produced within the body may play a role in sexual attraction and love.

- **What are the major phases of sexual activity?**

During sexual activity both males and females move through a series of distinct phases: excitement, plateau, orgasm, and resolution.

- **What is a key difference between human beings and other species with respect to sexual arousal?**

In contrast to other species, human beings can be sexually aroused by self-generated sexual fantasies and by exposure to erotic materials.

- **What factors appear to play a role in determining sexual orientation?**

At present, there is no clear evidence relating either hormonal levels or family background and early experience to sexual orientation. However, recent findings indicate that genetic factors may play a role in homosexuality.

- **What is aggressive motivation?**

Aggressive motivation involves the desire to inflict harm on others.

- **What are achievement and power motivation?**

Achievement motivation is the desire to meet standards of excellence, to outperform others, and to accomplish difficult tasks. Power motivation is the desire to be in charge and to influence others.

- **Do males and females differ in terms of achievement motivation?**

Contrary to initial findings, women do not fear success and they are equal to men with respect to achievement motivation.

- **Under what conditions can extrinsic rewards reduce intrinsic motivation?**

Extrinsic rewards can reduce intrinsic motivation when they are perceived as rewards or bribes for engaging in certain activities. Extrinsic rewards do not always reduce intrinsic motivation, however.

KEY TERMS: *motivation, p. 335; instinct theory, p. 335; instincts, p. 335; drive theory, p. 335; homeostasis, p. 335; arousal theory, p. 336; expectancy theory, p. 337; incentives, p. 337; work motivation, p. 337; hierarchy of needs, p. 338; hunger motivation, p. 339; obesity, p. 340; anorexia nervosa, p. 341; bulimia, p. 341; body-mass index, p. 342; sexual motivation, p. 342; gonads, p. 342; sexual jealousy, p. 345; homosexual, p. 346; bisexual, p. 346; heterosexual, p. 346; aggressive motivation, p. 347; aggression, p. 347; frustration, p. 348; achievement motivation, p. 351; power motivation, p. 351; Thematic Apperception Test (TAT), p. 351; intrinsic motivation, p. 352*

EMOTIONS: THEIR NATURE, EXPRESSION, AND IMPACT

- **What is the Cannon-Bard theory of emotion?**

The Cannon-Bard theory of emotion suggests that emotion-provoking stimuli simultaneously elicit physiolog-ical arousal and the subjective cognitive states we label as emotions.

- **What is the James-Lange theory of emotion?**

The James-Lange theory contends that emotion-provoking stimuli induce physiological reactions and that these form the basis for the subjective cognitive states we label as emotions.

- **What is the Schachter-Singer theory of emotion?**

The Schachter-Singer theory suggests that when we are aroused by emotion-provoking stimuli, we search the external environment for the causes of our feelings of arousal. The causes we select then determine the emotions we experience.

- **What is the opponent-process theory of emotion?**

According to the opponent-process theory, strong emotional reactions are followed by opposite emotional reactions.

- **What portions of the brain are associated with positive and negative emotional reactions?**

Research findings indicate that positive emotional reactions are associated with greater activation of the left cerebral hemisphere, while negative emotional reactions are associated with greater activation of the right cerebral hemisphere.

- **Through what nonverbal cues do we communicate emotional states to others?**

Emotional states are communicated to others through facial expressions, eye contact, body language, and touching.

- **What is the impact of our affective states on memory?**

We tend to remember information consistent with our moods more easily than information inconsistent with these moods.

- **What other effects do our affective states exert on cognitive processes?**

Our moods have also been shown to influence decision making, creativity, and resistance to persuasion.

- **How do cognitive processes influence our affective states?**

Cognition influences affect in several ways. Activation of schemas containing an affective component can strongly influence our current moods. Our interpretations of potentially emotion-provoking events can strongly influence our emotional reactions to them. Expectancies exert strong effects on emotional reactions and may even alter memories of actual experiences.

KEY TERMS: *emotions, p. 354; Cannon-Bard theory, p. 354; James-Lange theory, p. 354; facial feedback hypothesis, p. 355; Schachter-Singer theory, p. 355; opponent-process theory of emotion, p. 355; nonverbal cues, p. 359; body language, p. 360; gestures, p. 361; affect, p. 362*

CRITICAL THINKING QUESTIONS

APPRAISAL	Ultimately, emotions are a private experience: No one can ever share them with us directly. Despite this fact, psychologists have attempted to investigate emotions scientifically. Do you think a scientific understanding of emotions is possible? If so, why? If not, why not?
CONTROVERSY	Not long ago, a large U.S. federal agency planned to fund research designed to study the possibility that aggressive tendencies are inherited. Vigorous objections to this plan were voiced by many political groups, fearing that the proposed research would yield findings very unfavorable to minority groups. The plan was shelved. Do you think this was appropriate? Or should the research have been funded, no matter how unpopular its results might be?
MAKING PSYCHOLOGY PART OF YOUR LIFE	Now that you understand the basic nature of hunger motivation and the many factors that affect it, can you think of ways you can use this knowledge to regulate your own weight better? Describe at least three concrete steps, based on the research findings discussed in this chapter, you can take to help ensure that your weight stays at desirable levels in the decades ahead.

Individual Differences:
Personality

*A*ccording to one old saying, "Variety is the spice of life." Whether that's true or not, there's certainly no doubt that the people around us provide us with plenty of variety: They differ tremendously in their behavior, their preferences, their outlook on life, and their emotional volatility, and in a thousand and one other ways too. We have already considered several important aspects of such individual differences in chapter 7. Here, we'll continue our exploration of this important topic by focusing on another key aspect of individual differences: *personality*.

PERSONALITY: CONSISTENCY IN THE BEHAVIOR OF INDIVIDUALS

We generally assume that people show consistency in at least some aspects of their behavior across time and in a wide range of contexts.
(*Source:* ZIGGY copyright 1982 ZIGGY AND FRIENDS, INC. Dist. by UNIVERSAL PRESS SYNDICATE. Reprinted with permission. All rights reserved.)

Personality: Individuals' unique and relatively stable patterns of behavior, thoughts, and feelings.

Personality can be defined as an individual's unique and relatively stable patterns of behavior, thoughts, and emotions (Burger, 1990; Carver & Scheier, 1992; Wallace, 1993). In daily life, we generally act as though personality is a fact. We expect others to demonstrate consistency in their behavior across different situations and over long periods of time. Once we conclude that a person possesses certain traits—that he or she is, for example, *friendly, sloppy,* and *generous*, we expect that person to behave in ways consistent with these traits in many situations. This raises an intriguing question: Does such consistency really exist? Some psychologists have argued that it does not—that behavior is largely determined by external factors rather than by stable traits or dispositions (Mischel, 1977, 1985). According to these critics of the concept of personality, individuals actually behave very differently in different situations; our perception that they act consistently across situations and over time is largely an error stemming from our desire to simplify the task of predicting their actions (Kunda & Nisbett, 1986; Reeder, Fletcher, & Furman, 1989.)

While these arguments are intriguing ones, the weight of existing evidence suggests that personality, defined in terms of stable behavior tendencies, is indeed real. Long-term studies of individual behavior indicate that people *do* show a fair amount of consistency with respect to many aspects of behavior (e.g., Woodall & Matthews, 1993). In other words, if someone tends to be friendly, sloppy, and generous today, the chances are quite good that that individual will also be friendly, sloppy, and generous tomorrow, next month, next year, or even ten years from today. Indeed, several recent investigations indicate that measures of personality gathered with children are often good predictors of their behavior as adults forty or even fifty years later (e.g., Friedman et al., 1993).

It's important to be aware, however, that such consistency over long periods of time does *not* exist for all traits and for all persons (Baumeister & Tice, 1988; Tice, 1989). In fact, the extent to which people show such consistency across time and situations may itself be an important aspect of personality (Koestner, Bernieri, & Zuckerman, 1992). Also, the existence of stable traits in no way implies that situational factors are *not* important determinants of behavior. On the contrary, most psychologists now agree that *both* traits and situations are important. In other words, behavior in a given context is often a function of both internal, dispositional factors—factors people bring with them to that situation—*and* external ones. Further, there are many instances in which situational factors overwhelm dispositions or strongly influence their expression. For instance, even people with wild tempers tend to behave politely when stopped for speeding by a state trooper. So, behavior is generally influenced both by situational factors and by internal ones; and among the internal factors, the stable tendencies included in the concept of personality appear to be quite important.

In the remainder of this chapter, then, we'll assume that personality does indeed exist and can exert important effects on behavior. But what, precisely, is the nature of personality? How do individual differences in it arise? And which personal dispositions or traits are the most important? In order to provide you with an overview of psychology's insights concerning these issues, I'll proceed as follows.

First, I'll survey several *theories of* personality—theoretical frameworks, many of them grand and sweeping in nature, designed to explain the origins and nature of personality. Few of these frameworks are currently accepted as accurate, but as a group they *have* called attention to important issues and so are worthy of our attention. For each theory, I'll first describe it, then present some research evidence relating to it, and finally offer an evaluation of its current status in psychology. After examining these theories, we'll focus on the nature and impact of several specific *personality traits*—key dimensions along which individuals differ in consistent, stable ways (Wallace, 1993).

KEY QUESTIONS

- What is the modern definition of personality?
- What are the roles of situational factors and personal dispositions in human behavior?

THE PSYCHOANALYTIC APPROACH: *Messages from the Unconscious*

When asked to name the three people who have exerted the greatest influence on intellectual developments during the twentieth century, many historians reply without hesitation: Albert Einstein, Karl Marx, and Sigmund Freud. So, by this measure, a psychologist—or at least someone who operated as a psychologist for much of his career—is one of the key figures of modern history. Why is Freud credited with having such an important effect on our intellectual heritage? Much of the answer lies in his influential theories, which focus on personality and other important topics, such as the roots of psychological disorders. Before turning to his theories, however, it seems appropriate to spend a moment or two on Freud's background—*his* personality, if you will.

FREUD THE PERSON: *A Capsule Memoir*

Freud was born in what is now part of the Czech Republic, but when he was four years old, his family moved to Vienna, and he spent almost his entire life in that city. As a young man, Freud was highly ambitious and decided to make a name for himself as a medical researcher. He became discouraged with his prospects in this respect, however, and soon after receiving his medical degree he entered private practice. It was during this period that he formulated his theories of human personality and psychological disorders.

Freud's mother was his father's second wife, and she was much younger than her husband. In fact, she was only twenty-one when Freud was born. Although she had several other children, Sigmund was the first and always his mother's favorite. Among the Freud children only Sigmund had his own room, and when his sister's piano practice disturbed his study, her lessons were stopped and the piano sold. Freud's relationship with his father, in contrast, was cold and distant. Indeed, he even arrived late at his father's funeral and missed most of the service. At the age of twenty-six, Freud married Martha Bernays. The marriage was a happy one and produced six children. Freud had a powerful personality, and as he developed his controversial theories, he attracted numerous followers. In many cases these people began as ardent supporters but then came to question some aspects of his work. Freud was intolerant of such criticism, and this often led to angry breaks with once-cherished students. One disciple, however, never broke with his views: his daughter Anna, who became a famous psychoanalyst in her own right.

Freud loved antiques and collected them throughout his life. His collection filled the walls and shelves of his office—even the top of his desk. Each morning the first thing he did was to reach over and affectionately pat one or more of his stone sculptures. Freud recognized a connection between his hobby and

Learning Objective 10.1
Survey the different levels of consciousness and the three personality structures proposed by Freudian theory.

Learning Objective 10.2
List the psychosexual stages of development proposed by Freud and discuss the consequences of fixation at each stage of development.

Learning Objective 10.3
Provide an evaluation of Freudian theory.

his work: He told many of his patients that his search for hidden memories in their unconscious minds was similar to the excavation of a buried ancient city. Freud smoked heavily (he is often shown with a large cigar in his hand), and he contracted oral cancer. This caused him great pain, and starting in 1923 he underwent numerous operations for his disease. Ultimately these interfered with his speech and ended his career as a public speaker.

Like many people of Jewish descent, Freud found it necessary to flee the Nazis, and in 1938 he left Vienna for England. He died there of throat cancer the next year. Many biographies of Freud have been written, and several draw connections between his theories and his personal life experiences—for example, his close relationship with his mother and distant relationship with his father. Whether such links actually exist remains open to debate. What *is* certain, however, is that this complex, brilliant, and dominating man changed Western ideas about human behavior and personality in a lasting way.

FREUD'S THEORY OF PERSONALITY

As noted earlier, Freud entered private practice soon after obtaining his medical degree. A turning point in his early career came when he won a research grant to travel to Paris in order to observe the work of Jean-Martin Charcot, who was then using hypnosis to treat several types of mental disorders. When Freud returned to Vienna, he worked with Joseph Breuer, a colleague who was using hypnosis in the treatment of *hysteria*—a condition in which individuals experienced physical symptoms, such as blindness, deafness, or paralysis of arms or legs, for which there seemed to be no underlying physical cause. Out of these experiences, and out of his growing clinical practice, Freud gradually developed his theories of human personality and mental illness. His ideas were complex and touched on many different issues. With respect to personality, however, four topics are most central: levels of consciousness, the structure of personality, anxiety and defense mechanisms, and psychosexual stages of development.

SIGMUND FREUD

Freud is clearly a major figure in the history of psychology. His theories of personality had a profound effect on intellectual thought for many decades.

LEVELS OF CONSCIOUSNESS: BENEATH THE ICEBERG'S TIP Freud viewed himself as a scientist, and he was well aware of research on thresholds for sensory experience (refer to chapter 3). Freud applied some of these ideas to the task of understanding the human mind, and reached the startling conclusion that most of the mind lies below the surface—below the threshold of conscious experience. Above this threshold is the realm of the *conscious*. This includes our current thoughts: whatever we are thinking about or experiencing at a given moment. Beneath the conscious realm is the much larger *preconscious*. This contains memories that are not part of current thoughts but can readily be brought to mind if the need arises. Finally, beneath the preconscious, and forming the bulk of the human mind, is the *unconscious*: thoughts, desires, and impulses of which we remain largely unaware (see Figure 10.1). Although some of this material has always been unconscious, Freud believed, much of it was once conscious but has been actively *repressed*—driven from consciousness because it was too anxiety-provoking. For example, according to Freud, shameful experiences or unacceptable sexual or aggressive urges are often driven deep within the unconscious. The fact that we are not aware of the unconscious, however, in no way prevents it from affecting our behavior. Indeed, Freud believed that many of the symptoms experienced by his patients were disguised and indirect reflections of repressed

FIGURE 10.1

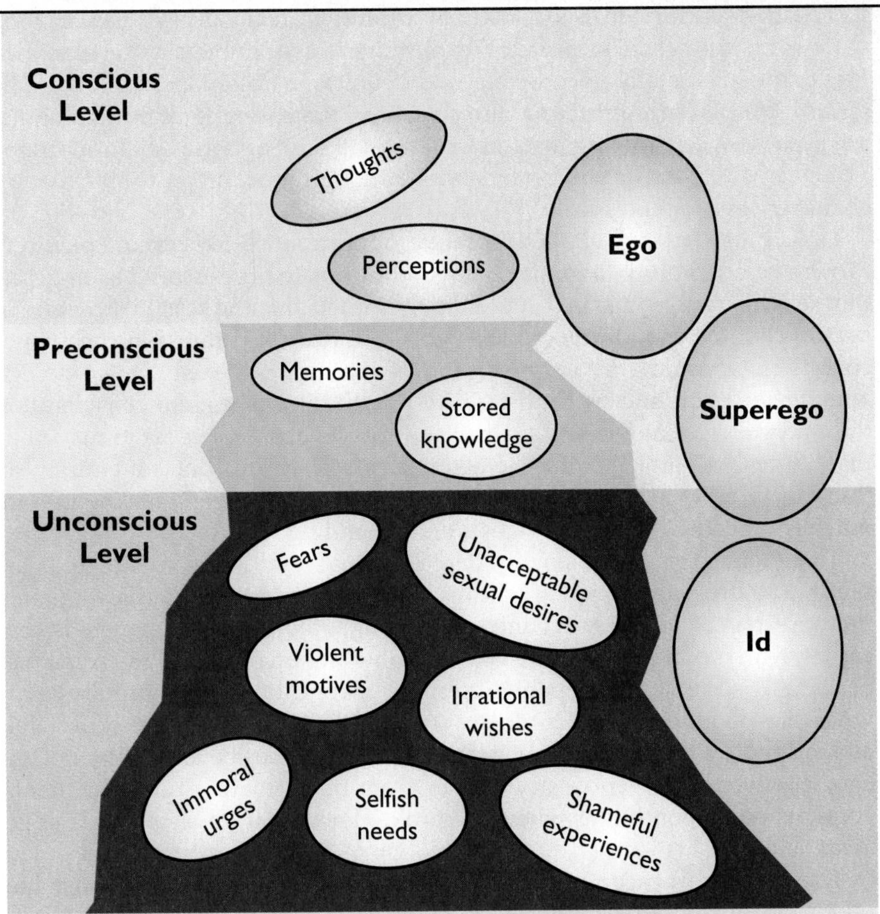

Conscious Level

Thoughts

Perceptions

Ego

Preconscious Level

Memories

Stored knowledge

Superego

Unconscious Level

Fears

Unacceptable sexual desires

Violent motives

Irrational wishes

Id

Immoral urges

Selfish needs

Shameful experiences

Aspect of Personality	Level of Consciousness	Description/Function
Ego	Mostly conscious	Mediates between id impulses and superego inhibitions; reality principle; rational
Superego	All levels, but mostly preconscious	Ideals and morals; conscience; incorporated from parents
Id	Unconscious	Basic impulses (sex and aggression); pleasure principle; seeks immediate gratification; irrational, impulsive

Freud's Views about Levels of Consciousness and Structures of Personality

Freud believed that the human mind has three distinct levels of consciousness: the *unconscious*, the *preconscious*, and the *conscious*. He also believed that personality involves three important structures: *ego*, *superego*, and *id*, which serve different but related functions and operate at different levels of consciousness.

thoughts and desires. This is why one major goal of **psychoanalysis**—the method of treating psychological disorders devised by Freud—is to bring repressed material back into consciousness. Presumably, once this material is made conscious, it can be dealt with more effectively, and important causes of mental illness may be eliminated.

THE STRUCTURE OF PERSONALITY: ID, EGO, AND SUPEREGO Do you know the story of Dr. Jekyll and Mr. Hyde? If so you already have a basic idea of some of the key structures of personality described by Freud. He suggested that personality consists largely of three parts: the *id*, the *ego*, and the *superego* (refer to Figure 10.1). As we'll soon see, these correspond, roughly, to *desire*, *reason*, and *conscience*.

√**Psychoanalysis:** *A method of therapy based on Freud's theory of personality, in which the therapist attempts to bring repressed unconscious material into consciousness.*

The **id**, or desire, consists of all of our primitive, innate urges. These include various bodily needs, sexual desire, and aggressive impulses. According to Freud, the id is totally unconscious and operates in accordance with what he termed the **pleasure principle**: It wants immediate, total gratification and is not capable of considering the potential costs of seeking this goal. In short, the id is the Mr. Hyde of our personality—although, in contrast to this literary character, it is not necessarily evil.

Unfortunately, the world offers few opportunities for instant pleasure. Moreover, attempting to gratify many of our innate urges would soon get us into serious trouble. It is in response to these facts that the second structure of personality, the **ego**, develops. The ego's task is to hold the id in check until conditions appropriate for satisfaction of its impulses exist. Thus, the ego operates in accordance with the **reality principle**: It takes into consideration the external consequences of actions and directs behavior so as to maximize pleasure *and* minimize pain. The ego is partly conscious but not entirely so; thus, some of its actions—for example, its eternal struggle with the id—are outside our conscious knowledge or understanding.

The final aspect of personality described by Freud is the **superego**. It too seeks to control satisfaction of id impulses, permitting their gratification only under certain conditions. In contrast to the ego, though, the superego is concerned with morality: It can tell right from wrong according to the principles of a given society. The superego permits gratification of id impulses only when it is morally correct to do so—not simply when it is safe or feasible, as required by the ego. So, for example, it would be the superego, not the ego, that would prevent a stockbroker from manipulating funds in clients' accounts under conditions where the broker knew that it was possible to get away with such actions.

The superego is acquired from our parents and through experience and represents our internalization of the moral teachings and norms of our society. Unfortunately, such teachings are often quite inflexible and leave little room for gratification of our basic desires: They require us to be good at all times, like Dr. Jekyll. Because of this fact, the ego faces another difficult task: It must mediate between the id and superego, striking a balance between our primitive urges and our learned moral constraints. Freud felt that this constant struggle among id, ego, and superego plays a key role in the development of personality and in the development of many forms of psychological disorder.

ANXIETY AND DEFENSE MECHANISMS: SELF-PROTECTION BY THE EGO   In its constant struggle to prevent outbreak of unbridled impulses from the id, the ego faces a difficult task. Yet for most people, most of the time, the ego is capable of performing this crucial function. Sometimes, though, id impulses grow so strong that they threaten to get out of control. For example, consider the case of a middle-aged widow who finds herself strongly attracted to her daughter's boyfriend. She hasn't had a romantic attachment in years, so her sexual desire quickly rises to powerful levels. What happens next? According to Freud, when her ego senses that unacceptable impulses are about to get out of hand, it experiences **anxiety**—unpleasant feelings of nervousness, tension, or worry. These feelings occur because the unacceptable impulses are getting closer and closer to consciousness, as well as closer and closer to the limits of the ego to hold them in check.

At this point, Freud contends, the ego may resort to one of several different **defense mechanisms**. These are all designed to keep unacceptable impulses from the id out of consciousness and so to prevent their open expression. Defense mechanisms take many different forms. For example, in **sublimation**, the unacceptable impulse is channeled into some socially ac-

DEFENSE MECHANISM	ITS BASIC NATURE	EXAMPLE
Repression	"Forgetting"—or pushing from consciousness into unconsciousness—unacceptable thoughts or impulses	A woman fails to recognize her attraction to her handsome new son-in-law.
Rationalization	Conjuring up socially acceptable reasons for thoughts or actions based on unacceptable motives	A young woman explains that she ate an entire chocolate cake so that it wouldn't spoil in the summer heat.
Displacement	Redirection of an emotional response from a dangerous object to a safe one	Anger is redirected from one's boss to one's child.
Projection	Transfer to others of unacceptable motives or impulses	A man sexually attracted to a neighbor perceives the neighbor as being sexually attracted to him.
Regression	Responding to a threatening situation in a way appropriate to an earlier age or level of development	A student asks a professor to raise his grade; when she refuses, the student throws a temper tantrum.

TABLE 10.1

Defense Mechanisms: Reactions to Anxiety

According to Freud, when the ego feels that it may be unable to control impulses from the id, it experiences anxiety. To reduce such feelings, the ego employs various *defense mechanisms*, such as the ones described here.

ceptable action. Instead of making love to the young man, as Freud would say she really wants to do, the widow may "adopt" him as a son and provide financial support for furthering his education. Another mechanism, known as **reaction formation**, consists of efforts to hide from a threatening impulse by behaving in a manner directly opposite to the impulse. For example, the widow might convince herself that she intensely dislikes the young man and urge her daughter to stop seeing him. Table 10.1 describes additional defense mechanisms. While they differ greatly in specific form, all serve the function of reducing anxiety by keeping unacceptable urges and impulses from breaking into consciousness.

PSYCHOSEXUAL STAGES OF DEVELOPMENT   Now we come to what is perhaps the most controversial aspect of Freud's theory of personality. Many people find Freud's ideas about levels of consciousness to be quite reasonable: After all, as we saw in chapter 4, we do seem to move through distinct levels of consciousness during the course of a single day. Similarly, many find appealing the idea of distinct aspects of personality reflecting primitive urges, conscience, and the mediation between these forces. When we turn to Freud's ideas about the formation of personality, however, the situation changes radically. Even a hundred years after he proposed them, Freud's views concerning this issue offend some people and seem totally absurd to others. These views can be grouped under the heading **psychosexual stages of development**: innately determined stages of sexual development through which, presumably, we all pass.

To understand Freud's ideas concerning psychosexual development we must first grasp his concepts of *libido* and *fixation*. According to Freud, the **libido** is the instinctual life force that energizes the id. Release of libido is closely related to pleasure, but the focus of such pleasure—and the expression of libido—changes as we move through discrete stages of development. As we move through these stages, and obtain different kinds of pleasure in

✓*Reaction Formation: A defense mechanism in which people act in a manner directly opposite to their unconscious wishes.*

✓*Psychosexual Stages of Development: According to Freud, an innate sequence of stages through which all human beings pass. At each stage, pleasure is focused on a different region of the body.*

✓*Libido: According to Freud, the psychic energy that powers all mental activity.*

FREUD'S ANAL STAGE OF DEVELOPMENT

Freud believed that fixation during the anal stage, resulting from traumatic toilet training experiences, could lead to an excessive need for order and a stubborn personality in adults.

✓**Fixation:** *Excessive investment of psychic energy in a particular stage of psychosexual development, which results in various types of psychological disorders.*

✓**Oral Stage:** *In Freud's theory, a stage of psychosexual development during which pleasure is centered in the region of the mouth.*

✓**Anal Stage:** *In Freud's theory, a psychosexual stage of development in which pleasure is focused primarily on the anal zone.*

✓**Phallic Stage:** *In Freud's theory, a psychosexual stage of development during which pleasure is centered in the genital region. It is during this stage that the Oedipus complex develops.*

✓**Oedipus Complex:** *In Freud's theory, a crisis of psychosexual development in which children must give up their sexual attraction to their opposite-sex parent.*

✓**Latency Stage:** *In Freud's theory, the psychosexual stage of development that follows resolution of the Oedipus complex. During this stage, sexual desires are relatively weak.*

them, we leave behind small amounts of our libido. But if an excessive amount of energy is tied to a particular stage, **fixation** is said to result. This can stem from either too little or too much gratification during this stage, and in either case the result is harmful. Since the individual has left too much "psychic energy" behind, less of it is available for full adult development. The outcome may be an adult personality reflecting the stage or stages at which fixation has occurred. To put it another way, if too much energy is drained away by fixation at earlier stages of development, the amount remaining may be insufficient to power movement to full adult development. Then, an individual may develop an immature personality and so be subject to several important forms of psychological disorder.

Now back to the actual stages themselves. According to Freud, as we grow and develop, different parts of the body serve as the focus of the constant quest for pleasure. In the initial **oral stage**, lasting until we are about eighteen months old, we seek pleasure primarily through the mouth. If too much or too little gratification occurs during this stage, an individual may become *fixated* at it. Too little gratification results in a personality that is overly dependent on others; too much, especially after the child has developed some teeth, results in a personality that is excessively hostile, especially through verbal sarcasm and similar "biting" forms of behavior.

The next stage occurs in response to efforts by parents to toilet train their children. During the **anal stage**, the process of elimination becomes the primary focus of pleasure. Fixation at this stage, stemming from traumatic toilet-training experiences, may result in individuals who are excessively orderly and stubborn or, alternatively, excessively generous and undisciplined.

At about age four, the genitals become the primary source of pleasure, and children enter the **phallic stage**. Freud speculated that at this time we fantasize about sexual relations with our opposite-sex parent—a phenomenon he termed the **Oedipus complex**. (The complex is named after Oedipus, a character in ancient Greek literature who unknowingly killed his father and then married his mother. When he discovered the true nature of these monstrous acts, he blinded himself.) Fear of punishment for such desires then enters the picture. Among boys, the feared punishment is castration, leading to *castration anxiety*; among girls, the feared punishment is loss of love. In both cases these fears bring about resolution of the Oedipus complex and identification with the same-sex parent. This, in turn, stimulates development of the superego. Because fear of castration is more vivid and threatening than fear of loss of love, Freud contended that resolution of the Oedipus complex is more complete in boys than girls. Thus, in his theory, the superego is, supposedly, stronger for males than for females.

Even more controversial is Freud's suggestion that little girls experience *penis envy*: feelings of envy upon seeing the male organ and realizing that they do not possess it. Freud suggested that confronted with this realization, girls experience strong feelings of inferiority and jealousy—feelings they may carry with them in disguised form even in adult life. As you can readily guess, these ideas now are strongly rejected by virtually all psychologists.

After resolution of the Oedipus conflict, children enter the **latency stage**, in which they remain until the onset of puberty. During the latency period, Freud contended, sexual urges are largely repressed. After puberty, individuals enter the final stage—the **genital stage**. During this stage, pleasure is

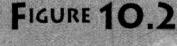
FIGURE 10.2

Oral 0–2
Infant achieves gratification through oral activities such as feeding, thumb sucking, and babbling.

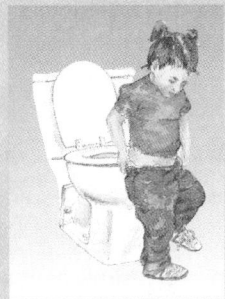

Anal 2–3
The child learns to respond to some of the demands of society (such as bowel and bladder control).

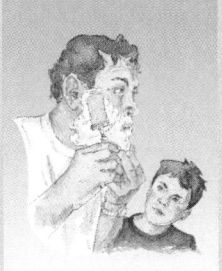

Phallic 3–7
The child learns to realize the differences between males and females and becomes aware of sexuality.

Latency 7–11
The child continues his or her development but sexual urges are relatively quiet.

Genital 11–adult
The growing adolescent shakes off old dependencies and learns to deal maturely with the opposite sex.

Psychosexual Stages of Development: Freud's View

According to Freud, all human beings pass through a series of discrete *psychosexual stages of development*. At each stage, pleasure is focused on a particular part of the body. Too much or too little gratification at any stage can result in *fixation* and can lead to psychological disorders.

again focused on the genitals. Now, however, lust is blended with affection, and the person becomes capable of adult love in its fullest meaning. Please remember: progression to the genital stage is possible only if serious fixation has *not* occurred at the earlier stages of development. If such fixation has occurred, then the normal pattern of development is blocked, and various forms of psychological disorder result.

Figure 10.2 summarizes the various stages of psychosexual development that Freud proposed.

RESEARCH EVIDENCE CONCERNING FREUD'S THEORY: *Freudian Slips*

Freud's theory of personality is filled with provocative ideas and suggestions. Moreover, there can be little doubt that it is now part of our general culture. It is equally clear, however, that many of the ideas and concepts introduced by Freud are difficult to assess through empirical research. This is one of the key criticisms of his theory. Yet over the years, many investigators have developed ingenious ways of testing some of Freud's ideas and hypotheses (Deckers &

KEY QUESTIONS

- According to Freud, what are the three levels of consciousness?
- In Freud's theory, what are the three basic parts of personality?
- According to Freud, what are psychosexual stages of development?

Genital Stage: *In Freud's theory, the final psychosexual stage of development—one in which individuals acquire the adult capacity to combine lust with affection.*

Carr, 1986; Hall, 1984). For example, researchers have attempted to study what have come to be known as **Freudian slips**—occasions on which we say something quite different from our intended meaning. Consider the following examples:

GUEST TO HOSTESS: "The food is really inedible . . . I mean *incredible!*"

SALESPERSON TO CUSTOMER: "You can't get a better deal everywhere . . . I mean *anywhere!*"

Are these merely slips of the tongue? Perhaps. But according to Freud, these errors may also reflect hidden, unconscious thoughts, which is why they are often known as *Freudian slips*. This intriguing suggestion has been subjected to careful empirical test. For example, in one study on the nature of Freudian slips (Motley & Camden, 1985), male students were asked to complete innocent-sounding sentences. Half performed this task in the presence of a male experimenter and half performed it in the presence of an attractive and seductively clad female experimenter. Results indicated that the participants made more slips of the tongue with a sexual connotation in the presence of the female experimenter. For example, when asked to complete the sentence "With the telescope, the details of the distant landscape were easy to . . . ," they were more likely to say "make out" in the presence of the female. And many of the participants found their words, once uttered, to be embarrassing. At first glance this study seems to support Freud's contention that slips of the tongue are revealing of unconscious motives or desires—although it seems more likely that the desires were quite conscious! However, other interpretations exist. For instance, in the presence of the strong sex-related cues provided by the attractive experimenter, activation of sex-related words may have been stronger than activation of other, more neutral words. Thus, it is not surprising that the sex-related words were selected more frequently by subjects. Unfortunately, similar ambiguity with respect to interpretation is present in many other studies designed to test various aspects of Freud's theory (e.g., Dworkin & Efran, 1967; Zillmann, 1988).

FREUD'S THEORY: *An Overall Evaluation*

As noted earlier, Freud's place in history seems assured: His ideas and writings have had a profound impact on twentieth-century intellectual trends. But what about his theory of personality? Is it currently accepted by most psychologists? As you can probably guess from my earlier comments, the answer is *definitely not*. The reasons for this rejection, too, are clear. First, many critics have noted that Freud's theory is really not a theory at all, at least in the scientific sense of this term. Several of the concepts it contains cannot be measured, even indirectly. How, for example, does one go about observing an *id*, a *fixation*, or the psychic energy contained in the *libido*? Similarly, the theory offers few if any testable hypotheses about human behavior. As you will recall from chapter 1, a theory that cannot be tested is largely useless.

Second, as we have already seen, several of Freud's proposals are not consistent with the findings of modern research. For example, he believed that dreams reflect unconscious urges and desires. As chapter 4 explained, there is little evidence for this view.

Third, in constructing his theory, Freud relied heavily on a small number of case studies—no more than a dozen at most. Almost all of these individuals came from wealthy backgrounds and lived in a large and sophisticated city in a single culture. Thus, they were hardly representative of human beings generally. (See the **Perspectives on Diversity** section for more information on this

✓**Freudian Slips:** *Statements that seem to be simple errors in speech, but which in fact reveal unconscious thoughts or impulses.*

point.) Moreover, Freud indicated that he accepted for study and treatment only persons he viewed as particularly good candidates for successful therapy, and he himself recorded and later analyzed all of the information about these cases. Thus, there were many opportunities for unconscious forms of bias to enter the process through which he constructed his theories.

Finally, and perhaps most important of all, Freud's theories contain so many different concepts that they can explain virtually any pattern of behavior in an after-the-fact manner. Imagine, for example, that someone suffering from an "anal" personality is very messy rather than neat, as the theory would initially predict. Freudian psychoanalytic theory is not at a loss: It might suggest that the person's messiness is a defense reaction against anxiety stemming from the need to be neat. In short, no matter what pattern of behavior is demonstrated, Freudian concepts can "explain" them. As you can see, this fact leaves little room for disconfirmation, and thus for testing the theory adequately.

For these and other reasons, Freud's theory of personality is not currently accepted by most psychologists. Yet I should add that several of Freud's insights—especially his ideas about levels of consciousness and the importance of anxiety in various psychological disorders—*have* contributed to our understanding of human behavior in general and personality in particular. There can be no doubt that he has had a major and lasting impact on psychology.

PERSPECTIVES ON DIVERSITY

Love and Intimacy in Different Cultures

According to Freud, all human beings pass through a fixed series of stages with respect to sexuality—stages of *psychosexual development*. If this is true, then we might expect human beings all over the world, even in sharply divergent cultures, to express love and intimacy in similar ways. This would be so because if Freud's theory is correct, all human beings would move through the same stages of development and ultimately attain the same final stage.

In fact, however, this is definitely not the case. On the contrary, ideas about love and intimacy and the overt forms these take vary greatly from culture to culture. For example, in one study on this topic, Simmons, vom Kolke, and Shimizu (1986) compared attitudes about love among Japanese, German, and American college students. Important differences emerged. Japanese students rated romantic love as being less important to personal and marital happiness than did their German and American counterparts. Further, Japanese students described the state of being in love in more negative terms—as a dazed condition filled with feelings of jealousy. American and German students, however, described being in love in comparatively positive terms. Finally, Japanese students expected marriage to result in disillusionment, while American and German students were more optimistic about the possibility of long-lasting romantic relationships.

Important cultural differences also emerge with respect to the expression of intimacy. According to Ting-Toomey (1991), a researcher who has studied many cultural differences, individuals learn to express intimacy toward a romantic partner in ways viewed as acceptable by their society. For example, Ting-Toomey predicted that societies differing along the cultural dimension of *individualism-collectivism* would also differ with respect to the expression of intimacy in love relationships. The individualism-collectivism dimension (Hofstede, 1980) refers to the extent to which a society focuses on the individual or, instead, on the family and other groups. The United States is generally described as a highly individualistic culture, while Japan is described as a collectivist culture. France falls in between these two on the individualism-collectivism dimension.

LOVE IN DIFFERENT CULTURES

Research suggests that love and intimacy are expressed in sharply different ways in various cultures. These findings appear to contradict Freud's belief that all human beings pass through the same stages of psychosexual development.

To see if persons in these cultures do indeed express intimacy differently, Ting-Toomey (1991) surveyed university students in all three countries, asking them to answer questions concerning perceived interdependence, communication about the relationship, and conflict (overt arguments and disagreements). She predicted that all types of intimacy expression would be greater in individualistic than in collectivistic societies. The findings of the study confirmed her predictions: Students in the United States reported higher feelings of interdependence, communication with their romantic partner, and conflict than students in France; those in Japan reported the lowest levels on all measures.

Together, these findings and those of related research suggest that there are indeed important cultural differences both in ideas about love and intimacy and in their overt expression. To the extent such differences exist, any theory that assumes that all human beings move through an identical series of psychosexual stages—such as Freud's—must be called into question. In short, where the study of personality is concerned, wearing cultural blinders can severely limit our understanding of important aspects of human behavior.

OTHER PSYCHOANALYTIC VIEWS: *Freud's Disciples . . . and Dissenters*

Neo-Freudians: Personality theorists who accepted basic portions of Freud's theory but rejected or modified other portions.

Whatever else Freud was, he was certainly an intellectual magnet. Over the course of several decades, he attracted as students or colleagues many brilliant and creative people. Most of these scholars began by accepting Freud's views. Later, however, they often disagreed with some of his major assumptions. For example, while many of these **neo-Freudians** accepted the importance of the unconscious, they objected to Freud's contention that personality is fully formed during the first years of life and to his emphasis on instinctual rather than social influences on personality. As I mentioned earlier, these disagreements sometimes led to angry breaks between Freud and his followers; the master, it seems, was unwilling to accept even slight deviations from what he defined as the only true path to greater knowledge. Let's consider some of the intriguing views proposed by these one-time protégés of Freud.

JUNG: *The Collective Unconscious*

Perhaps the most bitter of all the defections from Freud's inner circle was the departure of Carl Jung. Freud viewed Jung as his heir apparent and was deeply upset when his former disciple broke with him. Jung shared Freud's views concerning the importance of the unconscious. Jung contended, however, that there is another part to this aspect of personality that Freud overlooked: the **collective unconscious**. According to Jung, the material in the collective unconscious is shared by all human beings and is part of our biological heritage. Of what does the collective unconscious consist? For one thing, **archetypes**—images that predispose us to perceive the external world in certain ways. Included among the archetypes we all share, Jung maintained, are these: *mother, father, wise old man, the sun, the moon, God, death,* and *the hero*. It is because of these shared innate images, Jung contended, that the folklore of many different cultures often contains similar figures and themes.

Two especially important archetypes in Jung's theory are known as the **animus** and the **anima**. The animus is the masculine side of females, while the anima is the feminine side of males. Jung believed that in looking for a mate, we search for the person onto whom we can best project these hidden sides of our personality. When there is a good match between such projections and another person, attraction occurs.

Another aspect of Jung's theory was his suggestion that we are all born with innate tendencies to be concerned primarily either with ourselves or with the outside world. Jung labeled persons in the first category **introverts** and described them as being hesitant and cautious; they do not make friends easily and prefer to observe the world rather than become involved in its many activities. He labeled persons in the second category **extroverts**. Such persons are open and confident, make friends readily, enjoy high levels of stimulation, and take part in a wide range of activities. While many aspects of Jung's theory have been rejected by psychologists, the dimension of *introversion-extroversion* appears to be a basic one and continues to be the subject of a considerable amount of research (Eysenck & Eysenck, 1985).

ARCHETYPES: A KEY CONCEPT IN JUNG'S THEORY OF PERSONALITY

According to Jung, all human beings possess *archetypes*—shared images of figures such as heros. What other archetypes can you think of?

Learning Objective 10.6
Describe Adler's view on the roles of social factors and feelings of inferiority in shaping adult personality.

HORNEY: *The Importance of Social and Cultural Factors*

Why do men and women differ to some extent in some aspects of behavior? Almost all modern psychologists would answer: largely because of contrasting experiences during childhood, exposure to different kinds of social models, and so on. Freud, as you already know, held a sharply different view. In many of his writings, he attributed behavioral differences between men and women to innate factors—for example, anatomical differences between the sexes and the resulting *penis envy* he believed all females experience.

Karen Horney, one of the few females in the early psychoanalytic movement, disagreed strongly. She contended that differences between males and females were largely the result of social factors, *not* innate inferiority on the part of females. In fact, Horney (1967) countered Freud's concept of penis envy with one of her own: *womb envy*—males' envy of women's ability to bear and nurse children! Her point was not that males are inferior to females. Rather, she wished to emphasize the fact that each sex has attributes admired by the other and that neither should be viewed as superior *or* inferior.

While well-reasoned objections to some of Freud's negative ideas about women constitute an important contribution, Horney also focused on other issues. She emphasized that psychological disorders stem not from the fixation of psychic energy, as Freud saw it, but from disturbed interpersonal relationships during childhood. In particular, Horney contended that parents often generate feelings of isolation and helplessness in their children—feelings that interfere with healthy development. Unfortunately, parents can produce such outcomes in many ways—by being too dominant, by showing

Collective Unconscious: *In Jung's theory, a portion of the unconscious shared by all human beings.*

Archetypes: *According to Jung, inherited images in the collective unconscious that shape our perceptions of the external world.*

Animus: *According to Jung, the archetype representing the masculine side of females.*

Anima: *According to Jung, the archetype representing the feminine side of males.*

Introverts: *Individuals who are quiet, cautious, and reclusive, and who generally inhibit expression of their impulses and feelings.*

Extroverts: *Individuals who are talkative and sociable, and who often give free rein to their impulses and feelings.*

indifference, by providing too much approval and admiration or too little. When such conditions exist, individuals do not develop adequately and may adopt ineffective styles of interacting with others.

Horney described one of these styles as *moving toward people*. This pattern involves compulsively seeking affection and acceptance from others. Persons who show it need desperately to be liked and loved but are often unable to return true affection to those who fill these needs. Another pattern is termed *moving against people*. Individuals who show this pattern assume that others are hostile and that it is appropriate to manipulate and take advantage of them. A third pattern, *moving away from people*, centers on striving for independence and privacy. Persons who show this pattern form few friendships and prefer privacy and isolation to social contacts. To summarize, persons with the three patterns seem to go through life asking, respectively, these questions: "Will he/she like me?" or "Can he/she be useful to me?" or "Will he/she interfere with me or leave me alone?" All of these patterns are ineffective and lead to considerable unhappiness. Only if people can overcome them through appropriate therapy can they recover from the damage produced by their early experiences with disturbed interpersonal relations.

ADLER: *Striving for Superiority*

Do the views of personality theorists reflect their own life experiences? I raised this possibility when I described Freud's early life. If there is a theorist for whom these potential links seem even stronger, however, it is Alfred Adler. Like Freud, Adler lived in or near Vienna. But unlike Freud, he was a pampered and sickly child. He suffered from a series of childhood illnesses that made him feel weak and awkward, especially in comparison with his strong and healthy older brother. Indeed, Adler recalled an incident in which a physician informed his father: "Your boy is lost." (He was suffering from pneumonia at the time.) In later childhood Adler worked very hard to overcome his physical disabilities. Ultimately, he was so successful in doing so that he rose to leadership among his friends.

These early experiences had a profound impact on Adler and led him to formulate a theory in which feelings of inferiority play a central role. According to Adler's theory, we are motivated by feelings of inferiority, which stem initially from our small size and physical weakness during early childhood. In reaction to these feelings, we try to overcome them through **striving for superiority**. In other words, we engage in *compensation*; we strive to overcome real or imagined inferiorities by developing our abilities. If we succeed, healthy development may follow. If we overcompensate, however, we may conceal our feelings of inferiority even from ourselves, and so develop a distorted self-image.

Like several other neo-Freudians, Adler emphasized the importance of social factors in personality development. For example, he felt that birth order was an important variable: Only children are spoiled by too much parental attention, while first-borns are "dethroned" by a second child. Second-borns, Adler felt, are often competitive, since they have to struggle to catch up with an older sibling. The *family constellation*—our early perceptions of the dynamics within our family—is important, too. Later, we develop a distinctive *style of life*, in which our emotions, thoughts, and actions are directed toward the achievement of life goals we have formulated out of our strivings to overcome feelings of inferiority. In sum, in contrast to Freud, Adler believed that personality development is driven by forces other than the quest for pleasure, and that an understanding of adult personality must be focused on these diverse factors.

Striving for Superiority: *Attempting to overcome feelings of inferiority. According to Adler, this is the primary motive for human behavior.*

THE NEO-FREUDIANS:
An Evaluation

Several neo-Freudians paid a high price for their objections to features of Freud's theory: They were literally drummed out of the group for daring to dissent. Was this high personal cost justified by the magnitude of their contributions? Some modern psychologists would answer yes.

The theories proposed by the neo-Freudians are subject to some of the same criticisms applied to Freud's views. For example, they are *not* based on the kind of hard data science requires; they are difficult if not impossible to test through actual research. And since these theories were often derived from case studies from the neo-Freudians' own clinical practice, they are subject to the same potential types of bias as Freud's original theories.

But—and this is an important point—the theories proposed by some neo-Freudians have served as a kind of bridge between the psychoanalytic approach and later, modern theories of personality. In particular, two of the neo-Freudians' ideas—that the ego is the most important aspect of personality and that human relationships are a key part of life and strongly affect personality—are similar to views proposed by *humanistic theorists*, a group to which we turn next. Please don't misunderstand: The neo-Freudians did not seek to build bridges to modern psychology. Most were trained in medicine, and they focused their attention on Freud's theories, *not* on the research and thinking of academic psychologists (Carver & Scheier, 1992). However, there was some degree of contact between these two groups of scholars, and it seems possible that the neo-Freudians contributed to the advancement of personality theory. So, in a sense, the intellectual—and sometimes personal—battles waged by the neo-Freudians were not in vain. They never toppled the edifice erected by Freud, but did help connect it to important developments that followed.

> ### KEY QUESTIONS
>
> - According to Jung, what is the collective unconscious?
> - To what aspects of Freud's theory did Horney object?
> - According to Adler, what role do feelings of inferiority play in personality?

HUMANISTIC THEORIES: *Emphasis on Growth*

*I*d versus ego, Jekyll versus Hyde—on the whole, psychoanalytic theories of personality take a dim view of human nature, contending that we must struggle constantly to control our brutish impulses if we are to function as healthy, rational adults. Is this view accurate? Many psychologists think it isn't. They believe that human strivings for growth, dignity, and self-determination are just as strong as, if not stronger than, the more primitive motives Freud emphasized. Several theories of personality, because of their more optimistic views concerning human nature, are known as **humanistic theories** (Maslow, 1970; Rogers, 1977, 1982). These theories differ widely in the concepts they employ and the aspects of personality on which they focus but share the following characteristics.

First, they emphasize *personal responsibility*. Each of us, these theories contend, is largely responsible for what happens to us. Our fate is mostly in our own hands; we are *not* at the mercy of dark forces within our personalities that leave us little choice but to act in certain ways. Second, while these theories don't deny the importance of past experience, they generally focus on the present. True, we may be influenced by traumatic early experiences. Yet these do

Humanistic Theories:
Theories of personality emphasizing personal responsibility and innate tendencies toward personal growth.

Learning Objective 10.7
Survey the central assumptions of Rogers's theory.

Learning Objective 10.8
Describe Maslow's concept of the self-actualizing person.

Learning Objective 10.9
Evaluate the humanistic perspective on personality development.

not have to shape our entire adult lives, and the capacity to overcome them and to go on from there is both real and potent. Third, humanistic theories stress the importance of *personal growth*. People are not, such theories argue, content with merely having their current needs met. They wish to continue their development and to progress toward becoming the best they can be. Only when obstacles interfere with such growth is the process interrupted. A key goal of therapy, therefore, should be to help remove obstacles so that natural growth processes can continue. As examples of humanistic theories, we'll now consider the influential views of Carl Rogers and Abraham Maslow.

ROGERS'S SELF THEORY: *Becoming a Fully Functioning Person*

Carl Rogers planned to become a minister, but after exposure to several courses in psychology, he changed his mind. He decided, instead, to focus on efforts to understand the nature of human personality—and why it sometimes goes off the track. The theory Rogers formulated played an important role in the emergence of humanistic psychology and remains influential today.

One central assumption of Rogers's theory was this: Left to their own devices, human beings show many positive characteristics and move, over the course of their lives, toward becoming **fully functioning persons**. What are such persons like? Rogers suggests that they are people who strive to experience life to the fullest, who live in the here and now, and who trust their own feelings. They are sensitive to the needs and rights of others, but do not allow society's standards to shape their feelings or actions to an excessive degree. "If it feels like the right thing to do," such people reason, "then I should do it." Fully functioning people aren't saints; they can—and do—lose their tempers or act in ways they later regret. But throughout life, their actions become increasingly dominated by constructive impulses. They are in close touch with their own values and feelings and experience life more deeply than most other persons.

If all human beings possess the capacity to become fully functioning persons, why don't they all succeed? Why, in short, aren't we surrounded by models of health and happy adjustment? The answer, Rogers contends, lies in the anxiety generated when life experiences are inconsistent with our ideas about ourselves—in short, when a gap develops between our **self-concept** (our belief and knowledge about ourselves) and reality, or our perceptions of it. For example, imagine an individual who believes that she is very likable and that she makes friends easily. One day she happens to overhear a conversation between two other people who describe her as moody, difficult to get along with, and definitely *not* very likable. She is crushed; here is information that is highly inconsistent with her self-concept. As a result of this experience, anxiety occurs, and she adopts one or more psychological defenses to reduce it. The most common of these is *distortion*; for example, the woman convinces herself that the people discussing her do not really know her very well or that they have misinterpreted her behavior. Another defense process is *denial*. Here, the woman may refuse to admit to herself that she heard the conversation or that she understood what the other people were saying.

In the short run, such maneuvers are successful: They help reduce anxiety. Ultimately, however, they produce sizable gaps between an individual's self-concept and reality. The larger such gaps, Rogers contends, the greater an individual's maladjustment—and personal unhappiness (see Figure 10.3). Rogers suggests that distortions in the self-concept are common because most people grow up in an atmosphere of *conditional positive regard*. They learn that others, such as their parents, will approve of them only when they behave in certain ways and express certain feelings. As a result, many people are forced

Fully Functioning Persons: In Rogers's theory, psychologically healthy persons who enjoy life to the fullest.

Self-Concept: All the information and beliefs individuals have about their own characteristics and themselves.

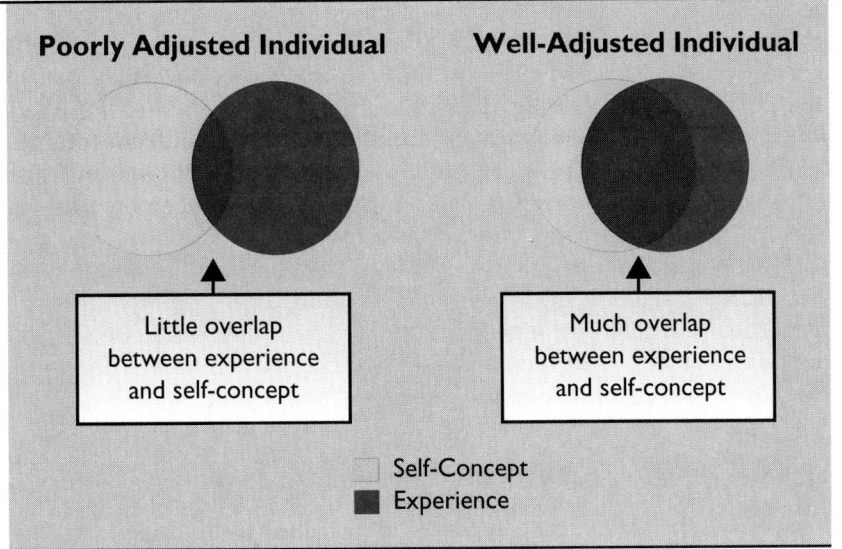

FIGURE **10.3**

Rogers's View of Adjustment

According to Rogers, the larger the gap between an individual's self-concept and reality, the poorer the person's psychological adjustment.

Poorly Adjusted Individual   **Well-Adjusted Individual**

Little overlap between experience and self-concept

Much overlap between experience and self-concept

☐ Self-Concept
■ Experience

to deny the existence of various impulses and feelings, and their self-concepts become badly distorted.

How can such distorted self-concepts be repaired—brought more closely into alignment with reality? Rogers suggests that therapists can help accomplish this by placing individuals in an atmosphere of **unconditional positive regard**—a setting in which they realize that they will be accepted by another person *no matter what they say or do*. Such conditions are provided by *client-centered therapy*, a form of therapy developed by Rogers and his colleagues. We'll consider client-centered therapy in detail in chapter 13. Here, I wish simply to note that such therapy does seem to be effective in helping at least some people attain enhanced levels of personal happiness and adjustment.

MASLOW AND THE STUDY OF SELF-ACTUALIZING PEOPLE

Another influential humanistic theory of personality is one proposed by Abraham Maslow (1970). We have already encountered a portion of Maslow's theory, his concept of a *needs hierarchy*, in chapter 9. As you may recall, this concept suggests that human needs exist in a hierarchy, ranging from *physiological needs* on the bottom through *safety needs, belongingness needs, esteem needs*, and finally, *self-actualization needs* at the top. According to Maslow, lower-order needs in the hierarchy must be satisfied before we can turn to more complex, higher-order needs. Thus, our basic biological needs must be at least partially met before we can become concerned about belonging to social networks or enhancing our self-esteem.

The needs hierarchy, however, is only part of Maslow's theory of personality. Maslow has also devoted much attention to the study of people who, in his terms, are *psychologically healthy*. These are individuals who have attained high levels of **self-actualization**—a state in which they have reached their own fullest true potential. What are such people like? In essence, they are very similar to the fully functioning persons described by Rogers. Self-actualized people accept themselves for what they are; they recognize their shortcomings as well as their strengths. Being in touch with their own personalities, they are less conformist or inhibited than most of us. Self-actualized

✓**Unconditional Positive Regard:** *In Rogers's theory, communicating to others that they will be respected or loved regardless of what they say or do.*

✓**Self-Actualization:** *A stage of personal development in which individuals reach their maximum potential.*

HARRIET TUBMAN: AN EXAMPLE OF SELF-ACTUALIZATION

According to Maslow, only a few people become fully self-actualized. Harriet Tubman, who dedicated her life to ending slavery, is one example; can you think of others?

people are well aware of the rules imposed by society but feel greater freedom to ignore them than is typical. Two additional characteristics of self-actualized persons are also worthy of note. Unlike most of us, they seem to retain their childhood wonder and amazement with the world. For them, life continues to be an exciting adventure rather than a humdrum routine. And finally, self-actualized persons sometimes experience what Maslow describes as **peak experiences**—instances in which they experience powerful feelings of unity with the universe and tremendous waves of power and wonder. Such experiences appear to be linked to personal growth, for after them, individuals report feeling more spontaneous, more appreciative of life, and less concerned with the problems of everyday life. Examples of people Maslow describes as being fully self-actualized are Thomas Jefferson, Albert Einstein, Eleanor Roosevelt, and Albert Schweitzer.

HUMANISTIC THEORIES: An Evaluation

Humanistic theories of personality hit psychology like a cyclone in the 1960s and 1970s. Large numbers of psychologists quickly adopted them as a framework for understanding personality and a basis for new forms of psychotherapy. Like all storms, however, their impact first rose to a peak and then gradually diminished. Have these theories left a lasting impact? Definitely. Many of the ideas first proposed by Rogers, Maslow, and other supporters of the humanistic perspective have entered into the mainstream of psychology. For example, interest in the *self* as a central concept of personality has persisted and even spilled over into several other branches of the field (e.g., Baumeister, Heatherton, & Tice, 1993). Similarly, the contention that behavior stems more from positive forces, such as tendencies toward personal growth, than from primitive sexual and aggressive urges has done much to restore a sense of balance to current views of personality. And the importance of maintaining close contact with one's own feelings, emphasized in several humanistic theories, is seen as a positive development by many psychologists.

But humanistic theories have also been subject to strong criticism. Many psychologists are uncomfortable with their strong emphasis on personal responsibility, or *free will*. As you may recall, humanistic theories propose that individuals are responsible for their own actions and can readily change these if they wish to do so. To an extent, this notion is true. Yet it conflicts with *determinism:* the idea that behavior is determined by numerous different factors and can be predicted from them. And such determinism is one of the cornerstones of modern scientific psychology.

Second, many key concepts of humanistic theories are loosely defined. What, precisely, is self-actualization? A peak experience? A fully functioning person? Until such terms are clearly defined, it is difficult to know exactly what they mean and to conduct systematic research designed to test their validity.

Third, humanistic theorists have been criticized for making what some view as naive or overly optimistic assumptions about human nature. Are people really basically good? Many psychologists would answer that they are neither bad *nor* good. Rather, their behavior is a product of their past experience, current situations, and many other factors. Assuming that people are innately good, therefore, is as untenable as assuming that they are filled with innate destructive impulses.

Despite these criticisms, however, the impact of humanistic theories has persisted. One reason this is so is that, in contrast to the psychoanalytic approach, such theories have stimulated a considerable amount of research. One line of research related to, if not always stimulated by, humanistic theories of personality is described below.

Peak Experiences: In Maslow's theory, intense emotional experiences during which individuals feel at one with the universe.

SELF-DISCLOSURE: *The Potential Benefits of Revealing Ourselves to Others*

Have you ever experienced the "stranger on the bus effect"—an incident in which a total stranger sitting next to you on a bus or plane reveals many details of her or his life? If so, you may have wondered whether engaging in such **self-disclosure**—revealing information about oneself to another person—provides any benefits. Humanistic theories such as Rogers's (1977, 1982) suggest that it may, since self-disclosure can, potentially, increase our self-knowledge and, perhaps, help us to close any gaps between our self-concept and external reality.

Research findings tend to support this possibility (Dindia & Allen, 1992; Meleshko & Alden, 1993). For example, consider a study by Pennebaker, Kiecolt-Glaser, and Glaser (1988). These researchers asked college students to spend about twenty minutes each day writing either about some traumatic event they had experienced or about their feelings and thoughts concerning superficial topics (for instance, a description of their living room). Among the traumatic events disclosed by the students in the first group were instances of rape, child abuse, and the death of loved ones. Participants in both groups gave blood samples before they started writing, after the last writing session, and six weeks later. Analysis of these samples indicated increased functioning of the immune system among those who wrote about traumatic events, both at the end of the study and six weeks later. In addition, persons who wrote about traumatic events had fewer visits to the campus health center for illness than those who wrote about trivial events. Finally, and perhaps most revealing, persons who indicated that they had revealed things in their essays that they had previously kept secret from others showed the greatest improvement in immune functioning—they benefited most from written self-disclosure.

Needless to say, such results must be repeated before they can be accepted with confidence. Still, these and other findings indicate that, as suggested by humanistic theories of personality, self-disclosure can, under some conditions, yield important beneficial effects.

KEY QUESTIONS

- According to humanistic theories of personality, what forces lie behind human development?
- According to Rogers, why do many individuals fail to become fully functioning persons?
- In Maslow's theory, what is self-actualization?

TRAIT THEORIES: *Seeking the Key Dimensions of Personality*

When we describe other persons, we often do so in terms of specific **personality traits**—stable dimensions of personality along which people can vary. This strong tendency to think about others in terms of specific characteristics is reflected in **trait theories** of personality. Such theories focus on identifying key dimensions of personality—the most important ways in which people differ. The basic idea behind this approach is as follows: Once we know *how* people differ, we can measure how *much* they differ, and can then relate such differences to behavior in a wide range of settings.

Unfortunately, this task sounds easier than it actually is. Human beings differ in an almost countless number of ways. How can we determine which of these are most important and perhaps most stable? The scope of the problem was first suggested by a famous study conducted by Allport and Odbert (1936). By consulting a standard dictionary, these researchers identified fully *17,953* words in English that referred to specific traits. Even when words with

Self-Disclosure: The act of revealing information about oneself to another person.

Personality Traits: Specific dimensions along which individuals' personalities differ in consistent, stable ways.

Trait Theories: Theories of personality that focus on identifying the key dimensions along which people differ.

Learning Objective 10.10
Discuss the trait approach to personality and outline the trait theories of Allport and Cattell.

Learning Objective 10.11
List and define the "big five" robust factors of personality.

Learning Objective 10.12
Evaluate the trait approach to the study of personality.

similar meanings were combined, 171 distinct traits remained. How can we hope to deal with this multitude of traits? One solution is to search for *clusters*—groups of traits that seem to go together. Let's now examine some theories that have adopted this approach. Then we'll turn to recent evidence suggesting that in the final analysis, the number of key traits or dimensions we must consider is actually relatively small.

ALLPORT'S CENTRAL, SECONDARY, AND CARDINAL TRAITS

If you have a successful older sister or brother, you can empathize with Gordon Allport: He grew up in the long shadow of his brother Floyd. By the time Gordon entered Harvard as a freshman, his brother was already a graduate student; later, Gordon actually took a course from his older brother—something few universities would permit today. But the two brothers chose different specialties in psychology: Floyd became a well-known social psychologist, while Gordon chose the study of personality.

Allport concluded that personality traits could be divided into several major categories. Of least importance are **secondary traits**, which exert relatively weak effects on behavior. More important are **central traits**: the five to ten traits that together best account for the uniqueness of an individual's personality. Finally, Allport noted that a few people are dominated by a single all-important **cardinal trait**. A few examples of such persons and the cardinal traits that seemed to drive their personalities: Alexander the Great (ambition), Machiavelli (lust for power), and Don Juan (just plain lust).

Perhaps an even more important aspect of Allport's theory of personality is his concept of **functional autonomy** (Allport, 1965)—the idea that patterns of behavior that are initially acquired under one set of circumstances, and which satisfy one set of motives, may later be performed for very different reasons or motives. For example, initially, a child may learn to read because this pleases his teachers and parents and because failure to do so is punished. Later in life, however, the same person may read because he has come to enjoy this activity in and of itself. Notice how this contrasts with Freud's view that the roots of adult personality are planted firmly in the soil of childhood—that, as Freud himself put it, "The child is the father [mother] of the man [woman]." For Allport, such connections are not necessarily present. On the contrary, our adult behavior may spring from roots entirely different from those that gave rise to our childhood behavior.

CATTELL'S SURFACE AND SOURCE TRAITS

Another well-known advocate of the trait approach is Raymond Cattell. He and his colleagues have focused firmly on the task described earlier: identifying the basic dimensions of personality. Instead of beginning with hunches or insights, however, Cattell has followed a very different approach. He has conducted extensive research in which literally thousands of persons responded to measures designed to reflect individual differences on hundreds of traits. These responses were then subjected to a statistical technique known as *factor analysis*. This technique reveals patterns in the extent to which various traits are correlated. In this manner, it can help to identify important *clusters* of traits—ones that seem to be closely linked to one another. As such clusters are identified, Cattell reasoned, the number of key traits in human personality can be reduced until we are left with those that are truly central.

Using this approach, Cattell and his associates (e.g., Cattell & Dreger, 1977) have identified sixteen basic **source traits**—ones he believes underlie differences in many other, less important *surface traits*. It is not yet clear whether

Secondary Traits: According to Allport, traits that exert relatively specific and weak effects upon behavior.

Central Traits: According to Allport, the five or ten traits that best describe an individual's personality.

Cardinal Trait: According to Allport, a single trait that dominates an individual's entire personality.

Functional Autonomy: In Allport's theory, maintenance of patterns of behavior by motives other than the ones originally responsible for the behavior's occurrence.

Source Traits: According to Cattell, key dimensions of personality that underlie many other traits.

TABLE 10.2

END POINTS ON SIXTEEN DIMENSIONS OF PERSONALITY

Cool, reserved	Warm, easygoing
Concrete thinking	Abstract thinking
Easily upset	Calm, stable
Not assertive	Dominant
Sober, serious	Happy-go-lucky
Expedient	Conscientious
Shy, timid	Venturesome
Tough-minded	Tender-minded
Trusting	Suspicious
Practical	Imaginative
Forthright	Shrewd
Self-assured	Apprehensive
Conservative	Experimenting
Group-oriented	Self-sufficient
Undisciplined	Self-disciplined
Relaxed	Tense, driven

Cattell's Sixteen Basic Dimensions of Personality

According to Cattell, the sixteen *source traits* shown here are the most important or basic ones and underlie differences in many other, less crucial *surface traits*. The two columns in the table list the extremes or end points for each trait (dimension).

(*Source*: Adapted from the *Sixteen Personality Factor Questionnaire*, Cattell and the Institute for Personality and Ability Testing, 1983.)

this is actually the case, but at least the list Cattell proposes is more manageable in length than previous ones. (See Table 10.2 for a list of these traits.)

FIVE ROBUST FACTORS: *A Modern Framework*

I began this discussion of trait theories with what seemed to be a fairly straightforward question: What are the key traits or dimensions of human personality? By now you realize that this issue is more complex than it seems. Fortunately, though, this is one instance in which we do *not* have to leave matters dangling. Sophisticated research conducted since the 1970s has begun to converge on a refreshingly simple conclusion: In fact, there may be only five key or central dimensions of personality (Costa & McCrae, 1994; Digman, 1990; McCrae, 1989). These are sometimes labeled the five robust dimensions:

1. **Extraversion**: A dimension ranging from sociable, talkative, fun-loving, affectionate, and adventurous at one end to retiring, sober, reserved, silent, and cautious at the other.

2. **Agreeableness**: A dimension ranging from good-natured, gentle, cooperative, trusting, and helpful at one end to irritable, ruthless, suspicious, uncooperative, and headstrong at the other.

3. **Conscientiousness**: A dimension ranging from well-organized, careful, self-disciplined, responsible, and scrupulous at one end to disorganized, careless, weak-willed, and unscrupulous at the other.

4. **Emotional stability**: A dimension ranging from poised, calm, composed, and not hypochondriacal at one end to nervous, anxious, excitable, and hypochondriacal at the other.

5. **Openness to experience**: A dimension ranging from imaginative, sensitive, intellectual, and polished at one end to down-to-earth, insensitive, crude, and simple at the other.

Extraversion: One of the "big five" dimensions of personality; ranges from sociable, talkative, fun-loving at one end to sober, reserved, cautious at the other.

Agreeableness: One of the "big five" dimensions of personality; ranges from good-natured, cooperative, trusting at one end to irritable, suspicious, uncooperative at the other.

Conscientiousness: One of the "big five" dimensions of personality; ranges from well-organized, careful, responsible at one end to disorganized, careless, unscrupulous at the other.

Emotional Stability: One of the "big five" dimensions of personality; ranges from poised, calm, composed at one end to nervous, anxious, excitable at the other.

Openness to Experience: One of the "big five" dimensions of personality; ranges from imaginative, sensitive, intellectual at one end to down-to-earth, insensitive, crude at the other.

WHOOPI GOLDBERG: AN EXAMPLE OF EXTRAVERSION

According to the five-factor theory of personality, there are only five key dimensions that make up personality; extraversion is one of them. How would you describe yourself on each trait?

How basic, and therefore important, are the "big five" robust dimensions? Many researchers believe that the answer is clear: *very basic*. This is indicated, in part, by the fact that these dimensions are ones to which most people in many different cultures refer in describing themselves (Funder & Colvin, 1991). In addition, these dimensions are readily apparent to total strangers, even in a very brief meeting (Watson, 1989). Compelling evidence for this latter conclusion is provided by an important study conducted recently by Funder and Sneed (1993).

These researchers videotaped pairs of unacquainted college students as they interacted with one another for the first time. The researchers coded sixty-two different behaviors, including "has high enthusiasm and energy level," "says or does interesting things," "shows lack of interest in the interaction," "appears relaxed and comfortable," "expresses hostility," and "speaks fluently." A second group of participants then rated each of these behaviors in terms of how useful they thought they were for determining where others stood on each of the "big five" personality dimensions—conscientiousness, extraversion, agreeableness, and so on. Finally, two persons very familiar with each participant described each participant's personality. On the basis of these descriptions, a rating of each participant for each of the big five dimensions was obtained.

With all these data in hand, Funder and Sneed (1993) could address the following questions: (1) Are the behaviors people believe are important in rating others' personalities the ones we actually use in judging others' personalities? (2) Are these behaviors actually useful in making accurate judgments about others' personalities? The answer to both questions was a clear *yes*. Strangers did tend to use the behaviors identified by participants as useful in making judgments of others' personalities. And these behaviors were indeed useful in making such judgments: They were closely related to the descriptions of participants' personalities provided by persons who knew them well. This was especially true for three of the big five dimensions—extraversion, agreeableness, and conscientiousness—although it was less true for emotional stability and did not seem to hold for openness. In sum, where people stand on several of the big five dimensions is readily apparent in their behavior, and we can make fairly accurate judgments about people's standing on each of these dimensions even on the basis of very brief meetings with them.

TRAIT THEORIES: *An Evaluation*

In the 1990s, most research on personality reflects the trait approach. Instead of seeking to propose and test grand theories such as the ones offered by Freud, Jung, and Rogers, most personality psychologists currently direct their effort to the task of understanding specific traits—ones that appear to exert important effects on behavior in key areas of life (Friedman et al., 1993; Kring, Smith, & Neale, 1994). This trend is due both to the success of the trait approach and to the obvious shortcomings of the theories described in earlier sections of this chapter.

This is not to imply that the trait approach is perfect, however. On the contrary, it, too, can be criticized in several respects. First, the trait approach is largely *descriptive* in nature. It seeks to describe the key dimensions of personality but does not attempt to determine *how* various traits develop or *how* they influence behavior. Thus, in a sense, the trait approach has not generated fully developed theories of personality in the way that other approaches have. Second, despite several decades of careful research, there is still no final agreement concerning the traits that are most important and that constitute the basic dimensions of personality. The five robust factors described above come closest to this goal, but acceptance of these is by no means universal, and they have not emerged as separate and distinct aspects of personality in all research projects (Church & Burke, 1994; Waller & Ben-Porath, 1987).

As you can readily see, these criticisms relate primarily to what the trait approach has not yet accomplished rather than to its findings or proposals. All in all, we can conclude that this approach to personality has generally been a valuable one. Attempting to understand how people differ appears to be a useful strategy for understanding the uniqueness and consistency of key aspects of human behavior.

LEARNING APPROACHES TO PERSONALITY

Whatever their focus, all personality theories must ultimately come to grips with two basic questions: What accounts for the *uniqueness*, and what underlies the *consistency*, of human behavior? Freud's answer focused almost entirely on *internal* factors—hidden conflicts between the id, ego, and super-ego and the active struggle to keep unacceptable impulses out of consciousness. At the other end of the continuum are approaches to personality that emphasize the role of learning and experience. While such views were not originally presented as formal theories of personality, they are often described as *learning theories of personality* to distinguish them from other perspectives (Bandura, 1986; Rotter, 1982; Skinner, 1974).

How can a learning perspective account for the uniqueness and the consistency of human behavior? Very readily. Uniqueness, the learning approach contends, merely reflects the fact that we have all experienced distinctive life (and learning) experiences. Similarly, the learning approach can explain consistency in behavior over time and across situations by noting that the responses, associations, and habits acquired through learning tend to persist. Moreover, since individuals often find themselves in situations very similar to the ones in which they acquired these tendencies, their behavior, too, tends to remain quite stable.

Early learning-oriented views of personality demonstrated another important characteristic. In general, learning theorists denied the importance of considering virtually *any* internal causes of behavior—motives, traits, intentions, goals (Skinner, 1974). The only things that matter, these theorists suggested, are external conditions determining patterns of reinforcement; recall the discussion of this topic in chapter 5. At present, few psychologists agree with this position. Most now believe that internal factors play a crucial role in behavior. Moreover, several theorists contend that these internal factors must be carefully considered if we are ever to understand both uniqueness and consistency in human behavior. As an example of this approach, which more accurately reflects the flavor of modern psychology, let's consider the *social cognitive theory* proposed by Bandura (1986).

SOCIAL COGNITIVE THEORY: Reciprocal Causality in Human Behavior

In his **social cognitive theory**, Albert Bandura, a past president of the American Psychological Association, notes that people do indeed acquire many forms of

Learning Objective 10.13
Discuss how learning approaches to personality can account for the consistency and uniqueness of human behavior.

Learning Objective 10.14
Describe and evaluate the social learning approaches of Bandura and Rotter.

Learning Objective 10.15
Evaluate the learning approach to personality.

Social Cognitive Theory: *A theory of behavior suggesting that human behavior is influenced by many cognitive factors as well as by reinforcement contingencies, and that human beings have an impressive capacity to regulate their own actions.*

TV AND VIOLENCE

According to Bandura, children learn that aggression is acceptable—and sometimes even admirable—through watching violent models on television.

Self-Reinforcement: The delivery of rewards to oneself for reaching one's self-set goals.

Self-Efficacy: Individuals' expectations concerning their ability to perform various tasks.

Internals: In Rotter's terms, individuals who believe that they exert considerable control over the outcomes they experience.

Externals: In Rotter's terms, individuals who believe that they have little control over the outcomes they experience.

behavior through basic processes of learning—operant conditioning and classical conditioning. He adds, however, that a third form—*observational learning,* described in chapter 5—is of special importance. In observational learning, individuals acquire both information and new forms of behavior through observing others (Bandura, 1977). And such learning plays a role in a very wide range of human activities—everything from aggression, which can be acquired by observing violent models in daily life or in television shows and movies, to many types of task performance, which can be acquired from watching other persons at work or from instructional videotapes and manuals.

Bandura also calls attention to the fact that learning is far from the entire story where human behavior and personality are concerned. In addition, many cognitive factors play a role. Unlike many other animals, Bandura notes, human beings do not respond passively or automatically to the external conditions around them. Instead, they plan, form expectancies, set goals, imagine possible outcomes, and so on. In short, people's actions are often strongly determined by a wide range of cognitive factors that were totally ignored by both early behaviorists and early learning theories of personality.

In addition, Bandura (1986) notes, human beings often demonstrate impressive capacity for the *self-regulation* of their own behavior. While people may often respond to external factors such as positive reinforcement and punishment, they sometimes choose to ignore these and to operate in terms of internal standards and values. We set our own goals, and we often provide our own rewards when we reach them—a process known as **self-reinforcement**. Moreover, these rewards range from a direct pat on our own backs, through more generalized feelings of personal accomplishment. For example, consider the hundreds of amateur runners who participate in major marathons. Few believe that they have any chance of winning and obtaining the external reinforcements offered—status, fame, cash prizes. Why, then, do they run? Because, Bandura would contend, they have *self-determined goals,* such as finishing the race, or merely going as far as they can. And meeting these goals is sufficient to initiate what is obviously very effortful behavior.

Another important concept in Bandura's theory is **self-efficacy**—perceived ability to carry out a desired action (Bandura, 1986). The higher a person's feelings of self-efficacy, the better that person tends to do at a wide range of tasks. And such success, of course, can ultimately lead to more generalized positive feelings about oneself. We'll return to such feelings (often termed *self-esteem*) below.

Other learning-oriented approaches to personality share a similar perspective. For example, the *social learning theory* proposed by Julian Rotter (1954, 1982) suggests that the likelihood that a given behavior will occur in a specific situation depends on individuals' *expectancies* concerning the outcomes the behavior will produce and the *reinforcement value* they attach to such outcomes—the degree to which they prefer one reinforcer over another. According to Rotter, on the basis of their experience, individuals also form *generalized expectancies* concerning the extent to which their own actions determine the outcomes they experience. Rotter calls persons who strongly believe that they shape their own destinies **internals** and those who believe their outcomes are largely the result of forces outside their control **externals**. As you can probably guess, internals are often happier and better adjusted than externals. Note again how in this theory, internal factors such as subjective estimates concerning the likelihood of various outcomes, subjective reactions to these, and generalized expectancies of personal control play an important role in behavior. Certainly, such contentions contrast very sharply with the view, stated in early learning approaches to personality, that only external reinforcement contingencies should be taken into account.

EVALUATION OF THE LEARNING APPROACH

Do all human beings confront an Oedipus conflict? Are peak experiences real, and do they in fact constitute a sign of growing self-actualization? Considerable controversy exists with respect to these and many other aspects of psychoanalytic and humanistic theories of personality. In contrast, virtually all psychologists agree that behaviors are acquired and modified through basic processes of learning. Moreover, in the 1990s, after the "cognitive revolution" of the 1970s and 1980s (see chapters 6 and 7), there is general agreement about the importance of cognitive factors in human behavior. Thus, a key strength of the learning approach is obvious: It is based on widely accepted principles in psychology, principles for which there is an impressive amount of evidence.

Another positive feature of this framework for understanding personality lies in the fact that it has been put to effective, practical use in efforts to modify maladaptive forms of behavior. Such efforts have proved to be quite effective in treating a wide range of psychological disorders (Sherman, 1990); we'll consider these therapies in detail in chapter 13. Finally, it should be noted that in contrast to other major theories of personality, learning approaches have been put to empirical test in ongoing research and rest on an extensive body of research findings.

Turning to criticisms, most of these have focused on older behaviorist approaches rather than on the more sophisticated theories proposed by Bandura (1986) and others. Those early behaviorist theories generally ignored the role of cognitive factors in human behavior and frequently assumed that principles uncovered in research with animals would transfer readily to human beings. Such views ignored human capacities for self-regulation of behavior and the important fact that cognitive factors such as beliefs and expectancies may often be more important determinants of overt actions than reinforcement contingencies.

As you can readily see, these criticisms do not apply to new learning approaches such as social cognitive theory. In fact, it seems fair to state that at present these social cognitive theories of personality are more in tune with the eclectic approach of modern psychology than any others. As such, they are certain to play an important role in continuing efforts to understand many aspects of personality. Please see the **Key Concept** on page 394 for an overview of several major theories of personality discussed in this chapter.

KEY QUESTIONS

- According to learning approaches, how does personality develop?
- What is Bandura's social cognitive theory?
- What is Rotter's social learning approach to personality?

KEY ASPECTS OF PERSONALITY: A Sample of Recent Research

*I*n recent decades efforts to understand personality have undergone a major shift. Rather than attempting to construct grand theories, psychologists have focused on efforts to identify and investigate key aspects of personality. One idea behind this approach is that a fuller understanding of personality will

Major Theories of Personality: An Overview

Theory	Major Focus	Key Concepts

Psychoanalytic Theory

Freud

Levels of consciousness

States of psychosexual development

Anxiety and defense mechanisms

Conscious, preconscious, unconscious

Oral, anal, phallic, latency, genital

Repression, rationalization, displacement, projection, regression

Humanistic Theories

Rogers

Personal growth, personal responsibility

The present rather than the past

Self-concept, self-actualization

Maslow

Trait Theories

Stable dimensions of personality along which people vary

Cardinal traits, central traits, surface and source traits; the "big five" dimensions of personality

Recent findings indicate that individual differences in *shyness*—one aspect of temperament—are present shortly after birth and tend to persist through life.

Even in a brief meeting, it would be apparent to you that Whoopi Goldberg rates high on *extraversion*—one of the "big five" dimensions of personality.

Learning Approaches

Role of basic learning processes in establishing the uniqueness and stability of individual behavior

Self-regulation of behavior

Operant conditioning, observational learning

Self-efficacy

Internal versus external locus of control

gradually emerge from knowledge about these factors and the ways in which they interact. Reflecting this modern approach, let's look at modern research findings concerning several intriguing aspects of personality.

Learning Objective 10.16
Discuss the research on self-esteem and self-monitoring and discuss their impact on behavior.

Learning Objective 10.17
Describe the characteristics of high and low sensation-seekers.

TWO ASPECTS OF THE SELF: *Self-Esteem and Self-Monitoring*

Many different theorists have suggested that in several respects, our *self-concept*—our beliefs and knowledge about ourselves—plays a crucial role in our total personality (Benesch & Page, 1989). Reflecting this emphasis, much current research on personality is concerned with various aspects of the self. Here, we'll focus on two aspects of the self that have been the focus of special attention: *self-esteem* and *self-monitoring*.

SELF-ESTEEM: SOME EFFECTS OF FEELING GOOD—OR BAD—ABOUT OURSELVES

How do you feel about yourself? Generally good? Generally bad? Most people tend to hold relatively favorable views of themselves; they realize that they aren't perfect, but in general they conclude that their good points outweigh their bad ones. Large individual differences with respect to such self-evaluations exist, however, so one important aspect of the self is **self-esteem**: the extent to which our self-evaluations are favorable or unfavorable (Campbell, 1990; Epstein, 1983). Such self-evaluations generally reflect individuals' assessments of their own attributes—how they compare with others on various dimensions. In addition, however, there is a *collective* aspect to self-esteem: It is often influenced by our evaluations of the groups to which we belong (Crocker et al., 1994; Miller & Prentice, 1994). For example, our self-esteem may be boosted if we perceive that other people view the groups to which we belong favorably, but it may be undermined if we perceive that others view our groups negatively.

Whether self-esteem derives primarily from individual attributes or from group membership, it is related to many forms of behavior. Persons who are high in self-esteem tend to report fewer negative emotions and less depression than persons who are low in self-esteem (Straumann & Higgins, 1988). Similarly, persons high in self-esteem are better able to handle stress, and they experience fewer negative health effects when exposed to it (Brown & McGill, 1989).

Findings reported recently by Straumann, Lemieux, and Coe (1993) help explain why this may be so. These researchers induced anxious, depressed, or control participants to think about themselves by asking them to consider questions about various traits; for example, "Is it important for you to be . . . ?" "Would your parents say that they want you to be . . . ?" Participants' answers to other questions were used to measure the gap between their ideal and actual selves. As expected, this gap was larger for depressed and anxious persons than for controls. In addition, both anxious and depressed persons (who, presumably, were lower in self-esteem than controls) showed signs of reduced efficiency in their immune system when they thought about themselves: Activity in the immune system's natural "killer cells" decreased. Controls (who, presumably, had higher self-esteem) did *not* experience such effects. These findings are consistent with the view that low self-esteem, or states linked to it, can reduce the effectiveness of the immune system, thus placing low-self-esteem persons at increased risk for many illnesses.

Other findings indicate that persons high in self-esteem, as compared to those low in self-esteem, are less susceptible to influence (Wylie, 1974), more confident of achieving their goals (Wells & Marwell, 1976); and more effective in social situations—that is, they make more favorable impressions on others (Baron & Byrne, 1994).

✓**Self-Esteem:** *The extent to which individuals have positive or negative feelings about themselves and their own worth.*

Finally, persons low and high in self-esteem also differ with respect to the clarity of their own self-concepts. Those low in self-esteem report less confidence in their judgments when asked to rate themselves on various traits and show less tendency to report the same ratings over time than do high self-esteem persons (Campbell, 1990). In addition, persons low in self-esteem show less consistency in their self-ratings. When asked to rate the extent to which adjectives that are opposite in meaning describe them, they are more likely than high self-esteem persons to say that both opposite adjectives apply (Campbell, 1990). Together, these findings suggest that persons low in self-esteem have self-concepts that are less clear or well-developed than those of persons high in self-esteem. Such uncertainty has been found to be negatively related to resistance to stress: People who have less clear-cut self-concepts are more vulnerable to the harmful effects of stress (Brown & Smart, 1989). This interesting finding has direct applications for people's health. We'll discuss individual differences in resistance to stress in chapter 11.

Looking back over these diverse findings, it is easy to conclude that high self-esteem is desirable, while low self-esteem is undesirable—and perhaps even dangerous to one's health. In general, these conclusions are true. But recent findings indicate that high self-esteem, too, can sometimes have its costs. Persons high in self-esteem may sometimes suffer from *overconfidence*— unrealistically optimistic expectations. For example, they may set unrealistic goals or commit themselves to doing more than they can actually accomplish (Vallone et al., 1990). Direct evidence for such effects is provided by research carried out by Baumeister, Heatherton, and Tice (1993).

These investigators reasoned that under normal conditions, persons high in self-esteem have an edge over those low in self-esteem with respect to performing many tasks, because they have more complete and consistent self-knowledge and can do a better job at choosing the most desirable goals —ones that are challenging but within their reach. However, the situation changes radically when high-self-esteem persons are exposed to threats to their ego from negative feedback. Under these conditions, they may become unduly concerned with protecting their favorable self-concept, and this may interfere with their performance. In contrast, persons low in self-esteem do not react as strongly to ego threats and so should suffer smaller decrements in performance in negative-feedback situations.

To test these predictions, Baumeister et al. (1993) had high- and low-self-esteem participants play a computer game in which they navigated an airplane through an obstacle course. Before playing the game, participants worked on another task: coming up with as many uses as possible for a doughnut. Some were told that they did very well on this task and were highly creative, while others received negative feedback. While playing the computer game, participants were told that they must bet on the outcome. They had to bet at least 25¢ of a $3.00 payment they received, but they could bet anything up to the full amount. If they met a criterion based on their doughnut performance, they would receive triple their bet; if they failed to meet it, they would lose the entire bet. Baumeister and his colleagues predicted that after receiving failure feedback (an ego threat), high-self-esteem participants would be more likely to make inappropriate bets and would actually do worse than those low in self-esteem. After receiving success feedback, however, they would do better than low-self-esteem persons. As shown in Figure 10.4, this is precisely what happened.

While high self-esteem is generally a plus, then, this is not always true. Under most conditions, high-self-esteem persons do a better job of regulating their own behavior than low-self-esteem persons. As a result, they may well set themselves up for confirmation of their favorable self-concept: One success, stemming from wisely chosen goals, follows another. When their egos are threatened, however, such persons may focus their attention on the task

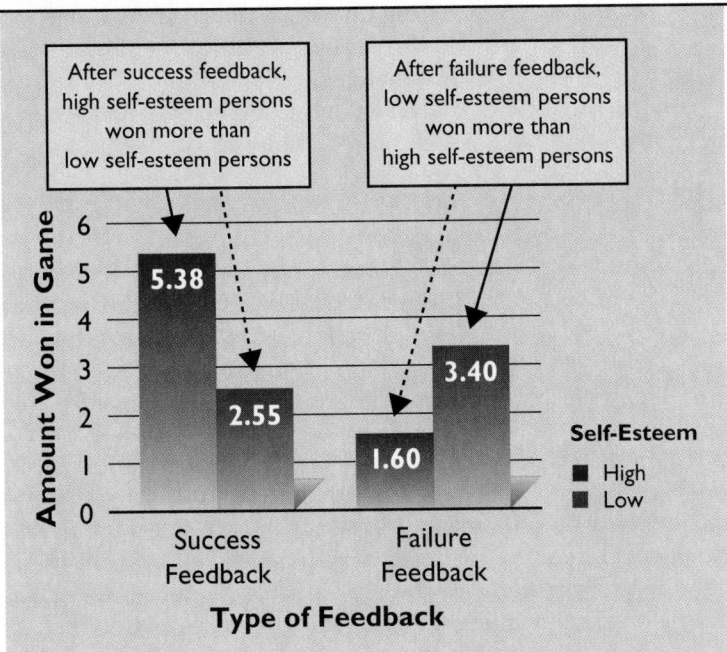

FIGURE 10.4

When High Self-Esteem Can Hurt

When they received feedback indicating they had failed at a preliminary task, persons high in self-esteem actually did worse in terms of making appropriate bets, and so won less money, than persons low in self-esteem. In contrast, when both groups received feedback indicating they had succeeded, persons high in self-esteem did better than those low in self-esteem. These findings indicate that in situations involving ego threat, high self-esteem can actually interfere with performance. (*Source:* Based on data from Baumeister, Heatherton, & Tice, 1993.)

of protecting or restoring their self-esteem, with the result that they may slip into ineffective, self-defeating strategies. In contrast, low-self-esteem persons are accustomed to being kicked around in life and may not suffer equal decrements in performance. In such situations, then, self-esteem may fail to confer the kind of benefits with which it is usually associated.

SELF-MONITORING: PUBLIC APPEARANCE AND PRIVATE REALITY   Respond to each of the following statements with *true* or *false*:

When I am uncertain how to act in social situations, I look to the behavior of others for cues.

In different situations and with different people, I often act like very different persons.

My behavior is usually an expression of my true inner feelings, attitudes, and beliefs.

I would not change my opinions or the way I do things to please someone else or to win their favor.

If you answered *true* to the first two statements but *false* to the remaining two, you may well be high in another interesting dimension of personality. In contrast, if you answered *false* to the first two and *true* to the others, you may well be relatively low on this dimension. This trait, **self-monitoring**, relates primarily to the ability to adapt one's behavior to the demands of a current social situation. Persons high in self-monitoring are like social chameleons— they can change their behavior to match the current situation. (Chameleons are small lizards capable of altering their skin color to match different backgrounds.) If high self-monitors find themselves among beer-drinking construction workers, they roll up their sleeves and swig some beer. If, instead, they find themselves among wine conoisseurs, they roll *down* their sleeves and sip with the best of them. In short, they adjust what they say and what they do to the current situation in order to make a positive impression on others (Snyder, 1987; Snyder & Gangestad, 1986). In contrast, persons low in

Self-Monitoring: A personality trait involving sensitivity to social situations and an ability to adapt one's behavior to the demands of those situations in order to make favorable impressions on others.

"Why, you swine!"

FAILURE TO REGULATE ONE'S EXPRESSIVE BEHAVIOR

There are many situations in which people are required to conceal their true feelings from others. (This therapist is clearly violating one such rule.) High self-monitors are generally more successful at this task than low self-monitors.
(*Source:* Drawing by Richter; © 1952, 1980 The New Yorker Magazine, Inc.)

KEY QUESTIONS

- How do persons high in self-esteem differ from those low in self-esteem?

- Under what conditions is high self-esteem not beneficial?

- What are the characteristics of persons who are high self-monitors?

Sensation Seeking: A trait relating to the extent to which individuals seek and enjoy high levels of stimulation.

self-monitoring tend to show a higher degree of consistency: They act much the same across a wide range of situations.

Self-monitoring also involves several other factors, such as the ability to control and modify one's own behavior, or skill in what might be termed *acting*; sensitivity to the expressive behaviors of others (Lennox & Wolfe, 1984); willingness to serve as the center of attention; and concern with being liked by others (Briggs & Cheek, 1988). High self-monitors exceed low self-monitors on all of these dimensions.

Self-monitoring plays a role in many different aspects of behavior. First, consider choice of friends. Low self-monitors are often closely attuned to their own attitudes and values. Thus, it seems reasonable to expect that they will often like others who resemble themselves in various ways—people who share their views and beliefs. In contrast, high self-monitors realize that they often act differently in different situations. As a result, they may like and choose as friends others who share their preferences for specific activities—people who enjoy doing the same things (Jamiesen, Lydon, & Zanna, 1987).

Next, consider dating and sexual relationships. Do you think high or low self-monitors will have a larger number of different partners? The answer is clear: High self-monitors report having had a greater number of different sexual partners and expect to have more partners in the future than do low self-monitors (Snyder, Simpson, & Gangestad, 1987).

Finally, high self-monitors are much better at certain kinds of social deception than low self-monitors. For example, they are better at managing their own nonverbal cues so as to conceal their true reactions from others (Friedman & Miller-Herringer, 1991). There are many situations in which such self-regulation of both verbal and nonverbal cues is necessary. Athletes aren't supposed to gloat openly after defeating their opponents; and therapists are supposed to refrain from acting like the character in the cartoon, no matter what their patients say!

SENSATION SEEKING: The Desire for Stimulation

When I was in high school, I had a friend named Lonny who had an insatiable desire for stimulation. I don't think I was timid, but where risk taking was concerned, I was definitely *not* in Lonny's league. One example: There was a high dam near where we lived. On one side was an artificial lake; on the other, a sheer drop of about eighty feet onto jagged rocks. The top of the dam was narrow and slippery: When the water was high, it flowed over the top, and the plants that grew there made the dam slimy. One look at the rocks was enough to convince me that crossing the dam wasn't worth it. But Lonny insisted on crossing over and over again. In fact, to show us how easy it was, he even hopped across on one leg! When he wanted to cross blindfolded, though, we talked him out of it; that was too much even for a bunch of fifteen-year-old boys.

Today I'd describe Lonny as someone high in what psychologists term **sensation seeking**—the desire for new, exciting experiences (Zuckerman, 1990). Lonny liked high levels of arousal, and if the only way to achieve these was by exposing himself to danger, then that's the way it had to be. The dimension of *sensation seeking* is an aspect of personality that has received increasing attention from psychologists. Research on sensation seeking indicates that, compared to low sensation-seekers, high sensation-seekers drive faster (Zuckerman & Neeb, 1980) and are more likely to engage in substance abuse (Teichman, Barnea, & Rahav, 1989), more likely to get into trouble with the law while teenagers (Hamilton, 1983), and more likely to engage in high-risk sports such as skydiving (Humbaugh & Garrett, 1974). In short, they often lead lives in which they actively seek thrills and adventure wherever and however they can find them.

What accounts for this preference for dangerous behaviors and the high levels of arousal they produce? Zuckerman (1984, 1990), the psychologist who first called attention to this aspect of personality, believes that it has important roots in biological processes. High sensation-seekers, he suggests, are persons whose nervous systems operate best at high levels of arousal. Thus, for them, the optimal level of arousal is much higher than is true for other persons, and so they seek situations and activities that will generate such reactions.

Considerable evidence supports these views. First, high sensation-seekers show stronger *orienting response* to the initial presentation of an unfamiliar auditory or visual stimulus (Zuckerman, Simons, & Como, 1988). In other words, they seem to pay more attention to such stimuli than other persons. Second, high sensation-seekers show greater ability to ignore irrelevant information (Martin, 1986). So, in sum, they are better able than low sensation-seekers to zero in on new stimuli and give them their full attention. Such effects are clearly illustrated by a study conducted by Ball and Zuckerman (1992). These researchers asked high and low sensation-seekers to perform a *shadowing* task in which different lists of words were presented simultaneously to each ear. They were to repeat out loud only the words they heard in one ear. Results indicated that high sensation-seekers made fewer errors in this task than low sensation-seekers. Moreover, their performance improved more quickly than that of low sensation-seekers, thus indicating that they could establish a focus of attention more quickly.

Additional evidence for the view that sensation seeking is closely related to biological processes comes from research on patients undergoing treatment for pain. Among the patients studied, high sensation-seekers had lower levels of *endorphins*—natural substances produced within our brains that act somewhat like opiates—than low sensation-seekers (Johansson et al., 1979). Since endorphins are released by the body after painful experiences, one interpretation of these findings is that the bodies of high sensation-seekers were working less hard to counteract pain—one source of high arousal and stimulation.

Whatever the precise basis for high sensation seeking, it is clear that persons demonstrating this characteristic often engage in behaviors that expose them to danger. Does high sensation seeking always have negative implications for personal health or safety? There are some grounds for predicting that this may not be true. It seems possible, for example, that people high in sensation seeking might be better able to tolerate the emotional arousal produced by stressful life events. After all, their nervous systems operate best under high arousal, so they may be able to cope with stress more effectively than persons low in sensation seeking. Research by Smith, Ptacek, and Smoll (1992) provides support for this prediction. These psychologists found that high school athletes high in sensation seeking were *less* likely than athletes low in sensation seeking to experience injuries following stress (such as strong criticism from their coaches). One interpretation of these findings is that the high sensation-seekers

HIGH-RISK SPORTS: A FAVORITE PASTIME OF HIGH SENSATION-SEEKERS

People who rate high in sensation seeking are attracted to activities like white-water kayaking.

were indeed better able to cope with stress than the low sensation-seekers and so had fewer injuries.

As is true for other aspects of personality, therefore, the effects of high sensation seeking are neither uniformly negative nor uniformly positive. In many cases, being high on this dimension does appear to have negative implications for one's health and well-being; but this is not always the case. In fact, in one area of life—participation in sports—being high in sensation seeking may confer important benefits.

KEY QUESTIONS

• What are high sensation-seekers?
• In what ways does the behavior of high and low sensation-seekers differ?

MAKING PSYCHOLOGY PART OF YOUR LIFE

How Accurate Is Your Self-Concept?

Self-knowledge is a useful thing; the better we understand ourselves, the better the choices we can make in many contexts and the more accurately we can predict our reactions to many events or situations. In addition, several theories of personality suggest that the more accurate our self-concept is, the happier and better adjusted we will be (Maslow, 1970; Rogers, 1982). How well do you know *yourself*? Follow the procedures below and find out.

First, make about ten copies of the questionnaire given here. Next, complete one copy yourself. The third step is to give copies (blank, of course, except for your name in the space for it) to several people who know you well—good friends, family members, romantic partners. Try to have at least five to ten people provide ratings. Finally, average their ratings on each dimension and then compare these averages with your own ratings. The larger the differences, the less accurate your self-concept.

Do you find any dimensions on which your perceptions of yourself are sharply different from those of others—showing scale differences of one point or more? If so, consider why these differences exist. The insight you gain into your own traits and personality may prove very valuable.

Rate _____ on each of the dimensions below. Circle one number to indicate where she/he falls on this dimension (4 is the middle of the scale).

1. Cautious   Adventurous
   1   2   3   4   5   6   7

2. Insensitive   Sensitive
   1   2   3   4   5   6   7

3. Calm   Anxious
   1   2   3   4   5   6   7

4. Cooperative   Uncooperative
   1   2   3   4   5   6   7

5. Irresponsible   Responsible
   1   2   3   4   5   6   7

6. Composed   Excitable
   1   2   3   4   5   6   7

7. Sociable   Shy
   1   2   3   4   5   6   7

8. Suspicious   Trusting
   1   2   3   4   5   6   7

9. Imaginative   Down-to-earth
   1   2   3   4   5   6   7

10. Careless   Careful
   1   2   3   4   5   6   7

Note: Items on this scale relate to four of the five robust factors of personality described earlier in this chapter as follows: extraversion (items 1 and 7); agreeableness (4 and 8); conscientiousness (5 and 10); openness to experience (2, 7, and 9).

How well do you know yourself? Awareness of our own thoughts, feelings, and abilities can help us become happier and better adjusted.

- *What is the modern definition of personality?*

Personality consists of the unique and stable patterns of behavior, thoughts, and emotions shown by individuals.

- *What are the roles of situational factors and personal dispositions in human behavior?*

Behavior is influenced by both situational factors and personal dispositions. In many situations, complex interactions between these factors determine behavior.

KEY TERM: *personality, p. 370*

THE PSYCHOANALYTIC APPROACH: MESSAGES FROM THE UNCONSCIOUS

- *According to Freud, what are the three levels of consciousness?*

According to Freud, three distinct levels of consciousness exist: conscious, preconscious, and unconscious.

- *In Freud's theory, what are the three basic parts of personality?*

Freud believed that personality consists of three basic parts: id, ego, and superego, which correspond roughly to desire, reason, and conscience.

- *According to Freud, what are psychosexual stages of development?*

Freud believed that all human beings move through a series of psychosexual stages during which the id's search for pleasure is focused on different regions of the body.

KEY TERMS: *psychoanalysis, p. 373; id, p. 374; pleasure principle, p. 374; ego, p. 374; reality principle, p. 374; superego, p. 374; anxiety, p. 374; defense mechanisms, p. 374; sublimation, p. 374; reaction formation, p. 375; psychosexual stages of development, p. 375; libido, p. 375; fixation, p. 376; oral stage, p. 376; anal stage, p. 376; phallic stage, p. 376; Oedipus complex, p. 376; latency stage, p. 376; genital stage, p. 377; Freudian slips, p. 378*

OTHER PSYCHOANALYTIC VIEWS: FREUD'S DISCIPLES . . . AND DISSENTERS

- *According to Jung, what is the collective unconscious?*

Jung believed that all human beings share a collective unconscious: memories and images that strongly influence our perceptions of the world and our behavior.

- *To what aspects of Freud's theory did Horney object?*

Horney rejected Freud's suggestion that females experience penis envy. She also contended that many psychological disorders stem from social factors rather than from fixation at various stages of psychosexual development.

- *According to Adler, what role do feelings of inferiority play in personality?*

Adler believed that human beings experience strong feelings of inferiority during early life and must struggle to overcome these through compensation.

KEY TERMS: *neo-Freudians, p. 380; collective unconscious, p. 381; archetypes, p. 381; animus, p. 381; anima, p. 381; introverts, p. 381; extroverts, p. 381; striving for superiority, p. 382*

HUMANISTIC THEORIES: EMPHASIS ON GROWTH

- *According to humanistic theories of personality, what forces lie behind human development?*

Humanistic theories of personality suggest that human beings strive for personal development and growth, not merely the satisfaction of biological needs.

- *According to Rogers, why do many individuals fail to become fully functioning persons?*

Rogers believed that many individuals fail to become fully functioning persons because distorted self-concepts interfere with their personal growth.

- *In Maslow's theory, what is self-actualization?*

Self–actualization is a state in which an individual has reached his or her maximum potential. Maslow suggests that when lower-level needs are met, human beings strive to attain self-actualization.

KEY TERMS: *humanistic theories, p. 383; fully functioning persons, p. 384; self-concept, p. 384; unconditional positive regard, p. 385; self-actualization, p. 385; peak experiences, p. 386; self-disclosure, p. 387*

TRAIT THEORIES: SEEKING THE KEY DIMENSIONS OF PERSONALITY

- *According to Allport, what are central traits?*

Allport suggested that human beings possess a small number of central traits that account for much of their uniqueness as individuals.

- *What are source traits?*

According to Cattell, there are sixteen source traits that underlie differences between individuals on many specific dimensions.

- *What are the five robust dimensions of personality?*

Research findings point to the conclusion that there are only five basic dimensions of personality: extraversion, agreeableness, conscientiousness, emotional stability, and openness to experience.

LEARNING APPROACHES TO PERSONALITY

- *According to learning approaches, how does personality develop?*

Learning approaches to personality suggest that personality is strongly influenced by learning and experience.

- *What is Bandura'a social cognitive theory?*

Bandura's social cognitive theory assumes that behavior is influenced by cognitive factors and personal dispositions as well as by reinforcement contingencies and the social and physical environment.

- *What is Rotter's social learning approach to personality?*

Rotter's social learning approach calls attention to the importance of generalized expectancies concerning the internal or external control of outcomes.

KEY ASPECTS OF PERSONALITY: A SAMPLE OF RECENT RESEARCH

- *How do persons high in self-esteem differ from those low in self-esteem?*

Persons high in self-esteem are generally happier, healthier, and more successful at many tasks than are persons low in self-esteem. They also have more consistent and well-developed self-concepts.

- **Under what conditions is high self-esteem not beneficial?**

Under conditions involving ego threat, persons high in self-esteem may experience larger decrements in performance than do persons low in self-esteem.

- *What are the characteristics of persons who are high self-monitors?*

High self-monitors are better at reading others, better at regulating their own expressive behavior, more successful in making favorable impressions on others, and better at social deception than are low self-monitors.

- *What are high sensation-seekers?*

High sensation-seekers are persons who prefer high levels of arousal and stimulation.

- *In what ways does the behavior of high and low sensation-seekers differ?*

High sensation-seekers show stronger orienting responses, and are better able to focus their attention on new stimuli and to handle stressful life events than are low sensation-seekers.

CRITICAL THINKING QUESTIONS

APPRAISAL	Some would say that people differ in so many ways that it is impossible ever to obtain solid, scientific understanding of personality. Do you agree or disagree? Why?
CONTROVERSY	Growing evidence indicates that some aspects of personality, like some aspects of physical appearance, are influenced by genetic factors. Does this mean that personality, like eye color or height, is predetermined and can't be changed? Or, even if genetic factors *do* play a role, do you think that personality remains open to change throughout life?
MAKING PSYCHOLOGY PART OF YOUR LIFE	Different jobs or careers seem to require different traits for their successful performance. For example, a timid, shy person would probably *not* be successful as an emergency-room physician or as a politician. What kind of jobs or careers do you think might provide a good match to *your* personality? Why? Do you think that taking careful account of your own traits and dispositions might help you to choose the right career?

Health, Stress, and Coping

_I_magine that you've been granted three wishes. How will you use them? Will you request fame and power? Immense wealth? Irresistible charm or beauty? Obviously, the possibilities are endless. But what about good health—will this be among your choices? For many people, especially young people, the answer is probably no. In one sense, this is somewhat surprising, for without good health it would be impossible for you to enjoy the benefits you gained from your other wishes.

Fortunately, over the past several decades, a growing number of people all over the world have become increasingly aware of the importance of good health and the value of taking active steps to ensure it. Many of us are trying to eat healthier foods, to refrain from smoking, to drink alcohol only in moderation, and to engage in regular physical exercise. Psychologists, too, have become increasingly interested in the issue of personal health and have made it the focus of a growing volume of research. This certainly seems appropriate. After all, mental health has always been a central topic in psychology, and it is increasingly clear that mental and physical health are intimately linked.

As a case in point, consider an example from my own life: the different ways in which members of my own family reacted to a critical health-related event. The event was the news that my grandfather had developed a serious form of cancer. Curiously, the person least affected by the diagnosis was my grandfather himself; he remained calm and collected, despite the implications for him personally. Why? Because, as he told me, he felt that he had done his part; he had done everything he could to stay healthy. In contrast, my grandmother took the news badly—but not just because of the discovery of the illness. Shortly before the examination in which doctors detected the cancer, she had given my grandfather a hard time about wasting time and money getting annual checkups. In particular, she felt that he paid too many visits to his life-long friend Herb, who also happened to be his personal physician. Each time he went for one of these check-ups, she had complained, Herb would tell him the same thing: "Good news, you're the picture of health—see you next time." Now, the uncertainty of my grandfather's future, coupled with the guilt she felt over her earlier behavior, weighed heavily on my grandmother's conscience. The result: *she* became physically ill and remained that way for several months.

The story has a happy ending, however. The cancer was detected at an early stage and treated successfully. Apparently my grandfather's faithful adherence to annual medical checkups, his careful attention to diet and exercise, and his positive outlook on life paid off. My grandmother, too, regained her former resilience, although it is interesting to note that her return to health occurred gradually and seemed to mirror my grandfather's recovery. Both of them went on to enjoy many more years of happy, fulfilling life, and my grandfather's cancer never recurred.

In this chapter we'll explore important ways in which our increasing knowledge of important mind-body interactions can be applied to promote health and wellness. We'll begin by considering the exciting new branch of psychology known as *health psychology*. The primary aim of health psychology is to determine important relationships between psychological variables and health (Gatchel, Baum, & Krantz, 1989; Matarazzo, 1980). Second, we'll consider the nature of *stress*, a major health-related problem in the hectic 1990s. We'll focus on both the causes of stress and some of its major effects—how it influences health and performance. In addition, we'll examine recent evidence regarding the short- and long-term effects of *environmental stressors,* such as the floods that devastated large areas of the midwestern United States in 1993. Next, we'll consider how some of our *beliefs and attitudes* influence the way in which we interpret certain health symptoms, and thus affect our willingness to seek necessary medical assistance. Fourth, we'll look at *behaviors* that can directly affect our risk of contracting certain lifestyle-related illnesses, such as cancer, cardiovascular diseases, and AIDS. Finally, we'll consider various ways in which psychologists work to promote personal health by encouraging healthy lifestyles.

INDIVIDUAL DIFFERENCES IN REACTIONS TO STRESS AND ILLNESS

It is often difficult to predict how people will react to bad news, such as learning that a family member or friend has a life-threatening illness. Sometimes the stress caused by these events can even lead to the development of a physical illness.

HEALTH PSYCHOLOGY:
An Overview

*H*ealth psychology, the branch of psychology that studies the relation be-tween psychological variables and health, reflects the view that both mind and body are important determinants of health and illness (Feuerstein, Labbe, & Kuczmierczyk, 1986). Health psychologists believe that our beliefs, attitudes, and behavior contribute significantly to the onset or prevention of illness (Engel, 1980). A closely related field, known as *behavioral medicine,* combines behavioral and biomedical knowledge for the prevention and treatment of disorders usu-ally thought of as being within the domain of medicine (Epstein, 1992).

Health psychology and behavioral medicine have experienced tremendous growth since their beginnings in the early 1970s. Perhaps the most fundamen-tal reason for the increased interest in health psychology and behavioral med-icine is the dramatic shift observed in the leading causes of death throughout the world during this century. In 1900, many of the leading causes of death could be traced to infectious diseases, such as influenza and pneumonia, tuberculosis, nephritis, and diphtheria (see Figure 11.1 on page 408). How-ever, because of advances in medical technology and a greater focus on pre-vention, only five of the ten leading causes of death in 1900 were still among the top ten in 1988.

Interestingly, most of the current leading causes of premature death can be attributed to characteristics that make up **lifestyle**: the overall pattern of deci-sions and behaviors that determines a person's health and quality of life (Lalonde, 1974). This fact suggests that psychologists, now more than ever, can make a difference in people's quality of life by helping them to eliminate behaviors that lead to illness and to adopt behaviors that lead to wellness. Indeed, a majority of the conditions that now constitute the leading causes of death (as illustrated in Figure 11.1) could be prevented if peo-ple would simply eat healthier foods, reduce alcohol con-sumption, practice safe sex, eliminate smoking, and exercise regularly. One encouraging piece of information is that during the 1980s declines occurred in the death rates from lifestyle-related causes, with the exception of deaths from smoking (U.S. Department of Health and Human Services, 1991).

A dramatic example of the impact of behavior on health was observed in a classic decade-long research project con-ducted in Alameda County, California (Wiley & Camacho, 1980). Adult participants were asked whether they followed certain health practices, including sleeping seven to eight hours each night, eating breakfast regularly, refraining from smoking, drinking alcohol in moderation or not at all, maintaining their weight within normal limits, and exercising regularly. Interestingly, participants who reported practicing all or most of these behaviors were much less likely to die during the study period than those who practiced few or none of these behaviors. Although these results are based on correlations and are therefore not conclusive, they do suggest a relationship between our lifestyle and our life span. Indeed, in the United States lifestyles contribute to a significant proportion of premature deaths (those that occur before age sixty-five)—in fact more than half.

Another important finding that has contributed to the rapid development of health psychology and behavioral medicine is the evidence that lifestyle factors that can be described as stressful can have adverse effects on our physical health. Let's turn now to the nature and causes of stress.

KEY QUESTIONS

- What is the aim of health psychologists?
- What is behavioral medicine?
- To what can many of today's leading causes of premature death be attributed?

Health Psychology: The study of the relation between psychological variables and health; reflects the view that both mind and body are important determinants of health and illness.

Lifestyle: In the context of health psychology, the overall pattern of decisions and be-haviors that determine health and quality of life.

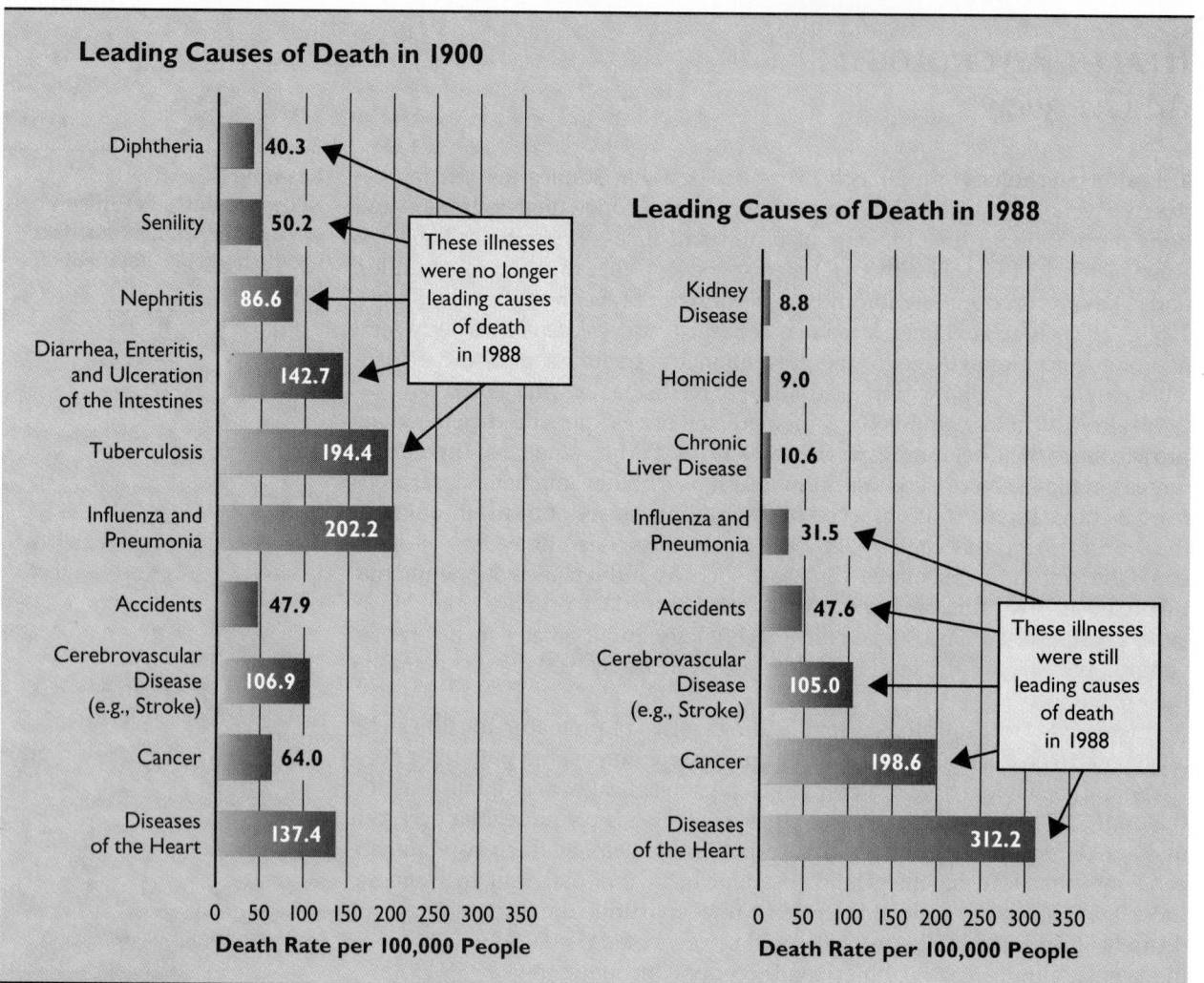

Leading Causes of Death in 1900

Death Rate per 100,000 People

Diphtheria	40.3
Senility	50.2
Nephritis	86.6
Diarrhea, Enteritis, and Ulceration of the Intestines	142.7
Tuberculosis	194.4
Influenza and Pneumonia	202.2
Accidents	47.9
Cerebrovascular Disease (e.g., Stroke)	106.9
Cancer	64.0
Diseases of the Heart	137.4

These illnesses were no longer leading causes of death in 1988

Leading Causes of Death in 1988

Death Rate per 100,000 People

Kidney Disease	8.8
Homicide	9.0
Chronic Liver Disease	10.6
Influenza and Pneumonia	31.5
Accidents	47.6
Cerebrovascular Disease (e.g., Stroke)	105.0
Cancer	198.6
Diseases of the Heart	312.2

These illnesses were still leading causes of death in 1988

FIGURE 11.1

Leading Causes of Death in the United States

The leading causes of death in the United States in 1900 (left) compared with those in 1988 (right).
(*Source:* Based on data from Wiley & Camacho, 1980, and the National Center for Health Statistics, 1988.)

STRESS: Its Causes, Effects, and Control

*A*s described earlier, the news of my grandfather's cancer affected each of my grandparents quite differently. My grandfather remained surprisingly unaffected, while my grandmother couldn't cope with the possible outcomes and in fact became very sick shortly after the diagnosis. Have you ever felt this way—felt that you were right at the edge of being overwhelmed by negative events in your life? Or felt so overwhelmed that you just gave up? If so, you are already quite familiar with **stress**: our response to events that disrupt, or threaten to disrupt, our physical or psychological functioning (Lazarus & Folkman, 1984; Taylor, 1991). Unfortunately, stress is a common part of life in the 1990s—something few of us can avoid altogether. Partly for this reason, and partly because it seems to exert negative effects on both

✓**Stress:** *The process that occurs in response to events that disrupt, or threaten to disrupt, our physical or psychological functioning.*

physical health and psychological well-being, stress has become an important topic of research in psychology. Let's examine the basic nature of stress and some of its major causes.

STRESS: *Its Basic Nature*

Stress is a many-faceted process that occurs in reaction to events or situations in our environment termed **stressors**. An interesting feature of stress is the wide range of physical and psychological reactions that different people have to the same event; some may interpret an event as stressful, whereas others simply take it in stride. Moreover, a particular person may react quite differently to the same stressor at different points in time.

STRESSORS: THE ACTIVATORS OF STRESS

What are stressors? Although we normally think of stress as stemming from negative events in our lives, positive events such as getting married or receiving an unexpected job promotion can also produce stress (Brown & McGill, 1989). Despite the wide range of stimuli that can potentially produce stress, it appears that many events we find stressful share several characteristics: (1) They are so intense, in some respect, that they produce a state of overload—we can no longer adapt to them. (2) They evoke incompatible tendencies in us, such as tendencies both to approach and to avoid some object or activity. (3) They are uncontrollable—beyond our limits of control. Indeed, a great deal of evidence suggests that when people can predict, control, or terminate an aversive event or situation, they perceive it to be less stressful than when they feel less in control (Karasek & Theorell, 1990; Rodin & Salovey, 1989).

PHYSIOLOGICAL RESPONSES TO STRESSORS

When exposed to stressors in our environment, we generally experience many physiological reactions. If you've been caught off-guard by someone who appears out of nowhere and grabs you while screaming "Gotcha," then you are probably familiar with some common physical reactions to stress. Initially, your blood pressure soars, your pulse races, and you may even begin to sweat. These are part of a general pattern of reactions referred to as the *fight-or-flight syndrome,* a process controlled through the sympathetic nervous system. As we saw in chapter 2, the sympathetic nervous system prepares our bodies for immediate action. Usually these responses are brief, and we soon return to normal levels. When we are exposed to chronic sources of stress, however, this reaction is only the first in a longer sequence of responses activated by our efforts to adapt to a stressor. This sequence, termed by Hans Selye (1976) the **general adaptation syndrome (GAS)**, consists of three stages.

As shown in Figure 11.2 (on page 410), the first is the *alarm* stage, in which the body prepares itself for immediate action; arousal of the sympathetic nervous system releases hormones that help prepare our body to meet threats or dangers (Selye, 1976). If stress is prolonged, however, the *resistance* stage begins. During this second stage, arousal is lower than during the alarm stage, but our bodies continue to draw on resources at an above-normal rate in order to cope effectively with the stressor. Continued exposure to the same stressor or additional stressors drains the body of its resources and leads to the third stage, *exhaustion*. During this stage our capacity to resist is depleted, and our susceptibility to illness increases. In severe cases of prolonged physical stress, the result can be death.

COGNITIVE APPRAISAL OF OUR STRESSORS

Selye's general adaptation syndrome provides a framework for understanding our physiological responses to stressful events and suggests at least one reasonable explanation for the

Learning Objective 11.2
Understand the basic nature and causes of stress, including the general adaptation syndrome and the cognitive appraisal process.

Learning Objective 11.3
Describe how stress can affect health and task performance and cause burnout.

Learning Objective 11.4
Identify the individual characteristics that are related to resistance to stress.

Stressors: *Events or situations in our environment that cause stress.*

General Adaptation Syndrome (GAS): *A three-phase model of how organisms respond to stress: (1) alarm or mobilization, (2) resistance, and (3) exhaustion.*

FIGURE 11.2

Selye's General Adaptation Syndrome

According to Hans Selye (shown here), the body's reaction to prolonged stress progresses through three stages: alarm, resistance, and, finally, exhaustion.

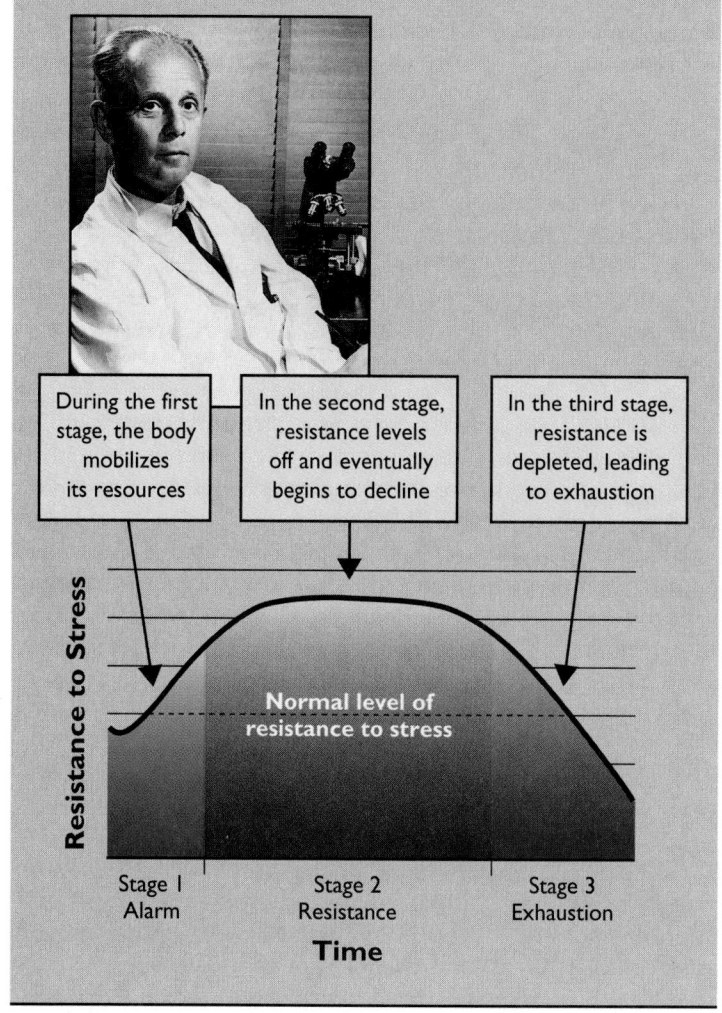

During the first stage, the body mobilizes its resources

In the second stage, resistance levels off and eventually begins to decline

In the third stage, resistance is depleted, leading to exhaustion

Normal level of resistance to stress

Stage 1 Alarm

Stage 2 Resistance

Stage 3 Exhaustion

Resistance to Stress

Time

relation between stress and illness. Indeed, few experts would disagree that chronic stress can lead to a lowered resistance to disease. However, a critical weakness with Selye's model is that it fails to consider the importance of cognitive processes in determining whether we interpret a specific event as stressful. The importance of these processes is made clear by the following fact: When confronted with the same potentially stress-inducing situation, some persons experience stress, whereas others do not. Why? One reason involves individuals' cognitive appraisals (Figure 11.3). In simple terms, stress occurs only to the extent that the persons involved perceive (1) that the situation is somehow threatening to their important goals (often described as *primary appraisal*) and (2) that they will be unable to cope with these dangers or demands (often described as *secondary appraisal*) (Croyle, 1992; Lazarus & Folkman, 1984).

An example will illustrate this point. Let's consider a recent study of the cognitive appraisal process by Tomaka and his colleagues (1993). Participants in this study were initially told that the researchers were interested in measuring their physiological responses (heart rate, pulse) while they performed a mental task: counting backward from the value 2,737 by sevens—that is, 2,730, 2,723, 2,716, and so on. The participants were instructed to perform the activity as quickly and as accurately as possible. Just before they began, the researchers assessed participants' primary and secondary appraisals of the

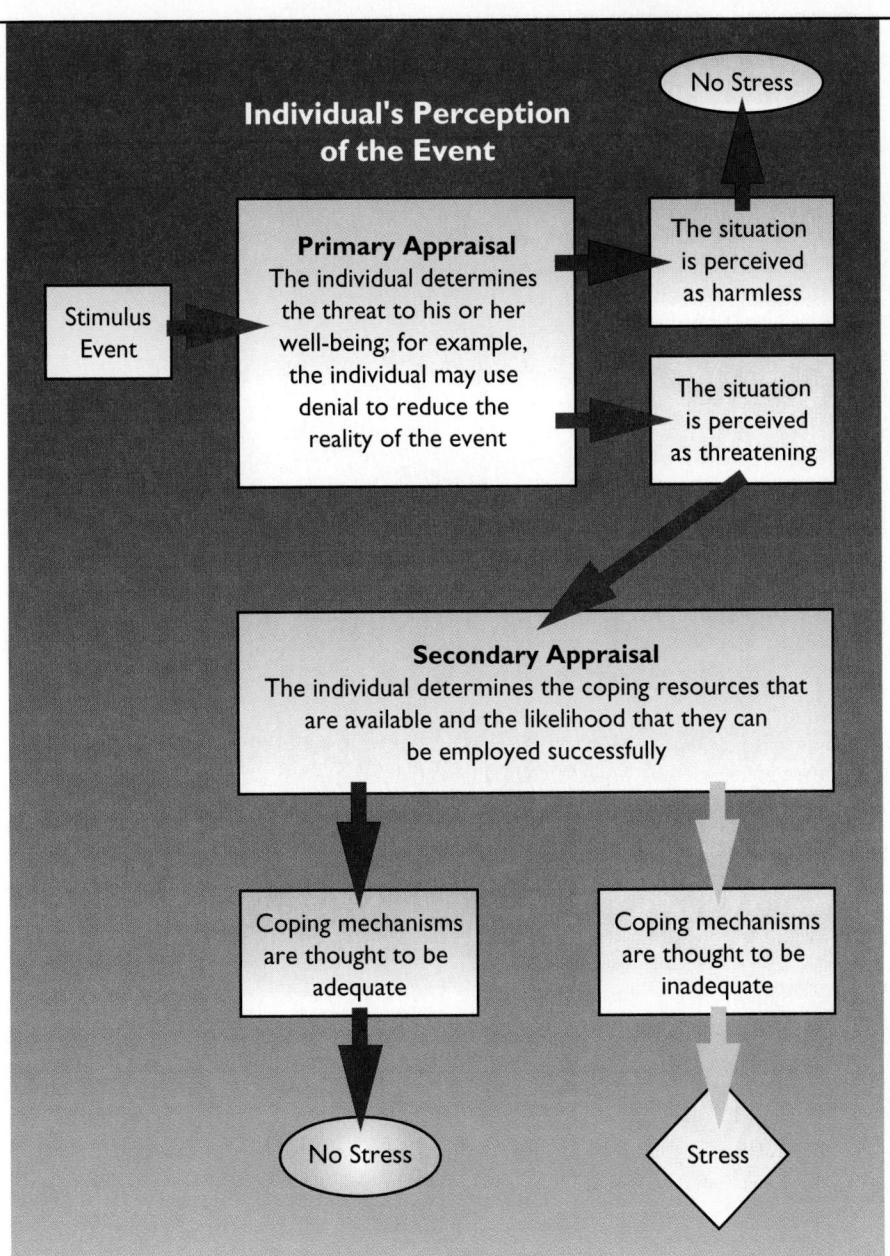

FIGURE 11.3

Stress: The Role of Cognitive Appraisals

The amount of stress you experience depends in part on your cognitive appraisals of the event or situation—the extent to which you perceive it as threatening and perceive that you will be unable to cope with it.
(*Source:* Based on data from Hingson et al., 1990.)

task. They assessed primary appraisals by asking them, "How threatening do you expect the upcoming task to be?" They assessed secondary appraisals by asking, "How able are you to cope with this task?" The researchers predicted that persons who felt they could not successfully perform the task would perceive it as threatening ("threat group") and would therefore experience stress. In contrast, they reasoned, persons who were more confident in their abilities might perceive the task as a challenge ("challenge group"); while these persons would not experience stress, they would in fact exhibit greater physiological arousal as they prepared to meet the challenge. All predictions were confirmed. Participants in the threat group reported *feeling* greater stress, and participants in the challenge group actually showed greater physiological arousal. Moreover, the challenge group scored higher on both perceived and actual measures of performance. The **Key Concept** on page 412 provides an overview of both the physical and cognitive aspects of stress.

The Two Sides of Stress

The Physical Side of Stress

Selye's *GAS model* provides a framework for understanding how stress affects us physically.

Stage 1

During the *alarm stage* the body prepares itself for immediate action (increased heart rate, blood pressure, and energy consumption).

Stage 2

During the *resistance stage* the body draws on resources at an above-normal rate to cope with a prolonged stressor.

Stage 3

During the *exhaustion stage* the body's capacity to cope with stress is depleted and susceptibility to illness increases dramatically.

After finishing a race, long-distance runners may find themselves in the *exhaustion stage* of Selye's GAS model: They have totally drained their body's capacity to cope with stress.

The Cognitive Side of Stress

The *cognitive appraisal model* illustrates how our interpretation of potentially stressful events greatly affects our reactions to them.

Primary appraisal addresses the following question: How threatening is a potentially stressful event?

- If the event is not perceived as threatening, then we experience no stress.
- If the event is perceived as threatening, then we engage in secondary appraisal of the situation.

Secondary appraisal addresses the following question: Given that an event is viewed as a threat, do we have the resources to cope with it effectively?

- If the answer is yes, we do not experience stress.
- If the answer is no, we experience stress.

If we interpret an event, such as news conveyed in a letter, as threatening, it will tend to be more stressful than if we interpret the same event as nonthreatening.

Additional research suggests that other cognitive factors also play a role in our interpretation of potentially stressful events, including the reactions of those around us and the extent of our experience in similar situations (Mendolia & Kleck, 1993; Tomaka et al., 1993). In short, these results and the results of related research provide evidence for the important role of cognitive and social processes in shaping our response to the stressors in our environment. We'll turn next to some of the causes of stress.

KEY QUESTIONS

- What is stress?
- What is the GAS model?
- What determines whether we interpret an event as stressful or as a challenge?

STRESS: *Some Major Causes*

What factors contribute to stress? Unfortunately, the list is a long one. A wide range of conditions and events seem capable of generating such feelings. Among the most important of these are major stressful life events, such as the death of a loved one or a painful divorce; the all-too-frequent minor hassles of everyday life; certain aspects of the physical environment; and conditions and events relating to one's job or career.

STRESSFUL LIFE EVENTS   Death of a spouse, injury to one's child, war, failure in school or at work, an unplanned pregnancy—unless we lead truly charmed lives, most of us experience traumatic events and changes at some time or other. What are their effects on us? This question was first investigated by Holmes and Rahe (1967), who asked a large group of persons to assign arbitrary points (to a maximum of one hundred) to various life events according to how much readjustment each had required. It was reasoned that the greater the number of points assigned to a given event, the more stressful it was for the persons experiencing it.

As you can see from Table 11.1 (on page 414), participants in Holmes and Rahe's study assigned the greatest number of points to such serious events as death of a spouse, divorce, and marital separation. In contrast, they assigned much smaller values to such events as change in residence, vacation, and minor violations of the law, such as a parking ticket.

Holmes and Rahe (1967) then related the total number of points accumulated by individuals during a single year to changes in their personal health. The results were dramatic—and did much to stir psychologists' interest in the effects of stress. The greater the number of "stress points" people accumulated, the greater was their likelihood of becoming seriously ill. For example, Cohen, Tyrrell, and Smith (1993) asked a group of volunteers to report all significant stressful events that had affected them negatively during the previous twelve months. Then the researchers gave these persons nose drops containing a virus known to cause the common cold. A control group received uncontaminated nose drops. The results? Volunteers who reported two or more negative life events during the previous year and felt that they were under a lot of stress were more likely to develop a cold than less-stressed volunteers who had experienced fewer than two negative life events.

This picture is complicated, however, by the existence of large differences in individuals' ability to withstand the impact of stress (Oulette-Kobasa & Puccetti, 1983). While some persons suffer ill effects after exposure to a few mildly stressful events, others remain healthy even after prolonged exposure to high levels of stress; they are described as being *stress-resistant* or *hardy*. I'll return to such differences later in this chapter. For the moment, I wish merely to emphasize the fact that in general, the greater the number of stressful life

TABLE 11.1

Life Events, Stress, and Personal Health

When individuals experience stressful life events, such as those near the top of this list, their health often suffers. The greater the number of points for each event, the more stressful it is perceived as being.

(*Source:* Based on data from Holmes & Masuda, 1974.)

RANK	LIFE EVENT	LIFE CHANGE UNIT VALUE
1	Death of spouse	100
2	Divorce	73
3	Marital separation	65
4	Jail term	63
5	Death of close family member	63
6	Personal injury or illness	53
7	Marriage	50
8	Getting fired at work	47
9	Marital reconciliation	45
10	Retirement	45
11	Change in health of family member	44
12	Pregnancy	40
13	Sex difficulties	39
14	Gain of new family member	39
15	Business readjustment	39
16	Change in financial state	38
17	Death of close friend	37
18	Change to different line of work	36
19	Change in number of arguments with spouse	35
20	Taking out mortgage for major purchase (e.g., home)	31
21	Foreclosure of mortgage or loan	30
22	Change in responsibilities at work	29
23	Son or daughter leaving home	29
24	Trouble with in-laws	29
25	Outstanding personal achievement	28
26	Wife beginning or stopping work	26
27	Beginning or ending school	26
28	Change in living conditions	25
29	Revision of personal habits	24
30	Trouble with boss	23
31	Change in work hours or conditions	20
32	Change in residence	20
33	Change in schools	20
34	Change in recreation	19
35	Change in church activities	19
36	Change in social activities	18
37	Taking out a loan for a lesser purchase (e.g., car or TV)	17
38	Change in sleeping habits	16
39	Change in number of family get-togethers	15
40	Change in eating habits	15
41	Vacation	13
42	Christmas	12
43	Minor violation of the law	11

events experienced by an individual, the greater the likelihood that the person's subsequent health will be adversely affected (Rowlison & Felner, 1988).

THE HASSLES OF DAILY LIFE While certain events, such as the death of someone close to us, are clearly stressful, they occur relatively infrequently. Does this mean that people's lives are mostly a serene lake of tranquility? Hardly. As you know, daily life is filled with countless minor sources of stress that seem to make up for their relatively low intensity by their much higher frequency. That such daily hassles are an important cause of stress is suggested by the findings of several studies by Lazarus and his colleagues (DeLongis, Folkman, & Lazarus, 1988; Kanner et al., 1981; Lazarus et al., 1985). These researchers have developed a Hassles Scale on which individuals indicate the extent to which they have been "hassled" by common events during the past month. The items included in this scale deal with a wide range of everyday events, such as having too many things to do at once, shopping, and concerns over money. While such events may seem relatively minor when compared with the life changes studied by Holmes and Rahe (1967), they appear to be quite important. When scores on the Hassles Scale are related to reports of psychological symptoms, strong positive correlations are obtained (Lazarus et al., 1985). In short, the more stress people report as a result of daily hassles, the poorer their psychological well-being.

And such effects may also apply to physical health as well, as indicated by a study conducted by Williams, Zyzanski, and Wright (1992). These researchers asked Navajo patients at a U.S. Indian Health Service facility about major life events during the preceding six months and about the daily hassles and "uplifts" (pleasant experiences) they'd experienced during the previous week. The measures were designed to include culturally relevant measures of daily irritation or satisfaction. Two years later, the researchers reviewed each participant's medical chart to determine the number of inpatient admissions and outpatient visits that had occurred. Consistent with the researchers' predictions, increased numbers of major life events and daily hassles, or an excess of hassles compared to uplifts, were associated with an increased risk of hospitalization during the two-year period. Additionally, participants' daily hassles scores predicted how frequently they used outpatient services during this time period.

These results, combined with those of previous studies, suggest the following possibility. Major life events can exert adverse effects on health; but for many individuals, the more minor hassles of everyday life—perhaps because of their frequent, repetitive nature—may actually prove even more important in this respect.

ENVIRONMENTAL SOURCES OF STRESS Have you ever experienced a flood—such as the one that devastated the midwestern United States in 1993? Lived through an earthquake—like the one that rocked Los Angeles in 1994? Even if you didn't experience these or other disasters directly, you've probably witnessed on television the scope of destruction resulting from each of these events. If so, you can no doubt appreciate that such natural events or disasters can be highly stressful. Until recently, catastrophic environmental events were not studied systematically, because of their infrequent and unpredictable occurrence (Solomon & Maser, 1990). However, because the survivors of these devastating events often experience the severe psychological aftermath termed **posttraumatic stress disorder** (see chapter 12), psychologists have taken a renewed interest in studying them (Kaniasty & Norris, 1993; Kasl, 1990). Commonly reported psychological problems that follow large-scale disasters include nightmares and flashbacks, distress at exposure to reminders of the event, irritability, difficulty concentrating, and a general unresponsiveness (Lindy, Green, & Grace, 1987).

Whether large-scale natural disasters produce lasting psychological effects, however, remains a source of controversy. Some research shows evidence of long-term psychological effects, whereas other studies show that the psychological impact of natural disasters is minimal. The most common finding is mild, transient distress that subsides soon after the visible effects of the

DAILY HASSLES AS A SOURCE OF STRESS

Many everyday hassles are stressful. Would you experience stress in the situation shown here?

✓*Posttraumatic Stress Disorder: Psychological disorder resulting from a very stressful experience; includes nightmares and flashbacks, distress at exposure to reminders of the event, irritability, difficulty concentrating, and a general unresponsiveness.*

disaster are no longer apparent (Bravo et al., 1990). Recent evidence suggests that the disparities among these findings may be attributable to the indirect effects of natural disasters—most importantly, the extent to which disaster victims experience deterioration in the amount and the availability of social support from their friends, family, and community (Kaniasty & Norris, 1993; Norris & Uhl, 1993). In other words, persons experiencing many forms of stress can usually expect to receive support from one or more of these resources. Unfortunately, large-scale disasters often impact entire communities. As a result, important sources of social support are virtually eliminated, which, in turn, sharply reduces their potential buffering effects.

Human-produced disasters, such as the meltdown of the Chernobyl nuclear reactor in the former Soviet Union, can also exert such effects. And in certain respects, the psychological trauma that results from human-produced disasters can be more dramatic and long-term in its scope (Baum & Fleming, 1993). Why should this be so? Several factors seem to play a role. One important factor appears to be control. Human-produced disasters are usually the result of human error; but we expect that adequate precautions will be taken to prevent human error. Thus, when disaster strikes, our expectations are violated, leading to a sense of loss of control. In contrast, we do not expect to have control over hurricanes, earthquakes, or other types of natural disasters.

A second factor has to do with the consequences associated with each type of disaster. Natural disasters, while large in scope, tend to be clearly marked and limited in time. In contrast, human-produced disasters—such as the contamination of groundwater with toxic chemicals—can potentially exert their effects for many years. For example, exposure to toxic chemicals can increase people's risk of developing cancer or produce genetic damage (Vaughan, 1993). Moreover, the psychological trauma combined with the uncertainty regarding when or if these consequences will appear can produce chronic stress-related problems. Consider what happened when the nuclear reactor at Three-Mile Island in Pennsylvania released small amounts of radioactivity into the environment in March 1979. People living nearby reported much higher levels of stress than those living far away. More importantly, however, these effects were still evident six years later (Gatchel, Schaeffer, & Baum, 1985). Similar outcomes have been observed for accidents involving toxic chemicals (Baum & Fleming, 1993).

WORK-RELATED STRESS   Most adults spend more time at work than in any other single activity. It is not surprising, then, that jobs or careers are a central source of stress. Some of the factors producing stress in work settings are obvious; for example, blatant sexual harassment or discrimination, or extreme *overload*—being asked to do too much in too short a time. Interestingly, being asked to do too little can also cause stress. Such *underload* produces intense feelings of boredom, and these, in turn, can be very stressful.

Several other factors that play a role in work-related stress may be less apparent. One of these is *role conflict*—being the target of conflicting demands or expectations from different groups of people. For example, consider the plight of many first-line managers. Their subordinates often expect these managers to go to bat for them with the company to improve their work assignments, pay, and conditions. In contrast, the managers' own bosses often expect them to do the opposite: somehow to induce the employees to work harder for fewer rewards. The result: a stressful situation for the managers.

Another work-related factor that can sometimes generate intense levels of stress involves *performance appraisals*, the procedures used for evaluating employees' performance. If employees perceive these procedures as fair, employee stress tends to be low; if employees view them as arbitrary or unfair, it is almost certain to be high. After all, no one wants to feel that rewards such as raises, promotions, or bonuses are being distributed in an unjust manner.

At this point, it should be clear that workplace stressors can exert powerful—and often negative—effects on those who experience them. Fortunately, recent research on this topic suggests that the damaging effects of workplace stress can be reduced when employees take an active role in developing effective coping strategies and when adequate sources of social support are available to them (Chay, 1993; Koeske et al., 1993). You are certain to encounter several sources of stress in your own job and career. For additional information on what can be done to combat the effects of stress in the workplace, see the **Point of It All** section.

KEY QUESTIONS

- What are stressors?
- What is posttraumatic stress disorder?
- What are some sources of work-related stress?

THE POINT OF IT ALL

Putting Psychology to Work: Reducing Stress in the Workplace

As I've already pointed out, many aspects of the workplace can be potential sources of stress. Moreover, a stressful working environment can lead to the development of psychological and physical problems or contribute to a worsening of existing health problems. Can anything be done to reduce such effects? Fortunately, the results of several lines of research suggest the answer is yes.

First, employers can help reduce stress in the workplace by considering the **person-environment (P-E) fit** (Edwards & Harrison, 1993). Growing evidence suggests that "misfits" between characteristics of workers and characteristics of their jobs or work environments are associated with a host of negative outcomes, including psychological disturbances, job dissatisfaction, and increases in stress and stress-related illnesses (Harrison, 1985). For example, consider the potential negative outcomes that might result from placing persons with a low tolerance for anxiety into high-pressure work environments or assigning persons who require variety and challenge to jobs consisting of simple repetitive tasks. Employers can often reduce stress in the workplace by incorporating the idea of P-E fit into their selection procedures. In other words, employers can minimize the potential for P-E "misfits"—and thereby reduce the potential for creating stressful situations—by hiring workers with characteristics that closely match the demands of the job for which they are being considered (Landsbergis et al., 1992).

Second, research suggests that the amount and availability of social support, both on and off the job, is also a crucial determinant of workplace stress (Cohen & Wills, 1985). Apparently, the presence of social support helps reduce the outcomes of stress by serving as a buffer against stressful events that occur at work (Landsbergis et al., 1992). Why is this important? Because it is not possible to eliminate all potential sources of stress in the workplace; nor is it possible to arrange a perfect P-E fit for every worker. Thus, the availability of strong sources of social support may help reduce the consequences of unavoidable workplace stressors.

Third, companies can implement interventions to improve employees' ability to cope with workplace stress and to change unhealthy practices that can intensify the effects of stress (Maturi, 1992). A rapidly growing literature suggests that the most effective interventions are those that are (1) designed

Person-Environment (P-E) Fit: *The approach that suggests that a misfit between a person and his or her work environment may produce stress.*

FIGURE **11.4**

Reducing Workplace Health Risks: The Beneficial Effects of Wellness Programs

The greatest reductions in health risk measures were observed among participants having three or more follow-up contacts with their wellness counselors. In contrast, participants who had no contact with their counselors actually worsened on some measures of health risk.

(*Source:* Based on data from Gregg et al., 1990.)

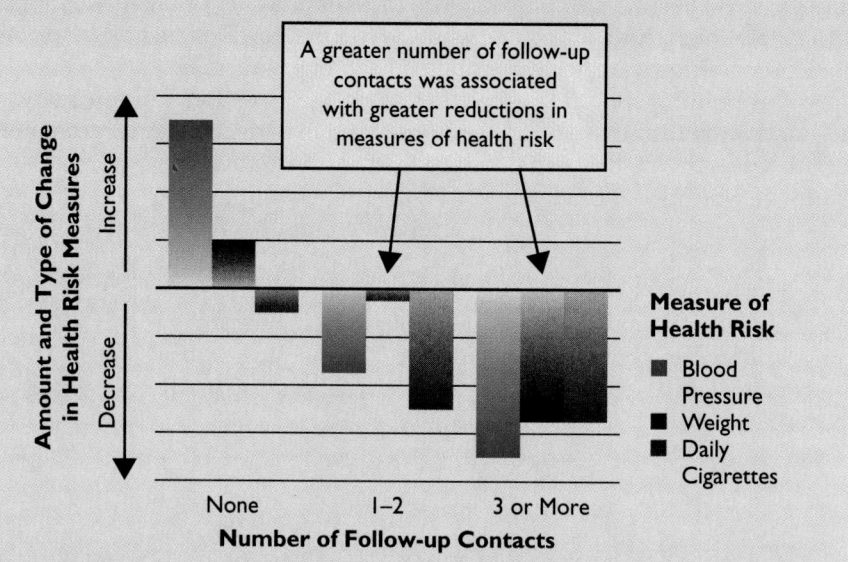

to meet the specific needs of individuals and (2) comprehensive and long-term in their focus.

For example, consider the results of one intriguing study conducted by Gregg and his colleagues (1990). These researchers began by interviewing more than 7,800 employees working in four manufacturing plants. Their survey revealed the presence of a substantial number of health risks among these workers: 19 percent had high blood pressure, 34 percent were overweight, and 44 percent were identified as smokers. Next, in two of the plants, wellness counselors contacted employees identified as having one or more health risks and designed individualized wellness programs specific to their needs. Then, over a three-year period, the counselors attempted to meet with each of the workers periodically to assess their progress, made changes to their programs if needed, and served as a support system to try to keep them motivated to stay with the program. At the end of the three-year study period, the researchers reassessed some of the at-risk workers identified at the beginning of the study to evaluate their progress in reducing their health risks.

As shown in Figure 11.4, results indicated that the program's effectiveness closely mirrored the amount of contact between the workers and the wellness counselors. Workers who had three or more follow-up contacts with a counselor showed the greatest reduction in their level of health risks. In contrast, workers who had no follow-up contacts actually increased their health risk on two of the measures, blood pressure and weight gain—reflecting the need for significant social support and follow-up in wellness programs.

The point of it all is that the results of systematic psychological research can have important applications, in this case to the reduction of the potentially devastating effects of stress in the workplace. As psychologists continue to refine their arsenal of techniques in this area, they will no doubt discover additional ways to help workers cope more effectively with the stressors they encounter at work.

STRESS: *Some Major Effects*

By now you may be convinced that stress stems from many different sources and exerts important effects on persons who experience it. What is sometimes difficult to grasp, though, is just how far-reaching these effects can be. Stress can influence our physical and psychological well-being, our performance on many tasks, and even the ultimate course of our careers.

STRESS AND HEALTH: THE SILENT KILLER The link between stress and personal health, according to medical experts, is very strong indeed (Kiecolt-Glaser & Glaser, 1992). In fact, some authorities estimate that stress plays some role in 50 to 70 percent of all physical illness (Frese, 1985). Moreover, included in these percentages are some of the most serious and life-threatening ailments known to medical science. To list just a few, stress has been implicated in the occurrence of heart disease, high blood pressure, hardening of the arteries, ulcers, and even diabetes.

How does stress produce such effects? The mechanisms involved remain to be determined precisely, but growing evidence suggests that the process goes something like this: By draining our resources and keeping us off balance physiologically, stress upsets our complex internal chemistry. In particular, it may interfere with efficient operation of our immune system—the elaborate internal mechanism through which our bodies recognize and destroy potentially harmful substances and intruders, such as bacteria, viruses, and cancerous cells. Foreign substances that enter our bodies are known as *antigens*. When they appear, certain types of white blood cells (called lymphocytes) begin to multiply. These attack the antigens, often destroying them by engulfing them. Other white blood cells produce antibodies, chemical substances that combine with antigens and so neutralize them. When functioning normally, the immune system is nothing short of amazing: Each day it removes or destroys many potential threats to our health and well-being.

Unfortunately, prolonged exposure to stress seems to disrupt this system. For example, in studies with animals, subjects exposed to inescapable shocks demonstrated reduced production of lymphocytes relative to subjects exposed to shocks from which they could escape (Ader & Cohen, 1984). Studies of the effects of stress on animals and humans suggest that a variety of stressors, including disruptions in interpersonal relationships, loneliness, academic pressure, daily hassles, and the lack of social support, can interfere with our immune systems (Cohen et al., 1992; Jemmott & Magloire, 1988; Levy et al., 1989).

For example, persons who are divorced or separated from their spouses often experience reduced functioning in certain aspects of their immune system, compared to individuals who are happily married (Kiecolt-Glaser et al., 1987, 1988). Additionally, some recent evidence suggests that the effects of stress on our immune system may be less for people who have effective ways of dealing with their stressors than for those who do not. For example, some studies have shown that optimism, regular exercise, and feelings of control over stressful events are associated with reduced suppression of our immune system under stress (Taylor, 1991). Such findings are both unsettling and encouraging. On the one hand, they suggest that our complex, high-stress lifestyles may be undermining our ability to resist many serious forms of illness, at least to a degree. On the other hand, they indicate that reductions in such stress may be of major benefit to our overall health.

STRESS AND TASK PERFORMANCE Psychologists once believed that stress actually improves performance on a wide range of tasks. They thought that the relationship between stress and task performance takes the form of an upside-down U: At first, performance improves as stress increases, presumably because the stress is arousing or energizing. Beyond some point, though, stress becomes distracting, and performance actually drops.

While this relationship may hold true under some conditions, growing evidence suggests that even low or moderate levels of stress can interfere with task performance (Motowidlo, Packard, & Manning, 1986; Steers, 1984). There are several reasons why this is so. First, even relatively mild stress can be distracting. People experiencing stress may focus on the unpleasant feelings and emotions it involves, rather than on the task at hand. Second, prolonged or repeated exposure to even mild levels of stress may exert harmful effects on health, and this may interfere with effective performance. Finally, a large body of research indicates that as arousal increases, task performance may rise at first, but at some point it falls (Berlyne, 1967). The precise location of this turning, or *inflection*, point seems to depend to an important extent on the complexity of the task performed. The greater the complexity, the lower the level of arousal at which the downturn in performance occurs. Are the tasks performed by today's working people more complex than those in the past? Many observers believe they are (Mitchell & Larson, 1987). For this reason, even relatively low levels of stress may interfere with performance in today's complex work world.

Together, these factors help explain why stress, even at fairly moderate levels, may interfere with many types of performance. However, stress does not always produce adverse effects. For example, people sometimes do seem to rise to the occasion and turn in sterling performances at times when stress is intense. Perhaps the most reasonable conclusion, then, is that while stress can indeed interfere with task performance in many situations, its precise effects depend on many different factors, such as the complexity of the task being performed and personal characteristics of the individuals involved. As a result, generalizations about the impact of stress on work effectiveness should be made with considerable caution.

BURNOUT: WHEN STRESS CONSUMES Most jobs involve at least a degree of stress. Yet somehow the persons performing them manage to cope: They continue to function despite their daily encounters with various stressors. Some individuals, though, are not so lucky. Over time, they seem to be worn down (or out) by repeated encounters with stress. Such persons are said to be suffering from *burnout*, and they show several distinctive characteristics (Maslach, 1982; Pines & Aronson, 1988).

First, victims of burnout often suffer from *physical exhaustion*. They have low energy and always feel tired. In addition, they report many symptoms of physical strain, such as frequent headaches, nausea, poor sleep, and changes in eating habits. Burnout may also be associated with risk factors for cardiovascular disease (Melamed, Kushnir, & Shirom, 1992). Second, they experience *emotional exhaustion*. Depression, feelings of hopelessness, and feelings of being trapped in one's job are all part of the picture. Third, persons suffering from burnout often show *mental or attitudinal exhaustion*, often known as depersonalization. They become cynical, hold negative attitudes toward others, and tend to derogate themselves, their jobs, and life in general. To put it simply, they come to view the world around them through dark gray rather than rose-colored glasses. Finally, they often report feelings of *low personal accomplishment* (Maslach & Jackson, 1984)—feelings that they haven't been able to accomplish much in the past and probably won't be successful in the future, either. Studies conducted in work settings (Lee & Ashforth, 1990) seem to confirm that these factors actually provide an accurate description of burnout. (Please see Figure 11.5 for a summary.)

What are the causes of burnout? The primary factor, of course, is prolonged exposure to stress, but other factors, too, seem to play a role. Job conditions implying that one's efforts are useless, ineffective, or unappreciated seem to contribute to burnout (Jackson, Schwab, & Schuler, 1986). In particular, such conditions contribute to the feelings of low personal accomplishment that are an important part of burnout.

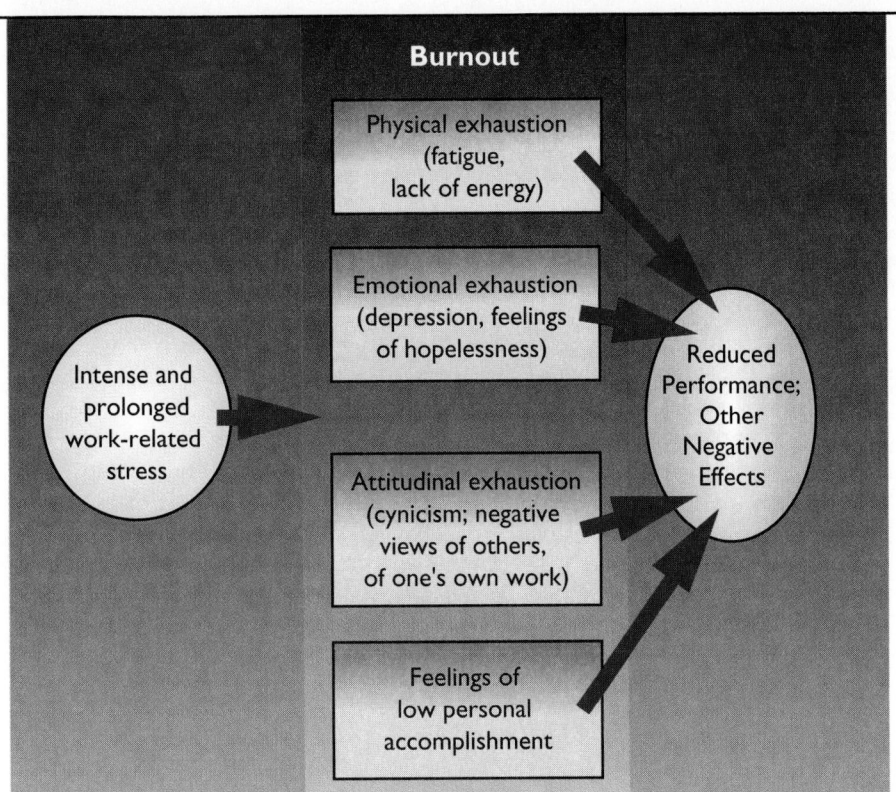

Burnout

Physical exhaustion
(fatigue,
lack of energy)

Emotional exhaustion
(depression, feelings
of hopelessness)

Intense and
prolonged
work-related
stress

Attitudinal exhaustion
(cynicism; negative
views of others,
of one's own work)

Feelings of
low personal
accomplishment

Reduced
Performance;
Other
Negative
Effects

FIGURE **11.5**

Burnout: An Overview

Individuals exposed to high levels of work-related stress over long periods of time may suffer from *burnout*. This state involves *physical*, *emotional*, and *mental*, or *attitudinal*, exhaustion, as well as feelings of *low personal accomplishment.*

Similarly, poor opportunities for promotion and the presence of inflexible rules and procedures lead individuals to feel that they are trapped in an unfair system and to develop negative views of their jobs (Gaines & Jermier 1983). Personal factors also play a role. People with satisfying lives outside work settings, such as stable love relationships, are less likely to experience burnout than ones without these social buffers.

Whatever its precise causes, once burnout develops, its victims seem either to change jobs or to withdraw psychologically, marking time until retirement. Fortunately, however, growing evidence suggests that the effects of burnout can be overcome. With appropriate help, victims of burnout can recover from their physical and psychological exhaustion. If ongoing stress is reduced, if individuals gain added support from friends and coworkers, and if they cultivate hobbies and other outside interests, at least some persons can return to positive attitudes and high levels of productivity.

INDIVIDUAL DIFFERENCES IN RESISTANCE TO STRESS: OPTIMISM, PESSIMISM, AND HARDINESS

It is clear that individuals differ in their resistance to stress. While some people suffer ill effects from even mild levels of stress, others are able to function effectively even in the face of intense, ongoing stress. How do such persons differ?

One difference involves the familiar dimension of *optimism–pessimism*. Optimists are people who see the glass as half full; pessimists are those who see it as half empty. Some evidence indicates that optimists—people who have general expectancies for good outcomes (Scheier & Carver, 1988)—seem to be much more stress-resistant than pessimists—people who have general expectancies for poor outcomes. For example, optimists are much less likely than pessimists to report physical illnesses and symptoms during highly stressful periods such as final exams. Additional evidence helps explain why

TABLE **11.2**	STRATEGIES PREFERRED BY OPTIMISTS	DESCRIPTION
Optimists and Pessimists: Contrasting Strategies for Coping with Stress	Problem-focused coping	Making specific plans for dealing with the source of stress; implementing such plans
Optimists and pessimists employ different strategies in coping with stress. The strategies used by optimists seem to be more effective than those adopted by pessimists.	Suppressing competing activities	Refraining from other activities until the problem is solved and stress is reduced
	Seeking social support	Obtaining the advice of others; talking the problem over with others

	STRATEGIES PREFERRED BY PESSIMISTS	DESCRIPTION
	Denial/distancing	Ignoring the problem or source of stress; refusing to believe that it exists or is important
	Disengagement from the goal	Giving up on reaching the goal that is being blocked by stress
	Focusing on the expression of feelings	Letting off steam instead of working on the problem directly

this is the case. Briefly, optimists and pessimists seem to adopt different tactics for coping with stress (Scheier & Carver, 1992). Optimists focus on problem-focused coping: making and enacting specific plans for dealing with sources of stress. They also seek to obtain social support—the advice and help of others (Carver et al., 1993). In contrast, pessimists tend to adopt different strategies, such as giving up the goal with which stress is interfering or denying that the stress exists (Scheier, Weintraub, & Carver, 1986). Needless to say, the former strategies are often more effective than the latter. Table 11.2 presents a summary of the different strategies adopted by optimists and pessimists.

Interestingly, recent research indicates that males tend to use the strategies adopted by optimists to a greater extent than females do. When confronted with an upcoming, stressful event (for example, giving a lecture in front of a class), males engage in more problem-focusing coping; females

tend to seek social support from friends or to engage in emotion-focused strategies such as wishful thinking (Ptacek, Smith, & Dodge, 1994). While these findings do *not* imply that men are necessarily more optimistic than women with respect to dealing with stressful situations, they do indicate that important gender differences seem to exist in terms of preferences for coping strategies.

Another characteristic that seems to distinguish stress-resistant people from those who are more susceptible to its harmful effects is **hardiness** (Kobasa, 1979). Actually, this term refers to a cluster of characteristics, rather than just

Hardiness: A personality style characterized by high levels of commitment, a view of change as an opportunity for growth, and a strong sense of being in control.

one. Hardy persons, those who are relatively stress-resistant, seem to differ from others in three respects. First, hardy individuals show higher levels of *commitment*—deeper involvement in whatever they do and stronger tendencies to perceive such activities as worth doing. Second, hardy persons tend to view change as a *challenge*—an opportunity for growth and development—rather than as a threat or a burden. Third, hardy persons have a stronger sense of *control* over events in their lives and over the outcomes they experience. Research findings indicate that persons high in hardiness report better health than those low in hardiness, even when they encounter major stressful life changes (Oulette-Kobasa & Puccetti, 1983).

These and other findings indicate that individuals differ greatly in terms of their ability to deal with stress. Understanding the reasons for such differences can be of considerable practical value. We'll return to various techniques for coping with stress in **Making Psychology Part of Your Life** at the end of this chapter.

UNDERSTANDING AND COMMUNICATING OUR HEALTH NEEDS

*T*here is no doubt that modern medicine has provided us with the means to alleviate many types of disease and illness considered incurable until this century. Yet all the available medicine and technology still does not ensure that we will seek proper treatment when necessary, or that we possess the knowledge or skills necessary to realize when help is required. Moreover, because of the beliefs and attitudes we hold, it's often difficult for health professionals to get us to comply with good health-promoting advice.

Consider, for example, the results of an Australian study in which people were asked to identify the lifestyle or behavior patterns responsible for health problems in their country (Hetzel & McMichael, 1987). The most frequently cited examples were alcohol and drug abuse, poor diet, lack of exercise, and smoking—a clear indication that respondents were aware of the health risks associated with these behaviors. Similarly, when asked to name the changes that would most likely improve their own future health, the respondents cited better diet, more exercise, stopping or reducing smoking, reducing alcohol consumption, and coping better with their worries—again proof that they knew what they were supposed to do to improve their health. Yet when they were asked why they had not made changes in the behaviors they considered most essential to improving their own health, their answers—including "laziness," "lack of time," "not worthwhile," "too difficult or expensive," or "lack of social support"—suggested that sufficient motivation to change was simply not there. This suggests an important role for health psychologists: not only to help people achieve a better understanding of their health needs and inform them about the risks of specific unhealthy behaviors, but also to identify techniques to reduce or eliminate unhealthy behaviors and to promote the adoption of healthier lifestyles.

SYMPTOM PERCEPTION: *How Do We Know When We're Ill?*

As we discovered in chapter 3, we all experience bodily sensations, such as the steady beating of our heart or the rush of air flowing in and out of our lungs as we breathe. But certain sensations—like irregularities in heartbeat, tiny aches and pains, a slight queasiness, or a backache—are often termed *symptoms*, because they may reflect an underlying medical problem. But what factors determine how people experience symptoms?

Important factors, research seems to indicate, are individual differences in attention to our bodies and certain situational factors that influence our

Learning Objective 11.5
Describe the factors that influence reporting and interpretation of symptoms, including the health belief model of seeking medical advice.

Learning Objective 11.6
Discuss the nature of the communication process between doctors and patients.

attention (Taylor, 1991). Those who focus their attention on themselves tend to notice symptoms more quickly than those who focus on the external environment. People who live with others, have interesting jobs, and lead exciting lives may be less likely to notice symptoms than are less active people who have boring jobs and/or who live alone (Pennebaker, 1983). In other words, we are most likely to notice symptoms when there are few distractions. Situational factors, such as our moods, can also determine the direction of our attention and thus affect whether we notice symptoms. People who are in a good mood report fewer symptoms and rate themselves as more healthy than people who are in a bad mood (Salovey & Birnbaum, 1989). Some symptoms, however, are difficult or almost impossible to notice on one's own. For example, the early detection of my grandfather's cancer led to successful treatment and a full recovery. The early diagnosis was possible not because my grandfather experienced any obvious symptoms, but rather because of his insistence on regular annual medical examinations.

Psychological factors also determine how we interpret symptoms. We often interpret the meaning of our current symptoms by comparing them with those we have experienced in the past. We recognize a runny nose, watery eyes, and tiredness as symptoms of the onset of a cold. In these instances our experience, or the experience of others, tells us that the underlying illness is probably not fatal and that the treatment of choice may include lots of rest, plenty of water, and staying dry and warm. Finally, our expectations can influence our interpretation of symptoms by causing us to focus on symptoms we are expecting and ignore those we are not expecting. After you visit a sick friend, a barely noticeable tickle in your throat may lead you to believe you are catching her cold. Because you expect to get sick, you interpret the tickle as a sign of illness.

HEALTH BELIEFS: *When Do We Seek Medical Advice?*

How do we decide that a symptom is severe enough to require medical attention? A number of factors may help determine the conditions under which we actually go to a doctor, clinic, or emergency room. Surprisingly, some evidence suggests that people may not seek help even when they know that something is seriously wrong (Locke & Slaby, 1982). Why is this so?

The **health belief model**, initially developed to help explain why people don't use medical screening services, may help us to understand the reasons. As shown in Figure 11.6, this model suggests that our willingness to seek medical help depends on: (1) the extent to which we perceive a threat to our health; and (2) the extent to which we believe that a particular behavior will effectively reduce that threat (Rosenstock, 1974). The perception of a personal threat is influenced by our health values, our specific beliefs about our susceptibility to a health problem, and our beliefs concerning the seriousness of the problem. For example, we may decide to stop smoking if we value our health, if we feel that our smoking might lead to fatal lung cancer, and if we don't like what we hear about death from lung cancer.

Our perceptions that our behavior will be effective in reducing a health threat—in this case the risk of lung cancer—depend on whether we believe that a particular practice will reduce the chances we will contract a particular illness and whether the perceived benefits of the practice are worth the effort. For example, whether a smoker concerned about developing cancer will actually quit depends on two beliefs: that giving up smoking will reduce the risk of cancer and that the benefits of doing so will outweigh the immediate pleasures of smoking.

Health Belief Model: A model predicting that whether a person practices a particular health behavior depends on the degree to which the person believes in a personal health threat and believes that practicing the behavior will reduce that threat.

424   CHAPTER 11

FIGURE **11.6**

Belief in the health threat posed by smoking depends on our:
• Health values
• Specific beliefs about susceptibility to cancer
• Beliefs about the potential severity of cancer

Belief that our behavior can reduce the health threat of cancer depends on our:
• Belief that a specific behavior (quitting smoking) will be effective in reducing the threat of cancer
• Belief that the benefits of quitting will outweigh the pleasures of smoking

Smoking Behavior Stops

The Health Belief Model

The health belief model suggests that whether a person practices a particular health behavior depends on the degree to which she or he believes in a personal health threat—and believes that practicing the behavior will reduce that threat. Each of these beliefs is influenced by additional variables. Here, the health belief model is applied to smoking.

The health belief model helps explain why certain people, especially young persons and adults who have never experienced a serious illness or injury, often fail to engage in actions that would be effective in preventing illness or injury—such as using a safety belt when driving a car or wearing a condom during sexual intercourse (Taylor & Brown, 1988). They don't engage in such preventive, health-protecting actions because, in their minds, the likelihood of experiencing illness or injury is very low—so why bother? (See the discussion of adolescent invulnerability in chapter 8 for more information on this topic.)

The health belief model also suggests that if people believe that their actions will be ineffective in changing their health status, they will be less likely to seek help or engage in healthy behaviors. For example, suppose you are overweight and have a family history of high blood pressure. Because you do not believe that anything can be done to lessen your genetic predisposition for heart attacks, you may refuse to adhere to a recommended diet and exercise program, even when you begin to experience symptoms.

DOCTOR-PATIENT INTERACTIONS:
Why Can't We Talk to Our Doctors?

Imagine the following situation: You are waiting in a crowded doctor's office. It's already forty-five minutes beyond your scheduled appointment time, and you are growing more impatient by the minute. Then, just before you reach the end of your rope, the nurse calls your name. Relieved finally to get away from the congestion of the waiting room, you swallow the choice words you've been saving for the doctor. But then, adding insult to injury, she sticks her head in the door of the examining room, says, "Please be seated, I'll be right back," and leaves! Fully twenty minutes pass before she returns. She offers no apology for the delay. After a rapid succession of questions, pokes, and prods, the doctor scribbles a prescription onto a piece of paper and says, "Take two of these four times a day, and call my office in a week if you have further problems." Then she promptly leaves once more.

If aspects of the preceding scene sound familiar, then you may have experienced the frustration that stems from ineffective doctor-patient interactions. Indeed, research has repeatedly documented the existence of communication problems between physicians and their patients (Roter & Ewart, 1992;

DOCTOR-PATIENT INTERACTIONS: COMMUNICATION IS THE KEY

Both physicians and their patients play an important role in the communication process.
(*Source:* CLOSE TO HOME © Copyright 1993 John McPherson. Reprinted with permission of UNIVERSAL PRESS SYNDICATE. All rights reserved.)

"Exhale."

Waitzkin, 1984). Although health care experts have long recognized the need for improving this process, it is only since the 1970s that researchers have systematically examined the doctor-patient communication process (Roter & Hall, 1989).

Duffy, Hamerman, and Cohen (1980) attempted to quantify aspects of the communication that takes place between patients and their doctor. These researchers selected ten communication skills they considered crucial to the communication process and then observed how often doctors exhibited these skills during actual medical examinations. The most frequently observed communication skills were those dealing with the mechanics of patients' illnesses, such as direct physical examination of illness-relevant areas and explanation of the nature of prescribed medication and therapy. In contrast, the skills observed least frequently were those related to the psychosocial aspects of patients' problems, such as asking patients what they knew or how they felt about their illnesses.

Although not conclusive, results like these have suggested that it may be important for physicians to receive as part of their medical education communication skills training—training in both people skills and technical skills. Indeed, growing evidence suggests that rapport and the quality of information communicated are critical factors in successful treatment of the disease and the person (Roter & Ewart, 1992).

Also, because communication is a two-way process, researchers now believe that both patients and doctors have important responsibilities during medical examinations. In one study, Hall, Roter, and Katz (1987) examined the relation of communication to patient outcomes such as satisfaction, recall of important medical information, and compliance. They quantified the communication process by categorizing behaviors observed during doctor-patient interactions into six categories: information giving, question asking, social talk, positive talk, negative talk, and partnership building. They subdivided these categories, for both physician and patient, into either task-focused or socioemotional dimensions of behavior (Roter, Hall, & Katz, 1988). The results of their investigation showed that both physicians and their patients have important roles in task-focused *and* socioemotional communication. All of the patient outcomes considered—satisfaction, recall of important medical information, and compliance—were strongly related to the amount of information given by the doctor during the medical encounter, particularly when the interaction included positive social conversation.

Together, these studies underscore the importance of training in communication skills for health care professionals. In order to be effective in treating patients and promoting their wellness, doctors, nurses, and other health professionals need to know how to get their message across—how to communicate effectively with the persons who come to them for

KEY QUESTIONS

- Why are symptoms and sensations important?

- According to the health belief model, what factors determine our willingness to make lifestyle changes or seek medical help?

- Why is it important for psychologists to study aspects of doctor-patient interactions?

help. The important benefits include increased patient satisfaction and improved quality of diagnostic information (Macguire, Fairburn, & Fletcher, 1986).

BEHAVIORAL AND PSYCHOLOGICAL CORRELATES OF ILLNESS: The Effects of Thoughts and Actions on Health

Consider this surprising chain of events. During the 1950s a terminally ill cancer patient learned of an experimental anticancer drug. Though the odds were slim, this patient requested treatment with the drug, hoping it would result in a cure. Amazingly, following treatment with the drug, the patient's cancer went into remission and he was able to leave the hospital, even returning to work. Then a curious and unfortunate thing happened: Evidence appeared indicating the anticancer drug he had taken was ineffective as a cancer treatment. When the patient learned about the ineffectiveness of his "wonder drug," his cancer returned. Understandably concerned, his doctor deceived him with the promise of an effective treatment—an improved and purer drug. Actually, the new drug was a placebo; the doctor reasoned that if it was the patient's will and not the drug that had produced the first remission, then there was every reason to believe that this strategy would succeed again. As predicted, the patient made a second recovery, and the cancer was again in remission. Unfortunately, a few months later another government report stated that the new anticancer drug he had supposedly taken was of no value for the treatment of cancer. Within a few days, the man died (Levy, 1990).

Although one should be skeptical about reports of miraculous remissions or even cures of cancer or other serious illness like the one I've just described, a possible basis for such events is becoming clear. **Cancer**, any illness in which proliferating abnormal cells overwhelm normal tissue, is often viewed as a physical illness with a definite genetic component; but mounting evidence suggests that psychological variables interact in important ways with physical conditions to determine cancer's progression. In other words, aspects of our behavior, perceptions, and personality contribute to this disease process.

One common characteristic among individuals from families with high cancer rates is a diminished efficiency of their natural killer cells—those designed specifically for the surveillance and destruction of cancerous tumor cells (Kiecolt-Glaser & Glaser, 1992). In most cases, however, whether we develop a cancer or other illness is moderated by **risk factors**—aspects of our lifestyle that affect our chances of developing or contracting a particular disease, within the limits established by our genes (American Cancer Society, 1989).

A deadly class of risk factors are the behaviors within our lifestyle that increase our exposure to **carcinogens**—cancer-producing agents in our environment. Tobacco and the smoke it produces, chemicals in the food that we eat, air that we breathe, alcohol in the beverages we drink, and the radiation we receive from overexposure to the sun have all been implicated to some extent as carcinogens. It was because of concerns about exposure to such substances that in 1994, many people in the United States protested about plans

Learning Objective 11.7
Know the biological nature of cancer and the role of physical and psychological variables in its progression.

Learning Objective 11.8
Describe the reasons for smoking and the effects of smoking, including those associated with passive smoking.

Learning Objective 11.9
Describe the relationships of diet and nutrition to health and disease.

Learning Objective 11.10
Know the effects of excessive alcohol consumption.

Cancer: A group of illnesses in which abnormal cells are formed that are able to proliferate, invade, and overwhelm normal tissues and to spread to distant sites in the body.

Risk Factors: Aspects of our environment or behavior that influence our chances of developing or contracting a disease, within the limits set by our genetic structure.

Carcinogens: Cancer-producing agents.

Learning Objective 11.11
Outline the influence of emotions and personality type on health.

Learning Objective 11.12
Understand the nature and causes of AIDS.

to sell milk from cows fed large amounts of growth hormones: The protesters didn't want such substances in their milk.

Because many risk factors involve people's behaviors, psychologists can play a crucial role in cancer prevention by developing techniques to reduce unsafe behaviors like smoking and to promote healthy behaviors like exercise and a proper diet. We'll now consider several behavioral risk factors that may contribute to the development of certain illnesses.

SMOKING: *Risky for You and Everyone around You*

Smoking is the largest preventable cause of illness and premature death (before age sixty-five) in the United States, accounting for about 125,000 deaths annually (American Cancer Society, 1989). It is the leading cause of several types of cancer, including cancers of the larynx, bladder, cervix and lung; indeed, a large body of evidence suggests that cigarette smoking is the principal cause of lung cancer (Lubin & Blot, 1993). Smoking also causes **cardiovascular disease** (disease of the heart and blood vessels).

Despite the risks associated with smoking, 25 percent of adults in the United States continue to smoke (Blume, 1993). Fortunately, recent evidence from the 1992 U.S. Census Bureau's Current Population Survey suggests that, in general, increasing numbers of people in the United States are learning to "break" their smoking habit. For example, the percentage of people who smoke decreased, especially among men, from about 50 percent in 1965 to about 30 percent in 1989. Similarly, cigarette smoking among high school students dropped from 71 percent in 1980 to 61.8 percent in 1992. Yet the overall number of smokers has remained constant, largely because of increases in the U.S. population over this period. One cause for alarm is the observed increase in smoking among some subgroups—especially young women in the United States and people in developing nations (Rothenberg & Koplan, 1990). The increased incidence of smoking has been accompanied by a parallel increase in the incidence of lung and other types of cancer among persons in these groups (Giovannucci et al., 1994). We'll explore this intriguing trend further in the **Perspectives on Diversity** section.

Why do people smoke? Genetic, psychosocial, and cognitive factors seem to play a role. Individual differences in our reaction to **nicotine**, the addictive substance in tobacco, suggest that some people are biologically predisposed to become addicted to nicotine, whereas others remain unaffected—evidence that our genes play a role in determining who will become a smoker (Pomerleau & Pomerleau, 1984). Nicotine enhances the availability of certain neurotransmitter substances, such as acetylcholine, norepinephrine, dopamine, and endogenous opioids. As you may recall from chapter 2, these substances produce temporary improvements in concentration, recall, alertness, arousal, and psychomotor performance that can be extremely pleasurable for some people. Other evidence suggests that psychosocial factors play a role in establishing smoking behavior, especially among young persons. Adolescents may be more likely to smoke if their parents or other role models smoke, or if they experience peer pressure to do so. Some researchers suggest, however, that smoking among adolescents is only part of a larger problem-behavior syndrome that may include problem drinking, drug use, and other delinquent behaviors (Donovan & Jessor, 1985). Finally, cognitive factors also appear to influence people's tendency to continue smoking. Most smokers recognize that smoking is harmful to their health, yet many continue to smoke. One possible explanation for this gap between their beliefs and their actions is that smokers may hold a set of false beliefs that serve to exempt them from per-

Cardiovascular Disease: All diseases of the heart and blood vessels.

Nicotine: The addictive substance in tobacco.

sonalizing their knowledge regarding the harmful consequences of smoking. To test this possibility Chapman and his colleagues (1993) asked two groups of people—smokers and ex-smokers—to indicate their agreement or disagreement with a series of self-exempting belief statements such as "smoking fewer than 20 cigarettes a day is safe." Smokers were more likely to agree with these beliefs than ex-smokers. While these results are preliminary, they do seem to suggest that developing ways to change the erroneous beliefs of smokers may be one important tool to help these persons kick the habit.

PERSPECTIVES ON DIVERSITY

Global Equality: Susceptibility to the Adverse Effects of Smoking

There are many ways in which people from around the globe differ, but one way in which they appear to be the same is in their susceptibility to the adverse health effects of smoking. This is an important point, since recent assessments of the prevalence of smoking show that the number of smokers worldwide—and hence the incidence of lung and other forms of cancer—continues to climb (LaVecchia et al., 1992, 1993). For example, since 1950 deaths from lung cancer in Japan have increased tenfold among men and eightfold among women. Even more disturbing is the prediction that rates of smoking-related deaths among men in Central and Eastern Europe will soon exceed the highest rates ever recorded (Boyle, 1993).

The percentage of deaths attributable to smoking has traditionally been higher for males than for females in many parts of the world (Peto et al., 1992). However, growing evidence suggests that this difference is disappearing—especially for female smokers in the United States. The percentage of deaths attributed to smoking in 1985 was higher for women in the United States than for women in other parts of the world—though still less than for their male counterparts. Scientists anticipate that over the next few years the percentage of deaths due to smoking among U.S. men and women will become increasingly similar. What is the reason for this swift rise in smoking-related deaths among women? Although scientists are not certain, part of the reason may be the large increase in the number of women who smoke in the United States and throughout the world (Boyle, 1993). And as women in the United States continue to move into high-pressure occupations that encourage some people to smoke, this trend is expected to continue.

The dangers of smoking are not limited to the smoker, however. Inhaling second-hand smoke, referred to as **passive smoking,** can also increase the incidence of respiratory disease and cardiovascular disease for smokers' family members and coworkers (Environmental Protection Agency, 1992). The effects of passive smoking can be particularly devastating for certain groups, including women and children. For example, nonsmoking women who live or work in an environment with a spouse or coworkers who smoke are at significantly greater risk of developing lung cancer than women who are not exposed to these conditions (Stockwell et al., 1992). In fact, the results of one study showed that nonsmoking women living with a smoking spouse

SMOKING: NO CULTURAL BOUNDARIES

The adverse effects of smoking are seen worldwide. In Japan, deaths from lung cancer have increased tenfold since 1950.

Passive Smoking: Inhaling other people's cigarette smoke.

experienced a 50 percent increase in their risk of developing lung cancer (Fontham, Correa, & Wu-Williams, 1991).

Passive smoking also adversely affects children: It causes more frequent and more severe attacks of asthma in children who already have the disease, and it may even produce brain tumors (Chilmonczyk et al., 1993; Gold et al., 1993). Further evidence shows decreased test performance among adolescents regularly exposed to their parent's smoking. Apparently, mental performance is affected by the carbon monoxide in tobacco smoke. Increasing concern over the many possible effects of passive smoking has prompted many companies to institute restrictive smoking policies and, in some cases, workplace smoking bans to reduce the health risks to nonsmoking coworkers (Borland et al., 1990).

These findings, and others, suggest that smoking is indeed the great equalizer. As smoking rates continue to soar worldwide, increases in the rates of cancer and cardiovascular diseases can be expected to follow among smokers and, unfortunately, those around them.

DIET AND NUTRITION: *What You Eat May Save Your Life*

Poor diet has been most closely linked with cancer of the colon and rectum. Fortunately, regular consumption of certain foods may *reduce* your risk of developing these cancers. Eating vegetables like broccoli and cauliflower may reduce the risk of cancer by inhibiting tumor formation and growth. Similarly, vitamin A—found in carrots, spinach, and cantaloupe—facilitates proper cell division and inhibits the destruction of healthy cells by carcinogens (Willet & MacMahon, 1984). Dietary fiber has also been proposed as a possible inhibitor of colorectal cancer (Graham, 1983).

Disturbing increases in the rates of breast cancer among women in the United States and other countries has led to large-scale multicultural studies to determine the cause. Growing evidence suggests that lifestyle factors, including the amount of fat consumed, may be among the culprits (Freedman et al., 1993; Makita & Sakamoto, 1990). For example, Howe and his colleagues (1990) examined the combined results of twelve previously conducted studies of diet and breast cancer including data from Australia, Canada, China, Greece, Hawaii, Israel, and Italy. Their analysis showed a consistent positive association between breast cancer risk and saturated fat intake for postmenopausal women, though not for premenopausal women. Additionally, as expected, these studies showed an inverse association between fruit and vegetable intake and risk for breast cancer.

Diet is also a significant risk factor in the development of *cardiovascular disease*, a term used to describe all diseases of the heart and blood vessels, including arteriosclerosis (hardening of the arteries), coronary heart disease (reduced blood flow to the heart), and stroke (bursting of a blood vessel in the brain). Most cardiovascular diseases affect the amount of oxygen and nutrients that reach organs and other tissues; prolonged oxygen and nutrition deficiency can result in permanent damage to the organs or tissues and even death. Arteriosclerosis, the major cause of heart disease in the United States, is caused by the buildup of cholesterol and other substances on arterial walls, which leads to a narrowing of those blood vessels. A large body of evidence shows that high levels of **serum cholesterol**, or blood cholesterol, are strongly associated with increased risk of cardiovascular diseases (Allred, 1993; Klag et al., 1993).

Serum Cholesterol: *The amount of cholesterol in the blood.*

Interestingly, the level of cholesterol in our blood is greatly affected by the amount of fat, especially saturated fat, and cholesterol in our diets. Serum cholesterol can be greatly reduced through a diet that is low in fats, cholesterol, and calories, and high in fiber, fruits, and vegetables (Carmody, Matarazzo, & Istvan, 1987). Unfortunately, it is difficult to get people to adhere to proper diets. Interventions designed to change people's eating habits, such as mass media campaigns, are often effective initially, but do not maintain the change over time. One approach that shows substantial promise for helping high-risk individuals to make long-term changes in their eating habits calls for the active involvement of the person's family in designing and implementing behavior change programs.

ALCOHOL CONSUMPTION: *Here's to Your Health?*

Although strong evidence suggests that biological and genetic factors contribute to alcoholism and problem drinking (Reid & Carpenter, 1990), psychosocial factors, including stress, environmental cues, and social pressure from peers, also play a significant role in determining drinking behavior. And even though evidence suggests that a daily glass of red wine may be associated with health benefits, too much alcohol can be harmful and can lead to a variety of social and physical disorders. The consequences of drinking can include stomach disease; cirrhosis of the liver; cancer; impaired sexual functioning; cognitive impairment; and, as we saw in chapter 8, *fetal alcohol syndrome*, a condition of retardation and physical abnormalities that occurs in children of mothers who are heavy drinkers. The amount of alcohol we drink is directly related to our risk for developing certain disorders. For example, drinking an average of 1.5 or more beers per day has been linked to subsequent development of colon and rectum cancer (Pollack et al., 1984). Drinking alcohol may also interact with smoking to increase cancer risk. Drinkers of alcohol who are also heavy smokers have twenty-two times greater risk of developing cancer than individuals who neither smoke nor drink (Rothman et al., 1980).

KEY QUESTIONS

- What is cancer?
- What determines who will become addicted to smoking?
- What are the potential consequences of smoking and exposure to second-hand smoke?
- What are the effects of poor dietary practices?
- What are the consequences of heavy consumption of alcohol?

EMOTIONS: *Mood and Health*

Inadequate emotional expression—especially of negative feelings—can have an adverse effect on the progression of certain types of illness, such as cancer. Individuals who cope with stress by keeping their negative emotions to themselves are likely to experience suppressed immune systems, greater recurrence of cancer, and higher mortality rates (Levy et al., 1985). In contrast, patients who demonstrate positive affect—especially joy, well-being, and happiness—increase the likelihood of recovery (Levy et al., 1988).

A curious point is the relation between expression of distress and treatment outcome. Open expression of negative affect and a willingness to fight illness are sometimes associated with greater immune function, decreased recurrence rates, and increased survival time, even among patients at advanced stages of cancer. For example, combative individuals—those who express anger about getting cancer and hostility toward their doctors and family members—often live longer than patients who passively accept their fate and quietly undergo treatment (Levy, 1990).

Emotion can also play a role in the progression of **hypertension**, or high blood pressure, a condition in which the pressure within the blood vessels is

Hypertension: High blood pressure, a condition in which the pressure within the blood vessels is abnormally high.

TYPE A BEHAVIOR PATTERNS AND HEALTH PROBLEMS

Type A persons tend to be always in a hurry, competitive, aggressive, hostile, and impatient. They are more than twice as likely as Type B persons to have coronary problems. Research shows that one aspect of Type A behavior—*cynical hostility*—may be particularly detrimental.

Type A Behavior Pattern: A cluster of traits such as competitiveness, aggressiveness, urgency, and hostility; related to important aspects of health, social behavior, and task performance.

abnormally high. Prolonged hypertension, when untreated, can result in extensive damage to the entire circulatory system. Indeed, about 30 percent of deaths due to cardiovascular disease each year are attributable to hypertension. Some evidence suggests that emotional stressors can affect the regulation of blood pressure through neurohormonal mechanisms (Krakoff et al., 1985). For example, anxiety and hostility can increase general arousal and facilitate the release of *catecholamines*—a class of neurotransmitters that play an important role in the sympathetic nervous system. The release of the catecholamine epinephrine has the effect of boosting our overall readiness to act, including our blood pressure. Although the effects of emotional stressors are usually brief, extreme reactivity to anxiety, hostility, and anger may indicate a predisposition to develop hypertension (Rosenman, 1988). Not surprisingly, the strongest relations between emotions and blood pressure have been found for unexpressed anger and hostility.

PERSONALITY AND HEALTH: TYPE A BEHAVIOR PATTERN   Think about the people you know. Can you name one person who always seems to be in a hurry, is extremely competitive, and is often hostile and irritable? Now, in contrast, can you name one who shows the opposite pattern—someone who is relaxed, relatively uncompetitive, and easygoing in relations with others? If you succeeded, you now have in mind two people who could be described as showing Type A and Type B behavior patterns, respectively.

Interest in the **Type A behavior pattern** was first stimulated by medical research. Several physicians (Jenkins, Zyzanski, & Rosenman, 1979, and their colleagues) noticed that many patients who had suffered heart attacks seemed to share certain personality traits (please refer to chapter 10). Individuals who tend to be competitive, aggressive, hostile, and impatient are displaying a pattern of behaviors termed Type A. They are likely to be hard workers and tend to seek out the most challenging and stressful work conditions. Often, their efforts are rewarded with additional work from their superiors and coworkers (Feather & Volkmer, 1988). But some researchers now believe that only certain aspects of the Type A pattern may be related to increased risk of heart disease. Recent findings suggest it may be only those Type A individuals who fail to express their emotions—especially anger, cynicism, and hostility—and fail to ignore early symptoms of cardiovascular disease who are at risk (Matthews, 1988). A particular type of hostility—*cynical hostility*, characterized by suspiciousness, resentment, anger, antagonism, and distrust of others—may be especially detrimental.

How can a Type A profile promote heart disease? The emotional reactions among Type A individuals may result in constriction of peripheral blood flow, higher blood pressure, and increased pulse rate (Lyness, 1993). Such changes in the cardiovascular system may produce excessive wear on the arteries of the heart, leading to the development of cardiovascular disease (Contrada, 1989). Additional evidence suggests that the emotional responses of Type A individuals are accompanied by increased hormone levels in the bloodstream, such as the catecholamines adrenaline and noradrenaline. These increased hormonal levels may lead to greater fatty deposits on the walls of blood vessels and ultimately to heart disease (Dembrowski & Williams, 1989).

Yet there may also be some health benefits to being Type A. In a thirteen-year longitudinal study of Type A and Type B men, researchers found that although the Type As had significantly more heart attacks than Type Bs, they were more likely to survive those heart attacks (Ragland & Brand, 1988). It appears that the personality style that drove them to heart attacks may also include behaviors that increase adherence to post–heart attack treatment. In short, the very characteristics that threaten to kill Type As may, under certain circumstances, be the same ones that save their lives.

AIDS: *The Assault on Public Health*

Acquired immune deficiency syndrome (AIDS) is a viral disease that reduces the immune system's ability to defend itself against the introduction of foreign matter. The first cases of AIDS in the United States were reported in 1981, although we now know there were cases that occurred before that date. It was not until 1984 that the cause of AIDS was isolated—a virus labeled *human immunodeficiency virus,* or *HIV*—and an antibody test was developed to detect infection.

THE FACTS ABOUT AIDS Since 1981 researchers have discovered a number of frightening facts about AIDS. First, the incubation period—the time it takes for the disease to develop—can be as long as ten years (Bachetti, 1990). This means that infected individuals can spread the disease to others without even realizing that they are infected. Thus, it is not surprising that the incidence of AIDS increased rapidly in the United States—from 250 cases documented in the early 1980s to an estimated 300,000 new cases occurring in 1993 alone (Centers for Disease Control, 1993). AIDS is now the second leading cause of death among American men between the ages of 18 and 44 and the sixth leading cause of death for American women in this age group (Kelly et al., 1993).

Second, growing evidence suggests that most—although not all—individuals infected with HIV will eventually develop AIDS. Since there are presently no effective vaccines or treatments for HIV, it is estimated that millions of people will die from AIDS-related illnesses (Cohen, 1993). Recent estimates suggest that over 17 million people worldwide, mostly in developing nations, are already infected with HIV (Gorman, 1994).

Third, an individual can only be infected if the virus is introduced directly into the bloodstream. This means that the disease cannot be contracted through casual contact, such as shaking hands with or hugging an infected person, and therefore can only be spread if the blood or semen of an infected person directly contacts the blood system of the potential recipient. There are two primary ways in which HIV is spread: through *unprotected sexual intercourse* and *use of infected blood or blood products.* The process by which HIV produces AIDS symptoms is complex, but essentially involves the devastation of aspects of the infected person's immune system, making the person extremely vulnerable to a host of infections, and ultimately resulting in death (Weiss, 1993).

AIDS: AN OUNCE OF PREVENTION IS THE ONLY KNOWN CURE Why are psychologists so interested in AIDS? One reason, aside from the tragic consequences of this disease, is that people contract HIV as a result of certain behaviors. Although initially researchers thought AIDS was a disease restricted to homosexuals and intravenous drug users, AIDS is currently being spread mainly through unprotected *heterosexual* rather than homosexual intercourse. The number of HIV infections in heterosexual populations in Africa, India, and Asia has risen sharply over the past several years and is expected to reach 110 million by 2000 (Mann, 1992).

Acquired Immune Deficiency Syndrome (AIDS): A fatal viral infection that reduces the immune system's ability to defend itself against the introduction of foreign matter.

Another reason for psychologists' interest in this problem is that effective preventive or therapeutic treatments for HIV have not yet been developed. Evaluations of drugs used to treat persons infected with HIV suggest that their beneficial effects are limited and short-lived because the HIV quickly mutates into drug-resistant forms (Cohen, 1993). Therefore, at present, the only effective means of combating AIDS are *primary prevention programs* aimed at changing people's attitudes, beliefs, and, most importantly, risky behaviors.

During the past decade, behavioral scientists have made substantial discoveries about the psychology of AIDS and its transmission. For example, initial research in this area revealed that many of the individuals not using condoms were those who were at greatest risk for contracting AIDS: homosexuals and intravenous drug users. Why were these persons ignoring warnings from the medical community and not practicing safe sex? One of the reasons involves **social norms**—rules that tell us how to act in social situations. Among homosexual men, for instance, the greater their reported involvement in social networks whose norms support using condoms to prevent AIDS transmission, the more likely the men are to engage in such behavior (Fisher & Misovich, 1989).

Beliefs, too, seem to play a role in determining why some groups of people engage in risky behaviors. In one study, Hingson and his colleagues (1990) assessed whether beliefs about AIDS and condom use were related to frequency of unprotected sex among sexually active adolescents—a group whose risk of contracting AIDS is rising. The results showed that adolescents who believed (1) they were highly susceptible to AIDS, (2) there is no cure for AIDS, and (3) condoms are effective in preventing AIDS were more likely to report the consistent use of condoms than those who did not share these beliefs.

DEVELOPING EFFECTIVE INTERVENTIONS TO PREVENT THE SPREAD OF AIDS

The results of these, and related studies, have led researchers to the conclusion that developing effective AIDS-prevention programs will be extremely challenging. Researchers also recognize that techniques effective for a particular target group may not necessarily be effective for all groups of people. Thus, for each population of interest, it will be important to perform *elicitation research*. This type of research assesses a given population's existing level of AIDS risk-reduction knowledge, the factors that determine their motivation to reduce AIDS risk, and their existing AIDS-prevention behavioral skills, such as the ability to communicate with and to be appropriately assertive with a potential sexual partner (Fisher & Fisher, 1992). Growing evidence suggests that prevention programs that provide not only knowledge but also motivation and behavioral skills are generally more effective in increasing AIDS-preventive behaviors than programs that do not (please refer to Figure 11.7).

Because scientists are still years, perhaps decades, away from finding a cure, the role of psychologists in designing effective interventions to change risky behaviors, and thereby prevent the spread of HIV, will become increasingly important in the decades ahead.

Social Norms: Rules that tell us how to act in certain social situations.

KEY QUESTIONS

- How is the expression of emotions related to health?
- What are the characteristics of Type A persons? What diseases have been linked to the Type A behavior pattern?
- What is AIDS and how is it transmitted?

PROMOTING WELLNESS:
Developing a Healthier Lifestyle

*H*ave you ever wondered why some individuals live to be more than one hundred years old, while most people live only sixty or seventy years?

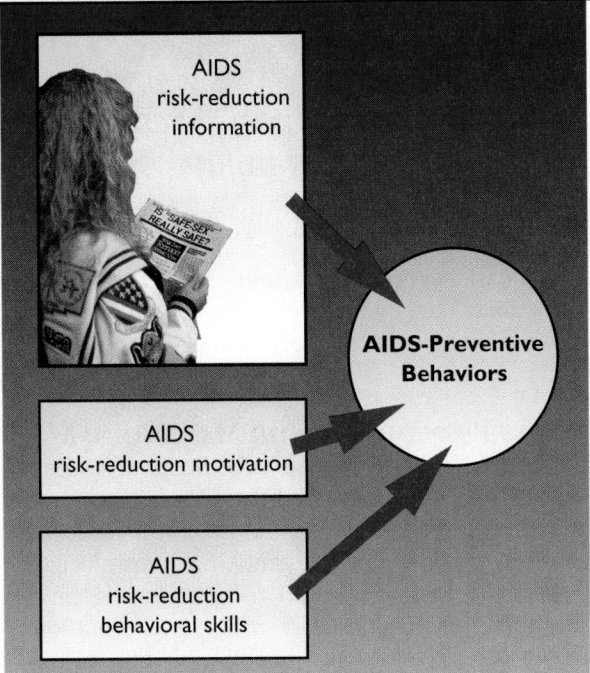

FIGURE 11.7

AIDS-Preventive Behaviors: A Model

Growing evidence suggests that prevention programs are more effective when they are tailored to meet the needs of specific target groups and when they provide people with information, motivation, and behavioral skills. (*Source:* Based on Fisher & Fisher, 1992.)

Studies of persons who live to be more than one hundred years old indicate that several factors may play a role in their extended life spans. (Chapter 8 addressed many issues relevant to lifestyles of older adults.) One of these factors is diet: Long-lived persons often show a pattern involving greater-than-average consumption of grains, leafy green and root vegetables, fresh milk, and fresh fruits, and they tend to eat low to moderate amounts of meat and animal fat. In addition, they maintain low to moderate levels of daily caloric intake (1,200 to 3,000 calories) and consume only moderate amounts of alcohol each day. Physical activity is perhaps the most important factor contributing to longevity and good health among long-lived people. Many work outdoors and walk a great deal. That is, regular physical activity is an integral part of their lives, continuing well into old age. Additional factors that may contribute to their extended life span are continued sexual activity and continued involvement in family and community affairs during their advanced years (please refer to chapter 8).

On the basis of such findings, a growing number of health professionals and psychologists have adopted an approach to health and wellness that is based on **prevention strategies,** techniques designed to reduce the occurrence of illness and other physical and psychological problems.

Primary prevention is considered the optimal prevention approach. Its goal is to reduce or eliminate altogether the incidence of preventable illness and injury. Primary prevention strategies usually involve one or more of the following components: educating people about the relation between their behaviors and their health, promoting motivation and skills to practice healthy behaviors, and directly modifying poor health practices through intervention.

Secondary prevention focuses on early detection to decrease the severity of illness that is already present. Thus, individuals learn about their health status through medical tests that screen for the presence of disease. Although early detection of certain diseases is traditionally carried out by health professionals and often requires sophisticated medical tests, exciting research is under way to

Learning Objective 11.13
Discuss the use and effectiveness of primary prevention strategies such as health promotion in the mass media, control of alcohol consumption, and exercise.

Learning Objective 11.14
Understand the role of early detection in disease and illness.

Prevention Strategies: Techniques designed to reduce the occurrence of physical and psychological problems.

teach patients methods of self-examination, especially for early detection of breast and testicular cancer.

PRIMARY PREVENTION: *Decreasing the Risks of Illness and Injury*

In most instances, our initial attempts to change our health behaviors are unsuccessful. Typically, we become aware of the need to change behaviors; we initiate change; we experience a series of failed attempts to change these behaviors; and sometimes—only sometimes—we succeed. The nature of this process indicates that we need help—a variety of intervention programs to meet our varied needs and purposes.

HEALTH PROMOTION AND THE MASS MEDIA: MARKETING HEALTHY LIFESTYLES IN THE COMMUNITY   We are constantly bombarded with messages about health risks. Numerous nonprofit organizations use television commercials, newspaper articles, magazine ads, and radio advertising to warn us about unhealthy behaviors like smoking, unprotected sex, and alcohol and drug abuse, and their associated risks, including cancer, heart disease, and AIDS. These campaigns typically provide information about symptoms that may indicate the presence of a health problem, such as shortness of breath or chest pains in the case of heart attacks, and information about the relation between specific behaviors and disease; for example, "Smoking is the number one cause of heart disease."

But can mass media campaigns alone produce widespread changes in behavior? There is little evidence that they can (Meyer, Maccoby, & Farquhar, 1980). One reason for the limited success of these programs may be the media's depiction and promotion of unhealthy habits, which counteract health promotion messages. An analysis of food and beverage commercials presented during prime-time television indicates that their messages are inconsistent with recommended dietary guidelines. For example, Story and Faulkner (1990) computed the frequency of commercials advertising healthy versus unhealthy food and beverages. Most of the prime-time commercials are for unhealthy foods and beverages. The clearest example is the difference in numbers of commercials for fast-food versus family-style restaurants. Despite these findings, it is interesting that many companies use health messages to sell their products.

The mass media can be a very effective tool for promoting behavior change, however, when combined with other intervention programs. For example, the Stanford Heart Disease Prevention Project investigated the combined effects of a media campaign and a program designed to change health-related behaviors (Farquhar, Maccoby, & Solomon, 1984). Three communities were chosen for the study. One community received an intense media campaign focusing on the risk factors associated with heart disease; a second group received the same media campaign plus a personal instruction program on modifying health habits for people in high-risk groups; a third community served as a control. Although the media campaign alone produced modest changes in health behavior, the program that included both a media campaign and behavior therapy was most effective. Another successful program, which used a combination of mass media, community antismoking programs, and physician intervention—termed the Quit for Life Project—was able to reduce smoking prevalence in two major cities by 6.5 percent over a four-year period (Pierce et al., 1990).

Some evidence suggests that our beliefs may affect our responses to advertisements. For example, individuals with high fear of contracting AIDS rate advertisements about AIDS as more effective than people with low fear of contracting AIDS (Struckman-Johnson et al., 1990). This finding is consistent with the health belief model described earlier, which predicts that people who believe they are more susceptible to disease will be more likely to accept an advertisement's intended message. During the 1980s and 1990s the mass media have been the primary tool for disseminating information about the AIDS crisis. The spread of information may help explain why sales of condoms recommended specifically for the prevention of AIDS transmission increased dramatically (116 percent) from 1984 to 1988 (Moran et al., 1990).

OVERCONSUMPTION OF ALCOHOL: INJURY CONTROL ON THE ROAD One of the biggest public health concerns facing our nation stems from the overconsumption of alcohol. The costs associated with alcohol-related accidents, crime, and lost production are enormous. Recently, psychologists and other health care experts have begun to recognize the need for primary prevention efforts to deal with alcohol-related problems; efforts that focus, for example, on reducing the chances that someone will drink to excess or drive drunk. This focus on prevention is particularly important for high-risk groups such as college students. It has been estimated that as many as 90 percent of college students consume alcohol to some degree (Kivlahan et al., 1990). Therefore, it is likely that some of these individuals will occasionally drink too much and thus place themselves or someone else at risk if they get behind the wheel of an automobile.

Psychologists have begun to investigate the environments in which drinking takes place, such as private social gatherings and fraternity parties (Geller & Kalsher, 1990; Kalsher et al., 1988). This kind of investigation includes a systematic assessment of environmental determinants of alcohol consumption: factors that tend to increase or decrease actual drinking behavior and the outcome of drinking (blood alcohol concentration) under naturalistic circumstances. Exploration of the environmental determinants of alcohol consumption among college drinkers may lead to practical ways to decrease the level of intoxication at college parties and perhaps, most importantly, to reduce the chances that students will be injured or injure someone else once they leave the party.

THE WORK OF STAYING HEALTHY: MOTIVATING THE COUCH POTATO Research evidence suggests that only one in five Americans exercises regularly and intensely enough to reduce his or her risk for chronic disease and premature death (Dubbert, 1992). This is surprising, since it is now very well known that regular and vigorous exercise can significantly reduce coronary heart disease, even in the presence of other health risk factors, including smoking, obesity, high blood pressure, and high blood cholesterol (Dishman, 1988). Moreover, some evidence suggests that even less vigorous forms of activity can be beneficial if done consistently. For example, people who walk regularly—at least four hours per week—have less than half the incidence of elevated cholesterol of those who do not (Tucker & Friedman, 1990).

Research also indicates that exercise can have a significant impact on our mental health. For example, exercise has been found to improve self-concept, alleviate feelings of depression, and reduce anxiety (Dubbert, 1992). These effects are particularly apparent just after a workout, but there may also be some benefits from long-term participation in exercise. Changes in mood following exercise may result from socializing and being involved with others (Plante & Rodin, 1990); running with a friend may improve mood because of the companionship the exercise provides. Mood may also

EXERCISING THE COUCH POTATO

Evidence suggests that regular and vigorous exercise reduces the risk of coronary heart disease.

improve because of exercise's effect on self-efficacy—enhanced confidence in our ability to perform a behavior, such as running a mile or completing an aerobics workout (Rodin & Plante, 1989).

So how can we get the rest of the couch potatoes off the couch? Some research suggests that starting and then maintaining an exercise program requires that people arrange their environment so that it supports the desired exercise behavior and weakens competing behaviors. First, it is important to arrange effective cues that become a signal to exercise. Working out in the same location, doing a similar warm-up routine, and recording and posting the results of one's physical activity can be effective in cueing future exercise behavior. It is also important to arrange when exercise occurs, to minimize the effects of the cues for competing behaviors. For example, individuals who have a tendency to work late should establish a morning training routine to minimize competition with a busy work schedule. Second, it is also important to arrange for consequences that maintain exercise behavior. Initially, it is critical for new exercisers to seek out sources of rewards for their exercise behavior and avoid potential sources of punishment, including muscle soreness, fatigue, and injury. Paradoxically, those most in need of consistent exercise, such as obese or extremely out-of-shape persons or older individuals, may be those most subject to punishing consequences—including the possibility of a heart attack if they overdo it (Curfman, 1993; Knapp, 1988). Finally, the presence of a strong social support network can greatly increase adherence to a lifelong exercise habit.

SECONDARY PREVENTION: *The Role of Early Detection in Disease and Illness*

Psychologists are taking an increasingly active role in developing motivational strategies to get people to take part in *early detection* procedures—techniques used to screen for the presence of high blood pressure, high blood cholesterol, and some forms of cancer. The identification of these conditions at an early stage can make an enormous difference in the chances for treatment success—in some cases the difference between life and death.

SCREENING FOR DISEASE: SEEKING INFORMATION ABOUT OUR HEALTH STATUS   The fact that early detection and treatment of an illness is more effective than later detection and treatment is the foundation for screening programs. Evidence suggests that the widespread use of available screening techniques could decrease the incidence of cardiovascular disease through the early detection of high blood pressure and cholesterol, and could significantly reduce the number of cervical, colon, and prostate cancer deaths. For example, it is estimated that 10 to 20 percent of invasive cervical cancer in females could be prevented by widespread Pap smear testing (Rothenberg et al., 1987).

Many companies, colleges, community organizations, and hospitals have screening programs to test for high blood pressure and serum cholesterol. Unfortunately, many people either do not take advantage of screening programs at all or fail to get screened regularly. Indeed, forgetting and underestimating the time since the last test are the primary reasons people wait too long between screenings. Interventions that heighten awareness or serve a reminder function, such as physician reminder systems and local advertising campaigns, can increase the frequency of screening visits (Mitchell, 1988).

The most significant factors governing the use of screening, as indicated by the health belief model, appear to be beliefs about the possible benefits of screening, the perceived severity of possible illnesses, perceived vulnerability to disease, and beliefs about what other people (friends, family) think about screening (Hennig & Knowles, 1990).

SELF-EXAMINATION: DETECTING THE EARLY SIGNS OF ILLNESS Self-examination can be instrumental for the early detection of both testicular and breast cancer. Testicular cancer is among the leading causes of death in men between the ages of fifteen and forty in the United States (Droller, 1980). The cure rate associated with testicular cancer is extremely high—if the cancer is detected early (Dahl, 1985). Unfortunately, in nearly half of the testicular cancers diagnosed, the presence of the disease is not detected until it has spread from the testes to the abdomen and other organs (Cummings et al., 1983), and the chances of a full recovery are significantly less (Bosl et al., 1981). Despite the fact that testicular self-examination techniques are available and are effective in detecting the early signs of cancer, many males are unaware of their existence (Goldenring & Putrell, 1984; Steffen, 1990).

The dangers associated with breast cancer present a similar challenge for females. Some researchers suggest that breast cancers detected early through secondary prevention programs, such as breast self-examination, clinical breast examination, and mammography, have an 85 to 90 percent chance of being cured (American Cancer Society, 1989). Skills training programs for the detection of the symptoms and signs of breast cancer were developed many years before those for testicular self-examination. Interestingly, knowledge of breast self-examination is much greater among females than is knowledge of testicular self-examination among males.

KEY QUESTIONS
• What role do the mass media play in promoting wellness?
• How have psychologists attempted to reduce the amount of alcohol consumed at social events?
• What are the effects of regular exercise on health?
• What are primary prevention and secondary prevention?

MAKING PSYCHOLOGY PART OF YOUR LIFE

Managing Stress: Some Useful Tactics

Stress is a fact of life. It's all around us: at work, in our environment, and in our personal lives. Because stress arises from so many different factors and conditions, it's probably impossible to eliminate it completely. But we *can* apply techniques to lessen its potentially harmful effects (Carver, Scheier, & Weintraub, 1989; Folkman et al., 1986). Let's consider several of these techniques, dividing them into three major categories: *physiological, cognitive,* and *behavioral.*

PHYSIOLOGICAL COPING TECHNIQUES

Common physiological responses to stress include tense muscles, racing pulse, pounding heart, dry mouth, queasy stomach, and sweating. But several coping techniques can be effective.

One of the most effective procedures is learning to reduce the tension in our own muscles through *pro-gressive relaxation* (Jacobson, 1938). To use this technique, begin by alternately flexing and relaxing your muscles to appreciate the difference between relaxed and tense muscles. Next, you might shake out your arms and then let them flop by your sides. Then relax your shoulders by slowly rolling them up and down. Now, relax your neck. Step by step, you extend this process until your body is completely relaxed from head to toe. Controlled breathing is also important. When you are tense, you tend to take in relatively short, shallow breaths. However, as your body slows down during relaxation, notice that your breathing changes to deeper, longer breaths. Relaxation procedures are effective in reducing emotional as well as physical tension. A related technique that is often effective for achieving a relaxed state is *meditation*, described in detail in chapter 4.

TABLE 11.3	**BASIC PRINCIPLES OF TIME MANAGEMENT**

Getting the Most Out of Your Day: Psychology in Action

One behavioral coping strategy is time management. Here are some tips to help you get the most out of your day.

1. Each day, make a list of things you want to accomplish.
2. Prioritize your list. Plan to do the toughest things first and save the easier tasks for later in the day when you are low on energy.
3. Arrange your work schedule to take best advantage of those hours when you work best.
4. Always set aside a block of time when you can work without any interruptions.
5. Be flexible about changes in your schedule so that you can handle unexpected events.
6. Plan for some leisure activity during your day—everybody needs a break.
7. Set aside some times each day or week in which you always do some planned leisure activity.

Vigorous physical exercise is another important technique for coping with stress and its adverse effects. I've been using this technique myself for more than fifteen years (mainly through running), and it has certainly done wonders for me. I still remember what finally got me started. I was working at the National Science Foundation in Washington, D.C., where my job focused on helping to determine which psychologists would receive research grants. Suddenly, after Ronald Reagan was elected president, the budget for my program was cut by more than 80 percent. As a result, I had to tell many colleagues that their research could no longer be supported. I found being the bearer of ill tidings so stressful that my health was affected. My physician suggested exercise, and he was right. Running didn't solve the serious problems I faced at work, but it certainly increased my capacity to cope with this stress, and definitely made me feel better.

BEHAVIORAL COPING TECHNIQUES

We're all guilty of behaving in ways that bring stress on ourselves. We overload our schedules with too many responsibilities; we procrastinate; it all adds up to stress. There are plenty of things we can do to reduce the stress in our lives. One method is *time management:* learning how to make time work for us instead of against us. Adhering to a well-planned schedule can help us make more efficient use of our time and eliminate behaviors that interfere with our main goals. An important—but often ignored—principle of time management is to balance work time and play time. Table 11.3 offers several tips to help you get the most out of your day.

COGNITIVE COPING TECHNIQUES

We don't always have control over all the stressors in our lives. We *can*, however, gain some control over our cognitive reactions to them. In other words, when exposed to a stressful situation, we can think about it in different ways, and some of these are much more beneficial than others. The process of replacing negative appraisals of stressors with more positive ones is

called *cognitive restructuring* (Meichenbaum, 1977). To use this technique successfully, begin by monitoring what you say to yourself during periods of stress. Begin to modify these thoughts by thinking more adaptive thoughts. For example, try to discover something humorous about the situation, or imagine creative ways to reduce or eliminate the source of stress. Also, as mentioned earlier, social support is important. Others—family, friends, or associates—can often help you to restructure stressors (Bruhn & Phillips, 1987): to perceive stressful events as less threatening and more under control than you might otherwise do. As you may recall, cognitive appraisal plays a crucial role in the way we interpret stressors. It's a good idea to be in contact with people who can suggest strategies for dealing with the sources of stress that you might not generate yourself and can help reduce the negative feelings that often accompany stressful events or situations (Costanza, Derlega, & Winstead, 1988).

Research shows that there are a number of steps you can take to help reduce stress, including relaxation, time management, and cognitive restructuring.

Summary and Review of Key Questions

Health Psychology: An Overview

• *What is the aim of health psychologists?*

The primary aim of health psychologists is to determine important relationships between psychological variables and health.

• *What is behavioral medicine?*

Behavioral medicine, a field of health psychology, combines behavioral and biomedical science knowledge to prevent and treat disorders.

• *To what can many of today's leading causes of premature death be attributed?*

Many of today's leading causes of premature death can be attributed to people's lifestyles.

Key Terms: *health psychology, p. 407; lifestyle, p. 407*

Stress: Its Causes, Effects, and Control

• *What is stress?*

Stress is the process that occurs in response to situations or events (stressors) that disrupt, or threaten to disrupt, our physical or psychological functioning.

• *What is the GAS model?*

The general adaptation syndrome (GAS) model, developed by Hans Selye, describes how our bodies react to the effects of prolonged stress in three distinct stages: alarm, resistance, and, finally, exhaustion.

• *What determines whether we interpret an event as stressful or as a challenge?*

Cognitive appraisals play an important role in determining whether we interpret a potentially stressful event as stressful or as a challenge.

• *What are stressors?*

Stressors can be major life events, such as the death of a spouse, or minor hassles of everyday life, such as receiving a traffic ticket or having to wait in a line at the grocery store.

• *What is posttraumatic stress disorder?*

Posttraumatic stress disorder is a stress-related psychological disturbance that often affects survivors of large-scale natural disasters, such as earthquakes and floods, or human-produced disasters, such as the meltdown of a nuclear reactor.

• *What are some sources of work-related stress?*

Sources of work-related stress include work overload and underload, role conflict, and performance appraisals.

• *Does stress play a role in physical illness?*

Stress may play a role in 50 to 70 percent of all physical illness, primarily through its effect on the immune system.

• *What are the effects of exposure to low levels of stress? To high levels?*

Even relatively low levels of stress may interfere with task performance. Prolonged exposure to high levels of stress may cause burnout.

• *Why are some people better able to cope with the effects of stress?*

Individual differences in optimism and hardiness help explain the ability of some people to cope with stress better than others. Optimists generally use problem-focused ways of coping with stress and actively seek out social support. Hardy people generally show high levels of commitment, view change as an opportunity for growth, and have a sense of control over events in their lives.

Key Terms: *stress, p. 408; stressors, p. 409; general adaptation syndrome (GAS), p. 409; posttraumatic stress disorder, p. 415; person-environment (P-E) fit, p. 417; hardiness, p. 422*

Understanding and Communicating Our Health Needs

• *Why are symptoms and sensations important?*

Symptoms and sensations, such as irregularities in heartbeat, are useful because they may help alert us to underlying health problems.

• *According to the health belief model, what factors determine our willingness to make lifestyle changes or seek medical help?*

According to the health belief model, our willingness to make lifestyle changes or seek medical help depends on our beliefs concerning our susceptibility to an illness, the severity of the illness, and the effectiveness of steps taken to deal with the illness.

• *Why is it important for psychologists to study aspects of doctor-patient interactions?*

Physicians are often more effective in dealing with the technical aspects of treating patients than the psychosocial aspects. Because of this fact, psychologists have begun to develop interventions aimed at improving the nature of doctor-patient interactions, which in turn can have a beneficial impact on important medical outcomes.

Key Term: *health belief model, p. 424*

Behavioral and Psychological Correlates of Illness: The Effects of Thoughts and Actions on Health

• *What is cancer?*

Cancer is a group of diseases characterized by rapidly multiplying abnormal cells that invade and overwhelm normal tissue.

- **What determines who will become addicted to smoking?**

Individual differences in people's reaction to nicotine, the addictive substance in tobacco, help determine who will become a smoker.

- **What are the potential consequences of smoking and exposure to second-hand smoke?**

Both smoking and exposure to second-hand smoke have been implicated in many types of cancer, in cardiovascular disease, and in a host of pathologies in children, including brain tumors.

- **What are the effects of poor dietary practices?**

Poor dietary practices can increase the risks of colon and rectal cancer, breast cancer, and cardiovascular disease.

- **What are the consequences of heavy consumption of alcohol?**

Heavy drinking can cause a variety of health problems including stomach, liver, and intestinal cancer. It can also impair mental and sexual functioning, and it can result in fetal alcohol syndrome.

- **How is the expression of emotions related to health?**

Failure to express emotions can adversely affect the progression of a cancer. Unexposed emotions can also lead to an increase in a person's blood pressure.

- **What are the characteristics of Type A persons? What disease has been linked to the Type A behavior pattern?**

Type A persons tend to be competitive, aggressive, hostile, and impatient. Persons who fit this pattern and fail to express their emotions are at the highest risk for cardiovascular disease.

- **What is AIDS, and how is it transmitted?**

Acquired immune deficiency syndrome (AIDS) is a reduction in the immune system's ability to defend the body against invaders and is caused by the HIV virus.

AIDS is transmitted primarily through unprotected sex and infected blood.

KEY TERMS: cancer, p. 427; risk factors, p. 427; carcinogens, p. 427; cardiovascular disease, p. 428; nicotine, p. 428; passive smoking, p. 429; serum cholesterol, p. 430; hypertension, p. 431; Type A behavior pattern, p. 432; acquired immune deficiency syndrome (AIDS), p. 433; social norms, p. 434

PROMOTING WELLNESS: DEVELOPING A HEALTHIER LIFESTYLE

- **What role do the mass media play in promoting wellness?**

The mass media, with other health promotion programs, can have a beneficial impact on health behaviors.

- **How have psychologists attempted to reduce the amount of alcohol consumed at social events?**

By systematically manipulating aspects of the social environment, psychologists have successfully reduced the amount of alcohol consumption that takes place at social events.

- **What are the effects of regular exercise on health?**

Regular and vigorous exercise promotes both physical and psychological health. Starting and maintaining an exercise habit requires that people arrange their environment in a way that supports the desired exercise behaviors and weakens competing behaviors.

- **What are primary prevention and secondary prevention?**

Primary prevention emphasizes disease prevention through educating people about the relation between their behavior and their health, promoting healthy behavior, and directly modifying poor health practices. Secondary prevention emphasizes early detection of disease to decrease the severity of illness that is already present.

KEY TERM: prevention strategies, p. 435

CRITICAL THINKING QUESTIONS

APPRAISAL	Throughout this chapter you've seen that lifestyle factors—what we choose to eat, drink, or smoke, and whether we choose to exercise regularly—greatly influence our health. If one can achieve good health simply by changing one's own behaviors, then why aren't more people doing so?
CONTROVERSY	The number of persons infected with HIV in the United States and throughout the world is increasing at an alarming rate. Since it is clear that many infections result from unprotected sex with an infected person, behavioral researchers have developed interventions that effectively promote the use of condoms—particularly among high-risk populations. Others argue, however, that these interventions simply promote promiscuity and thereby worsen the problem. Which perspective is correct? What are your views on this issue?
MAKING PSYCHOLOGY PART OF YOUR LIFE	Now that you know something about the many practices that can improve physical and psychological health, will you be more likely to follow these practices yourself? Why or why not?

Psychological Disorders:

Their Nature and Causes

12

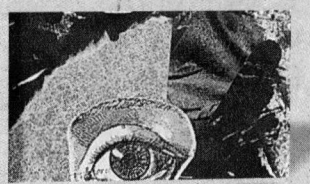

*T*hink back over all the people you have known. Can you remember ones who experienced any of the following problems?

• Wild swings in mood, from deep despair to the heights of elation

• Excessive dependence on alcohol, tranquilizers, or other drugs

PSYCHOLOGICAL DISORDERS: ATYPICAL AND MALADAPTIVE

Is the homeless man shown here suffering from a psychological disorder? We can't be sure without careful diagnosis, but his behavior certainly meets some of the key criteria defining such disorders.

- Intense and seemingly unjustifiable fear of certain situations, such as being in a crowd, being alone, or traveling by airplane

- Unusual preoccupation with illness, health, and various (perhaps largely imaginary) symptoms

- Tremendous concern about being overweight, coupled with a near-starvation diet and an emaciated body

If you *haven't* known someone who experienced one or more of these problems, then you have certainly led a charmed life, for disorders like these are experienced by many millions of human beings in every corner of the earth every year. It is on these and other **psychological disorders**—maladaptive patterns of behavior and thought that cause the persons who experience them considerable distress—that we will focus in this chapter and chapter 13.

But what, precisely, are such disorders? I have just offered a brief definition, but it is far from complete. In fact, psychologists and other professionals concerned with psychological disorders have debated this question for decades, for there appear to be no simple ways of distinguishing *abnormal* behavior from *normal* behavior. The two lie on a continuum, and one often shades into the other. Most psychologists agree, however, that psychological disorders (and, by extension, all forms of behavior described as "abnormal") often share some, if not all, of the following features.

First, these disorders usually generate *distress*—anxiety, internal conflict, depression, confusion, and other negative feelings—in the persons who experience them. Second, psychological disorders involve patterns of behavior or thought that are judged to be unusual or *atypical*. People with these disorders don't behave or think like most others in their society, and this fact is noticed—often with discomfort—by the persons around them. Third, psychological disorders involve behaviors that are *maladaptive*—ones that interfere with individuals' ability to function normally and to meet the demands of daily life. People suffering from such disorders find it difficult to carry out their work, to interact with friends or strangers, to meet family obligations, or to accomplish the countless small tasks of daily life.

Finally, psychological disorders are associated with behavior that is evaluated negatively by the members of a particular society. In other words, persons suffering from such disorders often behave in ways that are viewed as objectionable or unacceptable by the people around them. Of course, ideas about what forms of behavior are acceptable and what forms are unacceptable can and often do vary between cultures, and can also change greatly within the same culture over time. For example, when I was in college in the early 1960s, a young man who pierced his ears and wore two or more earrings would have been viewed as strange indeed. Today, such adornments hardly receive a second glance on most campuses; what might have been labeled as weird or abnormal in the 1960s is nothing out of the ordinary today.

Taking these points into account, we can define psychological disorders as *patterns of behavior and thought that are atypical, that are viewed as undesirable or unacceptable within a given culture, that are maladaptive, and that usually (although not always) cause the persons who demonstrate them considerable distress.* As I have already noted, such problems are far from rare. In fact, recent surveys indicate that perhaps as many as half of all human beings experience a psychological disorder at some point during their lives (Kessler, 1994; Robins & Regier, 1991). Fortunately, this need not be cause for alarm; as we will see in chapter 13, many effective techniques for dealing with such difficulties exist and can greatly reduce their negative effects.

In the present chapter, we'll consider a number of different psychological disorders. Before turning to specific disorders, however, it's essential to com-

Psychological Disorders: Behaviors or thoughts that are unusual in a given society, that are maladaptive, and that cause the persons who experience them considerable distress.

plete two preliminary tasks. First, we'll review contrasting perspectives on the nature of psychological disorders and indicate how views concerning such disorders have changed over the centuries. Second, we'll examine a widely used system for diagnosing various psychological disorders—the *DSM-IV*. After that, we'll turn to psychological disorders themselves, considering both the symptoms they produce and potential causes for their occurrence.

CHANGING CONCEPTIONS OF PSYCHOLOGICAL DISORDERS: *A Brief Historical Perspective*

*A*re psychological disorders a product of the stress and turmoil of modern life? Existing evidence suggests that, in fact, such disorders existed long before the dawn of civilization. Stone Age skulls containing neatly drilled holes have been uncovered by archaeologists in Europe and South America. One colorful explanation for such operations, known as **trephining**, is that they were performed in order to permit the escape of evil spirits that, it was believed, were causing certain people to behave in bizarre ways (Maher & Maher, 1985). However, it is also possible that such operations were performed simply to treat various types of head injuries. The fact that most skulls showing trephining are those of adult males—the members of primitive societies most likely to be injured by accidents or warfare—suggests that this less colorful interpretation may actually be correct. Still, there is indirect evidence that psychological disorders existed even in the distant past, and that people in primitive societies attempted to deal with these problems as best they could.

FROM DEMONS TO DISEASE: *Changing Concepts of Abnormal Behavior*

While the precise meaning of the holes in ancient skulls is open to interpretation, the earliest written descriptions of psychological disorders are clear as to the causes of these maladies: They lay the blame for such disorders squarely on supernatural forces. In societies ranging from China to ancient Babylon, possession by demons or evil spirits was the explanation commonly accepted for bizarre forms of behavior.

This view of abnormal behavior persisted into the fifteenth and sixteenth centuries. Indeed, even during the Renaissance, a period of dazzling advances in European art, music, and science, the supernatural theory endured. It was during the fifteenth and sixteenth centuries—the heart of the Renaissance—that more than 100,000 people in Europe were convicted of being witches and executed for their supposed crimes (Deutsch, 1949). While some of these executions were probably carried out for political or economic reasons, it appears that many of the victims were persons whose only crime was bizarre or unusual behavior stemming from psychological problems.

Gradually, however, the scientific approach emerged. This led many scholars and physicians to search for the roots of abnormal behavior in natural causes. The result was a shift toward the idea that psychological disorders are a form of illness or disease, a perspective that remains highly influential today.

Learning Objective 12.1
Know the definition and general characteristics of psychological disorders and describe how the concept of "abnormal" behavior has changed over time.

TREPHINING: EARLY TREATMENT FOR PSYCHOLOGICAL DISORDERS?

Stone Age skulls with neatly drilled holes may provide an example of early psychological treatment—or they may be the result of medical procedures for treating various types of head injuries.

Trephining: *An ancient surgical procedure in which holes are cut into the skull.*

HUMANE TREATMENT OF PEOPLE WITH PSYCHOLOGICAL DISORDERS

Until the eighteenth century, people suffering from psychological disorders were subject to harsh conditions. Philippe Pinel was one reformer who introduced more humane procedures in a large Paris hospital, with very positive results.

Learning Objective 12.2
Discuss the biological/medical perspective, the psychodynamic perspective, and the modern psychological approach to psychological disorders.

Medical Perspective: The view that psychological disorders have a biological basis and should be viewed as treatable diseases.

Psychiatry: A branch of medicine that focuses on the diagnosis and treatment of psychological disorders.

THE BIOLOGICAL/MEDICAL PERSPECTIVE: *Psychological Disorders as Disease*

Prior to the eighteenth century, persons suffering from mental disorders were often subjected to harsh "treatment." Patients in so-called mental hospitals were shackled to walls in dark, unlighted cells that they were never permitted to leave. Sanitation was primitive or nonexistent, and little if any attention was paid to diet.

But change was in the wind. Disturbed by these conditions, Jean-Baptiste Pussin, superintendent of a large hospital in Paris, established new and more humane rules for the treatment of inmates. No beatings were allowed, and patients who had been chained for years were freed from their shackles in the hope that they would become more manageable. Many *did* respond favorably to this improved treatment, so the reforms were continued by Philippe Pinel, who became chief physician of the hospital's ward for the mentally ill in 1793. Like Pussin, Pinel believed that psychologically disturbed persons were suffering from a form of illness, and that moving them from dungeons to bright, sunny rooms and treating them with kindness rather than violence would help them to recover. The results were impressive: Many patients (those, we must assume, who were less seriously disturbed) responded to this new treatment with rapid improvements. Indeed, many recovered to the point where they could be released—some after decades of confinement.

Similar actions by enlightened physicians in other nations produced parallel encouraging results. The view that abnormal behavior is the result of *mental illness* gradually gained in strength until it was, at least in Western nations, the dominant approach. This **medical perspective** remains highly influential today. Indeed, it is the basis for the field of **psychiatry**, a branch of modern medicine specializing in the treatment of psychological disorders.

Within psychology, there is less emphasis on abnormal behavior as a disease and more on its potential *biological* or *biochemical bases* (e.g. Cromwell, 1992; Heinrichs, 1993). Evidence suggests that changes in the structure or functioning of the brain may play an important role in several forms of abnormal behavior (Raz, 1993). It also appears that the tendency to develop some psychological disorders may be inherited (Faraone, Kremen, & Tsuang, 1990). Thus, while many psychologists prefer to avoid describing psychological disorders in strictly medical terms—as diseases requiring treatment—they do accept the view that such disorders often involve or stem from biological causes.

THE PSYCHODYNAMIC PERSPECTIVE: *Desires, Anxieties, and Defenses*

A very different perspective on abnormal behavior was offered by Freud and several other important figures in the history of psychology. According to this *psychodynamic perspective*, which we discussed in detail in chapter 10, many mental disorders can be traced to unconscious urges or impulses and to the struggle over their expression that takes place in the hidden depths of human personality. Remember that in Freud's theory the *id* (repository of our primitive desires) demands instant gratification, while the *superego* (conscience) denies it. The *ego* (consciousness) must strive to maintain a balance between these forces.

According to Freud, mental disorders arise when the ego, sensing that it may soon be overwhelmed by the id, experiences *anxiety*. To cope with such anxiety, the ego employs different *defense mechanisms*, as described in chapter 10. These serve to disguise the nature of the unacceptable impulses and so reduce the anxiety experienced by the ego; but they may also generate maladaptive behavior.

While few psychologists currently accept Freud's views about the origins of psychological disorders, his suggestion that unconscious thoughts or impulses can play a role in abnormal behavior remains influential. Thus, in this respect, the psychodynamic perspective has contributed to our modern understanding of abnormal behavior.

THE MODERN PSYCHOLOGICAL APPROACH: *Recognizing the Multiple Roots of Abnormal Behavior*

"Mental illness" is a term that makes some psychologists uneasy. Why? Because it implies acceptance of the medical model described above. To call an individual "mentally ill" implies that her or his problems constitute a disease that can be cured through appropriate medical treatment. In one respect, this view makes sense: As I have noted, many psychological problems do seem to have a biological basis. In another sense, though, the medical perspective is somewhat misleading. Decades of research suggest that full understanding of many psychological disorders requires careful attention to *psychological* processes such as learning, perception, and cognition, *plus* recognition of the complex interplay between environmental influences and heredity that seems to affect all forms of behavior.

For example, consider what is perhaps the most common form of psychological disorder—*depression*—which involves intense sadness, lack of energy, and feelings of hopelessness and despair. What are the roots of this complex problem? Evidence suggests that biochemical and genetic factors probably play an important role (Henriques & Davidson, 1990). But so do cognitive and social factors. As we'll see in more detail later in this chapter, depressed persons seem to process information about the external world differently from nondepressed persons; they are, for example, much more likely to notice negative information (Segal, 1988) and to hold unfavorable perceptions of themselves and others (Gara et al., 1993). Taking account of these factors adds appreciably to our understanding of the nature of depression and also suggests effective new ways of treating this disorder.

Finally, most psychologists also attach considerable importance to *social* or *cultural factors* in their efforts to understand abnormal behavior. Some disorders—especially those that are quite severe—appear to be universal, occurring in all or most cultures (Al-Issa, 1982). Others, however, vary greatly across cultures in terms of frequency, severity, and precise form. For example, depression appears to be more common in Western nations than in Asian ones (Kleinman, 1986). Moreover, some disorders seem to be restricted to specific cultures. In isolated rural areas of Japan, for instance, some individuals suffer from a disorder known as *kitsunetsuki*—the belief that they are possessed by foxes; this problem is largely unknown elsewhere. While the role of biological factors should not be overlooked in such disorders, it seems likely that

CULTURAL FACTORS AND ABNORMAL BEHAVIOR

Normal behavior in one culture may be considered abnormal in another. The Ashura ritual, practiced in the Middle East, involves self flagellation, a behavior that many other cultures would consider abnormal.

cultural beliefs, values, and conditions play a key role in their occurrence and specific form.

In sum, as the modern psychological perspective on abnormal behavior suggests that such problems can best be understood in terms of complex and often subtle interactions between biological, psychological, and sociocultural factors. This perspective is certainly more complex than one that views such disorders as biologically produced mental illnesses. However, as we'll discover in later sections of this chapter, it is probably also considerably more accurate. Please see the **Key Concept** page for an overview of contrasting perspectives on abnormal behavior.

KEY QUESTIONS

- How were psychological disorders viewed in the past?

- What is the modern psychological view of such disorders?

IDENTIFYING PSYCHOLOGICAL DISORDERS: The DSM-IV

Learning Objective 12.3
Describe the features of the DSM-IV and discuss how it differs from previous versions.

No physician would attempt to treat a common cold through surgery or internal injuries with a Band-Aid. The first and often most crucial step in medical practice is *diagnosis*—identifying the nature of the problem that brought the patient to the doctor's office in the first place. Even if we do not choose to view psychological disorders as medical illnesses, the need to identify such problems in a clear and reliable manner remains. Without an agreed-upon system of *classification*, different psychologists or psychiatrists might refer to the same disorder with different terms or might use the same term to describe very different problems (Millon, 1991).

Recognizing these issues, the American Psychiatric Association has for many years published guides for the diagnosis of mental disorders. These guides or manuals are primarily *descriptive* in nature; they are designed to help practitioners recognize and correctly identify (diagnose) specific disorders. The most recent edition of this guide is the **Diagnostic and Statistical Manual of Mental Disorders-IV** (or *DSM-IV* for short) (American Psychiatric Association, 1993). The major diagnostic categories of the DSM-IV are shown in Table 12.1 (on page 452). Within the manual, hundreds of specific disorders are described. These descriptions focus on observable features and include *diagnostic features*—symptoms that must be present before an individual is diagnosed as suffering from a particular problem. In addition, the manual includes information on *associated features and disorders*—clinical features that are frequently associated with the disorder but not considered essential to its diagnosis; *associated laboratory findings* and *physical examination signs*—biological factors associated with the condition; and information on *age-related*, *culture-related*, and *gender-related features*—variations in each disorder that may be related to age, cultural background, and gender.

Another important feature of the DSM-IV is that it classifies disorders along five *axes*, rather than merely assigning them to a given category. One of these (Axis I) relates to major disorders themselves. Another (Axis II) relates to what are known as *personality disorders*—maladaptive aspects of personality that exert powerful effects on individuals' behavior and lives. (We'll return to this topic in a later section.) A third axis pertains to general medical conditions relevant to each disorder, while a fourth axis considers psychosocial and environmental problems that may affect the diagnosis, treatment, or prognosis of various disorders. Finally, a fifth axis relates to a global assessment of current functioning. By evaluating people along these various axes,

✓*Diagnostic and Statistical Manual of Mental Disorders-IV (DSM-IV): The latest version of a manual widely used for diagnosing various psychological disorders.*

Contrasting Perspectives on Abnormal Behavior

Supernatural View

Abnormal behavior stems from supernatural causes—possession by demons, evil spirits, goddesses, or gods. This view was popular in ancient times, lost favor in the civilizations of Greece and Rome, and then had a resurgence during the Middle Ages.

Some evidence indicates that many of the persons burned at the stake during the fifteenth and sixteenth centuries because they were thought to be witches were actually suffering from psychological disorders.

Psychodynamic View

Abnormal behavior stems from hidden inner forces: conflict between unconscious impulses and aspects of personality that restrain them. This view, which was strongly supported by Freud, remains influential today.

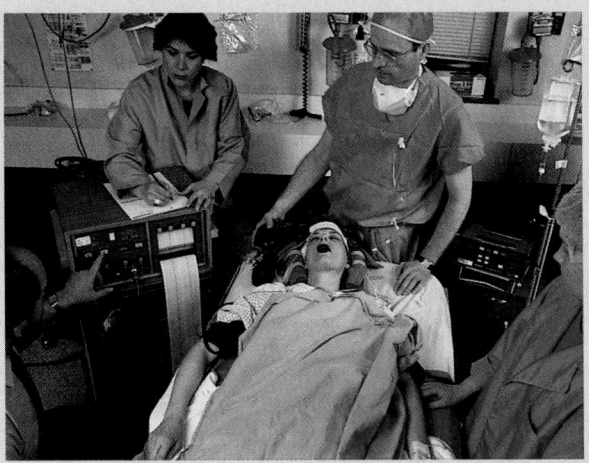

Medical Model

Abnormal behavior is a treatable disease that, like other diseases, stems from biological causes. This perspective serves as the foundation for the field of psychiatry.

Electroconvulsive therapy, which involves the delivery of strong shocks to the patient's head, reflects the view that psychological disorders stem primarily from biological causes.

Modern Psychological View

Abnormal behavior stems from multiple causes. These include *psychological factors* such as learning, perception, and cognition; *sociocultural factors;* and *biological factors.* This view is more complex than earlier perspectives on psychological disorders, but most psychologists believe that it provides a more accurate account of the nature and origins of such problems.

TABLE 12.1

**Major Diagnostic
Categories of the DSM-IV**

The DSM-IV classifies psychological
disorders according to the categories listed here.

DIAGNOSTIC CATEGORY	EXAMPLES
Disorders usually first diagnosed in infancy, childhood, or adolescence	Mental retardation, learning disorders, disruptive behavior
Delerium, dementia, and other cognitive disorders	Disturbance of consciousness
Mental disorders due to a general medical condition	Delerium due to a high fever
Substance-related disorders	Alcohol dependence, amphetamine dependence, cocaine-use disorders
Schizophrenia and other psychotic disorders	Schizophrenia, delusional disorder
Mood disorders	Depression, bipolar disorders
Anxiety disorders	Panic attacks, agoraphobia
Somatoform disorders	Somatization disorder, conversion disorder
Factitious disorders	Intentional feigning of symptoms
Dissociative disorders	Dissociative amnesia, dissociative fugue, dissociative identity disorder (multiple personality disorder)
Sexual and gender identity disorders	Sexual desire disorders, sexual arousal disorders, paraphilias
Eating disorders	Anorexia nervosa, bulimia nervosa
Sleep disorders	Primary insomnia, nightmare disorder
Impulse control disorders not elsewhere classified	Intermittent explosive disorder, kleptomania, pathological gambling
Adjustment disorder	Development of emotional or behavioral symptoms in response to an identifiable stressor
Personality disorders	Paranoid personality disorder, schizoid personality disorder, antisocial personality disorder
Other conditions that may be a focus of clinical attention	Medication-induced movement disorders, problems related to abuse or neglect

the DSM-IV offers a fuller and more sophisticated picture of individuals' current psychological condition than earlier systems of diagnosis.

How does the DSM-IV differ from earlier versions of the DSM? In several important respects. Perhaps most important, it is the first version of the DSM to which psychologists have had major input (Barlow, 1991). Partly as a result of this fact, and partly as a result of changes within psychiatry, strenuous efforts were made to base the DSM-IV more firmly than ever on empirical evidence concerning the nature and prevalence of psychological disorders. Thus, the task force of psychiatrists, psychologists, and other professionals who worked on this new version drew heavily on published studies and re-analysis of existing data in order to refine descriptions of each disorder. The task force also conducted special field trials in which they compared new descriptions and categories with existing ones to determine if proposed changes would indeed improve the reliability of diagnosis—the consistency with which specific disorders could be identified. On the basis of these procedures, many changes were made in the DSM-IV—changes intended to assist psychiatrists and psychologists in accurately recognizing, and therefore effectively treating, a wide range of psychological disorders.

Additional changes in the DSM-IV reflect efforts to take fuller account of the potential role of cultural factors in psychological disorders. Information on these changes is presented in the **Perspectives on Diversity** section. One further point: it is important to realize that the DSM-IV merely describes various disorders; it makes no attempt to explain them. This is deliberate, for the DSM-IV is designed to be neutral with respect to theories about the origins of psychological disorders. But since psychology, as a science, seeks *explanation*, not simply description, many psychologists view this aspect of the DSM-IV as a shortcoming that limits its value.

PERSPECTIVES ON DIVERSITY

Taking Account of Cultural Factors in Psychological Disorders: Improvements in the DSM-IV

There is little doubt that some psychological disorders take much the same form throughout the world. Depressed persons, for example, demonstrate negative moods, lack of energy, and feelings of hopelessness no matter where they happen to live and regardless of the specific cultural group to which they belong. But in many cases, cultural factors *are* reflected in psychological disorders in important ways. The specific symptoms shown by individuals, the terms in which they describe their discomfort, and even the frequency of various types of disorder can differ appreciably from one culture to another (American Psychiatric Association, 1993). This is an important point, because the DSM-IV, like earlier versions of the DSM, will be used all over the world, and with persons from highly diverse backgrounds and societies (Maser, Kaelber, & Weise, 1991). Thus, it is crucial that professionals using the DSM be aware of and sensitive to these cultural differences.

The DSM-IV attempts to foster this crucial awareness in several different ways. First, a new section of the description of each disorder focuses on *culturally related features*. Culturally specific symptoms, ways of describing distress, and similar information are included whenever available. This information is designed to help professionals recognize the many ways in which an individual's culture can influence the form of psychological disorders.

Second, certain disorders that seem to appear only in specific cultures are described where they are relevant. For example, do you remember *kitsunetsuki*—the belief, among certain villagers in rural areas of Japan, that they are possessed by foxes? Such disorders are included in the descriptions of various psychological disorders to which they seem to be related. Third, a new appendix describes culture-bound disorders. As stated by the task force charged with developing the DSM-IV: "It is hoped that these new features will increase sensitivity to variations in how mental disorders present in different cultures and will reduce the possible effect of unintended bias stemming from the clinician's own cultural background" (American Psychiatric Association, 1993, p. A:11).

This is a valuable goal, because some evidence suggests that a psychologist's or psychiatrist's cultural background *can* sometimes influence clinical judgment. In the past, most research designed to uncover *clinical bias* focused on *overpathologizing*—the tendency to perceive women, blacks, and other disadvantaged groups as being more disturbed than they actually are. Such research yielded little evidence for this type of bias (e.g., Abramowitz & Murray, 1983). However, more recent research has examined clinical diagnoses for

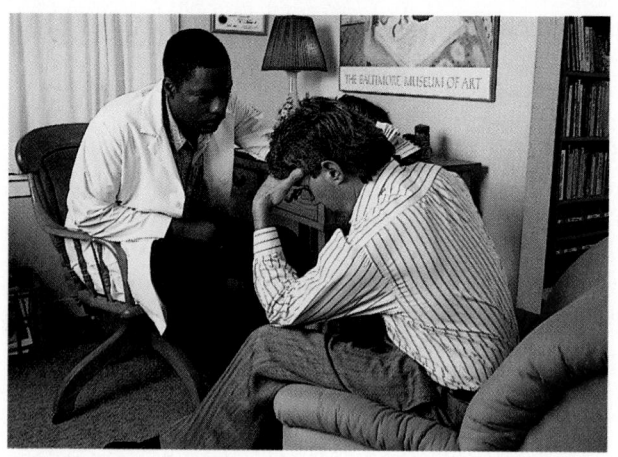

CULTURE AND THE DIAGNOSIS OF PSYCHOLOGICAL DISORDERS

Clinical judgments about psychological disorders can be influenced by cultural factors, including differences in ethnic or racial background between therapists and clients. Such factors are given increased attention in the DSM-IV.

signs of an opposite form of bias—a tendency to diagnose members of nonmale, nonwhite groups as showing *less* disturbance than they actually do. For example, depression may be perceived as more "normal" among women than among men, and drug abuse may be perceived as more "normal" among blacks than among whites, with the result that these disorders (depression and substance abuse) are perceived as less serious than they actually are, or are less likely to be recognized when they do in fact exist.

In recent research applying this broadened definition of clinical bias, Lopez (1989) has found considerable evidence for its existence. These findings suggest that important clinical judgments can sometimes be influenced by culture gaps between psychologists or psychiatrists and the persons they seek to help. Certainly such effects don't often arise from overt prejudice or bias on the part of clinicians; rather, they probably stem from the influence of unconscious assumptions or the kind of errors in memory and judgment we encountered in chapters 6 and 7. Whatever their origins, however, culturally related errors in the diagnosis of psychological disorders can have adverse effects on persons belonging to disadvantaged groups—persons who need all the help they can get. Thus, efforts to increase cultural sensitivity in the DSM-IV and other diagnostic procedures seem to be necessary as well as timely.

DESCRIBING PSYCHOLOGICAL DISORDERS: An Explanatory Note

As I mentioned earlier, the DSM-IV lists and describes literally hundreds of different psychological disorders. All of these are important, but space limitations make it impossible to cover all of them here. Instead, therefore, we'll focus on those disorders that are most common and hence have received most attention in systematic research by psychologists. In discussing these disorders, I'll generally follow the order in which they are described in the DSM-IV, with one major exception: I'll reserve discussion of what is in some ways the most serious disorder, *schizophrenia*, for a final section.

KEY QUESTIONS

• What is the DSM-IV?

• In what ways is it an improvement over earlier versions?

MOOD DISORDERS: *The Downs and Ups of Life*

*E*veryone experiences swings in mood or emotional state—these are a normal part of life. For most people, extreme moods are short-lived; most of the time, they find themselves somewhere in between feelings of elation and of sadness or despair. But in contrast to this typical pattern, some persons experience disturbances in mood that are both extreme and prolonged. Their highs are higher, their lows are lower, and the periods they spend at these emotional heights and depths are lengthy. Such persons are described as suffering from **mood disorders**, which the DSM-IV describes under two major categories: depressive disorders and bipolar disorders.

DEPRESSIVE DISORDERS: *Probing the Depths of Despair*

Unless we lead a truly charmed existence, our daily lives bring some events that make us feel sad or disappointed. An unexpectedly poor grade, breaking up with one's lover or spouse, failure to get a promotion or a raise—these and countless other events tip our emotional balance toward sadness. When do such reactions constitute depression? Most psychologists agree that several criteria are useful for reaching this decision.

First, persons suffering from **depression** experience truly profound unhappiness, and they experience it much of the time. Second, persons experiencing depression report that they have lost interest in all the usual pleasures of life. Eating, sex, sports, hobbies—all fail to provide the enjoyment and satisfaction people expect and, usually, derive from them. Third, persons suffering from depression experience major loss of energy. Everything becomes an effort, and feelings of exhaustion are common. Additional symptoms of depression include loss of appetite, followed by actual loss of weight; disturbances of sleep; difficulties in thinking—depressed people are indecisive and find that they cannot think, concentrate, or remember; recurrent thoughts of death; feelings of worthlessness or excessive guilt; and frequent feelings of agitation. As one depressed person described it:

> I began not to be able to manage . . . the kinds of things I really had always been able to do easily, such as cook, wash, take care of the children, play games. . . . Another thing that was frightening to me was that I couldn't read any more. And if awakened early, I sometimes would lie in bed two hours trying to make myself get up. . . . Then when I did, I felt that I couldn't get dressed. And whatever the next step was, I felt I couldn't do that either . . . (Educational Broadcasting Corporation, 1975).

When individuals experience five or more of these symptoms at once, they are classified by the DSM-IV as showing a *major depressive episode*.

Unfortunately, depression is all too common. It is by far the most frequent type of psychological disorder, although, for reasons that are not yet entirely clear, it is considerably more common among women than among men (Nolen-Hoeksema, 1987).

BIPOLAR DISORDERS: *Riding the Emotional Roller-Coaster*

If depression is the emotional black hole of life, then **bipolar disorder** is its emotional roller-coaster. People suffering from bipolar disorder experience wide swings in mood. They move, over varying periods of time, between deep depression and an emotional state known as *mania*, in which they are extremely excited, elated, and energetic. During manic periods, such persons speak rapidly, show a sharply decreased need for sleep, jump from one idea or activity to another, and show excessive involvement in pleasurable activities that have a high potential for painful consequences; for example, they may engage in uncontrolled buying sprees or make extremely risky investments. Clearly, bipolar disorders are very disruptive not only to the individuals who experience them but to other people in their lives as well.

Mood Disorders: Psychological disorders involving intense and prolonged mood shifts.

Depression: A psychological disorder involving intense feelings of sadness, lack of energy, and feelings of hopelessness and despair.

Bipolar Disorder: A mood disorder involving swings between depression and mania.

THE CAUSES OF DEPRESSION: Its Biological and Psychological Roots

Depression and other mood disorders tend to run in families (Egeland et al., 1987). Thus, if one identical twin experiences depression, the other has a substantial (perhaps as much as 40 percent) chance of developing a similar disorder. In contrast, among nonidentical twins, who don't share all of the same genes, this figure drops to 20 percent (Kolata, 1986).

Other findings suggest that mood disorders may involve abnormalities in brain biochemistry. For example, it has been found that levels of two neurotransmitters, *norepinephrine* and *serotonin,* are lower in the brains of depressed than in those of nondepressed persons. Similarly, levels of such substances are higher in the brains of persons demonstrating mania. Further, when persons who have recovered from depression undergo procedures that reduce the levels of serotonin in their brains, their depressive symptoms return within twenty-four hours (Delgado et al., 1990). Finally, drugs that produce depression as a side effect—such as reserpine, used in the treatment of high blood pressure—tend to reduce concentrations of norepinephrine, while drugs that counter depression act to increase brain levels of norepinephrine (Whybrow et al., 1984).

Unfortunately, this relatively neat picture is complicated by the following facts: Not all persons suffering from depression show reduced levels of norepinephrine or serotonin; and not all persons demonstrating mania have increased levels of these neurotransmitters. In addition, drugs used to treat both types of disorders produce many effects in addition to changing the presence or activity of these neurotransmitters. At present, then, it is clear that biological factors play a role in depression, but the precise nature of these effects remains to be determined.

While growing evidence indicates that depression involves subtle changes in biochemical processes, additional findings point to the importance of psychological mechanisms in this disorder. One of these is known as **learned helplessness** (Seligman, 1975). When individuals are exposed to situations in which they cannot control their own outcomes, they often develop negative expectancies: They conclude that nothing they do really matters and that no actions on their part will permit them to avoid unpleasant outcomes. It is a short step from such beliefs to serious feelings of depression.

An important addition to this learned-helplessness view of depression concerns individuals' *attributions* about the causes behind such lack of control (Abramson, Seligman, & Teasdale, 1978; Alloy et al., 1988). According to this modified theory, sometimes known as the *hopelessness model,* depression is related not simply to the belief that one cannot influence one's outcomes, but also to the tendency to attribute unfavorable events to stable internal causes. In other words, when negative events happen to depressed persons, they take the blame for their occurrence; they attribute the events to their own lasting shortcomings, such as lack of intelligence, laziness, poor judgment, and so on (Seligman et al., 1988).

Another factor that appears to play a crucial role in depression is the negative views that depressed persons seem to hold about themselves (Beck, 1976; Beck et al., 1979). Individuals suffering from depression seem to possess negative **self-schemas**—negative conceptions of their own characteristics, abilities, and behavior. As a result of negative self-schemas, depressed persons tend to be exquisitely sensitive to negative information about themselves; for example, negative feedback from others (Bradley & Mathews, 1983). This, in turn, often leads them excessively to seek reassurance from others that those persons "truly care" about them. As you can readily guess, these repeated

√Learned Helplessness: *Feelings of helplessness that develop after exposure to situations in which nothing individuals do affects their outcomes. Learned helplessness appears to play a role in the occurrence of depression.*

Self-Schemas: *Cognitive frameworks that serve to organize information about the self.*

456 CHAPTER 12

requests for reassurance can be annoying, and so tend to backfire: Ultimately, they lead to increased *rejection* by others—precisely the outcome depressed persons want to avoid (Joiner, Alfano, & Metalsky, 1993).

In addition to holding negative views about themselves, depressed persons often seem to hold negative views about others, too. This fact is illustrated very clearly by a study conducted recently by Gara and his colleagues (1993). In this investigation, both depressed and nondepressed persons were asked to describe nine people in their lives: mother, father, a significant other, three other people important to them, and three acquaintances who were less important. Then participants were asked to describe ten different aspects of their self-image: "me as I actually am," "how I am with my father," "how I am with my mother," and so on for the nine persons they described earlier. Finally, they were asked to rate themselves and each of the nine people in terms of attributes they mentioned in their descriptions.

On the basis of this information, Gara and his colleagues constructed measures of the extent to which individuals described themselves and others in positive or negative terms. It was predicted that the depressed persons would describe both themselves and others more negatively than the nondepressed persons, and as you can see from Figure 12.1, this is precisely what occurred.

Finally, depressed persons are prone to several types of faulty or distorted thinking (Persad & Polivy, 1993). For example, they tend to dwell on and amplify the importance of negative events while ignoring and minimizing the importance of positive outcomes. As a result, they often show better memory for failures and other unpleasant events than for successes or other ego-boosting experiences (Kuiper, Olinger, & MacDonald, 1987). In sum, several psychological mechanisms and tendencies seem to play a key role in depression.

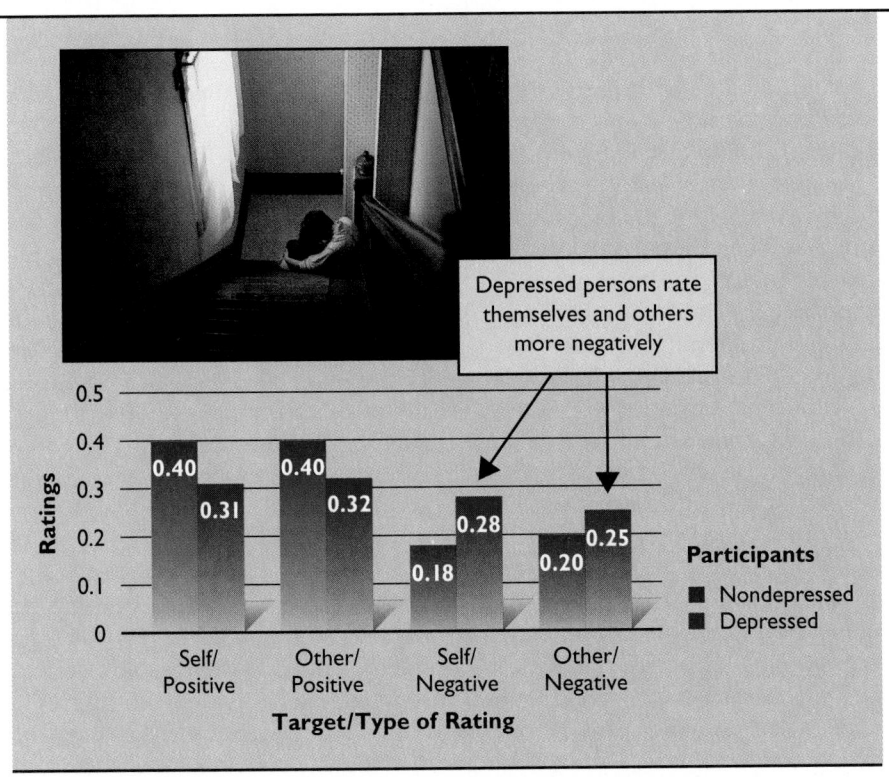

Depression: Negative Views of the Social World

Depressed persons reported more negative views of themselves and of other persons in their lives than did nondepressed persons.
(*Source:* Based on data from Gara et al., 1993.)

SUICIDE: *When Life Becomes Unbearable*

Hopelessness, despair, negative views about oneself and others—these are some of the hallmarks of depression. Given such reactions, it is not surprising that many persons suffering from this disorder seek a drastic solution to their problems—**suicide**. While not all persons who attempt or actually commit suicide are deeply depressed, a large percentage of them are (Goodstein & Calhoun, 1982). And given that depression is the most common psychological disorder, this translates into alarmingly large numbers. For example, in the United States, more than two million persons have attempted suicide—almost 1 percent of the entire population. And many persons who attempt suicide succeed in carrying it out. Suicide is the tenth or eleventh most frequent cause of death in the United States, and among young persons aged fifteen to twenty-four it actually ranks *second* in this respect, behind only accidents. More than three times as many women as men attempt suicide, but men more frequently succeed in ending their own lives. This difference stems from the fact that the two sexes use different methods. Men are more likely to use a gun or jump off a building, while women tend to use less certain methods, such as overdoses of sleeping pills or slashing their wrists. Suicide rates also vary with age and by nation. The highest suicide rates occur among older people, but suicide has been on the rise among young people for several decades and is now disturbingly high even among teenagers.

Can suicide be predicted? While there are no hard and fast rules for determining who may choose this path or when they may make the attempt, there do appear to be several important warning signs. First, suicide often seems to occur not when individuals are in the depths of despair—most depressed—but rather when they show some improvement. Apparently, deeply depressed persons lack the energy or will to commit suicide. When they feel somewhat better, however, they become capable of this act. Another clue to suicidal plans involves a period of calm following considerable agitation; the person may have made his or her decision and now feels calm or even relieved that an end to the suffering is in sight.

Additional, and often highly useful, clues to potential suicide are provided by cognitive factors. For example, persons who are seriously contemplating suicide report fewer and weaker reasons for living than do others (Steede & Range, 1989). Perhaps even more surprising, they also report different patterns of thoughts about death and its effects. When people contemplate their own deaths, they report several distinct types of fear relating to this event: fear of loss of self-fulfillment (it will bring an end to their plans); fear of self-annihilation or of loss of social identity (they will be forgotten by others); fear of consequences to their family; and fear of the unknown. Some findings indicate that persons who have actually attempted suicide report roughly equal fear of each of these outcomes (Orbach et al., 1993). In contrast, individuals who have not attempted suicide report contrasting levels of fear for these components: They are most frightened of loss of self-fulfillment and of the unknown, and least frightened about loss of social identity.

CAUSES OF SUICIDE: CONTRASTING PERSPECTIVES   Why, precisely, do some individuals choose to end their own lives? As noted previously, only *some* depressed persons adopt this course of action; so depression itself can be only part of the answer. Several different theories have been offered to account for suicide. Freud contended that suicide stems from the *death instinct*, an urge to return to nothingness, which he believed to be part of our basic biological heritage.

Suicide: *The act of taking one's own life.*

458   CHAPTER 12

A sharply different explanation of suicide, and one more consistent with the principles and findings of modern psychology, has been offered by Baumeister (1990). He suggests that suicide is the result of efforts by individuals to escape themselves—or, more accurately, to escape from awareness of their own faults and shortcomings. A considerable amount of evidence lends support to this newer view of suicide. For example, persons who attempt or actually commit suicide have been found to have less favorable views of themselves than others. Similarly, other evidence suggests that many persons who commit suicide are indeed in a state of heightened self-awareness. For instance, the notes left by suicides mention themselves more often than the notes left by people who are facing involuntary death—through disease or executions (Hull et al., 1983). Finally, the fact that persons who have attempted suicide report roughly equal fear of all aspects of death is also consistent with this view. Baumeister suggests that in the final stages, people trying to escape from themselves enter a state in which they don't bother to invest much mental effort in thinking about the consequences of suicide. Viewing all aspects of death as equally frightening is suggestive of such a "low mental effort" pattern.

In sum, considerable evidence is consistent with the view that suicide sometimes, and to some degree, stems from efforts by individuals to escape from a self they can no longer bear. However, other factors, too, probably play a role, for suicide is too complex—and too drastic—an action to be explained by one or even a few basic causes.

KEY QUESTIONS

- What are the major symptoms of depression? Of bipolar disorders?
- What factors seem to play a role in the occurrence of mood disorders?
- What are important warning signs of suicide?

ANXIETY DISORDERS: *When Dread Debilitates*

At one time or another we all experience **anxiety**—increased arousal accompanied by generalized feelings of fear or apprehension. If such feelings become very intense and persist for long periods of time, however, they can produce harmful effects. Such **anxiety disorders** take several different forms.

PANIC ATTACK: *The Body Signals "Danger!" But Is It Real?*

Have you ever experienced *panic*—very high levels of physical arousal coupled with the intense fear of losing control? If you have, don't worry: Almost everyone has had this experience at some time or other. But persons who suffer from a psychological condition known as **panic attack disorder** experience such reactions often, and sometimes without any specific triggering event. Such attacks can involve all or several of the following symptoms: pounding heart, chest pains, nausea, dizziness, trembling or shaking, fear of losing control or going crazy, chills, hot flashes, and numbness.

For some persons, panic attacks occur out of the blue—without any apparent cause. For others, however, they are linked with specific situations. In that case, panic disorder is associated with **agoraphobia**—intense fear of specific situations in which, individuals fear, they will experience panic attacks. Common patterns for agoraphobia include fear of being in a crowd; standing in a line; being on a bridge; traveling in a bus, train, or car; or merely leaving home (American Psychiatric Association, 1993). Persons suffering from such

Anxiety: Increased arousal accompanied by generalized feelings of fear or apprehension.

√Anxiety Disorders: Psychological disorders that center on the occurrence of anxiety and include generalized anxiety, phobias, and obsessive-compulsive disorders.

√Panic Attack Disorder: Anxiety disorder characterized by relatively brief periods during which individuals experience unbearably intense anxiety.

√Agoraphobia: Fear of losing control and experiencing a panic attack in specific situations, such as in open places, in a crowd, or on an airplane.

MUNCH'S *THE SCREAM*

This famous painting seems to evoke the feelings associated with panic attack disorder.

Learning Objective 12.7
Know the characteristics and potential causes of panic attacks and phobias.

Learning Objective 12.8
Describe the obsessive-compulsive disorder and the posttraumatic stress disorder.

Learning Objective 12.9
Discuss the research concerning how anxious persons may differ in how they use their information-processing capacity.

Obsessive-Compulsive Disorder: Anxiety disorder in which an individual is unable to stop thinking the same thoughts or performing the same ritualistic behaviors.

disorders often experience anticipatory anxiety—they are terrified of becoming afraid! I have a good friend who suffers from one form of agoraphobia: He is totally unwilling to travel by airplane. Since he has an active career, this condition causes him great difficulties. He has to drive or take trains even to distant locations. Yet he resists all suggestions that he seek professional help. Apparently the mere thought of discussing his problem is so anxiety-provoking that he prefers to leave matters as they are, despite the inconvenience and discomfort he is experiencing.

What causes panic attacks? Existing evidence indicates that both biological factors and conditioning play a role (Barlow, 1988, 1992; Clark, 1988). For example, some persons have a tendency to view their own emotions as unpredictable and uncontrollable. As a result, when they experience panic, they also experience anxiety that the panic will be repeated. This anxiety in itself may lead to additional panic attacks. The result: a vicious circle of panic–anxiety–panic–anxiety is established. Other findings indicate that persons suffering from panic disorder process threatening information differently than do other individuals; in particular, they seem more likely to notice and remember words (e.g., "madness," "choke," "faint," etc.) or other stimuli related to panic (Becker, Rinck, & Margraf, 1994). So, cognitive factors, too, seem to play a role.

Phobias: Fear That Is Focused

Most people will express some fear of snakes, heights, violent storms, and buzzing insects such as bees or wasps. Since all of these can pose real threats to our safety, such reactions are adaptive, up to a point. Some persons, though, experience intense anxiety when in the presence of these objects or even when they merely think about them. Such *phobias* can be so strong that they interfere with everyday activities. Thus, persons suffering from animal phobias may avoid visiting friends who own dogs or may cross the street to avoid passing a person walking a pet. Similarly, those with *social phobias*—fear of social situations—may avoid a wide range of situations in which they fear they will be exposed to and scrutinized by unfamiliar persons.

What accounts for such strong and irrational fears? One possibility involves the process of *classical conditioning*, described in chapter 5. Through such learning, stimuli that could not initially elicit strong emotional reactions can often come to do so. For example, consider the case of an individual who has a snake phobia. Perhaps as a child he witnessed one of his playmates actually being bitten by a snake. Although he himself experienced no harm, he reacted to the intense fear of his friend with strong arousal. The snake, a stimulus that was previously fairly neutral, now came, through classical conditioning, to evoke a similar reaction. (As you can readily see, observational learning, too, played a role in this example.) As we saw in chapter 5, classical conditioning is especially likely to occur with respect to certain stimuli: ones for which we are biologically *prepared* to acquire associations. Thus, phobias directed toward pencils, rabbits, and palm trees are virtually nonexistent, while those toward snakes and spiders are much more common.

Obsessive-Compulsive Disorder: Behaviors and Thoughts outside One's Control

Have you ever left your home, gotten halfway down the street, and then returned to see if you really locked the door or turned off the stove? Most of us have had such experiences, and they are completely normal. But for some persons, such anxieties are so intense that the individuals become trapped in repetitive behaviors known as *compulsions* that they seem unable to prevent, or in recurrent modes of thought called *obsessions*. Consider the following description of a person suffering from an **obsessive-compulsive disorder** of this kind:

> When George wakes in the morning . . . he feels that his hands are contaminated so he cannot touch his clothing. He won't wash in the bathroom because he feels that the carpet is contaminated. . . . I have to dress him, having first cleaned his shoes and got out a clean shirt, underclothes, socks and trousers. He holds his hands above his head . . . to make sure that he doesn't contaminate the outside of his clothing. Any error or mishap and he will have to have clean clothes. . . . George then goes downstairs, washes his hands in the kitchen and thereafter spends about twenty minutes in the toilet. . . . Basically he has to be completely sure that there is no contamination around because if he is not then he will start to worry about it later on . . . (Rachman & Hodgson, 1980, pp. 66–67).

What is the cause of such reactions? We all have repetitive thoughts occasionally. For example, after watching a film containing disturbing scenes of violence, we may find ourselves thinking about these over and over again. Most of us soon manage to distract ourselves from such unpleasant thoughts. But individuals who develop an obsessive-compulsive disorder are unable to do so. They are made anxious by their obsessional thoughts, yet they can't dismiss them readily from their minds. As a result, they become even more anxious, and the cycle builds. Only by performing specific actions can they ensure their "safety" and reduce this anxiety. Therefore, they engage in complex repetitive rituals that can gradually grow to fill most of their day. Since these rituals do generate reductions in anxiety, the tendency to perform them grows stronger. Thus, unless they receive effective outside help, persons suffering from obsessive-compulsive disorders have little chance of escaping from their anxiety-ridden prisons.

POSTTRAUMATIC STRESS DISORDER

Imagine what it is like to be sleeping in your own bed and then suddenly to be thrown out onto the floor as the ground under your home heaves and shakes. Once awakened, you find yourself surrounded by the sounds of objects, walls, and even entire buildings crashing to the ground—accompanied by shrieks of fear and cries of pain from your neighbors or perhaps even your own family. This is precisely the kind of experience reported by many persons during the California earthquake of 1994.

Such experiences are described as *traumatic* by psychologists because they are extraordinary in nature—and extraordinarily disturbing. It is not surprising, then, that some persons exposed to them experience *posttraumatic stress disorder*—a disorder, as described in chapter 11, in which people persistently reexperience the traumatic event in their thoughts or dreams, persistently avoid stimuli (places, people, thoughts) linked with the trauma, and persistently experience symptoms of increased arousal such as difficulty falling asleep, irritability, or difficulty in concentrating. Posttraumatic stress disorder can stem from

NATURAL DISASTERS: ONE CAUSE OF POSTTRAUMATIC STRESS DISORDER

When individuals live through natural disasters, such as the 1994 California earthquake, they sometimes develop posttraumatic stress disorder.

a wide range of traumatic events—natural disasters, accidents, rape and other assaults, or the horrors of wartime combat (Pitman et al., 1990). For example, survivors of the Khmer Rouge atrocities in Cambodia during the 1970s and 1980s witnessed such events as the murder of their families, men crushing infants by swinging them against trees, and many forms of torture. The result: many developed the symptoms of posttraumatic stress disorder and are still suffering from it many years later (Wilkinson, 1994). To compound their suffering, many persons who have survived atrocities or natural disasters also experience intense guilt; the fact they have survived while those they loved have died weighs heavily on their conscience. Clearly, then, posttraumatic stress disorder is a painful condition.

ANXIETY: *The Role of Subliminal Processing*

For persons suffering from anxiety disorders, the world is often a threatening place. They perceive danger everywhere, in contexts and actions that most people view as quite harmless. Why? What accounts for this distorted view of the physical and social environment? One answer seems to involve a tendency on the part of anxious persons to direct a larger-than-usual portion of their information-processing capacity to anxiety-relevant information. In other words, they "see" danger everywhere because, in a sense, they actively search for it (Mathews, 1990). Many studies offer support for this view, indicating that persons suffering from anxiety disorders are indeed more likely to notice and process information relating to their anxieties (Martin, Williams, & Clark, 1991). And at least one recent investigation, conducted by Mogg and her colleagues (Mogg et al., 1993), suggests that anxious persons are more sensitive than other persons to stimuli relevant to their anxiety even *before* such information has entered conscious awareness, even when it is presented *subliminally*.

To test this possibility, Mogg and her coworkers asked three groups of participants—anxious persons, depressed persons, and normal controls—to perform a color-naming task. Briefly, they asked the participants to name the colors of patches on which words appeared while ignoring the words themselves. In one condition (*subliminal*), the words were shown so briefly that they could not be recognized; indeed, exposure was so brief (14 milliseconds) that participants could not even tell whether a word had been presented. In another (*supraliminal*) condition, in contrast, the words were shown until participants named the color of the background. Some of the words shown were related to anxiety (such as "embarrassed," "candor"), while others were related to depression (such as "misery," "discouraged"). The others were either neutral ("carpet," "domestic") or positive ("adorable," "bliss").

Mogg and her associates reasoned that if anxious persons automatically devote more of their information-processing capacity to anxiety-related words, then anxious participants would respond more slowly than the depressed or control participants on trials when these words were presented. In contrast, neither depressed nor controls would show such effects. This is precisely what happened. Anxious persons responded more slowly to both kinds of negative words—both anxiety-related and depression-related—than the other two groups. Moreover, this was true in both the subliminal and supraliminal condition.

These findings, and those of related studies (e.g., Williams et al., 1988) indicate that persons suffering from anxiety disorder do indeed direct more of their information-processing resources toward threatening information than other persons,

KEY QUESTIONS

- What are anxiety disorders?
- What are panic attacks?
- What are phobias?

even before such information enters conscious awareness. To the extent this is true, it may be difficult to eliminate anxiety through forms of therapy focused on conscious thoughts and reactions. Rather, this underlying tendency to notice threatening information must be overcome, too.

SOMATOFORM DISORDERS: Physical Symptoms without Physical Causes

Several of Freud's early cases, ones which played an important role in his developing theory of personality, involved the following puzzling situation. An individual would show some physical symptom (such as deafness, or paralysis of some part of the body); yet careful examination would reveal no underlying physical causes for the problem. Such disorders are known as **somatoform disorders**—disorders in which psychological conflicts or other problems take on a *somatic,* or physical, form. The DSM-IV recognizes several distinct somatoform disorders.

One of these is known as **somatization disorder**, a condition in which individuals report physical complaints and symptoms that may include aches and pains, problems with their digestive systems, and sexual problems (such as sexual indifference or irregular menstruation). Another is **hypochondriasis**—preoccupation with fears of disease. Such persons do not actually have the diseases they fear, but they persist in worrying about them despite repeated reassurance by their doctors that they are healthy. It is important to note that hypochondriacs are not simply faking; they feel the pain and discomfort they report and are truly afraid that they are about to fall ill.

Another type of somatoform disorder is known as **conversion disorder**. In hypochondria, there are no apparent physical disabilities—just the feeling that they will develop. In conversion disorders, however, there are actual impairments. Individuals suffering from such disorders may experience blindness, deafness, paralysis, or loss of sensation in various body parts. Yet while these disabilities are quite real to the persons experiencing them, there is no underlying medical condition that would produce them.

What is the origin of somatoform disorders? Freud suggested that persons experiencing unacceptable impulses or conflicts converted these into various symptoms. By doing so, they reduced the anxiety generated by the impulses or conflicts, and at the same time gained much sympathy and attention. A behavioral interpretation of these disorders, in contrast, emphasizes the rewards individuals often obtain by adopting the *sick person role.* Being ill elicits sympathy and caring from others, and for some persons these benefits seem to have an irresistible charm. A third interpretation emphasizes cognitive factors, suggesting that individuals who experience somatoform disorders have a tendency to focus excessively on normal bodily sensations and to misinterpret them, attributing them to various serious conditions (Barsky & Wyshak, 1989). Thus, for example, when such persons experience increased heart rate, they interpret this as "I'm having a heart attack" rather than as "I'm excited or nervous," the kind of interpretation most people would adopt. Whatever their origins, somatoform disorders appear to be quite common. It has been estimated that as much as 20 percent of all patients admitted to hospitals may be suffering from symptoms produced by somatoform conditions (Jones, 1980).

Learning Objective 12.10
Describe the different somatoform disorders as well as their possible origins.

KEY QUESTION

• What are somatoform disorders?

✓*Somatoform Disorders:*
Category of disorders in which psychological conflicts or other problems take on a physical form.

Somatization Disorder: A psychological condition in which individuals report physical complaints and symptoms, including aches and pains, problems with their digestive systems, and sexual problems such as sexual indifference or irregular menstruation.

✓*Hypochondriasis: A psychological disorder in which individuals convert anxiety into chronic preoccupations with their health and bodily functions.*

✓*Conversion Disorder: Psychological disorder in which individuals experience real motor or sensory symptoms for which there is no known organic cause.*

DISSOCIATIVE DISORDERS:
When Memory Fails

Learning Objective 12.11
Know the meaning of "dissociative disorder" and the different types of this disorder.

*H*ave you ever awakened during the night and, just for a moment, been uncertain about where you were? Such temporary disruptions in our normal cognitive functioning are far from rare; many persons experience them from time to time as a result of fatigue, illness, or the use of alcohol or other drugs. Some individuals, however, undergo much more profound and lengthy losses of identity or memory. These are known as **dissociative disorders** and, like several other psychological disorders, can take several different forms.

In chapter 6, we saw that *amnesia*—loss of memory—can sometimes be produced by illnesses or injuries to the brain. Sometimes, however, amnesia seems to occur in the absence of any clear-cut physical cause. This **dissociative amnesia** appears to stem from the active motivation to forget. After experiencing some traumatic event, violating their own standards, or undergoing intense stress, individuals sometimes go blank with respect to these events and cannot recall them. Such amnesia can involve all events within a particular period of time (*localized amnesia*) or only some events occurring during this period (*selective amnesia*). Alternatively, it can erase memories for a person's entire life prior to a specific date (*generalized amnesia*). While individuals suffering from such disorders truly cannot remember past events, many aspects of their behavior remain intact: habits, tastes, previously learned skills. Musicians can continue to play their instruments, computer programmers can still operate computers, and beauticians can still give permanents; they may not remember that they once earned a living through such activities, however.

A second type of dissociative disorder is known as **dissociative fugue**. This is a sudden and extreme disturbance of memory in which individuals wander off, adopt a new identity, and are unable to recall their own past. Newspapers often report accounts of individuals who simply vanish one day, only to reappear years later in a new location living a new life—often with a new spouse and family.

Such reactions can truly be described as *dissociative* in nature, for they seem to represent disorders in which some portion of memory is split off, or dissociated, from conscious awareness. Please see the **Point of It All** section for discussion of another form of dissociative disorder.

KEY QUESTIONS

- What are dissociative disorders, such as dissociative amnesia?
- What is dissociative identity disorder?

THE POINT OF IT ALL

Dissociative Identity Disorder: Multiple Personalities in a Single Body?

*P*erhaps the most dramatic form of dissociative disorder is **dissociative identity disorder**, a condition labeled *multiple personality disorder* in earlier versions of the DSM. In this rare disorder, a single person seems to possess two, three, or even many distinct personalities. Some of these personalities are dominant, and alternately take control of the person's behavior. In addition, persons suffering from this type of dissociative disorder report selective amnesia: Information retained by one personality is not necessarily available to the others.

A dramatic illustration of dissociative identity disorder is provided by the case of William Milligan, a man arrested in 1977 for the rapes of three women. Milligan was identified by two of the victims, and his fingerprints matched those at the scene of one of the crimes, so it appeared to be an open-and-shut case. Only when he twice attempted suicide was he examined by psychiatrists. The results of their examinations were remarkable, to say the least. Milligan appeared to possess not one or two distinct personalities but at least *ten*. One was "Billy" Arthur, an emotionless Englishman who dominated the others. A second was Ragen, a powerful Yugoslavian. Additional personalities included Tommy, a belligerent teenager; Christene, a three-year-old English girl; and Christopher, her disturbed thirteen-year-old brother. On the basis of psychiatric testimony concerning his disorder, Milligan was found not guilty by reason of insanity—a legal category suggesting that he was not responsible for his actions. Thus, he was sent for treatment to a mental health center, where it was discovered that he had still more personalities, including a thug with a Brooklyn accent, a practical joker, and, surprisingly, a social snob! Milligan underwent treatment in a state facility for several years and was released when his separate personalities appeared to fuse. After his release he worked for a child-abuse prevention agency and later developed a career as an artist (Kihlstrom, Tataryn, & Hoyt, 1993).

Another bizarre case of dissociative identity disorder came to light some years ago when a multiple-personality patient accused a man she had dated, Mark Peterson, of rape. She claimed that only one of her personalities had given consent. Another had watched the event, and still another went to the police to report the assault. Peterson was convicted under a law that makes having sexual intercourse with a mental patient equivalent to rape (Kihlstrom et al., 1993).

These and other striking cases of dissociative identity disorder raise an intriguing question: Is multiple personality genuine—a real form of psychological disorder? Or are persons like William Milligan merely clever fakers? No final answer to this question currently exists. Some evidence, however, suggests that there is more to multiple personality than simple faking: Persons showing this disorder sometimes demonstrate distinctive patterns of brain activity when each of their supposedly separate personalities appear (Kaplan & Sadock, 1991). Similarly, each personality often scores differently on standardized personality tests (Kaplan & Sadock, 1991). Even the need for eyeglasses, or being right- or left-handed, may vary among different personalities.

Interestingly, dissociative identity disorder is nine times more common in women than men (Putnam, 1991; Putnam et al., 1986). Its causes have not yet been clearly identified, but many persons suffering from this disorder report that they experienced traumatic events, such as physical or sexual abuse, early in life (Ross et al., 1990). This has led to the suggestion that perhaps such persons use multiple personalities as a means of distancing themselves from the painful realities of their early lives. Unfortunately, it is often very difficult to determine whether reports of early sexual or physical abuse are accurate: Many years have passed since these events supposedly took place (Kihlstrom et al., 1993). And, as noted in our discussion of *repressed memories* in chapter 6, the seeds for some reports of such experiences may actually be planted by unwary therapists who mention this possibility to their patients (Loftus, 1993). For this reason, this interpretation of the origins of multiple personality must be viewed mainly as an intriguing but as yet unverified possibility. Whatever its specific origins, however, one fact is clear: Dissociative identity disorder is one of the most bizarre forms of psychological disorder studied—and treated—by psychologists.

MULTIPLE PERSONALITY: REAL OR FRAUD?

William Milligan, a convicted rapist, appeared to possess more than ten distinct personalities, including the one whose writing appears here. Although many cases of multiple personality (now termed *dissociative identity disorder*) are faked, others do appear to represent genuine psychological disorders.

√**Dissociative Disorder:** *Psychological disorder in which individuals experience profound and lengthy losses of identity or memory.*

√**Dissociative Amnesia:** *Amnesia for which there is no organic cause.*

√**Dissociative Fugue:** *Form of dissociative amnesia in which individuals forget their identity and virtually all of their past life.*

Dissociative Identity Disorder: *Multiple personality disorder, in which a single individual seems to possess more than one personality.*

SEXUAL AND GENDER IDENTITY DISORDERS

Learning Objective 12.12
Survey the different types of sexual disorders and gender identity disorders.

As we saw in chapter 10, Freud believed that many psychological disorders can be traced to disturbances in *psychosexual development*—our progression through a series of stages in which our quest for pleasure is centered on different parts of the body and different activities. While this theory is not currently accepted by most psychologists, there is little doubt that problems relating to sexuality and gender identity constitute an important group of psychological disorders. Several of these are considered below.

SEXUAL DYSFUNCTIONS: *Disturbances in Desire and Arousal*

Sexual dysfunctions comprise disturbances in sexual desire, sexual arousal, and/or the ability to attain orgasm. Such problems are classified according to when, in the normal pattern of sexual activity discussed in chapter 9, they occur. **Sexual desire disorders** involve a lack of interest in sex or active aversion to sexual activities. Persons suffering from these disorders report that they rarely have the sexual fantasies most persons generate, that they avoid all or almost all sexual activity, and that these reactions cause them considerable distress.

In contrast, **sexual arousal disorders** involve the inability to attain or maintain an erection (males) or the absence of vaginal swelling and lubrication (females). *Orgasm disorders* involve the delay or absence of orgasm in both sexes, and may also include *premature ejaculation* (reaching orgasm too quickly) in males.

PARAPHILIAS: *Disturbances in Sexual Object or Behavior*

What is sexually arousing? For most people, the answer has to do with the sight or touch of another human being—one they find sexually attractive. But human beings may also be aroused by other stimuli, too. Many men report that they find certain types of women's lingerie arousing. Similarly, members of both sexes are sometimes aroused by specific aromas—perfumes or other scents they associate with past enjoyable sexual experiences (Levine & McBurney, 1982). Still others find that either inflicting or receiving some slight pain increases their arousal and sexual pleasure. Do such reactions constitute sexual disorders? According to most psychologists they do not. Such disorders are indicated only when unusual or bizarre imagery or acts are *necessary* for sexual arousal. In other words, **paraphilias** (from the Greek *para*, meaning "amiss," and *philia*, meaning "love") may be said to exist only when unusual images, acts, or objects are required for sexual arousal and fulfillment.

Several types of paraphilias exist. In *fetishes*, individuals become aroused exclusively by inanimate objects. Often these are articles of clothing, such as shoes or underwear; in more unusual cases they can involve human waste, dirt, animals, or even dead bodies. *Frotteurism*, another paraphilia, involves fantasies and urges focused on touching or rubbing against a nonconsenting person. The touching, not the coercive nature of the act, is what persons with this disorder find sexually arousing. Perhaps more disturbing is *pedophilia*, in which individuals experience sexual urges and fantasies involving sexual activity with children, generally ones younger than thirteen. When such urges are translated into overt activity, the effects on the young victims can, of course, be devastating. Two other paraphilias are *sexual sadism* and *sexual*

Sexual Desire Disorders: Psychological disorders involving a lack of interest in sex or active aversion to sexual activities.

Sexual Arousal Disorders: Psychological disorders involving inability to attain an erection (males) or absence of vaginal swelling and lubrication (females).

✓*Paraphilias:* Sexual disorders involving choices of inappropriate sexual objects, such as young children, or the inability to experience arousal except in the presence of specific objects or fantasies.

PARAPHILIA	DESCRIPTION/SYMPTOMS
Exhibitionism	Sexual urges or arousing fantasies involving exposure of one's genitals to an unsuspecting stranger
Voyeurism	Recurrent sexual urges or arousing fantasies involving the act of observing an unsuspecting person who is naked, disrobing, or engaging in sexual activity
Transvestic fetishism	Intense sexual urges and arousing fantasies involving cross-dressing (dressing in the clothing of the other sex)
Other paraphilias	Telephone scatologia (lewdness) Necrophilia (sexual arousal to corpses) Zoophilia (sexual contact with or fantasies concerning animals)

TABLE 12.2

Paraphilias

Paraphilias—disorders in which unusual or bizarre imagery or acts are necessary for sexual arousal—take many different forms. A few are listed here.

masochism. In the former, individuals become sexually aroused by inflicting pain or humiliation on others. In the latter, they are aroused by receiving such treatment. Looking back, I now realize that one of my friends in college probably suffered from a mild form of sexual sadism; he frequently stated that hurting his girlfriends in some manner turned him on. It's interesting to note that he never lacked for willing partners, even in the (supposedly) repressed early 1960s. See Table 12.2 for other paraphilias.

GENDER IDENTITY DISORDER

Have you ever read about a man who altered his gender to become a woman, or vice versa? Such individuals feel, often from an early age, that they were born with the wrong sexual identity. They are often displeased with their bodies and request—again, often from an early age—medical treatment to alter their primary and secondary sex characteristics. In the past there was little that medicine could do to satisfy these desires on the part of persons suffering from *gender identity disorder.* However, advances in surgical techniques have made it possible for such persons to undergo *sex-change operations,* in which their sexual organs are altered to approximate those of the other sex. Before their operations these individuals receive extended counseling, learning the mannerisms of the other gender, how to wear its clothes, and so on; then the operations are performed. Several thousand individuals have undergone such operations, and evidence indicates that most report being satisfied with the results and happier than they were before (Green & Fleming, 1990). However, follow-up studies suggest that some of these persons experience regrets and continued unhappiness, sometimes to the point that they commit suicide or experience serious psychological disorders (Abramowitz, 1986). So it appears that such operations have a serious potential "downside" that should be carefully considered.

KEY QUESTIONS

- What are sexual disorders?
- What is gender identity disorder?

Learning Objective 12.13
Compare and contrast the characteristics of the two most common types of eating disorders.

EATING DISORDERS

*I*n our discussion of motivation (chapter 9), we encountered two serious **eating disorders**: *anorexia nervosa* and *bulimia nervosa*. These disorders are very common at the present time and adversely affect the health and well-being

Eating Disorders: *Serious disturbances in eating habits or patterns that pose a threat to individuals' physical health and well-being.*

ANOREXIA NERVOSA

People who suffer from anorexia nervosa often starve themselves to the point where their health is seriously endangered. What societal factors play a role in this disorder?

of millions of young persons. Thus, it seems important to return to these disorders here and to expand somewhat on the earlier discussion.

As you will recall, anorexia nervosa is a disorder in which individuals, intensely fearful of being or becoming "fat," literally starve themselves, failing to maintain a normal body weight. In contrast, bulimia nervosa involves episodes of binge eating followed by various forms of compensatory behavior designed to avoid weight gain—such as self-induced vomiting or overuse of laxatives. As noted in chapter 9, both of these eating disorders are much more common among females than among males (Hinsz & Williamson, 1987). Both disorders seem to stem at least in part from dissatisfaction with one's personal appearance and efforts to match the thin-is-in model promoted strongly in the mass media (Thompson, 1992; Williamson, Cubic, & Gleaves, 1993).

While both of these disorders are disturbing, bulimia nervosa is perhaps, the more puzzling of the two. Typical bulimics report purging about twelve times per week. How can persons with this disorder stand the repeated binge-purge cycles that they adopt as a basic aspect of their daily lives? One possibility is that as a result of their repeated purging, bulimics experience reduced taste sensitivity (Ramirez & Bartoshuk, 1987). This, in turn, makes vomiting less unpleasant, or at least more bearable. In fact, research by Rodin and her colleagues (1990) supports this reasoning: Persons suffering from bulimia nervosa do indeed show reduced taste sensitivity relative to other persons.

The research on bulimia nervosa, then, suggests that it is even more complex than was at first assumed. Social pressures to be slim may indeed contribute to its initiation, but once it is established, changes in the sense of taste may strengthen its occurrence and permit it to continue. One implication of these findings seems clear: Effective treatment for bulimia nervosa must include attention to sensory factors as well as to strong cultural pressures to be, and remain, slim.

KEY QUESTIONS

- What are anorexia nervosa and bulimia nervosa?
- What factors play a role in the occurrence of these disorders?

PERSONALITY DISORDERS:
Traits That Prove Costly

*H*ave you ever known someone who was highly suspicious and mistrustful of others in virtually all situations? Someone who had no close friends and was a true loner in all respects? Someone who showed a strong need to be taken care of by others, coupled with a dependent, clinging approach to relationships? If so, you may have already met people with **personality disorders**. Such persons possess specific personality traits (recall our discussion of traits in chapter 10) that are inflexible and maladaptive and cause them major difficulties in many respects. Personality disorders, in other words, are longstanding habits of thought and behavior that color an individual's whole life and also impair it, by making the person unhappy, interfering with his/her functioning, or both. More formally, personality disorders can be defined as extreme personality variation associated with the failure to achieve the universal tasks of establishing a personal identity, forming attachments to others, experiencing intimacy with them, and seeking affiliation (Livesley et al.,

Personality Disorders:
Extreme personality variation associated with the failure to achieve the universal tasks of establishing a personal identity, forming attachments to others, experiencing intimacy with them, and seeking affiliation.

1994). Many such disorders exist; but since the DSM-IV combines these into several major categories, we'll follow this pattern here.

Learning Objective 12.14
Know the characteristics of the paranoid, schizoid, and antisocial personality disorders.

PARANOID AND SCHIZOID PERSONALITY DISORDERS: *Cut Off from Human Contact*

From time to time, we all feel as though others are out to get us and that they can't be trusted. For persons suffering from **paranoid personality disorder**, however, such feelings are pervasive. They suspect that virtually everyone around them is trying to deceive or take advantage of them in some way. Consistent with this tendency, they perceive hidden, threatening meanings in ordinary remarks and bear strong grudges for these imaginary slights or injuries. I once had a very frightening experience with such a person. He was a coworker at one of the summer jobs I had in college, and he was convinced that everyone in the office was out to get him. For some reason he singled me out as the source of all these imaginary plots, and he threatened me with dire consequences. "Don't worry," he muttered through gritted teeth, "You'll get *yours!*" I think he meant what he said, because one evening he followed me home from work, clenched fists at his side. He didn't do anything that night, but I was relieved when, a couple of days later, he was arrested for assaulting a neighbor—another person he was convinced was engaged in deadly plots against him.

A related pattern is shown by persons suffering from **schizoid personality disorder**. They are truly detached from the social world, showing little interest in friendships, love affairs, or any other kind of intimate contact with other persons. They are indifferent to praise and criticism and often show emotional coldness and detachment. In short, contact with other persons is of little interest to them, and they often tend to perceive the people around them as mere nuisances, obstacles to the goals they wish to reach—without others' help, of course!

THE ANTISOCIAL PERSONALITY DISORDER

The personality disorder that has received by far the most attention is one known as the **antisocial personality disorder**. Individuals with this disorder show an almost total disregard for the rights and well-being of others. In addition, they demonstrate several characteristics that make them dangerous to others. Rules and regulations are not for them, so they often have a history of antisocial behavior: delinquency, theft, vandalism, lying, drug abuse, and the like. They are often irritable and aggressive, highly impulsive, seemingly fearless in the face of danger, and highly deceitful—they will lie to anyone, anytime, if they perceive this as advantageous. And after performing actions that harm others, they typically show no remorse.

The impulsiveness shown by such persons, coupled with several of their other traits, often lends a random, seemingly purposeless character to their antisocial behavior. Thus, the crimes committed by people with this disorder often seem to lack any rational purpose or goal. For example, consider the following chilling statement by Gary Gilmore, a convicted multiple murderer:

> I pulled up near a gas station I told the service station guy to give me all his money. I then took him to the bathroom and told him to kneel down and then I shot him in the head twice. The guy didn't give me any trouble but I just felt like I had to do it.

Why did Gilmore kill this innocent victim? He had no idea—and he didn't care. Because of their almost total lack of feelings of responsibility, individuals

Paranoid Personality Disorder: A personality disorder in which individuals feel that others are out to get them and cannot be trusted.

Schizoid Personality Disorder: A personality disorder in which individuals become almost totally detached from the social world.

✓*Antisocial Personality Disorder:* A personality disorder involving a lack of conscience and sense of responsibility, impulsive behavior, irritability, and aggressiveness.

showing the antisocial personality disorder engage unhesitatingly in actions other persons only daydream about: They walk off jobs if they get bored, readily desert spouses and children, and simply disappear when debts mount. For such persons, the term *obligation* has little if any meaning. Little wonder, then, they often become petty thieves, confidence artists, pimps, drug pushers, and prostitutes.

What are the origins of this pattern? What factors lead some individuals to develop this disturbing collection of traits? This is a complex issue, and existing evidence suggests that many factors probably play a role. From a behavioral perspective, such persons may learn as children, through exposure to violent models, that impulsive, aggressive behavior is appropriate: After all, the adults and older children they see around them regularly engage in such actions. As noted in our discussion of aggression (see chapter 9), such **modeling** influences can exert powerful effects on behavior (Bandura, 1986).

Cognitive factors, too, may play a role. Persons showing the antisocial personality disorder may fail to acquire the kinds of *schemas*, or cognitive frameworks, that help other persons to regulate their own behavior—schemas relating to impulse control, a sense of responsibility, and the reciprocal nature of human relationships.

Finally, growing evidence suggests that individuals suffering from the antisocial personality disorder may show weaker emotional reactions to negative stimuli—stimuli relating to the possibility of punishment, pain, or imminent danger—than do other persons (Ogloff & Wong, 1990; Patrick, Bradley, & Lang, 1993). For example, in one recent study (Patrick, Cuthbert, & Lang, 1994), male prisoners were asked to imagine neutral scenes (e.g., "I am relaxing on my living room couch") or fearful scenes (e.g., "Taking a shower,

Modeling: A basic learning process in which individuals acquire new behaviors by observing others and then put these into action.

TABLE 12.3	**PERSONALITY DISORDER**	**DESCRIPTION**
Personality Disorders As shown here, *personality disorders* take a wide range of forms.	Borderline personality disorder	Instability in interpersonal relationships, self-image, and moods. Relationships often alternate between idealization and devaluation of others.
	Histrionic personality disorder`	Excessive emotionality and attention seeking, beginning in early adulthood. Discomfort when not center of attention; inappropriate seductive or provocative behavior; exaggerated expression of emotion.
	Narcissistic personality disorder	Grandiosity in fantasy and behavior, coupled with need for admiration and lack of empathy. A grandiose sense of self-importance and preoccupation with fantasies of unlimited success, brilliance, or beauty.
	Avoidant personality disorder	Social inhibition, feelings of inadequacy, and hypersensitivity to negative evaluation. Unwillingness to get involved with people in new interpersonal situations.
	Dependent personality disorder	Excessive need to be taken care of, leading to submissive and clinging behavior and fears of separation. Difficulty expressing disagreement with others; feeling of discomfort and helplessness when alone.

alone in the house, I hear the sound of someone forcing the door and I panic"). While the prisoners were imagining these scenes, their physiological reactions were recorded, and the reactions of prisoners suffering from the antisocial personality disorder were compared with those of prisoners not suffering from this disorder. Results were clear: The control group of prisoners showed much higher arousal in response to the fearful scenes than to the neutral scenes. In contrast, this difference was much smaller among prisoners suffering from the antisocial personality disorder. In the light of these and related findings, it is hardly surprising that persons with this disorder often act in a reckless manner: they simply don't experience the high levels of fear that dangerous situations tend to evoke in most of us. (Please see Table 12.3 for a description of several other personality disorders.)

KEY QUESTIONS

- What are personality disorders?
- What characteristics and behaviors are shown by persons suffering from the antisocial personality disorder?

SCHIZOPHRENIA: *Out of Touch with Reality*

All of the disorders we've considered cause distress for the persons who experience them. Yet for the most part these persons can continue with their lives. Like people loaded down with lead weights, they toil and suffer, but generally can struggle on somehow. In contrast, individuals afflicted with **schizophrenia** are so disturbed that they usually cannot live ordinary lives. Indeed, in many cases, they must be removed from society, at least temporarily, for their own protection and to undergo treatment. Schizophrenia means "split mind," and modern definitions of the disorder reflect this meaning: All agree that it is a very serious disorder involving profound distortions of thought, perceptions, and affect (mood). What is the nature of schizophrenia? What are its major causes? These are the questions we'll now examine.

Learning Objective 12.15
Know the general nature and subtypes of schizophrenia as well as the major symptoms and origins of this disorder.

THE BASIC NATURE OF SCHIZOPHRENIA

Schizophrenia involves severe disruptions in virtually all aspects of psychological functioning. As noted recently by Heinrichs (1993, p. 221), schizophrenia depletes the mind's resources, just as severe brain damage depletes these resources. But while persons suffering from brain damage experience a world that is stripped of its meaning in many respects, those suffering from schizophrenia experience a world that has become, in Heinrich's words, ". . . excessively, terrifyingly rich in semantic possibilities. Instead of an inability to interpret experience, schizophrenia yields spurious experience in the form of hallucinations, or leads to . . . unwarranted interpretations of experience in the form of delusions. Instead of an inability to reason, schizophrenia produces a reasoning that it is so cryptic and obscure, it strikes the observer as incoherent." Let's look more closely at the major symptoms of this serious disorder. But first, one additional point: Although I'll discuss schizophrenia as though it is a single disorder, it's important to note that many experts believe that it may actually involve several different—and distinct—disturbances (Bellak, 1994; Heinrichs, 1993). Please keep this point in mind when we return to potential causes of schizophrenia below.

√**Schizophrenia:** *A group of serious psychological disorders characterized by severe distortions in thought and language, perceptions, and emotion.*

DISTURBANCES OF THOUGHT AND LANGUAGE First, and perhaps foremost, schizophrenics do not think or speak like others. Their words jump about in a fragmented and disorganized manner. There is a loosening of associations, so that one idea does not follow logically from another; indeed, ideas often seem totally unconnected. In addition, schizophrenics often create words of their own—neologisms such as "littlehood" for childhood, or "crimery" for bad actions. Indeed, in extreme cases, their words seem to be totally jumbled into what psychologists term a *word salad*.

These problems, and several others, seem to stem from a breakdown in the capacity for *selective attention*. Normally we can focus our attention on certain stimuli while largely ignoring others. This is not true for schizophrenics. They are easily distracted by anything and everything. Even the sound of their own words may disrupt their train of thought and send them wandering off into a mysterious world of their own creation.

Schizophrenics also frequently suffer from **delusions**—firmly held beliefs that have no basis in reality. Such delusions can take many different forms. One common type is *delusions of persecution*—the belief that one is being plotted against, spied on, threatened, or otherwise mistreated. For example, Leopold Bellak (1994), a scientist who has studied schizophrenia for more than fifty years, describes a female patient who would shout "Here comes Bellak, the Russian spy!" from her window every morning as he approached the hospital building. Another common type is *delusions of grandeur*—the belief that one is extremely famous, important, or powerful. Persons suffering from such delusions may claim that they are the president, a famous movie or rock star, or even Jesus, Mohammed, or Buddha. Finally, schizophrenics also sometimes suffer from *delusions of control*—the belief that other people, evil forces, or perhaps even beings from another planet are controlling their thoughts, actions, or feelings, often by means of electronic devices implanted in or aimed at their brains. As you can see, schizophrenics' ties to reality are tenuous at best, and may seem almost nonexistent in some cases.

DISTURBANCES OF PERCEPTION   Schizophrenics also show many signs of disturbed perceptions. Simply put, they do not perceive the world in the same way as other people do. Many experience **hallucinations** (described in chapter 4): vivid sensory experiences that have no basis in physical reality. The most common type of hallucinations are auditory. Schizophrenics "hear" voices, music, or other sounds that aren't present. Visual hallucinations are also quite frequent; and, again, these experiences can be quite intense. Hallucinations of smells and tastes are sometimes also reported.

In addition, schizophrenics often experience deficits with respect to *social perception*—their ability to recognize the emotions of others (Morrison, Bellack, & Mueser, 1988). For example, they are less successful than normal persons in identifying others' facial expressions and in recognizing others' emotions from the tone of their voices (Kerr & Neale, 1993). However, since schizophrenics are also less successful than normal people in recognizing nonsense syllables and in recognizing faces generally, it appears that their difficulties in social perception reflect more general deficits in perception.

DISTURBANCES OF EMOTION OR MOOD   A third key symptom of schizophrenia involves inappropriate or unusual emotional reactions. Some schizophrenics show almost no emotion at all: They remain impassive in the face of events that evoke strong reactions from others. Others do show emotion, but their reactions are inappropriate. They may giggle when describing a painful childhood experience or when receiving tragic news. In sum, schizophrenics' disturbed patterns of thought, perception, and emotion weaken their grip on reality, and virtually ensure that they will live in a private world largely of their own creation.

✓**Delusions:** *Irrational but firmly held beliefs about the world that have no basis in reality.*

✓**Hallucinations:** *Vivid sensory experiences that occur in the absence of any external stimuli.*

DISTURBANCES OF MOTOR BEHAVIOR A fourth symptom of schizophrenia involves unusual actions. These can take an incredible range of forms, as the following description of a hospital ward for schizophrenics suggests:

> Lou stands hour after hour . . . just rubbing the palm of his hand around the top of his head. Jerry spends his days rubbing his hand against his stomach and running around a post. . . . Helen paces back and forth . . . mumbling about enemies who are coming to get her, while Vic grimaces and giggles over in the corner. . . . Nick tears up magazines, puts bits of paper in his mouth, and then spits them out. . . . Bill sits immobile for hours, staring at the floor . . . (Hagen, 1993).

DISTURBANCES IN SOCIAL FUNCTIONING Given the difficulties outlined above, it is far from surprising that schizophrenics also frequently show seriously impaired social functioning. Their relationships with others deteriorate, and they experience increasing social isolation and withdrawal (Bellack et al., 1990). Further, they show severe deficits in basic social skills, such as solving problems through conversation, compromising with others, and negotiating with them (Bellack et al., 1994). These problems and deficits play an important role in the poor quality of life experienced by most schizophrenics.

POSITIVE VERSUS NEGATIVE SYMPTOMS As you can readily see, schizophrenia is a complex disorder. Are there any underlying dimensions that can help us make sense out of this vast range of diverse symptoms? One dimension that has proved useful—and that has provided insights into the nature of this disorder—divides symptoms into two types. *Positive symptoms* involve the presence of something that is normally absent, such as hallucinations and delusions. *Negative symptoms* involve the absence of something that is normally present and include withdrawal, apathy, absence of emotion, and so on. (These two groups are sometimes referred to as *Type I* and *Type II* schizophrenia, respectively.) Patients with negative symptoms generally have a poorer prognosis: They remain hospitalized longer and are less likely to recover than patients with positive symptoms (Fenton & McGlashan, 1991). In addition, patients with positive and negative symptoms appear to experience different kinds of cognitive deficits. Those with negative symptoms do worse on tests that measure visual and spatial skills; for example, they have more difficulty in recognizing visual stimuli. In contrast, patients with positive symptoms do worse on tests of short-term memory (Braff, 1989). These findings, as well as many others, indicate that there may be two distinct types of schizophrenia; and in fact, many experts believe that there may be several types (Heinrichs, 1993).

SUBTYPES OF SCHIZOPHRENIA

Although all schizophrenics show some of the symptoms outlined above, the overall pattern of these problems differs greatly. Largely on the basis of such differences, schizophrenia can be divided into several subtypes.

PARANOID TYPE As its name suggests, persons in this category have delusions of persecution—they see plots to harm them everywhere. These delusions are sometimes coupled with delusions of grandeur. Thus, such persons may claim that they possess tremendous power or wisdom or maintain that they are a famous figure from history, such as Napoleon, and are being persecuted by dangerous enemies.

CATATONIC SCHIZOPHRENIA

People who suffer from catatonic schizophrenia may remain totally immobile, frozen in a single posture for long periods of time.

DISORGANIZED TYPE Persons suffering from this type of schizophrenia show disorganized speech, disorganized behavior, and flat or inappropriate affect. They are the ones most likely to use neologisms and to produce a word salad. They sometimes have hallucinations or delusions, but these tend to be fuzzy or poorly developed. More common for this type are fits of giggling, making faces, and other childlike behavior.

CATATONIC SCHIZOPHRENIA In some respects this is the most bizarre form of all. Persons suffering from *catatonic schizophrenia* show marked disturbances in motor behavior. Many alternate between total immobility—they sit for days or even weeks frozen in a single posture—and wild, excited activity. In the latter state they sometimes engage in violent behavior, so this condition can be quite dangerous. When immobile, some catatonic schizophrenics show *waxy flexibility*. Their limbs can be moved and remain in the position into which they are arranged. Yet persons suffering from this form of schizophrenia also seem to be aware of the world around them. Sometimes they do not merely refuse requests—they do the opposite.

THE ORIGINS OF SCHIZOPHRENIA

Schizophrenia is certainly one of the most bizarre—and serious—psychological disorders. It is also more common than you might guess: Between 1 and 2 percent of all people in the United States have had or will have a schizophrenic episode during their lives (Robins et al., 1984). What are the causes of this disorder? Systematic research suggests that many different factors play a role.

GENETIC FACTORS Schizophrenia, like several other psychological disorders, tends to run in families. The closer the family relationship between two individuals, the higher the likelihood that if one develops schizophrenia, the other will show this disorder too (Nicole & Gottesman, 1983); see Figure 12.2.

FIGURE 12.2

Family Relationship and Schizophrenia

The more closely two individuals are related, the greater the likelihood that if one develops schizophrenia, the other will too. This finding suggests that genetic factors play a role in the occurrence of schizophrenia. (The babies shown here are the Genain quadruplets, a classic example of genetic influence.)

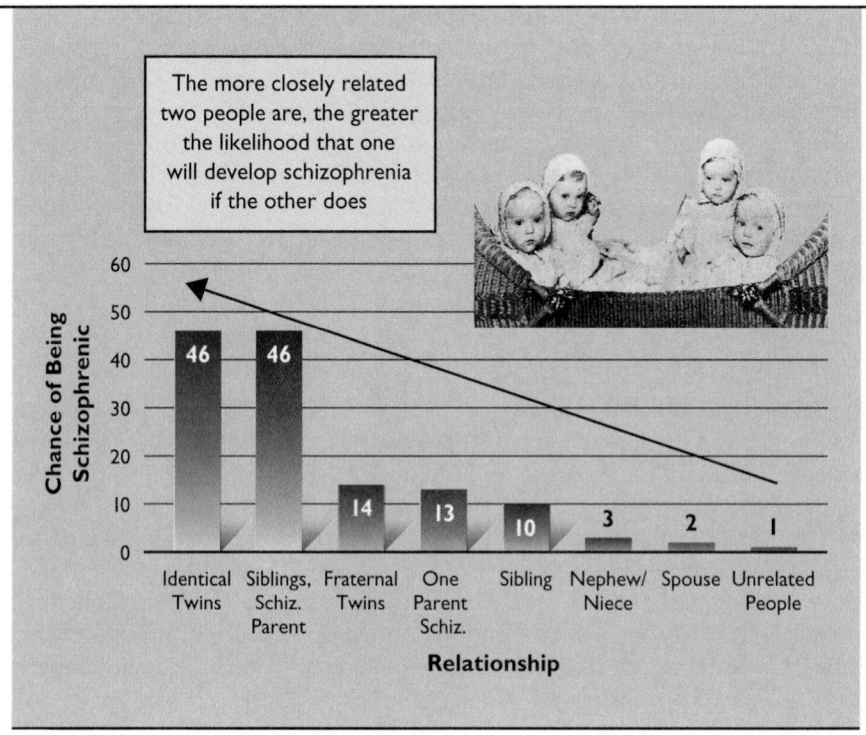

The more closely related two people are, the greater the likelihood that one will develop schizophrenia if the other does

Evidence suggesting that genetic factors play a role in schizophrenia is provided by studies of twins (Kendler & Robinette, 1983). For example, researchers have studied the children of twin pairs in which one twin is schizophrenic and the other is not. Clearly, being raised by a schizophrenic parent is very different from being raised by a nonschizophrenic parent. Thus, if cousins show similar rates of schizophrenia despite this difference, strong evidence for the role of genetic factors would be obtained. In fact, this is just what such studies have shown (Gottesman & Bertelsen, 1989). The rates of schizophrenia among children raised by schizophrenic and nonschizophrenic twins were 16.8 and 17.4 percent, respectively. These and other large-scale studies of twins and families (e.g, Kety, 1988) provide convincing evidence for the importance of genetic factors in schizophrenia.

At this point I should emphasize that what is inherited with respect to schizophrenia is not this disorder itself, but rather a predisposition (a *diathesis*) to develop it under conditions of high environmental stress. In other words, even if an individual is at high risk for developing schizophrenia because of genetic factors, she or he may not do so if the environment in which the person lives is relatively supportive and benign. Only when a genetically inherited predisposition is coupled with stressful conditions does schizophrenia develop. This is known as the **diathesis-stress model** and is accepted by many researchers investigating the nature of schizophrenia.

FAMILY FACTORS As we have already seen, the fact that schizophrenia seems to run in families provides evidence for the role of genetic factors in this disorder. It also raises the possibility that some families create social environments that place their children at risk—environments that increase the likelihood of their developing schizophrenia. What are these environments like? Research findings provide some intriguing answers.

First, it appears that in such families, children are exposed either to high levels of conflict between the parents (*schismatic families*) or to a situation in which all power rests with one parent and calm prevails for this reason (*skewed families*) (Arieti, 1974). Apparently, for at least some children, both conditions are disturbing and increase their risk of developing schizophrenia.

Second, families with a greater than expected incidence of schizophrenia are ones in which patterns of communication are confusing and upsetting to children. Several studies indicate that the families of schizophrenics express high levels of criticism and emotional overinvolvement toward them (e.g., Miklowitz et al., 1989). In short, family members appear to be very concerned about the patients' well-being but, at the same time, are highly critical of them—often, for their illness!

COGNITIVE FACTORS Earlier, we saw that schizophrenics are less accurate than normal people in judging the emotions of others (Kerr & Neale, 1993). Actually, this is just one piece of a larger pattern suggesting that schizophrenia involves—and may partly stem from—deficits in cognitive functioning. First, schizophrenics, especially those with positive symptoms (Type I schizophrenia), show reduced ability to ignore irrelevant or distracting stimuli (e.g., Braff & Geyer, 1990; Elkins, Cromwell, & Asarnow, 1992; Grillon et al., 1990).

In contrast, schizophrenics suffering from negative symptoms (Type II schizophrenia) seem to show opposite problems: They are *under*attentive to external stimuli. For example, they often show weaker than normal *orienting responses*—physiological reactions indicative of attention—when unfamiliar stimuli are presented (Bernstein, 1987).

It appears that schizophrenics experience several kinds of cognitive deficits. Moreover, the precise pattern of these deficits seems to vary with

Diathesis-Stress Model: *A model of schizophrenia suggesting that persons with inherited dispositions to develop this disorder do so only when subjected to stressful environmental conditions.*

their symptoms, and especially with whether these are positive or negative in nature.

BIOCHEMICAL FACTORS Consider the following observations: (1) Large doses of *amphetamines* produce patterns of behavior highly similar, in some respects, to those observed in some types of schizophrenia—for example, delusions of persecution and hallucinations. (2) Amphetamines seem to produce such effects by increasing levels of, or sensitivity to, the neurotransmitter *dopamine*. (3) Drugs effective in treating schizophrenia, such as the phenothiazines, block the brain's receptor sites for dopamine (e.g., Farde et al., 1988). When these observations are combined, it seems reasonable to suggest that schizophrenia may stem, at least in part, from excess activity in those parts of the brain that use dopamine as a neurotransmitter. This is the **dopamine hypothesis** of schizophrenia.

Evidence for this hypothesis is provided by the finding that the brains of deceased schizophrenics show increased dopamine and a higher than normal number of dopamine receptors (Mackay et al., 1982). Further, PET scans of the brains of living schizophrenics have sometimes (though not always) indicated an increased number of dopamine receptors in the limbic system (Wong et al., 1986). Such findings seem to apply primarily to schizophrenics with Type I schizophrenia.

I should hasten to add that while such evidence supports the dopamine hypothesis, not all findings are consistent with it. For example, schizophrenics who show improvement after taking dopamine-blocking drugs improve gradually over a period of about six weeks—not immediately. Yet it takes only a few hours for such drugs to block dopamine receptors within the brain. If schizophrenia resulted solely from dopamine-stimulated activity, the effects of these drugs should be visible very quickly (Pickar, 1988). Similarly, antipsychotic drugs that block the activity of dopamine relieve the symptoms of many serious forms of psychological disorder, not just schizophrenia. These findings suggest that while the dopamine hypothesis may provide important insights into the biochemical nature of schizophrenia, it by no means offers a complete picture of the biochemical imbalances that contribute to this disorder.

BRAIN STRUCTURE Finally, growing evidence suggests that schizophrenia may also stem from subtle but important damage to various portions of the brain. In particular, it appears that among schizophrenics, brain *ventricles*—cavities within the brain containing cerebrospinal fluid—are enlarged relative to those of persons not suffering from this disorder (Raz & Raz, 1990). Moreover, the longer individuals have been hospitalized for schizophrenia, and therefore the more serious their condition, the greater the degree of ventricular enlargement. Such enlargement, which may stem from damage to or atrophy of brain tissue in adjoining areas, seems to be quite general, involving many areas of the brain (e.g., Raz, 1993).

Additional evidence suggests that it is damage in the frontal lobes and in certain subcortical regions (temporal limbic structures) that may be most closely linked to the symptoms of schizophrenia (e.g., Barta et al., 1990; Jernigan et al., 1991). Once again, however, the pattern may be different for persons with Type I and Type II schizophrenia; definite conclusions are not yet possible.

In sum, it appears that genetic factors, certain types of home environments, and brain structure and function may all be related to the occurrence of schizophrenia. It remains for future research to determine the precise manner in which such factors combine to place specific persons at risk for the development of this serious psychological disorder.

Dopamine Hypothesis: The hypothesis that schizophrenia is associated with excess activity in those parts of the brain in which dopamine is the primary neurotransmitter.

476 CHAPTER 12

CHRONIC MENTAL ILLNESS AND THE HOMELESS

In the mid 1990s a visit to the downtown area of almost any large American city can be a shock. Huddled in doorways, sprawled on park benches, clustered around open fires in winter are the *homeless*—people who live on the street, without any permanent home of their own. Such persons are there for many reasons, including economic dislocation and lack of affordable housing, but one important factor is certainly mental illness. Many homeless persons are suffering from schizophrenia, mood disorders, and other serious psychological problems (Burt, 1992). Perhaps as many as one-third previously received care in hospitals, but were released when drug therapy reduced their symptoms. With nowhere to go, they ended up on the streets, where they soon succumbed to the temptations of alcohol and other drugs that were *not* part of their treatment. Given the number of persons released from large state institutions in recent decades (see chapter 13), it is hardly surprising that the ranks of the homeless—and the *chronically mentally ill*—have swelled greatly.

Of course, not all homeless persons fit this description; but enough do to suggest the need for new programs designed to get those in need of psychological help into settings where they can receive it. The cost of doing so may be high, but ignoring this problem in the hope that it will go away by itself does not seem to be either a humane solution or a viable one.

KEY QUESTIONS
• What is schizophrenia?
• What are the major subtypes of schizophrenia?
• What are the origins of schizophrenia?
• What is the relationship between schizophrenia and homelessness?

MAKING PSYCHOLOGY PART OF YOUR LIFE

Preventing Suicide: Some Basic Steps

When terminally ill persons choose to end their lives rather than endure continued pain and suffering, their actions are understandable, even if we disapprove of them on moral or religious grounds. But when young persons whose lives have just begun follow the same route, nearly everyone would agree that the death is tragic. Preventing such suicides is *crucial*. Is there anything you as an individual can do to help prevent suicide? Research findings suggest that there is.

1. *Take all suicide threats seriously.* One common myth about suicide is that people who threaten to kill themselves really won't; only those who tell no one about their plans will actually commit this act. *This is untrue!* Approximately 70 percent of all suicides communicate their intentions to others within a few months of their deaths. Thus, whenever someone talks about suicide, you should take it seriously.

2. *If someone mentions suicide, don't be afraid to discuss it.* Another common myth about suicide—and a dangerous one—is that one should never discuss suicide with another person; this will only add to the person's suicidal tendencies. This belief, too, is false. Encouraging people to talk about such thoughts gets them out into the open and can be helpful. It lets these people know that you are interested, and allows you to gather information you can pass on to counselors and others. So don't be afraid to discuss this matter with potential suicides if it arises.

3. *Recognize the danger signs.* These signs include (a) statements by someone that he or she has no strong or compelling reasons for living; (b) agitation or excitement followed by a period of calm resignation; (c) sudden efforts to give valued possessions away to others; (d) direct statements such as "I don't want to be a burden any more" or "I don't really want to go on living"; (e) revival from a deeply depressed state. If you observe these changes in others, along with other indications that they are contemplating suicide, the situation may well be a serious one.

4. *Discourage others from blaming themselves for failure to attain unrealistic standards.* Many persons who at-

tempt suicide do so because they feel that they have fallen far short of their own expectations and standards. Unfortunately, in many cases, these are unrealistically high—so high that almost no one could hope to attain them. If you hear someone you know criticizing herself or himself for such "failure," try to intervene by pointing out that these standards are exceptionally high, and by calling attention to the person's successes and good points. This may help break a downward cycle that can ultimately lead to thoughts of suicide.

5. *If a friend or family member shows the danger signs described above, don't leave him or her alone.* With rare exceptions, suicide is a solitary act. So if you are concerned that someone you know is seriously contemplating such an action, don't leave him or her alone. If you can't stay with the person, get others to help or bring the person with you.

There are a number of steps you can take to help someone who may be in danger of taking his or her own life.

6. *Most important of all: Get help!* Perhaps the most important point to keep in mind is this: Determining whether someone is at risk for suicide is a complex judgment—one that is difficult even for trained experts. Thus, you should definitely *not* try to make this judgment for yourself. Rather, if you have even the slightest concern that someone you know is seriously thinking of suicide, *seek professional help.* Call a local suicide hot line; or discuss your concerns with a physician, psychologist, counselor, or member of the clergy. And, if possible, try to get the person to seek help from one or more of these sources. Don't be afraid of overreacting. In signal-detection theory terms, this is one of those cases where a miss (failing to notice suicidal tendencies when they are present) is *much* worse than a false alarm (concluding that suicidal tendencies are present when in fact they are not).

Summary and Review of Key Questions

Changing Conceptions of Psychological Disorders: A Brief Historical Perspective

- *How were psychological disorders viewed in the past?*

Psychological disorders were viewed as the result of supernatural forces until well into the eighteenth century. This view was replaced by the medical model, which sees psychological disorders as forms of mental illness.

- *What is the modern psychological view of such disorders?*

Psychologists recognize the importance of biological factors in many forms of abnormal behavior, but they also emphasize the key role of psychological processes, such as cognition and learning, and the impact of sociocultural factors.

Key Terms: *psychological disorders, p. 446; trephining, p. 447; medical perspective, p. 448; psychiatry, p. 448*

Identifying Psychological Disorders: The DSM-IV

- *What is the DSM-IV?*

The DSM-IV—Diagnostic and Statistical Manual of Mental Disorders—is a guide published by the American Psychiactric Association and widely used by mental health professionals. It provides descriptions of a wide range of psychological disorders and associated conditions.

- *In what ways is it an improvement over earlier versions?*

The material in the DSM-IV rests on a firmer basis of published research than did the earlier versions. In addition, it directs increased attention to the impact of cultural factors on psychological disorders.

Key Term: *Diagnostic and Statistical Manual of Mental Disorders, p. 450*

Mood Disorders: The Downs and Ups of Life

- **What are the major symptoms of depression? Of bipolar disorders?**

Persons suffering from depression experience negative moods, reduced energy, feelings of hopelessness, loss of interest in previously satisfying activities, difficulties in sleep, and recurrent thoughts of death. Individuals with bipolar disorders experience wide swings in mood between depression and mania.

- **What factors seem to play a role in the occurrence of mood disorders?**

Mood disorders tend to run in families, so genetic factors play a role. In addition, depression involves disturbances in brain activity and biochemistry. Psychological factors such as learned helplessness, tendencies to attribute negative outcomes to internal causes, and negative perceptions of oneself and others are also involved.

- **What are important warning signs of suicide?**

Individuals are more likely to attempt suicide when they have recovered to some extent from depression than when they are in the depths of despair. Persons contemplating suicide show less concern about certain aspects of death than other persons.

Key Terms: mood disorders, p. 455; depression, p. 455; bipolar disorder, p. 455; learned helplessness, p. 456; self-schemas, p. 456; suicide, p. 458

Anxiety Disorders: When Dread Debilitates

- **What are anxiety disorders?**

Anxiety disorders involve increased arousal accompanied by generalized feelings of fear or apprehension.

- **What are panic attacks?**

Panic attacks involve symptoms of arousal coupled with intense fear—often of losing control in some specific situation.

- **What are phobias?**

Phobias are excessive fears focused on specific objects or situations.

Key Terms: anxiety, p. 459; anxiety disorders, p. 459; panic attack disorder, p. 459; agoraphobia, p. 459; obsessive-compulsive disorder, p. 460

Somatoform Disorders: Physical Symptoms without Physical Causes

- **What are somatoform disorders?**

In somatoform disorders, psychological problems find expression in physical symptoms for which there are no apparent biological causes.

Key Terms: somatoform disorders, p. 463; somatization disorder, p. 463; hypochondriasis, p. 463; conversion disorder, p. 463

Dissociative Disorders: When Memory Fails

- **What are dissociative disorders, such as dissociative amnesia?**

Dissociative disorders involve profound losses of memory or identity. In dissociative amnesia, individuals are unable to remember various events, especially ones they found traumatic or disturbing.

- **What is dissociative identity disorder?**

In dissociative identity (multiple personality) disorder, individuals seem to possess several distinct personalities which alternate in controlling their behavior.

Key Terms: dissociative disorder, p. 465; dissociative amnesia, p. 465; dissociative fugue, p. 465; dissociative identity disorder, p. 465

Sexual and Gender Identity Disorders

- **What are sexual dysfunctions and paraphilias?**

Sexual dysfunctions involve disturbances in sexual desire, sexual arousal, or the ability to attain orgasm. Paraphilias are disturbances in which unusual imagery or acts are necessary for sexual arousal.

- **What is gender identity disorder?**

Persons suffering from gender identity disorder feel that they were born with the wrong sexual identity and seek to change this through medical treatment or other means.

Key Terms: sexual desire disorders, p. 466; sexual arousal disorders, p. 466; paraphilias, p. 466

Eating Disorders

- **What are anorexia nervosa and bulimia nervosa?**

Persons suffering from anorexia nervosa are afraid of being or becoming fat, so they starve themselves and experience dangerous weight loss. Persons suffering from bulimia nervosa engage in repeated cycles of binge eating and purging.

- **What factors play a role in the occurrence of these eating disorders?**

Both anorexia nervosa and bulimia nervosa stem in part from dissatisfaction with one's appearance.

Key Terms: eating disorders, p. 467

Personality Disorders: Traits That Prove Costly

- **What are personality disorders?**

Personality disorders involve traits that are inflexible and maladaptive and cause serious difficulties for the persons who have them.

- *What characteristics and behaviors are shown by persons suffering from the antisocial personality disorder?*

Persons with the antisocial personality disorder show total disregard for the rights of others coupled with reckless behavior, fearlessness, and inability to form close relationships.

KEY TERMS: *personality disorders, p. 468; paranoid personality disorder, p. 469; schizoid personality disorder, p. 469; antisocial personality disorder, p. 469; modeling, p. 470*

SCHIZOPHRENIA: OUT OF TOUCH WITH REALITY

- *What is schizophrenia?*

Schizophrenia is a very serious psychological disorder involving severe disturbances in thought, perception, affect, social relations, and motor behavior.

- *What are the major subtypes of schizophrenia?*

Schizophrenics can be divided into those showing positive symptoms (reactions that are not present in normal persons) and those showing negative symptoms (the absence of normal reactions). Several distinct subtypes of schizophrenia exist, including paranoid, disorganized, and catatonic.

- *What are the origins of schizophrenia?*

Schizophrenia has complex origins involving genetic factors, certain aspects of family structure, biochemical factors, and cognitive deficits. Schizophrenia may also be related to damage in several regions of the brain.

- *What is the relationship between schizophrenia and homelessness?*

Many homeless persons appear to be individuals suffering from serious psychological disorders such as schizophrenia or mood disorders.

KEY TERMS: *schizophrenia, p. 471; delusions, p. 472; hallucinations, p. 472; diathesis-stress model, p. 475; dopamine hypothesis, p. 476*

CRITICAL THINKING QUESTIONS

APPRAISAL	Psychologists generally agree that only behavior that is atypical and evaluated negatively in a given society should be labeled as "abnormal." This implies that there are no absolutes in distinguishing between abnormal and normal behavior. As long as a behavior is viewed as acceptable within a culture, it will be described as "normal." Do you agree with this perspective? If not, why?
CONTROVERSY	Growing evidence indicates that genetic factors can predispose individuals to develop certain forms of psychological disorder. In other words, some persons are at "high risk" in this respect. This evidence leads to the suggestion that perhaps we should invest resources in identifying those persons and taking steps to prevent their inherited dispositions from developing into serious psychological disorders. In order to do so, it would first be necessary to gather information on the genetic background of many people. Do you think that doing so is justified? Or should this kind of information be viewed as too private to allow for such projects?
MAKING PSYCHOLOGY PART OF YOUR LIFE	Near the beginning of this chapter I noted that many psychologists are uneasy with the term "mental illness." Now that you know much more about the many causes of psychological disorders, I hope you can appreciate more fully why this is so. Such disorders are not simply "diseases" in the classic sense of this word; they involve much more than the ravages of harmful microorganisms. In view of this fact—and it certainly is a fact—will you think differently about persons suffering from such disorders than you did before you read this chapter? And do you think that your greater understanding of the many causes of psychological disorders will change your reactions to those who are experiencing these problems, perhaps increasing your level of sympathy for them?

Therapy:

Diminishing the Pain of Psychological Disorders

SPECIAL SECTION

PERSPECTIVES ON DIVERSITY
Psychotherapy: The Necessity for a Multicultural Perspective 504

*O*ne of my favorite old songs starts "I beg your pardon, I never promised you a rose garden." I like the melody, but it's really the lyrics that stand out in my mind. Life is good, the song suggests, but it's definitely no rose garden—no Eden free of problems. A few statistics help to drive this point home:

- More than half of all college students report that they have thought about suicide at least once (Meehan et al., 1992), and about 10 percent of adolescents indicate that they have actually attempted suicide (Shaffer et al., 1991).

- About 10 percent of adults suffer from depression or related disorders at any given time (Strickland, 1992); almost half report that they have experienced a major depressive episode at some time in their life (Kessler et al., 1994).
- More than six million persons in the United States alone are currently involved in various kinds of self-help groups—groups focused on problems ranging from alcoholism and drug abuse to stuttering and the trauma of losing one's spouse.

Yes, there's certainly a lot of pain in life—more than enough psychological discomfort to go around. Yet there's no reason to despair, because there are also many effective techniques for alleviating such discomfort. Many procedures for treating various psychological disorders exist. To acquaint you with the most important of these, this chapter will proceed as follows.

First, we'll begin with **psychotherapies**—procedures in which a trained person establishes a professional relationship with the patient in order to remove or modify existing symptoms, change disturbed patterns of behavior, and promote personal growth and development (Wolberg, 1977). As you'll soon see, many forms of psychotherapy exist, ranging from *psychoanalysis*, the famous procedures devised by Freud, through modern procedures firmly founded on basic principles of learning and cognition. Next, we'll explore several forms of therapy that involve several persons rather than a single individual—*group therapies*. Third, we'll consider therapies focused on interpersonal relations—*marital* and *family therapy*. After reviewing these various forms of therapy, we'll turn to some basic questions about all these approaches: Are they successful in alleviating psychological disorders? And if so, are some more helpful than others? Next, we'll examine several *biologically based therapies*—efforts to deal with psychological disorders through biological means. Finally, we'll look at various *settings* for therapy. These range from large state institutions or other facilities providing full-time care through community health centers and other locations in which individuals generally receive treatment on a part-time outpatient basis.

PSYCHOTHERAPIES: *Psychological Approaches to Psychological Disorders*

Say the word *psychotherapy* and many people quickly conjure up this image: A "patient" lies on a couch in a dimly lit room, while a therapist sits in the background. The therapist urges the patient to reveal the deepest secrets of her or his mind—hidden urges, frustrated desires, traumatic early experiences. As these painful revelations are brought to the surface, the patient, suffering much emotional turmoil, moves toward psychological health.

This popular image, however, has little to do with many modern forms of psychotherapy. In fact, it applies primarily to only one type, an approach developed by Freud that is now rarely used by psychologists (although it is still used by some psychiatrists). Psychotherapy, as it is currently practiced by psychologists and other professionals, actually occurs in many different settings, employs a tremendously varied range of procedures, and can be carried out with groups as well as with individuals.

What do these diverse procedures have in common? Most psychologists agree that two features are crucial: (1) establishment of a special relationship, sometimes known as the **therapeutic alliance**, between a person experiencing

Psychotherapies: Procedures designed to eliminate or modify psychological disorders through the establishment of a special relationship between a client and a trained therapist.

√Therapeutic Alliance: The special relationship between therapist and client that contributes to the effectiveness of many forms of psychotherapy.

psychological distress and a trained therapist—a relationship in which the distressed person feels free to reveal important and often embarrassing facts and has confidence in the therapist's genuine desire to help; and (2) efforts by the therapist to bring about beneficial changes in the client's behavior, feelings, or thoughts. In short, whatever form it takes, psychotherapy strives to place disturbed individuals in an environment in which they feel free to confide in another human being who is specially trained to help them change in beneficial ways. Let's take a closer look.

PSYCHODYNAMIC THERAPIES: *From Repression to Insight*

Psychodynamic therapies are based on the assumption that abnormal behavior stems primarily from the complex inner workings of personality. More specifically, psychological disorders occur because something has gone seriously wrong with the balance of these hidden inner forces. Several forms of therapy are based on these assumptions, but the most famous is *psychoanalysis,* the approach developed by Sigmund Freud.

PSYCHOANALYSIS   If Freud had known how many movies, television shows, and even cartoons would be based on his method of psychotherapy, he just might have changed it in several respects. He was a serious person who viewed himself as essentially scientific in orientation, and he would probably have found popular representations of his work thoroughly distasteful. But, as is often the case, there is a grain of truth in media representations of psychoanalysis: Freud *did* use a couch, and he *did* employ several other techniques that have become part of our conception of psychotherapy.

In order to understand Freud's methods, let's begin by briefly reviewing the reasoning that lay behind them. As you may recall from chapter 10, Freud believed that personality consists of three major parts: *id, ego,* and *superego,* which correspond roughly to desire, reason, and conscience. Freud suggested that psychological disorders stem from the fact that many impulses of the id are unacceptable to the ego or the superego and are therefore *repressed*—driven into the depths of the unconscious. There they persist, and individuals must devote a considerable portion of their psychic energy to keeping them in check and out of conscious experience—and to various *defense mechanisms* that protect the ego from feelings of anxiety. In short, Freud believed that hidden conflicts among the basic components of personality, if left unresolved, interfere with normal psychosexual development and so cause psychological disorders.

How can such problems be relieved? Freud felt that the crucial task was for people to overcome repression and come face to face with their hidden feelings and impulses. Having gained such insight into their inner conflicts, they would experience a release of emotion known as *abreaction,* and then, with their energies at last freed from the task of repression, they could direct these into healthy growth. Figure 13.1 (on page 486) summarizes these suggestions.

These ideas concerning the causes and cure of mental illness are reflected in the specific procedures used in psychoanalysis. As popular images suggest, the patient undergoing psychoanalysis lies on a couch in a partly darkened room and engages in **free association**. This involves reporting everything that passes through her or his mind, no matter how trivial it may appear to be. Freud believed that the repressed impulses and inner conflicts present in the unconscious would ultimately be revealed by these mental wanderings, at least to the trained ear of the analyst. As we saw in chapter 4, he felt that dreams were especially useful in this respect, since they often represented

✓*Psychodynamic Therapies: Therapies based on the assumption that psychological disorders stem primarily from hidden inner conflicts with repressed urges and impulses.*

✓*Free Association: A key procedure in psychoanalysis in which individuals spontaneously report all thoughts to the therapist.*

FIGURE **13.1**

Psychoanalysis: An Overview of Its Major Goals

According to Freud's theory, psychotherapists can overcome psychological disorders by helping individuals gain insight into their hidden inner conflicts. Once such insight is obtained, presumably, it will no longer be necessary to devote "psychic energies" to repressing unacceptable impulses, and the disorders caused by these conflicts and their repression will disappear.

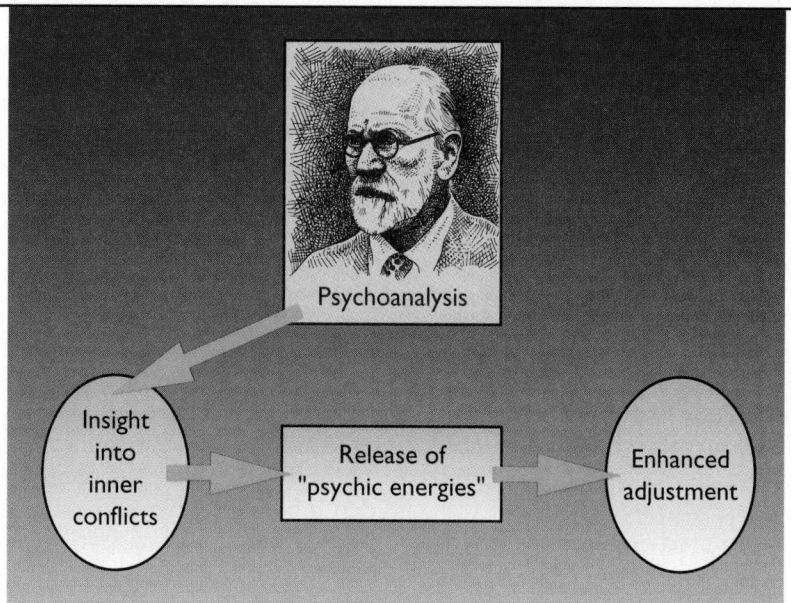

Psychoanalysis

Insight into inner conflicts → Release of "psychic energies" → Enhanced adjustment

FREUD'S FAMOUS COUCH

This scene of Freud's London office, which he opened after fleeing Nazi persecution in Germany, shows the famous couch.

✓*Resistance: Efforts by individuals undergoing psychoanalysis to prevent repressed impulses or conflicts from entering consciousness.*

✓*Transference: Strong positive or negative feelings toward the therapist on the part of individuals undergoing psychoanalysis.*

inner conflicts and hidden impulses in disguised form. As psychoanalysis progresses and the analyst gains understanding of the patient's problems, he or she asks questions and offers suggestions designed to enhance the patient's awareness of inner conflicts. It is through this process of *interpretation* that the patient finally gains increased insight.

During the course of psychoanalysis, Freud reported, several intriguing phenomena often occur. The first of these is **resistance**—a patient's refusal to report certain thoughts, motives, and experiences or his or her overt rejection of the analyst's interpretations (Strean, 1985). Presumably, resistance occurs because of patients' desire to avoid the anxiety produced as threatening or painful thoughts come closer and closer to consciousness.

Another aspect of psychoanalysis is **transference**—intense emotional feelings of love or hate toward the analyst on the part of the patient. Often, patients react toward their analyst as they did to an earlier crucial person in their lives—for example, one of their parents. Freud believed that the transference relationship could be an important tool for helping individuals work through conflicts regarding their parents, this time in a setting where the harm done by undesirable early relationships could be effectively countered. As patients' insight increases, transference gradually decreases and ultimately fades away.

PSYCHOANALYSIS: AN EVALUATION Psychoanalysis is probably the best-known form of psychotherapy. As noted by Hornstein (1992), early efforts by psychologists to ignore it (through the 1920s) and later to discredit it (in the 1930s and 1940s) largely failed: Psychoanalysis gained a firm grip on the public consciousness and refused to vanish, no matter how fervently psychologists trying to build a scientific field wished it to do so. Indeed, even one of the founders of experimental psychology—Edwin Boring—chose to undergo psychoanalysis when he experienced deep depression. To protect his reputation at the time (1934), Boring claimed that he was studying the relationship between psychology and psychoanalysis; in reality, though, he hoped for major benefits from this form of treatment (Hornstein, 1992). But he was bitterly disappointed. After ten months during which he saw his analyst four times a week, he concluded that the therapy had failed: He was no better off than before he entered treatment.

Unfortunately, Boring's experience seemed to be typical of the outcome of classical psychoanalysis: In general, its effectiveness has failed to match its fame. In the form proposed by Freud, it suffers from several major drawbacks that lessen its value. First, psychoanalysis is a costly and time-consuming process. Several years and large amounts of money are usually required for its completion. Second, it is based largely on Freud's theories of personality and psychosexual development. As chapter 10 explained, these theories are provocative but difficult to test scientifically. Third, Freud designed psychoanalysis for use with educated persons who already possessed high verbal skills. This limits the usefulness of psychoanalysis to what some have described as YAVIS patients— young, attractive, verbal, intelligent, and successful (Schofield, 1964). Other people, including many who may be desperately in need of psychological assistance, are left largely out in the cold (Snowden & Cheung, 1990). Finally, and perhaps most important, psychoanalysis has often adopted the posture of a closed logical system: A critic who raises questions about its validity or effectiveness is described as suffering from resistance and as showing severe psychological problems that prevent him or her from recognizing the obvious value of psychoanalysis! So, in sum, psychoanalysis has not turned out to be the major breakthrough that Freud predicted. While it may help some persons gain insights into their own personalities, it does not appear to be practical or highly effective in treating a wide range of psychological disorders.

BEYOND PSYCHOANALYSIS: PSYCHODYNAMIC THERAPY TODAY Because of such problems, classical psychoanalysis is a relatively rare type of therapy today. However, modified versions introduced by Freud's students and disciples, including the neo-Freudians we discussed in chapter 10, are in more common use. These modified forms of psychodynamic therapy are generally briefer than classical psychoanalysis, requiring months rather than many years of treatment (Strupp & Binder, 1984), and focus less on the past than on patients' present life and personal relationships. A couch is seldom used; instead, client and therapist sit face to face. And the therapist plays a more active role than in classical psychoanalysis, directing and advising rather than merely listening most of the time. Modern forms of psychodynamic therapy put less emphasis on the role of unconscious inner conflicts and devote more attention to current ego functioning—how the ego acts as a controlling agent in the individual's life. In addition, social factors in the environment in which clients live are considered, and efforts are made to change these in beneficial ways. Despite these differences, however, the basic goal remains the same: helping patients gain insight into their hidden motives and conflicts.

<table>
<tr><td>KEY QUESTIONS</td></tr>
</table>

- What do psychodynamic therapies see as the basis for psychological disorders?
- Is the widespread public acceptance of psychoanalysis justified?

HUMANISTIC THERAPIES: Emphasizing the Positive

Freud was something of a pessimist about basic human nature. He felt that we must constantly struggle with primitive impulses from the id. As we saw in chapter 10, many psychologists reject this view. They contend that people are basically good and that our strivings for growth, dignity, and self-control are just as strong as—if not stronger than—the powerful aggressive and sexual urges Freud described. According to such *humanistic* psychologists, psychological disorders do not stem from unresolved inner conflicts. Instead, they arise because the environment somehow interferes with personal growth and fulfillment.

Such views, of course, lead to forms of psychotherapy that are very different, both in purpose and procedure, from those developed by Freud.

FIGURE **13.2**

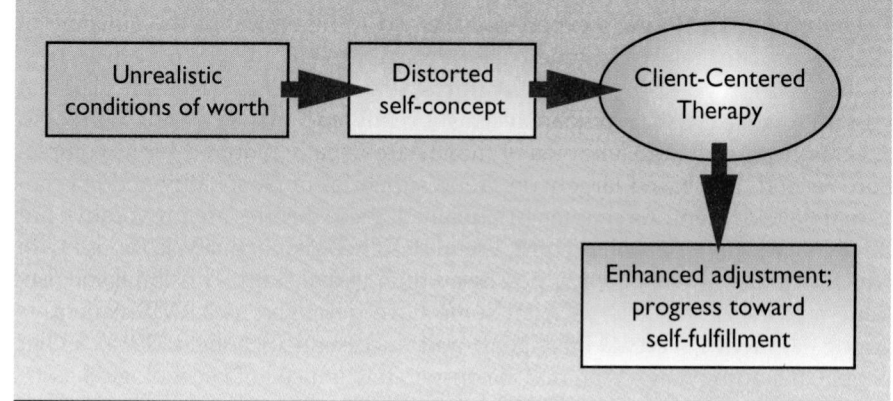

The Nature of Client-Centered Therapy

Rogers (1959) believed that psychological disorders stem from unrealistic *conditions of worth*—conditions people believe they must fulfill in order to be loved and accepted. These produce distortions in the self-concept. Client-centered therapy is designed to eliminate such distortions by placing clients in an environment in which they receive *unconditional positive regard* from the therapist and feel valued as persons.

✓*Humanistic Therapies:*
Forms of psychotherapy based on the assumption that psychological disorders stem from environmental conditions that block normal growth and development.

✓*Client-Centered Therapy: A form of psychotherapy that concentrates on eliminating irrational conditions of worth—conditions people believe they must meet in order to be loved or accepted.*

Conditions of Worth: In Rogers's theory, individuals' beliefs that they must meet certain unrealistic conditions in order to be loved or accepted.

✓*Gestalt Therapy: A form of humanistic psychotherapy designed to increase individuals' awareness and understanding of their own feelings.*

Humanistic therapies focus on the task of helping *clients* (note that humanistic therapists dislike the term "patient") to become more truly themselves—to find meaning in their lives and to live in ways consistent with their own inner values and traits. Unlike psychoanalysts, humanistic therapists believe that clients, not they, must take essential responsibility for the success of therapy. The therapist is primarily a guide and facilitator, *not* the one who runs the show. Let's take a closer look at several major types of humanistic therapy.

PERSON-CENTERED THERAPY: THE BENEFITS OF BEING ACCEPTED   Perhaps the most influential humanistic approach is the **client-centered therapy** developed by Carl Rogers (1970, 1980). Rogers strongly rejected Freud's view that psychological disorders stem from conflicts over the expression of primitive, instinctive urges. On the contrary, he argued that such problems arise primarily out of a distorted *self-concept*. According to Rogers, individuals often acquire what he terms unrealistic **conditions of worth** early in life. That is, they learn that they must be something other than what they really are in order to be loved and accepted. For example, they come to believe that they will be rejected by their parents if they harbor hostility toward their siblings. In response to such beliefs, people refuse to recognize large portions of their experience and emotions—any portions that violate their implicitly accepted conditions of worth. This in turn interferes with normal development of the self and causes people to suffer from various forms of maladjustment.

Person-centered therapy, as explained in chapter 10, focuses on eliminating such unrealistic conditions of worth through creation of a psychological climate in which clients feel valued as persons. Person-centered therapists offer *unconditional acceptance*, or *unconditional positive regard*, of the client and her or his feelings; a high level of *empathetic understanding;* and accurate reflection of the client's feelings and perceptions. In the context of this warm, caring relationship, freed from the threat of rejection, individuals can come to understand their own feelings and accept even previously unwanted aspects of their own personalities. As a result, they come to see themselves as unique human beings with many desirable characteristics. To the extent such changes occur, Rogers suggests, many psychological disorders disappear and individuals can resume their normal progress toward self-fulfillment (see Figure 13.2).

GESTALT THERAPY: BECOMING WHOLE   The theme of faulty or incomplete self-awareness so prominent in client-centered therapy is echoed in a second humanistic approach, **Gestalt therapy** (Perls, 1969). As noted in chapter 3, the

German word *gestalt* means "whole," and this word captures the essence of Gestalt therapy. According to Fritz Perls (1969), originator of this form of psychotherapy, individuals often experience difficulties because key aspects of their emotions are not acknowledged in consciousness. In short, they have, in a sense, psychologically disowned parts of their own being. They must recapture these before they can attain an accurate and complete self-concept.

How can progress toward this goal be achieved? Gestalt therapists use many different tactics. They may directly challenge their clients to give up their "phony games" and see themselves accurately. They may ask them to portray unresolved conflicts, a process referred to as *taking care of unfinished business*. At such times, clients are urged to reexperience their emotions vividly—to scream, swear, or weep as the need arises. Presumably, once such feelings are recognized and released, the unfinished business will be completed and the client will become whole once again.

Some of the techniques Gestalt therapists have developed for helping individuals recognize their own feelings are quite ingenious. For example, in the *two-chair exercise*, clients move back and forth between two chairs. While sitting in one they play themselves, while in the other they assume the role of some important person in their life—wife, husband, mother, father. The ultimate goal, of course, is to increase their awareness of their feelings toward, and relations with, these important persons in their lives.

HUMANISTIC PSYCHOTHERAPY: AN OVERVIEW While humanistic psychotherapies differ in many respects, they share a basic orientation: All reject the views, so powerfully promoted by Freud, that psychological disorders stem from repressed urges and hidden conflicts and that a therapist's key task is to force unwilling patients to gain insight into these conflicts. Further, all assume that human beings have the capacity to reflect on their own problems, to control their own behavior, and to make choices that will lead them toward more satisfying, fulfilling lives. And finally, all suggest that gaps in our self-concepts—flaws in our understandings of ourselves, our feelings, and our experiences—lie at the heart of much psychological distress.

Humanistic therapies have been criticized for their lack of a unified theoretical base and for being vague about precisely what is supposed to happen between clients and therapists. They have, however, helped to alter the dismal picture of human nature painted by Freud by calling attention to our capacities for growth and self-fulfillment. In addition, some of the central assumptions underlying humanistic approaches have been subjected to direct empirical test. For example, Rogers's view that the gap between an individual's self-image and his or her "ideal self" plays a crucial role in maladjustment has been investigated and often confirmed in many studies (e.g., Bootzin, Acocella, & Alloy, 1993). Also, research findings tend to confirm that therapists' personal warmth and ability to express empathy are predictive of their success, as suggested by Rogers's theory (e.g., Beutler, Crago, & Arizmendi, 1986). In these respects, then, humanistic therapies have made important and lasting contributions.

KEY QUESTIONS

- How do humanistic therapies explain the occurrence of psychological disorders?
- What is the major focus of Rogers's client-centered therapy?
- What is the major focus of Gestalt therapy?

BEHAVIOR THERAPIES: *Psychological Disorders and Faulty Learning*

While psychodynamic and humanistic therapies differ in many important ways, they both place considerable emphasis on early events in clients' lives as a key source of current disturbances. In contrast, another major group of

SYSTEMATIC DESENSITIZATION: USING THE PRINCIPLES OF CLASSICAL CONDITIONING

After learning how to induce relaxation, this client, who has a fear of airplanes, is gradually exposed to stimuli that make her anxious.

Behavior Therapies: Forms of psychotherapy that focus on changing maladaptive patterns of behavior through the use of basic principles of learning.

Systematic Desensitization: A form of behavior therapy in which individuals imagine scenes or events that are increasingly anxiety-provoking and at the same time engage in procedures that induce feelings of relaxation.

therapies, known collectively as **behavior therapies**, focus primarily on individuals' current behavior. These therapies are based on the belief that many psychological disorders stem from faulty learning. Either the persons involved have failed to acquire the skills and behaviors they need for coping with the problems of daily life, or they have acquired *maladaptive* habits and reactions—ones that cause them considerable distress. Within this context, the key task for therapy is to change current behavior: to provide clients with the skills they need or to alter learned patterns of behavior that are causing them distress. In addition, behavior therapy often seeks to provide individuals with behaviors and strategies they can use to overcome their problems when they are not in the presence of the therapist—through guided *self-care* (Marks, 1994). Self-care is obviously important in the treatment of many medical conditions—for example, persons with some forms of diabetes must inject themselves with insulin every day or face the real threat of death. Similarly, many behavior therapists believe that persons with psychological disorders must practice the skills they acquire during therapy in appropriate situations; this, too, constitutes a kind of self-care and can play a major role in overcoming many psychological disorders.

What kinds of learning play a role in behavior therapy? As we saw in chapter 5, there are several forms of learning. Reflecting this fact, various forms of behavior therapy focus on specific types of faulty learning involving these basic processes.

THERAPIES BASED ON CLASSICAL CONDITIONING As you may recall from chapter 5, *classical conditioning* is a process in which organisms learn that the occurrence of one stimulus will soon be followed by the occurrence of another. As a result, reactions that are at first elicited only by the second stimulus gradually come to be evoked by the first as well (one example: your salivation to the beep of a microwave oven into which you've placed a container of popcorn). What does classical conditioning have to do with psychological disorders? According to behavior therapists, quite a bit (Bandura, 1969). Behavior therapists suggest, for example, that many *phobias* may be acquired in this manner. Stimuli associated with real dangers may acquire the capacity to evoke the intense fear reactions that at first were elicited only by the actual dangers. As a result, individuals experience intense fears in situations that really pose no threat to their well-being. In order to reduce such fears, behavior therapists sometimes employ the technique known as *flooding* (refer to chapter 5). This involves prolonged exposure to the feared stimuli, or to mental representations of them, under conditions where the persons suffering from the phobias can't avoid these stimuli. Under these conditions, *extinction* of fear can occur, and the phobias fade away (Levis, 1985).

Another technique based at least in part on principles of classical conditioning is known as **systematic desensitization**. In systematic desensitization, which is also used to treat various phobias, individuals first learn to how to induce a relaxed state in their own bodies—often by learning how to relax their muscles. Then, while in a relaxed state, they are exposed to stimuli that elicit anxiety. Since they are now experiencing relaxation, the conditioned link between these stimuli and anxiety is weakened, and extinction of anxiety reactions can occur.

A third behavioral technique based on principles of classical conditioning is known as *aversion therapy* (Lovaas, 1977). Here, stimuli that have previously been associated with positive feelings, and so are conditioned stimuli for them, are associated instead with negative feelings. For example, consider the case of a man who is sexually aroused by young children and finds it difficult to resist making advances to them. How can such a person be helped—assuming that he *wants* to change? One possibility is as follows. The therapist shows the man color slides of attractive children, precisely the kind that he finds arousing. A few seconds after each slide appears, the man receives a harmless but painful electric shock. As the process continues, the man's emotional reactions to these stimuli change. Initially his feelings are positive; but as the slides of the children are paired over and over again with shocks, his feelings begin to take on a distinctly negative tone. After all, the slides are now signals for the occurrence of a very unpleasant event.

If such treatment is successful, as it has been in several studies (Bucher & Lovaas, 1968), the man may find that he is no longer sexually excited by children and can seek more appropriate sexual partners. Many psychologists find delivering unpleasant stimuli to their clients unacceptable, however, and so an alternative procedure known as *covert desensitization* has gained increasing use. In this procedure, clients are merely asked to imagine aversive stimuli; they never actually receive them. Yet research with this technique suggests that it can often prove highly effective (e.g., Cautela, 1985).

Therapies Based on Operant Conditioning   Behavior is often shaped by the consequences it produces; actions are repeated if they yield positive outcomes or if they permit individuals to avoid or escape from negative ones. In contrast, actions that lead to negative results are suppressed. These basic principles are incorporated in several forms of therapy based on *operant conditioning*. These differ considerably in specific procedures, but all incorporate the following basic steps: (1) clear identification of undesirable or maladaptive behaviors currently shown by individuals; (2) identification of events that reinforce and so maintain such responses; (3) efforts to change the environment so that these maladaptive behaviors no longer receive reinforcement.

Several techniques incorporate these principles. One of these is based on the principle of *shaping* discussed in chapter 5. This involves helping individuals to acquire desired responses not currently in their repertoire by offering them reinforcement for responses that more and more closely resemble the desired ones. An illustration of this procedure is provided by the following case:

> A three-year-old . . . boy lacked normal verbal and social behavior. He did not eat properly, engaged in self-destructive behavior such as banging his head and scratching his face, and manifested ungovernable tantrums. He had recently had a cataract operation, and required glasses. . . . He refused to wear his glasses and broke pair after pair. The technique of shaping was decided upon to counteract the problem of glasses. Initially, the boy was trained to expect a bit of candy or fruit at the sound of a toy noisemaker. Then training was begun with empty eyeglass frames. First the boy was reinforced with candy or fruit for picking them up, then for holding them, then for carrying them around, then for bringing the frames closer to the eyes, and then for putting the empty frames on his head. . . . Through successive approximation, the boy . . . learned to wear his glasses up to twelve hours a day (Wolf, Risley, & Mees, 1964).

Operant principles have also been used in hospital settings, where a large degree of control over patients' reinforcements is possible (Kazdin, 1982). Several projects have involved the establishment of **token economies**—systems under which patients earn tokens they can exchange for various rewards, such as television-watching privileges, candy, or trips to town. These tokens are awarded for various forms of adaptive behavior that will help a patient function effectively after leaving the hospital. Thus, keeping one's room neat, participating in group meetings or therapy sessions, coming to meals on time, and eating neatly all yield tokens. The results of such programs have been impressive. When individuals learn that they can acquire various rewards by

√***Token Economies:*** *Forms of behavior therapy based on operant conditioning, in which hospitalized patients earn tokens they can exchange for valued rewards when they behave in ways the hospital staff consider to be desirable.*

behaving in certain adaptive ways, they often do so, with important benefits to them as well as to hospital staff (Paul, 1982; Paul & Lentz, 1977).

Another technique based on principles of operant conditioning involves decreasing the probability of an undesirable response by increasing the likelihood of another response that is *incompatible* with it. For example, persons suffering from insomnia can learn various techniques for inducing relaxation, a state incompatible with feeling tense and wide awake; this can help them to get to sleep (e.g., Borkovec, 1982). Similarly, persons trying to quit smoking can learn to pop a piece of gum into their mouths whenever the craving for a cigarette arises. Since gum chewing is clearly incompatible with smoking, this response may help them avoid slipping back into smoking unintentionally—the kind of *absent-minded transgression* we considered in chapter 4.

Finally, I should mention the relationship between another principle of operant conditioning—*punishment*—and criminal behavior. While these principles have not been incorporated into specific forms of therapy, a growing body of evidence indicates that punishment *can* be effective in deterring a wide range of crimes (e.g., Schneider, 1990). Perhaps the most dramatic evidence in this respect has been reported recently by Brennan and Mednick (1994). These researchers obtained data on criminal arrests and subsequent punishment for a very large sample—all the men born in Copenhagen, Denmark, during 1944 (a total of 28,879 individuals). Results indicated that when offenders received some form of punishment (a fine, probation, or prison), the likelihood that they would be arrested again for another crime was significantly lower than when they did not receive any punishment. Further, and also consistent with learning theory principles, Brennan and Mednick found that the greater the proportion of arrests resulting in punishment, the lower the rates of future criminal recidivism (further arrests). In other words, punishment for various crimes did seem to deter the people convicted of them from engaging in additional crimes. Finally, recidivism rates increased among persons for whom punishment was discontinued—those who, for example, were released from prison before serving their entire sentence.

In sum, although punishment for criminal behavior does not constitute a form of therapy, the findings obtained by Brennan and Mednick (1994) suggest that it can be effective in deterring such behavior, as basic aspects of learning theory predict. However, in order to produce these effects, punishment must be applied in a manner consistent with learning theory principles—a criterion that is, unfortunately, often not met by the criminal justice systems of many nations.

MODELING: CHANGING BEHAVIOR THROUGH OBSERVING OTHERS

Seeing other people act in fearless ways can often help individuals overcome phobias.

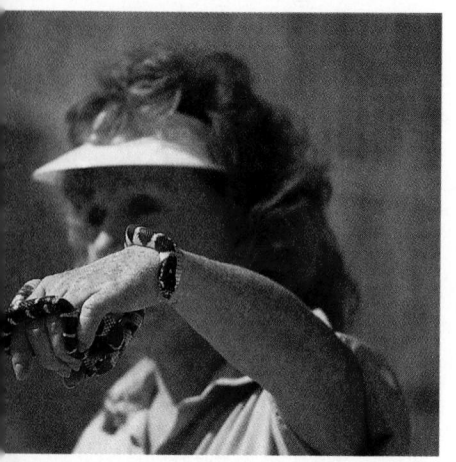

MODELING: BENEFITING FROM EXPOSURE TO OTHERS Chapter 5 explained how we sometimes acquire new forms of behavior through observational learning—observing the actions and outcomes of others (Bandura, 1977, 1986). This is not the only way in which we are affected by exposure to others' behavior, however. Seeing other persons act in various ways can weaken or strengthen our tendencies to engage in or avoid certain behaviors. For example, a motorist driving at 55 miles per hour in a 55-mph zone may soon speed up to 65 if she notices that everyone else is passing her. In this case, her restraints against engaging in a prohibited behavior are weakened when she sees others break the prohibition. Conversely, a student talking to a friend in class may quickly fall silent if he notices that everyone else is quiet and listening carefully to the instructor. In this case, restraints are strengthened by exposure to the actions of others. Even emotional reactions can be intensified or reduced when we observe outward signs of emotion—or their absence—in others (Izard, 1992). The process through which exposure to others affects our behavior is known as *modeling*, and the effects it produces are varied and far-ranging in scope.

A substantial body of evidence indicates that modeling principles can be used effectively in treating several different psychological disorders. Modeling has been used to change a wide range of maladaptive behaviors, ranging from sexual dysfunctions (Kelley & Byrne, 1992) to the inability to control one's temper (Bandura, 1986). Perhaps the most impressive application of modeling, however, has been in efforts to alleviate various phobias (Bandura, Adams, & Beyer, 1977; Bandura, 1986). Many carefully conducted studies indicate that individuals who experience intense fear of relatively harmless objects can be helped to overcome such fears through exposure to appropriate fearless social models (Bandura, Blanchard, & Ritter, 1969).

Modeling techniques have also been found to be very successful in modifying the behavior of highly aggressive children and adolescents (Schneider & Byrne, 1987). These youngsters often behave aggressively because they lack basic social skills: They don't know how to ask for what they want in a nonaggressive manner, how to refuse a request without angering the requester, and so on. The results of many studies indicate that modeling can be used to teach such skills quickly and efficiently (Schneider, 1991). A dramatic illustration is provided by a study conducted recently by Bienert and Schneider (1993).

These researchers exposed highly aggressive sixth graders to social skills training aimed specifically at teaching them how to deal with feelings of anger, stay out of fights, and respond nonaggressively to teasing. The children watched videotapes in which models showed both effective and ineffective actions, and also read passages in which other children coped successfully or unsuccessfully with problem situations. After only ten one-hour sessions, the participants showed significantly lower levels of aggression and significant improvements in the ratings they received from peers and teachers. In contrast, a control group of highly aggressive children who were *not* exposed to the modeling procedures showed no improvements in these respects. Further, the benefits of the modeling procedures were still visible one year later when the children moved to junior high schools. Findings such as these indicate that modeling can be effective in helping individuals deal with a wide range of psychological problems.

INADEQUATE SOCIAL SKILLS: ONE CAUSE OF AGGRESSION

Highly aggressive children are often lacking in basic social skills. When they learn appropriate social skills through modeling therapy, their tendency to behave aggressively toward others often decreases.

KEY QUESTIONS

- According to behavior therapies, what is the basis for psychological disorders?

- On what principles of learning are behavior therapies based?

- What specific changes do behavior therapies based on operant conditioning attempt to produce?

COGNITIVE THERAPIES: *Changing Disordered Thought*

A central theme in modern psychology—one I've emphasized at several points in this book—is this: Cognitive processes exert powerful effects on emotions and behavior. In other words, what we *think* strongly affects how we *feel* and what we *do*. This principle forms the foundation for another major approach to psychotherapy: **cognitive therapy**. The basic idea behind cognitive therapy is that many psychological disorders stem from faulty or distorted modes of thought. Change these, it is reasoned, and the disorders, too, can be alleviated. We'll now consider several popular forms of such therapy.

RATIONAL-EMOTIVE THERAPY: OVERCOMING IRRATIONAL BELIEFS Examine the list of beliefs or assumptions below:

Everyone who meets me should like me.
I should be perfect (or darn near perfect) at everything I do.

Cognitive Therapy: Psychotherapy that concentrates on altering faulty or distorted modes of thought so as to alleviate psychological disorders.

Because something once affected my life, it will always affect it.

It is unbearable and horrible when things are not the way I would like them to be.

It is impossible to control my emotions, and I can't help feeling the way I do about certain things.

Be honest: Do such assumptions ever underlie your own thinking? You may strongly protest that they do not, but Albert Ellis (1987), originator of one influential form of cognitive therapy, believes that thoughts like these are extremely common. Having been through psychotherapy myself, I realize that such assumptions have certainly influenced my own thinking—especially the first two listed above. I really *did* want to be liked by everyone—including all the students in my classes. And I *did* believe, implicitly, that I had to be perfect (or darn near perfect, anyway).

Ellis contends that such *irrational thoughts* lie behind many psychological disorders. He suggests that there are compelling reasons for having such thoughts. Most persons, he reasons, have strong desires for success, love, and a safe, comfortable existence. Life, however, often fails to gratify these desires. Irrational thinking, then, is a harmful but understandable reaction to the unavoidable disappointments and frustrations of life.

Ellis asserts that while such irrational beliefs take many different forms, most center on the tendency to escalate reasonable desires into "musts," as in "I *must* be loved by everyone" or "I *must* experience continuous success to be happy." Closely linked to such ideas are tendencies Ellis describes as *awfulizing* or *catastrophizing*—beliefs that if a certain event occurs or fails to occur, it will be a calamity of unbearable proportions from which one can never hope to recover. Here are two examples: "If I don't get that promotion, *my career will be completely over.*" "If I can't get into that course, *my semester will be totally ruined.*"

Ellis maintains that people are often their own worst enemies. They cause their own disturbances by worrying about their inability to reach impossible goals and by convincing themselves that they simply cannot tolerate the normal frustrations and disappointments of life. To make matters worse, once such thoughts take hold, negative feelings and maladaptive behaviors soon follow; as Ellis puts it, irrational ideas create disruptive feelings and behavior, which then serve to sustain and even intensify the irrational beliefs (see Figure 13.3).

FIGURE **13.3**

Rational-Emotive Therapy

According to Ellis, many psychological disorders stem from irrational thoughts. These create disruptive feelings and maladaptive behaviors, which in turn sometimes trap people in a vicious circle. Rational-emotive therapy seeks to break this cycle.

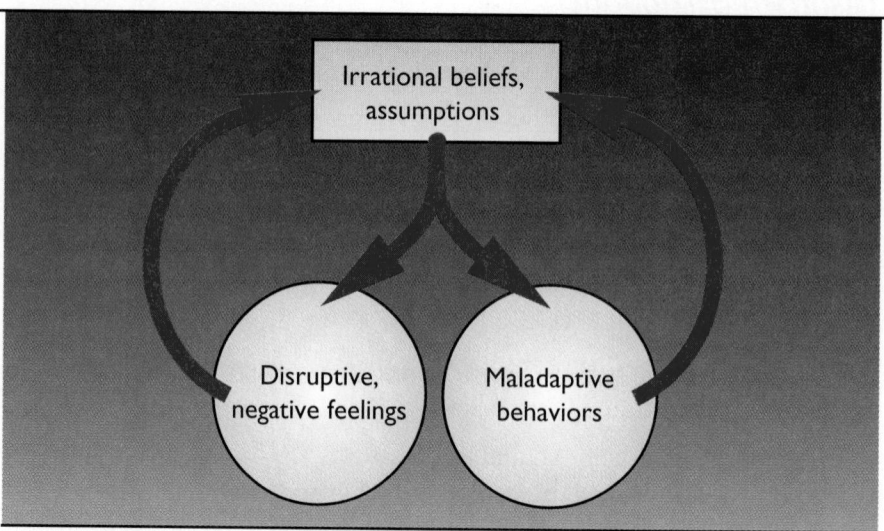

How can this self-defeating cycle be broken? Ellis suggests that the answer involves forcing disturbed individuals to recognize the irrationality of their views. **Rational-emotive therapy (RET)** is designed to accomplish this task. During this procedure the therapist first attempts to identify irrational thoughts and then tries to persuade clients to recognize them for what they are—badly distorted views of reality. For example, imagine that a therapist practicing RET is confronted with a client who says, "I just had an important article rejected for publication. It's so depressing. All that work down the tubes. I *can't stand it* when that happens!" The therapist might reply, "So you had an article rejected. Doesn't that happen to other people too? Why do you think your colleagues have to love everything you do, or that you have to be perfect?" Actually, my therapist said many things like this to me during my own rational-emotive therapy; his comments helped me recognize the irrational assumptions that were interfering with my adjustment.

BECK'S COGNITIVE BEHAVIOR THERAPY FOR DEPRESSION   The discussion of depression in chapter 12 noted that this common and serious psychological disorder has an important cognitive component: It stems, at least in part, from distorted and often self-defeating modes of thought. Recognizing this important fact, Beck and his colleagues (Beck, 1985) have devised a **cognitive behavior therapy** for alleviating this problem. Like Ellis, Beck assumes that depressed individuals' problems result from illogical thinking about themselves, the external world, and the future. Moreover, he contends, these illogical ideas and tendencies are often maintained in the face of evidence that contradicts them. In an important sense, then, they are both self-defeating and self-fulfilling. What are the cognitive tendencies that foster depression? Among the most important are these:

1. A tendency to overgeneralize on the basis of limited information—for example, to see oneself as totally worthless because of one or a few setbacks.
2. A tendency to explain away any positive occurrences by interpreting them as exceptions to the general rule of failure and incompetence.
3. A tendency toward selective perception—especially, perception of the world as a dangerous, threatening place.
4. A tendency to magnify the importance of undesirable events—to perceive them as the end of the world and unchangeable.
5. A tendency to engage in absolutistic, all-or-none thinking—for example, to interpret a mild rejection as final proof of one's undesirability.

How can such tendencies be altered? In contrast to rational-emotive therapy, Beck's cognitive behavior therapy does not attempt to disprove them. Rather, the therapist and client work together to identify the individual's assumptions, beliefs, and expectations and to formulate ways of testing them. For example, if a client voices the belief that she is a total failure, the therapist may suggest that this assumption should be evaluated. Together, the client and therapist then determine ways to test the assumption's accuracy. These tests are designed to provide the client with success experiences, thereby refuting her negative views, helping her toward enhanced self-esteem, and alleviating her depression.

Considerable evidence suggests that these procedures are highly effective in overcoming depression and helping depressed persons return to healthy,

KEY QUESTIONS

- What do cognitive therapies see as the basis for psychological disorders?
- What is the major focus of rational-emotive therapy? How do cognitive behavior therapies attempt to alleviate depression?

✓**Rational-Emotive Therapy:** *A cognitive therapy that focuses on changing irrational beliefs.*

Cognitive Behavior Therapy: *A form of psychotherapy designed to overcome depression by changing self-defeating patterns of thought.*

active lives (Clark, Beck, & Brown, 1989; Robinson, Berman, & Neimeyer, 1990). So there seems to be a grain of truth to the old belief that the problems experienced by many depressed persons are "all in their minds." Depression often *does* seem to stem from maladaptive patterns of thought, and for this reason forms of therapy focused on changing these aspects of cognition can often prove highly effective.

GROUP THERAPIES: *Working with Others to Solve Personal Problems*

*A*ll of the therapies we have considered so far are conducted on a one-on-one basis: One therapist works with one client. As you may already know, however, this is not the only approach to helping individuals deal with psychological problems. In recent decades, **group therapies**, in which treatment takes place in groups, have grown tremendously in popularity. We'll now examine several important types of group therapy, beginning with types that are closely linked to the individual therapies we considered earlier.

PSYCHODYNAMIC GROUP THERAPIES

Techniques developed by Freud for individual therapy have also been modified for use in group settings. Perhaps the most popular form of psychodynamic group therapy is **psychodrama**—a form of therapy in which group members act out their problems in front of other group members, often on an actual stage. Psychodrama also involves such techniques as *role reversal*, in which group members switch parts, and *mirroring*, in which they portray one another on the stage. In each case the goal is to show clients how they actually behave and to help them understand *why* they behave that way—what hidden inner conflicts lie behind their overt actions (Olsson, 1989). While psychodrama is highly appealing to many persons, it is subject to the same criticisms as all psychodynamic therapies, so its potential benefits may be somewhat overstated by its often ardent supporters.

BEHAVIORAL GROUP THERAPIES

In contrast, there is very compelling evidence for the effectiveness of *behavioral group therapies*—group approaches in which basic principles of learning are applied to solving specific behavioral problems. Such therapy has been found to be especially successful in teaching individuals basic *social skills* and in helping them learn how to stand up for their own rights—*assertiveness training*. In assertiveness training, for example, individuals practice such skills as expressing their feelings: verbally communicating their reactions to others, demonstrating their emotions nonverbally, expressing disagreement with others, and accepting praise by agreeing with it. By practicing these skills with and in front of other group members, people can often achieve major gains quite rapidly. In many cases the therapist first models the appropriate behavior and then provides group members with opportunities to practice these actions. During therapy sessions individuals also learn that no catastrophe will follow if they don't do it "right"—other members and the therapist are there to help them, not to damage their egos. This, too, is an important advantage.

Group Therapies: Therapies conducted with groups of clients.

Psychodrama: A form of psychodynamic group therapy in which people act out their problems in front of fellow group members.

HUMANISTIC GROUP THERAPIES

Psychologists who practice humanistic therapies have been by far the most enthusiastic about the potential benefits of adapting their therapeutic techniques to group settings. Indeed, interest in group therapy originated among humanistic therapists, who developed two forms of this type of therapy—**encounter groups** and **sensitivity-training groups**. Both of these techniques focus on the goals of personal growth, increased understanding of one's own behavior, and increased openness and honesty in personal relations. In both, group members are encouraged to talk about the problems they encounter in their lives. The reactions they receive from other group members are then crucial in helping them understand their own responses to these problems. The major difference between encounter groups and sensitivity-training groups lies in the fact that encounter groups carry the goal of open exchange of views to a greater extreme: Members in these groups are encouraged to yell, cry, touch each other, and generally act completely uninhibited. In contrast, sensitivity-training groups are somewhat more subdued.

Humanistic group therapies use any of several ingenious warming-up exercises to get the process of open exchange of views started. In one, for example, participants are blindfolded and wander around the room communicating only by touch. These procedures are designed to help members realize that normal restraints and rules don't operate in the group setting: that they are free to say and do almost anything—and so to come face to face with their own distorted self-concepts and perceptions.

Do such groups actually produce beneficial changes? Many persons who have participated in them attest that they do, but most research on this issue has been relatively informal in nature, so it is hard to reach firm conclusions (Kaplan, 1982). In any case, literally millions of people have participated in such groups; their sheer popularity may indicate that they are meeting a real need of some kind.

SELF-HELP GROUPS: SUPPORTING ONE ANOTHER

Members of self-help groups meet to discuss shared problems and find ways of coping with them.

SELF-HELP GROUPS: Help from Our Peers

When we are anxious, upset, or otherwise troubled, we often seek comfort and support from others. Long before there were psychologists or psychiatrists, people sought informal help with their personal difficulties from family, friends, or clergy. This natural tendency has taken a new form in **self-help groups** (Christensen & Jacobson, 1994). These are groups of persons who are experiencing the same kinds of problems and meet to help each other in their efforts to cope with their difficulties. Self-help groups are a fact of life in the 1990s; indeed, it has been estimated that at any given time, almost 4 percent of all American adults are involved in such groups (Jacobs & Goodman, 1989). What kinds of problems do self-help groups address? Almost everything you can imagine—and then some. Self-help groups have been formed to help their members cope with alcoholism (Alcoholics Anonymous is perhaps the most famous of all self-help groups), the death of a spouse, rape, AIDS, childhood sexual abuse, being a single parent, divorce, stuttering, abusive spouses, breast cancer—the list is almost endless.

✓**Encounter Groups:** *A form of group therapy in which people are urged to tell other group members exactly how they feel; designed to foster personal growth through increased understanding of one's own behavior and increased honesty and openness in personal relations.*

Sensitivity-Training Groups: *A form of group therapy designed to foster personal growth through increased understanding of one's own behavior and increased honesty and openness in personal relations.*

Self-Help Groups: *Groups of individuals experiencing the same kinds of difficulties that meet to discuss their shared problems and find solutions.*

- What is the major focus of psychodynamic group therapies such as psychodrama?
- What is the major focus of behavioral group therapies?
- What is the major focus of humanistic group therapies?
- What are self-help groups, and what do they provide?

A guiding principle behind these groups is that people who share a problem have a unique understanding of it and can offer one another a level of empathy that those who have not experienced the problem—no matter how concerned—can provide. Do self-help groups succeed? Few scientific studies of the impact of such groups have yet been conducted, but there is some indication that they can yield important benefits (Christensen & Jacobson, 1994; Stuart, 1977). In any case, these groups do provide their members with emotional support and help them to make new friends. Given the frequency with which many people relocate, this in itself can be beneficial.

THERAPIES FOCUSED ON INTERPERSONAL RELATIONS: *Marital and Family Therapy*

Learning Objective 13.7
Discuss the basic assumptions of therapies focusing on interpersonal relations and the characteristics of marital and family therapy.

*T*he therapies we have considered so far differ greatly in many respects, yet in one sense they are all related: They search for the roots of psychological disorders in processes operating within individuals. Another group of therapies adopts a sharply different perspective. According to practitioners of this *interpersonal* approach, disturbed or maladaptive interpersonal relationships lie at the heart of many psychological disorders (Gurman, Kniskern, & Pinsof, 1986). In other words, individuals experience personal difficulties because their relations with others are ineffective, unsatisfying—or worse. Several forms of therapy based on this idea are described below.

MARITAL THERAPY: *When Spouses Become the Intimate Enemy*

In the United States more than 50 percent of all marriages now end in divorce, and several million Americans have been married three or more times (Brody, Neubaum, & Forehand, 1988). Keeping people who are poorly matched in joyless marriages is certainly not a useful goal or one likely to promote favorable psychological adjustment. However, growing evidence indicates that in many cases the downward spiral that characterizes failing marriages can be stopped, and even reversed, if intervention occurs early enough in the process (Hendrick, 1989). Then the pain to both spouses and children can be reduced. What are the goals of such **marital therapy**, or *couple therapy*? These are closely linked to the factors that tend to disrupt such intimate relationships.

First, it appears that many couples get into serious difficulties largely because of a lack of appropriate *communication skills*. Happy couples, married or otherwise, tend to keep the channels of communication open. They talk to each other more often and more easily, sharing feelings, concerns, goals, and plans. They provide each other with more positive, and less negative, feedback than do unhappy couples (Lauer & Lauer, 1985). They have more problem-solving sessions in which they discuss how to deal with difficulties in their relationships and get along better (Margolin & Wampold, 1981). An important task for couple therapy, then, is improving the communication skills of both partners. The therapist works to foster such improvements in many different ways, including having each partner play the role of the other person so as to see their relationship as the other

Marital Therapy: Psychotherapy that attempts to improve relations and understanding in couples.

does, and having couples watch videotapes of their interactions. The latter procedure often leads to remarkable insights into just how poorly the couple has been communicating.

A second problem demonstrated by poorly adjusted couples involves *attributions*—explanations each partner offers for the other's behavior. Unhappy couples tend to explain each other's behavior in unflattering terms (Brehm, 1992; Holtzworth-Munroe & Jacobson, 1985). For example, they explain negative actions by their spouse, such as coming home late or failing to do agreed-upon chores, as stemming from *internal* causes such as stable traits: "She's irresponsible," or "He's just lazy." In contrast, happy couples faced with the same behaviors give the partner an out, assuming that some external factor beyond her or his control is to blame: "She must have missed the train," or "He's been so busy, he couldn't get to the chores." Couple therapy, therefore, is often directed toward the goals of helping both partners to recognize and change these destructive attributional patterns.

In sum, various forms of couple therapy focus on the task of arming couples with basic social skills they need to live together in a more harmonious manner. As a result of such training, couples' interpersonal relations can improve dramatically, and the overall adjustment—and happiness—of both partners may be substantially improved.

FAMILY THERAPY: *Changing Environments That Harm*

Let's begin with a disturbing fact: When individuals who have been hospitalized for the treatment of serious psychological disorders and who have shown marked improvements finally return home, they often experience a relapse. All the gains they have made through individual therapy seem quickly to vanish (Carson, Butcher, & Coleman, 1988). This fact points to an unsettling possibility: Perhaps the problems experienced by such persons can be traced, at least in part, to their families—or more specifically, to disturbed patterns of interaction among family members (Hazelrigg, Cooper, & Borduin, 1987). To the extent this is true, attempting to help one member of a family makes little sense. Once he or she is back in the same disordered home environment, any benefits of therapy may be very short-lived. In one respect, returning such persons to their families is akin to throwing a person who has just been saved from drowning back into deep, icy waters (Goldenberg & Goldenberg, 1985).

Recognition of this important fact has spurred the development of several types of **family therapy**—therapies designed to change the relationships among family members in constructive ways. One type of family therapy is known as the *communications approach* (e.g., Selvini-Palazzoli et al., 1978). This approach focuses on the fact that family members often send each other contradictory messages: "I forgive you—but don't touch me!" or "I don't care if you win; just do your best—but don't expect any hugs if you lose!" The primary goal of the communications approach is helping members of the family to recognize such conflicted messages and change them.

Another type of family therapy is known as *structural family therapy*. Here, it is assumed that relations *between* family members are more important in producing psychological disorders than aspects of personality or other factors operating largely *within* individuals (Minuchin & Fishman, 1981). Careful analysis of patterns of interaction within families often reveals key causes of distress. In one common pattern, a mother and child form a close relationship or *subsystem* within the family that all but excludes

> **Family Therapy:** *A form of psychotherapy that focuses on changing interactions or relations among family members.*

FAMILY THERAPY

Family therapy is based on the view that many psychological disorders stem from disturbed interpersonal relations among family members.

the father. This, in turn, may strain the relationship between the two parents to the point where the child, sensing conflict, develops various symptoms, such as disruptive behavior at school or illness that has no apparent physical cause. Another frequent pattern is one in which hostility between the parents is reflected in rivalry between siblings, who take sides in each dispute and may, as a result, bear most of the distress produced.

How can such destructive patterns be changed? In structural family therapy, the therapist may interact with the family almost as an insider and so gain insight into repeated patterns occurring within it. Thus, the therapist tries to determine who dominates the power structure, who gets blamed when things go wrong, who usually tries to patch things up, and so forth. Then, armed with this information, the therapist employs a wide range of techniques to facilitate positive change. In many cases, this involves efforts to alter specific behaviors (Gurman, Kniskern, & Pinsof, 1986). In others, the therapist may use modeling procedures to demonstrate more effective means of interacting. And in still other cases, the therapist tries to induce family members to recognize distorted thinking about one another or unfavorable patterns of attributions (Duck & Barnes, 1992).

Research on family therapy indicates that in many cases it is quite successful. For example, after undergoing such therapy, family members are rated by therapists, teachers, and other observers as demonstrating more adaptive behavior and better relations with each other than was true before (Hazelrigg, Cooper, & Borduin, 1987). The stability of such changes remains to be determined (Wellisch & Trock, 1980), but family therapy does seem to offer a promising new approach to dealing with psychological disorders when these seem to stem from interactions among family members.

Please see the **Key Concept** page for an overview of the major forms of psychotherapy discussed in this section.

KEY QUESTIONS

- What is the major focus of marital or couple therapy?
- What is the major focus of family therapy?

PSYCHOTHERAPY: *Some Current Issues*

Learning Objective 13.8
Discuss the major findings concerning the effectiveness of psychotherapy and whether some forms of therapy are more successful than others.

Learning Objective 13.9
Discuss the importance of including multicultural awareness in psychotherapy.

*P*sychotherapy has definitely arrived. While some people continue to view it with skepticism, ever-growing numbers of distressed individuals seek it out. Perhaps the magnitude of this shift is best illustrated by the following fact: In the 1950s only 1 percent of the U.S. population had ever had contact with a trained therapist; currently this figure is approaching 10 percent.

What accounts for this change? Part of the answer involves shifting attitudes toward the idea of participating in psychotherapy. Once, there was a stigma attached to this process. People spoke about it in hushed tones and did their best to conceal the fact that someone in their family—or they themselves—had received therapy. This was certainly true in my own family when my grandmother, suffering from deep depression, received prolonged medical care. I was ten years old at the time and knew quite well that something important was happening; but my parents refused to discuss it with me and brought the topic up only when they thought I was out of earshot—which wasn't always the case!

Major Forms of Psychotherapy

Therapy	Major Focus	Key Procedures
Psychoanalysis (Freudian)	Bringing repressed feelings and impulses into consciousness	Free association Dream interpretation Analysis of resistance

Freud's office in Vienna

Humanistic Therapies (Client-Centered Therapy)	Eliminating unrealistic conditions of worth	Therapist's expression of unconditional positive regard for client
	Correcting distortions in self-concept	Therapist's empathy toward client and reflection of client's feelings and reactions
Behavior Therapies	Changing maladaptive patterns of behavior Overcoming/changing past faulty learning	Systematic desensitization Shaping of adaptive behavior through reinforcement Modeling

Systematic desensitization in process

Cognitive Therapy	Changing faulty or distorted modes of thought Changing irrational beliefs and assumptions	Clarification of the irrational nature of client's beliefs Evaluation of self-defeating ideas and assumptions to demonstrate that they are false
Group Therapies	Inducing beneficial individual change or change in important interpersonal relations (e.g., family, couple) in context of group setting	Group activities, mutual empathy, and guidance to increase individuals' self-insight and help them to learn new social skills

A family therapy session

While negative attitudes about psychotherapy have not entirely vanished, they have certainly weakened considerably. As a result, growing numbers of people are now willing to seek assistance in dealing with psychological problems that threaten their happiness and adjustment. Another factor is the growing sophistication—and effectiveness—of psychotherapy itself. In recent decades many new forms of therapy have been introduced, and these are applicable to a wider range of disorders and a broader range of people than was true in the past. These trends, too, have contributed to the veritable boom in psychotherapy.

This is not to suggest, however, that important questions no longer exist. On the contrary, as psychotherapy has grown in popularity, such questions have become increasingly crucial and have received growing attention. Several of these issues are considered below.

DOES PSYCHOTHERAPY REALLY WORK?
An Optimistic Conclusion

In 1952 Hans Eysenck, a prominent psychologist, dropped a bombshell on his colleagues: He published a paper that reported data indicating that psychotherapy is ineffective. Specifically, Eysenck reported that about 67 percent of patients with a wide range of psychological disorders improve after therapy, but that *about the same proportion of persons receiving no treatment also improve.* This was a disturbing conclusion for psychologists and quickly led to a great deal of soul-searching—and research—within the field. After all, if the same proportion of people recover from psychological disorders with and without therapy, why bother?

Fortunately, the findings of subsequent studies pointed to a very different conclusion: Contrary to what Eysenck suggested, psychotherapy *is* helpful (Bergin & Lambert, 1978; Clum & Bowers, 1990; Shapiro & Shapiro, 1982). Apparently, Eysenck had overestimated the proportion of persons who recover spontaneously without any therapy. And he also *under*estimated the proportion who improve as a result of therapy. For example, in a major review of evidence on this issue, Smith, Glass, and Miller (1980) found that in almost five hundred separate studies, the average person receiving therapy showed fewer symptoms or difficulties than 80 percent of those who had not yet received therapy (persons who were still on waiting lists for such help). These findings have been confirmed over and over again in more recent reviews conducted with increasingly sophisticated procedures such as meta-analysis (e.g., Elkin et al., 1989).

Additional support for the effectiveness of therapy is provided by studies indicating that the more treatment individuals receive, the greater the improvement they demonstrate. In other words, as therapy progresses, persons receiving it continue to improve and show fewer symptoms and less and less distress (Howard et al., 1986; Orlinsky & Howard, 1987).

Such effects are not limited to therapy conducted with adults. Recent reviews indicate that therapy is also successful with children and adolescents (e.g., Kazdin, 1993; Weisz et al., 1992). Again, these reviews indicate that youngsters receiving therapy show greater improvements than most who do not receive treatment. Indeed, the average young person receiving therapy tends to score better, on various measures of adjustment, than 70 to 80 percent of those not receiving therapy.

Finally, additional studies have compared the effectiveness of psychotherapy with drug therapy, which we'll consider in the next section. Results indicate that certain forms of psychotherapy are at least as effective as drug therapy and may be superior to it in some respects. For example, in a review of existing evidence concerning the relative benefits of cognitive therapy and drug therapy for depression, Hollon, Shelton, and Loosen (1991) found that these two forms of treatment were about equally effective in alleviating the symptoms of this disorder. However, cognitive therapy appeared to be superior to drug therapy in terms of rates of relapse—the proportion of persons who become depressed again after treatment has been completed. Fewer persons who received cognitive therapy showed relapse into depression than persons who received drug therapy, and cognitive therapy alone was about as effective in this respect as a combination of both drug and cognitive therapy.

One note of caution: many of these findings are based on the results of carefully controlled studies in which participants voluntarily entered treatment, in which efforts were focused on dealing with specific problems, and in which therapists were trained in using certain techniques immediately before therapy was administered. As noted by Weisz, Weiss, and Donenberg (1992), these conditions tend to load the dice in favor of positive outcomes for the types of therapy studied, and it is not clear whether similar positive outcomes would be obtained under more normal clinical conditions. However, even in the face of such concerns, existing evidence seems to suggest that psychotherapy really does work. It is certainly not equally effective for all persons or for all disorders and does not necessarily totally eliminate various psychological problems (Robinson, Berman, & Neimeyer, 1990); but overall, it is considerably better than hoping that these problems will go away by themselves.

ARE SOME FORMS OF THERAPY MORE SUCCESSFUL THAN OTHERS? *Solving a Persistent Puzzle*

The procedures used in various forms of therapy differ sharply. It seems only reasonable, then, to expect that some types of therapy will be more effective than others. But brace yourself for a surprise: Comparisons among therapies have generally yielded inconclusive results. Despite the contrasting procedures various forms of therapy employ, they all seem to yield roughly equivalent benefits (Hollon, DeRubeis & Evans, 1987; Hollon, Shelton, & Loosen, 1991; Kiesler, 1985; Luborsky, Singer, & Luborsky, 1975). How can therapies employing sharply different procedures yield similar results? Here are two possibilities.

DIFFERENCES AMONG VARIOUS THERAPIES EXIST, BUT WE HAVE TO SEARCH FOR THEM IN THE RIGHT PLACES
First, it is possible that some forms of therapy *are* more effective than others, but only with respect to certain types of disorders. As Kiesler (1966) put it, in comparing various psychotherapies we should not ask, "Which is better?" Rather, we should inquire, "What type of treatment by what type of therapist is most effective in dealing with what specific problems among specific persons?" In short, it would be surprising if one type of psychotherapy was superior to others in all cases. It is much more likely that some types will prove to be more useful in dealing with certain types of psychological disorders and when administered by certain therapists. Many psychologists accept this view, although they realize that from a practical perspective, comparing the success of many types of therapy in overcoming a wide range of psychological disorders is a huge task (Stiles, Shapiro, & Elliott, 1986).

VARIOUS TYPES OF PSYCHOTHERAPY YIELD EQUIVALENT BENEFITS BECAUSE THEY HAVE A COMMON CORE
Another possibility is that while various forms of therapy do differ in rationale and procedures, these differences, from a practical point of view, are relatively unimportant. Under the surface,

all share common, crucial features, and it is this shared core that accounts for their similar effectiveness. What is this common nucleus? It may consist of several key features.

First, all major forms of psychotherapy provide troubled individuals with a special type of setting—one in which they interact closely, usually one-on-one with a highly trained, empathetic, professional. For many clients this exposure to another person who seems to understand their problems and genuinely to care about them may be a unique experience or at least one they have rarely encountered. The experience is very reassuring and may play an important role in the benefits of many forms of therapy.

Second, every form of therapy provides individuals with an explanation for their problems. No longer do these seem to be mysterious and, perhaps, the result of hidden character flaws. Rather, as therapists explain, psychological disturbances stem from understandable causes, many of which lie outside the individual. This is something of a revelation to many persons who have sought in vain for a clue as to the origins of their difficulties.

Third, all forms of therapy specify actions that individuals can take to cope more effectively with their problems. No longer must they merely suffer silently or wring their hands in despair. Rather, they are now actively involved in doing specific things that the confident, expert therapist indicates will help.

Fourth, as I mentioned at the start of this chapter, all forms of therapy involve clients in what has been termed the *therapeutic alliance*—a partnership in which powerful emotional bonds are forged between client and therapist, and in which both work to solve the client's problems.

Combining all of these points, the themes of *hope* and *personal control* seem to emerge very strongly. Perhaps diverse forms of therapy succeed because all provide people with increased hope about the future plus a sense of heightened personal control. At least individuals in therapy have taken their fate into their own hands and are doing something constructive about it. To the extent this is the case, it is readily apparent why therapies that seem so different on the surface can all be effective. All cast a bright, comforting light into the emotional darkness of troubled people and in this manner help bring about positive change.

KEY QUESTIONS

- Is psychotherapy effective?
- Are some types of psychotherapy more effective than others?

While many forms of therapy appear to be effective, it is important to note that all were first developed for use with white, middle-class patients. Is psychotherapy effective for other, ethnically and culturally diverse groups, too? And if not, how must therapeutic methods be altered to encompass such diversity? For information on these and related issues, please see the **Perspectives on Diversity** section.

PERSPECTIVES ON DIVERSITY

Psychotherapy: The Necessity for a Multicultural Perspective

In chapter 12, we saw that subtle forms of bias may play a role in the diagnosis of many psychological disorders. Individuals' race, sex, ethnic background, and social class all seem to influence the specific disorders attributed to them as well as judgments concerning the severity of such problems (Lopez, 1989). Thus, for example, blacks are more likely to be diagnosed as schizophrenic and less likely to be diagnosed as showing affective (mood) disorders than whites. Similar patterns occur for Hispanics, Native Americans, and individuals of Asian descent (Snowden & Cheung, 1990). While such findings may reflect actual differences in the underlying incidence of these disorders, growing evidence suggests that subtle—and usually unconscious—bias also plays a role (Lopez, 1989).

If racial and ethnic factors can influence the diagnosis of psychological disorders, it seems possible that they may play a role in psychotherapy as well. For example, therapists and clients may find it difficult to communicate with one another across substantial cultural gaps, with the result that the therapeutic process is slowed or even brought to a halt. Even worse, most forms of psychotherapy were originally developed for, and have been largely used with, persons of European descent. As a result, such procedures may not be entirely suitable for use with individuals from very different backgrounds. This possibility has received considerable attention from psychologists in recent years and has led to the suggestion that psychotherapies must be made more *culturally sensitive* (Rogler et al., 1987). This suggestion, in turn, involves three major points.

First, efforts must be made to make psychotherapy accessible to members of various ethnic groups, especially groups that are economically disadvantaged. Such persons seek psychological help far less often than other members of society, despite the fact that their need for it is just as great, possibly greater (Snowden & Cheung, 1990). Special efforts are needed to overcome language barriers and to place government-supported programs in minority communities where they will be accessible to people who don't have cars.

Second, the types of therapy employed should be consistent with the cultural, economic, and educational background of individuals to whom they are applied. For example, it would probably be quite inappropriate to employ psychoanalysis or other techniques requiring a high degree of verbal skills in a community where most people have not completed high school.

Third, therapy should take account of established values and traditions within minority cultures. For example, therapists working with people of Hispanic descent should consider the fact that Hispanics' views concerning the roles of males and females can be quite different from those of other groups in U.S. society (Rogler et al., 1987).

Finally, therapy—and other forms of social intervention—should be designed to deal with the unique problems of various ethnic groups. While basic psychological disorders appear to be much the same throughout the world, different cultural and ethnic groups often confront unique sets of circumstances and threats to their well-being. A prime example of such a circumstance is the tragically high rate of assaultive violence among young African-American men (Rodriguez, 1990; Rosenberg & Mercy, 1991). While violent crime has increased dramatically in all ethnic groups, the risk of becoming the victim of such assaults is far higher for African-American men than for any other group in the United States. Indeed, homicide is the leading cause of death among male *and* female African Americans ages fifteen to thirty-four. While other ethnic groups are also at risk, the mortality rate for young African-American men is almost ten times that for white males of the same age (Hammond & Yung, 1993).

As a result of these alarming rates of violent death, many urban African-American children grow up in an environment in which they must confront fears that other children largely escape—the very real fear of being shot, often as an innocent bystander to others' disputes. Needless to say, this can be a negative factor for psychological development. To bring these points into focus, consider the following fact: One survey found that more than 55 percent of eighth-grade boys and 45 percent of eighth-grade girls living in an impoverished Chicago neighborhood had personally seen someone shot (Shakoor & Chalmers, 1991).

What can psychologists do to help end this tragic carnage and its negative effects on African-Americans' emotional well-being? Two researchers who have studied this issue, Hammond and Yung (1993), offer several suggestions. For example, they recommend that young African Americans be given training in specific social skills—skills that may help them defuse violence and prevent its occurrence. Several programs of this type have been adopted by schools (Hammond, 1991), and while it is still too early to determine whether they will be successful, they do seem to offer one promising approach to this problem.

Similarly, Hammond and Yung (1993) suggest that psychologists and other health professionals must be trained to understand ethnic diversity and the cultures of the persons they seek to help. Only then can they comprehend the fact that young African Americans face a very different set of circumstances from those facing young Americans in many other ethnic groups, and gain crucial insights into the causes behind the alarming rates of violence.

In sum, all forms of psychotherapy, as well as other intervention techniques, should be conducted against a backdrop of awareness of cultural differences. If important ethnic and cultural differences are overlooked, much effort may be wasted, and even dedicated, talented therapists may fail to accomplish their major goals.

BIOLOGICALLY BASED THERAPIES

Mind and body are intimately linked, so in one sense everything we think, remember, feel, or do reflects activity in the central nervous system. This basic fact has led some researchers to conclude that all psychological disorders ultimately stem from, or at least involve, biological causes. In this section we'll consider forms of therapy deriving from this belief—approaches generally known as **biologically based therapies**.

EARLY FORMS OF BIOLOGICAL THERAPY

Early efforts to treat psychological disorders through biological means were described in chapter 12. As you may recall, such procedures were quite primitive and included skull surgery, beatings, and restraining devices. Lacking scientific knowledge, people were willing to try almost anything to free persons suffering from psychological disorders from the evil influences believed to cause their bizarre behavior.

It is somewhat more unsettling to realize that crude efforts at biological intervention continued even into the present century. The device shown in the photo (part of the author's collection of antiques) was in common use by physicians in the late nineteenth and early twentieth centuries. The physician would apply the electrodes to various portions of patients' anatomy and deliver electric shocks in efforts to counter anxiety, depression, and many other psychological disorders. Needless to say, such efforts were largely ineffective.

ELECTROCONVULSIVE THERAPY

The idea of using electric shock to treat psychological problems did not disappear in the twentieth century; it merely reentered psychiatry in another form. In the 1930s, many physicians believed that schizophrenics rarely had epileptic seizures. This observation, it turned out, was false. However, it led a Hungarian psychiatrist, Von Meduna, to suggest that inducing such seizures artificially might be an effective means of treating this serious disorder. At first psychiatrists produced convulsions by the injection of a drug such as camphor, but after observing the use of shock to render animals unconscious in slaughterhouses, two Italian physicians, Cerletti and Bini, proposed using powerful electric shocks instead (Bini, 1938). This procedure—known as **electroconvulsive therapy (ECT)**—became quite common, and it remains in fairly widespread use today. In fact, more than 90,000 patients receive ECT each year in the United States alone (Weiner, 1985).

EARLY BIOLOGICAL THERAPY

Electrical devices such as this one (from the author's collection of antiques) were widely used by physicians in the late nineteenth century to "treat" many psychological disorders.

Biologically Based Therapies: *Forms of therapy that attempt to reduce psychological disorders through biological means such as drug therapy or surgery.*

√*Electroconvulsive Therapy (ECT): A treatment for depression in which patients receive powerful electric shocks to the head.*

ECT involves placing electrodes on the patient's temples and delivering shocks of 70–130 volts for brief intervals (less than one second). These are continued until the patient has a seizure, a bodywide muscle contraction lasting at least thirty seconds. In order to prevent broken bones and other injuries, a muscle relaxant and a mild anesthetic are usually administered before the start of the shocks. Patients typically receive three treatments a week for several weeks.

Surprisingly, ECT seems to work, at least with certain disorders. It is especially effective with severe depression and appears to help many persons who have failed to respond to other forms of therapy (National Institutes of Mental Health, 1985). My grandmother received this treatment for severe depression in the early 1950s. After a number of ECT sessions, she returned, more or less, to her old self. But she clearly found these treatments very disturbing; she refused to discuss them even with me, her favorite grandson. All she would say was, "I only pray, Bobby, that it never happens to *you!*"

Unfortunately, there are important risks connected with ECT. It is designed to alter the brain, and it does, apparently producing irreversible damage in at least some cases. This has led many researchers to criticize its use and to call for its elimination as a form of therapy (Breggin, 1979). In addition, although the procedure itself is painless (patients are anesthetized before the shocks are delivered), many, like my grandmother, find it very frightening. ECT continues in use because it yields rapid improvements among depressed persons who might otherwise be at considerable risk for suicide (Martin et al., 1985). Clearly, however, it is a form of therapy that should be used with caution, and only when other, less drastic forms of therapy fail.

PSYCHOSURGERY

In 1935 a Portuguese psychiatrist, Egas Moniz, attempted to reduce aggressive behavior in psychotic patients by severing neural connections between the prefrontal lobes and the remainder of the brain. The operation, known as *prefrontal lobotomy*, seemed to be successful: Aggressive behavior by unmanageable patients did decrease. Moniz received the 1949 Nobel Prize in Medicine for his work—but, in one of those strange twists of history, he was later shot by one of his lobotomized patients!

Encouraged by Moniz's findings, psychiatrists all over the world rushed to treat a wide range of disorders through various forms of **psychosurgery**—brain operations designed to change abnormal behavior. Tens of thousands of patients were subjected to prefrontal lobotomies and related operations. Unfortunately, it soon became apparent that results were not always positive. While some forms of objectionable or dangerous behavior did decrease, serious side effects sometimes occurred: Some patients became highly excitable and impulsive; others slipped into profound apathy and a total absence of emotion; a few became living vegetables, requiring permanent care.

In view of these harmful outcomes, most physicians stopped performing prefrontal lobotomies. Totally banned in the Soviet Union as early as 1951, prefrontal lobotomies had all but faded from the scene worldwide by the 1960s. This dramatic decline also stemmed from the development of drugs for treating psychoses—substances we'll consider in detail below. Today psychosurgery, when it is performed, takes a much more limited form than prefrontal lobotomy. Instead of cutting connections between whole areas of the brain, modern-day brain surgery focuses on destroying tiny areas or on interrupting specific neural circuits.

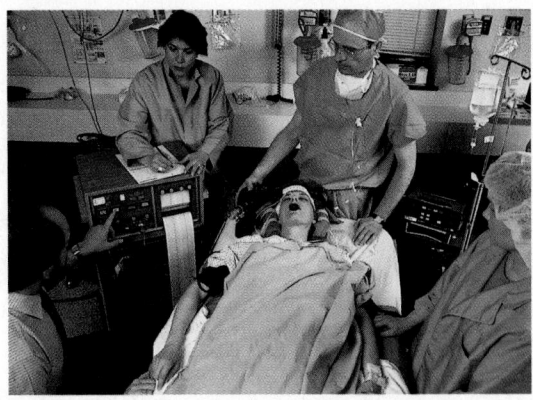

ELECTROCONVULSIVE THERAPY TODAY

In electroconvulsive therapy, an electric current passes through the brain for less than a second, causing a brief seizure.

Learning Objective 13.10
Discuss the basic assumption that underlies the biological approach to psychotherapy and survey the early forms of biological therapy.

Learning Objective 13.11
List the types of drugs used in therapy and discuss their effectiveness.

✓Psychosurgery: Efforts to alleviate psychological disorders by surgical means.

While such operations sometimes seem to be effective in treating depression and uncontrollable aggression, even this limited type of psychosurgery raises important ethical questions. Is it right to destroy healthy tissue in a person's brain in the hope that this will relieve symptoms of psychological disorder? And since the benefits are uncertain, should such irreversible procedures be permitted? These and related issues have led many to view psychosurgery as a very drastic form of treatment—something to be tried only when everything else has failed. As a result, fewer than one hundred such operations are now performed in the United States each year, and psychosurgery is no longer an important form of treatment for psychological disorders.

DRUG THERAPY: *The Pharmacological Revolution*

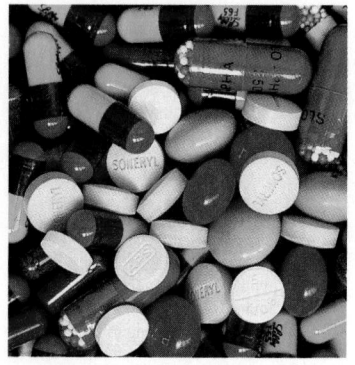

THE PHARMACOLOGICAL REVOLUTION

Drugs effective in treating a wide range of psychological disorders were developed during the 1950s and 1960s. As a result, the number of full-time patients in psychiatric hospitals decreased dramatically.

In 1955, almost 600,000 persons were full-time resident patients in psychiatric hospitals in the United States. Twenty years later, this number had dropped below 175,000. Were Americans achieving mental health at a dizzying pace? Absolutely not. What happened in those years was something many describe as a *pharmacological revolution:* A wide range of drugs effective in treating many serious psychological disorders was developed and put to use. So successful was **drug therapy** in reducing major symptoms that hundreds of thousands of persons who had previously been hospitalized for their own safety (and that of others) could now be sent home for treatment as outpatients. What are these wonder drugs, and how do they produce their beneficial effects? It is to these questions that we turn next.

ANTIPSYCHOTIC DRUGS If you had visited the wards of a psychiatric hospital for seriously disturbed persons before about 1955, you would have observed some pretty wild scenes—screaming, bizarre actions, nudity. If you had returned just a year or two later, however, you would have observed a dramatic change: peace, relative tranquillity, and many patients now capable of direct, sensible communication. What accounted for this startling change? The answer involves development of *antipsychotic drugs,* sometimes known as the *major tranquilizers.* The first of these was *reserpine,* which, as early as the 1950s, was found to exert a calming effect on mental patients. But reserpine produced harmful side effects such as low blood pressure and, in some patients, severe depression. Thus, its usefulness was quite restricted.

Much more effective relief of psychotic symptoms was provided by a family of drugs known as *phenothiazines.* The antipsychotic effects of these drugs were discovered by accident. Phenothiazine is also found in antihistamines—drugs widely used to relieve the symptoms of colds and allergies. As antihistamines came into widespread use for colds, it was found that they also had tranquilizing effects. This led chemists to examine other phenothiazines; and in 1950 a new derivative called *chlorpromazine* (trade name Thorazine) was produced. It was an immediate success, and within a few months it had been given to almost two million patients. Chlorpromazine was soon followed by many other related drugs in the same chemical family, although today, there are also some antipsychotic drugs that are not phenothiazines.

Antipsychotic drugs relieve a wide range of symptoms, including hallucinations, thought disorders, anxiety, and extreme hostility. The overall result is nothing short of amazing. Patients who are almost totally out of touch with reality and must be given custodial care can, after receiving the drugs, communicate with others and care for themselves. Perhaps even more important, they improve to the point where they become candidates for vari-

Drug Therapy: Efforts to treat psychological disorders through administration of appropriate drugs.

ous forms of psychotherapy. The scope of the changes produced is perhaps best summarized by the following statistic: In the mid 1950s, 70 percent of all persons diagnosed as suffering from schizophrenia spent most of their lives in mental hospitals. At present, this figure is less than 5 percent.

How do the antipsychotics produce such remarkable effects? Current evidence suggests that they block dopamine receptors in the brain. As noted in chapter 12, the presence of an excess of this neurotransmitter, or increased sensitivity to it, may play a role in the development of schizophrenia. Whatever the precise mechanisms involved, there can be little doubt that the development of antipsychotic drugs has helped transform many previously hopeless patients into ones responsive to psychotherapy.

The use of these drugs, however, is not without drawbacks. They often produce fatigue and apathy as well as calming effects. And after receiving antipsychotic drugs for prolonged periods of time, many patients develop a side effect called **tardive dyskinesia**: loss of motor control, especially in the face. As a result, they experience involuntary muscle movements of the tongue, lips, and jaw. These motor reactions produce difficulties with speech and sometimes result in bizarre facial expressions. In order to avoid such side effects, many psychiatrists no longer place patients on maintenance doses of the drug. Rather, they employ *target dosing:* They administer drugs only when serious symptoms appear and discontinue medication when the symptoms are eliminated. One new antipsychotic drug, *clozapine,* seems to be effective without producing tardive dyskinesia. It is very expensive, however, and this limits its potential use.

While the antipsychotic drugs are certainly of great value, they do not provide a total answer to schizophrenia and other serious psychological disorders. True, the most bizarre symptoms of schizophrenia decrease under medication. However, this does not usually result in an individual who can return to normal life. Persons on antipsychotic drug therapy often remain somewhat withdrawn and show relatively slow reactions and reduced levels of affect. And more serious symptoms often reappear if the drug therapy is stopped. In short, antipsychotic drugs seem to relieve the major symptoms of schizophrenia but don't deal with the causes that underlie them. Thus, it is imperative that persons receiving drug therapy also receive other forms of psychotherapy if they are capable of participating in them. Otherwise they may remain seriously disturbed, and unless they have families willing to care for them when they are released from mental institutions, they may join the ranks of homeless street people, of which there are already several million in the United States alone.

ANTIDEPRESSANT DRUGS   Shortly after the development of chlorprmazine, drugs effective in reducing depression also made their appearance. There are two basic types of such compounds: the *tricyclics* and the *monoamine oxidase inhibitors* (MAO inhibitors). Both seem to exert their antidepressant effects by increasing the concentration of certain neurotransmitters, primarily serotonin and norepinephrine, in the synaptic gap. It appears, however, that there may be several different types of depression and that antidepressant drugs may exert their effects through a wide range of biochemical mechanisms. While these drugs influence neurotransmitter concentrations very quickly, their antidepressant effects are delayed, often taking several days or longer to appear. This suggests that the biochemical mechanisms underlying depression are complex, to say the least.

Both tricyclics and MAO inhibitors produce potentially dangerous side effects. For trycyclics, these include drowsiness, irregularity in heartbeat, blurred vision, and constipation. For MAO inhibitors, the most important side effect is *hypertension*—a rise in blood pressure above normal levels. In

√Tardive Dyskinesia: A side effect of prolonged exposure to antipsychotic drugs in which individuals experience involuntary muscular movements, especially of the face.

some cases MAO inhibitors can trigger a *hypertensive crisis* involving severe headache, intracranial bleeding, and even death. Because of such side effects, MAO inhibitors are used less frequently than tricyclics in the treatment of depression.

Since both tricyclics and MAO inhibitors show delayed action and because of their potential side effects, several other, even more effective drugs have been developed. Among these, *fluoxetine* (Prozac) is perhaps the most widely used. This drug, which seems to operate by blocking the reuptake of serotonin, has fewer and milder side effects than older antidepressants. Yet it matches or exceeds the tricyclics in terms of countering depression. For these reasons, it is now the most widely prescribed antidepressant in the United States (Grilly, 1989). Prozac has been the subject of controversy, however, because a small number of persons experience dangerous side effects from it: They become manic, hyperactive, or even dangerously violent (Angier, 1990). A newer drug, Zoloft, seems less likely to produce such effects.

One final point: while drugs *are* often effective in treating depression, research evidence suggests that they are not necessarily more effective than several forms of psychotherapy, especially cognitive behavioral and cognitive therapies (Robinson, Berman, & Neimeyer, 1990). Since psychotherapy avoids the potential dangers involved in the use of any drug, it appears to be the more conservative form of treatment.

ANTIANXIETY DRUGS Alcohol, a substance used by many people to combat anxiety, has been available for thousands of years. As I'm sure you know, however, it has important negative side effects. Synthetic drugs with antianxiety effects—sometimes known as *minor tranquilizers*—have been manufactured for several decades. The most widely prescribed at present are the *benzodiazepines*. This group includes Valium, Ativan, Xanax, and Librium. In 1989, over 52 million prescriptions for these drugs were written in the United States alone (Shader, Greenblatt, & Balter, 1991). Another widely used antianxiety drug is *propanediol* (meprobamate); this drug seems to exert antianxiety effects mainly by reducing muscular tension. Yet another drug that has recently attained favor among physicians in treating mild anxiety is BuSpar.

The most common use for antianxiety drugs, at least ostensibly, is as an aid to sleep. At first glance, they seem safer for this purpose than *barbiturates*, since they are less addicting. However, substances deriving from the benzodiazepines remain in the body for longer periods of time than do those from barbiturates and can cumulate until they reach toxic levels. Thus, long-term use of these antianxiety drugs can be quite dangerous. In addition, when they are taken with alcohol, their effects may be magnified; this is definitely a combination to avoid. The benzodiazepines seem to produce their effects by chemically binding to receptors at synapses, thus blocking neural transmission. Common side effects of these antianxiety drugs include fatigue, drowsiness, and impaired motor coordination, so people taking them should avoid driving or operating power tools.

KEY QUESTIONS

- What is electroconvulsive therapy?
- What is psychosurgery?
- What drugs are used in the treatment of psychological disorders?

LITHIUM AND MOOD DISORDERS In the late 1940s, findings were reported indicating that compounds of lithium, such as lithium carbonate, could be effective in treating *manic disorders.* For more than twenty years this evidence was largely ignored, mainly because researchers could not conceive of any mechanisms through which this simple substance could produce these changes. Now, however, it seems clear that lithium *is* indeed helpful in treating manic disorders. About 60 to 80 percent of manic states can be quickly brought to a close by administration of lithium (Campbell, Perry, & Green, 1984). It can sometimes terminate depressive episodes, especially in persons with bipolar disorders. Lithium can be quite dangerous: Excessive doses can cause convulsions, delirium, and even death—and for many patients the effective dose is close to the overdose level. Thus, it is crucial that blood levels of lithium be closely monitored in persons who take it. Another problem is that after people have taken the drug for two years or more, manic episodes occur again when it is discontinued. Since it *is* effective in diminishing wild mood swings, though, lithium continues in widespread use.

THE SETTING FOR THERAPY: *From Institutional Care to the Community*

*E*arlier I noted that during the 1950s and 1960s, there was literally an outpouring of patients from psychiatric hospitals, produced in large measure by the *pharmacological revolution*. Where did these people go? How are they receiving treatment today? These are the issues we'll now consider.

STATE INSTITUTIONS: *Custodial Care*

When large state institutions for treating psychological disorders were founded, in the nineteenth century, they offered a major breakthrough: No longer would persons suffering from mental afflictions be chained, tortured, and abused. Instead, they would receive enlightened medical care. The promise of these institutions, however, was not fulfilled. Most were built in isolated rural areas, mainly because land was less expensive there than in cities; as a result, attracting competent medical staff was a serious problem. Further, budgets rarely kept pace with growing patient populations. The result was predictable: These large state-supported facilities soon became largely *custodial*. They provided little in the way of active treatment, and few patients ever left "cured" of their problems. Yet despite this fact, there was little choice for the families of seriously disturbed individuals: It was either commitment to one of these large institutions or remaining at home. Nothing in between existed.

Partly in response to these conditions, many private institutions for the treatment of psychological disorders were founded. Depending on the physicians who ran them, they adopted different methods of treatment, and provided sharply contrasting *therapeutic environments*—different settings for interactions with staff and different living conditions. Many of these institutions were *psychodynamic* in orientation, since psychiatry as a field was heavily influenced by Freudian concepts. In such institutions the staff endeavored to provide an environment in which early damage to the patients' personalities could be repaired. They conducted therapy with all patients who could participate in these procedures and assigned patients to living quarters on the basis of their problems. Other private institutions adopted different approaches. For example, in some, *milieu therapy* was practiced. This approach, which had important ties to humanistic therapies, provided an environment designed to foster independence and self-respect among patients. The atmosphere was warm and accepting, and

INSTITUTIONS FOR TREATING PSYCHOLOGICAL DISORDERS

Large state institutions for treating psychological disorders were placed far from urban areas and operated on limited budgets. As a result, they were often able to provide only custodial care to patients.

Learning Objective 13.12
Survey the different types of
environments that were created
as alternatives to psychiatric
hospitals.

Learning Objective 13.13
Know the goals of the different
types of prevention programs
and be able to discuss the
research concerning their effectiveness.

patients were kept busy with occupational therapy, recreational activities, and other projects.

Needless to say, only relatively wealthy persons were fortunate enough to enter such private facilities. For most persons suffering from psychological disorders, hospitalization meant being sent—often against their will—to the large custodial state institutions described above.

COMMUNITY MENTAL HEALTH CENTERS: *Bringing Care to Where It's Needed*

As large mental hospitals discharged more and more patients who responded well to drug therapy, the question of where these persons should go for continued treatment rose to prominence. That many patients required further treatment was obvious, but in the 1950s there was nowhere for them to receive it. In the United States and in other countries, the answer was the founding of **community mental health centers**. Distributed throughout the country geographically, these centers were designed to bring treatment for psychological disorders directly to the community—to where people lived.

What kind of services do community mental health centers deliver? A broad range. First, such centers provide *outpatient services*—treatment for patients who live at home and come to the mental health center once or twice a week, or as the need arises. Such treatment includes *aftercare*—treatment for persons newly released from the hospital—as well as various kinds of assessment and therapy. The basic goal is simple: to provide these services to people without disturbing their daily routines.

In addition, some community mental health centers offer *inpatient services:* They provide a place where persons requiring further hospitalization can receive it—again, in a location close to their homes. This makes it much easier for friends and relatives to visit than was true for the geographically isolated state institutions. And in keeping with the philosophy of active treatment rather than custodial care, patients receive therapy during their stays.

Third, community mental health centers provide *emergency services*—places to which people can turn in moments of crisis, even late at night and over weekends. These services are delivered by satellite storefront clinics that remain open at night or at the emergency rooms of local hospitals, to which community mental health centers provide teams of trained professionals.

Finally, these centers provide *consultation services*—advice and training to help members of the community deal with psychological problems. For example, such programs have trained physicians, teachers, and clergy in how to deal with psychologically disturbed persons. And they have taught police skills valuable in dealing with family violence and other situations in which people's emotions run high.

PREVENTION: *Heading Off Trouble before It Begins—or Becomes Serious*

Community Mental Health Centers: *Facilities for the delivery of mental health services located in communities where clients live.*

Primary Prevention: *Techniques aimed at preventing the occurrence of psychological disorders.*

Secondary Prevention: *Techniques that focus on early detection of psychological disorders so that minor disturbances will not develop into major ones.*

Tertiary Prevention: *Techniques designed to minimize the harm done by psychological disorders.*

Therapies, whatever their nature, are designed to correct or repair damage that has already occurred: They swing into action *after* individuals have begun to experience psychological disorders. A different approach to psychological problems is *prevention*. When psychologists use this term, they refer to one of three goals: (1) **primary prevention**, or preventing disorders from developing; (2) **secondary prevention**, or early detection and treatment so that minor disorders do not become major ones; and (3) **tertiary prevention**, or efforts to minimize the harm done to the individual and to society. In an important

Parent's History	Current Family Situation	Parent's Approach to Child Rearing	Table 13.1
Experience of abuse or neglect	Social isolation	Infrequent praise	**Factors Related to Child Abuse**
Lack of affection from own parents	Marital discord	Strict demands	The greater the extent to which a parent experiences the factors and conditions shown here, the greater the likelihood that the parent will abuse his or her children. (*Source:* Based on data from Nietzel & Himelein, 1986.)
Large family	Parental retardation or illiteracy	Low level of supervision	
Teenage marriage	Stressful living conditions	Early toilet training	
		Disagreements with partner over child-rearing practices	

sense, prevention is where a considerable part of the action promises to be in the mental health field in the years ahead. Efforts are now underway to help prevent many serious psychological disorders—and social problems—through a wide range of programs. The scope of these efforts and of the problems they address is extremely broad (e.g., Berman & Jobes, 1991). As an example of such work, let's look at recent efforts aimed at preventing child abuse.

CHILD ABUSE Each year many thousands of children are physically abused by their parents. Indeed, in the United States alone, more than 1 million cases of child abuse are reported each year (Krugman & Davidson, 1990). Can anything be done to reduce this tragedy? Growing evidence provides a mildly encouraging answer. Conditions associated with child abuse by parents have been identified (see Table 13.1), and programs designed to help counter the effects of these conditions—and so to reduce the incidence of child abuse—have been devised and tested (e.g., Wolfe, Sandler, & Kaufman, 1981). The results obtained have been encouraging. Consider, for example, a project involving 400 pregnant women who, because of a cluster of factors such as those in Table 13.1, were at risk for abusing their children. One group received free transportation to medical appointments. A second received nine visits to the home by a nurse during pregnancy in addition to the free transportation. Women in a third group also received regular visits by a nurse that extended to the child's second birthday. Moreover, during these visits, the nurse provided health consultations and information about parenting. In contrast, women in a control group received none of these benefits. Results were clear: 19 percent of those in the control group abused or neglected their children within the first two years of life. In contrast, only 4 percent of those receiving the maximum intervention showed such behavior. (The other two groups were in between.) These findings, and similar results in other research, indicate that appropriate preventive programs can substantially reduce the incidence of child abuse.

KEY QUESTIONS

- What kind of care have psychologically disturbed persons received in large state institutions?
- Why is the number of persons in such institutions much lower now than it was?

MAKING PSYCHOLOGY PART OF YOUR LIFE

How to Choose a Therapist: A Consumer's Guide

The odds are quite high that at some point during your life, you or someone very close to you will experience a psychological disorder. Depression, phobias, anxiety—these are very common patterns. If there's one point I hope this chapter has made clear, it is this: Effective help is available. When psychological problems occur, don't hesitate to seek assistance. But how should you go about obtaining such help—choosing a therapist? Here are some basic pointers.

1. *Where to go first.* The first question—how to start the process—is perhaps the trickiest. While you are a student, this task is fairly simple. Virtually every college or university has a department of psychology and a student health center, and in these locations, you are almost certain to find someone who can direct you to valuable sources of help—clinics, individual practitioners, referral services. So don't be shy. If you feel that you or someone close to you needs help, make an appointment to see someone.

But what if you are no longer a student and have no contact with university campuses? Can you still phone and ask for help from the nearest department of psychology? Absolutely. Psychology, after all, has a dual nature: It is both a branch of science *and* a helping profession. So the fact that you are not a student should not prevent you from asking for assistance in locating a therapist.

If for some reason this is not practical, there are other routes you can follow. First, you can ask your physician or some member of the clergy to direct you to the help you need. Both will almost certainly know someone you can contact in this regard. If you have no local physician and don't know any clergy, you can contact your local Mental Health Association. This organization is listed in the phone book and can direct you to the help you need. In short, there are several ways to proceed. Not knowing where to begin is definitely *not* a good excuse for delay.

2. *Choosing a therapist.* Let's assume that by following one of the routes outlined above, you have obtained the names of several different therapists. How can you choose among them? Several guidelines are useful.

First, always check for *credentials.* Therapists should generally be trained professionals. Before you consult one, be sure that this person has a PhD in psychology, an MD degree plus a residency in psychiatry, or other equivalent training. While such credentials don't guarantee that the therapist can help you, they are an important step in this direction.

Second, try to find out something about the kind of disorders in which each therapist specializes. Most will readily give you this information, and what you are looking for is a good *match* between your needs and the therapist's special competence.

Third, it is often helpful to know something about a therapist's preferred techniques of therapy. Most psychologists are quite eclectic: They use a wide variety of treatment procedures and tailor these to the needs of individual clients. Still, many therapists are most familiar with, and most highly trained in, the use of specific procedures. If you are uncomfortable with the particular type of therapy favored by a given therapist, then by all means look elsewhere.

3. *Signs of progress: How long should therapy take?* If therapy is going well, both you and the therapist will know it. You'll be able to see the beneficial changes in your behavior, your thoughts, and your feelings. But what if it is not going well? When and how should you decide to go elsewhere? This is a difficult decision, but a rough rule of thumb is this: If you have been visiting a therapist regularly (once a week or more) for three months and see no change, it may be time to ask the therapist whether she or he is satisfied with your progress. Most forms of therapy practiced by psychologists at present are relatively short-term in nature: They are designed to produce results relatively quickly. If several months have passed and your distress has not decreased, it is probably time to raise this issue with your therapist. In fact, it is a good idea to ask about the length of treatment when you first begin. Given the fact that all individuals differ, length of treatment is hard to predict. Still, an experienced therapist should have a general idea of how long therapy should take and will gladly share this information with you.

4. *Danger: When to quit.* Therapy is designed to help—to relieve the distress of psychological disorders. Unfortunately, though, there are instances in which it can actually hurt. Estimates indicate that negative effects may occur as often as 10 percent of the time (Lambert, Shapiro, & Bergin, 1986). How can you tell that you are in danger of such outcomes? Several basic points can help.

First, and most obvious, if you or people around you notice that you are actually becoming more distressed—more depressed, more anxious, and/or more nervous—you should take a step back and ask yourself whether you are satisfied with what is happening. It may be that these trends are only temporary. Still, signs that things are actually getting worse are certainly grounds for concern, and this is an issue you should raise with your therapist.

Second, never, under any circumstances, should you agree to performing activities during therapy that run counter to your own moral or ethical principles. A very large majority of therapists adopt extremely high standards and would never dream of making such requests. Sad to relate, however, there are a few who will take advantage of the therapeutic relationship to exploit their patients. The most common forms of such exploitation are sexual in nature. Unprincipled therapists may suggest that their clients engage in sexual relations with them as part of their "treatment." *This is never appropriate and is strongly censured by all professional associations.* So if your therapist makes such suggestions, it's time to leave.

Third, beware of exaggerated claims. If a therapist tells you that she or he can guarantee to remake your life, to convert you into a powerhouse of human energy, or to assure you of total happiness, be cautious. This is probably a sign that you are dealing with an unprincipled—and probably poorly trained—individual. Again, beat a hasty retreat.

All of these suggestions are merely *guidelines* you can follow in order to be a sophisticated consumer of psychological services. There may be cases, for exam-

ple, in which therapy requires considerably longer than the time period noted above; in which a therapist has valid reasons for being reluctant to discuss the procedures she or he will use; or in which someone without full credentials can be very helpful. These guidelines, however, should help you to avoid some of the pitfalls that exist with respect to finding a competent, caring therapist. Remember: *Effective help is definitely out there if you take the trouble to look for it.*

How would you seek help for psychological problems, if it became needed?

SUMMARY AND REVIEW OF KEY QUESTIONS

PSYCHOTHERAPIES: PSYCHOLOGICAL APPROACHES TO PSYCHOLOGICAL DISORDERS

• *What do psychodynamic therapies see as the basis for psychological disorders?*

Psychodynamic therapies such as psychoanalysis suggest that psychological disorders stem largely from hidden conflicts.

• *Is the widespread public acceptance of psychoanalysis justified?*

Although classical Freudian psychoanalysis is very famous, there is little evidence for its effectiveness.

• *How do humanistic therapies explain the occurrence of psychological disorders?*

Humanistic therapies assume that psychological disorders stem from interference by elements in one's environment with personal growth.

• *What is the major focus of Rogers's client-centered therapy?*

Rogers's client-centered therapy focuses on eliminating unrealistic conditions of worth in a therapeutic environment of unconditional positive regard.

• *What is the major focus of Gestalt therapy?*

Gestalt therapy focuses on helping clients acknowledge disowned parts of their own personalities and feelings.

• *What do behavior therapies see as the basis for psychological disorders?*

Behavior therapies assume that psychological disorders stem from faulty learning.

• *On what principles of learning are behavior therapies based?*

Behavior therapies are based on principles of classical conditioning such as extinction and desensitization.

They may also be based on principles of operant conditioning such as positive reinforcement and punishment.

- *What specific changes do behavior therapies based on operant conditioning attempt to produce?*

Behavior therapies based on operant conditioning attempt to strengthen adaptive behaviors or weaken and replace maladaptive ones.

- *What do cognitive therapies see as the basis for psychological disorders?*

Cognitive therapies assume that psychological disorders stem from irrational thoughts.

- *What is the major focus of rational-emotive therapy?*

Rational-emotive therapy focuses on inducing individuals to recognize and reject irrational assumptions and thoughts.

- *How do cognitive behavior therapies attempt to alleiviate depression?*

Cognitive behavior therapies seek to eliminate self-defeating modes of thought that seem to play an important role in depression.

KEY TERMS: psychotherapies, p. 484; therapeutic alliance, p. 484; psychodynamic therapies, p. 485; free association, p. 485; resistance, p. 486; transference, p. 486; humanistic therapies, p. 488; client-centered therapy, p. 488; conditions of worth, p. 488; Gestalt therapy, p. 488; behavior therapies, p. 490; systematic desensitization, p. 490; token economies, p. 491; cognitive therapy, p. 493; rational emotive therapy, p. 495; cognitive behavior therapy, p. 495

GROUP THERAPIES: WORKING WITH OTHERS TO SOLVE PERSONAL PROBLEMS

- *What is the major focus of psychodynamic group therapies such as psychodrama?*

Such therapies are designed to help individuals bring inner conflicts to the surface.

- *What is the major focus of behavioral group therapies?*

Behavioral group therapies focus on changing specific aspects of behavior, such as social skills or assertiveness.

- *What is the major focus of humanistic group therapies?*

Humanistic group therapies focus on enhancing personal growth and improving self-knowledge.

- *What are self-help groups, and what do they provide?*

Self-help groups consist of persons who share a problem. Such groups provide social support for their members and can be helpful in some instances.

KEY TERMS: group therapies, p. 496; psychodrama, p. 496; encounter groups, p. 497; sensitivity-training groups, p. 497; self-help groups, p. 497

THERAPIES FOCUSED ON INTERPERSONAL RELATIONS: MARITAL AND FAMILY THERAPY

- *What is the major focus of marital or couple therapy?*

Marital or couple therapy focuses on improving communication and changing faulty attributions within couples.

- *What is the major focus of family therapy?*

Family therapy focuses on improving relations among family members by reducing contradictory communication and altering family structure.

KEY TERMS: marital therapy, p. 498; family therapy, p. 499

PSYCHOTHERAPY: SOME CURRENT ISSUES

- *Is psychotherapy effective?*

Growing evidence indicates that psychotherapy is effective.

- *Are some types of psychotherapy more effective than others?*

Surprisingly, existing evidence suggests that various types of psychotherapy do not differ in overall success, perhaps because all forms of therapy share certain crucial features.

BIOLOGICALLY BASED THERAPIES

- *What is electroconvulsive therapy?*

Electroconvulsive therapy involves delivery of strong shocks to the brain. It is used to treat depression.

- *What is psychosurgery?*

Psychosurgery is any of various types of surgery performed on the brain in an attempt to reduce or eliminate psychological disorders.

- *What drugs are used in the treatment of psychological disorders?*

Drugs are used to treat a wide range of psychological disorders. Antipsychotic drugs reduce many symptoms, including hallucinations and extreme hostility. Antidepressant drugs counter depression but can produce side effects such as hypertension. Antianxiety drugs are effective in reducing anxiety, but may be habit-forming.

KEY TERMS: biologically based therapies, p. 506; electroconvulsive therapy, p. 506; psychosurgery, p. 507; drug therapy, p. 508; tardive dyskinesia, p. 509

THE SETTING FOR THERAPY: FROM INSTITUTIONAL CARE TO THE COMMUNITY

- *What kind of care have psychologically disturbed persons received in large state institutions?*

Such institutions have provided mainly custodial care for patients.

- *Why is the number of persons in state institutions much lower now than it was?*

The number of persons in such institutions has sharply decreased largely because of the availability of effective drug therapies. In addition, many persons with psychological problems are now treated in community mental health centers.

KEY TERMS: *community mental health centers, p. 512; primary prevention, p. 512; secondary prevention, p. 512; tertiary prevention, p. 512*

CRITICAL THINKING QUESTIONS

APPRAISAL	If various forms of therapy are as effective as suggested in this chapter, then why are psychological disorders so common? Why, in short, don't more people seek out appropriate treatment for their psychological problems?
CONTROVERSY	Most bookstores have a large self-help section—an area for books that promise to help individuals deal with their psychological problems. Do you believe that such books are useful? Or do you think that in many cases they can actually do more harm than good?
MAKING PSYCHOLOGY PART OF YOUR LIFE	Now that you know something about how various forms of therapy work, do you think you are more likely to seek out the help of a trained psychologist or other professional if *you* experience psychological distress? If not, what factors would deter you from doing so?

Social Thought and Social Behavior

*B*eing totally cut off from other people—that's the theme of many books and stories. Can you imagine what that would be like? Whether the story takes place on a desert island or in space, our reactions are much the same: We sympathize with the person experiencing such isolation, and we shudder at the thought of experiencing it ourselves. Our reactions in this respect are far from surprising, for other people truly play a crucial role in our lives. They are the source and focus of our most important emotions—love, anger, envy, jealousy. They are the source of many of our most valued forms of reward—praise, approval, sympathy, affection; *and* of our most devastating forms of punishment—criticism, rejection, disapproval. Life without other people is, in a very real sense, unimaginable. Yet, despite this fact, other persons often remain something of a mystery to us. They say and do things we don't expect; have motives we don't understand; and, as noted in chapter 3, often see the world through very different eyes than we do. For this reason, we do not merely *interact* with others; we also spend lots of time *thinking* about them. These two topics—social thought and social behavior—serve as the major focus of **social psychology**, the branch of psychology that investigates all aspects of social thought and social behavior.

Social psychology is an extremely diverse field. Indeed, when I teach this course, I describe it to my students as "the field that covers everything from love to hate, and whatever's in between." To provide you with an overview of this intriguing field, I'll proceed as follows. First, I'll introduce several aspects of *social thought: attribution*—our efforts to understand the causes behind others' behavior; *social cognition*—how we notice, store, remember, and process social information; and *attitudes*—our cognitive representations and evaluations of various features of the social or physical world.

After considering social thought, we'll turn to important aspects of *social behavior: prejudice*—negative attitudes toward the members of various social groups; *social influence*—the many ways in which individuals attempt to change others' behavior; *prosocial behavior*—actions we perform that benefit others; and *attraction, love,* and *close relationships*—the questions of why we like or dislike other persons, why we fall in (and out) of love, and how we form close relationships with others. We'll conclude by briefly examining effects of the physical environment on social behavior and how social behavior, in turn, affects the physical environment. These are important issues in the field of *environmental psychology.* Another aspect of social psychology—aggression—is covered in chapter 9.

SOCIAL THOUGHT: *Thinking about Other People*

Learning Objective 14.1
Be able to define attribution and identify the conditions leading to internal and external causal attributions according to Kelley's model.

Learning Objective 14.2
Describe the various attributional biases.

*H*ow much time do you spend thinking about other people? Probably, much more than you realize. Whenever you try to figure out why people have acted in various ways, or whenever you try to make various judgments about them (for example, will someone make a good roommate, or like one of your friends?), you are engaging in *social thought*. In short, there are many different aspects to this basic process. In this discussion we'll focus on three that have been identified by social psychologists as among the most important: *attribution, social cognition,* and *attitudes*.

ATTRIBUTION: *Understanding the Causes of Others' Behavior*

Imagine the following situation. You're standing at a counter in a store waiting your turn, when suddenly another customer walks up and hands the clerk an item he wishes to purchase. How do you react? While your first response is probably "with anger!", the way you react really depends on your perceptions of *why* this person has cut in front of you. Did he do it on purpose? In that case you are almost certain to get angry. But perhaps he just didn't see you, or maybe he is from another culture and is unfamiliar with the concept of waiting in line. In short, it's not just what this person did that matters; your perception of *why* he did it is important, too. This question—*why* others act the way they do—is one we face every day in a wide range of contexts. The process through which we attempt to answer this question—to determine the causes behind others' behavior—is known as **attribution**.

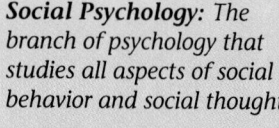

Social Psychology: The branch of psychology that studies all aspects of social behavior and social thought.

Attribution: The processes through which we seek to determine the causes behind others' behavior.

CAUSAL ATTRIBUTION: HOW WE ANSWER THE QUESTION "WHY?" Our efforts to understand the causes behind others' behavior take many forms. For example, we are often interested in identifying people's major traits—what kind of persons they really are (Gilbert et al., 1992; Jones & Davis, 1965). One of the most important questions we ask, however, is this: "Do others' actions stem mainly from *internal* causes (their own char-

"I'll be straight with you. I was put on this planet to make your life miserable."

acteristics, motives, intentions), largely from *external* factors (some aspect of the physical or social world), or from some combination of the two?" How do we go about reaching such conclusions? A theory proposed by Kelley (1972; Hilton & Slugoski, 1986) provides some intriguing insights.

According to Kelley, we seek to determine whether other persons' actions stem mainly from internal or external causes by focusing on three types of information. First, we consider **consensus**—the extent to which others react in the same manner to some stimulus or event as the person on whom we are focusing. Second, we consider **consistency**—the extent to which this person reacts to this stimulus or event in the same way on *other occasions.* And finally, we consider **distinctiveness**—the extent to which the person reacts in the same manner to other, different stimuli or events.

Kelley suggests that we are most likely to attribute another's behavior to internal causes under conditions where consensus and distinctiveness are *low*, but consistency is *high*. In contrast, we are most likely to attribute another's behavior to external causes under conditions where consensus, consistency, and distinctiveness are all *high*. Finally, we attribute behavior to a combination of these factors when consensus is *low*, but consistency and distinctiveness are *high*. Let's apply these suggestions to the "cutting in line" example above.

First, imagine that consistency is high, while both consensus and distinctiveness are low. That is, the person who cuts in front of you does so on other occasions, too (high consistency); few other people engage in such behavior (low consensus); and this person pushes ahead of others in different contexts, such as while driving or in grocery stores (low distinctiveness). Here, Kelley's theory predicts that you will attribute the individual's behavior to *internal factors*, concluding, perhaps, that he is a rude, inconsiderate person who needs to learn some manners.

In contrast, imagine that consistency, consensus, and distinctiveness are all high. That is, this person pushes ahead of you on other occasions (high consistency); many other people also push ahead of you (high consensus); and this person does not push ahead of others in different contexts (high distinctiveness). Here, Kelley's theory predicts that you will attribute the person's behavior to external factors—something about the current situation, perhaps the fact that you act in ways that seem to *invite* other people to cut in line ahead of you (see Figure 14.1 on page 522 for a summary of these suggestions).

Do we really think about others and the causes behind their actions in this manner? Performing the kind of analysis described by Kelley requires a lot of effort, and as I've noted repeatedly in this text, people tend to avoid unnecessary cognitive effort. So it's not surprising that studies that have investigated this issue (e.g., Hansen, 1980; Lupfer, Clark, & Hutcherson, 1990), point to the

---

ATTRIBUTION: DETERMINING THE CAUSES BEHIND OTHERS' BEHAVIOR

Why do other people act as they do? This is a question we often ask during social interaction. This woman has received a clear-cut answer to this question—but we doubt that she likes it!
(*Source:* Drawing by Bruce Eric Kaplan; © 1993 The New Yorker Magazine, Inc.)

Learning Objective 14.3
Know the definition of social cognition and sources of error in social thought, including the false consensus effect, automatic vigilance, motivated skepticism, and counterfactual thinking.

Learning Objective 14.4
Know the general definition of an attitude and the influence of conditioning.

Learning Objective 14.5
Describe the general conclusions derived from the early work on persuasion.

Learning Objective 14.6
Discuss the role of cognitive dissonance in attitude change and the practical implications of cognitive dissonance theory.

Consensus: The extent to which behavior by one person is shown by others as well.

Consistency: The extent to which a given person responds in the same way to a given stimulus across time.

Distinctiveness: The extent to which a given person reacts in the same manner to different stimuli or situations.

FIGURE **14.1**

Kelly's Theory of Causal Attribution: An Overview

Kelley's theory indicates that when consensus, distinctiveness, and consistency are all high, we attribute others' behavior to external causes (upper diagram). When consensus and distinctiveness are low while consistency is high, however, we attribute others' behavior to internal causes (lower diagram).

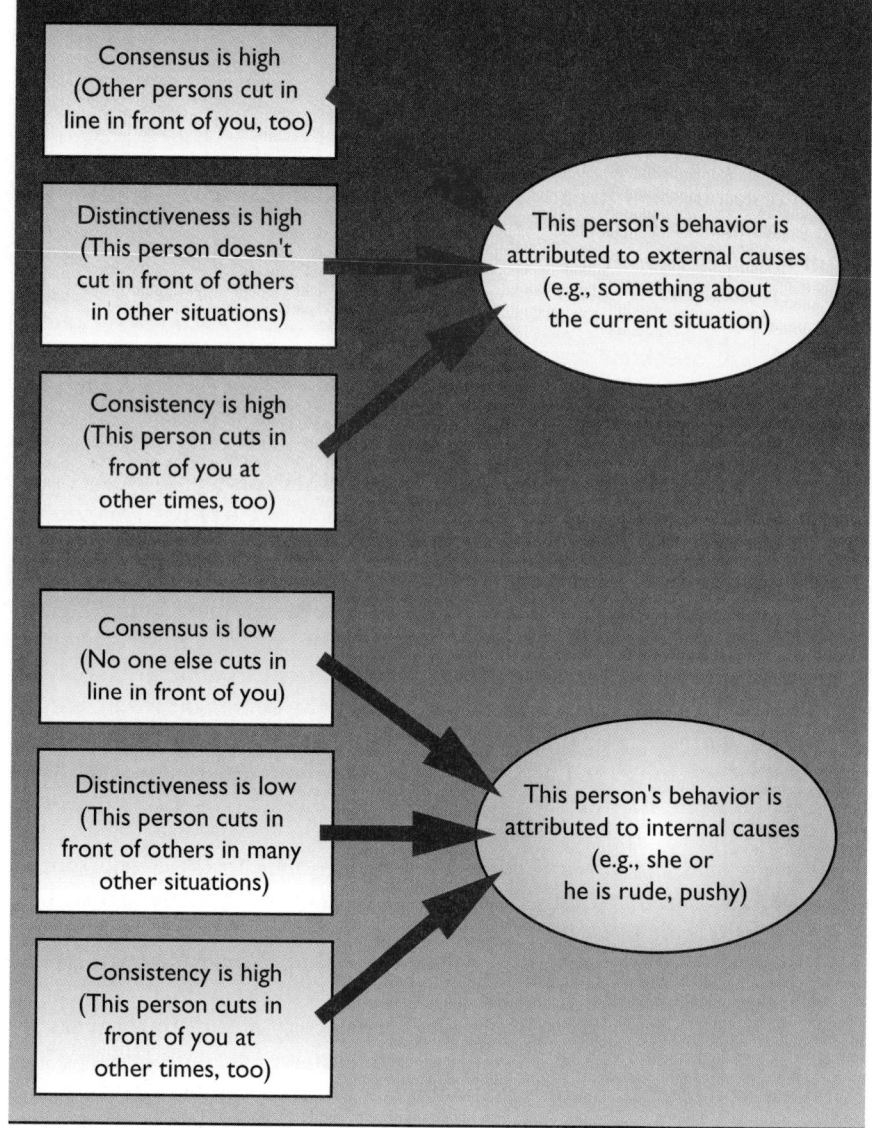

following conclusions: We *do* use the kind of information emphasized by Kelley in situations where we feel that high levels of cognitive effort are justified—primarily in situations where it's important to us to understand why others acted as they did, or when we can't readily explain their actions in terms of what we know about a specific situation or specific persons. In many other cases, however, we don't bother to perform this kind of analysis because, quite simply, it involves too much effort.

ATTRIBUTION: SOME BASIC SOURCES OF BIAS   Our discussion so far seems to imply that attribution is a highly rational process in which individuals seek to identify the causes of others' behavior by following orderly cognitive steps. In general, it is. However, attribution is also subject to several forms of bias—tendencies that can lead us into serious errors concerning the causes of others' behavior. Let's consider several of these.

The fundamental attribution error: Overestimating the role of dispositional causes.   Imagine that you witness the following scene: A man arrives at a meeting thirty minutes late. On entering the room he drops his notes on the floor. While attempting to pick them up, he falls over and breaks his glasses. How would you explain these events? Probably by concluding that this person is disorganized, clumsy, and generally inept. In other words, you would emphasize *internal* causes in your explanation. Are such attributions accurate? Perhaps. But it is also possible that the individual was late because of unavoidable delays in traffic, that he dropped his notes because they were printed on extremely slick paper, and that he fell down because the floor had just been waxed and was very slippery. The fact that you would be less likely to mention such *external* potential causes reflects what is often described as the **fundamental attribution error**—our strong tendency to explain others' actions in terms of dispositional (internal) rather than situational (external) causes. In sum, we tend to perceive others as acting as they do because they are "that kind of person" rather than because of situational factors that may well have affected their behavior.

Why do we show this tendency? One explanation suggests that when we observe others' behavior, we focus on their actions rather than on the context in which such actions take place. As a result, we tend to downplay potential situational causes of people's behavior. Another, related possibility is that we do notice situational factors but tend to assign insufficient importance to them (Gilbert & Jones, 1986). Whatever the precise basis for the fundamental attribution error, it has important implications. For example, it suggests that even if individuals are made aware of the situational forces that adversely affect disadvantaged groups in society—forces such as poor diet, disrupted family life, and exposure to lawless and violent peer models—they may still perceive such persons as "bad" and responsible for their own plight. In this respect, the fundamental attribution error can have important social consequences.

Interestingly, our tendency to attribute others' actions to internal causes tends to weaken over time (Burger, 1986; Frank & Gilovich, 1988). In other words, while we tend to attribute someone's action to internal causes soon after it has occurred, we take greater and greater account of situational causes with the passage of time. It seems that over time, the ease of remembering personal information diminishes more rapidly than the ease of remembering situational information. This kind of shift is illustrated clearly by research conducted by Burger and Pavelich (1993).

These investigators examined explanations for the outcome of various U.S. presidential elections printed on the editorial pages of major newspapers (the *New York Times, Wall Street Journal,* and *Christian Science Monitor)* within five days of the elections and much later—two or three years after the elections in question. Their object was to see whether the editorials attributed outcomes to personal characteristics of one or both candidates (internal causes) or to circumstances surrounding the election or events outside the candidates' control (external factors). An example of personal causes is: "Mondale made the outcome worse by the ineptitude of his campaign." An example of situational causes is: "The shadows of Watergate . . . cleared the way for Carter's climb to the presidency." Results were clear: Explanations printed a few days after the election emphasized internal causes; nearly two-thirds mentioned such causes. Two or three years later, however, the opposite was true: Two-thirds of the explanations referred to situational factors. So, over time, the fundamental attribution error does indeed tend to vanish, even in the realm of politics.

The self-serving bias: "I can do no wrong; you can do no right."
Suppose that you write a term paper for one of your classes. After reading it, your instructor provides very positive feedback. To what will you attribute such success? If you are like most people, the chances are good that you will explain it in terms of *internal* causes—your own talent or the high level of effort you put into preparing the report.

Fundamental Attribution Error: *The tendency to attribute behavior to internal causes to a greater extent than is actually justified.*

Now, in contrast, imagine that your instructor dislikes the report and criticizes it harshly. How will you explain *this* outcome? Here, it is likely that you will focus mainly on situational causes—the difficulty of the task, the instructor's unrealistically high standards, and so on. In short, you may well show another type of attributional error known as the **self-serving bias** (Miller & Ross, 1975). This is our tendency to take credit for positive behavior or outcomes by attributing them to internal causes, but to blame negative ones on external causes, especially on factors beyond our control (Baumgardner, Hepner, & Arkin, 1986; Brown & Rogers, 1991). Why does this slant in our attributions occur? While several factors may play a role, the most important seem to involve our need to protect and enhance our self-esteem, or the related desire to look good to others (Brown & Rogers, 1991; Greenberg, Pyszczynski, & Solomon, 1982). Attributing our successes to internal causes while attributing failures to external causes permits us to accomplish these ego-protective goals.

Whatever the precise origins of the self-serving bias, it can be the cause of much interpersonal friction. It often leads persons who work with others on a joint task to perceive that *they*, not their partners, have made the major contributions. Similarly, it leads individuals to perceive that while their own successes stem from internal causes and are well deserved, the successes of others stem from external factors and are less appropriate. Also, because of the self-serving bias, many persons tend to perceive negative actions on their part as justified and excusable, but identical actions by others as irrational and inexcusable (Baumeister, Stillwell, & Wotman, 1990). In these ways the self-serving bias can have important effects on interpersonal relations.

KEY QUESTIONS

- According to a theory proposed by Kelley, what kinds of information do we use in deciding whether others' actions stem from internal or external causes?

- What is the fundamental attribution error?

- What is the self-serving bias?

SOCIAL COGNITION: *How We Process Social Information*

Identifying the causes behind others' behavior is an important part of social thought; yet it is far from the entire picture. In thinking about other persons, we must also determine which information about them is most important and so worthy of further processing; we must enter this information into long-term memory; we must be able to retrieve it at later times, when needed; and we must be able to combine it in various ways in order to reach various judgments and decisions about others. These tasks are known in social psychology as **social cognition**—the processes through which we notice, interpret, remember, and then use social information (Gilovich, 1990; Ross, 1989).

Thinking about other persons occupies a considerable portion of our time, and the judgments and conclusions we make about them are of crucial importance in many aspects of our lives. These facts raise an intriguing question: Just how effective *are* we at social cognition—at processing information about others?

The answer provided by research is somewhat mixed. On the one hand, we do seem to be quite efficient in sorting, combining, and remembering a wealth of information about other persons (Fiske & Taylor, 1991). Considering the amount of input provided by people's words and deeds, this is no simple accomplishment! On the other hand, our social thought is subject to a number of intriguing forms of error. Most of these involve *mental shortcuts*—strategies we use to extract the maximum value from the widest range of information with the least amount of mental effort.

We have already examined some of these shortcuts in chapter 7, where *heuristics* were discussed. As you may recall, these are mental rules of thumb we use for making judgments or decisions very quickly. In this section, there-

✓Self-Serving Bias: The tendency to attribute positive outcomes to our own traits or characteristics but negative outcomes to factors beyond our control.

Social Cognition: The processes through which we notice, interpret, remember, and later use social information.

fore, we'll focus on other aspects of social thought—additional tendencies that play important roles in our efforts to make sense out of other people and the social world (Beggan, 1992; Forgas, 1991; Pratto & John, 1991).

BASIC ASPECTS OF SOCIAL THOUGHT: HOW WE THINK ABOUT OTHER PERSONS Human beings are definitely *not* computers. While we can imagine a person who reasons in a perfectly logical manner, like Mr. Spock of "Star Trek" fame, we are unlikely to ever meet one. Being human, we are fallible where the cognitive side of life is concerned, and social thought is no exception to this rule. Let's consider some of the ways in which social cognition departs from the total rationality of a computer.

The false consensus effect: Availability and the tendency to assume that others think as we do. Be honest: On a scale ranging from 1 (strongly against) to 7 (strongly favor), what is your view about permitting persons with openly homosexual lifestyles to join the military? Now, out of one hundred other students at your college, how many do you think share your view? That is, how many are on the same side of the neutral point on this scale (4) as you are? If you are like most people, the number you indicated is higher than what would be revealed by an actual survey. In other words, you assume that people agree with you to a greater extent than is actually true. This tendency is known as the **false consensus effect,** and it occurs in many contexts. For example, college students tend to overestimate the proportion of other students who agree with their attitudes about drugs, abortion, seat-belt use, university policies, politics, ethnic foods, and even Ritz crackers or Oreo cookies (Gilovich, 1990; Marks & Miller, 1987; Suls, Wan, & Sanders, 1988). So, though this error is not very large in absolute terms—people don't grossly overestimate the extent to which others agree with them—it does appear to be quite common (see Figure 14.2).

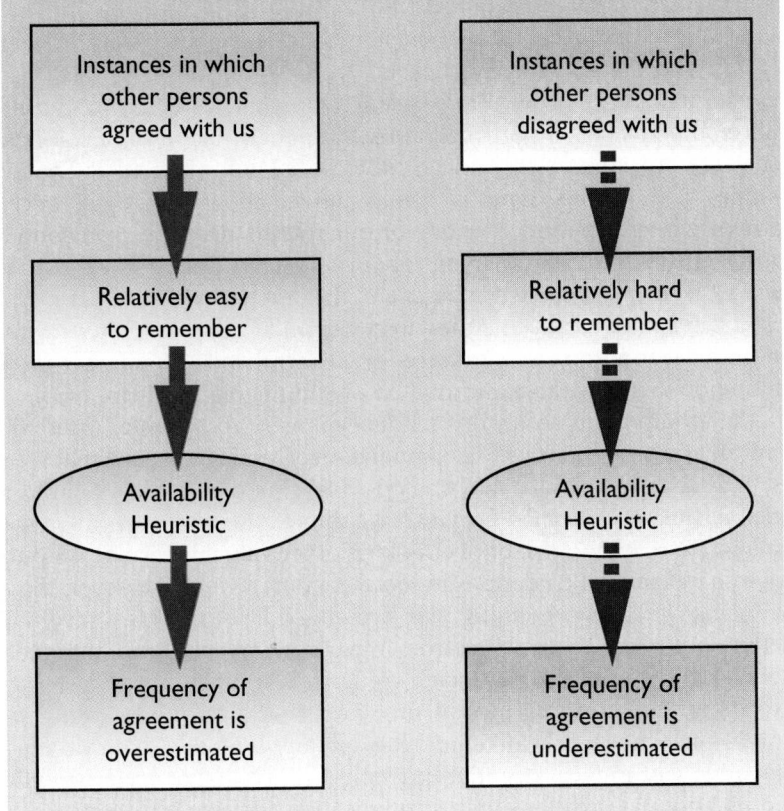

FIGURE 14.2

One Possible Basis for the False Consensus Effect

We often find it easier to remember instances in which others agreed with us than instances in which they disagreed with us. The availability heuristic indicates that the easier it is to remember information, the more weight we attach to it. As a result, we tend to overestimate the extent to which others share our opinions—the *false consensus effect.*

False Consensus Effect: The tendency to believe that other persons share our attitudes to a greater extent than is true.

What is the basis for this tendency to assume that others think as we do? Several factors seem to play a role, but the most important involves the *availability heuristic* described in chapter 7. As you may recall, the availability heuristic suggests that the easier it is to bring information to mind, the more important we judge that information to be. Applying this principle to the false consensus effect, it appears that most people find it easier to remember instances in which others have agreed with them than instances in which others have disagreed. As a result, people tend to overestimate the extent to which others share their views.

While the false consensus effect is very common, it's also important to note that it does not occur in all situations. Where highly *desirable* attributes are concerned, people wish to perceive themselves as *unique*—more different from others, in a positive direction, than they actually are (Suls & Wan, 1987). As a result, they tend to perceive themselves as happier, more intelligent, more ethical, and less prejudiced than the people around them (Miller & McFarland, 1987). If you'd like to demonstrate this for yourself, just ask ten of your friends to rate themselves on leadership ability; chances are good that almost all will rate themselves as above average on this dimension.

Automatic vigilance: Noticing the negative. Read the following information about someone named Jim:

> Jim, a junior at State U, is a biology major with an A– grade point average. He hopes to enter medical school after graduation. He is a friendly and humorous person, so his friends think that he'll make a great doctor. Jim's hobby is music, and he has a large collection of CDs. He works part-time to help pay for his education and to cover the insurance on his car, which is high because of several speeding tickets. Jim grew up in a small town and has one sister who is a junior in high school. He is neat and easygoing, so he never has any trouble getting roommates and is currently living with two other men at his college.

Quick: what piece of information stands out most when you think about Jim? If you said "those speeding tickets," you are reacting like most persons, because in general, we seem to pay much more attention to *negative* information about others than to positive information about them. In fact, it is fair to say that we are *ultrasensitive* to negative social information. If another person smiles at us twenty times during a conversation but frowns once, it is the frown we tend to notice. If one of our friends describes someone to us and mentions fifteen positive things about this individual but one negative thing, *this* is the item on which we focus and the one we tend to remember. So strong is this tendency to pay attention to negative information that some researchers describe it as **automatic vigilance**—a powerful and automatic tendency to pay attention to undesirable information or stimuli (e.g., Shiffrin, 1988).

In an important sense, this tendency is very reasonable. After all, negative information may alert us to potential danger, and it is crucial that we recognize it and respond to it as quickly as possible (Pratto & John, 1991). But our attentional capacity is limited, so when we direct attention to negative social information, we run the risk of overlooking other valuable forms of input. Thus, as is true with all the tendencies in social cognition we will discuss, the automatic vigilance effect is something of a two-edged sword: It may save us cognitive effort, but it can lead us into errors in our perceptions or judgments of others.

One final point: the automatic vigilance effect helps explain why it is often so important to make a good first impression on others. Since people are highly sensitive to negative information, anything we say or do during a first meeting that triggers negative reactions is likely to have a strong effect on the impression we create—much stronger than positive information. In this and

Automatic Vigilance: *The strong tendency to pay attention to negative social information.*

CHAPTER 14

many other respects, the automatic vigilance effect can have important effects on key aspects of social thought.

Motivated skepticism: In reaching conclusions, how much information is enough? Suppose that you are listening to a political debate between two candidates. You haven't made up your mind as to which one you'll vote for, but you are leaning toward one because her views seem closer to your own. How much information consistent with your views will it take for you to make up your mind to vote for this candidate? And how does this compare with the amount of information it would require to make you change your mind and switch to the other candidate? If you think about this situation for a moment, you'll probably realize that since you already have a preference for the first candidate, it won't take much to move you firmly into her camp: A relatively small amount of information will suffice. But what about the other candidate? Clearly, this person has a tough job ahead: She or he will have to say a lot of things with which you agree before you reverse your initial preference and decide to vote for this candidate.

This situation illustrates another basic aspect of our social thought: In general, we are skeptical about information that is inconsistent with our initial preferences but quite open to information that supports these views. Put another way, we examine information that supports our preferred conclusions much less carefully—and less skeptically—than information that is inconsistent with what we want to believe or decide. Evidence for this tendency to be more skeptical about information that doesn't support our current views—**motivated skepticism**—is provided by the findings of many studies (e.g., Ditto et al., 1988; Ditto & Lopez, 1992; Kruglanski, 1990). Thus, motivated skepticism appears to be yet another important "tilt" in social cognition. Because of its operation, we tend to require relatively little supporting information to arrive at the conclusions we *want* to reach, but a great deal of disconfirming information to arrive at conclusions opposite to our initial inclinations. This does not mean that we never acknowledge the accuracy or usefulness of information contrary to our preferences; we do accept such input in some cases. But, in general, we seem to possess several kinds of *cognitive filters* that make it more difficult for such input to enter into our social thought and to shape our conclusions. Motivated skepticism is one of these filters. When it operates, the answer to the question "How much information do we require before making a decision?" is "That depends on how closely it matches what we already believe."

Counterfactual thinking: The effects of considering "what might have been." Consider the following incidents:

> Ms. Caution never picks up hitchhikers. Yesterday, however, she gave a stranger a ride. He robbed her and stole her car.

> Ms. Risk frequently picks up hitchhikers. Yesterday, she gave a stranger a ride. He robbed her and stole her car.

Which of these two persons will experience greater regret? Both individuals have had precisely the same outcomes, but if you are like most people, you probably answered, "Ms. Caution will be more upset." Why? The answer involves some intriguing facts about social thought and the judgments and reactions stemming from it. Briefly, our reactions to various events depend not only on the events themselves, but also on what these events bring to mind (Kahneman & Miller, 1986). When we have an experience, we do not only think about the experience itself; we also engage in **counterfactual thinking**—imagining events and outcomes *different* from the ones we actually experienced (Gleicher et al., 1990). In this particular instance, we think, "If

Motivated Skepticism: The tendency to require more information to make a decision contrary to one's initial preferences than a decision consistent with one's initial preferences.

Counterfactual Thinking: The tendency to evaluate events by thinking about alternatives to them—"what might have been."

only Ms. Caution had not violated her usual rule against picking up hitchhikers, she would have avoided this frightening incident." Alternatively, we may imagine, "If only Ms. Risk had read the papers, she might have realized how dangerous it is to pick up hitchhikers. Then she might have acted differently."

But why does such counterfactual thinking lead us to conclude that Ms. Caution will experience greater regret? In part because it is easier to imagine alternatives to *unusual* forms of behavior than to *usual* or typical forms of behavior. In other words, it requires less mental effort to imagine Ms. Caution driving right by the hitchhiker—her usual behavior—than to imagine Ms. Risk *not* stopping for him—an unusual action for her. So we conclude that Ms. Caution experienced more regret because it is easier to imagine her acting in a different way—sticking to her rule—than it is to imagine Ms. Risk acting differently. After all, Ms. Risk always picks up hitchhikers; it was just her bad luck that it finally caught up with her.

This reasoning about counterfactual thinking leads to the following prediction: Negative outcomes that follow unusual behavior will generate more sympathy for the persons who experience them than negative outcomes that follow usual or typical behavior. This prediction has been confirmed by research findings (e.g., Miller & McFarland, 1987). For example, in one study on counterfactual thinking, Macrae (1992) had two groups of students read different versions of an incident in which a young woman got food poisoning after eating in a restaurant. In one condition the restaurant was one she regularly visited. In the other it was described as her first visit to this particular restaurant; in other words, her behavior in going there was unusual. Participants were then asked to indicate how much compensation the victim should receive and how large a fine the restaurant should pay for its negligence. Both amounts were larger in the "unusual behavior" (exceptional) condition than in the "usual behavior" (routine) condition.

In sum, our tendency to imagine events other than those that actually occurred is another important aspect of social cognition. Thinking about "what might have been" may sometimes be just as important in terms of our judgments and conclusions about others as thinking about what *did* occur.

SOME POSITIVE THOUGHTS ON SOCIAL COGNITION Looking back, this discussion of social cognition seems to paint a fairly bleak picture. In our efforts to make sense out of the social world, it seems, we use many mental shortcuts; and these can often lead us to false conclusions and inaccurate judgments or decisions. While this is certainly true in some instances, growing evidence also supports a somewhat more positive conclusion. The tendencies I've described do sometimes cause us to make errors, but this seems to be the exception rather than the rule. More typically, our mental shortcuts allow us to have our cake and eat it too—to process complex information quickly and efficiently without making serious errors. In this sense, it is useful to view the tendencies and effects we have considered here not as errors, but as useful working compromises we adopt in order to deal with persistent *information overload*—more social input than we can easily handle (Funder, 1987).

KEY QUESTIONS

• What is the false consensus effect?

• What is the automatic vigilance effect?

• What is motivated skepticism?

• What is counterfactual thinking?

ATTITUDES: Evaluating the Social World

Consider the following list:

Bill Clinton	AIDS
Michael Jackson	Sharon Stone
2 Live Crew	pizza

Do you have any reactions to each item? Unless you have been living a life of total isolation, you probably do. You may like or dislike President Clinton, be very worried or unconcerned about the spread of AIDS, and find Sharon Stone attractive or unattractive. At one time or other you have probably thought about every item on this list and have developed feelings and beliefs about them. Together, such reactions are generally known as **attitudes**—mental representations and evaluations of various aspects of the social world (Judd et al., 1991).

Attitudes are formed through basic processes of learning we considered in chapter 5. For example, they often stem from *operant conditioning*, since we are frequently rewarded by our parents, teachers, or friends for expressing the "correct views"—the ones *they* hold. Similarly, attitudes also derive from *observational learning*. Throughout life, we tend to emulate the views and preferences expressed by people we like or respect simply because we are exposed to these views. Even *classical conditioning* plays a role; it may be especially influential in shaping the *emotional,* or *affective,* aspect of attitudes (e.g., Betz & Krosnick, 1993; Krosnick et al., 1992).

Whatever their precise origins, attitudes are an important aspect of social thought and have long been the subject of systematic study by social psychologists. In this discussion we'll focus on certain key aspects of attitudes: *persuasion*—how attitudes can sometimes be changed; and *cognitive dissonance*—a process through which we sometimes actually seem to change our attitudes.

PERSUASION IN ACTION

Efforts to change attitudes and behavior through persuasion are all around us.

PERSUASION: THE PROCESS OF CHANGING ATTITUDES As the twentieth century draws to a close, the business of changing attitudes—or at least trying to change them—seems to grow ever more intense. Television commercials, magazine ads, giant billboards, political campaigns, public service announcements urging people to wear seat belts, stop smoking, or exercise—the messages and media vary, but the goal remains the same: to change people's attitudes and so, ultimately, their behavior. To what extent are such efforts at **persuasion** effective? And what factors determine whether and to what extent persuasion succeeds?

Persuasion: The traditional approach. In most cases, efforts at persuasion involve the following basic elements: Some *source* directs some type of *message,* or communication, to some target *audience.* Early research on persuasion, therefore, focused on these basic components, by addressing various aspects of the question "*Who* says *what* to *whom* and with what *effect?*" (Hovland, Janis, & Kelley, 1953). The findings of such research were complex, but among the most important were these:

1. Experts are more persuasive than nonexperts (Hovland & Weiss, 1951).

2. Messages that do not appear to be designed to change our attitudes are often more successful than ones that seem intended to manipulate us (Walster & Festinger, 1962).

3. Popular and attractive sources are more effective in changing attitudes than unpopular or unattractive ones (Kiesler & Kiesler, 1969).

4. Persons who are relatively low in self-esteem are often easier to persuade than persons high in self-esteem (Janis, 1954).

5. When an audience holds attitudes contrary to those of a would-be persuader, it is often more effective to adopt a *two-sided approach,* in which both sides of an issue are presented, rather than a *one-sided approach,* in which only one is described. When members of an audience hold attitudes consistent with those of a would-be persuader, however, a one-sided approach is often more effective.

Attitudes: Mental representations and evaluations of features of the social or physical world.

Persuasion: The process through which one or more persons attempt to alter the attitudes of one or more others.

SOCIAL THOUGHT AND SOCIAL BEHAVIOR

6. As we saw in chapter 1, people who speak rapidly are generally more persuasive than ones who speak slowly (Miller et al., 1976), partly because they seem more competent—and confident.

One word of caution: changing attitudes is a complex and tricky business. Many different factors play a role, including all of those listed above and others as well. Moreover, these variables can and often do interact with one another. For this reason, simple generalizations about persuasion are risky at best. However, the findings reported above have generally withstood the test of time and additional research, so they appear to represent useful basic principles. As such, they constitute an important part of our knowledge about the process of persuasion.

Persuasion: The cognitive approach. The traditional approach to understanding persuasion has certainly been useful; it provided a wealth of information about the "who" and the "how" of persuasion. This approach was less helpful, however, in terms of answering the question "why"—why do people change their attitudes in response to persuasive messages?

This issue has been brought into sharp focus in a more modern approach to understanding persuasion known as the **cognitive perspective on persuasion** (Petty & Cacioppo, 1986). This cognitive perspective focuses on the following question: What cognitive processes determine when someone is actually persuaded? In other words, this newer perspective seeks to understand (1) what people think about when they are exposed to persuasive appeals, and (2) how these thoughts and cognitive processes determine whether, and to what extent, attitude change occurs.

One theory that adopts this perspective is known as the **elaboration likelihood model (ELM)** (Petty & Cacioppo, 1986). According to this model, when individuals receive a persuasive message, they think about it, the arguments it makes, and (perhaps) the arguments it has left out. It is these thoughts—not the message itself—that then lead either to attitude change or to resistance. The model also suggests that persuasion can take place through different processes. When persuasive messages deal with issues that are important or personally relevant to recipients, these persons are likely to devote careful attention to the message and the arguments it contains. In that case, persuasion occurs through what is known as the **central route**—which includes such activities as evaluating the strength or rationality of the argument and deciding whether its content agrees or disagrees with current beliefs. When messages are processed via this central route, attitude change will occur only to the extent that the arguments presented are convincing and the facts marshaled on their behalf are strong.

In contrast, when messages deal with issues that are relatively unimportant and not personally relevant to recipients, persuasion occurs through the **peripheral route**. Here, little cognitive work is performed, and attitude change, when it takes place, involves a seemingly automatic response to *persuasion cues*—information relating to the source's prestige, credibility, or likability, or to the style or form of the message the would-be persuader presents. Attitude change is more likely to occur through the peripheral route when audience members are distracted and can't engage in a careful analysis of the speaker's message (see Figure 14.3).

A growing body of evidence indicates that the ELM analysis is accurate (e.g., DeBono, 1992; Roskos-Ewoldsen & Fazio, 1992). In any case, the cognitive perspective it represents has certainly added much to our understanding of persuasion. As a result of this approach, we now know more than merely when persuasion is likely to occur; in addition, we are beginning to understand *why* this process actually takes place.

Cognitive Perspective on Persuasion: An approach that seeks to understand persuasion by identifying the cognitive processes that play a role in it.

Elaboration Likelihood Model (of persuasion): A theory suggesting that there are two distinct routes to persuasion involving different amounts of cognitive elaboration in response to a persuasive message.

Central Route (to persuasion): Attitude change resulting from systematic processing of information contained in persuasive messages.

Peripheral Route (to persuasion): Attitude change resulting from peripheral persuasion cues—information concerning the expertise, status, or attractiveness of would-be persuaders.

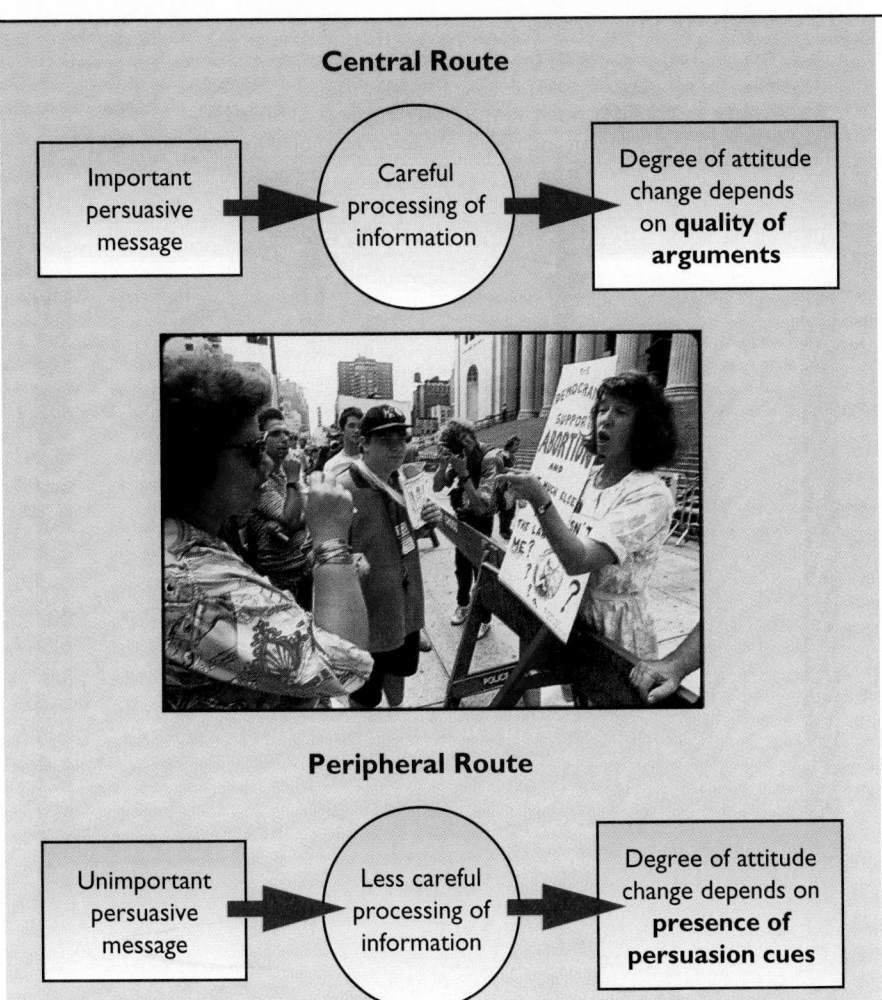

Central Route

| Important persuasive message | → | Careful processing of information | → | Degree of attitude change depends on **quality of arguments** |

Peripheral Route

| Unimportant persuasive message | → | Less careful processing of information | → | Degree of attitude change depends on **presence of persuasion cues** |

FIGURE **14.3**

The Elaboration Likelihood Model: An Overview

According to the ELM, persuasion can occur through two different processes. If persuasive messages are important or personally relevant to us, we pay careful attention to the arguments, and persuasion can occur through the *central route.* If we find messages unimportant or irrelevant, however, persuasion occurs through the *peripheral route,* largely in response to *persuasion cues.*
(*Source:* Based on suggestions by Petty & Cacioppo, 1986.)

COGNITIVE DISSONANCE: HOW WE SOMETIMES CHANGE OUR ATTITUDES
There are many occasions in everyday life when we feel compelled to say or do things inconsistent with our true attitudes. Here are two examples of these occasions:

> Your friend buys a car and proudly asks how you like it. You have just read an article indicating that this model is such a lemon that the manufacturer puts a ten-pound bag of sugar in the trunk. What do you say?

> You are writing a term paper, and your professor has given you one of his own articles to read. You found it murky beyond belief. Later he asks you, "How did you like my paper?" What do you answer?

Unless you are an especially courageous (foolhardy?) person, the chances are good that in these situations, and many others like them, you will say the polite thing: You will tell your friend that you like the car and will comment favorably on the professor's article. The reasons for doing so are so obvious that social psychologists describe such situations as ones involving **forced compliance**—situations where we practically feel compelled to say or do things inconsistent with our true attitudes. Does forced compliance have any effect on our underlying attitudes? According to a theory known as *cognitive dissonance*, it may (Festinger, 1957).

Forced Compliance: A situation in which we feel compelled to say or do things inconsistent with our true attitudes.

FIGURE **14.4**

Cognitive Dissonance

When people notice that two attitudes they hold are somehow inconsistent, they may experience *cognitive dissonance*—an unpleasant motivational state. In order to reduce cognitive dissonance, individuals may change one or both of the inconsistent attitudes.

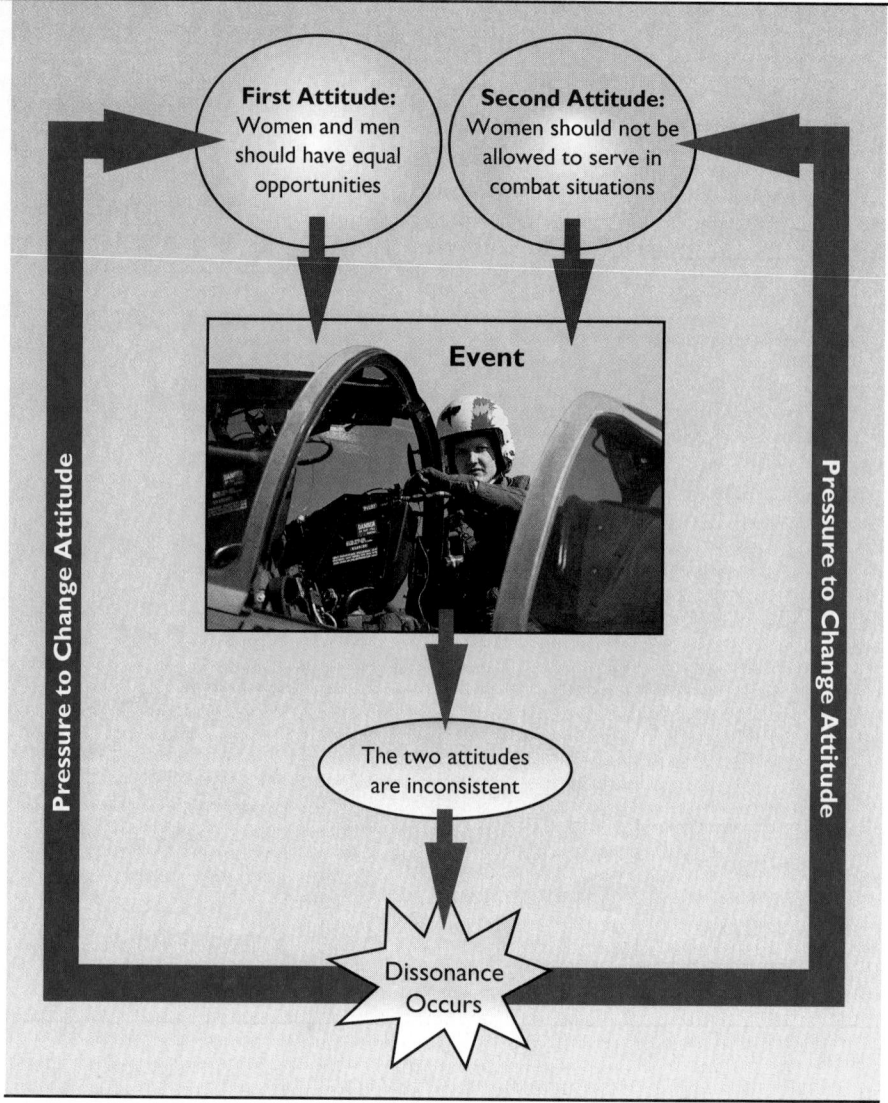

√ **Cognitive Dissonance:** *The state experienced by individuals when they discover inconsistency between two attitudes they hold or between their attitudes and their behavior.*

The term **cognitive dissonance** refers to the unpleasant state we experience in such situations—discomfort stemming from an obvious gap between our attitudes and our actions, or between two attitudes that we hold (see Figure 14.4). Such dissonance, the theory holds, is a *motivational state:* People experiencing it want to reduce it. In fact, people report considerable discomfort when they have said or done something inconsistent with their actual attitudes (Elliot & Devine, 1994). How do they diminish these unpleasant feelings? Several possibilities exist, such as minimizing the importance of the inconsistency in question; but by far the most intriguing is this: *Persons experiencing dissonance because they have said or done something inconsistent with their attitudes may experience change in these attitudes, because this helps to reduce dissonance.* In short, after praising your friend's lemon or your professor's jargon-studded paper, you may actually develop more favorable attitudes toward these items. Doing so helps to reduce dissonance, which, as I noted earlier, is an uncomfortable state.

Dissonance and the less-leads-to-more effect. This prediction—that people sometimes change their own attitudes—is surprising enough. But according to dissonance theory, there is more to the process than this. In any

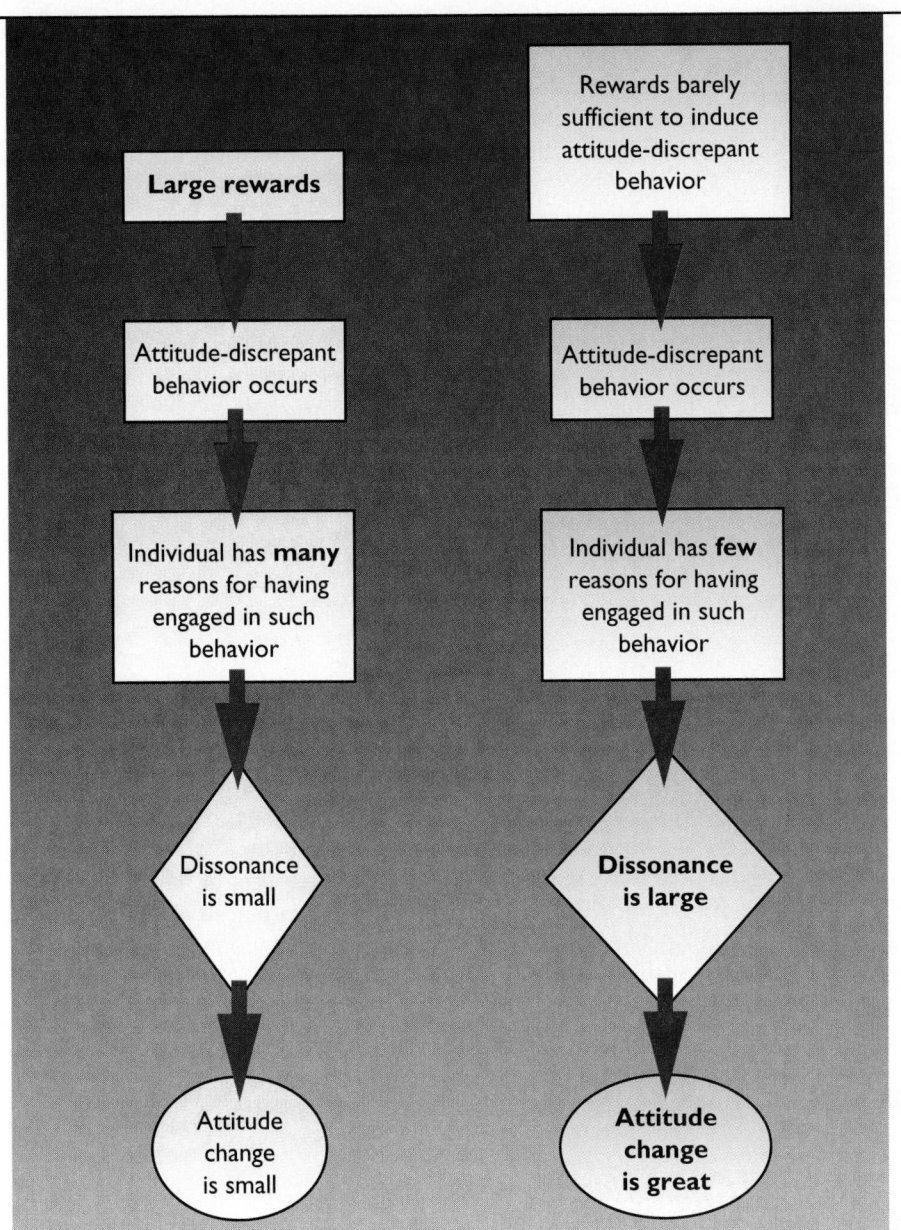

FIGURE **14.5**

Rewards and Forced Compliance: Why Less Sometimes Leads to More

When individuals receive *large* rewards for engaging in attitude-discrepant behavior, they experience little or no dissonance. Thus, there is little pressure for them to change their attitudes (shown on the left). In contrast, when individuals receive *small* rewards for engaging in attitude-discrepant behavior (ones just barely sufficient to induce them to perform such actions), they experience much greater dissonance and much greater pressure to change their attitudes (shown on the right). In short, less (smaller rewards) can really be more (produce more attitude change) in such situations.

situation where people say or do things inconsistent with their own views, we must consider another factor: How strong are the reasons for behaving in these ways? If these reasons are very good, then little or no dissonance will be generated. After all, telling your friend that his new car is a lemon or telling your professor that his paper was boring and muddled may prove very costly in terms of embarrassment and in other respects. So, in short, the better the reasons for saying what you don't believe, the less dissonance you will experience, and the weaker the pressure to change your own views.

Social psychologists describe this paradoxical state of affairs as the **less-leads-to-more effect:** the fact that the stronger the reasons for engaging in attitude-discrepant behavior, the weaker the pressures toward changing the underlying attitudes (see Figure 14.5), and vice versa. Surprising as it may seem, this effect has been confirmed in many different studies (e.g., Riess & Schlenker, 1977). In all these investigations, people provided with a small reward for stating attitudes contrary to their own views changed

Less-Leads-to-More Effect: *The fact that rewards just barely sufficient to induce individuals to state positions contrary to their own views often generate more attitude change than larger rewards.*

- What are attitudes?
- What factors received most attention in early research on persuasion?
- What factors are emphasized in modern cognitive models of persuasion?
- What is cognitive dissonance, and when does it occur?
- What is the less-leads-to-more effect?

these attitudes so that they later became closer to the false views they expressed.

The less-leads-to-more effect doesn't occur in all cases, however. In order for it to take place, people must feel that they had a choice as to whether to perform the attitude-discrepant behavior and must believe that they were personally responsible both for the chosen course of action and any negative effects it produced (Cooper & Scher, 1990; Goethals, Cooper, & Naficy, 1979). When these conditions exist—and they often do—then the less-leads-to-more effect occurs, and offering individuals small rewards for saying or doing what they don't believe will produce greater attitude change than offering them larger rewards.

SOCIAL BEHAVIOR: Interacting with Others

Learning Objective 14.7
Understand the different views on the origins of prejudice and discrimination and be aware of methods that can be used to reduce prejudice and its impact.

Learning Objective 14.8
Describe the three components of racial identification and the factors that influence its strength.

Learning Objective 14.9
Discuss the nature and predominance of conformity as well as the factors that influence it.

Learning Objective 14.10
Define compliance and understand the various techniques for gaining compliance.

Learning Objective 14.11
Define obedience and discuss the factors that increase the extent of obedience to authority.

*T*hinking about other people is an important aspect of our social existence; but as you know from your own life, we also *interact* with others in many ways. We work with them on various tasks; we offer them assistance and receive help from them; we attempt to influence others and are on the receiving end of *their* efforts at influence; we fall in and out of love, form and end relationships—the list is almost endless.

In this section, we'll look at several important aspects of *social interaction*. We'll begin with a topic that could readily have been placed either here or in our discussion of social thought: *prejudice,* or negative views of specific social groups that often lead to harmful actions against them. Next, we'll consider *social influence:* the many ways in which individuals seek to change the behavior of others. Then, we'll turn to *prosocial behavior*—actions that benefit others. Finally, we'll examine three closely related topics that play a key role in everyone's life: *attraction, love,* and *close relationships*.

PREJUDICE: Distorted Views of the Social World . . . and Their Consequences

"Ethnic cleansing" in Bosnia; racially motivated violence in South Africa, the United States, and many other countries; bombings in Northern Ireland—every day seems to bring new evidence of the tragic consequences of racial, ethnic, or religious hatred. Such actions often stem from **prejudice**—negative attitudes toward the members of a specific social group based solely on their membership in that group. Where do such attitudes come from? And what can be done to reduce their impact on behavior? These are the issues we'll now examine (Dovidio & Gaertner, 1986).

THE ORIGINS OF PREJUDICE: CONTRASTING PERSPECTIVES   Many different explanations for the origins of prejudice have been proposed. Here, I'll touch on the four that have received the most attention.

Direct intergroup conflict: Competition as a source of bias.   It is sad but true that many of the things we value most—a good job, a nice home, high status—are always in short supply; there's never quite enough to go around. This fact serves as the basis for what is perhaps the oldest explanation of prej-

✓Prejudice: Negative attitudes toward the members of some social group based on their membership in this group.

udice—**realistic conflict theory**. According to this view, prejudice stems from competition between social groups over valued commodities or opportunities. The theory further suggests that as such competition persists, the members of the groups involved come to view each other in increasingly negative ways (White, 1977). They label the people in the other group as enemies, view their own group as morally superior, and draw the boundaries between themselves and their opponents more and more firmly. In short, what starts out as economic competition gradually turns into full-scale prejudice, with the hatred and anger this usually implies.

Please don't misunderstand: The fact that conflict between groups *can* be a source of prejudice doesn't mean that this is always the case. However, it does seem to be true that groups in competition with one another tend to perceive each other in increasingly negative ways, so that such competition is often the starting point for the development of prejudice.

The us-versus-them effect: Social categorization as a basis for prejudice.
A second perspective on the origins of prejudice begins with a basic fact: Individuals generally divide the social world into two distinct categories—*us* and *them* (Turner et al., 1987). They view other persons as belonging either to their own social group, usually termed the *ingroup,* or to another group, an *outgroup.* Such distinctions involve many dimensions, including race, religion, sex, age, ethnic background, occupation, and even the town or neighborhood in which people happen to live.

If this process of **social categorization**—dividing the world into distinct social categories—stopped there, it would have little connection to prejudice. Unfortunately, it does not. Sharply contrasting feelings and beliefs are usually attached to members of one's ingroup and members of various outgroups. Persons in the former (us) category are viewed in largely favorable terms, while those in the latter (them) category are perceived negatively. Outgroup members are assumed to possess undesirable traits, are perceived as being "all alike" to a greater degree than members of one's own ingroup, and are often strongly disliked (Judd, Ryan, & Park, 1991; Linville, Fischer, & Salovey, 1989). Because of such tendencies (e.g., Tajfel, 1982), categorizing the social world into distinct ingroups and outgroups can be an important basis for prejudice.

The role of social learning.
A third perspective on the origins of prejudice begins with the obvious fact that infants do *not* show such reactions. This suggests that children acquire negative reactions to others as they grow older through the process of *social learning.* Prejudice emerges out of experiences in which children hear or observe their parents, friends, teachers, and others expressing prejudiced views; or because they are directly rewarded, with praise and approval, for adopting them.

While persons with whom children interact certainly play a key role in this process, the mass media, too, are important. What kind of views about African Americans would children obtain from the media portrayals illustrated on page 536? Obviously, very different ones. Where acquisition of prejudiced views is concerned, the impact of many hours of television viewing should not be overlooked.

Cognitive sources of prejudice: The role of stereotypes.
The final potential source of prejudice we'll consider is in some ways the most unsettling of all. It involves the possibility that prejudice stems at least in part from basic aspects of social thought itself—from basic ways in which we think about others and process social information (Bodenhausen, 1988). While several processes may play an important role, perhaps the most important of these involves the formation and impact of **stereotypes** (e.g., Bodenhausen, 1988; Devine, 1989; Gilbert & Hixon, 1991).

Learning Objective 14.12
Define prosocial behavior and the factors that influence it.

Learning Objective 14.13
Discuss the factors that influence interpersonal attraction.

Learning Objective 14.14
Discuss the nature and varieties of love as well as factors that influence it.

Learning Objective 14.15
Understand how the field of environmental psychology investigates interactions between human behavior and the physical environment.

Realistic Conflict Theory: A theory proposing that prejudice stems, at least in part, from economic competition between social groups.

Social Categorization: Our tendency to divide the social world into two distinct categories: "us" and "them."

✓*Stereotypes: Cognitive frameworks suggesting that all members of specific social groups share certain characteristics.*

Children seeing these two media portrayals of African Americans would obtain sharply contrasting views.

Stereotypes are cognitive frameworks consisting of knowledge and beliefs about specific social groups—frameworks suggesting that by and large, all members of these groups possess certain traits (Judd, Ryan, & Park, 1991). Like other cognitive frameworks, or schemas, stereotypes exert strong effects on the ways in which we process social information. For example, information relevant to a particular stereotype is processed more quickly than information unrelated to it (Dovidio, Evans, & Tyler, 1986). Similarly, stereotypes lead us to pay attention to specific types of information—usually information consistent with the stereotypes. And they may actually block our ability to pay attention to stereotype-inconsistent information (Sanbonmatsu, Akimoto, & Gibson, 1994). Finally, stereotypes also determine what we remember—usually, again, information that is consistent with these frameworks (Seta & Hayes, 1994).

What is the relevance of such effects to prejudice? Together, they tend to make stereotypes somewhat self-confirming. Once an individual has acquired a stereotype about some social group, she or he tends to notice information that fits readily into this cognitive framework and to remember "facts" that are consistent with it more readily than "facts" inconsistent with it. As a result, the stereotype strengthens with time. Indeed, even exceptions to it tend to make it stronger, for they simply induce the persons holding the stereotype to bring more supporting information to mind. In short, our tendency to create cognitive frameworks to hold and organize social information may contribute to the development and persistence of many forms of prejudice.

CHALLENGING PREJUDICE: SOME POTENTIAL PLANS OF ACTION Whatever the precise roots of prejudice, there can be no doubt about one fact: It is a brutal—and brutalizing—force. Reducing prejudice and countering its impact, therefore, are important tasks. Fortunately there are some effective strategies for combating prejudice. None is capable of totally eliminating prejudice, but together, they *can* help.

Breaking the cycle of prejudice: Learning not to hate. Bigots are made, not born. Children acquire negative attitudes toward specific social groups from their parents, friends, teachers, and others. Given this basic fact, one useful way to reduce prejudice would be to discourage the transmission of bigoted views and to encourage more positive attitudes toward others. But how can we encourage parents who are themselves highly prejudiced to change the message they transmit to their youngsters from "People in those groups are *bad*" to "People should be judged on their own merits—not on the basis of the groups to which they belong"? One possibility involves calling parents' and others' attention to their own prejudiced views. Few persons are willing to describe themselves as prejudiced. Instead, they view *their* negative attitudes toward others as justified. A key initial step, therefore, is convincing parents that the problem exists. Once they realize that it does, many are willing to modify their words and actions. True, some die-hard bigots *want* to turn their children into hate-filled fanatics. Most people, however, genuinely wish to provide their children with a more positive view of the social world. Thus, campaigns designed to enhance parents' awareness of prejudice and its harmful effects can sometimes yield desirable results (Aronson, 1990).

Schools and teachers, too, can play a positive role. By calling attention to the existence—and evils—of prejudice, they can help to increase children's awareness of this problem. And where prejudice is concerned, awareness of the problem is often a crucial first step toward its elimination.

Direct intergroup contact: The potential benefits of becoming acquainted. Prejudice tends to build social walls between people. Once it exists, members of different ethnic, racial, or religious groups have restricted contact with one another. Such limited contact, in turn, makes it easier for stereotypes to persist. Can this pattern be broken by direct intergroup contact? The **contact hypothesis** suggests that it can (Stephan, 1987). According to this hypothesis, increased contact between members of various groups can be effective in reducing prejudice, provided that it occurs under the following conditions:

1. The groups that interact are roughly equal in social, economic, or task-related status.
2. The contact situation involves cooperation and interdependence so that the groups work toward shared goals.
3. Contact between the groups is informal, so they can get to know one another on a one-to-one basis.
4. Contact occurs in a setting where existing norms favor group equality.
5. The persons involved view one another as typical members of their respective groups.

When contact between initially hostile groups occurs under these conditions, prejudice between them does seem to decrease (Cook, 1985). For example, increased contact between Jews of Middle Eastern origin and Jews of European or American origin has been found to reduce ingroup bias among Israeli soldiers (Schwarzwald, Amir, & Crain, 1992). Similarly, increased contact between African Americans and whites has been found to reduce prejudice between them in the United States (Aronson, Bridgeman, & Geffner, 1978). Thus, increased social contact, under appropriate conditions, offers another useful means for reducing prejudice.

Dissonance: Reducing prejudice through counter-attitudinal behavior. Earlier, we noted that cognitive dissonance can be a powerful force for attitude change. When people are somehow induced to say or do something inconsistent with their attitudes, they often experience strong pressure to change these views. Can this fact be applied to reducing prejudice? Recent research by Leippe and Eisenstadt (1994) suggests that it can. These researchers induced white college students to write essays supporting a policy that would benefit African-American students at some cost to the white students, by reserving a larger proportion of scholarship funds for African Americans. Students either wrote these essays by choice or were simply assigned to do so, and either signed them (high publicity) or remained anonymous (low publicity). Then, they expressed their attitudes toward the new policy and toward African Americans generally. Results indicated that participants' views did become more favorable as a result of engaging in the attitude-discrepant behavior. Moreover, this was especially true in the high

Contact Hypothesis: *The suggestion that increased contact between members of different social groups will reduce prejudice between them.*

RECATEGORIZATION: THE BOUNDARY BETWEEN "US" AND "THEM"

The greater the extent to which students at a multicultural school perceive themselves as part of a single group, the more positive their feelings toward other students outside their own cultural group.

Recategorization: Shifting the boundary between "us" and "them" so that persons previously seen as belonging to outgroups are now seen as belonging to the ingroup.

KEY QUESTIONS

- What is prejudice, and what factors contribute to its existence?
- How can prejudice be reduced?

publicity condition, where participants signed their essays. These findings suggest that under some conditions, cognitive dissonance can indeed be a useful means for reducing prejudice.

Recategorization: Redrawing the boundary between "us" and "them." Suppose that a team from your college played against a team from a rival college: Which would be "us" and which would be "them"? The answer is obvious: Your own school's team would constitute your ingroup, while the other school's team would be the outgroup. But now imagine that the team from the other school had won a whole series of games and was chosen to represent your state in a national tournament. When it played against a team from another state, would you now perceive it as "us" or "them"? Under these circumstances, many people would shift to viewing the other school's team as their ingroup. This suggests that the boundary between "us" and "them" is not fixed or inflexible. On the contrary, it can be shifted so as to include—or exclude—various groups of people. Can such a shift or **recategorization** of the social world be used to reduce prejudice in other contexts? Studies conducted by Gaertner and his colleagues (1989, 1990) suggest that it can.

For example, in one project, Gaertner and his coworkers (Gaertner et al., in press) investigated the attitudes of students at a multicultural high school in the United States. Students came from many different backgrounds—African-American, Chinese, Hispanic, Japanese, Korean, Vietnamese, and Caucasian. More than thirteen hundred young people completed a survey designed to measure their perceptions of the extent to which the student body at the school was a single group, consisted of distinct groups, or was composed of separate individuals. Results offered strong support for the view that redrawing the boundaries between "us" and "them" can have very beneficial effects. The stronger participants' belief that the student body was a single integrated group, the stronger their perception that students from all groups worked well together, and the more positive their feelings toward students from ethnic groups other than their own. Indeed, the stronger the students' beliefs that they all belonged to one group, the smaller the difference between their feelings about members of their own ethnic group (ingroup) and their feelings about other ethnic groups (outgroups). When combined with the results of systematic laboratory studies (Gaertner et al., 1989, 1990), these findings suggest that efforts to induce persons belonging to different groups to engage in recategorization can be an important first step toward reducing many forms of prejudice.

What are the effects of prejudice on groups who are its victims? For information on this important question, please see the **Perspectives on Diversity** section.

PERSPECTIVES ON DIVERSITY

The Effects of Prejudice: Racial Identification among African Americans

Many of the effects of prejudice on the groups toward whom it is directed are obvious: exclusion from jobs, housing, and schools; second-class treatment by the courts and other public institutions; stereotyping in the mass media; and, of course, senseless acts of violence. In addition to these effects, however, there are others that, while more subtle in form, may be equally important in their impact. These effects relate to the *reactions* of victims of prejudice to their mistreatment. What does prejudice do to their self-concept, their self-esteem, and their identification with their own group? How do they cope with prejudice—with being "outsiders" in their own society?

The idea of investigating such questions is far from new. Indeed, classic studies of the effects of prejudice on the self-concept of African Americans were conducted by the famous black psychologist Kenneth Clark in the 1940s (e.g., Clark & Clark, 1947). After this early work, however, the issue of reactions to prejudice on the part of its victims was largely neglected; it has reappeared—in much more sophisticated form—only in the past decade (McMillan, 1988). Since much of this work has focused on the reactions of African Americans to racial prejudice, we'll emphasize this topic here. But investigations of the reactions to prejudice of other minority groups is equally important and is currently proceeding.

While racial prejudice can potentially influence its victims in many different ways, one that seems especially important involves **racial identification**—the extent to which African Americans (or members of any other racial minority) are conscious of belonging to a specific racial group. That such feelings are indeed part of the experience of many African Americans seems obvious (e.g., Asante, 1980; Williams, 1976). But what, precisely, does racial identification involve? Does it consist of distinct components? And what factors affect it? Systematic research has begun to address all of these issues (e.g., Hilliard, 1985).

In what is perhaps the most influential current model of racial identification, Sanders Thompson (1991), a noted African-American researcher, suggests that racial identification among African Americans involves three components: *physical, psychological,* and *sociocultural.*

The physical component refers to a sense of acceptance and comfort with the physical attributes of blacks (skin color, hair texture, and so on). The psychological component refers to the individual's sense of concern and commitment to the racial group. Group pride and feelings of group membership are central to this aspect of racial identity. Finally, the sociocultural aspect refers to individuals' attitudes toward cultural, social, and economic issues. These include expressions of cultural heritage, as well as attitudes concerning the economic and political advancement of African Americans. According to Sanders Thompson (1990, 1991), all three are essential components of African Americans' racial identification (see Figure 14.6 on page 540).

What factors determine the extent to which individuals develop the physical, psychological, and sociocultural reactions described above? In order to find out, Sanders Thompson conducted a study in which almost two hundred African Americans provided information, through interviews and a questionnaire, concerning numerous variables that might influence racial identification. These included demographics (age, income, level of education, and so on) plus many variables relating to social factors, such as when and to what extent respondents had personally experienced racism; whether there had been conflict within their families relating to skin color or social class; and the extent to which respondents interacted with white Americans—the proportion of whites in their neighborhood and school, their experience with interracial dating, and so on.

Results indicated that by far the most important predictor of all three aspects of racial identification was the extent to which respondents had personal experience with racial prejudice. The greater such experience, the stronger their racial identification. Demographic factors such as age, income, and education were less important, although they did play some role in the psychological aspect of racial identification. Not surprisingly, conflicts within one's own family related to skin color or social class significantly predicted physical racial identification.

What do these findings mean? For one thing, that exposure to white prejudice is a key factor in the development of a strong sense of racial identification among African Americans. Such experiences seem to drive home the fact that blacks are viewed as different—as a definite outgroup—by the majority. This,

Racial Identification: *The extent to which individuals identify with their own racial group.*

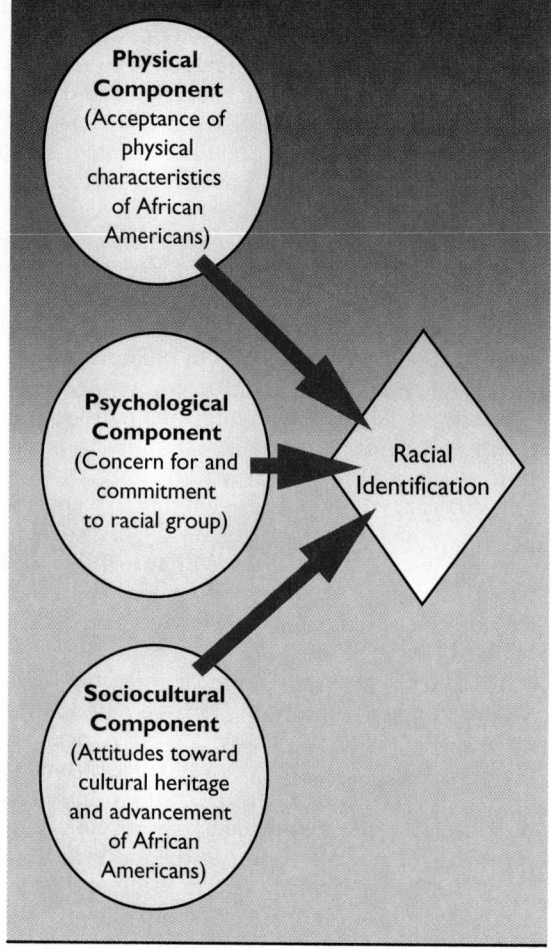

FIGURE 14.6

Racial Identification

According to Sanders Thompson (1991), racial identification involves three basic components: physical, psychological, and sociocultural. Her research indicates that the greater the exposure African Americans have had to racial prejudice, the stronger their racial identification.

Physical Component (Acceptance of physical characteristics of African Americans)

Psychological Component (Concern for and commitment to racial group)

Sociocultural Component (Attitudes toward cultural heritage and advancement of African Americans)

Racial Identification

in turn, leads many African Americans to identify strongly with their own group. Such identification can then serve as a source of personal strength and support for the individuals involved (White & Parham, 1990).

So in one crucial respect, majority prejudice may have surprising—and certainly unintended—effects: It can actually serve to strengthen the sense of group cohesion of many African Americans and thus enhance their ability to resist the impact of bigotry. Of course, heightened racial identification among African Americans, or among any other group in a culturally diverse society, is not an unmixed blessing. The ultimate goal in such a society is a high degree of tolerance and cooperation, *not* a series of groups fortified inside their own cultures. Still, if strong racial identification among African Americans boosts their pride and self-esteem, then the benefits may well outweigh any potential harm. More generally, such effects illustrate once again the resiliency and adaptiveness shown by human beings in the face of adversity.

SOCIAL INFLUENCE: *Changing Others' Behavior*

Social Influence: *Efforts by one or more individuals to change the attitudes or behavior of one or more others.*

How many times each day do others try to influence you in some way? And how often do *you* try to influence them? If you stop and count, you'll probably obtain a surprisingly large number, for efforts at **social influence**—attempts by one or more persons to change the attitudes or behavior of one or more others—are very common. Moreover they take many different forms. In this section we'll examine some of the most common, and most important, of these social influence techniques.

"Gotta run, Peter. A new client is on his way up."

CONFORMITY: TO GET ALONG, OFTEN, WE MUST GO ALONG

Have you ever been in a social situation where you felt that you stuck out like a sore thumb? If so, you know how unpleasant the experience can be. In these circumstances we encounter powerful pressures to act or think like those around us. Such pressures toward **conformity**—toward thinking or acting like most other persons—stem from the fact that in many contexts there are spoken or unspoken rules indicating how we *should* or *ought to* behave. These rules are known as **social norms.** Some norms can be both detailed and precise—for example, written constitutions, athletic rule books, traffic signs. In contrast, other norms, such as "Don't stare at strangers on the street" and "Never show up for a party exactly on time" are implicit, yet they still exert powerful effects on us. Whatever form they take, social norms are obeyed by most persons most of the time (Cialdini, 1988).

Is this necessarily bad? Not at all; if most people didn't follow such rules on most occasions, we would live in social chaos. Persons waiting to pay for their purchases in stores would fail to form lines; motorists would drive on whichever side of the road they preferred; people would come to work or show up for meetings whenever they felt like it. So norms and the conformity they produce are a necessary part of social life. Only when they enforce needless uniformity—for example, with respect to styles of dress or personal grooming—do norms and other pressures toward conformity seem objectionable.

How strong are pressures toward conformity? Research findings suggest the following answer: *powerful indeed.* The fact that we conform to most social norms most of the time is hardly surprising; failure to do so can lead to disapproval or rejection from others. More unexpected, however, is the fact that pressures toward conformity are so strong that we surrender to them even in situations where the costs of failing to conform are minimal—for example, mild embarrassment. This fact was first uncovered by Asch (1951) in research that is now a true classic in social psychology.

To investigate the tendency to succumb to conformity pressures, Asch asked male students to respond to a series of simple perceptual problems in which they were to indicate which of three comparison lines matched a standard line in length (see Figure 14.7). Six to eight other persons were also present, but, unknown to each participant, all were accomplices of the experimenter. These other persons gave their answers before the participant gave his, and on twelve out of the eighteen problems, these answers were clearly wrong. On such occasions, participants faced a dilemma. Should they follow the evidence of their own eyes and disagree with the unanimous group? Or should they go along with these persons even though they believed them to be wrong? The answer was clear: Fully 76 percent of the participants went along with the group's wrong answers at least once. In contrast, only 5 percent of persons in

ONE UNUSUAL FORM OF SOCIAL INFLUENCE

Social influence—efforts to change others' behavior—take many different forms.

(*Source:* Drawing by Shanahan; © 1993 The New Yorker Magazine, Inc.)

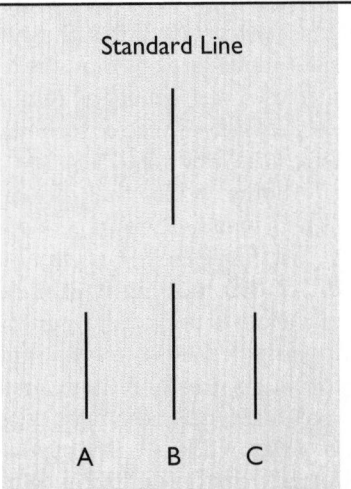

Standard Line

A B C

FIGURE **14.7**

Asch's Line-Judging Task: An Example

In one of the problems used by Asch in his famous research on conformity, the participants' task was to indicate which of the three comparison lines (A, B, or C) best matched the standard line in terms of length.

✓**Conformity:** *A type of social influence in which individuals experience pressure to adhere to existing social norms.*

✓**Social Norms:** *Rules in a given group or society indicating how individuals ought to behave in specific situations.*

a control group—one that responded to the same problems in the absence of any accomplices—made such errors.

These findings indicate that our tendency to conform is indeed strong; faced with a group of strangers who unanimously voice one opinion, most people tend to agree, even when doing so requires them to contradict the evidence of their own senses!

Does being a psychologist and knowing about such pressures make one immune to them? Far from it. Several years ago, when I was chair of the Department of Psychology at my university, I attended a meeting where the dean described a plan to create a new course for freshmen—a course that would combine psychology, sociology, philosophy, and economics. I took such a course when *I* was a freshman and strongly disliked it, so I was dead-set against the plan. But as I listened with growing horror, the chairs of the other departments all voiced their approval. When it was my turn to comment, I faced the same kind of dilemma as the subjects in Asch's research: Should I express my real views or go along with the group consensus? What I did, I'm sad to report, is waffle. I said something like "Very interesting . . . but I'd like some time to discuss it with my department." Later, I did voice my objections strongly, and in writing. But at that moment, the social pressure was too strong for me to resist.

Factors affecting the degree of conformity. Asch's research demonstrated the existence of powerful pressures toward conformity. Even a moment's reflection indicates, however, that conformity does not occur to the same degree in all settings or among all persons. Several factors have been found to be important in determining when, and to what extent, it occurs.

One of these is *group size*—the number of persons exerting such pressure. Up to a point, the more people around us who agree on or follow a given social norm, the stronger our own tendency to do so. There are definite limits to this effect, however. After the number of persons exerting conformity pressure rises above three or four, the tendency to go along (to conform) flattens out and increases very little. The reason is that beyond this point we often begin to suspect *collusion*—we conclude that other persons are working together to influence us (Wilder, 1977).

Another factor that influences our tendency to yield to conformity pressure is whether we are alone in our efforts to resist group pressure or have an *ally* in this respect. Participants in Asch's studies faced a *unanimous group* (as I did at that meeting with the dean). But what would have happened if some of the other persons present had given correct answers? Several studies have investigated this question, and results are clear: Under such conditions, conformity is greatly reduced (Allen & Levine, 1971; Morris & Miller, 1975).

A third factor that was once assumed to have a strong effect on conformity is *gender*. Early studies reported that females were more likely to show conformity than were males (e.g., Crutchfield, 1955). However, more recent investigations have failed to find such a difference (e.g., Sistrunk & McDavid, 1971; Maupin & Fisher, 1989). One reason for the difference in these findings seems to involve the kinds of items used in the two sets of studies. Those conducted during the 1950s and 1960s tended to use items that were more familiar to males than to females. Since individuals of both genders are more likely to yield to social pressure when they are uncertain about their judgments, it is not surprising that initial studies found greater conformity among females. More recent studies, in contrast, have used items and situations equally familiar to males and females (e.g., Sistrunk & McDavid, 1971). The result: equal levels of conformity among females and males.

Of course, it's also possible that the different findings reported in these two groups of studies reflect shifting roles for females in many societies.

Large numbers of women in the United States now work outside the home, and many occupy high-status, high-responsibility jobs. These changes have weakened stereotypes that suggest that females are more conforming than males. And since stereotypes often exert a self-confirming impact on behavior, these changes, too, may be responsible for the decline in the tendency for females to be perceived as more susceptible to influence than males (Maupin & Fisher, 1989). Whatever its basis, recent research indicates that males and females do *not* differ in terms of the tendency to yield to conformity pressure.

KEY QUESTIONS

- What is social influence?
- What factors influence the occurrence of conformity?

COMPLIANCE: TO ASK—SOMETIMES—IS TO RECEIVE   How many times a day do you receive requests? If you kept a record, you'd probably be surprised at the total, for friends, coworkers, family members, and roommates frequently ask us to change various aspects of our behavior. Social psychologists call this form of social influence **compliance,** and in its simplest form, it involves one person accepting a request from another—doing something that the requester wants. The situation is often more complex than this, however. Persons wishing to obtain compliance often take preliminary steps designed to increase the likelihood that the target person will say yes. Let's consider several of these tactics.

Ingratiation: Liking as an entering wedge for gaining compliance. For whom would you be more likely to do a favor—someone you like or someone you dislike? The former, of course. This fact is the basis for one important technique for gaining compliance: **ingratiation.** Briefly, ingratiation involves efforts to increase one's appeal to a target person before asking that person to grant a request (Liden & Mitchell, 1988; Wortman & Linsenmeier, 1977). What tactics are most successful in this respect? Research on ingratiation and on the related process of **impression management**—steps people take to enhance the impression they make on others—suggests that the following procedures are often useful: (1) indicating that we agree with target persons or share their views on various issues; (2) praising or flattering them (without overdoing it, of course!); (3) enhancing our personal appearance through dress, grooming, makeup, and other tactics; (4) associating ourselves with important or respected people (by name dropping, for example); (5) emitting many positive nonverbal cues, such as smiles and other signs that we like and are interested in the target person; and (6) making self-deprecating remarks—mild put-downs of ourselves, indicating that we realize we aren't perfect and that we have an appropriate sense of humility. Would you like a stranger who engaged in such tactics more than one who did not? Research findings suggest that you would (e.g., Baron et al., 1990; Godfrey, Jones, & Lord, 1986; Liden & Mitchell, 1988). So when salespersons and others who have something to gain from influencing you use such tactics, beware: Efforts to gain compliance may soon follow.

Multiple requests: Compliance as a two-step process. Suppose you wanted a fairly large favor from one of your friends. Would you approach this person and make your request cold, or would you try to do something to tip the balance in your favor first? Probably you would choose the latter course of action, especially if the favor were an important one. But what specific steps would help? Three different tactics seem to be effective.

In the first, known as the **foot-in-the-door technique,** you would start with a small request and then, once this was granted, escalate to a larger one. The results of many studies indicate that starting with the small request does increase the chances that the target person will also agree to the second, larger request (Beaman et al., 1983; Freedman & Fraser, 1966). Apparently this is so because once people have agreed to a small request, they feel that saying no to

✓ Compliance: A form of social influence in which one or more persons accepts direct requests from one or more others.

Ingratiation: A technique of social influence based on inducing increased liking in the target person before influence is attempted.

Impression Management: Efforts by individuals to enhance the impression they make on others.

Foot-in-the-Door Technique: A technique for gaining compliance in which a small request is followed by a larger one.

another request would threaten their enhanced self-image—their image of themselves as a helpful, considerate person (Eisenberg et al., 1987).

A second and exactly opposite technique for gaining increased compliance is known as the **door-in-the-face technique.** Here, you would start with a very large request; then, when this was rejected, you'd "back down" to a much smaller one—the one you wanted all along. This technique, too, seems to be effective in gaining increased compliance, primarily because when you retreat to the smaller request, this puts subtle pressure on the target person to make a similar concession; after all, it seems only reasonable to reciprocate in some manner (Cialdini et al., 1975; Pendleton & Batson, 1979).

A third tactic for gaining compliance is known as the **that's-not-all approach.** The basic idea here is to throw something extra into the situation *before* the target person has had a chance to say yes or no. This extra "deal-sweetener" can be very trivial in scope. For example, automobile dealers often offer to include an inexpensive option such as floor mats when they sense that a potential customer is hesitating. In economic terms, they are offering something that costs them about $35 in order to close a sale of $15,000 or more. Yet this technique often works (Burger, 1986). The small "extra" is often enough to increase the likelihood that the target person will say yes. Again, the reason seems to be that the target person feels the need to make a concession in response to the improved offer, and this translates into agreeing to accept the deal being offered.

In sum, there are many ways of gaining compliance from others, and persons skilled in the use of these tactics can often substantially increase the odds of getting what they want.

Complaining: Griping one's way to compliance. Before concluding this discussion of compliance, I should add one additional tactic that many persons use to exert such social influence: **complaining**—expressing discontent or dissatisfaction with yourself or some aspect of the social world. Research on complaining indicates that it is often quite effective in gaining compliance (Alicke et al., 1992). While most complaints seem to serve the function of emotional "venting," a sizable proportion (almost 10 percent) are aimed at changing others' behavior. And such complaints do succeed, at least part of the time (see Figure 14.8). Indeed, when asked to keep a diary of their own complaints,

Door-in-the-Face Technique: *A technique for gaining compliance in which a large request is followed by a smaller one.*

That's-Not-All Approach: *A technique for gaining compliance in which a small extra incentive is offered before the target person has agreed to or rejected a request.*

Complaining: *Expressing discontent or dissatisfaction with oneself or with some aspect of the external world.*

FIGURE 14.8

Complaining as a Technique for Gaining Compliance

Individuals often complain to others as a means of changing others' behavior. As shown here, students who kept a diary of their complaints reported that other persons often complied with the changes requested implicitly or explicitly in the complaints.
(*Source:* Based on data from Alicke et al., 1992.)

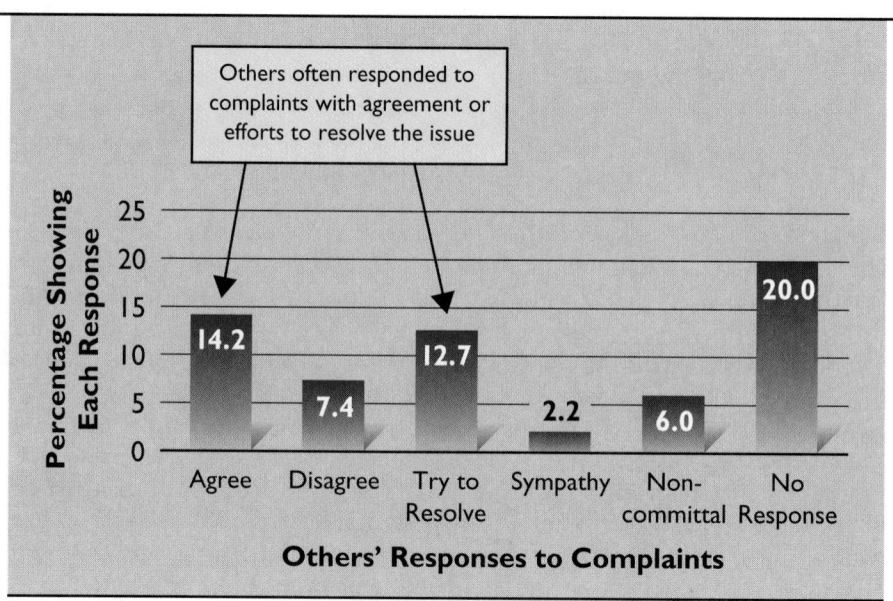

college students reported that complaining helped them gain compliance with their wishes about 25 percent of the time (Alicke et al., 1992).

Interestingly, females and males appear to complain about somewhat different topics. Females complain about themselves—their appearance or feelings—more often than males do, while males complain more often about other persons (Klotz & Alicke, 1993). And females show more supportive reactions to others' complaints than do males. They offer more suggestions for dealing with the topic of the complaints and more emotional support ("I know exactly how you feel"). In contrast, males are more likely to ignore others' complaints or to reject them ("Big deal!"). So, while both sexes use complaints in their dealings with others, there appear to be some differences in precisely *how* they use this technique.

OBEDIENCE: SOCIAL INFLUENCE BY DEMAND   What is the most direct technique one person can use to change the behavior of another? One answer is *direct orders*—simply telling the other person to do something. This approach is less common than either conformity pressure or tactics for gaining compliance, but it is far from rare. Executives issue orders to their subordinates; military officers shout commands that they expect to be obeyed; parents, police officers, and sports coaches all influence others in the same manner. **Obedience** to the commands of sources of authority is far from surprising: Such sources have powerful means for enforcing their orders. More surprising, though, is the fact that even persons lacking in such authority can sometimes induce high levels of obedience in others. Unsettling evidence for such effects was first reported by Stanley Milgram in a series of famous and controversial experiments (Milgram, 1963, 1974).

Destructive obedience: Basic findings.   In order to find out whether individuals would obey commands from a relatively powerless stranger, Milgram designed an ingenious set of procedures. Participants were told that they were taking part in a study on the effects of punishment on learning. Their role was to deliver electric shocks to a male "learner," actually an assistant of the experimenter, each time he made an error in a simple learning task. These shocks were delivered by means of switches on special equipment shown in the photo, and participants were told to move to the next higher switch each time the learner made an error. The first switch delivered a shock of 15 volts, the second a shock of 30, and so on up to the last switch, which supposedly delivered a shock of fully 450 volts. In reality, *the accomplice never received any shocks during the study.* The only real shock was a mild demonstration pulse from button number three used to convince participants that the equipment was real.

During the session the learner seemed to make many errors, so participants soon faced a dilemma: Should they continue punishing this person with increasingly painful shocks, or should they refuse to continue? The experimenter pressured them to continue, so the choice wasn't easy. Since participants were volunteers and were paid in advance, you might predict that they would quickly refuse such orders. In reality, though, *fully 65 percent showed total obedience*, continuing through the entire series to the final 450-volt shock (see Figure 14.9 on page 546). Of course, many persons protested and expressed concern over the learner's welfare. When ordered to proceed, however, most yielded to social influence and continued to obey. Indeed, they did so even when the victim pounded on the wall as if in protest against the painful shocks he was receiving. Similar findings have been obtained in studies conducted around the world (Jordan, Germany, Australia) and with children as well as adults, so this tendency to obey seemingly dangerous commands from a relatively powerless source of authority appears to be quite general (e.g., Kilham & Mann, 1974; Shanab & Yahya, 1977).

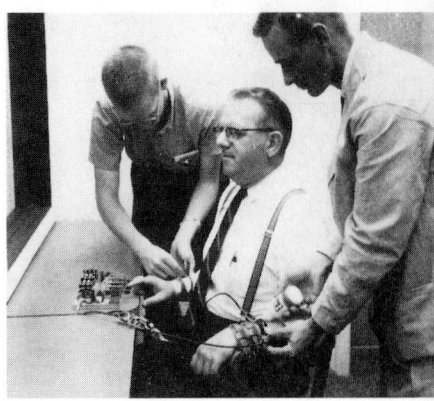

MILGRAM'S EQUIPMENT AND PROCEDURE

The photo on the top shows the apparatus used by Milgram in his famous studies of obedience. The photo on the bottom shows the experimenter (Milgram, in a white coat) and a participant (rear) attaching the electrodes to the learner's (accomplice's) wrists. (*Source:* From the film *Obedience*, distributed by the New York University Film Library, Copyright 1965 by Stanley Milgram. Reprinted by permission of the copyright holder.)

▾ **Obedience:** *A form of social influence in which one individual issues orders to another to behave in a specific way.*

FIGURE **14.9**

Milgram's Research on Obedience

This graph illustrates the proportion of participants who obeyed the experimenter's commands at various levels of shock. Fully 65 percent obeyed at the highest shock level—supposedly 450 volts!
(*Source:* Based on data from Milgram.)

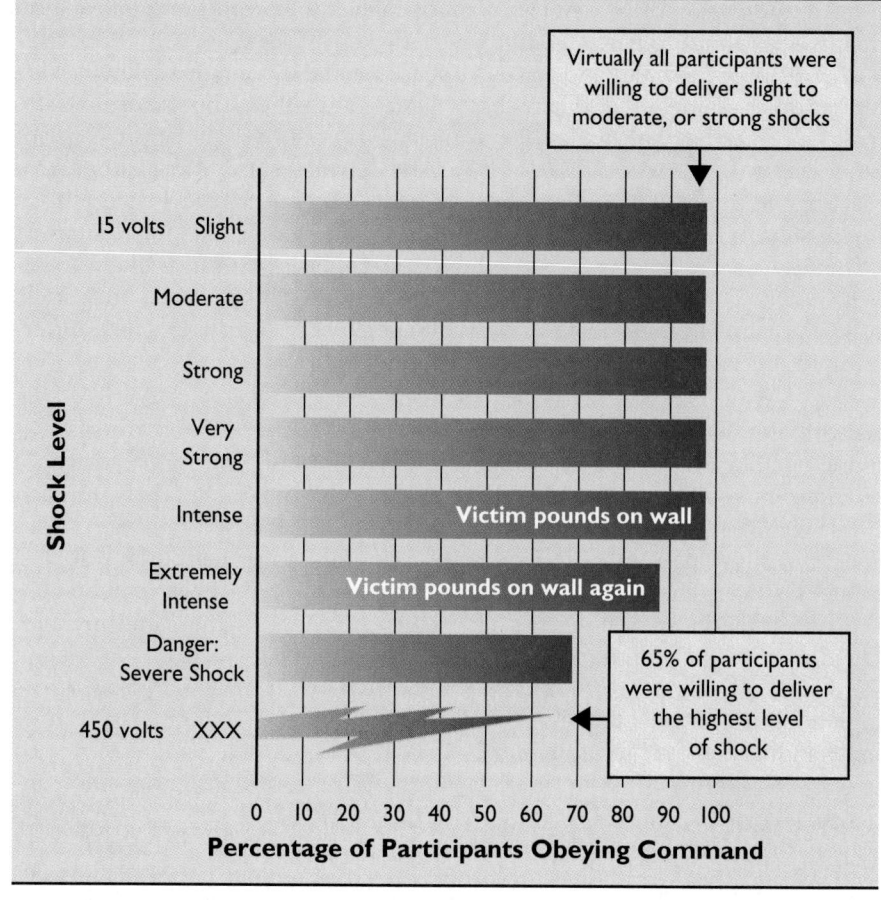

Destructive obedience: Why does it occur, and how can it be resisted? The results obtained by Milgram are very disturbing. The parallels between the behavior of participants in his studies and atrocities against civilians during times of war or civil unrest are clear. But why, precisely, do such effects occur? Why were participants in these experiments so willing to yield to the commands of a relatively powerless person? Several factors seem to play a role.

First, in each case the experimenter relieved participants of all personal responsibility. He indicated that he, not they, would be responsible for the victim's welfare. So, just as in many real-life situations where soldiers or police commit atrocities, participants could say, "I was only following orders." An analysis of situations in which people obey commands that cause them to violate widely accepted moral or ethical standards (Kelman & Hamilton, 1989) suggests that the absence or diffusion of personal responsibility plays a major role. Indeed, this may be a central factor in the occurrence of what Kelman and Hamilton (1989) term *crimes of obedience* (Hans, 1992).

Second, the experimenter possessed clear signs of authority, and existing social norms suggest that persons holding authority are to be obeyed (Bushman, 1984, 1988).

Third, the experimenter's commands were gradual in nature. He didn't request that participants jump to the 450-volt shock immediately; rather, he moved toward this request one step at a time. Again, this is similar to many real-life situations in which police or military personnel are initially ordered merely to question, arrest, or threaten potential victims. Only later are they ordered to beat, torture, or even kill unarmed persons.

In sum, several factors probably contributed to the high levels of obedience observed in Milgram's research and related studies. Together, these factors merge into a powerful force—one that most persons find difficult to resist. But this does not mean that commands from authority figures *cannot* be resisted. In fact, events in 1989 and afterwards in Germany, the former Soviet Union, Poland, and many other countries suggest that *dis*obedience is sometimes a real option. In these countries, repressive Communist regimes that had ruled for decades disappeared overnight when large numbers of citizens refused to obey their commands. What factors contributed to these dramatic events? Systematic research indicates that important factors in disobedience include exposure to *disobedient models*—persons who refuse to obey; increased personal responsibility for the outcome produced (Hamilton, 1978); and clear evidence that authorities are pursuing selfish rather than prosocial goals (Saks, 1992). When such conditions prevail, the power of authorities to command may be sharply curtailed, despite their possession of guns, planes, and tanks; and victory may ultimately go to those on the side of freedom and decency.

Please see the **Key Concept** on page 548 for an overview of major techniques of social influence.

> **KEY QUESTIONS**
>
> - What is compliance, and how can it be increased?
> - What is destructive obedience, and how can it be reduced?

PROSOCIAL BEHAVIOR: *When We Help . . . and When We Don't*

In chapter 9 we examined *aggression,* a form of social behavior in which individuals attempt to harm others (Baron & Richardson, 1994). Here, to balance the picture, we'll focus on behavior that is in some respects precisely opposite: **prosocial behavior.** Such behavior involves actions that benefit others without necessarily providing any direct benefit to the person performing them (Spacapan & Oskamp, 1992).

Fortunately, prosocial behavior is a common part of social life. Each day most of us perform favors for others and help them in various ways. Further, we often do so without demanding direct or immediate repayment for such aid. Yet while prosocial behavior is common, there are many instances in which it fails to occur. People sometimes *don't* help others who need assistance very badly, and even ignore direct pleas for aid. If you've ever ignored charity workers seeking donations or walked by a homeless person begging for small change, you are quite familiar with this fact (Steinfels, 1992).

So prosocial behavior is neither automatic nor assured. This fact has led social psychologists to focus much attention on the following question: What factors determine whether and to what extent people offer help to others? As we'll now see, several factors play an important role.

PROSOCIAL BEHAVIOR: NOT A CERTAINTY

Prosocial behavior is common, but far from guaranteed. In many instances, people ignore direct requests for help from others.

THE BYSTANDER EFFECT: WHY THERE'S NOT ALWAYS SAFETY IN NUMBERS

Research in social psychology, like that in other fields, usually stems from carefully developed theories. Occasionally, however, it is stimulated by a dramatic incident that captures the attention of social psychologists. One such incident occurred in New York City one night in the mid 1960s. A young woman named Catherine (Kitty) Genovese was returning home from her job when she was attacked by a man with a knife. She ran, but he chased her and stabbed her when he caught her. Genovese screamed for help, and lights came on in many windows in nearby buildings. Seeing these, the attacker fled. When no one actually came to her aid, however, he returned and stabbed her again. Once more Genovese screamed for help, but not a single person came to her aid. The attack continued until she lay dead.

> **Prosocial Behavior:** Actions that benefit others without necessarily providing any direct benefit to the persons who perform them.

Major Forms of Social Influence

Conformity

Being required to wear uniforms or follow some other dress code is one way that individuals experience pressure to "stay in line"—to adhere to widely accepted social norms. Although many persons object to such pressures, evidence indicates that most of us do conform in many situations.

Many social groups exert strong pressure on their members to conform in terms of style of dress.

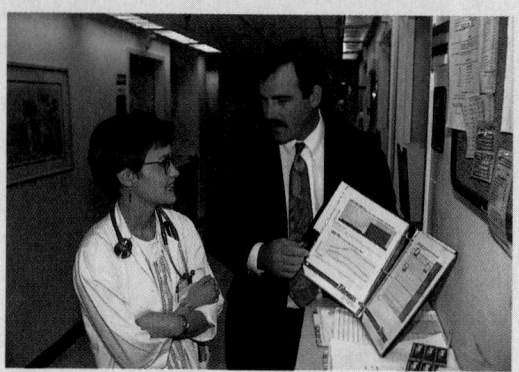

Salespersons use many different techniques to gain compliance from potential customers.

Compliance

Ingratiation

An individual tries to get a target person to like her/him and then uses this liking as a basis for exerting influence (e.g., making requests).

Foot-in-the-Door Technique

Requester makes initial, small request with which target person is almost certain to comply. This is followed by a larger request—the one the requester really wants.

Door-in-the-Face Technique

Requester makes large initial request, one the target person is certain to reject. This is followed by a smaller request—the one the requester really wants.

That's-Not-All Approach

Initial request or offer is made and then, before the target person can respond, a small "extra" is added.

Obedience

One person issues direct orders to another. Tendencies toward obedience are strong; indeed, many persons obey commands from sources of authority having no means of enforcing those orders.

Authority figures, such as judges, can simply order other persons to obey.

Why did no one help or even phone the police? What invisible barriers prevented all those law-abiding citizens who witnessed the crime from offering assistance? Two social psychologists offered an answer. Darley and Latané (1968) reasoned that perhaps no one had come to Kitty Genovese's aid because all the witnesses assumed that someone else would rush to her rescue; after all, there were many other potential helpers. In short, Darley and Latané suggested that where helping in emergencies is concerned, there may be *danger*, not safety, in numbers. Was this hypothesis correct? To find out, they conducted a famous experiment (Darley & Latané, 1968) in which male participants seated alone in separate rooms overheard another person experience what seemed to be an intense epileptic seizure. The incident was staged by means of a special tape recording, but to participants it seemed frighteningly real.

To examine the potential effects of the presence of other bystanders on bystanders' willingness to help, participants in three conditions were led to believe that (1) only they and the victim were present; (2) they, the victim, and one other bystander were present; or (3) they, the victim, and four other persons were present. Results offered strong support for what has come to be known as the **bystander effect**—a reduced tendency of witnesses to an emergency to help when they believe that there are other potential helpers present. As the number of supposed bystanders increased, the percentage of participants who rushed from their room to offer assistance dropped sharply, from 85 percent to 31 percent, and the time that passed before help was offered increased, from 52 to 166 seconds.

These results were soon confirmed in many other studies, so it appeared that **diffusion of responsibility**—a sharing of responsibility among all potential helpers—plays an important role in determining whether and how quickly victims receive aid in emergencies. Moreover, recent findings indicate that the higher the population density of various cities, the lower the incidence of spontaneous helping behavior in them (Levine et al., 1994). This same research indicates that it is not the size of a city that is crucial; rather, it is *population density*—the number of people per square mile, and thus the number of potential helpers in the immediate vicinity. But diffusion of responsibility, important as it is, is far from the entire story; several other factors also play significant roles in people's tendency to help others. One of the most important of these is potential helpers' present mood.

FEELING GOOD OR FEELING BAD AND HELPING: MOOD AND PROSOCIAL BEHAVIOR   Are you more likely to offer help to others when in a good mood or in a bad mood? The answer seems obvious: when you are in a good mood. And in fact, many studies offer support for this view (Isen, 1987). People exposed to virtually any event or condition that elevates their mood—finding a coin in a phone booth, watching a funny comedy film, or even smelling pleasant aromas—are more willing to help others than persons not exposed to such mood-elevating events (Baron & Thomley, 1994; Wilson, 1981). This is not always the case, however. When the consequences of helping look unpleasant—for example, when the victim is bleeding or might be sick—people in a good mood actually appear to be *less* likely to help than others. Apparently this is because they are reluctant to undertake actions that will interfere with their good mood (Shaffer & Graziano, 1983).

What about being in a bad mood; can this, too, influence helping? Common sense suggests that negative moods might inhibit prosocial behavior, and research findings confirm this suggestion—but again, only under some conditions. Specifically, being in a bad mood tends to reduce helping when potential helpers focus on their own needs or misfortunes (e.g., Thompson, Cowan, & Rosenhan, 1980). Under other conditions, in contrast, being in a bad mood can have the opposite effect—it can increase the tendency to help. How can

Bystander Effect: A reduced tendency of witnesses to an emergency to help when they believe that there are other potential helpers present.

Diffusion of Responsibility: *A sharing of responsibility among all potential helpers who witness an emergency; the result is that each feels less responsible for helping victims.*

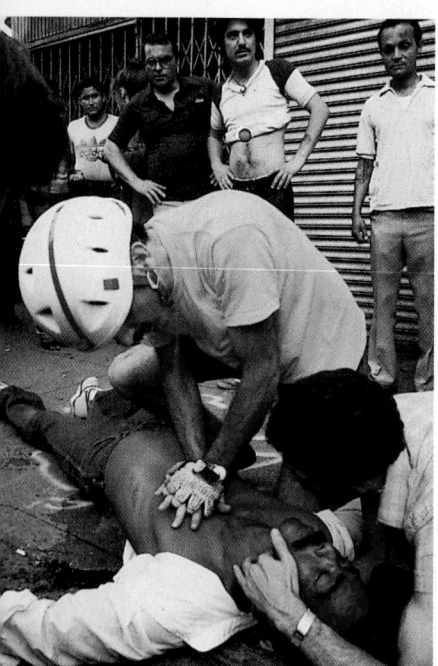

WHO HELPS IN EMERGENCIES? PERSONAL CHARACTERISTICS DO MATTER

Persons who rush forward to help the victims of accidents appear to differ from those who fail to help in several important respects.

this be so? The answer has to do with the fact that helping others sometimes makes us feel good. They thank us, and we can observe the good effects of our aid and can also pat ourselves on the back for engaging in prosocial behavior. Such reactions can serve to counter negative moods—an effect social psychologists describe as *negative state relief*. Helping, then, can sometimes be motivated by this factor: by the desire to counter our own negative moods (Cialdini, Kenrick, & Bauman, 1982; Cunningham et al., 1990).

In sum, the tendency to engage in prosocial behavior is often strongly affected by our current moods. However, the direction of such effects depends on several factors, such as the consequences of helping and the extent to which we focus on our own moods or the plight of the victims.

PERSONAL CHARACTERISTICS AND HELPING My grandfather was on the mailing list of every major charity; he donated to all of them regularly. Interestingly, he did this over the protests of my grandmother, who often proclaimed that she didn't believe in giving money to strangers. This sharp contrast in my grandparents' attitudes, and in their charitable donations, emphasizes the fact that there are large individual differences in the tendency to help. In other words, some persons are much more likely to engage in prosocial behavior than others. What characteristics are related to these differences? An intriguing study conducted by Bierhoff, Klein, and Kramp (1991) provides some answers.

These researchers obtained the names of persons who had administered first aid to accident victims before the ambulance arrived. Then they contacted these persons and asked them to complete a questionnaire that measured many personal characteristics the researchers believed might be linked to such helping. A second group, who had witnessed accidents but failed to help, also completed the questionnaire. When the responses of the two groups were compared, interesting differences emerged. For example, those who offered first aid had stronger beliefs in a *just world;* they tended to believe that the world is a fair and predictable place in which good behavior is rewarded and bad behavior is punished. In addition, they were higher in *internal locus of control*—the belief that people can control their own outcomes or fate. Third, the persons who engaged in helping were higher in *social responsibility*—the idea that we are responsible for others and should help them when the need arises. Finally, those who had helped were *lower* than the control group in *egocentrism*, or concern with themselves and their own problems. In sum, it appears that because of a combination of beliefs and characteristics, some persons are much more likely than others to engage in prosocial behavior. Clearly, these are the kind of individuals we all hope will be around if *we* are unfortunate enough to become the victim of an accident, crime, or natural disaster.

KEY QUESTIONS

- What is prosocial behavior?
- What is the bystander effect?
- How do the moods of potential helpers influence their tendency to engage in prosocial behavior?

ATTRACTION, LOVE, AND CLOSE RELATIONSHIPS

According to the lyrics of one old song, "Love makes the world go round." And most people agree: **Love**—an intense emotional state involving attraction, sexual desire, and deep concern for another person—exerts a profound influence on our lives (Hatfield & Rapson, 1993; Hendrick & Hendrick, 1992). Here, we'll consider what psychologists have discovered not only about love, but also about *interpersonal attraction*—the extent to which we like or dislike others—and about *close relationships*—long-term relationships with other persons (Baron & Byrne, 1994).

Love: *A strong emotional state involving attraction, sexual desire, and concern for another person.*

INTERPERSONAL ATTRACTION: LIKING AND DISLIKING OTHERS Think of someone you like very much, someone you strongly dislike, and someone you'd place in the middle of this dimension. Now, ask yourself this question: *Why* do you have these reactions? Research on the nature and causes of **interpersonal attraction** provides some interesting answers.

Propinquity: Nearness makes the heart grow fonder. Many friendships and romances start when individuals are brought into contact with one another, often by chance. Thus, in a key sense, **propinquity**—physical proximity and the interpersonal contact it produces—is a necessary condition for interpersonal attraction. Many studies confirm this basic fact (Festinger, Schachter, & Back, 1950). In general, the closer to one another people live, work, or even sit in a college classroom, the more likely they are to form friendships and grow to like each other.

Why does propinquity often lead to attraction? In part because the more frequently we are exposed to almost any stimulus, the more positive our reactions toward it tend to be. This is known as the **repeated exposure effect,** and it seems to operate as strongly in relation to people as with many aspects of the physical world (Bornstein, 1989; Zajonc, 1968). The more often we are exposed to others, the more familiar they become, the more comfortable we feel in their presence, and the more we tend to like them (e.g., Moreland & Beach, 1992). For this reason, propinquity is one important basis for interpersonal attraction.

Similarity: Liking others who are like ourselves. You've probably heard both of these proverbs: "Birds of a feather flock together" and "Opposites attract." Which is true? A large amount of evidence leaves little room for doubt: Similarity wins hands down (Byrne, 1971; Park & Fink, 1989). Moreover, this is so whether such similarity relates to attitudes and beliefs, to personality traits, to success in school, to personal habits such as drinking and smoking, or even to whether others are morning or evening persons (see chapter 4) (Jamieson, Lydon, & Zanna, 1987).

Why do we like others who are similar to ourselves? The most plausible explanation is that such persons provide validation for our views or our personal characteristics (Goethals, 1986). If they agree with us, this indicates that our views are correct; and if they share our traits, this indicates that these are desirable ones—or at least ones shared by other persons. Whatever the precise mechanisms involved, though, it is clear that similarity is another important determinant of interpersonal attraction.

Reciprocity: Liking others who like us. When we examined the topic of *ingratiation,* we saw that one way of getting others to like us is to express positive feelings toward them. This suggests that one important determinant of attraction may be others' feelings toward us. In fact, many studies indicate that this is the case: The more others like us, the more, in general, we tend to like them (Condon & Crano, 1988; Curtis & Miller, 1986). Why is this the case? Largely because we enjoy receiving positive evaluations and strongly dislike negative ones. Thus, we tend to like others who express positive sentiments about us. Indeed, this tendency is so strong that it prevails even in situations where we believe that others' assessments of us are inaccurate (Swann et al., 1987) or represent an obvious attempt at flattery (Drachman, DeCarufel, & Insko, 1978)!

Physical attractiveness: Beauty may be only skin deep, but we pay lots of attention to skin. Perhaps the most obvious factor affecting interpersonal attraction is *physical beauty.* Are we really suckers for a pretty or hand-

Interpersonal Attraction: *The extent to which we like or dislike other persons.*

Propinquity: *Physical proximity and the interpersonal contact it produces.*

Repeated Exposure Effect: *The fact that the more frequently we are exposed to various stimuli (at least up to a point), the more we tend to like them.*

some face? A large body of research findings indicates that we are (Hatfield & Rapson, 1993). Moreover, this is true for both women and men, although the effects seem to be somewhat stronger for males (Feingold, 1990; Pierce, 1992). Interestingly, the effects of physical attractiveness are visible across the entire life span. For example, twelve-month-old infants demonstrate more positive reactions to a stranger wearing an attractive mask than to a stranger wearing an unattractive mask (Langlois & Roggman, 1990); and persons in their seventies and eighties still report a preference for others who are high in physical attractiveness (Pittenger, Mark, & Johnson, 1989).

But what, precisely, *is* physical attractiveness? What makes someone physically attractive to others? Clearly, this varies greatly from culture to culture; but within Western societies several characteristics have been found to be closely related to ratings of attractiveness. With respect to facial features, it appears that most men find two facial types attractive in women: youthful, childlike features (large, widely spaced eyes; small nose and chin) or bolder, more "mature" features (prominent cheekbones, narrow cheeks, high eyebrows, large pupils, a big smile) (Cunningham, 1986). Additional findings suggest that faces are perceived as attractive when they don't depart in any pronounced way from the "typical" face in their culture. To test this assertion, Langlois and Roggman (1990) constructed composite faces from photos of different individuals. They found that the more faces they used in constructing these composites, the more attractive the composites were rated as being (Langlois & Roggman, 1990). So, like Goldilocks in the nursery story, we seem to prefer faces that are "just right"—ones that do not depart from average by too much in any direction.

Turning to body features, it appears that many men find medium-size breasts and a slim figure attractive in women (Franzoi & Herzog, 1987), while women find men with broad shoulders, small backsides, and a narrow waist attractive (Lavrakas, 1975). Height, too, is important, especially for women: They don't necessarily prefer tall men, but do prefer ones who are taller than themselves (Pierce, 1992). This preference is weaker among men, but they tend to prefer women somewhat shorter than themselves.

Keep in mind that these findings are averages across thousands of people; huge differences exist with respect to individual preferences. And the findings are based mainly on research conducted in Western cultures; as we noted earlier, standards of physical beauty vary greatly around the world, so these may not generalize to all societies.

PHYSICAL ATTRACTIVENESS IN DIFFERENT CULTURES

Different cultures may have sharply contrasting views about what makes a person physically attractive.

LOVE: THE MOST INTENSE FORM OF ATTRACTION And now at last we come to what many would consider the heart of the matter: love. Countless poets, novelists, and philosophers, as well as billions of ordinary human beings, have pondered the nature of love since the dawn of civilization. Yet, surprisingly, it is only within the past few decades that love has become the topic of systematic research by psychologists (e.g., Hatfield & Rapson, 1993; Hendrick & Hendrick, 1992). While this research has certainly not answered all our questions about love, it *has* added significantly to our understanding of this important topic. Since most research has focused on romantic or passionate love, I'll also emphasize those aspects of love here. But please remember that passionate love is not the only kind of love or necessarily the most important kind. Any theory that attempts to explain love must also consider other types, too, such as the love of parents for their children and the kind of love that remains in stable marriages long after the first flames of passion have subsided (Borello & Thompson, 1990; Hatfield, 1988).

Romantic love: Its basic nature. One approach to understanding the nature of **romantic love** is to begin by asking the following question: What conditions are necessary before individuals are willing to conclude that they are in love? Research on this issue indicates that three basic conditions may be necessary (Hatfield, 1988; Hatfield & Walster, 1981).

First, the persons involved must experience strong emotional arousal; love, after all, is an intense emotional state. Second, they must experience such feelings in the presence of an appropriate person—someone defined by their culture as a suitable object for such feelings. Third, the concept of romantic love must be present in the individuals' culture. Not all cultures have this concept; and when it is lacking, it is difficult for persons to state that they have "fallen in love," since they don't have a clear idea of what this involves. In cultures where the idea of romantic love is absent, people do not marry for love and do not regard it as important for a happy relationship (Kaufman, 1980). They expect positive feelings to develop over time rather than being there at the start.

But once people report that they are in love, what do they experience? Love obviously means different things to different people; and such differences are reflected in modern theories of love, which describe several rather than only one type of love (e.g., Jacobs, 1992; Sternberg, 1988). Several theories, for example, distinguish among various forms of *passionate* love—love dominated by strong physical attraction—and *companionate* love—love, in the words of one noted researcher, that reflects "the affection we feel for those with whom our lives are deeply entwined" (Hatfield, 1988, p. 205). **Companionate love** emphasizes commitment and concern for the loved one's well-being. Other models describe several additional aspects of love; one of these models is summarized in Table 14.1 (on page 554). As you can see, it calls attention to six distinct types of love.

Love: A biochemical interpretation. At this point I should briefly mention one additional approach to understanding love—an approach based largely on biochemical reactions. Some evidence indicates that the shift from passionate love to companionate love may have roots in basic biological systems. According to this view (Gray, 1993), romantic love, which involves intense attraction to another person, triggers the release of amphetamine-like substances within the body, especially *phenylethylamine* (PEA). These substances, in turn, play an important role in the emotional high of love—the rush of excitement and pleasant feelings we experience when we first fall in love. Over time, however, the production of such substances in response to the presence of one's lover decreases. In some cases this leads to the decline of

Romantic Love: *A form of love in which feelings of strong attraction and sexual desire toward another person are dominant.*

Companionate Love: *A form of love involving a high degree of commitment and deep concern for the well-being of the beloved.*

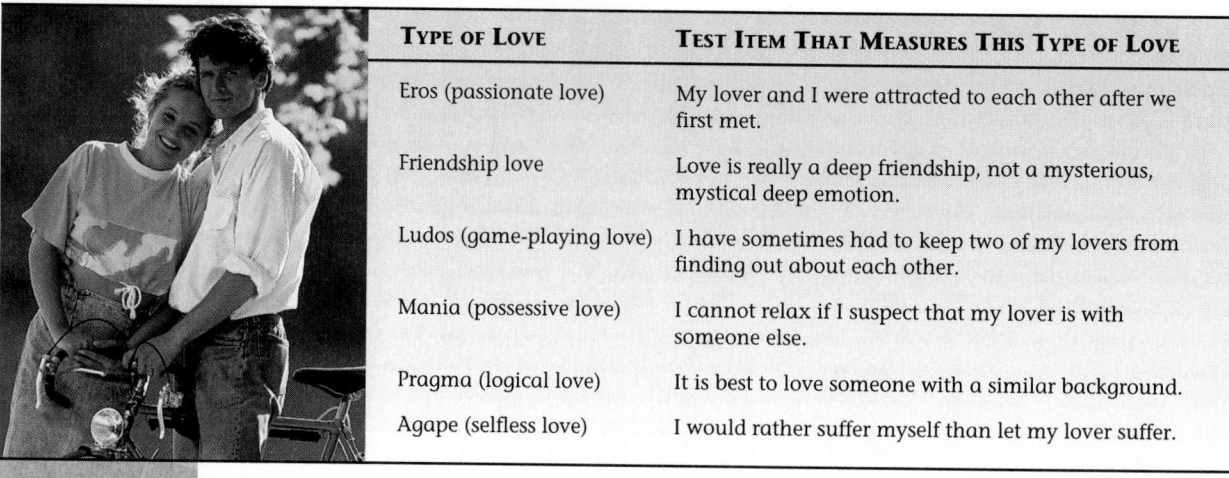

TYPE OF LOVE	TEST ITEM THAT MEASURES THIS TYPE OF LOVE
Eros (passionate love)	My lover and I were attracted to each other after we first met.
Friendship love	Love is really a deep friendship, not a mysterious, mystical deep emotion.
Ludos (game-playing love)	I have sometimes had to keep two of my lovers from finding out about each other.
Mania (possessive love)	I cannot relax if I suspect that my lover is with someone else.
Pragma (logical love)	It is best to love someone with a similar background.
Agape (selfless love)	I would rather suffer myself than let my lover suffer.

TABLE 14.1

Types of Love: One Model

A model of love proposed by Hendrick and Hendrick (1986) suggests that there are distinct types of love. Test items designed to measure each of these types are shown in the right-hand column.
(*Source:* Based on suggestions by Hendrick & Hendrick, 1986, and Lasswell & Lobsenz, 1980.)

romantic relationships: When the excitement is gone, one or both partners seek a new love, perhaps because they value most of all the emotional high of falling in love. In many other cases, however, the presence of one's lover becomes a stimulus for the production of *endorphins*, substances that are soothing and generate feelings of calmness or contentment. These feelings, in turn, serve as one basis for companionate love. The intense misery many happily married people suffer when their spouse dies is a result of the sharp reduction in endorphins they experience in the absence of this person.

Is this biochemical theory of love accurate? At present, there is not sufficient scientific evidence to tell. But there can be no doubt that love, like all other aspects of human experience, is closely linked to biological processes and that full understanding of this powerful reaction will certainly involve these processes.

Troubled relationships: When love dies. ". . . And they lived happily ever after." This is the way many fairy tales end—with the characters riding off into a glowing, love-filled future. Alas—if only life could match these high hopes. Some romantic relationships do blossom into lifelong commitment; my own parents, for example, recently celebrated their fifty-first anniversary, and my wife and I have just celebrated our twentieth. But all too often, the glow of love fades and leaves behind empty relationships from which one or both partners soon withdraw. What causes such outcomes? Research on intimate relationships suggests that several factors are often at work.

We have already considered one of these factors in chapter 9: *jealousy*. Obviously, if one or both partners in a romantic relationship experience high levels of jealousy, the relationship is in jeopardy. Another factor is romantic partners' increasing discovery of *dissimilarities* between them. Such differences are often hidden by the flames of passion, only to emerge as the persons involved get on with the task of living together (Byrne & Murnen, 1988). In addition, some differences don't develop until after the relationship has lasted for several years. One or both partners may change their religious views, political beliefs, drinking behavior, or sexual preference, while the other does not. In such cases, initial similarity gradually shifts into dissimilarity (Levinger, 1988), with negative implications for the relationship.

Another key problem faced by many couples is simple *boredom*. Over time, the unchanging routines of living may lead people to feel that they are in a rut. The feelings of boredom that result, often a major cause of marital dissatisfaction, contribute to the dissolution of many relationships (Fincham & Bradbury, 1992). I should emphasize that boredom is *not* inevitable in stable

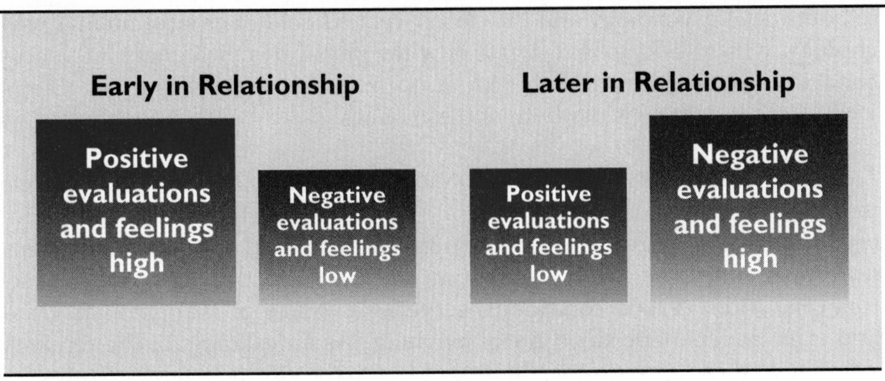

FIGURE 14.10

Self-Defeating Behavior: One Reason Why Relationships Dissolve

Initially, dating couples and newly-weds express mostly positive evaluations and feelings to one another. Over time this pattern may change so that a couple expresses mostly negative evaluations and feelings. If this change goes too far, the relationship may dissolve.

relationships. Happily married couples report that they avoid boredom by seeking new stimulation together—new projects they can share, new learning experiences, joint vacations, to mention just a few.

Finally, as relationships persist, patterns of behavior that can only be described as *self-defeating* in nature sometimes develop. Dating couples and newlyweds frequently express positive evaluations and feelings to one another. As time passes, however, these sometimes decrease and are replaced by negative statements and interactions. "It's all your fault!"—either stated or implicit—becomes a frequent form of exchange, and couples spend less time praising and more time criticizing each other (Miller, 1991); see Figure 14.10. When a relationship slips into this pattern, it is in serious trouble. Existing evidence suggests that this pattern of negative interactions is literally deadly: When it develops, love doesn't simply die but is murdered by caustic, biting remarks.

Fortunately, additional research suggests that persons committed to maintaining a happy long-term relationship can avoid all of these pitfalls (Hatfield & Rapson, 1993). The effort required is far from trivial, but the rewards of maintaining love, and remaining in loving relationships, make this one of the most important tasks we can ever undertake.

> ### KEY QUESTIONS
>
> - What factors influence interpersonal attraction?
> - Under what conditions do people conclude that they are in love?
> - What kinds of love exist?
> - What factors contribute to the dissolution of intimate relationships?

ENVIRONMENTAL PSYCHOLOGY: *How the Physical Environment Affects Social Behavior—and Vice Versa*

When I was a graduate student, the newspaper at my university ran an editorial complaining bitterly about the fact that the new psychology laboratories were air-conditioned while many dorms were not. I was so incensed by the harsh tone of this article that I wrote a reply, pointing out that it would be impossible to study behavior scientifically if environmental conditions that can strongly affect it, such as temperature, were allowed to vary greatly and at random, depending on the current weather. I didn't realize it at the time, but this was the start of my career-long interest in how the physical environment influences behavior. Some of my earliest research was concerned with the "long-hot-summer" effect—the possibility that high temperatures make people irritable and aggressive (Baron, 1972; Baron & Bell, 1975). And my recent research on air quality, lighting, and fragrance (Baron, 1994) centers on the same question: How does the physical environment influence our behavior, and especially, our social behavior? This issue has been of major interest to both social psychology and the closely related field of **environmental psychology,** which seeks to investigate how the physical environment influences behavior and how human behavior, in turn, affects the environment (Stern, 1992). Let's briefly consider both of these issues.

EFFECTS OF THE PHYSICAL ENVIRONMENT ON SOCIAL BEHAVIOR While many different aspects of the physical environment might potentially influence behavior, most research attention has been focused on three: *temperature, noise,* and *air quality* (Bell, Fisher, Baum, and Greene, 1990). Each of these factors can, under certain conditions, serve as a source of *environmental stress* and exert adverse effects on social behavior. As an example of the research pointing to these conclusions, I'll focus here on the effects of temperature.

Heat and aggression: Do tempers really rise when temperature goes up?
During the late 1960s and 1970s, major riots erupted in large cities in the United States and elsewhere. These riots were primarily related to social factors such as prejudice and efforts to overcome it, but psychologists soon noticed that most occurred during warm summer months. Did this mean that commonsense notions connecting heat and aggression are correct—that people really do become "hot under the collar" when exposed to high temperatures? Initial laboratory studies designed to test this notion yielded mixed results: Up to a point—about the mid-80s Fahrenheit—rising temperature did increase aggression. When temperatures rose above this point, however, aggression actually declined, perhaps because the persons involved became more concerned with minimizing their own discomfort than with behaving aggressively against others who had previously annoyed them (Baron, 1978). And in laboratory studies, they could only accomplish this goal by reducing their aggression and so, perhaps, speeding the end of the session (Bell, 1992).

Other research, which examined the relationship between heat and aggression outside the laboratory, pointed to somewhat different conclusions, however. These studies found a correlation between temperature and violent crimes (Anderson & Anderson, 1984; Anderson & DeNeve, 1992). As temperatures rose, so too did the incidence of violent crimes (murder, rape) in many large cities. Moreover, there was no indication of a downturn in crime at very high temperatures. And as shown in Figure 14.11, corresponding effects were even observed on baseball fields: More players were hit by pitched balls on hot days than on cool ones (Reifman, Larrick, & Fein, 1991).

Environmental Psychology:
The branch of psychology that investigates the effects of the physical environment on human behavior and the effects of that behavior on the environment.

p

p

So where does all this leave us? On the one hand, it appears that aggression does increase as temperatures rise. Moreover, such effects seem to occur even as temperatures rise to very high levels—into the 90s Fahrenheit. However, it is also clear that at some point, increasing heat may induce lethargy or even *heat exhaustion*—muscular weakness, nausea, dizziness, and fainting stemming from physiological causes (Sanders & McCormick, 1993). To the extent that individuals experience such effects, of course, their liklihood of engaging in aggression will be reduced. So why didn't field studies of the heat-aggression relationship observe this pattern? Perhaps because people are so good at countering the effects of heat: They drink cold liquids, douse themselves with water, and so on. In the laboratory studies, where aggression did decline at very high temperatures, participants couldn't engage in these tactics, so, perhaps, their discomfort rose to levels high enough to reduce aggression. Additional research is necessary to resolve this issue, but at present one important conclusion is clear: In a wide range of situations and settings, high temperatures can, indeed, contribute to increased aggression.

EFFECTS OF HUMAN BEHAVIOR ON THE ENVIRONMENT: WHAT WE ARE DOING TO PLANET EARTH

When I was in junior high school (in the late 1950s), the population of the earth was about three billion; now, it is six billion. As human numbers rise and as more societies industrialize, the impact of human activities on our planet also increases—with perhaps dangerous implications (e.g., Stevens, 1992). Let's consider two of these potential effects.

The greenhouse effect: A coming climatic disaster?

Hundreds of millions of automobiles; an ever-increasing number of factories and electricity generating plants that burn coal or oil—some of the effects of these aspects of human activity are obvious. Aside from air pollution, however, it is possible that these aspects of human activity could have another, and even more important, effect: The tremendous amounts of *carbon dioxide* released by these and other sources may actually change the global climate. You've probably heard the term *greenhouse effect*; it refers to the fact that carbon dioxide and other gases produced by industry and by the billions of cattle we raise for milk, meat, and leather may serve to trap heat in the earth's atmosphere, thus producing global warming. While scientists do not agree about the size of this effect, most do expect some warming to occur as a result of human activity (Havel, 1992). The results of such change may be catastrophic. Patterns of rainfall may be altered so that, for example, droughts strike the American Midwest—the true "breadbasket" of the planet—with increasing frequency; the monsoons, which bring needed rain to India and many other countries, may fail; and the Sahara desert may spread over larger areas of Africa. In addition, sea level will rise as the polar ice caps melt, thus producing serious flooding around the world.

Again, scientists don't all agree that such effects are likely; but merely the possibility that they may occur should be enough to spur vigorous action to prevent or at least slow this process. The Earth Summit Conference held in Rio de Janeiro, Brazil, in 1992 represented an attempt to encourage coordinated action by many different nations, and it is clear that additional meetings and concrete actions are necessary if we are to address this serious problem adequately.

How can emissions of carbon dioxide and other gases that contribute to the greenhouse effect be reduced? Primarily through steps that encourage *energy efficiency*: increased insulation in all buildings; more efficient equipment for heating, cooling, and manufacturing processes; and vehicles that deliver more miles for every gallon or liter of fuel used. In addition, increased *recycling* of waste materials is crucial. Paper, glass, metals—all these

INCREASED USE OF FOSSIL FUELS: A FACTOR IN THE GREENHOUSE EFFECT

Increased use of fossil fuels such as oil and coal may be contributing to rising levels of air pollution and, ultimately, to the *greenhouse effect.*

can be recovered from used products for reuse in new ones. For example, consider one simple fact: In the United States alone, more than 250 million tires are thrown away each year. Until recently, little effort was made to recycle this potentially valuable resource. Now, however, one company—Cycletech, Inc.—has developed a new process in which used tires are frozen and then ground into tiny particles. From these, valuable materials such as rubber, steel, and nylon fiber can be recovered and used in making new products. Since less energy is required to recover and reuse these materials than to make them from scratch, recycling of tires not only removes unsightly "eyesores" from the environment and prevents polluting tire fires, it also helps to reduce energy consumption and thus to slow development of the greenhouse effect.

Destruction of the rainforest and the spread of viral diseases. Each year, millions of acres of virgin rainforest are cut down, either to make room for farming by growing populations or to harvest the timber. The effects of this human activity may also prove catastrophic. Many scientists believe that the rainforests play an important role in moderating the earth's climate, lessening wide swings in temperature or patterns of rainfall (Toufexis, 1992). Perhaps even more important, however, is the fact that as such rainforests are eliminated, contact between humans and animals that once lived within them is increased. Unfortunately, many of these animals carry viruses to which they are relatively immune, but to which human beings are highly susceptible. For example, consider the *Ebola virus*, unknown to medical science until the 1970s. It first came to the attention of scientists in 1976, when residents of fifty-five villages in Africa near the Ebola River became ill with an unknown disease. More than 88 percent died, and researchers soon determined that the cause was a virus not recognized until that time—a virus that may well have been passed to the human population from animals living in the nearby forest. Efforts to prevent the spread of the virus succeeded, and so the threat of a major epidemic was averted. But this tragic incident raises an alarming question: How many other potentially deadly viruses lurk in the rainforests we are currently destroying? The answer is unknown, but many scientists believe that as the process of cutting down rainforests continues, the risk of human contact with new viruses—and new diseases—will continue to mount (Preston, 1992).

In view of such frightening possibilities, coordinated efforts to deal with this problem seem essential. And, again, there are hopeful signs that such action *is* beginning. For example, organizations have been established for the purpose of purchasing millions of acres of rainforest, not to exploit them, but to preserve them in their natural state forever. If enough actions of this type occur, then perhaps disaster can be avoided—perhaps, but only time will tell whether humanity will pass this ultimate test of its capacity for rational thought and planning.

KEY QUESTIONS

- What is environmental psychology?
- What are the effects of heat on aggression?
- In what important ways is human behavior influencing the environment?

Are You in Love? One Way of Telling

One question almost everyone has pondered is this: "Am I really in love?" Despite many songs suggesting that love is readily visible in one's eyes or on one's face, this is a difficult question to answer. Love has several different components, and one really can't measure it directly!

One answer, however, is provided by systematic research on love and its various components. Draw-ing on the findings of such work, social psychologists have devised questionnaires that reliably measure the intense emotional reactions characteristic of romantic love. One of these scales (in modified form) is printed below. Follow the instructions to obtain a rough measure of your own love for any specific per-son you wish to consider.

Think of a person with whom you believe you are or have been in love. Insert that person's name in each of the state-ments below and then respond to each by writing a number in the space next to it. Responses to each item are made along the following scale:

Not at all true		Moderately true			Definitely true	
1	2	3	4	5	6	7	8	9

For example, if you feel that a statement is definitely true, enter a nine; if you feel that it is completely false, enter a one.

After answering all the questions, add the numbers you have entered. The highest score—indicating very intense love—is 120; the lowest is 15.

The items on this scale are based on one developed by Hatfield and Sprecher (1986). They are designed to measure romantic or passionate love. Remember that there are sev-eral other kinds of love as well.

_____ 1. I would feel deep despair if _____ left me.

_____ 2. Sometimes I feel I can't control my thoughts, they are obsessively on _____.

_____ 3. I feel happy when I am doing something to make _____ happy.

_____ 4. I would rather be with _____ than anyone else.

_____ 5. I'd get jealous if I thought _____ were falling in love with someone else.

_____ 6. I yearn to know all about _____.

_____ 7. I want _____—physically, emotionally, mentally.

_____ 8. I have an endless appetite for affection from _____.

_____ 9. For me, _____ is the perfect romantic partner.

_____ 10. I sense my body responding when _____ touches me.

_____ 11. _____ always seems to be on my mind.

_____ 12. I want _____ to know me—my thoughts, my fears, and my hopes.

_____ 13. I eagerly look for signs indicating _____'s desire for me.

_____ 14. I possess a powerful attraction for _____.

_____ 15. I get extremely depressed when things don't go right in my relationship with _____.

Systematic research on the nature of romantic love has led to ques-tionnaires designed to measure its characteristics. How do you score?

Social Thought: Thinking about Other People

- *According to a theory proposed by Kelley, what kinds of information do we use in deciding whether others' actions stem from internal or external causes?*

According to Kelley's theory, we decide whether others' actions have internal or external causes by focusing on information relating to consensus, consistency, and distinctiveness.

- *What is the fundamental attribution error?*

The fundamental attribution error is our tendency to overestimate the importance of dispositional (internal) causes of others' behavior.

- *What is the self-serving bias?*

The self-serving bias is our tendency to attribute our own positive outcomes to internal causes and to attribute negative outcomes to external factors.

- *What is the false consensus effect?*

The false consensus effect refers to our tendency to assume that others share our views to a greater extent than is really true.

- *What is the automatic vigilance effect?*

The automatic vigilance effect refers to our tendency to be especially sensitive to negative social information.

- *What is motivated skepticism?*

Motivated skepticism is the tendency to be much more open to information consistent with our initial preferences than to information inconsistent with these preferences.

- *What is counterfactual thinking?*

Counterfactual thinking involves imagining events and outcomes that didn't occur.

- *What are attitudes?*

Attitudes are lasting beliefs about and evaluations of aspects of the world.

- *What factors received most attention in early research on persuasion?*

Early research on persuasion focused primarily on how aspects of the source, the message, and the audience influence this process.

- *What factors are emphasized in modern cognitive models of persuasion?*

Modern cognitive models of persuasion emphasize the role of cognitive processes such as the processing of information contained in messages.

- *What is cognitive dissonance, and when does it occur?*

Cognitive dissonance is an unpleasant motivating state experienced by individuals when they notice that either two attitudes they hold or their attitudes and their behavior are inconsistent.

- *What is the less-leads-to-more effect?*

The less-leads-to-more effect refers to the fact that providing individuals with small rewards for expressing views they don't really hold sometimes leads to greater attitude change than providing them with relatively large rewards.

KEY TERMS: *social psychology, p. 520; attribution, p. 520; consensus, p. 521; consistency, p. 521; distinctiveness, p. 521; fundamental attribution error, p. 523; self-serving bias, p. 524; social cognition, p. 524; false consensus effect, p. 525; automatic vigilance, p. 526; motivated skepticism, p. 527; counterfactual thinking, p. 527; attitudes, p. 529; persuasion, p. 529; cognitive perspective on persuasion, p. 530; elaboration likelihood model, p. 530; central route, p. 530; peripheral route, p. 530; forced compliance, p. 531; cognitive dissonance, p. 532; less-leads-to-more effect, p. 533*

Social Behavior: Interacting with Others

- *What is prejudice, and what factors contribute to its existence?*

Prejudice involves negative attitudes toward members of specific social groups. It stems from many sources, including economic competition between the groups, social categorization, social learning, and cognitive factors such as stereotypes.

- *How can prejudice be reduced?*

Prejudice can be reduced by socialization of children for tolerance, greater intergroup contact, cognitive dissonance, and recategorization—shifting the boundaries between ingroups and outgroups so as to include people previously excluded from one's own group.

- *What is social influence?*

Social influence involves attempts to change others' behavior.

- *What factors influence the occurrence of conformity?*

Several factors have been found to influence conformity, including group size and unanimity of the influencing group. However, gender does not appear to have an effect on the tendency to conform.

- *What is compliance, and how can it be increased?*

Compliance involves social influence through acceptance of direct requests. It is often gained through the use of multiple requests, as in the foot-in-the-door or door-in-the-face techniques.

- *What is destructive obedience, and how can it be reduced?*

Destructive obedience occurs when individuals follow direct orders from others to engage in some form of antisocial behavior. It can be reduced through exposure to disobedient models, acceptance of personal responsibility, and evidence that authority figures are seeking selfish ends.

- **What is prosocial behavior?**

Prosocial behavior involves actions that benefit others without necessarily providing any direct benefit to the persons who perform them.

- **What is the bystander effect?**

The bystander effect refers to the fact that the more persons present at the scene of an accident, the less likely the victim is to receive aid.

- **How do the moods of potential helpers influence their tendency to engage in prosocial behavior?**

The moods of potential helpers can exert strong effects on prosocial behavior. However, the direction of these effects—toward increased or reduced helping—depends on several factors, such as the consequences of engaging in such behavior.

- **What factors influence interpersonal attraction?**

Interpersonal attraction is influenced by many factors, including propinquity, similarity, reciprocity, and physical attractiveness.

- **Under what conditions do people conclude that they are in love?**

People generally conclude that they are in love when they experience strong emotional arousal in the presence of an appropriate person and when the concept of romantic love is present in their culture.

- **What kinds of love exist?**

Several distinct types of love exist, including passionate love and companionate love.

- **What factors contribute to the dissolution of intimate relationships?**

Factors that can lead to the dissolution of intimate relationships include jealousy, boredom, growing dissimilarity, and a pattern in which negative statements and interactions replace positive ones.

- **What is environmental psychology?**

Environmental psychology is the branch of psychology that investigates how the physical environment influences behavior and how human behavior affects the environment.

- **What are the effects of heat on aggression?**

Growing evidence indicates that aggression increases as temperature rises.

- **In what important ways is human behavior influencing the environment?**

Human behavior appears to be influencing global climate through the greenhouse effect. In addition, destruction of the rainforest may bring human beings into contact with viruses against which they have little or no immunity.

KEY TERMS: prejudice, p. 534; realistic conflict theory, p. 535; social categorization, p. 535; stereotypes, p. 535; contact hypothesis, p. 537; recategorization, p. 538; racial identification, p. 539; social influence, p. 540; conformity, p. 541; social norms, p. 541; compliance, p. 543; ingratiation, p. 543; impression management, p. 543; foot-in-the-door technique, p. 543; door-in-the-face technique, p. 544; that's-not-all approach, p. 544; complaining, p. 544; obedience, p. 545; prosocial behavior, p. 547; bystander effect, p. 549; diffusion of responsibility, p. 549; love, p. 550; interpersonal attraction, p. 551; propinquity, p. 551; repeated exposure effect, p. 551; romantic love, p. 553; companionate love, p. 553; environmental psychology, p. 556

CRITICAL THINKING QUESTIONS

APPRAISAL	Social thought and social interaction occur together in a seamless fashion in everyday life. Do you think that studying them separately, as social psychologists have often done, makes any sense? If so, why? If not, how could they be studied simultaneously?
CONTROVERSY	Many people believe that love is beyond the realm of science—that we will never be able to understand it fully through scientific research. Do you agree? Or do you think that love can be investigated in a systematic manner through the methods of modern psychology?
MAKING PSYCHOLOGY PART OF YOUR LIFE	Now that you know more about the many techniques people use to influence each other, do you think that you can use this information to (1) be more effective in exerting influence over others and (2) resist such influence yourself? What techniques do you think might be most useful to you in your own life? Which do you feel might be hardest to resist when used by other persons?

Appendix

Statistics: Uses—
and Potential Abuses

At many points in this text, I've noted that one benefit you should gain from your first course in psychology is the ability to think about human behavior in a new way. This appendix will expand on that theme by offering a basic introduction to one essential aspect of psychological thinking: **statistics**.

What does this special form of mathematics have to do with psychology or thinking like a psychologist? The answer involves the fact that all fields of science require two major types of tools. First, scientists need various kinds of equipment to gather the data they seek. Obviously, this equipment differs from field to field; for example, biologists use microscopes, astronomers employ telescopes, and geologists wield hammers (or even dynamite!) in their work.

Second, all scientists need some means for interpreting the findings of their research—for determining the *meaning* of the information they have acquired and its relationship to important theories in their field. Again, this varies from one science to another. In most cases, though, some type of mathematics is involved. Psychology is no exception to this general rule: To understand the findings of their research (and, hence, important aspects of human behavior), psychologists make use of *statistics*—or, more accurately, *statistical analysis* of the data they collect.

As you'll soon see, statistics are a flexible tool and can be used for many different purposes. In psychology, however, they are usually employed to accomplish one or more of the following tasks: (1) *summarizing* or *describing* large amounts of data; (2) *comparing* individuals or groups of individuals in various ways; (3) determining whether certain aspects of behavior are *related* (whether they vary together in a systematic manner); and (4) *predicting* future behavior from current information. In the pages that follow we'll consider each of these major uses of statistics by psychologists. After doing so, we'll explore several ways in which statistics can be abused—how they can be employed to disguise or conceal important facts rather than to clarify them.

DESCRIPTIVE STATISTICS:
Summarizing Data

Suppose that a psychologist conducts an experiment concerned with the effects of staring at others in public places. The procedures of the study are simple. He stares at people in stores, airports, and a variety of other locations, and he records the number of seconds until they look away—or until they approach to make him stop! After carrying out these procedures twenty times, he obtains the data shown in Table A.1. Presented in this form, the scores seem meaningless. If they are grouped together in the manner shown in Figure A.1, however, a much clearer picture emerges. Now we can see at a

Statistics: *Mathematical procedures used to describe data and draw inferences from them.*

glance that the most frequent score is 4 seconds; that fewer people look away after 3 or 5 seconds; and that even fewer look away very quickly (after 2 seconds) or after a longer delay (6 seconds). This graph presents a **frequency distribution**: It indicates the number of times each score occurs within an entire set of scores. Here, the frequency distribution indicates how many times scores of 1, 2, 3, 4, 5, and 6 seconds were recorded in the study of staring.

A graph such as the one in Figure A.1 provides a rough idea of the way a set of scores is distributed. In science, however, a rough idea is not sufficient: More precision is required. In particular, it would be useful to have an index of (1) the middle score of the distribution of scores (their **central tendency**) and (2) the extent to which the scores spread out around this point (their **dispersion**). Such measures are provided by **descriptive statistics.**

	NUMBER OF SECONDS UNTIL PERSON EITHER LOOKS AWAY OR APPROACHES
Person 1	4
Person 2	4
Person 3	1
Person 4	4
Person 5	3
Person 6	2
Person 7	5
Person 8	3
Person 9	6
Person 10	5
Person 11	4
Person 12	4
Person 13	3
Person 14	3
Person 15	5
Person 16	4
Person 17	4
Person 18	2
Person 19	6
Person 20	5

TABLE **A.1**

Raw Data from a Simple Experiment

When a psychologist stares at strangers in a public place, these persons either look away or approach him in the number of seconds shown. Note that more people look away or approach after 4 seconds than any other value.

Frequency Distribution: The frequency with which each score occurs within an entire distribution of scores.

Central Tendency: The middle (center) of a distribution of scores.

Dispersion: The extent to which scores in a distribution spread out or vary around the center.

Descriptive Statistics: Statistics that summarize the major characteristics of an array of scores.

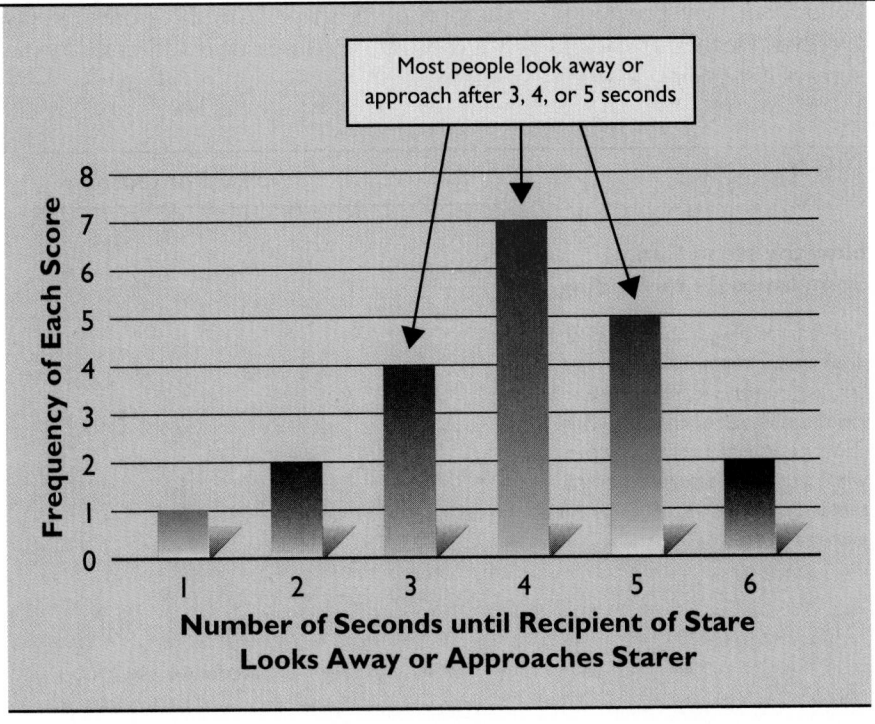

FIGURE **A.1**

A Frequency Distribution

In a *frequency distribution,* scores are grouped together according to the number of times each occurs. This one suggests that most persons react to being stared at within about four seconds.

Most people look away or approach after 3, 4, or 5 seconds

MEASURES OF CENTRAL TENDENCY: Finding the Center

You are already familiar with one important measure of central tendency: the **mean**, or average. We calculate a mean by adding all scores and then dividing by the total number of scores. The mean represents the typical score in a distribution and in this respect is often quite useful. Sometimes, though, it can be misleading. This is because the mean can be strongly affected by one or a few extreme scores. To see why this is so, consider the following example. Ten families live on a block. The number of children in each family is shown in Table A.2. Adding these numbers together and dividing by ten yields a mean of four. Yet, as you can see, *not one family actually has four children.* Most have none or two, but one has eight and another has nineteen.

In cases such as this, it is better to refer to other measures of central tendency. One of these is the **mode**—the most frequently occurring score. As you can see, the mode of the data in Table A.2 is 2: More families have two children than have any other number. Another useful measure of central tendency is the **median**—the midpoint of the distribution. Fifty percent of the scores fall at or above the median, while 50 percent fall at or below this value. Returning to the data in Table A.2, the median also happens to be 2: Half the scores fall at or below this value, while half fall at or above it.

As you can readily see, both the mode and the median provide more accurate descriptions of the data than does the mean in this particular example. But please note that this is *not* always, or even usually, the case. It is true only in instances where extreme scores distort the mean. In fact, there is no single rule for choosing among these measures. The decision to employ one over the others should be made only after careful study of frequency distributions such as the one shown in Figure A.1.

MEASURES OF DISPERSION: Assessing the Spread

The mean, median, and mode each tell us something about the center of a distribution, but they provide no indication of its shape. Are the scores bunched together? Do they spread out over a wide range? This issue is addressed by measures of *dispersion.*

Mean: *A measure of central tendency derived by adding all scores and dividing by the number of scores.*

Mode: *A measure of central tendency indicating the most frequent score in an array of scores.*

Median: *A measure of central tendency indicating the midpoint of an array of scores.*

TABLE A.2		NUMBER OF CHILDREN
How the Mean Can Sometimes Be Misleading	Family 1	0
	Family 2	0
Ten families have a total of 40 children among them. The mean is 4.0, but, as you can see, not one family has this number of children. This illustrates the fact that the *mean,* while a useful measure of central tendency, can be distorted by a few extreme scores.	Family 3	2
	Family 4	2
	Family 5	2
	Family 6	2
	Family 7	2
	Family 8	3
	Family 9	19
	Family 10	8
		Total = 40 children
		Mean = 40/10 = 4.0

The simplest measure of dispersion is the **range**—the difference between the highest and lowest scores. For example, the range for the data on number of children per family in Table A.2 is 19 (19 – 0 = 19). Although the range provides some idea of the extent to which scores vary, it suffers from one key drawback: It does not indicate how much the scores spread out around the center. Information on this important issue is provided by the **variance** and **standard deviation**.

The variance provides a measure of the average distance between scores in a distribution and the mean. It indicates the extent to which, on average, the scores depart from (vary around) the mean. Actually, the variance refers to the average *squared* distance of the scores from the mean; squaring eliminates negative numbers. The *standard deviation* then takes account of this operation of squaring by calculating the square root of the variance. So the standard deviation, which is widely used in psychology, represents the average distance between scores and the mean in any distribution. The larger the standard deviation, the more the scores are spread out around the center of the distribution.

THE NORMAL CURVE: *Putting Descriptive Statistics to Work*

Despite the inclusion of several examples, this discussion so far has been somewhat abstract. As a result, it may have left you wondering about the following question: Just what do descriptive statistics have to do with understanding human behavior or thinking like a psychologist? One important answer involves their relationship to a special type of frequency distribution known as the **normal curve**.

While you may never have seen this term before, you are probably quite familiar with the concept it describes. Consider the following characteristics: height, size of vocabulary, strength of motivation to attain success. Suppose you obtained measurements of each among thousands of persons. What would be the shape of each of these distributions? If you guessed that they would all take the form shown in Figure A.2, you are correct. In fact, on each

Range: The difference between the highest and lowest scores in a distribution of scores.

Variance: A measure of dispersion reflecting the average squared distance between each score and the mean.

Standard Deviation: A measure of dispersion reflecting the average distance between each score and the mean.

Normal Curve: A symmetrical, bell-shaped frequency distribution. Most scores are found near the middle, and fewer and fewer occur toward the extremes. Many psychological characteristics are distributed in this manner.

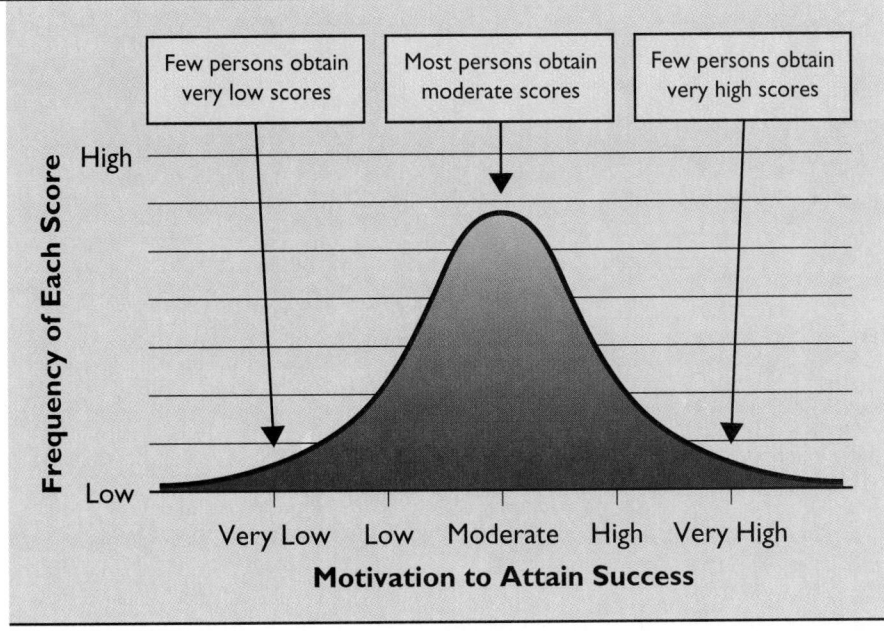

Few persons obtain very low scores

Most persons obtain moderate scores

Few persons obtain very high scores

Frequency of Each Score

High

Low

Very Low   Low   Moderate   High   Very High

Motivation to Attain Success

FIGURE A.2

The Normal Curve

On many dimensions relating to behavior, scores show the kind of frequency distribution illustrated here: the *normal* curve. Most scores pile up in the middle, and fewer and fewer occur toward the extremes.

dimension most scores would pile up in the middle, and fewer and fewer scores would occur farther away from this value. In short, most people would be found to be average height, would have average vocabularies, and would show average desire for success; very few would be extremely high or low on these characteristics. We should add, by the way, that the normal curve applies to an amazingly wide range of human characteristics—everything from personality traits to cognitive abilities and physical attributes.

What does the normal curve have to do with the use of descriptive statistics? A great deal. One key property of the normal curve is as follows: Specific proportions of the scores within it are contained in certain areas of the curve; moreover, these portions can be defined in terms of the standard deviation of all of the scores. Therefore, once we know the mean of a normal distribution and its standard deviation, we can determine the relative standing of any specific score within it. Perhaps a concrete example will help clarify both the nature and the value of this relationship.

Figure A.3 presents a normal distribution with a mean of 5.0 and a standard deviation of 1.0. Let's assume that the scores shown are those on a test of desire for power. Suppose that we now encounter an individual with a score of 7.0. We know that she is high on this characteristic, but *how* high? On the basis of descriptive statistics—the mean and standard deviation—plus the properties of the normal curve, we can tell. Statisticians have found that 68 percent of the scores in a normal distribution fall within one standard deviation of the mean, either above or below it. Similarly, fully 96 percent of the scores fall within two standard deviations of the mean. Given this information, we can conclude that a score of 7 on this test is very high indeed:

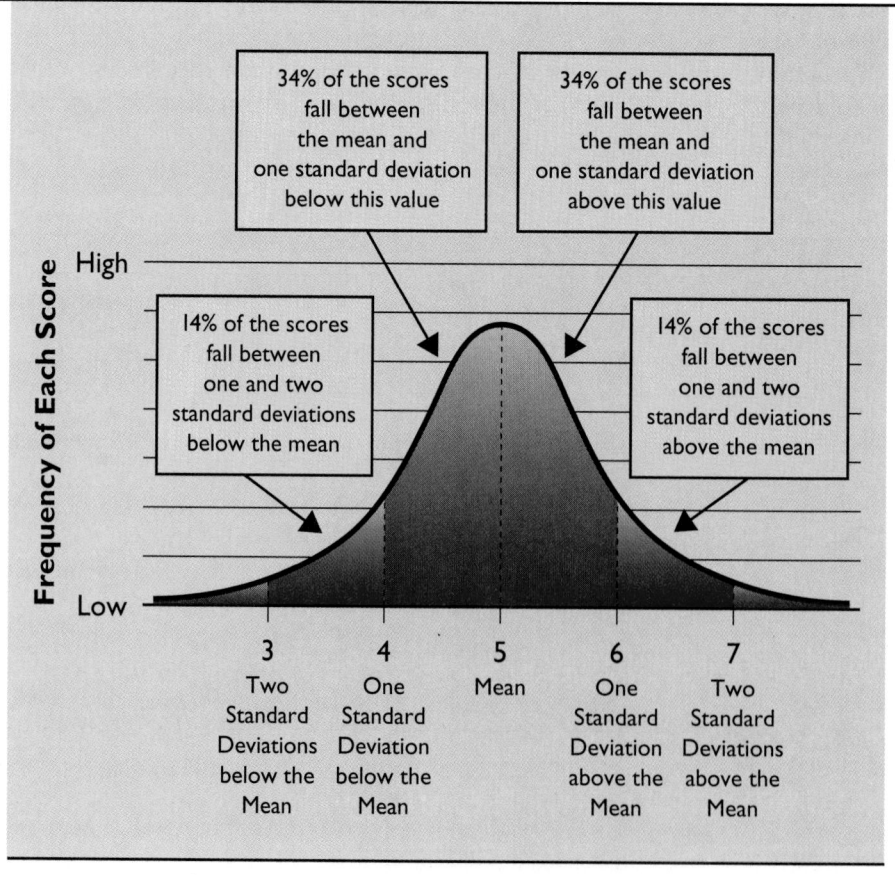

FIGURE A.3

Interpreting Scores by Means of the Normal Distribution

Sixty-eight percent of the scores in a normal distribution fall within one standard deviation of the mean (above or below it). Similarly, fully 96 percent of the scores fall within two standard deviations of the mean. Thus, on a test with a mean of 5.0 and a standard deviation of 1.0, only 2 percent of persons attain a score of 7.0 or higher.

34% of the scores fall between the mean and one standard deviation below this value

34% of the scores fall between the mean and one standard deviation above this value

14% of the scores fall between one and two standard deviations below the mean

14% of the scores fall between one and two standard deviations above the mean

High

Frequency of Each Score

Low

3 — Two Standard Deviations below the Mean

4 — One Standard Deviation below the Mean

5 — Mean

6 — One Standard Deviation above the Mean

7 — Two Standard Deviations above the Mean

Only 2 percent of persons taking the test attain a score equal to or higher than this one.

In a similar manner, descriptive statistics can be used to interpret scores in any other distribution, providing it approaches the normal curve in form. As noted above, a vast array of psychological characteristics and behaviors do seem to be distributed in this manner. The result: we can readily determine an individual's relative standing on any of these dimensions from just two pieces of information—the mean of all scores in the distribution and the standard deviation. Little wonder, then, that the normal curve has sometimes been described as a statistician's or psychologist's delight.

Now imagine that your first psychology test contains fifty multiple-choice items. You obtain a score of 40. Did you do well or poorly? If your instructor provides two additional pieces of information—the mean of all the scores in the class and the standard deviation—you can tell. Suppose the mean is 35, and the standard deviation is 2.50. The mean indicates that most people got a lower score than you did. The relatively small standard deviation indicates that most scores were quite close to the mean—only about twice this distance *above* the mean. Further—and here is a key point—this conclusion would be accurate whether there were 30, 100, or 500 students in the class, assuming the mean and standard deviation remained unchanged. It is precisely this type of efficiency that makes descriptive statistics so useful for summarizing even large amounts of information.

INFERENTIAL STATISTICS: Determining Whether Differences Are or Are Not Real

*T*hroughout this book, the results of many experiments have been described. When these studies were discussed, differences between various conditions or groups were often mentioned. For example, we saw that participants exposed to one set of conditions or one level of an independent variable behaved differently from participants exposed to another set of conditions or another level of an independent variable. How did we know that such differences were real ones rather than differences that might have occurred by chance alone? The answer involves the use of **inferential statistics**. These methods allow us to reach conclusions about just this issue: whether a difference we have actually observed is large enough for us to conclude (to *infer*) that it is indeed a real or *significant* one. The logic behind inferential statistics is complex, but some of its key points can be illustrated by the following example.

Suppose that a psychologist conducts an experiment to examine the impact of mood on memory. (As you may recall, such research was discussed in chapter 6.) To do so, he exposes one group of participants to conditions designed to place them in a good mood: They watch a very funny videotape. A second group, in contrast, is exposed to a neutral tape—one that has little impact on their mood. Both groups are then asked to memorize lists of words, some of which refer to happy events, such as "party," "success." Later, both groups are tested for recall of these words. Results indicate that those who watched the funny tape remember more happy words than those who watched the neutral tape; in fact, those in the first group remember twelve happy words, while those in the second remember only eight—a difference of 4.0. Is this difference a real one?

Inferential Statistics: Statistical procedures that permit us to determine whether differences between individuals or groups are ones that are likely or unlikely to have occurred by chance.

One way of answering this question would be to repeat the study over and over again. If a difference in favor of the happy group were obtained consistently, our confidence that it is indeed real (and perhaps due to differences in subjects' mood) would increase. As you can see, however, this would be a costly procedure. Is there any way of avoiding it? One answer is provided by inferential statistics. These methods assume that if we repeated the study over and over again, the size of the difference between the two groups obtained each time would vary; moreover, these differences would be normally distributed. Most would fall near the mean, and only a few would be quite large. When applying inferential statistics to the interpretation of psychological research, we make a very conservative assumption: We begin by assuming that there is no difference between the groups—that the mean of this distribution is zero. Through methods that are beyond the scope of this discussion, we then estimate the size of the standard deviation. Once we do, we can readily evaluate the difference obtained in an actual study. If an observed difference is large enough that it would occur by chance only 5 percent (or less) of the time, we can view it as significant. For example, assume that in the study we have been discussing, this standard deviation (a standard deviation of mean differences) is 2.0. This indicates that the difference we observed (4.0) is two standard deviations above the expected mean of zero (please refer to Figure A.4). As you'll recall from our discussion of the normal curve, this means that the difference is quite large and would occur by chance less than 2 percent of the time. Our conclusion: the difference between the two groups in our study is *probably* real. Thus, mood does indeed seem to affect memory.

Please note the word *probably* above. Since the tails of the normal curve never entirely level off, there is always some chance—no matter how

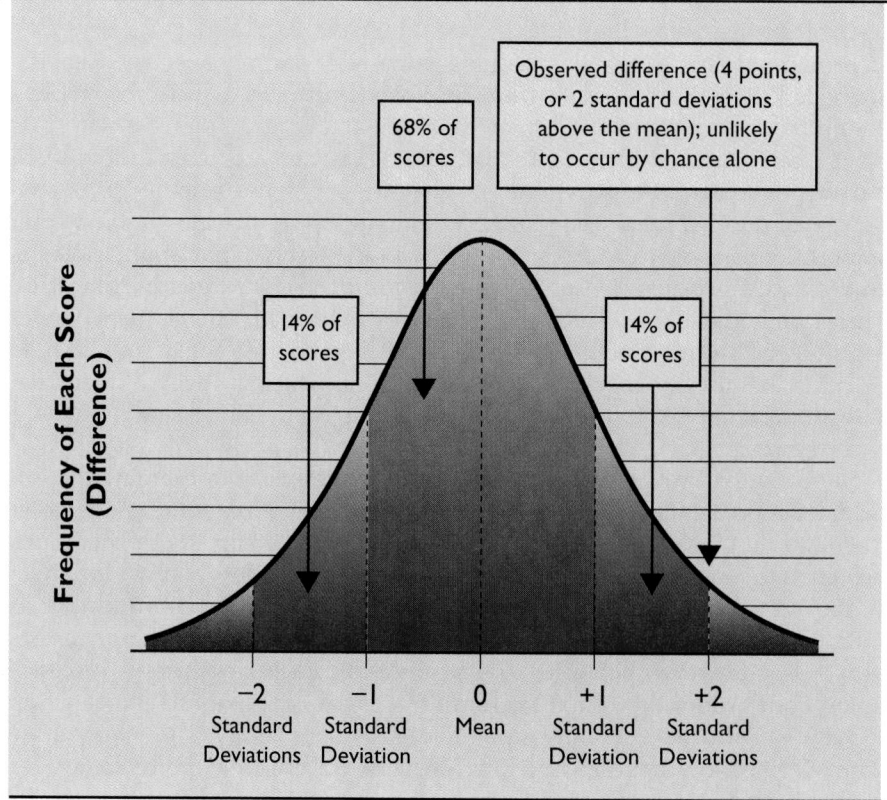

Figure A.4

Using Inferential Statistics to Determine Whether an Observed Difference Is a Real One

Two groups in a study concerned with the effects of mood on memory attain mean scores of 12.0 and 8.0, respectively. Is this difference *significant* (real)? Through inferential statistics, we can tell. If the study were repeated over and over, and the two groups did not really differ, the mean difference in their scores would be zero. Assuming that the standard deviation is 2.0, we know that the probability of a difference this large is very small—less than 2 percent. In view of this fact, we conclude that this finding is indeed significant.

Within the figure:

68% of scores

Observed difference (4 points, or 2 standard deviations above the mean); unlikely to occur by chance alone

14% of scores

14% of scores

Frequency of Each Score (Difference)

−2 Standard Deviations   −1 Standard Deviation   0 Mean   +1 Standard Deviation   +2 Standard Deviations

APPENDIX

slight—that even a huge observed difference is due to chance. If we accept a difference that really occurred by chance as being real, we make what statisticians describe as a Type I error. If, in contrast, we interpret a real difference as being one that occurred by chance, we make a Type II error. Clearly, both kinds can lead us to false conclusions about the findings of a research project.

CORRELATION AND PREDICTION

Does crime increase as temperatures rise? Does the chance of winning elections increase with a candidate's height? Does our ability to solve certain kinds of problems change with age? Psychologists are often interested in such questions. In short, they are concerned with whether two or more variables are *related*, so that changes in one are associated with changes in the other. Remember: this is quite different from the issue of whether changes in one variable *cause* changes in another. (If you're unclear about this distinction, refresh your memory by referring to chapter 1.)

In order to answer such questions, we must gather information on each variable. For example, assume that we wanted to find out if political fortunes are indeed related to height. To do so, we might obtain information on (1) the height of hundreds of candidates and (2) the percentage of votes they obtained in recent elections. Then we'd plot these two variables, height against votes, by entering a single point for each candidate on a graph such as those in Figure A.5 (on page 570). As you can see, the first graph in this figure indicates that tallness is positively associated with political success. The second graph points to the opposite conclusion, and the third suggests that there is no relationship at all between height and political popularity.

While such graphs, known as *scatterplots,* are useful, they don't by themselves provide a precise index of the strength of the relationship between two or more variables. To obtain such an index, we often calculate a statistic known as a **correlation coefficient**. Such coefficients can range from –1.00 to +1.00. Positive numbers indicate that as one variable increases, so does the other. Negative numbers indicate that as one factor increases, the other decreases. The greater the difference from 0.00 in either direction, the stronger the relationship between the two variables. Thus, a correlation of +0.80 is stronger than one of +0.39. Similarly, a correlation of –0.76 is stronger than one of –0.51.

Once we've computed a correlation coefficient, we can test its significance: We can determine whether it is large enough to be viewed as unlikely to occur by chance alone. Further, we can also compare correlations to determine if, in fact, one is significantly larger or smaller than another. The methods used for completing these tasks are somewhat different from those used for comparing means, but the logic is much the same.

In addition to determining the extent to which two or more variables are related, statistical procedures also exist for determining the degree to which a specific variable can be *predicted* from one or more others. These methods of *regression analysis* are complex, but they are of great practical value. Knowing the extent to which performance can be predicted from currently available information—such as grades, past performance, or scores on psychological tests—can aid companies, schools, and many other organizations in selecting the best persons for employment or educational opportunities.

Correlation Coefficient: A statistic indicating the degree of relationship between two or more variables.

Illustrating Relationships through Scatterplots

Is height related to success in politics? To find out, we measure the height of many candidates and obtain records of the percentage of votes they obtained. We then plot height against votes in a *scatterplot*. Plot A indicates a positive relationship between height and political success: the taller candidates are, the more votes they get. Plot B indicates a negative relationship between these variables. Plot C suggests that there is no relationship between these variables.

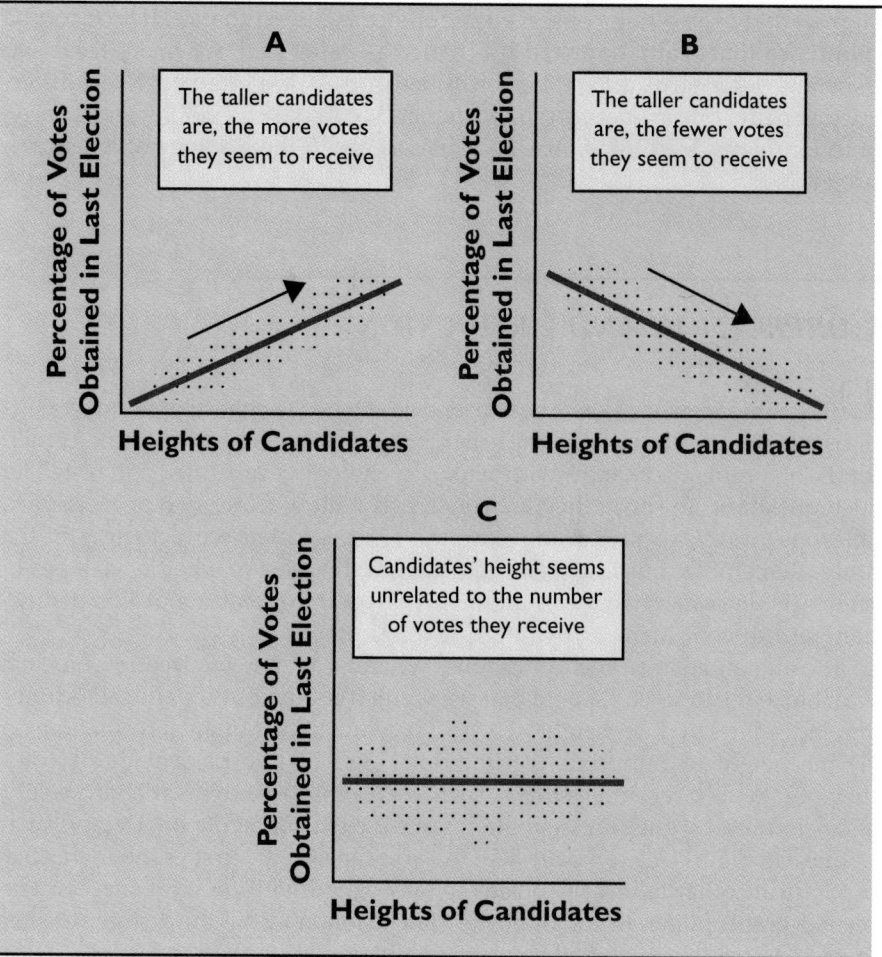

THE MISUSE OF STATISTICS:
Numbers Don't Lie . . . or Do They?

A public figure once remarked, "There are lies, damned lies, and statistics!" By this, he meant that statistics are often used for purposes quite different from the ones we've discussed here. Instead of serving as a valuable basis for understanding scientific data, interpreting test scores, or making predictions about behavior, statistics are sometimes employed to confuse, deceive, or mislead their intended victims. To make matters worse, in the wrong hands statistics can be quite effective in this role. The reason for such success lies in the fact that most of us firmly accept another popular saying: "Numbers don't lie." Thus, when confronted with what appear to be mathematical data and facts, we surrender our usual skepticism and readily accept what we are told. Since the costs of doing so can be quite high, let's conclude this brief discussion of statistics by examining some of the more common—and blatant—*mis*uses of statistics. Here, too, thinking like a psychologist can be of considerable practical value. If you keep the principles outlined here firmly in mind, you'll often be able to spot such statistical abuses and can avoid being deceived by them.

RANDOM EVENTS DON'T ALWAYS SEEM RANDOM

You pick up the paper and read an account of a young woman who won more than one million dollars at a gambling casino. She placed sixteen bets in a row at a roulette table and won on every spin of the wheel. Why? Was she incredibly lucky? Did she have a system? If you are like many people, you may jump to the conclusion that there is indeed something special about her. After all, how else can this incredible series of events be explained?

If you do jump to such conclusions, you are probably making a serious mistake. Here's why. For any single player, the odds of winning so many times in succession are indeed slight. But consider the vast number of players and the number of occasions on which they play; some casinos remain open around the clock. Also, remember the shape of the normal curve. The mean number of wins in a series of sixteen bets is indeed low—perhaps one or two. But the tails of the curve never level off, so there is some probability, however slight, of even sixteen wins occurring in a row. In short, even events that would be expected to occur by chance very rarely *do* occur. The moral is clear: Don't overinterpret events that seem, at first glance, to border on impossible. They may actually be rare chance occurrences with no special significance of their own.

LARGE SAMPLES PROVIDE A BETTER BASIS FOR REACHING CONCLUSIONS THAN SMALL ONES

Many television commercials take the following form. A single consumer is asked to compare three unlabeled brands of facial tissue or to compare the whiteness of three loads of wash. She then makes the "right" choice, selecting the sponsor's product as softest, brightest, or whitest. The commercial ends with a statement of the following type: "Here's proof. Our brand is the one most shoppers prefer." Should you take such evidence seriously? I doubt it. In most cases, it is not possible to reach firm statistical conclusions on the basis of the reactions of a single individual, or even of several individuals. Rather, a much larger number of cooperative participants is necessary. After watching such a commercial, then, you should ask what would happen if the same procedures were repeated with 20, 50, or 500 shoppers. Would the sponsor's brand actually be chosen significantly more often than the others? The commercials leave the impression that it would; but, as I'm sure you now realize, jumping to such conclusions is risky. So be skeptical of claims based on very small samples. They are on shaky grounds at best, and they may be designed to be purposely misleading.

UNBIASED SAMPLES PROVIDE A BETTER BASIS FOR REACHING CONCLUSIONS THAN BIASED ONES

Here's another popular type of commercial, and another common misuse of statistics. An announcer, usually dressed in a white coat, states: "Three out of four dentists surveyed recommend *Jawbreak* sugarless gum." At first glance, the meaning of this message seems clear: Most dentists prefer that their patients chew a specific brand of gum. But look more closely: There's an important catch. Notice that the announcer says, "Three out of four dentists *surveyed.* . . ." Who were these people? A fair and representative sample of all dentists? Major stockholders in the Jawbreak company? Close relatives of the person holding the patent on this product? From the information given, it's impossible to tell. To the extent these or many other possibilities are true, the dentists surveyed represent a *biased* sample; they are *not* representative of the population to which the sponsor wishes us to generalize: all dentists.

So whenever you encounter claims about the results of a survey, ask two questions: (1) Who were the persons surveyed? (2) How were they chosen? If these questions can't be answered to your satisfaction, be on guard: Someone may be trying to mislead you.

UNEXPRESSED COMPARISONS ARE OFTEN MEANINGLESS

Another all-too-common misuse of statistics involves what might be described as "errors of omission." Persons using this tactic mention a comparison but then fail to specify all of the groups or items involved. For example, consider the following statement: "In recent laboratory tests, *Plasti-spred* was found to contain fully 82 percent less cholesterol! So, if you care about your family's health, buy Plasti-spred, the margarine for modern life." Impressive, right? After all, Plasti-spred seems to contain much less of a dangerous substance than—what? There, in fact, is the rub: We have no idea as to the identity of the other substances in the comparison. Were they other brands of margarine? Butter? A jar of bacon drippings? A beaker full of cholesterol?

The lesson offered by such claims is clear. Whenever you are told that a product, candidate, or anything else is better or superior in some way, always ask the following question: Better than *what*?

SOME DIFFERENCES AREN'T REALLY THERE

Here's yet another type of commercial you've probably seen before. An announcer points to lines on a graph that diverge before your eyes and states, "Here's proof! *Gasaway* neutralizes stomach acid twice as fast as the other leading brand." And in fact, the line labeled Gasaway does seem to rise more quickly, leaving its poor competitor in the dust. Should you take such claims seriously? Again, the answer is no. First, such graphs are usually unlabeled. As a result, we have no idea as to what measure of neutralizing acids or how much time is involved. It is quite possible that the curves illustrate only the first few seconds after the medicine is taken and that beyond that period the advantage for the sponsor's product disappears.

Second, and even more important, there are no grounds for assuming that the differences shown are *significant*—that they could not have occurred by chance. Perhaps there is no difference whatsoever in the speed with which the two products neutralize acid, but the comparison was run over and over again until—by chance—a seemingly large difference in favor of the sponsor's brand occurred. This is not to say that all advertisers, or even most, engage in such practices. Perhaps the differences shown in some commercials are indeed real. Still, given the strong temptation to stress the benefits of one's own product, the following policy is probably best: Assume that all differences reported in ads and similar sources are *not* significant—that is, not real—unless specific information to the contrary is provided.

GRAPHS MAY DISTORT (OR AT LEAST BEND) REALITY

The results of psychological research are often represented in graphs; graphs can communicate major findings efficiently and can readily present complex relationships that are difficult to describe verbally. Unfortunately, however, graphs are often used for another purpose: to alter the conclusions drawn from a given set of data. There are many ways to do this, but the most common involves altering the meaning of the axes—the horizontal or vertical boundaries of the graph. A specific example may help clarify this process.

Consider how two political candidates, a Democrat and a Republican, might choose to represent the budget deficit in the United States. The Democrat, eager to convince voters that the deficit rose alarmingly under Republican rule, might choose the graph shown on the left in Figure A.6. In contrast, the Republican might prefer to use the graph shown on the right. Notice that in both the same numbers are represented: The deficit rose from $165 billion in 1989 to more than $300 billion in 1991. Yet this rise seems larger and more dramatic in the left-hand graph. As you can readily see, these contrasting patterns are produced by shifts in the size of the units along the vertical axis. These are small in the left-hand graph, but very large in the right-hand one. Would you reach different conclusions about the growth in the deficit if you were exposed to one graph or the other? If you are like most people, the answer is yes, especially if the graph was accompanied by appropriate verbal commentary. For example, Democrat: "The growth in the deficit under Republican rule was nothing short of *alarming!*" Republican: "There was indeed a modest increase in the deficit, but weighed against the economic benefits obtained, this is a small price to pay."

Sadly, such fine-tuning of graphs is common in magazines, political mailings, and many other sources. Thus, it is important to pay careful attention to the scale employed in any graph, the precise quantities being measured, and all labels employed. If you overlook such factors, you may be a sitting duck for those who wish to lead you to false conclusions.

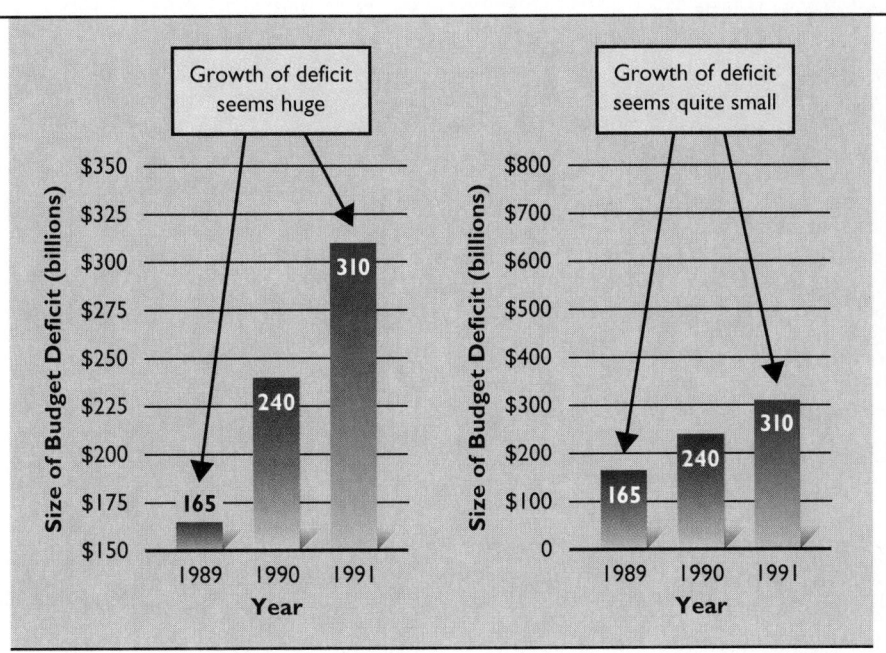

FIGURE A.6

Misleading Graphs: One Common Technique

A change in the scale of the vertical axis can make graphs representing the same data seem to convey very different information. The growth of the budget deficit appears to be huge in the left-hand graph but quite modest in the right-hand graph.

Summary and Review of Key Points

Descriptive Statistics

All scientists require two types of tools in their research: equipment for collecting data and some means of interpreting their findings. In psychology statistics are often used for the latter purpose.

Large quantities of data can be grouped into frequency distributions indicating the number of times each score occurs. Two important facts about any frequency distribution are its central tendency—its center—and its dispersion, or the extent to which scores spread out around this value.

Common measures of central tendency include the mean, mode, and median. Dispersion is often measured in terms of variance and the standard deviation. This latter term refers to the average distance of each score from the mean.

The frequency distributions for many behavioral characteristics show a bell-shaped form known as the normal distribution or normal curve. Most scores fall near the middle, and fewer occur at increasing distances from this value. Specific proportions of the scores are found under certain parts of the curve.

Key Terms: statistics, p. 562; frequency distribution, p. 563; central tendency, p. 563; dispersion, p. 563; descriptive statistics, p. 563; mean, p. 564; mode, p. 564; median, p. 564; range, p. 565; variance, p. 565; standard deviation, p. 565; normal curve, p. 565

Inferential Statistics

Psychologists use inferential statistics to determine whether differences between individuals or groups are significant, or real. Inferential statistics assume that the mean difference in question is zero and that observed differences are distributed normally around this value.

If an observed difference is large enough that it would occur by chance only 5 percent of the time, it is viewed as significant.

Key Term: inferential statistics, p. 567

Correlation and Prediction

To determine whether two or more variables are related, psychologists compute correlation coefficients. These range from −1.00 to +1.00. The larger the departure from 0.00, the stronger the correlation between the variables in question.

Correlations, and statistics derived from them, can be used to predict future behavior from current information. Such predictions are of great practical benefit to schools, companies, and others wishing to predict future performance from current behavior.

Key Term: correlation coefficient, p. 569

Misuse of Statistics

Although statistics have many beneficial uses, they are often employed to deceive or mislead.

Misuse of statistics can involve the use of extremely small or biased samples, unexpressed comparisons, and misleading graphs and presentations.

REFERENCES

Aaronson, L. S., & MacNee, C. L. (1989). Tobacco, alcohol, and caffeine use during pregnancy. *Journal of Obstetrics, Gynecology, and Neonatal Nursing, 18*, 279–287.

Abelson, R. P., Loftus, E. F., & Greenwald, A. G. (1992). Attempts to improve the accuracy of self-reports of voting. In J. M. Tanur (Ed.), *Questions about survey questions: Meaning, memory, expression, and social interactions in surveys* (pp. 138–153). New York: Russell Sage Foundation.

Abramowitz, S. I. (1986). Psychosocial outcomes of sexual reassignment surgery. *Journal of Consulting and Clinical Psychology, 54*, 183–189.

Abramowitz, S. I., & Murray, J. (1983). Race effects in psychotherapy. In J. Murray & P. R. Abramson (Eds.), *Bias in psychotherapy* (pp. 215–255). New York: Academic Press.

Abramson, L. Y., Seligman, M. E. P., & Teasdale, J. D. (1978). Learned helplessness in humans: Critique and reformation. *Journal of Abnormal Psychology, 87*, 49–74.

Adams, R. J. (1987). An evaluation of color preference in early infancy. *Infant Behavior and Development, 10*, 143–150.

Ader, R., & Cohen, N. (1984). Behavior and the immune system. In W. D. Gentry (Ed.), *Handbook of behavioral medicine.* New York: Guilford.

Adler, N. J., & Bartholomew, S. (1992). Managing globally competent people. *Academy of Management Executive, 6*, 52–65.

Aiello, J. R. (1993). Computer-based work monitoring: Electronic surveillance and its effects. *Journal of Applied Social Psychology, 23*, 499–507.

Aiello, J. R., & Svec, C. M. (1993). Computer monitoring of work performance: Extending the social facilitation framework to electronic presence. *Journal of Applied Social Psychology, 23*, 537–548.

Aiken, L. R. (1991). *Psychological testing and assessment* (7th ed.). Boston: Allyn and Bacon.

Ainsworth, M. D. S. (1969). Object relations, dependency, and attachment: A theoretical review of the infant-mother relationship. *Child Development, 40*, 969–1025.

Ainsworth, M. D. S. (1973). The development of infant-mother attachment. In B. Caldwell & H. Riciutti (Eds.), *Review of child development research* (Vol. 3, pp. 1–94). Chicago: University of Chicago Press.

Ainsworth, M. D. S., Blehar, M. C., Waters, E., & Wall, S. (1978). *Patterns of attachment.* Hillsdale, NJ: Erlbaum.

Akerstedt, T., & Froberg, J. E. (1976). Interindividual differences in circadian pattern of catecholamine excretion, body temperature, performance, and subjective arousal. *Biological Psychology, 4*, 277–292.

Akil, J., Watson, S. J., Young, E., Lewis, M. E., Kachaturian, H., & Walker, M. W. (1984). Endogenous opiates: Biology and function. *Annual Review of Neuroscience, 7*, 223–256.

Alagna, F. J., Whitcher, S. J., & Fisher, J. D. (1979). Evaluative reactions to interpersonal touch in a counseling interview. *Journal of Counseling Psychology, 26*, 465–472.

Alberts-Corush, J., Firestone, P., & Goodman, J. T. (1986). Attention and impulsivity characteristics of the biological and adoptive parents of hyperactive and normal control children. *American Journal of Orthopsychiatry, 56*, 413–423.

Alicke, M. D., Braun, J. C., Glor, J. E., Klotz, N. L., Nagee, J., Sederhold, H., & Siegel, R. (1992). Complaining behavior in social interaction. *Personality and Social Psychology Bulletin, 18*, 286–292.

Al-Issa, I. (1982). Does culture make a difference in psychopathology? In I. Al-Issa (Ed.), *Culture and psychopathology.* Baltimore: University Park Press.

Allen, V. L., & Levine, J. M. (1971). Social support and conformity: The role of independent assessment of reality. *Journal of Experimental Social Psychology, 4*, 48–58.

Allgood-Merton B., Lewinsohn, P. M., & Hops, H. (1990). Sex differences and adolescent depression. *Journal of Abnormal Psychology, 99*, 55–63.

Alloy, L., Abramson, L., Metalsky, G., & Bartlage, S. (1988). The hopelessness theory of depression: Attributional aspects. *British Journal of Clinical Psychology, 27*, 5–21.

Allport, G. W. (1965). *Letters from Jenny.* New York: Harcourt, Brace & World.

Allport, G. W., & Odbert, H. S. (1936). Trait names: A psycholexical study. *Psychological Monographs, 47*, 211.

Allred, J. B. (1993). Lowering serum cholesterol: Who benefits? *Journal of Nutrition, 123*, 1453–1459.

Altman, I., & Taylor, D. A. (1973). *Social penetration: The development of interpersonal relationships.* New York: Holt, Rinehart & Winston.

Altshuler, J. L., & Ruble, D. N. (1989). Developmental changes in children's awareness of strategies for coping with uncontrollable stress. *Child Development, 60*, 1337–1349.

Amato, P. R. (1990). Parental divorce and attitudes toward marriage and family life. *Journal of Marriage and the Family, 50*, 453–461.

American Cancer Society. (1989). *Cancer facts and figures—1989.* Atlanta, GA: Author.

American Psychiatric Association. (1993). DSM-IV Draft Criteria. Washington, DC: Author.

American Psychological Association, (1992). Ethical principles of psychologists and code of conduct. *American Psychologist, 47*, 1597–1611.

American Psychological Association. (1993). 1993 Membership Register. Washington, D.C.: American Psychological Association.

American Psychological Association. (1993). Guidelines for providers of psychological services to ethnic, linguistic, and culturally diverse populations. *American Psychologist, 48*, 45–48.

American Psychological Association. (1994). Office of Demographic Employment, and Educational Research. Washington, D.C.: American Psychological Association.

Amoore, J. (1970). *Molecular basis of odor.* Springfield, IL: Thomas.

Amoore, J. (1982). Odor theory and odor classification. In E. Theimer (Ed.), *Fragrance chemistry—the science of the sense of smell.* New York: Academic Press.

Anderson, C. A., & Anderson, D. C. (1984). Ambient temperature and violent crime: Tests of the linear and curvilinear hypotheses. *Journal of Personality and Social Psychology, 46*, 91–97.

Anderson, C. A., & DeNeve, K. M. (1992). Temperature, aggression, and the negative affect escape model. *Psychological Bulletin, 111*, 347–351.

Andre, A. D., & Segal, L. D. (1993, April). Design functions. *Ergonomics in Design*, pp. 5–7.

Andreasen, N. C., Flaum, M., Swayze, V., II, O'Leary, D. S., Alliger, R., Cohen, G., Ehrhardt, J., & Yuhn, W. T. C. (1993). Intelligence and brain structure in normal individuals. *American Journal of Psychiatry, 150*, 130–134.

Andrews, J. D. W. (1967). The achievement motive and advancement in two types of organization. *Journal of Personality and Social Psychology, 6*, 163–168.

Angerspach, D., Knauth, P., Karvonen, M. J., & Undeutsch, K. (1980). A retrospective cohort study comparing complaints and diseases in day and shift workers. *International Archives of Occupational and Environmental Health, 45*, 127–140.

ANSI. (1988). *American national standard on product safety signs: Z535.4—draft.* New York: American National Standards Institute.

Anson, A. R., Cook, T. D., Habib, F., Grady, M. K., Haynes, N., & Comer, P. (1991). The Comer school development program: A theoretical analysis. *Urban Education, 26*, 56–82.

Antrobus, J. (1991). Dreaming: Cognitive processes during cortical activation and high afferent thresholds. *Psychological Review, 98*, 96–212.

Arieti, S. (1974). *Interpretation of schizophrenia.* New York: Basic Books.

Arkes, H. R., Herren, L. T., & Isen, A. M. (1988). The role of potential loss in the influence of affect on risk-taking behavior. *Organizational Behavior and Human Decision Processes, 42*, 181–193.

Arkin, R. M., Lake, E. A., & Baumgardner, A. H. (1986). Shyness and self-presentation. In W. Jones, J. Cheek, & S. Briggs (Eds.), *Shyness: Perspectives on research and treatment* (pp. 189–203). New York: Plenum Press.

Armstrong, C. (1991). Emotional changes following brain injury: Psychological and neurological components of depression, denial and anxiety. *Journal of Rehabilitation, 2*, 15–22.

Aronoff, J., Woike, B. A., & Hyman, L. M. (1992). Which are the stimuli in facial displays of anger and happiness? Configurational bases of emotional recognition. *Journal of Personality and Social Psychology, 62*, 1050–1066.

Aronoff, S. R., & Spilka, B. (1984–1985). Patterning of facial expressions among terminal cancer patients. *Omega, 15,* 101–108.

Aronson, E. (1990). Applying social psychology to desegregation and energy conservation. *Personality and Social Psychology Bulletin, 16,* 118–132.

Aronson, E. (1992). The return of the repressed: Dissonance theory makes a comeback. *Psychological Inquiry, 3*(4), 303–311.

Aronson, E., Bridgeman, D. L., & Geffner, R. (1978). Independent interactions and prosocial behavior. *Journal of Research and Development in Education, 12,* 16–27.

Arterberry, M. E., & Granrud, C. E. (1987). Four-month-old infants' sensitivity to binocular and kinetic information for three-dimensional object shape. *Child Development, 58,* 910–927.

Arvey, R. D., Bouchard, T. J., Jr., Segal, N. L., & Abraham, L. M. (1989). Job satisfaction: Genetic and environmental components. *Journal of Applied Psychology, 74,* 187–192.

Asante, M. K. (1980). Afrocentricity: The theory of social change. Buffalo, NY: Amulefi Publishing Company.

Asch, S. E. (1951). Effects of group pressure upon the modification and distortion of judgment. In H. Guetzkow (Ed.), *Groups, leadership, and men.* Pittsburgh, PA: Carnegie.

Ashford, S. J., & Tsui, A. S. (in press). Self-regulation for managerial effectiveness: The role of active feedback seeking. *Academy of Management Journal.*

Astley, S. J., Claaren, S. K., Little, R. E., Sampson, P. D., & Daling, J. R. (1992). Analysis of racial shape in children gestationally exposed to marijuana, alcohol, and/or cocaine. *Pediatrics, 89,* 67–77.

Atkinson, J. W., & Litwin, G. H. (1960). Achievement motive and test anxiety conceived as motive to approach success and motive to avoid failure. *Journal of Abnormal and Social Psychology, 60,* 52–63.

Atkinson, R. C., & Shiffrin, R. M. (1968). Human memory: A proposed system and its control processes. In K. W. Spence (Ed.), *The psychology of learning and motivation: Advances in research and theory* (Vol. 2, pp. 89–195). New York: Academic Press.

Aubé, J., & Koestner, R. (1992). Gender characteristics and adjustment: A longitudinal study. *Journal of Personality and Social Psychology, 63,* 485–493.

Austin, J., Hatfield, D. B., Grindle, A. C., & Bailey, J. S. (1993). Increasing recycling in office environments: The effects of specific, informative cues. *Journal of Applied Behavior Analysis, 26,* 247–253.

Babcock, R. L., & Salthouse, T. A. (1990). Effects of increased processing demands on age differences in working memory. *Psychology and Aging, 5,* 421–428.

Bachetti, P. (1990). Estimating the incubation period of AIDS by comparing population infection and diagnosis patterns. *Journal of the American Statistical Association, 85,* 1002–1008.

Bachman, J. G. (1987, February). An eye on the future. *Psychology Today,* pp. 6–7.

Baddeley, A. (1990). *Human memory: Theory and practice.* Boston: Allyn and Bacon.

Bahrick, H. P. (1984). Memory for people. In J. E. Harris & P. E. Morris (Eds.), *Everyday memory actions and absent-mindedness* (pp. 19–34). London: Academic Press.

Bailey, M. J., & Pillard, R. C. (1991). A genetic study of male sexual orientation. *Archives of General Psychiatry, 48,* 1089–1096.

Bailey, M. J., Pillard, R. C., Neale, M. C., & Agyei, Y. (1993). Heritable factors influence sexual orientation in women. *Archives of General Psychiatry, 50,* 217–223.

Baillargeon, R. (1987). Object permanence in 3.5- and 4.5-month-old infants. *Developmental Psychology, 23,* 655–664.

Baker, A. G., & Mackintosh, N. J. (1977). Excitatory and inhibitory conditioning following uncorrelated presentations of CS and US. *Animal Learning and Behavior, 5*(3), 315–319.

Baker-Ward, L., Ornstein, P. A., & Holden, D. J. (1984) The expression of memorization in early childhood. *Journal of Experimental Child Psychology, 37,* 555–575.

Ball, S. A., & Zuckerman, M. (1992). Sensation seeking and selective attention: Focused and divided attention on a dichotic listening task. *Journal of Personality and Social Psychology, 63,* 825–831.

Balogh, R. D., & Porter, R. H. (1986). Olfactory preferences resulting from mere exposure in human neonates. *Infant Behavior and Development, 9,* 395–401.

Balzer, W. K., & Sulsky, L. M. (1990). Performance appraisal effectiveness. In K. Murphy & F. Saal (Eds.), *Psychology in organizations: Integrating science and practice* (pp. 133–156). Hillsdale, NJ: Erlbaum.

Bandura, A. (1969). *Principles of behavior modification.* New York: Holt, Rinehart & Winston.

Bandura, A. (1977). *Social learning theory.* Englewood Cliffs, NJ: Prentice-Hall.

Bandura, A. (1986). *Social foundations of thought and action: A social cognitive theory.* Englewood Cliffs, NJ: Prentice-Hall.

Bandura, A., Adams, N. E., & Beyer, J. (1977). Cognitive processes mediating behavioral change. *Journal of Personality and Social Psychology, 35,* 125–139.

Bandura, A., Blanchard, E. B., & Ritter, B. (1969). Relative efficacy of desensitization and modeling approaches for inducing behavioral, affective, and attitudinal change. *Journal of Personality and Social Psychology, 13,* 173–199.

Bandura, A., Ross, D., & Ross, S. (1963). Imitation of film-mediated aggressive models. *Journal of Abnormal and Social Psychology, 66,* 3–11.

Banich, M. T., & Belger, A. (1990). Inter-hemispheric interaction: How do the hemispheres divide and conquer a task? *Cortex, 26,* 77–94.

Banks, C. G., & Murphy, K. R. (1985). Toward narrowing the research-practice gap in performance appraisal. *Personnel Psychology, 38,* 335–345.

Bardwell, J. R., Cochran, S. W., & Walker, S. (1986). Relationship of parental education, race, and gender to sex role stereotyping in five-year-old kindergarteners. *Sex Roles, 15,* 275–281.

Bargones, J. Y., & Werner, L. A. (1994). Adults listen selectively; infants do not. *Psychological Science, 5,* 170–174.

Barkley, R. A. (1990). *Attention deficit hyperactivity disorder: A handbook for diagnosis and treatment.* New York: Guilford.

Barlow, D. H. (1988). *Anxiety and its disorders: The nature and treatment of anxiety and panic.* New York: Guilford Press.

Barlow, D. H. (1991). Introduction to the special issue on diagnoses, dimensions, and DSM-IV: The science of classification. *Journal of Abnormal Psychology, 100,* 243–244.

Barlow, D. H. (1992). An integrated model of panic. Described in Antony, M. M., Brown, T. A., & Barlow, D. H. Current perspectives on panic and panic disorder. *Journal of Abnormal Psychology, 100,* 79–82.

Baron, J. (1988). *Thinking and deciding.* Cambridge, England: Cambridge University Press.

Baron, J., & Brown, R. (Eds.). (1991). *Teaching decision making to adolescents.* Hillsdale, NJ: Erlbaum.

Baron, R. A. (1970). Attraction toward the model and model's competence as determinants of adult imitative behavior. *Journal of Personality and Social Psychology, 14,* 335–344.

Baron, R. A. (1972). Aggression as a function of ambient temperature and prior anger arousal. *Journal of Personality and Social Psychology, 21,* 183–189.

Baron, R. A. (1978). Aggression and heat: The "long hot summer" revisited. In A. Baum, S. Valins, and J. E. Singer (Eds.), *Advances in environmental research* (Vol. 1). Hillsdale, NJ: Erlbaum.

Baron, R. A. (1983). The "sweet smell of success"? The impact of pleasant artificial scents (perfume or cologne) on evaluations of job applicants. *Journal of Applied Psychology, 68,* 709–713.

Baron, R. A. (1986). Self-presentation in job interviews: When there can be "too much of a good thing." *Journal of Applied Social Psychology, 16,* 16–28.

Baron, R. A. (1987). Mood of interviewer and the evaluation of job candidates. *Journal of Applied Social Psychology, 17,* 911–926.

Baron, R. A. (1989). Impression management by applicants during employment interviews: The "too much of a good thing" effect. In R. W. Eder & G. R. Ferris (Eds.), *The employment interview* (pp. 204–216). Newbury Park, CA: Sage.

Baron, R. A. (1990). Environmentally induced positive affect: The impact on self-efficacy, task performance, negotiation, and conflict. *Journal of Applied Social Psychology, 20,* 368–384.

Baron, R. A. (1993). Interviewers' moods and evaluations of job applicants: The role of applicant qualifications. *Journal of Applied Social Psychology, 23,* 253–271.

Baron, R. A. (1994). The physical environment of work settings: Effects on task performance, interpersonal relations, and job satisfaction. In B. M. Staw and L. L. Cummings (Eds.), *Research in organizational behavior* (Vol. 16, pp. 1–46). Greenwich, CT: JAI Press.

Baron, R. A., & Bell, P. A. (1975). Aggression and heat: Mediating effects of prior provocation and exposure to an aggressive model. *Journal of Personality and Social Psychology, 31,* 825–832.

Baron, R. A., & Bronfen, M. I. (1994). A whiff of reality: Empirical evidence concerning the effects of pleasant fragrances on work-related behavior. *Journal of Applied Social Psychology, 24,* 1179–1203.

Baron, R. A., & Byrne, D. (1994). *Social psychology: Understanding human interaction* (7th ed.). Boston: Allyn and Bacon.

Baron, R. A., Fortin, S. P., Frei, R. L., Haver, L. A., & Shack, M. L. (1990). Reducing organizational conflict: The potential role of socially induced positive affect. *International Journal of Conflict Management, 1,* 133–152.

Baron, R. A., Rea, M. S., & Daniels, S. G. (1992). Effects of indoor lighting (illuminance and spectral distribution) on the performance of cognitive tasks and interpersonal behavior: The potential mediating role of positive affect. *Motivation and Emotion, 16,* 1–33.

Baron, R. A., & Richardson, D. (1994). *Human aggression* (2nd ed.). New York: Plenum.

Baron, R. A., & Thomley, J. (1994). *A whiff of reality: Positive affect as a potential mediator of the effects of pleasant fragrances on task performance and helping.* Environment and Behavior, 26, 766–784.

Barrera, M. E., & Maurer, D. (1981a). Discrimination of strangers by the three-month-old. *Child Development, 52,* 559–563.

Barrera, M. E., & Maurer, D. (1981b). Recognition of mother's photographed face by the three-month-old infant. *Child Development 52,* 714–716.

Barsky, A. J., & Wyshak, G. (1989). Hypochondriasis and related health attitudes. *Psychosomatics, 330,* 412–420.

Barta, P. E., Pearlson, G. D., Powers, R. E., Richards, S. S., & Tune, L. E. (1990). Auditory hallucinations and smaller superior temporal gyral volume in schizophrenia. *American Journal of Psychiatry, 147,* 1457–1462.

Barth, R. J., & Kinder, B. N. (1988). A theoretical analysis of sex differences in same-sex friendships. *Sex Roles, 19,* 343–363.

Baruch, G. (1984). The psycological well-being of women in the middle years. In G. Baruch & J. Brooks-Gunn (Eds.), *Women in midlife* (pp. 161–180). New York: Plenum Press.

Baruch, G., Barnett, R., & Rivers, C. (1983). *Lifeprints.* New York: McGraw-Hill.

Bates, S., & Bates, D. F. (1971). . . . And a child shall lead them. Stephanie's chart story. *Teaching Exceptional Children, 3,* 24–27.

Bauer, P. J., & Mandler, J. M. (1992). Putting the horse before the cart: The use of temporal order in recall of events by one-year-old children. *Developmental Psychology, 28,* 441–452.

Baum, A., & Fleming, I. (1993). Implications of psychological research on stress and technological accidents. *American Psychologist, 48,* 665–672.

Baum, D. R., & Jonides, J. J. (1979). Cognitive maps: Analysis of comparative judgments of distance. *Memory and Cognition, 7,* 462–468.

Baumeister, R. F. (1990). Suicide as escape from self. *Psychological Review, 97,* 90–113.

Baumeister, R. F., & Heatherton, T. D. (1993). When ego threats lead to self-regulation failure: Negative consequences of high self-esteem. *Journal of Personality and Social Psychology, 64,* 141–156.

Baumeister, R. F., Heatherton, T. F., & Tice, D. M. (1993). When ego threats lead to self-regulation failure: Negative consequences of high self-esteem. *Journal of Personality and Social Psychology, 64,* 141–156.

Baumeister, R. F., & Scher, S. J. (1988). Self-defeating behavior patterns among normal individuals: Review and analysis of common self-destructive tendencies. *Psychological Bulletin, 104,* 3–22.

Baumeister, R. F., & Steinhilber, A. (1984). Paradoxical effects of supportive audiences on performance under pressure: The home field disadvantage in sports championships. *Journal of Personality and Social Psychology, 47,* 85–93.

Baumeister, R. F., Stillwell, A., & Wotman, S. R. (1990). Victim and perpetrator accounts of interpersonal conflict: Autobiographical narratives about anger. *Journal of Personality and Social Psychology, 59,* 994–1003.

Baumeister, R. F., & Tice, D. M. (1988). Metatraits. *Journal of Personality, 64,* 141–156.

Baumgardner, A. H., Hepner, P. P., & Arkin, R. M. (1986). Role of causal attribution in personal problem solving. *Journal of Personality and Social Psychology, 40,* 165–174.

Baumrind, D. (1984). A developmental perspective on adolescent drug use. Unpublished manuscript, University of California, Berkeley.

Baumrind, D. (1985). Research using intentional deception: Ethical issues revisited. *American Psychologist, 40,* 165–174.

Beaman, A. L., Cole, N., Preston, M., Glentz, B., & Steblay, N. M. (1983). Fifteen years of the foot-in-the-door research: A meta-analysis. *Personality and Social Psychology Bulletin, 9,* 181–186.

Beck, A. T. (1976). *Cognitive therapy and the emotional disorders.* New York: International Universities Press.

Beck, A. T. (1985). *Anxiety disorders and phobias: A cognitive perspective.* New York: Basic Books.

Beck, A. T., Rush, A. J., Shaw, B. F., & Emery, G. (1979). *Cognitive theory of depression.* New York: Guilford Press.

Becker, E., Rinck, M., & Margraf, J. (1994). Memory bias in panic disorder. *Journal of Abnormal Psychology, 103,* 396–399.

Becklen, R., & Cerone, D. (1983). Selective looking and the noticing of unexpected events. *Memory & Cognition, 11,* 601–608.

Beckstead, J. W. (1991). Psychological factors influencing judgments and attitudes regarding animal research: An application of functional measurement and structural equation modeling. Unpublished doctoral dissertation, State University of New York, Albany.

Beggan, J. K. (1992). On the social nature of nonsocial perception: The mere ownership effect. *Journal of Personality and Social Psychology, 62,* 229–237.

Behrend, D. A., Rosengren, K. S., & Perlmutter, M. (1988, April). *Parental style and children's private speech: Relations between two sources of regulation.* Paper presented at the biannual meeting of the Society for Research in Child Development, Kansas City.

Behrend, D.A., Rosengren, K. S., & Perlmutter, M. (1992). The relation between private speech and parental interactive style. In R. M. Diaz & L. E. Berk (Eds.), *Private speech: From social interaction to self-regulation* (pp. 85–100). Hillsdale, NJ: Erlbaum.

Békésy, G. von. (1960). *Experiments in hearing.* New York: McGraw-Hill.

Bell, A. P., Weinberg, M. S., & Hammersmith, S. K. (1981). *Sexual preference: Its development in men and women.* Bloomington: Indiana University Press.

Bell, P. A. (1992). In defense of the negative affect escape model of heat and aggression. *Psychological Bulletin, 111,* 342–346.

Bell, P. A., Fisher, J. D., Baum, A., & Green, T. E., (1990). *Environmental psychology* (3rd ed.). New York: Holt, Rinehart, & Winston.

Bellack, A. S., Morrison, R. L., Mueser, K. T., Wade, J. H. & Sayers, S. L. (1990). Role play for assessing the social competence of psychiatric patients. *Psychological Assessment: A Journal of Consulting and Clinical Psychology, 2,* 248–255.

Bellack, A. S., Sayers, M., Mueser, K. T., & Bennett, M. (1994). Evaluation of social problem solving in schizophrenia. *Journal of Abnormal Psychology, 103,* 371–378.

Bellak, L. (1994). The schizophrenic syndrome and attention deficit disorder. *American Psychologist, 49,* 25–29.

Bellisimo, A., & Tunks, E. (1984). *Chronic pain.* New York: Praeger.

Belsky, J., & Braungart, J. M. (1991). Are insecure-avoidant infants with extensive day-care experience less stressed by and more independent in the Strange Situation? *Child Development, 662,* 567–571.

Bem, D. J., & Honorton, C. (1994). Does psi exist? Replicable evidence for an anomalous process of information transfer. *Psychological Bulletin, 115,* 4–18.

Bem, S. L. (1974). The measurement of psychological androgyny. *Journal of Consulting and Clinical Psychology, 42,* 155–162.

Bem, S. L. (1981). Gender schema theory: A cognitive account of sex typing. *Psychological Review, 88,* 354–364.

Bem, S. L. (1984). Adrogyny and gender schema theory: A conceptual and empirical integration. In R. A. Dientsbier & T. B. Sondregger (Eds.), *Nebraska Symposium on Motivation* (Vol. 34, pp. 179–226). Lincoln: University of Nebraska Press.

Bem, S. L. (1989). Genital knowledge and gender constancy in preschool children. *Child Development, 60,* 649–662.

Bemis, K. M. (1987). The present status of operant conditioning for the treatment of anorexia nervosa. *Behavior Modification, 11,* 432–463.

Benesch, K. F., & Page, M. M. (1989). Self-construct systems and interpersonal congruence. *Journal of Personality, 57,* 139–173.

Benson, D. F. (1985). Aphasia. In K. M. Heilman & E. Valenstein (Eds.), *Clinical neuropsychology* (pp. 17–47). New York: Oxford University Press.

Benson, H., & Friedman, R. (1985). A rebuttal to the conclusions of David S. Holmes's article: "Meditation and somatic arousal reductions." *American Psychologist, 40,* 725–728.

Bentall, R. P. (1990). The illusion of reality: A review and integration of psychological research on hallucinations. *Psychological Bulletin, 107,* 82–95.

Berenbaum, S. A., & Hines, M. (1992). Early androgens are related to childhood sex-typed toy preferences. *Psychological Science, 3,* 203–206.

Bergin, A. E., & Lambert, M. J. (1978). The evaluation of therapeutic outcomes. In S. L. Garfield & A. E. Bergin (Eds.), *Handbook of psychotherapy and behavior change: An empirical analysis,* (2nd ed., pp. 139–190). New York: Wiley.

Berk, L. E. (1993). *Infants, children and adolescents.* Boston: Allyn and Bacon.

Berkowitz, L. (1984). Some effects of thoughts on anti- and pro-social influences of media events: A cognitive-neoassociation analysis, *Psychological Bulletin, 95,* 410–427.

Berkowitz, L. (1989). Frustration-aggression hypothesis: Examination and reformulation. *Psychological Bulletin, 106,* 59–73.

Berkowitz, L. (1990). On the formation and regulation of anger and aggression. *American Psychologist, 45,* 494–503.

Berlyne, D. E. (1967). Arousal and reinforcement. In D. Levine (Ed.), *Nebraska Symposium on Motivation* (Vol. 15, pp. 279–286). Lincoln: University of Nebraska Press.

Berman, A. L., & Jobes, D. A. (1991. *Adolescent suicide: Assessment and intervention.* Washington, DC: American Psychological Association.

Berndt, T. J. (1992). Friendship and friends' influence in adolescence. *Current Directions in Psychological Science, 1,* 156–159.

Bernstein, A. S. (1987). Orienting response research in schizophrenia: Where we have come and where we might go. *Schizophrenia Bulletin, 13,* 623–641.

Bernstein, I. L. (1978). Learned taste aversion in children receiving chemotherapy. *Science, 200,* 1302–1303.

Berry, D. S. (1991). Attractive faces are not all created equal: Joint effects of facial babyishness and attractiveness on social perception. *Personality and Social Psychology Bulletin, 17,* 523–531.

Berry, D. S., & McArthur, L. Z. (1986). Perceiving character in faces: The impact of age-related craniofacial changes on social perception. *Psychological Bulletin, 100,* 3–18.

Berry, D. S., & Zebrowitz-McArthur, L. (1988). What's in a face? Facial maturity and the attribution of legal responsibility. *Personality and Social Psychology Bulletin, 14,* 23–33.

Berry, D. T. R., & Webb, W. B. (1985). Mood and sleep in aging women. *Journal of Personality and Social Psychology, 49,* 1724–1727.

Berscheid, E., Dion, K., Walster, E., & Walster, G. W. (1971). Physical attractiveness and dating choice: A test of the matching hypothesis. *Journal of Experimental Social Psychology, 7,* 173–189.

Besson, J., & Chaouch, A. (1987). Peripheral spinal mechanisms of nociception. *Psychological Review, 67,* 67–186.

Best, D. L., Williams, J. E., Cloud, J. M., Davis, S. W., Robertson, L. S., Edwards, J. R., Giles, H., & Fowles, J. (1977). Development of sex-trait stereotypes among young children in the United States, England, and Ireland. *Child Development, 48,* 1375–1384.

Bettencourt, B. N., & Miller, N. (in press). Sex differences in aggression as a function of provocation: A meta-analysis. *Psychological Bulletin.*

Betz, A. I., & Krosnick, J. A. (1993). *A test of the primacy of affect: Does detection of the affective tone of a stimulus precede detection of stimulus presence or content?* Unpublished manuscript, Ohio State University.

Betz, E. L. (1982). Need fulfillment in the career development of women. *Journal of Vocational Behavior, 20,* 53–66.

Beutler, L. E., Crago, M., & Arizmendi, T. G. (1986). Research on therapist variables in psychotherapy. In S. L. Garfield & A. E. Bergin (Eds.), *Handbook of psychotherapy and behavior change: An evaluative analysis* (3rd ed.). New York: Wiley.

Beyth-Marom, R., Austin, L., Fischoff, B., Palmgren, C., & Quadrel, M. (in press). Perceived consequences of risky behaviors: Adolescents and adults. *Developmental Psychology.*

Bickford, E. W. (1988). *Human circadian rhythms: A review.* (Lighting Research Institute Project 88 DR NEMA2.) Morris Plains, NJ: Lighting Research Institute.

Bienert, H., & Schneider, B. H. (1993). Diagnosis-specific social skill: Training with peer-nominated aggressive-disruptive and sensitive-isolated preadolescents. *Journal of Applied Developmental Psychology.*

Bierhoff, H. W., Klein, R., & Kramp, P. (1991). Evidence for the altruistic personality from data on accident research. *Journal of Personality, 59,* 263–280.

Binet, A., & Simon, T. (1905). Methodes nouvelles pour le diagnostic du niveau intellectual des anormaux. *L'Année Psychologique, 11,* 191–244.

Bini, L. (1938). Experimental researches on epileptic attacks induced by the electric current. *American Journal of Psychiatry* (Suppl. 94), 172–183.

Binning, J. H., Goldstein, M. A., Garcia, M. F., & Scattaregia, J. H. (1988). Effects of preinterview impressions on questioning strategies in same- and opposite-sex employments. *Journal of Applied Psychology, 73,* 239–244.

Birnbaum, I. M., & Parker, E. D. (Eds.). (1977). *Alcohol and human memory.* Hillsdale, NJ: Erlbaum.

Bivens, J. A., & Berk, L. E. (1990). A longitudinal study of the development of elementary school children's private speech. *Merrill-Palmer Quarterly, 36,* 443–463.

Bixler, E. O., Kales, A., Soldatos, C. R., Kales, J. D., & Healey, S. (1979). Prevalence of sleep disorders in the Los Angeles metropolitan area. *American Journal of Psychiatry, 136,* 1257–1262.

Bjorklund, D. F. (1987). How age changes in knowledge base contribute to the development of children's memory: An interpretive review. *Developmental Review, 7,* 93–130.

Bjorklund, D. F., & Muir, J. E. (1988). Children's development of free recall memory: Remembering on their own. In R. Vasta (Ed.), *Annals of child development* (Vol. 5, pp. 79–123). Greenwich, CT: JAI Press.

Bjorkqvist, K., Lagerspetz, K. M. J., & Kaukiainen, A. (1992). Do girls manipulate and boys fight? Developmental trends in regard to direct and indirect aggression. *Aggressive Behavior, 18,* 117–128.

Black, J. S., & Mendenhall, M. (1990). Cross-cultural training effectivness: A review and a theoretical framework for future research. *Academy of Management Review, 15,* 113–136.

Blackmore, S. (1986). A critical guide to parapsychology. *Skeptical Inquirer, 11*(1), 97–102.

Blake, R. R., & Mouton, J. S. (1985). *The managerial grid III.* Houston: Gulf.

Blakemore, C., & Cooper, G. F. (1970). Development of the brain depends on the visual environment. *Nature, 228,* 477–478.

Blakeslee, S. (1993, September 7). Human nose may hold an additional organ for a real sixth sense: Odorless skin chemicals may draw or repel other people. *New York Times,* pp. C1, C3.

Bless, H., Bohner, G., Schwarz, N., & Stracik, F. (1990). Mood and persuasion: A cognitive response analysis. *Personality and Social Psychology Bulletin, 16,* 331–345.

Bliss, R. E., Garvey, A. J., Heinhold, J. W., & Hitchcock, J. L. (1989). The influence of situation and coping on relapse crisis outcomes after smoking cessation. *Journal of Consulting and Clinical Psychology, 57,* 443–449.

Blume, E. (1993). Smoking control effort moves to second phase. *Journal of the National Cancer Institute, 85,* 1720.

Blyth, D. A., Bulcroft, R., & Simmons, R. G. (1981, August). *The impact of puberty on adolescents: A longitudinal study.* Paper presented at the annual meetings of the American Psychological Association, Los Angeles.

Bobocel, D. R., & Meyer, J. P. (1994). Escalating commitment to a failing course of action: Separating the roles of choice and justification. *Journal of Applied Psychology, 79,* 360–363.

Bodenhausen, G. V. (1988). Stereotypic biases in social decision making and memory: Testing process models of stereotype use. *Journal of Personality and Social Psychology, 55,* 726–737.

Bogard, N. (1990). Why we need gender to understand human violence. *Journal of Interpersonal Violence, 5,* 132–135.

Boles, D. B. (1992). Factor analysis and the cerebral hemispheres: Temporal, occipital and frontal functions. *Neuropsychologia, 30,* 963–988.

Boles, D. B., & Law, M. B. (1992). *Orthogonal lateralized processes have* orthogonal attentional resources. Paper presented at the annual meeting of the Psychonomic Society, St. Louis, MO.

Bootzin, R. R., Acocella, J. R., & Alloy, L. B. (1993). Abnormal psychology (6th ed.). New York: McGraw-Hill.

Borbely, A. A., Achermann, P., Trqachsel, L., & Tobler, I. (1989). Sleep initiation and initial sleep intensity: Interactions of homeostatic and circadian mechanisms. Journal of Biological Rhythms, 4, 149–160.

Borello, G. M., & Thompson, B. (1990). An hierarchical analysis of the Hendrick-Hendrick measure of Lee's typology of love. Journal of Social Behavior and Personality, 5, 327–342.

Borkovec, T. D. (1982). Insomnia. Journal of Consulting and Clinical Psychology, 50, 880–895.

Borland, R., Chapman, S., Owen, N., & Hill, D. (1990). Effects of workplace smoking bans on cigarette consumption. American Journal of Public Health, 80, 178–180.

Bornstein, R. F. (1989). Subliminal techniques as propaganda tools: Review and critique. Journal of Mind and Behavior, 10, 231–262.

Bosl, G. J., Vogelzang, N. J., Goldman, A., Fraley, E. E., Lange, P. H., Lewitt, S. H., & Kennedy, B. J. (1981). Impact of delay in diagnosis on clinical stage of testicular cancer. Lancet, 2, 970–973.

Bothwell, R. K. (1989). Hypnosis and episodic recall. Paper presented at the meetings of the American Psychological Association, New Orleans.

Bouchard, T. J., Jr. (1987). Information about the Minnesota Center for Twin and Adoption Research. Minneapolis: University of Minnesota.

Bouchard, T. J., Jr., Lykken, D. T., McGue, M., Segal, N. L. & Tellegen, A. (1990). Sources of human psychological differences: The Minnesota Study of Twins Reared Apart. Science, 250, 223–228.

Bouchard, T. J., Jr., & McGue, M. (1981). Familial studies of intelligence: A review. Science, 212, 1055–1059.

Bouchard, T. J., Jr., & Segal, N. L. (1985). Environment and IQ. In B. B. Wolman (Ed.), Handbook of intelligence: Theories, measurements, and applications. New York: Wiley.

Bower, G. H., Clark, M. C., Lesgold, A. M., & Winzenz, D. (1969). Hierarchical retrieval schemes in recall of categorized word lists. Journal of Verbal Learning and Verbal Behavior, 8, 323–343.

Bowers, K. S. (1990). Unconscious influences and hypnosis. In J. L. Singer (Ed.)., Repression and dissociation: Implications for personality theory, psychopathology, and health (pp. 143–178). Chicago: University of Chicago Press.

Bowlby, J. (1969). Attachment and loss: Vol. 1. Attachment. New York: Basic Books.

Bowles, N., & Hynds, F. (1978). Psy search: The comprehensive guide to psychic phenomena. New York: Harper & Row.

Boyes, M. C., & Walker, L. J. (1988). Implications of cultural diversity for the universality claims of Kohlberg's theory of moral reasoning. Human Development, 31, 44–59.

Boyle, P. (1993). The hazards of passive—and active—smoking. New England Journal of Medicine, 328, 1708–1709.

Bozarth, M. A. (1987). Intracranial self-administration procedures for the assessment of drug reinforcement. In M. A. Bozarth (Ed.), Methods of assessing the reinforcing properties of abused drugs (pp. 173–187). Berlin: Springer-Verlag.

Bradbury, T. N., & Fincham, F. D. (1992). Attributions and behavior in marital interaction. Journal of Personality and Social Psychology, 63, 613–628.

Bradley, B., & Mathews, A. (1983). Negative self-schemata in clinical depression. British Journal of Clinical Psychology 22, 173–181.

Braff, D. L. (1989). Sensory input deficits and negative symptoms in schizophrenic patients. American Journal of Psychiatry, 146, 1006–1011.

Braff, D. L., & Geyer, M. A. (1990). Sensorimotor gating and schizophrenia: Human and animal model studies. Archives of General Psychiatry, 47, 181–188.

Braverman, N. S., & Bronstein, P. (Eds.). (1985). Experimental assessments and clinical applications of conditioned food aversions. Annals of the New York Academy of Sciences, 443, 1–41.

Bravo, M., Rubio-Stipec, M., Canino, G. J., Woodbury, M. A., & Ribera, J. C. (1990). The psychological sequelae of disaster prospectively and retrospectively evaluated. American Journal of Community Psychology, 18, 661–680.

Brean, H. (1958, March 31). What hidden sell is all about. Life, pp.104–114.

Breggin, P. R. (1979). Electroshock: Its brain-disabling effects. New York: Springer.

Brehm, J. W., & Self, E. A. (1989). The intensity of motivation. Annual Review of Psychology, 40, 109–131.

Brehm, S. (1992). Intimate relationships. New York: McGraw-Hill.

Breland, K., & Breland, M. (1961). The misbehavior of organisms. American Psychologist, 16, 681–684.

Brennen, P. A., & Mednick, S. A. (1994). Learning theory approach to the deterrence of criminal recidivism. Journal of Abnormal Behavior, 103, 430–440.

Brennan, W. M., Ames, E. W., & Moore, R. W. (1966). Age differences in infants' attention to patterns of different complexities. Science, 151, 354–356.

Briesacher, P. (1971). Neuropsychological effects of air pollution. American Behavioral Scientist, 14, 837–864.

Briggs, R. (1990). Biological aging. In J. Bond & P. Coleman (Eds.), Aging in society. Newbury Park, CA: Sage.

Briggs, S. R., & Cheek, J. M. (1988). On the nature of self-monitoring: Problems with assessment, problems with validity. Journal of Personality and Social Psychology, 54, 663–678.

Britt, T. W. (1992). The self-consciousness scale: On the stability of the three-factor structure. Personality and Social Psychology Bulletin, 18, 748–755.

Brockner, J., & Rubin, J. Z. (1985). Entrapment in escalating conflicts. New York: Springer-Verlag.

Brody, G. H., Neubaum, E., & Forehand, R. (1988). Serial marriage: A heuristic analysis of an emerging family form. Psychological Bulletin, 103, 211–222.

Brothers, K. J., Krantz, P. J., & McClannahan, L. E. (1994). Office paper recycling: A function of container proximity. Journal of Applied Behavior Analysis, 27, 153–160.

Brown, J. D., & McGill, K. L. (1989). The cost of good fortune: When positive life events produce negative health consequences. Journal of Personality and Social Psychology, 57, 1103–1110.

Brown, J. D., & Rogers, R. J. (1991). Self-serving attributions: The role of physiological arousal. Personality and Social Psychology Bulletin, 17, 501–506.

Brown, J. D. & Smart, S. A. (1989). Role of self-concept certainty in buffering the adverse impact of stressful life events. Unpublished manuscript, University of Washington, Seattle.

Brown, N. R., Shevell, S. K., & Rips, L. J. (1986). Public memories and their personal context. In D. C. Rubin (Ed.), Autobiographical memory (pp. 137–158). Cambridge, England: Cambridge University Press.

Brown, R. (1973). A first language: The early stages. Cambridge, MA: Harvard University Press.

Brown, R. W., & Kulik, J. (1977). Flashbulb memories. Cognition, 5, 73–99.

Brown, R. W., & McNeill, D. (1966). The "tip of the tongue" phenomenon. Journal of Verbal Learning and Verbal Behavior, 5, 325–337.

Bruhn, J. G., & Phillips, B. U. (1987). A developmental basis for social support. Journal of Behavioral Medicine, 10, 213–229.

Bryden, J. P., Ley, R. G., & Sugarman, J. H. (1982). A left ear advantage for identifying the emotional quality of tonal sequences. Neuropsychologia, 20, 83–87.

Bucher, B., & Lovaas, O. N. I. (1968). Use of aversive stimulation in behavior modification. In M. R. Jones (Ed.), Miami symposium on the prediction of behavior, 1967: Aversive stimulation. Coral Gables, FL: University of Miami Press.

Burger, J. M. (1986). Temporal effects on attributions: Actor and observer differences. Social Cognition, 4, 377–387.

Burger, J. M. (1990). Personality, (2nd ed.). Belmont, CA: Wadsworth.

Burger, J. M., & Pavelich, J. L. (1993). Attributions for presidential elections: The situational shift over time. Unpublished manuscript, Santa Clara University.

Burish, T. G., & Carey, M. P. (1986). Conditioned aversive response in cancer chemotherapy patients: Theoretical and developmental analysis. Journal of Consulting and Clinical Psychology, 54, 593–600.

Burt, M. (1992). Over the edge: The growth of homelessness in the 1980's. New York: Russell Sage Foundation.

Bushman, B. J. (1984). Perceived symbols of authority and their influence on compliance. Journal of Applied Social Psychology, 14, 501–508.

Bushman, B. J. (1988). The effects of apparel on compliance: A field experiment with a female authority figure. Personality and Social Psychology Bulletin, 14, 459–467.

Buss, D. M. (1989). Sex differences in human mate preferences: Evolutionary hypotheses tested in 37 cultures. Behavioral and Brain Sciences, 12, 1–49.

Buss, D. M. (1990). Evolutionary social psychology: Prospects and pitfalls. *Motivation and Emotion, 14,* 265–286.

Buss, D. M., et al. (1990). International preferences in selecting mates: A study of 37 cultures. *Journal of Cross-Cultural Psychology, 21,* 5–47.

Buss, D. M., Larsen, R. J., Westen, D., & Semmelroth, J. (1992). Sex differences in jealousy: Evolution, physiology, and psychology. *Psychological Science, 3,* 251–258.

Byrne, D. (1971). *The attraction paradigm.* New York: Academic Press.

Byrne, D. (1982). Predicting human sexual behavior. In A. G. Kraut (Ed.), *The G. Stanley Hall Lecture Series* (Vol. 2, pp. 363–364, 368). Washington, DC: American Psychological Association.

Byrne, D., & Murnen, S. K. (1988). Maintaining loving relationships. In R. J. Sternberg & M. I. Barnes (Eds.), *The psychology of love* (pp. 293–310). New Haven, CT: Yale University Press.

Cacioppo, J. T., Petty, R. E., & Quintanar, L. R. (1982). Individual differences in relative hemisphere alpha abundance and cognitive responses persuasive communications. *Journal of Personality and Social Psychology, 43,* 623–626.

Cain, W. S. (1988). Olfaction. In R. C. Atkinson, R. J. Herrnstein, G. Lindzey, & R. D. Luce (Eds.), *Stevens' handbook of experimental psychology: Vol. 1. Perception and motivation* (rev. ed., pp. 409–459). New York: Wiley.

Callan, V. J. (1993). Subordinate-manager communication in different sex dyads: Consequences for job satisfaction. *Journal of Occupational and Organizational Psychology, 66,* 13–27.

Campbell, J. D. (1990). Self-esteem and clarity of the self-concept. *Journal of Personality and Social Psychology, 59,* 538–549.

Campbell, J. N., & LaMotte, R. H. (1983). Latency to detection of first pain. *Brain Research, 266,* 203–208.

Campbell, M., Perry, R., & Green, W. H. (1984). Use of lithium in children and adolescents. *Psychosomatics, 25,* 95–106.

Campbell, P. E., Batsche, C. J., & Batsche, G. M. (1972). Spaced-trials reward magnitude effects in the rat: Single versus multiple food pellets. *Journal of Comparative and Physiological Psychology, 81,* 360–364.

Campion, M. A., & McClelland, C. L. (1991). Interdisciplinary examination of the costs and benefits of enlarged jobs: A job design quasi-experiment. *Journal of Applied Psychology, 76,* 186–198.

Cannon, W. B., Lewis, J. T., & Britton, S. W. (1927). The dispensability of the sympathetic division of the autonomic nervous system. *Boston Medical Surgery Journal, 197,* 514.

Capaldi, E. J. (1978). Effects of schedule and delay of reinforcement on acquisition speed. *Animal Learning and Behavior, 6,* 330–334.

Capaldi, E. J., & Miller, D. J. (1988). Counting in rats: Its functional significance and the independent cognitive processes that constitute it. *Journal of Experimental Psychology: Animal Behavior Processes, 14,* 3–17.

Carlson, N. R. (1993). *Foundations of physiological psychology* (4th ed.). Boston: Allyn and Bacon.

Carlson, N. R. (1994). *Physiology of behavior* (5th ed.). Boston: Allyn and Bacon.

Carmody, T. P., Matarazzo, J. D., & Istvan, J. A. (1987). Promoting adherence to heart-healthy diets: A review of the literature. *Journal of Compliance in Health Care, 2,* 105–124.

Carr, E. G. (1977). The motivation of self-injurious behavior: A review of some hypotheses. *Psychological Bulletin, 84,* 800–816.

Carson, R. C., Butcher, J. N., & Coleman, J. C. (1988). *Abnormal psychology and modern life* (8th ed.). Glenview, IL: Scott, Foresman.

Carsten, J. M., & Spector, P. E. (1987). Unemployment, job satisfaction, and employee turnover: A meta-analytic test of the Muchinsky model. *Journal of Applied Psychology, 72,* 75–80.

Carver, C. S., Pozo, C., Harris, S. D., Noriega, V., Scheier, M. F., Robinson, D. S., Ketcham, A. S., Moffat, F. L., & Clark, K. C. (1993). How coping mediates the effect of optimism on distress: A study of women with early stage breast cancer. *Journal of Personality and Social Psychology, 65,* 375–390.

Carver, C. S., & Scheier, M. F. (1981). *Attention and self-regulation: A control-theory approach to human behavior.* New York: Springer-Verlag.

Carver, C. S., & Scheier, M. F. (1990). Origins and functions of positive and negative affect: A control-process view. *Journal of Personality and Social Psychology, 97,* 19–35.

Carver, C. S., & Scheier, M. F. (1992). *Perspectives on personality* (2nd ed.). Boston: Allyn and Bacon.

Carver, C. S., Scheier, M. F., & Weintraub, J. K. (1989). Assessing coping strategies: A theoretically based approach. *Journal of Personality and Social Psychology, 56,* 267–283.

Case, R. (1991). *The mind's staircase: Exploring the conceptual underpinnings of children's thought and knowledge.* Hillsdale, NJ: Erlbaum.

Casper, R. C. (1990). Personality features of women with good outcome from restricting anorexia nervosa. *Psychosomatic Medicine, 52,* 156–170.

Cattell, R. B. (1963). Theory of fluid and crystallized intelligence: A critical experiment. *Journal of Educational Psychology, 54,* 1–22.

Cattell, R. B. (1987). *Intelligence: Its structure, growth and action.* Amsterdam: North-Holland.

Cattell, R. B., & Dreger, R. M. (Eds.). (1977). *Handbook of modern personality theory.* Washington, DC: Hemisphere.

Cautela, J. R. (1985). Covert modeling. In A. S. Bellack & M. Hersen (Eds.), *Dictionary of behavior therapy techniques.* New York: Pergamon.

Ceci, S. J. (1991) How much does schooling influence general intelligence and its cognitive components? A reassessment of the evidence. *Developmental Psychology, 27,* 703–722.

Ceci, S. J., Baker, J. E., & Bronfenbrenner, U. (1988). Prospective remembering, temporal calibration, and context. In M. M. Gruneberg, P. E. Morris, & R. N. Sykes (Eds.), *Practical aspects of memory: Current research and issues* (pp. 360–365). Chichester, England: John Wiley & Sons.

Centers for Disease Control and Public Health Service. (1993). *HIV/AIDS surveillance.* Atlanta, GA: Centers for Disease Control.

Centerwall, B. S. (1989). Exposure to television as a cause of violence. In G. Comstock (Ed.), *Public communication and behavior* (Vol. 2). San Diego: Academic Press.

Cerelli, E. (1989). *Older drivers, the age factor in traffic safety* (DOT HS-807-402). Washington, DC: National Highway Traffic and Safety Administration.

Chance, P. (1988). *Learning and behavior* (2nd ed.). Belmont, CA: Wadsworth Publishing Company.

Chapman, S., Wong, W. L., & Smith, W. (1993). Self-exempting beliefs about smoking and health: Differences between smokers and ex-smokers. *American Journal of Public Health, 83,* 215–219.

Charness, N. (1989). Age and expertise: Responding to Talland's challenge. In L. W. Poon, D. C. Rubin, & B. A. Wilson (Eds.), *Everyday cognition in adulthood and old age.* New York: Cambridge University Press.

Chasnoff, I. J., Griffith, D. R., MacGregor, S., Dirkes, K., & Burns, K. S. (1989). Temporal patterns of cocaine use in pregnancy: Perinatal outcome. *Journal of the American Medical Association, 261,* 1741–1744.

Chaves, J. F., & Brown, J. M. (1987). Spontaneous cognitive strategies for the control of clinical pain and stress. *Journal of Behavioral Medicine, 10,* 263–276.

Chay, Y. W. (1993). Social support, individual differences and well-being: A study of small business entrepreneurs and employees. *Journal of Occupational and Organizational Psychology, 66,* 285–302.

Cherry, E. C. (1953). Some experiments on the recogniton of speech with one and with two ears. *Journal of Acoustical Society of America, 25,* 975–979.

Cherry, F., & Deaux, K. (1975). *Fear of success versus fear of gender-inconsistent behavior: A sex similarity.* Paper presented at the meetings of the Midwestern Psychological Association, Chicago.

Chess, S., & Thomas, A. (1984). *Origins and evolution of behavior disorders.* New York: Brunner/Mazel.

Chilmonczyk, B. A., Salmun, L. M., Megathlin, K. N., Neveux, L. M., Palomaki, G. E., Knight, G. J., Pulkkinen, M. S., & Haddow, J. E. (1993). Association between exposure to environmental tobacco smoke and exacerbations of asthma in children. *New England Journal of Medicine, 328,* 1665–1669.

Chipman, S. F., Brush, L. R., & Wilson, D. M. (Eds.). (1985). *Women and mathematics: Balancing the equation.* Hillsdale, NJ: Erlbaum.

Chipman, S. F., Krantz, D. H., & Silver, R. (1992). Mathematics anxiety and science careers among able college women. *Psychological Science, 3,* 292–295.

Chomsky, N. (1968). *Language and mind.* New York: Harcourt Brace.

Christensen, A., & Jacobson, N. S. (1994). Who (or what) can do psychotherapy: The status and challenge of nonprofessional therapies. *Psychological Science, 5,* 8–14.

Church, A. T., & Burke, P. J. (1994). Exploratory and confirmatory tests of the big five and Tellegen's three- and four-dimensional models. *Journal of Personality and Social Psychology, 66,* 93–114

Church, G. J. (1993). Jobs in an age of insecurity. *Time,* November 22, pp. 34–37.

Cialdini, R. B. (1988). *Influence: Science and practice* (2nd ed.). Glenview, IL: Scott, Foresman.

Cialdini, R. B., Kenrick, D. T., & Bauman, D. J. (1982). Effects of mood on prosocial behavior in children and adults. In N. Eisenberg-Berg (Ed.), *Development of prosocial behavior.* New York: Academic Press.

Cialdini, R. B., Vincent, J. E., Lewis, S. K., Catalan, J., Wheeler, D., & Darby, B. L. (1975). Reciprocal concession procedure for inducing compliance: The door-in-the-face technique. *Journal of Personality and Social Psychology, 31,* 206–215.

Clark, D. A., Beck, A. T. , & Brown, G. (1989). Cognitive mediation in general psychiatric outpatients: A test of the content-specificity hypothesis. *Journal of Personality and Social Psychology, 56,* 958–964.

Clark, D. M. (1988). A cognitive model of panic attacks. In S. Rachman & J. D. Maser (Eds.), *Panic: Psychological perspectives.* Hillsdale, NJ: Erlbaum.

Clark, E. V. (1973). Nonlinguistic strategies and the acquisition of word meanings. *Cognition, 2,* 161–182.

Clark, H. H., & Chase, W. G. (1972). On the process of comparing sentences against pictures. *Cognitive Psychology, 3,* 472–517.

Clark, K., & Clark, M. (1947). Racial identification and racial preferences in Negro children. In T. M. Newcomb & E. L. Hartley, *Readings in social psychology* (pp. 169–178). New York: Holt.

Clark, W., & Clark, S. (1980). Pain response in Nepalese porters. *Science, 209,* 410–412.

Clarke, S., Kraftsik, R., Van der Loos, H., & Innocenti, G. M. (1989). Forms and measures of adult and developing human corpus callosum: Is there sexual dimorphism? *Journal of Comparative Neurology, 280,* 213–230.

Clum, G. A., & Bowers, T. G. (1990). Behavior therapy better than placebo treatments: Fact or artifact? *Psychological Bulletin, 107,* 110–113.

Cohen, J. (1993). AIDS research: The mood is uncertain. *Science, 260,* 1254–1265.

Cohen, R. J., Montague, P., Nathanson, L. S., & Swerdlik, M. E. (1988). *Psychological testing: An introduction to test & measurement.* Mountain View, CA: Mayfield Publishing Company.

Cohen, S., Kaplan, J. R., Cunnick, J. E., Manuck, S. B., & Rabin, B. S. (1992). Chronic social stress, affiliation, and cellular immune response in nonhuman primates. *Psychological Science, 3,* 301–304.

Cohen, S., Tyrrell, D. A., & Smith, A. P. (1993). Negative life events, perceived stress, negative affect, and susceptibility to the common cold. *Journal of Personality and Social Psychology, 64,* 131–140.

Cohen, S., & Wills, T. A. (1985). Stress, social support, and the buffering hypothesis. *Psychological Bulletin, 98,* 310–357.

Colby, A., Kohlberg, L., Feonton, E., Speicher-Dubin, B., & Lieberman, M. (1983). A longitudinal study of moral judgment. *Monographs of the Society for Research in Child Development, 48,* (1–2, Serial No. 200).

Cole, M., & Scribner, S. (1974). *Culture and thought: A psychological introduction.* New York: John Wiley.

Colwill, R. M. (1993). An associative analysis of instrumental learning. *Current Directions in Psychological Science, 2,* 111–116.

Colwill, R. M., & Rescorla, R. A. (1985). Postconditioning devaluation of a reinforcer affects instrumental responding. *Journal of Experimental Psychology, 11,* 120–132.

Colwill, R. M., & Rescorla, R. A. (1988). Associations between the discriminative stimulus and the reinforcer in instrumental learning. *Journal of Experimental Psychology, 14,* 155–164.

Condon, J. W., & Crano, W. D. (1988). Inferred evaluation and the relation between attitude similarity and interpersonal attraction. *Journal of Personality and Social Psychology, 54,* 789–797.

Conger, J. A. (1991). Inspiring others: The language of leadership. *Academy of Management Executive, 5,* 31–45.

Constanza, R. S., Derlega, V. J., & Winstead, B. A. (1988). Positive and negative forms of social support: Effects of conversational tactics on coping with stress among same-sex friends. *Journal of Experimental Social Psychology, 24,* 182–193.

Contrada, R. J. (1989). Type A behavior, personality hardiness, and cardiovascular responses to stress. *Journal of Personality and Social Psychology, 57,* 895–903.

Cook, R. G. (1993). The experimental analysis of cognition in animals. *Psychological Science, 4,* 174–178.

Cook, S. W. (1985). Experimenting on social issues: The case of school desegregation. *American Psychologist, 40,* 452–460.

Cooper, J., & Scher, S. J. (1990). Actions and attitude: The role of responsibility and aversive consequences in persuasion. In T. Brock & S. Shavitt (Eds.), *The psychology of persuasion.* San Francisco: Freeman.

Coren, S., & Girgus, J. S. (1978). *Seeing is deceiving: The psychology of visual illusion.* Hillsdale, NJ: Lawrence Erlbaum.

Coren, S., Girgus, J. S., Erlichman, H., & Hakstean, A. R. (1976). An empirical taxonomy of visual illusions. *Perception & Psychophysics, 20,* 129–137.

Coren, S., & Ward, L. M. (1989). *Sensation and perception* (3rd ed.). San Diego: Harcourt Brace Jovanovich.

Cornelius, S. W., & Caspi, A. (1987). Everyday problem solving in adulthood and old age. *Psychology and Aging, 2,* 144–153.

Corso, J. F. (1977). Auditory perception and communication. In J. E. Birren & K. W. Schaie (Eds.), *Handbook of the psychology of aging* (pp. 535–553). New York: Van Nostrand Reinhold.

Costa, P. T., Jr., & McCrae, R. R. (1988). Personality in adulthood: A six-year longitudinal study of self-reports and spouse ratings on the NEO Personality Inventory. *Journal of Personality and Social Psychology, 54,* 853–863.

Costa, P. T., Jr., & McCrae, R. R. (1994). The Revised NEO Personality Inventory (NEO-PI-R). In R. Briggs & J. M. Cheek (Eds.), *Personality measures: Development and evaluation* (Vol. 1.). Greenwich, CT: JAI Press.

Cottrell, N., Eisenberg, R., & Speicher, H. (1992). Inhibiting effects of reciprocation wariness on interpersonal relationships. *Journal of Personality and Social Psychology, 62,* 658–668.

Covino, N. A., Jimeson, D.C., Wolfe, B. E., Franko, D. L., & Frankel, F. H. (1994) Hypnotiziability, dissociaton, and bulimia nervosa. *Journal of Abnormal Psychology, 103,* 455–458

Cowan, N. (1984). On short and long auditory stores. *Psychological Bulletin, 96,* 341–370.

Cowan, N., Day, L., Saults, J. S., Keller, T. A., Johnson, T., & Flores, L. (1992). The role of verbal output time in the effects of word length on immediate memory. *Journal of Memory and Language, 31,* 1–17.

Cowan, N., Wood, N. L., & Borne, D. N. (1994). Reconfirmation of the short-term storage concept. *Psychological Science, 5,* 103–106.

Coyle, J. T. (1987). Alzheimer's disease. In G. Adelman (Ed.), *Encyclopedia of neuroscience* (pp. 29–31). Boston: Birkhauser.

Coyle, J. T., Price, D. L., & DeLong, M. R. (1983). Alzheimer's disease: A disorder of cortical cholinergic innervation. *Science, 219,* 1184–1190.

Craig, K. D., & Prkachin, K. M. (1978). Social modeling influences on pain thresholds influenced by social modeling. *Journal of Personality and Social Psychology, 36,* 805–815.

Craik, F. I. M., & Lockhart, R. S. (1972). Levels of processing: A framework for memory research. *Journal of Verbal Learning and Verbal Behavior, 11,* 671–684.

Craik, F. I. M., & Tulving, E. (1975). Depth of processing and the retention of words in episodic memory. *Journal of Experimental Psychology: General, 104,* 268–294.

Crespi, L. P. (1942). Quantitative variation of incentive and performance in the white rat. *American Journal of Psychology, 55,* 467–517.

Cristofalo, V. J. (1988). An overview of the theories of biological aging. In J. E. Birren & V. L. Bengtson (Eds.), *Emergent theories of aging* (pp. 118–127). New York: Springer.

Crocker, J., Luhtanen, R., Blaine, B., & Broadnax, S. (1994). Collective self-esteem and psychological well-being among White, Black, and Asian college students. *Personality and Social Psychology Bulletin, 20,* 503–513.

Cromwell, R. L. (1992). Searching for the original of schizophrenia. *Psychological Science, 4,* 276–279.

Cropanzano, R. (Ed.). (1993). *Justice in the workplace: Approaching fairness in human resource management.* Hillsdale, NJ: Erlbaum.

Cropanzano, R., & James, K. (1990). Some methodological considerations for the behavioral-genetic analysis of work attitudes. *Journal of Applied Psychology, 21,* 433–439.

Cropanzano, R., & Randall, M. L. (1993). Injustice and work behavior: A historical review. In R. Cropanzano (Ed.), *Justice in the workplace* (pp. 3–20). Hillsdale, NJ: Erlbaum.

Crouch, A., & Yetton, P. (1987). Manager behavior, leadership style, and subordinate performance: An empirical extension of the Vroom-Yetton conflict rule. *Organizational Behavior and Human Decision Processes, 39,* 384–396.

Crowder, R. G. (1993). Short-term memory: Where do we stand? *Memory and Cognition, 21,* 142–145.

Croyle, R. T. (1992). Appraisal of health threats: Cognition, motivation, and social comparison. *Cognitive Therapy and Research, 16,* 165–182.

Crusco, A. H., & Wetzel, C. G. (1984). The Midas touch: The effects of interpersonal touch on restaurant tipping. *Personality and Social Psychology Bulletin, 10,* 512–517.

Crutchfield, R. A. (1955). Conformity and character. *American Psychologist, 10,* 191–198.

Csikszentmihalyi, M., & Larson, R. (1984). *Being adolescent: Conflict and growth in the teenage years.* New York: Basic Books.

Cummings, M. K., Lampone, D., Mettlin, C., & Pontes, J. E. (1983). What young men know about testicular cancer. *Preventive Medicine, 12,* 326–330.

Cuneo, D. O. (1980). A general strategy for quantity judgment: The height and width rule. *Child Development, 50,* 170–179.

Cunningham, M. R. (1986). Measuring the physical in physical attractiveness: Quasi-experiments on the sociobiology of female facial beauty. *Journal of Personality and Social Psychology, 50,* 925–935.

Cunningham, M. R., Shaffer, D. R., Barbee, A., Wolff, P. L., & Kelley, D. J. (1990). Separate processes in the relation of elation and depression to helping: Social versus personal concerns. *Journal of Experimental Social Psychology, 26,* 13–33.

Curfman, G. O. (1993). Is exercise beneficial—or hazardous—to your heart? *The New England Journal of Medicine, 329,* 173.

Curtis, R. C., & Miller, K. (1986). Believing another likes or dislikes you: Behavior making the beliefs come true. *Journal of Personality and Social Psychology, 50,* 284–290.

Czeisler, C. A., Moore-Ede, M. C., & Coleman, R. M. (1982). Rotating shift work schedules that disrupt sleep are improved by applying Circadian principles. *Science, 217,* 460–462.

Dahl, O. (1985). Testicular carcinoma: A curable malignancy. *Acta Radiology and Oncology, 24,* 3–15.

Daniel, J., & Potasova, A. (1989). Oral temperature and performance in 8 hour and 12 hour shifts. *Ergonomics, 32,* 689–696.

Darley, J. M., & Latane, B. (1968). Bystander intervention in emergencies: Diffusion of responsibility. *Journal of Personality and Social Psychology, 8,* 377–383.

Datan, N., Antonovsky, A., & Moaz, B. (1984). Love, war, and the life cycle of the family. In K. A. McCluskey & H. W. Reese (Eds.), *Life-span developmental psychology: Historical and generational effects* (pp. 143–159). New York: Academic Press.

Daum, I., Ackermann, H., Schugens, M. M., Reimold, C., Dichgans, J., & Birbaumer, N. (1993). The cerebellum and cognitive functions in humans. *Behavioral Neuroscience, 104,* 411–419.

Davey, G. C. L. (1992). Classical conditioning and the acquisition of human fears and phobias: A review and synthesis of the literature. *Advances in Behavior Research Therapy, 14,* 29–66.

Davidson, J. K., Sr., & Hoffman, L. E. (1986). Sexual fantasies and sexual satisfaction: An empirical analysis of erotic thought. *Journal of Sex Research, 22,* 184–205.

Davidson, K., & Hopson, J. L. (1988). Gorilla business. *Image* (San Francisco Chronicle), 14–18.

Davidson, R. J. (1992). Emotion and affective style: Hemispheric substrates. *Psychological Science, 3,* 39–43.

Davidson, R. J., Finman, R., Straus, A., & Kagan, J. (1991). *Childhood temperament and frontal lobe activity: Patterns of asymmetry differentiate between wary and outgoing children.* Manuscript submitted for publication.

Davidson, R. J., & Fox, N. A. (1988). Cerebral asymmetry and emotion: Developmental and individual differences. In D. L. Molfese & S. J. Segalowitz (Eds.), *Brain lateralization in children: Developmental implications* (pp. 191–206). New York: Guilford Press.

Davies, M. F. (1987). Reduction of hindsight bias by restoration of foresight perspective. *Organizational Behavior and Human Decision Processes, 40,* 50–68.

Davis, M. H., & Franzoi, S. L. (1986). Adolescent loneliness, self-disclosure and private self-consciousness: A longitudinal investigation. *Journal of Personality and Social Psychology, 51,* 595–608.

De Villiers, J. G., & De Villiers, P. A. (1978). *Language acquisition.* Cambridge, MA: Harvard University Press.

Deaux, K. (1993). Commentary: Sorry, wrong number—a reply to Gentile's call. *Psychological Science, 4,* 125–126.

Deaux, K., & Lewis, L. L. (1986). The structure of gender stereotypes: Interrelationships among components and gender label. *Journal of Personality and Social Psychology, 46,* 991–1005.

DeBono, K. G. (1992). Pleasant scents and persuasion: An information processing approach. *Journal of Applied Social Psychology, 22,* 910–919.

DeCasper, A. J., & Fifer, W. P. (1980). Of human bonding: Newborns prefer their mothers' voices. *Science, 208,* 991–1004.

DeCasper, A. J., & Spence, M. J. (1986). Prenatal maternal speech influences newborns' perception of speech sounds. *Infant Behavior and Development, 9,* 133–150.

Deci, E. L. (1975). *Intrinsic motivation.* New York: Plenum.

Deci, E. L., & Ryan, R. M. (1985). *Intrinsic motivation and self-determination in human behavior.* New York: Plenum Press.

Deckers, L., & Carr, D. E. (1986). Cartoons varying in low-level pain ratings, not aggression ratings, correlate positively with funniness ratings. *Motivation and Emotion, 10,* 207–216.

Delgado, P. L., Charney, D. S., Price, L. H., Aghajanian, G. K., Landis, H., & Heninger, G. R. (1990). Serotonin function and mechanism of antidepressant action: Reversal of antidepressant-induced remission by rapid depletion of plasma atryptophan. *Archives of General Psychiatry, 47,* 411–418.

DeLongis, A., Folkman, S., & Lazarus, R. S. (1988). The impact of daily stress on health and mood: Psychological and social resources as mediators. *Journal of Personality and Social Psychology, 54,* 486–495.

Dembrowski, T. M., & Williams, R. B. (1989). Definition and assessment of coronary-prone behavior. In N. Schneiderman, P. Kaufmann, & S. M. Wiess (Eds.), *Handbook of research methods in cardiovascular behavioral medicine.* New York: Plenum.

Dement, W. C. (1975). *Some must watch while some must sleep.* San Francisco: W. H. Freeman.

Dement, W. C., & Kleitman, N. (1957). The relation of eye movement during sleep to dream activity: An objective method for the study of dreaming. *Journal of Experimental Psychology, 53,* 339–353.

Dement, W. C., & Wolpert, E. A. (1958). The relation of eye movements, body mobility and external stimuli to dream content. *Journal of Experimental Psychology, 55,* 543–553.

DeNisi, A. S., Cafferty, T. P., & Meglino, B. M. (1984). A cognitive view of the performance appraisal process: A model and research proposition. *Organizational Behavior and Human Performance, 33,* 360–396.

Denney, N. W., & Palmer A. M. (1981). Adult age differences on traditional and practical problem-solving measures. *Journal of Gerontology, 36,* 323–328.

Denning, P. J. (1992). Neural networks. *American Scientist, 80,* 426–429.

DePaulo, B. M. (1992). Nonverbal behavior and self-presentation. *Psychological Bulletin, 111,* 230–243.

Deutsch, A. (1949). *The mentally ill in America* (2nd ed.). New York and London: Columbia University Press.

DeValois, R. L., & DeValois, K. K. (1975). Neural coding of color. In E. C. Carterette & M. P. Friedman (Eds.), *Handbook of perception* (pp. 117–166). New York: Academic Press.

Devine, P. O. (1989). Stereotypes and prejudice: Their automatic and controlled components. *Journal of Personality and Social Psychology, 56,* 5–18.

Dickerson, C. A., Thibodeau, R., Aronson, E., & Miller, D. (1992). Using cognitive dissonance to encourage water conservation. *Journal of Applied Social Psychology, 22,* 841–854.

Digman, J. M. (1990). Personality structure: Emergence of the five-factor model. *Annual Review of Psychology, 41,* 417–440.

Dillard, J. P. (1991). The current status of research on sequential-request compliance techniques. *Personality and Social Psychology Bulletin, 17,* 283–288.

Dindia, K., & Allen, M. (1992). Sex differences in self-disclosure: A meta-analysis. *Psychological Bulletin, 112,* 106–124.

Dishman, R. K. (1988). *Exercise adherence: Its impact on public health.* Champaign, IL: Human Kinetic Books.

Ditto, P. H., Jemmot, J. B., III, & Darley, J. M. (1988). Appraising the threat of illness: A mental representational approach. *Health Psychology, 7,* 183–200.

Ditto, P. H., & Lopez, D. F. (1992). Motivated skepticism: Use of differential decision criteria for preferred and nonpreferred conclusions. *Journal of Personality and Social Psychology, 63,* 568–584.

Donovan, J. E., & Jessor, R. (1985). Structure of problem behavior in adolescence and young adulthood. *Journal of Consulting and Clinical Psychology, 53,* 890–904.

Doty, R. L., Shaman, P., Applebaum, S. L., Giberson, R., Sikorski, L., & Rosenberg, L. (1984). Smell identification ability: Changes with age. *Science, 226,* 141–143.

Douek, E. (1988). Olfaction and medicine. In S. Van Toller & G. Doll (Eds.), *Perfumery: The psychology and biology of fragrance.* London: Chapman Hall.

Dovidio, J. F., Evans, N., & Tyler, R. B. (1986). Racial stereotypes: The contents of their cognitive representations. *Journal of Experimental Social Psychology, 22,* 22–37.

Dovidio, J. F., & Gaertner, S. L. (Eds.). (1986). *Prejudice, discrimination, and racism.* Orlando, FL: Academic Press.

Drachman, D., DeCarufel, A., & Insko, C. A. (1978). The extra credit effect in interpersonal attraction. *Journal of Experimental Social Psychology, 14,* 458–465.

Droller, M. J. (1980). Cancer of the testes: An overview. *Urologic Clinics of North America, 7,* 731–733.

Dubbert, P. M. (1992). Exercise in behavioral medicine. *Journal of Consulting and Clinical Psychology, 60,* 613–618.

Duck, S., & Barnes, M. H. (1992). Disagreeing about agreement: Reconciling differences about similarity. *Communication Monographs, 59,* 199–208.

Duffy, D. L., Hamerman, D., & Cohen, M. A. (1980). Communication skills of house officers: A study in a medical clinic. *Annals of Internal Medicine, 93,* 354–357.

Duffy, R. D., Kalsher, M. J., & Wogalter, M. S. (1993). The effectiveness of an interactive warning in a realistic product-use situation. *Proceedings of the Human Factors and Ergonomics Society, 37th Annual Meeting,* 935–939.

Duncker, K. (1945). On problem solving. *Psychological Monographs* (whole No. 270).

Durso, F. T., Rea, C. B., & Dayton, T. (1994). Graph-theoretic confirmation of restructuring during insight. *Psychological Science, 5,* 94–98.

Dutton, D. G., & Aron, A. P. (1974). Some evidence for heightened sexual attraction under conditions of high anxiety. *Journal of Personality and Social Psychology, 30,* 510–517.

Dweck, C. S., & Licht, B. G. (1980). Learned helplessness and intellectual achievement. In M. E. P. Seligman & J. Garber (Eds.), *Human helplessness: Theory and application.* New York: Academic Press.

Dworkin, E. S., & Efran, J. S. (1967). The angered: Their susceptibility to varieties of humor. *Journal of Personality and Social Psychology, 34,* 510–518.

Dwyer, W. O., Leeming, F. C., Cobern, M. K., Porter, B. E., & Jackson, J. M. (1993). Critical review of behavioral interventions to preserve the environment. *Environment and Behavior, 25,* 275–321.

Dyer, F. C. (1991). Bees acquire route-based memories but not cognitive maps in a familiar landscape. *Animal Behaviour, 41,* 239–246.

Eagly, A. E., & Carli, L. (1981). Sex of researchers and sex-typed communications as determinants of sex differences in influence ability: A meta-analysis of social influence studies. *Psychological Bulletin, 90,* 1–20.

Eagly, A. H. (1987). *Sex differences in social behavior: A social-role interpretation.* Hillsdale, NJ: Erlbaum.

Eagly, A. H., & Johnson, B. T. (1990). Gender and leadership style: A meta-analysis. *Psychological Bulletin, 108,* 233–256.

Eagly, A. H., Makhijani, M. G., & Klonsky, B. G. (1992). Gender and the evaluation of leaders: A meta-analysis. *Psychological Bulletin, 111,* 3–22.

Ebbinghaus, H. (1885). *Uber das Gedachtnis.* Leipzig: Dunker. (Translation by H. Ruyer & C. E. Bussenius [1913], *Memory.* New York: Teachers College, Columbia University.)

Eberhardt, C. A., & Schill, T. (1984). Differences in sexual attitudes and likeliness of sexual behavior of black lower-socioeconomic father-present vs. father-absent female adolescents. *Adolescence, 19,* 99–105.

Eder, R. W., & Gerris, R. G. (Eds.). (1989). *The employment interview: Theory, research, and practice.* Newbury Park, CA: Sage.

Edwards, J. R., & Harrison, R. V. (1993). Job demands and worker health: Three-dimensional reexamination of the relationship between person-environment fit and strain. *Journal of Applied Psychology, 78,* 628–648.

Egeland, J. A., Gerhard, D. S., Pauls, D. L., Sussex, J. N., Kidd, K. K., Allen, C. R., Hostetter, A. M., & Housman, D. E. (1987). Bipolar affective disorders linked to DNA markers on chromosome 11. *Nature, 325,* 783–787.

Ehrhardt, A. A., & Meyer-Bahlberg, H. F. L. (1981). Effects of prenatal sex hormones on gender-related behavior. *Science, 211,* 1312–1317.

Ehrlichman, H., & Bastone, L. (1990). Olfaction and emotion. In M. Serby & K. Chobor (Eds), *Olfaction and the central nervous system.* Hillsdale, NJ: Erlbaum.

Ehrman, R. N., Robbins, S. J., Childress, A. R., & O'Brien, C. P. (1992). Conditioned responses to cocaine-related stimuli in cocaine abuse patients. *Psychopharmacology, 107,* 523–529.

Eich, J. E. (1985). Levels of processing, encoding specificity, elaboration, and CHARM. *Psychological Review, 92,* 1–38.

Eichar, D. M., Brady, E. M., & Fortinsky, R. H. (1991). The job satisfaction of older workers. *Journal of Organizational Behavior, 12,* 609–620.

Eimas, P. D., & Tarter, V. C. (1979). The development of speech perception. In H. W. Reese & L. P. Lipsitt (Eds.), *Advances in child development and behavior* (Vol. 13, pp. 155–193). New York: Academic Press.

Eisenberg, N., Cialdini, R. B., McCreath, H., & Shell, R. (1987). Consistency-based compliance: When and why do children become vulnerable? *Journal of Personality and Social Psychology, 52,* 1174–1181.

Ekman, P. (1992). Facial expressions of emotion: New findings, new questions. *Psychological Science, 3,* 34–38.

Ekman, P., Davidson, R. J., & Friesen, W. V. (1990). The Duchenne smile: Emotional expression and brain physiology II. *Journal of Personality and Social Psychology, 58,* 231–242.

Ekman, P., & Friesen, W. V. (1975). *Unmasking the face.* Englewood Cliffs, NJ: Prentice Hall.

Elkin, J., Shea, T., Watkins, J. T., Imber, S. D., Stotsky, S. M., Collins, J. F., Glass, D. R., Pilkonis, P. A., Leber, W. R., Docherty, J. P., Fiester, S. J., & Parloff, M. B. (1989). National Institutes of Mental Health treatment of depression and collaborative research program. *Archives of General Psychiatry, 46,* 971–982.

Elkind, D. (1967). Egocentrism in adolescence. *Child Development, 38,* 1025–1034.

Elkins, I. J., Cromwell, R. L., & Asarnow, R. F. (1992). Span of apprehension in schizophrenic patients as a function of distracter masking and laterality. *Journal of Abnormal Psychology, 101,* 53–60.

Elkins, L. E., & Peterson, C. (1993). Gender differences in best friendships. *Sex Roles, 29,* 497–508.

Ellington, R. J. (1954). Incidence of EEG abnormality among patients with mental disorders of apparently nonorganic origin: A criminal review. *American Journal of Psychiatry, 3,* 263–275.

Elliot, A. J. (1981) *Child language.* Cambridge, England: Cambridge University Press.

Elliot, A. J., & Devine, P. G. (1994). On the motivational nature of cognitive dissonance: Dissonance as psychological discomfort. *Journal of Personality and Social Psychology, 67,* 382–394.

Ellis, A. (1987). The impossibility of achieving consistently good mental health. *American Psychologist, 42,* 364–375.

Ellsworth, P. C., & Carlsmith, J. M. (1973). Eye contact and gaze aversion in aggressive encounter. *Journal of Personality and Social Psychology, 33,* 117–122.

Elmer-Dewitt, P. (1985, October 28). Kings, queens, and silicon chips. *Time.*

Empson, J. A. C. (1984). Sleep and its disorders. In R. Stevens (Ed.), *Aspects of consciousness.* New York: Academic Press.

Engel, G. L. (1980). The clinical application of a biopsychosocial model. *American Journal of Psychiatry, 137,* 535–544.

Engen, T. (1982). *The perception of odors.* New York: Academic Press.

Engen, T. (1986). *Remembering odors and their names.* Paper presented at the First International Conference on the Psychology of Perfumery, University of Warwick, England.

Engen, T. (1987). Remembering odors and their names. *American Scientist, 75,* 497–503.

Engen, T., & Ross, B. M. (1973). Long-term memory of odors with and without verbal descriptions. *Journal of Experimental Psychology, 100,* 221–227.

Environmental Protection Agency. (1990). *The environmental consumer's handbook.* Washington, DC: EPA.

Environmental Protection Agency. (1992). *Respiratory health effects of passive smoking: Lung cancer and other disorders.* Washington, DC: Author.

Epstein, L. H. (1992). Role of behavior theory in behavioral medicine. Special Issue: Behavioral medicine: An update for the 1990s. *Journal of Consulting and Clinical Psychology, 60,* 493–498.

Epstein, R. (1992) The quest for the thinking computer. *AI Magazine,* pp. 81–91.

Epstein, S. (1983). Aggregation and beyond: Some basic issues on the prediction of behavior. *Journal of Personality, 51,* 360–392.

Erikson, E. H. (1950). *Childhood and society.* New York: Norton.

Erikson, E. H. (1987). *A way of looking at things: Selected papers from 1930 to 1980* (S. Schlein, Ed.). New York: Norton.

Erlenmeyer-Kimling, L., & Jarvik, L. F. (1963). Genetics and intelligence. *Science, 142,* 1477–1479.

Eron, L. D. (1987). The development of aggressive behavior from the perspective of a developing behaviorist. *American Psychologist, 42,* 435–442.

Estrada, C. A., Isen, A. M., & Young, M. J. (in press). Positive affect improves creative problem solving and influences reported source of practice satisfaction in physicians. *Motivation and Emotion.*

Etaugh, C., & Liss, M. B. (1992). Home, school, and playroom: Training grounds for adult gender roles. *Sex Roles, 26,* 129–147.

Evans, C. (1985). *Landscapes of the night.* New York: Viking.

Eysenck, H. J. (1952). The effects of psychotherapy: An evaluation. *Journal of Consulting Psychology, 16,* 319–324.

Eysenck, H. J., & Eysenck, M. W. (1985). *Personality and individual differences.* New York: Plenum.

Fagot, B. I., & Kavanagh, K. (1990). The prediction of antisocial behavior from avoidance attachment classifications. *Child Development, 60,* 663–672.

Fallon, A. E., & Rozin, P. (1985). Sex differences in perceptions of desirable body shape. *Journal of Abnormal Psychology, 94,* 102–105.

Fantz, R. L. (1961). The origin of form perception. *Scientific American, 204,* 66–72.

Faraone, S. V., Kremen, W. S., & Tsuang, M. T. (1990). Genetic transmission of major affective disorders: Quantitative models and linkage analyses. *Psychological Bulletin, 108,* 109–127.

Farde, L., Wiesel, F., Halldin, C., & Sevdall, G. (1988). Central D2-dopamine receptor occupancy in schizophrenic patients treated with antipsychotic drugs. *Archives of General Psychiatry, 45,* 71–76.

Farquhar, J. W., Maccoby, N., & Solomon, D. S. (1984). Community applications of behavioral medicine. In W. D. Gentry (Ed.), *Handbook of behavioral medicine.* New York: Guilford Press.

Feather, N. T., & Volkmer, R. E. (1988). Preference for situations involving effort, time pressure, and feedback in relation to Type A behavior, locus of control, and test anxiety. *Journal of Personality and Social Psychology, 55,* 266–271.

Fechner, G. T. (1860). *Elementse der psychophysik.* Leipzig: Breitkops & Harterl.

Feingold, A. (1992a). Gender differences in mate selection preferences: A test of the parental investment model. *Psychological Bulletin, 112,* 125–139.

Feingold, A. (1992b). Cognitive gender differences: A developmental perspective. *Sex roles, 29,* 91–112.

Feingold, A. J. (1990). Gender differences in the effects of physical attractiveness on romantic attraction: A comparison across five research paradigms. *Journal of Personality and Social Psychology, 59,* 981–993.

Feldman, D. C., & Arnold, H. J. (1985). Personality types and career patterns: Some empirical evidence on Holland's model. *Canadian Journal of Administraive Sciences, 2,* 192–210.

Feldman, D. C., & Tompson, H. B. (1993). Entry shock, culture shock: Socializing the new breed of global managers. *Human Resource Management, 31,* 345–362.

Fenton, W. S., & McGlashan, T. H. (1991). Natural history of schizophrenia subtypes: II. Positive and negative symptoms and long-term course. *Archives of General Psychiatry, 48,* 978–986.

Fernandez, E., & Turk, D. C. (1992). Sensory and affective components of pain: Separation and synthesis. *Psychological Bulletin, 113,* 205–217.

Ferster, C. B., & Skinner, B. F. (1957). *Schedules of reinforcement.* New York: Appleton-Century-Crofts.

Festinger, L. (1957). *A theory of cognitive dissonance.* Evanston, IL: Row, Peterson.

Festinger, L., Schachter, S., & Back, K. (1950). *Social pressures in informal groups: A study of a housing community.* New York: Harper.

Feuerstein, M., Labbé, E. E., & Kuczmierczyk, A. R. (1986). *Health psychology: A psychobiological perspective.* New York: Plenum.

Fibiger, H. C., Murray, C. L., & Phillips, A. G. (1983). Lesions of the nucleus basalis magoncellularis impair long-term memory in rats. *Society for Neuroscience Abstracts, 9,* 332.

Field, R. H. G., & House, R. J. (1990). A test of the Vroom-Yetton model using manager and subordinate reports. *Journal of Applied Psychology, 75,* 362–366.

Fielder, F. E., Mitchell, T., & Triandis, H. C. (1971). The culture assimilator: An approach to cross-cultural training. *Journal of Applied Psychology, 55,* 95–102.

Fields, H. L., & Basbaum, A. (1984). Endogenous pain control mechanisms. In P. D. Wall & R. Melzack (Eds.), *Textbook of pain* (pp. 142–152). Edinburgh: Churchill Livingstone.

Fiez, J. A., & Petersen, S. E. (1993). PET as part of an interdisciplinary approach to understanding processes involved in reading. *Psychological Science, 4,* 287–293.

Fincham, F. D., & Bradbury, T. N. (1992). Assessing attributions in marriage: The relationship attribution measure. *Journal of Personality and Social Psychology, 62,* 457–468.

Fischoff, B. (1975). Hindsight-foresight: The effect of outcome knowledge on judgment under uncertainty. *Journal of Experimental Psychology: Human Perception and Performance, 1,* 288–299.

Fischoff, B. (1992). Risk taking: A developmental perspective. In J. F. Yates (Ed.), *Risk taking.* New York: Wiley.

Fisher, J. D., & Fisher, W. A. (1992). Changing AIDS-risk behavior. *Psychological Bulletin, 3,* 455–474.

Fisher, J. D., & Misovich, S. J. (1989). Social influence and AIDS-preventive behavior. In J. Edwards (Ed.), *Applied social psychology annual* (Vol. 9). New York: Plenum.

Fisher, R. P., & Geiselman, R. E. (1988). Enhancing eyewitness memory with the cognitive interview. In M. M. Gruneberg, P. E. Morris, & R. N. Sykes (Eds.), *Practical aspects of memory: Current research and issues: Vol. 1. Memory in everyday life* (pp. 34–39). Chichester, England: John Wiley & Sons.

Fiske, S. T., & Neuberg, S. L. (1990). A continuum model of impression formation, from category based to individuating processes: Influences of information and motivation in attention and interpretation. In M. P. Zanna (Ed.), *Advances in experimental social psychology* (Vol. 23). New York: Academic Press.

Fiske, S. T., & Taylor, S. (1991). *Social cognition* (2nd ed.). New York: Random House.

Flaherty, C. F., & Largen, J. (1975). Within-subjects positive and negative contrast effects in rats. *Journal of Comparative and Physiological Psychology, 88,* 653–664.

Flavell, J. H. (1973). The development of inferences about others. In T. Misebel (Ed.), *Understanding other persons.* Oxford: Blackwell, Basic, & Mott.

Flavell, J. H. (1982). Structures, stage and sequences in cognitive development. In W. A. Collins (Ed.), *Minnesota Symposia on Child Psychology* (Vol. 15, pp. l–28). Hillsdale, NJ: Erlbaum.

Flavell, J. H. (1985). *Cognitive development* (2nd ed.). Englewood Cliffs, NJ: Prentice-Hall.

Flynn, J. R. (1987). Massive IQ gains in 14 nations: What IQ tests really measure. *Psychological Bulletin, 101,* 171–191.

FMC Corporation. (1985). *Product safety sign and label system.* Santa Clara, CA: FMC Corporation.

Foderaro, L. W. (1988, February 4). The fragrant house: An expanding market for every mood. *The New York Times,* pp. C1, C10.

Folkman, S., Lazarus, R. S., Dunkel-Schetter, C., DeLongis, A., & Gruen, R. J. (1986). Dynamics of a stressful encounter: Cognitive appraisal, coping, and encounter outcomes. *Journal of Personality and Social Psychology, 50,* 992–1003.

Fontham, E. T., Correa, P., & Wu-Williams, A. (1991). Lung cancer in nonsmoking women: A multicenter case-control study. *Cancer Epidemiology, Biomarkers & Prevention, 1,* 35–43.

Forgas, J. P. (1991). Affect and social perception: Research evidence and an integrative theory. In W. Stroebe & M. Newstone (Eds.), *European review of social psychology.* New York: Wiley.

Forgas, J. P. (1991). Affective influences on partner choice: Role of mood in social interviewer's selection decisions. *Journal of Applied Psychology, 70,* 374–378.

Forgas, J. P. (1993). On making sense of odd couples: Mood effects on the perception of mismatched relationships. *Personality and Social Psychology Bulletin, 19,* 59–70.

Forgas, J. P. (in press). The role of emotion in social judgments: An introductory review and an affect infusion model (AIM). *European Journal of Social Psychology.*

Forgas, J. P., & Bower, G. H. (1988). Affect in social and personal judgments. In K. Fiedler & J. P. Forgas (Eds.), *Affect, cognition, and social behavior.* Toronto: Hogrefe.

Foulkes, D. (1985). *Dreaming: A cognitive-psychological analysis.* Hillsdale, NJ: Erlbaum.

Fowler, R. D. (1993). 1992 report of the chief executive officers. *American Psychologist, 48,* 726–735.

Fox, R., Aslin, R. N., Shea, S. L., & Duais, S. T. (1979). Stereopsis in human infants. *Science, 207,* 323–324.

Fraczek, A., & Kirwil, L. (1992). Living in the family and child aggression: Studies on some socialization conditions of development of aggression. In A. Fraczek & H. Zumky (Eds.), *Socialization and aggression.* Berlin: Springer-Verlag.

Frank, M. G., & Gilovich, T. (1988). The dark side of self and social perception: Black uniforms and aggression in professional sports. *Journal of Personality and Social Psychology, 54,* 74–85.

Franks, J. J., & Bransford, J. D. (1971). Abstraction of visual patterns. *Journal of Experimental Psychology, 90,* 65–74.

Franzoi, S. L., & Herzog, M. E. (1987). Judging physical attractiveness: What body aspects do we use? *Personality and Social Psychology Bulletin, 13,* 19–33.

Frederick, D., & Libby, R. (1986). Expertise and auditors' judgments of conjunctive events. *Journal of Accounting Research, 24,* 270–290.

Freedman, J. L. (1986). Television violence and aggression: A rejoinder. *Psychological Bulletin, 100,* 372–378.

Freedman, J. L., & Fraser, S. C. (1966). Compliance without pressure: The foot-in-the-door technique. *Journal of Personality and Social Psychology, 4,* 195–202.

Freedman, L. S., Prentice, R. L., Clifford, C., Harlan, W., Henderson, M., & Rossouw, J. (1993). Dietary fat and breast cancer: Where we are. *Journal of the National Cancer Institute, 85,* 764–765.

Frese, M. (1985). Stress at work and psychosomatic complaints: A causal interpretation. *Journal of Applied Psychology, 70,* 314–328.

Freud, S. (1901/1915). The interpretation of dreams. In J. Strachey (Ed.), *The standard edition of the complete psychological works of Sigmund Freud* (Vol. 4, 5). London: Hogarth.

Freud, S. (1908). *The interpretation of dreams.* In J. Strachey (Ed.), *Standard edition of the complete psychological works of Sigmund Freud* (Vols. 4, 5). London: Hogarth.

Freud, S. (1915). Instincts and their vicissitudes. In E. Jones (Ed.), *The Collected papers of Sigmund Freud* (Vol. 4). New York: Basic Books.

Fricko, M. A. M., & Beehr, T. A. (1992). A longitudinal investigation of interest congruence and gender concentration as predictors of job satisfaction. *Personnel Psychology, 45,* 99–117.

Friedman, H., & Zebrowitz, L. A. (1992). The contribution of typical sex differences in facial maturity to sex role stereotypes. *Personality and Social Psychology Bulletin, 18,* 430–438.

Friedman, H. S., & Miller-Herringer, T. (1991). Nonverbal display of emotion in public and private: Self-monitoring, personality, and expressive cues. *Journal of Personality and Social Psychology, 62,* 766–775.

Friedman, H. W., Tucker, J. S., Tomlinson-Keasey, C., Schwartz, J. E., Wingard, D. L., & Criqui, M. H. (1993). Does childhood personality predict longevity? *Journal of Personaltiy and Social Psychology, 65,* 176–185.

Friedman, W. J. (1993). Memory for the time of past events. *Psychological Bulletin, 113,* 44–66.

Friedmann, K. (1988). The effect of adding symbols to written warning labels on user behavior and recall. *Human Factors, 30,* 507–515.

Fry, D. P. (1990, August). Aggressive interaction among Zapotec children in two different microcultural environments. *Proceedings of the Ninth World Meeting of the International Society for Research on Aggression,* Banff, Canada.

Fuchs, I., Eisenberg, N., Herz-Lazarowitz, R., & Sharabany, R. (1986). Kibbutz, Israeli city, and American children's moral reasoning about prosocial moral conflicts. *Merrill-Palmer Quarterly, 32,* 37–50.

Funder, D. C. (1987). Errors and mistakes: Evaluating the accuracy of social judgment. *Psychological Bulletin, 101,* 75–90.

Funder, D. C., & Colvin, C. R. (1991). Explorations in behavioral consistency: Properties of persons, situations, and behavior. *Journal of Personality and Social Psychology, 60,* 773–794.

Funder, D. C., & Sneed, C. D. (1993). Behavioral manifestations of personality: An ecological approach to judgmental accuracy. *Journal of Personality and Social Psychology, 64,* 479–490.

Furomoto, L., & Scarborough, E. (1986). Placing women in the history of psychology. *American Psychologist, 41,* 35–42.

Furstenberg, F. F., Jr. (in press). How families manage risk and opportunity in dangerous neighborhoods. In W. J. Wilson (Ed.), *Sociology and the public agenda.* Newbury Park, CA: Sage.

Gaertner, S. L., Dovidio, J. F., Anastasio, P. A., Bachman, B. A., & Rust, M. C. (in press). The common ingroup identity model: Recategorization and the reduction of intergroup bias. In W. Stroebe & H. Hewstone (Eds.), *European Review of Social Psychology.*

Gaertner, S. L., Mann, J. A., Dovidio, J. F., & Murrell, J. A. (1990). How does cooperation reduce intergroup bias? *Journal of Personality and Social Psychology, 57,* 239–249.

Gaertner, S. L., Mann, J., Murrell, A., & Dovidio, J. F. (1989). Reducing intergroup bias: The benefits of recategorization. *Journal of Personality and Social Psychology, 57,* 239–249.

Gaines, J., & Jermier, J. M. (1983). Emotional exhaustion in a high stress organization. *Academy of Management Journal, 26,* 567–586.

Galambos, N. I. (1992). Parent-adolescent relations. *Current Directions in Psychological Science, 1,* 146–149.

Galanter, E. (1962). Contemporary psychophysics. In R. Brown, E. Galanter, E. G. Hess, & G. Mandler (Eds.), *New Directions in Psychology.* New York: Holt, Rinehart, & Winston.

Galotti, K. (1989). Approaches to studying formal and everyday reasoning. *Psychological Bulletin, 105,* 331–351.

Galotti, K. M., Kozberg, S. F., & Farmer, M. C. (1991). Gender and developmental differences in adolescents. conceptions of moral reasoning. *Journal of Youth and Adolescence, 20,* 13–30.

Gannon, L., Luchetta, T., Rhodes, K., Pardie, L., & Segrist, D. (1992). Sex bias in psychological research: Progress or complacency? *American Psychologist, 47,* 389–396.

Gans, J. E., & Blyth, D. A. (1990). *America's adolescents: How healthy are they?* (AMA Profiles of Adolescent Health series.) Chicago: American Medical Association.

Gara, M. A., Woolfolk, R. L., Cohen, B. D., Goldston, R. B., Allen, L. A., & Novalany, J. (1993). Perception of self and other in major depression. *Journal of Abnormal Psychology, 102,* 93–100.

Garb, J. L., & Stunkard, A. J. (1974). Taste aversion in man. *American Journal of Psychiatry, 131,* 1204–1207.

Garcia, J., Hankins, W. G., & Rusiniak, K. W. (1974). Behavioral regulation of the milieu interne in man and rat. *Science, 185,* 824–831.

Garcia, J., & Koelling, R. A. (1966). Relation of cue to consequence in avoidance learning. *Psychonomic Science, 4,* 123.

Garcia, J., Rusiniak, K. W., & Brett, L. P. (1977). Conditioning food-illness aversions in wild animals: Caveat Canonici. In H. Davis & H. M. B. Hurwitz (Eds.), *Operant-Pavlovian interactions.* Hillsdale, NJ: Erlbaum.

Gardner, B. T., & Gardner, R. A. (1975). Evidence for sentence constituents in the early utterances of child and chimpanzee. *Journal of Experimental Psychology: General, 4,* 244–267.

Gardner, H. (1983). *Frames of mind: The theory of multiple intelligences.* New York: Basic Books.

Garland, H., & Newport, S. (1991). Effects of absolute and relative sunk costs on the decision to persist with a course of action. *Organizational Behavior and Human Decision Processes, 48,* 55–69.

Gatchel, R. J., Baum, A., & Krantz, D. S. (1989). *An introduction to health psychology* (2nd ed.). New York: Random House.

Gatchel, R. J., Schaeffer, M. A., & Baum, A. (1985). A psychophysiological field study of stress at Three Mile Island. *Psychophysiology, 22,* 175–181.

Gauvain, M., & Rogoff, B. (1989). Collaborative problem solving and children's planning skills. *Developmental Psychology, 25,* 139–151.

Gazzaniga, M. S. (1984). Right hemisphere language: Remaining problems. *American Psychologist, 39,* 1494–1495.

Gazzaniga, M. S. (1985, November). The social brain. *Psychology Today,* pp. 29–38.

Geary, D. C., Fan, L., & Bow-Thomas, C. C. (1992). Numerical cognition: Loci of ability differences comparing children from China and the United States. *Psychological Science, 3,* 180–185.

Geary, D. C., & Widaman, K. F. (1992). Numerical cognition: on the convergence of componential and psychometric models. *Intelligence, 16,* 47–80.

Geen, R. G. (1989). Alternative conceptions of social facilitation. In P. B. Paulus (Ed.), *Psychology of group influence* (2nd ed., pp. 1–37). New York: Academic Press.

Geen, R. G., Beatty, W. W., & Arkin, R. M. (1984). *Human motivation.* Boston: Allyn and Bacon.

Gehring, R. E., & Toglia, M. P. (1989). Recall of pictorial enactments and verbal descriptions with verbal and imagery study strategies. *Journal of Mental Imagery, 13,* 83–98.

Geiselman, R. E., Fisher, R. P., Mackinnon, D. P., & Holland, H. L. (1985). Eyewitness memory enhancement in the police interview: Cognitive retrieval mnemonics versus hypnosis. *Journal of Applied Psychology, 70,* 401–412.

Geller, E. S. (1988). A behavioral science approach to transportation safety. *Bulletin of the New York Academy of Medicine, 64*(7), 632–661.

Geller, E. S., & Kalsher, M. J. (1990). Environmental determinants of party drinking: Bartenders versus self-service. *Environment and Behavior, 22,* 74–90.

Geller, E. S., Kalsher, M. J., Rudd, J. R., Streff, F. M., & Lehman, G. R. (1989). Promoting safety belt use on a university campus: An integration of incentive and commitment strategies. *Journal of Applied Social Psychology, 19,* 3–19.

Geller, E. S., Rudd, J. R., Kalsher, M. J., Streff, F. M., & Lehman, G. R. (1987). Employer-based programs to motivate safety belt use: A review of short and long-term effects. *Journal of Safety Research, 18,* 1–17.

Geller, E. S., Winett, R. A., & Everett, P. B. (1982). *Preserving the environment: New strategies for behavior change.* New York: Pergamon Press.

George, J., & Brief, A. P. (1992). Feeling good—doing good: A conceptual analysis of the mood at work—organizational spontaneity relationship. *Psychological Bulletin, 112,* 310–329.

George, J. T., & Hopkins, B. L. (1989). Multiple effects of performance-contingent pay for waitpersons. *Journal of Applied Behavior Analysis, 22,* 131–142.

Gerrard, M. (1986). Are men and women really different? In K. Kelley (Ed.), *Females, males, and sexuality.* Albany, NY: SUNY Press.

Geschwind, N. (1972). Language and the brain. *Scientific American, 226,* 76–83.

Gibbons, B. (1986). The intimate sense of smell. *National Geographic, 170,* 324–361.

Gibbons, L. J., Stiles, D. A., & Shkodriani, G. M. (1991). Adolescents' attitudes toward family and gender roles: An international comparison. *Sex Roles, 25,* 625–643.

Gibbs, N. R. (1993, June 28). Bringing up father. *Time,* pp. 53–61.

Gibson, E. J., & Walk, R. D. (1960). The "visual cliff." *Scientific American, 202,* 64–71.

Gilbert, A. N., & Wysocki, C. J. (1987). The smell survey results. *National Geographic, 172,* 514–525.

Gilbert, D. T., & Hixon, J. O. (1991). The trouble of thinking: Activation and application of stereotypic beliefs. *Journal of Personality and Social Psychology, 6,* 509–517.

Gilbert, D. T., & Jones, E. E. (1986). Perceiver-induced constraint: Interpretations of self-generated reality. *Journal of Personality and Social Psychology, 50,* 269–280.

Gilbert, D. T., McNulty, S. E., Guiliano, T. A., & Benson, J. E. (1992). Blurry words and fuzzy deeds: The attribution of obscure behavior. *Journal of Personality and Social Psychology, 62,* 18–25.

Gill, J. (1985, August, 22). Czechpoints. *Time Out,* p. 15.

Gilligan, C. F. (1982). *In a different voice.* Cambridge, MA: Harvard University Press.

Gilovich, T. (1990). Differential construal and the false consensus effect. *Journal of Personality and Social Psychology, 59,* 623–634.

Giovannucci, E., Colditz, G. A., Stampfer, M. J., Hunter, D., Rosner, B. A., Willett, W. C., & Speizer, F. E. (1994). A prospective study of cigarette smoking and risk of colorectal adenoma and colorectal cancer in U.S. women. *Journal of the National Cancer Institute, 86,* 192–199.

Gisiner, R., & Schusterman, R. J. (1992). Sequence, syntax, and semantics: Responses of a language-trained sea lion (*Zalophus californianus*) to novel sign combinations. *Journal of Comparative Psychology, 106,* 78–91.

Gladue, B. A. (1991). Aggressive behavioral characteristics, hormones, and sexual orientation in men and women. *Aggressive Behavior, 17,* 313–326.

Glazer, S. (1993). Intelligence testing. *CQ Researcher, 3,* 651–659.

Gleicher, F., Kost, K. A., Baker, S. M. Strathma, A. J., Richman, S. A., & Sherman, S. J. (1990). The role of counterfactual thinking in judgments of affect. *Personality and Social Psychology Bulletin, 16,* 284–295.

Glenn, N. D., & Kramer, K. B. (1987). The marriages and divorces of the children of divorce. *Journal of Marriage and the Family, 48,* 737–747.

Glick, P. (1989). Remarried families, stepfamilies, and stepchildren: A brief demographic analysis. *Family Relations, 38,* 24–27.

Godden, D., & Baddeley, A. D. (1975). Context-dependent memory in two natural environments: On land and under water. *British Journal of Psychology, 66,* 325–331.

Godden, D., & Baddeley, A. D. (1980). When does context influence recognition memory? *British Journal of Psychology, 71,* 99–104.

Godfrey, D. R., Jones, E. E., & Lord, C. C. (1986). Self-promotion is not ingratiating. *Journal of Personality and Social Psychology, 50,* 106–115.

Goethals, G. R., (1986). Fabricating and ignoring social reality: Self-serving estimates of consensus. In J. Olson, C. P. Herman, & N. P. Zanna (Eds.), *Relative deprivation and social comparison: The Ontario symposium on social cognition IV.* Hillsdale, NJ: Erlbaum.

Goethals, G. R., Cooper, J., & Naficy, A. (1979). Role of foreseen, foreseeable, and unforeseeable behavioral consequences in the arousal of cognitive dissonance. *Journal of Personality and Social Psychology, 37,* 1179–1185.

Gold, E. B., Leviton, A., Lopez, R., Gilles, F. H., Hedley-White, E. T., Kolonel, L. N., Lyon, J. L., Swanson, G. M., Weiss, N. S., West, D., Aschenbrener, C., & Austin, D. F. (1993). Parental smoking and risk of childhood brain tumors. *American Journal of Epidemiology, 137,* 620–628.

Goldberg, J. (1992, May). The empty mirror. *Omni,* p. 16.

Goldenberg, I., & Goldenberg, H. (1985). *Family therapy: An overview,* (2nd ed.). Monterey, CA: Brooks/Cole.

Goldenring, J. M., & Purtell, E. (1984). Knowledge of testicular cancer risk and need for self-examination in college students: A call for equal time for men in teaching early cancer detection techniques. *Pediatrics, 74,* 1093–1096.

Goleman, D. (1993, June 11). Studies reveal suggestibility of very young as witnesses. *New York Times,* pp. A1, A23, A24.

Goleman, D. (1993, November 9). The secret of long life? Be dour and dependable. *New York Times,* p. C3.

Goleman, O. (1980, February). 1,528 little geniuses and how they grew. *Psychology Today,* pp. 28–53.

Goode, E. (1990, May 14). Getting slim. *U.S. News & World Report,* pp. 56–59.

Goodman, G. S., Hirschman, J. E., Hepps, D., & Rudy, L. (1991). Children's memory for stressful events. *Merrill-Palmer Quarterly, 37,* 109–158.

Goodstein, L. D., & Calhoun, J. F. (1982). *Understanding abnormal behavior.* Reading, MA: Addison-Wesley.

Gordon, W. C. (1989). *Learning and memory.* Belmont, CA: Brooks/Cole Publishing Company.

Gorman, C. (1994, August). Battle fatigue: Scant hope emerges from this year's AIDS meeting. *Time,* p. 63.

Gottesman, I. I., & Bertelsen, A. (1989). Confirming unexpressed genotypes for schizophrenia. *Archives of General Psychiatry, 46,* 867–872.

Gottfried, A. W. (Ed.). (1984). *Home environment and early cognitive development.* San Francisco: Academic.

Gould, R. L. (1978). *Transformations, growth, and change in adult life.* New York: Simon & Schuster.

Graf, P., & Schacter, D. L. (1985). Implicit and explicit memory for new associations in normal and amnesic subjects. *Journal of Experimental Psychology: Learning, Memory, and Cognition, 11,* 501–518.

Graham, C. H., & Hsia, Y. (1958). Color defect and color theory. *Science, 127*, 675–682.

Graham, S. (1983). Diet and cancer: Epidemiologic aspects. *Review of Cancer Epidemiology, 2*, 2–45.

Graham, S. (1992). "Most of the subjects were white and middle class": Trends in published research on African Americans in selected APA journals, 1970–1989. *American Psychologist, 47*, 629–639.

Graham, T., & Perry, M. (1993). Indexing transitional knowledge. *Developmental Psychology, 29*, 778–788.

Granchrow, J. R., Steiner, J. E., & Daher, M. (1983). Neonatal facial expressions in response to different qualities and intensities of gustatory stimuli. *Infant Behavior and Development, 6*, 189–200.

Gray, P. (1993, February 15). What is love? *Time*, pp. 47–51.

Gray, T. A., & Morley, J. E. (1986). Minireview: Neuropeptide Y: Anatomical distribution and possible function in mammalian nervous system. *Life Sciences, 38*, 389–401.

Graziano, W. G., Jensen-Campbell, L. A., Shebilske, L. J., & Lundgren, S. R. (1993). Social influence, sex differences, and judgments of beauty: Putting the interpersonal back in interpersonal attraction. *Journal of Personality and Social Psychology, 65*, 522–531.

Green, L., Fry, A. F., & Myerson, J. (1994). Discounting of delayed rewards: A life-span comparison. *Psychological Science, 5*, 33–36.

Green, R., & Fleming, D. T. (1990). Transsexual surgery follow-up: Status in the 1990s. *Annual Review of Sex Research, 1*, 163–174.

Greenberg, J. (1990). Employee theft as a reaction to underpayment inequity: The hidden cost of pay cuts. *Journal of Applied Psychology, 75*, 561–568.

Greenberg, J., & Baron, R. A. (1995). *Behavior in organizations* (5th ed.). Englewood Cliffs, NJ: Prentice Hall.

Greenberg, J., Pyszcynski, T., & Solomon, S. (1982). The self-serving attributional bias: Beyond self-presentation. *Journal of Experimental Social Psychology, 18*, 56–67.

Greenberg, J. S. (1991). *Comprehensive stress management* (3rd ed.). Madison, WI: William C. Brown.

Greene, B. F., Winett, R. A., Van Houten, R., Geller, E. S., & Iwata, B. A. (Eds.). (1987). *Behavior analysis in the community: Volume 2.* Lawrence, KS: Journal of Applied Behavior Analysis.

Greenwald, A. G. (1992). New look 3: Unconscious cognition reclaimed. *American Psychologist, 47*, 766–779.

Greenwald, A. G., Spangenberg, E. R., Pratkanis, A. R., & Eskenazi, J. (1991). Double-blind tests of subliminal self-help audiotapes. *Psychological Science, 2*, 119–122.

Gregg, W., Foote, A., Erfurt, J. C., & Heirich, M. A. (1990). Worksite follow-up and engagement strategies for initiating health risk behavior changes. *Health Education Quarterly, 17*, 455–478.

Greist-Bousquet, S., Watson, M., & Schiffman, H. R. (1990). *An examination of illusion decrement with inspection of wings-in and wings-out Müller-Lyer figures: The role of corrective and contextual information perception.* New York: Wiley.

Griffin, R. W., & McMahan, G. C. (in press). Motivation through job design. In J. Greenberg (Ed.), *Organizational behavior: The state of the science.* Hillsdale, NJ: Erlbaum.

Griffith, T. L. (1993). Monitoring and performance: A comparison of computer and supervisor monitoring. *Journal of Applied Social Psychology, 23*, 549–572.

Grillon, C., Courchesne, E., Ameli, R., Geyer, M. A., & Braff, D. L. (1990). Increased distractibility in schizophrenic patients: Electrophysiologic and behavioral evidence. *Archives of General Psychiatry, 47*, 171–179.

Grilly, D. M. (1989). *Drugs and human behavior.* Boston: Allyn and Bacon.

Grivel, F., & Candas, V. (1991). Ambient temperatures preferred by young European males and females at rest. *Ergonomics, 34*, 365–378.

Gruneberg, M. M. (1978). The feeling of knowing, memory blocks, and memory aids. In M. M. Gruneberg & P. Morris (Eds.), *Aspects of memory.* London: Methuen.

Gruneberg, M. M., Morris, P., & Sykes, R. N. (1988). *Practical aspects of memory: Current research and issues* (Vols. 1 & 2). Chichester, England: John Wiley & Sons.

Guilford, J. (1967). *The nature of human intelligence.* New York: McGraw-Hill.

Guilford, J. (1985). Cognitive psychology's ambiguities: Some suggested remedies. *Psychological Review, 89*, 48–59.

Gurman, A. S., Kniskern, D. P., & Pinsof, W. M. (1986). Research on marital and family therapies. In S. L. Garfield & A. E. Bergin (Eds.), *Handbook of psychotherapy and behavior change* (pp. 565–626). New York: Wiley.

Gustavson, C. R., Garcia, J., Hawkins, W. G., & Rusiniak, K. W. (1974). Coyote predation control by aversive conditioning. *Science, 184*, 581–583.

Gutek, B. A., & Winter, S. J. (1992). Consistency of job satisfaction across situations: Fact or framing artifice? *Journal of Vocational Behavior, 41*, 61–78.

Haas, K., & Haas, A. (1993). *Understanding sexuality.* St. Louis, MO: Mosby.

Hagen, R. (1993). Clinical files, Florida State University. Quoted in R. R. Bootzin, J. R. Acocella, & L. B. Alloy, *Abnormal psychology* (6th ed.). New York: McGraw-Hill.

Hagenzeiker, M. (1991). Enforcement or incentives? Promoting safety belt use among military personnel in the Netherlands. *Journal of Applied Behavior Analysis, 24*, 23–30.

Haier, R. J., Siegel, B. V., Tang, C., Abel, L., & Buchsabum, M. S. (in press). Intelligence and changes in regional cerebral glucose metabolic rate following learning. *Intelligence.*

Hajek, P., & Belcher, M. (1991). Dream of absent-minded transgression: An empirical study of a cognitive withdrawal symptom. *Journal of Abnormal Psychology, 100*, 487–491.

Hall, C. S. (1984). "A ubiquitous sex difference in dreams" revisited. *Journal of Personality and Social Psychology, 46*, 1109–1117.

Hall, J. A., Roter, D. L., & Katz, N. R. (1987). Task versus socioemotional behaviors in physicians. *Medical Care, 25*, 399–412.

Hall, J. A., & Veccia, E. M. (1990). More "touching" observations: New insights on men, women, and interpersonal touch. *Journal of Personality and Social Psychology, 59*, 1155–1162.

Halpern, S. (1992, May 6). Big boss is watching you. *Details*, pp. 18–23.

Hamer, D. H., Hu, S., Magnuson, V. L., Hu, N., & Pattatucci, A. J. (1993). A linkage between DNA markers on the X chromosome and male sexual orientation. *Science, 261*, 321–327.

Hamilton, G. V. (1978). Obedience and responsibility: A jury simulation. *Journal of Personality and Social Psychology, 36*, 126–146.

Hamilton, J. A. (1983). Development of interest and enjoyment in adolescence: II. Boredom and psychopathology. *Journal of Youth and Adolescence, 12*, 363–372.

Hammersmith, S. K. (1982). *Sexual preference: An empirical study from the Alfred C. Kinsey Institute for Sex Research.* Paper presented at the meetings of the American Psychological Association, Washington, D.C.

Hammond, R. (1991). *Dealing with anger: Givin' it, takin' it, workin' it out.* Champaign, IL: Research Press.

Hammond, W. R., & Yung, B. (1993). Psychology's role in the public health response to assaultive violence among young African-American men. *American Psychologist, 48*, 142–154.

Hans, V. P. (1992). Obedience, justice, and the law: PS reviews recent contributions to a field ripe for new research efforts by psychological scientists. *Psychological Science, 3*, 218–221.

Hansen, R. D. (1980). Common sense attribution. *Journal of Personality and Social Psychology, 17*, 398–411.

Harder, J. W. (1992). Play for pay: Effects of inequity in a pay-for-performance context. *Administrative Science Quarterly, 37*, 321–335.

Harlow, H. F., & Harlow, M. H. (1966). Learning to love. *American Scientist, 54*, 244–272.

Harpur, T. J., & Hare, R. D. (1990). Psychopathy and attention. In J. Enns (Ed.) *The development of attention: Research and theory* (pp. 429–444). New York: North Holland.

Harrigan, J. A. (1987). Self-touching as indicator of underlying affect and language processing. *Social Science and Medicine, 20*, 1161–1168.

Harris, J., & Wilkins, A. J. (1982). Remembering to do things: A theoretical framework and illustrative experiment. *Human Learning, 1*, 1–14.

Harris, M. B. (1992). Sex, race, and experiences of aggression. *Aggressive Behavior, 18*, 201–217.

Harris, M. B. (1994). Gender of subject and target as mediators of aggression. *Journal of Applied Social Psychology, 24*, 453–471.

Harris, P. L. (1991). The work of the imagination. In A. Whiten (Ed.), *Natural theories of mind* (pp. 283–304). Oxford: Blackwell.

Harris, P. R. (1979, March). Cultural awareness training for human resource development. *Training and Development Journal*, 64–74.

Harris, R. L., Ellicott, A. N. M., & Holmes, D. S. (1986). The timing of psychosocial transitions and changes in women's lives: An examination of women aged 45 to 60. *Journal of Personality and Social Psychology, 51*, 409–416.

Harrison, J. K. (1992). Individual and combined effects of behavior modeling and the cultural assimilator in cross-cultural management training. *Journal of Applied Psychology, 77,* 952–962.

Harrison, R. V. (1985). The person-environment fit model and the study of job stress. In T. A. Beehr & R. S. Bhagat (Eds.), *Human stress and cognition in organizations* (pp. 23–55). New York: Wiley.

Hartel, C. E. (1993). Rating format research revisited: Format effectiveness and acceptability depend on rater characteristics. *Journal of Applied Psychology, 78,* 212–217.

Hartley, J. T. (1986). Reader and text variables as determinants of discourse memory in adulthood. *Psychology and Aging, 1,* 150–158.

Hartmann, E. L. (1973). *The functions of sleep.* New Haven: Yale University Press.

Harvey, S. M. (1987). Female sexual behavior: Fluctuations during the menstrual cycle. *Journal of Psychosomatic Research, 31,* 101–111.

Haskins, R. (1989). Beyond metaphor: The efficacy of early childhood education. *American Psychologist, 44,* 274–282.

Hassett, J. (1978). Sex and smell. *Psychology Today, 11,* 40, 42, 45.

Hatfield, E. (1988). Passionate and companionate love. In R. J. Sternberg & M. I. Barnes (Eds.), *The psychology of love* (pp. 191–217). New Haven, CT: Yale University Press.

Hatfield, E., & Rapson, R. L. (1993). *Love, sex, and intimacy: Their psychology, biology, and history.* New York: HarperCollins.

Hatfield, E., & Sprecher, S. (1986). *Mirror, mirror . . . The importance of looks in everyday life.* Albany, NY: SUNY Press.

Hatfield, E., & Walster, G. W. (1981). *A new look at love.* Reading, MA: Addison-Wesley.

Hauenstein, N. A. (1992). An information-processing approach to leniency in performance judgments. *Journal of Applied Psychology, 77,* 485–493.

Haugaard, J. J., Repucci, N. D., Laurd, J., & Nauful, T. (1991). Children's definitions of the truth and their competency as witnesses in legal proceedings. *Law and Human Behavior, 15,* 253–273.

Havel, V. (1992, June 3). Rio and the new millennium. *New York Times,* p. A21.

Hawkins, S. A., & Hastie, R. (1990). Hindsight: Biased judgments of past events after the outcomes are known. *Psychological Bulletin, 107,* 311–327.

Haynes, B. F. (1993). Scientific and social issues of human immunodeficiency virus vaccine development. *Science, 260,* 1279–1286.

Hazelrigg, M. D., Cooper, H. M., & Borduin, C. M. (1987). Evaluating the effectiveness of family therapies: An integrative review and analysis. *Psychological Bulletin, 101,* 428–442.

Hecaen, H., & Angelergues, R. (1964). Localization of symptoms in aphasia. In A. V. S. de Reuck & M. O'Connor (Eds.), *CIBA foundation symposium on the disorders of language* (pp.222–256). London: Churchill Press.

Heider, F. (1958). *The psychology of interpersonal relations.* New York: Wiley.

Heilman, M. E., & Martell, R. F. (1986). Exposure to successful women: Antidote to sex discrimination in applicant screening decisions? *Organizational Behavior and Human Decision Processes, 37,* 376–390.

Heilman, M. E., Martell, R. F., & Simon, M. C. (1988). The vagaries of sex bias: Conditions regulating the undervaluation, equivaluation, and overvaluation of female job applicants. *Organizational Behavior and Human Decision Processes, 41,* 98–110.

Heinrichs, R. W. (1993). Schizophrenia and the brain: Conditions for a neuropsychology of madness. *American Psychologist, 48,* 221–233.

Hellige, J. B. (1993). Unity of thought and action: Varieties of interaction between the left and right cerebral hemispheres. *Current Directions in Psychological Sciences, 2,* 21–25.

Helms, J. E. (1989). Oral and literate traditions among black Americans living in poverty. *American Psychologist, 44,* 367–373.

Helms, J. E. (1992). Why is there no study of cultural equivalence in standardized cognitive ability testing? *American Psychologist, 47,* 1083–1101.

Hendrick, C. (Ed.). (1989). *Close relationships.* Newbury Park, CA: Sage.

Hendrick, C., & Hendrick, S. S. (1986). A theory and method of love. *Journal of Personality and Social Psychology, 50,* 392–402.

Hendrick, S. S., & Hendrick, C. (1992). *Romantic love.* Newbury Park, CA: Sage.

Heneman, R. L., Greenberger, D. B., & Anonyuo, C. (1989). Attributions and exchanges: The effects of interpersonal factors on the diagnosis of employee performance. *Academy of Management Journal, 32,* 466–476.

Henker, B., & Whalen, C. K. (1989). Hyperactivity and attention deficits. *American Psychologist, 44,* 216–223.

Hennig, P., & Knowles, A. (1990). Factors influencing women over 40 years to take precautions against cervical cancer. *Journal of Applied Social Psychology, 20,* 1612–1621.

Henriques, J. B., & Davidson, R. J. (1990). Regional brain electrical asymmetries discriminate between previously depressed and healthy control subjects. *Journal of Abnormal Psychology, 99,* 22–31.

Henriques, J. B., & Davidson, R. J. (1991). Left frontal hypoactivation in depression. *Journal of Abnormal Psychology, 100,* 535–545.

Henry, W. A., III. (1993, July 26). Born gay? *Time,* pp. 36–39.

Herman, L. M., Kuczaj, S. A., & Holder, M. D. (1993). Responses to anomalous gestural sequences by a language-trained dolphin: Evidence for processing of semantic relations and syntactic information. *Journal of Experimental Psychology: General, 122,* 184–194.

Herman, L. M., Richards, D. G., & Wolz, J. P. (1984). Comprehension of sentences by bottlenosed dolphins. *Cognition, 16,* 129–219.

Herrnstein, R. J. (1973). *IQ in the meritocracy.* Boston: Little, Brown.

Hersey, P., & Blanchard, K. (1982). *Management of organizational behavior* (4th ed.). Englewood Cliffs, NJ: Prentice Hall.

Hershberger, S. L., Lichtenstein, P., & Knox, S. S. (1994). Genetic and environmental influences on perceptions of organizational climate. *Journal of Applied Psychology, 79,* 24–33.

Hetzel, B., & McMichael, T. (1987). *The LS factor: Lifestyle and health.* Ringwood, Victoria: Penguin.

Higgins, A. T., & Turnure, J. E. (1984). Distractibility and concentration of attention in children's development. *Child Development, 55,* 1799–1810.

Hilgard, E. R. (1977). *Divided consciousness: Multiple controls in human thought and action.* New York: Wiley.

Hilgard, E. R. (1979). Divided consciousness in hypnosis: Implications of the hidden observer. In E. Fromm & R. E. Shor (Eds.), *Hypnosis: Developments in research and new perspectives* (2nd ed). Chicago: Aldine.

Hill, R. (1945). Campus values in mate selection. *Journal of Home Economics, 37,* 554–558.

Hilliard, A. (1985). *Parameters affecting the African-American child.* Paper presented at the Black Psychology seminar, Duke University, Durham, NC.

Hilton, D., & Slugoski, B. R. (1986). Knowledge-based causal attribution: The abnormal conditions focus model. *Psychological Review, 93,* 75–88.

Hilton, M. E. (1993). An overview of recent findings on alcoholic beverage warning labels. *Journal of Public Policy and Marketing, 12,* 1–9.

Hines, M., Chiu, L., McAdams, L. A., Bentler, P. M., & Lipcamon, J. (1992). Cognition and the corpus callosum: Verbal fluency, visuospatial ability, and language lateralization related to midsagittal surface areas of callosal subregions. *Behavioral Neuroscience, 106,* 3–14.

Hingson, R., Strunin, L., Berlin, B., & Heeren, T. (1990). Beliefs about AIDS, use of alcohol and drugs, and unprotected sex among Massachusetts adolescents. *American Journal of Public Health, 80,* 295–299.

Hinsz, L. D., & Williamson, D. A. (1987). Bulimia and depression: A review of the affective variant hypothesis. *Psychological Bulletin, 102,* 150–158.

Hinz, L. D., & Williamson, D. A. (1987). Bulimia and depression: A review of the affective variant hypothesis. *Psychological Bulletin, 102,* 150–158.

Hirsch-Pasek, K., Treiman, R., & Schneiderman, M. (1984). Brown and Hanlon revisited: Mothers' sensitivity to ungrammatical forms. *Journal of Child Language, 11,* 81–88.

Hixon, J. G., & Swann, W. B., Jr. (1993). When does introspection bear fruit? Self-reflection, self-insight, and interpersonal choices. *Journal of Personality and Social Psychology, 64,* 35–43.

Hobson, J. A. (1988). *The dreaming brain.* New York: Basic Books.

Hodges, J., & Tizard, B. (1989). Social and family relationships of ex-institutional adolescents. *Journal of Child Psychology and Psychiatry, 30,* 77–97.

Hofstede, G. (1980). *Culture's consequences: International differences in work-related values.* Beverly Hills, CA: Sage.

Holland, J. L. (1973). *Making vocational choices: A theory of careers.* Englewood Cliffs, NJ: Prentice Hall.

Hollon, S. D., DeRubeis, R. J., & Evans, M. D. (1987). Causal mediation of change in treatment for depression: Discriminating between nonspecificity and noncausality. *Psychological Bulletin, 102,* 139–149.

Hollon, S. D., Shelton, R. C., & Loosen, P. T. (1991). Cognitive therapy and pharmacotherapy for depression. *Journal of Consulting and Clinical Psychology, 59,* 88–99.

Holmes, D. (1990). The evidence for repression: An examination of sixty years of research. In J. Singer (Ed.), *Repression and dissociation: Implications for personality theory, psychopathology, and health* (pp. 85–102). Chicago: University of Chicago Press.

Holmes, D. S. (1984). Meditation and somatic arousal reduction: A review of the experimental evidence. *American Psychologist, 39,* 1–10.

Holmes, T. H., & Masuda, M. (1974). Life change and illness susceptibility. In B. S. Dohrenwend and B. P. Dohrenwend (Eds.), *Stressful life events: Their nature and effects.* New York: Wiley.

Holmes, T. H., & Rahe, R. H. (1967). The social readjustment rating scale. *Journal of Psychosomatic Research, 11,* 213–218.

Holstein, C. B. (1976). Irreversible, stepwise sequence in the development of moral judgement: A longitudinal study of males and females. *Child Development, 47,* 51–61.

Holtzworth-Munroe, A., & Jacobson, N. S. (1985). Causal attributions of married couples: When do they search for causes? What do they conclude when they do? *Journal of Personality and Social Psychology, 50,* 537–542.

Honig, W. K., & Staddon, J. E. R. (Eds.). (1977). *Handbook of operant behavior.* Englewood Cliffs, NJ: Prentice-Hall.

Honig, W. K., & Urcuioli, P. J. (1981). The legacy of Guttman and Kalish: Twenty-five years of research on stimulus generalization. *Journal of the Experimental Analysis of Behavior, 36,* 405–445.

Honts, C. R. (1994). Psychophysiological detection of deception. *Current Direction in Psychological Science, 3,* 77–82.

Hoppe, R. B. (1988). In search of a phenomenon: Research in parapsychology. *Contemporary Psychology, 33,* 129–130.

Hopson, J., & Rosenfeld, A. (1984, August). PMS: Puzzling monthly symptoms. *Psychology Today,* 30–35.

Horner, M. (1970). Femininity and successful achievement: A basic inconsistency. In J. M. Bardwicks, E. Douvan, M. Horner, & D. Gutmann (Eds.), *Feminine personality and conflict.* Belmont, CA: Wadsworth.

Horner, M. (1972). Toward an understanding of achievement-related conflicts in women. *Journal of Social Issues, 28,* 157–176.

Horney, K. E. (1967). *Feminine psychology.* New York: Norton.

Hornstein, G. A. (1992). The return of the repressed: Psychology's problematic relations with psychoanalysis, 1909–1960. *American Psychologist, 47,* 254–263.

Hosman, L. A. (1986). *A meta-analysis of sex differences in self-disclosure.* Paper presented at the meetings of the Southern Speech Communication Association, Houston.

Houfman, L. G., House, M., & Ryan, J. B. (1981). Dynamic visual acuity: A review. *Journal of the American Optometric Association, 52,* 883–887.

House, R. J. (1977). A theory of charismatic leadership. In J. G. Hunt & L. L. Larson (Eds.), *Leadership: The cutting edge* (pp. 189–207). Carbondale, IL: Southern Illinois University Press.

House, R. J., Spangler, W. D., & Woycke, J. (1991). Personality and charisma in the U.S. presidency: A psychological theory of leader effectiveness. *Administrative Science Quarterly, 36,* 263–296.

Hovland, C., Janis, I. L., & Kelley, H. H. (1953). *Communication and Persuasion: Psychological studies of one on one.* New Haven, CT: Yale University Press.

Hovland, C. I., & Weiss, W. (1951). The influence of source credibility on communication effectiveness. *Public Opinion Quarterly, 1,* 635–650.

Howard, G. S. (1985). The role of values in the science of psychology. *American Psychologist, 40,* 255–265.

Howard, K. I., Kopta, S. M., Krause, M. S., & Orlinsky, D. E. (1986). The dose-effect relationship in psychotherapy. *American Psychologist, 41,* 159–164.

Howe, G. R., Hirohata, T., Hislop, T. G., Iscovich, J. M., Yuan, J., Katsouyanni, K., Lubin, F., Marubini, E., Modan, B., Rohan, T., Toniolo, P., & Shunzhang, Y. (1990). Dietary factors and risk of breast cancer: Combined analysis of 12 case-control studies. *Journal of the National Cancer Institute, 82,* 561–569.

Howe, M. L., & Courage, M. L. (1993). On resolving the enigma of infantile amnesia. *Psychological Bulletin, 113,* 305–326.

Howell, J. M. & Frost, P. J. (1989). A laboratory study of charismatic leadership. *Organizational Behavior and Human Decision Processes, 43,* 243–269.

Howell, W. C. (1994). Human factors and the challenges of the future. *Psychological Science, 5,* 1, 4–7.

Hoyseth, K., & Jones, P. J. H. (1989). Ethanol induced teratogenesis: Characterization, mechanisms, and diagnostic approaches. *Life Sciences, 44,* 643–649.

Hsu, L. K. G. (1986). The treatment of anorexia nervosa. *American Journal of Psychiatry, 143,* 573–581.

Hubble, L. M., & Groff, M. G. (1982). WISC-R verbal performance IQ discrepancies among Quay-classified adolescent male delinquents. *Journal of Youth and Adolescence, 11,* 503–508.

Hubel, D. H., & Wiesel, T. N. (1979). Brain mechanisms of vision. *Scientific American, 241,* 150–162.

Hughes, J. R., Smith, T. W., Kosterlitz, H. W., Fothergill, L. A., Morgan, B. A., & Morris, H. R. (1975). Identification of two related pentapeptides from the brain with potent opiate agonist activity. *Nature, 258,* 577–581.

Hull, C. L. (1943). *Principles of behavior theory.* New York: Appleton-Century-Crofts.

Hull, J. G., Levenson, R. W., Young, R. D., & Sher, K. J. (1983). Self-awareness-reducing effects of alcohol consumption. *Journal of Personality and Social Psychology, 44,* 461–473.

Hulse, S. H. (1993). The present status of animal cognition: An introduction. *Psychological Science, 4,* 154–155.

Hultsch, D. F., & Dixon, R. A. (1990). Learning and memory in aging. In J. E. Birren & K. W. Schaie (Eds.), *Handbook of the psychology of aging* (3rd ed., pp. 359–374). San Diego: Academic Press.

Humbaugh, K., & Garrett, J. (1974). Sensation seeking among skydivers. *Perceptual and Motor Skills, 38,* 103–111.

Hunn, B. P., & Dingus, T. A. (1992). Interactivity, information and compliance cost in a consumer product warning scenario. *Accident Analysis and Prevention, 24,* 497–505.

Hurvich, L. M. (1981). *Color vision.* Sunderland, MA: Sinauer Associates.

Hwang, K. (1986). Behavior of Swedish primary and secondary caretaking fathers in relation to mother's presence. *Developmental Psychology, 22,* 739–751.

Hyde, J. S., Fennema, E., & Lamon, S. J. (1990). Gender differences in mathematics performance: A meta-analysis. *Psychological Bulletin, 107,* 130–155.

Hyde, J. S., & Linn, M. (1988). Gender differences in verbal stability: A meta-analysis. *Psychological Bulletin, 104,* 53–69.

Hyman, R. (1994). Anomaly or artifact? Comments on Bem and Honorton. *Psychological Bulletin, 115,* 19–24.

Intons-Peterson, M. J., & Roskos-Ewoldsen, B. (1988). *Sensory/perceptual qualities of images.* Paper presented at the 29th annual meeting of the Psychonomics Society, Chicago.

Isabella, R., & Belsky, J. (1991). Interactional synchrony and the origins of infant-mother attachment: A replications study. *Child Development, 62,* 373–384.

Isen, A. M. (1987). Positive affect, cognitive processes, and social behavior. In L. Berkowitz (Ed.), *Advances in experimental social psychology* (Vol. 20, pp. 203–253). New York: Academic Press.

Isen, A. M., & Baron, R. A. (1991). Positive affect and organizational behavior. In B. M. Staw & L. L. Cummings (Eds.), *Research in organizational behavior* (Vol. 14, pp. 1–48). Greenwich, CT: JAI Press.

Isen, A. M., & Daubman, K. A. (1984). The influence of affect on categorization. *Journal of Personality and Social Psychology, 47,* 1206–1217.

Isen, A. M., & Daubman, K. A., & Nowicki, G. P. (1987). Positive affect facilitates creative problem solving: When we are glad, we feel as if the light has increased. *Journal of Personality and Social Psychology, 52,* 1122–1131.

Isen, A. M., & Johnson, N. M. S., Merz, E., & Robinson, G. (1985). The influence of positive affect on the usualness of word associations. *Journal of Personality and Social Psychology, 48,* 1413–1426.

Isen, A. M., & Shalker, T. E. (1982). Do you "accentuate the positive, eliminate the negative" when you are in a good mood? *Social Psychology Quarterly, 41,* 345–349.

Iwahashi, M. (1992). Scents and science. *Vogue,* pp. 212–214.

Iwata, B. A., Dorsey, M. F., Slifer, K. J., Bauman, K. E., & Richman, G. S. (1982). Toward a functional analysis of self-injury. *Analysis and Intervention in Developmental Disabilities, 2,* 3–20.

Iwata, B. A., Pace, G. M., Kalsher, M. J., Cowdery, G. E., & Cataldo, M. F. (1990). Experimental analysis and extinction of self-injurious escape behavior. *Journal of Applied Behavior Analysis, 23,* 11–27.

Izard, C. E. (1992). *Human emotions* (2nd ed.). New York: Plenum.

Izard, C. E., Hembree, E. A., & Huebner, R. R. (1987). Infants' emotion expressions to acute pain. *Developmental Psychology, 23,* 105–113.

Izard, C. I. (1992). *The psychology of emotion.* New York: Plenum.

Jaccard, J. (1992, November). *Women and AIDS.* Paper presented at the meetings of the Society for the Scientific Study of Sex, San Diego.

Jackson, S. E., Schwab, R. L., & Schuler, R. S. (1986). Toward an understanding of the burnout phenomenon. *Journal of Applied Psychology, 71,* 630–640.

Jacobs, J. R. (1992.) Facilitators of romantic attraction and their relation to lovestyle. *Social Behavior and Personality, 20,* 227–234.

Jacobs, M. K., & Goodman, G. (1989). Psychology and self-help groups: Predictions on a partnership. *American Psychologist, 44,* 536–545.

Jacobson, E. (1938). *Progressive relaxation.* Chicago: University of Chicago Press.

Jacobson, S., Fein, G., Jacobson, J., Schwartz, P., & Dowler, J. (1984). Neonatal correlates of prenatal exposure to smoking, caffeine, and alcohol. *Infant Behavior and Development, 7,* 253–265.

Jako, R. A., & Murphy, K. R. (1990). Distributional ratings, judgment decomposition, and their impact on interrater agreement and rating accuracy. *Journal of Applied Psychology, 75,* 500–505.

James, W. J. (1890). *Principles of psychology.* New York: Holt.

Jameson, D., & Hurvich, L. M. (1989). Essay concerning color constancy. *Annual Review of Psychology, 40,* 1–22.

Jamieson, D. W., Lydon, J. E., & Zanna, M. P. (1987). Attitude and activity preference similarity: Different bases of interpersonal attraction for low and high self–monitors. *Journal of Personality and Social Psychology, 53,* 1052–1060.

Janis, I. L. (1954). Personality correlates of susceptibility to persuasion. *Journal of Personality, 22,* 504–518.

Jefferson, D. J. (1993, August 12). Dr. Brown treats what ails the rides at amusement parks. *The Wall Street Journal,* p. 1.

Jemmott, J. B., III, & Magloire, K. (1988). Academic stress, social support, and secretory immunoglobulin A. *Journal of Personality and Social Psychology, 55,* 803–810.

Jencks, D. (1972). *Inequality: A reassessment of the effect of family and school in America.* New York: Basic Books.

Jenkins, C. D., Zyzanski, S. J., & Rosenman, R. H. (1979). *Jenkins Activity Survey.* Cleveland, OH: Psychological Corp.

Jenkins, J. G., & Dallenbach, K. M. (1924). Obliviscence during sleep and waking. *American Journal of Psychology, 35,* 605–612.

Jernigan, T. L., Zisook, S., Heaton, R. K., Moranville, J. T., Hesselkink, J. R., & Braff, D. L. (1991). Magnetic resonance imaging abnormalities in lenticular nuclei and cerebral cortex in schizophrenia. *Archives of General Psychiatry, 48,* 881–890.

Jessor, R. (1993). Successful adolescent development among youth in high-risk settings. *American Psychologist, 48,* 117–126.

Johansson, F., Almay, B. G. L., von Knorring, L., Terenius, L., & Astrom, M. (1979). Personality traits in chronic pain patients related to endorphin levels in cerebrospinal fluid. *Psychiatry Research, 1,* 231–239.

Johnson, E. J. (1985). Expertise and decision under uncertainty: Performance and process. In M. Chi, R. Glasse, & M. Farr (Eds.), *The nature of expertise.* Columbus, OH: National Center for Research in Vocational Education.

Johnson-Laird, P. N., Byrne, R. M. J., Tabossi, P. (1989). Reasoning by model: The case of multiple quantification. *Psychological Review, 96,* 658–673.

Johnston, W., & Dark, V. (1986). Selective attention. *Annual Review of Psychology, 37,* 43–75.

Joiner, T. E., Jr., Alfano, M. S., & Metalsky, G. I. (1993). When depression breeds contempt: Reassurance seeking, self-esteem, and rejection of depressed college students by their roommates. *Journal of Abnormal Psychology, 101* 165–173.

Jones, D. M., & Broadbent, D. E. (1987). Noise. In G. Salvendy (Ed.), *Handbook of human factors.* New York: John Wiley & Sons.

Jones, E. E., & Davis, K. E. (1965). From acts to dispositions: The attribution process in person perception. In L. Berkowitz (Ed.), *Advances in experimental social psychology* (Vol. 2, pp. 219–266). New York: Academic Press.

Jones, M. M. (1980). Conversion reaction: Anachronism or evolutionary form? Review of the neurological, behavioral, and psychoanalytic literature. *Psychological Bulletin, 87,* 427–441.

Jourard, S. M. (1971). *Self-disclosure.* New York: Wiley.

Judd, C. M., Drake, R. A, Downing, J. W., & Krosnick, J. A. (1991). Some dynamic properties of attitude structures: context-induced response facilitation and polarization. *Journal of Personality and Social Psychology, 60,* 193–202.

Judd, C. M., Ryan, C. N., & Park, B. (1991). Accuracy in the judgment of in-group and out-group variability. *Journal of Personality and Social Psychology, 61,* 366–379.

Judge, T. A. (1993). Does affective disposition moderate the relationship between job satisfaction and voluntary turnover? *Journal of Applied Psychology, 78,* 395–401.

Just, M. A., & Carpenter, P. A. (1987). *The psychology of reading and language comprehension.* Newton, MA: Allyn and Bacon.

Kagan, J., Reznick, J. S., & Gibbons, J. (1989). Inhibited and uninhibited types of children. *Child Development, 60,* 838–845.

Kagan, J., Reznick, J. S., & Snidman, M. (1988). Biological bases of childhood shyness. *Science, 240,* 167–171.

Kagan, J., & Snidman, N. (1991). Temperamental factors in human development. *American Psychologist, 46,* 856–862.

Kagan, J., Snidman, N., & Arcus, D. M. (1992). Initial reactions to unfamiliarity. *Current Directions in Psychological Science, 1,* 171–174.

Kahneman, D., & Tversky, A. (1982). Judgment under uncertainty: Heuristics and biases. In D. Kahneman, P. Slovic, & A. Tversky (Eds.), *Judgment under uncertainty: Heuristics and biases* (pp. 3–22). Cambridge, England: Cambridge University Press.

Kahnemann, D., & Miller, D. T. (1986). Norm theory: Comparing reality to its alternatives. *Psychological Review, 93,* 136–153.

Kalick, S. M., & Hamilton, T. E. (1986). The matching hypothesis reexamined. *Journal of Experimental Social Psychology, 24,* 469–489.

Kalivas, P. W., & Samson, H. H. (Eds.). (1992). *The neurobiology of drug and alcohol addiction.* Annals of the New York Academy of Sciences, Vol. 654. New York: Academy of Sciences.

Kalsher, M. J., Clarke, S. W., & Wogalter, M. S. (1993). Communication of alcohol facts and hazards by a warning poster. *Journal of Public Policy and Marketing, 12,* 78–90.

Kalsher, M. J., Geller, E. S., Clarke, S. W., & Lehman, G. R. (1989). Safety belt promotion on a naval base: A comparison of incentives vs. disincentives. *Journal of Safety Research, 20,* 103–113.

Kalsher, M. J., Glindemann, K., Geller, E. S., & Clarke, S. W. (1988). *Situational determinants of excessive alcohol consumption at parties.* Paper presented at the American Psychological Association Conference, Atlanta.

Kalsher, M. J., Pucci, S., Wogalter, M. S., & Racicot, B. M. (1994). Enhancing the perceived readability of pharmaceutical container labels and warnings: The use of alternative designs and pictorials. In *Proceedings of the Human Factors and Ergonomics Society, 38th Annual Meeting.* Santa Monica, CA.

Kalsher, M. J., Rodocker, A. J., Racicot, B. M., & Wogalter, M. S. (1993). Promoting recycling behavior in office environments. *Proceedings of the Human Factors and Ergonomics Society, 37,* 484–488.

Kamin, L. J. (1965). Temporal and intensity characteristics of the conditioned stimulus. In W. F. Prokasy (Ed.), *Classical conditioning: A symposium.* New York: Appleton-Century-Crofts.

Kamin, L. J. (1978). Comment on Munsinger's review of adoption studies. *Psychological Bulletin, 85,* 194–201.

Kaniasty, K., & Norris, F. H. (1993). A test of the social support deterioration model in the context of natural disaster. *Journal of Personality and Social Psychology, 64,* 395–408.

Kanner, A. D., Coyne, J. C., Schaefer, C., & Lazarus, R. S. (1981). Comparison of two modes of stress measurement: Daily hassles and uplifts versus major life events. *Journal of Behavioral Medicine, 4,* 1–39.

Kantrowitz, B., Rosenberg, D., Rogers, P., Beachy, L., & Holmes, S. (November 1, 1993). Heroin makes an ominous comeback. *Newsweek,* p. 53.

Kaplan, H. I., & Sadock, B. J. (1991). *Synopsis of psychiatry: Behavioral sciences, clinical psychiatry* (6th ed.). Baltimore: Williams & Wilkins.

Kaplan, R. E. (1982). The dynamics of injury in encounter groups: Power, splitting, and the mismanagement of resistance. *International Journal of Group Psychotherapy, 32,* 163–187.

Karacan, I., Goodenough, D. R., Shapiro, A., & Starker, S. (1966). Erection cycle during sleep in relation to dream anxiety. *Archives of General Psychiatry, 15,* 183–189.

Karasek, R., & Theorell, T. (1990). *Healthy work: Job stress, productivity, and the reconstruction of working life.* New York: Basic Books.

Kasl, S. V. (1990). Some considerations in the study of traumatic stress. *Journal of Applied Social Psychology, 20,* 1655–1665.

Kaufman, A., Baron, A., & Kopp, R. E. (1966). Some effects of instructions on human operant behavior. *Psychonomic Monographs Supplement, 1,* 243–250.

Kaufman, A. S. (1983). Some questions and answers about the Kaufman Assessment Battery for Children (K-ABC). *Journal of Psychoeducational Assessment, 1,* 205–218.

Kaufman, A. S. (1990). V-PIQ discrepancies in brain-damaged adults: Interactions with gender, race, and other patient variables. In *Assessing adolescent and adult intelligence* (pp. 301–343). Boston: Allyn and Bacon.

Kaufman, K., Gregory, W. L., & Stephan, W. G. (1990). Maladjustment in statistical minorities within ethnically unbalanced classrooms. *American Journal of Community Psychology, 18,* 757–765.

Kaufman, M. T. (1980, November 16). Love upsetting Bombay's view of path to altar. *New York Times,* p. 12.

Kazdin, A. E. (1982). The token economy: A decade later. *Journal of Applied Behavior Analysis, 15,* 431–446.

Kazdin, A. E. (1993). Psychotherapy for children and adolescents: Current progress and future research directions. *American Psychologist, 48,* 644–657.

Keller, L. M., Bouchard, T. J., Jr., Arvey, R. D., Segal, N. L., & Dawis, R. V. (1992). Work values: Genetic and environmental influences. *Journal of Applied Psychology, 77,* 79–88.

Kelley, H. H. (1972). Attribution in social interaction. In E. E. Jones et al. (Eds.), *Attribution: Perceiving the causes of behavior.* Morristown, NJ: General Learning Press.

Kelley, K., & Byrne, D. (1992). *Exploring human sexuality.* Englewood Cliffs, NJ: Prentice Hall.

Kelley, K., & Byrne, D. (1992). *Human sexual behavior.* Englewood Cliffs, NJ: Prentice Hall.

Kelly, D. D. (1981). Disorders of sleep and consciousness. In E. Kandel & J. Schwartz (Eds.), *Principles of neural science.* New York: Elsevier–North Holland.

Kelly, J. A., Murphy, D. A., Sikkema, K. J., & Kalichman, S. C. (1993). Psychological interventions to prevent HIV infection are urgently needed. *American Psychologist, 48,* 1023–1034.

Kelman, H. C. (1967). Human use of human subjects: The problem of deception in social psychological experiments. *Psychological Bulletin, 67,* 1–11.

Kelman, H. C., & Hamilton, V. L. (1989). *Crimes of obedience.* New Haven, CT: Yale University Press.

Kelsey, F. O. (1969). Drugs and pregnancy. *Mental Retardation, 7,* 7–10.

Kendall-Tackett, K. A. (1991). Characteristics of abuse that influence when adults molested as children seek treatment. *Journal of Interpersonal Violence, 6,* 486–493.

Kendall-Tackett, K. A., Williams, L. M., & Finkelhor, D. (1993). Impact of sexual abuse on children: A review and synthesis of recent empirical studies. *Psychological Bulletin, 113,* 164–180.

Kendler, H. S., & Robinette, C. D. (1983). Schizophrenia in the National Academy of Sciences' National Research Council twin registry: A 16-year update. *American Journal of Psychiatry, 1140,* 1551–1563.

Kenrick, D. T., Groth, G. E., Trost, M. R., & Sadalla, E. K. (1993). Integrating evolutionary and social exchange perspectives on relationships: Effects of gender, self-appraisal, and involvement level on mate selection criteria. *Journal of Personality and Social Psychology, 64,* 951–969.

Kenrick, D. T., & Keefe, R. C. (1992). Age preferences in mates reflect sex differences in human reproductive strategies. *Behavioral and Brain Science, 15,* 75–133.

Kenrick, D. T., Neuberg, S. L., Zierk, K.L., & Krones J. M. (1994). Evolution and social cognition: Contrast effects as a function of sex, dominance, and physical attractiveness. *Personality and Social Psychology Bulletin, 20,* 210–217.

Kerr, S. L., & Neale, J. M. (1993). Emotion perception in schizophrenia: specific deficit or further evidence of generalized poor performance? *Journal of Abnormal Psychology, 102,* 312–318.

Kessler, C. R. (1994). Incidence of mental disorders in a non-institutionalized population. *Archives of General Psychiatry, 50,* in press.

Kessler, R. C., McGonagle, K. A., Zhao, S., Nelson, C. B., Hughes, M., Eshleman, S., Witchen, H-U., & Kendler, K. S. (1994). Lifetime and 12–month prevalence of DSM-III-R psychiatric disorders in the United States. *Archives of General Psychiatry, 5,* 8–19.

Kety, S. S. (1988). Schizophrenic illness in the families of schizophrenic adoptees: Findings from the Danish national sample. *Schizophrenic Bulletin, 14,* 217–222.

Kiecolt-Glaser, J. K., Fisher, L., Ogrocki, P., Stout, J. C., Speicher, C. E., & Glaser, R. (1987). Marital quality, marital disruption, and immune function. *Psychosomatic Medicine, 49,* 13–34.

Kiecolt-Glaser, J. K., & Glaser, R. (1992). Psychoneuroimmunology: Can psychological interventions modulate immunity? *Journal of Consulting and Clinical Psychology, 60,* 569–575.

Kiecolt-Glaser, J. K., Kennedy, S., Malkoff, S., Fisher, L., Speicher, C. E., & Glaser, R. (1988). Marital discord and immunity in males. *Psychosomatic Medicine, 50,* 213–229.

Kiesler, C. A., & Kiesler, S. B. (1969). *Conformity.* Reading, MA: Addison-Wesley.

Kiesler, D. J. (1966). Some myths of psychotherapy research and the search for a paradigm. *Psychological Bulletin, 65,* 110–136.

Kiesler, D. J. (1985). Meta-analysis, clinical psychology, and social policy. *Clinical Psychology Review, 5,* 3–12.

Kihlstrom, J. F., Tataryn, D. J., & Hoyt, I. P. (1993). Dissociative disorders. In P. B. Sutker & H. E. Adams (Eds.), *Comprehensive handbook of psychopathology* (2nd ed.). New York: Plenum Press.

Kilham, W., & Mann, L. (1974). Level of destructive obedience as function of transmitter and executant roles in the Milgram obedience paradigm. *Journal of Personality and Social Psychology, 29,* 696–702.

Kinnunen, T., Zamansky, T., & Block, M. (1994). Is the hypnotized subject lying? *Journal of Abnormal Psychology, 103,* 184–191.

Kinsey, A. C., Pomeroy, W., & Martin, C. (1984). *Sexual behavior in the human male.* Philadelphia: W. B. Saunders.

Kinsey, A. C., Pomeroy, W., Martin, C., & Gebhard, P. (1953). *Sexual behavior in the human female.* Philadelphia: W. B. Saunders.

Kirkpatrick, S. A., & Locke, E. A. (1991). Leadership: Do traits matter? *Academy of Management Executive, 5*(2), 48–60.

Kivlahan, D. R., Coppel, D. B., Fromme, K., Williams, E., & Marlatt, G. A. (1990). Secondary prevention of alcohol-related problems in young adults at risk. In K. D. Craig & S. M. Weiss (Eds.), *Prevention and early interventions: Biobehavioral perspectives.* New York: Springer.

Klag, M. J., Ford, D. E., Mead, L. A., He, J., Whelton, P. K., Liang, K., & Levine, D. M. (1993). Serum cholesterol in young men and subsequent cardiovascular disease. *New England Journal of Medicine, 328,* 313–318.

Klayman, J., & Ha, Y. W. (1987). Confirmation, disconfirmation, and information in hypothesis testing. *Psychological Review, 94,* 211–228.

Klein, H. J. (1991). Further evidence on the relationship between goal setting and expectancy theories. *Organizational Behavior and Human Decision Processes, 49,* 230–257.

Kleinke, C. L. (1986). Gaze and eye contact: A research review. *Psychological Bulletin, 100,* 78–100.

Kleinman, A. (1986). *Social origins of distress and disease.* New Haven, CT: Yale University Press.

Klotz, M. L., & Alicke, M. D. (1993). *Complaining in close relationships.* Manuscript under review.

Knapp, D. N. (1988). Behavioral management techniques and exercise promotion. In R. K. Dishman (Ed.), *Exercise adherence: Its impact on public health.* Champaign, IL: Human Kinetics Books.

Knowlton, B. J., Ramus, S. J., & Squire, L. R. (1992). Intact artificial grammar learning in amnesia: Dissociation of classification learning and explicit memory for specific instances. *Psychological Science, 3,* 172–179.

Kobasa, S. C. (1979). Stressful life events, personality, and health: An inquiry into hardiness. *Journal of Personality and Social Psychology, 37,* 1–11.

Koeske, G. F., Kirk, S. A., & Koeske, R. D. (1993). Coping with job stress: Which strategies work best? *Journal of Occupational and Organizational Psychology, 66,* 319–335.

Koestner, R., Bernieri, F., & Zuckerman, M. (1992). Self-regulation and consistency between attitudes, traits, and behaviors. *Personality and Social Psychology Bulletin, 18*, 52–59.

Kohlberg, L. (1984). *Essays on moral development: Vol. 2. The Psychology of moral development.* San Francisco: Harper & Row.

Kohler, I. (1962, May). Experiments with goggles. *Scientific American,* pp. 62–72.

Kolata, G. (1985). Obesity declared a disease. *Science, 227*, 1019–1020.

Kolata, G. B. (1986). Manic depression: Is it inherited? *Science, 232*, 448–450.

Komaki, J. L. (1986). Toward effective supervision: An operant analysis and comparison of managers at work. *Journal of Applied Psychology, 36*, 271–279.

Konovsky, M. A., & Brockner, J. (1993). Managing victim and survivor layoff reactions: A procedural justice perspective. In R. Cropanzano (Ed.), *Justice in the workplace* (pp. 133–155). Hillsdale, NJ: Erlbaum.

Kosslyn, S. M. (1980). *Image and mind.* Cambridge, MA: Harvard University Press.

Kosslyn, S. M. (1987). Seeing and imagining in the cerebral hemispheres: A computational approach. *Psychological Review, 14*, 148–175.

Kosslyn, S. M., Segar C., Pani, J., & Hilger, L. A. (1991). When is imagery used? A diary study. *Journal of Mental Imagery.*

Krakoff, L. R., Dziedzic, S., Mann, S. J., Felton, K., & Yeager, K. (1985). Plasma epinephrine concentrations in healthy men: Correlation with systolic blood pressure and rate-pressure product. *Journal of American College of Cardiology, 5*, 352.

Kring, A. M., Smith, D. A., & Neale, J. M. (1994). Individual differences in dispositional expressiveness: Development and validation of the emotional expressivity scale. *Journal of Personality and Social Psychology, 66*, 934–949.

Kroger, W. S., & Douce, R. G. (1979). Hypnosis in criminal investigation. *International Journal of Clinical and Experimental Hypnosis, 27*, 358–384.

Krosnick, J. A., Betz, A. L., Jussim, L. J., & Lynn, A. R. (1992). Subliminal conditioning of attitudes. *Personality and Social Psychology Bulletin, 18*, 152–162.

Kruglanski, A. W. (1990). Motivations for judging and knowing: Implications for causal attribution. In E. T. Higgins & R. M. Sorrentino (Eds.), *The handbook of motivation and cognition: Foundations of social behavior* (Vol. 2, pp. 333–368). New York: Guilford Press.

Krugman, R., & Davidson, H. (1990). *Child abuse and neglect: Critical first steps in response to a national emergency.* Washington, DC: U.S. Advisory Board on Child Abuse and Neglect.

Kuhn, D. (1989). Children and adults as intuitive scientists. Psychological Review, 96, 674–689.

Kuiper, N. A., Olinger, L. J., & MacDonald, M. R. (1987). Depressive schemata and the processing of personal and social information. In L. B. Alloy (Ed.), *Cognitive processes in depression.* New York: Guilford Press.

Kulik, C. T., & Ambrose, M. L. (1992). Personal and situational determinants of referent choice. *Academy of Management Review, 17*, 212–237.

Kunce, J. T., Ryan, J., & Eckelman, C. C. (1976). Violent behavior and differential WAIS characteristics. *Journal of Consulting and Clinical Psychology, 44*, 42–45.

Kunda, Z., & Nisbett, R. E. (1986). The psychometrics of everyday life. *Cognitive Psychology, 18*, 195–224.

Kunzinger, E. L., III. (1985). A short-term longitudinal study of moral development during early grade school. *Developmental Psychology, 21*, 642–646.

Kurdek, L. A. (1993). Predicting marital dissolution: A 5-year longitudinal study of newlywed couples. *Journal of Personality and Social Psychology, 64*, 221–242.

Kutchinsky, B. (1992). The child sexual abuse panic. *Nordisk Sexologist, 10*, 30–42.

Kübler-Ross, E. (1974). *Questions and answers on death and dying.* New York: Macmillan.

Labouvie-Vief, G. M., & Hakim-Larson, J. (1989). Developmental shifts in adult thought. In S. Hunter & M. Sundel (Eds.), *Midlife myths: Issues, findings, and practical implications* (pp. 690–696). Newbury Park, CA: Sage.

Lagerspetz, K. M., Bjorkqvist, K., & Peitonen, T. (1988). Is indirect aggression typical of females? Gender differences in aggressiveness in 11–12 year old children. *Aggressive Behavior, 14*, 403–414.

Laird, J. D. (1984). The real role of facial response in the experience of emotion: A reply to Tourangeua and Ellsworth, and others. *Journal of Personality and Social Psychology, 47*, 909–917.

Lalonde, M. (1974). *A new perspective on the health of Canadians.* Ottawa: Canadian Government Printing Office.

Lamb, M. E. (1977). Father-infant and mother-infant interactions in the first year of life. *Child Development, 48*, 167–181.

Lambert, M. J., Shapiro, D. A., & Bergin, A. E. (1986). The effectiveness of psychotherapy. In S. L. Garfield & A. E. Bergin (Eds.), *Handbook of psychotherapy and behavior change: An evaluative analysis,* (3rd ed.). New York: Wiley.

Lambert, S. (1991). The combined effect of job and family characteristics on the job satisfaction, job involvement, and intrinsic motivation of men and women workers. *Journal of Organizational Behavior, 12*, 341–363.

Landau, S., Milich, R., & Lorch, E. P. (1992). Visual attention to and comprehension of television in attention-deficit hyperactivity disordered and normal boys. *Child Development, 63*, 928–937.

Landsbergis, P. A., Schnall, P. L., Deitz, D., Friedman, R., & Pickering, T. (1992). The patterning of psychological attributes and distress by job strain and social support in a sample of working men. *Journal of Behavioral Medicine, 15*, 379–405.

Landy, F. J., & Farr, J. L. (1983). *The measurement of work performance: Methods, theory, and applications.* New York: Academic Press.

Lange, J. D., Brown, W. A., Wincze, J. P., & Zwick W. (1980). Serum testosterone concentration and penile tumescence changes in men. *Hormones and Behavior, 14*, 267–270.

Langlois, J. H., & Roggman, L. A. (1990). Attractive faces are only average. *Psychological Science, 1*, 115–121.

Langlois, J. H., Roggmann, L. A., & Reisser-Danner, L. A. (1990). Infants' differential social responses to attractive and unattractive faces. *Developmental Psychology, 26*, 153–159.

Larrick, R. P. (1993). Motivational factors in decision theories: The role of self-protection. *Psychological Bulletin, 113*, 440–450.

Lashley, K. S., Chow, K. L., & Semmes, J. (1951). An examination of the electrical field theory of cerebral integration. *Psychological Review, 58*, 123–136.

Laswell, M. E., & Lobsenz, N. M. (1980). *Styles of loving.* New York: Ballantine.

Latham, G., & Baldes, J. (1975). The practical significance of Locke's theory of goal setting. *Journal of Applied Psychology, 60*, 122–124.

Lauer, J., & Lauer, R. (1985, June). Marriages made to last. *Psychology Today,* pp. 22–26.

LaVecchia, C., Lucchini, F., Negri, E., Boyle, P., & Levi, F. (1993). Trends in cancer mortality in the Americas, 1955–1989. *European Journal of Cancer, 29*, 431–470.

LaVecchia, C., Lucchini, F., Negri, E., Boyle, P., Maisonneuve, P., & Levi, F. (1992). Trends of cancer mortality in Europe, 1955-1989: II, Respiratory tract, bone, connective and soft tissue sarcomas, and skin. *European Journal of Cancer, 23*, 514–599.

Lavrakas, P. J. (1975). Female preferences for male physiques. *Journal of Research in Personality, 9*, 324–334.

Law, D. J., Pellegrino, J. W., & Hunt, E. B. (1993). Comparing the tortoise and the hare: Gender differences and experience in dynamic spatial reasoning tasks. *Psychological Science, 4*, 35–40.

Lawless, H., & Engen, T. (1977). Associations to odors: Interference, mnemonics, and verbal labeling. *Journal of Experimental Psychology: Human Learning and Memory, 3*, 52–59.

Lazarus, R. S., & Folkman, S. (1984). *Stress, appraisal, and coping.* New York: Springer.

Lazarus, R. S., Opton, E. M., Nomikos, M. S., & Rankin, N. O. (1985). The principle of short-circuiting of threat: Further evidence. *Journal of Personality, 33*, 622–635.

Lee, P. C., Senders, C. W., Gantz, B. J., & Otto, S. R. (1985). Transient sensorineural hearing loss after overuse of portable headphone cassette radios. *Otolaryngology, 93*, 622–625.

Lee, R. T., & Ashforth, B. E. (1990). On the meaning of Maslach's three dimensions of burnout. *Journal of Applied Psychology, 75*, 743–747.

Lehman, H. C. (1953). *Age and achievement.* Philadelphia: W. B. Saunders.

Leippe, M. R., & Eisenstadt, D. (1994). Generalization of dissonance reduction: Decreasing prejudice through induced compliance. *Journal of Personality and Social Psychology, 67*, 395–413.

Lempers, J. D., Flavell, E. R., & Flavell, J. H. (1977). The development in very young of tacit knowledge concerning visual perception. *Genetic Psychology Monographs 95,* 3–53.

Lennox, R. D., & Wolfe, R. N. (1984). Revision of the self-monitoring scale. *Journal of Personality and Social Psychology, 46,* 1349–1364.

Lepper, M., & Green, D. (Eds.). (1978). *The hidden costs of reward.* Hillsdale, NJ: Erlbaum.

Lepper, M. R., & Cordova, D. I. (1992). A desire to be taught: Instructional consequences of intrinsic motivation. *Motivation and Emotion, 16,* 187–208.

Lepper, M. R., & Hoddell, M. (1992). *Instructional games: Effects of sex-typed fantasy contexts on boys' and girls' learning and instruction.* Unpublished manuscript, Stanford University.

Lerner, R. M. (1990). Plasticity, person-context relations, and cognitive training in the aged years: A developmental contextual perspective. *Developmental Psychology, 26,* 911–915.

Lerner, R. M. (1993). The demise of the nature-nurture dichotomy. *Human Development, 36,* 119–124.

LeVay, S. (1991). A difference in hypothalamic structure between heterosexual and homosexual men. *Science, 253,* 1034–1037.

Levenson, R. W. (1992). Autonomic nervous system differences among emotions. *Psychological Science, 3,* 23–27.

Levenson, R. W., Carstensen, L. L., Friesen, W. V., & Ekman, P. (1991). Emotion, physiology, and expression in old age. *Psychology and Aging, 6,* 28–35.

Levine, D. S. (1991). *Introduction to neural and cognitive modeling.* Hillsdale, NJ: Erlbaum.

Levine, J. M., & McBurney, D. H. (1982). *The role of olfaction in social perception and behavior.* Paper presented at the Third Ontario Symposium in Personality and Social Psychology, Toronto.

Levine, R. V., Martinez, T. S., Brase, G., & Sorenson, K. (1994). Helping in 36 U. S. cities. *Journal of Personality and Social Psychology, 67,* 69–82.

Levinger, G. (1988). Can we picture "love"? In R. J. Sternberg & M. I. Barnes (Eds.), *The psychology of love* (pp. 139–158). New Haven, CT: Yale University Press.

Levinson, D. J. (1986). A conception of adult development. *American Psychologist, 41,* 3–13.

Levis, D. J. (1985). Implosive theory: A comprehensive extension of conditioning theory of fear/anxiety to psychology. In S. Reiss & R. R. Bootzin (Eds.), *Theoretical issues in behavior therapy.* New York: Academic Press.

Levy, B., & Langer, E. (1994). Aging free from negative stereotypes: Successful memory in China and among the American deaf. *Journal of Personality and Social Psychology, 66,* 989–997.

Levy, S. M. (1990). Psychosocial risk factors and cancer progression: Mediating pathways linking behavior and disease. In K. D. Craig & S. M. Weiss (Eds.), *Health enhancement, disease prevention, and early intervention: Biobehavioral perspectives.* New York: Springer.

Levy, S. M., Herberman, R., Maluish, A., Achlien, B., & Lippman, M. (1985). Prognostic risk assessment in primary breast cancer by behavioral and immunological parameters. *Health Psychology, 4,* 99–113.

Levy, S. M., Herberman, R. B., Simons, A., Whiteside, T., Lee, J., McDonald, R., & Beadle, M. (1989). Persistently low natural killer cell activity in normal adults: Immunological, hormonal and mood correlates. *Natural Immune Cell Growth Regulation, 8,* 173–186.

Levy, S. M., Lee, J., Bagley, C., & Lippman, M. (1988). Survival hazards analysis in first recurrent breast cancer patients: Seven-year follow-up. *Psychosomatic Medicine, 50,* 520–528.

Lewandowsky, S., & Murdock, B. B., Jr. (1989). Memory for serial order. *Psychological Review, 96,* 25–57.

Lewin, K. (1947). Group decision and social change. In T. N. Newcomb & E. L. Hartley (Eds.), *Readings in social psychology.* New York: Holt, Rinehart, & Winston.

Lewis, M., Sullivan, M. W., Stanger, C., & Weiss, M. (1989). Self-development and self-consciousness emotions. *Child Development, 60,* 146–156.

Ley, P. (1988). *Communicating with patients.* London: Croom Helm.

Liddell, F. D. K. (1982). Motor vehicle accidents (1973–6) in a cohort of Montreal drivers. *Journal of Epidemiological Community Health, 36,* 140–145.

Liden, R. C., & Mitchell, T. R. (1988). Ingratiatory behaviors in organizational settings. *Academy of Management Review, 13,* 572–587.

Lieberman, D. A. (1990). *Learning: Behavior and cognition.* Belmont, CA: Wadsworth Publishing Company.

Lightdale, J. R., & Prentice, D. A. (1994). Rethinking sex differences aggression: Aggressive behavior in the absence of social roles. *Personality and Social Psychology Bulletin, 20,* 34–44.

Linden, E. (1993, March 22). Can animals think? *Time.*

Lindsley, O. (1992). Precision teaching: Discoveries and effects. *Journal of Applied Behavior Analysis, 25,* 51–57.

Lindy, J. D., Green, B. L., & Grace, M. C. (1987). Commentary: The stressor criterion and post–traumatic stress disorder. *Journal of Nervous and Mental Disease, 175*(5), 269–272.

Linton, M. (1975). Memory for real-world events. In D. A. Norman & D. E. Rumelhart (Eds.), *Explorations in cognition,* chapter 14. San Francisco: Freeman.

Linville, P. W., Fischer, O. W., & Salovey, P. (1989). Perceived distributions of the characteristics of in-group and out-group members: Empirical evidence and a computer simulation. *Journal of Personality and Social Psychology, 57,* 165–188.

Livesley, W. J., Schroeder, M. L., Jackson, D. N., & Jang, K. L. (1994). Categorial distinctions in the study of personality disorder: Implications for classification. *Journal of Abnormal Psychology, 103,* 6–17.

Locke, B. Z., & Slaby, A. E. (1982). Preface. In D. Mechanic (Ed.), *Symptoms, illness behavior, and help-seeking* (pp. xi–xv). New York: Prodist.

Locke, E. A., & Latham, G. P. (1990). *A theory of goal setting and task performance.* Englewood Cliffs, NJ: Prentice Hall.

Locke, E. A., & Schweiger, D. M. (1979) Participation in decision-making: One more look. In B. M. Staw & L. L. Cummings (Eds.), *Research on organizational behavior* (Vol. 1, pp. 265–339). Greenwich, CT: JAI Press.

Loebner, H. G. (1994). In response to Shieber. *Communications of the Association of Computing Machinery, 37,* 79–82

Loftus, E. F. (1991). The glitter of everyday memory . . . and the gold. *American Psychologist, 46,* 16–18.

Loftus, E. F. (1992). When a lie becomes memory's truth: Memory distortion after exposure to misinformation. *Current Directions in Psychological Science, 1,* 121–123.

Loftus, E. F. (1993). The reality of repressed memories. *American Psychologist, 48,* 518–537.

Loftus, E. F., & Coan, D. (in press). The construction of childhood memories. In D. Peters (Ed.), *The child in context: Cognitive, social and legal perspectives.* New York: Kluwer.

Loftus, E. F., & Herzog, C. (1991). Unpublished data, University of Washington. Cited in Loftus, E. F. (1993). The reality of repressed memories. *American Psychologist, 48,* 518–537.

Logan, G. D. (1985). Skill and automaticity: Relations, implications, and future directions. *Canadian Journal of Psychology, 39,* 367–386.

Logan, G. D. (1988). Toward an instance theory of automotization. *Psychological Review, 95,* 492–527.

Logue, A. W. (1979). Taste aversion and the generality of the laws of learning. *Psychological Bulletin, 86,* 27–296.

Logue, A. W., Logue, K. R., & Strauss, K. E. (1983). The acquisition of taste aversion in humans with eating and drinking disorders. *Behavioral Research and Therapy, 21,* 275–289.

Logue, A. W., Ophir, I., & Strauss, K. E. (1981). The acquisition of taste aversion in humans. *Behavior Research and Therapy, 19,* 319–333.

Long, G. M., & Crambert, R. F. (1990). The nature and basis of age-related change in dynamic visual acuity. *Psychology and Aging, 5,* 138–143.

Lonner, W. J., & Malpass, R. (Eds.) (1994). *Psychology and Culture.* Boston: Allyn and Bacon.

Lopez, S. R. (1989). Patient variable biases in clinical judgment: Conceptual overview and methodological considerations. *Psychological Bulletin, 106,* 184–203.

Lovaas, O. I. (1977). *The autistic child: Language development through behavior modification.* New York: Halsted Press.

Lovaas, O. I. (1982). Comments on self-destructive behaviors. *Analysis and Intervention in Developmental Disabilities, 2,* 115–124.

Lubin, J. H., & Blot, W. J. (1993). Lung cancer and smoking cessation: Patterns of risk. *Journal of the National Cancer Institute, 85,* 422–423.

Luborsky, L., Singer, B., & Luborsky, L. (1975). Comparative studies of psychotherapies: Is it true that "everyone has won and all must have prizes"? *Archives of General Psychiatry, 32,* 49–62.

Luchins, A. S. (1942). Mechanization in problem solving. *Psychological Monographs, 54* (whole No. 248).

Lupfer, M. B., Clark, L. F., & Hutcherson, H. W. (1990). Impact of context on spontaneous trait and situational attributions. *Journal of Personality and Social Psychology, 58,* 239–249.

Luthans, F., Paul, R., & Baker, D. (1981). An experimental analysis of the impact of a contingent reinforcement intervention on salespersons' performance behaviors. *Journal of Applied Psychology, 66,* 314–323.

Lykken, D. I. (1957). A study of anxiety in the sociopathic personality. *Journal of Abnormal and Social Psychology, 55,* 6–10.

Lykken, D. T. (1985). The probity of the polygraph. In S. M. Kassin & L. S. Wrightsman (Eds.), *The psychology of evidence and trial procedure.* Beverly Hills, CA: Sage.

Lykken, D. T., McGue, M., Tellegen, A., & Bouchard, T. J. (1992). Emergenesis: Genetic traits that may not run in families. *American Psychologist, 47,* 1565–1577.

Lyman, B. J., & McDaniel, M. A. (1986). Effects of encoding strategy on long-term memory for odours. *Quarterly Journal of Experimental Psychology, 38A,* 753–765.

Lyman, B. J., & McDaniel, M. A. (1987, April). *Effects of experimenter and subject provided verbal and visual elaborations on long-term memory for odors.* Paper presented at the annual meeting of the Eastern Psychological Association, Arlington, VA.

Lyness, S. A. (1993). Predictors of differences between Type A and B individuals in heart rate and blood pressure reactivity. *Psychological Bulletin, 114,* 266–295.

Lynn, S. J., & Rhue, J. W. (1986). The fantasy-prone person: Hypnosis, imagination, and creativity. *Journal of Personality and Social Psychology, 51,* 404–408.

Lynn, S. J., Rhue, J. W., & Weekes, J. R. (1990). Hypnotic involuntariness: A social cognitive analysis. *Psychological Review, 974,* 169–184

Maccoby, E. E. (1990). Gender relationships: A developmental account. *American Psychologist, 45,* 513-520.

Maccoby, E. E., & Jacklin, C. N. (1987). Gender segregation in childhood. In H. W. Reese (Ed.), *Advances in child development and behavior* (Vol. 20, pp. 239–288). New York: Academic Press.

Macguire, P., Fairburn, S., & Fletcher, C. (1986). Consultation skills of young doctors: I. Benefits of feedback training in interviewing as students persists. *British Medical Journal, 292,* 1573–1576.

Mackay, A. V. P., Iversen, L. L., Rossor, M., Spokes, E., Bird, E., Arregui, A., Creese, I., & Snyder, S. (1982). Increased brain dopamine and dopamine receptors in schizophrenia. *Archives of General Psychiatry, 39,* 991–997.

Mackie, D. M., & Worth, L. T. (1989). Processing deficits and the mediation of positive affect in persuasion. *Journal of Personality and Social Psychology, 57,* 27–40.

Macrae, C. N. (1992). A tale of two curries: Counterfactual thinking and accident-related judgments. *Personality and Social Psychology Bulletin, 18,* 84–87.

Maher, B. A., & Maher, W. B. (1985). Psychopathology: II. From the eighteenth century to modern times. In G. A. Kimble & K. Schlesinger (Eds.), *Topics in the history of psychology* (Vol. 2). Hillsdale, NJ: Erlbaum.

Mahoney, M. J. (1991). *Human change process: The scientific foundations of psychotherapy.* New York: Basic Books.

Maier, S. F., & Jackson, R. L. (1979). Learned helplessness: All of us were right (and wrong): Inescapable shock has multiple effects. In G. H. Bower (Ed.), *The psychology of learning and motivation* (Vol. 13). New York: Academic Press.

Major, B., Carnevale, P. J. D., & Deaux, K. (1981). A different perspective on androgyny: Evaluation of masculine and feminine personality characteristics. *Journal of Personality and Social Psychology, 41,* 988–1001.

Makita, M., & Sakamoto, G. (1990). Natural history of breast cancer among Japanese and Caucasian females. *Gan-To-Kagaku-Ryoho, 17,* 1239–1243.

Malinowski, B. (1927). *Sex and repression in savage society.* London: Humanities Press.

Malpass, R. S., & Devine, P. G. (1981). Guided memory in eyewitness identification research. *Journal of Applied Psychology, 66,* 343–350.

Mann, J. (1992). *AIDS in the world 1992: A global epidemic out of control?* Report of the Global AIDS Policy Coalition. Cambridge, MA: Harvard University School of Public Health.

Mann, L. M., Chassin, L., & Sher, K. J. (1987). Alcohol, expectancies and risk for alcoholism. *Journal of Consulting and Clinical Psychology, 55,* 411–417.

Mann, T. (1994). Informed consent for psychological research: Do subjects comprehend consent forms and understand their legal rights? *Psychological Science, 5,* 140–143.

Marek, G. R. (1975). *Toscanini.* London: Vision Press.

Margolin, G., & Wampold, B. E. (1981). Sequential analysis of conflict and accord in distressed and non-distressed marital partners. *Journal of Consulting and Clinical Psychology, 49,* 554–567.

Marks, G., & Miller, N. (1987). Ten years of research on the false-consensus effect: An empirical and theoretical review. *Psychology Bulletin, 8,* 728–735.

Marks, I. (1994). Behavior therapy as an aid to self-care. *Current Directions in Psychological Science, 3,* 19–22.

Markus, H. M. & Nurius, P. (1986). Possible selves. *American Psychologist, 41,* 954–969.

Marlatt, G. A., Baer, J. S., Donovan, D. M., & Kivlahan, D. R. (1988). Addictive behaviors: Etiology and treatment. *Annual Review of Psychology, 58,* 265–272.

Marr, D. (1982). *Vision: A computational investigation into the human representation and processing of visual information.* San Francisco: W. H. Freeman.

Martin, C. L., & Little, J. K. (1990). The relation of gender understanding to children's sex-typed preferences and gender stereotypes. *Child Development, 61,* 1427–1439.

Martin, M. (1986). Individual differences in sensation seeking and attentional ability. *Personality and Individual Differences, 6,* 637–649.

Martin, M., Williams, R., & Clark, D. (1991). Does anxiety lead to selective processing of threat-related information? *Behaviour Research and Therapy, 29,* 147–160.

Martin, R. L., Cloninger, R., Guze, S. B., & Clayton, P. J. (1985). Mortality in a follow-up of 500 psychiatric outpatients: I. Total mortality. *Archives of General Psychiatry, 42,* 47–54.

Marzetta, B. R., Benson, H., & Wallace, R. K. (1972). Combatting drug dependency in young people: A new approach. *Medical Counterpoint, 4,* 13–37.

Maser, J. D., Kaelber, C., & Weise, R. E. (1991). International use and attitudes toward DSM-III and DSM-III-R: Growing consensus in psychiatric classification. *Journal of Abnormal Psychology, 100,* 271–279.

Maslach, C. (1982). *Burnout: The cost of caring.* Englewood Cliffs, NJ: Prentice-Hall.

Maslach, C., & Jackson, S. E. (1984). Burnout in organizational settings. In S. Oskamp (Ed.), *Applied social psychology annual* (Vol. 5, pp. 135–154). Beverly Hills: Sage.

Maslow, A. H. (1970). *Motivation and personality* (2nd ed.). New York: Harper & Row.

Masters, W. H., & Johnson, V. E. (1966). *Human sexual response.* Boston: Little, Brown.

Matarazzo, J. D. (1980). Behavioral health and behavioral medicine: Frontiers for a new health psychology. *American Psychologist, 35,* 807–817.

Matarrazo, J. D. (1992). Psychological testing and assessment in the 21st century. *American Psychologist, 47,* 1007–1018.

Mathews, A. (1990). Why worry? The cognitive function of anxiety. *Behavior Research and Therapy, 28,* 455–468.

Matlin, M. E. (1990). *Cognition* (3rd ed.). New York: Holt, Rinehart & Winston.

Matlin, M. W., & Foley, H. J. (1992). *Sensation and perception* (3rd ed.). Needham Heights, MA: Allyn and Bacon.

Matthews, K. A. (1988). Coronary heart disease and Type A behaviors: Update on and alternative to the Booth-Kewley and Friedman (1987) quantitative review. *Psychological Bulletin, 104,* 373–380.

Maturi, R. (1992, July 20). Stress can be beaten. *Industry Week,* pp. 23–26.

Maupin, H. E., & Fisher, R. J. (1989). The effects of superior female performance and sex-role orientation on gender conformity. *Canadian Journal of Behavioral Science, 21,* 55–69.

Maurer, D., & Barrera, M. (1981). Infants' perception of natural and distorted arrangements of a schematic face. *Child Development, 52,* 196–202.

Maurice, P., & Trudel, G. (1982). Self-injurious behavior prevalence and relationships to environmental events. In J. H. Hollis & C. E. Meyers (Eds.), *Life-threatening behavior: Analysis and intervention.*

Washington, DC: American Association on Mental Deficiency, Monograph No. 5, 81–103.

May, C. P., Hasher, L., & Stoltzfus, E. R. (1993). Optimal time of day and the magnitude of age differences in memory. *Psychological Science, 4*, 326–330.

Mayer, R. E., Tajika, H., & Stanley, C. (1991). Mathematical problem solving in Japan and the United States: A controlled comparison. *Journal of Educational Psychology, 1*, 69–72.

Mazursky, D., & Ofir, C. (1990). "I could never have expected it to happen": The reversal of the hindsight bias. *Organizational Behavior and Human Decision Processes, 46*, 20–33.

McCall, R. B. (1994). Academic underachievers. *Current Directions in Psychological Science, 3*, 13–19.

McCann, S. J. H. (1992). Alternative formulas to predict the greatness of U.S. presidents: Personological, situational, and zeitgeist factors. *Journal of Personality and Social Psychology, 62*, 469–479.

McCanne, T. R., & Anderson, J. A. (1987). Emotional responding following experimental manipulation of facial electromyographic activity. *Journal of Personality and Social Psychology, 52*, 759–768.

McCarley, R. W., & Hobson, R. W. (1981). REM sleep dreams and the activation hypothesis. *American Journal of Psychiatry, 138*, 904–912.

McCarthy, R. L., Finnegan, J. P., Krumm-Scott, S., & McCarthy, G. E. (1984). Product information presentation, user behavior, and safety. In *Proceedings of the Human Factors Society 28th Annual Meeting* (pp. 81–85). Santa Monica, CA: Human Factors Society.

McClearn, G. E., Plomin, R., Gora-Maslak, G., & Crabbe, J. C. (1991). The gene chase in behavioral science. *Psychological Science, 2*, 222–229.

McClelland, D. C. (1961). *The achieving society.* Princeton, NJ: Van Nostrand.

McClelland, D. C. (1975). *Power: The inner experience.* New York: Irvington.

McClelland, D. C., Atkinson, J. W., Clark, R. W., & Lowell, E. L. (1953). *The achievement motive.* New York: Appleton-Century-Crofts.

McConkie, G. W., Kerr, P. W., Reddix, M. D., Zola, D., & Jacobs, A. M. (1989). Eye movement control during reading: II. Frequency of refixating a word. *Perception & Psychophysics, 46*, 245–253.

McConkie, G. W., & Zola, D. (1984). Eye movement control during reading. The effect of word units. In W. Prinz & A. F. Sanders (Eds.), *Cognition and motor processes* (pp. 63–74). Berlin: Springer-Verlag.

McCrae, R. R. (1989). Why I advocate the five-factor model. Joint factor analyses of the NEO-PI with other instruments. In D. M. Buss & N. Cantor (Eds.), *Personality psychology: Recent trends and emerging directions* (pp. 237–245). New York: Springer-Verlag.

McEwan, N. H., & Yuille, J. C. (1982). *The effect of hypnosis as an interview technique on eyewitness memory.* Paper presented at annual meeting of the Canadian Psychological Association, Montreal.

McFarland, C., Ross, M., & DeCourville, N. (1989). Women's theories of menstruation and biases in recall of menstrual symptoms. *Journal of Personality and Social Psychology, 576*, 522–531.

McGinnis, R. (1958). Campus values in mate selection: A repeat study. *Social Forces, 36*, 368–373.

McGrath, J. E., & Cohen, D. B. (1978). REM sleep facilitation of adaptive waking behavior: A review of the literature. *Psychological Bulletin, 85*, 24–57.

McGue, M., & Lykken, D. T. (1992). Genetic influence on risk of divorce. *Psychological Science, 3*, 368–373.

McGuire, J. (1988). Gender stereotypes of parents with two-year-olds and beliefs about gender differences in behavior. *Sex Roles, 19*, 233–240.

McKenna, S. P., & Glendon, A. I. (1985). Occupational first aid training: Decay in cardiopulmonary resuscitation (CPR) skills. *Journal of Occupational Psychology, 58*, 109–117.

McKenry, P. C., Kotch, J. B., & Browne, D. H. (1991). Correlates of dysfunctional parenting attitudes among low-income adolescent mothers. *Journal of Adolescent Research, 6*, 212–234.

McKey, R., Condelli, L., Ganson, H., Barrett, B., McConkey, C., & Plantz, M. (1985). *The impact of Head Start on children, families, and communities: Final report of the Head Start Evaluation, Synthesis and Utilization Project* (No. OHDS 85-31193). Washington, DC: U.S. Government Printing Office.

McMillan, M. (1988). The doll test studies—from cabbage patch to self-concept. *Journal of Black Psychology, 25*, 69–72.

McNeal, E. T., & Cimbolic, P. (1986). Antidepressants and biochemical theories of depression. *Psychological Bulletin, 99*, 361–374.

McReynolds, W. T. (1980). Learned helplessness as a schedule-shift effect. *Journal of Research in Personality, 14*, 139–157.

Medin, D. L., & Ross, B. H. (1992). *Cognitive psychology.* Fort Worth, TX: Harcourt Brace Jovanovich.

Meehan, P. J., Lamb, J. A., Saltzman, L. E., & O'Carroll, P. W. (1992). Attempted suicide among young adults: Progress towards a meaningful estimate of prevalence. *American Journal of Psychiatry, 149*, 41–44.

Meichenbaum, D. H. (1977). *Cognitive-behavior modification.* New York: Plenum.

Meier, S. T. (1991). Vocational behavior, 1988–1990: Vocational choice, decision-making, career development interventions, and assessment. *Journal of Vocational Behavior, 39*, 459–484.

Melamed, S., Kushnir, T., & Shirom, A. (1992). Burnout and risk factors for cardiovascular diseases. *Behavioral Medicine, 18*, 53–60.

Meleshko, K. G. A., & Alden, L. E. (1993). Anxiety and self-disclosure: Toward a motivational model. *Journal of Personality and Social Psychology, 64*, 1000–1009.

Meltzoff, A. N. (1990). Towards a developmental cognitive science: The implications of cross-modal matching and imitation for the development of representation and memory in infancy. In A. Diamond (Ed.), *Annals of the New York Academy of Sciences: Vol. 608. The development and neural bases of higher cognitive functions* (pp. 1–37). New York: New York Academy of Sciences.

Meltzoff, A. N., & Moore, M. K. (1977). Imitation of facial and manual gestures by human neonates. *Science, 198*, 75–78.

Meltzoff, A. N., & Moore, M. K. (1989). Imitation in newborn infants: Exploring the range of gestures imitated and the underlying mechanisms. *Developmental Psychology, 25*, 954–962.

Melzack, R. (1976). Pain: Past, present, and future. In M. Weisenberg & B. Tursky (Eds.), *Pain: New perspectives in therapy and research.* New York: Plenum.

Melzack, R. (1990, Special Issue). The tragedy of needless pain. *Medicine,* pp. 45–51.

Melzack, R., & Wall, P. D. (1982). *The challenge of pain.* New York: Basic.

Mendolia, M., & Kleck, R. E. (1993). Effects of talking about a stressful event on arousal: Does what we talk about make a difference? *Journal of Personality and Social Psychology, 64*, 283–292.

Merikle, P. M. (1992). Perception without awareness. *American Psychologist, 47*, 792–795.

Merritt, T. A. (1981). Smoking mothers affect little lives. *American Journal of Diseases of Children, 135*, 501–502.

Merson, M. H. (1993). Slowing the spread of HIV: Agenda for the 1990s. *Science, 260*, 1266–1268.

Mestre, D. R., Brouchon, M., Ceccaldi, M., & Poncet, M. (1992). Perception of optical flow in cortical blindness: A case report. *Neuropsychologia, 30*, 783–795.

Metzger, A. M. (1980). A methodological study of the Kübler-Ross stage theory. *Omega, 10*, 291–301.

Meyer, A. J., Maccoby, N., & Farquhar, J. W. (1980). Skills training in a cardiovascular health education campaign. *Journal of Consulting and Clinical Psychology, 48*, 129–142.

Meyer, J. P., Allen, J. J., & Smith, C. A. (1993). Commitment to organizations and occupations: Extension and test of a three-component conceptualization. *Journal of Applied Psychology, 78*, 538–551.

Miceli, M. P., & Lane, M. C. (1991). Antecedents of pay satisfaction: A review and extensions. In K. Rowland & O. R. Ferris (Eds.), *Research in personnel and human resources management* (Vol. 9, pp. 235–309). Greenwich, CT: JAI Press.

Miklowitz, D. J., Goldstein, M. J., Doane, J. A., Neuchterlein, K. H., Strachan, A. M., Snyder, K. S., & Magana-Amato, A. (1989). Is expressed emotion an index of a transactional process? I. Parents' affective style. *Family Process, 22*, 153–167.

Milgram, S. (1963). Behavioral study of obedience. *Journal of Abnormal and Social Psychology, 67*, 371–378.

Milgram, S. (1974). *Obedience to authority.* New York: Harper.

Millan, M. J. (1986). Multiple opioid systems and pain. *Pain, 27*, 303–347.

Miller, D. T., & McFarland, C. (1987). Counterfactual thinking and victim compensation: A test of norm theory. *Personality and Social Psychology Bulletin, 12*, 513–519.

Miller, D. T., & Prentice, D. B. (1994). The self and the collective. *Personality and Social Psychology Bulletin, 20,* 451–453.

Miller, D. T., & Ross, M. (1975). Self-serving biases in attribution of causality: Fact or fiction? *Psychological Bulletin, 82,* 313–325.

Miller, K. (1994, March 17). Safety quiz: Insurance-claims data don't show advantage of some auto devices. *Wall Street Journal,* pp. Al, A7.

Miller, L. (1987). The emotional brain. *Psychology Today, 22,* 35–42.

Miller, L. L., Cornelius, T., & McFarland, D. (1978). Marijuana: An analysis of storage and retrieval deficits in memory with the technique of restricted reminding. *Pharmacology, Biochemistry, and Behavior, 8,* 441–457.

Miller, M. E., & Bowers, K. S. (1993). Hypnotic analgesia: Dissociated experience or dissociated control? *Journal of Abnormal Psychology, 102,* 29–38.

Miller, N. E. (1985). The value of behavioral research on animals. *American Psychologist, 40,* 423–440.

Miller, N., Maruyama, G., Beaber, R. J., & Valone, K. (1976). Speed of speech and persuasion. 615–624.

Miller, P. H., & Zalenski, R. (1982). Preschoolers' knowledge about attention. *Developmental Psychology, 18,* 871–875.

Miller, R. S. (1991). On decorum in close relationships: Why aren't we polite to those we love? *Contemporary Social Psychology, 15,* 63–65.

Millon, T. (1991). Classification psychopathology: Rationale, alternatives, and standards. *Journal of Abnormal Psychology, 100,* 245–261.

Milner, B. (1974). Hemispheric specialization: Scope and limits. In F. O. Schmitt & F. G. Worden (Eds.), *The neurosciences: Third study program* (pp. 75–89). Cambridge, MA: MIT Press.

Milner, B., Corkin, S., & Teuber, H. L. (1968) Further analysis of the hippocampal amnesic syndrome: 14-year follow-up study of H. M. *Neuropsychologia, 6,* 317–338.

Minami, H., & Dallenbach, K. M. (1946). The effect of activity upon learning and retention in the cockroach. *American Journal of Psychology, 59,* 1–58.

Minkoff, H., Deepak, N., Menez, R., & Fikrig, S. (1987). Pregnancies resulting in infants with acquired immunodeficiency syndrome or AIDS-related complex: Follow-up of mothers, children, and subsequently born siblings. *Obstetrics and Gynecology, 69,* 288–291.

Minuchin, P., & Shapiro, E. K. (1983). The school as a context for social development. In P. Mussen & E. M. Heatherington (Eds.), *Handbook of child psychology* (Vol. 4, 4th ed., pp. 197–172). New York: Wiley.

Minuchin, S., & Fishman, H. C. (1981). *Family therapy techniques.* Cambridge, MA: Harvard University Press.

Mischel, W. (1977). On the future of personality measurement. *American Psychologist, 32,* 246–254.

Mischel, W. (1985). *Personality: Lost or found? Identifying when individual differences make a difference.* Paper presented at the meetings of the American Psychological Association, Los Angeles.

Mistler-Lachman, J. L. (1975). Queer sentences, ambiguity, and levels of processing. *Memory and Cognition, 3,* 395–400.

Mitchell, D. J., Russo, J. E., & Pennington, N. (1989). Back to the future: Temporal perspective in the explanation of events. *Journal of Behavioral Decision Making. 2,* 25–38.

Mitchell, H. (1988, February). Why are women still dying of cervical cancer? *Australian Society,* pp. 34–35.

Mitchell, T. R. (1983). Expectancy-value models in organizational psychology. In N. Feather (Ed.), *Expectancy, incentive, and action* (pp. 293–314). Hillsdale, NJ: Erlbaum.

Mitchell, T. R., Green, S. G., & Wood, R. S. (1982). An attributional model of leadership and the poor performing subordinate: Development and validation. In B. M. Staw and L. L. Cummings (Eds.), *Research in organizational behavior* (Vol. 3). Greenwich, CT: JAI Press.

Mitchell, T. R., & Larson, J. R., Jr. (1987). *People in organizations: An introduction to organizational behavior* (3rd ed.). New York: McGraw-Hill.

Miura, I., & Okamoto, Y. (1989). Comparisons of U.S. and Japanese first graders' cognitive representation of number and understanding of place value. *Journal of Educational Psychology, 81,* 109–113.

Mogg, K., Bradley, B. P., Williams, R., & Mathews, A. (1993). Subliminal processing of emotional information in anxiety and depression. *Journal of Abnormal Psychology, 102,* 304–311.

Money, J. (1980). *Love and love sickness.* Baltimore: Johns Hopkins University Press.

Money, J. (1985). *Pornography as related to criminal sex offenses and the history of medical degeneracy theory.* Paper presented at the U.S. Justice Department Hearings, Houston.

Money, J., & Ehrhardt, A. A. (1972). *Man and woman, boy and girl.* Baltimore: Johns Hopkins University Press.

Monk, T. H., & Folkard, S. (1983). Circadian rhythms and shiftwork. In G. R. J. Hockey (Ed.), *Stress and fatigue in human performance* (pp. 97–121). New York: Wiley.

Monroe, L. R. (1990, January 3). Listen to the music: Headsets for children strike a harmful note. *Los Angeles Times,* p. 3.

Moore, B. C. J. (1982). *An introduction to the psychology of hearing* (2nd ed.). New York: Academic.

Moore, R. Y., & Card, J. P. (1985). Visual pathways and the entrainment of circadian rhythms: The medical and biological effects of light. In R. J. Wurtman, M. J. Baum, J. T. Potts, Jr. (Eds.), *Annals of the New York Academy of Science, 453,* 123–133.

Moore-Ede, M. C., Sulzman, F. M., & Fuller, C. A. (1982). *The clocks that time us.* Cambridge, MA: Harvard University Press.

Moran, J. S., Janes, H. R., Peterman, T. A., & Stone, K. M. (1990). Increase in condom sales following AIDS education and publicity, United States. *American Journal of Public Health, 80,* 607–608.

Moray, N. (1959). Attention in dichotic listening: Affective cues and the influence of instruction. *Quarterly Journal of Experimental Psychology, 11,* 59–60.

Moreland, R. L., & Beach, S. R. (1992). Exposure effects in the classroom: the development of affinity among students. *Journal of Experimental Social Psychology, 28,* 255–276.

Morganstern, K. P. (1973). Implosive therapy and flooding procedures: A critical review. *Psychological Bulletin, 79,* 318–334.

Morinaga, Y., Frieze, I. H., & Ferligoj, A. (1993). Career plans and gender-role attitudes of college students in the United States, Japan, and Slovenia. *Sex Roles, 29,* 317–334.

Morris, C. G. (1990). *Contemporary psychology and effective behavior* (7th ed.). New York: Harper Collins Publishers.

Morris, W. N., & Miller, R. S. (1975). The effects of consensus-breaking and consensus-preempting partners on reduction of conformity. *Journal of Personality and Social Psychology, 11,* 215–223.

Morrison, R. L., Bellack, A. S., & Mueser, K. T. (1988). Deficits in facial-affect recognition in schizophrenia. *Schizophrenia Bulletin, 14,* 67–83.

Morrongiello, B. A., & Clifton, R. K. (1984). Effects of sound frequency on behavioral and cardiac orienting in newborn and five-month-old infants. *Journal of Experimental Child Psychology, 38,* 429–446.

Morrow, K. B., & Sorell G. T. (1989). Factors affecting self-esteem, depression, and negative behaviors in sexually abused female adolescents. *Journal of Marriage and the Family, 51,* 677–686.

Morse, J. M., & Morse, R. M. (1988). Cultural variation in the inference of pain. *Journal of Cross Cultural Psychology, 19,* 232–242.

Moscovitch, M. (1985). Memory from infancy to old age: Implications for theories of normal and pathological memory. *Annals of the New York Academy of Sciences, 444,* 79–96.

Motley, M. T., & Camden, C. T. (1985). Nonlinguistic influences on lexical selection: Evidence from double entendres. *Communication Monographs, 52,* 124–135.

Motowidlo, S. J., Packard, J. S., & Manning, M. R. (1986). Occupational stress: Its causes and consequences for job performance. *Journal of Applied Psychology, 71,* 618–629.

Mowrer, O. H., & Jones, H. M. (1945). Habit strength as a function of the pattern of reinforcement. *Journal of Experimental Psychology, 35,* 293–311.

Mullaney, D. J., Johnson, L. C., Naitoh, P., Friedman, J. K., & Globus, G. G. (1977). Sleep during and after gradual sleep reduction. *Psychophysiology, 14,* 237–244.

Mumford, M. D., O'Connor, J., Clifton, T. C., Connelly, M. S., & Zaccaro, S. J. (in press). Background data constructs as predictors of leadership behavior. *Human Performance.*

Munakata, T. (1994). Commercial and Industrial AI. *Communications of the Association of Computing Machinery, 37,* 23–25.

Munsinger, H. A. (1978). The adopted child's IQ: A crucial review. *Psychological Bulletin, 82,* 623–659.

Murdoch, D. D., & Pihl, R. O. (1988). The influence of beverage type on aggression in males in the natural setting. *Aggressive Behavior, 14,* 325–335.

Murphy K. R., & Cleveland, N. J. (1991). *Performance appraisal: An organizational perspective.* Boston: Allyn and Bacon.

Murphy, K. R., Jako, R. A., & Anhalt, R. L. (1993). Nature and consequences of halo error: A critical analysis. *Journal of Applied Psychology, 78,* 218–225.

Murrey, G. J., Cross, H. J., & Whipple, J. (1992). Hypnotically created pseudomemories: Further investigation into the "memory distortion or response bias" question. *Journal of Abnormal Psychology, 101,* 75–77.

Nadis, S. (1992, February). The energy-efficient brain: PET scans reveal how the brain delegates mental tasks. *Omni,* p. 16.

Naeser, M. A., Hayward, R. W., Laughlin, S. A., & Zatz, L. M. (1981). Quantitative CT scan studies in aphasia. *Brain and Language, 12,* 140–164.

Nagar, D., & Pandey, J. (1987). Affect and performance on cognitive task as a function of crowding and noise. *Journal of Applied Social Psychology, 17,* 141–157.

Nagar, D., Pandey, J., & Paulus, P. B. (1988). The effects of residential crowding experience on reactivity to laboratory crowding and noise. *Journal of Applied Social Psychology, 18,* 1423–1442.

Naglieri, J. A., & Das, J. P. (1990). Planning, attention, simultaneous and successive (PASS) cognitive processes. *Journal of Psychoeducational Assessment, 8,* 303–337.

Nash, J. E., & Persaud, T. V. N. (1988). Embryopathic risks of cigarette smoking. *Experimental Pathology, 33,* 65–73.

Nathan, B. R., & Tippins, N. (1990). The consequences of halo "error" in performance ratings: A field study of the moderating effects of halo on test validation results. *Journal of Applied Psychology, 75,* 290–296.

Nathans, J. (1989). The genes for color vision. *Scientific American, 260,* 42–49.

Nathans, J., Thomas, D., & Hogness, D. S. (1986). Molecular genetics of human color vision: The genes encoding blue, green, and red pigments. *Science, 232,* 193–202.

National Association of Secondary School Principals. (1984). *The mood of American youth.* Reston, VA: Author.

National Center for Education in Maternal and Child Health. (1990). *The health of America's youth.* Washington, DC: Author.

National Institutes of Mental Health. (1985). *Electroconvulsive therapy: Consensus development conference statement.* Bethesda, MD: Office of Medical Applications of Research.

Navarro, R. (1990). *Sound pressure levels of portable stereo headphones.* Indianapolis: Ear Institute of Indiana.

Neale, J. H., Barker, J. L., Uhl, G. R., & Snyder, S. H. (1978). Enkephalin-containing neurons visualized in spinal cord cultures. *Science, 201,* 467–469.

Neale, M. A., & Bazerman, M. H. (1985). The effects of framing and negotiator overconfidence on bargaining behaviors and outcomes. *Academy of Management Journal, 28,* 34–49.

Nebeker, D. M., & Tatum, B. C. (1993). The effects of computer monitoring, standards, and rewards on work performance, job satisfaction, and stress. *Journal of Applied Social Psychology, 23,* 508–536.

Neimeyer, G. J., & Banikiotes, P. G. (1981). Self-disclosure flexibility, empathy, and perceptions of adjustment and attraction. *Journal of Counseling Psychology, 28,* 272–275.

Neisser, U. (1991). A case of misplaced nostalgia. *American Psychologist, 46,* 34–36.

Nelson, M. J., Lamke, T. A., & French, J. L. (1973). *The Henmon-Nelson Tests of Mental Ability.* Riverside, CA: Riverside Publishing.

Neugarten, B. L. (1979). Time, age, and the life cycle. *American Journal of Psychiatry, 136,* 887–894.

Neugarten, B. L. (1987). The changing meaning of age. *Psychology Today, 21,* 29–33.

Newell, A., & Rosenbloom, P. S. (1981). Mechanisms of skill acquisition and the law of practice. In J. R. Anderson (Ed.), *Cognitive skills and their acquisition* (pp. 1–55). Hillsdale, NJ: Erlbaum.

Newman, J. P., Widom, C. S., & Nathan, S. (1985). Passive avoidance in syndromes of disinhibition: Psychopathy and extraversion. *Journal of Personality and Social Psychology, 48,* 1316–1327.

Nicole, S. E., & Gottesman, I. I. (1983). Clues to the genetics and neurobiology of schizophrenia. *American Scientist, 71,* 398–404.

Niedenthal, P. M. (1990). Implicit perception of affective information. *Journal of Experimental Social Psychology, 26,* 505–527.

Nietzel, M. T., & Himelein, M. J. (1986). Prevention of crime and delinquency. In B. A. Edelstein and L. Mitchelson (Eds.), *Handbook of prevention.* New York: Plenum.

Nilsson, L. G., & Cohen, R. L. (1988). Enrichment and generation in the recall of enacted and non-enacted instructions. In M. M. Gruneberg, P. E. Morris, & R. N. Sykes (Eds.), *Practical aspects of memory: Current research and issues: Vol. 1. Memory in everyday life* (pp. 427–432). Chichester, England: John Wiley & Sons.

Nisbett, R. E. (1990). Evolutionary psychology, biology, and cultural evolution. *Motivation and Emotion, 14,* 255–263.

Noble, B. P. (1993, June 13). Staying bright-eyed in the wee hours. *New York Times,* pp. F1, F11.

Nolen-Hoeksema, S. (1987). Sex differences in unipolar depression: Evidence and theory. *Psychological Bulletin, 101,* 259–282.

Nolen-Hoeksema, S. (1990). *Sex differences in depression.* Stanford, CA: Stanford University Press.

Noller, P., Law, H., & Comrey A. L. (1987). Cattell, Comrey, and Eysenck personality factors compared: More evidence for the five robust factors? *Journal of Personality and Social Psychology, 53,* 775–782.

Norman, D. A., & Shallice, T. (1985). Attention to action: Willed and automatic control of behavior. In R. J. Davidson, G. E. Schwartz, & D. Shapiro (Eds.), *Consciousness and self-regulation: Vol. 4. Advances in research and theory* (pp. 2–18). New York: Plenum Press.

Norris, F. H., & Murrell, S. A. (1990). Social support, life events, and stress as modifiers of adjustment to bereavement by older adults. *Psychology and Aging, 5,* 429–436.

Norris, F. H., & Uhl, G. A. (1993). Chronic stress as a mediator of acute stress: The case of hurricane Hugo. *Journal of Applied Social Psychology, 23,* 1263–1284.

Northcraft, G. B., & Neale, M. A. (1987). Experts, amateurs, and real estate: An anchoring-and-adjustment perspective on property pricing in decision. *Organizational Behavior and Human Decision Processes, 39,* 94–97.

Norton, A., & Moorman, J. E. (1987). Current trends in marriage and divorce among American women. *Journal of Marriage and the Family, 49,* 3–14.

Novick, B. E. (1989). Pediatric AIDS: A medical overview. In J. M. Seibert & R. A. Olson (Eds.), *Children, adolescents, and AIDS* (pp. 1–23). Lincoln: University of Nebraska Press.

Nyhan, W. L. (1987). Phenylalanine and mental retardation (PKU). In G. Adelman (Ed.), *Encyclopedia of neuroscience* (Vol. 2, pp. 940–942). Boston: Birkhauser.

Offer, D., & Sabshin, M. (1984). Adolescence: empirical perspectives. In D. Offer & M. Sabshin (Eds.), *Normality and the life cycle.* New York: Basic Books.

Ofshe, R. J. (1992). Inadvertent hypnosis during interrogation: False confession due to dissociative state, misidentified multiple personality, and the satanic cult hypothesis. *International Journal of Clinical and Experimental Hypnosis, 40,* 125–156.

Ogloff, J. R., & Wong, S. (1990). Electrodermal and cardiovascular evidence of a coping response in psychopaths. *Criminal Justice and Behavior, 17,* 231–245.

Oliver, M. B., & Hyde, J. S. (1993). Gender differences in sexuality: A meta-analysis. *Psychological Bulletin, 114,* 29–51.

Olsson, P. A. (1989). Psychodrama and group therapy approaches to alexithymia. In D. A. Halperin (Ed.), *Group Psychodynamics: New paradigms and new perspectives.* Chicago: Year Book Medical.

O'Neill, P., Duffy, C., Enman, M., Blackmer, E., & Goodwin, J. (1988). Cognition and citizen participation in social action. *Journal of Applied Social Psychology, 18,* 1067–1083.

Orbach, I., Kedem, P., Gorchover, O., Apter, A., & Tyano, S. (1993). Fears of death in suicidal and nonsuicidal adolescents. *Journal of Abnormal Psychology, 102,* 553–558.

Organ, D. W. (1988). *Organizational citizenship behavior: The good soldier syndrome.* Lexington, MA: Lexington Books.

Orlinsky, D. E., & Howard, K. E. (1987). The relation of process to outcome in psychotherapy. In S. L. Garfield & A. E. Bergin (Eds.), *Handbook of psychotherapy and behavior change* (3rd ed.). New York: Wiley.

Orlofsky, J. L., & O'Heron, C. A. (1987). Stereotypic and nonstereotypic sex role trait and behavior orientations: Implications for personal adjustment. *Journal of Personality and Social Psychology, 52,* 1034–1042.

Osborne, D., & Ellingstad, V. (1987). Using sensory lines to show control-display linkages on a four-burner stove. *Proceedings of the Human Factors Society 31st Annual Meeting* (pp. 581–584). Santa Monica, CA: Human Factors Society.

Osterwell, Z., & Nagano-Nakamura, I. K. (1992). Maternal views on aggression: Japan and Israel. *Aggressive Behavior, 18,* 263–270.

Ostroff, C. (1992). The relationship between satisfaction, attitudes and performance: An organizational level analysis. *Journal of Applied Psychology, 77,* 963–974.

Otaki, M., Durrett, M., Richards, P., Nyquist, L., & Pennebaker, J. (1986). Maternal and infant behavior in Japan and America: A partial replication. *Journal of Cross-Cultural Psychology, 17,* 251–268.

Otis, A. S., & Lennon, R. T. (1967). *The Otis-Lennon Mental Ability Tests.* Los Angeles: Psychological Corp.

Otsubo, S. M. (1988). A behavioral study of warning labels for consumer products: Perceived danger and use of pictographs. *Proceedings of the Human Factors Society, 32,* 536–540.

Oulette-Kobasa, S. C., & Puccetti, M. C. (1983). Personality and social resources in stress resistance. *Journal of Personality and Social Psychology, 45,* 836–850.

Pace, G. M., Iwata, B. A., Cowdery, G. E., Andree, P. J., & McIntyre, T. (1993). Stimulus (instructional) fading during extinction of self-injurious escape behavior. *Journal of Applied Behavior Analysis, 26,* 205–212.

Page, J. B., Fletcher, J., & True, W. R. (1988). Psychosociocultural perspectives on chronic cannabis use: The Costa Rica follow-up. *Journal of Psychoactive Drugs, 20,* 57–65.

Page, N. R., & Wiseman, R. L. (1993). Supervisory behavior and worker satisfaction in the United States, Mexico, and Spain. *Journal of Business Communication, 30,* 161–180.

Pagelow, M. D. (1984). *Family violence.* New York: Praeger.

Palmer, S. E. (1992). Common region: A new principle of perceptual grouping. *Cognitive Psychology, 24,* 436–447.

Park, B., & Fink, C. (1989). A social relations analysis of agreement in liking judgments. *Journal of Personality and Social Psychology, 56,* 506–518.

Parker, L. E., & Lepper, M. R. (1992). The effects of fantasy contexts on children's learning and motivation: Making learning more fun. *Journal of Personality and Social Psychology, 62,* 625–633.

Passman, R. H., & Weisberg, P. (1975). Mothers and blankets as agents for promoting play and exploration by young children in a novel environment: The effects of social and nonsocial attachment objects. *Developmental Psychology, 11,* 170–177.

Pastor, D. L. (1981). The quality of mother-infant attachment and its relationship to toddlers' initial sociability with peers. *Developmental Psychology, 17,* 326–335.

Patrick, C. J., Bradley, M. M., & Lang, P. J. (1993). Emotion in the criminal psychopath: Startle reflex modulation. *Journal of Abnormal Psychology, 102,* 83–92.

Patrick, C. J., Cuthbert, B. N., & Lang, P. J. (1994). Emotion in the criminal psychopath: Fear image processing. *Journal of Abnormal Behavior, 103,* 523–534.

Patterson, F. (1978). Conversations with a gorilla. *National Geographic, 154,* 438–465.

Paul, G. L. (1982). *The development of a "transportable" system of behavioral assessment for chronic patients.* Invited address, University of Minnesota, Minneapolis.

Paul, G. L., & Lentz, R. J. (1977). *Psychosocial treatment of chronic mental patients: Milieu versus social-learning programs.* Cambridge, MA: Harvard University Press.

Paul, J. (1990). *Critical thinking: What every person needs to survive in a rapidly changing world.* Rohnert Park, CA: Sonoma State University.

Paul, S. M. (1985). The Advanced Raven's Progressive Matrices: Normative data for an American university population and an examination of the relationship with Spearman's "g." *Journal of Experimental Education, 54,* 95–100.

Pavio, A. (1969). Mental imagery in associative learning and memory. *Psychological Review, 76,* 241–263.

Pavlov, I. P. (1927). Conditioned reflexes. (G. V. Anrep, Trans.). London: Oxford University Press.

Payne, D. G. (1987). Hypermnesia and reminiscence in recall: A historical and empirical review. *Psychological Bulletin, 101,* 5–27.

Pearce, J. M. (1986). A model for stimulus generalization in Pavlovian conditioning. *Psychological Review, 94,* 61–73.

Pelletier, K. R. (1986). Longevity: What can centenarians teach us? In K. Dychtwald (Ed.), *Wellness and health promotion for the elderly.* Rockville, MD: Aspen Publishers.

Pendleton, M. G., & Batson, C. D. (1979). Self-presentation and the door-in-the-face technique for inducing compliance. *Personality and Social Psychology Bulletin, 5,* 77–81.

Pennebaker, J. W. (1983). Accuracy of symptom perception. In A. Baum, S. E. Taylor, & J. Singer (Eds.). *Handbook of psychology and health* (Vol. 4, pp. 189–218). Hillsdale, NJ: Erlbaum.

Pennebaker, J. W. (1990). *Opening up: The healing power of confiding in others.* New York: William Morrow.

Pennebaker, J. W., Hughes, C. F., & O'Heeron, R. C. (1987). The psychophysiology of confession: Linking inhibitory and psychosomatic processes. *Journal of Personality and Social Psychology, 52,* 718–793.

Pennebaker, J. W., Kiecolt-Glaser, J. K., & Glaser, R. (1988). Disclosure of traumas and immune function: Health implications for psychotherapy. *Journal of Consulting and Clinical Psychology, 56,* 239–245.

Perls, F. S. (1969). *Gestalt therapy verbatim.* Lafayette, CA: Real People Press.

Persad, S. M., & Polivy, J. (1993). Differences between depressed and nondepressed individuals in the recognition of and response to facial emotional cues. *Journal of Abnormal Psychology, 102,* 358–368.

Peterson, A. C. (1987, September). Those gangly years. *Psychology Today,* pp. 28–34.

Peterson, L. R., & Peterson, M. J. (1959). Short-term retention of individual verbal items. *Journal of Experimental Psychology, 58,* 193–198.

Peterson, S. E., Fox, P. T., Mintun, M. A., Posner, J. I., & Raichle, M. E. (1989). Studies of the processing of single words using averaged positron emission tomographic measurements of cerebral blood flow change. *Journal of Cognitive Neuroscience, 1,* 153–170.

Peto, R., Lopez, A. D., Boreham, J., Thun, M., & Heath, C. (1992). Mortality from tobacco in developed countries: Indirect estimation from national vital statistics. *Lancet, 339,* 1268–1278.

Petty, M. M., Singleton, B., & Connell, D. W. (1992). An experimental evaluation of an organizational incentive plan in the electric utility industry. *Journal of Applied Psychology, 77,* 427–436.

Petty, R. E., & Cacioppo, J. T. (1981). *Attitudes and persuasion: Classic and contemporary approaches.* Dubuque, IA: W. C. Brown.

Petty, R. E., & Cacioppo, J. T. (1986). The elaboration likelihood model of persuasion. In L. Berkowitz (Ed.), *Advances in experimental social psychology* (Vol. 19, pp. 123–205). New York: Academic Press.

Pfaffman, C. (1978). The vertebrate phylogeny, neural code, and integrative processes of taste. In E. C. Carterrette & M. P. Friedman (Eds.), *Handbook of perception* (vol. 6A). New York: Academic.

Phares, V., & Compas, B. E. (1992). The role of fathers in child and adolescent psychopathology: Make room for daddy. *Psychological Bulletin, 111,* 387–412.

Phillips, A. G., & Fibiger, H. C. (1989). Neuroanatomical bases of intracranial self-stimulation: Untangling the Gordian knot. In J. M. Leibman & S. J. Cooper (Eds.), *The neuropharmacological bases of reward* (pp. 66–105). Oxford, England: Clarendon Press.

Phillips, D. P., & Brugge, J. F. (1985). Progress in neurophysiology of sound localization. *Annual Review of Psychology, 36,* 245–274.

Piaget, J. (1952). *The origins of intelligence in children.* New York: International Universities Press.

Piaget, J. (1965). *The moral judgment of the child.* New York: Free Press. (Original work published 1932.)

Piaget, J. (1975). *The child's conception of the world.* Totowa, NJ: Littlefield, Adams. (Originally published in 1929.)

Pickar, D. (1988). Perspectives on a time-dependent model of neuroleptic action. *Schizophrenia Bulletin 14,* 255–265.

Pierce, C. A. (1992). *The effects of physical attractiveness and height on dating choice: Meta-analysis.* Unpublished masters thesis, University at Albany, State University of New York, Albany.

Pierce, J. P., Macaskill, P., & Hill, D. (1990). Long-term effectiveness of mass media led antismoking campaigns in Australia. *American Journal of Public Health, 80,* 565–569.

Pinel, J. P. J. (1993). *Biopsychology* (2nd ed.). Boston: Allyn and Bacon.

Pines, A., & Aronson, E. (1988). *Career burnout: Causes and cures.* New York: Free Press.

Pinker, S. (1984). Visual cognition: An introduction. *Cognition: International Journal of Cognitive Science, 18*, 1–63.

Pitman, R. K., Orr, S. P., Forgue, D. F., Altman, B., deJong, J. B., & Hgerz, L. R. (1990). Psychophysiologic responses to combat imagery of Vietnam veterans with posttraumatic stress disorder versus other anxiety disorders. *Journal of Abnormal Psychology, 99*, 49–54.

Pittenger, J. B., Mark, L. S., & Johnson, D. F. (1989). Longitudinal stability of facial attractiveness. *Bulletin of the Psychonomic Society, 27*, 171–174.

Plante, T. G., & Rodin, J. (1990). Physical fitness and enhanced psychological health. *Current Psychology: Research & Reviews, 9*, 3–24.

Plomin, R. (1989). Environment and genes: Determinants of behavior. *American Psychologist, 44*, 105–111.

Polich, J. (1993). Cognitive brain potentials. *Current Directions in Psychological Science, 3*, 175–178.

Pollack, E. S., Nomura, A. M., Heilbrun, L. K., Stemmermann, G. N., & Green, S. B. (1984). Prospective study of alcohol consumption and cancer. *New England Journal of Medicine, 310*, 617–621.

Pomerleau, O. F., & Pomerleau, C. S. (1984). Neuro-regulators and the reinforcement of smoking: Towards a biobehavioral explanation. *Neuroscience and Biobehavioral Reviews, 8*, 503–513.

Poon, L. W., & Fozard, J. L. (1980). Age and word frequency effects in continuous recognition memory. *Journal of Gerontology, 35*, 77–86.

Pope, K. S., & Vetter, V. A. (1992). Ethical dilemmas encountered by members of the American Psychological Association. *American Psychologist, 47*, 397–411.

Popper, K. (1959). *The logic of scientific discovery.* London: Hutchinson.

Porter, L. W., & Lawler, E. E., III. (1968). *Managerial attitudes and performance.* Homewood, IL: Dorsey Press.

Porter, L. W., & Steers, R. M. (1973). Organizational work and personal factors in employee turnover and absenteeism. *Psychological Bulletin, 80*, 151–176.

Posner, M. I., & McCandliss, B. D. (1993). Converging methods for investigating lexical access. *Psychological Science, 4*, 305–309.

Postman, L., & Phillips, L. W. (1965). Short-term temporal changes in free recall. *Quarterly Journal of Experimental Psychology, 17*, 132–138.

Poucet, B. (1993). Spatial cognitive maps in animals: New hypotheses on their structure and neural mechanisms. *Psychological Review, 100*, 163–182.

Powell, G. N. (1990). One more time: Do female and male managers differ? *Academy of Management Executive, 4*(3), 68–75.

Powley, T. L., Opsahl, C. A., Cox, J. E., & Weingarten, H. P. (1980). The role of the hypothalamus in energy homeostasis. In P. J. Morgane & J. Panksepp (Eds.), *Handbook of the hypothalamus. 3A: Behavioral studies of the hypothalamus* (pp. 211–298). New York: Marcel Dekker.

Pratto, F., & John, O. P. (1991). Automatic vigilance: The attention-grabbing power of negative social information. *Journal of Personality and Social Psychology, 51*, 380–391.

Preston, R. (1992, October 26). Crisis in the hot zone. *New Yorker,* pp. 58–62, 64–76, 78–81.

Prigatano, G. P. (1992). Personality disturbances associated with traumatic brain injury. *Journal of Consulting and Clinical Psychology, 3*, 360–368.

Pritchard, R. (1991). The effects of cultural schemata on reading processing strategies. *Reading Research Quarterly, 24*, 273–293.

Pritchard, R. D., Dunnette, M. D., & Jorgenson, D. O. (1972). Effects of perceptions of equity and inequity on work performance and satisfaction. *Journal of Applied Psychology, 57*, 75–94.

Pruitt, D. G., & Rubin, J. Z. (1986). *Social conflict: Escalation, stalemate, settlement.* New York: Random House.

Ptacek, J. T., Smith, R. E, & Dodge, K. L. (1994). Gender differences in coping with stress: When stressor and appraisals do not differ. *Personality and Social Psychology Bulletin, 20*, 421-430.

Purvis, A. (1993, December 6). Cursed, yet blessed. *Time,* p. 67.

Putnam, F. W. (1991). Dissociative phenomena. In A. Tasman & S. M. Goldfinger (Eds.), *Review of psychiatry* (Vol. 10, pp. 144–164). Washington, D.C.: American Psychiatric Press.

Putnam, F. W., Guroff, J. J., Silberman, E. K., Barban, L., & Post, R. M. (1986). The clinical phenomenology of multiple personality disorder: Review of 100 recent cases. *Journal of Clinical Psychiatry, 47*, 285–293.

Pylyshyn, Z. W. (1981). The imagery debate: Analogue media versus tacit knowledge. *Psychological Review, 88*, 16–45.

Quadrel, M. J. (1990). *Elicitations of adolescents' risk perceptions: Qualitative and quantitative dimensions.* Unpublished doctoral dissertation, Carnegie Mellon University.

Quadrel, M. J., Fischoff, B., & Davis, W. (1993). Adolescent (in)vulnerability. *American Psychologist, 48*, 102–116. Rabin, M. D., & Cain, W. S. (1984). Determinants of measured olfactory sensitivity. *Perception & Psychophysics, 39*, 281–286.

Rabin, M. D., & Cain, W. S. (1984). Determinants of measured olfactory sensitivity. *Perception & Psychophysics, 39*, 281–286.

Rachman, S. J., & Hodgson, R. J. (1980). *Obsessions and compulsions.* Englewood Cliffs, NJ: Prentice-Hall.

Ragland, D. R., & Brand, R. J. (1988). Type A behavior and mortality from coronary heart disease. *New England Journal of Medicine, 318*, 65–69.

Rainie, H., Streisand, B., Guttman, M., & Witkin, G. (1993, July 12). Warning shots at TV. *U.S. News & World Report,* pp. 48–50.

Ramirez, V., & Bartoshuk, L. M. (1987). *Effects of HCl on taste: Possible role in bulimia.* Poster presented at the 95th annual meeting of the American Psychological Association, New York.

Ramsey, J., & Kwon, Y. (1988). Simplified decision rules for predicting performance loss in the heat. *Proceedings on heat stress indices.* Luxembourg: Commission of the European Communities.

Raphael, B., Cubis, J., Dunne, M., Lewin, T., & Kelly, B. (1990). The impact of parental loss on adolescents' psychosocial characteristics. *Adolescence, 25*, 689–700.

Rasmussen, T., & Milner, B. (1975). Excision of Broca's area without persistent aphasia. In K. J. Zulch, O. Creutzfeldt, & G. C. Gailbraith (Eds.), *Central localization* (pp. 258–263). New York: Springer-Verlag.

Raven, J. C. (1977). *Raven Progressive Matrices.* Los Angeles: Psychological Corp.

Raynor, J. O. (1970). Relationships between achievement-related motives, future orientation, and academic performance. *Journal of Personality and Social Psychology, 15*, 28–33.

Raz, S. (1993). Structural cerebral pathology in schizophrenia: Regional or diffuse? *Journal of Abnormal Psychology, 102*, 445–452.

Raz, S., & Raz, N. (1990). Structural brain abnormalities in the major psychoses: A quantitative review of the evidence from computerized imaging. *Psychological Bulletin, 108*, 93–108.

Reason, J. T., & Lucas, D. (1984). Using cognitive diaries to investigate naturally occurring memory blocks. In J. E. Harris & P. E. Morris (Eds.), *Everyday memory actions and absent-mindedness* (pp. 53–70). London: Academic Press.

Rechtschaffen, A., Gilliland, M. A., Bergmann, B. M., & Winter, J. B. (1983). Physiological correlates of prolonged sleep deprivation in rats. *Science, 221*, 182–184.

Reed, T. E., & Jensen, A. R. (in press). Conduction velocity in a brain nerve pathway of normal adults correlates with intelligence level. *Intelligence.*

Reeder, G. D., Fletcher, G. J. O., & Furman, K. (1989). The role of observers: Expectations in attitude attribution. *Journal of Experimental Social Psychology, 25*, 168–188.

Reese, H. W., & Rodeheaver, D. (1985). Problem solving and complex decision making. In J. E. Birren & K. W. Schaie (Eds.), *Handbook of the psychology of aging* (2nd ed., pp. 474–499). New York: Van Nostrand Reinhold.

Reeves, A., & Sperling, G. (1986). Attention gating in short-term retention of individual verbal items. *Psychological Review, 93*, 180–206.

Reid, L. D. (1990). Rates of cocaine addiction among newborns. Personal communication, Rensselaer Polytechnic Institute.

Reid, L. D. (Ed.). (1990). *Opioids, bulimia, and alcohol abuse and alcoholism.* New York: Springer-Verlag.

Reid, L. D., & Carpenter, D. J. (1990). Alcohol-abuse and alcoholism. In L. D. Reid (Ed.), *Opioids, bulimia, and alcohol abuse & alcoholism* (pp. 23–48). New York: Springer-Verlag.

Reifman, A. S., Larrick, R. P., & Fein, S. (1991). Temper and temperature on the diamond: The heat-aggression relationship in major league baseball. *Personality and Social Psychology Bulletin, 17*, 580–585.

Reis, H. T., Senchak, M., & Solomon, B. (1985). Sex differences in the intimacy of social interaction: Further examination of potential explanations. *J, 48*, 1204–1217.

Reisenzein, R. (1983). The Schachter theory of emotion: Two decades later. *Psychological Bulletin, 94*, 239–264.

Reissland, N. (1988). Neonatal imitation in the first hour of life: Observations in rural Nepal. *Developmental Psychology, 24*, 464–469.

Reitman, J. S. (1974). Without surreptitious rehearsal, information in short-term memory decays. *Journal of Verbal Learning and Verbal Behavior, 13*, 365–377.

Rensberger, B. (1993, May 3). The quest for machines that not only listen, but also understand. *Washington Post*, p.3.

Rescorla, R. A. (1988). Pavlovian conditioning: It's not what you think it is. *American Psychologist, 43*, 151–160.

Rescorla, R. A., & Wagner, A. R. (1972). A theory of Pavlovian conditioning: Variations in the effectiveness of reinforcement and nonreinforcement. In A. Black & W. F. Prokasy (Eds.), *Classical conditioning: II. Current research and theory*. New York: Appleton.

Resnick, S. (1993, Fall Special Issue). The young and the gifted: Are our schools nurturing talented kids? *Time*, 73–78.

Resnick, S. M. (1992). Positron emission tomography in psychiatric illness. *Current Directions in Psychological Science, 1*, 92–98.

Rest, J. R. (1986). *Moral development: Advances in research and theory*. New York: Praeger.

Rest, J. R., & Thomas, S. J. (1985). Relation of moral judgment to formal education. *Developmental Psychology, 21*, 709–714.

Rice, C. G., Breslin, M., & Roper, R. G. (1987). Sound levels from personal cassette players. *British Journal of Audiology, 21*, 273–278.

Rice, F. P. (1992). *Intimate relationships, marriages, and families*. Mountain View, CA: Mayfield.

Richardson, J. T. E., & Zucco, G. M. (1989). Cognition and olfaction: A review. *Psychological Bulletin, 105*, 352–360.

Riess, M., & Schlenker, B. R. (1977). Attitude changes and responsibility avoidance as modes of dilemma resolution in forced-compliance situations. *Journal of Personality and Social Psychology, 35*, 21–30.

Rigby, C. S., Deci, E. L., Patrick, B. C., & Ryan, R. M. (1992). Beyond the intrinsic-extrinsic dichotomy: Self-determination in motivation and learning. *Motivation and Emotion, 16*, 165–185.

Rix, S. E. (1990). *The American woman: 1990–91: A status report*. New York: Norton.

Robbins, T. L., & DeNisi, A. S. (1994). A closer look at interpersonal affect as a distinct influence on cognitive processing in performance evaluations. *Journal of Applied Psychology, 79*, 341–353.

Roberts, P., & Newton, P. M. (1987). Levinsonian studies of women's adult development. *Psychology and Aging, 2*, 154–163.

Roberts, T. A. (1991). Gender and the influence of evaluations on self-assessments in achievement settings. *Psychological Bulletin, 109*, 297–308.

Roberts, T. A., & Nolen-Hoeksema, S. (1990). *Gender differences in construals of and responsiveness to evaluations in an achievement situation*. Unpublished manuscript, Stanford University.

Robins, L. N. (1966). *Deviant children grow up*. Baltimore: Williams & Wilkins.

Robins, L. N., Helzer, J. E., Weissman, M. M., Orvaschel, H., Gruenberg, E., Burke, J. D., & Regier, D. (1984). Lifetime prevalence of specific psychiatric disorders in three sites. *Archives of General Psychiatry, 41*, 954–958.

Robins, L. N., & Regier, D. A. (1991). *Psychiatric disorders in America: The epidemiological catchment area*. New York: The Free Press.

Robinson, L. A., Berman, J. S., & Neimeyer, R. A. (1990). Psychotherapy for the treatment of depression: A comprehensive review of controlled outcome research. *Psychological Bulletin, 108*, 30–49.

Robinson, R. G., Kubos, K. L., Starr, L. B., Rao, K., & Price, T. R. (1984). Mood disorders in stroke patients: Importance of location of lesion. *Brain, 107*, 81–93.

Robotics Institute. (1984). *Some common types of defects in printed wiring*. Pittsburgh, PA: Carnegie Mellon University.

Rodin, J. (1984, April). A sense of control. *Psychology Today*, 38–45.

Rodin, J., Bartoshuk, L., Peterson, C., & Schank, D. (1990). Bulimia and taste: Possible interactions. *Journal of Abnormal Psychology, 99*, 32–39.

Rodin, J., & Plante, T. (1989). The psychological effects of exercise. In R. S. Williams & A. Wellece (Eds.), *Biological effects of physical activity*. Champaign, IL: Human Kinetics.

Rodin, J., & Salovey, P. (1989). Health psychology. *Annual Review of Psychology, 40*, 533–580.

Rodin, J., & Slochower, J. (1976). Externality in the nonobese: Effects of environmental responsiveness on weight. *Journal of Personality and Social Psychology, 33*, 338–344.

Rodriquez, J. (1990). Childhood injuries in the United States. *American Journal of Diseases of Childhood, 144*, 627–646.

Roediger, H. L., III, & Wheeler, M. A. (1993). Hypermnesia in episodic and semantic memory: Response to Bahrick and Hall. *Psychological Science, 4*, 207–208.

Rogers, C. R. (1959). A theory of therapy, personality, and interpersonal relationships as developed in the client-centered framework. In S. Koch (Ed.), *Psychology: A study of a science* (Vol. 3, pp. 184–256). New York: McGraw-Hill.

Rogers, C. R. (1970). *Carl Rogers on encounter groups*. New York: Harper & Row.

Rogers, C. R. (1977). *Carl Rogers on personal power: Inner strength and its revolutionary impact*. New York: Delacorte.

Rogers, C. R. (1980). *A way of being*. Boston: Houghton Mifflin.

Rogers, C. R. (1982, August). Nuclear war: A personal response. *American Psychological Association*, pp. 6–7.

Rogers, R. W. (1980). Subjects' reactions to experimental deception. Unpublished manuscript, University of Alabama.

Rogler, L. H., Malgady, R. G., Constantino, G., & Blumenthal, R. (1987). What do culturally sensitive mental health services mean? The case of Hispanics. *American Psychologist, 42*, 565–570.

Roopnarine, J. L., Talukuder, E., Jain, D., Josi, P. & Srivastav, P. (1990). Characteristics of holding, patterns of play, and social behaviors between parents and infants in New Delhi, India. *Developmental Psychology, 26*, 667–673.

Rosch, E. H. (1973). Natural categories. *Cognitive Psychology, 4*, 328–349.

Rosch, E. H. (1975). The nature of mental codes for color categories. *Journal of Experimental Psychology: Human Perception and Performance, 1*, 303–322.

Rosenberg, M., & Mercy, J. (1991). Assaultive violence. In M. Rosenberg & J. Mercy (Eds.), *Violence in America: A public health approach* (pp. 14–50). New York: Oxford University Press.

Rosenfield, D., Folger, R., & Adelman, H. F. (1980). When rewards reflect competence: A qualification of the overjustification effect. *Journal of Personality and Social Psychology, 39*, 368–376.

Rosenman, R. H. (1988). The impact of certain emotions in cardiovascular disorders. In M. P. Janisse (Ed.), *Individual differences, stress, and health psychology* (pp. 1–23). New York: Springer-Verlag.

Rosenstock, I. M. (1974). The health belief model and preventive health behavior. *Health Education Monographs, 2*, 354–386.

Rosenthal, N. E. (1985). Antidepressant effects of light in seasonal affective disorder. *American Journal of Psychiatry, 142*, 163–170.

Rosenthal, R. R., & DePaulo, B. M. (1979). Sex differences in eavesdropping on nonverbal cues. *Journal of Personality and Social Psychology, 37*, 273–285.

Rosenzweig, J. M., & Darley, D. M. (1989) Dyadic adjustment/sexual satisfaction in women and men as a function of psychological sex role self-perception. *Journal of Sex and Marital Therapy, 15*, 42–56.

Rosenzweig, M. R. (1992). Psychological science around the world. *American Psychologist, 47*, 718–722.

Roskies, E. (1987). *Stress management for the healthy Type A*. New York: Guilford Press.

Roskos-Ewoldsen, D. R., & Fazio, R. H. (1992). The accessibility of source likabilty as a determinant of persuasion. *Personality and Social Psychology Bulletin, 18*, 19–25.

Ross, C. A., Miller, S. D., Reagor, P., Bjornson, L., Fraser, G. A., & Anderson, G. (1990). Structured interview data on 102 cases of multiple personality disorder from four centers. *American Journal of Psychiatry, 147*, 596–601.

Ross, N. (1989). Relation of implicit theories to construction of personal histories. *Psychological Review, 96*, 341–357.

Roter, D. L., & Ewart, C. K. (1992). Emotional inhibition in essential hypertension: Obstacle to communication during medical visits? *Health Psychology, 11*, 163–169.

Roter, D. L., & Hall, J. A. (1989). Studies of doctor-patient interaction. *Annual Review of Public Health, 10*, 163–180.

Roter, D. L., Hall, J. A., & Katz, N. R. (1988). Doctor-patient communication: A descriptive summary of the literature. *Patient Education Counselor, 12*, 99–119.

Rothenberg, R., Nasca, P., Mikl, J., Burnett, W., & Reynolds, B. (1987). In R. W. Amler & H. B. Dull (Eds.), *Closing the gap: The burden of unnecessary Illness*. New York: Oxford University Press.

Rothenberg, R. B., & Koplan, J. P. (1990). Chronic disease in the 1990s. *Annual Review of Public Health, 11*, 267–296.

Rothman, K. R., Cristina, I. C., Flanders, D., & Fried, M. P. (1980). Epidemiology of laryngeal cancer. In P. E. Sartwell (Ed.), *Epidemiologic reviews* (Vol. 2, pp. 195–209). Baltimore: Johns Hopkins University Press.

Rotter, J. B. (1954). *Social learning and clinical psychology*. Englewood Cliffs, NJ: Prentice-Hall.

Rotter, J. B. (1982). *The development and applications of social learning theory: Selected papers*. New York: Praeger.

Rovee-Collier, C. K. (1987). Learning and memory. In J. D. Osofky (Ed.), *Handbook of infant development* (2nd ed., pp. 98–148). New York: Wiley.

Rowlison, R. T., & Felner, R. D. (1988). Major life events, hassles, and adaptation in adolescence: Confounding in the conceptualization and measurement of life stress and adjustment revisited. *Journal of Personality and Social Psychology, 55*, 432–444.

Royce, J. M., Darlington, R. B., & Murray, H. W. (1983). Pooled analyses: Findings across studies. In Consortium for Longitudinal Studies, *As the twig is bent . . . Lasting effects of preschool programs*. Hillsdale, NJ: Erlbaum.

Rubin, J. Z. (1985). Deceiving ourselves about deception: Comment on Smith and Richardson's "Amelioration of deception and harm in psychological research." *Journal of Personality and Social Psychology, 48*, 252–253.

Ruff, H. A., Lawson, K. R., Parrinello, R., & Weissberg, R. (1990). Long-term stability of individual differences in sustained attention in the early years. *Child Development, 61*, 60–75.

Rumelhart, D. E. (1975). Notes on a schema for stories. In D. G. Bobrow & A. Collins (Eds.), *Representation and understanding* (pp. 211–236). New York: Academic Press.

Rushton, J. P. (1989a). Genetic similarity, human altruism, and group selection. *Behavioral and Brain Sciences, 12*, 503–559.

Rushton, J. P. (1989b). Genetic similarity in male friendships. *Ethology and Sociobiology, 10*, 361–373.

Rushton, W. A. H. (1975). Visual pigments and color blindness. *Scientific American, 232*, 64–74.

Russell, G. W. (Ed.). (1988). *Violence in interpersonal relationships*. New York: PMA Publishing.

Russell, J. A. (1994). Is there universal recognition of emotion from facial expression? A review of the cross-cultural studies. *Psychological Bulletin, 115*, 102–141

Ryan, R. M. (1982). Control and information in the intrapersonal sphere: An extension of cognitive evaluation theory. *Journal of Personality and Social Psychology, 43*, 450–561.

Sacks, O. (1993, May 10). To see and not see: A neurologist's notebook. *The New Yorker*, pp. 59–73.

Saks, M. J. (1992). Obedience versus disobedience to legitimate versus illegitimate authorities issuing good versus evil directions. *Psychological Science, 3*, 221–223.

Salame, P., & Baddeley, A. D. (1982). Disruption of short-term memory by unattended speech: Implications for the structure of working memory. *Journal of Verbal Learning and Verbal Behavior, 21*, 150–164.

Salovey, P. (Ed.). (1991). *The psychology of jealousy and envy*. New York: Guilford Press.

Salovey, P. (1992). Mood-induced self-focused attention. *Journal of Personality and Social Psychology, 62*, 699–707.

Salovey, P., & Birnbaum, D. (1989). Influence of mood on health-relevant cognitions. *Journal of Personality and Social Psychology, 57*, 539–551.

Samson, L. F. (1988). Perinatal viral infections and neonates. *Journal of Perinatal and Neonatal Nursing, 1*, 56–65.

Samuels, M., & Samuels, N. (1986). *The well pregnancy book*. New York: Summit.

Sanbonmatsu, D. M., Akimoto, S. A., & Gibson, B. D. (1994). Stereotype-based blocking in social explanation. *Personality and Social Psychology Bulletin, 20*, 71–81.

Sanders, M. S., & McCormick, E. J. (1993). *Human factors in engineering and design*. New York: McGraw-Hill.

Sanders Thompson, V. L. (1990). Factors affecting the level of African American identification. *Journal of Black Psychology, 17*, 14–23.

Sanders Thompson, V. L. (1991). Perceptions of race and race relations which affect African American identification. *Journal of Applied Social Psychology, 21*, 1502–1516.

Sargent, C. (1984). Between death and shame: Dimensions in pain in Bariba culture. *Social Science Medicine, 19*, 1299–1304.

Savage-Rumbaugh, E. S., Sevcik, R. A., Brakke, K. E., & Rumbaugh, D. M. (1992). Symbols: Their communicative use, communication, and combination by bonobos (*Pan paniscus*). In L. P. Lipsitt & C. Rovee-Collier (Eds.), *Advances in infancy research* (Vol. 7, pp. 221–278). Norwood, NJ: Ablex.

Saxe, L. (1994). Detection of deception: Polygraph and integrity tests. *Current Directions in Psychological Science, 3*, 69–73.

Scarr, S., & Weinberg, R. A. (1976). IQ test performance of black children adopted by white families. *American Psychologist, 31*, 726–739.

Schab, F. R. (1991). Odor memory: Taking stock. *Psychological Bulletin, 109*, 242–251.

Schachter, D. L., Church, B., & Treadwell, J. (1994). Implicit memory in amnesic patients: Evidence for spared auditory priming. *Psychological Science, 5*, 20–25.

Schachter, S., & Singer, J. E. (1962). Cognitive, social, and physiological determinants of emotional states. *Psychological Review, 69*, 379–399.

Schaie, K. W. (1974). Translations in gerontology—from lab to life: Intellectual functioning. *American Psychologist, 29*, 802–807.

Schaie, K. W. (1986). *Adult development and aging* (2nd ed.). Boston: Little, Brown.

Schaie, K. W. (1990). Intellectual development in adulthood. In J. E. Birren & K. W. Schaie (Eds.), *Handbook of the psychology of aging* (3rd ed., pp. 291–309). San Diego: Academic Press.

Schaie, K. W. (1993). The Seattle longitudinal studies of adult intelligence. *Current Directions in Psychological Science, 2*, 171–175.

Schaller, G. G. (1986). Secrets of the wild panda. *National Geographic, 169*, 284–309.

Schank, R. (1988). *The creative attitude*. New York: Macmillan.

Scheier, M. F, & Carver, C. S. (1986). A model of self-regulation: Translating intention into action. In L. Berkowitz (Ed.), *Advances in experimental social psychology* (Vol. 20). New York: Academic Press.

Scheier, M. F., & Carver, C. S. (1987). Dispositional optimism and physical well-being: The influence of generalized outcome expectancies in health. *Journal of Personality, 55*, 169–210.

Scheier, M. F., & Carver, C. S. (1988). *Perspectives on personality*. Boston: Allyn and Bacon.

Scheier, M. F., & Carver, C. S. (1992). Effects of optimism on psychological and physical well-being: Theoretical overview and empirical update. *Cognitive Therapy and Research, 16*, 201–228.

Scheier, M. F., Weintraub, J. K., & Carver, C. S. (1986). Coping with stress: Divergent strategies of optimists and pessimists. *Journal of Personality and Social Psychology, 51*, 1257–1264.

Schiffman, H. R. (1990). *Sensation and perception: An integrated approach* (3rd ed). New York: John Wiley & Sons.

Schmidt, U. (1989). Behavioural psychotherapy of eating disorders. *International Review of Psychiatry, 1*, 245–256.

Schneider, A. L. (1990). *Deterrence and juvenile crime*. New York: Springer-Verlag.

Schneider, B. H. (1991). A comparison of skill-building and desensitization strategies for intervention with aggressive children. *Aggressive Behavior, 17*, 301–311.

Schneider, B. H., & Byrne, B. M. (1987). Individualizing social skills training for behaviour-disordered children. *Journal of Consulting and Clinical Psychology, 55*, 444–445.

Schneider, W., & Shiffrin, R. M. (1977). Controlled and automatic human information processing. I: Detection, search, and attention. *Psychological Review, 84*, 1–66.

Schofield, W. (1964). *Psychotherapy: The purchase of friendship*. Englewood Cliffs, NJ: Prentice-Hall.

Schwarzwald, J., Amir, Y., & Crain, R. L. (1992). Long-term effects of school desegregation experiences on interpersonal relations in the Israeli defense forces. *Personality and Social Psychology Bulletin, 18*, 357–368.

Scott, J. P. (1992). Aggression: Functions and control in social systems. *Aggressive Behavior, 18*, 1–20.

Scribner, S. (1977). Recall of classical syllogisms: A cross-cultural investigation of error on logical problems. In R. J. Falmagne (Ed.), *Reasoning: Representation and process*. Hillsdale, NJ: Erlbaum.

Scrivner, E., & Safer, M. A. (1988). Eyewitnesses show hypermnesia for details about a violent event. *Journal of Applied Psychology, 73,* 371–377.

Searle, J. (1980). Minds, brains, and programs. *Behavioral and Brain Science, 3,* 417–457.

Segal, N. L., & Bouchard, T. J. (1993). Grief intensity following the loss of a twin and other relatives: Test of kinship-genetic hypotheses. *Human Biology, 65,* 87–105.

Segal, Z. (1988). Appraisal of the self-schema construct in cognitive models of depression. *Psychological Bulletin, 103,* 147–162.

Segall, M. H., Dasen, P. R., Berry, J. W., & Poortinga, Y. H. (1990). *Human behavior in global perspective: An introduction to cross-cultural psychology.* Boston: Allyn and Bacon.

Sekuler, R., & Blake, R. (1990). *Perception.* New York: Alfred A. Knopf.

Seligman, M. E. P. (1975). *Helplessness: On depression, development, and death.* San Francisco: W. H. Freeman.

Seligman, M. E. P., Castellon, C., Cacciola, J., Schulman, P., Luborsky, L., Ollove, M., & Downing, R. (1988). Explanatory style change during cognitive therapy for unipolar depression. *Journal of Abnormal Psychology, 97,* 13–18.

Seligman, M. E. P., & Hager, J. L. (1972). *Biological boundaries of learning.* New York: Appleton-Century-Crofts.

Selvini-Palazzoli, M., Boscolo, L., Cecchin, G., & Prata, G. (1978). *Paradox.* New York: Aronson.

Selye, H. (1976). *The stress of life* (2nd ed.). New York: McGraw-Hill.

Seminara, J. L. (1993, July). Taking control of controls. *Ergonomics in Design,* pp. 5–7.

Seta, C. E., & Hayes, N. (1994). The influence of impression formation goals on the accuracy of social memory. *Personality and Social Psychology Bulletin, 20,* 93–101.

Sewitch, D. E. (1987). Slow wave sleep deficiency insomnia: A problem in thermo-downregulation at sleep onset. *Psychophysiology, 24,* 200–215.

Sexton, V. S., & Hogan, J. (Eds.). (1992). *International psychology: Views from around the world* (2nd ed.). Lincoln: University of Nebraska Press.

Shaffer, D., Garland, A., Vieland, V., Underwood, M., & Busner, C. (1991). The impact of curriculum-based suicide prevention programs for teenagers. *Journal of the American Academy of Child and Adolescent Psychiatry, 30,* 588–596.

Shaffer, D. R., & Graziano, W. G. (1983). Effects of positive and negative moods on helping tasks having pleasant or unpleasant consequences. *Motivation and Emotion, 7,* 269–278.

Shafir, E. (1993). Choosing versus rejecting: Why some options are both better and worse than others. *Memory and Cognition, 21,* 546–556.

Shakoor, B., & Chalmers, D. (1991). Co-victimization of African American children who witness violence: Effects on cognitive, emotional, and behavioral development. *Journal of the National Medical Association, 83,* 233–237.

Shanab, M. E., & Spencer, R. E. (1978). Positive and negative contrast effects obtained following shifts in delayed water reward. *Bulletin of the Psychonomic Society, 12,* 199–202.

Shanab, N. E., & Yahya, K. A. (1977). A behavioral study of obedience in children. *Journal of Personality and Social Psychology, 35,* 530–536.

Shantz, C. U., & Hartup, W. W. (Eds.) (1993). *Conflict in child and adolescent development.* Cambridge: Cambridge University Press.

Shapiro, D. A., & Shapiro, D. (1982). Meta-analysis of comparative therapy outcome studies: A replication and refinement. *Psychological Bulletin, 92,* 581–604.

Shapiro, D. H. (1980). *Meditation: Self-regulation strategy and altered states of consciousness.* New York: Aldine.

Shapiro, I. (1993). Quoted in Gibbs, N. R. (1993, June 28). Bringing up father. *Time,* pp. 53–61.

Sharpe, D., Adair, J. G., & Roese, N. J. (1992). Twenty years of deception research: A decline in subjects' trust? *Personality and Social Psychology Bulletin, 18,* 585–590.

Shepard, R. N. (1964). Circularity in judgments of relative pitch. *Journal of the Acoustical Society of America, 36,* 2346–2353.

Shepard, R. N., & Metzler, J. (1971). Mental rotation of three-dimensional objects. *Science, 171,* 701–703.

Sherif, M. (1935). A study of some social factors in perception. *Archives of Psychology, 27,* 187.

Sherman, W. M. (1990). *Behavior modification.* New York: Harper Collins.

Shettleworth, S. J. (1993). Where is the comparison in comparative cognition? *Psychological Science, 4,* 179–183.

Shieber, S. M. (1994). Lessons from a restricted Turing test. *Communications of the Association of Computing Machinery, 37,* 70–78.

Shiffrin, R. M. (1988). Attention. In R. C. Atkinson, R. J. Herrnstein, G. Lindzey, & R. D. Luce (Eds.), *Stevens' handbook of experimental psychology: Vol. 2. Learning and cognition* (pp. 739–811). New York: Wiley.

Shiffrin, R. M., & Dumais, S. T. (1981). The development of automatism. In J. R. Anderson (Ed.), *Cognitive skills and their acquisition.* Hillsdale, NJ: Erlbaum.

Shiffrin, R. M., & Schneider, W. (1977). Controlled and automatic human information processing. II: Perceptual learning, automatic attending, and a general theory. *Psychological Review, 84,* 127–190.

Shore, B. (1991). Twice-born, once conceived: Meaning construction and cultural cognition. *American Anthropologist, 32,* 9–23.

Siegel, S. (1975). Evidence from rats that morphine tolerance is a learned response. *Journal of Comparative and Physiological Psychology, 89,* 598–606.

Siegel, S. (1983). Classical conditioning, drug tolerance, and drug dependence. In R. G. Smart, F. B. Glaser, Y. Israel, H. Kalant, R. E. Popham, & W. Schmidt (Eds.), *Research advances in alcohol and drug problems* (Vol. 7). New York: Plenum.

Siegel, S. (1984). Pavlovian conditioning and heroin overdose: Reports by overdose victims. *Bulletin of the Psychonomic Society, 22,* 428–430.

Siegel, S., Hinson, R. E., Krank, M. D., & McCully, J. (1982). Heroin "overdose" death: The contribution of drug-associated environmental cues. *Science, 216,* 436–437.

Siegler, R. S. (1994). Cognitive variability: A key to understanding cognitive development. *Current Directions in Psychological Science, 3,* 1–5.

Siegler, R. S., & Crowley, K. (in press). Goal sketches constrain children's strategy discoveries. *Cognitive Psychology.*

Siegler, R. S., & Jenkins, E. (1989). *How children discover new strategies.* Hillsdale, NJ: Erlbaum.

Silva, C. E., & Kirsch, I. (1992). Interpretive sets, expectancy, fantasy proneness, and dissociation as predictors of hypnotic response. *Journal of Personality and Social Psychology, 63,* 847–856.

Silver, S., Mitchell, R. M., & Gist, B. (in press). Responses to successful and unsuccessful performance: The relationship between self-efficacy and causal attributions. *Organizational Behavior and Human Decision Processes.*

Simmons, C. H., von Kolke, A., & Shimizu, H. (1986). Attitudes toward romantic love among American, German, and Japanese students. *Journal of Social Psychology, 126,* 327–336.

Simonton, D. K. (1986). Presidential personality: Biographical uses of the Gough Adjective Check List. *Journal of Personality and Social Psychology, 51,* 149–160.

Simonton, D. K. (1990). Creativity and wisdom in aging. In J. E. Birren & K. W. Schaie (Eds.), *Handbook of the psychology of aging* (3rd ed., pp. 320–329). San Diego: Academic Press.

Simpson, J. A. (1990). Influence of attachment styles on romantic relationships. *Journal of Personality and Social Psychology. 59,* 971–980.

Sinclair, R. C., Hoffman, C., Mark, M. M., Martin, L. L., & Pickering, T. L. (1994). Construct accessibility and the misattribution of arousal: Schachter and Singer revisited. *Psychological Science, 5,* 15–19.

Singer, J. L. (1975). Navigating the stream of consciousness: Research in daydreaming and related inner experience. *American Psychologist, 30,* 727–738.

Sinott, J. D. (1986). Prospective/intentional and incidental everyday memory: Effects of age and passage of time. *Psychology and Aging, 1,* 110–116.

Sistrunk, F., & McDavid, J. W. (1971). Sex variable in conforming behavior. *Journal of Personality and Social Psychology, 29,* 200–207.

Skeels, H. M. (1938). Mental development of children in foster homes. *Journal of Consulting Psychology, 2,* 33–43.

Skeels, H. M. (1966). Ability status of children with contrasting early life experience. *Society for Research in Child Development Monographs, 31*(3), 1–65.

Skinner, B. F. (1938). *The behavior of organisms.* New York: Appleton-Century-Crofts.

Skinner, B. F. (1953). *The behavior of organisms.* New York: Appleton-Century-Crofts.

Skinner, B. F. (1969). *Contingencies of reinforcement.* New York: Appleton-Century-Crofts.

Skinner, B. F. (1974). *About behaviorism.* New York: Vintage Books.

Slobin, D. I. (1979). *Psycholinguistics* (2nd ed.). Glenview, IL: Scott, Foresman.

Slovic, P., Fischoff, B., & Lichtenstein, S. (1977). Behavioral decision theory. *Annual Review of Psychology, 28,* 1–39.

Smeaton, D., Byrne, D., & Murnen, S. K. (1989). The revulsion hypothesis revisited: Similarity irrelevance or dissimilarity bias? *Journal of Personality and Social Psychology, 56,* 54–59.

Smith, D. E., Gier, J. A., & Willis, F. N. (1982). Interpersonal touch and compliance with a marketing request. *Basic and Applied Social Psychology, 3,* 35–38.

Smith, J., & Baltes, P. B. (1990). Wisdom-related knowledge: Age/cohort differences in response to life-planning problems. *Developmental Psychology, 26,* 494–505.

Smith, J. F., & Kida, T. (1991). Heuristics and biases: Expertise and task realism in auditing. *Psychological Bulletin, 109,* 472–489.

Smith, M. C. (1983). Hypnotic memory enhancement of witnesses: Does it work? *Psychological Bulletin, 94,* 387–407.

Smith, M. L., Glass, G. V., & Miller, T. J. (1980). *The benefits of psychotherapy.* Baltimore: Johns Hopkins.

Smith, P. B., & Bond, N. H. (1993). *Social psychology across cultures.* Boston: Allyn and Bacon.

Smith, R. E., Ptacek, J. T., & Smoll, F. L. (1992). Sensation seeking, stress, and adolescent injuries: A test of stress-buffering, risk-taking, and coping skills hypotheses. *Journal of Personality and Social Psychology, 62,* 1016–1024.

Smith, S. M. (1979). Remembering in and out of context. *Journal of Experimental Psychology: Human Learning and Memory, 5,* 460–471.

Smith, S. M., & Shaffer, D. R. (1991). Celerity and cajolery: Rapid speech may enhance or inhibit persuasion through its impact on message elaboration. *Personality and Social Psychology Bulletin, 17,* 663–669.

Smith, S. M., & Shaffer, D. R. (1991). The effects of good moods on systematic processing: "Willing but not able, or able but not willing?" *Motivation and Emotion, 15,* 243–279.

Smith, S. S., & Richardson, D. (1983). Amelioration of deception and harm in psychological research: The important role of debriefing. *Journal of Personality and Social Psychology, 44,* 1075–1082.

Smith, S. S., & Richardson, D. (1985). On deceiving ourselves about deception: Reply to Rubin. *Journal of Personality and Social Psychology, 48,* 254–255.

Snowden, L. R., & Cheung, F. K. (1990). Use of inpatient mental health services by members of ethnic minority groups. *American Psychologist, 45,* 347–355.

Snyder, M. (1987). *Public appearances/private realities: The psychology of self-monitoring.* New York: W. H. Freeman.

Snyder, M., & Gangestad, S. (1986). On the nature of self-monitoring: Matters of assessment, matters of validity. *Journal of Personality and Social Psychology, 51,* 125–139.

Snyder, M., Simpson, J. A., & Gangestad, S. (1986). Personality and sexual relations. *Journal of Personality and Social Psychology, 51,* 181–190.

Snyder, S. (1991). Movies and juvenile delinquency: An overview. *Adolescence, 26,* 121–132.

Snyder, S. H. (1977). The brain's own opiates. *Chemical & Engineering News, 55,* 26–35.

Solomon, R. L. (1982). The opponent-process in acquired motivation. In D. W. Pfaff (Ed.), *The physiological mechanisms of motivation.* New York: Springer-Verlag.

Solomon, S. D., & Maser, J. D. (1990). Defining terms and instruments for assessing traumatic stress. *Journal of Applied Social Psychology, 20*(2), 1623–1631.

Solso, R. L. (1991). *Cognitive psychology* (3rd ed.). Boston: Allyn and Bacon.

Spacapan, S., & Oskamp, S. (Eds.). (1992). *Helping and being helped.* Newbury Park, CA: Sage.

Spanos, N. P. (1991). A sociocognitive approach to hypnosis. In S. J. Lynn & J. R. Rhue (Eds.), *Hypnosis theories: Current models and perspectives* (pp. 324–361). New York: Guilford Press.

Spanos, N. P., Burgess, C. A., & Perlini, A. H. (in press). Compliance and suggested deafness in hypnotic and nonhypnotic subjects. *Imagination, Cognition, and Personality.*

Spanos, N. P., Perlini, A. H., Patrick, L., Bell, S., & Gwynne, M. I. (1990). The role of compliance in hypnotic and nonhypnotic analgesia. *Journal of Research in Personality, 24,* 433–453.

Spearman, C. E. (1927). *The abilities of man.* London: Macmillan.

Spence, A. P. (1989). *Biology of human aging.* Englewood Cliffs, NJ: Prentice Hall.

Spence, J. T., & Helmreich, R. L. (1972). The Attitudes toward Women Scale: An objective instrument to measure attitudes toward the rights and roles of women in contemporary society. *JSAS Catalog of Selected Documents in Psychology, 2,* 66 (Ms. No. 153).

Spence, J. T., Helmreich, R., & Stapp, J. A. (1975). A short version of the Attitudes toward Women Scale (AWS). *Bulletin of the Psychonomic Society, 2,* 219–220.

Spencer, J. (1990). Collective violence and everyday practice in Sri Lanka. *Journal of Asian Studies, 24,* 603–623.

Sperling, G. (1960). The information available in brief visual presentations. *Psychological Monographs: General and Applied, 74,* 1–29.

Sperry, R. W. (1968). Hemisphere deconnection and unity of conscious experience. *American Psychologist, 29,* 723–733.

Spirduso, W. W., & MacRae, P.G. (1990). Motor performance and aging. In J. E. Birren & K. W. Schaie (Eds.), *Handbook of the psychology of aging* (3rd ed., pp. 184–200). San Diego: Academic Press.

Springer, S. P., & Deutsch, G. (1985). *Left brain, right brain.* San Francisco: Freeman.

Squire, L. R. (1991). Closing remarks. In L. R. Squire & E. Lindenlaub (Eds.), *The biology of memory* (pp. 643–664). Stuttgart, Germany: F. K. Schattauer Verlag.

Squire, L. R., & McKee, R. (1992). The influence of prior events on cognitive judgments in amnesia. *Journal of Experimental Psychology: Learning, Memory, and Cognition, 18,* 106–115.

Squire, L. R., & Spanis, C. W. (1984). Long gradient of retrograde amnesia in mice: Continuity with the findings in humans. *Behavioral Neuroscience, 98,* 345–348.

Sroufe, L. A., & Waters, E. (1976). The ontogenesis of smiling and laughter on the organization of development in infancy. *Psychological Review, 83,* 173–189.

Stager, J. M. (1988). Menarche and exercise. *Medical Aspects of Human Sexuality, 22,* 118, 133.

Standing, L. G., Canezio, J., & Haber, N. (1970). Perception and memory for pictures: Single-trial learning of 2500 visual stimuli. *Psychonomic Science, 19,* 73–74.

Stangor, C., & Ruble, D. N. (1989). Strength of expectancies and memory for social information: What we remember depends on how much we know. *Journal of Experimental Social Psychology, 39,* 1408–1423.

Stanley, B. G., & Gillard, E. R. (1994). Hypothalamic neuropeptide Y and the regulation of eating behavior and body weight. *Current Directions in Psycological Science, 3,* 1, 9–15.

Stanton, A. L., & Dunckel-Schetter, C. A. (1991). Psychological adjustment to infertility: An overview of conceptual approaches. In A. L. Standon & C. A. Dunkel-Schetter (Eds.), *Infertility: Perspectives from stress and coping research.* New York: Plenum.

Staw, B. M., & Ross, J. (1985). Stability in the midst of change: A dispositional approach to job attitudes. *Journal of Applied Psychology, 70,* 56–77.

Staw, B. M., & Ross, J. (1987). Behavior in escalation situations: Antecedents, prototypes, and solutions. In L. L. Cummings & B. M. Staw (Eds.), *Research in organizational behavior* (Vol. 9, pp. 29–78). Greenwich, CT: JAI Press.

Staw, B. M., & Ross, J. (1989). Understanding behavior in escalation situations. *Science, 246,* 216–220.

Stearns, H. L., Barrett, G. V., & Alexander, R. A. (1985). Accidents and the aging individual. In J. E. Birren & K. W. Schaie (Eds.), *Handbook of the psychology of aging* (2nd ed.) (pp. 703–724). New York: Van Nostrand Reinhold.

Steede, K. C., & Range, L. M. (1989). Does television induce suicide contagion with adolescents? *Journal of Community Psychology, 15,* 24–28.

Steele, C. M., & Josephs, R. A. (1990). Alcohol myopia: Its prized and dangerous effects. *American Psychologist, 45,* 921–933.

Steers, R. M. (1984). *Organizational behavior* (2nd ed.). Glenview, IL: Scott Foresman.

Steffen, V. J. (1990). Men's motivation to perform the testicular self-exam: Effect of prior knowledge and an educational brochure. *Journal of Applied Social Psychology, 20,* 681–702.

Steffen, V. J., & Eagly, A. H. (1985). Implicit theories about influence style: The effects of status and sex. *Personality and Social Psychology Bulletin, 11,* 191–201.

Steiner, D. D., Rain, J. S., & Smalley, M. M. (1993). Distributional ratings of performance: Further examination of new rating format. *Journal of Applied Psychology, 78,* 438–442.

Steinfels, P. (1992, January 20). Apathy is seen toward agony of the homeless. *New York Times,* pp. A1, B7.

Stellar, E. (1985, April). *Hunger in animals and humans.* Lecture to the Eastern Psychological Association, Boston.

Stephan, W. G. (1987). The contact hypothesis in intergroup relations. In C. Hendrick (Ed.), Group processes and intergroup relations. *Review of Personality and Social Psychology, 9,* 41–67.

Stern, J. M., & Stewart, G. G., III. (1993, June). Pay for performance: Only the theory is easy. *HR Magazine,* pp. 48–49.

Stern, P. C. (1992). Psychological dimensions of global environmental change. In M. R. Rosenzweig & L. W. Porter (Eds.), *Annual review of psychology* (Vol. 43, pp. 269–302). Palo Alto, CA: Annual Reviews.

Sternberg, R. J. (1985). *Beyond IQ.* Cambridge: Cambridge University Press.

Sternberg, R. J. (1986). *Intelligence applied.* New York: Harcourt Brace Jovanovich.

Sternberg, R. J. (1988). Mental self-government: A theory of intellectual styles and their development. *Human Development, 31,* 197–224.

Sternberg, R. J. (1988). Triangulating love. In R. J. Sternberg & H. J. Barnes (Eds.), *The psychology of love* (pp. 119–138). New Haven, CT: Yale University Press.

Sternberg, R. J. (1989). Domain-generality versus domain-specificity: The life and impending death of a false dichotomy. *Merrill-Palmer Quarterly, 35,* 115–130.

Stevens, W. K. (1992, February 25). Global warming threatens to undo decades of conservation efforts. *New York Times,* p. C4.

Stevenson, H. W., Lee, S-Y., & Stigler, J. W. (1986). Mathematics achievement of Chinese, Japanese, and American children. *Science, 321,* 593–699.

Stiles, W. B., Shapiro, D. A., & Elliott, R. (1986). "Are all psychotherapies equivalent?" *American Psychologist, 41,* 165–180.

Stipp, D. (1990, May 17). Einstein bird has scientists atwitter over mental feats. *Wall Street Journal,* pp. 1, 7.

Stockwell, H. G., Goldman, A. L., Lyman, G. H., Noss, C. I., Armstrong, A. W., Pinkham, P. A., Candelora, E. C., & Brusa, M. R. (1992). Environmental tobacco smoke and lung cancer risk in nonsmoking women. *Journal of the National Cancer Institute, 18,* 1417–1422.

Stone, J., Aronson, E., Crain, A. L., Winslow, M. P., & Fried, C. B. (1994). Inducing hypocrisy as a means of encouraging young adults to use condoms. *Personality and Social Psychology Bulletin, 20,* 116–128.

Stoppard, J. M., & Gruchy, C. D. G. (1993). Gender, context, and expression of positive emotion. *Personality and Social Psychology Bulletin, 19,* 143–150.

Storms, M. D. (1981). Theories of sexual orientation. *Journal of Personality and Social Psychology, 38,* 783–792.

Story, M., & Faulkner, P. (1990). The prime time diet: A content analysis of eating behavior and food messages in television program content and commercials. *American Journal of Public Health, 80,* 738–740.

Straumann, T. J., & Higgins, E. G. (1988). Self-discrepancies as predictors of vulnerability to distinct syndromes of chronic emotional distress. *Journal of Personality, 56,* 685–707.

Straumann, T. J., Lemieux, A. M., & Coe, C. L. (1993). Self-discrepancy and natural killer cell activity: Immunological consequences of negative self-evaluation. *Journal of Personality and Social Psychology, 64,* 1042–1052.

Strean, H. S. (1985). *Resolving resistances in psychotherapy.* New York: Wiley Interscience.

Strickland, B. R. (1992). Women and depression. *Current Direction in Psychological Science, 1,* 132–134.

Striegel-Moore, R. H., Silberstein, L. R., & Rodin, J. (1993). The social self in bulimia nervosa: Public self-consciousness, social anxiety, and perceived fraudulence. *Journal of Abnormal Psychology, 102,* 297–303.

Stroh, L. K., Brett, J. M., & Reilly, A. H. (1992). All the right stuff: A comparison of female and male managers' career progression. *Journal of Applied Psychology, 77,* 251–260.

Struckman-Johnson, C. J., Gilliland, R. C., Struckman-Johnson, D. L., & North, T. C. (1990). The effects of fear of AIDS and gender on responses to fear-arousing condom advertisements. *Journal of Applied Social Psychology, 20,* 1396–1410.

Strupp, H. H., & Binder, J. L. (1984). *Psychotherapy in a new key: A guide to time-limited dynamic psychotherapy.* New York: Basic Books.

Strydom, N., Kotze, H., van der Walt, W., & Rogers, G. (1986) Effect of ascorbic acid on rate of heat acclimatization. *Journal of Applied Physiology, 41,* 202–205.

Stuart, R. B. (1977). Self-help group approach to self-management. In R. B. Stuart (Ed.), *Behavioral self-management: Strategies, techniques, and outcome.* New York: Brunner/Mazel.

Suls, J., & Wan, C. K. (1987). In search of the false uniqueness phenomenon: Fear and estimates of social consensus. *Journal of Personality and Social Psychology, 52,* 211–217.

Suls, J., Wan, C. K., & Sanders, C. L. (1988). False consensus and false uniqueness in estimating the prevalence of health-protective behaviors. *Journal of Applied Social Psychology, 19,* 66–79.

Sulsky, L. M., & Day, D. V. (1992). Frame-of-reference training and cognitive categorization: An empirical investigation of rater memory issues. *Journal of Applied Psychology, 77,* 501–510.

Sundstrom, E., & Sundstrom, M. G. (1986). *Work places: The psychology of the physical environment in offices and factories.* Cambridge, England: Cambridge University Press.

Swann, W. B., Jr., Griffin, J. J., Jr., Predmore, S. C., & Gaines, B. (1987). Cognitive-affective crossfires: When self-consistency meets self-enhancement. *Journal of Personality and Social Psychology, 52,* 881–889.

Swann, W. B., Jr., Stein-Seroussi, A., & Giesler, R. B. (1992). Why people self-verify. *Journal of Personality and Social Psychology, 62,* 392–401.

Swartzentruber, D. (1991). Blocking between occasion setters and contextual stimuli. *Journal of Experimental Psychology: Animal Behavior Processes, 12,* 163–173.

Swets, J. A. (1992). The science of choosing the right decision threshold in high-stakes diagnostics. *American Psychologist, 47,* 522–532.

Tajfel, H. (1982). *Social identity and intergroup relations.* Cambridge, England: Cambridge University Press.

Takanishi, R. (1993). The opportunities of adolescence—research, interventions, and policy. *American Psychologist, 48,* 85–87.

Taylor, R. L. (1991). Poverty and adolescent Black males: The subculture of disengagement. In P. B. Edelman & J. Ladner (Eds.), *Adolescence and poverty: Challenge for the 1990s* (pp. 139–162). Washington, DC: Center for National Policy Press.

Taylor, S. E. (1991). *Health psychology* (2nd ed.). New York: McGraw-Hill.

Taylor, S. E., & Brown, J. (1988). Illusion and well-being: A social psychological perspective on mental health. *Psychological Bulletin, 103,* 193–210.

Teichman, M., Barnea, Z., & Rahav, G. (1989). Sensation seeking, state and trait anxiety, and depressive mood in adolescent substance abusers. *International Journal of the Addictions, 24,* 87–99.

Tellegen, A., Lykken, D. T., Bouchard, T. J., Wilcox, K. J., Segal, N. L., & Rich, S. (1988). Personality similarity in twins raised apart and together. *Journal of Personality and Social Psychology, 54,* 1031–1039.

Tennen, H., & Eller, S. J. (1977). Attributional components of learned helplessness. *Journal of Personality and Social Psychology, 35,* 265–271.

Terman, L. M. (1954). The discovery and encouragement of exceptional talent. *American Psychologist, 9,* 221–230.

Terrace, H. S. (1985). In the beginning was the "name." *American Psychologist, 40,* 1011–1028.

Tett, R. P., & Meyer, J. P. (1993). Job satisfaction, organizational commitment, turnover intention, and turnover: Path analyses based on meta-analytic findings. *Personnel Psychology, 46,* 259–293.

Teyler, T. J., & DiScenna, P. (1984). Long-term potentiation as a candidate mnemonic device. *Brain Research Reviews, 7,* 15–28.

Thomas, A., & Chess, S. (1977). *Temperament and development.* New York: Brunner/Mazel.

Thomas, J. L. (1992). *Adulthood and aging.* Boston: Allyn and Bacon.

Thomas, M. H. (1982). Physiological arousal, exposure to a relatively lengthy aggressive film, and aggressive behavior. *Journal of Research in Personality, 16,* 72–181.

Thompson, J. K. (1992). Body image: Extent of disturbance, associated features, theoretical models, assessment methodologies, intervention strategies, and a proposal for a new DSM-IV diagnostic category—Body Image Disorder. In M. Hesen, R. M. Eisler, & P. M. Miller (Eds.), *Progress in behavior modification* (pp. 3–54). Sycamore, IL: Sycamore Publishing.

Thompson, R. A. (1988). The effects of infant day care through the prism of attachment theory: A critical appraisal. *Early Childhood Research Quarterly, 3,* 273–283.

Thompson, R. F. (1989). A model system approach to memory. In P. R. Solomon, G. R. Goethals, C. M. Kelley, & B. R. Stephens (Eds.), *Memory: Interdisciplinary approaches.* New York: Springer-Verlag.

Thompson, W. C., Cowan, C. L., & Rosenhan, D. L. (1980). Focus of attention mediates the impact of negative affect on altruism. *Journal of Personality and Social Psychology, 38,* 291–300.

Thorndike, R. L., & Hagen, E. (1982). *Ten thousand careers.* New York: Wiley.

Thurstone, E. L. (1938). *Primary mental abilities.* Chicago: University of Chicago Press.

Tice, D. M. (1989). Metatraits: Interitem variance as personality assessment. In D. M. Buss & N. Cantor (Eds.), *Personality psychology: Recent trends and emerging directions* (pp. 194–200). New York: Springer-Verlag.

Tiffany, S. T. (1990). A cognitive model of drug urges and drug-use behavior: Role of automatic and nonautomatic processes. *Psychological Review, 97,* 147–168.

Time-CNN Poll. (1993, November 22). Cited in G. J. Church, Jobs in an age of insecurity. *Time,* pp. 32–39.

Ting-Toomey, S. (1991). Intimacy expressions in three cultures: France, Japan, and the United States. *International Journal of Intercultural Relations, 15,* 29–46.

Tisserand, R. B. (1977). *The art of aromatherapy.* Rochester, VT: Healing Arts Press.

Tobin, D., Johnson, C., Steinberg, S., Staats, M., & Enright, A. B. (1991). Multifactorial assessment of bulimia nervosa. *Journal of Abnormal Psychology, 100,* 14–21.

Tolman, E. C., & Honzik, C. H. (1930). Introduction and removal of reward, and maze performance in rats. *University of California Publications in Psychology, 4,* 257–275.

Tomaka, J., Blascovich, J., Kelsey, R. M., & Leitten, C. L. (1993). Subjective, physiological, and behavioral effects of threat and challenge appraisal. *Journal of Personality and Social Psychology, 65,* 248–260.

Tomarken, A. J., Davidson, R. J., & Henriques, J. B. (1990). Resting frontal brain asymmetry predicts affective responses to films. *Journal of Personality and Social Psychology, 59,* 791–801.

Toufexis, A. (1992, April 27). Endangered species. *Time,* pp. 49–51.

Toufexis, A. (1993, February 15). The right chemistry. *Time,* pp. 49–51.

Trinder, J. (1988). Subjective insomnia without objective findings: A pseudo diagnostic classification? *Psychological Bulletin, 103,* 87–94.

Trivers, R. (1985). *Social evolution.* Menlo Park, CA: Benjamin/Cummings.

Tronick, E. Z. (1989). Emotions and emotional communication in infants. *American Psychologist, 44,* 112–119.

Tschann, J. M., Johnston, J. R., & Wallerstein, J. S. (1989). Resources, stressors, and attachment as predictors of adult adjustment after divorce: A longitudinal study. *Journal of Marriage and the Family, 51,* 1033–1046.

Tubbs, M. E., Boehne, D., & Dahl, J. G. (1993). Expectancy, valence, and motivational force functions in goal-setting research: An empirical test. *Journal of Applied Psychology, 78,* 361–373.

Tucker, L. A., & Friedman, G. M. (1990). Walking and serum cholesterol in adults. *American Journal of Public Health, 80,* 1111–1113.

Tulving, E. (1993). What is episodic memory? *Current Directions in Psychological Science, 2,* 67–70.

Tulving, E., & Psotka, L. (1971). Retroactive inhibition in free recall: Inaccessibility of information available in the memory store. *Journal of Experimental Psychology, 87,* 1–8.

Tulving, E., & Schachter, D. L. (1990). Priming and human memory systems. *Science, 247,* 301–396

Tulving, E., & Thomson, D. M. (1973). Encoding specificity and retrieval processes in episodic memory. *Psychological Review, 80,* 352–373.

Turk, D. C., & Rudy, T. E. (1992). Cognitive factors and persistent pain: A glimpse into Pandora's box. *Cognitive Therapy and Research, 16,* 99–122.

Turkheimer, E., & Farace, A. (1992). A reanalysis of gender differences in IQ scores following unilateral brain lesions. *Psychological Assessment, 4,* 498–501.

Turner, J. A., & Clancy, S. (1986). Strategies for coping with chronic low back pain: Relationship to pain and disability. *Pain, 24,* 355–362.

Turner, J. C., Hogg, M. A., Oakes, P. J., Richer, S. D., & Wetherell, M. S. (1987). *Rediscovering the social group: A self-categorization theory.* Oxford, England: Blackwell.

Turtle, J. W., & Yuille, J.C. (1994). Lost but not forgotten details: Repeated eyewitness recall leads to reminiscence but not hypermnesia. *Journal of Applied Psychology, 79,* 260–271.

Tversky, A., & Kahneman, D. (1974). Judgment under uncertainty: Heuristics and biases. *Science, 185,* 1124–1131.

Tversky, A., & Kahneman, D. (1981). The framing of decisions and the psychology of choice. *Science, 211,* 453–458.

Tyler, T. R., & Cook, F. L. (1984). The mass media and judgment of risk: Distinguishing impact on personal and societal level judgments. *Journal of Personality and Social Psychology, 47,* 693–708.

Uhlarik, J., & Joseph, K. M. (1992). Spatial and temporal (Rapcom) visual display formats and the proximity compatibility principle. *Proceedings of the Human Factors Society, 36th Annual Meeting,* 1383–1387.

Unger, R. K. (in press). Alternative conceptions of sex (and sex differences). In M. Haug, R. Whalen, C. Aron, & K. L. Olsen (Eds.), *The development of sex differences and similarities in behavior.* Dordrecht, The Netherlands: Kluwer Academic.

Unger, R. K., & Crawford, M. (1992). *Women and gender: A feminist psychology.* Philadelphia: Temple University Press.

United States Bureau of the Census. (1991). *Statistical Abstract of the United States, 1991.* Washington, DC: U.S. Government Printing Office.

United States Department of Health and Human Services. (1989). *Aging in the eighties: The prevalence of comorbidity and its associations with disability* (DHHS Publication No. PHS 89-1250). Washington, DC: U.S. Government Printing Office.

United States Department of Health and Human Services. (1991). *Healthy people 2000. National health promotion and disease prevention objectives.* Washington, DC: DHHS publication PHS 91-50212.

United States Government Printing Office. (1987). Premature mortality in the United States. *Morbidity and Morality Weekly Reports* (suppl.), *35,* 1–11.

United States Office of Technology Assessment. (1991). *Adolescent health: Vol. 3. Crosscutting issues in the delivery of health and related services* (Publication No. OTA-H-467). Washington, DC: U.S. Congress.

Urban, M. J. (1992) Auditory subliminal stimulation: A reexamination. *Perceptual and Motor Skills, 74,* 515–541.

Usher, J. A, & Neisser, U. (in press). Childhood amnesia and the beginnings of memory for four early life events. *Journal of Experimental Psychology: General.*

Vallone, R. P., Griffin, D. W., Lin, S., & Ross, L. (1990). Overconfident prediction of future actions and outcomes by self and others. *Journal of Personality and Social Psychology, 58,* 582–592.

Van Houten, R. (1993). The use of wrist weights to reduce self-injury maintained by sensory reinforcement. *Journal of Applied Behavior Analysis, 26,* 197–204.

Van Vianen, A. E. M., & Willemsen, T. M. (1992). The employment interview: The role of sex stereotypes in the valuation of male and female job applicants in the Netherlands. *Journal of Applied Social Psychology, 22,* 471–491.

Vance, J., et al. v. Judas Priest et al., No. 86-5844 (2nd Dist. Ct. Nev. 1990).

Vasudev, J., & Hummel, R. C. (1987). Moral stage sequence and principled reasoning in an Indian sample. *Human Development, 30, 105–118*

Vauclair, J., Fagot, J., & Hopkins, W. D. (1993). Rotation of mental images in baboons when the visual input is directed to the cerebral hemisphere. *Psychological Science, 4,* 99–103.

Vaughan, E. (1993). Individual and cultural differences in adaptation to environmental risks. *American Psychologist, 48,* 673–680.

Vitz, P. C. (1990). The use of stories in moral development: New psychological reasons for an old education method. *American Psychologist, 45,* 709–720.

Volpicelli, J. R., Alterman, A. I., Hayashida, M., & O'Brien, C. P. (1992). Naltrexone in the treatment of alcohol dependence. *Archives of General Psychiatry, 49,* 876–880.

Von Senden, M. (1960). *Space and sign.* Trans. by P. Heath. New York: Free Press.

Vormbrock, J. K. (1993). Attachment theory as applied to wartime and job-related marital separation. *Psychological Bulletin, 114,* 122–144.

Vredenburgh, A. G. & Cohen, H. H. (1993). Compliance with warnings in high risk recreational activities: Skiing and scuba. *Proceedings of the Human Factors and Ergonomics Society, 37th Annual Meeting,* 945–949.

Vroom, V. H. (1964). *Work and motivation.* New York: Wiley.

Vroom, V. H., & Yetton, P. W. (1973). *Leadership and decision-making.* Pittsburgh: University of Pittsburgh Press.

Vygotsky, L. S. (1987). Thinking and speech. In R. W. Rieber, A. S. Carton (Eds.), & N. Minick (Trans.), *The collected works of L. S. Vygotsky: Vol 1. Problems of general psychology* (pp. 37–285). New York: Plenum. (Original work published in 1934.)

Wagenaar, W. A., (1986). My memory: A study of autobiographical memory over six years. *Cognitive Psychology, 18,* 225–252.

Waitzkin, H. (1984). Doctor-patient communication: Clinical implications of social scientific research. *Journal of the American Medical Association, 252,* 2441–2446.

Walden, T. A., & Ogan, T. A. (1988). The development of social referencing. *Child Development, 29,* 1230–1240.

Walker, L. J. (1988). The development of moral reasoning. In R. Vasta (Ed.), *Annals of child development* (Vol. 5, pp. 33–78). Greenwich, CT: JAI Press.

Walker, L. J. & DeVries, B. (1985). *Moral stages/moral orientations: Do the sexes really differ?* Paper presented at the meetings of the American Psychological Association, Los Angeles.

Walker, L. J. & Taylor, J. H. (1991). Family interactions and the development of moral reasoning. *Child Development, 62,* 264–283.

Wallace, B. (1993). Day persons, night persons, and variability in hypnotic susceptability. *Journal of Personality and Social Psychology, 64,* 827–833.

Wallace, R. K., & Benson, H. (1972). The physiology of meditation. *Scientific American, 236,* 84–90.

Wallace, R. K., & Fisher, L. E. (1987). *Consciousness and behavior* (2nd ed.). Boston: Allyn and Bacon.

Waller, N. G., & Ben-Porath, Y. S. (1987). Is it time for clinical psychology to embrace the five-factor model of personality? *American Psychologist, 42,* 887–889.

Walsh, S. (1993). Cited in Toufexis, A. (1993, February 15), *Time,* pp. 49–51.

Walster, E., & Festinger, L. (1962). The effectiveness of "overheard" persuasive communication. *Journal of Abnormal and Social Psychology, 65,* 395–402.

Walton, G. E., & Bower, T. G. R. (1993). Newborns form "prototypes" in less than 1 minute. *Psychological Science, 4,* 203–205.

Walton, G. E., Bower, N. J. A., & Bower, T. G. R. (1992). Recognition of familiar faces by newborns. *Infant Behavior and Development, 15,* 265–269.

Warm, J. S., Dember, W. N., & Parasuraman, R. (1991). Effects of olfactory stimulation on performance and stress in a visual sustained attention task. *Journal of the Society of Cosmetic Chemists, 12,* 1–12.

Wasserman, D., Lempert, R. O., & Hastie, R. (1991). Hindsight and causality. *Personality and Social Psychology Bulletin, 17,* 30–35

Wasserman, E. A. (1993). Comparative cognition: Toward a general understanding of cognition in behavior. *Psychological Science, 4,* 156–161.

Watson, D. (1989). Strangers' ratings of the five robust personality factors: Evidence of a surprising convergence with self-report. *Journal of Personality and Social Psychology, 57,* 120–128.

Watson, J. B. (1924). The unverbalized in human behavior. *Psychological Review, 31,* 273–280

Watson, J. B., & Raynor, R. (1920). Conditioned emotional reactions. *Journal of Experimental Psychology, 3,* 1–14.

Watson, J. S., & Ramey, C. T. (1972). Reactions to response-contingent stimulation in early infancy. *Merrill-Palmer Quarterly, 18,* 219–229.

Wayne, S. J., & Ferris, G. R. (1990). Influence tactics, affect, and exchange quality in supervisor-subordinate interactions: A laboratory experiment and field study. *Journal of Applied Psychology, 75,* 487–499.

Webb, W. (1975). *Sleep: The gentle tyrant.* Englewood Cliffs, NJ: Prentice-Hall.

Webb, W., & Agnew, H. W. (1967). Sleep cycling within the twenty-four hour period. *Journal of Experimental Psychology, 74,* 167–169.

Weekes, J. R., Lynn, S. J., Green, J. P., & Brentar, J. T. (1992). Pseudomemory in hypnotized and task-motivated subjects. *Journal of Abnormal Psychology, 101,* 356–360.

Wehner, R., & Menzel, R. (1990). Do insects have cognitive maps? *Annual Review of Neuroscience, 13,* 403–414.

Weinberg, R. A. (1989). Landmark issues and great debates. *American Psychologist, 44*(2), 98–104.

Weiner, B. (1989). *Human motivation.* Hillsdale, NJ: Erlbaum.

Weiner, R. D. (1985). Convulsive therapies. In H. I. Kaplan & B. J. Sadock (Eds.), *Comprehensive textbook of psychiatry,* 4th ed. (pp. 1558–1562). Baltimore: Williams & Wilkins.

Weisberg, R., & Suls, J. M. (1973). An information-processing model of Duncker's candle problem. *Cognitive Psychology, 4,* 255–276.

Weisenberg, M. (1982). Cultural and ethnic factors in reaction to pain. In I. Al-Issa (Ed.), *Culture and psychopathology.* Baltimore: University Park Press.

Weisner, T. S., & Wilson-Mitchell, J. E. (1990). Nonconventional family life-styles and sex typing in six-year-olds. *Child Development, 61,* 1915–1933.

Weiss, R. A. (1993). How does HIV cause AIDS? *Science, 260,* 1273–1278.

Weisz, J. R., Weiss, B., & Donenberg, G. R. (1992). The lab versus the clinic: Effects of child and adolescent psychotherapy. *American Psychologist, 47,* 1578–1585.

Weisz, J. R., Weiss, B., Morton, T., Granger, D., & Han, S. (1992). *Metaanalysis of psychotherapy outcome research with children and adolescents.* Unpublished manuscript, University of California, Los Angeles.

Wellisch, D. K., & Trock, G. K. (1980). A three-year follow-up of family therapy. *International Journal of Family Therapy, 2,* 169–175.

Wellman, H. M., Somerville, S. C., & Haake, R. J. (1979). Development of search procedures in real-life spatial environments. *Developmental Psychology, 15,* 530–542.

Wells, G. L. (1993). What do we know about eyewitness identification? *American Psychologist, 48,* 553–571.

Wells, L. E., & Marwell, G. (1976). *Self-esteem.* Beverly Hills, CA: Sage.

White, G. L., & Mullen, P. E. (1990). *Jealousy: Theory, research, and clinical strategies.* New York: Guilford Press.

White, J. L., & Parham, T. (1990). *The psychology of Blacks: An African-American perspective.* Englewood Cliffs, NJ: Prentice Hall.

White, R. K. (1977). Misperception in the Arab-Israeli conflict. *Journal of Social Issues, 25,* 41–78.

Whorf, B. L. (1956). Science and linguistics. In J. B. Carroll (Ed.), *Language, thought, and reality: Selected writings of Benjamin Whorf.* Cambridge, MA: MIT Press.

Whybrow, P. C., Akiskal, H. S., & McKinney, W. T., Jr. (1984). *Mood disorders: Toward a new psychophysiology.* New York: Plenum.

Whyte, G. (1991). Diffusion of responsibility: Effects on the escalation tendency. *Journal of Applied Psychology, 76,* 408–415.

Wickelgren, W. A. (1965). Acoustic similarity and intrusion errors in short-term memory. *Journal of Experimental Psychology, 70,* 102–108.

Widom, C. S. (1989). Does violence beget violence? A critical examination of the literature. *Psychological Bulletin, 106,* 3–28.

Wielkiewicz, R. M., & Calvert, C. R. X. (1989). *Training and habilitating developmentally disabled people: An introduction.* Newbury Park, CA: Sage.

Wiesel, T. N. (1982). Postnatal development of the visual cortex and the influence of environment. *Nature, 299,* 583–591.

Wilcoxon, H. C., Dragoin, W. B., & Kral, P. A. (1971). Illness-induced aversions in rats and quail: Relative salience of visual and gustatory cues. *Science, 171,* 826–828.

Wilder, D. A. (1977). Perception of groups, size of opposite, and social influence. *Journal of Experimental Social Psychology, 13,* 253–268.

Wiley, J. A., & Camacho, T. C. (1980). Life-style and future health: Evidence from the Alameda County study. *Preventive Medicine, 9,* 1–21.

Wilkinson, A. (1994, January 24). A changed vision of God. *New Yorker,* p. 68.

Willett, W. C., & MacMahon, B. (1984). Diet and cancer—an overview. *New England Journal of Medicine, 310,* 633–638.

Williams, D. E., & Page, M. M. (1989). A multi-dimensional measure of Maslow's hierarchy of needs. *Journal of Research in Personality, 23,* 192–213.

Williams, J. M. G., Watts, F. N., MacLeod, C., & Matthews, A. (1988). *Cognitive psychology and emotional disorders.* New York: Wiley.

Williams, K. J., Suls, J., Alliger, G. M., Learner, S. M., & Wan, C. K. (1991). Multiple role juggling and daily mood states in working mothers: An experience sampling study. *Journal of Applied Psychology, 76,* 664–674.

Williams, R., Zyzanski, S. J., & Wright, A. L. (1992). Life events and daily hassles and uplifts as predictors of hospitalization and outpatient visitation. *Social Science Medicine, 34,* 763–768.

Williams, R. L. (1976). *Manual of direction for Williams awareness sentence completion.* St. Louis, MO: Robert L. Williams & Associates.

Williamson, D. A. (1990). *Assessment of eating disorders: Obesity, anorexia, and bulimia nervosa.* New York: Pergamon Press.

Williamson, D. A., Cubic, B. A., & Gleaves, D. H. (1993). Equivalence of body image disturbances in anorexia and bulimia nervosa. *Journal of Abnormal Psychology, 102,* 177–180.

Willis, S. L., & Nesselroade, C. S. (1990). Long-term effects of fluid ability training in old-old age. *Developmental Psychology, 26,* 905–910.

Willis, W. D. (1985). *The pain system. The neural basis of nociceptive transmission in the mammalian nervous system.* Basel: Karger.

Wilson, D. W. (1981). Is helping a laughing matter? *Psychology, 18,* 6–9.

Wilson, T. D., DePaulo, B. M., Mook, D. G., & Klaaren, K. J. (1993). Scientists' evaluations of research: The biasing effects of the importance of the topic. *Psychological Science, 4,* 322–325.

Wilson, T. D., & Klaaren, K. J. (1992). *Effects of affective expectations on willingness to relive pleasant and unpleasant events.* Unpublished data. Cited in Wilson, T. D., & Klaaren, K. J., "Expectation whirls me round": The role of affective expectations in affective experience. In M. S. Clark (Ed.), *Emotion and social behavior* (pp. 1–31). Newbury Park, CA: Sage.

Wilson, T. D., Lisle, D. J., Kraft, D., & Wetzel, C. G. (1989). Preferences as expectation-driven inferences: Effects of affective expectations on affective experience. *Journal of Personality and Social Psychology, 56,* 519–530.

Wilson, T. D., & Schooner, J. (1991). Thinking too much: Introspection can reduce the quality of preferences and decisions. *Journal of Personality and Social Psychology, 60,* 181–192.

Winefield, A. H., & Tiggemann, M. (1991). Employment status and psychological well-being: A longitudinal study. *Journal of Applied Psychology, 75,* 455–459.

Winett, R. A., & Neale, M. S. (1981). Flexible work schedules and family time allocation: Assessment of a system change on individual behavior using self-report logs. *Journal of Applied Behavior Analysis, 14,* 39–46.

Winograd, E. (1988). Some observations on prospective remembering. In M. M. Gruneberg, P. E. Morris, & R. N. Sykes (Eds.), *Practical aspects of memory: Current research and issues: Vol. 1* (pp. 348–353). Chichester, England: John Wiley & Sons.

Winter, D. G. (1973). *The power motives.* New York: Free Press.

Winter, D. G. (1983). *Development of an integrated system for scoring motives in verbal running text.* Unpublished manuscript, Wesleyan University.

Wise, R. A., & Bozarth, M. A. (1987). A psychomotor stimulant theory of addiction. *Psychological Review, 94,* 469–492.

Wogalter, M. S., & Kalsher, M. J. (1994). Increasing the correct connection of automobile battery jumper cables with an enhanced warning. In H. Zwaga & T. Boersema (Eds.) , *Proceedings of Public Graphics Symposium: Visual Information for Everday Use.* Lunteren, Netherlands.

Wogalter, M. S., Kalsher, M. J., & Racicot, B. M. (1993). Behavioral compliance with warnings: Effects of voice, context, and location. *Safety Science, 16,* 637–654.

Wogalter, M. S., Racicot, B. M., Kalsher, M. J., & Simpson, S. N. (1993). Behavioral compliance to personalized warning signs and the role of perceived relevance. *Proceedings of the Human Factors and Ergonomics Society, 37th Annual Meeting,* 950–954.

Wogalter, M. S., & Young, S. L. (1991). Behavioural compliance to voice and print warnings. *Ergonomics, 34,* 79–89.

Wogalter, M. S., & Young, S. L. (1993). Using warnings to increase safe behavior: A process approach. *Best's safety directory.* Oldwick, NJ: A. M. Best Company.

Wolberg, L. R. (1977). *The technique of psychotherapy.* New York: Grune & Stratton.

Wolf, M., Risley, T., & Mees, H. (1964). Application of operant conditioning procedures to the behavior problems of an autistic child. *Behavior Research and Therapy, 1,* 305–312.

Wolfe, D. A., Sandler, J., & Kaufman, K. (1981). Competency-based parent training program for child abusers. *Journal of Consulting and Clinical Psychology, 49,* 633–640.

Wolpe, J. (1958). *Psychotherapy by reciprocal inhibition.* Stanford, CA: Stanford University Press.

Wolpe, J. (1969). *The practice of behavior therapy.* Oxford: Pergamon Press.

Wong, D. F., Gjedde, A., Wagner, H. N., Jr., Tune, L. E., Dannals, R. F., Pearlsson, G. D., Links, J. M., Tamminga, C. A., Broussolle, E. P., Ravert, H. T., Wilson, A. A., Toung, J. K. T., Malat, J., Williams, F. A., O'Touma, L. A., Snyder, S. H., & Kuhar, M. J. (1986). Positron emission tomography reveals elevated D2 dopamine receptors in drug-naive schizophrenics. *Science, 234,* 1558–1563.

Wood, R. A., & Locke, E. A. (1990). Goal setting and strategy effects on complex tasks. In B. M. Staw & L. L. Cummings (Eds.), *Research in organizational behavior* (Vol. 12, pp. 73–110). Greenwich, CT: JAI Press.

Wood, W., Wong, F. Y., & Chachere, J. G. (1991). Effects of media violence on viewers' aggression in unconstrained social interaction. *Psychological Bulletin, 109,* 373–383.

Woodall, K. L., & Matthews, K. A. (1993). Changes in and stability of hostile characteristics: Results from a 4-year longitudinal study of children. *Journal of Personality and Social Psychology, 64,* 491–499.

Wortman, C. B., & Linsenmeier, H. A. W. (1977). Interpersonal attraction and techniques of ingratiation in organizational settings. In B. N. Staw & G. R. Salancik (Eds.), *New directions in organizational behavior* (pp. 133–178). Chicago: St. Clair Press.

Wright, P. L. (1990). Teller job satisfaction and organization commitment as they relate to career orientations. *Human Relations, 43,* 369–381.

Wright, R. W. (1982). *The sense of smell.* Boca Raton, FL: CRC Press.

Wrightsman, L. S. (1988). *Personality development in adulthood.* Newbury Park, CA: Sage.

Wylie, R. (1974). *The self-concept* (Vol. 1). Lincoln: University of Nebraska Press.

Yankner, J., Johnson, S. T., Menerdo, T., Cordell, B., & Firth, C. L. (1990). Relations of neural APP-751/APP-695 in RNA ratio and neuritic plaque density in Alzheimer's disease. *Science, 248,* 854–856.

Yogman, M. W. (1981). Development of the father-infant relationship. In H. Fitzgerald, B. Lester, & M. W. Yogman (Eds.), *Theory and research in behavioral pediatrics* (Vol. 1, pp. 221–279). New York: Plenum.

Yonas, A., Arterberry, M. E., & Granrud, C. E. (1987). Four-month-old infants' sensitivity to binocular and kinetic information for three-dimensional object shape. *Child Development, 58,* 910–927.

Young, A. M., & Herling, S. (1986). Drugs as reinforcers: Studies in laboratory animals. In S. R. Goldberg & I. P. Stolerman (Eds.), *Behavioral analysis of drug dependence* (pp. 9–67). New York: Academic Press.

Yuille, J. C., & Cutshall, J. L. (1986). A case study of eyewitness memory of a crime. *Journal of Applied Psychology, 71,* 291–301.

Yuille, J. C., & Tollestrup, P. A. (1990). Some effects of alcohol on eyewitness memory. *Journal of Applied Psychology, 75,* 268–273.

Yukl, G. (1989). *Leadership in organizations* (2nd ed.). Englewood Cliffs, NJ: Prentice Hall.

Zaccaro, S. J., Foti, R. J., & Kennedy, D. A. (1991). Self-monitoring and trait-based variance in leadership: An investigation of leader-flexibility across multiple group situations. *Journal of Applied Psychology, 76,* 308–315.

Zacks, R. T., & Hasher, L. (1988). Capacity theory and the processing of inferences. In L. Light & D. Burke (Eds.), *Language, memory, and aging.* New York: Cambridge University Press.

Zaidel, D. W. (1994). Worlds apart: Pictorial semantics in the left and right cerebral hemispheres. *Current Directions in Psychological Science, 3,* 5–8.

Zajonc, R. B. (1968). Attitudinal effects of mere exposure. *Journal of Personality and Social Psychology Monograph Supplement, 9,* 1–27.

Zajonc, R. B. (1976). Family configuration and intelligence. *Science, 192,* 226–236.

Zajonc, R. B. (1985). Emotion and facial efference: A theory reclaimed. *Science, 228,* 15–21.

Zajonc, R. B. (1986, February). Mining new gold from old research. *Psychology Today.*

Zajonc, R. B., & Markus, G. B. (1975). Birth order and intellectual development. *Psychological Review, 82,* 74–88.

Zajonc, R. B., & McIntosh, D. N. (1992). Emotions research: Some promising questions and some questionable promises. *Psychological Science, 3,* 70–74.

Zajonc, R. B., Murphy, S. T., & Inglehart, M. (1989). Feeling and facial efference: Implications of the vascular theory of emotions. *Psychological Review, 96,* 395–416.

Zatzick, D. F., & Dimsdale, J. E. (1990). *Psychosomatic Medicine, 52,* 544–557.

Zeki, S. (1992, September). The visual image in mind and brain. *Scientific American,* pp. 69–76.

Zigler, E., & Berman, W. (1983). Discerning the future of early childhood intervention. *American Psychologist, 38,* 894–906.

Zillmann, D. (1984). *Connections between sex and aggression.* Hillsdale, NJ: Erlbaum.

Zillmann, D. (1988). Cognition-excitation interdependencies in aggressive behavior. *Aggressive Behavior, 14,* 51–64.

Zillmann, D., Baron, R. A., & Tamborini, R. (1981). Social costs of smoking: Effects of tobacco smoke on hostile behavior. *Journal of Applied Social Psychology, 11,* 548–561.

Zillmann, D., & Bryant, J. (1984). Effects of massive exposure to pornography. In N. M. Malamuth & E. Donnerstein (Eds.), *Pornography and sexual aggression.* New York: Academic Press.

Zillmann, D., & Bryant, J. (1988). Pornography's impact on sexual satisfaction. *Journal of Applied Social Psychology, 18,* 438–453.

Zimbardo, P. G. (1977). *Shyness: What it is and what you can do about it.* Reading, MA: Addison-Wesley.

Zuckerman, M. (1984). Sensation seeking: A comparative approach to a human trait. *Behavioral and Brain Sciences, 7,* 413–471.

Zuckerman, M. (1990). The psychophysiology of sensation seeking. *Journal of Personality, 58,* 313–345.

Zuckerman, M., & Neeb, M. (1980). Demographic influences in sensation seeking and expression of sensation seeking in religion, smoking, and driving habits. *Personality and Individual Differences, 1,* 197–206.

Zuckerman, M., Simons, R. F., & Como, P. (1988). Sensation seeking and stimulus intensity as modulators of cortical, cardiovascular, and electrodermal responses: A cross-modality study. *Personality and Individual Differences, 9,* 361–372.

GLOSSARY

Absolute Threshold: The smallest amount of a stimulus that we can detect 50 percent of the time.

Accommodation: In Piaget's theory, the modification of existing mental frameworks to take account of new information.

Achievement Motivation: The desire to accomplish difficult tasks and meet standards of excellence.

Acquired Immune Deficiency Syndrome (AIDS): A fatal viral infection that reduces the immune system's ability to defend itself against the introduction of foreign matter.

Acquisition: The process by which a conditioned stimulus acquires the ability to elicit a conditioned response through repeated pairings of an unconditioned stimulus with the conditioned stimulus.

Action Potential: A rapid shift in the electrical charge across the cell membrane of neurons. This disturbance along the membrane communicates information within neurons.

Acuity: The visual ability to see fine details.

Adaptation: In Piaget's theory of cognitive development, building mental representations of the world through interaction with it.

Adolescence: A period beginning with the onset of puberty and ending when individuals assume adult roles and responsibilities.

Adolescent Invulnerability: Adolescents' belief that they are immune from the potential harm of high-risk behaviors.

Affect: A person's current mood.

Aggression: Behavior directed toward the goal of harming another living being who wishes to avoid such treatment.

Aggressive Motivation: The desire to inflict harm on others.

Agoraphobia: Fear of losing control and experiencing a panic attack in specific situations, such as in open places, in a crowd, or on an airplane.

Agreeableness: One of the "big five" dimensions of personality; ranges from good-natured, cooperative, trusting at one end to irritable, suspicious, uncooperative at the other.

Algorithm: A rule that guarantees a solution to a specific type of problem.

Alpha Waves: Brain waves that occur when individuals are awake but relaxed.

Alzheimer's Disease: An illness primarily afflicting individuals over the age of sixty-five and involving severe mental deterioration, including retrograde amnesia.

Amnesia: Loss of memory stemming from illness, accident, drug abuse, or other causes.

Amphetamines: Drugs that act as stimulants, increasing feelings of energy and activation.

Anal Stage: In Freud's theory, a psychosexual stage of development in which pleasure is focused primarily on the anal zone.

Analogy: A strategy for solving problems based on applying solutions that were previously successful with other problems similar in underlying structure.

Anchoring-and-Adjustment Heuristic: A cognitive rule of thumb for decision making in which existing information is accepted as a reference point but then adjusted in light of various factors.

Anima: According to Jung, the archetype representing the feminine side of males.

Animus: According to Jung, the archetype representing the masculine side of females.

Anorexia Nervosa: An eating disorder in which persons starve themselves and often lose a dangerous amount of weight.

Anterograde Amnesia: The inability to store in long-term memory information that occurs after an amnesia-inducing event.

Antisocial Personality Disorder: A personality disorder involving a lack of conscience and sense of responsibility, impulsive behavior, irritability, and aggressiveness.

Anxiety: In Freudian theory, unpleasant feelings of tension or worry experienced by individuals in reaction to unacceptable wishes or impulses; increased arousal accompanied by generalized feelings of fear or apprehension.

Anxiety Disorders: Psychological disorders that center on the occurrence of anxiety and include generalized anxiety, phobias, and obsessive-compulsive disorders.

Apnea: Cessation of breathing during sleep.

Archetypes: According to Jung, inherited images in the collective unconscious that shape our perceptions of the external world.

Arousal Theory: A theory of motivation suggesting that human beings seek an optimal level of arousal, not minimal levels of arousal.

Artificial Intelligence: A branch of science that studies the capacity of computers to demonstrate performance that, if it were produced by human beings, would be described as showing intelligence.

Assimilation: In Piaget's theory, the tendency to understand new information in terms of existing mental frameworks.

Attachment: A strong affectional bond between infants and their caregivers.

Attention-Deficit Hyperactivity Disorder: A psychological disorder in which children are unable to concentrate their attention on any task for more than a few minutes.

Attitudes: Mental representations and evaluations of features of the social or physical world.

Attribution: The processes through which we seek to determine the causes behind others' behavior.

Automatic Processing: Processing of information with minimal conscious awareness.

Automatic Vigilance: The strong tendency to pay attention to negative social information.

Autonomic Nervous System: The part of the peripheral nervous system that connects internal organs, glands, and involuntary muscles to the central nervous system.

Availability Heuristic: A cognitive rule of thumb in which the importance or probability of various events is judged on the basis of how readily they come to mind.

Avoidant Attachment: A pattern of attachment in which infants don't cry when their mother leaves them alone during the strange situation test.

Axon Terminals: Structures at the end of axons that contain transmitter substances.

Axons: The parts of the neurons that conduct the action potential away from the cell body.

Babbling: An early stage of speech development in which infants emit virtually all known sounds of human speech.

Backward Conditioning: A type of conditioning in which the presentation of the unconditioned stimulus precedes and does not overlap with the presentation of the conditioned stimulus.

Barbiturates: Drugs that act as depressants, reducing activity in the nervous system and behavior output.

Behavior Therapies: Forms of psychotherapy that focus on changing maladaptive patterns of behavior through the use of basic principles of learning.

Behaviorism: The view that psychology should study only observable behavior.

Binocular Cues: Cues to depth or distance provided by the use of both eyes.

Biological Constraints on Learning: Tendencies of some species to acquire some forms of conditioning less readily than other species do.

Biological Rhythms: Cyclic changes in bodily processes.

Biologically Based Therapies: Forms of therapy that attempt to reduce psychological disorders through biological means such as drug therapy or surgery.

Biopsychology: The branch of psychology concerned with discovering the biological bases of our thoughts, feelings, and behaviors.

Bipolar Disorder: A mood disorder involving swings between depression and mania.

Bisexual (sexual orientation): A sexual orientation in which individuals seek sexual relations with members of both their own and the other sex.

Blended Families: Families resulting from remarriage, consisting of biological parents, step-parents, and biological children of one or both spouses.

Blind Spot: The point in the back of the retina through which the optic nerve exits the eye. This exit point contains no rods or cones and is therefore insensitive to light.

Body Language: Nonverbal cues involving body posture or movement of body parts.

Body-Mass Index: A measure of degree of obesity, based on the ratio between height and weight.

Braille Alphabet: Representation of letters by a system of raised dots, used in reading materials for blind persons.

Brightness: The physical intensity of light.

Brightness Constancy: The tendency to perceive objects as having a constant brightness even when they are viewed under different conditions of illumination.

Bulimia: An eating disorder in which periods of binge eating alternate with periods of self-induced purging.

Bystander Effect: A reduced tendency of witnesses to an emergency to help when they believe that there are other potential helpers present.

Cancer: A group of illnesses in which abnormal cells are formed that are able to proliferate, invade, and overwhelm normal tissues and to spread to distant sites in the body.

Cannon-Bard Theory: A theory of emotion suggesting that various emotion-provoking events simultaneously produce subjective reactions labeled as emotions and physiological arousal.

Carcinogens: Cancer-producing agents.

Cardinal Trait: According to Allport, a single trait that dominates an individual's entire personality.

Cardiovascular Disease: All diseases of the heart and blood vessels.

Case Method: A method of research in which detailed information about individuals is used to develop general principles about behavior.

Central Nervous System: The brain and the spinal cord.

Central Route (to persuasion): Attitude change resulting from systematic processing of information contained in persuasive messages.

Central Tendency: The middle (center) of a distribution of scores.

Central Traits: According to Allport, the five or ten traits that best describe an individual's personality.

Cerebellum: A part of the brain concerned with the regulation and coordination of basic motor activities.

Cerebral Cortex: The outer covering of the cerebral hemispheres.

Chaining: A procedure that establishes a sequence of responses, which lead to a reward following the final response in the chain.

Childhood: The period between birth and adolescence.

Choking under Pressure: The tendency to perform less well at times when pressures for excellent performance are especially high.

Chromosomes: Threadlike structures containing genetic material, found in nearly every cell of the body.

Chunk: Stimuli perceived as a single unit or a meaningful grouping. Most people can retain seven to nine chunks of information in short-term memory at a given time.

Circadian Rhythms: Cyclic changes in bodily processes occurring within a single day.

Classical Conditioning: A basic form of learning in which one stimulus comes to serve as a signal for the occurrence of a second stimulus. During classical conditioning, organisms acquire information about the relations between various stimuli, not simple associations between them.

Client-Centered Therapy: A form of psychotherapy that concentrates on eliminating irrational conditions of worth—conditions people believe they must meet in order to be loved or accepted.

Climacteric: A period during which the functioning of the reproductive system, and various aspects of sexual activity, change greatly.

Cocaine: A powerful stimulant that produces pleasurable sensations of increased energy and self-confidence.

Cochlea: A portion of the inner ear containing the sensory receptors for sound.

Cognition: The activities involved in thinking, reasoning, decision making, memory, problem solving, and all other forms of higher mental processes.

Cognitive Behavior Therapy: A form of psychotherapy designed to overcome depression by changing self-defeating patterns of thought.

Cognitive Development: Changes in cognitive abilities and functioning occurring as individuals grow older.

Cognitive Dissonance: The state experienced by individuals when they discover inconsistency between two attitudes they hold or between their attitudes and their behavior.

Cognitive Perspective on Persuasion: An approach that seeks to understand persuasion by identifying the cognitive processes that play a role in it.

Cognitive Therapy: Psychotherapy that concentrates on altering faulty or distorted modes of thought so as to alleviate psychological disorders.

Cohort Effects: Differences between persons of different ages stemming from the contrasting social or cultural conditions of the periods in which they grew up.

Collective Unconscious: In Jung's theory, a portion of the unconscious shared by all human beings.

Community Mental Health Centers: Facilities for the delivery of mental health services located in communities where clients live.

Companionate Love: A form of love involving a high degree of commitment and deep concern for the well-being of the beloved.

Complaining: Expressing discontent or dissatisfaction with oneself or with some aspect of the external world.

Complex Cells: Neurons in the visual cortex that respond to stimuli moving in a particular direction and having a particular orientation.

Compliance: A form of social influence in which one or more persons accepts direct requests from one or more others.

Componential Intelligence: The ability to think analytically.

Concrete Operations: In Piaget's theory, a stage of cognitive development occurring roughly between the ages of seven and eleven. It is at this stage that children grasp such principles as conservation and the capacity for logical thought emerges.

Concurrent Validity: The relationship between test scores and current performance relative to some criterion.

Conditioned Response (CR): In classical conditioning, the response to the conditioned stimulus.

Conditioned Stimulus (CS): In classical conditioning, the stimulus that is repeatedly paired with an unconditioned stimulus.

Conditioned Taste Aversion: A type of conditioning in which the UCS (usually internal cues associated with nausea or vomiting) occurs several hours after the CS (often a novel food), leading to a strong CS–UCS association in a single trial.

Conditions of Worth: In Rogers's theory, individuals' beliefs that they must meet certain unrealistic conditions in order to be loved or accepted.

Cones: Sensory receptors in the eye that play a crucial role in sensations of color.

Confirmation Bias: The tendency to pay attention primarily to information that confirms existing views or beliefs.

Conformity: A type of social influence in which individuals experience pressure to adhere to existing social norms.

Conscientiousness: One of the "big five" dimensions of personality; this dimension ranges from well-organized, careful, responsible at one end to disorganized, careless, unscrupulous at the other.

Consensus: The extent to which behavior by one person is shown by others as well.

Conservation: Principle that states that certain physical attributes of an object remain unchanged even though its outward appearance changes.

Consistency: The extent to which a given person responds in the same way to a given stimulus across time.

Consolidation of Memory: The process of shifting new information from short-term to long-term storage.

Constancies: Our tendency to perceive physical objects as unchanging despite shifts in the pattern of sensations these objects induce.

Construct Validity: The extent to which a test measures a variable or concept described by a psychological theory.

Contact Hypothesis: The suggestion that increased contact between members of different social groups will reduce prejudice between them.

Content Validity: The extent to which the items on a test sample the skills or knowledge needed for achievement in a given field or task.

Context-Dependent Memory: The greater ease of recall of information entered into memory in one context or setting in that same context than in others.

Contextual Intelligence: The ability to adapt to a changing environment.

Continuous Reinforcement Schedule: A schedule of reinforcement in which every occurrence of a particular behavior is reinforced.

Control Theory of Self-Consciousness: A theory suggesting that people compare their current behavior and states with important goals and values. They then alter their behavior to close any gaps they observe.

Controlled Processing: Processing of information with relatively high levels of conscious awareness.

Conventional Level (of morality): According to Kohlberg, a stage of moral development during which individuals judge morality largely in terms of existing social norms or rules.

Convergent Thinking: Thinking that applies existing knowledge and rules of logic so as to zero in on a single correct solution to a problem.

Conversion Disorder: Psychological disorder in which individuals experience real motor or sensory symptoms for which there is no known organic cause.

Cornea: The curved, transparent layer through which light rays enter the eye.

Corpus Callosum: A band of nerve fibers connecting the two hemispheres of the brain.

Correlation Coefficient: A statistic indicating the degree of relationship between two or more variables.

Correlational Method: A research method in which investigators observe two or more variables to determine whether changes in one are accompanied by changes in the other.

Counterfactual Thinking: The tendency to evaluate events by thinking about alternatives to them—"what might have been."

Crack: A cocaine derivative that can be smoked. It acts as a powerful stimulant.

Creativity: Cognitive activity resulting in new or novel ways of viewing or solving problems.

Criterion-Related Validity: A measure of the validity of any psychological test, determined by correlations between scores on the test and some standard of the characteristic the test supposedly assesses.

Critical Thinking: Careful assessment of available evidence in order to evaluate claims and statements in an objective and reasoned manner.

Cross-Sectional Research: Research comparing groups of persons of different ages in order to determine how some aspect of behavior or cognition changes with age.

Cross-Tolerance: Increased tolerance for one drug that develops as a result of taking another drug.

Crystallized Intelligence: Aspects of intelligence that draw on previously learned information to make decisions or solve problems.

Cultural Bias: The tendency of items on a test of intelligence to require specific cultural experience or knowledge.

Dark Adaptation: The process by which the visual system increases its sensitivity to light under low illumination.

Daydreams: Imaginary scenes or events that occur while a person is awake.

Debriefing: In psychological research, the provision of complete and accurate information about a study to participants after they have taken part in it.

Deception: Withholding information about a study from participants. Deception is used in situations where the information that is withheld is likely to alter participants' behavior.

Decision Making: The process of choosing among various courses of action or alternatives.

Defense Mechanisms: Techniques used by the ego to keep threatening and unacceptable material out of consciousness and so to reduce anxiety.

Delayed Conditioning: A form of forward conditioning in which presentation of the conditioned stimulus precedes, but overlaps with, presentation of the unconditioned stimulus.

Delta Waves: High-amplitude, slow brain waves that occur during several stages of sleep, but especially Stage 4.

Delusions: Irrational but firmly held beliefs about the world that have no basis in reality.

Demand Characteristics: Implicit pressure on research participants to act in ways consistent with a researcher's expectations.

Dendrites: The parts of neurons that conduct action potentials toward the cell body.

Dependence: Strong physiolgical or psychological need for particular drugs.

Dependent Variable: The aspect of behavior that is measured in an experiment.

Depressants: Drugs that reduce activity in the nervous system and therefore slow many bodily and cognitive processes. Depressants include alcohol and barbiturates.

Depression: A psychological disorder involving intense feelings of sadness, lack of energy, and feelings of hopelessness and despair.

Descriptive Statistics: Statistics that summarize the major characteristics of an array of scores.

Developmental Psychology: The branch of psychology that studies all types of changes occurring throughout the life span.

Diagnostic and Statistical Manual of Mental Disorders-IV (DSM-IV): The latest version of a manual widely used for diagnosing various psychological disorders.

Diathesis-Stress Model: A model of schizophrenia suggesting that persons with inherited dispositions to develop this disorder do so only when subjected to stressful environmental conditions.

Difference Threshold: The amount of change in a stimulus required before a person can detect the shift.

Diffusion of Responsibility: A sharing of responsibility among all potential helpers who witness an emergency; the result is that each feels less responsible for helping victims.

Discriminative Stimulus: Stimulus that signals the availability of reinforcement if a specific response is made.

Disorganized (or Disoriented) Attachment: A pattern of attachment in which infants show contradictory reactions to their mother after being reunited with her during the strange situation test.

Dispersion: The extent to which scores in a distribution spread out or vary around the center.

Dissociative Amnesia: Amnesia for which there is no organic cause.

Dissociative Disorder: Psychological disorder in which individuals experience profound and lengthy losses of identity or memory.

Dissociative Fugue: Form of dissociative amnesia in which individuals forget their identity and virtually all of their past life.

Dissociative Identity Disorder: Multiple personality disorder, in which a single individual seems to possess more than one personality.

Distinctiveness: The extent to which a given person reacts in the same manner to different stimuli or situations.

Divergent Thinking: Thinking that moves outside conventional solutions or knowledge in an effort to develop novel solutions to a problem.

Door-in-the-Face Technique: A technique for gaining compliance in which a large request is followed by a smaller one.

Dopamine Hypothesis: The hypothesis that schizophrenia is associated with excess activity in those parts of the brain in which dopamine is the primary neurotransmitter.

Double-Blind Procedure: Procedure in which neither the persons collecting data nor research participants have knowledge of the experimental conditions to which they have been assigned.

Down Syndrome: A disorder caused by an extra chromosome and characterized by varying degrees of retardation and physical disorders.

Dream: In Levinson's theory of adult development, a vision of future accomplishments.

Dreams: Cognitive events, often vivid but disconnected, that occur during sleep; most dreams take place during REM sleep.

Dreams of Absent-Minded Transgression: Dreams in which persons attempting to change their own behavior, as in quitting smoking, see themselves unintentionally slipping into the unwanted behavior.

Drive Theory: A theory of motivation suggesting that behavior is "pushed" from within by drives stemming from basic biological needs.

Drug Abuse: Instances in which individuals take drugs purely to change their moods, and in which they experience impaired behavior or social functioning as a result of doing so.

Drug Therapy: Efforts to treat psychological disorders through administration of appropriate drugs.

Drugs: Chemical substances that change the structure or function of biological systems.

Dysfunctional Families: Families that do not meet the needs of children and in fact do them serious harm.

Eating Disorders: Serious disturbances in eating habits or patterns that pose a threat to individuals' physical health and well-being.

Ego: In Freud's theory, the part of personality that takes rational account of external reality in the expression of instinctive sexual and aggressive urges.

Egocentrism: The inability of young children to distinguish their own perspective from that of others.

Elaboration Likelihood Model (of persuasion): A theory suggesting that there are two distinct routes to persuasion involving different amounts of cognitive elaboration in response to a persuasive message.

Elaborative Rehearsal: Rehearsal in which the meaning of information is considered and the information is related to other knowledge already present in memory.

Electroconvulsive Therapy (ECT): A treatment for depression in which patients receive powerful electric shocks to the head.

Electroencephalogram (EEG): A record of electrical activity within the brain. EEGs play an important role in the scientific study of sleep.

Electroencephalography (EEG): A technique for measuring the electrical activity of the brain via electrodes placed at specified locations on the skull.

Embryo: The developing child during the second through the eighth week of prenatal development.

Emotional Stability: One of the "big five" dimensions of personality; ranges from poised, calm, composed at one end to nervous, anxious, excitable at the other.

Emotions: Reactions consisting of physiological changes, subjective cognitive states, and expressive behaviors.

Encoding: The process through which information is converted into a form that can be entered into memory.

Encoding Specificity Principle: The fact that only cues encoded at the time information is entered into memory can later contribute to the retrieval of such information.

Encounter Groups: A form of group therapy in which people are urged to tell other group members exactly how they feel; designed to foster personal growth through increased understanding of one's own behavior and increased honesty and openness in personal relations.

Endocrine Glands: Glands that secrete hormones directly into the bloodstream.

Endorphins: Morphine-like substances produced by the body.

Environmental Psychology: The branch of psychology that investigates the effects of the physical environment on human behavior and the effects of that behavior on the environment.

Episodic Memory: Memories of events that we have experienced personally (sometimes termed autobiographical memory).

Escalation of Commitment: The tendency to become increasingly committed to bad decisions even as losses associated with them increase.

Ethological Theory (of attachment): A theory suggesting that infants are born with a set of behaviors that elicit parental care and so increase the infants' chances of survival.

Evolutionary Psychology: A branch of psychology that studies the adaptive problems humans faced over the course of evolution and the behavioral mechanisms that evolved in response to these environmental pressures.

Expectancy Theory: A theory of motivation suggesting that behavior is elicited by expectations of desirable outcomes.

Experiential Intelligence: The ability to formulate new ideas or to combine seemingly unrelated information.

Experimentation: A research method where investigators systematically alter one or more variables in order to deter-mine whether such changes will influence some aspect of behavior.

Experimenter Effects: Unintentional influence exerted by researchers on research participants.

Explicit (Declarative) Memory: A memory system that permits us to express the information it contains verbally. It includes both semantic and episodic memory.

Externals: In Rotter's terms, individuals who believe that they have little control over the outcomes they experience.

Extinction: The process through which a conditioned stimulus gradually loses the ability to elicit conditioned responses when it is no longer followed by the unconditioned stimulus.

Extrasensory Perception (ESP): Perception without a basis in sensory input.

Extraversion: One of the "big five" dimensions of personality; ranges from sociable, talkative, fun-loving at one end to sober, reserved, cautious at the other.

Extroverts: Individuals who are talkative and sociable, and who often give free rein to their impulses and feelings.

Eyewitness Testimony: Information provided by witnesses to crimes or accidents.

Facial Feedback Hypothesis: A hypothesis indicating that facial expressions can influence as well as reflect emotional states.

False Consensus Effect: The tendency to believe that other persons share our attitudes to a greater extent than is true.

Family Therapy: A form of psychotherapy that focuses on changing interactions or relations among family members.

Fantasies: Imaginary events or scenes that a person experiences while awake.

Farsightedness: A condition in which the visual image of a nearby object is focused behind rather than directly on the retina. Therefore close objects appear out of focus, while distant objects are seen clearly.

Fast Mapping: A process through which children attach a new word to an underlying concept on the basis of a single encounter with it.

Feature Detectors: Neurons at various levels within the visual cortex that respond primarily to stimuli possessing certain features.

Fetus: The developing child during the last seven months of prenatal development.

Figure-Ground Relationship: Our tendency to divide the perceptual world into two distinct parts: discrete figures and the background against which they stand out.

Fixation: Excessive investment of psychic energy in a particular stage of psychosexual development, which results in various types of psychological disorders.

Fixed-Interval Schedule: A schedule of reinforcement in which a specific interval of time must elapse before a response will yield reinforcement.

Fixed-Ratio Schedule: A schedule of reinforcement in which reinforcement occurs only after a fixed number of responses have been emitted.

Flashbulb Memories: Vivid memories of what we were doing at the time of an emotion-provoking event.

Flooding: A procedure for eliminating conditioned fears that is based on principles of classical conditioning. During flooding an individual is exposed to fear-inducing objects or events. Since no unconditioned stimulus then follows, extinction of fears eventually takes place.

Fluid Intelligence: Aspects of intelligence that involve forming concepts, reasoning, and identifying similarities.

Foot-in-the-Door Technique: A technique for gaining compliance in which a small request is followed by a larger one.

Forced Compliance: A situation in which we feel compelled to say or do things inconsistent with our true attitudes.

Formal Operations: In Piaget's theory, the final stage of cognitive development, during which individuals may acquire the capacity for deductive or propositional reasoning.

Fovea: The area in the center of the retina in which cones are highly concentrated.

Framing: Presentation of information concerning potential outcomes in terms of gains or losses.

Free Association: A key procedure in psychoanalysis in which individuals spontaneously report all thoughts to the therapist.

Frequency Distribution: The frequency with which each score occurs within an entire distribution of scores.

Frequency Theory: A theory of pitch perception suggesting that sounds of different frequencies, heard as differences in pitch, induce different rates of neural activity in the hair cells of the inner ear.

Freudian Slips: Statements that seem to be simple errors in speech, but which in fact reveal unconscious thoughts or impulses.

Frontal Lobe: The portion of the cerebral cortex that lies in front of the central fissure.

Frustration: The blocking of ongoing goal-directed behavior.

Fully Functioning Persons: In Rogers's theory, psychologically healthy persons who enjoy life to the fullest.

Functional Autonomy: In Allport's theory, maintenance of patterns of behavior by motives other than the ones originally responsible for the behavior's occurrence.

Functional Fixedness: The tendency to think of using objects only as they have been used in the past.

Functionalism: An early view of psychology suggesting that psychology should study the ways in which the ever-changing stream of conscious experience helps us adapt to a complex and challenging world.

Fundamental Attribution Error: The tendency to attribute behavior to internal causes to a greater extent than is actually justified.

Gate-Control Theory: A theory suggesting that the spinal cord contains a mechanism that can block transmission of pain signals to the brain.

Gender: An individual's membership in one of the two sexes; all the attributes, behaviors, and expectancies associated with each sex in a given society.

Gender Constancy: Children's understanding that gender is stable over time.

Gender Roles: Beliefs about how males and females are expected to behave in many situations.

Gender Schema Theory: A theory that children develop a cognitive framework, or schema, reflecting the beliefs of their society concerning the characteristics and roles of males and females; this gender schema then strongly affects the processing of new social information.

General Adaptation Syndrome (GAS): A three-phase model of how organisms respond to stress: (1) alarm or mobilization, (2) resistance, and (3) exhaustion.

Genes: Biological "blueprints" that shape development and all basic bodily processes.

Genetic Theories of Aging: Theories suggesting that aging results from genetic programming that regulates the aging process.

Genital Stage: In Freud's theory, the final psychosexual stage of development—one in which individuals acquire the adult capacity to combine lust with affection.

Gestalt Psychologists: German psychologists intrigued by our tendency to perceive sensory patterns as well-organized wholes rather than as separate, isolated parts.

Gestalt Therapy: A form of humanistic psychotherapy designed to increase individuals' awareness and understanding of their own feelings.

Gestures: Movements of various body parts that convey a specific meaning to others.

Glial Cells: Cells in the nervous system that surround, support, and protect neurons.

Gonads: The primary sex glands.

Graded Potential: A basic type of signal within neurons that results from external physical stimulation of the dendrite or cell body. Unlike the all-or-nothing nature of action potentials, graded potentials vary in proportion to the size of the stimulus that produced them.

Grammar: Rules within a given language indicating how words can be combined into meaningful sentences.

Group Therapies: Therapies conducted with groups of clients.

Hallucinations: Vivid sensory experiences that occur in the absence of external stimuli yet have the full force of impact of real events or stimuli.

Hallucinogens: Drugs that profoundly alter consciousness, such as marijuana and LSD.

Hardiness: A personality style characterized by high levels of commitment, a view of change as an opportunity for growth, and a strong sense of being in control.

Health Belief Model: A model predicting that whether a person practices a particular health behavior depends on the degree to which the person believes in a personal health threat and believes that practicing the behavior will reduce that threat.

Health Psychology: The study of the relation between psychological variables and health; reflects the view that both mind and body are important determinants of health and illness.

Heredity: Biologically inherited characteristics.

Heterosexual (sexual orientation): A sexual orientation in which individuals engage in sexual relations only with members of the other sex.

Heuristics: Mental rules of thumb that permit us to make decisions and judgments in a rapid and efficient manner.

Hierarchy of Needs: In Maslow's theory of motivation, an arrangement of needs from the most basic to those at the highest levels.

Hindsight Effect: The tendency to assume that we would have been better at predicting actual events than is really true.

Homeostasis: A state of physiological balance within the body.

Homosexual (sexual orientation): A sexual orientation in which individuals prefer sexual relations with members of their own sex.

Hormones: Substances secreted by endocrine glands that regulate a wide range of bodily processes.

Hue: The color that we experience due to the dominant wavelength of a light.

Humanistic Perspective: A perspective in modern psychology suggesting that human beings have free will and are not simply under the control of various internal and external factors.

Humanistic Theories: Theories of personality emphasizing personal responsibility and innate tendencies toward personal growth.

Humanistic Therapies: Forms of psychotherapy based on the assumption that psychological disorders stem from environmental conditions that block normal growth and development.

Hunger Motivation: The motivation to obtain and consume food.

Huntington's Disease: A genetically based fatal neuromuscular disorder characterized by the gradual onset of jerky, uncontrollable movements.

Hypercomplex Cells: Neurons in the visual cortex that respond to complex aspects of visual stimuli, such as width, length, and shape.

Hypersomnias: Disorders involving excessive amounts of sleep or an overwhelming urge to fall asleep.

Hypertension: High blood pressure, a condition in which the pressure within the blood vessels is abnormally high.

Hypnosis: An interaction between two persons in which one (the hypnotist) induces changes in the behavior, feelings, or cognitions of the other (the subject) through suggestions. Hypnosis involves subjects' expectations and their attempts to conform to the role of the hypnotized person.

Hypochondriasis: A psychological disorder in which individuals convert anxiety into chronic preoccupations with their health and bodily functions.

Hypothalamus: A small structure deep within the brain that plays a key role in the regulation of the autonomic nervous system and of several forms of motivated behavior such as eating and aggression.

Hypothesis: In psychology, a prediction about behavior that is to be investigated in a research project.

Hypothetico-Deductive Reasoning: In Piaget's theory, a type of reasoning first shown during the stage of formal operations. It involves formulating a general theory and deducing specific hypotheses from it.

Id: In Freud's theory, the portion of personality concerned with immediate gratification of primitive needs.

Illusions: Instances in which perception yields false interpretations of physical reality.

Implicit Memory: A memory system that stores information that we cannot express verbally; sometimes termed procedural memory.

Impression Management: Efforts by individuals to enhance the impression they make on others.

Incentives: Rewards individuals seek to attain.

Independent Variable: The variable that is systematically altered in an experiment.

Infantile Amnesia: Inability to remember the first two or three years of life, probably because we did not possess a well-developed self-concept during that period.

Inferential Statistics: Statistical procedures that provide information on the probability that an observed event is due to chance and that permit us to determine whether differences between individuals or groups are ones that are likely or unlikely to have occurred by chance.

Information-Processing Approach: An approach to understanding human memory that emphasizes the encoding, storage, and later retrieval of information.

Informed Consent: Participants' agreement to take part in a research project after they are provided with information about the nature of such participation.

Ingratiation: A technique of social influence based on inducing increased liking in the target person before influence is attempted.

Insomnia: Disorder involving the inability to fall asleep or remain asleep.

Instinct Theory: A theory of motivation suggesting that many forms of behavior stem from innate urges or tendencies.

Instincts: Patterns of behavior assumed to be universal in a species.

Intelligence: The ability to think abstractly and to learn readily from experience.

Internals: In Rotter's terms, individuals who believe that they exert considerable control over the outcomes they experience.

Interpersonal Attraction: The extent to which we like or dislike other persons.

Intrinsic Motivation: The desire to perform activities because they are rewarding in and of themselves.

Introverts: Individuals who are quiet, cautious, and reclusive, and who generally inhibit expression of their impulses and feelings.

IQ: A numerical value that reflects the extent to which an individual's score on an intelligence test departs from the average for other people of the same age.

Iris: The colored part of the eye that adjusts the amount of light that enters by constricting or dilating the pupil.

James-Lange Theory: A theory of emotion suggesting that emotion-provoking events produce various physiological reactions and that recognition of these is responsible for subjective emotional experiences.

Just Noticeable Difference (jnd): The smallest amount of change in a physical stimulus necessary for an individual to notice a difference in the intensity of the stimulus.

Kinesthesia: The sense that gives us information about the location of our body parts with respect to each other and allows us to perform movements.

Korsakoff's Syndrome: An illness caused by long-term abuse of alcohol that often involves profound retrograde amnesia.

Language: A system of symbols, plus rules for combining them, used to communicate information.

Late-Adult Transition: In Levinson's theory of adult development, a transition in which individuals must come to terms with their impending retirement.

Latency Stage: In Freud's theory, the psychosexual stage of development that follows resolution of the Oedipus complex. During this stage, sexual desires are relatively weak.

Latent Content: In Freud's theory, the hidden content of dreams.

Lateralization of Function: Specialization of the two hemispheres of the brain for the performance of different functions.

Laws of Grouping: Simple principles describing how we tend to group discrete stimuli together in the perceptual world.

Learned Helplessness: Feelings of helplessness that develop after exposure to situations in which nothing individuals do affects their outcomes. Learned helplessness appears to play a role in the occurrence of depression.

Learning: Any relatively permanent change in behavior (or behavior potential) resulting from experience.

Lens: A curved structure behind the pupil that bends light rays, focusing them on the retina.

Less-Leads-to-More Effect: The fact that rewards just barely sufficient to induce individuals to state positions contrary to their own views often generate more attitude change than larger rewards.

Levels of Processing View: A view of memory suggesting that the greater the effort expended in processing information, the more readily it will be recalled at later times.

Libido: According to Freud, the psychic energy that powers all mental activity.

Life Structure: In Levinson's theory of adult development, the underlying pattern or design of a person's life.

Lifestyle: In the context of health psychology, the overall pattern of decisions and behaviors that determine health and quality of life.

Limbic System: Several structures deep within the brain that play a role in emotional reactions and behavior.

Linguistic Relativity Hypothesis: The view that language shapes thought.

Localization: The ability of our auditory system to determine the direction of a sound source.

Longitudinal Research: Research in which the same individuals are studied across relatively substantial periods of time, such as years.

Longitudinal-Sequential Design: A research approach in which several groups of individuals of different ages are studied across time.

Long-Term Memory: A memory system for the retention of large amounts of information over long periods of time.

Love: A strong emotional state involving attraction, sexual desire, and concern for another person.

LSD: A powerful hallucinogen that produces profound shifts in perception; many of these are frightening in nature.

Magnetic Resonance Imaging (MRI): A method for studying the intact brain in which images are obtained by exposure of the brain to a strong magnetic field.

Make-Believe Play: Play in which children pretend to be engaging in various familiar activities, such as eating or going to sleep.

Manifest Content: In Freud's theory, the overt or reported content of dreams.

Marital Therapy: Psychotherapy that attempts to improve relations and understanding in couples.

Mean: A measure of central tendency derived by adding all scores and dividing by the number of scores.

Means-Ends Analysis: A technique for solving problems in which the overall problem is divided into parts and efforts are made to solve each part in turn.

Median: A measure of central tendency indicating the midpoint of an array of scores.

Medical Perspective: The view that psychological disorders have a biological basis and should be viewed as treatable diseases.

Medulla: A brain structure concerned with the regulation of vital bodily functions such as breathing and heartbeat.

Memory: The capacity to retain and later retrieve information.

Menopause: Cessation of the menstrual cycle.

Mental Retardation: Intellectual functioning that is considerably below average.

Mental Set: The impact of past experience on present problem solving; specifically, the tendency to retain methods that were successful in the past even if better alternatives now exist.

Mentor: In Levinson's theory of adult development, an older and more experienced individual who helps to guide younger adults.

Meta-Analysis: Statistical procedures for combining the results of many studies in order to determine whether their findings provide support for specific hypotheses.

Metacognition: Awareness and understanding of our own cognitive processes.

Midbrain: A part of the brain containing primitive centers for vision and hearing. It also plays a role in the regulation of visual reflexes.

Midlife Transition: In Levinson's theory of adult development, a turbulent transitional period occurring between the ages of forty and forty-five.

Mitosis: Cell division in which chromosome pairs split and then replicate themselves so that the full number is restored in each of the cells produced by division.

Mode: A measure of central tendency indicating the most frequent score in an array of scores.

Modeling: A basic learning process in which individuals acquire new behaviors by observing others and then put these into action.

Monocular Cues: Cues to depth or distance provided by one eye.

Mood Disorders: Psychological disorders involving intense and prolonged mood shifts.

Moral Development: Changes in the capacity to reason about actions' rightness or wrongness that occur with age.

Motivated Skepticism: The tendency to require more information to make a decision contrary to one's initial preferences than a decision consistent with one's initial preferences.

Motivation: An inferred internal process that activates, guides, and maintains behavior over time.

Multicultural Perspective: In modern psychology, a perspective that takes note of the fact that many aspects of behavior are strongly influenced by factors related to culture and ethnic identity.

Narcolepsy: A sleep disorder in which individuals are overcome by uncontrollable periods of sleep during waking hours.

Naturalistic Observation: A research method in which various aspects of behavior are carefully observed in the settings where such behavior naturally occurs.

Nearsightedness: A condition in which the visual image of a distant object is focused slightly in front of the retina rather than directly on it. Therefore distant objects appear fuzzy or blurred, whereas near objects can be seen clearly.

Negative Afterimage: A sensation of complementary color that we experience after staring at a stimulus of a given hue.

Negative Reinforcers: Stimuli that strengthen responses that permit an organism to avoid or escape from their presence.

Neodissociation Theory: A theory of hypnosis suggesting that hypnotized individuals enter an altered state of consciousness in which consciousness is divided.

Neo-Freudians: Personality theorists who accepted basic portions of Freud's theory but rejected or modified other portions.

Nervous System: The complex structure that regulates bodily processes and is responsible, ultimately, for all aspects of conscious experience.

Neural Networks: Computer systems modeled after the brain and made up of highly interconnected elementary computational units that work together in parallel.

Neurons: Cells specialized for communicating information, the basic building blocks of the nervous system.

Neurotransmitters: Chemicals, released by neurons, that carry information across the synapse.

Nicotine: The addictive substance in tobacco.

Night Terrors: Extremely frightening dreamlike experiences that occur during non-REM sleep.

Nodes of Ranvier: Small gaps in the myelin sheath surrounding the axons of many neurons.

Nonverbal Cues: Outward signs of others' emotional states. Such cues involve facial expressions, eye contact, and body language.

Normal Curve: A symmetrical, bell-shaped frequency distribution. Most scores are found near the middle, and fewer and fewer occur toward the extremes. Many psychological characteristics are distributed in this manner.

Obedience: A form of social influence in which one individual issues orders to another to behave in a specific way.

Obesity: The state of being significantly overweight.

Object Permanence: An understanding of the fact that objects continue to exist when they pass from view.

Observational Learning: The acquisition of new information, concepts, or forms of behavior through exposure to others and the consequences they experience.

Obsessive-Compulsive Disorder: Anxiety disorder in which an individual is unable to stop thinking the same thoughts or performing the same ritualistic behaviors.

Occipital Lobe: A portion of the cerebral cortex involved in vision.

Oedipus Complex: In Freud's theory, a crisis of psychosexual development in which children must give up their sexual attraction to their opposite-sex parent.

Omission Training: A procedure in which a response is weakened through the removal of a desired object or activity.

Openness to Experience: One of the "big five" dimensions of personality; ranges from imaginative, sensitive, intellectual at one end to down-to-earth, insensitive, crude at the other.

Operant Conditioning: A process through which organisms learn to repeat behaviors that yield positive outcomes or permit them to avoid or escape from negative outcomes.

Opiates: Drugs that induce a dreamy, relaxed state and, in some persons, intense feelings of pleasure. Opiates exert their effects by stimulating special receptor sites within the brain.

Opponent-Process Theory: A theory that describes the processing of sensory information related to color at levels above the retina. The theory suggests that we possess six types of neurons, each of which is either stimulated or inhibited by red, green, blue, yellow, black, or white.

Opponent-Process Theory of Emotion: A theory suggesting that an emotional reaction to a stimulus is followed automatically by an opposite reaction.

Optic Nerve: A bundle of nerve fibers that exit the back of the eye and carry visual information to the brain.

Oral Stage: In Freud's theory, a stage of psychosexual development during which pleasure is centered in the region of the mouth.

Oversight Bias: The tendency to overlook flaws if the overall topic or issue is perceived as important.

Panic Attack Disorder: Anxiety disorder characterized by relatively brief periods during which individuals experience unbearably intense anxiety.

Parallel Distributed Processing Model: A model suggesting that our memory systems process information in several different ways simultaneously.

Paranoid Personality Disorder: A personality disorder in which individuals feel that others are out to get them and cannot be trusted.

Paraphilias: Sexual disorders involving choices of inappropriate sexual objects, such as young children, or the inability to experience arousal except in the presence of specific objects or fantasies.

Parapsychologists: Individuals who study psi and other paranormal events.

Parasympathetic Nervous System: The portion of the autonomic nervous system that readies the body for restoration of energy.

Parietal Lobe: A portion of the cerebral cortex, lying behind the central fissure, that plays a major role in the skin senses: touch, temperature, pressure.

Passive Smoking: Inhaling other people's cigarette smoke.

Peak Experiences: In Maslow's theory, intense emotional experiences during which individuals feel at one with the universe.

Perception: The process through which we select, organize, and interpret input from our sensory receptors.

Peripheral Nervous System: The portion of the nervous system that connects internal organs and glands, as well as voluntary and involuntary muscles, to the central nervous system.

Peripheral Route (to persuasion): Attitude change resulting from peripheral persuasion cues—information concerning the expertise, status, or attractiveness of would-be persuaders.

Person-Environment (P-E) Fit: The approach that suggests that a misfit between a person and his or her work environment may produce stress.

Personality: Individuals' unique and relatively stable patterns of behavior, thoughts, and feelings.

Personality Disorders: Extreme personality variation associated with the failure to achieve the universal tasks of establishing a personal identity, forming attachments to others, experiencing intimacy with them, and seeking affiliation.

Personality Traits: Specific dimensions along which individuals' personalities differ in consistent, stable ways.

Persuasion: The process through which one or more persons attempt to alter the attitudes of one or more others.

Phallic Stage: In Freud's theory, a psychosexual stage of development during which pleasure is centered in the genital region, and during which the Oedipus complex develops.

Phenylketonuria (PKU): A genetically based disorder in which a person lacks the enzyme to break down phenylalanine, a substance present in many foods. The gradual buildup of phenylalanine contributes to subsequent outcomes that include retardation.

Phobias: Intense, irrational fears of objects or events.

Phonological Development: Development of the ability to produce recognizable speech.

Phonological Strategies: Simplifications used by young children to facilitate the task of producing recognizable speech.

Physical Growth and Development: Physical changes in the size and structure of our bodies between conception and adulthood.

Physiological Dependence: Strong urges to continue using a drug based on organic factors such as changes in metabolism.

Pinna: The external portion of the ear.

Pitch: The characteristic of a sound that is described as high or low. Pitch is mediated by the frequency of a sound.

Pituitary Gland: An endocrine gland that releases hormones to regulate other glands and several basic biological processes.

Place Theory: A theory suggesting that sounds of different frequency stimulate different areas of the basilar membrane.

Pleasure Principle: The principle on which the id operates—immediate pleasure with no attention to possible consequences.

Pons: A portion of the brain through which sensory and motor information passes and which contains structures relating to sleep, arousal, and the regulation of muscle tone and cardiac reflexes.

Positive Reinforcers: Stimuli that strengthen responses that precede them.

Positron Emission Tomography (PET): An imaging technique that detects the activity of the brain by measuring glucose utilization or blood flow.

Postconventional Level (of morality): According to Kohlberg, the final stage of moral development, in which individuals judge morality in terms of abstract principles.

Posttraumatic Stress Disorder: Psychological disorder resulting from a very stressful experience; includes nightmares and flashbacks, distress at exposure to reminders of the event, irritability, difficulty concentrating, and a general unresponsiveness.

Power Motivation: Motivation to be in charge, have high status, and exert influence over others.

Preconventional Level (of morality): According to Kohlberg, the earliest stage of moral development, in which individuals judge morality in terms of the effects produced by various actions.

Predictive Validity: The relationship between scores on a test and later performance relative to a criterion.

Prejudice: Negative attitudes toward the members of some social group based on their membership in this group.

Premack Principle: The principle that a more preferred activity can be used to reinforce a less preferred activity.

Preoperational Stage: In Piaget's theory, a stage of cognitive development during which children become capable of mental representations of the external world.

Prevention Strategies: Techniques designed to reduce the occurrence of physical and psychological problems.

Primary Aging: Aging due to the passage of time and, to some extent, inherited biological factors.

Primary Prevention: Techniques aimed at preventing the occurrence of psychological disorders.

Private Speech: The instructions about what to do next that young children often give themselves as they perform various activities.

Proactive Interference: Interference with the learning or storage of current information by information previously entered into memory.

Problem Solving: Efforts to develop or choose among various responses in order to attain desired goals.

Procedural Memory: A memory system that retains information we cannot readily express verbally—for example, information necessary to perform skilled motor activities such as riding a bicycle.

Propinquity: Physical proximity and the interpersonal contact it produces.

Propositions: Sentences that relate one concept to another and can stand as separate assertions.

Prosocial Behavior: Actions that benefit others without necessarily providing any direct benefit to those who perform them.

Prosopagnosia: A rare condition in which brain damage impairs a person's ability to recognize faces.

Prospective Memory: Remembering to perform certain activities at specific times.

Prototypes: Representations in memory of various objects or stimuli in the physical world; the best or clearest examples of various objects or stimuli in the physical world.

Psi: Unusual processes of information or energy transfer that are currently unexplained in terms of known physical or biological mechanisms. Included under the heading of psi are such supposed abilities as telepathy (reading others' thoughts) and clairvoyance (perceiving unseen objects or unknowable events).

Psychedelics: Drugs that alter sensory perception and so may be considered mind-expanding.

Psychiatry: A branch of medicine that focuses on the diagnosis and treatment of psychological disorders.

Psychoanalysis: A method of therapy based on Freud's theory of personality, in which the therapist attempts to bring repressed unconscious material into consciousness.

Psychodrama: A form of psychodynamic group therapy in which people act out their problems in front of fellow group members.

Psychodynamic Perspective: An approach suggesting that many aspects of behavior stem from hidden forces within our personalities.

Psychodynamic Therapies: Therapies based on the assumption that psychological disorders stem primarily from hidden inner conflicts with repressed urges and impulses.

Psychological Dependence: Strong desires to continue using a drug even though it is not physiologically addicting.

Psychological Disorders: Behaviors or thoughts that are unusual in a given society, that are maladaptive, and that cause the persons who experience them considerable distress.

Psychology: The science of behavior and cognitive processes.

Pysochosexual Stages of Development: According to Freud, an innate sequence of stages through whcih all human beings pass. At each stage, pleasure is focused on a different region of the body.

Psychosurgery: Efforts to alleviate psychological disorders by surgical means.

Psychotherapies: Procedures designed to eliminate or modify psychological disorders through the establishment of a special relationship between a client and a trained therapist.

Puberty: The period of rapid change during which individuals reach sexual maturity and become capable of reproduction.

Punishment: The application or removal of a stimulus so as to decrease the strength of a behavior.

Pupil: An opening in the eye, just behind the cornea, through which light rays enter the eye.

Racial Identification: The extent to which individuals identify with their own racial group.

Random Assignment of Participants to Experimental Conditions: Assuring that all research participants have an equal chance of being assigned to each of the experimental conditions.

Range: The difference between the highest and lowest scores in a distribution of scores.

Rational-Emotive Therapy: A cognitive therapy that focuses on changing irrational beliefs.

Reaction Formation: A defense mechanism in which people act in a manner directly opposite to their unconscious wishes.

Realistic Conflict Theory: A theory proposing that prejudice stems, at least in part, from economic competition between social groups.

Reality Principle: The principle on which the ego operates, according to which the external consequences of behavior are considered in the regulation of expression of impulses from the id.

Reasoning: Cognitive activity that transforms information in order to reach specific conclusions.

Recategorization: Shifting the boundary between "us" and "them" so that persons previously seen as belonging to out-groups are now seen as belonging to the ingroup.

Reconditioning: The rapid recovery of a conditioned response to a CS–UCS pairing following extinction.

Reinforcement: The application or removal of a stimulus so as to increase the strength of a behavior.

Relative Size: A visual cue based on comparison of the size of an unknown object to one of known size.

REM Sleep: A state of sleep in which brain activity resembling waking restfulness is accompanied by deep muscle relaxation and movements of the eyes. Most dreams occur during periods of REM sleep.

Repeated Exposure Effect: The fact that the more frequently we are exposed to various stimuli (at least up to a point), the more we tend to like them.

Representativeness Heuristic: A mental rule of thumb suggesting that the more closely an event or object resembles typical examples of some concept or category, the more likely it is to belong to that concept or category.

Repression: A theory of forgetting that suggests that memories of experiences or events we find threatening are sometimes pushed out of consciousness so that they can no longer be recalled.

Resistance: Efforts by individuals undergoing psychoanalysis to prevent repressed impulses or conflicts from entering consciousness.

Resistant Attachment: A pattern of attachment in which infants reject their mother and refuse to be comforted by her after she leaves them alone during the strange situation test.

Reticular Activating System: A structure within the brain concerned with sleep, arousal, and the regulation of muscle tone and cardiac reflexes.

Retina: The surface at the back of the eye containing the rods and cones.

Retrieval: The process through which information stored in memory is located.

Retrieval Cues: Stimuli associated with information stored in memory that can aid in its retrieval.

Retroactive Interference: Interference with retention of information already present in memory by new information being entered into memory.

Retrograde Amnesia: The inability to store in long-term memory information that occurred before an amnesia-inducing event.

Risk Factors: Aspects of our environment or behavior that influence our chances of developing or contracting a disease, within the limits set by our genetic structure.

Rods: One of the two types of sensory receptors for vision found in the eye.

Romantic Love: A form of love in which feelings of strong attraction and sexual desire toward another person are dominant.

Saccadic Movements: Quick movements of the eyes from one point of fixation to another.

Saturation: The degree of concentration of the hue of light. We experience saturation as the purity of a color.

Schachter-Singer Theory (two-factor theory): A theory of emotion suggesting that our subjective emotional states are determined, at least in part, by the cognitive labels we attach to feelings of arousal.

Schedules of Reinforcement: Rules determining when and how reinforcements will be delivered.

Schemas: Cognitive frameworks representing our knowledge about aspects of the world.

Schizoid Personality Disorder: A personality disorder in which individuals become almost totally detached from the social world.

Schizophrenia: A group of serious psychological disorders characterized by severe distortions in thought and language, perceptions, and emotion.

Script: Mental representation of the sequence of events in a given situation.

Seasonal Affective Disorder (SAD): Depression experienced during the winter months, supposedly stemming from a lack of exposure to sunlight.

Secondary Aging: Aging due to the effects of disease, disuse, or abuse of the body.

Secondary Prevention: Techniques that focus on early detection of psychological disorders so that minor disturbances will not develop into major ones.

Secondary Traits: According to Allport, traits that exert relatively specific and weak effects upon behavior.

Secure Attachment: A pattern of attachment in which infants actively seek contact with their mother and take comfort from her presence when they are reunited with her during the strange situation test.

Selective Attention: Our ability to pay attention to only some aspects of the world around us while largely ignoring others.

Self-Actualization: A stage of personal development in which individuals reach their maximum potential.

Self-Concept: All the information and beliefs individuals have about their own characteristics and themselves.

Self-Consciousness: Increased awareness of oneself as a social object or of one's own values and attitudes.

Self-Disclosure: The act of revealing information about oneself to another person.

Self-Efficacy: Individuals' expectations concerning their ability to perform various tasks.

Self-Esteem: The extent to which individuals have positive or negative feelings about themselves and their own worth.

Self-Help Groups: Groups of individuals experiencing the same kinds of difficulties that meet to discuss their shared problem and find solutions to it.

Self-Monitoring: A personality trait involving sensitivity to social situations and an ability to adapt one's behavior to the demands of those situations in order to make favorable impressions on others.

Self-Reinforcement: The delivery of rewards to oneself for reaching one's self-set goals.

Self-Schemas: Cognitive frameworks that serve to organize information about the self.

Self-Serving Bias: The tendency to attribute positive outcomes to our own traits or characteristics but negative outcomes to factors beyond our control.

Semantic Development: Development of understanding of the meaning of spoken or written language.

Semantic Memory: The content of our general, abstract knowledge about the world.

Semicircular Canals: Fluid-filled structures that provide information about rotational acceleration of the head or body around three principal axes of rotation.

Sensation: Input about the physical world provided by our sensory receptors.

Sensation Seeking: A trait relating to the extent to which individuals seek and enjoy high levels of stimulation.

Sensitivity-Training Groups: A form of group therapy designed to foster personal growth through increased understanding of one's own behavior and increased honesty and openness in personal relations.

Sensorimotor Stage: In Piaget's theory, the earliest stage of cognitive development.

Sensory Adaptation: Reduced sensitivity to unchanging stimuli over time.

Sensory Memory: A memory system that retains representations of sensory input for brief periods of time.

Sensory Receptors: Cells specialized for the task of transduction—converting physical energy (light, sound) into neural impulses.

Serial Position Curve: The greater accuracy of recall of words or other information early and late in a list than words or information in the middle of the list.

Serum Cholesterol: The amount of cholesterol in the blood.

Sexual Abuse: Sexual contact or activities forced on children or adolescents by other persons, usually adults.

Sexual Arousal Disorders: Psychological disorders involving inability to attain an erection (males) or absence of vaginal swelling and lubrication (females).

Sexual Desire Disorders: Psychological disorders involving a lack of interest in sex or active aversion to sexual activities.

Sexual Jealousy: A negative state aroused by a perceived threat to one's sexual relationship with another person.

Sexual Motivation: Motivation to engage in various forms of sexual activity.

Shape Constancy: The tendency to perceive a physical object as having a constant shape even when the image it casts on the retina changes.

Shaping: A technique in which closer and closer approximations of desired behavior are required for the delivery of positive reinforcement.

Short-Term Memory: A memory system that holds limited amounts of information for relatively short periods of time.

Signal Detection Theory: A theory suggesting that there are no absolute thresholds for sensations. Rather, detection of stimuli depends on their physical energy and on internal factors such as the relative costs and benefits associated with detecting their presence.

Simple Cells: Cells within the visual system that respond to specific shapes presented in certain orientations (horizontal, vertical, etc.).

Simultaneous Conditioning: A form of conditioning in which the conditioned stimulus and the unconditioned stimulus begin and end at the same time.

Size Constancy: The tendency to perceive a physical object as having a constant size even when the size of the image it casts on the retina changes.

Sleep: A process in which important physiological changes (including shifts in brain activity and slowing of basic bodily functions) are accompanied by major shifts in consciousness.

Social and Emotional Development: Changes in emotional experiences and expressions, and in behaviors and attitudes toward others, occurring with age.

Social Categorization: Our tendency to divide the social world into two distinct categories: "us" and "them."

Social Cognition: The processes through which we notice, interpret, remember, and later use social information.

Social Cognitive Theory: A theory of behavior suggesting that human behavior is influenced by many cognitive factors as well as by reinforcement contingencies, and that human beings have an impressive capacity to regulate their own actions.

Social Influence: Efforts by one or more individuals to change the attitudes or behavior of one or more others.

Social Norms: Rules in a given group or society indicating how individuals ought to behave in specific situations.

Social Psychology: The branch of psychology that studies all aspects of social behavior and social thought.

Somatic Nervous System: The portion of the peripheral nervous system that connects the brain and spinal cord to voluntary muscles.

Somatization Disorder: A psychological condition in which individuals report physical complaints and symptoms, including aches and pains, problems with their digestive systems, and sexual problems such as sexual indifference or irregular menstruation.

Somatoform Disorders: Category of disorders in which psychological conflicts or other problems take on a physical form.

Somnambulism: A sleep disorder in which individuals actually get up and move about while still asleep.

Source Traits: According to Cattell, key dimensions of personality that underlie many other traits.

Split-Half Reliability: The extent to which an individual attains equivalent scores on two halves of a psychological test.

Spontaneous Recovery: Following extinction, return of a conditioned response upon reinstatement of CS–UCS pairings.

SQUID (Superconducting Quantum Interference Device): An imaging device that captures images of the brain through its ability to detect tiny changes in magnetic fields in the brain.

Stage Theory: Any theory proposing that all human beings move through an orderly and predictable series of changes.

Standard Deviation: A measure of dispersion reflecting the average distance between each score and the mean.

Stanford-Binet Test: A popular test for measuring individual intelligence.

State-Dependent Retrieval: Retrieval of information stored in long-term memory cued by aspects of one's physical state.

States of Consciousness: Varying degrees of awareness of ourselves and the external world.

Statistics: Mathematical procedures used to describe data and draw inferences from them.

Stereotypes: Cognitive frameworks suggesting that all members of specific social groups share certain characteristics.

Stimulants: Drugs that increase activity in the nervous system, including amphetamines, caffeine, and nicotine.

Stimulus: A physical event capable of affecting behavior.

Stimulus Control: Consistent occurrence of a behavior in the presence of a discriminative stimulus.

Stimulus Discrimination: The process by which organisms learn to respond to certain stimuli but not to others.

Stimulus Generalization: The tendency of stimuli similar to a conditioned stimulus to elicit a conditioned response.

Storage: The process through which information is retained in memory.

Strange Situation Test: A procedure for studying attachment in which mothers leave their children alone with a stranger for several minutes and then return.

Stress: The process that occurs in response to events that disrupt, or threaten to disrupt, our physical or psychological functioning.

Stressors: Events or situations in our environment that cause stress.

Striving for Superiority: Attempting to overcome feelings of inferiority. According to Adler, this is the primary motive for human behavior.

Structuralism: An early view suggesting that psychology should focus on conscious experience and on the task of analyzing such experience into its basic parts.

Sublimation: A defense mechanism in which threatening unconscious impulses are channeled into socially acceptable forms of behavior.

Subliminal Perception: The presumed ability to perceive a stimulus that is below the threshold for conscious experience.

Suicide: The act of taking one's own life.

Superego: According to Freud, the portion of human personality representing the conscience.

Suprachiasmatic Nucleus: A portion of the hypothalamus that seems to play an important role in the regulation of circadian rhythms.

Survey Method: A research method in which large numbers of people answer questions about aspects of their views or their behavior.

Syllogistic Reasoning: A type of formal reasoning in which two premises are used as the basis for deriving logical conclusions.

Sympathetic Nervous System: The portion of the autonomic nervous system that readies the body for energy expenditure.

Synapse: A region where the axon of one neuron closely approaches other neurons or the cell membrane of other types of cells such as muscle cells.

Synaptic Vesicles: Structures in the axon terminals that contain various neurotransmitters.

Systematic Desensitization: A form of behavior therapy in which individuals imagine scenes or events that are increasingly anxiety-provoking and at the same time engage in procedures that induce feelings of relaxation.

Tardive Dyskinesia: A side effect of prolonged exposure to antipsychotic drugs in which individuals experience involuntary muscular movements, especially of the face.

Temperament: Stable individual differences in the quality and intensity of emotional reactions.

Templates: Specific patterns stored in our memories for various visual stimuli that we encounter.

Temporal Lobe: The lobe of the cerebral cortex that is involved in hearing.

Teratogens: Factors in the environment that can harm the developing fetus.

Tertiary Prevention: Techniques designed to minimize the harm done by psychological disorders.

Test-Retest Reliability: The extent to which a psychological test yields similar scores when taken by the same person on different occasions.

Thalamus: A structure deep within the brain that receives sensory input from other portions of the nervous system and then transmits this information to the cerebral hemispheres and other parts of the brain.

That's-Not-All Approach: A technique for gaining compliance in which a small extra incentive is offered before the target person has agreed to or rejected a request.

Thematic Apperception Test (TAT): A psychological test used to assess individual differences in several motives, such as achievement motivation and power motivation.

Theories: In science, frameworks for explaining various phenomena. Theories consists of two major parts: basic concepts and assertions concerning relationships between these concepts.

Therapeutic Alliance: The special relationship between therapist and client that contributes to the effectiveness of many forms of psychotherapy.

Timbre: The quality of a sound, resulting from the complex makeup of a sound wave; timbre helps us to distinguish the sound of a trumpet from that of a saxophone.

Tip-of-the-Tongue Phenomenon: The feeling that we can almost remember some information we wish to retrieve from memory.

Token Economies: Forms of behavior therapy based on operant conditioning, in which hospitalized patients earn tokens they can exchange for valued rewards when they behave in ways the hospital staff consider to be desirable.

Tolerance: Habituation to a drug, causing larger and larger doses to be required to produce effects of the same magnitude.

Trace Conditioning: A form of forward conditioning in which the presentation of the conditioned stimulus precedes and does not overlap with the presentation of the unconditioned stimulus.

Trait Theories: Theories of personality that focus on identifying the key dimensions along which people differ.

Transduction: The translation of physical energy into electrical signals by specialized receptor cells.

Transference: Strong positive or negative feelings toward the therapist on the part of individuals undergoing psychoanalysis.

Trephining: An ancient surgical procedure in which holes are cut into the skull.

Trial and Error: A method of solving problems in which possible solutions are tried until one succeeds.

Triarchic Theory: A theory suggesting that there are actually three distinct kinds of intelligence.

Trichromatic Theory: A theory of color perception suggesting that we have three types of cones, each primarily receptive to particular wavelengths of light.

Type A Behavior Pattern: A cluster of traits such as competitiveness, aggressiveness, urgency, and hostility; related to important aspects of health, social behavior, and task performance.

Unconditional Positive Regard: In Rogers's theory, communicating to others that they will be respected or loved regardless of what they say or do.

Unconditioned Response (UCR): In classical conditioning, the response elicited by an unconditioned stimulus.

Unconditioned Stimulus (UCS): In classical conditioning, a stimulus that can elicit an unconditioned response the first time it is presented.

Validity: The extent to which tests actually measure what they claim to measure.

Variable-Interval Schedule: A schedule of reinforcement in which a variable amount of time must elapse before a response will yield reinforcement.

Variable-Ratio Schedule: A schedule of reinforcement in which reinforcement is delivered after a variable number of responses have been performed.

Variance: A measure of dispersion reflecting the average squared distance between each score and the mean.

Vestibular Sacs: Fluid-filled sacs in our inner ear that provide information about the positions and changes in linear movement of our head and body.

Vestibular Sense: Our sense of balance.

Wavelength: The peak-to-peak distance in a sound or light wave.

Wear-and-Tear Theories of Aging: Theories suggesting that aging results from continuous use of cells and organs within our bodies.

Wernicke-Geschwind Theory: A theory of how the brain processes information relating to speech and other verbal abilities. Although the theory has generated a considerable amount of research, recent evidence suggests that it does not provide an adequate picture of this process.

Work Motivation: Motivation to perform and complete various tasks.

Subject Index

Mood, prosocial behavior and, 549–550
Mood disorders, 454–459. *See also*
    Depression
    bipolar, 455, 510–511
    definition of, 455
    depressive, 455–457
    lithium and, 510–511
    suicide, 458–459
Moon illusion, 109–110
Moral development, 294–299
Moral understanding, stages of, 294–297
Morphine, 50–51, 148, 150, 169
Motion parallax, 112
Motivated skepticism, 527
Motivation, 334–353
    achievement, 351–353
    aggressive, 347–350
    definition of, 334
    health and, 424
    hunger, 339–342
    intrinsic, 352–353
    in observational learning, 186
    role of brain in, 58
    sexual, 342–347
    techniques for enhancing, 364–365
    theories of, 335–339
    and traumatic brain injury, 74
    work, 7, 36, 337–338, 364
Motivational state, 531
Motor cortex, 59, 60
Motor development. *See* Physical development
Mourning, stages in, 325
Mr. Yuk, 179
Müller-Lyer illusion, 108–109
Multicultural perspective, 10–13. *See also*
    Cultural differences
Multiple personalities, 464–465
Multiple resource theory, 65–66
Mumps, 283
Myelin sheath, 45–46

Naive hedonistic orientation, 294, 297
Narcissistic personality disorder, 470
Narcolepsy, 136–137
Natural concepts, 231
Natural killer cells, 427
Naturalistic observation, 18–19
Nature-nurture controversy, 9, 72,
    113–114
Nearsightedness, 87
Needs hierarchy, Maslow's, 338–339,
    385–386, 394
Negative afterimages, 89
Negative reinforcement, 172–173, 174
Negative reinforcers, 172, 173
Negative state relief, 550
Neo-Freudian theories
    Adler's striving for superiority, 382
    evaluation of, 383
    Horney's social factors, 381–382
    Jung's collective unconscious, 380–381
Neo-Freudians, 380
Neocortex, 221
Neodissociation theory, 143
Nerves, 52
Nervous system
    damage to, 54
    definition of, 51
    divisions of, 51–53
    emotions and, 357
    structure and functions of, 51–56
    study of, 54–55
Neural networks, 223, 247
Neurohormones, 66

Neurons, 45, 46–48
Neuroscience approach, 256–257
Neurotransmitters. *See also* specific transmitters
    definition of, 47
    effects of drugs on, 147
    memory and, 223
    types of, 49–51
Newborns. 285, 292. *See also* Infants
Nicotine, 148, 428
Night terrors, 136
Nightmares, 136
Nocturnal myoclonus, 136
Nodes of Ranvier, 46
Noise pollution, 117
Nonverbal cues, 359–362
Noradrenaline, 432
Norepinephrine
    depression and, 456, 509
    effects of drugs on, 147
    location and effects of, 50
    nicotine and, 428
Normal curve, 565–567
Nutrition, health and, 430–431

Obedience, 545–547, 548
Obesity, 340–341
Object permanence (Piaget), 289, 291
Observation
    naturalistic, 18–19
    systematic, 13
Observational learning, 185–188
    aggression and, 187
    attitude formation and, 529
    definition of, 185
    gender identity and, 304
    personality and, 392
    principles of, 185–186
    as type of learning, 158
Obsessive-compulsive disorder, 55–56,
    460–461
Occipital lobe, 60
Oedipus complex, 139, 376
Olfactory epithelium, 98
Omission, errors of, 572
Omission training, 172
One-trial learning, 166
Openness to experience, 389
Operant conditioning, 170–184
    application of, 182–184
    attachment and, 301
    attitude formation and, 529
    cognitive perspective on, 180–182
    definition of, 171
    gender identity and, 304
    nature of, 171–172
    of newborns, 285
    principles of, 174–179
    therapies based on, 491–492
    as type of learning, 158
Operating principles, of language, 249
Opiate(s), 148, 150
Opiate receptors, 97–98
Opioid peptides, 51, 148, 428
Opium, 148, 150
Opponent-process theory, 89, 355, 357
Optic nerve, 86
Optimism, stress resistance and, 421–422
Oral stage, 376, 377
Organization, 224
Orgasm disorders, 466
Orgasmic phase, 344
Orienting responses, 476
Otis-Lennon School Ability test, 263
Outpatient services, 512

Ovaries, 68
Overconfidence, 396
Overload, stress and, 416
Overpathologizing, 453
Oversight bias, 233–234

Pain, 51, 96–98
Pain threshold, 97
Pancreas, 68
Panic attack disorder, 459–460
Papillae, 99
Parallel distributed processing model,
    196–197
Paranoid personality disorder, 469
Paranoid schizophrenia, 473
Paraphilias, 466–467
Parapsychologists, 115
Parasympathetic nervous system, 53,
    357
Parathyroid, 68
Parent-absent families, 311
Parietal lobe, 60
Partial reinforcement, 177–178
Partial reinforcement effect, 179
Passive smoking, 429–430
Passive touch, 96
Pattern recognition, 110–112
Peak experiences, 386
Pedophilia, 466
Penis envy, 376–377, 381
Perception, 103–116
    constancies in, 106, 108
    definition of, 80
    of distance, 112–113
    effect of hypnosis on, 143
    extrasensory, 115–116
    illusions in, 108–110
    learning and, 114
    nature of, 113–114
    pattern recognition, 110–112
    principles of, 105–106
    schizophrenic disturbances in, 472
    selectiveness of, 104
Perceptual development, 285–286
Perceptual organization, 105
Performance appraisals, 416–417
Peripheral nervous system, 51–52
Peripheral route, 530
Permanent threshold shift (PTS), 117
Person-environment (P-E) fit, 417
Personal identity, 308
Personality. *See also* Personality disorders
    definition of, 370
    Freud's theories on, 371–379, 394
    health and, 432–433
    humanistic theories of, 383–387, 394
    key aspects of, 393–400
    learning approaches to, 391–393, 394
    Neo-Freudian theories of, 380–383
    trait theories of, 387–391, 394
Personality disorders, 468–471
    antisocial, 263, 469–471
    paranoid and schizoid, 469
Personality traits, 371, 387
Persuasion, 529–530
Persuasion cues, 530
Pessimism, stress resistance and, 421–422
Phallic stage, 376, 377
Phenothiazines, 476, 508
Phenylalanine, 71
Phenylethylamine, (PEA), 342, 553
Phenylketonuria (PKU), 71
Pheromones, 344–345
Philosophy, 3–4
Phobias, 169, 460, 490, 493

Reorganization, 325
Repeated exposure effect, 551
Representativeness heuristic, 238, 240
Repressed memories, 465
Repression, 208–209
    in Freud's theory, 372–373, 375, 485
    nature of, 375
Reserpine, 456, 508
Resistance, 486
Resistance stage, 409, 410, 412
Resistant attachment, 302
Resolution phase, 344
Responsibility, 383, 549
Resting potential, 46
Retention, 186
Reticular activating system, 57, 58
Retina, 85
Retinal disparity, 113
Retrieval, 195
Retrieval cues, 205–206, 210, 224
Retroactive interference, 207–208
Retrograde amnesia, 220, 222
Reuptake, 47, 49
Reversibility, 290
Reward, compliance and, 532–534
Reward delay, 176
Risk averse, 239
Risk factors, 427
Risk prone, 239
Risk-taking, emotions and, 362
Rods, 86
Role conflict, 416
Role reversal, 496
Romantic love, 553
Rubella, 283

Saccadic movements, of eye, 88
Sadism, 466
Sadomasochism, 344
Safety needs, 338, 385
Sample, 571–572
Saturation, 86
Scatterplots, 569
Schacter-Singer theory of emotions, 355,
    356
Schedules of reinforcement, 176–179
Schemas
    cultural, 216–217
    development of, 292
    emotions and, 363
    gender, 304
    memory and, 215–217
    personality disorders and, 470
    self-, 310, 456–457
Schismatic families, 475
Schizoid personality disorder, 469
Schizophrenia, 471–477
    intelligence scores and, 263
    nature of, 471–473
    origins of, 474–476
    treatment of, 508–509
    types of, 473–474
Science, 3–4, 13–15
Scripts, 293
Seasonal affective disorder (SAD), 124
Secondary aging, 316
Secondary appraisal, 410–411
Secondary prevention, 434–435, 438–440,
    512
Secondary traits, 388
Secure attachment, 301
Selective amnesia, 464
Selective attention, 104, 196
Self-absorption, 309, 313

Self-actualization, 338, 385–386
Self-care, 490
Self-concept
    distortions in, 488
    gender schema and, 304
    memory and, 214
    prejudice and, 538–540
    Rogers' theory of, 384–385
    self-disclosure and, 387
    stress and, 396
    test of accuracy of, 400
Self-consciousness, 129–131
Self-defeating behavior, 555
Self-disclosure, 387
Self-efficacy, 392, 438
Self-esteem, 392, 395–397
Self-examination, 439
Self-help groups, 497–498
Self-identity, 309–310
Self-image, 241–242
Self-injurious behavior (SIB), 184
Self-insight, 131
Self-justification, 241–242
Self-monitoring, 397–398
Self-perception, 350
Self-regulation, 294, 392
Self-reinforcement, 392
Self-schemas, 310, 456–457
Self-serving bias, 523–524
Semantic coding, 201
Semantic development, 250
Semantic memory, 197–198, 221
Semicircular canals, 103
Sensation
    definition of, 80
    just noticeable difference in, 82
    raw materials of, 80–84
Sensation seeking, 398–400
Sensitivity-training groups, 497
Sensorimotor stage (Piaget), 289, 295
Sensory abilities, and aging, 316
Sensory adaptation, 84
Sensory cortex, 61
Sensory deprivation, 81
Sensory memory, 195, 196, 198–199, 213
Sensory processing, 292, 295
Sensory receptors, 80
Sensory thresholds, 81–84
Sequential processing, 269
Serial position curve, 200
Seriation, 289
Serotonin
    aggression and, 348
    depression and, 456, 509
    location and effects of, 50
Serum cholesterol, 430–431, 438
Setting, for therapy, 511–513
Sex-stereotyped behavior, 304–305
Sexual abuse, 208–209, 311
Sexual arousal disorders, 466
Sexual behavior
    arousal stimulation and, 344–345
    effects of hormones on, 342–343
    facts on, 343–345
    gender differences in, 344, 345–346
    risk prevention and, 433–434
Sexual desire disorders, 466
Sexual dysfunctions, 466
Sexual jealousy, 345–346
Sexual motivation, 342–347
Sexual orientation, 72, 346–347
Shadowing task, 399
Shame, versus autonomy, 308, 309
Shape constancy, 106

Shaping
    in operant conditioning, 175–176
    use of, 183, 491
    for weight-loss program, 189
Shift work, 126
Shock, 325
Short-term memory, 199–202, 213
    children's development of, 293–295
    definition of, 199–202
    effects of aging on, 317
    evidence for, 200–201
    limitations of, 204–206
    in modal model, 195, 196
    operation of, 201–202
Shyness, 300, 357–358
Signal detection theory, 82, 104
Significant difference, 567, 572
Similarity, law of, 107
Simple cells, 90
Simplicity, law of, 107
Simultaneous conditioning, 161, 163
Simultaneous processing, 269
Size constancy, 106, 108–109
Size cues, 112
Size-distance invariance, 106
Skewed families, 475
Skin senses, 94–97
Skinner box, 174–175
Sleep, 132–141
    definition of, 132
    disorders of, 135–137
    functions of, 134–135
    stages of, 132–133
Sleep efficiency, 135
Sleep spindles, 133
Smell, 98–101
Smoking, 428–430
Social and emotional development
    in adolescence, 307–308
    of children, 299–305
    definition of, 282
    and temperament, 299–303
Social behavior, 534–557
    attraction, 550–555
    changing others', 540–547
    environment and, 555–558
    prejudice, 534–540
Social categorization, 535
Social clock, 314
Social cognition, 524–528
Social cognitive theory, 391–393
Social-cognitive view, of hypnosis,
    142–144
Social contract/legalistic orientation, 296,
    297
Social influence, 540–547
    compliance, 543–545
    conformity, 541–543
    obedience and, 545–547
Social learning theory, 248–249, 303–304,
    391–393
Social needs, 338, 385
Social norms, 434, 541
Social-order-maintaining orientation, 296,
    297
Social perspective, on drug abuse, 145
Social psychology, 17, 520
Social referencing, 300
Social rejection, 352
Social role, hypnotized subject's, 142
Social selves, 310
Social smiling, 299
Social thought, 520–534
    aspects of, 525–528

Violence, effects of, 505–506
Viruses, 558
Vision, 84–91
    and brain's processing of information, 89–91
    color, 88–89
    stimulus for, 86
    and vestibular information, 103
Visual acuity, dynamic, 87, 316
Visual cliff, 286
Visual cortex, 90
Visual imagery, 232, 224
Visual perception, 113–114
Visual system, 87–88
Vitamin A, 430
Volley principle, 93–94
Voyeurism, 467

Warnings, 104
Washoe, 252
Wavelength, 86
Wear-and-tear theories of aging, 323
Wechsler Adult Intelligence Scale, 257, 262–263
Wechsler Intelligence Scale for Children (WISC), 263
Weight-loss program, 189
Wellness, promotion of, 434–439
Wernicke-Geschwind theory of speech, 61–63
Wernicke's area, 61, 62
Withdrawal, effects of, 148
Womb envy, 381
Word-length effect, 200
Work, stress from, 416–418

Work motivation, 7, 36, 337–338, 364
Workaholics, 333
Working memory. *See* Short-term memory
Worth, conditions of, 488

Xanax, 510

Yogis, 151

Zoloft, 510